The British
BOXING
Board of Control
YEARBOOK
1996

C000048243

Edited and Compiled by
Barry J. Hugman

Robson Books

First published in Great Britain in 1995 by Robson Books Ltd,
Bolsover House, 5-6 Clipstone Street, London W1P 8LE

© Barry J. Hugman 1995
The right of Barry J. Hugman to be identified as author of
this work has been asserted by him in accordance with the
Copyright, Designs and Patents Act 1988

British Library Cataloguing in Publication Data
A catalogue record for this title is available from the British
Library

ISBN 1 86105 000 3

All rights reserved. No part of this publication may be
reproduced, stored in a retrieval system, or transmitted in any
form or by any means, electronic, mechanical, photocopying,
recording or otherwise, without the prior permission in
writing of the publishers.

Typesetting & Artwork by Typecast (Artwork & Design), 8
Mudford Road, Yeovil, Somerset BA21 4AA.
Printed in Great Britain by Butler & Tanner Ltd, Frome &
London

Contents

TARA PROMOTIONS & MANAGEMENT

headquarters:
TARA SPORTS & LEISURE CENTRE,
Grains Road, Shaw, Oldham, Lancs.
Tel: (01706) 841460   Fax: (01706) 882810
STAGING REGULAR SHOWS THROUGHOUT THE NORTH-WEST

*Our gymnasium includes:-
2 Rings, Spacious Weights Room, Showers, Sauna and Sunbeds*

*Other facilities include:-
Toning Salon, Badminton Courts, Snooker Hall, 3 Bars, Restaurant, Function Rooms, Cabaret Lounge and Large Enclosed Car Park*

BOXERS

Glenn Campbell (Bury) Super-Middleweight (Central Area Champion)
Derek "Cheyenne" Wormald (Rochdale) Middleweight
Warren Stowe (Burnley) Middleweight
Darren Swords (Manchester) Middleweight
Jeff Finlayson (Manchester) Light-Middleweight
Wayne Shepherd (Carlisle) Welterweight
Kevin McKillan (Manchester) Lightweight
Scott Walker (Oldham) Lightweight
Bobbie Vanzie (Bradford) Lightweight
Charles Shepherd (Carlisle) Super-Featherweight
Wayne Rigby (Manchester) Super-Featherweight
Dave Clavering (Bury) Super-Featherweight
Henry Armstrong (Manchester) Featherweight
Des Gargano (Middleton) Super-Bantamweight
Marcus Duncan (Lancaster) Bantamweight
Ady "The Mighty Atom" Lewis (Bury) Flyweight

Licenced Manager: Jack Doughty *Matchmaker:* Graham Lockwood
Trainers: Peter McElhinney, Bob Shannon,
Godfrey Brown, Frank Harrington and Kenny Daniels

Acknowledgements

Even though this is the 12th edition, it never seems to get any easier and I continue to rely heavily upon my willing team of helpers. This year we have a new publisher, Robson Books, hopefully, an ideal choice, particularly when taking into account their growing reputation in the field of specialist boxing books.

Once again I am indebted to John Morris, the General Secretary of the BBBoC, for all the help and support I have received from him and his team at Jack Petersen House over the years. My relationship with John, and most of those I come into contact within boxing, goes way beyond that of author and the garnering in of information neccessary to compile a book of this kind. That is why the *British Boxing Yearbook*, is a special book for me to be involved in. Regarding this year's tome, I would again wish to publicly thank John, Simon Block (Assistant Secretary), Paula Gibson, Mary Farnan, Joanne Landers and especially, Karyn Locke, who co-ordinated a whole range of requirements on my behalf, including updates on licensed officials, Area title bouts and boxers' manager details, just to name a few.

Where would I be without Ron Olver. A "lovely" man, who has spent a lifetime in boxing and puts back far more than he takes out, he can still be found keeping regularly in touch with the many ex-boxers and their associations that he, more than anyone else, has helped to support and encourage. Indeed, he continues to present the "Old Timers" feature in *Boxing News*, something he has done for the past 28 years. Quite rightly, his services to boxing have recently been rewarded by both the Boxing Writers' Club and the BBBoC. A former Assistant Editor of both *Boxing News* and *Boxing World*, Ron is also recognised as having been the British correspondent for *The Ring*; author of *The Professionals*, the boxing section within *Encyclopedia Britannica*, and *Boxing*, Foyle's Library Service; former co-editor of the *Boxing News Annual*; Chairman of the BBBoC Benevolent Fund Grants Committee; Vice-President of many ex-boxers' associations; Public Relations Officer of the London Ex-Boxers' Association; and a member of the Commonwealth Boxing Council and the International Hall of Fame Committee.

As in last year's book, I would like to thank Bob Lonkhurst, Derek O'Dell and Ralph Oates, well-known for his quiz books on the sport and with *Boxing Clever* still on sale, for their help in creating a balanced range of articles and for their special support in aiming to keep the *British Boxing Yearbook* at the forefront of boxing publications. Bob, who will shortly be looking to publish a book on Tommy Farr that gives a fresh insight into a Welsh hero who will never be forgotten, has produced a healthy defence of why the British referee and the British system of scoring a fight is second to none, while Derek takes us on an interesting journey in detailing the rise of "Jersey" Joe Walcott to the advent of Rocky Marciano, and Ralph looks at the importance of Charlie Magri to the British flyweight division.

I would also like to thank John Jarrett, the Northern Area Secretary; Eric Armit, an expert in the field of co-ordinating boxers' records on a world-wide basis; and David Prior, who covers amateur boxing for the *Amateur Boxing Scene* and *Boxing News*. These three men are regular contributors to the *Yearbook*, producing the annual features: Home and Away with British Boxers, A-Z of Current World Champions, and Highlights from the Amateur Season, respectively.

As in last year's book, the biggest single area of research was in the World Title Bouts Since Gloves section. For this edition we concentrate on light-welters through to heavyweights. In repeating what I said last year, without the expert help of Professor Luckett Davis, Bob Soderman and Hy Rosenberg (America) and Harold Alderman, Bill Matthews, author of *The English Boxing Champions*, and Derek O'Dell, at home, I could not have started, let alone begun to complete what has been such a complex area of research down the ages. Certainly, without the tremendous help of Luckett Davis, with hours upon hours of detailed research, early day boxing in America would still remain a mystery. Harold Alderman is Luckett's British equivalent, spending over 30 years researching boxing at the National Newspaper Library in an effort to track down the early history of boxing in this country. Although there are no obvious parameters, I would have thought that the three leading experts this side of the Atlantic are Bill Matthews (bare-fists), Harold Alderman (gloves through to the 1920s), and Vic Hardwicke (master compiler of boxers' records from the 1920s to date).

Other editorial help has come in the shape of Neil Blackburn (world-wide obituaries), Mrs Enza Jacoponi (IBU data), Patrick Mylor (Irish amateur boxing), Bob Yalen (world title data), Frank Hendry, Jim Robertson, Ray Allen and Alston Alsop (amateur boxing), and Dai Corp, Brian McAllister, Stanley Anderson, John Jarrett, Paul Thomas, Simon Block and Harry Warner (Area title data).

As in previous years, the *British Boxing Yearbook* has relied extensively for photos from Les Clark, who, over the past few seasons, has built up quite a library of both action shots and poses. If anyone requires a photo that has appeared in the book, he can be reached at 352 Trelawney Avenue, Langley, Bucks SL3 7TS. This time round, although predominately among the amateurs, Steve Parkin has assisted and will continue to help out, especially in the north, or if Les is unavailable. Other photographs were supplied by my good friends Harry Goodwin and Derek Rowe, Penny Bracey, Chris Bevan, and George Ashton of Sportapics.

Others I would like to make mention of are Bernard Hart, the Managing Director of Lonsdale Sports Equipment Ltd, who sponsor the BBBoC Awards that coincide with the launch of the *British Boxing Yearbook*; Jean Bastin, of Typecast (Artwork & Design), for continuing to set such high standards with the typesetting and design; my wife, Jennifer, who looks after the proof-reading side of things, and the sponsor, Jonathan Ticehurst, Managing Director of the Sports Division of Windsor Insurance Brokers, whose generous support has helped the *Yearbook* to maintain the quality that has come to be expected.

Barry J. Hugman (Editor)

GUS ROBINSON

GEORGE BOWES

GUS ROBINSON

Promotions

**PROMOTING & MANAGING
NORTH-EAST FIGHTERS
GYM & VENUE - HARTLEPOOL
BOROUGH HALL**

CONTACT GUS ROBINSON

on
**(01429) 234221 - OFFICE
(01429) 869822 - OFFICE FAX
(0191) 587 0336 - HOME**

6

Introduction

by Barry J. Hugman

As in previous years, I have done my level best to maintain the high standards of the *British Boxing Yearbook*, now in its 12th edition, both in quality and information. Current boxers' records are meticulously updated and the team and myself continue to appraise old records and, at the same time, introduce fresh new features and articles.

Last year, part one of World Title Bouts Since Gloves was introduced, starting with mini-flys through to the lightweight division, while this edition concentrates on light-welters to heavyweights. If you found yourself dipping into this section, you will probably know by now how difficult it is to evaluate what was a title bout and what was not, especially before the 1920s when commissions began to be set up and the weight classes standardised. The common problem was that of billing, with many champions (claimants) increasing their weight and still being advertised as defending their title claims. Title claims you might say, but that was really all they were in the days before the existence of governing bodies. The reality was that there were always plenty of claimants at any given time, and many of them were in billed title fights, but it was only when all the leading contenders had been eliminated that a man could rightly be called a champion. Thus for example, when Tommy Ryan failed to make 158 lbs after 1902, the middleweight limit in those days, there were several leading claimants, including Hugo Kelly, Jack and Mike "Twin" Sullivan, Joe Thomas, Billy Papke and Stanley Ketchel, and it was only after the last two named met in June 1908, having eliminated the rest of the pack, that Ketchel was generally recognised as champion in America. Hopefully, that will give you a taste for what you might find in the section.

Yet again, there are several topical articles on tap, featuring, among others, the benefits of insuring boxers against injuries, Sky Sports and their boxing aspirations, the fine tradition of British referees, how "Jersey" Joe Walcott got to meet Rocky Marciano, and how little Charlie Magri rescued the British flyweight division from extinction. Added to ongoing articles, such as Home and Away with British Boxers, Highlights from the Amateur Season, an A-Z of Current World Champions, and Obituaries, and the fact that the complete record can be found for every active British boxer, plus much more, it is to be hoped you find the book well structured and to your liking.

If you are one of the many fans who are sick and tired of the way world championship boxing is going in this day and age of 68 possible world champions – that is if you recognise the IBF, WBA, WBC and WBO as being much of a muchness, although there are many more titles on offer if you care to accept the existence of others less well known – just take a look at the World Champions Since Gloves section. Interestingly, in the light of the slogan, "I wish we could go back to the good old days", looking at the divisional listings since the early 1890s, you will

probably be surprised to find so few universally recognised champions. Even allowing for that, today is abysmal by comparison and the game cries out for an international controlling body, encompassing everything from rules and championships to medical care. Here are the totals: Fly (15), Bantam (29), Feather (20), Light (28), Welter (39), Middle (29), L. Heavy (18), Cruiser (1) and Heavy (25). Since 1980, the only men to have achieved universal status are:- Sugar Ray Leonard, Don Curry and Lloyd Honeyghan (Welter); Vito Antuofermo, Alan Minter and Marvin Hagler (Middle); Michael Spinks (L. Heavy); Evander Holyfield (Cruiser); and Mike Tyson (Heavy). You do not need me to tell you that with just nine universally recognised champions in the last 15 years, and none at present, as opposed to 204 in 105 years of gloved fighting, things could be better.

Finally, I would like to make mention of Babs Spear-Adair, the first woman in this country to be licensed by the BBBoC as a chief second. It would have been nice to have included her in last year's article, Women in Boxing, but we had already gone to press when advised. We wish her well.

Abbreviations and Definitions used in the record sections of the Yearbook: PTS (Points), CO (Count Out), RSC (Referee Stopped Contest), RTD (Retired), DIS (Disqualified), NC (No Contest), ND (No Decision).

British Boxing Board of Control Ltd: Structure

(Members of the World Boxing Council, World Boxing Association, International Boxing Federation, World Boxing Organisation, Commonwealth Boxing Council and European Boxing Union)

PRESIDENT	Sir David Hopkin
VICE PRESIDENT	Leonard E. Read, QPM
CHAIRMAN	Sir David Hopkin
VICE CHAIRMAN	Leonard E. Read, QPM
GENERAL SECRETARY	John Morris
ADMINISTRATIVE STEWARDS	Sir David Hopkin Leonard E. Read QPM Dr Adrian Whiteson, OBE Dr Oswald Ross William Sheeran Dennis Lockton Lincoln Crawford Frank Butler, OBE Tom Pendry, MP Cliff Curvis Bill Martin Robert Graham, BEM Lord Brooks of Tremorfa Gerald Woolard Charles Giles Sebastian Coe, OBE, MP Judge Alan Simpson
HONORARY STEWARD*	Dr James Shea
STEWARDS OF APPEAL*	Robin Simpson, QC John Mathew, QC Nicholas Valios, QC Robert Harman, QC William Tudor John Geoffrey Finn Judge Brian Capstick, QC Colin Ross Munro, QC Peter Richards Lord Meston
HONORARY CONSULTANT*	Ray Clarke, OBE
HEAD OFFICE	Jack Petersen House 52a Borough High Street London SE1 1XW Tel. 0171 403 5879 Fax. 0171 378 6670 Telegrams: BRITBOX, LONDON

* Not directors of the company

AREA COUNCILS - AREA SECRETARIES

AREA NO 1 (SCOTLAND)
Brian McAllister
11 Woodside Crescent, Glasgow G3 7UL
Telephone 0141 332 0392

AREA NO 2 (NORTHERN IRELAND)
Stanley Anderson
5 Ardenlee Avenue, Ravenhill Road, Belfast,
Northern Ireland BT6 0AA
Telephone 01232 453829

AREA NO 3 (WALES)
Dai Corp
113 Hill Crest, Brynna, Llanharan, Mid Glamorgan
CF7 9SN
Telephone 01443 226465

AREA NO 4 (NORTHERN)
(Northumberland, Cumbria, Durham, Cleveland, Tyne and Wear, North Yorkshire [north of a line drawn from Whitby to Northallerton to Richmond, including these towns].)
John Jarrett
5 Beechwood Avenue, Gosforth, Newcastle NE3 5DM
Telephone 0191 2856556

AREA NO 5 (CENTRAL)
(North Yorkshire [with the exception of the part included in the Northern Area - see above], Lancashire, West and South Yorkshire, Greater Manchester, Merseyside and Cheshire, Isle of Man, North Humberside.)
Harry Warner
14 St Christopher's Road,
The 18th Fairway, Ashton under Lyme, Lancashire
OL6 9EO
Telephone 0161 330 4572

AREA NO 6 (SOUTHERN)
(Bedfordshire, Berkshire, Buckinghamshire, Cambridgeshire, Channel Islands, Isle of Wight, Essex, Hampshire, Kent, Hertfordshire, Greater London, Norfolk, Suffolk, Oxfordshire, East and West Sussex.)
Simon Block
British Boxing Board of Control
Jack Petersen House, 52a Borough High Street, London
SE1 1XW
Telephone 0171 403 5879

AREA NO 7 (WESTERN)
(Cornwall, Devon, Somerset, Dorset, Wiltshire, Avon, Gloucestershire.)
Dai Corp
113 Hill Crest, Brynna, Llanharan, Mid Glamorgan
CF7 9SN
Telephone 01443 226465

AREA NO 8 (MIDLANDS)
(Derbyshire, Nottinghamshire, Lincolnshire, Salop, Staffordshire, Herefordshire and Worcestershire, Warwickshire, West Midlands, Leicestershire, South Humberside, Northamptonshire.)
Alec Kirby
105 Upper Meadow Road, Quinton, Birmingham B32
Telephone 0121 421 1194

Foreword

by John Morris *(General Secretary, British Boxing Board of Control)*

A wind of change is running through world boxing, a steady blow if not yet a genuine whirlwind, as editor Barry Hugman presents us with his annual super-mix of fistic facts, both current and historical. Last year he fascinated us with the first stage of his breakdown of the world championships and now completes a study that throws a whole new light on the performances of so many legendary names.

This year, the *British Boxing Yearbook* has a new publisher in Robson Books and its principal Jeremy Robson takes another step in his ascendancy within the sports field. We believe this is a partnership that will be a major boost to both the book and the annual Awards that run alongside, which are once again sponsored by the Lonsdale International Sporting Club.

The new edition reflects the excellent state of British professional boxing, thanks to the host of thrilling contests over the past 12 months, the performances of our champions, and the steady emergence of fine young prospects.

A top Commissioner from the United States joined me at ringside recently as championship boxing returned to the magnificent Royal Albert Hall, and he told me how much he envies us just at the moment. "You have so many fine young fighters who really want to entertain and your matchmakers put together so many exciting domestic contests".

I agree, but I wish promoters would give more thought to the standard of opponents they import from abroad. Despite all the restrictions the Board has imposed, and the way we vet visitors before they arrive, I am still disappointed. Of course there are exceptions, but we may have to toughen up even more to make these contests at least competitive.

But where blows this wind you ask? Hopefully, in the initiative that the British Board has started, to standardise both the boxing rules and the medical and safety regulations. The Board has circulated the State commissions, national federations and championship organisations of the world seeking copies of their rules and regulations.

These will be placed on computer by a British research team and a comparative study produced. It is the hope of the Board that this will lead within two years to a world conference of professional boxing when we hope agreement can be reached for the sport to be officiated in exactly the same way for all international boxing.

If this leads on to a world controlling body then one of my own great ambitions will have been achieved. Even a year ago I would have pushed this dream aside as naive and

impossible, but so many world figures in boxing have offered support and encouragement, I believe that before we move into the 21st Century boxing could have an organisation in place along the same lines as FIFA in football. I must stress, this is not an attempt to create yet another world championship organisation – there are far too many of those already.

Here in Britain, one of the most exciting contests we have seen for years was marred when Gerald McClellan from the United States collapsed in the ring after his defeat by Nigel Benn at the London Arena in February and needed brain surgery. The reaction of the Board's medical team was widely praised and, after surgery by Mr John Sutcliffe at the Royal London Hospital, McClellan's life was saved. Now he is home in the United States, we wish him well and hope his recovery continues.

The Board's work continues behind the scenes in many areas. Boxers have a new accident insurance policy in place which they can supplement individually, the boxer/manager contract has been revised and the Board's medical system is under review. There remains much to do, with a great deal depending on boxing people realising this and doing their utmost to keep British boxing the envy of the world in so many ways.

Sporting Club

LONSDALE

INTERNATIONAL

THE LONSDALE INTERNATIONAL SPORTING CLUB

President: The Earl Grey
Vice-President: Lord Addington
Patrons: Reg Gutteridge, OBE (UK); Tom Pendry, MP (UK);
                  Angelo Dundee (USA); Thomas Hauser (USA);
                  Kepler Wessels (SA); Joe Koizumi (Japan)

The club is now accepting applications for membership for the new season. If you are interested in becoming a member of the world's No. 1 boxing fan club please contact the club administrator.

Join us on 2nd November 1995 at Madison Square Garden (in The Hall of Fame Banqueting Suite) to honour Leroy Neiman in the presence of the New York State Athletic Commissioner, Floyd Patterson, and many past and present boxing champions worldwide.

The club fixture list is complete until March 1997.

Office address: 21 Beak Street, London W1R 3LB.
                  Tel: 0171 434 1741   Fax: 0171 734 2094

British Boxing Board of Control Awards

The Awards, inaugurated in 1984, in the form of statuettes of boxers, and designed by Morton T. Colver, the manufacturer of the Lonsdale Belt, are supplied by Len Fowler Trophies of Holborn. Len was an early post-war light-heavyweight favourite. Right from the start, the winners have been selected by an Award's Committee, which currently comprises John Morris, Simon Block, Frank Butler OBE, Bill Martin, Doctor Adrian Whiteson OBE, Ray Clarke OBE, and Barry J. Hugman, the editor of the *British Boxing Yearbook*. For 1995, the Awards Ceremony, which is reverting back to a luncheon format, is due to be held this coming Autumn in London, and will be hosted by the Lonsdale International Sporting Club's Bernard Hart, the managing Director of Lonsdale Sports Equipment Ltd, and sponsor of the Awards.

British Boxer of the Year: The outstanding British Boxer at any weight. 1984: Barrry McGuigan. 1985: Barry McGuigan. 1986: Dennis Andries. 1987: Lloyd Honeyghan. 1988: Lloyd Honeyghan. 1989: Dennis Andries. 1990: Dennis Andries. 1991: Dave McAuley. 1992: Colin McMillan. 1993: Lennox Lewis. 1994: Steve Robinson.

British Contest of the Year: Although a fight that took place in Europe won the 1984 Award, since that date, the Award, presented to both participants, has applied to the best all-action contest featuring a British boxer in a British ring. 1984: Jimmy Cable v Said Skouma. 1985: Barry McGuigan v Eusebio Pedroza. 1986: Mark Kaylor v Errol Christie. 1987: Dave McAuley v Fidel Bassa. 1988: Tom Collins v Mark Kaylor. 1989: Michael Watson v Nigel Benn. 1990: Orlando Canizales v Billy Hardy. 1991: Chris Eubank v Nigel Benn. 1992: Dennis Andries v Jeff Harding. 1993: Andy Till v Wally Swift Jnr. 1994: Steve Robinson v Paul Hodkinson.

Overseas Boxer of the Year: For the best performance by an overseas boxer in a British ring. 1984: Buster Drayton. 1985: Don Curry. 1986: Azumah Nelson. 1987: Maurice Blocker. 1988: Fidel Bassa. 1989: Brian Mitchell. 1990: Mike McCallum. 1991: Donovan Boucher. 1992: Jeff Harding. 1993: Crisanto Espana. 1994: Juan Molina.

Special Award: Covers a wide spectrum, and is an appreciation for services to boxing. 1984: Doctor Adrian Whiteson. 1985: Harry Gibbs. 1986: Ray Clarke. 1987: Hon. Colin Moynihan. 1988: Tom Powell. 1989: Winston Burnett. 1990: Frank Bruno. 1991: Muhammad Ali. 1992: Doctor Oswald Ross. 1983: Phil Martin. 1994: Ron Olver.

Sportsmanship Award: This Award recognises boxers who set a fine example, both in-and-out of the ring. 1986: Frank Bruno. 1987: Terry Marsh. 1988: Pat Cowdell. 1989: Horace Notice. 1990: Rocky Kelly. 1991: Wally Swift Jnr. 1992: Duke McKenzie. 1993: Nicky Piper. 1994: Francis Ampofo.

Steve Robinson (right), who won the 1994 "British Boxer of the Year" Award, poses with Ron Olver, the winner of the "Special" Award
Tony Fitch

Insure You Keep Your Guard Up

Insurance Brokers and Insurance Consultants to the:-
British Boxing Board of Control, Football Association,
F.A. Premier League, Football League, British Olympic Association,
Professional Board Sailors Association, Cricketer's Association,
Spanish Basketball Association, St Moritz Tobogganing Club.

Windsor is one of the world's largest specialist sports, leisure and entertainment brokers, servicing national sports associations, leagues, clubs and players throughout the U.K., Europe, and North America.

While Personal Accident forms the major part of our sports related business, the group can also offer many other types of insurance cover, including Stadium Risks, Commercial Fire, High-Risk Liability, Professional Indemnity, Marine and Aviation - at highly competitive rates.

For sponsors and event organisers we offer wide experience of contingency risks such as Event Cancellation/Abandonment, Prize Indemnity, Death and Disgrace, Bonus Protection, and other insurance-protected sponsorship enhancements and marketing initiatives.

A separate group company provides consultancy on Life Assurance, Group Pensions and Personal Financial Planning.

Windsor Insurance Brokers Ltd

Lyon House, 160/166 Borough High Street, London SE1 1JR
Tel: 0171 - 407 7144 Fax: 0171 - 378 6676 Telex: 889360
For further infomation ring Jonathan Ticehurst on:
+44(0)171 - 407 7144

Boxing and the Need for Insurance

by Jonathan Ticehurst (Managing Director Sports Division of Windsor Insurance Brokers Ltd)

To all of us in the insurance industry, our clients are of paramount importance. But, in our case, not only are they important, they are also in the public eye – because our speciality is professional sports and, in particular, boxing.

Boxing is, of course, a national sport, enjoyed at amateur level through schools and clubs by thousands of people and watched at top professional level by millions worldwide through the eyes of television.

How many of us see claims, or potential claims, occurring on television, or read about them in the papers before we get to the office? Millions have seen both promising, mature and lucrative careers ended in a matter of seconds as we have watched late night title fights and supporting bouts from our sitting room chairs.

Many people might wonder how such a direct contact sport can possibly qualify for Accident and Injury insurance cover. The answer lies in the definition of "injury" and the definition of "disablement". For many years, the British Boxing Board of Control has provided and paid for a Personal Accident Policy for every one of its licensed boxers. This includes overseas boxers who have acquired a temporary licence for the purposes of fighting in this country in specific bouts. Traditionally, that policy provided cover for death, blindness, deafness and loss of limbs or parts of limbs whilst the licensed boxer was in the ring or climbing into or out of the ring.

Windsor have been managing the insurance affairs of the world of professional football and cricket for 20 years or more. During this time, various policies have paid out millions of pounds against claims by the national associations, the leagues, the clubs and counties, in respect of players who have gone out of the game early through injury. Some names you will only remember, others you may well have seen or, in early days, even played with, like Ian Storey-Moore, Steve Coppell, Gary Bailey, Alan Brazil, John O'Neill, Norman Whiteside, Gary Stevens, Siggi Jonsson, Mick McCarthy, Paul Elliott, John Fashanu, "Syd" Lawrence, Paul Downton, Nigel Felton, Rodney Ontong and many others.

It was, perhaps, no surprise, therefore, that the Board should turn to Windsor in the course of its review of the insurance cover which has been available historically for boxers. The London insurance market is nothing if not imaginative and when brokers who are experts in their field put their heads together with underwriters who have made it their business to specialise in a particular class of insurance worldwide, then almost anything is possible at an affordable premium. The result was that the Board has now been able to include within their policy the all-important additional cover of Permanent & Total Disablement.

Experience has taught us that where an association, a federation, or affinity body takes out insurance for the benefit of its membership, then any individual member who needs additional or more wide-ranging cover for his own particular needs, should be able to buy his or her own cover as an extension to the group cover. That is what happens in football, cricket and many other sports. The Board's policy provides basic benefits for its licensed members and, although the benefits could not be, and, as is generally known, was never intended to be, regarded as a "retirement fund", the policy is a very important starting point.

The Professional Boxers' Association recognised the hard work and imagination that the Board put into their new policy and were quick to endorse its value to all their members. Perhaps, more importantly, the PBA then worked closely with Windsor in designing tailor-made additional insurance cover which could be purchased, through their association, by members individually.

It is an ideal arrangement. The British Boxing Board of Control, through their own funds, are providing a general benefit for all their licensed boxers which can act as a platform for individual members to buy top-up cover, at their own expense, to suit their own particular requirements and financial obligations. The insurance wraps itself around the actual business of boxing and those in it and responds directly to the risks associated with it. It may be marginally more expensive than "off the shelf" Accident & Injury policies, but then "off the shelf" policies will not respond to the peculiarities and the particular risks associated with a sport having such pugnacious characteristics.

Between them, the Board and the PBA have taken a giant leap forward for the benefit of all professional boxers. We, at Windsor, are happy that another high profile professional sport has the protection from the insurance market that it needs and deserves.

Hand in glove

Boxing & Sky Sports
the biggest fights on the box
call Sky
now on 0990 123 123

SKY
NO TURNING BACK

Sky Sports, Boxing – "Bottom"!

by Roger Moody (Deputy Head of Sky Sports)

Two hundred years ago, Michael Brander, in his book "The Georgian Gentleman", reminds us that the 18th century was a transitional age for sport between the primitive methods of bygone ages and the more sophisticated methods and ideas of the 19th century.

Today, almost on the eve of the millennium, we find ourselves, yet again, in a period of major change within the sporting world.

Rugby Union has thrown off its dubious cloak of amateurism; the code's 100-year-old offspring, Rugby League, changes, at least in England, from a winter sport to a summer sport in the guise of the "Super League"; football has already seen the breakaway of the Premier League and cricket has succumbed to its alternative World Series and coloured clothing.

All, I believe, for the better, but what about your sport? What about boxing? Is it in a transitional stage and, if so, for better or worse? Far more qualified followers of the noble art can answer better than I the questions that all of us – promoters, managers, matchmakers, referees, trainers, governing bodies, fight fans, press and television, and, of course, the boxers themselves – should perhaps give a little more thought to.

Do we really need so many different championships at the same weight – indeed, do we need so many weights? Should the few well-to-do in the business get richer and the many less well off continue to struggle? Must fighters, even when psyching themselves up for a bout, threaten to "kill" opponents, or allegedly use hypnosis, or brawl in dirty puddles in pre-fight press conferences? Should rings be bigger or smaller, gloves lighter or heavier; headguards obligatory; rounds shorter or longer; championships with less rounds or more; or fights taking place when the boxers' body clocks say they are peaking and not at the demand of other forces? Does the sport need the supposed fan who runs amuck inside the arena? A better policy for encouraging the young and talented? More direction from the top and more enthusiasm at the bottom?

If all this seems a little heavy it is because the sport cannot afford to let itself fall behind the changes that are taking place in the wider arena of the cricket pitch, the soccer field, or the rugby ground.

And so to a world I know marginally better and one, too, that is going through massive changes – the world of television.

With really only four "conventional" channels – two BBC, two commercial – until the late '80s, broadcasting in the United Kingdom was dragging its heels behind continental Europe and light years behind America.

The last half decade has seen a massive explosion, not only in television choice but also in production techniques and standards, certainly as far as sport is concerned. The additional channels offered by satellite and cable operators have forced the old guard to realise that it should move with the times or be left behind forever.

There is no question that if the sports fan does not subscribe to "Sky Sports" he's being denied the best action – live Premier League, FA Cup and International soccer games; live overseas cricket tours; live club championship rugby union and rugby league; live golf, including the Ryder Cup; tennis, darts, snooker, motorbikes . . . the list is endless. And, of course, live Benn, Eubank, Bruno, Nassem, Collins, Lewis and, equally important, the up-and-coming fighters on the British undercards, as well as fascinating overseas action with Tyson, Holyfield, Jones, Whittaker, and so on.

Television and boxing are made for each other. The game pulls fighters from all walks of life and television is in everyone's home. Boxing is hard and sometimes unforgiving but is essentially entertainment – and entertainment is what "Sky Sports" is all about.

Do we need the Harley Davidson entries? The fireworks, lasers and pulsating music? Should cameramen stare up from every angle, replays expose every weakness, microphones grab every sound? Well why not!

Years ago, I was stopped from putting cameras in the corners during rounds because a handful of spectators allegedly had a slightly obstructed view; ring walks started on a promoter's whim rather than on a cue from live television when really it didn't matter a few seconds here or there and corner microphones were definitely de rigeuer. How things have changed.

And the fighters themselves – what about them? Superb athleticism is not enough. They must be entertainers, performers, personalities and, thankfully, most of them are. I grovelled at the feet of Ali on his Ovaltine tour as a radio reporter in the Midlands in the '70s just to coax the great Muhammad to rhyme Birmingham with "then you'll know who I am"; bulged with pride at walking out with McGuigan to the Wembley ringside at the Bruno v Witherspoon fight; marvelled at Las Vegas world heavyweight title show-downs – and I don't even specialise in your game.

So what of the future? Well, there is going to be a lot more of you and us – boxing and television. Could there be a boxing channel? Who knows! There is certainly enough old footage to run and re-run time and again, let alone hundreds of big and small time fights taking place every year. Could there be the opportunities for the viewer to select his camera shots and not the television director? Will the armchair fight fan – in his new high tech television sitting room – flick a switch and watch bouts of *his* choice at almost a moments notice? Could he feel the punches, smell the fear, fight the fight? All is possible, most of it probable. After all this is the age of virtual reality.

What we all need – boxing and television – is more "Bottom". Bottom, our "Georgian Gentleman" scribe tells us, was an alternative term for courage in those far off days. "It was a virile age," writes Michael Brander, "when the weakest went to the wall and 'Bottom' was an essential quality in survival".

The toast then, gentlemen, is – to "Bottom"!

CHARLIE MAGRI SPORTS

345 BETHNAL GREEN ROAD
LONDON E2 6LG
TEL: 0171-739-9035
FAX: 0171-729-2515

LONDON'S BIGGEST STOCKIST OF BOXING EQUIPMENT

TOP
TEN

adidas®

RINGSIDE

FOR ALL YOUR BOXING REQUIREMENTS. WE HAVE SOMETHING TO SUIT EVERYBODY FROM AMATEUR THROUGH TO TOP PROFESSIONALS

Charlie Magri: The Saviour of British Flyweights

by Ralph Oates

It may be the smallest professional boxing poundage on our shores, as recognised by the British Boxing Board of Control, but the flyweights have given Britain more world title claimants than any other weight division (18 in total - role of honour: Sid Smith, Bill Ladbury, Percy Jones, Tancy Lee, Joe Symonds, Jimmy Wilde, Johnny Hill, Jackie Brown, Benny Lynch, Peter Kane, Jackie Paterson, Rinty Monaghan, Terry Allen, Walter McGowan, Charlie Magri, Duke McKenzie, Dave McAuley and Pat Clinton). Indeed, a number of years ago, Britain dominated this weight category in much the same way as the American's rule the heavyweights today. We even produced the first man to gain recognition as world champion in the able shape of Sid Smith and can proudly lay claim to producing two really great champions in Welshman, Jimmy Wilde, and Scotland's Benny Lynch.

What an exciting prospect it would have been had Wilde and Lynch boxed in the same era, since a meeting between the two would most certainly have produced a classic encounter of breathtaking proportions. The big question being of course, who would have won? Well it would be tough attempting to pick a victor from such a pairing, just like it would be trying to predict a winner from a Joe Louis-Muhammad Ali contest or a Rocky Marciano-Joe Frazier match. You constantly come up with a good argument for either man winning on the night.

In truth, we will never really know for certain. We can only imagine the results of such pairings based on the evidence of the respective boxer's record and, even then, such findings are often inconclusive. All we can be sure of is that both Wilde and Lynch were magnificent fighters, who greatly enhanced the reputation of the British flyweight. However, despite our record of past flyweight success, it appeared that the 1970s would be the final decade for the poundage, which was created in England in 1910. It seemed that the division was set to follow the trail of the dinosaur into extinction. Fighters from the Orient and South America, who had always been a force, started to make an even bigger impact. The active British flyweight was becoming a truly rare species, and at the time one would have been most hard pressed to have found four boxers in the domestic ratings.

The then British champion, John McCluskey, from Scotland, won the Lonsdale Belt outright on 14 October 1974 with a one round stoppage over his challenger, Tony Davies, from Wales. The contest which took place at Swansea, looked like being the very last domestic title fight at the weight. There just were not any more challengers for McCluskey to defend against. It looked very likely that the division would be abolished when the champion decided to retire. However, McCluskey did not hang up his gloves until 1977 and in that very same year a glimmer of hope emerged. A young man by the name of Charlie Magri, with an excellent amateur pedigree (1974 ABA light-flyweight champion and 1975, 1976 & 1977 ABA flyweight title holder), turned professional under top manager, Terry Lawless. Even before throwing his first punch in the paid ranks, Magri looked as if he was the fighter with the class to keep the division alive.

Charlie's first contest without the amateur vest took place on 25 October 1977 against Neil McLaughlin and he made short work of his opponent, when blasting him out in two rounds. The little dynamo from Stepney, by way of Tunisia, was wasting no time at all in breathing new life into a division, which, at one time, appeared to have less chance of survival than a fly caught in a spiders web. His second pro fight took place on 15 November 1977 against Bryn Griffiths, Charlie despatching his man in round two, giving further evidence of not only his boxing ability but his impressive punching power. Then amazingly, Magri was nominated to fight for the vacant British title in just his third contest.

The bout was to take place at the Albert Hall on 6 December 1977 against Dave Smith. While Charlie was the clear favourite to win the championship, the match was not considered a walk-over. Smith, who had taken part in his first professional contest on the 22 November 1976, knocking out Ray Dodd in the first round, was coming into the title fight undefeated in eight bouts. Dave was full of ambition and he was not going into the ring just to make up the numbers – he wanted to win. However, while Smith had the definite edge in professional experience, Magri clearly had the advantage in punching power. Smith had been held to a draw over eight rounds in his first meeting with Neil McLaughlin, before winning on a seven round retirement in a return bout, while Bryn Griffiths was outpointed over eight rounds by Smith soon after the McLaughlin encounters. Charlie of course terminated his bouts with both men in the second round.

On the night, Magri won the championship when a brave and game Smith was stopped in round seven, having given his all. But Magri had too much of everything for him, boxing and punching in a way which made it difficult to believe that he was having just his third contest in the pro ranks. The performance confirmed the view of many that here was a man with the potential to go all the way to the top of the flyweight ladder and thus put the domestic division back on the international map. A few sceptic's took the side of caution, with the opinion that it was too early and a little foolish to make such grandiose claims for a fighter with so few fighting miles on the professional clock. There was also the factor that many of the ranked fighters in the world's top ten were really tough individuals, some of whom looked as if they could punch holes in a brick wall with ultimate ease.

However, all agreed that 21-year-old Magri was more than entitled to enjoy his moment of glory as the first English holder of the British eight stone title since Terry

Allen, who retired in 1954. Thereafter, the crown passed to Welshman, Dai Dower, Scotland's Frankie Jones and Ireland's John Caldwell, before it went back to Scotland with Jackie Brown, then Walter McGowan and finally, John McCluskey. So an English holder of the championship was well overdue. Charlie was now attracting his share of attention from both the public and the media, which of course in turn provided the flyweight division with a much needed boost. For so long, the domestic poundage had been overshadowed by the other weight divisions, but now it was again becoming a force to be reckoned on with an exciting champion who was fast becoming a box office magnet.

Terry Lawless was well aware that he had to pick Magri's future opponents with care, for while his charge was a British champion, he was still only a three fight professional novice with a great deal to learn, and the ring was the blackboard where the lessons could be very painful against the wrong kind of fighter. Matching a boxer is a precarious business to say the least. The standard of each opponent should improve very gradually, so, that over a period of time, the said boxer is able to gain experience against various styles and thus learn his trade thoroughly. When the time comes for the boxer to meet the best it is to be hoped that the lessons will have been well and truly learned and he will be able to defeat the opposition or, at the very least, trade with them on equal terms without looking out of his league. It is not just the defeat, but the way it is inflicted.

Too many bouts over soft and past their best fighters, create a false impression and often produces an undefeated record of no real substance, which does not stand up to close scrutiny. In many ways this can be "Fools Gold", since the record may lead to a world title shot, but the end result can be a devastating defeat from which the boxer may never recover career wise. There is also the danger of being over ambitious by matching your boxer against an opponent who he is not yet ready for. Once again, a bad defeat can destroy his confidence for all-time. So making the right fight for your boxer is like walking a minefield without directions, one wrong move and everything can blow up in your face.

In 1978, Charlie had six bouts, winning five inside the distance. Spain's Manuel Carrasco was the first man to take him the full distance of eight rounds and although he lost clearly enough, he made Charlie work for the points, in putting up a good show.

Magri won his first two bouts in 1979 inside the distance, then it was time to step up in class, the European Boxing Union nominating him to challenge Italy's Franco Udella. Udella was a classy boxer who had put his name in the record books by becoming the first WBC world light-flyweight champion (7st 10lbs). This historic event took place on 4 April 1975, the Italian winning the vacant crown with a disqualification in round 12 over opponent, Valentin Martinez, in Milan.

Udella's success at the weight was short lived when, in August of the same year, the World Boxing Council stripped him of the title, due to his failure to defend against the then number one contender, Rafael Lovera. Franco had won the vacant European flyweight title on 25 October 1974, knocking out Pedro Molledo of Spain in round five. The defence against Magri would be the ninth by the Italian, who was, without doubt, the most experienced fighter the British boxer had met to-date and would prove a stern test.

On the night of 1 May 1979, much to the delight of the fans at Wembley, Udella became a former champion, when Charlie boxed his way to a 12 round points decision. 32-year-old Franco fought well enough, but he did not have the necessary ammunition in his gloves to contain his younger challenger. During a career which started in 1972, Udella had taken part in 42 bouts prior to his meeting with Magri. He had even challenged for the WBC flyweight crown in 1974 against world champion, Betulio Gonzalez, the contest ending in a ten round stoppage defeat for the Italian. However, this was by no means a disgrace for Udella, since Gonzalez was an outstanding title-holder who, during the course of his career, held both versions of the championship, the WBC and WBA.

There was no doubt that Udella was a genuine world class fighter and the victory by Magri in just his 12th contest was a remarkable achievement. Charlie had also become the first British-European flyweight champion since Dai Dower, who had both won and lost the crown in 1955. Men like Derek Lloyd, Walter McGowan and John McCluskey (three times) had challenged and failed to bring the continental crown back to these shores. Magri was doing an excellent revival job with the domestic division and he was fast becoming a major player amongst the world's top flyweights.

During the following months, he kept active, having three bouts, all of which ended inside the scheduled distance, before making the first defence of the European title. The challenger was a former opponent, Manuel Carrasco, who had taken Magri the full distance of eight rounds. Since that occasion, the Spaniard had challenged and failed in a previous bid for the EBU title against Franco Udella, losing a 12 round points decision.

On 4 December, Carrasco boxed well against Magri, showing both courage and resistance to the heavy blows which came his way with constant regularity, but, at the end of the 12 round contest, the Englishman was still the champion of Europe. At least, the challenger had the satisfaction of going the distance with a fighter whose reputation as a puncher was growing daily.

Many fans were now calling for Charlie to challenge for a world title but the question had to be asked, was the European champion really ready to tackle title-holders', Luis Ibarra (WBA) and Chan-Hee Park (WBC), after just 16 bouts! So many past events had shown that there was often a huge gulf in class between European and world title-holders. To rush in too quickly could be counter-productive at this stage and there were signs that, despite his good performances, Charlie still had a few more moves to learn before going up against the big guns of the division. It seemed good sense to wait just a little longer for his championship chance.

Charlie opened his account in January 1980 with a three round knockout over Aniceto Vargas, followed by a second defence of the EBU title in June against Giovanni Camputaro. The Italian was brushed aside in three rounds by Charlie, a performance that confirmed that he was head and shoulders above the flyweights in Europe.

Next came Alberto Lopez, a former WBA flyweight champion from Panama. This was an interesting match for Magri, since Lopez had exchanged punches with many of the best in the world at the weight and was clearly no pushover. During the September contest, Lopez revealed the class and the various skills which had taken him to the very top, but Magri fought with great gusto and was always one or two paces in front of the former world champion, taking a deserved ten round points decision. The victory over Lopez further cemented his position in the world top ten.

Charlie destroyed his next opponent Enrique Castro inside a round in October, but, while that bout was exceptionally easy, the next contest was to prove the exact opposite.

Argentina's Santos Benigno Laciar, a talented fighter, was signed to meet Magri in a contest which was to take place in December. Laciar, who had his first professional contest in 1976, would be taking part in his 49th bout against Magri, having won 37, drawn seven and lost four, and had yet to be stopped. The 21-year-old ironman had won both the Argentinian and South American flyweight titles, so his credentials were more than adequate for the task which lay ahead of him.

The contest proved to be an excellent encounter between two ambitious and talented boxers, who would not give an inch to each other during the course of battle – the ring was an out-and-out war zone. Although both gladiators gave their all and deserved every penny of their respective purses, at the end of the ten rounds, Magri's weary arm was raised in victory to take his undefeated record to 21 bouts. The encounter against Laciar had been difficult, and had tested Charlie to the full, but, to his credit, he proved his mettle and came through over the most dangerous opponent he had faced.

Later events confirmed the worth of Magri's victory over Laciar, when, in his second contest of 1981, the Argentinian travelled to South Africa to challenge Peter Mathebula for the WBA flyweight title. Mathebula had won the championship in December 1980, outpointing Tae-Shik Kim over 15 rounds in Los Angeles, and on the surface his defence against Laciar looked to be a safe one.

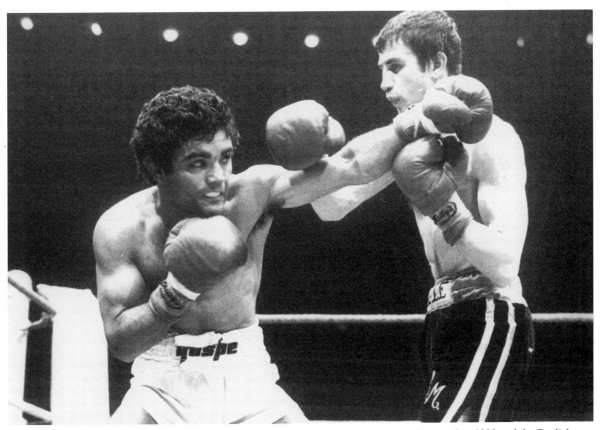

According to Charlie, Santos Laciar (left) was his toughest opponent. The pair met on 8 December 1980 and the Englishman took the "nod" after ten hard-fought rounds

19

However, the fans in Soweto watched in shock as the crown changed hands on 28 March, the referee stepping in to stop the bout in Laciar's favour during round seven. From this point the Argentinian went on to become one of the better champions at the weight, making a number of defences during his reign. There was some speculation for a time that Magri might get a shot at Laciar's newly won championship, but for various reasons the fight did not come off. Such is the oddity of boxing, that it was the loser and not the victor who went on to get a crack at a world title.

Charlie was now marking time, waiting for his golden opportunity to contest a version of the world championship and, in order to maintain his position in the ratings, he had to stay active and keep punch sharp. Ring rust can be just as damaging to a boxer's career as an opponents left-hook.

His first contest in 1981 was an EBU title defence in the month of February against Spain's Enrique Rodriguez Cal. The proceedings, which took place at the Albert Hall, came to an abrupt end in round two, with the referee's intervention. Magri had made a successful defence of his crown without even raising a sweat and, at this moment in time, it appeared that he was now light years ahead of all the other flyweights in Europe.

At Wembley in June, Charlie indulged in a routine bout, knocking out Jose Herrera in just one round. He now had the confident look of a genuine world title contender, his boxing and punching ability making him a real threat to the top men in the division. The fans were now talking in terms of – not if Charlie wins the world title, but when he wins the world title.

Single-handedly, Magri had made the British flyweight division a commodity of both value and respect, and it was now quite noticeable that the weight class was slowly beginning to increase in number. It was, as if the various amateurs who boxed at the weight, had been inspired by his success and could see that there could be a future among the eight stone men in the professional ranks, even in these days of heavyweight obsession. Charlie had given a vital transfusion to a division which was close to death and it was now obvious that the poundage had well and truly responded to treatment. On 6 August, he decided to relinquish his British title, while maintaining his grip on the European crown.

Bout number 24 took place on 13 October against Juan Diaz, a fighter who was not expected to give him any undue problems. Yet a stunning upset occurred, as the Mexican handed Charlie his first defeat in the professional ranks, knocking him out inside six rounds. Up to that stage of the contest the British fighter had taken a commanding points lead. This was a serious set-back for a man who was on the verge of a world title challenge.

Charlie did not box again until 2 March 1982, his opponent being Cipriano Arreola. Winning the ten round points decision he followed that up in April with a third round stoppage against Ron Cisneros.

Then, just as it was beginning to look as if the Diaz defeat was no-more than an aberration, a fluke to be written off as just one of those things, disaster struck once again.

This time his career looked in tatters, as Jose Torres stopped him in nine rounds at Wembley in the month of May. It now seemed that his chance of ever becoming a world champion was, to say the least, remote. Many critics were now claiming that Magri did not have the durability to take on the top men in the division. He could hand out punishment. But just couldn't take it.

The golden future was tarnished – the dream, it seemed, was over and Charlie did not put the gloves on again for battle until September when ordered to defend his EBU title against a former opponent, Enrique Rodriguez Cal.

On the surface, this contest may have appeared to be a pointless exercise, but Enrique had earned his second chance at the title, having outpointed Welshman, Kelvin Smart, over 12 rounds of a final eliminator. Smart, in his very next bout won the British crown which had been vacated by Magri, when he knocked out Dave George, also from Wales, in six rounds. For the defence against Cal, Magri had to travel abroad for the first time in his professional career, the place of combat being Aviles in Spain. While Charlie was able to handle the Spaniard with no problems what-so-ever in their first meeting, how would he fare fighting in the other man's backyard, where an opponent had all the advantages. Certainly, he would not be given any favours in a bout he had to win to keep his career alive. Although he had to be favoured, even away from home, there was a nagging doubt at the back of the mind, in that coming back from a bad defeat, the psychological effect on him could prove to be a crucial factor during the heat of battle. Enrique was also now aware that the man he was crossing gloves with could be hurt and stopped.

However, just when his back was against the ropes career-wise, Charlie once again produced the old magic, defeating the Spanish fighter by a knockout in two rounds. At the same time he again proved that he had the punch to put almost anyone away if catching them right. Magri was not yet ready to surrender his throne of Europe. On the continent he was still the king.

The victory over Cal may not have sent shock waves through the world of boxing, but it was clear confirmation that the flame of desire and ambition still burnt with a warrior's passion inside the Londoner's heart. At the same time he became the first British flyweight to make four official successive defences of the European title. Not surprisingly, Charlie left Spain with his fighting stock far higher than when he first arrived. The big question now being what next?

That was soon answered when, in the following November, Charlie had the chance of revenge when a return bout was arranged with his former conqueror, Jose Torres. It was said that if Charlie won he would be given a shot at the world title, while a defeat would finally put an end to his championship aspirations at world level. On a night filled with both tension and dire apprension, Magri fought his way to a well deserved ten round points decision over the Mexican, to put him on the road to a world championship challenge.

The chance for Charlie to rule the world came on 15 March 1983, against the WBC champion, Eleoncio Mercedes, of the Dominican Republic. Mercedes had won the title when outpointing Freddie Castillo over 15 rounds in Los Angeles on 6 November 1982, but while his record indicated that he could be beaten, a Magri victory was by no means a foregone conclusion.

The Dominican was a well schooled boxer who knew his way around the ring and would be able to exploit any weakness in the British fighter's defence and durability. Even with the help of the partisan fans cheering him on at Wembley, the Englishman had a difficult night ahead of him. The contest itself made history to some degree since it was the first World Boxing Council flyweight title fight to be held over the new distance of 12 rounds, rather than the traditional 15.

The atmosphere was electric as the bell sounded to start round one and, if the challenger had any self-doubts or nerves on this, the biggest occasion of his fighting life, they didn't show. Magri was relentless as he pushed forward, driving the champion back with an assortment of punches to both head and body. Yet it was not all one-way traffic. Mercedes, a clever boxer, dished out his share of punishment in a contest which was full of excitement and drama. In round seven the bout was all over when the referee stopped the battle, with the champion's left-eye being too badly cut for him to continue. With the result, his number one fan, the irrepressible Joe Meade, made his own presentation to Charlie, a privately commissioned cup already inscribed to Charlie Magri: World Flyweight Champion.

Charlie had made it in his 30th contest, he was the world flyweight champion. He was also the first British boxer to hold this title since Scotland's Walter McGowan, who won and lost the championship in 1966. A British flyweight was once again on top of the world.

How much brighter the domestic scene now looked when compared to the dull dismal early 1970s. There was Keith Wallace, who took the Commonwealth flyweight crown from defending champion, Steve Muchoki, with a ninth round stoppage. At the time many thought that Wallace also had the potential to go on and reach world level. Then there was British champion, Kelvin Smart, who was progressing at a steady rate. The British flyweight division was back with a bang, with Magri well and truly at the helm.

In Europe, Antoine Montero of France won the EBU title which had been vacated by Magri when Spain's Mariano Garcia retired in round eight. After enjoying all the well deserved praise and glory it was soon time for Magri to go back to work with a title defence.

The man to challenge Charlie was Frank Cedeno of the Philippines. While Cedeno was a worthy challenger, it was felt that Charlie would have a safe passage in his first defence.

However, on 27 September, Cedeno upset the odds and brought down the curtain on Magri's short reign when he stopped the champion in six rounds. It seemed so hard to believe that after overcoming all the obstacles and setbacks to win the title, such a defeat could happen. The fans who were expecting to see Charlie punch his way to an inside the distance victory were shocked at the spectacle they had just witnessed. The world title had once again left British hands.

Charlie didn't box again until the following year when he travelled to Cagliari, Italy, to meet Franco Cherchi for the vacant European title. The contest was to take place on 24 August 1984. Frenchman, Antoine Montero, who had made two successful title defences against Italy's Giovanni Camputaro, and Britain's Keith Wallace, had been stripped of the crown because he was unable to defend in the time stipulated by the European Boxing Union.

If anyone had been of the view that Magri was a spent force ready for the taking they were mistaken. Charlie stopped Cherchi in the first round, when the Italian received a badly cut left-eye. Magri thus became the first Briton to regain the EBU flyweight title. Once again, when the chips were down, Charlie had come through with a victory which kept him amongst the contenders and, in so doing, continued to boost the reputation of the British flyweight.

Charlie later relinquished the European crown without defending it. Then another chance developed for him to have one more bite at the golden apple when he was given an opportunity to challenge for the world crown. Charlie had regained his EBU title, could he possibly go one step further and regain the world championship!

The odds were stacked heavily against it. Since taking the WBC crown from Magri, Cedeno had lost it to Japan's Koji Kobayashi, who was followed in rapid succession by Mexico's Gabriel Bernal and Thailand's Sot Chitalada.

Chitalada was a "bit" special, having won the world championship in just his eighth professional contest with a 12 round points decision over Bernal on 8 October 1984 in Bangkok. His bout against Magri would be his ninth and also his first defence. The champion had lost just once and that was in his fifth contest when he was outpointed over 12 rounds by the Korean, Jung-Koo Chang, when duly challenging for the WBC light-flyweight title in 1984.

While Magri made an aggressive start on the night of 20 February 1985, Chitalda proved to be much too strong and retained his crown when Charlie retired in round four. It was a disappointment for both Magri and his many fans, but there was no shame in defeat, since it was clear that the fighter from Thailand was destined to become one of the best world champions in the division.

Charlie did not resume his boxing career until 30 October. Once again the Briton had to travel to Italy to meet former rival, Franco Cherchi, who had won the vacant European flyweight crown after Charlie had relinquished it, when outpointing Frenchman Alain Limarola over 12 rounds on 27 February 1985. This was followed by a title defence on 4 August against Lorenzo Pacheco of Spain, which saw Cherchi retain the crown with a 12 round points decision.

Magri faced the Italian at the Sports Palace, Alessandria and proved once again that he was still the best flyweight in Europe when he knocked out Cherchi in round two. A certain amount of history was made in this contest, for Magri was the first man to regain the European flyweight title twice.

While Charlie had been fighting for world and European championships, a talented boxer by the name of Duke McKenzie had been making a certain amount of progress in the domestic ranks. The boxer from Croydon had been learning his trade both in Britain and in American rings, with bouts in places like Las Vegas, Los Angeles, Reno and Atlantic City. Then, in his 11th contest, he won the vacant British title when he stopped Danny Flynn in four rounds. For the first time in his professional career Charlie appeared to have a real challenger on the domestic front in McKenzie. The two fighters signed to meet on 20 May 1986 in a double championship battle.

Magri's European crown would be on the line against Duke's British title. Charlie was of course a former holder of the British championship, having relinquished the title in 1981 without making a single defence. A British champion cannot of course make a Lonsdale Belt his own property until he has achieved three title victories. However, Charlie had been allowed to keep the much valued and respected prize even though he only had one notch on the belt. This was made possible on the three year no available challengers rule. (Former WBC world champion, Walter McGowan, was also awarded the belt under the same circumstances).

The Magri v McKenzie confrontation was a match which prompted various opinions with regards to the eventual winner. Going into the contest, 23-year-old McKenzie was undefeated in 13 bouts, eight of them coming inside the distance. Duke was both fresh and full of ambition. However, would these attributes be enough to defeat the experienced former world title holder, who would be having his 35th contest.

At the age of almost 30 it was possible that Charlie's best fighting days were behind him. Yet he could still punch and it was generally felt that he would be at his most dangerous in the early rounds. If Duke could survive the early stages, he might well be able to defeat Charlie and thus become a double champion. So it was no surprise when Magri attacked from the first bell, throwing punches from every conceivable angle. A lesser man than McKenzie would have folded under the pressure, but the British champion showed strength of character by remaining cool and not getting drawn into a war.

Duke, a clever boxer, was able to avoid many of the blows which came his way and, at the same time, took those which landed without too much difficulty, before starting to land his own punches. In round five the contest was over. Charlie was sent down to the canvas for a count and upon rising to commence battle, his corner promptly retired him from the proceedings. Duke McKenzie had retained the British title, won the European championship and, in so doing, became the first British fighter in the professional ranks to defeat Magri. It was also the last time that Charlie appeared in the ring as a boxer, for he later retired with a record of 35 bouts – 30 wins, with just five defeats.

Without a doubt, it was a sad occasion, since it heralded the end of an era – the end of a fighting man who was for so long the mainstay of the British flyweight division. In fact he was the British flyweight division. Yet, if Charlie had to bow out of the business with a defeat, then there was no disgrace in losing to Duke McKenzie, who later went on to win world titles in three different weight divisions (IBF flyweight, WBO bantamweight and WBO super-bantamweight).

Recently, on behalf of the British Boxing Board of Control Yearbook, I arranged to meet Charlie and his wife Jackie at their sports shop, which is situated in Bethnal Green Road. Charlie and Jackie have now been married for 16 years and have been blessed with two children, Emma (13) and Charlie junior (9).

Upon my conversation with the former champion I was really astonished to learn that he has not yet received either an OBE or MBE. Surely this is an injustice to a man who did so much for the sport of boxing, in both the amateur and professional ranks. Let us hope this situation is soon corrected and Charlie is awarded the medal which would mean so very much to him. It is an honour which is so very long overdue. Charlie also pointed out that his winning of the British flyweight crown in just his third contest deserved a mention in the Guinness Book of Records.

These days, he is kept busy, not only with his shop, but with his charity work. The former champion is also a boxing manager and trainer who would like to take a fighter to the world flyweight championship.

When looking back at his fine career, Charlie has no hesitation in stating that former WBA flyweight and WBC super-flyweight champion, Santos Benigno Laciar, was his most difficult opponent. Of today's fighters, he names WBC super-middleweight champion, Nigel Benn, his favourite, with his all-action style. Of yesteryear the incredible hard-punching former world bantamweight and former WBA and WBC featherweight king, Ruben Olivares, from Mexico, rates number one with Charlie.

After saying goodbye to both Charlie and Jackie, I thought once more about the way the sinking 112 lb division had been salvaged by Magri and how healthy the poundage looks today, with 25 men recently rated by Boxing News, the trade paper. It appears that the flyweights are set to exist for many more years to come, with some fine competitors in the ranks. Hopefully, another Wilde, Lynch, McGowan or Magri, will emerge to once again put a British flyweight on top of the world. Thanks to Charlie Magri such an event is more than possible.

The Third Man in British Rings

by Bob Lonkhurst

Whatever the sport, officials at all levels come in for varying degrees of criticism and abuse. Whether it be football, cricket, or boxing, there are always plenty of "know-alls" ready to challenge the split-second decisions of the men in charge. Whilst a bad umpiring call can sometimes effect the balance of a cricket match, and a dubious penalty cause an injustice at football, a serious mis-judgement by a boxing referee could have fatal consequences. In the heat of battle when the fans are screaming at fever pitch, he is the one man who must keep his head and retain his concentration at all times.

Britain is one of the few countries within world boxing where the judging system doesn't operate. Instead, the referee not only controls the action in the ring, but acts as the sole judge in all contests except those under the rules of the European Boxing Union and various world governing bodies. Whether the three judges system is better or not is open to opinion, but followers of boxing will know that there have been countless occasions where two judges have scored conclusively in favour of one fighter, whilst the third saw it the other way.

Each judge sees the action from a fixed position at ringside, and unless a contest is very one-sided, differences in scoring will always occur. Consider the situation where a boxer is under heavy pressure and backed up against the ropes immediately above one judge. It is virtually impossible for that official to see which are scoring punches. The view of another judge may also be obscured by the referee as he moves closer to the action. This could occur several times during the course of a fight and thus lead to a variance in scoring. The referee, however, apart from being closest to the action, will always be in a better position to identify the scoring blows.

Every so often there are rumours that the judging system is being considered for Britain in order to fall in line with Europe and America. As long ago as December 1957, promoter Jack Solomons asked the Board of Control to try out the American system, where the referee and two judges scored a fight. Jack had a big show coming up at Harringay with Dick Richardson and Brian London meeting Americans, and considered it was an ideal occasion to test the system. The Board took the view that it would be turning the clock back, because years earlier they had condemned the system of refereeing from outside the ring which occurred prior to the 1930s.

The British system of the referee being the sole judge of a contest should always be maintained. Not only is "the third man" closest to the action, but he sees a fight from every conceivable angle. The majority of British referees favour this system and would oppose a move towards introducing judges.

Each referee must be the holder of a valid license issued by the British Boxing Board of Control and there are three grades of license:

CLASS "B": Referees who, following application, interviews, and practical and oral examinations, have satisfied the Board as to their competence and suitability to referee a contest not exceeding 24 minutes of actual boxing.

CLASS "A": Referees who have satisfied the Board through it's committees as to their competence and suitability to officiate in all contests, including those for Area championships, but excluding eliminators and contests for championships of Great Britain and Northern Ireland, the Commonwealth, Europe, and the world.

CLASS "A" STAR: Referees who have satisfied the Board through its committees, as to their competence and suitability to officiate in all or any contests.

Before being appointed, an applicant referee will be required to undergo practical tests both in and outside the ring. Once the Board are satisfied as to his competence and suitability, a provisional Class "B" license may be issued. Applications for upgrading must be made in the first instance to the Area Council of the referee concerned. All recommendations will be considered by the Referees' Committee before submission to the Board, but nothing shall prevent an Area Council making a recommendation to the committee on its own account.

Apart from having a sound knowledge of the sport, the boxing referee must be alert, quick-thinking, prompt, and decisive. It is important that he has a personality to gain the respect of the boxers and get them to accept that he is the man in charge.

Eugene Corri

23

Eugene Corri, a legend amongst British referees, once remarked, "The referee is a most important personage of the trio in the ring. Yet he must be the least conspicuous. An officious referee is a bad referee, not sometimes, but all the time." It was an accurate assessment because nothing incenses a boxing crowd more than a busy-body of a referee who won't let the action flow.

A stockbroker from Westcliffe on Sea, Eugene Corri was one of the most celebrated referees of all time. Apart from officiating in more than 1,000 fights, he claimed to have watched three times that number, and was the man largely responsible for Bombardier Billy Wells becoming a professional. His splendid career within boxing, which spanned more than 50 years, was highlighted in his books, "Thirty Years a Boxing Referee", "Refereeing a 1,000 Fights", "Gloves and the Man", and "Fifty Years in the Ring". The tremendous respect held for Corri within boxing circles was once highlighted by Lord Lonsdale when he said, "You have built up an international reputation as a referee. Your efficiency and your unstained integrity stand, and have always stood, above any suggestion of adverse criticism."

Apart from Corri, there were a number of good responsible officials at the turn of the century. Joe Palmer is believed to have refereed as many as 3,000 fights, whilst Mr Bernard "B. J." Angle officiated with great dignity for more than 40 years. In those early days, referees were engaged by the promoters as opposed to the modern day system where all officials are appointed by the British Boxing Board of Control.

Until about 1930, the "third man" invariably occupied a seat outside the ring beside the timekeeper. He only climbed through the ropes as a last resort if it was impossible to control the contestants at long range. To actually officiate within the ropes was in fact a practice very much frowned upon by the old National Sporting Club.

The standard of refereeing set by Eugene Corri at the turn of the century was an example for his successors to follow. They have done so with great credit, with the result that British referees are recognised today as being amongst the finest in the world. There have been a succession of highly respected men whose skills and understanding of the sport have been inherited from their predecessors. Before discussing some of our modern day officials, mention must therefore be made of some of the men who have kept the tradition going over the years, their skills and integrity combining to gain the respect of the fighters and fans alike.

Mr C. H. "Pickles" Douglas was a character known and respected by everyone in the sport and many outside it as well. Teddy Waltham held a referee's license from 1933 until 1950, when he surrendered it to take up the post of General Secretary of the British Boxing Board of Control; Pat Floyd, a three times ABA heavyweight champion, the first back in 1929, was one of the most loved and respected officials of all time; Moss Deyong refereed for over 30 years until retiring in 1951 at the age of 73; Bill Williams, a former RSM, was also a civil servant and school teacher outside the ring.

Andrew Smythe of Belfast, who always gave his fee to charity, handled top fights all over Britain and Europe in the 1950s and '60s, whilst Jack Smith of Manchester was highly respected, not only in Britain, but also in America during the 1930s. When Max Baer travelled to London in 1937 to meet Tommy Farr at Harringay, his manager, Ancil Hoffman, asked the Board of Control to appoint Jack as the referee because of his international reputation.

Mr C. B. Thomas of Porthcawl in fact took charge of the Farr v Baer fight, and was one of a long line of fine referees from Wales. Others included Ben Hardwicke of Tylorstown and Billy Moore of Penygraig who, between them, handled thousands of fights in the valleys back in the 1920s and '30s. More recently, the tradition has progressed through Ike Powell, James Brimmell, an "A" Star official who retired in 1985, and Adrian Morgan, who reached international status before his enforced retirement at the age of 65 in 1994.

Other top names of days gone by, include W. Barrington Dalby, Tommy Little, Jack Hart, Eugene Henderson and George Smith of Edinburgh, Frank Wilson of Glasgow, Wally Thom and Roland Dakin. More recently there were Harry Gibbs and Syd Nathan who, although forced to retire at 65, are still recognised by the European and World bodies, who continue to engage them as judges at title fights. Gibbs, a modern day Eugene Corri, has officiated all over the world, including Zambia, Ghana, Korea, Japan, Chile, North and South America, and the Philippines. The highlight of his career was undoubtedly when he was awarded the OBE "for services to boxing".

For some years the Board of Control have enforced a ruling which compels referees to relinquish their licenses upon reaching the age of 65. Yet it is a rule which confuses many followers of boxing because it has deprived the sport of some of its top officials whilst they were apparently still at their peak. Harry Gibbs and Syd Nathan are prime examples.

One alternative to the current rule would be to review referees every six months after they reached the age of 65. That, however, would leave the Board open to suggestions of bias and unfairness in the event of one official being allowed to continue, whilst another was not. Without doubt, the Board of Control have far greater responsibilities than the controlling bodies in many other sports. They cannot therefore take risks. If a referee's misjudgement was ever contributory to a boxer being seriously injured, the controlling body would have to assume ultimate responsibility.

As long ago as November 1950, the Board expressed concern about officials carrying on too long. When Moss Deyong refereed a fight at Leicester between Tommy Farr and Piet Wilde of Belgium, he counted Wilde out whilst in the act of rising. The controversial ending brought about ugly crowd scenes and resulted in an immediate Board enquiry. It was established that Deyong, who was 73-years-old, was in fact two seconds ahead of the timekeeper in his count, meaning that the Belgian actually got to his feet at "eight". Although Deyong was a top-class referee, the Board made a recommendation that all officials retired at 65.

Reg Thompson (centre), who has now retired, is seen here giving instructions to the fighters   Pennie Bracey

The most recent casualty of the retirement rule is Reg Thompson, a Southern Area referee since 1985. Having started boxing at the age of 14, when he was in the Sea Cadets, Reg had a total of 108 amateur contests. He won a Naval Cadet eight stone championship and later a Naval Command nine stone title. For most of his career he boxed for the Lynn Amateur Boxing Club in south-east London.

After hanging up his gloves, Reg became an ABA judge in 1954 and later graduated to an international class amateur referee. In 1985 he was granted a Board of Control license, permitting him to officiate in the professional ring. Born and raised in Clapham, Reg was introduced to boxing when he was just ten years old. A neighbour, who was a professional, was boxing on a show at the Snooker Hall in Clapham High Street and took Reg along. Despite his tender age, he fell in love with the sport and has been connected with it for 51 years.

During his days as an amateur official, Reg had occasion to disqualify a young boxer named Frank Maloney, who is now one of the countries leading promoters. One of Reg's last engagements was on a Maloney show at the Ipswich Corn Exchange, and to the amusement of the crowd and officials, the incident was referred to by the MC when announcing Reg's forthcoming retirement.

Away from boxing, Reg Thompson spent 12 years as a licensee in the Clapham and Walworth areas and worked as a casino manager with London clubs before taking early retirement in 1992. Reg has been a fine servant to boxing, and his enforced retirement through age is a great loss to the sport he loves.

Billy Rafferty of Glasgow did not reach retirement age because he sadly passed away suddenly in 1994 at the age of 61, while on a holiday cruise. After stopping off at Miami and going on a training run, he collapsed and died from a heart-attack. Billy had been the "third man" in many championship contests throughout Britain.

As a boxer, he lost just four of his 30 contests in a two year amateur career, and, despite failing to win a title, was a Scottish International. He turned professional in March 1956, and, when he retired in 1962, had lost six and drawn one of his 31 fights, but again a title had eluded him. Billy will always be remembered for his two epic contests with Freddie Gilroy for the British, European, and Empire bantamweight titles. The first was in Belfast in March 1960, but injuries to the Scotsman's ear and right-eye caused him to be stopped in the 13th round. In 1961, he beat George Bowes in a final eliminator for Gilroy's titles, and the pair met again in Belfast in March 1962. Again, Rafferty gave everything but was knocked out in the 12th round, in what was to be his last contest.

Following his retirement, Billy successfully applied to become a referee and was eventually promoted to Class "A" Star status in 1989. Outside the ring he was heavily involved in charity work and was a member of the Scottish Ex-Boxers' Association. He had a blacksmiths business in

Glasgow and a house at Stewarton, Ayrshire. Long may he be remembered.

John Coyle of Wolverhampton is currently one of the most respected British officials. He has been a Class "A" Star official for 13 years, reaching that status just nine years after being appointed a referee.

Born in 1938, John grew up at Greenford in Middlesex before moving to the midlands in 1964. At the time he was employed as a chief draughtsman with an engineering company, and the move provided him with an opportunity for promotion. It is a move he has never regretted because, despite being a "southerner", he loves the midlands and the people there.

John has enjoyed boxing ever since the early 1950s when his father took him to Harringay and Earls Court to see great fighters, including the likes of Freddie Mills. Although he never belonged to a boxing club, he had a limited number of fights at school and in the services whilst doing his National Service with the Royal Military Police.

After moving to the Midlands, John was a regular at shows promoted by Alex Griffiths and Reg King, and desperately wanted to become involved. His chance came in 1968 when he read an article in a local paper about Arthur Musson, who, at the time, was Midlands Area Secretary of the British Boxing Board of Control. There was mention that two Area referees, Mickey Fox and Chris Meggs, were approaching retirement, but no replacements were lined up. Becoming a referee appealed to John so he telephoned Musson and was offered an interview. He completed his first practical tests at the Midlands Sporting Club at Solihull in 1970, and since being appointed has not looked back.

Apart from refereeing dozens of British and Commonwealth title fights, John Coyle has been in charge of about 40 European title contests. At world level, he works for the World Boxing Association, and has officiated at 34 world title bouts, the last 29 as referee. His first world title contest as "third man" was at St Tropez in August 1987 when Evander Holyfield beat Ossie Ocasio for the WBA cruiserweight title. Yet it had been seven years earlier, in March 1980, when he first acted as a judge in a world title contest. On that occasion, Jim Watt beat Charlie Nash for the lightweight title in Glasgow. Two weeks earlier, John took charge of his first British title fight, again in Glasgow, when Ray Cattouse beat Dave McCabe to win the lightweight title.

Although British referees have been in charge of world title fights in many parts of the Americas, John Coyle was the first to be appointed on the mainland. That was on 10 December 1994 when he refereed the lightweight title fight between Orzubek "Gussie" Nazarov of Russia and Joey Gamache of Lewiston, at Portland, Maine. Another "first" for John was when he became the first British referee to take charge of a Latin-American championship contest. Whilst attending the WBA Convention in Venezuela in 1993, he was invited to referee one of three title bouts scheduled to take place a few days later. It was an honour he readily accepted.

John insists that he has developed his own style as a referee, and when talking to young referees he always advises them to do the same. He does, however, suggest that they pick out the good things they see in established officials. In his early days John had great respect for Syd Nathan, and admired the smooth way he moved around the ring. He is also grateful for considerable advice and guidance he was given by Roland Dakin, a former member of the Midlands Area Council.

For the past 21-years, John has operated his own company, "Penn Sports - Contender Boxing", which manufactures and distributes sportswear from premises in Wolverhampton. In his leisure time, he relates his experiences in after-dinner speeches. Although he refers to his travels to South Africa, Japan, Korea, Thailand, and the Americas, he includes a number of amusing stories as well. One relates to a night when he was refereeing a small hall fight in the midlands where one of the contestants was Birmingham lightweight, Des Gwilliam, who was known for his sharp sense of humour. Des indicated to Coyle on a number of occasions that his opponent was being careless with his head. Suddenly, in the fourth round he stopped boxing and shouted "watch his head ref". John promptly pulled Des aside and asked, "Who's refereeing this fight, you or me?" Without a seconds hesitation Des replied, "neither of us at the moment."

Operating a retail food shop just outside Derby is the full time occupation of "A" Star referee, Paul Thomas. His boyhood hero was "Sugar" Ray Robinson, and, although he loved the sport of boxing as a youngster, his career was limited to just one amateur contest in which he was knocked out in the first round. He started going to the fights when he was about 14, both in London and the midlands. The contest he remembers best was the classic welterweight title fight between Peter Waterman and Frank Johnson at Birmingham in 1956.

As he got older, Paul was anxious to become involved in the sport as an official. He wrote to the Board of Control on three occasions but received no reply. Eventually, his wife persuaded him to write to Area Secretary, Arthur Musson, who had a pub in the midlands. Just as he did with John Coyle, Musson invited Paul along for an interview. Everything went well and he was appointed as a "B" Grade referee in 1978 and reached "A" Star status in 1991. In that capacity he has refereed numerous British, European, and Commonwealth title bouts. At world level, Paul works for the WBO and has taken charge of eight title contests. Away from boxing, he counts jazz amongst his hobbies. He also loves old movies, and Frank Sinatra is his favourite singer. Paul is married with one son aged 14, and two others who are grown up. His eldest boxed as an amateur and, like his father, loves the sport.

Although many of Britain's top sportsmen now come from ethnic backgrounds, there is a noticeable shortage of black officials at the top level. Boxing is no exception, and despite the fact that many professional fighters are of West Indian parentage, there are currently only three referees from similar backgrounds. Jeffrey Hinds is of Barbadian parentage, Ian John-Lewis has a Dominican-born father and an English mother, whilst Ken Curtis' father is from Trinidad and his mother is English. All are Class "B" referees operating in the Southern Area.

Reading-born Jeff Hinds is 34-years-old, his parents having settled in Britain in 1956. Now in his fifth season as a referee, his boxing career was limited to just two amateur contests with Reading ABC. "They were sufficient to convince me to become an official," he remarked when we discussed his career.

For the past 15 years, Jeffrey has been employed in the accounts department of a large motoring company and, apart from officiating within professional boxing, leads a full and active life. He is involved in many local community events at Reading, and sits on various community management committees, particularly those involving the welfare of the elderly.

Apart from refereeing, Jeffrey is a keen boxing fan, but away from the sport his main hobby is music. He is the leader of a steel band which performs all over Britain and on the Mediterranean. He is also a "calypsonian" which involves him in folk music of the Caribbean, depicting current or recent events within society, government, and the world, as well as social and domestic happenings. He is also involved with the British Association of Calypsonians, based in Kensal Green, which comes into its own at the Notting Hill Carnival.

Although Jeffrey takes his ring responsibilities very seriously, he does smile when recalling a situation involving Hackney boxer, Paul "Scrap Iron" Ryan. He had occasion to lecture the boxer for an infringement, but when he gave the order to "box on", Ryan walked behind his back and stuck out his tongue. A Board of Control inspector saw the gesture and after the fight suggested to Ryan that he apologised to the referee. When the boxer did so with great sincerity, Jeff was completely bemused because he had been totally unaware of what had occurred.

Ken Curtis, a 48-year-old roofer, was born and brought up at Hayes in Middlesex. After an amateur career at both junior and senior levels with Hayes ABC, he became an official. He was an ABA judge for two years and then a referee for a further 12. He joined the professional ranks in 1992.

Ian John-Lewis from Stroud in Kent is the only active coloured referee to have been a professional boxer. As an amateur, Ian boxed for the Chatham based St Mary's Club from the age of 15. He had an amateur record of 53 fights, losing only 13. He won the first 11, eight of which were by knockout. Ian was Kent ABA welterweight champion five times, Southern Area ABA champion in 1985, and beaten finalist in 1986.

Having lost his first two professional contests, he then went undefeated in the next nine and was rewarded with a fight for the vacant Southern Area welterweight title. Unfortunately, for Ian, he was stopped in eight rounds by Trevor Smith. When he retired from the ring in 1992, he had won 13 and lost seven of his 20 professional fights.

He was appointed as a referee the following year and will always reflect on an occasion when as a boxer he was stopped on a cut eye. He protested bitterly to referee, Roy

Ian John-Lewis   Pennie Bracey

Francis, who told him, "Son, you can still come another day." It is a remark he will remember during his career as a referee.

Born in Kent in 1962, Ian is married with a four-year-old daughter, Kelsey, and is an electrician by trade. He loves all aspects of boxing, recently giving a talk about his involvement in the sport to inmates at Maidstone Prison, and this is an area he feels he can develop.

One of the most interesting characters amongst British boxing officials is "A" Star referee, Mickey Vann. Although he has lived in Leeds for most of his life, he was born at Camberwell in south London during the Second World War. He was just two-months-old when his parents went to America, leaving him to be brought up in a private home until he was seven.

Mickey comes from a circus background and has seen life from many sides. He spent five years working with clowns and on the trapeze, and also on side-shows where he acted as a "Giraffe Headed Woman". His father was recognised as the world's number one knife thrower and even had a spot on the famous Ed Sullivan Show in America, alongside The Platters and Mickey Rooney.

It was whilst working in the fairgrounds in the days when the booths were a common feature that Mickey first became interested in boxing. Although he liked the game as a schoolboy, he was a brilliant all-round sportsman, representing Buckinghamshire at gymnastics and football, and going on to play for Leeds United juniors as a goalkeeper. At the age of nine he also represented Bucks at dancing.

Despite his many talents, boxing became Mickey's favourite sport, and he boxed for Market District, Lincoln

Green, and Burtons Amateur Boxing Clubs, all in Leeds, representing Yorkshire as a featherweight, and having an amateur career of more than 60 contests. Although he turned professional during the late 1960s, he retired from the ring after about a dozen contests.

Mickey stayed in touch with boxing and in 1979 was appointed by the Board of Control as a referee. He became a Class "A" Star in 1987 and currently works for the WBC, who have appointed him to officiate at more than 30 world title fights at venues in Japan, Thailand, Trinidad, Argentina, Mexico, Italy, France and the United States. He has also refereed many British, European and Commonwealth title fights.

A married man, Mickey Vann has two sporting sons. One has played Rugby League for Bramley, whilst the other was a member of the north of England athletics squad at hurdling and also won a junior bronze medal for sprinting at the Dunlop English Schools Games.

Mickey owns and runs a transport cafe situated on Whitehall Road about a mile from Leeds city-centre. The walls are lavishly decorated with more than 200 framed boxing photos, and the establishment is appropriately named "Ringside Diner".

Terry O'Connor, a "B" Grade referee from Birmingham, was a solid heavyweight boxer in his day. As an amateur he boxed for the Thurmaston club and was a losing finalist in the Midland Counties final of 1975. He turned professional in March, the following year, and within the first 12 months had won 12 of his 14 contests.

Then, in April 1977, he faced the former British and Commonwealth champion, Danny McAlinden, before a packed house at Dudley. After a hectic opening couple of minutes there was a crack of heads and Terry came away with blood streaming from a terrible gash above his left-eye. The bout was immediately stopped and the injury required five stitches.

Defeats by Les Stevens (pts), George Butzbach (pts in Hamburg), Bruce Grandham (rtd 4), Stan McDermott (rsc 5), and Gordon Ferris (pts), followed, but all were good class opponents. In September 1978, Terry travelled to Cape Town where he lost on points to the promising South African, Jimmy Abbott. He then challenged for the vacant Midlands Area heavyweight title but was outpointed by Brian Huckfield. Referee John Coyle's decision, by half a point, was loudly booed.

In 1979, Terry had the satisfaction of wins in Oslo and Zaragosa, and, the following year, lost on points to Rudi Lubbers in Rotterdam, and to Felipe Rodriguez in Pontevedne. He also drew with Louis Hendricks in Welkom. In 1980, Terry won the vacant Midlands Area title by stopping Rocky Burton in six rounds and although losing it to Ricky James in 1981, he continued to face quality opposition. A stoppage defeat in Paris was followed by a points victory in Milan. In October 1981 he travelled to Madrid and held former European heavyweight champion, Alfredo Evangelista, to a draw. The following month he was beaten in Johannesburg by Bennie Knoetze.

Terry's last fight before retiring from the ring was in February 1983 when he was outpointed in Copenhagen by

Anders Eklund, a man who would become European champion just two years later. As a fighter, O'Connor ducked nobody, and was prepared to travel all over the world if the money was right. He was the ideal candidate to become a referee.

The Southern Area is privileged to have three "A" Star referees in Larry O'Connell, Roy Francis, and Dave Parris, all of whom were experienced fighters. O'Connell started boxing at the age of 11 and carried on until he was 27. Although he never turned professional, he won a host of titles during a long and accomplished amateur career with the famous Fitzroy Lodge Club.

In 1960, whilst doing his National Service with the Royal West Kent Regiment, he was Army and Imperial Services champion, and, in 1962, won the London South-East Division light-welterweight title. The following year he made it all the way to the ABA final, only to lose narrowly on points to Dick McTaggart. Larry represented England against Ireland, Scotland (twice), Hungary, West Germany, and Russia (twice), and boxed for London against Paris, the Army, and Italy "B", where he was the sole winner in a 9-1 defeat in Venice.

Although he had to pull out of the 1964 London South-East Divisional finals due to injury, Larry was back to his best in 1965. Apart from beating McTaggart on a Fitzroy Lodge Club show, he again made it all the way to the ABA light-welterweight final. Once more, McTaggart was in the opposite corner, but this time the Londoner was boxing so well that "Boxing News" made him favourite to win the title. Despite an aggressive display, Larry again found himself on the wrong end of a points decision, and ended up in hospital with a damaged shoulder.

Larry O'Connell   Pennie Bracey

Larry did not turn professional because he didn't feel his style was suited. Instead, he coached at the Fitzroy Lodge Club for four years. He eventually became a referee in 1977 and was appointed as Class "A" Star just eight years later. Working for the WBC, he has officiated in 28 world title fights, 14 as a referee, and has travelled to Korea, Japan, Ghana, Italy, France, Mexico, and the United States. He has been in charge of more than 60 other championship contests throughout Britain, Europe and the Commonwealth.

Already a Freeman of Goldsmiths Hall, Larry was made a Freeman of the City of London in 1994. He has been an engraver since 1953, and has his own company, O'Connell & Yardley, situated in Mayfair. His skills have brought him work for the Royal Family and Royalty from the Middle-East. His hobbies include oil painting and golf. He plays in many charity tournaments, and does after-dinner speaking about his exploits in the ring.

As a youngster, Roy Francis was a fine all-round sportsman. By the age of 15 he was a good swimmer, had won Schoolboy and Federation of Boys Club Boxing Championships, and represented London Schools at football. He was then invited for a trial at Chelsea Football Club. The great Ted Drake, the club manager at the time, was suitably impressed, but told Roy that he would have to choose between football and boxing. He chose the latter, and it is a decision he has never regretted.

Roy started boxing at the age of 12, and, before he was 20, was one of the finest amateur light-middleweights in Europe. He won BAOR and Imperial Services titles, was champion of London in 1953, ABA finalist the same year, and semi-finalist in 1955. Boxing for the Brixton Ivy Leaf Club, Roy Francis came on the scene with a bang in 1953. Not only did he beat the talented Bruce Wells on a cut eye, but won the London South-East Division light-middle-weight title on a first round stoppage, having knocked out the reigning champion, Terry Wakeling, in the semi-final. The following month his big punching brought him the London title with second round wins in both the semi and final stages. He was just 17 and already in sight of an ABA title, but, despite winning the semi-final on a third round stoppage, the skill of Corporal Bruce Wells was just too much for him.

The defeat was no disgrace, because Wells' class was confirmed the following month when he went on to win the European title in Warsaw. Roy's ability was also recognised and during the same season he represented the London ABA against the Army, and celebrated his first international with a points win for England against Wales.

Roy joined the Army in 1954 to do his National Service, and reached the rank of Corporal with The Royal Tank Regiment. In 1955, he won the Army light-middle-weight title and the Imperial Services Championship. He also reached the ABA semi-finals, only to be knocked out in 50 seconds in what was only his second loss in 30 fights that season.

When representing England against Scotland, Russia, Wales and America, his only defeat, a terrible decision against a Russian, sparked off crowd demonstrations lasting several minutes. Roy also represented The Army against Wales and London, the ABA against Scotland, and London against Berlin. Yet it was on 25 October that year which was the high point of his fine amateur career. Boxing for England against the United States, Roy faced Frankie Davis, the star of the American team. A tremendous hitter, who had won 66 fights in a row, Davis was expected to add the Brixton man to his long list of victims. Although he was under pressure, Roy landed a mighty left-hook, which sensationally ended the fight after just 56 seconds, causing one of the great amateur upsets of all-time.

Although he turned professional under Jim Wicks in 1956, Roy retired after only three fights (two losses). He had just got married, and admits, "You have to be honest with yourself if you don't think you will make it." With boxing in his blood, Roy became coach at the Robert Browning Boys Club in Walworth, which he ran for 26 years. He became one of the finest amateur coaches in Britain, trained the England team for six years, and toured the world with the team. Amongst the lads he trained were Johnny Clark and John H. Stracey.

In 1980, Roy turned to refereeing, and was appointed an "A" Star official in 1991. Working for the WBO, he has been a judge or referee at about 20 world title fights, those duties taking him to South Africa (twice), America (twice), Italy, Germany and France. He is a commanding, no-nonsense figure in the ring, with the bark of a Sergeant Major and has been in the thick of the action on more than one occasion. In 1992, he was hit solidly on the chin (accidentally) by Herbie Hide in his fight at Norwich with Jean Chanet. "The biggest surprise to Herbie was the fact that I didn't go down," said Roy dryly when recalling the incident. He did, however, finish on the floor at the Albert Hall on 1 July 1995 (the fight came too late to make our record section), amidst a rough and tumble between heavyweights, Julius Francis and Scott Welch.

Roy's courage in the ring has been matched outside as well, and in 1956 he was awarded the Queens Commendation for Bravery. He was with a friend in Wood Green when they spotted a man hanging by his collar from scaffolding, which was starting to collapse from the side of high building. Risking their lives, Roy and his pal climbed the building only to find that the victim had a scaffold pole impaled into the back of his head. Nevertheless, they managed to strap him to some boards and get him inside the building before the scaffolding collapsed. The man was removed to hospital but sadly died later the same day.

Outside boxing, Roy was employed as a security officer with the De Beer Diamond Company at Hatton Garden for more than 20 years, until he retired in March 1995. Married with three grown-up children, and five grand-children, he is a member of the London Ex-Boxers' Association, and amongst his hobbies is golf. In 1991 he played the part of a boxing referee in the classic movie "The Power of One", which was filmed at Charterhouse School.

Dave Parris, a 50-year-old Class "A" Star referee from Tottenham in north London, is another ex-professional fighter. Boxing with the Harris Lebus and Enterprise Amateur Boxing Clubs, Dave packed more than 100 fights into four seasons before turning professional as a light-heavyweight in 1969. Five years later he moved up to heavyweight, and, when he retired in 1976, had won 23, lost 30, and drawn 7, in a 60 fight professional career.

Very much the solid journeyman fighter, Dave boxed at venues in Glasgow, Bristol, Blackpool, Cleethorpes, and the midlands, as well as London. Most of his fights went the distance. Amongst his trainers were Al Phillips and Ernie Fossey,who prepared him for his last 20 contests.

Dave was a late starter and only got into boxing after sustaining a series of serious injuries at football. He was playing at a good level but, after two broken legs, realised he had no future in the game. He loved boxing, and, despite only having had a few minor bouts at school, went to the gym and put in some intensive training before joining the amateur ranks in 1965 at the age of 20.

After being appointed as a referee in 1978, Dave graduated to "A" Star Class in 1989. He has refereed four world title contests, and judged 30 others. He has also been in charge of four European title fights as well as many others with British and Commonwealth titles at stake.

Outside boxing, Dave is a driver for an asphalt company. He is married with three grown-up children and nine grand-children.

Nobody within boxing disputes that it is a highly dangerous sport. Boxers know and accept the risks involved, but to a certain extent they are very much in the hands of the "third man". Although fatalities have occurred in recent years from injuries sustained from boxing, none could be attributed to negligence on behalf of the referee. Indeed, Michael Watson and his handlers accused Roy Francis of stopping his ill-fated bout with Chris Eubank too early. Bradley Stone protested when John Keane pulled him out in the tenth round of his fatal contest with Richie Wenton at Bethnal Green in April 1994. Even Steve Watt questioned Syd Nathan's decision to stop his fight with Rocky Kelly in March 1986. None of the officials in any of those contests could have envisaged what lay ahead, and none could be faulted in any way.

Like Eugene Corri at the turn of the century, a number of our modern day officials have international reputations. They have maintained the tradition of the British referee being the finest in the world. Most boxing fans recognise the top officials, but know very little about their backgrounds. I hope this story has enlightened them about the men whose split-second decisions continue to keep Britain at the very top in world boxing.

The three grades covering licensed BBBoC referees are represented in this photo by (left to right): Jeff Hinds (Class "B"), Roy Francis (Class "A" Star) and Reg Thompson (Class "A")

Pennie Bracey

Home and Away with British Boxers during 1994-95

by John Jarrett

JULY

The guy at Sky Sports who inked the £10m deal for eight fights with Chris Eubank and Barry Hearn did not sleep very well after watching the Brighton boxer struggle through bout number one to retain his WBO super-middleweight title against the rather limited talents of the boy from Brazil, Mauricio Amaral, at Olympia. In fact, practically everyone who saw the fight was of the opinion that Eubank had not retained the title at all, well, everyone bar Chris, Barry and three judges, that is.

Press reaction the following morning said it all. The Times: "The quality of Eubank's boxing was scarcely above novice level." The Sun: "The few genuine boxing people at ringside knew damn well that Amaral had been robbed of a deserved victory." Daily Mail: "Even the wisest sages shook their heads in dismay at the unanimous verdict for the champion." What made Eubank's lacklustre performance even worse was the fact that the 22-year-old challenger, with a modest pro log of 15-1-1, was no more than a hand-picked journeyman. Yet at the end of 12 rounds, most observers were ready to hail him as the new champion.

There was another WBO title bout on the Olympia bill, West Ham's Garry Delaney defending his Penta-Continental light-heavyweight crown against Argentine veteran, Sergio Merani, but this too was a rather pedestrian affair that ran its full course, with the Londoner scoring a lop-sided decision to keep his title and take his unbeaten record to 17-0-1. Garry's big punch, which had accounted for 11 of his 16 victims, failed to disturb the visitor. Brother Mark had better luck in a super-middleweight undercard bout, as he racked up his eighth straight inside the distance win with a fourth round stoppage over Eddie Knight. Making the first London appearance of his 14-fight career, British bantamweight champion, Drew Docherty, got back on the winning trail after suffering defeat when trying for Vincenzo Belcastro's European championship last time out. Irishman, Conn McMullen, gave the Scot a brisk workout, but finished in second place after eight rounds.

Win some, lose some. Two European championship contests involving British boxers took place in the other guy's backyard and both ended in round seven. At Solofra, near Naples, British middleweight champion, Neville Brown, went up against Agostino Cardamone, the undefeated (21-0) EBU titleholder. The Italian southpaw proved too strong for Brown, who was decked three times before the referee stopped it halfway through the seventh.

A few days later, big Henry Akinwande took his European heavyweight title back to Berlin to give Mario Schiesser the chance to succeed where Axel Schulz had failed. With a moderate 22-1-1 pro log, the German could not get to grips with the 6' 7" Peckham puncher and was poleaxed in the seventh round.

Revenge was sweet, if somewhat unsatisfactory for the Nigerian veteran, Hunter Clay, as he regained the WBC International super-middleweight championship with a ninth round technical decision over Lou Gent at Tooting Leisure Centre. The Streatham crowd pleaser suffered a cut left-eye in an accidental clash of heads and, when referee Larry O'Connell waved the fight over, the scorecards indicated Clay as winner and new champion. Although the verdict did not sit too well with Lou, or his supporters, the Nigerian looked headed for victory anyway, with Gent showing the rust of 13 months inactivity.

Having fought his way back to a third crack at the British flyweight championship, Scot, James Drummond, took a fight with Zolile Mbityi at East London, South Africa. Bad move! Nice trip, good purse, shame about the fight. The South African champion got Drummond's attention in the fourth with a stunning left-hook, dropped him in the seventh, and knocked him out in round eight.

Northern Ireland super-bantamweight, John Lowey, having settled in Chicago, continued his winning run with a seventh round stoppage of Texan Albert Rendon, taking his record to 18-0. It was the fifth straight stoppage win for the former amateur star since re-locating to the Windy City after a three-year break from boxing.

Welshman, J. T. Williams, reached for the moon and fell flat on his face at York Hall on the Kotey-del Valle WBO bantamweight title card, as Tony Pep, the tall and talented Canadian, retained his Commonwealth super-featherweight championship. Williams was down twice before the referee called it off after just 92 seconds of round one.

Chris Eubank (left) boxed well below par when successfully defending his WBO super-middles title against the untried Brazilian, Mauricio Amaral   Les Clark

Ross Hale (right) had to rely on his big punch to dismiss the British light-welterweight challenge of Hugh Forde

Les Clark

AUGUST

You had to feel sorry for Antonio Picardi when the EBU nominated him as their number one challenger for the European bantamweight title, for that normally coveted appointment meant the 31-year-old Italian would have to tangle with the sensational southpaw talents of Prince Nassem Hamed. That was bad enough, but worse was to follow. Promoter Frank Warren bagged the fight for Sheffield, Hamed's hometown. There's more! In taking the crown from the veteran Vincenzo Belcastro three months earlier, Hamed had drawn flak from the critics for his outlandish showboating tactics against the champion. So you had to figure the Prince would waste no time in getting rid of an opponent who really had no right to be in there with him, a man Belcastro had beaten three times in four fights.

When the first bell rang, Signor Picardi found it every bit as hot inside the ring as it was back home in Naples. It was Hamed's 13th fight, but all the bad luck was with the visitor as he was felled three times before it was called off halfway through the third round. The Yemeni-Yorkshireman turned in a brilliant performance and, at 20, is surely a world champion just waiting to happen.

In an undercard bout, Duke McKenzie stopped Mark Hargreaves inside three rounds. The former three-time world champion was already lined up to go for a fourth title against Steve Robinson and had a free ride against the overmatched lad from Burnley, who was a 24-hour substitute. Right-hands dropped Hargreaves twice before it was stopped.

Clifton Mitchell started his professional career as "Paddy Reilly" and hopes to finish it as heavyweight champion. Already lined up to meet James Oyebola for the WBC International and vacant British titles, Mitchell took out Carl Gaffney with a right-uppercut in just 56 seconds of round one and broke Carl's nose for good measure. It was the Derby man's 12th win inside the distance in 13 fights.

Two Olympic boxers maintained their winning form on the Sheffield bill, welterweight gold medallist, Michael Carruth, belting out Mark Antony inside three rounds, making it 3-0 for the Dublin southpaw, and Robin Reid, light-middleweight bronze winner in Barcelona, who took his pro log to 8-0-1 as he stopped Andrew Jervis in just 1.45 of the first.

The Chris Eubank roadshow pitched its tent in Cardiff at the new International Arena and Belfast-Irishman, Sammy Storey, stepped up to challenge the champion for his WBO super-middleweight title. Southpaw Sammy, with a 22-3 record, and four years past his time as British champion, was not expected to win and he didn't, but he made a fight of it while it lasted. Storey twisted his left-ankle when he was knocked down in round six, and it gave out again in the seventh. He struggled upright, but when a punch-push had him over again, his corner threw the towel in as the referee called it off. It was the first fight in his last ten that Eubank went home early, and the drums were already beating for Sun City and Dan Schommer. Dan who?

With his countrymen cheering him on, Swansea's former British featherweight champion, Peter Harris, looked as though he had done enough to take the WBO Penta-Continental title off Wilson Docherty. But the three British judges decreed otherwise, handing a unanimous decision to the Scottish youngster, having only his eighth pro fight. The 32-year-old Welsh veteran paced himself well and was gutted at the verdict.

It was a bridge too far for Commonwealth flyweight champion, Daren Fifield, when he tried to capture the European title from Luigi Camputaro at Whitchurch Leisure Centre in Bristol. The tough little Italian had too much of everything for the Oxford lad, who was having only his tenth pro fight (6-2-2) against the 26-7 pro log of Camputaro. The Italian had mixed with some of the best little men in the world, including Johnny Tapia, Vincenzo Belcastro, and Jake Matala, and it showed in everything he did. Fifield took a hammering around the body and did well to finish on his feet, as the referee and two judges scored Luigi an easy winner.

In the chief supporting contest, former British and Commonwealth super-featherweight champion, Hugh

Forde, somehow landed a title shot against British and Commonwealth light-welter titleholder, Ross Hale. The man from Birmingham had fought only three times in two-and-a-half years since moving up to light-welter and the Commonwealth Council refused to recognise the fight as being for their title. Well, you can never tell in this business! As the seventh round drew to a close, Forde had survived Hale's early onslaughts to take charge and the local favourite was looking anything but a winner. But, if nothing else, Ross Hale is a puncher. The Bristol southpaw stunned Forde with a left-hand, then smashed him to the floor with another left to the jaw. It was all over, and Hughie talked of retirement when he pulled himself together. A much-relieved Hale saw his record move to 23-1, but his crown was at a crooked angle when he looked in the dressing room mirror!

A couple of our boys retained their unbeaten slates in American rings. Adrian Stone stopped Wayne Richards in five rounds at New York for his tenth win, and Irish heavyweight, Kevin McBride, took his record to 8-0-1 as he halted James Truesdale in three rounds in Maryland.

SEPTEMBER

The "Atomic Bull" exploded at London's Wembley Arena and the sound sent shock waves reverberating throughout the boxing world. With one stick of dynamite, American demolition man, Oliver McCall, raised the beautiful Lennox Lewis building to the ground in just three minutes and 31 seconds, and when the resin dust settled the WBC had a new heavyweight champion.

So what happened at Wembley? Was Lewis too focused on the proposed big money battle with Riddick Bowe? Did he take too lightly a man who had only a modest 24-5 pro log and who had worked regularly as a sparmate for Tyson, and even our own Frank Bruno? Whatever happened, it probably started in the dressing room. Motivated by ace trainer Emanuel Steward, McCall came into the ring straining at the leash, a pit bull rather than the "Atomic Bull" he was known as back home. Half-a-minute into the second round he had Lewis by the throat and they had to pull him off. It was actually a crushing right-hook that dropped Lennox on his back and when he got up the referee rightly decided he was not able to go on. Oliver McCall's dream had become Lennox Lewis' worst nightmare.

Britain's other WBC champion, super-middleweight Nigel Benn, had a rough night at Birmingham's National Exhibition Centre, though not with substitute challenger, Juan Carlos Giminez, whom he outpointed comfortably in the sixth defence of his title. During the fourth and fifth rounds, a chair-tossing battle broke out between fans of Robert McCracken and Steve Foster, who were to contest the former's British light-middleweight title later that night. This brawl should have been listed on the programme because everyone knew it was going to happen! And it did.

McCracken's fans had caused trouble on the night he beat Andy Till, as had the supporters of Foster in his fight with Kevin Sheeran, and they gave boxing another black-eye on this night in Birmingham. It was such a pity, because the sportsmanship of the men in the ring could not be faulted as they waged a competitive struggle, McCracken retaining his title and taking his unbeaten record to 20-0 with a hard-earned decision.

In another British title bout on the Birmingham bill, welterweight champion, Del Bryan, contained the challenge of Lindon Scarlett, who found the Nottingham southpaw too much on what could have been his big night. The fact that the fight went on at midnight, in a by-then half empty arena, did not help either man, but the champion deserved his victory.

The Commonwealth super-middleweight champion, Henry Wharton, was also in action at the NEC, although his title was not on the line. American journey-man, Guy Stanford, was bleeding from his nose and cut over his left-eye when his corner pulled him out after three rounds. European cruiserweight champion, Carl Thompson, didn't even work up a decent sweat against Brazil's Dionosio Lazario, who was on his way to the showers after just 66 seconds of round one. Another wasted journey was that made by heavyweight Jeff Williams, from Louisiana, who was down and out in just 70 seconds after Clifton Mitchell hit him. Light-middleweight, Adrian Dodson, had stopped eight of his ten pro victims, but found lanky Colin Pitters a bit of a handful and had to go the distance to get his win.

Three is not a lucky number for the Kilmarnock flyweight, James Drummond. In front of his "ain" folk at Musselburgh, the Scot made his third attempt to win the British title, having previously failed against Robbie Regan and Francis Ampofo. Facing champion Ampofo again, Drummond won the first two rounds, only to be cut, dropped, and stopped, in round three!

Johnny Armour was all set to make the fourth defence of his Commonwealth bantamweight title against his fifth African opponent, but Steve Mwema failed to pass the Board's medical and Scot, Shaun Anderson, got an unexpected crack at the title. The Glasgow man travelled to London and gave Armour and the York Hall fans a run for their money before being pulled out by the referee in round 11. The Chatham southpaw remained unbeaten after 16 fights, but he had seen better nights.

A bantamweight who would love to fight Armour is Belfast's Wayne McCullough, making his way up the ladder, via Las Vegas, where he set up base after his Olympic silver medal success. "Mac" hammered Mexican, Andres Cazares, into a third round knockout to stay unbeaten in 14 fights. A couple of days later, McCullough's Barcelona buddy, Michael Carruth, arrived in town to make his American debut a success, a fourth round knockout of Indiana welter-weight, Kim-Ken Jackson. Former British heavyweight champion, Gary Mason, was also in action in Nevada, scoring his second comeback win over Martin Foster in three rounds.

Big-punching Garry Delaney gained a somewhat hollow victory over mismatched African, Arigoma Chiponda, who was kayoed in round two at York Hall. The win took Delaney's record to 18-0-1 and added the Commonwealth crown to his WBO Penta-Continental belt.

Veteran Kirkland Laing took another fight at 40 and had a rough night before Swindon-based South African, Chris Peters, was pulled out by the referee after an accidental clash of heads left him too badly cut to continue.

OCTOBER

Fiasco in the Far East! Professional boxing is all about money, dreams come second, and when the money fell short in Hong Kong, the dream became a nightmare. Twenty years after hatching Ali-Foreman in Zaire, Londoner, John Daly, tried to bring big-time boxing to Hong Kong, with American, Bob Arum, as the promoter of record. Herbie Hide would defend his WBO heavyweight title against former champion, Tommy Morrison, Billy Schwer would challenge IBF lightweight champion, Rafael Ruelas, Lonnie Beasley going for Steve Collins' WBO middle crown, and big Frank Bruno tackling Ray Mercer. But the day before the show, as the fighters gathered for the weigh-in, Barry Hearn pulled Hide and Collins out as the $1.5m guarantee for their purses was not forthcoming. Arum refused to make up the shortfall and the show fell apart.

The Cardiff Ice Rink made a perfect stage for that cool craftsman Steve Robinson to display his growing repertoire of punches. This time it was a beautiful short left-hook to the body of Duke McKenzie that ended the challenge of the former three-time world champion in round nine, and gave Steve his fifth successful defence of the WBO feather-weight title. Having cleaned up the domestic opposition, Robinson served notice on the rest of the world's nine-stone men that he is a force to be reckoned with.

One guy who is looking forward to meeting "Robbo" is Prince Nassem Hamed. In front of his hometown fans at Sheffield, he added the WBC International super-bantam-weight title to his European bantamweight belt, dismantling Freddy Cruz in six rounds, the same Cruz who had taken Robinson the distance when challenging for his title four months previously. Hamed gave a virtuoso perform-ance that had world class stamped all over it.

Dan Schommer, a 34-year-old southpaw from Minneapolis, beat Chris Eubank in their WBO super-middleweight championship contest in Sun City, but when the judges' scorecards were added up, surprise, surprise, Eubank was announced as the winner, and still champion! Even Barry Hearn thought his boy had lost it this time.

On the undercard, Billy Hardy fought like a champion to retain his Commonwealth featherweight title against the spirited challenge of South African titleholder, Stanford Ngcebeshe, coming out with the unanimous vote of all three officials. The Sunderland red-head dedicated his victory to his South African trainer, Richard Smith, who was murdered earlier in the year.

In his unbeaten 14-fight career (1 draw), Maurice Core had won and relinquished the British light-heavyweight title, but when he tried to move up in class against European champion, Fabrice Tiozzo, he found the French-man more than equal to the challenge. With cuts over both eyes, Maurice from Manchester was floored twice before it was stopped in round four.

The ability of some Commonwealth title aspirants leaves a lot to be desired. Sipho Moyo from Zimbabwe was on his way back home after just 38 seconds of his futile challenge against big-punching Henry Wharton at Leeds Town Hall. Already matched with Eubank for his title in December, Wharton needed only one punch, a terrific left-hook to the body, to end this farce.

At least Canadian, Jacques Le Blanc, stood up to Richie Woodhall for 12 rounds. But Richie is not a banger, he is a boxer, as he ably demonstrated in retaining his Commonwealth middleweight title for the third time in the Wolverhampton ring. In a support, European welterweight champion, Gary Jacobs, stopped the American import, Rusty DeRouen, inside six rounds.

It was a traumatic outing for British super-bantam-weight champion, Richie Wenton, having his first fight since the death of Bradley Stone following their title bout some six months previously. In the Cardiff ring, Neil Swain was matching Richie punch-for-punch until round five when the champion suddenly walked to his corner and quit. "For every second of every minute of every round, I was seeing Bradley," he said afterwards.

More non-title action saw British light-middleweight champion, Robert McCracken, stop Bristol's Dean Cooper in four rounds at York Hall. . . British middleweight titleholder, Neville Brown, got his gloves out again after his European title defeat and racked up lanky Colin Pitters for a second round knockout at Cannock. . . European cruiserweight kingpin, Carl Thompson, took his big punch to Paris, stuck it on hapless American, Tim Knight, and the referee let it go into round five before calling time.

Former champions kept their names in the frame as Robbie Regan beat Shaun Norman inside two rounds at Cardiff. Shaun was no match for the former British and European flyweight titleholder. . . Ex-British and Common-wealth lightweight champion, Paul Burke, had an easy ride against Rudy Valentino in a six-rounder in Mayfair, but former British super-featherweight champion, Michael Armstrong, was not so fortunate in another bout on the bill when stopped with a cut *arm*! Stitches in a previous injury burst during round three and the fight was stopped, leaving Bamana Dibateza the winner. . . Golden oldie Dennis Andries supplemented his pension with a job in the south of France, stopping American, Sylvester White, in five rounds, and looked forward to fighting Anaclet Wamba for his WBC cruiser title.

NOVEMBER

The big fight boom continued in Cardiff with four title bouts at the Ice Rink. Two years almost to the day since winning the European flyweight championship, Robbie Regan won it again, beating Italian tough guy, Luigi Camputaro, on a split decision after 12 rounds of blistering action. Regan's feet were even blistered, but that was from a pair of new boots. At the final bell both men wore the scars of battle, but as the Welsh lad took his record to 15-1-3, his world title hopes did not look good.

In one of two vacant British title bouts on the card, Crawford Ashley outlasted Nicky Piper in a bruising war of attrition that saw the Leeds man reclaim the light-heavyweight title he held in 1991-92. It was third-time unlucky for Piper in his quest for a major title, yet he almost pulled it off as a desperate final round rally saw Ashley out on his feet.

An ambitious heavyweight needs a knockout punch if he is going all the way, something like the thunderous right-cross James Oyebola used to separate Clifton Mitchell from his senses in round four of their contest for the heavyweight title. The Derby man had won 14 on the trot, but he didn't win this one! Oyebola may not be the best British heavyweight champion (yet), but at 6' 8½" he must be the biggest!

It wouldn't be a show without Punch! Prince Nassem Hamed gave Steve Robinson's supporters something to think about as he stopped Laureano Ramirez, a Dominican based in Spain, in round three to retain his WBC International super-bantamweight title. Ramirez was unbeaten in 18 fights, but the only thing he had in common with Hamed was a southpaw stance.

Tancy Lee, Benny Lynch, Jackie Paterson, Walter McGowan and Paul Weir. The little man from Irvine may not yet belong up there with those legendary wee warriors from north of the border, but it's early days. Weir was having only his *ninth* pro fight when he whipped South African, Paul Oulden, for the vacant WBO light-flyweight championship in front of his hometown fans. And this was Weir's *second* world title, having previously worn the WBO strawweight crown, and his *fourth* world title bout as recognised by the WBO! Yes that's right, *nine* pro fights. Crazy!

British bantamweight champion, Drew Docherty, realised an ambition as he comprehensively outboxed Dewsbury challenger, Ady Benton, to retain his title and make the Lonsdale Belt his own. Benton had retired Pat Clinton on his last visit to Scotland, but there was no way Drew was going to let Ady rain on his parade and he didn't.

Another Lonsdale Belt to find a permanent home was that worn by British middleweight champion Neville Brown. Antonio Fernandez made a fight of it for seven rounds at Cannock, but when he sustained a bad cut over his left-eye in the eighth, Brown turned the volume up and it was stopped in the ninth. Surprise of the night was the hard-earned victory of scrappy little Midlands lightweight champion, Karl Taylor, over former double world champion, Dingaan Thobela. The South African was streets ahead in class, but Taylor took him down a back lane and mugged him.

European middleweight champion, Agostino Cardamone, was unbeaten in 23 fights and ranked "numero uno" by the WBC, but he had to haul himself off the canvas and dig deep to hang on to those credentials when Shaun Cummins came looking for him in San Remo. The Leicester hardman hurt Cardamone several times and dropped him heavily in the eighth, but the Italian southpaw kept his boxing together to retain his crown and his rating.

Belfast bantamweight, Wayne McCullough, risked his position as official challenger for the WBC title when he tackled former IBF super-bantamweight champion, Fabrice Benichou, in front of a sellout 6,000 crowd in Dublin. The Olympic silver medallist had earned his crack at the world title with a tough win over Victor Rabinales and he had another tough night with the hard little man from France, even if the scoring (100-91) made it look easy.

Back in London after his aborted world title fight in Hong Kong, British and Commonwealth lightweight champion, Billy Schwer, took out his frustration on hapless Mexican, Manuel Hernandez, who was decked in round two and knocked out in the sixth. Also on the York Hall show, European welterweight champion, Gary Jacobs, chased Argentinian, Marcelo di Croce, for ten rounds to take the points and raise his record to 36-5.

The extrovert skills of Kirkland Laing made him a champion, of Britain and of Europe, but that was then and this was now and, at the Sports Centre at Whitchurch, the 40-year-old veteran of 55 fights stared retirement in the face after being stopped inside five rounds by Glenn Catley, a boy from Bristol with only ten bouts on his card.

At Wolverhampton, Richie Woodhall put his Commonwealth middleweight title up for grabs for the fourth time, but Art Serwano was not equal to the task. The California-based Ugandan was not big enough and not good enough as Richie punched out a methodical victory, Serwano being rescued by a compassionate John Coyle in round 11. In a supporting bout, bomber Joe Calzaghe hammered Trevor Ambrose to second round defeat for his eighth straight win since winning three ABA titles. The Hammersmith-born Welsh-based super-middleweight likes to go home early. . . six wins in the first and two in the second!

DECEMBER

Chris Eubank was still undefeated, officially anyway, with 40 wins and two draws in 42 pro fights, and his fight with Henry Wharton at Manchester's G-Mex Centre was his 19th WBO championship contest involving first the middleweight title and now the super-middleweight crown. Impressive stats whatever combination of letters they stick in front of your title. But the man himself had not been too impressive in recent outings and it had gotten so that Eubank's entrance into the arena, culminating in that vault over the top rope, was the best part of his fights. There had also been several dubious decisions which had the fans holding their noses and his opponents crying out, "We wuz robbed!"

Speculation was rife that Chris was ready for the taking and that Henry Wharton was the man to take him. The Commonwealth champion was a strong winning fighter with a big punch that could have won him Nigel Benn's WBC version of the title, had not the big occasion got to him. As it turned out, it was Wharton's big heart that got him through to the final bell against the best Eubank we had seen in four years. Chris turned in a vintage performance to come out with the decision and this time everyone agreed that he deserved it.

It takes more than ten fights and a bit of hype to make a champion, as Dave McHale learned to his cost at Ilford when he tried to take Floyd Havard's British super-featherweight title. The Swansea southpaw outboxed the Glasgow man, then outpunched him to bring the referee's intervention in round ten, with McHale running on empty. Floyd's victory was sweetened as he took the Lonsdale Belt home to keep.

Little Francis Ampofo showed Daren Fifield the way to go home when they clashed at the York Hall in Bethnal Green. Both men brought a title to the table, Ampofo hoping to add Daren's Commonwealth flyweight crown to his British bauble. He accomplished his task with consummate ease, crushing Fifield inside two rounds to become a double champion.

British welterweight champion, Del Bryan, was not so fortunate when he went after the European title against Jose Luis Navarro in Cordoba. The heavy-handed Spaniard had stopped all 17 of his victims and he made "Del Boy" number 18 with a relentless attack that finally bore fruit in the tenth round. The Nottingham road warrior got away to a good start and had the unbeaten champion bloodied and bruised before being run over.

An official eliminator for the British lightweight title turned into a war of attrition as local favourite, Dave Anderson, clashed with Peter Till in Glasgow. In taking his unbeaten run to 15, Dave racked up his hat-trick over the Walsall warrior, but came out of the ring looking more a loser than a winner, his face bruised and battered and his right hand injured.

Doncaster's Jonjo Irwin breezed to an easy victory over Dagenham-based African, Bamana Dibateza, at Potters Bar, to record the second defence of his WBO Penta-Continental super-featherweight title with a runaway points victory and take his record to 11-2.

WBO welterweight champion, Eamonn Loughran, retained his title against former champion, Manning Galloway, on a technical decision at Manchester on the Eubank-Wharton card. Both men suffered facial cuts in a clash of heads and the referee halted the action in the fifth, going to the scorecards, which showed the Ballymena battler to be ahead and therefore the winner and still champion. The Irishman deserved his victory as he had outpunched the American from the first bell.

Cordwell Hylton was the Midland Area cruiserweight champion but he was 36 and this was his 70th pro fight and, as he said after his gruelling ten rounds with John Foreman, "It's a hard way to make a living." That observation was echoed by Foreman, who won the decision and the title but knew he had been in a battle that night in Birmingham. Hylton gave it everything, but maybe it was time to look for another line of work.

At the other end of the spectrum, young Brian Carr stepped into the professional ring for the first time in Glasgow. After a glittering amateur career, the young featherweight tangled with Fred Reeve of Hull in a scheduled six-twos. Brian scored a second round knockout, but, as the referee held up his hand in victory, blood was running from a gash over his left-eye. Like the man said, "It's a hard way to make a living."

Overseas action saw Bristol-born welterweight, Adrian Stone, campaigning in America since coming second in the

1992 ABA light-welter final, take his pro log to 13-0 (1 draw) with an easy two-rounds stoppage over Israel Figueroa in Boston. . . It was Christmas Day in Belgium, but there was little joy for Manchester's former British and European light-welterweight champion, Pat Barrett, as he turned in yet another disappointing performance to take the decision over Marino Monteyne. . . In Cagliari, manager Brendan Ingle inspired southpaw Chris Saunders to a fine points win over former European amateur champion, Roberto Welin. The Barnsley welterweight took his record to a modest 15-16-1, but it was his sixth straight win over good opposition and maybe he was now doing something right. . . In Portland, Maine, Frank Maloney's big Irish heavyweight, Kevin McBride, disposed of John Lamphrey in 62 seconds of round one for his 11th win against one draw.

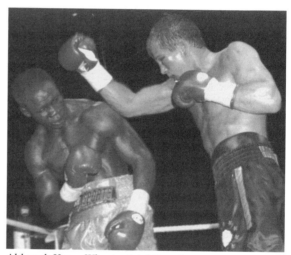

Although Henry Wharton (right) made a game attempt to win the WBO super-middleweight crown, he was comprehensively outscored by a seemingly rejuvenated Chris Eubank
Les Clark

JANUARY

Billy Schwer's only defeat in a 27-bout pro career had been a cut eye stoppage against Paul Burke, a defeat that cost Billy his British and Commonwealth lightweight titles. Loss number two also came about through badly cut eyes and this time it cost the lad from Luton the IBF lightweight title. Rafael Ruelas is a fine champion and maybe he would have won their fight in Las Vegas anyway, but Schwer had given him a helluva scrap for eight rounds before the bout was stopped. This was one of the fights aborted in the Hong Kong debacle some three months previously and the shift in venues did Billy no favours. Nor, unfortunately, did Ruelas.

At home, the big fight action was in Glasgow where Prince Nassem Hamed packed them in to see how long it would take him to deal with the challenge of Mexican tough guy, Armando Castro, a veteran of distance fights with men like Khaosai Galaxi, Greg Richardson, and most recently, Alfred Kotey. He didn't go the distance with the

Yemeni-Yorkshireman who, as usual, was in brilliant form, dumping Castro twice before the referee called it off in round four. Hamed's WBC International super-bantamweight belt was on the line but, like its owner, was never in any danger.

Like "Old Father Time", Dennis Andries keeps rolling along. Admitting to 41 years, the former WBC three-time light-heavyweight champion won his second British title when he stopped Denzil Browne in round 11 for the vacant cruiserweight championship on the Glasgow card. Victory marked the Hackney veteran as the oldest man to win a British title, beating the previous record held by heavyweight champion, Gunner Moir, back in the gaslight days.

Irish Olympic champion, Michael Carruth, slumped to his first defeat after six wins as Glasgow's Gordon Blair hustled him out of the decision in a six-threes. . . Southpaw James Murray outpunched veteran Louis Veitch for a three rounds stoppage to hold on to his Scottish bantamweight title. . . Lightweight, Dave Anderson, easily handled his first foreign opponent, Carlos Javier Pena Lopez, walking away with the decision to make the Spaniard his 16th straight victim since joining the pro ranks.

A couple of days later, Glasgow was again the scene of championship boxing as Mike Deveney and Wilson Docherty tangled for the British featherweight title left vacant by Billy Hardy. Docherty was favoured to join his brother Drew as British champion, thus emulating John and George Feeney as the only brothers to hold British titles at one and the same time. At the end of 12 absorbing rounds, however, referee, Dave Parris, awarded the decision and the title to Deveney!

The British super-middleweight Lonsdale belt handed back by Cornelius Carr, left the ring at York Hall strapped around the waist of Ali Forbes, much to the disgust of former champion, Fidel Castro Smith. For the third time in a British title match, Smith saw a tight decision go against him, yet he had only himself to blame as he allowed the 33-year-old Sydenham slugger to outwork him.

Defending his WBO Penta-Continental middleweight title for the first time, Paul Busby experienced little trouble with challenger, Warren Stowe, to come out with the decision and take his pro log to 17-3-1 in front of his hometown fans at Worcester. Another champion to come out a winner was Midlands middleweight titleholder, Antonio Fernandez, but he had to come off the deck to take a decision from the Leeds' puncher, Colin Manners.

Unbeaten in 15 pro fights (2 draws), Islington light-middleweight, Clay O'Shea, had stopped seven opponents inside two rounds and his supporters packed into Bethnal Green's York Hall expecting him to blow away Geoff McCreesh to claim the vacant Southern Area title. But the Bracknell boxer, unbeaten in seven bouts, came off his stool with both guns blazing to have Clay going up and down like a yo-yo, before the third man called a halt at 2.27 of round one, with O'Shea taking his fourth count.

Trainers were in the news this month. Lennox Lewis, having fired Pepe Correa, signed up with the "King of the Kronk", Emanuel Steward, the man who motivated Oliver McCall to take the WBC title from him in September. . . Jim McDonnell, the former European champion, having trained Herbie Hide for his startling upset WBO title win over Michael Bentt, could not agree on the size of his pay packet for Herbie's fight with Riddick Bowe in Las Vegas, so the two parted company. . . Money was also the cause of the split between Jimmy Tibbs and WBC super-middleweight champion, Nigel Benn, who was being trained for his title defence against American, Gerald McClellan, by Kevin Sanders of Peterborough.

Geoff McCreesh (right) blasted the unbeaten Clay O'Shea to a first round defeat on his way to the Southern Area light-middleweight title   Les Clark

FEBRUARY

Such was the fury and ferocity of the epic contest between Nigel Benn and Gerald McClellan that it must surely be added to anyone's list of Battles of the Century. Sadly, it was almost added to the list of boxing fatalities as the American collapsed in his corner after being counted out in a dramatic tenth round and was taken to hospital where he was operated on for the removal of a blood-clot from his brain. Thankfully, McClellan did not die, but his brilliant career ended in that brutal fight at London's Docklands Arena. Challenging Benn for his WBC super-

The new "kid on the block", Adrian Dodson (right), was far too fresh for former world champion, Lloyd Honeyghan, retiring him for good in round three

Les Clark

middleweight title, McClellan was a red-hot favourite to stop the champion and almost did in a frantic first round. Nigel, hammered through the ropes onto the ring apron, managed to scramble back in time to survive the round and stage a remarkable comeback. It was round seven before the American got back into the fight and Benn was in trouble again through the eighth and ninth. In the tenth it all went terribly wrong as McClellan suddenly came apart. The battle with Benn was over, the fight for life was beginning.

You can't blame Frank Bruno for carrying on with his career when he can pick up something in excess of £200,000 for knocking over reluctant stiffs like Rodolfo Marin. This one lasted a mere 65 seconds and left a capacity crowd of 5,000 at the Shepton Mallet Showgrounds holding their noses. Fortunately for the fans, there was a real fight on the card, Ross Hale retaining his British and Commonwealth light-welterweight titles against the gutsy challenge of Malcolm Melvin, who climbed off the deck three times in the first round to go the distance. Victory gave Hale the Lonsdale Belt to take home for good.

The world title aspirations of British bantamweight champion, Drew Docherty, were ruthlessly exposed by WBO champion, Alfred "Cobra" Kotey, at the Tryst Centre in Cumbernauld, where the little African lion tore the Scot to pieces inside four rounds, retaining his title for the second time.

In a career-best performance, Commonwealth middleweight champion, Richie Woodhall, thrilled his hometown fans at Telford when he outboxed and outpunched tough Italian, Silvio Branco, to win the vacant European title and put himself in line for better things. As a fine methodical boxer, Woodhall had won 18 pro bouts without setting the world on fire but, against Branco, he turned fighter and they had to stop it in round nine to save the Italian.

The way Steve Robinson is going, it may take surgery to separate the little Cardiff featherweight from his beloved WBO belt. The Argentine challenger, Domingo Damigella, was the sixth to try and the sixth to fail, even if he did manage to last the full 12 rounds. Robinson was a good winner, but he has looked better and was maybe a little stale.

Paul Burke was hoping to regain his British lightweight championship when he stepped in against Michael Ayers at the Crawley Leisure Centre, but the Tooting man had other ideas. By round six, the Preston puncher was bleeding from a bad cut on his left-eye and after he was rocked by a savage left-hook the referee stopped it and awarded the vacant title to Ayers.

It looked a safe fight for British light-middleweight champion, Robert McCracken, to secure permanent possession of his Lonsdale Belt. Paul Wesley had won only 15 of his 43 fights and hardly rated a title chance, at least on paper. But Paul was a much better fighter than his record suggested, as McCracken discovered in a blistering fight that was in doubt right to the final bell. The champion took this battle of the "Brummies" by half-a-point to stay undefeated in his 22 fights, but only just!

There is a maturity about Billy Hardy's work these days, crafted in rings around the world as the Sunderland lad challenged for world titles twice, European honours twice, and won British titles at bantamweight and feather. In front of his adoring hometown fans at Crowtree, Billy retained his Commonwealth featherweight championship against Percy Commey, stopping the African inside 11 rounds to keep his world title ambitions alive.

Commonwealth bantam champion, Johnny Armour, kept his crown, but he had to get off the deck to do it. South African southpaw, Tsitsu Sokutu, proved a stubborn foe at York Hall and dropped Armour in round four before the Chatham boxer repaid the compliment in the seventh. Sokutu got up but, under fire, was stopped as Armour took his pro log to 16-0.

He was a former world champion, but at 34-years-old and having seen better days, in round three the referee stopped it and sent Lloyd Honeyghan back to his corner, pointing to Adrian Dodson as the winner that night in London's Docklands Arena. Hugh Forde was another ex-champion to falter on the road back, the one-time British and Commonwealth super-featherweight titleholder losing a six-threes to Carl Wright at Barrow. At his best, Derek Williams was European and Commonwealth heavyweight champion, but he didn't have enough left to beat Michael Murray over eight rounds at Southwark and has nowhere left to go.

At the other end of the spectrum, Peter Richardson, Spencer Oliver, and Dean Pithie, took their first steps along the glory road. England captain and Commonwealth Games gold medallist, Richardson, outpunched John O.Johnson in a light-welter bout at Southwark, while at Cumbernauld, Commonwealth and ABA bantam champion, Oliver, beat Des Gargano, and ABA featherweight titleholder, Pithie, stopped Kid McAuley in three rounds.

MARCH

For almost ten years and 43 professional fights, Chris Eubank marched undefeated to the tune of "Simply The Best", although lately the performance has sometimes been out of tune with the orchestra. So maybe he was pushing his luck more than somewhat when he agreed to defend his WBO super-middleweight title against Irishman, Steve Collins, in a County Cork village called Millstreet, the day after St Patrick's Day. Already the WBO middleweight titleholder, Collins fought out of his skin, survived a knockdown in the tenth and, going into the final round, Ronnie Davies told Eubank he needed a knockout to save his precious title. He didn't get it and three minutes later the celebrations began. "Simply the Best," on this night anyway, simply wasn't good enough!

Over in Las Vegas, Herbie Hide wasn't good enough either and his WBO heavyweight crown found a new owner as Riddick Bowe simply overpowered the Nigerian from Norwich in six one-sided rounds. Herbie gave it a shot, but the former undisputed champ was just too big, too powerful, and too much of everything. Still only 23, Herbie will have better nights.

The pint-sized punchers have always found favour with the Scots and they have taken Nassem Hamed to their hearts, but then who wouldn't! Two months after taking out Armando Castro in Glasgow, Hamed was even more spectacular in Livingston, demolishing Argentine toughie, Sergio Liendo, in 69 seconds of round two in taking his record to 17-0. There was something for everyone on this 12-fight card, including a shock for new British featherweight champion, Mike Deveney, who lost a decision to five-fight Welsh novice, Dean Phillips.

There was a "trailer" for a forthcoming British title fight as cruiserweight champion, Dennis Andries, and contender, Terry Dunstan, displayed their fistic wares. The old man took a decision over American Mike Peak and Hackney's unbeaten Dunstan knocked out Art Stacey in the first round. Bring on the champ!

British and Commonwealth flyweight champion, Francis Ampofo, ran into a tartar in Mayfair and when he left the Grosvenor House later that night he had only his domestic bauble in his bag. South African, Danny Ward, turned in a major surprise as he outboxed Ampofo for 11 rounds, then knocked him out in the 12th to become his country's first Commonwealth title holder since re-admission.

Three months after losing that same Commonwealth flyweight title to Ampofo, Daren Fifield went after the vacant Southern Area championship at York Hall in Bethnal Green. On paper he looked a good thing against Ricky Beard, who came in with ten losses in his 16 fights, but the Dagenham man upset the odds by stopping Fifield inside eight rounds. Funny game, this!

New British lightweight champion, Michael Ayers, wasted no time sticking a second notch on his Lonsdale Belt as he squared accounts with Birmingham toughie, Karl Taylor, who had forced a draw in their previous fight. This time Ayers fought like a champion to stop his man in eight rounds. . . Another British champion to retain his title was super-bantamweight, Richie Wenton, who stormed back in style to stop fancied challenger, Paul Lloyd, inside five rounds at Chester. In his only outing since winning the title in that tragic contest with Bradley Stone, Wenton had given up against Neil Swain, but against Lloyd he was a winner all the way. . . British middleweight champion, Neville Brown, made hard work of his title defence against Welsh challenger, Carlo Colarusso, before stopping him in round seven.

Have gloves, will travel. Just 11 days after defending his Commonwealth featherweight title, Billy Hardy jumped at the chance of a fight with French veteran, Fabrice Benichou, in Saint-Quentin. After a tough ten rounds, Billy came out with two cut eyes and a draw. . . In Vitrolles, Noel Magee was not so fortunate when going up against Fabrice Tiozzo for the European light-heavyweight title. The Frenchman had the power and, in the fourth, he turned it on to floor Magee twice and force a stoppage. . . Gary Jacobs appeared in Atlantic City in preparation for his mandatory challenge to WBC welterweight champion, Pernell Whitaker, but had the misfortune to suffer a split knuckle on his right-hand in taking a decision over Jose Miguel Fernandez. . . Belfast bantamweight, Wayne McCullough, continued his American campaign in Louisiana when he buried Geronimo Cardoz in an avalanche of leather, before the Mexican's corner pulled him out after seven one-sided rounds.

Newcastle super-featherweight rivals, Frankie Foster and Dominic McGuigan, took their argument out of town to the High Pit Club in Cramlington where a full house saw them battle for Foster's Northern Area championship. Frankie got away to a good start, but McGuigan turned in his finest performance to force a sixth round stoppage and take the belt. . . Nigel Rafferty won the Midlands Area cruiserweight title in a bruising battle with champion, John Foreman, in Birmingham, putting an end to the local boxer's three-month reign and hopes of a British title challenge against Dennis Andries.

He used to be the WBC International bantamweight champion, but, at 31-years-of-age, Donnie Hood struggled to gain a disputed decision over Rowan Williams in Glasgow in a lack-lustre eight-twos. Nothing is forever!

APRIL

A fighter's hands are the tools of his trade, so it makes you wonder at the wisdom of Paul Weir going into a defence of his WBO light-flyweight title against Ric Magramo at Irvine knowing that his right-hand was virtually useless. The little Scot strained his right-wrist ten days before the fight and was still having treatment up to going into the ring. But there was no way he was pulling out of the fight! "I need the money after being idle for ten months," he said. Other financial factors involved were a sell-out at the venue and the television fee from BBC. Ric Magramo, the 33-year-old Filipino challenger, was apparently not such an important factor in the equation. "Even with this handicap," Weir told Boxing News, "after watching Magramo carefully on video, I still felt I could outbox him, even if it meant with just one hand!" In the event, Paul had to do just that. His right-hand was a passenger after two rounds, but his left was enough to bring him a unanimous decision. If and when he climbs in there with someone like "Baby Jake" Matlala or Michael Carbajal, let us hope that everything is in working order.

Another little man hoping for bigger things was Johnny Armour, who added the European bantamweight title to his Commonwealth crown at York Hall, when Antonio Picardi retired in the eighth round. A clash of heads left the Chatham southpaw with a cut above his right-eye, but the Italian, also cut in a previous round, was trailing on points and had suffered enough.

Welsh southpaw, Neil Swain, became the first Commonwealth super-bantamweight champion when he stopped Guyanan veteran, Mike Parris, in ten rounds at Llanelli. The right man in the right place at the right time. . .

The fates were also kind to Sammy Storey as he ended the brief reign of Ali Forbes as British super-middleweight champion, taking the decision, the title, and the Lonsdale Belt he had cut two notches on back in 1989. Forbes put in a storming finish to their fight at York Hall, but it was too late and the 31-year-old Belfast southpaw was back in business.

The luck of the Irish was not with Damien Denny, as the former amateur star made his challenge for the vacant WBO Continental light-middleweight title at home in Belfast. Sheffield's Paul "Silky" Jones didn't give Denny a chance, bombing him out in exactly three minutes to become champion. John Lowey gave the Irish something to cheer about as he stopped Juan Cardona in five rounds at Chicago to win the IBO super-bantamweight title, whatever that is.

In area title action, heavyweight Julius Francis was just too big, too heavy, and too good for Keith Fletcher, as he soundly outboxed the Reading man to retain his Southern Area championship at York Hall in Bethnal Green. The vacant Central Area cruiserweight title was on the line when Tony Booth tangled with tough Art Stacey at Hull. Both men were up for the job, with the skills of Booth, honed by Brendan Ingle, prevailing over the Leeds' man in a torrid ten-rounder.

Two men on the comeback trail were Darlington light-welterweight, Allan Hall, and Eltham flyweight, Mickey Cantwell. Hall, out for over two years, dumped Nigel Bradley with a cracking right to bring the referee's intervention in the second round of their Bloomsbury fight and take his record to 16-1. Cantwell, a loser against Luigi Camputaro in a European title challenge and to Lyndon Kershaw on his last two outings, hooked up with Anthony Hanna at York Hall to repeat the points victory he scored over the Birmingham man in November 1993.

Our boys met with mixed fortune when travelling abroad for fights this month. British light-heavyweight champion, Crawford Ashley, lasted the full distance when challenging Virgil Hill for his WBA title in Stateline, Nevada, but only just, surviving a rough final round as the American turned it on to complete his 17th successful defence in two reigns as champion. Henry Akinwande made a big impression in Las Vegas, which is not difficult when you stand 6' 7" in your socks and bounce the scales around $16\frac{1}{2}$ stones. In his first fight since joining the Don King camp, the former European and Commonwealth champion took his record to 25-0-1 with an easy second round knockout of Calvin Jones. At Salem, New Hampshire, Bristol-born Adrian Stone was on his way to taking the USBA welterweight title from James Hughes, when the champion saved his crown with some heavy leather in round ten to wipe out Stone's lead and bring the referee's intervention.

Duke McKenzie journeyed to the Paris suburb of Fontenay-Sous-Bois to challenge Mehdi Labdouni for his European featherweight championship and thought he had boxed well enough to come out a winner, as did his entourage, which included promoter, Frank Warren. But the three officials saw the champion a unanimous winner on a decision Warren called "diabolical." Duke boxed well enough, but allowed himself to be outfought by the Frenchman.

Let's hear the applause for unheralded Simon McDougall, who carried the flag in Berne, Switzerland. The Blackpool light-heavyweight loses more fights than he wins, but he did something right this time, stopping Stefan Angehrn inside five rounds. It was all going wrong for Condorrat featherweight, Wilson Docherty. After losing to Mike Deveney for the vacant British title he saw his hopes dashed again as former champion, Peter Harris, took the decision in their final eliminator in Glasgow.

MAY

Comebacks made the news this month as Lennox Lewis and Chris Eubank attempted to show that they were far from back numbers in their respective divisions. Heavyweight, Lewis, dramatically knocked off his WBC perch by Oliver McCall, worked with his new trainer, Emanuel Steward, for his bout with Lionel Butler, scheduled for Sacramento. Butler, at least on paper, was a tough assignment with 17 straight wins inside the distance, and the WBC labelled the fight an eliminator. Lewis duly eliminated Butler inside five rounds, overcoming a nervous start against a man who was sadly out of condition. Steward was pleased with Lennox, while admitting there was still work to do before, hopefully, getting another crack at the title.

Eubank's return to the ring after losing his WBO title to Steve Collins was over before it began, 2.45 of round one, with Argentine opponent, Bruno Godoy, ruled out with facial cuts, much to the disgust of the crowd at Belfast's King's Hall. While it lasted, Eubank was in charge of the action and the damage was inflicted by his fists, not his head, as claimed by the South American.

Also on the Belfast card, there was a disappointing ending to Eamonn Loughran's defence of his WBO welterweight title, as the challenger, Angel Beltre, of the Dominican Republic, came out of a clash of heads in round three with blood streaming from a cut on his right-eyebrow. The doctor needed only a glance before ruling Beltre out of the contest and the result was declared a no-decision, since three rounds had not been completed. Loughran had used his power to offset the cleverness of the Latin and appeared to be leading at the time of the unfortunate ending.

Another fighter coming back from a world title defeat was Billy Schwer, stepping out for the first time since losing an IBF title challenge to Rafael Ruelas in January. Billy had his hands full with Zambian, Stephen Chungu, who got away to a fine start before running out of ideas, and was eventually stopped in round 11 as the Luton man retained his Commonwealth crown at York Hall.

Making the fourth defence of his WBC International super-bantamweight title, Nassem Hamed ruthlessly destroyed Mexican, Enrique Angeles, inside two rounds at Shepton Mallet. Hamed's performance was truly awesome in its execution and he is on course for at least one major title. Probably more.

Making his own mark in the book, British lightweight champion, Michael Ayers, won his Lonsdale Belt outright in a record 95 days when he chopped down game, but overmatched challenger, Charles Shepherd, in three rounds at Potters Bar. Michael smashed the previous mark set by Colin McMillan, who won his belt in 160 days in 1991.

The case for a super-heavyweight division in pro boxing was further emphasised at Glasgow where Frank Bruno toppled American Mike Evans in two rounds to keep alive his world title crack at Oliver McCall, scheduled for London in July. Evans lacked ambition and, at a whopping 19st 4½lbs, certainly lacked condition. Bruno scaled 17st 10lbs and you had to fear for referee Dave Parris being crushed by one of these behemoths toppling to the canvas. Dave wisely kept his eye on Evans and was able to escape injury.

Possibly, referee, Paul Thomas, was in more danger from Dennis Andries after taking the old man's British cruiserweight title from him and awarding it to Terry Dunstan, who appeared just as surprised as the fans. The Hackney challenger had started well but Andries finished better and looked to have done enough to keep his crown. Not to Mr Thomas, however.

British super-featherweight champion, Floyd Havard, had designs on the WBO featherweight crown worn by fellow-Welshman, Steve Robinson, while former champion, Michael Armstrong, had his eye on his old title when they clashed at Swansea. The Manchester man was in superb condition and Havard had to dig deep before finding the punches to flatten Armstrong in the ninth.

Birmingham's Shaun Cogan jumped at the chance of fighting Ross Hale for his Commonwealth light-welterweight title after Ghanaian veteran, Razor Addo, pulled out of the match at Shepton Mallet. Cogan was floored twice and suffered left-eye damage, which ended his challenge in the fourth, but he gave the champ an argument while he was in there.

If at first you don't succeed, try, try again. Noel Magee became a firm believer in that old adage when he challenged unbeaten Garry Delaney for the Commonwealth light-heavyweight crown at Basildon. In four previous challenges for various titles, Magee had been stopped each time, and he was expected to fall against the big-punching West Hammer. Delaney had put together a 19-0-1 record, with 13 early wins, but after seven rounds it was he who was unable to go on, claiming a damaged left-hand. By then, it must be said, Magee was on top and looking all over a winner. At 29-years-of-age, and after ten years in the business, he was a champion!

When he became a professional boxer in 1989, Manchester's Delroy Waul looked a champion in the making. But he seemed to have lost his way during the last couple of years and even this fight with Roberto Welin, in Kiel for the WBU Global light-middleweight title, looked out of reach. But Waul turned in a fine performance to grab the title which, with a pound coin, will get him a ticket on the London Underground!

Birmingham's veteran light-middleweight, Paul Murray, lost a six-threes to Andrew Flute at Dudley Town Hall. It was Paul's 100th pro fight!

JUNE

It was blood, sweat, and tears for Robbie Regan when he finally got his shot at a world title, the WBO flyweight championship worn by the Mexican, Alberto Jimenez. The blood came in the fifth round of their fight at the Cardiff Ice Rink, from Robbie's left eye. The sweat came as Regan tried so hard to emulate his stablemate, Steve Robinson, by becoming the WBO champion. The tears came at the end of the ninth round as manager, Dai Gardiner, did the humane thing and pulled Robbie out of a fight he could no longer win. At 26, the former British and European champion still has some good fights left in him, but his world title limitations were cruelly exposed by the little man from Mexico.

Another former British and European champion going for a WBO title was Carl Thompson, and the Manchester puncher was favoured to pick up the vacant cruiserweight crown against Germany's Ralf Rocchigiani before his own fans at the G-Mex. By round 11, Carl had survived two knockdowns to build a solid points lead over his rugged opponent, only to be put out of the fight by a big right-hand punch. Ironically, it was a punch thrown by Carl himself that popped his right arm out of its socket and him out of the fight. The big puncher had knocked himself out!

It was victory for substance over style as Nottingham southpaw, Del Bryan, retained his British welterweight championship over Gary Logan at York Hall in Bethnal Green, the referee stopping the contest in round 11, with the Croydon challenger offering no resistance to Bryan's final assault. Logan had lost only two of 30 pro fights, but the champion had graduated from a tougher school, and it showed.

Three weeks later the York Hall showcased another champion, Commonwealth lightweight titleholder, Billy Schwer, of Luton, in action against tough Mexican, Bruno Rabanales, for ten rounds or less. It turned out to be less.

They were in round six when referee, Larry O'Connell, ruled the visitor out for persistently spitting out his gum-shield. Billy was winning it anyway, outboxing and out-punching the Mexican from the opening bell.

Say what you will, the WBO has been a Godsend for British boxing. On the same night, in Liverpool and Doncaster, their Continental titles were up for grabs and Richie Wenton and Jonjo Irwin cashed in. Already British super-bantamweight champion, Wenton won easily over Guyanese veteran, Mike Parris, in a fight that left a lot to be desired, while Irwin had a tougher job on his hands, but still boxed well enough to take the decision over the Spaniard, Manuel Calvo.

Up there in Musselburgh, Willie "The Mighty" Quinn latched on to a WBO label when he beat Paul Busby for the Worcester man's Continental middleweight title. Paul failed to come up for the ninth, claiming an injury to his right-ankle, but Willie and his army of fans went home happy in the thought that the better man had emerged triumphant.

One WBO title did get away from us, however, when Michael Alldis failed his big test at Basildon, being soundly beaten for the Continental super-bantamweight title by Laureano Ramirez, a Dominican Republican living in Spain. The Crawley boxer was in over his head after only a dozen fights and never looked like winning.

When two bangers get together it is not always who has the better punch, but who has the better chin. Kevin Lueshing had both and they brought him a third round victory over Michael Smyth in their British welterweight title eliminator at Cardiff. It was the Welshman's first loss in 17 fights.

Birmingham flyweight, Anthony Hanna, travelled to London as the Midlands Area champion, but found his road to the British title blocked by Mark Reynolds in an official eliminator at York Hall, the Sudbury boxer taking the decision in a competititve ten-rounder. Another "Brummie" hoping to parlay his Midlands Area title into a shot at the British championship was middleweight, Antonio Fernandez, but, like Hanna, he lost his eliminator to Derek Wormald in a tough scrap at Doncaster.

Thirty-seven is old for a professional fighter, 15 years is a long time in the hardest game of them all, and some 70-odd fights is more than enough. After losing his Midlands Area heavyweight title to Big Wayne Buck at the new Grimsby Auditorium, old Cordwell Hylton went home to Walsall and hung up his gloves for good.

Maybe he wasn't good enough to lick Julio Cesar Chavez, but he was British and Commonwealth light-welterweight champion before Ross Hale took his titles 13 months ago, and now Andy Holligan wants Hale again. He looked sharp in his comeback at Liverpool, dismantling Tony Foster inside two rounds, and maybe he can get back up there. He's trying anyway.

At Manchester, the 35-year-old veteran, John Smith, knocked out Wahid Fats in round three with a beautiful right-hook. It was only Smith's second win in his last 38 fights! Bring on the champ!

Facts and Figures, 1994-95

There were 676 British-based boxers who were active between 1 July 1994 and 30 June 1995, spread over 224 promotions held in Britain during the same period. The above figure comprised 544 boxers already holding licenses or having been licensed previously, five foreign-born boxers who started their careers elsewhere, and 127 new professionals. Although promotions were up by two shows on the previous season, there was a reduction of 36 on boxers used.

Unbeaten during season (minimum qualification: 6 contests) 10: Mark Delaney. 9: Michael Brodie. 8: Colin Dunne, Kevin McBride. 7: Dean Francis, Andy McVeigh, Nicky Thurbin. 6: Prince Nassem Hamed, Ady Lewis, James Murray, Willie Quinn, Robin Reid, Derek Roche, Paul Ryan, Georgie Smith, Darren Sweeney, Clinton Woods.

Longest unbeaten sequence (minimum qualification: 10 contests) 26: Henry Akinwande (1 draw). 23: Robert McCracken. 19: John Armour, Jason Rowland, Richie Woodhall. 18: Dave Anderson, Prince Nassem Hamed, Justin Juuko, Paul Ryan. 17: Mark Delaney, Willie Quinn. 16: Cornelius Carr, Kevin McBride (1 draw). 15: Gilbert Jackson, Bruce Scott. 14: Nigel Benn (1 draw), Robin Reid (1 draw). 13: Mark Bowers, Colin Dunne, Lester Jacobs, Shea Neary. 12: Adrian Dodson, Barry Jones, Mark Smallwood, Nicky Thurbin, 11: Joe Calzaghe, P. J. Gallagher, Gareth Jordan. 10: Tanveer Ahmed, Ross Hale, Ray Kane, James Murray, Robert Norton (1 draw).

Most wins during season (minimum qualification: 6 contests) 10: Mark Delaney. 9: Michael Brodie. 8: Colin Dunne, Keith Fletcher, Kevin McBride. 7: Howard Clarke, Dean Francis, Neil Swain, Nicky Thurbin. 6: Dave Battey, Prince Nassem Hamed, Ady Lewis, Graham McGrath, Andy McVeigh, Anthony Maynard, James Murray, Dean Phillips, Willie Quinn, Robin Reid, Derek Roche, Paul Ryan, Georgie Smith, Darren Sweeney, Clinton Woods.

Most contests during season (minimum qualification: 10 contests) 16: Graham McGrath. 14: Pete Buckley, Julian Eavis. 13: Garry Burrell, Shamus Casey. 11: Wayne Jones, Kid McAuley, Paul Murray, Steve Osborne, Andy Peach. 10: Mark Allen, Marty Chestnut, Brian Coleman, Mark Dawson, Mark Delaney, Martin Jolley, Rick North, Neil Parry, Art Stacey.

Most contests during career (minimum qualification: 50) 138: Shamus Casey. 108: Des Gargano. 101: Paul Murray. 92: Julian Eavis. 79: Miguel Matthews. 73: Cordwell Hylton. 72: Pete Buckley. 70: John Smith. 64: Steve Pollard. 62: Dennis Andries. 61: Dave Owens. 56: Kirkland Laing. 55: Tony Foster, Sugar Gibiluru, Trevor Meikle. 53: Migel Rafferty. 51: Mark Antony.

Diary of British Boxing Tournaments, 1994-95

Tournaments are listed by date, town, venue, and promoter and cover the period 1 July 1994 - 30 June 1995

Code: SC = Sporting Club

Date	Town	Venue	Promoters
02.07.94	Keynsham	Rugby Ground	Sanigar
02.07.94	Liverpool	Moat House Hotel	Vaughan
09.07.94	Earls Court	Olympia Grand Hall	Matchroom
21.07.94	Battersea	Town Hall	Carew
21.07.94	Edinburgh	Assembly Rooms	Morrison
28.07.94	Tooting	Leisure Centre	Anglo-Swedish Promotions
30.07.94	Bethnal Green	York Hall	Spensley
03.08.94	Bristol	Whitchurch Leisure Centre	Maloney/Sanigar
17.08.94	Sheffield	Hillsborough Leisure Centre	Warren
26.08.94	Barnsley	Metrodome	Gray
27.08.94	Cardiff	International Arena	Matchroom
02.09.94	Spitafields	Covered Market	Holdsworth
05.09.94	Brentwood	Heybridge Moat House Hotel	Matchroom
06.09.94	Stoke	Moat House Hotel	Brogan
08.09.94	Glasgow	Hospitality Inn	Morrison
10.09.94	Birmingham	National Exhibition Centre	Warren
12.09.94	Doncaster	Earl of Doncaster Hotel	Rushton
12.09.94	Mayfair	Marriott Hotel	National Promotions
17.09.94	Crawley	Leisure Centre	Matchroom
19.09.94	Glasgow	Forte Crest Hotel	St Andrew's SC
20.09.94	Musselburgh	Brunton Hall	St Andrew's SC
21.09.94	Cardiff	Star Leisure Centre	Warren
22.09.94	Bury	Castle Leisure Centre	Tara Boxing Promotions
23.09.94	Bethnal Green	York Hall	National Promotions
24.09.94	Wembley	Arena	Maloney
26.09.94	Bradford	Norfolk Gardens	Yorkshire Executive SC
26.09.94	Morecambe	Carlton Club	Tara Boxing Promotions
26.09.94	Liverpool	Everton Park Sports Centre	Vaughan
26.09.94	Cleethorpes	Winter Gardens	Gray
28.09.94	Glasgow	Forte Crest Hotel	St Andrew's SC
29.09.94	Walsall	Town Hall	Gray
29.09.94	Bethnal Green	York Hall	Maloney
29.09.94	Tynemouth	Park Hotel	St Andrew's SC
30.09.94	Bethnal Green	York Hall	Matchroom
01.10.94	Cardiff	National Ice Rink	Warren/Gardiner
03.10.94	Manchester	Piccadilly Hotel	Trickett
04.10.94	Mayfair	Grosvenor House	Matchroom
05.10.94	Wolverhampton	Civic Hall	National Promotions
06.10.94	Cramlington	High Pit Club	O'Brien
06.10.94	Hull	Royal Hotel	Hull & District SC
07.10.94	Taunton	Blackbrook Pavilion	Sanigar
11.10.94	Wolverhampton	Park Hall Hotel	Wolverhampton SC
11.10.94	Bethnal Green	York Hall	National Promotions
12.10.94	Sheffield	Ponds Forge Centre	Warren
12.10.94	Stoke	Trentham Gardens	North Staffs SC
13.10.94	Houghton le Spring	McEwan's Indoor Centre	Winning Combination
17.10.94	Birmingham	Grand Hotel	Cowdell
17.10.94	Mayfair	Marriott Hotel	National Promotions
20.10.94	Walsall	Saddlers' Club	Gray
20.10.94	Middleton	Civic Centre	Tara Boxing Promotions
21.10.94	Glasgow	Hospitality Inn	Morrison
24.10.94	Glasgow	Forte Crest Hotel	St Andrew's SC

Date	Town	Venue	Promoters
24.10.94	Bradford	Norfolk Gardens	Yorkshire Executive SC
25.10.94	Southwark	Elephant & Castle Leisure Centre	Maloney
25.10.94	Edgbaston	Tower Ballroom	Gray
25.10.94	Middlesbrough	Town Hall	Spensley
26.10.94	Leeds	Town Hall	National Promotions
26.10.94	Stoke	Moat House Hotel	Brogan
27.10.94	Bayswater	Royal Lancaster Hotel	Nordoff/Robbins Trust
27.10.94	Millwall	Britannia Hotel	Peacock Promotions
29.10.94	Cannock	Chase Leisure Centre	Gray
31.10.94	Liverpool	Moat House Hotel	Vaughan
02.11.94	Birmingham	Albion Hotel	Cowdell
02.11.94	Solihull	Conference Centre	Midland SC
07.11.94	Bethnal Green	York Hall	Matchroom
07.11.94	Piccadilly	Cafe Royal	Maloney
09.11.94	Stafford	Coliseum Night Club	Gray
09.11.94	Millwall	London Arena	National Promotions
16.11.94	Bloomsbury	Forte Crest Hotel	Brogan
17.11.94	Sheffield	Pinegrove County Club	Hobson
18.11.94	Glasgow	Hospitality Inn	Morrison
18.11.94	Bracknell	Leisure Centre	Evans
19.11.94	Cardiff	National Ice Rink	Warren/Gardiner
19.11.94	Heathrow	Park Hotel	Holland
21.11.94	Glasgow	Forte Crest Hotel	St Andrew's SC
22.11.94	Bristol	Whitchurch Leisure Centre	Maloney/Sanigar
23.11.94	Irvine	Magnum Centre	St Andrew's SC
23.11.94	Piccadilly	Cafe Royal	Maloney
24.11.94	Hull	Humberside Arena	Pollard
24.11.94	Newcastle	Mayfair Suite	Fawcett
27.11.94	Southwark	Elephant & Castle Leisure Centre	Gee
28.11.94	Northampton	Glenville's Nightclub	Cox
28.11.94	Manchester	Piccadilly Hotel	Trickett
29.11.94	Cannock	Chase Leisure Centre	Matchroom
29.11.94	Cardiff	Welsh Institute of Sport	Gardiner
29.11.94	Wolverhampton	Park Hall Hotel	Wolverhampton SC
30.11.94	Wolverhampton	Civic Hall	National Promotions
30.11.94	Solihull	Conference Centre	Midland SC
05.12.94	Bradford	Norfolk Gardens	Yorkshire Executive SC
05.12.94	Houghton le Spring	McEwan's Indoor Centre	Winning Combination
05.12.94	Birmingham	Grand Hotel	Cowdell
05.12.94	Cleethorpes	Beachcomber	Frater
07.12.94	Stoke	Moat House Hotel	Brogan
07.12.94	Stoke	Trentham Gardens	North Staffs SC
08.12.94	Hull	Royal Hotel	Hull & District SC
09.12.94	Bethnal Green	York Hall	National Promotions
10.12.94	Manchester	G-Mex Centre	Matchroom
12.12.94	Cleethorpes	Winter Gardens	Gray
12.12.94	Doncaster	Earl of Doncaster Hotel	Rushton
13.12.94	Ilford	Island Venue	Maloney
13.12.94	Potters Bar	Furzefield Leisure Centre	Matchroom
15.12.94	Evesham	Public Halls	Evesham SC
15.12.94	Walsall	Saddlers' Club	Gray
18.12.94	Glasgow	Hospitality Inn	Morrison
20.12.94	Bethnal Green	York Hall	Matchroom
12.01.95	Leeds	Queens Hotel	Sportsman Promotions
16.01.95	Musselburgh	Brunton Hall	St Andrew's SC
17.01.95	Worcester	Perdiswell Leisure Centre	Matchroom
18.01.95	Solihull	Conference Centre	Midland SC
20.01.95	Bethnal Green	York Hall	National Promotions

Date	Town	Venue	Promoters
21.01.95	Glasgow	Scottish Exhibition Centre	Warren
23.01.95	Bethnal Green	York Hall	Maloney
23.01.95	Glasgow	Forte Crest Hotel	St Andrew's SC
24.01.95	Piccadilly	Cafe Royal	Maloney
25.01.95	Cardiff	Welsh Institute of Sport	Gardiner
25.01.95	Stoke	Moat House Hotel	Brogan
25.01.95	Stoke	Trentham Gardens	North Staffs SC
30.01.95	Bradford	Norfolk Gardens	Yorkshire Executive SC
04.02.95	Cardiff	National Ice Rink	Warren/Gardiner
07.02.95	Ipswich	Corn Exchange	Maloney
07.02.95	Wolverhampton	Park Hall Hotel	Wolverhampton SC
09.02.95	Doncaster	Dome	Rushton
10.02.95	Birmingham	Aston Villa Leisure Centre	National Promotions
14.02.95	Bethnal Green	York Hall	National Promotions
16.02.95	Bury	Castle Leisure Centre	Tara Boxing Promotions
17.02.95	Crawley	Leisure Centre	Matchroom
17.02.95	Cumbernauld	Tryst Centre	Spensley
18.02.95	Shepton Mallet	Bath & West Country Showground	Warren
20.02.95	Manchester	Piccadilly Hotel	Trickett
20.02.95	Glasgow	Forte Crest Hotel	St Andrew's SC
21.02.95	Sunderland	Crowtree Leisure Centre	St Andrew's SC
22.02.95	Telford	Ice Rink	National Promotions
23.02.95	Hull	Royal Hotel	Hull & District SC
23.02.95	Southwark	Elephant & Castle Leisure Centre	Maloney
24.02.95	Irvine	Volunteer Rooms	St Andrew's SC
24.02.95	Weston super Mare	Winter Gardens	Queensberry Yeo Ltd
25.02.95	Millwall	London Arena	Warren
27.02.95	Barrow	Forum 28	Vaughan
01.03.95	Glasgow	Forte Crest Hotel	St Andrew's SC
02.03.95	Glasgow	Hospitality Inn	Morrison
02.03.95	Cramlington	High Pit Club	Fawcett
03.03.95	Bracknell	Leisure Centre	Evans
03.03.95	Bethnal Green	York Hall	National Promotions
04.03.95	Livingston	Forum	Warren
06.03.95	Leicester	Coliseum	Griffin
06.03.95	Mayfair	Grosvenor House	Matchroom
06.03.95	Bradford	Norfolk Gardens	Yorkshire Executive SC
06.03.95	Mayfair	Marriott Hotel	National Promotions
07.03.95	Edgbaston	Tower Ballrooms	Cowdell
08.03.95	Cardiff	City Hall	Gardiner
08.03.95	Bloomsbury	Forte Crest Hotel	Brogan
08.03.95	Solihull	Conference Centre	Midland SC
09.03.95	Walsall	Saddlers' Club	Gray
11.03.95	Barnsley	Metrodome	Doyle
15.03.95	Stoke	Moat House Hotel	Brogan
16.03.95	Sunderland	Crowtree Leisure Centre	Winning Combination
16.03.95	Basildon	Festival Hall	Matchroom
20.03.95	Birmingham	Grand Hotel	Cowdell
20.03.95	Glasgow	Forte Crest Hotel	St Andrew's SC
21.03.95	Swansea	Dillwyn Llewellyn Leisure Centre	Dragon Boxing Promotions
22.03.95	Stoke	Trentham Gardens	North Staffs SC
25.03.95	Chester	Northgate Arena	Vaughan
25.03.95	Rothwell	Leisure Centre	Sportsman Promotions
25.03.95	Millwall	Britannia Hotel	Peacock Promotions
28.03.95	Wolverhampton	Park Hall Hotel	Wolverhampton SC
30.03.95	Bethnal Green	York Hall	Maloney
31.03.95	Crystal Palace	National Sports Centre	Matchroom
03.04.95	Northampton	Glenville's Nightclub	Cox

Date	Town	Venue	Promoters
03.04.95	Manchester	Piccadilly Hotel	Trickett
05.04.95	Irvine	Magnum Leisure Centre	St Andrew's SC/Matchroom
06.04.95	Sheffield	Pinegrove Country Club	Hobson
12.04.95	Llanelli	Leisure Centre	Gardiner
13.04.95	Bloomsbury	Royal National Hotel	Matthews
14.04.95	Belfast	Ulster Hall	Matchroom
19.04.95	Bethnal Green	York Hall	National Promotions
20.04.95	Mayfair	Hilton Hotel	National Promotions
20.04.95	Liverpool	Everton Park Sports Centre	Vaughan
21.04.95	Dudley	Town Hall	National Promotions
21.04.95	Glasgow	Hospitality Inn	Morrison
24.04.95	Glasgow	Forte Crest Hotel	St Andrew's SC
26.04.95	Stoke	Moat House Hotel	Brogan
26.04.95	Solihull	Conference Centre	Midland SC
27.04.95	Hull	Royal Hotel	Hull & District SC
27.04.95	Bethnal Green	York Hall	Maloney
05.05.95	Swansea	Brangwyn Hall	Matchroom
05.05.95	Doncaster	Dome	Rushton
06.05.95	Shepton Mallet	Bath & West Country Showground	Warren
09.05.95	Basildon	Festival Hall	Matchroom
11.05.95	Sunderland	Crowtree Leisure Centre	Winning Combination
11.05.95	Dudley	Town Hall	Cowdell
12.05.95	Bethnal Green	York Hall	National Promotions
13.05.95	Glasgow	Kelvin Hall	Warren
15.05.95	Bradford	Norfolk Gardens	Yorkshire Executive SC
15.05.95	Cleethorpes	Winter Gardens	Gray
17.05.95	Ipswich	Corn Exchange	Maloney
18.05.95	Middleton	Civic Hall	Tara Boxing Promotions
19.05.95	Leeds	Queen's Hotel	Sportsman Promotions
19.05.95	Southwark	Elephant & Castle Leisure Centre	National Promotions
22.05.95	Morecambe	Carlton Club	Tara Boxing Promotions
23.05.95	Potters Bar	Furzefield Leisure Centre	Matchroom
25.05.95	Reading	Rivermead Leisure Centre	Maloney
26.05.95	Norwich	Lads' Club	Evans
27.05.95	Belfast	King's Hall	Matchroom
01.06.95	Musselburgh	Brunton Hall	St Andrew's SC
02.06.95	Bethnal Green	York Hall	Warren
04.06.95	Bethnal Green	York Hall	Maloney
05.06.95	Birmingham	Grand Hotel	Cowdell
05.06.95	Glasgow	Forte Crest Hotel	St Andrew's SC
06.06.95	Leicester	Aylestone Leisure Centre	Griffin
08.06.95	Glasgow	Hospitality Inn	Morrison
10.06.95	Manchester	G-Mex Centre	Warren
12.06.95	Bradford	Norfolk Gardens	Yorkshire Executive SC
12.06.95	Manchester	New Century Hall	Jewish Blind Society
13.06.95	Basildon	Festival Hall	Matchroom
14.06.95	Batley	Frontier Club	UK Pro Box Promotions
16.06.95	Southwark	Elephant & Castle Leisure Centre	Maloney
16.06.95	Liverpool	Everton Park Sports Centre	Hyland
17.06.95	Cardiff	National Ice Rink	Warren/Gardiner
20.06.95	Edgbaston	Tower Ballrooms	Cowdell
22.06.95	Houghton le Spring	McEwan's Indoor Centre	Winning Combination
23.06.95	Bethnal Green	York Hall	National Promotions
24.06.95	Cleethorpes	Grimsby Auditorium	Frater
30.06.95	Doncaster	Dome	Matchroom/Vaughan
30.06.95	Liverpool	Everton Park Sports Centre	Matchroom/Rushton

Current British-Based Champions: Career Records

Shows the complete record of all British champions, or British boxers holding Commonwealth, European, IBF, WBA, WBC and WBO titles, who have been active between 1 July 1994 and 30 June 1995. Names in brackets are real names, where they differ from ring names, and the first place name given is the boxer's domicile. Boxers are either shown as self managed, or with a named manager, the information being supplied by the BBBoC shortly before going to press. Included this year is the record for the Ghanaian, Alfred Kotey, the WBO bantamweight champion, who had three fights in Britain last season and currently holds a BBBoC licence.

Henry Akinwande

Walworth. *Born* London, 12 October, 1965
Former Undefeated European Heavyweight Champion. Commonwealth Heavyweight Champion. Ht. 6'7"
Manager Self

04.10.89	Carlton Headley W CO 1 Kensington
08.11.89	Dennis Bailey W RSC 2 Wembley
06.12.89	Paul Neilson W RSC 1 Wembley
10.01.90	John Fairbairn W RSC 1 Kensington
14.03.90	Warren Thompson W PTS 6 Kensington
09.05.90	Mike Robinson W CO 1 Wembley
10.10.90	Tracy Thomas W PTS 6 Kensington
12.12.90	Francois Yrius W RSC 1 Kensington
06.03.91	J. B. Williamson W RSC 2 Wembley
06.06.91	Ramon Voorn W PTS 8 Barking
28.06.91	Marshall Tillman W PTS 8 Nice, France
09.10.91	Gypsy John Fury W CO 3 Manchester *(Elim. British Heavyweight Title)*
06.12.91	Tim Bullock W CO 3 Dussledorf, Germany
28.02.92	Young Joe Louis W RSC 3 Issy les Moulineaux, France
26.03.92	Tucker Richards W RSC 2 Telford
10.04.92	Lumbala Tshimba W PTS 8 Carquefou, France
05.05.92	Kimmuel Odum W DIS 6 Marseille, France
18.07.92	Steve Garber W RTD 2 Manchester
19.12.92	Axel Schulz DREW 12 Berlin, Germany *(Vacant European Heavyweight Title)*
18.03.93	Jimmy Thunder W PTS 12 Lewisham *(Vacant Commonwealth Heavyweight Title)*
01.05.93	Axel Schulz W PTS 12 Berlin, Germany *(Vacant European Heavyweight Title)*
06.11.93	Frankie Swindell W PTS 10 Sun City, South Africa
01.12.93	Biagio Chianese W RSC 4 Kensington *(European Heavyweight Title Defence)*
05.04.94	Johnny Nelson W PTS 10 Bethnal Green
23.07.94	Mario Schiesser W CO 7 Berlin, Germany *(European Heavyweight Title Defence)*
08.04.95	Calvin Jones W CO 2 Las Vegas, USA

Career: 26 contests, won 25, drew 1.

Francis Ampofo

Bethnal Green. *Born* Ghana, 5 June, 1967
British Flyweight Champion. Former Commonwealth Flyweight Champion. Ht. 5'1½"
Manager B. Hearn

Henry Akinwande   Tony Fitch

30.01.90	Neil Parry W PTS 6 Bethnal Green
06.03.90	Robbie Regan L PTS 6 Bethnal Green
29.05.90	Eric George W RSC 3 Bethnal Green
12.09.90	Eric George W CO 2 Bethnal Green
26.03.91	Ricky Beard W PTS 8 Bethnal Green
22.06.91	Neil Johnston W RSC 2 Earls Court
03.09.91	Robbie Regan W RSC 11 Cardiff *(British Flyweight Title Challenge)*
17.12.91	Robbie Regan L PTS 12 Cardiff *(British Flyweight Title Defence)*
25.02.92	Ricky Beard W PTS 8 Crystal Palace
16.06.92	Shaun Norman RSC 4 Dagenham
12.12.92	James Drummond W PTS 12 Mayfair *(Vacant British Flyweight Title)*
17.02.93	Alberto Cantu W RSC 5 Bethnal Green
29.06.93	Albert Musankabala W RSC 3 Mayfair *(Vacant Commonwealth Flyweight Title)*
11.06.94	Jacob Matlala L RTD 9 Bethnal Green *(WBO Flyweight Title Challenge)*
20.09.94	James Drummond W RSC 3 Musselburgh *(British Flyweight Title Defence)*

47

Francis Ampofo   Les Clark

20.12.94	Daren Fifield W RSC 2 Bethnal Green	
	(British Flyweight Title Defence.	
	Commonwealth Flyweight Title	
	Challenge)	
06.03.95	Danny Ward L CO 12 Mayfair	
	(Commonwealth Flyweight Title	
	Defence)	

Career: 17 contests, won 13, lost 4.

John Armour

Chatham. *Born* Chatham, 26 October, 1968
European & Commonwealth Bantamweight
Champion. Ht. 5'4¾"
Manager M. Duff

24.09.90	Lupe Castro W PTS 6 Lewisham
31.10.90	Juan Camero W RSC 4 Crystal Palace
21.01.91	Elijro Mejia W RSC 1 Crystal Palace
30.09.91	Pat Maher W CO 1 Kensington
29.10.91	Pete Buckley W PTS 6 Kensington
14.12.91	Gary Hickman W RSC 6 Bexleyheath
25.03.92	Miguel Matthews W PTS 6 Dagenham
30.04.92	Ndabe Dube W RSC 12 Kensington
	(Vacant Commonwealth Bantamweight
	Title)
17.10.92	Mauricio Bernal W PTS 8 Wembley
03.12.92	Albert Musankabala W RSC 6
	Lewisham
	(Commonwealth Bantamweight Title
	Defence)

28.01.93	Ricky Romero W CO 1 Southwark
10.02.93	Morgan Mpande W PTS 12 Lewisham
	(Commonwealth Bantamweight Title
	Defence)
09.06.93	Boualem Belkif W PTS 10 Lewisham
01.12.93	Karl Morling W CO 3 Kensington
14.01.94	Rufus Adebayo W RSC 7 Bethnal
	Green
	(Commonwealth Bantamweight Title
	Defence)
23.09.94	Shaun Anderson W RSC 11 Bethnal
	Green
	(Commonwealth Bantamweight Title
	Defence)
14.02.95	Tsitsi Sokutu W RSC 7 Bethnal Green
	(Commonwealth Bantamweight Title
	Defence)
19.04.95	Antonio Picardi W RSC 8 Bethnal
	Green
	(Vacant European Bantamweight Title)
19.05.95	Matthew Harris W RSC 3 Southwark

Career: 19 contests, won 19.

John Armour   Les Clark

(Gary) Crawford Ashley (Crawford)

Leeds. *Born* Leeds, 20 May, 1964
British L. Heavyweight Champion. Former
Undefeated Central Area L. Heavyweight
Champion. Ht. 6'3"
Manager Self

26.03.87	Steve Ward W RSC 2 Merton
29.04.87	Lee Woolis W RSC 3 Stoke
14.09.87	Glazz Campbell L PTS 8 Bloomsbury
07.10.87	Joe Frater W RSC 5 Burnley
28.10.87	Ray Thomas W RSC 1 Stoke
03.12.87	Jonjo Greene W RSC 7 Leeds
04.05.88	Johnny Nelson L PTS 8 Solihull
15.11.88	Richard Bustin W CO 3 Norwich
22.11.88	Cordwell Hylton W CO 3 Basildon
24.01.89	John Foreman W RSC 4 Kings Heath

Crawford Ashley (left) looks to set up Hunter Clay with the jab at Millwall last February   Les Clark

08.02.89	Lavell Stanley W CO 1 Kensington
28.03.89	Blaine Logsdon L RSC 2 Glasgow
10.05.89	Serg Fame W RTD 7 Solihull
31.10.89	Carl Thompson W RSC 6 Manchester
	(Vacant Central Area L. Heavyweight Title)
24.01.90	Brian Schumacher W RSC 3 Preston
	(Central Area L. Heavyweight Title Defence)
25.04.90	Dwain Muniz W RSC 1 Brighton
26.11.90	John Williams W RSC 1 Mayfair
12.02.91	Melvin Ricks W CO 1 Belfast
01.03.91	Graciano Rocchigiani L PTS 12 Dusseldorf, Germany
	(Vacant European L. Heavyweight Title)
25.07.91	Roy Skeldon W RSC 7 Dudley
	(Vacant British L. Heavyweight Title)
30.01.92	Jim Peters W RSC 1 Southampton
	(British L. Heavyweight Title Defence)
25.04.92	Glazz Campbell W RSC 8 Belfast
	(British L. Heavyweight Title Defence)
23.09.92	Yawe Davis DREW 12 Campione d'Italia, Italy
	(Vacant European L. Heavyweight Title)
23.04.93	Michael Nunn L RSC 5 Memphis, USA
	(WBA S. Middleweight Title Challenge)

29.01.94	Dennis Andries L RTD 4 Cardiff
19.11.94	Nicky Piper W PTS 12 Cardiff
	(Vacant British L. Heavyweight Title)
25.02.95	Hunter Clay W RTD 3 Millwall
01.04.95	Virgil Hill L PTS 12 Stateline, USA
	(WBA L. Heavyweight Title Challenge)

Career: 28 contests, won 20, drew 1, lost 7.

Michael Ayers

Tooting. *Born* London, 26 January, 1965
British Lightweight Champion. Former
Undefeated WBC International & Southern
Area Lightweight Champion. Ht. 5'8"
Manager B. Hearn

16.05.89	Young Joe Rafiu W RSC 5 Wandsworth
27.06.89	Greg Egbuniwe W CO 1 Kensington
15.11.89	Mille Markovic W RSC 2 Lewisham
05.12.89	Darren Mount W RSC 2 Catford
26.04.90	Nick Hall W CO 3 Wandsworth
04.06.91	Stuart Rimmer W CO 1 Bethnal Green
22.06.91	Wayne Weekes W RSC 6 Earls Court
	(Vacant Southern Area Lightweight Title)
21.09.91	Peter Till W RSC 5 Tottenham
	(Elim. British Lightweight Title)

28.01.92	Jorge Pompey W PTS 8 Hamburg, Germany
19.02.92	Rudy Valentino W RSC 7 Muswell Hill
	(Southern Area Lightweight Title Defence. Elim. British Lightweight Title)
27.06.92	Sugar Gibiliru W RSC 6 Quinta do Lago, Portugal
13.10.92	Scott Brouwer W RSC 4 Mayfair
	(Vacant WBC International Lightweight Title)
20.02.93	Danny Myburgh W RSC 5 Earls Court
	(WBC International Lightweight Title Defence)
16.04.93	Giovanni Parisi L PTS 12 Rome, Italy
	(WBO Lightweight Title Challenge)
24.05.94	Karl Taylor DREW 8 Sunderland
30.09.94	John O. Johnson W RSC 3 Bethnal Green
07.11.94	Bamana Dibateza W PTS 6 Bethnal Green
17.02.95	Paul Burke W RSC 6 Crawley
	(Vacant British Lightweight Title)
31.03.95	Karl Taylor W RSC 8 Crystal Palace
	(British Lightweight Title Defence)
23.05.95	Charles Shepherd W RSC 3 Potters Bar
	(British Lightweight Title Defence)

Career: 20 contests, won 18, drew 1, lost 1.

Michael Ayers   Les Clark

Nigel Benn

Ilford. *Born* Ilford, 22 January, 1964
WBC S. Middleweight Champion. Former
WBO & Commonwealth Middleweight
Champion. Ht. 5'9½"
Manager P. De Freitas

28.01.87	Graeme Ahmed W RSC 2 Croydon
04.03.87	Kevin Roper W RSC 1 Basildon
22.04.87	Bob Niewenhuizen W RSC 1 Kensington
09.05.87	Winston Burnett W RSC 4 Wandsworth
17.06.87	Reggie Marks W RSC 1 Kensington
01.07.87	Leon Morris W CO 1 Kensington
09.08.87	Eddie Smith W CO 1 Windsor
16.09.87	Winston Burnett W RSC 3 Kensington
13.10.87	Russell Barker W RSC 1 Windsor
03.11.87	Ronnie Yeo W RSC 1 Bethnal Green
24.11.87	Ian Chantler W CO 1 Wisbech
02.12.87	Reggie Miller W CO 7 Kensington
27.01.88	Fermin Chirinos W CO 2 Bethnal Green
07.02.88	Byron Prince W RSC 2 Stafford
24.02.88	Greg Taylor W RSC 2 Aberavon
14.03.88	Darren Hobson W CO 1 Norwich
20.04.88	Abdul Amoru Sanda W RSC 2 Muswell Hill
	(Vacant Commonwealth Middleweight Title)
28.05.88	Tim Williams W RSC 2 Kensington
26.10.88	Anthony Logan W CO 2 Kensington
	(Commonwealth Middleweight Title Defence)
10.12.88	David Noel W RSC 1 Crystal Palace
	(Commonwealth Middleweight Title Defence)
08.02.89	Mike Chilambe W CO 1 Kensington
	(Commonwealth Middleweight Title Defence)
28.03.89	Mbayo Wa Mbayo W CO 2 Glasgow

21.05.89	Michael Watson L CO 6 Finsbury Park
	(Commonwealth Middleweight Title Defence)
20.10.89	Jorge Amparo W PTS 10 Atlantic City, USA
01.12.89	Jose Quinones W RSC 1 Las Vegas, USA
14.01.90	Sanderline Williams W PTS 10 Atlantic City, USA
29.04.90	Doug de Witt W RSC 8 Atlantic City, USA
	(WBO Middleweight Title Challenge)
18.08.90	Iran Barkley W RSC 1 Las Vegas, USA
	(WBO Middleweight Title Defence)
18.11.90	Chris Eubank L RSC 9 Birmingham
	(WBO Middleweight Title Defence)
03.04.91	Robbie Sims W RSC 7 Bethnal Green
03.07.91	Kid Milo W RSC 4 Brentwood
26.10.91	Lenzie Morgan W PTS 10 Brentwood
07.12.91	Hector Lescano W CO 3 Manchester
19.02.92	Dan Sherry W RSC 3 Muswell Hill
23.05.92	Thulani Malinga W PTS 10 Birmingham
03.10.92	Mauro Galvano W RTD 3 Marino, Italy
	(WBC S. Middleweight Title Challenge)
12.12.92	Nicky Piper W RSC 11 Muswell Hill
	(WBC S. Middleweight Title Defence)
06.03.93	Mauro Galvano W PTS 12 Glasgow
	(WBC S. Middleweight Title Defence)
26.06.93	Lou Gent W RSC 4 Earls Court
	(WBC S. Middleweight Title Defence)
09.10.93	Chris Eubank DREW 12 Manchester
	(WBC S. Middleweight Title Defence. WBO S. Middleweight Title Challenge)
26.02.94	Henry Wharton W PTS 12 Earls Court
	(WBC S. Middleweight Title Defence)
10.09.94	Juan Carlos Gimenez W PTS 12 Birmingham
	(WBC S. Middleweight Title Defence)
25.02.95	Gerald McClellan W CO 10 Millwall
	(WBC S. Middleweight Title Defence)

Career: 43 contests, won 40, drew 1, lost 2.

Nigel Benn   Les Clark

Neville Brown   Les Clark

Neville Brown

Burton. *Born* Burton, 26 February, 1966
British Middleweight Champion. Ht. 5'10"
Manager F. Warren

08.11.89	Spencer Alton W RSC 4 Wembley
10.01.90	Colin Ford W RTD 4 Kensington
27.03.90	Jimmy McDonagh W RSC 2 Mayfair
09.05.90	William Pronzola W RSC 3 Wembley
13.09.90	Anthony Campbell W RSC 2 Watford
10.10.90	Nigel Moore W CO 1 Kensington
13.12.90	Chris Richards W RSC 2 Dewsbury
17.01.91	Shamus Casey W RSC 4 Alfreton
13.02.91	Jimmy Thornton W RSC 1 Wembley
28.03.91	Tony Booth W PTS 6 Alfreton
12.04.91	Winston Wray W RSC 1 Willenhall
04.07.91	Paul Wesley L RSC 1 Alfreton
29.08.91	Paul Smith W RSC 3 Oakengates
03.10.91	Paul Wesley W PTS 8 Burton
21.11.91	Colin Pitters W RSC 3 Burton
26.03.92	Paul Murray W CO 3 Telford
01.10.92	Ernie Loveridge W CO 4 Telford
02.11.92	Horace Fleary W PTS 8 Wolverhampton
04.12.92	Karl Barwise W RSC 6 Telford
20.01.93	Graham Burton W CO 4 Wolverhampton
16.03.93	Paul Busby W PTS 10 Wolverhampton
	(Elim. British Middleweight Title)
10.11.93	Frank Grant W RSC 7 Bethnal Green
	(British Middleweight Title Challenge)
26.01.94	Andrew Flute W RTD 7 Birmingham
	(British Middleweight Title Defence)
16.03.94	Wallid Underwood W PTS 10 Birmingham
20.07.94	Agostino Cardamone L RSC 7 Solofra, Italy
	(European Middleweight Title Challenge)
29.10.94	Colin Pitters W CO 2 Cannock
29.11.94	Antonio Fernandez W RSC 9 Cannock
	(British Middleweight Title Defence)
10.02.95	Steve Goodwin W RSC 3 Birmingham
03.03.95	Carlo Colarusso W RSC 7 Bethnal Green
	(British Middleweight Title Defence)

Career: 29 contests, won 27, lost 2.

(Delroy) Del Bryan

Nottingham. *Born* Nottingham, 16 April, 1967
British Welterweight Champion. Former Undefeated Midlands Area Welterweight Champion. Ht. 5'8"
Manager W. Swift

21.04.86	Wil Halliday W PTS 6 Birmingham
15.05.86	Gary Sommerville L PTS 6 Dudley
28.05.86	Trevor Hopson W RTD 4 Lewisham
26.06.86	Gary Sommerville L PTS 8 Edgbaston
26.09.86	Gary Cass W PTS 6 Swindon
06.10.86	Gary Sommerville W PTS 8 Birmingham
14.10.86	Mickey Lerwill W PTS 8 Wolverhampton
04.11.86	George Collins L RSC 4 Oldham
16.12.86	Ray Golding W PTS 6 Alfreton
08.01.87	Darren Dyer W PTS 6 Bethnal Green
17.02.87	Tommy Shiels L RSC 2 Alfreton
30.09.87	Peter Ashcroft W PTS 8 Solihull
26.10.87	Gary Sommerville W RSC 7 Birmingham
	(Vacant Midlands Area Welterweight Title)
03.12.87	Mickey Hughes W PTS 8 Southend
15.12.87	Lloyd Christie W PTS 8 Bradford
24.02.88	Gary Jacobs L PTS 10 Glasgow
	(Final Elim. British Welterweight Title)
09.03.88	Michael Justin DREW 8 Wembley
20.04.88	Kelvin Mortimer W RSC 4 Stoke
04.05.88	Gary Sommerville W PTS 8 Solihull
09.08.88	Jimmy Thornton W PTS 6 St Helier
28.09.88	Ossie Maddix W PTS 8 Solihull
12.12.88	Michael Justin W RSC 8 Nottingham
	(Midlands Area Welterweight Title Defence)
22.03.89	Lenny Gloster W PTS 8 Solihull
10.05.89	Crisanto Espana L PTS 8 Kensington
19.08.89	Javier Castillejos W PTS 8 Benidorm, Spain
04.09.89	Joni Nyman L PTS 8 Helsinki, Finland
30.01.90	Simon Eubank W PTS 6 Battersea
16.02.90	Arvey Castro W RSC 1 Bilbao, Spain
17.04.90	Damien Denny W PTS 10 Millwall
	(Final Elim. British Welterweight Title)
30.09.90	Phumzile Madikane L RSC 6 Capetown, South Africa
16.01.91	Kirkland Laing W PTS 12 Wolverhampton
	(British Welterweight Title Challenge)
16.04.91	Anthony Ivory W PTS 10 Nottingham
26.11.91	Mickey Hughes W RSC 3 Bethnal Green
	(British Welterweight Title Defence)
20.02.92	Gary Jacobs L PTS 12 Glasgow
	(British Welterweight Title Challenge)
12.05.92	Darren Dyer L RSC 10 Crystal Palace
29.09.92	Chris Peters W PTS 10 Stok
02.01.93	Godfrey Nyakana L PTS 8 Differdange, Luxembourg
05.05.93	Oscar Checca W CO 2 Belfast
11.08.93	Sidney Msutu W PTS 10 Durban, South Africa
22.09.93	Pat Barrett W PTS 12 Bethnal Green
	(Vacant British Welterweight Title)
17.02.94	Derek Grainger W CO 7 Dagenham
	(British Welterweight Title Defence)
11.05.94	Paul Lynch W PTS 8 Sheffield
10.09.94	Lindon Scarlett W PTS 12 Birmingham
	(British Welterweight Title Defence)
17.12.94	Jose Luis Navarro L RSC 10 Cordoba, Spain
	(Vacant European Welterweight Title)
02.06.95	Gary Logan W RSC 11 Bethnal Green
	(British Welterweight Title Defence)

Career: 45 contests, won 32, drew 1, lost 12.

Del Bryan   Les Clark

Steve Collins

Dublin. *Born* Dublin, 21 July, 1964
WBO S. Middleweight Champion. Former Undefeated USBA, WBO, Penta-Continental & All-Ireland Middleweight Champion. Ht. 5'11"
Manager Self

24.10.86	Julio Mercado W RSC 3 Lowell, USA
26.11.86	Mike Bonislawski W PTS 4 Dorchester, USA
20.12.86	Richard Holloway W RSC 2 Dorchester, USA
10.10.87	Jim Holmes W CO 1 Attleboro, USA
29.10.87	Harold Souther W PTS 8 Lowell, USA
20.11.87	Mike Williams W PTS 6 Atlantic City, USA
09.12.87	Benny Sims W PTS 8 Atlantic City, USA
18.03.88	Sammy Storey W PTS 10 Boston, USA
	(Vacant All-Ireland Middleweight Title)
26.05.88	Lester Yarborough W PTS 10 Boston, USA
30.07.88	Mike Dale W PTS 8 Brockton, USA
22.10.88	Muhammad Shabbaz W RSC 4 Salem, USA
10.12.88	Jesse Lanton W PTS 10 Salem, USA
07.02.89	Paul McPeek W RSC 9 Atlantic City, USA
09.05.89	Kevin Watts W PTS 12 Atlantic City, USA
	(USBA Middleweight Title Challenge)
16.07.89	Tony Thornton W PTS 12 Atlantic City, USA
	(USBA Middleweight Title Defence)
21.11.89	Roberto Rosiles W RSC 9 Las Vegas, USA
03.02.90	Mike McCallum L PTS 12 Boston, USA
	(WBA Middleweight Title Challenge)
16.08.90	Fermin Chirino W RSC 6 Boston, USA
24.11.90	Eddie Hall W PTS 10 Boston, USA
11.05.91	Kenny Snow W RSC 3 Belfast
22.05.91	Jean-Noel Camara W CO 3 Brest, France
11.12.91	Danny Morgan W RSC 3 Dublin
22.04.92	Reggie Johnson L PTS 12 East Rutherford, USA
	(Vacant WBA Middleweight Title)
22.10.92	Sumbu Kalambay L PTS 12 Verbania, Italy
	(European Middleweight Title Challenge)
06.02.93	Johnny Melfah W RSC 3 Cardiff
20.02.93	Ian Strudwick W RSC 7 Kensington
26.06.93	Gerhard Botes W RSC 7 Kensington
	(Vacant Penta-Continental Middleweight Title)
30.11.93	Wayne Ellis W RSC 9 Cardiff
	(Penta-Continental Middleweight Title Defence)
22.01.94	Johnny Melfah W RSC 4 Belfast
09.02.94	Paul Wesley W PTS 8 Brentwood
11.05.94	Chris Pyatt W RSC 5 Sheffield
	(WBO Middleweight Title Challenge)
18.03.95	Chris Eubank W PTS 12 Millstreet, Eire
	(WBO S. Middleweight Title Challenge)

Career: 32 contests, won 29, lost 3.

Steve Collins   Les Clark

Mike Deveney

Paisley. *Born* Elderslie, 14 December, 1965
British Featherweight Champion. Ht. 5'5"
Manager N. Sweeney

18.02.91	John George W PTS 6 Glasgow
18.03.91	Frankie Ventura W PTS 6 Piccadilly
22.04.91	Neil Leitch W PTS 6 Glasgow

09.09.91	Pete Buckley W PTS 8 Glasgow
19.09.91	Noel Carroll L PTS 6 Stockport
14.11.91	Pete Buckley W PTS 6 Edinburgh
28.01.92	Graham O'Malley L RSC 1 Piccadilly
28.02.92	Gary Hickman W PTS 6 Irvine
14.09.92	David Ramsden L PTS 6 Bradford
07.10.92	Mark Hargreaves L RSC 7 Glasgow
07.12.92	Carl Roberts W PTS 6 Manchester
27.01.93	Barry Jones L PTS 6 Cardiff
26.02.93	Alan Graham W PTS 6 Irvine
23.03.93	Colin Lynch W PTS 6 Wolverhampton
29.05.93	Dave Buxton W PTS 6 Paisley
20.09.93	Ady Benton W PTS 8 Glasgow
30.11.93	Elvis Parsley L PTS 6 Wolverhampton
24.01.94	Ady Benton L PTS 6 Glasgow
02.03.94	Yusuf Vorajee W PTS 6 Solihull
21.03.94	Chris Jickells W RSC 5 Glasgow
15.04.94	Chris Clarkson W RSC 3 Hull
06.06.94	Mark Hargreaves W PTS 6 Manchester
15.06.94	Justin Murphy L PTS 6 Southwark
29.09.94	Henry Armstrong W PTS 8 Tynemouth
24.10.94	Henry Armstrong W PTS 10 Glasgow
	(Elim. British Featherweight Title)
23.01.95	Wilson Docherty W PTS 12 Glasgow
	(Vacant British Featherweight Title)
04.03.95	Dean Phillips L PTS 8 Livingston

Career: 27 contests, won 18, lost 9.

Mike Deveney   Chris Bevan

(Andrew) Drew Docherty

Croy. *Born* Glasgow, 29 November, 1965
British Bantamweight Champion. Ht. 5'6"
Manager T. Gilmour

14.09.89	Gordon Shaw W PTS 6 Motherwell
23.11.89	Chris Clarkson W PTS 6 Motherwell
09.05.90	Rocky Lawlor DREW 8 Solihull
03.10.90	Steve Robinson W PTS 8 Solihull
21.11.90	Pete Buckley W PTS 8 Solihull
14.11.91	Stevie Woods W RSC 1 Edinburgh
27.01.92	Neil Parry W RSC 4 Glasgow
27.04.92	Pete Buckley W PTS 8 Glasgow
01.06.92	Joe Kelly W RSC 5 Glasgow
	(British Bantamweight Title Challenge)
25.01.93	Donnie Hood W PTS 12 Glasgow
	(British Bantamweight Title Defence)

26.04.93	Russell Davison W PTS 8 Glasgow
25.10.93	Pete Buckley W PTS 8 Glasgow
02.02.94	Vincenzo Belcastro L PTS 12 Glasgow
	(European Bantamweight Title Challenge)
09.07.94	Conn McMullen W PTS 8 Earls Court
20.09.94	Miguel Matthews W PTS 8 Musselburgh
23.11.94	Ady Benton W PTS 12 Irvine
	(British Bantamweight Title Defence)
17.02.95	Alfred Kotey L RSC 4 Cumbernauld
	(WBO Bantamweight Title Challenge)

Career: 17 contests, won 14, drew 1, lost 2.

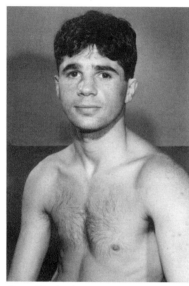

Drew Docherty
George Ashton, Sportapics Ltd

Terry Dunstan   Les Clark

Terry Dunstan

Vauxhall. *Born* London, 21 October, 1968
British Cruiserweight Champion. Ht. 6'3"
Manager F. Warren

12.11.92	Steve Osborne W PTS 6 Bayswater
25.11.92	Steve Yorath W PTS 8 Mayfair
31.03.93	Lee Prudden W PTS 6 Barking
15.09.93	Paul McCarthy W RSC 3 Ashford
02.12.93	Devon Rhooms W RSC 1 Sheffield
30.09.94	Michael Murray W PTS 8 Bethnal Green
20.12.94	Trevor Small W RTD 4 Bethnal Green
04.03.95	Art Stacey W CO 1 Livingston
13.05.95	Dennis Andries W PTS 12 Glasgow
	(British Cruiserweight Title Challenge)

Career: 9 contests, won 9.

Ross Hale

Bristol. *Born* Bristol, 28 February, 1967
British & Commonwealth L. Welterweight
Champion. Former Undefeated Western
Area Welterweight Champion. Ht. 5'9"
Manager C. Sanigar

16.11.89	Dave Jenkins W PTS 6 Weston super Mare
30.11.89	Tony Gibbs W PTS 6 Mayfair
12.12.89	Chris McReedy W RSC 4 Brentford
13.03.90	Davey Hughes W RSC 3 Bristol
30.04.90	Andy Robins W RSC 4 Bristol
12.09.90	Derrick Daniel W PTS 6 Bethnal Green
21.11.90	Mark Kelly W PTS 8 Chippenham
29.11.90	Chris Saunders W PTS 6 Bayswater
24.10.91	Greg Egbuniwe W RSC 4 Bayswater
22.01.92	Tony Borg W PTS 6 Cardiff
30.04.92	Jason Matthews W RSC 3 Bayswater
12.05.92	John Smith W CO 1 Crystal Palace
07.07.92	Julian Eavis W RSC 8 Bristol
	(Vacant Western Area Welterweight Title)
05.10.92	Malcolm Melvin W PTS 10 Bristol
	(Elim. British L. Welterweight Title)
01.12.92	Sugar Gibiliru W RSC 1 Bristol
27.01.93	Andreas Panayi L RSC 3 Cardiff
26.06.93	Mark Antony W RSC 1 Keynsham
28.07.93	Gary Barron W CO 2 Brixton
01.10.93	Carlos Chase W RTD 8 Cardiff
	(Elim. British L. Welterweight Title)
03.11.93	Regino Caceres W CO 2 Bristol
11.12.93	Stephen Schramm W RSC 4 Dusseldorf, Germany
22.01.94	Michael Driscoll W RSC 7 Cardiff
	(Elim. British L. Welterweight Title)
25.05.94	Andy Holligan W RSC 3 Bristol
	(British & Commonwealth L. Welterweight Title Challenge)
03.08.94	Hugh Forde W RSC 7 Bristol
	(British L. Welterweight Title Defence)
18.02.95	Malcolm Melvin W PTS 12 Shepton Mallet
	(British & Commonwealth Welterweight Title Defence)
06.05.95	Shaun Cogan W RSC 4 Shepton Mallet
	(Commonwealth L. Welterweight Title Defence)

Career: 26 contests, won 25, lost 1.

Ross Hale   Les Clark

Billy Hardy

Sunderland. *Born* Sunderland, 15
September, 1964
Commonwealth Featherweight Champion.
Former Undefeated British Featherweight
Champion. Former Undefeated British
Bantamweight Champion. Ht. 5'6"
Manager T. Gilmour

21.11.83	Kevin Downer W PTS 6 Eltham	
03.12.83	Brett Styles W PTS 6 Marylebone	
27.01.84	Keith Ward W PTS 6 Longford	
13.02.84	Johnny Mack W RSC 6 Eltham	
01.03.84	Graham Kid Clarke W PTS 8 Queensway	
27.03.84	Glen McLaggon W PTS 6 Battersea	
06.04.84	Graham Kid Clarke W RSC 7 Watford	
25.04.84	Anthony Brown W RSC 5 Muswell Hill	
04.06.84	Roy Webb L PTS 6 Mayfair	
06.09.84	Les Walsh W PTS 6 Gateshead	
10.10.84	Jorge Prentas L RSC 5 Shoreditch	
12.02.85	Ivor Jones W PTS 8 Kensington	
17.04.85	Ivor Jones W PTS 10 Bethnal Green	
08.06.85	Valerio Nati L RSC 4 Florence, Italy	
10.10.85	Keith Wallace W RSC 7 Alfreton *(Final Elim. British Bantamweight Title)*	
02.06.86	Rocky Lawlor W PTS 8 Mayfair	
19.02.87	Ray Gilbody W RSC 3 St Helens *(British Bantamweight Title Challenge)*	
23.04.87	Rocky Lawlor W RSC 7 Newcastle	
04.06.87	Brian Holmes W PTS 10 Sunderland	
17.03.88	John Hyland W CO 2 Sunderland *(British Bantamweight Title Defence)*	
11.05.88	Luis Ramos W RSC 2 Wembley	
29.09.88	Jose Gallegos W RSC 4 Sunderland	
02.11.88	Vincenzo Belcastro L PTS 12 Paolo, Italy *(European Bantamweight Title Challenge)*	
14.02.89	Ronnie Carroll W PTS 12 Sunderland *(British Bantamweight Title Defence)*	
29.03.89	Jose Soto W PTS 8 Wembley	
28.06.89	Vincenzo Belcastro DREW 12 Pavia, Italy *(European Bantamweight Title Challenge)*	
10.10.89	Brian Holmes W CO 1 Sunderland *(British Bantamweight Title Defence)*	
24.01.90	Orlando Canizales L PTS 12 Sunderland *(IBF Bantamweight Title Challenge)*	
22.05.90	Miguel Pequeno W RSC 4 Stockton	
29.11.90	Ronnie Carroll W RSC 8 Sunderland *(British Bantamweight Title Defence)*	
28.02.91	Francisco Ortiz W RSC 7 Sunderland	
04.05.91	Orlando Canizales L RSC 8 Laredo, USA *(IBF Bantamweight Title Challenge)*	
03.03.92	Chris Clarkson W RSC 5 Houghton le Spring	
07.10.92	Ricky Raynor W RSC 10 Sunderland *(Vacant Commonwealth Featherweight Title)*	
19.05.93	Barrington Francis W PTS 12 Sunderland *(Commonwealth Featherweight Title Defence)*	
15.06.93	Angel Fernandez W PTS 10 Hemel Hempstead	
30.11.93	Mustapha Hame L PTS 8 Marseilles, France	
24.05.94	Alan McKay W RSC 8 Sunderland *(Vacant British Featherweight Title)*	
15.10.94	Stanford Ngcebeshe W PTS 12 Sun City, South Africa *(Commonwealth Featherweight Title Defence)*	
21.02.95	Percy Commey W RSC 11 Sunderland *(Commonwealth Featherweight Title Defence)*	
04.03.95	Fabrice Benichou DREW 10 St Quentin, France	

Career: 41 contests, won 32, drew 2, lost 7.

Billy Hardy

Floyd Havard

Swansea. *Born* Swansea, 16 October, 1965
British S. Featherweight Champion.
Ht. 5'8"
Manager Self

30.11.85	Dean Brahmald W RSC 3 Cardiff	
22.01.86	Sugar Gibiliru W PTS 6 Muswell Hill	
20.02.86	Dean Brahmald W PTS 6 Halifax	
10.03.86	Russell Jones W PTS 8 Cardiff	
28.04.86	Tony McLaggon W CO 2 Cardiff	
24.05.86	Sugar Gibiliru W PTS 8 Manchester	
20.09.86	George Jones W RSC 4 Hemel Hempstead	
25.10.86	Joe Duffy W RSC 3 Stevenage	
29.11.86	Marvin P. Gray W RSC 2 Wandsworth	
14.03.87	Nigel Senior W RSC 5 Southwark	

Floyd Havard (left) forces Neil Haddock to cover up during his British super-featherweight title challenge   Les Clark

14.04.87	Ray Newby W RSC 7 Cumbernauld
28.04.87	Hector Clottey W RSC 5 Halifax
19.05.87	Kid Sumali W RTD 2 Cumbernauld
22.09.87	Frank Loukil W RSC 4 Bethnal Green
11.11.87	Cedric Powell W PTS 8 Usk
12.01.88	Mario Salazar W RSC 2 Cardiff
24.02.88	Richard Fowler W RSC 1 Aberavon
20.04.88	Benji Marquez W PTS 8 Muswell Hill
18.05.88	Pat Cowdell W RSC 8 Aberavon
	(British S. Featherweight Title Challenge)
15.11.88	John Kalbhenn W PTS 10 Norwich
11.04.89	Idabeth Rojas W PTS 10 Aberavon
06.09.89	John Doherty L RTD 11 Aberavon
	(British S. Featherweight Title Defence)
05.03.91	Tony Foster W PTS 8 Millwall
29.10.91	Thunder Aryeh W RTD 6 Cardiff
17.12.91	Patrick Kamy W DIS 5 Cardiff
17.03.92	Harry Escott W RSC 7 Mayfair
01.12.93	Harry Escott W PTS 8 Bethnal Green
22.01.94	Juan Molina L RTD 6 Cardiff
	(IBF S. Featherweight Title Challenge)
23.03.94	Neil Haddock W RSC 10 Cardiff
	(British S. Featherweight Title Challenge)
29.09.94	Edward Lloyd W RSC 4 Bethnal Green
13.12.94	Dave McHale W RSC 10 Ilford
	(British S. Featherweight Title Defence)
21.03.95	Elvis Parsley W RSC 6 Swansea
05.05.95	Michael Armstrong W CO 9 Swansea
	(British S. Featherweight Title Defence)

Career: 33 contests, won 31, lost 2.

Alfred Kotey

London. *Born* Accra, Ghana, 26 March, 1968
WBO Bantamweight Champion. Former Undefeated West African & Commonwealth Flyweight Champion. Ht. 5'3¾"
Manager M. Jacobs

26.11.88	Viper Tagoe W CO 1 Accra, Ghana
12.12.88	Mohammed Alimbey W CO 5 Accra, Ghana
11.03.89	Ramos Armah W CO 1 Accra, Ghana

Alfred Kotey   Les Clark

22.04.89	Danjumah Musah W RSC 5 Accra, Ghana
	(Vacant West Africa Flyweight Title)
10.06.89	Aristo Soweto W RSC 8 Accra, Ghana
21.10.89	George Freeman W RSC 2 Accra, Ghana
	(Vacant Commonwealth Flyweight Title)
28.04.90	Shaibu Annan W CO 2 Accra, Ghana
06.07.90	Danny Porter W PTS 12 Brentwood
	(Commonwealth Flyweight Title Defence)
09.07.91	Kenny Butts W CO 1 Philadelphia, USA
10.09.91	Pop Robinson W RSC 7 Philadelphia, USA
19.11.91	Nelson Vicioso W CO 2 Atlantic City, USA
10.03.92	Ramon Solis W CO 3 Philadelphia, USA
16.04.92	Francisco Montiel W PTS 10 Philadelphia, USA
25.06.92	Armando Diaz W PTS 10 Philadelphia, USA
14.07.92	Antonio Gastelum W RSC 2 Philadelphia, USA
28.07.92	Alex Sanabria W PTS 10 Atlantic City, USA
17.11.92	Julio Borboa L PTS 10 Philadelphia, USA
03.03.94	Chris Clarkson W PTS 8 Ebbw Vale
30.07.94	Rafael del Valle W PTS 12 Bethnal Green
	(WBO Bantamweight Title Challenge)
25.10.94	Armando Castro W PTS 12 Middlesbrough
	(WBO Bantamweight Title Defence)
17.02.95	Drew Docherty W RSC 4 Cumbernauld
	(WBO Bantamweight Title Defence)

Career: 21 contests, won 20, lost 1.

Eamonn Loughran

Ballymena. *Born* Ballymena, 5 June, 1970
WBO Welterweight Champion. Former Undefeated Commonwealth Welterweight Champion. Ht. 5'9"
Manager B. Hearn

03.12.87	Adam Muir W DIS 4 Belfast
08.06.88	Tony Britland W RSC 1 Sheffield
25.06.88	Antonio Campbell DREW 4 Panama City, Panama
19.10.88	Stan King W PTS 6 Belfast
19.09.89	Ricky Nelson W RSC 3 Belfast
31.10.89	Mark Pearce W PTS 6 Belfast
29.11.89	Ronnie Campbell W RSC 1 Belfast
24.11.90	Parrish Johnson W RSC 2 Benalmadena, Spain
12.12.90	Mike Morrison W PTS 6 Basildon
12.02.91	Nick Meloscia W CO 1 Cardiff
05.03.91	Julian Eavis W PTS 6 Cardiff
26.03.91	Stan Cunningham W RSC 2 Bethnal Green
24.04.91	Kevin Plant W RTD 1 Preston
28.05.91	Terry Morrill W CO 1 Cardiff
03.09.91	Marty Duke W PTS 6 Cardiff
21.09.91	Glyn Rhodes W PTS 8 Tottenham
15.10.91	Juan Carlos Ortiz W PTS 8 Hamburg, Germany
13.03.92	Tony Ekubia L DIS 5 Bury
	(Elim. British Welterweight Title)
19.05.92	Kelvin Mortimer W RSC 1 Cardiff
29.09.92	Judas Clottey W PTS 8 Hamburg, Germany
24.11.92	Donovan Boucher W RSC 3 Doncaster
	(Commonwealth Welterweight Title Challenge)
18.12.92	Desbon Seaton W RSC 2 Hamburg, Germany
06.02.93	Michael Benjamin W RSC 6 Cardiff
	(Commonwealth Welterweight Title Defence)
16.10.93	Lorenzo Smith W PTS 12 Belfast
	(Vacant WBO Welterweight Title)
22.01.94	Alessandro Duran W PTS 12 Belfast
	(WBO Welterweight Title Defence)
10.12.94	Manning Galloway W TD 4 Manchester
	(WBO Welterweight Title Defence)
27.05.95	Angel Beltre ND 3 Belfast
	(WBO Welterweight Title Defence)

Career: 27 contests, won 24, drew 1, lost 1, no decision 1.

Robert McCracken

Birmingham. *Born* Birmingham, 31 May, 1968
British L. Middleweight Champion. Ht. 6'0"
Manager M. Duff

24.01.91	Mick Mulcahy W RSC 1 Brierley Hill
13.02.91	Gary Barron W RTD 2 Wembley
06.03.91	Tony Britland W RSC 2 Wembley
12.04.91	Dave Andrews W RSC 4 Willenhall
08.05.91	Tony Gibbs W CO 1 Kensington
30.05.91	Paul Murray W RSC 2 Birmingham
04.07.91	Marty Duke W RSC 1 Alfreton
25.07.91	John Smith W RTD 1 Dudley
31.10.91	Newton Barnett W DIS 2 Oakengates
28.11.91	Michael Oliver W RSC 3 Liverpool
12.02.92	Paul Lynch W RSC 4 Wembley
01.10.92	Horace Fleary W PTS 8 Telford
02.11.92	Ensley Bingham W RSC 10 Wolverhampton
	(Elim. British L. Middleweight Title)
20.01.93	Leigh Wicks W PTS 8 Wolverhampton
17.02.93	Ernie Loveridge W CO 4 Bethnal Green
24.04.93	Martin Smith W RSC 10 Birmingham
	(Final Elim. British L. Middleweight Title)
29.06.93	Steve Langley W RSC 4 Edgbaston

Eamonn Loughran   Les Clark

01.12.93	Chris Peters W PTS 8 Kensington
23.02.94	Andy Till W PTS 12 Watford
	(British L. Middleweight Title
	Challenge)
10.09.94	Steve Foster W PTS 12 Birmingham
	(British L. Middleweight Title Defence)
11.10.94	Dean Cooper W RSC 4 Bethnal Green
10.02.95	Paul Wesley W PTS 12 Birmingham
	(British L. Middleweight Title Defence)
21.04.95	Sergio Medina W RSC 7 Dudley

Career: 23 contests, won 23.

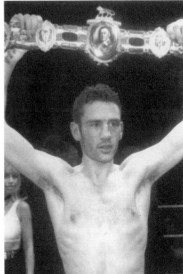

Robert McCracken   Les Clark

Noel Magee

Belfast. *Born* Belfast, 16 December, 1965
Commonwealth L. Heavyweight
Champion. Ht. 6'1"
Manager Self

22.05.85	Nigel Prickett W CO 1 Stoke
12.09.85	Dave Furneaux W RSC 3 Swindon
28.10.85	Eddie Chatterton W RSC 1 Stoke
06.11.85	Winston Burnett W PTS 8 Nantwich
11.12.85	Winston Burnett W PTS 8 Stoke
22.01.86	Blaine Logsdon W PTS 8 Stoke
20.02.86	Barry Ahmed W PTS 8 Newcastle
05.03.86	Winston Burnett W PTS 8 Stoke
23.04.86	Barry Ahmed W RSC 7 Stoke
30.05.86	Geoff Rymer W CO 1 Stoke
13.10.86	Jimmy Ellis W PTS 8 Dulwich
17.11.86	Serg Fame W PTS 8 Dulwich
24.02.87	Lennie Howard W RSC 1 Ilford
03.08.87	Jimmy Ellis W RSC 6 Stoke
20.10.87	Johnny Held L PTS 8 Stoke
13.02.88	Rufino Angulo DREW 8 Paris, France
03.05.88	Mike Brothers W CO 6 Stoke
15.11.88	Ian Bulloch DREW 10 Hull
15.02.89	Yves Monsieur L RSC 5 Stoke
02.10.89	Paul McCarthy W CO 2 Hanley
29.11.89	Sammy Storey L RSC 9 Belfast
	(British S. Middleweight Title
	Challenge)
15.09.90	Glazz Campbell W PTS 8 Belfast
30.10.90	Johnny Melfah W PTS 6 Belfast
12.02.91	R. F. McKenzie W PTS 6 Belfast
11.05.91	Simon Collins W PTS 8 Belfast
13.11.91	Frankie Minton W RSC 3 Belfast
11.12.91	Tony Wilson W RSC 3 Dublin
25.04.92	R. F. McKenzie W PTS 8 Belfast
28.09.92	Maurice Core L RSC 9 Manchester
	(Vacant British L. Heavyweight Title)
22.05.93	Dariusz Michalczewski L RSC 8
	Aachen, Germany
16.10.93	John Kaighin W PTS 6 Belfast
21.05.94	John J. Cooke W PTS 6 Belfast
05.03.95	Fabrice Tiozzo L RSC 4 Vitrolles,
	France
	(European L. Heavyweight Title
	Challenge)
09.05.95	Garry Delaney W RTD 7 Basildon
	(Commonwealth L. Heavyweight
	Challenge)

Career: 34 contests, won 26, drew 2, lost 6.

Noel Magee

James Oyebola

Paddington. *Born* Nigeria, 10 June, 1961
British & WBC International Heavyweight
Champion. Former Undefeated Southern
Area Heavyweight Champion. Ht. 6'9"
Manager Self

01.07.87	Andrew Gerrard W PTS 6 Kensington
16.09.87	Ian Priest W RSC 2 Kensington
03.11.87	Carl Timbrell W CO 2 Bethnal Green
24.11.87	Mike Jones L RSC 2 Wisbech
09.02.88	Denroy Bryan W RSC 6 Bethnal Green
10.05.88	Andrew Gerrard DREW 6 Tottenham
07.09.88	Tee Lewis W CO 1 Reading
01.11.88	Dorcey Gayman W RSC 1 Reading
23.11.88	Everton Christian W CO 1 Bethnal
	Green
31.01.89	John Westgarth W CO 3 Reading
15.02.89	Art Terry W CO 5 Bethnal Green
07.03.89	John Westgarth L RSC 5 Wisbech
12.04.91	Stan Campbell W CO 1 Greenville,
	USA
18.05.91	Bonyongo Destroyer W CO 1 Harare,
	Zimbabwe
	(Final Elim. African Heavyweight
	Title)
15.09.93	Denroy Bryan W RSC 5 Bethnal Green
13.10.93	R. F. McKenzie W RSC 1 Bethnal
	Green
	(Southern Area Heavyweight Title
	Challenge)
01.12.93	Jimmy Bills W PTS 8 Bethnal Green
09.02.94	Ladislao Mijangos W RSC 2 Bethnal
	Green
06.05.94	Scott Welch W CO 5 Atlantic City,
	USA
	(Vacant WBC International
	Heavyweight Title)

19.11.94 Clifton Mitchell W CO 4 Cardiff
(WBC International Heavyweight Title Defence & Vacant British Heavyweight Title)
07.02.95 Keith McMurray W RSC 7 Ipswich
Career: 21 contests, won 18, drew 1, lost 2.

James Oyebola   Les Clark

Steve Robinson

Cardiff. *Born* Cardiff, 13 December, 1968
WBO Featherweight Champion. Former
Undefeated Penta-Continental & Welsh
Featherweight Champion. Ht. 5'8"
Manager D. Gardiner

01.03.89 Alan Roberts W PTS 6 Cardiff
13.03.89 Terry Smith W RTD 4 Piccadilly
06.04.89 Nicky Lucas L PTS 8 Cardiff
04.05.89 John Devine W PTS 6 Mayfair
19.08.89 Marcel Herbert L PTS 6 Cardiff
13.11.89 Shane Silvester W RSC 2 Brierley Hill
10.07.90 Mark Bates L PTS 6 Canvey Island
12.09.90 Tim Driscoll L PTS 8 Bethnal Green
26.09.90 Russell Davison W PTS 8 Manchester
03.10.90 Drew Docherty L PTS 8 Solihull
22.10.90 Alan McKay L PTS 6 Mayfair
19.11.90 Neil Haddock W RSC 9 Cardiff
19.12.90 Brian Roche DREW 6 Preston
24.04.91 Russell Davison W RTD 6 Preston
28.05.91 Colin Lynch W RSC 6 Cardiff
18.07.91 Peter Harris W PTS 10 Cardiff
(Welsh Featherweight Title Challenge)
31.01.92 Henry Armstrong L RSC 6 Manchester
11.05.92 Neil Haddock L PTS 10 Llanelli
(Vacant Welsh S. Featherweight Title)
07.10.92 Edward Lloyd W RTD 8 Barry
30.10.92 Stephane Haccoun W PTS 8 Istres, France
01.12.92 Dennis Oakes W RTD 2 Liverpool
19.01.93 Paul Harvey W PTS 12 Cardiff
(Vacant Penta-Continental Featherweight Title)
13.02.93 Medhi Labdouni L PTS 8 Paris, France
17.04.93 John Davison W PTS 12 Washington
(Vacant WBO Featherweight Title)
10.07.93 Sean Murphy W CO 9 Cardiff
(WBO Featherweight Title Defence)
23.10.93 Colin McMillan W PTS 12 Cardiff
(WBO Featherweight Title Defence)
12.03.94 Paul Hodkinson W CO 12 Cardiff
(WBO Featherweight Title Defence)
04.06.94 Freddy Cruz W PTS 12 Cardiff
(WBO Featherweight Title Defence)
01.10.94 Duke McKenzie W CO 9 Cardiff
(WBO Featherweight Title Defence)
04.02.95 Domingo Damigella W PTS 12 Cardiff
(WBO Featherweight Title Defence)
Career: 30 contests, won 20, drew 1, lost 9.

Steve Robinson   Les Clark

Billy Schwer

Luton. *Born* Luton, 12 April, 1969
Commonwealth Lightweight Champion.
Former Undefeated British Lightweight
Champion. Ht. 5'8½"
Manager M. Duff

04.10.90 Pierre Conan W RSC 1 Bethnal Green
31.10.90 Mark Antony W RSC 2 Wembley
12.12.90 Sean Casey W RSC 1 Kensington
16.01.91 Dave Jenkins W PTS 6 Kensington
07.02.91 John Smith W RSC 2 Watford
06.03.91 Chubby Martin W RSC 3 Wembley
04.04.91 Andy Robins W RSC 2 Watford
17.04.91 Chris Saunders W RSC 1 Kensington
02.05.91 Karl Taylor W RSC 2 Northampton
30.06.91 Chris Saunders W RSC 3 Southwark
11.09.91 Tony Foster W PTS 8 Hammersmith
26.09.91 Felix Kelly W RSC 2 Dunstable
24.10.91 Patrick Kamy W CO 1 Dunstable
20.11.91 Marcel Herbert W PTS 8 Kensington
12.02.92 Tomas Quinones W CO 8 Wembley
25.03.92 Bobby Brewer W RSC 4 Kensington
03.09.92 Wayne Windle W CO 1 Dunstable
28.10.92 Carl Crook W RTD 9 Kensington
(British & Commonwealth Lightweight Title Challenge)
17.12.92 Mauricio Aceves W RSC 3 Wembley
24.02.93 Paul Burke L RSC 7 Wembley
(British & Commonwealth Lightweight Title Defence)
15.06.93 Farid Benredjeb W PTS 8 Hemel Hempstead
10.11.93 Paul Burke W PTS 12 Watford
(British & Commonwealth Lightweight Title Challenge)
16.02.94 Sean Murphy W RSC 3 Stevenage
(British & Commonwealth Lightweight Title Defence)
04.03.94 John Roby W RSC 2 Bethnal Green
22.03.94 Edgar Castro W CO 5 Bethnal Green
11.05.94 Howard Grant W RSC 9 Stevenage
(Commonwealth Lightweight Title Defence)
09.11.94 Manuel Hernandez W CO 6 Millwall

28.01.95 Rafael Ruelas L RTD 8 Las Vegas, USA
(IBF Lightweight Title Challenge)
12.05.95 Stephen Chungu W RSC 11 Bethnal Green
(Commonwealth Lightweight Title Defence)
23.06.95 Bruno Rabanales W DIS 6 Bethnal Green
Career: 30 contests, won 28, lost 2.

Billy Schwer   Les Clark

Sammy Storey

Belfast. *Born* Belfast, 9 August, 1963
British S. Middleweight Champion. Former
All-Ireland Middleweight Champion. Ht.
6'0"
Manager Self

03.12.85 Nigel Shingles W RSC 6 Belfast
05.02.86 Sean O'Phoenix W PTS 6 Sheffield
22.04.86 Karl Barwise W PTS 6 Belfast
29.10.86 Jimmy Ellis W RSC 5 Belfast
25.04.87 Rocky McGran W PTS 10 Belfast
(Vacant All-Ireland Middleweight Title)
19.10.87 Shamus Casey W PTS 6 Belfast
05.12.87 Paul Mitchell W PTS 6 Doncaster
27.01.88 Steve Foster W RSC 4 Belfast
18.03.88 Steve Collins L PTS 10 Boston, USA
(All-Ireland Middleweight Title Defence)
19.10.88 Tony Lawrence W RSC 3 Belfast
07.12.88 Darren Hobson W RSC 6 Belfast
25.01.89 Abdul Amoru Sanda W RSC 8 Belfast
08.03.89 Kevin Roper W RSC 3 Belfast
19.09.89 Tony Burke W PTS 12 Belfast
(Vacant British S. Middleweight Title)
29.11.89 Noel Magee W RSC 9 Belfast
(British S. Middleweight Title Defence)
17.03.90 Simon Collins W CO 7 Belfast
30.10.90 James Cook L RSC 10 Belfast
(British S. Middleweight Title Defence)
31.05.91 Saldi Ali L PTS 8 Berlin, Germany
07.09.91 Johnny Melfah W PTS 8 Belfast
13.11.91 Karl Barwise W PTS 6 Belfast
25.04.92 Nigel Rafferty W RSC 3 Belfast

03.02.93	Graham Jenner W RSC 4 Earls Court
28.04.93	Carlos Christie W RSC 8 Dublin
22.09.93	John Kaighin W PTS 6 Bethnal Green
21.05.94	Fidel Castro W PTS 6 Belfast
27.08.94	Chris Eubank L RSC 7 Cardiff
	(WBO S. Middleweight Title Challenge)
18.03.95	Colin Manners W PTS 8 Millstreet, Eire
27.04.95	Ali Forbes W PTS 12 Bethnal Green
	(British S. Middleweight Title Challenge)

Career: 28 contests, won 24, lost 4.

Sammy Storey   Les Clark

Neil Swain

Gilfach Goch. *Born* Pontypridd, 4
September, 1971
Commonwealth S. Bantamweight
Champion. Ht. 5'5"
Manager D. Gardiner

29.04.93	Vince Feeney W PTS 6 Mayfair
27.05.93	Marcus Duncan W PTS 6 Burnley
01.10.93	Rowan Williams W PTS 6 Cardiff
16.10.93	Philippe Desavoye W PTS 6 Levallois, France
10.11.93	Barry Jones L PTS 6 Ystrad
29.01.94	Alan Ley W RSC 3 Cardiff
12.03.94	Ceri Farrell W CO 1 Cardiff
09.04.94	Vince Feeney L PTS 6 Mansfield
06.05.94	Peter Culshaw L PTS 6 Liverpool
25.05.94	Paul Ingle L CO 4 Bristol
30.07.94	Jose Lopez L RTD 4 Bethnal Green
21.09.94	Yusuf Vorajee W RTD 1 Cardiff
01.10.94	Richie Wenton W RTD 5 Cardiff
19.11.94	Dave Hardie W RSC 2 Cardiff
29.11.94	Pete Buckley W PTS 6 Cardiff
25.01.95	Rowan Williams W PTS 6 Cardiff
04.02.95	Chris Jickells W PTS 6 Cardiff
12.04.95	Mike Parris W RSC 10 Llanelli
	(Vacant Commonwealth S. Bantamweight Title)

Career: 18 contests, won 13, lost 5.

Neil Swain

Paul Weir

Irvine. *Born* Glasgow, 16 September, 1967
Flyweight. WBO L. Flyweight Champion.
Former Undefeated WBO M. Flyweight
Champion. Ht. 5'3"
Manager T. Gilmour

27.04.92	Eduardo Vallejo W CO 2 Glasgow
09.07.92	Louis Veitch W PTS 6 Glasgow
21.09.92	Neil Parry W RSC 4 Glasgow
23.11.92	Shaun Norman W PTS 8 Glasgow
06.03.93	Kevin Jenkins W PTS 8 Glasgow
15.05.93	Fernando Martinez W RSC 7 Glasgow
	(Vacant WBO M. Flyweight Title)
25.10.93	Lindi Memani W PTS 12 Glasgow
	(WBO M. Flyweight Title Defence)
02.02.94	Josue Camacho L PTS 12 Glasgow
	(WBO L. Flyweight Title Challenge)
23.11.94	Paul Oulden W PTS 12 Irvine
	(Vacant WBO L. Flyweight Title)
05.04.95	Ric Magramo W PTS 12 Irvine
	(WBO L. Flyweight Title Defence)

Career: 10 contests, won 9, lost 1.

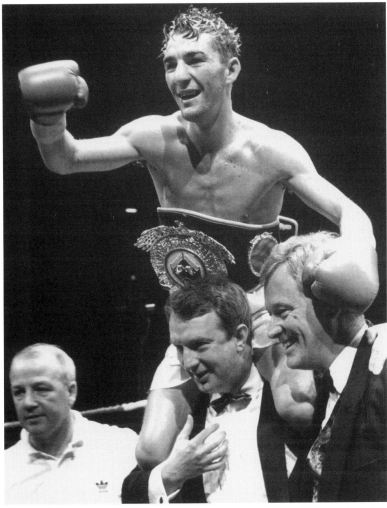

Paul Weir   George Ashton, Sportapics Ltd

Richie Wenton

Liverpool. *Born* Liverpool, 28 October, 1967
British & WBO Continental S. Bantamweight Champion. Ht. 5'8"
Manager F. Warren

14.12.88	Miguel Matthews W CO 2 Kirkby
25.01.89	Sean Casey W PTS 4 Belfast
10.04.89	Stuart Carmichael W RSC 2 Mayfair
13.12.89	Joe Mullen W RSC 5 Kirkby
21.02.90	Ariel Cordova W PTS 6 Belfast
17.03.90	Mark Johnston W PTS 4 Belfast
28.03.90	Jose Luis Vasquez W PTS 6 Manchester
23.05.90	Graham O'Malley W PTS 6 Belfast
09.07.90	Eugene Pratt W CO 1 Miami Beach, USA
15.09.90	Graham O'Malley W PTS 6 Belfast
30.10.90	Alejandro Armenta W RSC 2 Belfast
12.02.91	Sean Casey W PTS 4 Belfast
31.03.92	Graham O'Malley W PTS 6 Stockport
25.07.92	Ramos Agare W RSC 3 Manchester
26.09.92	Floyd Churchill L RSC 2 Earls Court
28.04.93	Kelton McKenzie W PTS 8 Dublin
13.11.93	Des Gargano W PTS 8 Cullompton
26.04.94	Bradley Stone W RSC 10 Bethnal Green *(Vacant British S. Bantamweight Title)*
01.10.94	Neil Swain L RTD 5 Cardiff
25.03.95	Paul Lloyd W RSC 5 Chester *(British S. Bantamweight Title Defence)*
30.06.95	Mike Parris W PTS 12 Liverpool *(Inaugural WBO Continental S. Bantamweight Title)*

Career: 21 contests, won 19, lost 2.

Richie Wenton   Les Clark

Henry Wharton   Les Clark

Henry Wharton

York. *Born* Leeds, 23 November, 1967
Commonwealth S. Middleweight Champion. Former Undefeated British S. Middleweight Champion. Ht. 5'10½"
Manager M. Duff

21.09.89	Dean Murray W RSC 1 Harrogate
25.10.89	Mike Aubrey W PTS 6 Wembley
05.12.89	Ron Malek W RSC 1 Dewsbury
11.01.90	Guillermo Chavez W CO 1 Dewsbury
03.03.90	Joe Potts W CO 4 Wembley
11.04.90	Juan Elizondo W RSC 3 Dewsbury
18.10.90	Chuck Edwards W RSC 1 Dewsbury
31.10.90	Dino Stewart W PTS 8 Wembley
21.03.91	Francisco Lara W CO 1 Dewsbury
09.05.91	Frankie Minton W CO 7 Leeds
27.06.91	Rod Carr W PTS 12 Leeds *(Vacant Commonwealth S. Middleweight Title)*
30.10.91	Lou Gent DREW 12 Leeds *(Commonwealth S. Middleweight Title Defence)*
23.10.92	Nicky Walker W PTS 10 York
19.03.92	Kenny Schaefer W CO 1 York
08.04.92	Rod Carr W RSC 8 Leeds *(Commonwealth S. Middleweight Title Defence)*
23.09.92	Fidel Castro W PTS 12 Leeds *(Commonwealth S. Middleweight Title Defence. British S. Middleweight Title Challenge)*
07.04.93	Ray Domenge W RSC 3 Leeds
01.07.93	Royan Hammond W RSC 3 York
07.10.93	Ron Amundsen W RSC 8 York
26.02.94	Nigel Benn L PTS 12 Earls Court *(WBC S. Middleweight Title Challenge)*
10.09.94	Guy Stanford W RTD 3 Birmingham
26.10.94	Sipho Moyo W CO 1 Leeds *(Commonwealth S. Middleweight Title Defence)*
10.12.94	Chris Eubank L PTS 12 Manchester *(WBO S. Middleweight Title Challenge)*

Career: 23 contests, won 20, drew 1, lost 2.

Richie Woodhall

Telford. *Born* Birmingham, 17 April, 1968
Commonwealth & European Middleweight Champion. Ht. 6'2"
Manager M. Duff

18.10.90	Kevin Hayde W RSC 3 Birmingham
30.11.90	Robbie Harron W RSC 2 Birmingham
16.01.91	Chris Haydon W RSC 3 Kensington
21.02.91	Shamus Casey W RSC 3 Walsall
30.05.91	Marty Duke W RSC 4 Birmingham
29.08.91	Nigel Moore W RSC 1 Oakengates
31.10.91	Colin Pitters W PTS 8 Oakengates
04.02.92	Graham Burton W RSC 2 Alfreton
26.03.92	Vito Gaudiosi W CO 1 Telford *(Vacant Commonwealth Middleweight Title)*
01.10.92	John Ashton W PTS 12 Telford *(Commonwealth Middleweight Title Defence)*
04.12.92	Horace Fleary W PTS 8 Telford
16.03.93	Carlo Colarusso W PTS 8 Wolverhampton
24.04.93	Royan Hammond W PTS 10 Birmingham
27.10.93	Garry Meekison W PTS 12 West Bromwich *(Commonwealth Middleweight Title Defence)*
01.03.94	Heath Todd W RSC 7 Dudley
16.03.94	Greg Lonon W RSC 6 Birmingham
05.10.94	Jacques le Blanc W PTS 12 Wolverhampton *(Commonwealth Middleweight Title Defence)*
30.11.94	Art Serwano W RSC 11 Wolverhampton *(Commonwealth Middleweight Title Defence)*
22.02.95	Silvio Branco W RSC 9 Telford *(Vacant European Middleweight Title)*

Career: 19 contests, won 19.

Richie Woodhall   Les Clark

Active British-Based Boxers: Career Records

Shows the complete record for all British-based boxers, excluding those currently holding British, Commonwealth, European, IBF, WBA, WBC and WBO titles, who have been active between 1 July 1994 and 30 June 1995. Names in brackets are real names, where they differ from ring names, and the first place name given is the boxer's domicile. Boxers are either shown as being self-managed or with a named manager, the information being supplied by the BBBoC shortly before going to press. Also included are foreign-born fighters who made their pro debuts in Britain, along with others like Bamana Dibateza (Zaire), Justin Juuko (Uganda), Yifru Retta (Ethiopia) and Newby Stevens (Zimbabwe), who, although starting their careers elsewhere, now hold BBBoC licenses and had three or more fights in this country last season in order to qualify for this section.

Ojay Abrahams

Watford. *Born* Lambeth, 17 December, 1964
Welterweight. Ht. 5'8½"
Manager Self

21.09.91	Gordon Webster W RSC 3 Tottenham
26.10.91	Mick Reid W RSC 5 Brentwood
26.11.91	John Corcoran W PTS 6 Bethnal Green
21.01.92	Dave Andrews DREW 6 Norwich
31.03.92	Marty Duke W RSC 2 Norwich
19.05.92	Michael Smyth L PTS 6 Cardiff
16.06.92	Ricky Mabbett W PTS 6 Dagenham
13.10.92	Vince Rose L RSC 3 Mayfair
30.01.93	Vince Rose DREW 6 Brentwood
19.05.93	Ricky Mabbett L RSC 4 Leicester
18.09.93	Ricky Mabbett L PTS 6 Leicester
09.12.93	Nick Appiah W PTS 6 Watford
24.01.94	Errol McDonald W RSC 2 Glasgow
09.02.94	Vince Rose W PTS 6 Brentwood
23.05.94	Spencer McCracken L PTS 6 Walsall
11.06.94	Darren Dyer W RSC 1 Bethnal Green
29.09.94	Gary Logan L PTS 10 Bethnal Green *(Southern Welterweight Title Challenge)*
13.12.94	Geoff McCreesh L PTS 6 Potters Bar
11.02.95	Gary Murray L PTS 8 Hammanskraal, South Africa

Career: 19 contests, won 9, drew 2, lost 8.

Kevin Adamson

Walthamstow. *Born* Hackney, 19 February, 1968
L. Middleweight. Ht. 6'0½"
Manager F. Warren

17.07.89	Carlton Myers W RSC 1 Stanmore
04.12.90	Darron Griffiths L RSC 4 Southend
12.11.91	Danny Shinkwin W RSC 4 Milton Keynes
30.04.92	Wayne Appleton W RSC 2 Bayswater
03.02.93	Joel Ani W RSC 6 Earls Court
27.02.93	Robert Whitehouse W RSC 1 Dagenham
31.03.93	Russell Washer W PTS 6 Barking
07.09.93	Bullit Andrews W PTS 6 Stoke
22.09.93	Russell Washer W PTS 6 Bethnal Green
27.10.93	Mick Duncan W RSC 3 Stoke
10.11.93	Clayon Stewart W RSC 1 Bethnal Green
01.12.93	Dave Maj W RSC 2 Stoke
19.01.94	Spencer Alton W RSC 1 Stoke
26.02.94	Lloyd Honeyghan L RSC 6 Earls Court *(Commonwealth L. Middleweight Title Challenge)*
25.05.94	Chris Richards W RSC 2 Stoke
17.08.94	Ernie Loveridge W RSC 2 Sheffield
25.02.95	Ensley Bingham L CO 5 Millwall

Career: 17 contests, won 14, lost 3.

Tanveer Ahmed (Niazi)

Glasgow. *Born* Glasgow, 25 October, 1968
Lightweight. Ht. 5'10"
Manager A. Morrison

22.10.92	John T. Kelly W PTS 6 Glasgow
01.12.92	Shaun Armstrong L PTS 6 Hartlepool
26.03.93	David Thompson W PTS 6 Glasgow
14.05.93	Dean Bramhald W PTS 6 Kilmarnock
09.09.93	Brian Wright W RTD 5 Glasgow
21.10.93	Martin Campbell W PTS 6 Glasgow
21.03.94	Chris Aston W CO 5 Glasgow
06.06.94	Chris Aston W CO 4 Glasgow
28.09.94	Norman Dhalie W CO 5 Glasgow
10.12.94	Kevin McKillan W PTS 6 Manchester
16.01.95	Micky Hall W RSC 4 Musselburgh
13.05.95	John O. Johnson W CO 3 Glasgow

Career: 12 contests, won 11, lost 1.

Rob Albon

Hayes. *Born* Hayes, 21 April, 1964
Heavyweight. Ht. 6'1½"
Manager Self

10.05.89	Massimo Mighaccio L RSC 3 Tallin, Estonia
15.09.89	L. A. Williams DREW 6 High Wycombe
20.02.90	Steve Osborne W PTS 6 Brentford
03.04.90	Dennis Bailey L RSC 4 Canvey Island
08.05.90	Steve Yorath W PTS 6 Brentford
12.09.90	Phil Soundy L RSC 1 Bethnal Green
18.02.91	Des Vaughan W PTS 6 Windsor
25.01.95	Darren Fearn L PTS 6 Cardiff
03.03.95	Keith Fletcher L RSC 3 Bracknell
09.05.95	Darren Westover L RSC 2 Basildon

Career: 10 contests, won 3, drew 1, lost 6.

Ojay Abrahams   Les Clark

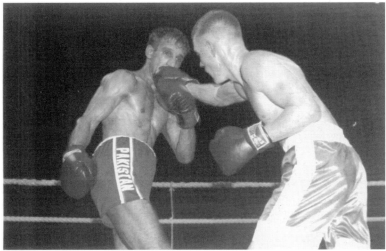

Tanveer Ahmed (left) looks set to counter Kevin McKillan   Les Clark

Michael Alexander　　　　Les Clark

Michael Alexander

Doncaster. *Born* Doncaster, 31 August, 1971
L. Welterweight. Ht. 5'9"
Manager T. Petersen

25.01.93 Tim Hill W PTS 6 Bradford
09.03.93 J. T. Kelly L PTS 6 Hartlepool
29.04.93 Pete Roberts W RSC 2 Hull
06.05.93 Ian Noble W PTS 6 Hartlepool
28.06.93 Mick Hoban W PTS 6 Morecambe
04.10.93 Micky Hall L CO 1 Bradford
28.11.93 Everald Williams L PTS 6 Southwark
28.02.94 Paul Hughes W PTS 6 Manchester
28.03.94 Laurence Roche W PTS 6 Cleethorpes
20.05.94 Andrew Morgan W PTS 6 Neath
13.06.94 Laurence Roche L PTS 6 Bradford
26.09.94 Derek Roche L RSC 6 Bradford
21.11.94 Alan Peacock L RSC 1 Glasgow
06.03.95 Brian Dunn L CO 5 Bradford
Career: 14 contests, won 7, lost 7.

Michael Alldis

Crawley. *Born* London, 25 May, 1968
S. Bantamweight. Ht. 5'6"
Manager B. Hearn

15.09.92 Ceri Farrell W RSC 3 Crystal Palace
10.11.92 Kid McAuley W PTS 6 Dagenham
12.12.92 Kid McAuley W CO 1 Muswell Hill
16.02.93 Ceri Farrell W CO 1 Tooting
29.06.93 Ady Benton L DIS 3 Mayfair
28.09.93 Alan Ley W PTS 6 Bethnal Green
06.11.93 Pete Buckley W PTS 8 Bethnal Green
09.04.94 Fernando Lugo W CO 1 Bethnal Green
11.06.94 Conn McMullen W PTS 8 Bethnal Green
20.12.94 Pete Buckley W PTS 6 Bethnal Green
17.02.95 Miguel Matthews W PTS 8 Crawley
25.03.95 Chip O'Neill W RSC 2 Chester
13.06.95 Laureano Ramirez L PTS 12 Basildon
　　　　　*(Inaugural WBO Continental
　　　　　S. Bantamweight Title)*
Career: 13 contests, won 11, lost 2.

Mark Allen (Hodgson)

Denaby. *Born* Mexborough, 11 January, 1970
L. Welterweight. Ht. 5'11"
Manager Self

24.03.92 Jamie Morris L PTS 6 Wolverhampton
04.06.92 Blue Butterworth L RSC 5 Burnley
10.11.92 Bobby Guynan L RSC 2 Dagenham
09.12.92 Simon Hamblett DREW 6 Stoke
09.02.93 Simon Hamblett W PTS 6 Wolverhampton
23.02.93 Simon Hamblett L PTS 6 Doncaster
11.03.93 Jamie Morris DREW 6 Walsall
20.04.93 Paul Knights L PTS 6 Brentwood
06.05.93 Brian Coleman L PTS 6 Walsall
28.05.93 Nick Boyd L CO 2 Middleton
29.06.93 Robbie Sivyer W PTS 6 Edgbaston
14.08.93 Cham Joof L RSC 3 Hammersmith
28.10.93 Paul Bowen L RSC 2 Walsall
09.02.94 Paul Knights L RSC 2 Brentwood
18.04.94 Patrick Parton L PTS 6 Walsall
23.05.94 Patrick Parton L PTS 6 Walsall
13.06.94 James Jiora L PTS 6 Bradford
21.07.94 Bradley Welsh L PTS 6 Edinburgh
11.10.94 Marc Smith L PTS 6 Wolverhampton
20.10.94 Marc Smith W PTS 6 Walsall
02.11.94 Mark Breslin LPTS 6 Solihull
29.11.94 Simon Hamblett L PTS 6 Wolverhampton
18.12.94 Gordon Blair L RSC 3 Glasgow
09.03.95 Patrick Parton L PTS 6 Walsall
16.03.95 Tim Hill L PTS 6 Sunderland
11.05.95 Shaun O'Neill L PTS 6 Sunderland
18.05.95 Scott Walker L RSC 2 Middleton
Career: 27 contests, won 3, drew 2, lost 22.

Jimmy Alston

Preston. *Born* Preston, 2 February, 1967
L. Middleweight. Ht. 5'9"
Manager Self

07.12.92 Spencer Alton W PTS 6 Manchester
25.02.93 Crain Fisher L RTD 2 Burnley
22.04.93 Crain Fisher L PTS 6 Bury
02.12.93 Japhet Hans W PTS 6 Sheffield
18.02.94 Stuart Dunn L RSC 1 Leicester
18.04.94 Carl Smith W PTS 6 Manchester
06.06.94 Carl Smith DREW 6 Manchester
22.09.94 Warren Stowe L CO 4 Bury
Career: 8 contests, won 3, drew 1, lost 4.

Spencer Alton

Alfreton. *Born* Derby, 4 October, 1966
S. Middleweight. Ht. 5'11"
Manager M. Shinfield

13.06.88 Ian Midwood-Tate W PTS 6 Manchester
10.07.88 Lou Ayres L PTS 6 Eastbourne
31.08.88 Ian Midwood-Tate L PTS 6 Stoke
30.09.88 Steve West L CO 3 Battersea
19.10.88 Wil Halliday W CO 6 Evesham
31.10.88 Michael Oliver W RSC 2 Leicester
14.11.88 G. L. Booth L RSC 7 Manchester
13.12.88 Paul Dolan W RTD 4 Glasgow
20.12.88 Wayne Ellis L RTD 4 Swansea
27.01.89 Neil Patterson W CO 1 Durham
31.01.89 Brian Robinson L PTS 6 Reading
15.02.89 Mark Holden DREW 6 Stoke
06.03.89 Mark Howell L PTS 8 Manchester
21.03.89 Ricky Nelson L PTS 6 Cottingham
04.04.89 Graham Burton W RSC 3 Sheffield

09.05.89 Wayne Ellis L RSC 3 St Albans
20.06.89 Peter Vosper L PTS 6 Plymouth
06.07.89 Ian Strudwick L PTS 8 Chigwell
26.09.89 Frank Eubanks W PTS 6 Oldham
10.10.89 Terry Morrill L PTS 6 Hull
17.10.89 Peter Vosper DREW 8 Plymouth
08.11.89 Neville Brown L RSC 4 Wembley
20.12.89 Mickey Morgan W RSC 5 Swansea
15.01.90 Andy Marlow DREW 6 Northampton
30.01.90 Darren Pilling L PTS 6 Manchester
13.02.90 Colin Pitters W PTS 6 Wolverhampton
26.02.90 Antoine Tarver L PTS 4 Crystal Palace
22.03.90 Richard Carter L PTS 6 Wolverhampton
24.05.90 Andrew Flute W RSC 1 Dudley
21.06.90 Paul Murray W PTS 6 Alfreton
10.09 92 Dave Johnson L PTS 6 Sunderland
23.10.92 Terry French L PTS 6 Gateshead
07.12.92 Jimmy Alston L PTS 6 Manchester
02.02.93 Chris Mulcahy W RSC 3 Derby
09.03.93 Mark Jay L RSC 4 Hartlepool
08.06.93 Eddie Collins W PTS 6 Derby
20.09.93 Sean Byrne L PTS 6 Northampton
03.11.93 Paul Busby L RTD 4 Worcester
16.12.93 Joe Calzaghe L RSC 2 Newport
19.01.94 Kevin Adamson L RSC 1 Stoke
28.03.94 Willie Quinn L RTD 3 Musselburgh
13.06.94 Craig Joseph L PTS 6 Bradford
02.07.94 Danny Peters L PTS 6 Liverpool
03.08.94 Dean Cooper L RSC 6 Bristol
06.10.94 Mark Jay L PTS 6 Cramlington
09.11.94 Andy McVeigh L RTD 3 Stafford
02.03.95 Mark Jay L PTS 6 Cramlington
18.03.95 Packie Collins L PTS 4 Millstreet, Eire
20.04.95 Steve McNess L RSC 2 Mayfair
Career: 49 contests, won 12, drew 3, lost 34.

Trevor Ambrose

Bournemouth. *Born* Leicester, 8 September, 1963
S. Middleweight. Ht. 5'11"
Manager J. Bishop

19.02.90 Ian Thomas L RSC 3 Kettering
06.04.90 Colin Pitters W PTS 6 Telford
24.04.90 Barry Messam W RSC 4 Stoke
14.05.90 Gordon Blair L CO 5 Northampton
12.09.90 Dave Fallon W CO 3 Battersea
23.10.90 David Lake W PTS 6 Leicester
04.11.90 Eddie King W RSC 3 Doncaster
21.11.90 Andreas Panayi W RSC 5 Solihull
14.02.91 Adrian Riley W CO 6 Southampton
28.03.91 Richard O'Brien W RSC 1 Alfreton
25.04.91 Gary Logan L PTS 8 Mayfair
03.07.91 Darren Dyer L PTS 6 Brentwood
24.09.91 Willie Beattie L PTS 8 Glasgow
11.03.92 John Davies L RSC 5 Cardiff
19.05.92 Paul Jones L PTS 6 Cardiff
19.03.93 Errol Christie W CO 2 Manchester
10.07.93 Nicky Piper L RSC 5 Cardiff
30.09.93 Simon Harris L PTS 6 Hayes
27.11.93 Cesar Kazadi L CO 4 Echirolles, France
23.02.94 W. O. Wilson W RSC 5 Watford
06.03.94 Ray Webb L RSC 6 Southwark
14.05.94 Bernard Bonzon L PTS 8 Sierre, Switzerland
04.06.94 Zdravko Kostic L RSC 4 Paris, France
30.11.94 Joe Calzaghe L RSC 2 Wolverhampton
31.03.95 Mark Delaney L RSC 1 Crystal Palace
Career: 25 contests, won 11, lost 15.

Dean Amory

Birmingham. *Born* Marston Green, 2 July, 1969
S. Featherweight. Ht. 5'7"
Manager W. Swift

21.10.92	Brian Hickey W PTS 6 Stoke
20.01.93	Dean Bramhald W PTS 6 Solihull
28.04.93	Elvis Parsley W PTS 6 Solihull
19.05.93	Neil Smith W PTS 6 Leicester
19.12.93	Alan McDowall L PTS 8 Glasgow
26.01.94	Kevin McKillan L PTS 8 Stoke
26.04.95	Joe Donohoe W PTS 6 Stoke
17.06.95	Gareth Lawrence L RSC 2 Cardiff

Career: 8 contests, won 5, lost 3.

Dave Anderson

Glasgow. *Born* Glasgow, 23 December, 1966
Lightweight. Ht. 5'8"
Managers F. Warren/A. Morrison

25.09.90	Junaido Musah W RSC 3 Glasgow
09.10.90	Alan Peacock W RSC 3 Glasgow
10.12.90	Chris Bennett W RSC 7 Glasgow
11.02.91	Steve Pollard W PTS 6 Glasgow
15.04.91	Tony Foster W PTS 8 Glasgow
24.09.91	Ian Honeywood W PTS 8 Glasgow
28.11.91	Pete Roberts W RSC 3 Glasgow
11.09.92	Kevin Toomey W PTS 8 Glasgow
22.10.92	Kevin McKenzie W RSC 3 Glasgow
10.06.94	Peter Till W PTS 6 Glasgow
21.07.94	John Stovin W CO 4 Edinburgh
01.10.94	Wayne Windle W RSC 2 Cardiff
21.10.94	Peter Till W PTS 8 Glasgow
19.11.94	Nigel Haddock W PTS 6 Cardiff
18.12.94	Peter Till W PTS 10 Glasgow
	(*Elim. British Lightweight Title*)
21.01.95	Carlos Javier Pena Lopez W PTS 8 Glasgow
04.03.95	Michael Hermon W PTS 8 Livingston
08.06.95	Floyd Churchill W PTS 8 Glasgow

Career: 18 contests, won 18.

Shaun Anderson

Maybole. *Born* Girvan, 20 September, 1969
Bantamweight. Ht. 5'5"
Manager A. Melrose

29.05.92	Tucker Thomas W RSC 1 Glasgow
11.09.92	Mark Hargreaves W PTS 6 Glasgow
10.12.92	Graham McGrath W PTS 6 Glasgow
29.01.93	Graham McGrath W PTS 6 Glasgow
26.03.93	Dave Campbell W RSC 5 Glasgow
30.04.93	Paul Kelly W RSC 5 Glasgow
14.05.93	Kid McAuley W PTS 8 Kilmarnock
29.05.93	Ronnie Stephenson W PTS 6 Paisley
09.09.93	Graham McGrath W PTS 6 Glasgow
19.12.93	Pete Buckley W PTS 6 Glasgow
13.04.94	Paul Wynn DREW 6 Glasgow
13.05.94	Paul Wynn L PTS 8 Kilmarnock
08.09.94	Graham McGrath W PTS 8 Glasgow
23.09.94	John Armour L RSC 11 Bethnal Green
	(*Commonwealth Bantamweight Title Challenge*)
18.11.94	James Murray L PTS 10 Glasgow
	(*Vacant Scottish Bantamweight Title*)
21.01.95	Brian Carr L PTS 6 Glasgow
04.03.95	Shaun Norman W PTS 6 Livingston
21.04.95	Donnie Hood W PTS 8 Glasgow
12.05.95	Mark Bowers L RSC 7 Bethnal Green

Career: 19 contests, won 13, drew 1, lost 5.

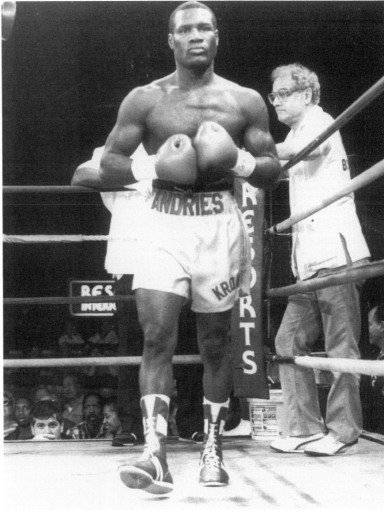

Dennis Andries   Peter Goldfield

Dennis Andries

Hackney. *Born* Guyana, 5 November, 1953
Former British Cruiserweight Champion.
Former WBC L. Heavyweight Champion.
Former Undefeated WBC Continental L.
Heavyweight Champion. Former
Undefeated British & Southern Area L.
Heavyweight Champion. Ht. 5'11"
Manager Self

16.05.78	Ray Pearce W CO 2 Newport
01.06.78	Mark Seabrook W RSC 1 Heathrow
20.06.78	Bonny McKenzie L PTS 8 Southend
18.09.78	Ken Jones W PTS 6 Mayfair
31.10.78	Neville Estaban W PTS 6 Barnsley
14.11.78	Les McAteer DREW 8 Birkenhead
22.11.78	Glen McEwan W RSC 7 Stoke
04.12.78	Tom Collins W PTS 8 Southend
22.01.79	Bunny Johnson L PTS 10 Wolverhampton
30.01.79	Tom Collins W CO 6 Southend
05.04.79	Francis Hand W RSC 8 Liverpool
06.06.79	Bonny McKenzie W PTS 8 Burslem

17.09.79	Johnny Waldron W RTD 10 Mayfair
	(*Southern Area L. Heavyweight Title Challenge*)
27.02.80	Bunny Johnson L PTS 15 Burslem
	(*British L. Heavyweight Title Challenge*)
17.04.80	Mustafa Wasajja L PTS 8 Copenhagen, Denmark
18.06.80	Chris Lawson W RSC 8 Burslem
23.03.81	Shaun Chalcraft W PTS 10 Mayfair
	(*Southern Area L. Heavyweight Title Challenge*)
16.09.81	Liam Coleman W RSC 6 Burslem
12.10.81	David Pearce L RSC 7 Bloomsbury
23.11.81	Alek Penarski W PTS 10 Chesterfield
15.03.82	Tom Collins L PTS 15 Bloomsbury
	(*Vacant British L. Heavyweight Title*)
10.08.82	Keith Bristol W PTS 10 Strand
	(*Southern Area L. Heavyweight Title Defence*)
28.02.83	Karl Canwell W CO 4 Strand
	(*Southern Area L. Heavyweight Title Defence & Elim. British L. Heavyweight Title*)

61

19.05.83	Chris Lawson W CO 4 Queensway
22.09.83	Keith Bristol W CO 4 Strand
	(Southern Area L. Heavyweight Title Defence & Elim. British L. Heavyweight Title)
26.01.84	Tom Collins W PTS 12 Strand
	(British L. Heavyweight Title Challenge)
06.04.84	Tom Collins W PTS 12 Watford
	(British L. Heavyweight Title Defence)
10.10.84	Devon Bailey W CO 12 Shoreditch
	(British L. Heavyweight Title Defence)
23.03.85	Jose Seys W RSC 3 Strand
07.05.85	Jeff Meacham W CO 4 New Orleans, USA
25.05.85	Tim Broady W RSC 5 Atlantic City, USA
06.06.85	Marcus Dorsey W CO 3 Lafayette, USA
11.12.85	Alex Blanchard DREW 12 Fulham
	(European L. Heavyweight Title Challenge)
13.02.86	Keith Bristol W RSC 6 Longford
	(British L. Heavyweight Title Defence)
30.04.86	J. B. Williamson W PTS 12 Edmonton
	(WBC L. Heavyweight Title Challenge)
10.09.86	Tony Sibson W RSC 9 Muswell Hill
	(WBC & British L. Heavyweight Title Defence)
07.03.87	Thomas Hearns L RSC 10 Detroit, USA
	(WBC L. Heavyweight Title Defence)
06.10.87	Robert Folley W PTS 10 Phoenix, USA
20.02.88	Jamie Howe W PTS 10 Detroit, USA
22.05.88	Bobby Czyz W PTS 10 Atlantic City, USA
10.09.88	Tony Harrison W RTD 7 Detroit, USA
17.10.88	Paul Maddison W RSC 4 Tucson, USA
21.02.89	Tony Willis W RSC 5 Tucson, USA
	(Vacant WBC L. Heavyweight Title)
24.06.89	Jeff Harding L RSC 12 Atlantic City, USA
	(WBC L. Heavyweight Title Defence)
26.10.89	Art Jimmerson W PTS 10 Atlantic City, USA
20.01.90	Clarismundo Silva W RSC 7 Auburn Hills, USA
	(Vacant WBC Continental L. Heavyweight Title)
28.07.90	Jeff Harding W CO 7 Melbourne, Australia
	(WBC L. Heavyweight Title Challenge)
10.10.90	Sergio Merani W RTD 4 Kensington
	(WBC L. Heavyweight Title Defence)
19.01.91	Guy Waters W PTS 12 Adelaide, Australia
	(WBC L. Heavyweight Title Defence)
11.09.91	Jeff Harding L PTS 12 Hammersmith
	(WBC L. Heavyweight Title Defence)
15.11.91	Ed Neblett W RSC 4 Tampa, USA
11.12.91	Paul Maddison W RTD 8 Duluth, USA
27.02.92	Akim Tafer L PTS 12 Beausoleil, France
	(Vacant European Cruiserweight Title)
27.02.93	David Sewell W PTS 10 Dagenham
31.03.93	Willie Jake W RTD 6 Barking
29.01.94	Crawford Ashley W RTD 4 Cardiff
26.02.94	Mike Peak W PTS 4 Earls Court
23.03.94	Chemek Saleta L PTS 12 Cardiff
	(Vacant WBC International Cruiserweight Title)
01.10.94	Sylvester White W RSC 5 Carpentras, France

21.01.95	Denzil Browne W RSC 11 Glasgow
	(Vacant British Cruiserweight Title)
04.03.95	Mike Peak W PTS 10 Livingston
13.05.95	Terry Dunstan L PTS 12 Glasgow
	(British Cruiserweight Title Defence)

Career: 62 contests, won 48, drew 2, lost 12.

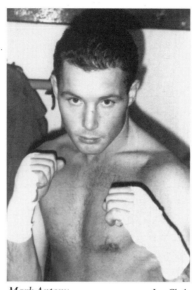

Mark Antony   Les Clark

Mark Antony (Brooks)

Doncaster. *Born* Worksop, 24 January, 1968
Welterweight. Ht. 5'8"
Manager Self

16.11.87	Robbie Bowen L CO 5 Stratford on Avon
22.03.88	Paul Bowen L RSC 3 Wolverhampton
14.11.88	Phil Lashley W RSC 2 Stratford on Avon
21.11.88	Paul Chedgzoy W CO 2 Leicester
01.12.88	Andrew Robinson W PTS 6 Stafford
14.12.88	Paul Bowen L PTS 6 Evesham
02.02.89	Shaun Cooper L CO 3 Wolverhampton
20.04.89	Andrew Brightman W PTS 6 Weston super Mare
17.05.89	Mark Tibbs L PTS 6 Millwall
29.05.89	Mike Close L PTS 6 Liverpool
04.09.89	Warren Bowers L PTS 6 Grimsby
04.10.89	Karl Taylor L CO 2 Stratford
06.12.89	Peter Bowen L PTS 6 Stoke
13.02.90	Peter Bowen W RSC 1 Wolverhampton
07.03.90	Stuart Rimmer W RSC 1 Doncaster
21.03.90	Nick Hall L PTS 6 Solihull
27.03.90	Shaun Cogan L CO 1 Wolverhampton
21.05.90	Tony Feliciello L RTD 2 Grimsby
21.06.90	Andrew Robinson W PTS 6 Alfreton
31.10.90	Billy Schwer L RSC 2 Wembley
03.12.90	Nigel Senior W PTS 8 Cleethorpes
12.12.90	Richard Woolgar L RSC 5 Basildon
05.03.91	Jim Moffat L PTS 6 Glasgow
12.03.91	Wayne Windle L CO 1 Mansfield
12.11.91	Shaun Cooper L CO 1 Wolverhampton
20.01.92	Jamie Morris W RSC 5 Coventry
11.02.92	Billy Robinson L RSC 5 Wolverhampton

11.03.92	Simon Hamblett W CO 1 Stoke
11.05.92	Pat Delargy L PTS 6 Coventry
04.06.92	Darren Powell W CO 2 Burnley
23.11.92	Darren McInulty L PTS 6 Coventry
07.12.92	Spencer McCracken L CO 1 Birmingham
30.04.93	Colin Wallace L PTS 6 Glasgow
18.05.93	Steve Levene W RSC 1 Edgbaston
29.05.93	Steve Boyle L PTS 6 Paisley
17.06.93	Darren McInulty W CO 2 Bedworth
26.06.93	Ross Hale L RSC 1 Keynsham
25.10.93	Shea Neary L RSC 1 Liverpool
01.12.93	P. J. Gallagher L PTS 4 Bethnal Green
11.12.93	Tony Mock L RSC 4 Liverpool
11.01.94	Patrick Gallagher L RSC 3 Bethnal Green
09.02.94	Bobby Guynan L DIS 5 Brentwood
11.03.94	Allan Logan L PTS 6 Glasgow
28.03.94	Steve McLevy L CO 1 Musselburgh
10.06.94	Alan McDowall L PTS 8 Glasgow
02.07.94	Floyd Churchill W RSC 1 Liverpool
21.07.94	Gordon Blair L PTS 6 Edinburgh
17.08.94	Michael Carruth L RSC 3 Sheffield
29.09.94	Gary Osborne L RSC 2 Walsall
09.11.94	Richard O'Brien DREW 6 Stafford
29.11.94	Andy Peach L PTS 6 Wolverhampton

Career: 51 contests, won 14, drew 1, lost 36.

Wayne Appleton

Pontefract. *Born* Hemsworth, 9 November, 1967
Welterweight. Ht. 5'10"
Manager T. Callighan

13.11.90	Bullit Andrews W RSC 5 Edgbaston
26.11.90	Stuart Good W CO 4 Lewisham
10.12.90	Wayne Timmins W CO 4 Birmingham
15.03.91	Andre Wharton L RSC 7 Willenhall
14.11.91	Dave Hindmarsh W RSC 8 Edinburgh
30.04.92	Kevin Adamson L RSC 2 Bayswater
01.03.93	Hughie Davey W PTS 6 Bradford
12.05.93	Richard O'Brien W RTD 2 Sheffield
25.10.93	Errol McDonald W PTS 8 Glasgow
04.12.93	Gary Murray L RTD 7 Sun City, South Africa
18.01.95	Delroy Waul L PTS 6 Solihull
10.06.95	Joni Nyman L PTS 6 Pori, Finland

Career: 12 contests, won 7, lost 5.

Lee Archer

Dudley. *Born* West Bromwich, 3 January, 1971
L. Heavyweight. Ht. 6'2"
Manager Self

12.11.91	Paul Murray W PTS 6 Wolverhampton
24.03.92	Darryl Ritchie W PTS 6 Wolverhampton
28.04.92	Carl Smallwood L PTS 6 Wolverhampton
18.05.92	Marc Rowley W PTS 6 Bardon
05.10.92	Paul Murray W PTS 6 Bardon
13.10.92	Paul Murray W PTS 6 Wolverhampton
23.10.92	Ian Henry L RTD 1 Gateshead
24.11.92	Zak Chelli L PTS 6 Wolverhampton
09.02.93	Zak Goldman W CO 3 Wolverhampton
22.03.93	Carl Smallwood W PTS 8 Bedworth
17.03.93	Ian Henry W PTS 6 Stoke
06.05.93	Tony Behan DREW 6 Walsall
28.10.93	Nigel Rafferty W PTS 8 Walsall
04.11.93	Greg Scott-Briggs W PTS 8 Stafford
08.12.93	Greg Scott-Briggs L RTD 6 Stoke
17.02.94	Greg Scott-Briggs W PTS 8 Walsall

17.03.94 Martin Langtry L CO 4 Lincoln
05.10.94 Stinger Mason W PTS 6 Wolverhampton
26.10.94 John Keeton L PTS 6 Stoke
Career: 19 contests, won 12, drew 1, lost 6.

(Kevin) Henry Armstrong (Morris)

Manchester. *Born* Manchester, 10 December, 1967
Featherweight. Ht. 5'6"
Managers J. Doughty/T. Gilmour

09.12.87 Sean Hogg W PTS 6 Stoke
28.03.88 Steve Bowles W RSC 5 Stoke
20.04.88 Dean Lynch L PTS 6 Stoke
03.05.88 Paul Charters W PTS 4 Stoke
16.05.88 Dean Dickinson W PTS 6 Manchester
09.08.88 Dean Dickinson L RSC 4 St Helier
20.09 88 Jimmy Vincent W PTS 6 Stoke
10.10.88 Jimmy Vincent W PTS 6 Manchester
12.12.88 Les Walsh L DIS 3 Manchester
25.01.89 Nigel Senior W PTS 8 Stoke
01.03.89 Derek Amory W PTS 8 Stoke
15.04.89 Keith Wallace L CO 7 Salisbury
20.09.89 Gary de Roux W PTS 8 Stoke
16.10.89 Graham O'Malley W PTS 8 Manchester
13.11.89 Gary Maxwell W PTS 8 Stratford on Avon
14.03.90 Mark Holt W PTS 8 Stoke
19.04.90 Gary de Roux L CO 8 Oldham
12.12.90 Colin Lynch W RSC 3 Stoke
12.04.91 Ray Newby W PTS 8 Manchester
31.01.92 Steve Robinson W PTS 6 Manchester
02.03.92 Jyrki Vierela DREW 6 Helsinki, Finland
15.09.92 Dean Lynch L RSC 5 Liverpool
26.04.93 Derek Amory W PTS 6 Manchester
29.09.94 Mike Deveney L PTS 8 Tynemouth
24.10.94 Mike Deveney L PTS 10 Glasgow
(*Elim. British Featherweight Title*)
Career: 25 contests, won 17, drew 1, lost 7.

Michael Armstrong (Morris)

Stoke. *Born* Moston, 18 December, 1968
Former British S. Featherweight Champion.
Ht. 5'4"
Manager J. Trickett

27.01.88 John Hales W RSC 1 Stoke
02.03.88 Gypsy Johnny W RSC 2 Stoke
20.04.88 Pepe Webber W PTS 6 Stoke
16.05.88 Steve Bowles W RSC 3 Manchester
13.06.88 Tony Heath W PTS 6 Manchester
09.08.88 G. G. Corbett W DIS 6 St Helier
20.09.88 Darren Weller W PTS 8 Stoke
26.10.88 Gary King DREW 8 Stoke
07.12.88 Mark Holt L PTS 8 Stoke
15.02.89 Gerry McBride W RSC 5 Stoke
19.04.89 Russell Davison W PTS 8 Stoke
24.05.89 Anthony Barcla W PTS 8 Hanley
04.09.89 Steve Pollard W PTS 8 Hull
06.12.89 Russell Davison L PTS 8 Stoke
06.03.90 Russell Davison W PTS 10 Stoke
18.09.90 Modest Napunyi L CO 9 Stoke
(*Commonwealth Featherweight Title Challenge*)
14.10.91 Barrie Kelley W CO 4 Manchester
07.12.91 Mark Holt W PTS 4 Manchester
21.01.92 Darren Elsdon W RSC 1 Stockport
(*Final Elim. British S. Featherweight Title*)

25.04.92 John Doherty W RSC 7 Manchester
(*British S. Featherweight Title Challenge*)
25.07.92 Karl Taylor W RSC 3 Manchester
13.10.92 Neil Haddock L RSC 6 Bury
(*British S. Featherweight Title Defence*)
10.05.94 Jonjo Irwin L PTS 12 Doncaster
(*Vacant Penta-Continental S. Featherweight Title*)
04.10.94 Bamana Dibateza L RSC 3 Mayfair
06.03.95 Miguel Matthews W PTS 6 Mayfair
05.05.95 Floyd Havard L CO 9 Swansea
(*British S. Featherweight Title Challenge*)
Career: 26 contests, won 18, drew 1, lost 7.

Graham Arnold

Bury St Edmonds. *Born* Fulford, 29 June, 1968
Heavyweight. Ht. 6'3"
Manager Self

24.09.91 John Palmer W CO 2 Basildon
26.10.91 Gary Charlton L RSC 1 Brentwood
21.01.92 Steve Yorath L PTS 6 Norwich
31.03.92 Steve Yorath W PTS 6 Norwich
08.09.92 Steve Stewart L RSC 3 Norwich
23.05.93 Julius Francis L RSC 5 Brockley
08.12.93 Gary Williams W PTS 6 Hull
29.03.94 Joey Paladino L RSC 5 Wolverhampton
24.09.94 Kevin McBride L RSC 2 Wembley
07.02.95 Pat Passley W RSC 3 Ipswich
Career: 10 contests, won 4, lost 6.

Darren Ashton

Stoke. *Born* Stoke, 26 June, 1969
S. Middleweight. Ht. 6'1"
Manager W. Swift

13.10.93 Tony Colclough W RSC 1 Stoke
08.12.93 Nigel Rafferty W PTS 6 Stoke
23.03.94 L. A. Williams W PTS 6 Stoke
23.05.94 Nigel Rafferty W PTS 6 Walsall
30.11.94 Carlos Christie L PTS 6 Solihull
04.03.95 John Wilson NC 3 Livingston
06.05.95 Dale Nixon W RSC 4 Shepton Mallet
13.05.95 Stefan Wright W PTS 6 Glasgow
Career: 8 contests, won 6, lost 1, no contest 1.

Chris Aston

Leeds. *Born* Huddersfield, 7 August, 1961
Lightweight. Ht. 5'7"
Manager Self

07.10.91 Mick Holmes W RSC 2 Bradford
28.10.91 Charles Shepherd L PTS 6 Leicester
21.11.91 Dean Hiscox W PTS 6 Stafford
09.12.91 David Thompson W PTS 6 Bradford
21.01.92 Rob Stewart L RSC 4 Stockport
28.02.92 Mark Legg L RSC 4 Stockport
29.04.92 Richard Swallow L RSC 3 Solihull
02.11.93 Jason Beard L RSC 3 Southwark
08.12.93 Kevin Toomey L PTS 6 Hull
26.01.94 Paul Hughes L PTS 6 Stoke
17.02.94 Nick Boyd L CO 3 Bury
21.03.94 Tanveer Ahmed L CO 5 Glasgow
20.05.94 Keith Marner L PTS 8 Acton
06.06.94 Tanveer Ahmed L CO 4 Glasgow
06.10.94 John T. Kelly DREW 6 Hull
17.11.94 Tim Hill W PTS 6 Sheffield
20.01.95 Colin Dunne L RSC 4 Bethnal Green

21.04.95 James Montgomerie L PTS 6 Glasgow
12.05.95 Colin Dunne L RSC 4 Bethnal Green
14.06.95 Robert Grubb W CO 1 Batley
Career: 20 contests, won 5, drew 1, lost 14.

(Mark) M. T. Atkin

Norwich. *Born* Scarborough, 13 November, 1969
Lightweight. Ht. 5'6"
Manager B. Lee

15.03.94 Jason Campbell W RSC 5 Mayfair
28.06.94 Andy Davidson L RSC 1 Mayfair
26.05.95 Anthony Campbell DREW 6 Norwich
Career: 3 contests, won 1, drew 1, lost 1.

Dennis Bailey

Liverpool. *Born* Liverpool, 23 February, 1963
Heavyweight. Ht. 6'0"
Manager Self

27.11.84 Ronnie Fraser W CO 1 Wolverhampton
12.03.85 Alex Romeo W PTS 6 Birmingham
20.03.85 Alex Romeo W PTS 6 Evesham
23.05.85 Alex Romeo W PTS 6 Dudley
12.03.86 Abner Blackstock L CO 2 Stoke
20.05.86 Tony Wilson L RSC 6 Wembley
25.09.86 Tommy Taylor L CO 4 Wolverhampton
(*Vacant Midlands Area L. Heavyweight Title*)
01.02.88 Johnny Nelson W PTS 8 Northampton
08.11.89 Henry Akinwande L RSC 2 Wembley
19.03.90 Steve Lewsam DREW 8 Grimsby
03.04.90 Rob Albon W RSC 4 Canvey Island
21.05.90 Steve Lewsam L PTS 8 Grimsby
23.10.90 Terry Dixon L PTS 6 Leicester
28.09.93 Albert Call DREW 6 Liverpool
11.12.93 Paul McCarthy W PTS 6 Liverpool
19.01.94 John Keeton L RSC 1 Stoke
17.02.95 Richard Bango L RSC 1 Cumbernauld
14.04.95 Darren Corbett L RSC 2 Belfast
Career: 18 contests, won 7, drew 2, lost 9.

Ian Baillie

Peterborough. *Born* Highgate, 23 July, 1966
Flyweight. Ht. 5'2"
Manager K. Whitney

10.12.92 Tiger Singh L PTS 6 Corby
23.02.93 Graham McGrath L PTS 6 Kettering
06.12.93 Lyndon Kershaw L PTS 6 Bradford
19.12.93 Mickey Bell L CO 1 Northampton
02.02.94 Louis Veitch L RSC 1 Glasgow
04.03.94 Keith Knox L CO 3 Irvine
09.05.94 Lyndon Kershaw L PTS 6 Bradford
24.05.94 Shaun Norman L RSC 2 Leicester
26.09.94 Terry Gaskin L RSC 3 Bradford
08.12.94 Terry Gaskin L RTD 3 Hull
23.01.95 Neil Parry L RTD 3 Glasgow
Career: 11 contests, lost 11.

David Bain

Walsall. *Born* Peterborough, 2 October, 1966
L. Middleweight. Ht. 5'8"
Manager C. Flute

29.03.94 Warren Stephens W PTS 6 Wolverhampton

23.05.94 Andy Peach W RSC 6 Walsall
11.10.94 Warren Stephens W PTS 6 Wolverhampton
07.02.95 Peter Reid L PTS 6 Wolverhampton
28.03.95 Prince Kasi Kiahau W PTS 6 Wolverhampton
11.05.95 Howard Clarke L RSC 1 Dudley
Career: 6 contests, won 4, lost 2.

Mark Baker

Bermondsey. *Born* Farnborough, 14 July, 1969
S. Middleweight. Ht. 5'9½"
Managers M. Duff/T. Lawless

07.09.92 Jason McNeill W RSC 2 Bethnal Green
15.10.92 Graham Jenner W RTD 4 Lewisham
03.12.92 Adrian Wright W RSC 1 Lewisham
10.02.93 Paul Hanlon W RSC 2 Lewisham
26.04.93 Karl Mumford W CO 1 Lewisham
15.06.93 Alan Baptiste W PTS 6 Hemel Hempstead
14.01.94 Karl Barwise L PTS 6 Bethnal Green
11.03.94 Graham Jenner W RSC 2 Bethnal Green
26.04.94 Jerry Mortimer W PTS 6 Bethnal Green
23.09.94 Alan Baptiste W RSC 1 Bethnal Green
17.10.94 Steve Thomas W RSC 5 Mayfair
27.10.94 Chris Richards W PTS 6 Millwall
13.12.94 Stinger Mason W RSC 4 Ilford
20.01.95 Mark Dawson W RSC 3 Bethnal Green
Career: 14 contests, won 13, lost 1.

Sean Baker

Bristol. *Born* Bristol, 21 February, 1969
L. Middleweight. Ht. 5'10"
Manager C. Sanigar

08.09.92 Delwyn Panayiotiou W RSC 2 Southend
05.10.92 Raziq Ali W PTS 6 Bristol
01.12.92 Wayne Panayiotiou W RSC 3 Bristol
27.01.93 Danny Harper W PTS 6 Cardiff
09.03.93 Rick North W PTS 8 Bristol
24.03.93 Steve Levene DREW 6 Belfast
27.05.93 Gavin Lane W PTS 8 Bristol
26.06.93 David Lake W PTS 4 Keynsham
13.09.93 Mark Pearce W PTS 4 Bristol
03.11.93 George Wilson W RSC 2 Bristol
13.12.93 Hughie Davey W PTS 4 Bristol
10.03.94 Paul Quarrie W RTD 3 Bristol
31.03.94 Paul Lynch L RSC 3 Bristol
25.05.94 Andrew Jervis DREW 4 Bristol
03.08.94 Colin Pitters L PTS 6 Bristol
22.11.94 Julian Eavis W PTS 6 Bristol
18.02.95 Dave Lovell W PTS 6 Shepton Mallet
06.05.95 John Janes W PTS 4 Shepton Mallet
Career: 18 contests, won 14, drew 2, lost 2.

Adam Baldwin

Nuneaton. *Born* Nuneaton, 20 March, 1976
Welterweight. Ht. 5'7"
Manager C. Gunns

08.03.95 Mike Watson L PTS 6 Bloomsbury
03.04.95 Jamie Gallagher W PTS 6 Northampton
02.06.95 Martin Holgate L PTS 6 Bethnal Green
Career: 3 contests, won 1, lost 2.

Adam Baldwin   Les Clark

Phil Ball

Doncaster. *Born* Doncaster, 23 May, 1968
S. Middleweight. Ht. 6'0½"
Manager J. Rushton

24.11.92 Martin Jolley DREW 6 Doncaster
23.02.93 Martin Jolley L RSC 5 Doncaster
01.04.93 Chris Nurse DREW 6 Evesham
29.05.93 Alan Smiles L PTS 6 Paisley
07.06.93 Justin Clements L PTS 6 Walsall
17.06.93 Mark Smallwood L RSC 1 Bedworth
13.10.93 Dean Ashton L PTS 6 Stoke
25.10.93 Peter Flint W RSC 3 Liverpool
30.11.93 Chris Nurse L PTS 6 Wolverhampton
10.02.94 Tim Robinson W PTS 6 Hull
07.03.94 Tim Robinson W PTS 6 Doncaster
10.05.94 Dave Proctor W PTS 6 Doncaster
26.08.94 Dave Battey L PTS 6 Barnsley
12.09.94 Shamus Casey W PTS 6 Doncaster
12.10.94 Mark Hale L RSC 3 Stoke
09.02.95 Pat Durkin W PTS 6 Doncaster
06.04.95 Dave Battey L RSC 5 Sheffield
Career: 17 contests, won 6, drew 2, lost 9.

Richard Bango

Crystal Palace. *Born* Ibadan, Nigeria, 21 April, 1968
Heavyweight. Ht. 6'5"
Manager M. Jacobs

30.07.94 Steve Garber W CO 1 Bethnal Green
25.10.94 John Pierre W RSC 3 Middlesbrough
05.11.94 Archie Perry W PTS 4 Las Vegas, USA
17.02.95 Dennis Bailey W RSC 1 Cumbernauld
Career: 4 contests, won 4.

Alan Baptiste

Luton. *Born* Luton, 17 October, 1960
S. Middleweight. Ht. 6'1"
Manager Self

29.10.84 Terry Gilbey W PTS 6 Lewisham
26.11.84 Sean O'Phoenix DREW 6 Sheffield
23.01.85 Tony Meszaros W PTS 6 Solihull

04.02.85 Oscar Angus L RSC 5 Lewisham
18.04.85 Paul Gamble W PTS 6 Mayfair
30.04.85 Karl Barwise DREW 8 Merton
16.06.85 John Graham L PTS 8 Bethnal Green
22.07.85 Dennis Boy O'Brien W PTS 6 Longford
10.10.85 Karl Barwise L PTS 8 Merton
21.10.85 Sean O'Phoenix L PTS 8 Nottingham
28.10.85 Gary Tomlinson W PTS 8 Stoke
19.11.85 Karl Barwise W PTS 6 Battersea
03.02.86 Paul Gamble W CO 8 Dulwich
17.03.86 Tony Meszaros W RSC 6 Birmingham
17.04.86 Tony Britton W PTS 8 Piccadilly
22.09.86 Tony Meszaros W RSC 7 Edgbaston
04.11.86 Michael Watson L PTS 8 Wembley
15.12.86 John Graham L PTS 8 Mayfair
23.03.87 T.P. Jenkins W RSC 3 Mayfair
07.05.87 Johnny Melfah L CO 1 Bayswater
26.10.87 John Graham L PTS 8 Piccadilly
03.11.87 Blaine Logsdon L RSC 3 Bethnal Green
29.11.88 Simon Harris L RSC 4 Battersea
07.02.89 Richard Bustin L PTS 6 Southend
16.02.89 Roland Ericsson L RSC 5 Battersea
03.10.89 Richard Bustin L PTS 6 Southend
30.04.90 Antonio Fernandez L PTS 6 Brierley Hill
14.05.90 Chris Walker L PTS 6 Leicester
08.10.90 Joe Frater DREW 6 Cleethorpes
12.11.90 Richard Bustin L RSC 1 Norwich
27.02.91 Gil Lewis L RSC 1 Wolverhampton
19.04.91 Tony Lawrence W RSC 5 Peterborough
02.05.91 Kevin Morton L RSC 2 Northampton
15.06.93 Mark Baker L PTS 6 Hemel Hempstead
06.09.93 Paul Wright L PTS 6 Liverpool
16.09.93 Gilbert Jackson L RSC 5 Southwark
23.09.94 Mark Baker L RSC 1 Bethnal Green
Career: 37 contests, won 12, drew 3, lost 22.

Nicky Bardle

Ware. *Born* Ware, 30 January, 1972
L. Welterweight. Ht. 5'9½"
Manager H. Holland

07.11.91 Michael Clynch W RSC 4 Peterborough
12.02.92 Steve Hearn W RSC 1 Watford
30.04.92 James Campbell L CO 1 Watford
17.09.92 Brian Coleman W RSC 4 Watford
19.11.94 Anthony Campbell W PTS 6 Heathrow
Career: 5 contests, won 4, lost 1.

Gavin Barker

Ipswich. *Born* Nottingham, 11 May, 1969
Welterweight. Ht. 5'9"
Manager G. Holmes

17.05.95 Seth Jones W PTS 4 Ipswich
Career: 1 contest, won 1.

Chris Barnett

Wolverhampton. *Born* Coventry, 15 July, 1973
Welterweight. Ht. 5.5½"
Manager F. Warren

18.02.95 Wayne Jones W RSC 5 Shepton Mallet
Career: 1 contest, won 1.

Chris Barnett　　　　　Harry Goodwin

Pat Barrett

Manchester. *Born* Manchester, 22 July, 1967
Welterweight. Former Undefeated British, European & Central Area L. Welterweight Champion. Ht. 5'9"
Manager Self

01.05.87	Gary Barron W RSC 6 Peterborough	
18.05.87	Jim Moffat W RSC 1 Glasgow	
01.06.87	Paul Burke L PTS 6 Bradford	
13.06.87	Eamonn Payne W RSC 3 Great Yarmouth	
01.07.87	Iskender Savas W CO 1 Interlaken, Switzerland	
03.08.87	Mike Russell W PTS 6 Stoke	
20.10.87	Michael Howell W PTS 4 Stoke	
08.02.88	Oliver Henry W RSC 2 Manchester	
01.03.88	Sugar Gibiliru DREW 8 Manchester	
22.03.88	Donnie Parker W PTS 6 Baltimore, USA	
12.04.88	Stanley Jones W RSC 2 Cardiff	
04.05.88	Lenny Gloster W PTS 8 Solihull	
08.06.88	Dave McCabe W RSC 2 Glasgow	
10.10.88	Dave Haggarty W RSC 7 Glasgow	
01.11.88	Jeff Connors W RSC 5 Glasgow	
29.11.88	Kevin Plant W PTS 10 Manchester	
	(Vacant Central Area L. Welterweight Title)	
06.03.89	Dean Bramhald W RSC 7 Glasgow	
28.03.89	Marc Delfosse W CO 1 Glasgow	
11.04.89	Sugar Gibiliru W CO 8 Oldham	
	(Central Area L. Welterweight Title Defence)	
09.05.89	Tony Willis W CO 9 St Albans	
	(Vacant British L. Welterweight Title)	
07.06.89	John Rafuse W CO 6 Wembley	
27.06.89	Roberto Trevino W CO 2 Glasgow	
19.09.89	Dana Roston W RSC 4 Millwall	
24.10.89	Robert Harkin W PTS 12 Wolverhampton	
	(British L. Welterweight Title Defence)	
21.11.89	Joey Ferrell W RSC 6 Glasgow	
02.06.90	Juan Nunez W RSC 1 Manchester	
24.08.90	Efren Calamati W CO 4 Salerno, Italy	
	(European L. Welterweight Title Challenge)	
04.10.90	Dwayne Swift W PTS 10 Bethnal Green	

15.11.90	Eduardo Jacques W RSC 1 Oldham	
16.01.91	Jimmy Harrison W RTD 1 Kensington	
13.02.91	Salvatore Nardino W CO 6 Wembley	
	(European L. Welterweight Title Defence)	
17.04.91	Mark McCreath W RSC 6 Kensington	
	(European L. Welterweight Title Defence)	
09.10.91	Racheed Lawal W RSC 4 Manchester	
	(European L. Welterweight Title Defence)	
19.12.91	Mike Johnson W RSC 2 Oldham	
25.07.92	Manning Galloway L PTS 12 Manchester	
	(WBO L. Welterweight Title Challenge)	
20.11.92	Tomas Quinones W RSC 1 Casino, Italy	
19.12.92	Sam Gervins W RSC 1 San Severo, Italy	
13.02.93	Juan Gonzalez W PTS 8 Manchester	
22.09.93	Del Bryan L PTS 12 Bethnal Green	
	(Vacant British Welterweight Title)	
01.11.93	Patrick Vungbo L PTS 12 Izegem, Belgium	
	(Vacant WBF L. Middleweight Title)	
11.03.94	Donnie Parker W RSC 4 Sharon, USA	
25.12.94	Marino Monteyne W PTS 8 Izegem, Belgium	

Career: 42 contests, won 37, drew 1, lost 4.

Dave Battey

Worksop. *Born* Gainsborough, 14 December, 1972
S. Middleweight. Ht. 6'1¼"
Manager G. Rhodes

24.05.94	Johnny Hooks L PTS 6 Leicester	
28.06.94	Justin Clements L RSC 2 Edgbaston	
26.08.94	Phil Ball W PTS 6 Barnsley	
26.09.94	Greg Scott-Briggs L RSC 4 Cleethorpes	
25.10.94	Darren Sweeney L CO 1 Edgbaston	
05.12.94	Dave Owens W PTS 6 Cleethorpes	
15.12.94	Andy McVeigh L RSC 3 Walsall	
09.02.95	Kevin Burton W PTS 6 Doncaster	
06.04.95	Phil Ball W RSC 5 Sheffield	
05.05.95	Kevin Burton W PTS 6 Doncaster	
15.05.95	Mark Hale W PTS 6 Bradford	

Career: 11 contests, won 6, lost 5.

Jason Beard　　　　　Tony Fitch

Jason Beard

Beckton. *Born* Whitechapel, 24 April, 1967
Welterweight. Ht. 5'8½"
Manager D. Mancini

03.12.92	Robert Whitehouse W RSC 3 Lewisham	
28.01.93	Jason Barker W RSC 3 Southwark	
24.02.93	Michael Dick W RSC 5 Wembley	
26.04.93	Brian Coleman W PTS 6 Lewisham	
09.06.93	Phil Found W PTS 6 Lewisham	
16.09.93	David Lake W PTS 6 Southwark	
02.11.93	Chris Aston W RSC 3 Southwark	
07.12.93	Jason Campbell W RSC 2 Bethnal Green	
14.01.94	Steve Phillips W RTD 3 Bethnal Green	
11.03.94	Dave Maj W PTS 6 Bethnal Green	
23.09.94	Mark McCreath L PTS 6 Bethnal Green	
09.09.94	Dewi Roberts W RSC 4 Millwall	
09.12.94	Marty Duke W PTS 6 Bethnal Green	
14.02.95	Richard Swallow W PTS 6 Bethnal Green	
19.04.95	Steve McGovern W PTS 6 Bethnal Green	

Career: 15 contests, won 14, lost 1.

Ricky Beard

Dagenham. *Born* Hackney, 1 March, 1963
Southern Area Flyweight Champion. Ht. 5'7½"
Manager Self

02.05.89	Ged Goodwin W RSC 1 Chigwell	
06.06.89	Ged Goodwin W RTD 1 Chigwell	
19.09.89	Eric George L PTS 6 Bethnal Green	
04.10.89	Gordon Shaw L PTS 6 Basildon	
03.10.90	Neil Johnston DREW 6 Basildon	
19.11.90	Robbie Regan L RSC 6 Cardiff	
26.03.91	Francis Ampofo L PTS 8 Bethnal Green	
30.09.91	Mickey Cantwell L PTS 8 Kensington	
25.02.92	Francis Ampofo L PTS 8 Crystal Palace	
14.04.92	Prince Nassem Hamed L CO 2 Mansfield	
20.04.93	Tim Yeates L PTS 6 Brentwood	
11.05.93	Mickey Bell W RSC 2 Norwich	
29.06.93	James Drummond W PTS 8 Mayfair	
05.09.94	Shaun Norman L PTS 8 Brentwood	
16.09.94	Jesper D. Jensen L RTD 2 Aalborg, Denmark	
23.11.94	James Drummond W RSC 2 Irvine	
30.03.95	Daren Fifield W RSC 8 Bethnal Green	
	(Vacant Southern Area Flyweight Title)	

Career: 17 contests, won 6, drew 1, lost 10.

Gary Beardsley

Belper. *Born* Belper, 18 July, 1968
Welterweight. Ht. 5'10"
Manager J. Ashton

09.02.95	Shaun Stokes W RSC 3 Doncaster	
01.03.95	Eddie Haley W RSC 1 Glasgow	
06.03.95	Stefan Scriggins L PTS 6 Leicester	
15.03.95	Jamie Gallagher W PTS 6 Stoke	

Career: 4 contests, won 3, lost 1.

Robbie Bell

Sunderland. *Born* Sunderland, 11 February, 1977
L. Middleweight. Ht. 5'9½"
Manager T. Conroy

11.05.95 Paul Webb W PTS 6 Sunderland
22.06.95 Nic Ingram W PTS 6 Houghton le Spring
Career: 2 contests, won 2.

Mervyn Bennett

Cardiff. *Born* Cardiff, 20 February, 1960
Welsh Lightweight Champion. Ht. 5'6½"
Manager Self

06.01.81 Geoff Smart W RSC 6 Bethnal Green
26.01.81 Paddy McGuire W RSC 2 Edgbaston
07.04.81 Philip Morris W PTS 6 Newport
25.09.81 Alec Irvine W PTS 6 Nottingham
12.10.81 Richie Foster W PTS 8 Bloomsbury
19.11.81 Don George L PTS 10 Ebbw Vale
(*Vacant Welsh Featherweight Title*)
26.10.82 Mike Rowley L PTS 8 Newport
24.11.82 Jimmy Duncan L PTS 8 Stoke
17.02.83 Kevin Pritchard L RSC 5 Coventry
18.04.83 Keith Foreman L RSC 6 Bradford
17.02.86 Dave Smith W PTS 8 Mayfair
10.04.86 Dave Pratt W CO 6 Leicester
29.10.86 Keith Parry L RSC 3 Ebbw Vale
19.01.87 John Mullen W CO 1 Glasgow
16.02.87 Ray Newby L CO 8 Glasgow
19.05.92 Edward Lloyd L RSC 5 Cardiff
28.10.92 Mike Morrison W PTS 6 Cardiff
14.12.92 Mike Morrison W PTS 6 Cardiff
27.01.93 Carl Hook W PTS 10 Cardiff
(*Vacant Welsh Lightweight Title*)
17.06.95 Vince Burns W CO 4 Cardiff
Career: 20 contests, won 12, lost 8.

Andrew Benson

Mile End. *Born* Islington, 8 May, 1969
Cruiserweight. Ht. 6'0"
Manager F. Warren

02.09.94 Trevor Small W PTS 6 Spitalfields
18.11.94 Gypsy Carman W PTS 6 Bracknell
26.04.95 Martin Langtry L PTS 6 Solihull
17.05.95 Paul Lawson L RSC 2 Ipswich
Career: 4 contests, won 2, lost 2.

(Adrian) Ady Benton

Bradford. *Born* Dewsbury, 26 August, 1973
Bantamweight. Ht. 5'6"
Manager K. Tate

27.04.92 Mark Hargreaves W PTS 6 Bradford
29.10.92 Vince Feeney DREW 6 Bayswater
09.11.92 Stevie Woods W PTS 6 Bradford
25.01.93 Neil Parry W RSC 6 Bradford
26.02.93 James Drummond DREW 6 Irvine
08.03.93 Dave Campbell W PTS 6 Leeds
29.06.93 Michael Alldis W DIS 3 Mayfair
20.09.93 Mike Deveney L PTS 8 Glasgow
08.11.93 Chip O'Neill W RSC 5 Bradford
24.01.94 Mike Deveney W PTS 6 Glasgow
25.02.94 Paul Lloyd L RSC 5 Chester
(*Vacant Central Area S. Bantamweight Title*)
25.04.94 Pat Clinton W RSC 1 Glasgow
16.09.94 Johnny Bredahl L PTS 8 Aalborg, Denmark
23.11.94 Drew Docherty L PTS 12 Irvine
(*British Bantamweight Title Challenge*)
21.04.95 James Murray L RSC 7 Glasgow
14.06.95 Louis Veitch L RSC 2 Batley
Career: 16 contests, won 8, drew 2, lost 6.

Dennis Berry

Alfreton. *Born* Birmingham, 4 April, 1967
Welterweight. Ht. 5'8"
Manager M. Shinfield

01.04.93 Lee Renshaw W RSC 3 Evesham
08.06.93 David Sumner W PTS 6 Derby
04.11.93 Andy Peach W PTS 6 Stafford
17.03.94 Rick North L PTS 6 Lincoln
16.05.94 Rick North W RSC 6 Cleethorpes
24.05.94 Norman Hutcheon W RSC 2 Leicester
28.06.94 Howard Clarke W RSC 3 Edgbaston
30.07.94 Kevin Lueshing L CO 2 Bethnal Green
07.11.94 Vince Rose L PTS 6 Bethnal Green
15.12.94 Warren Stephens W PTS 6 Evesham
25.01.95 Howard Clarke W PTS 8 Stoke
03.03.95 Geoff McCreesh W RTD 5 Bracknell
Career: 12 contests, won 9, lost 3.

Ensley Bingham

Manchester. *Born* Manchester, 27 May, 1963
L. Middleweight. Ht. 5'8½"
Managers F. Warren/N. Basso

20.11.86 Steve Ward W CO 5 Bredbury
16.12.87 Tony Britland W CO 1 Manchester
23.02.88 Franki Moro W PTS 6 Oldham
01.03.88 Kelvin Mortimer W PTS 8 Manchester
26.04.88 Clinton McKenzie L PTS 8 Bethnal Green
18.10.88 Kostas Petrou L RSC 7 Oldham
22.03.89 Gary Cooper L PTS 8 Reading
26.09.89 Wally Swift Jnr W PTS 10 Oldham
(*Elim. British L. Middleweight Title*)
28.03.90 Fernando Alanis L RSC 3 Manchester

Andrew Benson   Les Clark

Ensley Bingham   Harry Goodwin

06.06.90	Andy Till W DIS 3 Battersea
	(Final Elim. British L. Middleweight Title)
19.03.91	Wally Swift Jnr L RSC 4 Birmingham
	(Vacant British L. Middleweight Title)
29.11.91	Russell Washer W RSC 4 Manchester
29.05.92	Graham Jenner W CO 5 Manchester
18.07.92	Gordon Blair W CO 2 Manchester
02.11.92	Robert McCracken L RSC 10 Wolverhampton
	(Elim. British L. Middleweight Title)
28.05.93	Mark Kelly W RSC 5 Middleton
14.08.93	Robert Peel W RTD 3 Hammersmith
25.02.95	Kevin Adamson W CO 5 Millwall

Career: 18 contests, won 12, lost 6.

Gordon Blair   Les Clark

Gordon Blair

Glasgow. *Born* Glasgow, 26 February, 1969
Welterweight. Ht. 5'10"
Managers A. Melrose/A. Morrison

21.11.89	Gavin Fitzpatrick W RSC 3 Glasgow
18.12.89	John Ritchie W PTS 4 Glasgow
19.02.90	Trevor Meikle W PTS 6 Glasgow
26.02.90	Jim Conley W RSC 3 Bradford
26.04.90	Kid Sylvester L PTS 6 Halifax
14.05.90	Trevor Ambrose W CO 5 Northampton
25.09.90	Calum Rattray W RSC 3 Glasgow
22.10.90	Shamus Casey W RSC 3 Glasgow
06.11.90	Leigh Wicks L PTS 8 Mayfair
10.12.90	Quinn Paynter W PTS 6 Glasgow
25.01.91	Danny Quigg W PTS 6 Shotts
18.02.91	Gary Logan L CO 1 Mayfair
15.04.91	Rob Pitters L PTS 6 Glasgow
31.05.91	Paul King W PTS 8 Glasgow
20.06.91	Delroy Waul W CO 2 Liverpool
24.09.91	Bozon Haule W RSC 8 Glasgow
19.11.91	Tony McKenzie L RSC 5 Norwich
31.01.92	Willie Beattie L RSC 3 Glasgow
	(Vacant Scottish Welterweight Title)
12.03.92	Mark Jay DREW 8 Glasgow
29.05.92	Ossie Maddix L PTS 6 Manchester
18.07.92	Ensley Bingham L CO 2 Manchester

27.10.92	Howard Clarke W RSC 4 Cradley Heath
24.11.92	Errol McDonald L RSC 5 Doncaster
29.01.93	Mark Cichocki L PTS 8 Glasgow
15.02.93	Lindon Scarlett L CO 4 Mayfair
25.06.93	Gary Logan L RSC 6 Battersea
12.03.94	Michael Smyth L RSC 4 Cardiff
13.04.94	Gilbert Jackson L RTD 1 Glasgow
21.07.94	Mark Antony W PTS 6 Edinburgh
08.09.94	Lee Blundell DREW 6 Glasgow
18.12.94	Mark Allen W RSC 3 Glasgow
21.01.95	Michael Carruth W PTS 6 Glasgow
13.05.95	Kevin McKenzie W RTD 5 Glasgow
02.06.95	Maurice Forbes L RSC 4 Bethnal Green

Career: 34 contests, won 17, drew 2, lost 15.

Andrew Bloomer

Pontypridd. *Born* Pontypridd, 26 September, 1964
Featherweight. Ht. 5'8½"
Manager Self

30.06.91	Leigh Williams L PTS 6 Southwark
03.09.91	Alan Ley L PTS 6 Cardiff
02.10.91	Bradley Stone L PTS 6 Barking
17.10.91	Leigh Williams L PTS 6 Southwark
04.11.91	Ceri Farrell L PTS 6 Merthyr
20.11.91	Ceri Farrell L PTS 6 Cardiff
28.11.91	Chris Morris L PTS 6 Liverpool
24.02.92	Alex Docherty L PTS 6 Glasgow
08.04.92	Jacob Smith L PTS 6 Leeds
30.04.92	Tony Falcone L PTS 6 Mayfair
16.05.92	Bradley Stone L PTS 6 Muswell Hill
23.05.92	Prince Nassem Hamed L RSC 2 Birmingham
05.10.92	Tony Falcone L PTS 8 Bristol
12.11.92	Marcus Duncan L PTS 6 Burnley
29.03.93	Vince Feeney L PTS 6 Mayfair
26.04.93	Mark Bowers L PTS 6 Lewisham
04.05.93	Paul Lloyd L PTS 6 Liverpool
15.09.93	Justin Murphy L PTS 4 Bethnal Green
04.10.93	Marco Fattore L PTS 6 Mayfair
28.11.94	Chris Lyons L PTS 6 Northampton

Career: 20 contests, lost 20.

Lee Blundell

Wigan. *Born* Wigan, 11 August, 1971
Middleweight. Ht. 6'2"
Manager J. McMillan

25.04.94	Robert Harper W RSC 2 Bury
20.05.94	Freddie Yemofio W RSC 6 Acton
08.09.94	Gordon Blair DREW 6 Glasgow
07.12.94	Kesem Clayton W RTD 2 Stoke
18.02.95	Glenn Catley L RSC 6 Shepton Mallet

Career: 5 contests, won 3, drew 1, lost 1.

Stevie Bolt

Plymouth. *Born* Hanover, Germany, 13 April, 1968
Lightweight. Ht. 6'0"
Manager N. Christian

29.09.94	Alan Temple L CO 2 Bethnal Green
20.12.94	Georgie Smith L RSC 2 Bethnal Green
24.02.95	Trevor Royal L RSC 5 Weston super Mare

Career: 3 contests, lost 3.

Stevie Bolt   Les Clark

Tony Booth

Sheffield. *Born* Hull, 30 January, 1970
Central Area Cruiserweight Champion. Ht. 5'11¾"
Manager B. Ingle

08.03.90	Paul Lynch L PTS 6 Watford
11.04.90	Mick Duncan W PTS 6 Dewsbury
26.04.90	Colin Manners W PTS 6 Halifax
16.05.90	Tommy Warde W PTS 6 Hull
05.06.90	Gary Dyson W PTS 6 Liverpool
05.09.90	Shaun McCrory L PTS 6 Stoke
08.10.90	Bullit Andrews W RSC 3 Cleethorpes
23.01.91	Darron Griffiths DREW 6 Stoke
06.02.91	Shaun McCrory L PTS 6 Liverpool
06.03.91	Billy Brough L PTS 6 Glasgow
18.03.91	Billy Brough W PTS 6 Glasgow
28.03.91	Neville Brown L PTS 6 Alfreton
17.05.91	Glenn Campbell L RSC 2 Bury
	(Central Area S. Middleweight Title Challenge)
25.07.91	Paul Murray W PTS 6 Dudley
01.08.91	Nick Manners DREW 8 Dewsbury
11.09.91	Jim Peters L PTS 8 Hammersmith
28.10.91	Eddie Smulders L RSC 6 Arnhem, Holland
09.12.91	Steve Lewsam L PTS 8 Cleethorpes
30.01.92	Serg Fame W PTS 6 Southampton
12.02.92	Tenko Ernie W RSC 4 Wembley
05.03.92	John Beckles W RSC 6 Battersea
26.03.92	Dave Owens W PTS 6 Hull
08.04.92	Michael Gale L PTS 8 Leeds
13.05.92	Phil Soundy W PTS 6 Kensington
02.06.92	Eddie Smulders L RSC 1 Rotterdam, Holland
18.07.92	Maurice Core L PTS 6 Manchester
07.09.92	James Cook L PTS 8 Bethnal Green
30.10.92	Roy Richie DREW 6 Istrees, France
18.11.92	Tony Wilson DREW 8 Solihull
25.12.92	Francis Wanyama L PTS 6 Izegem, Belgium
09.02.93	Tony Wilson W PTS 8 Wolverhampton
01.05.93	Ralf Rocchigiani DREW 8 Berlin, Germany

03.06.93 Victor Cordoba L PTS 8 Marseille, France
23.06.93 Tony Behan W PTS 6 Gorleston
01.07.93 Michael Gale L PTS 8 York
17.09.93 Ole Klemetsen L PTS 8 Copenhagen, Denmark
07.10.93 Denzil Browne DREW 8 York
02.11.93 James Cook L PTS 8 Southwark
12.11.93 Carlos Christie W PTS 6 Hull
28.01.94 Francis Wanyama L RSC 2 Waregem, Belgium
(Vacant Commonwealth Cruiserweight Title)
26.03.94 Torsten May L PTS 6 Dortmund, Germany
21.07.94 Mark Prince L RSC 3 Battersea
24.09.94 Johnny Held L PTS 8 Rotterdam, Holland
09.10.94 Dirk Wallyn L PTS 6 Waregem, Belgium
27.10.94 Dean Francis L CO 1 Bayswater
23.01.95 Jan Lefeber L PTS 8 Rotterdam, Holland
07.03.95 John Foreman L PTS 6 Edgbaston
27.04.95 Art Stacey W PTS 10 Hull
(Vacant Central Area Cruiserweight Title)
04.06.95 Montell Griffin L RSC 2 Bethnal Green
Career: 49 contests, won 16, drew 6, lost 27.

John Bosco   Tony Fitch

John Bosco (Waigo)

Bermondsey. *Born* Uganda, 16 July, 1967
L. Middleweight. Ht. 5'8½"
Manager M. Duff

05.12.91 Tony Kosova W CO 2 Peterborough
17.02.92 Gilbert Jackson W PTS 6 Mayfair
03.09.92 Russell Washer W RSC 2 Dunstable
19.10.92 Steve Goodwin W RSC 2 Mayfair
07.12.92 Griff Jones W RSC 1 Mayfair
28.01.93 Jerry Mortimer W RSC 4 Southwark
15.02.93 Mark Dawson W PTS 6 Mayfair
29.03.93 Winston May W RSC 3 Mayfair
10.11.93 Mark Dawson W RTD 4 Watford
26.01.94 Julian Eavis W RSC 1 Birmingham

14.03.94 Carlo Colarusso W PTS 6 Mayfair
28.04.94 Chris Peters W PTS 8 Mayfair
05.10.94 Robert Wright L RSC 7 Wolverhampton
Career: 13 contests, won 12, lost 1.

Michael Bowen

West Ham. *Born* Forest Gate, 14 November, 1974
Middleweight. Ht. 6'1½"
Manager P. De Freitas

02.06.95 Robert Harper W PTS 6 Bethnal Green
Career: 1 contest, won 1.

Mark Bowers

Lock Heath. *Born* Fareham, 19 October, 1970
S. Bantamweight. Ht. 5'5"
Managers M. Duff/T. Lawless

13.05.92 Hamid Moulay W CO 1 Kensington
17.10.92 Miguel Matthews W PTS 6 Wembley
17.12.92 Chris Lyons W CO 2 Wembley
26.04.93 Andrew Bloomer W PTS 6 Lewisham
09.06.93 Kurt Griffiths W RSC 1 Lewisham
02.11.93 Chris Jickells W RSC 3 Southwark
07.12.93 Thomas Bernard W RSC 1 Bethnal Green
05.04.94 Pete Buckley W PTS 6 Bethnal Green
11.05.94 Dean Lynch W RSC 2 Stevenage
09.12.94 Ian Reid W PTS 6 Bethnal Green
14.02.95 Graham McGrath W PTS 6 Bethnal Green
03.03.95 Des Gargano W RTD 2 Bracknell
12.05.95 Shaun Anderson W RSC 7 Bethnal Green
Career: 13 contests, won 13.

Warren Bowers

Grimsby. *Born* Grimsby, 14 January, 1971
L. Middleweight. Ht. 5'7"
Manager L. Slater

08.05.89 Andrew Brightman W CO 5 Grimsby
04.09.89 Mark Antony W PTS 6 Grimsby
14.05.90 Barry North W RSC 4 Cleethorpes
02.03.91 Andy Kent L PTS 6 Cleethorpes
25.11.91 John Baxter L RSC 3 Cleethorpes
04.06.92 Peter Reid L RSC 2 Cleethorpes
26.04.93 Colin Anderson W RSC 5 Cleethorpes
07.10.93 Ron Hopley L PTS 6 York
19.10.93 Craig Hartwell W PTS 6 Cleethorpes
08.11.93 Hughie Davey L RSC 2 Bradford
28.02.94 Ron Hopley L RSC 1 Marton
24.06.95 Phil Epton L PTS 6 Cleethorpes
Career: 12 contests, won 5, lost 7.

Nigel Bradley

Sheffield. *Born* Sheffield, 24 February, 1968
L. Welterweight. Ht. 5'8"
Manager B. Ingle

14.12.87 Lee Amass L RSC 4 Piccadilly
29.01.88 John Townsley L PTS 6 Durham
23.03.88 Darren Darby W RSC 1 Sheffield
28.03.88 Adam Muir NC 4 Glasgow
18.04.88 Mark Kelly L PTS 6 Manchester
08.06.88 Mike Russell W PTS 6 Sheffield
09.09.88 David Bacon W RSC 5 Doncaster
26.10.88 Dean Dickinson W PTS 6 Sheffield

23.02.89 Chris Mulcahy W RSC 2 Stockport
09.03.89 Michael McDermott W RSC 5 Glasgow
04.04.89 John Mullen W RSC 6 Sheffield
08.10.90 John Townsley DREW 8 Glasgow
14.11.90 B. F. Williams W CO 2 Sheffield
29.01.91 Sugar Gibiliru L PTS 8 Stockport
11.02.92 Dean Hollington L PTS 6 Barking
18.03.92 Kris McAdam W CO 2 Glasgow
14.04.92 Dave Whittle W CO 3 Mansfield
29.09.92 Tony Swift L PTS 8 Stoke
08.02.94 Howard Clarke L RTD 6 Wolverhampton
17.11.94 John Smith W PTS 6 Sheffield
03.03.95 Jason Rowland L RSC 3 Bethnal Green
13.04.95 Allan Hall L RSC 2 Bloomsbury
Career: 22 contests, won 11, drew 1, lost 9, no contest 1.

Mark Breslin

Barrhead. *Born* Paisley, 5 January, 1972
L. Welterweight. Ht. 5'9½"
Manager T. Gilmour

10.09.94 Brian Coleman W CO 1 Glasgow
02.11.94 Mark Allen W PTS 6 Solihull
23.11.94 Kevin McKenzie W PTS 6 Irvine
05.04.95 T. J. Smith W PTS 6 Irvine
01.06.95 T. J. Smith W RSC 3 Musselburgh
Career: 5 contests, won 5.

Henry Brewer

Shipley. *Born* Bradford, 18 September, 1969
Cruiserweight. Ht. 6'0"
Manager K. Tate

16.05.89 Steve Osborne L PTS 6 Halifax
14.06.95 Cliff Elden W PTS 6 Batley
Career: 2 contests, won 1, lost 1.

Michael Brodie   Les Clark

Michael Brodie

Manchester. *Born* Manchester, 10 May, 1974
Featherweight. Ht. 5'6"
Manager J. Trickett

03.10.94	Graham McGrath W RSC 5 Manchester
20.10.94	Chip O'Neill W CO 3 Middleton
28.11.94	Muhammad Shaffique W RSC 2 Manchester
13.12.94	Pete Buckley W PTS 6 Potters Bar
16.02.95	G. G. Goddard W PTS 6 Bury
03.04.95	Garry Burrell W RSC 4 Manchester
05.05.95	G. G. Goddard W PTS 6 Swansea
17.05.95	Ian Reid W RSC 3 Ipswich
10.06.95	Chris Clarkson W PTS 6 Manchester

Career: 9 contests, won 9.

Roger Brotherhood
Mansfield. *Born* Mansfield, 10 June, 1971
Featherweight. Ht. 5'8"
Manager J. Ashton

07.04.94	Robert Grubb W PTS 6 Walsall
05.12.94	Garry Burrell W PTS 6 Bradford
09.02.95	Kid McAuley L PTS 6 Doncaster
06.04.95	Paul Wynn W RSC 5 Sheffield

Career: 4 contest, won 3, lost 1.

Clayton Brown
Wolverhampton. *Born* Wolverhampton, 14 September, 1966
Heavyweight. Ht. 5'10"
Manager F. Warren

10.09.94	Gary Williams W PTS 4 Birmingham
12.10.94	Shane Meadows W CO 1 Sheffield
06.05.95	Gary Williams W PTS 4 Shepton Mallet

Career: 3 contests, won 3.

Clayton Brown   Harry Goodwin

Jason Brown
Retford. *Born* Worksop, 12 November, 1970
S. Middleweight. Ht. 6'2¼"
Manager K. Richardson

05.12.94	Stinger Mason L RSC 2 Cleethorpes
12.01.95	Sean Hendry L CO 1 Leeds

Career: 2 contests, lost 2.

Matt Brown   Les Clark

Matt Brown
Walworth. *Born* Camberwell, 17 February, 1971
S. Featherweight. Ht. 5'6"
Manager F. Maloney

15.06.94	Chris Lyons W CO 3 Southwark
25.10.94	Jason Hutson W PTS 4 Southwark
23.01.95	Andrew Reed W PTS 4 Bethnal Green

Career: 3 contest, won 3.

Mike Anthony Brown
Brixton. *Born* Jamaica, 8 February, 1970
S. Featherweight. Ht. 5'8"
Manager Self

23.05.93	Norman Dhalie L PTS 4 Brockley
25.06.93	G.G. Goddard W CO 2 Battersea
14.08.93	Simon Frailing W RSC 4 Hammersmith
14.04.94	Norman Dhalie W PTS 6 Battersea
22.05.94	Miguel Matthews L RSC 5 Crystal Palace
21.07.94	Miguel Matthews W PTS 6 Battersea
31.03.95	Barrie Kellie W RSC 2 Crystal Palace

Career: 7 contests, won 5, lost 2.

Tony Brown
Liverpool. *Born* Liverpool, 10 August, 1961
Former Undefeated Central Area Welterweight & L. Welterweight Champion. Ht. 5'8"
Manager Self

29.03.82	Paul Murray W PTS 6 Liverpool
05.04.82	Glen Crump W PTS 6 Manchester
22.04.82	Mickey Williams W RSC 3 Liverpool
10.05.82	Gary Petty W RSC 5 Liverpool
17.05.82	Cecil Williams W RSC 4 Manchester
03.06.82	Errol Dennis DREW 6 Liverpool
21.06.82	Errol Dennis W CO 3 Liverpool
06.07.82	Danny Garrison W PTS 6 Leeds
23.09.82	Ian Chantler W PTS 8 Liverpool

05.10.82	Ian Chantler L PTS 8 Liverpool
18.10.82	Steve Early L PTS 6 Edgbaston
06.12.82	Steve Early L PTS 8 Edgbaston
14.03.83	Walter Clayton W PTS 10 Sheffield *(Vacant Central Area L. Welterweight Title)*
20.04.83	Martin McGough W PTS 8 Solihull
03.10.83	Steve Tempro W PTS 8 Liverpool
13.10.83	Vernon Vanriel W PTS 8 Bloomsbury
30.11.83	Tony Laing L PTS 8 Piccadilly
12.03.84	Mickey Bird W RSC 6 Liverpool
04.06.84	Tony Adams L RSC 2 Mayfair
29.08.84	Joseph Lala L PTS 10 Sebokeng, South Africa
24.10.84	Kostas Petrou L PTS 8 Birmingham
31.05.85	Cliff Domville W RSC 1 Liverpool *(Vacant Central Area Welterweight Title)*
22.10.85	Billy Ahearne W PTS 6 Hull
04.11.85	Phil Duckworth W RTD 5 Manchester
06.12.85	Ian Chantler W RSC 7 Liverpool *(Central Area Welterweight Title Defence)*
13.03.86	Kostas Petrou W PTS 8 Alfreton
29.11.86	Rocky Kelly L RSC 11 Wandsworth *(Final Elim. British Welterweight Title)*
07.04.87	Derek Wormald L RSC 6 Batley
09.05.87	George Collins L RSC 5 Wandsworth
25.04.88	Jim Kelly W PTS 8 Liverpool
10.11.89	Humphrey Harrison L PTS 6 Liverpool
13.06.94	Phil Found L RSC 4 Liverpool
06.09.94	Rick North DREW 8 Stoke
25.10.94	Sean Knight L RTD 1 Middlesbrough
08.12.94	Kevin Toomey L PTS 6 Hull
23.02.95	Kevin Toomey W RSC 10 Hull *(Vacant Central Area Welterweight Title)*

Career: 36 contests, won 20, drew 2, lost 14.

Denzil Browne
Leeds. *Born* Leeds, 21 January, 1969
Cruiserweight. Ht. 6'2½"
Manager M. Duff

18.10.90	Mark Bowen W PTS 6 Dewsbury
29.11.90	R. F. McKenzie L PTS 6 Sunderland
13.12.90	Gary Railton W RSC 2 Dewsbury
21.02.91	Mark Bowen W PTS 6 Walsall
21.03.91	R. F. McKenzie W PTS 6 Dewsbury
09.05.91	Darren McKenna W PTS 6 Leeds
27.06.91	Steve Yorath W PTS 6 Leeds
01.08.91	Tony Colclough W RSC 1 Dewsbury
09.10.91	R. F. McKenzie L PTS 6 Manchester
30.10.91	Gus Mendes W RSC 6 Leeds
23.01.92	Darren McKenna W PTS 6 York
19.03.92	Ian Bulloch W PTS 8 York
23.09.92	Steve Yorath W PTS 8 Leeds
29.10.92	Sean O'Phoenix W RSC 4 Leeds
25.02.93	Cordwell Hylton W PTS 8 Bradford
22.04.93	Dave Muhammed W PTS 8 Mayfair
01.07.93	Steve Osborne W RSC 1 York
07.10.93	Tony Booth DREW 8 York
01.12.93	Lennie Howard W RSC 6 Kensington
26.10.94	Steve Lewsam W CO 2 Leeds
21.01.95	Dennis Andries L RSC 11 Glasgow *(Vacant British Cruiserweight Title)*

Career: 21 contests, won 17, drew 1, lost 3.

Frank Bruno
Wandsworth. *Born* Hammersmith, 16 November, 1961
Former Undefeated European Heavyweight Champion. Ht. 6'3½"
Manager Self

17.03.82 Lupe Guerra W CO 1 Kensington
30.03.82 Harvey Steichen W RSC 2 Wembley
20.04.82 Tom Stevenson W CO 1 Kensington
04.05.82 Ron Gibbs W RSC 4 Wembley
01.06.82 Tony Moore W RSC 2 Kensington
14.09.82 George Scott W RSC 1 Wembley
23.10.82 Ali Lukasa W CO 2 Berlin, Germany
09.11.82 Rudi Gauwe W CO 2 Kensington
23.11.82 George Butzbach W RTD 1 Wembley
07.12.82 Gilberto Acuna W RSC 1 Kensington
18.01.83 Stewart Lithgo W RTD 4 Kensington
08.02.83 Peter Mulendwa W CO 3 Kensington
01.03.83 Winston Allen W RSC 2 Kensington
05.04.83 Eddie Neilson W RSC 3 Kensington
03.05.83 Scott Ledoux W RSC 3 Wembley
31.05.83 Barry Funches W RSC 5 Kensington
09.07.83 Mike Jameson W CO 2 Chicago, USA
27.09.83 Bill Sharkey W CO 1 Wembley
11.10.83 Floyd Cummings W RSC 7 Kensington
06.12.83 Walter Santemore W CO 4 Kensington
13.03.84 Juan Figueroa W CO 1 Kensington
13.05.84 James Smith L CO 10 Wembley
25.09.84 Ken Lakusta W CO 2 Wembley
(Elim. Commonwealth Heavyweight Title)
06.11.84 Jeff Jordan W RSC 3 Kensington
27.11.84 Phil Brown W PTS 10 Wembley
26.03.85 Lucien Rodriguez W RSC 1 Wembley
01.10.85 Anders Eklund W CO 4 Wembley
(European Heavyweight Title Challenge)
04.12.85 Larry Frazier W CO 2 Kensington
04.03.86 Gerrie Coetzee W CO 1 Wembley
(Final Elim. WBA Heavyweight Title)
19.07.86 Tim Witherspoon L RSC 11 Wembley
(WBA Heavyweight Title Challenge)
24.03.87 James Tillis W RSC 5 Wembley
27.06.87 Chuck Gardner W CO 1 Cannes, France
30.08.87 Reggie Gross W RSC 8 Marbella, Spain
24.10.87 Joe Bugner W RSC 8 Tottenham
25.02.89 Mike Tyson L RSC 5 Las Vegas, USA
(WBC Heavyweight Title Challenge)
20.11.91 John Emmen W CO 1 Kensington
22.04.92 Jose Ribalta W CO 2 Wembley
17.10.92 Pierre Coetzer W RSC 8 Wembley
(Elim. IBF Heavyweight Title)
24.04.93 Carl Williams W RSC 10 Birmingham
01.10.93 Lennox Lewis L RSC 7 Cardiff
(WBC Heavyweight Title Challenge)
16.03.94 Jesse Ferguson W RSC 1 Birmingham
18.02.95 Rodolfo Marin W RSC 1 Shepton Mallet
13.05.95 Mike Evans W CO 2 Glasgow
Career: 43 contests, won 39, lost 4.

Wayne Buck

Derby. *Born* Nottingham, 31 August, 1966
Midland Area Heavyweight Champion. Ht. 5'10¾"
Manager M. Shinfield

26.03.90 Tucker Richards W CO 1 Nottingham
30.04.90 Chris Hubbert L CO 4 Nottingham
04.06.92 Gary Charlton W PTS 6 Cleethorpes
08.09.92 David Jules W RSC 3 Doncaster
12.11.92 Gary Charlton W PTS 8 Stafford
02.02.93 John Harewood L RSC 3 Derby
11.03.93 Vance Idiens W PTS 8 Walsall
29.10.93 Mikael Lindblad L RTD 3 Kordoer, Denmark
28.03.94 Steve Lewsam L PTS 10 Cleethorpes
(Vacant Midlands Area Heavyweight Title)

11.05.94 J. A. Bugner DREW 6 Stevenage
05.12.94 Vance Idiens W PTS 6 Cleethorpes
24.06.95 Cordwell Hylton W RSC 6 Cleethorpes
(Vacant Midlands Area Heavyweight Title)

Career: 12 contests, won 7, drew 1, lost 4.

Pete Buckley

Adcocks Green. *Born* Birmingham, 9 March, 1969
Midlands Area S. Bantamweight Champion. Former Undefeated Midlands Area S. Featherweight Champion. Ht. 5'8"
Manager Self

04.10.89 Alan Baldwin DREW 6 Stafford
10.10.89 Ronnie Stephenson L PTS 6 Wolverhampton
30.10.89 Robert Braddock W PTS 6 Birmingham
14.11.89 Neil Leitch W PTS 6 Evesham
22.11.89 Peter Judson W PTS 6 Stafford
11.12.89 Stevie Woods W PTS 6 Bradford
21.12.89 Wayne Taylor W PTS 6 Kings Heath
10.01.90 John O'Meara W PTS 6 Kensington
19.02.90 Ian McGirr L PTS 6 Birmingham
27.02.90 Miguel Matthews DREW 6 Evesham
14.03.90 Ronnie Stephenson DREW 6 Stoke
04.04.90 Ronnie Stephenson L PTS 8 Stafford
23.04.90 Ronnie Stephenson W PTS 6 Birmingham
30.04.90 Chris Clarkson L PTS 8 Mayfair
17.05.90 Johnny Bredahl L PTS 6 Aars, Denmark
04.06.90 Ronnie Stephenson W PTS 8 Birmingham
28.06.90 Robert Braddock W RSC 5 Birmingham
01.10.90 Miguel Matthews W PTS 8 Cleethorpes
09.10.90 Miguel Matthews L PTS 8 Wolverhampton
17.10.90 Tony Smith W PTS 6 Stoke
29.10.90 Miguel Matthews W PTS 8 Birmingham
21.11.90 Drew Docherty L PTS 8 Solihull
10.12.90 Neil Leitch W PTS 8 Birmingham
10.01.91 Duke McKenzie L RSC 5 Wandsworth
18.02.91 Jamie McBride L PTS 8 Glasgow
04.03.91 Brian Robb W RSC 7 Birmingham
26.03.91 Neil Leitch DREW 8 Wolverhampton
01.05.91 Mark Geraghty W PTS 8 Solihull
05.06.91 Brian Robb W PTS 10 Wolverhampton
(Vacant Midlands Area S. Featherweight Title)
09.09.91 Mike Deveney L PTS 8 Glasgow
24.09.91 Mark Bates W RTD 5 Basildon
29.10.91 John Armour L PTS 6 Kensington
14.11.91 Mike Deveney L PTS 6 Edinburgh
28.11.91 Craig Dermody L PTS 6 Liverpool
19.12.91 Craig Dermody L PTS 6 Oldham
18.01.92 Alan McKay DREW 8 Kensington
20.02.92 Brian Robb W RSC 10 Oakengates
(Midlands Area S. Featherweight Title Defence)
27.04.92 Drew Docherty L PTS 8 Glasgow
15.05.92 Ruben Condori L PTS 10 Augsburg, Germany
29.05.92 Donnie Hood L PTS 8 Glasgow
07.09.92 Duke McKenzie L RTD 3 Bethnal Green
12.11.92 Prince Nassem Hamed L PTS 6 Liverpool

19.02.93 Harald Geier L PTS 12 Vienna, Austria
(Vacant Penta-Continental S. Bantamweight Title)
26.04.93 Bradley Stone L PTS 8 Lewisham
18.06.93 Eamonn McAuley L PTS 6 Belfast
01.07.93 Tony Silkstone L PTS 8 York
06.10.93 Jonjo Irwin L PTS 8 Solihull
25.10.93 Drew Docherty L PTS 8 Glasgow
06.11.93 Michael Alldis L PTS 8 Bethnal Green
30.11.93 Barry Jones L PTS 4 Cardiff
19.12.93 Shaun Anderson L PTS 6 Glasgow
22.01.94 Barry Jones L PTS 6 Cardiff
29.01.94 Prince Nassem Hamed L RSC 4 Cardiff
10.03.94 Tony Falcone L PTS 4 Bristol
29.03.94 Conn McMullen W PTS 6 Bethnal Green
05.04.94 Mark Bowers L PTS 6 Bethnal Green
13.04.94 James Murray L PTS 6 Glasgow
06.05.94 Paul Lloyd L RTD 4 Liverpool
03.08.94 Greg Upton L PTS 6 Bristol
26.09.94 John Sillo L PTS 6 Liverpool
05.10.94 Matthew Harris L PTS 6 Wolverhampton
07.11.94 Marlon Ward L PTS 4 Piccadilly
23.11.94 Justin Murphy L PTS 4 Piccadilly
29.11.94 Neil Swain L PTS 6 Cardiff
13.12.94 Michael Brodie L PTS 6 Potters Bar
20.12.94 Michael Alldis L PTS 6 Bethnal Green
10.02.95 Matthew Harris W RSC 6 Birmingham
(Midlands Area S. Bantamweight Title Challenge)
23.02.95 Paul Ingle L PTS 8 Southwark
20.04.95 John Sillo L PTS 6 Liverpool
27.04.95 Paul Ingle L PTS 8 Bethnal Green
09.05.95 Ady Lewis L PTS 4 Basildon
23.05.95 Spencer Oliver L PTS 4 Potters Bar

Career: 72 contests, won 20, drew 5, lost 47.

(Andrew) Stefy Bull (Bullcroft)

Denaby. *Born* Doncaster, 10 May, 1977
S. Bantamweight. Ht. 5'10"
Manager J. Rushton

30.06.95 Andy Roberts W PTS 4 Doncaster

Career: 1 contest, won 1.

Paul Burke

Preston. *Born* Preston, 25 July, 1966
Former British & Commonwealth Lightweight Champion. Ht. 5'10"
Manager J. Trickett

21.01.87 Steve Brown W CO 4 Stoke
30.01.87 Paul Marriott L PTS 6 Kirkby
02.03.87 Brian Murphy W CO 2 Marton
06.04.87 Paul Marriott W PTS 6 Newcastle
30.04.87 Paul Gadney W PTS 6 Bethnal Green
01.06.87 Pat Barrett W PTS 6 Bradford
15.09.87 Marvin P. Gray L RSC 6 Batley
18.11.87 Rudy Valentino W PTS 6 Bethnal Green
15.12.87 James Jiora L PTS 4 Bradford
11.02.88 Paul Gadney DREW 8 Gravesend
25.01.89 Paul Charters W PTS 6 Bethnal Green
23.02.89 Mark Kelly L DIS 5 Stockport
07.03.89 Tony Connellan W RSC 5 Manchester
11.04.89 Billy Buchanan W RSC 4 Oldham
21.10.89 Aaron Kabi DREW 8 Middlesbrough
09.12.89 Angel Mona L RSC 3 Toulouse, France
23.04.90 Tony Richards W PTS 10 Glasgow
(Elim. British Lightweight Title)
25.09.90 Robert Harkin W PTS 8 Glasgow

21.01.91 Peter Bradley W PTS 10 Glasgow
(Elim. British Lightweight Title)
31.05.91 Art Blackmore W RSC 3 Manchester
20.09.91 Tony Richards W PTS 8 Manchester
09.02.92 Dave Andrews W PTS 6 Bradford
28.04.92 Paul Charters W RSC 7 Houghton le
Spring
(Final Elim. British Lightweight Title)
28.09.92 Marcel Herbert W PTS 6 Manchester
17.11.92 Jean-Baptiste Mendy L PTS 12 Paris,
France
*(European Lightweight Title
Challenge)*
24.02.93 Billy Schwer W RSC 7 Wembley
*(British & Commonwealth Lightweight
Title Challenge)*
25.07.93 Lyndon Paul Walker W PTS 8 Oldham
10.11.93 Billy Schwer L PTS 12 Watford
*(British & Commonwealth Lightweight
Title Defence)*
22.04.94 Racheed Lawal L RSC 4 Aalborg,
Denmark
*(European Lightweight Title
Challenge)*
04.10.94 Rudy Valentino W PTS 6 Mayfair
17.02.95 Michael Ayers L RSC 6 Crawley
(Vacant British Lightweight Title)
27.05.95 Patrick Gallagher W PTS 8 Belfast
Career: 32 contests, won 20, drew 2, lost 10.

Paul Burns

Liverpool. *Born* Liverpool, 15 February,
1971
Welterweight. Ht. 5'9½"
Manager J. Hyland

16.06.95 Mick Mulcahy W RSC 3 Liverpool
Career: 1 contest, won 1.

Vince Burns

Pimlico. *Born* Paddington, 27 July, 1970
Lightweight. Ht. 5'7"
Manager P. Healy

29.04.93 Jason Hutson W RSC 1 Hayes
04.10.93 Yifru Retta L PTS 6 Mayfair
17.10.94 Danny Lutaaya L RSC 6 Mayfair
25.03.95 Lewis Reynolds L RSC 4 Millwall
17.06.95 Mervyn Bennett L CO 4 Cardiff
Career: 5 contests, won 1, lost 4.

Garry Burrell

Kirkcaldy. *Born* Musselburgh, 9 July, 1965
S. Featherweight. Ht. 5'7½"
Manager T. Gilmour

21.09.92 Alan Graham W PTS 6 Glasgow
09.11.92 Alan Graham W PTS 6 Bradford
22.02.93 Tim Hill L PTS 6 Glasgow
23.03.93 Yusuf Vorajee L PTS 6
Wolverhampton
26.04.93 Robbie Sivyer W PTS 6 Glasgow
20.09.93 Phil Found L RSC 4 Glasgow
25.11.93 Colin Innes L PTS 6 Newcastle
24.05.94 Alan Graham L PTS 6 Sunderland
29.09.94 Tim Hill L PTS 6 Tynemouth
07.10.94 Dennis Holbaek Pedersen L PTS 6
Copenhagen, Denmark
05.12.94 Roger Brotherhood L PTS 6 Bradford
23.01.95 Trevor George L PTS 6 Glasgow
24.02.95 Colin Innes L PTS 6 Irving
16.03.95 Liam Dineen L PTS 6 Sunderland
25.03.95 John Sillo L PTS 6 Chester

03.04.95 Michael Brodie L RSC 4 Manchester
15.05.95 Paul Goode W RSC 1 Bradford
22.05.95 Trevor Sumner L PTS 6 Morecambe
01.06.95 Marty Chestnut W RTD 3 Musselburgh
05.06.95 Robert Hay L PTS 6 Glasgow
16.06.95 Paul Lloyd L RSC 2 Liverpool
Career: 21 contests, won 5, lost 16.

Kevin Burton

Doncaster. *Born* Doncaster, 20 June, 1965
L. Heavyweight. Ht. 5'10½"
Manager J. Rushton

10.05.93 Pat McNamara W RSC 2 Cleethorpes
07.06.93 Tony Colclough W PTS 6 Walsall
20.09.93 Bullit Andrews W PTS 6 Cleethorpes
30.09.93 Tony Colclough W DIS 5 Walsall
13.12.93 Tony Colclough W RSC 3 Doncaster
07.03.94 Bullit Andrews W RSC 1 Doncaster
07.04.94 Johnny Hooks L PTS 6 Walsall
10.05.94 Declan Faherty L RSC 4 Doncaster
12.10.94 Tony Colclough W PTS 6 Stoke
25.10.94 Chris Nurse W RSC 1 Edgbaston
12.12.94 Jem Jackson W RSC 4 Doncaster
09.02.95 Dave Battey L PTS 6 Doncaster
05.05.95 Dave Battey L PTS 6 Doncaster
15.05.95 Clinton Woods L PTS 6 Cleethorpes
14.06.95 Clinton Woods L RSC 6 Batley
Career: 15 contests, won 9, lost 6.

Steve Burton

Pembroke. *Born* Pembroke, 29 August,
1970
L. Welterweight. Ht. 5'7"
Manager D. Davies

26.04.94 Colin Dunne L CO 2 Bethnal Green
29.05.94 Everald Williams DREW 6 Queensway
21.07.94 Adrian Chase L PTS 6 Battersea
05.09.94 Bobby Guynan W RTD 1 Brentwood
12.09.94 Jason Rowland L RSC 1 Mayfair
29.11.94 John Janes L PTS 6 Cardiff
13.12.94 Bernard Paul L PTS 6 Potters Bar
04.02.95 Trevor Smith L RSC 6 Cardiff
08.03.95 Malcolm Thomas W PTS 6 Cardiff
12.04.95 Nigel Haddock W PTS 6 Llanelli
12.06.95 Mark Haslam L PTS 6 Manchester
Career: 11 contests, won 3, drew 1, lost 7.

Paul Busby

Worcester. *Born* Worcester, 20 April, 1966
Former Penta-Continental Middleweight
Champion. Ht. 5'11½"
Manager B. Hearn

18.11.90 Carlos Christie W PTS 6 Birmingham
04.12.90 Marty Duke W PTS 6 Bury St
Edmunds
23.01.91 Tony Wellington W RSC 2 Brentwood
27.02.91 Paul Murray W PTS 6 Wolverhampton
19.03.91 Paul Smith W PTS 6 Leicester
10.09.91 Nigel Rafferty W RSC 6
Wolverhampton
12.11.91 Graham Burton W RSC 3
Wolverhampton
17.12.91 Paul Murray W CO 3 Cardiff
01.02.92 John Kaighin W PTS 4 Birmingham
23.05.92 Stinger Mason W RSC 2 Birmingham
06.10.92 Chris Richards W PTS 6 Antwerp,
Belgium
14.11.92 Paul Wesley W PTS 8 Cardiff
19.01.93 Stan King W PTS 8 Cardiff

16.03.93 Neville Brown L PTS 10
Wolverhampton
(Elim. British Middleweight Title)
10.07.93 Wayne Ellis L RSC 5 Cardiff
03.11.93 Spencer Alton W RTD 4 Worcester
19.01.94 Colin Manners DREW 8 Solihull
15.03.94 Colin Manners W PTS 8 Mayfair
28.06.94 Wayne Ellis L TD 4 Mayfair
*(Vacant Penta-Continental
Middleweight Title)*
29.10.94 Wayne Ellis W PTS 12 Cannock
*(Penta-Continental Middleweight Title
Challenge)*
17.01.95 Warren Stowe W PTS 12 Worcester
*(Penta-Continental Middleweight Title
Defence)*
01.06.95 Willie Quinn L RTD 8 Musselburgh
*(Inaugural WBO Continental
Middleweight Title)*
Career: 22 contests, won 17, drew 1, lost 4.

(Barrie) Blue Butterworth

Burnley. *Born* Lambeth, 5 October, 1970
L. Welterweight. Ht. 5'8½"
Manager Self

31.03.92 Brian Coleman W PTS 6 Stockport
04.06.92 Mark Allen W RSC 5 Burnley
14.09.92 Lee Soar W CO 4 Bradford
12.11.92 Dave Madden W RSC 2 Burnley
25.02.93 Ian Thomas W PTS 6 Burnley
27.05.93 Brian Coleman W PTS 6 Burnley
13.09.93 Kevin McKenzie L PTS 6 Middleton
11.11.93 Jamie Davidson W RSC 3 Burnley
25.04.94 Rob Stewart L PTS 6 Bury
20.10.94 Wahid Fats DREW 6 Middleton
03.04.95 Jay Mahoney L PTS 6 Manchester
Career: 11 contests, won 7, drew 1, lost 3.

Craig Byrne

Birmingham. *Born* Birmingham, 12 July,
1974
S. Middleweight. Ht. 6'1"
Manager E. Cashmore

23.05.94 Richard Guy L RSC 4 Walsall
29.09.94 Tony Colclough W PTS 6 Walsall
18.12.94 John Wilson L RSC 2 Glasgow
Career: 3 contest, won 1, lost 2.

Sean Byrne

Northampton. *Born* Manchester, 20
September, 1966
Middleweight. Ht. 6'0"
Manager Self

06.04.92 Martin Jolley W RSC 6 Northampton
28.04.92 John McKenzie W RSC 6 Corby
05.10.92 Russell Washer W PTS 6 Northampton
20.09.93 Spencer Alton W PTS 6 Northampton
23.11.93 John Rice W PTS 6 Kettering
19.12.93 Kessem Clayton W PTS 6
Northampton
28.11.94 Steve Thomas W PTS 6 Northampton
Career: 7 contests, won 7.

Damien Caesar

Stepney. *Born* Stepney, 2 October, 1965
Heavyweight. Ht. 6'5"
Manager T. Lawless

22.04.91 Larry Peart W RSC 2 Mayfair
30.05.91 Tony Colclough W RSC 1 Mayfair

17.02.92 Steve Stewart W RSC 5 Mayfair
27.04.92 Gary Williams W RSC 4 Mayfair
05.10.92 Denroy Bryan W RSC 5 Bristol
07.12.93 Joey Paladino W RSC 3 Bethnal Green
14.03.94 Vance Idiens W RSC 4 Mayfair
13.12.94 Gary Williams W RSC 2 Ilford
23.02.95 Julius Francis L RSC 8 Southwark
 (Vacant Southern Area Heavyweight
 Title)
Career: 9 contests, won 8, lost 1.

Joe Calzaghe

Newbridge. *Born* Hammersmith, 23 March,
1972
S. Middleweight. Ht. 5'11"
Managers M. Duff/T. Lawless

01.10.93 Paul Hanlon W RSC 1 Cardiff
10.11.93 Stinger Mason W RSC 1 Watford
16.12.93 Spencer Alton W RSC 2 Newport
22.01.94 Martin Rosamond W RSC 1 Cardiff
01.03.94 Darren Littlewood W RSC 1 Dudley
04.06.94 Karl Barwise W RSC 1 Cardiff
01.10.94 Mark Dawson W RSC 1 Cardiff
30.11.94 Trevor Ambrose W RSC 2
 Wolverhampton
14.02.95 Frank Minton W CO 1 Bethnal Green
22.02.95 Bobbi Joe Edwards W PTS 8 Telford
19.05.95 Robert Curry W RSC 1 Southwark
Career: 11 contests, won 11.

Joe Calzaghe   Les Clark

Anthony Campbell

Shepherds Bush. *Born* Kensington, 20
January, 1967
Lightweight. Ht. 5'6"
Manager D. Gunn

05.04.94 Andrew Reed W PTS 6 Bethnal Green
20.05.94 Malcolm Thomas W PTS 6 Acton
29.09.94 P. J. Gallagher L PTS 6 Bethnal Green
19.11.94 Nicky Bardle L PTS 6 Heathrow
25.01.95 Gareth Lawrence L PTS 6 Cardiff
07.02.95 Anthony Maynard L PTS 8
 Wolverhampton
26.05.95 M. T. Atkin DREW 6 Norwich
Career: 7 contests, won 2, drew 1, lost 4.

Dave Campbell

South Shields. *Born* South Shields, 13
December, 1968
S. Bantamweight. Ht. 5'4½"
Manager A. Walker

11.09.91 Mark Hargreaves L RSC 4 Stoke
14.11.91 Dave Martin W PTS 6 Bayswater
27.11.91 Shaun Norman W PTS 6 Marton
18.05.92 Glyn Shepherd W RSC 1 Marton
23.09.92 Tony Silkstone L RSC 4 Leeds
08.03.93 Ady Benton L PTS 6 Leeds
26.03.93 Shaun Anderson L RSC 5 Glasgow
30.04.93 James Murray L PTS 6 Glasgow
11.11.93 Marcus Duncan L PTS 6 Burnley
02.06.94 Adey Lewis L RSC 1 Middleton
21.07.94 James Murray L RSC 3 Edinburgh
26.09.94 Marcus Duncan L PTS 6 Morecambe
21.10.94 Dave Hardie L RTD 4 Glasgow
Career: 13 contests, won 3, lost 10.

Glenn Campbell

Bury. *Born* Bury, 22 April, 1970
Central Area S. Middleweight Champion.
Ht. 5'10"
Managers J. Doughty/T. Gilmour

19.04.90 Ian Vokes W CO 1 Oldham
01.05.90 Stevie R. Davies W RSC 2 Oldham
21.05.90 Andy Marlow W RSC 6 Hanley
11.06.90 Stinger Mason W RTD 5 Manchester
26.09.90 Tony Kosova W RSC 2 Manchester
22.10.90 Simon McDougall W RSC 4
 Manchester
26.11.90 Sean O'Phoenix W RSC 4 Bury
 (Vacant Central Area S. Middleweight
 Title)
28.02.91 Simon McDougall W PTS 10 Bury
 (Central Area S. Middleweight Title
 Defence)
17.05.91 Tony Booth W RSC 2 Bury
 (Central Area S. Middleweight Title
 Defence)
21.01.92 Nigel Rafferty W RSC 6 Stockport
10.03.92 Carlos Christie DREW 8 Bury
05.05.92 Ian Henry W RSC 1 Preston
22.04.93 Paul Wright W RSC 4 Bury
 (Elim. British S. Middleweight Title &
 Central Area S. Middleweight Title
 Defence)
17.02.94 Nigel Rafferty W RSC 7 Bury
15.03.94 Juan Carlos Scaglia L PTS 12 Mayfair
 (Vacant Penta-Continental
 S. Middleweight Title)
16.02.95 Simon McDougall W PTS 6 Bury
20.03.95 Stephen Wilson L PTS 10 Glasgow
 (Final Elim. British S. Middleweight
 Title)
Career: 17 contests, won 14, drew 1, lost 2.

Mickey Cantwell

Bermondsey. *Born* London, 23 November,
1964
Former Undefeated Southern Area
Flyweight Champion. Ht. 5'2½"
Manager Self

21.01.91 Eduardo Vallejo W RSC 4 Crystal
 Palace
26.03.91 Mario Alberto Cruz W PTS 6 Bethnal
 Green
30.09.91 Ricky Beard W PTS 8 Kensington

23.10.91 Carlos Manrigues W RSC 5 Bethnal
 Green
14.12.91 Shaun Norman W PTS 8 Bexleyheath
16.05.92 Louis Veitch W PTS 6 Muswell Hill
10.02.93 Louis Veitch DREW 8 Lewisham
14.04.93 Daren Fifield W PTS 10 Kensington
 (Vacant Southern Area Flyweight Title)
15.09.93 Pablo Tiznado L PTS 12 Bethnal Green
 (Vacant WBC International L.
 Flyweight Title)
03.11.93 Anthony Hanna W PTS 8 Bristol
27.04.94 Luigi Camputaro L PTS 12 Bethnal
 Green
 (European Flyweight Title Challenge)
15.06.94 Lyndon Kershaw L PTS 8 Southwark
27.04.95 Anthony Hanna W PTS 6 Bethnal
 Green
Career: 13 contests, won 9, drew 1, lost 3.

(George) Gypsy Carman

Norwich. *Born* Wisbech, 23 November,
1964
Cruiserweight. Ht. 6'0"
Manager Self

30.01.84 Dave Mowbray W PTS 6 Manchester
16.02.84 Lennie Howard L RTD 1 Basildon
03.04.84 Gordon Stacey W PTS 6 Lewisham
07.06.84 Deka Williams L PTS 6 Dudley
29.10.84 Wes Taylor W PTS 6 Streatham
04.02.85 Lee White W PTS 6 Lewisham
20.02.85 Charlie Hostetter L PTS 6 Muswell
 Hill
27.03.85 Glenn McCrory L PTS 8 Gateshead
09.05.85 Barry Ellis L PTS 8 Acton
10.06.85 Chris Jacobs DREW 6 Cardiff
02.09.85 Barry Ellis L PTS 8 Coventry
31.10.85 Tee Jay L PTS 6 Wandsworth
15.03.86 Mick Cordon W PTS 8 Norwich
24.03.86 Chris Harbourne W PTS 6 Mayfair
13.09.86 Tee Jay L RSC 4 Norwich
 (Vacant Southern Area Cruiserweight
 Title)
20.11.86 Lou Gent L CO 1 Merton
12.01.87 Patrick Collins W PTS 8 Glasgow
19.01.87 Johnny Nelson L PTS 6 Mayfair
19.02.87 Danny Lawford L PTS 6 Peterborough
04.03.87 Tommy Taylor L PTS 8 Dudley
24.11.87 Tommy Taylor W PTS 8 Wisbech
14.03.88 Blaine Logsdon L RSC 8 Norwich
25.04.88 Gerry Storey L PTS 6 Bethnal Green
15.09.89 Carlton Headley W PTS 6 High
 Wycombe
22.02.90 Lou Gent L PTS 10 Wandsworth
 (Southern Area Cruiserweight Title
 Challenge)
07.05.90 Eddie Smulders L RSC 4 Arnhem,
 Holland
26.11.90 Everton Blake L PTS 6 Bethnal Green
22.10.91 Tenko Ernie W PTS 6 Wandsworth
21.01.92 Dave Lawrence L PTS 6 Norwich
31.03.92 Richard Bustin W PTS 6 Norwich
27.10.92 Everton Blake L RSC 4 Hayes
 (Southern Area Cruiserweight Title
 Challenge)
29.04.93 Paul McCarthy W PTS 6 Hayes
28.09.93 Scott Welch L RSC 3 Bethnal Green
18.11.94 Andrew Benson L PTS 6 Bracknell
03.03.95 Steve Osborne W PTS 6 Bracknell
26.05.95 Art Stacey W PTS 6 Norwich
Career: 36 contests, won 15, drew 1, lost 20.

Brian Carr

Modiesburn. *Born* Glasgow, 20 June, 1969
Featherweight. Ht. 5'6"
Manager A. Morrison

18.12.94	Fred Reeve W CO 2 Glasgow	
21.01.95	Shaun Anderson W PTS 6 Glasgow	
04.03.95	G. G. Goddard W PTS 8 Livingston	
13.05.95	Paul Wynn W RTD 2 Glasgow	
08.06.95	Abdul Mannon W PTS 6 Glasgow	

Career: 5 contests, won 5.

Cornelius Carr Les Clark

(John) Cornelius Carr

Middlesbrough. *Born* Middlesbrough, 9
April, 1969
Former Undefeated British S. Middleweight
Champion. Ht. 5'9½"
Manager M. Duff

22.09.87	Paul Burton W RSC 5 Bethnal Green
28.11.87	Dave Heaver W RSC 2 Windsor
12.01.88	Shamus Casey W RSC 6 Cardiff
27.01.88	Kesem Clayton W PTS 6 Bethnal Green
29.03.88	Darren Parker W RSC 1 Bethnal Green
12.04.88	Franki Moro W PTS 6 Cardiff
10.05.88	Andy Catesby W RSC 5 Tottenham
15.11.88	Skip Jackson W CO 1 Norwich
20.12.88	Kevin Hayde W PTS 6 Swansea
22.03.89	Bocco George L RSC 3 Reading
24.10.89	Carlo Colarusso W RTD 4 Watford
20.02.90	Peter Gorny W RSC 4 Millwall
21.04.90	Franki Moro W PTS 8 Sunderland
26.09.90	John Maltreaux W CO 1 Metairie, USA
27.10.90	Jerry Nestor W CO 1 Greenville, USA
16.02.91	Frank Eubanks W RSC 5 Thornaby
02.03.91	Carlo Colarusso W PTS 8 Darlington
18.05.91	Paul Burton W RSC 3 Verbania, Italy
06.09.91	Marvin O'Brien W RSC 7 Salemi, Italy
29.10.92	Alan Richards W PTS 8 Bayswater
24.04.93	Graham Burton W PTS 6 Birmingham
19.05.93	Stan King W PTS 8 Sunderland
22.09.93	Horace Fleary W PTS 8 Wembley
11.03.94	James Cook W PTS 12 Bethnal Green *(British S. Middleweight Title Challenge)*
04.02.95	Colin Manners W PTS 8 Cardiff
13.05.95	Chris Richards W RTD 3 Glasgow

Career: 26 contests, won 25, lost 1.

Paul Carr Les Clark

Paul Carr

Sidcup. *Born* Basildon, 16 April, 1973
L. Middleweight. Ht. 5'10"
Manager F. Warren

02.06.95	Dave Curtis W PTS 6 Bethnal Green

Career: 1 contest, won 1.

Michael Carruth

Dublin. *Born* Dublin, 9 July, 1967
Welterweight. Ht. 5'8"
Manager F. Warren

26.02.94	George Wilson W PTS 6 Earls Court
21.05.94	Ricky Mabbett W CO 3 Belfast
17.08.94	Mark Antony W RSC 3 Sheffield
17.09.94	Kim-Ken Jackson W RSC 4 Las Vegas, USA
12.10.94	Rick North W PTS 6 Sheffield
19.11.94	Dave Lovell W RSC 2 Cardiff
21.01.95	Gordon Blair L PTS 6 Glasgow
17.03.95	Vernice Harvard W RSC 3 Worcester, USA
17.06.95	Steve McGovern W RSC 4 Cardiff

Career: 9 contests, won 8, lost 1.

Shamus Casey (West)

Alfreton. *Born* Pinxton, 13 January, 1960
Middleweight. Ht. 5'11"
Manager Self

25.01.84	Tony Burke L CO 1 Solihull
16.04.84	Ronnie Fraser L RSC 3 Nottingham
05.07.84	Craig Edwards L PTS 6 Prestatyn
21.09.84	Dave Foley W PTS 6 Alfreton
28.09.84	Dennis Boy O'Brien L PTS 6 Longford
11.10.84	Terry Gilbey L RSC 1 Barnsley
22.10.84	Dave King W PTS 6 South Shields
09.11.84	Reuben Thurley W CO 4 Alfreton
16.11.84	Tucker Watts L PTS 6 Leicester
26.11.84	Terry Gilbey L RSC 1 Liverpool
14.01.85	Mark Walker L PTS 6 Manchester
24.01.85	Tommy Campbell L PTS 8 Manchester
11.02.85	Paul Smith W PTS 6 Manchester
18.02.85	John Graham L PTS 6 Mayfair
01.03.85	Dennis Sheehan W PTS 6 Mansfield
11.03.85	Sean O'Phoenix L PTS 6 Manchester

20.03.85	Sean O'Phoenix L PTS 6 Stoke
15.04.85	Ronnie Tucker L PTS 6 Manchester
14.05.85	Dennis Sheehan L PTS 10 Mansfield *(Midlands Area L. Middleweight Title Challenge)*
05.06.85	Gary Stretch L RSC 2 Kensington
02.09.85	Newton Barnett DREW 8 Coventry
12.09.85	Cliff Curtis W RSC 7 Swindon
23.09.85	Danny Quigg L PTS 8 Glasgow
10.10.85	Davey Cox W PTS 6 Alfreton
22.10.85	Mick Mills L RSC 3 Hull
02.12.85	Newton Barnett DREW 8 Dulwich
09.12.85	Steve Ward L PTS 6 Nottingham
16.12.85	Robert Armstrong W PTS 6 Bradford
20.01.86	Billy Ahearne L PTS 8 Leicester
06.02.86	Denys Cronin L RSC 6 Doncaster
10.03.86	Neil Munn L PTS 8 Cardiff
20.03.86	Andy Wright L RSC 4 Merton
22.04.86	Franki Moro L PTS 8 Carlisle
29.04.86	John Graham L PTS 8 Piccadilly
08.05.86	Randy Henderson L PTS 8 Bayswater
19.05.86	Joe Lynch W RSC 3 Plymouth
28.05.86	Andy Wright L PTS 6 Lewisham
15.09.86	Gerry Sloof L PTS 6 Scheidam, Holland
23.09.86	Derek Wormald L PTS 8 Batley
06.10.86	David Scere L PTS 6 Leicester
21.10.86	David Scere W PTS 8 Hull
29.10.86	Peter Elliott W PTS 6 Stoke
25.11.86	Steve Foster L PTS 8 Manchester
15.12.86	Tucker Watts DREW 6 Loughborough
13.01.87	Robert Armstrong L PTS 6 Oldham
26.01.87	Richard Wagstaff W PTS 8 Bradford
05.02.87	Neil Patterson L PTS 6 Newcastle
20.02.87	Dennis Boy O'Brien L PTS 8 Maidenhead
02.03.87	Roddy Maxwell L PTS 6 Glasgow
24.03.87	Ian Chantler L PTS 8 Nottingham
07.04.87	Richard Wagstaff L PTS 8 Batley
28.04.87	Sean Leighton DREW 8 Manchester
05.05.87	Dave Owens L PTS 6 Leeds
12.05.87	Jason Baxter L PTS 6 Alfreton
23.06.87	Terry Magee L CO 6 Swansea *(Vacant All-Ireland L. Middleweight Title)*
31.07.87	Cyril Jackson L RSC 5 Wrexham
22.09.87	Brian Robinson L PTS 6 Bethnal Green
28.09.87	Sean Leighton L PTS 8 Bradford
19.10.87	Sammy Storey L PTS 6 Belfast
10.11.87	Peter Brown L PTS 8 Batley
19.11.87	Kid Murray W PTS 6 Ilkeston
26.11.87	Trevor Smith L CO 4 Fulham
12.01.88	Cornelius Carr L RSC 6 Cardiff
15.02.88	Leigh Wicks L PTS 6 Copthorne
25.02.88	R. W. Smith L RSC 3 Bethnal Green
28.03.88	Tony Britton L PTS 8 Birmingham
13.06.88	Jim Kelly L PTS 6 Glasgow
25.06.88	Wayne Ellis L PTS 6 Luton
12.09.88	Shaun Cummins L CO 3 Northampton
17.10.88	Jim Kelly L PTS 6 Glasgow
01.11.88	Brian Robinson L PTS 6 Reading
17.11.88	Mark Howell L CO 1 Ilkeston
16.12.88	Conrad Oscar L PTS 6 Brentwood
25.01.89	Tony Velinor L RTD 3 Basildon
22.02.89	Mickey Murray DREW 6 Doncaster
01.03.89	Nigel Fairbairn L PTS 6 Stoke
21.03.89	Dave Thomas L PTS 6 Cottingham
29.03.89	W. O. Wilson L RSC 5 Wembley
08.05.89	Antonio Fernandez L PTS 6 Edgbaston
31.05.89	Ossie Maddix L CO 3 Manchester
11.09.89	Terry French W PTS 6 Nottingham
18.09.89	Skip Jackson W PTS 6 Northampton
26.09.89	Theo Marius L PTS 8 Chigwell
05.10.89	Val Golding L PTS 6 Stevenage

73

17.10.89 Carl Harney L PTS 4 Oldham
13.11.89 Ian Vokes W RSC 5 Bradford
29.11.89 Ray Close L CO 2 Belfast
21.06.90 Skip Jackson W PTS 6 Alfreton
04.09.90 Pete Bowman W PTS 6 Southend
14.09.90 Chris Richards L PTS 6 Telford
08.10.90 Billy Brough W PTS 6 Leicester
22.10.90 Gordon Blair L RSC 3 Glasgow
22.11.90 Jimmy Thornton W PTS 6 Ilkeston
14.12.90 Stefan Wright L PTS 6 Peterborough
17.01.91 Neville Brown L RSC 4 Alfreton
21.02.91 Richie Woodhall L RSC 3 Walsall
28.03.91 Pete Bowman W PTS 6 Alfreton
12.04.91 Martin Rosamond W PTS 6 Willenhall
13.05.91 Paul King W PTS 6 Northampton
04.07.91 Dave Hall W PTS 6 Alfreton
11.09.91 Clay O'Shea L PTS 6 Hammersmith
10.10.91 Dave Johnson L PTS 6 Gateshead
17.10.91 Tyrone Eastmond L PTS 6 Mossley
14.11.91 Dave Johnson L PTS 6 Gateshead
28.11.91 Ian Vokes W PTS 6 Hull
07.12.91 Steve Foster L PTS 8 Manchester
17.03.92 Gary Osborne L RSC 5
Wolverhampton
*(Vacant Midlands Area
L. Middleweight Title)*
28.05.92 Mark Jay L PTS 8 Gosforth
25.07.92 Warren Stowe L CO 2 Manchester
16.10.92 Terry Morrill L PTS 6 Hull
23.10.92 Fran Harding L PTS 6 Liverpool
12.11.92 Gypsy Johnny Price L PTS 6 Burnley
14.12.92 Peter Wauby L PTS 6 Cleethorpes
22.02.93 Lee Ferrie L CO 3 Bedworth
07.06.93 Stephen Wilson L PTS 6 Glasgow
16.09.93 Peter Waudby L PTS 6 Hull
03.11.93 Warren Stephens W PTS 6 Worcester
13.11.93 Terry Morrill L PTS 8 Hull
30.11.93 Stuart Dunn L PTS 6 Leicester
12.12.93 Glenn Catley L PTS 4 Bristol
20.01.94 Darren Dorrington L PTS 6 Battersea
26.02.94 Adrian Dodson L CO 1 Earls Court
21.04.94 Mark Jay L PTS 6 Gateshead
16.05.94 Peter Waudby L PTS 6 Cleethorpes
02.06.94 Eric Noi L PTS 6 Middleton
02.07.94 Paul Wright L RSC 1 Liverpool
12.09.94 Phil Ball L PTS 6 Doncaster
20.09.94 Willie Quinn L RSC 3 Musselburgh
24.10.94 John Stronach L PTS 6 Bradford
31.10.94 Jon Stocks L PTS 6 Liverpool
07.11.94 Sven Hamer L PTS 4 Piccadilly
24.11.94 Peter Waudby L PTS 6 Hull
05.12.94 Derek Roche L PTS 6 Bradford
15.12.94 Ray Golding L PTS 6 Evesham
16.01.95 Billy Collins L PTS 6 Musselburgh
30.01.95 Shaun Hendry L PTS 6 Bradford
16.02.95 Darren Swords L PTS 6 Bury
04.03.95 Ryan Rhodes L CO 1 Livingston

Career: 138 contests, won 26, drew 5, lost 107.

Fidel Castro (Smith)

Sheffield. *Born* Nottingham, 17 April, 1963
Former British S. Middleweight Champion.
Former Undefeated Central Area
Middleweight Champion. Ht. 5'9"
Manager Self

06.04.87 Ian Bayliss W RSC 5 Newcastle
28.04.87 Nick Gyaamie W RSC 2 Manchester
29.04.87 Leigh Wicks L PTS 6 Hastings
11.05.87 Steve Foster W PTS 8 Manchester
23.09.87 Ian Jackson W PTS 6 Stoke
11.11.87 Denys Cronin W PTS 8 Usk

24.02.88 Ian Bayliss W RSC 6 Sheffield
*(Central Area Middleweight Title
Challenge)*
09.05.88 Franki Moro W RSC 2 Nottingham
18.05.88 Chris Galloway W PTS 6 Gillingham
23.05.88 Sean Heron W RSC 4 Mayfair
08.07.88 Francesco dell' Aquila L DIS 3 San
Remo, Italy
19.11.88 Paul Tchoue W RSC 3 Chateau
Thierry, France
23.01.89 Andre Mongalema L PTS 8 Paris,
France
22.06.89 Denys Cronin W RSC 7 Stevenage
27.01.90 Thomas Covington W PTS 8 Sheffield
12.03.90 Darren McKenna W PTS 6 Hull
20.05.90 Nigel Fairbairn W RSC 7 Sheffield
20.08.90 Elvis Parks W PTS 6 Helsinki, Finland
29.10.90 Dave Owens W PTS 6 Birmingham
24.11.90 Johnny Melfah W RSC 4
Benalmadena, Spain
24.09.91 Ian Strudwick W RSC 6 Basildon
(Vacant British S. Middleweight Title)
01.10.91 Johnny Melfah W RSC 7 Sheffield
25.02.92 Lou Gent W PTS 12 Crystal Palace
(British S. Middleweight Title Defence)
18.07.92 Frank Eubanks W RTD 6 Manchester
23.09.92 Henry Wharton L PTS 12 Leeds
*(British S. Middleweight Title Defence.
Commonwealth S. Middleweight Title
Challenge)*
16.12.92 Vincenzo Nardiello L PTS 12 Arricia,
Italy
*(Vacant European S. Middleweight
Title)*
14.08.93 Karl Barwise W RSC 6 Hammersmith
16.09.93 James Cook L PTS 12 Southwark
(Vacant British S. Middleweight Title)
21.05.94 Sammy Storey L PTS 6 Belfast
23.01.95 Ali Forbes L PTS 12 Bethnal Green
(Vacant British S. Middleweight Title)

Career: 30 contests, won 22, lost 8.

Glenn Catley

Bristol. *Born* Sodbury, 15 March, 1972
Middleweight. Ht. 5'8"
Manager C. Sanigar

27.05.93 Rick North W PTS 4 Bristol
26.06.93 Chris Vassiliou W CO 2 Keynsham
31.08.93 Marty Duke W RSC 2 Croydon
13.09.93 Barry Thorogood W PTS 4 Bristol
03.11.93 Marty Duke W RSC 1 Bristol
13.12.93 Shamus Casey W PTS 4 Bristol
10.03.94 Mark Cichocki W PTS 6 Bristol
23.03.94 Carlo Colarusso L RSC 5 Cardiff
25.05.94 Chris Davies W RSC 1 Bristol
02.07.94 Martin Jolley W RSC 1 Keynsham
22.11.94 Kirkland Laing W RSC 5 Bristol
18.02.95 Lee Blundell W RSC 6 Shepton Mallet
06.05.95 Mark Dawson W RSC 5 Shepton
Mallet

Career: 13 contests, won 12, lost 1.

Gary Charlton (Wilkes)

Leeds. *Born* Leeds, 6 April, 1968
Heavyweight. Ht. 6'0"
Manager P. Coleman

10.10.91 John Pierre L PTS 6 Gateshead
26.10.91 Graham Arnold W RSC 1 Brentwood
11.11.91 Gary Railton L PTS 6 Bradford
23.04.92 Wayne Llewelyn L RSC 4 Eltham
04.06.92 Wayne Buck L PTS 6 Cleethorpes

07.10.92 John Harewood L PTS 6 Sunderland
12.11.92 Wayne Buck L PTS 8 Stafford
17.12.92 Kevin McBride DREW 6 Barking
23.02.93 Scott Welch W RSC 3 Doncaster
26.03.93 Mark Hulstrom L DIS 5 Copenhagen,
Denmark
29.04.93 Manny Burgo L PTS 6 Newcastle
22.09.93 J. A. Bugner L RSC 1 Wembley
23.11.94 Julius Francis L RSC 1 Piccadilly

Career: 13 contests, won 2, drew 1, lost 10.

Adrian Chase

St Albans. *Born* St Albans, 18 October,
1968
L. Welterweight. Ht. 5'9"
Manager H. Holland

06.05.93 Jason Campbell W CO 2 Bayswater
24.06.93 Delwyn Panayiotiou W CO 1 Watford
23.02.94 Dennis Griffin W PTS 6 Watford
16.05.94 Tony Gibbs W PTS 6 Heathrow
21.07.94 Steve Burton W PTS 6 Battersea
19.11.94 Wayne Jones W PTS 6 Heathrow
21.04.95 Juha Temonen L PTS 4 Pori, Finland

Career: 7 contests, won 6, lost 1.

(Ivan) Carlos Chase

Bushey. *Born* Watford, 10 August, 1966
L. Welterweight. Ht. 5'6¼"
Manager H. Holland

28.09.89 Tony Gibbs W PTS 6 Wandsworth
12.12.89 Carl Brasier W PTS 6 Brentford
30.01.90 Barry North W RSC 1 Battersea
14.03.90 Trevor Meikle W PTS 6 Battersea
03.04.91 Seamus O'Sullivan W PTS 8 Bethnal
Green
01.06.91 Marcel Herbert W PTS 6 Bethnal
Green
12.11.91 Tony Swift L PTS 6 Milton Keynes
12.02.92 Gary Barron W RSC 5 Watford
30.04.92 Dave Pierre L RSC 7 Watford
*(Southern Area L. Welterweight Title
Challenge)*
17.09.92 Felix Kelly W RSC 2 Watford
14.04.93 Ian Honeywood W RSC 1 Kensington
01.10.93 Ross Hale L RTD 8 Cardiff
(Elim. British L. Welterweight Title)
23.02.94 Hugh Forde L PTS 6 Watford
16.05.94 Peter Judson L PTS 4 Heathrow
09.07.94 Bernard Paul L RSC 2 Earls Court
21.04.95 Joni Nyman L PTS 6 Pori, Finland

Career: 16 contests, won 9, lost 7.

(Martin) Marty Chestnut
(Concannon)

Birmingham. *Born* Birmingham, 8 March,
1968
Featherweight. Ht. 5'8"
Manager Self

29.04.93 Fred Reeve L PTS 6 Hull
07.06.93 Ian McGirr L PTS 6 Glasgow
30.10.93 Paul Lloyd L RSC 1 Chester
11.12.93 John Sillo L PTS 6 Liverpool
25.01.94 Anthony Hanna L PTS 4 Piccadilly
10.02.94 James Murray L PTS 6 Glasgow
01.03.94 Chris Lyons W PTS 6 Dudley
27.04.94 Chris Lyons L RSC 3 Bethnal Green
02.06.94 Des Gargano L PTS 6 Middleton
02.09.94 Tiger Ray W PTS 4 Spitalfields
17.09.94 Stephen Smith L RSC 5 Leverkusen,
Germany

27.10.94	Abdul Mannon W DIS 2 Millwall	
30.11.94	Matthew Harris L RSC 3 Wolverhampton	
23.01.95	Paul Webster L RSC 3 Bethnal Green	
20.02.95	Paul Hamilton W PTS 6 Manchester	
09.03.95	Graham McGrath W PTS 6 Walsall	
20.03.95	Graham McGrath L PTS 6 Birmingham	
13.04.95	Spencer Oliver L RSC 4 Bloomsbury	
01.06.95	Garry Burrell L RTD 3 Musselburgh	

Career: 19 contests, won 5, lost 14.

Roy Chipperfield

Bury. *Born* Radcliffe, 29 April, 1965
Middleweight. Ht. 5'10¾"
Manager B. Myers

22.09.94	Darren Swords L PTS 6 Bury
30.11.94	Eddie Haley L RSC 3 Solihull
27.02.95	Jon Stocks L RSC 3 Barrow

Career: 3 contests, lost 3.

(Peter) Carlos Christie

Birmingham. *Born* Birmingham, 17 August, 1966
Midlands Area S. Middleweight Champion. Ht. 6'0"
Manager Self

04.06.90	Roger Wilson L PTS 6 Birmingham
17.09.90	John Kaighin W PTS 6 Cardiff
27.09.90	Colin Manners W PTS 6 Birmingham
29.10.90	Paul Murray W PTS 6 Birmingham
18.11.90	Paul Busby L PTS 6 Birmingham
27.11.90	Nigel Rafferty W PTS 8 Wolverhampton
06.12.90	Nigel Rafferty W PTS 6 Wolverhampton
10.01.91	Ray Webb L PTS 6 Wandsworth
28.01.91	Gil Lewis W PTS 8 Birmingham
04.03.91	Nigel Rafferty W PTS 8 Birmingham
14.03.91	Michael Gale L PTS 8 Middleton
01.05.91	Peter Elliott W RSC 9 Solihull
	(Vacant Midlands Area S. Middleweight Title)
11.05.91	Ray Close L PTS 6 Belfast
07.09.91	Ray Close L PTS 6 Belfast
20.11.91	Nicky Piper L CO 6 Cardiff
10.03.92	Glenn Campbell DREW 8 Bury
15.09.92	Roland Ericsson W RSC 4 Crystal Palace
28.01.93	James Cook L PTS 8 Southwark
28.04.93	Sammy Storey L RSC 8 Dublin
31.08.93	Simon Harris L CO 3 Croydon
12.11.93	Tony Booth L PTS 6 Hull
28.11.93	Ali Forbes L CO 4 Southwark
22.01.94	Darron Griffiths L PTS 8 Cardiff
21.02.94	Stephen Wilson L RSC 2 Glasgow
15.06.94	William Joppy L PTS 6 Southwark
27.08.94	Antonio Fernandez L PTS 8 Cardiff
26.09.94	Paul Wright L PTS 6 Liverpool
29.10.94	Andrew Flute W PTS 8 Cannock
30.11.94	Darren Ashton W PTS 6 Solihull
23.01.95	Robert Allen L CO 2 Bethnal Green
16.03.95	Mark Delaney L CO 1 Basildon

Career: 31 contests, won 11, drew 1, lost 19.

Floyd Churchill

Kirkby. *Born* Liverpool, 19 January, 1969
Welterweight. Former Undefeated Central Area S. Featherweight Champion. Ht. 5'4"
Manager D. Isaaman

29.04.92	T. J. Smith W RSC 2 Liverpool

14.05.92	Jamie Davidson W RSC 4 Liverpool
12.06.92	Kevin McKillan L PTS 6 Liverpool
26.09.92	Richie Wenton W RSC 2 Earls Court
12.11.92	Brian Hickey W CO 1 Liverpool
04.05.93	Jimmy Owens W CO 1 Liverpool
	(Vacant Central Area S. Featherweight Title)
02.07.94	Mark Antony L RSC 1 Liverpool
09.11.94	Jason Rowland L RSC 2 Millwall
25.03.95	Tony Mock L PTS 6 Chester
08.06.95	Dave Anderson L PTS 8 Glasgow

Career: 10 contests, won 5, lost 5.

James Clamp

Selkirk. *Born* Hawick, 17 May, 1972
Welterweight. Ht. 5'9½"
Manager J. Murray

26.03.91	Jason Brattley L RSC 3 Bradford
13.05.95	Craig Lynch DREW 6 Glasgow

Career: 2 contests, drew 1, lost 1.

Howard Clarke

Warley. *Born* London, 23 September, 1967
L. Middleweight. Ht. 5'10"
Manager Self

15.10.91	Chris Mylan W PTS 4 Dudley
09.12.91	Claude Rossi W RSC 3 Brierley Hill
04.02.92	Julian Eavis W PTS 4 Alfreton
03.03.92	Dave Andrews W RSC 3 Cradley Heath
21.05.92	Richard O'Brien W CO 1 Cradley Heath
29.09.92	Paul King W PTS 6 Stoke
27.10.92	Gordon Blair L RSC 4 Cradley Heath
16.03.93	Paul King W PTS 6 Edgbaston
07.06.93	Dean Bramhald W RTD 2 Walsall
29.06.93	Paul King W PTS 6 Edgbaston
06.10.93	Julian Eavis L PTS 6 Solihull
30.11.93	Julian Eavis W PTS 8 Wolverhampton
08.02.94	Nigel Bradley W RTD 6 Wolverhampton
18.04.94	Andy Peach W PTS 6 Walsall
28.06.94	Dennis Berry L RSC 3 Edgbaston
12.10.94	Julian Eavis W PTS 8 Stoke
25.10.94	Andy Peach W RSC 3 Edgbaston
02.11.94	Julian Eavis W PTS 8 Birmingham
29.11.94	Julian Eavis W PTS 6 Cannock
07.12.94	Peter Reid W PTS 8 Stoke
25.01.95	Dennis Berry L PTS 8 Stoke
08.03.95	Andrew Jervis W PTS 6 Solihull
11.05.95	David Bain W RSC 1 Dudley

Career: 23 contests, won 19, lost 4.

Chris Clarkson

Hull. *Born* Hull, 15 December, 1967
Lightweight. Former Undefeated Central Area Bantamweight & Featherweight Champion. Ht. 5'4"
Manager M. Brooks

18.03.85	Gypsy Johnny L PTS 4 Bradford
09.04.85	Terry Allen W PTS 4 South Shields
30.04.85	Terry Allen W PTS 4 Chorley
30.05.85	Gypsy Johnny W PTS 4 Blackburn
17.10.85	Tony Heath W PTS 4 Leicester
13.02.86	Glen Dainty L RSC 4 Longford
17.03.86	Jamie McBride L PTS 4 Glasgow
03.11.86	Gerry McBride DREW 6 Manchester
13.11.86	Gordon Stobie W RSC 4 Huddersfield
01.12.86	Nigel Crook L RSC 6 Nottingham
27.01.87	Donnie Hood L PTS 6 Glasgow

23.02.87	Dave Boy Mallaby W PTS 4 Bradford
02.03.87	Dave Boy Mallaby W CO 3 Nottingham
16.03.87	Pepe Webber W PTS 6 Glasgow
24.03.87	Nigel Crook W PTS 6 Hull
06.04.87	Joe Kelly L PTS 8 Glasgow
14.04.87	Jamie McBride L PTS 6 Cumbernauld
28.04.87	John Green L RSC 6 Manchester
13.06.87	Ronnie Stephenson W PTS 8 Great Yarmouth
23.09.87	Mitchell King L PTS 6 Loughborough
15.11.88	Gordon Shaw W PTS 6 Hull
29.11.88	Des Gargano L PTS 6 Manchester
14.12.88	Dave George L PTS 6 Evesham
16.02.89	Johnny Bredahl L PTS 6 Copenhagen, Denmark
09.03.89	Mark Geraghty L PTS 6 Glasgow
20.03.89	George Bailey W PTS 6 Bradford
11.07.89	Des Gargano W PTS 6 Batley
11.10.89	Gerry McBride W PTS 10 Hull
	(Vacant Central Area Bantamweight Title)
23.11.89	Drew Docherty L PTS 6 Motherwell
15.03.90	Noel Carroll W PTS 6 Manchester
19.04.90	Gerry McBride W DIS 5 Oldham
	(Vacant Central Area Featherweight Title)
30.04.90	Pete Buckley W PTS 8 Mayfair
19.11.90	James Drummond W PTS 8 Glasgow
02.03.91	Francesco Arroyo L RSC 4 Darlington
	(Vacant IBF Intercontinental Bantamweight Title)
04.04.91	Duke McKenzie L RSC 5 Watford
09.10.91	Mark Geraghty L PTS 6 Glasgow
21.10.91	Ian McGirr DREW 6 Glasgow
16.12.91	Noel Carroll L PTS 6 Manchester
03.03.92	Billy Hardy L RSC 5 Houghton le Spring
14.12.92	David Ramsden W PTS 4 Bradford
24.02.93	Bradley Stone L PTS 8 Wembley
24.09.93	Prince Nassem Hamed L CO 2 Dublin
03.03.94	Alfred Kotei L PTS 8 Ebbw Vale
15.04.94	Mike Deveney L RSC 3 Hull
13.06.94	Wayne Rigby L PTS 6 Liverpool
26.09.94	Paul Lloyd W RSC 4 Liverpool
28.04.95	Julian Lorcy L RSC 1 Randers, Denmark
10.06.95	Michael Brodie L PTS 6 Manchester

Career: 48 contests, won 19, drew 2, lost 27.

Paul Clarkson

Ellesmere Port. *Born* Nantwich, 21 March, 1970
S. Middleweight. Ht. 5'7½"
Manager R. Jones

05.12.94	Darren Swords L RSC 3 Bradford
23.02.95	Clinton Woods L RSC 1 Hull

Career: 2 contests, lost 2.

Dave Clavering

Bury. *Born* Bury, 21 October, 1973
S. Featherweight. Ht. 5'6"
Manager J. Doughty

16.05.94	Al Garrett W RTD 4 Morecambe
22.09.94	Ian Richardson W RSC 1 Bury
26.09.94	Chris Jickells W PTS 6 Morecambe
16.02.95	Trevor George W PTS 6 Bury
18.05.95	Kid McAuley W PTS 6 Middleton

Career: 5 contests, won 5.

Kesem Clayton

Coventry. *Born* Coventry, 19 May, 1962
Middleweight. Ht. 5'9"
Manager P. Byrne

06.10.86	Rocky Reynolds W PTS 6 Birmingham
26.11.86	Kid Murray W PTS 6 Wolverhampton
21.01.87	Cecil Branch W RSC 4 Stoke
04.03.87	Ian John-Lewis W RSC 4 Dudley
30.03.87	Mark Howell L PTS 6 Birmingham
08.04.87	Kevin Hayde W PTS 6 Evesham
12.06.87	Mark Howell L PTS 6 Leamington
30.09.87	Theo Marius DREW 6 Mayfair
12.10.87	Andy Catesby W RSC 3 Mayfair
16.11.87	Rocky Feliciello W PTS 8 Stratford upon Avon
28.11.87	Mark Howell L PTS 6 Windsor
27.01.88	Cornelius Carr L PTS 6 Bethnal Green
09.03.88	Brian Robinson W PTS 6 Bethnal Green
21.03.88	Dean Barclay DREW 8 Bethnal Green
17.04.88	R. W. Smith W RSC 4 Peterborough
06.10.88	Kid Milo L RSC 4 Dudley
16.12.88	Tony Velinor W RSC 2 Brentwood
06.02.89	Michael Justin L PTS 8 Nottingham
15.03.89	Ian Chantler L CO 4 Stoke
15.07.89	Michele Mastrodonato L RSC 2 San Severo, Italy
04.10.89	Shaun Cummins W RSC 6 Solihull
22.11.89	Ian Chantler W PTS 8 Solihull
15.12.89	Benito Guida L PTS 8 Milan, Italy
24.01.90	John Ashton L PTS 10 Solihull
	(Vacant Midlands Area Middleweight Title)
12.10.90	Frederic Seillier L RSC 1 Toulon, France
22.02.91	Steve Foster L CO 6 Manchester
02.12.91	Nigel Rafferty L PTS 8 Birmingham
31.03.92	Stan King L RSC 4 Norwich
19.12.93	Sean Byrne L PTS 6 Northampton
09.04.94	Robin Reid L RSC 1 Mansfield
24.09.94	Robert Allen L RSC 1 Wembley
07.12.94	Lee Blundell L RTD 2 Stoke

Career: 32 contests, won 12, drew 2, lost 18.

Justin Clements

Birmingham. *Born* Birmingham, 25 September, 1971
L. Heavyweight. Ht. 5'11½"
Manager Self

02.12.91	Adrian Wright W PTS 6 Birmingham
03.03.92	Andy Manning DREW 6 Cradley Heath
16.03.93	Paul McCarthy W PTS 6 Edgbaston
18.05.93	Lee Sara W PTS 6 Edgbaston
07.06.93	Phil Ball W PTS 6 Walsall
30.09.93	Smokey Enison W PTS 6 Walsall
02.12.93	Paul Murray L PTS 6 Walsall
08.03.94	Zak Goldman W RSC 3 Edgbaston
28.06.94	Dave Battey W RSC 2 Edgbaston
25.10.94	Tony Colclough W PTS 4 Edgbaston
05.12.94	Steve Osborne W PTS 6 Birmingham
07.03.95	Stinger Mason W RSC 4 Edgbaston

Career: 12 contests, won 10, drew 1, lost 1.

Shaun Cogan

Birmingham. *Born* Birmingham, 7 August, 1967
L. Welterweight. Ht. 5'8"
Manager Self

25.09.89	Peter Bowen W RSC 1 Birmingham

24.10.89	Gary Quigley W RSC 2 Wolverhampton
06.12.89	George Jones W PTS 6 Stoke
14.03.90	Dean Bramhald W PTS 6 Stoke
27.03.90	Mark Antony W CO 1 Wolverhampton
23.04.90	Mike Morrison W PTS 8 Birmingham
21.02.91	Tony Britland W PTS 6 Walsall
19.03.91	Rocky Lawlor W RSC 2 Birmingham
25.07.91	David Thompson W CO 1 Dudley
05.12.91	Steve Pollard W PTS 6 Oakengates
27.11.92	Soren Sondergaard L PTS 6 Randers, Denmark
16.03.93	Malcolm Melvin L PTS 10 Edgbaston
	(Vacant All-Ireland L. Welterweight Title & Midlands Area L. Welterweight Title Challenge)
18.05.93	Seth Jones W RSC 2 Edgbaston
15.09.93	Paul Ryan L RSC 3 Ashford
06.11.93	Bernard Paul DREW 6 Bethnal Green
02.12.93	Kane White W RSC 1 Evesham
11.01.94	Bernard Paul W PTS 6 Bethnal Green
01.03.94	Karl Taylor W PTS 6 Dudley
10.05.94	Andreas Panayi L RSC 7 Doncaster
28.09.94	John Smith W PTS 8 Solihull
24.10.94	Charlie Kane L PTS 10 Glasgow
	(Elim. British L. Welterweight Title)
29.11.94	John Smith W RSC 4 Cannock
06.03.95	Delroy Leslie L RSC 1 Mayfair
06.05.95	Ross Hale L RSC 4 Shepton Mallet
	(Commonwealth L. Welterweight Title Challenge)

Career: 24 contests, won 16, drew 1, lost 7.

Mark Cokely

Port Talbot. *Born* Neath, 31 July, 1970
Bantamweight. Ht. 5'3"
Manager Self

27.04.94	Lyndon Kershaw L PTS 6 Solihull
20.05.94	Graham McGrath L PTS 6 Neath
06.03.95	Ady Lewis L RSC 5 Mayfair
05.05.95	Anthony Hanna L RSC 4 Swansea

Career: 4 contests, lost 4.

Carlo Colarusso

Llanelli. *Born* Swansea, 11 February, 1970
Welsh L. Middleweight Champion. Ht. 5'7"
Manager Self

14.09.89	Paul Burton W RSC 5 Basildon
11.10.89	Lindon Scarlett L PTS 8 Stoke
24.10.89	Cornelius Carr L RTD 4 Watford
22.11.89	Lindon Scarlett L PTS 8 Stoke
01.03.90	Kevin Hayde W RTD 3 Cardiff
14.03.90	Kevin Plant W PTS 8 Stoke
21.03.90	Sammy Sampson W RSC 3 Preston
06.04.90	Ray Webb W PTS 6 Telford
19.11.90	Gary Pemberton W RSC 3 Cardiff
29.11.90	Nigel Moore L PTS 6 Bayswater
24.01.91	Gary Pemberton W RSC 8 Gorseinon
	(Vacant Welsh L. Middleweight Title)
02.03.91	Cornelius Carr L PTS 8 Darlington
11.05.92	Russell Washer W RSC 5 Llanelli
	(Welsh L. Middleweight Title Defence)
27.06.92	Newton Barnett W RTD 5 Quinta do Lago, Portugal
28.10.92	Lloyd Honeyghan L RSC 6 Kensington
16.03.93	Richie Woodhall L PTS 8 Wolverhampton
30.03.93	Tony Velinor W RSC 3 Cardiff
14.03.94	John Bosco L PTS 6 Mayfair
23.03.94	Glenn Catley W PTS 5 Cardiff
03.03.95	Neville Brown L RSC 7 Bethnal Green
	(British Middleweight Title Challenge)

Career: 20 contests, won 11, lost 9.

Tony Colclough

Birmingham. *Born* Birmingham, 9 May, 1960
L. Heavyweight. Ht. 6'0"
Manager Self

15.04.91	Steve Yorath L PTS 6 Wolverhampton
30.05.91	Damien Caesar L RSC 1 Mayfair
01.08.91	Denzil Browne L RSC 1 Dewsbury
07.10.91	Karl Guest DREW 6 Birmingham
15.10.91	Jason McNeill W PTS 6 Dudley
02.12.91	Carl Guest W RSC 2 Birmingham
03.03.92	Greg Scott-Briggs L RSC 2 Cradley Heath
21.05.92	Mark Hale DREW 6 Cradley Heath
01.06.92	Mark Hale W PTS 6 Solihull
27.11.92	Mark Hulstrom L RSC 2 Randers, Denmark
27.02.93	Kenley Price L RSC 5 Ellesmere Port
26.04.93	Greg Scott-Briggs L RSC 4 Glasgow
07.06.93	Kevin Burton L PTS 6 Walsall
11.08.93	John Keeton L RSC 1 Mansfield
30.09.93	Kevin Burton L DIS 5 Walsall
13.10.93	Darren Ashton L RSC 1 Stoke
24.11.93	Greg Scott-Briggs L PTS 6 Solihull
01.12.93	Steve Loftus L PTS 6 Stoke
13.12.93	Kevin Burton L RSC 3 Doncaster
09.02.94	Mark Delaney L RSC 4 Brentwood
28.03.94	Dave Proctor L RSC 3 Birmingham
29.10.94	Craig Byrne L PTS 6 Walsall
12.10.94	Kevin Burton L PTS 6 Stoke
25.10.94	Justin Clements L PTS 4 Edgbaston

Career: 24 contests, won 3, drew 2, lost 19.

Brian Coleman

Birmingham. *Born* Birmingham, 27 July, 1969
L. Welterweight. Ht. 5'11"
Manager Self

21.11.91	Jamie Morris DREW 6 Stafford
11.12.91	Craig Hartwell DREW 6 Leicester
22.01.92	John O. Johnson L PTS 6 Stoke
20.02.92	Davy Robb L PTS 6 Oakengates
31.03.92	Blue Butterworth L PTS 6 Stockport
17.05.92	Korso Aleain L RSC 5 Harringay
17.09.92	Nicky Bardle L RSC 4 Watford
21.10.92	Jason Barker W PTS 6 Stoke
10.12.92	A. M. Milton DREW 4 Bethnal Green
31.03.93	A. M. Milton L PTS 4 Bethnal Green
26.04.93	Jason Beard L PTS 6 Lewisham
06.05.93	Mark Allen W PTS 6 Walsall
18.05.93	Sean Metherell DREW 6 Kettering
27.05.93	Blue Butterworth L PTS 6 Burnley
23.06.93	Jonathan Thaxton L PTS 8 Gorleston
11.08.93	Steve Howden L RSC 4 Mansfield
13.09.93	Mick Hoban L PTS 6 Middleton
01.12.93	A. M. Milton L PTS 4 Bethnal Green
08.12.93	Chris Pollock W PTS 6 Stoke
16.12.93	Mark Newton L PTS 6 Newport
11.01.94	Paul Knights L RSC 4 Bethnal Green
08.02.94	Andy Peach W PTS 6 Wolverhampton
18.02.94	Cam Raeside L PTS 6 Leicester
08.03.94	Chris Pollock L PTS 6 Edgbaston
29.03.94	P. J. Gallagher L PTS 6 Bethnal Green
14.04.94	Cham Joof L CO 3 Battersea
02.06.94	Scott Walker L CO 1 Middleton
12.09.94	Shaba Edwards L PTS 6 Mayfair
19.09.94	Mark Breslin L CO 1 Glasgow
09.11.94	Kenny Scott L PTS 6 Stafford
23.11.94	Billy McDougall W PTS 4 Piccadilly
29.11.94	Warren Stephens W PTS 6 Wolverhampton

09.12.94   Danny Stevens L RTD 2 Bethnal Green
24.01.95   Wayne Jones L PTS 6 Piccadilly
07.02.95   Alan Temple L PTS 4 Ipswich
23.02.95   Darren Covill L PTS 4 Southwark
16.03.95   Paul Knights L RSC 2 Basildon
Career: 37 contests, won 6, drew 4, lost 27.

Billy Collins

Stirling. *Born* Stirling, 20 May, 1968
L. Middleweight. Ht. 5'9"
Manager T. Gilmour

25.04.94   Raziq Ali W PTS 6 Glasgow
16.01.95   Shamus Casey W PTS 6 Musselburgh
23.01.95   Eddie Haley W RSC 4 Glasgow
24.02.95   Rob Stevenson W PTS 6 Irvine
24.04.95   Phil Epton W RSC 3 Glasgow
05.06.95   Ernie Loveridge W PTS 8 Glasgow
Career: 6 contests, won 6.

Hugh Collins

Stirling. *Born* Stirling, 17 August, 1969
Lightweight. Ht. 5'6"
Manager T. Gilmour

29.03.93   Tim Hill W PTS 6 Glasgow
20.09.93   Robert Braddock W PTS 8 Glasgow
24.11.93   Paul Bowen W PTS 6 Solihull
24.01.94   Colin Innes W PTS 6 Glasgow
21.02.94   Norman Dhalie W RTD 4 Glasgow
28.03.94   Trevor Royal W RSC 2 Musselburgh
25.04.94   Miguel Matthews W PTS 8 Glasgow
20.09.94   Russell Davison W RTD 4 Musselburgh
02.11.94   Michael Hermon L RSC 3 Solihull

16.01.95   John T. Kelly W PTS 6 Musselburgh
17.02.95   Paul Wynn W RSC 3 Cumbernauld
05.04.95   Kid McAuley W PTS 6 Irvine
05.06.95   Wayne Rigby L RSC 4 Glasgow
Career: 13 contests, won 11, lost 2.

John J. Cooke

Coventry. *Born* Coventry, 22 January, 1966
Midlands Area L. Heavyweight Champion.
Ht. 5'10"
Manager J. Griffin

05.10.92   Paul Hanlon W RSC 1 Bardon
23.11.92   Paul Murray W CO 1 Coventry
02.12.92   Nigel Rafferty W PTS 6 Bardon
22.02.93   Zak Chelli DREW 6 Bedworth
17.06.93   Gil Lewis W RSC 9 Bedworth
         (Vacant Midlands Area L. Heavyweight Title)
25.04.94   Stephen Wilson L PTS 6 Bury
21.05.94   Noel Magee L PTS 6 Belfast
20.10.94   Nigel Rafferty W RSC 7 Walsall
         (Midlands Area L. Heavyweight Title Defence)
Career: 8 contests, won 5. drew 1, lost 2.

Dean Cooper

Bristol. *Born* Southampton, 5 August, 1969
Western Area L. Middleweight Champion.
Ht. 6'0"
Manager C. Sanigar

15.09.90   Russell Washer W PTS 6 Bristol
08.10.90   Brian Keating W PTS 6 Bradford
29.10.90   Peter Reid W RSC 1 Nottingham

06.11.90   Tony Wellington W PTS 6 Southend
08.12.90   Lee Farrell W PTS 6 Bristol
04.02.91   Mike Phillips W PTS 6 Leicester
18.02.91   Andre Wharton W PTS 8 Birmingham
22.10.91   Nick Meloscia W PTS 6 Wandsworth
09.03.93   Winston May W PTS 8 Bristol
27.05.93   Robert Peel W PTS 6 Bristol
26.06.93   Julian Eavis W PTS 10 Keynsham
         (Vacant Western Area L. Middleweight Title)
28.07.93   Kirkland Laing L RSC 5 Brixton
20.01.94   Jerry Mortimer W PTS 8 Battersea
10.03.94   Terry Magee W PTS 8 Bristol
31.03.94   Julian Eavis W PTS 6 Bristol
02.07.94   Horace Fleary W PTS 10 Keynsham
03.08.94   Spencer Alton W RSC 6 Bristol
11.10.94   Robert McCracken L RSC 4 Bethnal Green
18.02.95   Stuart Dunn W RSC 1 Shepton Mallet
21.03.95   Paul Lynch L RSC 6 Swansea
Career: 20 contests, won 17, lost 3.

Darren Corbett

Belfast. *Born* Belfast, 8 July, 1972
Heavyweight. Ht. 5'11"
Manager B. Hearn

10.12.94   David Jules W RSC 1 Manchester
13.12.94   Carl Gaffney W RSC 1 Potters Bar
21.02.95   Steve Garber W PTS 6 Sunderland
18.03.95   Gary Williams DREW 6 Millstreet, Eire
14.04.95   Dennis Bailey W RSC 2 Belfast
27.05.95   R. F. McKenzie L PTS 6 Belfast
Career: 6 contests, won 4, drew 1, lost 1.

Dean Cooper (left) in non-title action against the British light-middleweight champion, Robert McCracken, last October

Les Clark

Darren Corbett   Les Clark

Darren Covill   Les Clark

Maurice Core (Coore)

Manchester. *Born* Manchester, 22 June, 1965
Former Undefeated British L. Heavyweight Champion. Ht. 6'5"
Manager Self

15.01.90	Dennis Banton W PTS 6 Mayfair
03.05.90	Everton Blake W PTS 8 Kensington
22.05.90	Nicky Piper DREW 6 St Albans
22.02.91	Everton Blake W RSC 8 Manchester
12.04.91	Glazz Campbell W CO 2 Manchester
31.05.91	Rodney Brown W RSC 6 Manchester
29.11.91	Steve Osborne W PTS 6 Manchester
31.01.92	Denroy Bryan W RSC 1 Manchester
05.04.92	Willie Ball W RSC 3 Bradford
18.07.92	Tony Booth W PTS 6 Manchester
28.09.92	Noel Magee W RSC 9 Manchester
	(Vacant British L. Heavyweight Title)
05.02.93	Larry Prather W PTS 10 Manchester
25.07.93	John Kaighin W PTS 6 Oldham
01.12.93	Simon Harris W RSC 11 Bethnal Green
	(British L. Heavyweight Title Defence)
25.10.94	Fabrice Tiozzo L RSC 4 Besancon, France
	(European L. Heavyweight Title Challenge)
10.06.95	Eric French W RSC 2 Manchester

Career: 16 contests, won 14, drew 1, lost 1.

Darren Covill

Welling. *Born* Welling, 11 April, 1970
Welterweight. Ht. 5'8"
Manager D. Powell

23.02.95	Brian Coleman W PTS 4 Southwark
19.05.95	Allan Gray L PTS 6 Southwark
04.06.95	Dick Hanns-Kat W RSC 3 Bethnal Green

Career: 3 contests, won 2, lost 1.

Dave Cranston

Streatham. *Born* Lambeth, 2 November, 1968
Middleweight. Ht. 5'9"
Manager G. Steene

02.06.94	Steve Thomas W PTS 6 Tooting
28.07.94	Ernie Loveridge W PTS 6 Tooting

Career: 2 contests, won 2.

Lee Crocker   Les Clark

Lee Crocker

Swansea. *Born* Swansea, 9 May, 1969
Middleweight. Ht. 6'0"
Manager Self

31.01.91	Colin Manners L PTS 6 Bredbury
12.02.91	Paul Evans W RSC 2 Cardiff

04.04.91	Johnny Pinnock W RSC 5 Watford
30.06.91	Andrew Furlong DREW 6 Southwark
30.09.91	Fran Harding L RSC 3 Kensington
11.03.92	Russell Washer W PTS 6 Cardiff
30.04.92	Winston May W RSC 2 Bayswater
23.09.92	Nick Manners L CO 1 Leeds
17.12.92	Jamie Robinson L RTD 2 Barking
20.01.93	Ernie Loveridge W PTS 6 Wolverhampton
28.01.93	Clay O'Shea L RSC 1 Southwark
14.06.93	Gilbert Jackson L RSC 2 Bayswater
07.10.93	David Larkin L RSC 5 York
23.03.94	Leif Keiski L CO 2 Cardiff
04.06.94	Derek Grainger W RSC 3 Cardiff
04.02.95	Ryan Rhodes L RSC 2 Cardiff
21.03.95	Darren Dorrington W PTS 6 Swansea
05.05.95	Carl Harney W CO 4 Swansea
16.06.95	Andy Ewen W RSC 3 Southwark

Career: 19 contests, won 8, drew 1, lost 10.

Peter Culshaw

Liverpool. *Born* Liverpool, 15 May, 1973
Flyweight. Ht. 5'6"
Manager S. Vaughan

02.07.93	Graham McGrath W PTS 6 Liverpool
28.09.93	Vince Feeney W PTS 6 Liverpool
11.12.93	Nick Tooley W RSC 1 Liverpool
25.02.94	Des Gargano W PTS 6 Chester
06.05.94	Neil Swain W PTS 6 Liverpool
26.09.94	Daryl McKenzie W PTS 6 Liverpool
20.04.95	Rowan Williams W CO 6 Liverpool

Career: 7 contests, won 7.

Ryan Cummings

Islington. *Born* Lancaster, 17 November, 1973
L. Heavyweight. Ht. 5'11"
Manager F. Warren

10.03.94	Terry Duffus W PTS 6 Watford
07.11.94	Mark Hale W RSC 6 Bethnal Green
10.06.95	Mark Dawson L PTS 6 Manchester

Career: 3 contests, won 2, lost 1.

Shaun Cummins

Leicester. *Born* Leicester, 8 February, 1968
Middleweight. Former Undefeated Penta-Continental L. Middleweight Champion. Ht. 6'1"
Manager Self

29.09.86	Michael Justin W PTS 6 Loughborough
24.11.86	Gary Pemberton W RSC 6 Cardiff
09.02.87	Rob Thomas W PTS 8 Cardiff
23.09.87	Chris Richards W PTS 6 Loughborough
07.03.88	Antonio Fernandez W PTS 6 Northampton
12.09.88	Shamus Casey W CO 3 Northampton
24.10.88	Frank Grant L RTD 7 Northampton
01.03.89	Gary Pemberton W CO 2 Cardiff
05.04.89	Efren Olivo W RSC 1 Kensington
04.10.89	Kesem Clayton L RSC 6 Solihull
31.01.90	Tony Velinor W PTS 8 Bethnal Green
20.02.90	Brian Robinson W RSC 5 Millwall
26.04.90	Wally Swift Jnr L PTS 10 Merthyr
	(Vacant Midlands Area L. Middleweight Title & Elim. British L. Middleweight Title)
18.09.90	Paul Wesley W RSC 1 Wolverhampton
31.10.90	Terry Morrill W RSC 1 Crystal Palace
23.01.91	Ian Chantler W PTS 10 Brentwood

19.03.91 Martin Smith DREW 8 Leicester
07.11.91 Jason Rowe W RSC 2 Peterborough
05.12.91 Winston May W RSC 2 Peterborough
18.06.92 Leroy Owens W RSC 2 Peterborough
26.09.92 John Kaighin W RTD 4 Earls Court
28.11.92 Steve Foster W PTS 12 Manchester
(Vacant Penta-Continental L. Middleweight Title)
20.04.93 Mickey Hughes W CO 11 Brentwood
(Penta-Continental L. Middleweight Title Defence)
16.02.94 John Kaighin W RSC 3 Stevenage
11.05.94 Colin Manners L RSC 6 Sheffield
09.11.94 Agostino Cardamone L PTS 12 San Remo, Italy
(European Middleweight Title Challenge)
06.05.95 Val Golding W RSC 7 Shepton Mallet
Career: 27 contests, won 21, drew 1, lost 5.

Dave Curtis

Hull. *Born* Hull, 19 January, 1967
L. Middleweight. Ht. 5'9"
Manager L. Billany

15.04.94 Brian Hickey W PTS 6 Hull
09.05.94 Laurence Roche L PTS 6 Bradford
20.09.94 Steve McLevy L RTD 3 Musselburgh
24.11.94 Steve Pollard L RTD 4 Hull
02.06.95 Paul Carr L PTS 6 Bethnal Green
12.06.95 Lee Murtagh L PTS 6 Bradford
Career: 6 contests, won 1, lost 5.

Dave Curtis   Les Clark

Hughie Davey

Wallsend. *Born* Wallsend, 27 January, 1966
Welterweight. Ht. 5'8"
Manager Self

30.03.92 Wayne Shepherd W PTS 6 Bradford
28.04.92 Benji Joseph W RSC 4 Houghton le Spring
10.09.92 Darren McInulty W PTS 6 Southwark
21.09.92 Rick North DREW 6 Cleethorpes
23.10.92 Richard O'Brien W PTS 6 Gateshead
01.03.93 Wayne Appleton L PTS 6 Bradford
29.04.93 Paul King L PTS 6 Newcastle
11.06.93 Wayne Shepherd W PTS 6 Gateshead

04.10.93 Steve Scott W PTS 6 Bradford
08.11.93 Warren Bowers W RSC 2 Bradford
13.12.93 Sean Baker L PTS 4 Bristol
03.03.94 Paul King L PTS 10 Newcastle
(Vacant Northern Area Welterweight Title)
06.10.94 Mick Hoban W PTS 6 Cramlington
24.11.94 John Stronach W PTS 6 Newcastle
10.12.94 Craig Winter L PTS 6 Manchester
21.02.95 David Maw W RSC 3 Sunderland
20.03.95 Joe Townsley W PTS 6 Glasgow
22.06.95 David Maw W PTS 6 Houghton le Spring
Career: 18 contests, won 12, drew 1, lost 5.

Andy Davidson

Salford. *Born* Salford, 11 March, 1972
L. Welterweight. Ht. 5'9"
Manager J. Trickett

18.04.94 Kevin McKenzie W RSC 1 Manchester
28.06.94 M. T. Atkin W RSC 1 Mayfair
03.10.94 Wahid Fats L RSC 4 Manchester
03.04.95 Andrew Jervis L CO 3 Manchester
Career: 4 contests, won 2, lost 2.

Kent Davis

Cwmbran. *Born* Stroud, 12 August, 1965
Cruiserweight. Ht. 6'2"
Manager M. Hill

27.10.93 Robert Norton L PTS 6 West Bromwich
16.12.93 L. A. Williams W RSC 2 Newport
12.03.94 Ray Kane L PTS 6 Cardiff
02.07.94 Newby Stevens L PTS 6 Keynsham
27.08.94 Steve Yorath L PTS 6 Cardiff
06.10.94 Slick Miller W PTS 6 Hull
25.01.95 Steve Yorath W PTS 6 Cardiff
Career: 7 contests, won 3, lost 4.

Kent Davis (right) in action against the Irishman, Ray Kane   Les Clark

Russell Davison

Salford. *Born* Salford, 2 October, 1961
S. Featherweight. Former Central Area
Featherweight Champion. Ht. 5'7"
Manager Self

22.05.86	Nigel Crook L PTS 6 Horwich
09.06.86	Gary Maxwell L PTS 6 Manchester
25.09.86	Nigel Crook L PTS 6 Preston
14.10.86	Davey Hughes W PTS 6 Manchester
25.11.86	Carl Gaynor W PTS 6 Manchester
10.12.86	Davey Hughes W PTS 8 Stoke
27.01.87	Nigel Senior DREW 8 Manchester
04.03.87	Tim Driscoll L PTS 8 Stoke
31.03.87	Stuart Carmichael W PTS 8 Oldham
26.05.87	Kevin Taylor L PTS 10 Oldham
	(Central Area S. Featherweight Title Challenge)
06.10.87	Gary Maxwell L PTS 8 Manchester
16.12.87	Mike Whalley W PTS 8 Manchester
16.03.88	Gary de Roux L PTS 8 Solihull
03.05.88	Rocky Lawlor L PTS 8 Stoke
29.11.88	Mike Whalley L RSC 7 Manchester
	(Vacant Central Area Featherweight Title)
25.01.89	Derek Amory W PTS 8 Solihull
19.04.89	Michael Armstrong L PTS 8 Stoke
06.12.89	Michael Armstrong W PTS 8 Stoke
23.12.89	Kevin Kelley L PTS 8 Hoogvleit, Holland
06.03.90	Michael Armstrong L PTS 10 Stoke
26.09.90	Steve Robinson L PTS 8 Manchester
19.11.90	Peter Judson W PTS 8 Manchester
17.12.90	Dave Buxton W PTS 8 Manchester
29.01.91	Peter Judson W PTS 10 Stockport
	(Vacant Central Area Featherweight Title)
05.03.91	Colin McMillan L PTS 6 Millwall
24.04.91	Steve Robinson L RTD 6 Preston
09.09.91	Jimmy Owens W PTS 10 Liverpool
	(Central Area Featherweight Title Defence)
29.02.92	Moussa Sangaree L RSC 5 Gravelines, France
13.10.92	Craig Dermody L PTS 10 Bury
	(Central Area Featherweight Title Defence)
24.03.93	Eamonn McAuley L PTS 6 Belfast
26.04.93	Drew Docherty L PTS 8 Glasgow
15.05.93	Alan Levene L PTS 6 Bradford
24.05.93	David Ramsden L PTS 6 Bradford
02.03.94	Ian McGirr W CO 1 Glasgow
10.04.94	Ian McGirr L PTS 6 Glasgow
06.06.94	Miguel Matthews L PTS 6 Glasgow
20.09.94	Hugh Collins L RTD 4 Musselburgh
03.04.95	Trevor Sumner L PTS 6 Manchester

Career: 38 contests, won 12, drew 1, lost 25.

Mark Dawson (Lee)

Burton. *Born* Burton, 26 February, 1971
S. Middleweight. Ht. 5'8"
Manager Self

03.06.92	Rick North W PTS 6 Newcastle under Lyme
09.09.92	Jimmy Vincent W PTS 6 Stoke
29.09.92	Steve Goodwin L RSC 1 Stoke
28.10.92	Steve McNess W RSC 2 Kensington
07.12.92	Steve Goodwin W PTS 6 Mayfair
27.01.93	Rick North W PTS 8 Stoke
15.02.93	John Bosco L PTS 6 Mayfair
27.02.93	Robin Reid L RSC 1 Dagenham
30.03.93	Matthew Turner L PTS 6 Cardiff

12.05.93	Steve Goodwin L PTS 10 Stoke
	(Vacant Midlands Area L. Middleweight Title)
27.05.93	Derek Wormald L RTD 5 Burnley
10.11.93	John Bosco L RTD 4 Watford
15.03.94	Stinger Mason W RSC 6 Stoke
22.03.94	Geoff McCreesh L PTS 6 Bethnal Green
05.09.94	Tony Griffiths W PTS 6 Brentwood
17.09.94	Mark Delaney L PTS 6 Crawley
01.10.94	Joe Calzaghe L RSC 1 Cardiff
29.11.94	Andrew Flute L PTS 8 Cannock
07.12.94	John Duckworth W PTS 6 Stoke
20.01.95	Mark Baker L RSC 3 Bethnal Green
08.03.95	Lester Jacobs L PTS 6 Bloomsbury
30.03.95	David Starie L RSC 1 Bethnal Green
06.05.95	Glenn Catley L RSC 5 Shepton Mallet
10.06.95	Ryan Cummings W PTS 6 Manchester

Career: 24 contests, won 9, lost 15.

Roy Dehara

Ashford. *Born* Lambeth, 17 September,
1963
L. Middleweight. Ht. 5'8"
Manager A. Urry

27.05.94	Nic Ingram L PTS 6 Ashford
02.09.94	Warren Stephens W RSC 6 Spitalfields
29.09.94	Paolo Roberto L RSC 1 Bethnal Green
14.02.95	Danny Stevens L RSC 6 Bethnal Green

Career: 4 contests, won 1, lost 3.

Roy Dehara   Les Clark

Garry Delaney

West Ham. *Born* Newham, 12 August,
1970
Penta-Continental & Southern Area L.
Heavyweight Champion. Former
Commonwealth L. Heavyweight
Champion. Ht. 6'3"
Manager Self

02.10.91	Gus Mendes W RSC 1 Barking

23.10.91	Joe Frater W RSC 1 Bethnal Green
13.11.91	John Kaighin W PTS 6 Bethnal Green
11.12.91	Randy B. Powell W RSC 1 Basildon
11.02.92	Simon Harris DREW 8 Barking
12.05.92	John Williams W PTS 6 Crystal Palace
16.06.92	Nigel Rafferty W CO 5 Dagenham
15.09.92	Gil Lewis W CO 2 Crystal Palace
06.10.92	Simon McDougall W PTS 8 Antwerp, Belgium
10.11.92	John Oxenham W CO 5 Dagenham
12.12.92	Simon McDougall W PTS 8 Muswell Hill
30.01.93	Simon Collins W PTS 8 Brentwood
28.09.93	Glazz Campbell W CO 6 Bethnal Green
	(Southern Area L. Heavyweight Title Challenge)
06.11.93	John Kaighin W CO 1 Bethnal Green
21.12.93	Ray Albert W RSC 3 Mayfair
	(Vacant Penta-Continental L. Heavyweight Title)
11.01.94	Jim Murray W RSC 7 Bethnal Green
	(Penta-Continental L. Heavyweight Title Defence)
09.04.94	Simon Harris W CO 6 Bethnal Green
	(Penta-Continental & Southern Area L. Heavyweight Title Defence)
09.07.94	Sergio Merani W PTS 12 Earls Court
	(Penta-Continental L. Heavyweight Title Defence)
30.09.94	Arigoma Chiponda W CO 2 Bethnal Green
	(Vacant Commonwealth L. Heavyweight Title)
18.03.95	Ernest Mateen W RTD 7 Millstreet, Eire
	(Inaugural WBO Continental L. Heavyweight Title)
09.05.95	Noel Magee L RTD 7 Basildon
	(Commonwealth L. Heavyweight Title Defence)

Career: 21 contests, won 19, drew 1, lost 1.

Mark Delaney

West Ham. *Born* London, 1 December,
1971
S. Middleweight. Ht. 5'11"
Manager B. Hearn

05.10.93	Lee Sara W RTD 5 Mayfair
11.01.94	Jason McNeill W RSC 2 Bethnal Green
22.01.94	Graham Jenner W RTD 3 Belfast
09.02.94	Tony Colclough W RSC 4 Brentwood
19.03.94	Paul Murray W CO 3 Millwall
09.04.94	Tim Robinson W RSC 2 Bethnal Green
11.06.94	Ernie Loveridge W RSC 5 Bethnal Green
09.07.94	Eddie Knight W CO 4 Earls Court
17.09.94	Mark Dawson W PTS 6 Crawley
30.09.94	Jerry Mortimer W RSC 3 Bethnal Green
07.11.94	Martin Jolley W RSC 3 Bethnal Green
23.11.94	Marvin O'Brien W RTD 1 Irvine
20.12.94	Martin Jolley W RSC 4 Bethnal Green
17.02.95	Peter Vosper W RSC 1 Crawley
16.03.95	Carlos Christie W CO 1 Basildon
31.03.95	Trevor Ambrose W RSC 1 Crystal Palace
09.05.95	Eddie Knight W RSC 2 Basildon

Career: 17 contests, won 17.

Mark Delaney seen knocking over Eddie Knight at Basildon in May Les Clark

Damien Denny

Belfast. *Born* Lisburn, 20 April, 1966
L. Middleweight. Ht. 5'9"
Manager Self

01.07.87	Manny Romain W CO 1 Kensington
09.08.87	Joe Lynch W RSC 1 Windsor
16.09.87	Billy Cairns W PTS 8 Kensington
13.10.87	Chris Richards W PTS 6 Windsor
27.01.88	Simon Lee W CO 7 Bethnal Green
07.02.88	Dean Bramhald W PTS 4 Stafford
09.03.88	Jimmy Thornton W PTS 8 Bethnal Green
25.06.88	Martin Smith NC 5 Luton
15.11.88	Tommy McCallum W RSC 2 Norwich
01.12.88	Kelvin Mortimer W RSC 1 Edmonton
28.03.89	Mickey Lloyd W RSC 4 Bethnal Green
11.04.89	Winston May W RSC 3 Aberavon
19.09.89	Mark Holden W RSC 2 Millwall
17.04.90	Del Bryan L PTS 10 Millwall *(Final Elim. British Welterweight Title)*
06.07.90	Parrish Johnson W RSC 4 Brentwood
22.09.90	Newton Barnett L RSC 6 Kensington
06.02.91	Newton Barnett W PTS 8 Bethnal Green
09.04.91	Jason Rowe L CO 7 Mayfair
01.12.92	Bozon Haule W PTS 6 Bristol
24.03.93	James McGee W CO 2 Belfast *(Elim. All-Ireland L. Middleweight Title)*
18.06.93	Rob Pitters W RSC 3 Belfast
12.11.94	Rick North W PTS 6 Dublin
14.04.95	Paul Jones L CO 1 Belfast *(Inaugural WBO Continental L. Middleweight Title)*

Career: 23 contests, won 18, lost 4, no contest 1.

Paul Denton (Ramsey)

Walthamstow. *Born* Birmingham, 12 April, 1970
Welterweight. Ht. 5'10"
Manager B. Ingle

18.03.93	Mark O'Callaghan W RSC 4 Lewisham
29.04.93	Dave Maj DREW 6 Mayfair
11.08.93	Billy McDougall W PTS 6 Mansfield
01.10.93	Ferid Bennecer W CO 3 Waregem, Belgium
01.12.93	Brian Hickey W CO 1 Kensington
28.01.94	Youssef Bakhouche L PTS 6 Waregem, Belgium
07.05.94	Viktor Fesechko L PTS 6 Dnepropetrousk, Ukraine
23.09.94	Roy Rowland W RSC 5 Bethnal Green
03.01.95	Patrick Charpentier L RSC 4 Epernay, France
25.02.95	Paul Ryan L RSC 4 Millwall

Career: 10 contests, won 5, drew 1, lost 4.

Norman Dhalie

Birmingham. *Born* Birmingham, 24 March, 1971
Lightweight. Ht. 5'7"
Manager Self

06.04.92	Karl Morling L PTS 6 Northampton
27.04.92	Wilson Docherty L RSC 2 Glasgow
02.07.92	John White L RSC 6 Middleton
29.09.92	Gary Marston DREW 6 Stoke
07.10.92	Jacob Smith W PTS 6 Sunderland
03.12.92	Bradley Stone L CO 4 Lewisham
26.01.93	Neil Smith L PTS 4 Leicester
13.02.93	John White L CO 2 Manchester
20.04.93	Bobby Guynan L PTS 6 Brentwood
29.04.93	Kevin Toomey L PTS 6 Hull
23.05.93	Mike Anthony Brown W PTS 4 Brockley
09.06.93	Joey Moffat L RTD 4 Liverpool
30.09.93	Simon Frailing W PTS 6 Hayes
06.10.93	Kevin McKillan L RSC 1 Solihull
06.12.93	Colin Innes W PTS 6 Bradford
16.12.93	Peter Till L PTS 8 Walsall
19.01.94	John Naylor L RSC 3 Stoke
21.02.94	Hugh Collins L RTD 4 Glasgow
14.04.94	Mike Anthony Brown L PTS 6 Battersea
28.04.94	John Stovin DREW 6 Hull
06.05.94	Sugar Gibiliru L RTD 5 Liverpool
02.09.94	Dave Fallon L DIS 4 Spitalfields
28.09.94	Tanveer Ahmed L CO 5 Glasgow
24.11.94	Tony Foster L RTD 7 Hull
17.02.95	Paul Knights L RTD 5 Crawley
16.06.95	George Naylor L PTS 6 Liverpool

Career: 26 contests, won 4, drew 2, lost 20.

(Hardip) Harry Dhami

Gravesend. *Born* Gravesend, 17 April, 1972
L. Middleweight. Ht. 5'10"
Manager M. Hill

29.10.92	Johnny Pinnock W PTS 6 Hayes	
20.05.94	Nick Appiah W RSC 4 Acton	
27.05.94	Chris Vassiliou W RSC 5 Ashford	
11.10.94	Steve McNess DREW 6 Bethnal Green	
09.11.94	Clay O'Shea L PTS 6 Millwall	
30.11.94	Robert Wright L PTS 8 Wolverhampton	

Career: 6 contests, won 3, drew 1, lost 2.

(Guillaume) Bamana Dibateza

Dagenham. *Born* Kinshasha, Zaire, 27 June, 1968
S. Featherweight. Ht. 5'5"
Manager R. Colson

13.12.88	Nicola Cara L PTS 6 San Pellegrino, Italy
27.12.88	Massimo Spinelli L PTS 6 San Pellegrino, Italy
21.01.89	Nicola Cara L PTS 6 Vasto, Italy
10.03.90	Djamel Ayed W PTS 6 Brest, France
20.04.90	Abdelac Lahmeri L PTS 6 Istres, France
30.09.90	Boualem Belkif L PTS 8 Calais, France
02.03.91	Pascal Ragaut W PTS 6 Salon, France
12.04.91	Didier Schaeffer W PTS 6 Elbeuf, France
25.05.91	Santiago Galan L PTS 8 Mondragon, Spain
07.06.91	Frederic Malesa W PTS 6 La Seyne, France
23.11.91	Mustapha Hame W PTS 6 Beziers, France
13.02.93	Alain Pernice W PTS 6 Narbonne, France
09.04.94	Justin Juuko L RSC 5 Mansfield
11.05.94	Yifru Retta L PTS 6 Stevenage
04.10.94	Michael Armstrong W RSC 3 Mayfair
07.11.94	Michael Ayers L PTS 6 Bethnal Green
13.12.94	Jonjo Irwin L PTS 12 Potters Bar *(Penta-Continental S. Featherweight Title Challenge)*
08.03.95	Charles Shepherd L PTS 8 Solihull
21.03.95	Dean Phillips L PTS 6 Swansea

Career: 19 contests, won 7, lost 12.

Liam Dineen

Horden. *Born* Horden, 17 October, 1972
Lightweight. Ht. 5'10"
Manager T. Conroy

24.05.94	Carl Roberts W PTS 6 Sunderland
05.12.94	Ram Singh W PTS 6 Houghton le Spring
21.02.95	T. J. Smith W PTS 6 Sunderland
16.03.95	Garry Burrell W PTS 6 Sunderland

Career: 4 contests, won 4.

Terry Dixon

West Ham. *Born* London, 29 July, 1966
Cruiserweight. Ht. 5'11"
Manager Self

21.09.89	Dave Mowbray W RSC 1 Southampton
30.11.89	Brendan Dempsey W RSC 8 Barking
08.03.90	Cordwell Hylton W PTS 8 Watford
06.04.90	Prince Rodney W RSC 7 Stevenage
23.10.90	Dennis Bailey W PTS 6 Leicester
07.03.91	Carl Thompson L PTS 8 Basildon
22.04.91	Everton Blake L RSC 8 Mayfair
25.03.92	Mark Bowen W RTD 1 Kensington
27.04.92	Ian Bulloch W RSC 4 Mayfair
17.10.92	Darren McKenna L RSC 3 Wembley

04.10.93	Steve Yorath W RSC 4 Mayfair
03.08.94	Chemek Saleta L PTS 8 Bristol

Career: 12 contests, won 8, lost 4.

Wilson Docherty

Croy. *Born* Glasgow, 15 April, 1968
Penta-Continental Featherweight Champion. Ht. 5'6"
Manager Self

27.04.92	Norman Dhalie W RSC 2 Glasgow
09.07.92	Graham McGrath W RSC 4 Glasgow
26.04.93	Des Gargano W PTS 6 Glasgow
07.06.93	Chris Jickells W RSC 5 Glasgow
14.07.93	Anton Gilmore L PTS 8 Marula, South Africa
07.11.93	Robert Braddock W RSC 3 Glasgow
24.01.94	Paul Harvey W PTS 12 Glasgow *(Vacant Penta-Continental Featherweight Title)*
27.08.94	Peter Harris W PTS 12 Cardiff *(Penta-Continental Featherweight Title Defence)*
23.01.95	Mike Deveney L PTS 12 Glasgow *(Vacant British Featherweight Title)*
24.04.95	Peter Harris L PTS 10 Glasgow *(Final Elim. British Featherweight Title)*

Career: 10 contests, won 7, lost 3.

Adrian Dodson Les Clark

Adrian Dodson

Islington. *Born* Georgetown, 20 September, 1970
L. Middleweight. Ht. 5'10"
Manager Self

31.03.93	Chris Mulcahy W RSC 1 Bethnal Green
14.04.93	Rick North W RTD 1 Kensington
06.05.93	Greg Wallace W RSC 3 Las Vegas, USA
23.06.93	Russell Washer W PTS 6 Edmonton
22.09.93	Robert Peel W CO 1 Bethnal Green
23.10.93	Julian Eavis W RSC 4 Cardiff

26.02.94	Shamus Casey W CO 1 Earls Court
12.03.94	Danny Juma W PTS 6 Cardiff
09.04.94	Stuart Dunn W RSC 1 Mansfield
04.06.94	Andrew Jervis W RSC 2 Cardiff
10.09.94	Colin Pitters W PTS 6 Birmingham
25.02.95	Lloyd Honeyghan W RSC 3 Millwall

Career: 12 contests, won 12.

Joe Donohoe

Walworth. *Born* London, 2 March, 1962
S. Featherweight. Ht. 5'4¾"
Manager Self

13.10.82	Shaun Shinkwin W PTS 6 Walthamstow
09.05.85	Gary King DREW 6 Acton
02.09.85	Billy Joe Dee W PTS 6 Coventry
07.10.85	Gary King W PTS 6 Dulwich
24.03.86	Nigel Senior W PTS 6 Mayfair
12.02.88	Lars Lund Jensen L PTS 6 Elsinore, Denmark
08.03.88	Kid Sumali W PTS 6 Holborn
18.03.88	Kid Sumali W PTS 6 Wandsworth
15.11.88	Derek Amory W PTS 8 Piccadilly
07.12.88	Roy Webb L CO 2 Belfast
25.11.89	Herve Jacob L DIS 6 Gravelines, France
19.03.90	Mark Geraghty W RSC 3 Glasgow
18.03.91	Derek Amory W PTS 8 Piccadilly
26.04.95	Dean Amory L PTS 6 Stoke

Career: 14 contests, won 9, drew 1, lost 4.

Darren Dorrington

Bristol. *Born* Bristol, 24 July, 1968
Middleweight. Western Area S.
Middleweight Champion. Ht. 5'11"
Manager C. Sanigar

13.09.93	Justin Smart DREW 4 Bristol
03.11.93	Russell Washer W PTS 4 Bristol
20.01.94	Shamus Casey W PTS 6 Battersea
29.01.94	Barry Thorogood DREW 6 Cardiff
10.03.94	Ray Price W RSC 6 Bristol
25.05.94	Steve Thomas W PTS 4 Bristol
02.07.94	Paul Murray W RSC 3 Keynsham
03.08.94	Gary Pemberton W CO 4 Bristol
07.10.94	Peter Vosper W RSC 6 Taunton *(Vacant Western Area S. Middleweight Title)*
27.10.94	Russell Washer W PTS 8 Bayswater
22.11.94	Robert Allen L RSC 5 Bristol
21.03.95	Lee Crocker L PTS 6 Swansea

Career: 12 contests, won 8, drew 2, lost 2.

Scott Doyle

Birmingham. *Born* Birmingham, 14 June, 1968
Welterweight. Ht. 5'8"
Manager Self

15.03.91	Chris Cooper W RSC 1 Millwall
12.04.91	Barry North W PTS 6 Willenhall
17.06.91	Tony Doyle W PTS 6 Edgbaston
07.10.91	Jason Brattley W PTS 6 Birmingham
21.11.91	Shane Sheridan W PTS 6 Ilkeston
09.12.91	Peter Till L CO 3 Brierley Hill
03.02.92	Ricky Sackfield L PTS 6 Manchester
03.03.92	Richard O'Brien W PTS 4 Cradley Heath
14.05.92	Joey Moffat L RSC 8 Liverpool
28.04.94	Andy Peach W PTS 6 Mayfair
06.05.94	Tony Mock L PTS 6 Liverpool
25.10.94	Michael Smyth L CO 1 Southwark

29.11.94 Anthony Huw Williams L PTS 6 Cardiff
24.02.95 Paul Wesley L PTS 8 Weston super Mare
03.03.95 Keith Marner L PTS 6 Bracknell
25.03.95 James Lowther L PTS 6 Rothwell
Career: 16 contests, won 7, lost 9.

Scott Doyle   Les Clark

James Drummond

Kilmarnock. *Born* Kilmarnock, 11 February, 1969
Scottish Flyweight Champion. Ht. 5'6"
Manager Self

18.09.89 Tony Smith W RSC 1 Glasgow
09.10.89 Kruga Hydes W RSC 3 Glasgow
22.01.90 Kevin Jenkins L PTS 6 Glasgow
08.03.90 Kevin Jenkins W RSC 5 Glasgow
19.03.90 Neil Parry W RSC 4 Glasgow
08.10.90 Derek Amory L PTS 8 Cleethorpes
19.11.90 Chris Clarkson L PTS 8 Glasgow
18.03.91 Stewart Fishermac W RSC 8 Piccadilly
07.05.91 Des Gargano W PTS 8 Glasgow
01.06.91 Mercurio Ciaramitaro DREW 6 Ragusa, Italy
15.11.91 Salvatore Fanni L PTS 12 Omegna, Italy
(European Flyweight Title Challenge)
19.05.92 Robbie Regan L RSC 9 Cardiff
(British Flyweight Title Challenge)
22.12.92 Francis Ampofo L PTS 12 Mayfair
(Vacant British Flyweight Title)
26.02.93 Ady Benton DREW 6 Irvine
29.06.93 Ricky Beard L PTS 8 Mayfair
25.10.93 Neil Parry W RSC 2 Glasgow
22.11.93 Louis Veitch W PTS 8 Glasgow
21.03.94 Neil Armstrong W RSC 5 Glasgow
(Elim. British Flyweight Title. Vacant Scottish Flyweight Title)
31.07.94 Zolile Mbityi L CO 8 East London, South Africa
20.09.94 Francis Ampofo L RSC 3 Musselburgh
(British Flyweight Title Challenge)
23.11.94 Ricky Beard L RSC 2 Irvine
Career: 21 contests, won 9, drew 2, lost 10.

John Duckworth

Burnley. *Born* Burnley, 25 May, 1971
Middleweight. Ht. 6'2"
Manager B. Myers

04.04.92 Warren Stephens W RSC 5 Cleethorpes
13.04.92 Steve Goodwin L PTS 6 Manchester
04.06.92 Phil Foxon W RSC 4 Burnley
05.10.92 Dave Maj DREW 6 Manchester
29.10.92 Tony Massey W RTD 4 Leeds
20.01.93 James McGee W PTS 6 Solihull
25.02.93 Tony Trimble W PTS 6 Burnley
31.03.93 Jamie Robinson L RSC 3 Barking
27.05.93 Warren Stephens W RSC 5 Burnley
15.09.93 Mark Jay W RSC 4 Newcastle
11.11.93 Darren Pilling W PTS 6 Burnley
02.03.94 Dave Johnson L PTS 8 Solihull
15.03.94 Andrew Jervis W PTS 6 Stoke
18.04.94 Craig Winter L RSC 5 Manchester
26.09.94 Danny Peters L PTS 6 Liverpool
26.10.94 Darren Littlewood L PTS 6 Stoke
07.11.94 Paolo Roberto DREW 6 Piccadilly
28.11.94 Carl Harney L PTS 6 Manchester
07.12.94 Mark Dawson L PTS 6 Stoke
27.02.95 Paul Wright DREW 6 Barrow
05.04.95 Willie Quinn L PTS 8 Irvine
12.06.95 Carl Smith W PTS 6 Manchester
20.06.95 Andy McVeigh DREW 6 Edgbaston
Career: 23 contests, won 10, drew 4, lost 9.

Marty Duke

Yarmouth. *Born* Yarmouth, 19 June, 1967
Welterweight. Ht. 5'9"
Manager Self

16.05.88 Wayne Timmins L PTS 6 Wolverhampton
06.09.88 Tony Cloak W PTS 6 Southend
26.09.88 Tony Cloak L RSC 2 Bedford
27.10.88 Matthew Jones L PTS 8 Birmingham
06.12.88 Peter Mundy W PTS 6 Southend
25.01.89 Tony Hodge W RSC 2 Basildon
07.02.89 Dennis White L PTS 6 Southend
04.04.89 Tony Cloak W PTS 6 Southend
27.04.89 Steve West L RSC 1 Southwark
03.10.89 Colin Ford L PTS 6 Southend
23.10.89 Andy Catesby W PTS 6 Mayfair
19.12.89 Mike Jay DREW 6 Southend
08.02.90 Dean Lake L RSC 4 Southwark
14.03.90 Ahmet Canbakis L RSC 6 Battersea
12.11.90 Chris Haydon W PTS 6 Norwich
04.12.90 Paul Busby L PTS 6 Bury St Edmunds
29.01.91 Paul Smith L PTS 6 Wisbech
15.04.91 James McGee W PTS 6 Leicester
08.05.91 Martin Rosamond DREW 8 Millwall
16.05.91 Danny Shinkwin L PTS 6 Battersea
30.05.91 Richie Woodhall L RSC 4 Birmingham
04.07.91 Robert McCracken L RSC 1 Alfreton
03.09.91 Eamonn Loughran L PTS 6 Cardiff
26.09.91 Adrian Riley L PTS 6 Dunstable
05.11.91 Tony McKenzie L RSC 7 Leicester
31.03.92 Ojay Abrahams L RSC 2 Norwich
08.09.92 Ricky Mabbett DREW 6 Norwich
14.11.92 Vince Rose L PTS 6 Gorleston
26.01.93 Ricky Mabbett W CO 1 Leicester
14.04.93 Kevin Lueshing L RSC 2 Kensington
23.06.93 Billy McDougall W PTS 6 Gorleston
31.08.93 Glenn Catley L RSC 2 Croydon
03.11.93 Glenn Catley L RSC 1 Bristol
28.03.94 Spencer McCracken L RSC 2 Birmingham
27.11.94 Maurice Forbes L PTS 6 Southwark
09.12.94 Jason Beard L PTS 6 Bethnal Green
20.01.95 Nicky Thurbin L PTS 6 Bethnal Green

06.03.95 Howard Eastman L RSC 1 Mayfair
14.04.95 Neil Sinclair L RSC 2 Belfast
12.05.95 Nicky Thurbin L RSC 3 Bethnal Green
Career: 40 contests, won 9, drew 3, lost 28.

Marcus Duncan

Lancaster. *Born* Blackpool, 9 January, 1971
Bantamweight. Ht. 5'6"
Manager J. Doughty

12.11.92 Andrew Bloomer W PTS 6 Burnley
22.04.93 Chris Lyons W RSC 2 Bury
27.05.93 Neil Swain L PTS 6 Burnley
28.06.93 Neil Parry L RSC 2 Morecambe
13.09.93 Neil Parry W PTS 6 Middleton
11.11.93 Dave Campbell W PTS 6 Burnley
17.02.94 Jason Morris W RSC 6 Bury
21.03.94 Graham McGrath W PTS 6 Bradford
16.05.94 Daryl McKenzie W PTS 6 Morecambe
13.06.94 Matthew Harris L RSC 1 Bradford
26.09.94 Dave Campbell W PTS 6 Morecambe
22.05.95 Robert Hay L RSC 3 Morecambe
Career: 12 contests, won 8, lost 4.

Brian Dunn

Immingham. *Born* Cleethorpes, 16 July, 1969
L. Middleweight. Ht. 5'10"
Manager L. Billany

15.04.94 Warren Stephens W PTS 6 Hull
16.05.94 Peter Reid W RSC 4 Cleethorpes
06.06.94 Eddie Haley L PTS 6 Glasgow
26.09.94 Japhet Hans L PTS 6 Cleethorpes
26.10.94 Ron Hopley W PTS 6 Leeds
12.12.94 Japhet Hans W PTS 6 Cleethorpes
06.03.95 Michael Alexander W CO 5 Bradford
05.04.95 Joe Townsley L RSC 3 Irvine
15.05.95 Andy Peach L RSC 2 Cleethorpes
Career: 9 contests, won 5, lost 4.

Robbie Dunn

Plymouth. *Born* Mexborough, 29 May, 1969
L. Middleweight. Ht. 5'10½"
Manager N. Christian

24.01.95 Chris Vassiliou L PTS 6 Piccadilly
03.03.95 Dennis Gardner L RSC 4 Bracknell
13.06.95 Steve Roberts L RSC 3 Basildon
Career: 3 contests, lost 3.

Stuart Dunn

Leicester. *Born* Leicester, 19 January, 1970
Middleweight. Ht. 5'10½"
Manager J. Baxter

15.10.91 Spencer McCracken DREW 6 Dudley
09.12.91 Wayne Panayiotiou W CO 4 Brierley Hill
23.01.92 Charlie Moore L RSC 3 York
27.10.92 Andy Peach W RSC 3 Leicester
26.01.93 Wayne Panayiotiou W RSC 2 Leicester
28.04.93 Barry Thorogood W RSC 2 Solihull
19.05.93 Matthew Turner W RSC 3 Leicester
18.09.93 Lee Ferrie L RSC 1 Leicester
10.11.93 Jamie Robinson L PTS 6 Bethnal Green
30.11.93 Shamus Casey W PTS 6 Leicester
18.02.94 Jimmy Alston W RSC 1 Leicester
09.04.94 Adrian Dodson L RSC 1 Mansfield
18.02.95 Dean Cooper L RSC 1 Shepton Mallet
20.04.95 Howard Eastman L RSC 2 Mayfair
Career: 14 contests, won 7, drew 1, lost 6.

Colin Dunne

Holloway. *Born* Liverpool, 19 September, 1970
Lightweight. Ht. 5'6"
Manager T. Toole

07.12.93	Mark O'Callaghan W RSC 1 Bethnal Green
14.01.94	Wayne Jones W RSC 3 Bethnal Green
04.03.94	Malcolm Thomas W CO 1 Bethnal Green
26.04.94	Steve Burton W CO 2 Bethnal Green
17.05.94	Phil Found W PTS 6 Kettering
23.09.94	Steve Howden W CO 1 Bethnal Green
11.10.94	Jimmy Phelan W PTS 6 Bethnal Green
09.11.94	Mark O'Callaghan W RSC 2 Millwall
09.12.94	David Thompson W RSC 3 Bethnal Green
20.01.95	Chris Aston W RSC 4 Bethnal Green
03.03.95	Marco Fattore W RSC 3 Bethnal Green
19.04.95	Rudy Valentino W PTS 6 Bethnal Green
12.05.95	Chris Aston W RSC 4 Bethnal Green

Career: 13 contests, won 13.

Pat Durkin

Southport. *Born* Southport, 15 February, 1969
L. Heavyweight. Ht. 6'2"
Manager N. Basso

28.10.87	Paul Jones L PTS 4 Sheffield
09.11.87	Michael Justin L PTS 4 Leicester
16.11.87	Michael McDermott L PTS 4 Glasgow
30.11.87	Mike Snagg W RSC 6 Manchester
14.12.87	Dave Kettlewell L PTS 4 Bradford
18.01.88	Frank Harrington L PTS 4 Bradford
29.01.88	Dave Kettlewell L PTS 4 Durham
08.02.88	Adrian Din L CO 2 Nottingham
11.03.88	Frank Mobbs L RSC 3 Cottingham
03.11.88	Chris Mulcahy L RSC 2 Manchester
09.10.90	Trevor Meikle L DIS 3 Liverpool
07.02.91	Phil Epton L PTS 6 Watford
25.02.91	Willie Yeardsley L PTS 6 Bradford
05.03.91	Chris Mulcahy L PTS 6 Leicester
06.06.94	Laurence Rowe L PTS 6 Manchester
15.12.94	Chris Nurse L PTS 6 Walsall
09.02.95	Phil Ball L PTS 6 Doncaster
15.03.95	Steve Loftus L PTS 6 Stoke

Career: 18 contests, won 1, lost 17.

Darren Dyer Les Clark

Darren Dyer

Islington. *Born* London, 31 July, 1966
Welterweight. Ht. 5'7½"
Manager B. Hearn

20.11.86	Trevor Grant W RSC 2 Bethnal Green
08.01.87	Del Bryan L PTS 6 Bethnal Green
26.02.87	Kid Murray W CO 3 Bethnal Green
18.04.87	Geoff Calder W RSC 2 Kensington
07.09.87	Kelvin Mortimer L RSC 1 Mayfair
25.02.88	Donald Gwynn W CO 1 Bethnal Green
13.04.88	Kent Acuff W CO 2 Bethnal Green
16.05.88	Thomas Garcia W RSC 2 Piccadilly
02.11.88	Harlein Holden W CO 2 Southwark
07.12.88	Jean-Marc Phenieux W RSC 3 Piccadilly
12.01.89	Anthony Travers W RSC 6 Southwark
29.03.89	Mario Coronado W RSC 1 Wembley
04.10.89	Efrom Brown W RSC 4 Kensington
11.01.90	Fernando Segura W CO 2 Dewsbury
14.03.90	Jorge Maysonet L RSC 2 Kensington
03.07.91	Trevor Ambrose W PTS 6 Brentwood
26.10.91	Kelvin Mortimer W RSC 2 Brentwood
26.11.91	Robert Wright W RSC 3 Bethnal Green
19.02.92	Ian John-Lewis W RSC 2 Muswell Hill
12.05.92	Del Bryan W RSC 10 Crystal Palace
10.11.92	Chris Peters W RSC 9 Dagenham
09.03.93	Marcelo Domingo di Croce L RSC 4 Hartlepool
	(Vacant Penta-Continental Welterweight Title)
09.04.94	Julian Eavis W PTS 8 Bethnal Green
11.06.94	Ojay Abrahams L RSC 1 Bethnal Green
15.10.94	Gary Murray L RSC 4 Sun City, South Africa

Career: 25 contests, won 19, lost 6.

Paul Dyer

Portsmouth. *Born* Portsmouth, 11 July, 1970
L. Welterweight. Ht. 5'11½"
Manager C. Sanigar

24.09.91	Mick Reid W PTS 6 Basildon
19.11.91	Dave Andrews W PTS 6 Norwich
23.02.93	Kevin Mabbutt L PTS 6 Kettering
17.06.94	Dewi Roberts W PTS 6 Plymouth
27.10.94	George Wilson W PTS 4 Bayswater
25.01.95	John Janes W PTS 6 Cardiff
08.03.95	Anthony Huw Williams W PTS 6 Cardiff
06.05.95	Wahid Fats W PTS 4 Shepton Mallet

Career: 8 contests, won 7, lost 1.

Howard Eastman Tony Fitch

Howard Eastman

Battersea. *Born* New Amsterdam, 8 December, 1970
Middleweight. Ht. 5'11"
Manager D. Mancini

06.03.94	John Rice W RSC 1 Southwark
14.03.94	Andy Peach W PTS 6 Mayfair
22.03.94	Steve Phillips W RSC 5 Bethnal Green
17.10.94	Barry Thorogood W RSC 6 Mayfair
06.03.95	Marty Duke W RSC 1 Mayfair
20.04.95	Stuart Dunn W RSC 2 Mayfair
23.06.95	Peter Vosper W RSC 1 Bethnal Green

Career: 7 contests, won 7.

Julian Eavis

Yeovil. *Born* Bourton, 3 December, 1965
L. Middleweight. Ht. 5'7¾"
Manager Self

12.10.88	Noel Rafferty W PTS 6 Stoke
17.10.88	Steve Taggart W PTS 6 Birmingham
17.11.88	Young Gully W PTS 6 Weston super Mare
07.12.88	Adrian Din L PTS 6 Stoke
14.12.88	Young Gully L PTS 6 Evesham
30.01.89	Frank Harrington W PTS 6 Leicester
06.02.89	Young Gully L RSC 4 Nottingham
15.03.89	Steve Taggart W PTS 6 Stoke
21.03.89	Steve Hogg W PTS 6 Wolverhampton
15.04.89	Andy Tonks W PTS 6 Salisbury
09.05.89	Mark Purcell L RSC 5 Plymouth
	(Western Area Welterweight Title Challenge)
25.09.89	Wayne Timmins L PTS 6 Birmingham
04.10.89	Barry Messam W PTS 8 Stafford
10.10.89	Robert Wright L PTS 8 Wolverhampton
30.10.89	Wayne Timmins L PTS 8 Birmingham
14.11.89	Bobby McGowan W PTS 8 Evesham
22.11.89	Ronnie Campbell W PTS 8 Solihull
06.12.89	Lindon Scarlett L PTS 8 Stoke
10.01.90	Gary Logan L PTS 8 Kensington
24.01.90	Kevin Plant L PTS 6 Solihull
06.02.90	Tony Connellan L PTS 8 Oldham
13.02.90	Kevin Thompson L PTS 8 Wolverhampton
27.02.90	Ernie Loveridge L PTS 6 Evesham
07.03.90	Kevin Plant L PTS 8 Doncaster
22.03.90	Wayne Timmins L PTS 8 Wolverhampton
26.04.90	Leigh Wicks DREW 8 Mayfair
24.05.90	Gary Osborne L PTS 8 Dudley
04.06.90	Paul Wesley L PTS 8 Birmingham
17.09.90	Dave Andrews L PTS 6 Cardiff
01.10.90	Kevin Plant L PTS 8 Cleethorpes
09.10.90	Ronnie Campbell DREW 6 Wolverhampton
17.10.90	Paul Wesley L PTS 6 Stoke
31.10.90	Mickey Lloyd L PTS 8 Wembley
14.11.90	Glyn Rhodes L RSC 5 Sheffield
12.12.90	Barry Messam L PTS 6 Leicester
19.12.90	Carl Wright L PTS 6 Preston
16.01.91	Gary Logan L RSC 5 Kensington
05.03.91	Eamonn Loughran L PTS 6 Cardiff
20.03.91	Kevin Plant L PTS 6 Solihull
10.04.91	Ernie Loveridge DREW 8 Wolverhampton
01.05.91	Humphrey Harrison L PTS 6 Solihull
28.05.91	Darren Liney L PTS 6 Cardiff
05.06.91	Wayne Timmins L PTS 6 Wolverhampton
11.06.91	James McGee L PTS 6 Leicester
03.07.91	Benny Collins L PTS 6 Reading

03.09.91 Michael Smyth L PTS 6 Cardiff
01.10.91 Lee Ferrie L PTS 6 Bedworth
23.10.91 Kevin Lueshing L RSC 2 Bethnal Green
26.11.91 James Campbell W PTS 8 Wolverhampton
04.12.91 Peter Reid W PTS 6 Stoke
11.12.91 James McGee DREW 6 Leicester
17.12.91 Michael Smyth L PTS 6 Cardiff
15.01.92 Robert Wright L PTS 8 Stoke
04.02.92 Howard Clarke L PTS 4 Alfreton
11.02.92 Jamie Robinson L PTS 6 Barking
24.02.92 Lee Ferrie L PTS 8 Coventry
11.03.92 Rob Pitters L PTS 6 Solihull
11.05.92 James McGee L RSC 3 Coventry
07.07.92 Ross Hale L RSC 8 Bristol
(Vacant Western Area Welterweight Title)
05.10.92 James McGee W PTS 6 Bardon
28.11.92 Warren Stowe L RSC 6 Manchester
27.01.93 Mark Kelly L PTS 8 Stoke
22.02.93 James McGee L PTS 6 Bedworth
06.03.93 Robin Reid L RSC 2 Glasgow
10.05.93 Peter Waudby L PTS 6 Cleethorpes
26.06.93 Dean Cooper L PTS 10 Keynsham
(Vacant Western Area L. Middleweight Title)
13.09.93 Crain Fisher L PTS 6 Middleton
06.10.93 Howard Clarke L PTS 8 Solihull
23.10.93 Adrian Dodson L RSC 4 Cardiff
30.11.93 Howard Clarke L PTS 6 Wolverhampton
08.12.93 Peter Reid L PTS 6 Stoke
19.01.94 Spencer McCracken L PTS 8 Solihull
26.01.94 John Bosco L RSC 1 Birmingham
08.03.94 Malcolm Melvin L PTS 6 Edgbaston
23.03.94 Peter Reid L PTS 8 Stoke
31.03.94 Dean Cooper L PTS 6 Bristol
09.04.94 Darren Dyer L PTS 8 Bethnal Green
11.05.94 Roy Rowland L RSC 4 Stevenage
02.07.94 Geoff McCreesh L PTS 4 Keynsham
28.07.94 Jason Hart L PTS 6 Tooting
26.08.94 Chris Saunders L PTS 6 Barnsley
26.09.94 Chris Saunders L PTS 6 Cleethorpes
12.10.94 Howard Clarke L PTS 8 Stoke
25.10.94 Spencer McCracken L PTS 6 Edgbaston
02.11.94 Howard Clarke L PTS 8 Birmingham
22.11.94 Sean Baker L PTS 6 Bristol
29.11.94 Howard Clarke L PTS 6 Cannock
09.12.94 Nicky Thurbin L PTS 6 Bethnal Green
17.01.95 Paul Jones L RSC 4 Worcester
23.02.95 Steve McNess L PTS 6 Southwark
16.03.95 Steve Roberts L PTS 6 Basildon
25.03.95 Sandy Katerega L PTS 6 Millwall
Career: 92 contests, won 14, drew 4, lost 74.

(Clive) Bobbi Joe Edwards

Manchester. *Born* Jamaica, 25 December, 1957
Cruiserweight. Ht. 5'10"
Manager Self

09.10.90 Doug McKay W RSC 1 Glasgow
26.11.90 Keith Inglis W RSC 1 Mayfair
22.02.91 Cordwell Hylton L RTD 6 Manchester
29.11.91 David Brown W RSC 4 Manchester
31.01.92 Richard Bustin W PTS 6 Manchester
29.05.92 John Foreman L RSC 4 Manchester
29.10.92 Michael Gale L PTS 10 Leeds
(Vacant Central Area L. Heavyweight Title)
30.03.93 Simon Collins W PTS 6 Cardiff
16.10.93 Ginger Tshabala L RSC 5 Belfast

25.12.93 Francis Wanyama L PTS 8 Izegem, Belgium
04.05.94 Dirk Walleyn L RSC 5 Bredene, Belgium
17.10.94 Bruce Scott L PTS 8 Mayfair
26.10.94 Michael Gale L PTS 8 Leeds
11.12.94 Eddy Smulders L PTS 8 Amsterdam, Holland
22.02.95 Joe Calzaghe L PTS 8 Telford
14.04.95 Ray Kane L PTS 6 Belfast
27.05.95 Ray Kane L PTS 6 Belfast
Career: 17 contests, won 5, lost 12.

Michael Edwards

Dudley. *Born* Swindon, 21 February, 1971
S. Bantamweight. Ht. 5'6"
Manager C. Flute

29.09.94 Jon Pegg L RSC 5 Walsall
07.02.95 Chris Lyons L PTS 6 Wolverhampton
22.03.95 Andy Roberts W PTS 6 Stoke
06.06.95 Jason Squire L RSC 1 Leicester
Career: 4 contests, won 1, lost 3.

Richie Edwards

Greenford. *Born* Ealing, 25 March, 1969
L. Welterweight. Ht. 5'8"
Manager F. Maloney

30.03.95 John O. Johnson W PTS 4 Bethnal Green
04.06.95 Seth Jones W RSC 4 Bethnal Green
16.06.95 Mikael Nilsson W PTS 4 Southwark
Career: 3 contests, won 3.

Shaba Edwards

Bermondsey. *Born* Clapham, 29 April, 1966
L. Welterweight. Ht. 5'7½"
Manager Self

12.05.93 Jason Barker L PTS 6 Stoke
23.06.93 Steve Howden L RSC 1 Gorleston
12.09.94 Brian Coleman W PTS 6 Mayfair
29.09.94 Everald Williams L CO 1 Bethnal Green
30.11.94 Clayton Hollingsworth L PTS 6 Wolverhampton
22.02.95 Clayton Hollingsworth L PTS 6 Telford
16.03.95 Georgie Smith L CO 2 Basildon
Career: 7 contests, won 1, lost 6.

Steve Edwards

Haverfordwest. *Born* Haverfordwest, 18 July, 1970
S. Featherweight. Ht. 5'4"
Manager Self

02.03.92 Nigel Burder W RSC 1 Merthyr
25.02.94 George Naylor L RTD 3 Chester
28.05.94 Sugar Free Somerville W RSC 2 Queensway
25.06.94 Greg Upton DREW 6 Cullompton
21.09.94 Dean Phillips L RTD 4 Cardiff
Career: 5 contests, won 2, drew 1, lost 2.

Cliff Elden

Norwich. *Born* Norwich, 6 September, 1967
Cruiserweight. Ht. 6'2"
Manager B. Lee

25.01.95 Johnny Moth L PTS 6 Stoke
26.05.95 Newby Stevens W RSC 3 Norwich
14.06.95 Henry Brewer L PTS 6 Batley
Career: 3 contests, won 1, lost 2.

Mark Elliot

Telford. *Born* Telford, 2 February, 1966
L. Welterweight. Ht. 5'9"
Manager M. Duff

10.09.91 Dean Bramhald W CO 5 Wolverhampton
12.11.91 John Smith W PTS 6 Wolverhampton
05.12.91 Mick Mulcahy W RSC 2 Cannock
17.03.92 Andrew Morgan W PTS 6 Wolverhampton
20.01.93 Wayne Windle W CO 3 Wolverhampton
16.03.93 Chris Saunders W PTS 6 Wolverhampton
27.10.93 Rob Stewart W PTS 6 West Bromwich
26.01.94 Dave Lovell W PTS 6 Birmingham
16.03.94 Phil Found W PTS 6 Birmingham
05.10.94 Tony Swift W PTS 8 Wolverhampton
30.11.94 Mark Ramsey L RSC 10 Wolverhampton
(Elim. British L. Welterweight Title)
Career: 11 contests, won 10, lost 1.

Wayne Ellis

Cardiff. *Born* Cardiff, 18 July, 1968
S. Middleweight. Former Penta-Continental Middleweight Champion. Former Undefeated Welsh Middleweight Champion. Ht. 6'0"
Manager B. Hearn

25.06.88 Shamus Casey W PTS 6 Luton
07.09.88 Kevin Hayde W PTS 6 Reading
01.11.88 Dennis White W CO 2 Reading
20.12.88 Spencer Alton W RTD 4 Swansea
11.04.89 Mark Howell W PTS 6 Aberavon
09.05.89 Spencer Alton W RSC 3 St Albans
06.09.89 Ian Chantler W RSC 4 Aberavon
14.02.90 Lindon Scarlett DREW 6 Millwall
22.05.90 Paul Jones W PTS 6 St Albans
10.10.90 Frank Eubanks W PTS 6 Millwall
05.03.91 Johnny Melfah W RSC 2 Cardiff
03.09.91 Colin Manners L RSC 1 Cardiff
11.02.92 Alan Richards W PTS 10 Cardiff
(Vacant Welsh Middleweight Title)
14.07.92 Mike Phillips W RSC 7 Mayfair
(Welsh Middleweight Title Defence)
10.07.93 Paul Busby W RSC 5 Cardiff
30.11.93 Steve Collins L RSC 9 Cardiff
(Penta-Continental Middleweight Title Challenge)
28.06.94 Paul Busby W TD 4 Mayfair
(Vacant Penta-Continental Middleweight Title)
29.10.94 Paul Busby L PTS 12 Cannock
(Penta-Continental Middleweight Title Defence)
05.05.95 Darron Griffiths L PTS 10 Swansea
(Welsh S. Middleweight Title Challenge)
Career: 19 contests, won 14, drew 1, lost 4.

Phil Epton (Hampton)

Doncaster. *Born* Doncaster, 14 June, 1968
L. Middleweight. Ht. 5'8"
Manager T. Petersen

18.10.90 Mark Jay W PTS 6 Dewsbury
15.11.90 Paul King L PTS 6 Oldham
07.02.91 Pat Durkin W PTS 6 Watford
21.03.91 Paul King L PTS 6 Dewsbury
13.06.91 Willie Yeardsley W RSC 3 Hull
23.01.92 Carl Hook W PTS 6 York
19.03.92 Ricky Mabbett L RSC 3 York
23.09.92 Jimmy Vincent L RSC 6 Leeds
08.12.94 David Maw L PTS 6 Hull
24.04.95 Billy Collins L RSC 3 Glasgow
24.06.95 Warren Bowers W PTS 6 Cleethorpes
Career: 11 contests, won 5, lost 6.

Harry Escott   Les Clark

Harry Escott

Sunderland. *Born* West Germany, 17
October, 1969
S. Featherweight. Ht. 5'8"
Manager P. Byrne

26.02.87 Kenny Walsh W RSC 4 Hartlepool
06.04.87 Gypsy Finch W PTS 4 Newcastle
23.04.87 Gypsy Finch W PTS 4 Newcastle
30.04.87 Craig Windsor W RSC 3 Washington
22.05.87 Ginger Staples W RSC 1 Peterlee
04.06.87 Barry Bacon W RSC 2 Sunderland
04.09.87 Kevin Plant L RSC 2 Gateshead
26.01.88 Michael Howell W RSC 4 Hartlepool
17.03.88 Ian Honeywood W RSC 4 Sunderland
25.04.88 Les Walsh W PTS 8 Bradford
23.05.88 Tony Foster L RSC 6 Bradford
22.09.88 Dave Kettlewell W PTS 6 Newcastle
14.11.88 John Townsley W PTS 8 Glasgow
30.01.89 Tony Dore DREW 8 Glasgow
14.02.89 Kevin Pritchard W RSC 3 Sunderland
13.03.89 Young Joe Rafiu W PTS 8 Glasgow
11.04.89 Muhammad Lovelock W PTS 6
Oldham
05.06.89 Gary Maxwell W PTS 8 Glasgow
11.09.89 Gary Maxwell W PTS 8 Nottingham
19.10.89 Rudy Valentino W RTD 4 Manchester
07.12.89 Joey Jacobs W PTS 6 Manchester
24.01.90 Tomas Arguelles W PTS 6 Sunderland
15.05.90 Kevin Pritchard W PTS 8 South Shields
13.11.90 Brian Roche L RSC 3 Hartlepool
02.03.91 Steve Walker DREW 6 Darlington
06.04.91 Darren Elsdon L RSC 2 Darlington

06.07.91 Jackie Gunguluza L CO 6 Imperia,
Italy
20.09.91 Steve Walker DREW 6 Manchester
04.02.92 Neil Smith W PTS 8 Alfreton
17.03.92 Floyd Havard L RSC 7 Mayfair
27.05.92 Wilson Rodriguez L PTS 10 Cologne,
Germany
07.10.92 Dominic McGuigan W RTD 5
Sunderland
30.10.92 Eugene Speed L PTS 8 Istres, France
01.12.92 Neil Haddock L PTS 10 Liverpool
18.06.93 Medhi Labdouni L PTS 8 Fontenay
Sous Bois, France
21.07.93 Phil Holliday L PTS 8 Marula, South
Africa
01.12.93 Floyd Havard L PTS 8 Bethnal Green
27.04.94 Kid McAuley W RTD 6 Solihull
10.05.94 Kelton McKenzie W PTS 6 Doncaster
04.10.94 Jonjo Irwin L PTS 12 Mayfair
*(Penta-Continental S. Featherweight
Title Challenge)*
04.02.95 Colin McMillan L PTS 8 Cardiff
01.04.95 Julien Lorcy L RSC 1 Levallois Perret,
France
Career: 42 contests, won 23, drew 3, lost 16.

Chris Eubank

Brighton. *Born* Dulwich, 8 August, 1966
Former WBO S. Middleweight Champion.
Former Undefeated WBO Middleweight
Champion. Former Undefeated WBC
International Middleweight Champion. Ht.
5'10"
Manager Self

03.10.85 Tim Brown W PTS 4 Atlantic City, USA
07.11.85 Kenny Cannida W PTS 4 Atlantic City,
USA
08.01.86 Mike Bragwell W PTS 4 Atlantic City,
USA
25.02.86 Eric Holland W PTS 4 Atlantic City,
USA
25.03.87 James Canty W PTS 4 Atlantic City, USA
15.02.88 Darren Parker W RSC 1 Copthorne
07.03.88 Winston Burnett W PTS 6 Hove
26.04.88 Michael Justin W RSC 5 Hove
04.05.88 Greg George W RSC 5 Wembley
18.05.88 Steve Aquilina W RSC 4 Portsmouth
31.01.89 Simon Collins W RSC 4 Bethnal Green
08.02.89 Anthony Logan W PTS 8 Kensington
01.03.89 Franki Moro W PTS 8 Bethnal Green
26.05.89 Randy Smith W PTS 10 Bethnal Green
28.06.89 Les Wisniewski W RSC 2 Brentwood
04.10.89 Ron Malek W RSC 5 Basildon
24.10.89 Jean-Noel Camara W RSC 2 Bethnal
Green
05.11.89 Johnny Melfah W CO 4 Kensington
20.12.89 Jose da Silva W RTD 6 Kirkby
16.01.90 Denys Cronin W RSC 3 Cardiff
06.03.90 Hugo Corti W RSC 8 Bethnal Green
*(WBC International Middleweight Title
Challenge)*
25.04.90 Eduardo Contreras W PTS 12 Brighton
*(WBC International Middleweight Title
Defence)*
05.09.90 Kid Milo W RSC 8 Brighton
*(WBC International Middleweight Title
Defence)*
22.09.90 Reginaldo Santos W CO 1 Kensington
18.11.90 Nigel Benn W RSC 9 Birmingham
(WBO Middleweight Title Challenge)
23.02.91 Dan Sherry W TD 10 Brighton
(WBO Middleweight Title Defence)

18.04.91 Gary Stretch W RSC 6 Earls Court
(WBO Middleweight Title Defence)
22.06.91 Michael Watson W PTS 12 Earls Court
(WBO Middleweight Title Defence)
21.09.91 Michael Watson W RSC 12 Tottenham
(Vacant WBO S. Middleweight Title)
01.02.92 Thulani Malinga W PTS 12
Birmingham
(WBO S. Middleweight Title Defence)
25.04.92 John Jarvis W CO 3 Manchester
(WBO S. Middleweight Title Defence)
27.06.92 Ronnie Essett W PTS 12 Quinta do
Lago, Portugal
(WBO S. Middleweight Title Defence)
19.09.92 Tony Thornton W PTS 12 Glasgow
(WBO S. Middleweight Title Defence)
28.11.92 Juan Carlos Giminez W PTS 12
Manchester
(WBO S. Middleweight Title Defence)
20.02.93 Lindell Holmes W PTS 12 Earls Court
(WBO S. Middleweight Title Defence)
15.05.93 Ray Close DREW 12 Glasgow
(WBO S. Middleweight Title Defence)
09.10.93 Nigel Benn DREW 12 Manchester
*(WBO S. Middleweight Title Defence,
WBC S. Middleweight Title Challenge)*
05.02.94 Graciano Rocchigiani W PTS 12
Berlin, Germany
(WBO S. Middleweight Title Defence)
21.05.94 Ray Close W PTS 12 Belfast
(WBO S. Middleweight Title Defence)
09.07.94 Mauricio Amaral W PTS 12 Earls
Court
(WBO S. Middleweight Title Defence)
27.08.94 Sammy Storey W RSC 7 Cardiff
(WBO S. Middleweight Title Defence)
15.10.94 Dan Schommer W PTS 12 Sun City,
South Africa
(WBO S. Middleweight Title Defence)
10.12.94 Henry Wharton W PTS 12 Manchester
(WBO S. Middleweight Title Defence)
18.03.95 Steve Collins L PTS 12 Millstreet, Eire
(WBO S. Middleweight Title Defence)
27.05.95 Bruno Godoy W RSC 1 Belfast
Career: 45 contests, won 42, drew 2, lost 1.

Andy Ewen

Ipswich. *Born* Ipswich, 12 January, 1966
Middleweight. Ht. 5'9"
Manager G. Holmes

12.10.94 Peter Mitchell W PTS 6 Sheffield
23.11.94 Sven Hamer L RSC 1 Piccadilly
07.02.95 Russell Washer W PTS 4 Ipswich
31.03.95 Jason Hart L PTS 6 Crystal Palace
17.05.95 Robert Peel W RSC 4 Ipswich
16.06.95 Lee Crocker L RSC 3 Southwark
Career: 6 contests, won 3, lost 3.

Barry Exton

Lincoln. *Born* Lincoln, 27 December, 1970
S. Middleweight. Ht. 6'0"
Manager J. Gaynor

20.06.95 Robert Harper W PTS 6 Edgbaston
Career: 1 contest, won 1.

Declan Faherty

Huddersfield. *Born* Leeds, 23 August, 1969
Cruiserweight. Ht. 6'4"
Manager P. Coleman

24.02.94 Lee Avery W RSC 2 Hull

Dave Fallon (left) seen here trading blows with Erwin Edwards   Les Clark

28.02.94	Shane Meadows W CO 3 Marton
28.03.94	Jem Jackson W RTD 5 Birmingham
28.04.94	Slick Miller W RSC 2 Hull
10.05.94	Kevin Burton W RSC 4 Doncaster
08.12.94	Art Stacey L PTS 6 Hull
15.05.95	John Pierre W PTS 6 Bradford

Career: 7 contests, won 6, lost 1.

(Antonio) Tony Falcone

Chippenham. *Born* Chippenham, 15 October, 1966
Western Area S. Bantamweight Champion. Ht. 5'6"
Manager C. Sanigar

22.10.90	Karl Morling L PTS 6 Mayfair
21.11.90	Barrie Kelley L PTS 6 Chippenham
18.02.91	Barrie Kelley W PTS 6 Windsor
28.02.91	Paul Wynn W PTS 6 Sunderland
21.03.91	Tony Silkstone L PTS 6 Dewsbury
22.04.91	Alan Smith L RSC 5 Mayfair
30.05.91	Alan Smith W PTS 6 Mayfair
11.12.91	Dennis Adams W RTD 4 Basildon
30.04.92	Andrew Bloomer W PTS 6 Mayfair
07.07.92	Miguel Matthews W PTS 6 Bristol
05.10.92	Andrew Bloomer W PTS 8 Bristol
13.12.93	Des Gargano W PTS 4 Bristol
23.02.94	Conn McMullen DREW 4 Watford
10.03.94	Pete Buckley L PTS 6 Bristol
29.03.94	Justin Murphy L RSC 2 Bethnal Green
22.11.94	Fred Reeve W PTS 6 Bristol

18.02.95	Danny Ruegg W PTS 10 Shepton Mallet
	(Vacant Western Area S. Bantamweight Title)
06.05.95	Danny Lawson W RSC 2 Shepton Mallet

Career: 18 contests, won 12, drew 1, lost 5.

Dave Fallon

Watford. *Born* Watford, 22 June, 1967
Welterweight. Ht. 6'0"
Manager Self

12.09.90	Trevor Ambrose L CO 3 Battersea
14.02.91	Richard Swallow L RSC 4 Southampton
12.11.91	Tim Harmey W PTS 6 Milton Keynes
05.12.91	Sean Cave W PTS 6 Peterborough
06.05.93	Noel Henry W PTS 6 Bayswater
24.06.93	Erwin Edwards L RSC 3 Watford
10.03.94	Dave Madden L PTS 6 Watford
02.09.94	Norman Dhalie W DIS 4 Spitalfields
26.05.95	Dennis Gardner L RSC 2 Norwich

Career: 9 contests, won 4, lost 5.

Andy Farr

Walworth. *Born* Erith, 6 March, 1965
S. Middleweight. Ht. 5'11"
Manager B. Padget

13.06.95	Tony Griffiths W RSC 4 Basildon

Career: 1 contest, won 1.

Ceri Farrell

Swansea. *Born* Swansea, 27 October, 1967
Bantamweight. Ht. 5'7"
Manager Self

14.05.90	Kruga Hydes L PTS 6 Cleethorpes
06.06.90	Conn McMullen L RSC 5 Battersea
03.10.90	Tim Yeates L PTS 6 Basildon
05.12.90	Paul Dever W RSC 2 Stafford
12.12.90	Tim Yeates L PTS 6 Basildon
19.12.90	Mercurio Ciaramitaro DREW 6 Rimini, Italy
24.01.91	Kevin Jenkins L PTS 6 Gorseinon
07.02.91	Mark Tierney L PTS 6 Watford
06.03.91	Mark Tierney L PTS 6 Wembley
25.04.91	Mark Loftus L RSC 3 Basildon
04.11.91	Andrew Bloomer W PTS 6 Merthyr
20.11.91	Andrew Bloomer W PTS 6 Cardiff
29.11.91	John Green L RTD 4 Manchester
08.01.92	Miguel Matthews L PTS 6 Burton
22.01.92	Alan Ley L PTS 6 Cardiff
09.02.92	Peter Judson L PTS 6 Bradford
15.09.92	Michael Alldis L RSC 3 Crystal Palace
16.02.93	Michael Alldis L CO 1 Tooting
12.03.94	Neil Swain L CO 1 Cardiff
01.10.94	Marcus McCrae L RTD 1 Cardiff

Career: 20 contests, won 3, drew 1, lost 16.

(Noor Alam) Wahid Fats

Manchester. *Born* Manchester, 2 September, 1971
L. Welterweight. Ht. 5'8"
Manager N. Basso

87

06.06.94 Ram Singh W RSC 3 Manchester
03.10.94 Andy Davidson W RSC 4 Manchester
20.10.94 Blue Butterworth DREW 6 Middleton
28.11.94 Scott Walker W RSC 4 Manchester
06.05.95 Paul Dyer L PTS 4 Shepton Mallet
12.06.95 John Smith L CO 3 Manchester
Career: 6 contests, won 3, drew 1, lost 2.

Marco Fattore

Watford. *Born* Italy, 17 October, 1968
Lightweight. Ht. 5'8"
Manager Self

03.09.92 Jason White W RSC 1 Dunstable
19.10.92 Carlos Domonkos W RTD 4 Mayfair
07.12.92 Steve Patton W RSC 6 Mayfair
15.02.93 Jason Hutson W PTS 6 Mayfair
29.03.93 T. J. Smith DREW 6 Mayfair
22.04.93 Jason Barker W PTS 6 Mayfair
04.10.93 Andrew Bloomer W PTS 6 Mayfair
10.11.93 Lee Fox W PTS 6 Watford
09.12.93 Jason Hutson DREW 6 Watford
10.03.94 Simon Frailing DREW 6 Watford
28.04.94 Andrew Reed DREW 6 Mayfair
12.09.94 Keith Jones W PTS 6 Mayfair
30.11.94 Kid McAuley L PTS 6 Solihull
03.03.95 Colin Dunne L RSC 3 Bethnal Green
25.05.95 P. J. Gallagher L RSC 5 Reading
Career: 15 contests, won 8, drew 4, lost 3.

Darren Fearn

Carmarthen. *Born* Carmarthen, 21
February, 1969
Heavyweight. Ht. 6'2"
Manager D. Gardiner

25.06.94 Keith Fletcher W PTS 6 Cullompton
25.01.95 Rob Albon W PTS 6 Cardiff
12.04.95 L. A. Williams W PTS 6 Llanelli
Career: 3 contests, won 3.

Vince Feeney

Sligo. *Born* Sligo, 12 May, 1973
Flyweight. Ht. 5'4"
Manager J. Griffin

29.10.92 Ady Benton DREW 6 Bayswater
04.02.93 Kevin Jenkins W PTS 6 Cardiff
29.03.93 Andrew Bloomer W PTS 6 Mayfair
29.04.93 Neil Swain L PTS 6 Mayfair
28.09.93 Peter Culshaw L PTS 6 Liverpool
30.11.93 Tiger Singh W PTS 6 Leicester
18.02.94 Shaun Norman W RSC 2 Leicester
09.04.94 Neil Swain W PTS 6 Mansfield
24.05.94 Louis Veitch W PTS 6 Leicester
07.10.94 Jesper D. Jensen L PTS 6 Copenhagen, Denmark
12.11.94 Mark Reynolds W PTS 6 Dublin
Career: 11 contests, won 7, drew 1, lost 3.

Richard Fenton

Cardiff. *Born* Cardiff, 20 September, 1972
Heavyweight. Ht. 6'0"
Manager F. Warren

04.02.95 Keith Fletcher L CO 1 Cardiff
Career: 1 contest, lost 1.

Richard Fenton   Les Clark

Antonio Fernandez (Golding)

Birmingham. *Born* Birmingham, 3 January, 1965
Midlands Area Middleweight Champion. Ht. 5'11¼"
Manager B. Lynch

10.03.87 David Heath W RSC 5 Manchester
29.04.87 Darren Hobson L PTS 6 Stoke
18.11.87 Tony White W PTS 6 Solihull
19.01.88 Malcolm Melvin W RSC 4 Kings Heath
07.03.88 Shaun Cummins L PTS 6 Northampton
10.10.88 Chris Richards W PTS 6 Edgbaston
23.11.88 Chris Richards W PTS 8 Solihull
24.01.89 Paul Murray W PTS 6 Kings Heath
08.05.89 Shamus Casey W PTS 6 Edgbaston
13.11.89 Cyril Jackson W PTS 8 Brierley Hill
03.12.89 Steve Foster L PTS 8 Birmingham
06.03.90 Paul Jones L PTS 8 Stoke
30.04.90 Alan Baptiste W PTS 6 Brierley Hill
04.06.90 Chris Richards W PTS 6 Edgbaston
13.11.90 Chris Walker W PTS 6 Edgbaston
24.01.91 Franki Moro W PTS 6 Brierley Hill
07.10.91 Paul Murray W RSC 7 Birmingham
09.12.91 Paul McCarthy W PTS 8 Brierley Hill
03.03.92 Paul Wesley W PTS 10 Cradley Heath
(Vacant Midlands Area Middleweight Title)
28.10.92 Darron Griffiths L PTS 10 Cardiff
(Elim. British Middleweight Title)
18.05.93 Ernie Loveridge W PTS 8 Edgbaston
28.07.93 Paul Wesley W RSC 3 Brixton
(Midlands Area Middleweight Title Defence)
27.08.94 Carlos Christie W PTS 8 Cardiff
29.11.94 Neville Brown L RSC 9 Cannock
(British Middleweight Title Challenge)
17.01.95 Colin Manners W PTS 8 Worcester
30.06.95 Derek Wormald L PTS 10 Doncaster
(Elim. British Middleweight Title)
Career: 26 contests, won 19, lost 7.

(Robert) Rocky Ferrari (Ewing)

Glasgow. *Born* Glasgow, 27 October, 1972
Lightweight. Ht. 5'7"
Managers A. Melrose/A. Morrison

25.01.91 James Hunter W CO 1 Stoke

11.02.91 Sol Francis W RSC 5 Glasgow
05.03.91 Chris Saunders W PTS 4 Glasgow
11.09.92 Mick Mulcahy W PTS 6 Glasgow
28.02.94 Kevin McKenzie L PTS 6 Marton
13.05.94 Colin Innes W PTS 6 Kilmarnock
02.03.95 Kevin McKenzie DREW 6 Glasgow
21.04.95 Jyrki Vierela L RTD 3 Glasgow
Career: 8 contests, won 5, drew 1, lost 2.

Daren Fifield

Oxford. *Born* Wantage, 9 October, 1969
Former Commonwealth Flyweight
Champion. Ht. 5'2"
Manager F. Maloney

22.10.92 Glyn Shepherd DREW 4 Bethnal Green
10.12.92 Anthony Hanna W RSC 6 Bethnal Green
14.01.93 Graham McGrath W PTS 4 Mayfair
17.02.93 Kevin Jenkins DREW 6 Bethnal Green
14.04.93 Mickey Cantwell L PTS 10 Kensington
(Vacant Southern Area Flyweight Title)
28.08.93 Eric Burton W CO 1 Bismark, USA
13.10.93 Danny Porter W RSC 9 Bethnal Green
(Vacant Commonwealth Flyweight Title)
09.02.94 Danny Porter W RSC 6 Bethnal Green
(Commonwealth Flyweight Title Defence)
15.06.94 Ladislao Vazquez W RSC 4 Southwark
03.08.94 Luigi Camputaro L PTS 12 Bristol
(European Flyweight Title Challenge)
20.12.94 Francis Ampofo L RSC 2 Bethnal Green
(Commonwealth Flyweight Title Defence. British Flyweight Title Challenge)
30.03.95 Ricky Beard L RSC 8 Bethnal Green
(Vacant Southern Area Flyweight Title)
Career: 12 contests, won 6, drew 2, lost 4.

Keith Fletcher   Les Clark

Keith Fletcher

Reading. *Born* Reading, 20 July, 1967
Heavyweight. Ht. 6'0"
Manager C. Sanigar

25.06.94 Darren Fearn L PTS 6 Cullompton
24.09.94 John Pettersson W RSC 1 Wembley
12.10.94 Dermot Gascoyne W PTS 6 Sheffield
18.11.94 Art Stacey W PTS 6 Bracknell
04.02.95 Richard Fenton W CO 1 Cardiff
03.03.95 Rob Albon W RSC 3 Bracknell
30.03.95 Pat Passley W RSC 6 Bethnal Green
27.04.95 Julius Francis L PTS 10 Bethnal Green
          *(Southern Area Heavyweight Title
          Challenge)*
25.05.95 John Williams W RSC 2 Reading
16.06.95 Derek Williams W RSC 5 Southwark
Career: 10 contests, won 8, lost 2.

David Flowers

Leeds. *Born* Leeds, 29 December, 1974
L. Heavyweight. Ht. 5'10½"
Manager G. Lockwood

25.03.95 Laurence Rowe W PTS 6 Rothwell
19.05.95 Michael Pinnock W PTS 6 Leeds
Career: 2 contests, won 2.

Andrew Flute

Coseley. Born Wolverhampton, 5 March,
1970
S. Middleweight. Ht. 6'1"
Manager B. Hearn

24.05.89 Stinger Mason W PTS 6 Hanley
24.10.89 Paul Murray W RSC 4 Wolverhampton
22.03.90 Dave Maxwell W RSC 5
          Wolverhampton
24.05.90 Spencer Alton L RSC 1 Dudley
18.09.90 Tony Hodge W CO 2 Wolverhampton
24.10.90 Nigel Rafferty W CO 6 Dudley
27.11.90 Paul Burton L PTS 6 Stoke
13.03.91 Robert Peel W PTS 6 Stoke
10.04.91 Russell Washer W PTS 6
          Wolverhampton
14.05.91 Alan Richards W PTS 8 Dudley
16.10.91 Karl Barwise L RSC 8 Stoke
05.12.91 Richard Okumu DREW 8 Cannock
17.03.92 Graham Burton W PTS 8
          Wolverhampton
28.04.92 Paul Smith W RSC 5 Wolverhampton
20.01.93 Glen Payton W RSC 4 Wolverhampton
16.03.93 Mark Hale W RSC 2 Wolverhampton
24.04.93 Steve Thomas W RSC 1 Birmingham
21.10.93 Terry Magee W RSC 6 Bayswater
26.01.94 Neville Brown L RTD 7 Birmingham
          (British Middleweight Title Challenge)
16.03.94 Graham Burton W PTS 6 Birmingham
29.10.94 Carlos Christie L PTS 8 Cannock
29.11.94 Mark Dawson W PTS 8 Cannock
17.01.95 Chris Richards W PTS 6 Worcester
11.05.95 Paul Murray W PTS 6 Dudley
Career: 24 contests, won 18, drew 1, lost 5.

Ali Forbes

Sydenham. *Born* London, 7 March, 1961
Former British S. Middleweight Champion.
Former Undefeated Southern Area S.
Middleweight Champion. Ht. 5'9"
Manager Self

16.02.89 David Haycock W RSC 4 Battersea
22.06.90 Andy Marlow W RTD 4 Gillingham
26.09.90 Peter Vosper W PTS 6 Mayfair
06.02.91 Adrian Wright W PTS 6 Battersea
03.04.91 Karl Barwise W RTD 4 Bethnal Green
16.05.91 Quinn Paynter DREW 6 Battersea
01.06.91 Paul McCarthy W CO 2 Bethnal Green

11.03.92 Ian Strudwick L PTS 10 Solihull
          *(Southern Area S. Middleweight Title
          Challenge)*
29.10.92 Nick Manners W RSC 3 Leeds
28.11.93 Carlos Christie W CO 4 Southwark
06.03.94 Richard Bustin W PTS 10 Southwark
          *(Vacant Southern Area S. Middleweight
          Title)*
29.09.94 Darron Griffiths W PTS 12 Bethnal
          Green
          *(Final Elim. British S. Middleweight
          Title)*
23.01.95 Fidel Castro W PTS 12 Bethnal Green
          (Vacant British S. Middleweight Title)
27.04.95 Sammy Storey L PTS 12 Bethnal
          Green
          (British S. Middleweight Title Defence)
Career: 14 contests, won 11, drew 1, lost 2.

Maurice Forbes

Brixton. *Born* Jamaica, 24 June, 1968
Welterweight. Ht. 5'10½"
Manager Self

23.05.93 Michael Dick W RSC 1 Brockley
25.06.93 Kenny Scott W RSC 2 Battersea
14.08.93 Phil Found W PTS 4 Hammersmith
14.04.94 Dave Maj W RTD 2 Battersea
22.05.94 Trevor Meikle W RTD 3 Crystal Palace
21.07.94 Michael Smyth L RSC 3 Battersea
27.11.94 Marty Duke W PTS 6 Southwark
31.03.95 Steve McGovern W PTS 6 Crystal
          Palace
02.06.95 Gordon Blair W RSC 4 Bethnal Green
Career: 9 contests, won 8, lost 1.

Hugh Forde

Birmingham. *Born* Birmingham, 7 May,
1964
L. Welterweight. Former British &
Commonwealth S. Featherweight
Champion. Former Undefeated Midlands
Area S. Featherweight Champion. Ht. 5'9"
Manager Self

13.05.86 Little Currie W PTS 6 Digbeth
26.06.86 Carl Cleasby W RSC 3 Edgbaston
22.09.86 Carl Gaynor W PTS 6 Edgbaston
25.10.86 Tony Graham W PTS 6 Stevenage
03.11.86 John Bennie W RSC 3 Edgbaston
08.12.86 Darren Connellan W PTS 6 Edgbaston
21.01.87 Craig Walsh W PTS 8 Solihull
07.04.87 Gary Maxwell W PTS 8 West
          Bromwich
24.04.87 Lambsy Kayani W PTS 8 Liverpool
14.12.87 Patrick Kamy W PTS 8 Edgbaston
19.01.88 Billy Cawley W PTS 8 Kings Heath
05.04.88 Rudy Valentino W RSC 2 Birmingham
17.06.88 Gary Maxwell W RSC 2 Edgbaston
          *(Vacant Midlands Area S.
          Featherweight Title)*
10.10.88 Wayne Weekes W RSC 7 Edgbaston
28.11.88 Brian Cullen W RTD 4 Edgbaston
08.05.89 Paul Bowen W RSC 4 Edgbaston
31.10.89 Brian Roche W RSC 2 Manchester
          *(Final Elim. British S. Featherweight
          Title)*
14.02.90 Harold Warren W PTS 8 Brentwood
25.04.90 Delfino Perez W RSC 2 Brighton
18.09.90 Joey Jacobs W RSC 11
          Wolverhampton
          *(British S. Featherweight Title
          Challenge)*

24.10.90 Kevin Pritchard L CO 4 Dudley
          *(British S. Featherweight Title
          Defence)*
27.02.91 Tony Pep L RSC 9 Wolverhampton
14.05.91 Richard Joyce W RTD 5 Dudley
10.09.91 Thunder Aryeh W PTS 12
          Wolverhampton
          *(Commonwealth S. Featherweight Title
          Challenge)*
12.11.91 Paul Harvey L RSC 3 Wolverhampton
          *(Commonwealth S. Featherweight Title
          Defence)*
02.11.92 Karl Taylor W PTS 6 Wolverhampton
28.09.93 Andreas Panayi L PTS 8 Liverpool
23.02.94 Carlos Chase W PTS 6 Watford
03.08.94 Ross Hale L RSC 7 Bristol
          *(British L. Welterweight Title
          Challenge)*
27.02.95 Carl Wright L PTS 6 Barrow
16.06.95 Shea Neary L RTD 6 Liverpool
Career: 31 contests, won 24, lost 7.

John Foreman

Birmingham. *Born* Birmingham, 6
November, 1967
Former Midlands Area Cruiserweight
Champion. Ht. 6'0"
Manager Self

26.10.87 Randy B. Powell W RSC 1
          Birmingham
18.11.87 Dave Owens L RSC 5 Solihull
16.03.88 John Fairbairn W RSC 6 Solihull
05.04.88 David Jono W CO 1 Birmingham
11.04.88 Byron Pullen W PTS 6 Northampton
17.06.88 Gus Mendes W RSC 5 Edgbaston
28.11.88 Dave Owens W CO 1 Edgbaston
24.01.89 Crawford Ashley L RSC 4 Kings Heath
13.11.89 Everton Blake W PTS 6 Brierley Hill
03.12.89 Chris Coughlin W RSC 2 Birmingham
19.03.90 Abner Blackstock W PTS 8 Brierley
          Hill
04.06.90 Brian Schumacher W RSC 4 Edgbaston
03.09.90 Roy Skeldon L RTD 6 Dudley
          *(Midlands Area L. Heavyweight Title
          Challenge & Elim. British L.
          Heavyweight Title)*
18.04.91 Richard Bustin L PTS 8 Earls Court
22.06.91 Gil Lewis DREW 6 Earls Court
16.12.91 Steve McCarthy L PTS 8 Southampton
26.01.92 Fabrice Tiozzo L RSC 6 Saint-Ouen,
          France
29.05.92 Bobbi Joe Edwards W RSC 4
          Manchester
06.10.92 Eddie Smulders L RSC 4 Antwerp,
          Belgium
20.03.93 Anthony Hembrick L RSC 6
          Dusseldorf. Germany
06.12.93 Zak Chelli W RSC 4 Birmingham
08.03.94 Simon McDougall L PTS 6 Edgbaston
07.04.94 L. A. Williams W RSC 7 Walsall
14.04.94 Mark Prince L CO 3 Battersea
17.10.94 Art Stacey W PTS 8 Birmingham
05.12.94 Cordwell Hylton W PTS 10
          Birmingham
          *(Midlands Area Cruiserweight Title
          Challenge)*
07.03.95 Tony Booth W PTS 6 Edgbaston
20.03.95 Nigel Rafferty L PTS 10 Birmingham
          *(Midlands Area Cruiserweight Title
          Defence)*
Career: 28 contests, won 16, drew 1, lost 11.

Frankie Foster

Newcastle. *Born* Newcastle, 25 May, 1968
Former Northern Area S. Featherweight
Champion. Ht. 5'6"
Manager Self

22.09.88	Mick Mulcahy W PTS 6 Newcastle
29.09.88	Paul Chedgzoy W PTS 6 Sunderland
07.11.88	Pete Roberts W PTS 4 Bradford
01.12.88	Peter English L PTS 8 Manchester
26.01.89	James Jiora W PTS 6 Newcastle
09.03.89	John Townsley W PTS 8 Glasgow
03.04.89	Jose Tuominen L PTS 4 Helsinki, Finland
24.04.89	Jim Moffat L PTS 8 Glasgow
21.06.89	Paul Gadney L PTS 6 Eltham
02.10.89	Shaun White DREW 6 Bradford
11.10.89	Lester James W PTS 6 Stoke
21.10.89	Chad Broussard L PTS 6 Middlesbrough
13.11.89	Steve Winstanley L PTS 6 Bradford
24.01.90	Kid Sumali W PTS 6 Sunderland
05.02.90	Muhammad Shaffique L PTS 6 Brierley Hill
20.03.90	Dominic McGuigan DREW 4 Hartlepool
26.04.90	Les Walsh W PTS 8 Manchester
04.06.90	Stuart Rimmer W PTS 6 Glasgow
18.10.90	Nigel Senior W CO 2 Hartlepool *(Vacant Northern Area S. Featherweight Title)*
19.11.90	Sugar Gibiliru DREW 8 Manchester
22.04.91	John Doherty L PTS 10 Glasgow *(Elim. British S. Featherweight Title)*
14.08.91	Gianni di Napoli L PTS 8 Alcamo, Italy
22.10.91	Darren Elsdon L RSC 7 Hartlepool *(Northern Area S. Featherweight Title Defence)*
31.03.92	Sugar Gibiliru L PTS 8 Stockport
10.09.92	Darren Elsdon W PTS 10 Sunderland *(Northern Area S. Featherweight Title Challenge)*
04.07.93	Stanford Ngcebeshe L PTS 10 Eldorado, South Africa
21.03.94	Dave McHale L PTS 8 Glasgow
29.09.94	Charles Shepherd L RSC 3 Tynemouth
02.03.95	Dominic McGuigan L RSC 6 Cramlington *(Northern Area S. Featherweight Title Defence)*

Career: 29 contests, won 11, drew 3, lost 15.

Steve Foster

Manchester. *Born* Salford, 28 December, 1960
L. Middleweight. Ht. 5'8½"
Manager F. Warren

09.02.81	Pat McCarthy W RSC 3 Manchester
16.03.81	Dave Dunn L PTS 6 Manchester
26.03.81	John Lindo L RSC 1 Newcastle
28.11.85	Malcolm Melvin DREW 6 Ilkeston
06.03.86	Taffy Morris L PTS 6 Manchester
17.04.86	Martin Kielty W RSC 4 Wolverhampton
25.11.86	Shamus Casey W PTS 8 Manchester
28.04.87	Cyril Jackson W RSC 7 Manchester
11.05.87	Fidel Castro L PTS 8 Manchester
19.10.87	Cyril Jackson W RTD 3 Manchester
14.12.87	Sean Leighton L PTS 8 Bradford
27.01.88	Sammy Storey L RSC 6 Belfast
20.04.88	Tony Collins L PTS 4 Muswell Hill

19.10.88	Ray Close L RSC 2 Belfast
14.12.88	Fran Harding L PTS 6 Kirkby
01.03.89	Dario Deabreu W RSC 2 Cardiff
06.03.89	Steve Aquilina W PTS 6 Manchester
03.12.89	Antonio Fernandez W PTS 8 Birmingham
06.02.90	Sean O'Phoenix W RSC 4 Oldham
14.03.90	Andy Till L RTD 5 Battersea
02.06.90	Ian Chantler DREW 4 Manchester
22.02.91	Kesem Clayton W CO 6 Manchester
20.09.91	Colin Pitters W RTD 5 Manchester
07.12.91	Shamus Casey W PTS 8 Manchester
10.03.92	Mike Phillips W RSC 4 Bury
25.04.92	Mark Jay W RSC 7 Manchester
28.11.92	Shaun Cummins L PTS 12 Manchester *(Vacant Penta-Continental L. Middleweight Title)*
25.07.93	Russell Washer W PTS 6 Oldham
18.12.93	Kevin Sheeran W RSC 4 Manchester
10.09.94	Robert McCracken L PTS 12 Birmingham *(British L. Middleweight Title Challenge)*
10.06.95	Tony Enna W RSC 6 Manchester

Career: 31 contests, won 17, drew 2, lost 12.

Tony Foster

Hull. *Born* Hull, 9 July, 1964
Central Area Lightweight Champion. Ht. 5'7"
Manager S. Pollard

04.09.87	Paul Kennedy L PTS 6 Gateshead
17.09.87	Ian Hosten L PTS 6 Gravesend
28.09.87	Steve Winstanley L PTS 6 Bradford
06.10.87	Roy Doyle L PTS 6 Manchester
03.11.87	Darren Darby L PTS 6 Cottingham
25.11.87	Kevin McCoy W RSC 4 Cottingham
02.12.87	Alan Roberts W RSC 5 Piccadilly
11.12.87	Mitchell King DREW 8 Coalville
11.01.88	Paul Chedgzoy W PTS 6 Manchester
25.01.88	Johnny Walker L PTS 6 Glasgow
01.02.88	Sean Hogg W PTS 6 Manchester
11.02.88	Lee Amass L RSC 6 Gravesend
28.03.88	Darryl Pettit W PTS 6 Bradford
22.04.88	Paul Charters L PTS 6 Gateshead
09.05.88	Gary Maxwell L PTS 6 Nottingham
17.05.88	Warren Slaney W PTS 6 Leicester
23.05.88	Harry Escott W RSC 6 Bradford
26.09.88	Peter Bradley L PTS 8 Piccadilly
17.10.88	John Townsley L PTS 8 Glasgow
15.11.88	Steve Pollard W RSC 3 Hull
12.12.88	Mark Kelly W PTS 6 Nottingham
08.02.89	Paul Gadney W PTS 6 Kensington
03.04.89	Jari Gronroos W PTS 4 Helsinki, Finland
15.04.89	Paul Moylett W PTS 6 Salisbury
27.06.89	Ian Honeywood L PTS 6 Kensington
10.10.89	Steve Pollard W RSC 3 Hull
16.11.89	Sugar Gibiliru W PTS 8 Manchester
30.11.89	Joey Jacobs L CO 4 Oldham
30.01.90	Sugar Gibiliru L PTS 10 Manchester *(Vacant Central Area Lightweight Title)*
21.04.90	Marvin P. Gray DREW 6 Sunderland
22.05.90	Marvin P. Gray L PTS 6 Stockton
15.06.90	Marcel Herbert L RSC 4 Telford
15.02.91	Jimmy Bredahl L PTS 6 Randers, Denmark
05.03.91	Floyd Havard L PTS 8 Millwall
15.04.91	Dave Anderson L PTS 8 Glasgow
12.05.91	Alain Simoes W PTS 8 Voiron, France
11.09.91	Billy Schwer L PTS 8 Hammersmith

21.11.91	Giovanni Parisi L RSC 6 Perugia, Italy
31.01.92	Angel Mona L PTS 8 Esch, Luxembourg
30.03.92	Ian Honeywood L RSC 4 Eltham
13.06.92	Pierre Lorcy L PTS 8 Levallois Perret, France
16.10.92	Tony Doyle W PTS 8 Hull
31.10.92	Dingaan Thobela L PTS 8 Earls Court
14.01.93	Allan Hall L PTS 6 Mayfair
27.02.93	Steve Foran DREW 6 Ellesmere Port
09.07.93	Giorgio Campanella L PTS 8 Barisardo, Italy
12.11.93	Micky Hall W PTS 8 Hull
10.02.94	Kid McAuley W RTD 4 Hull
18.02.94	Racheed Lawal L PTS 8 Randers, Denmark
21.04.94	Charles Shepherd W PTS 10 Hull *(Vacant Central Area Lightweight Title)*
24.11.94	Norman Dhalie W RTD 7 Hull
07.12.94	Shea Neary L RSC 2 Stoke
25.02.95	Cham Joof L PTS 8 Millwall
11.05.95	Spencer McCracken L PTS 6 Dudley
30.06.95	Andy Holligan L CO 2 Liverpool

Career: 55 contests, won 20, drew 3, lost 32.

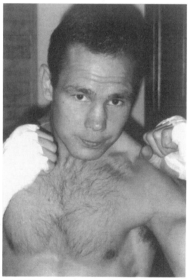

Phil Found   Les Clark

Phil Found

Hereford. *Born* Hereford, 9 June, 1967
L. Welterweight. Ht. 5'9"
Manager D. Gardiner

30.03.93	Paul Davies W PTS 6 Cardiff
29.04.93	Delroy Leslie L PTS 6 Mayfair
09.06.93	Jason Beard L PTS 6 Lewisham
26.06.93	Paul Knights L PTS 4 Earls Court
14.08.93	Maurice Forbes L PTS 4 Hammersmith
20.09.93	Garry Burrell W RSC 4 Glasgow
16.10.93	Julien Lorcy L PTS 6 Levallois, France
10.11.93	Robert Dickie W RTD 2 Ystrad
16.12.93	Gareth Jordan L PTS 6 Newport
20.01.94	Cham Joof L RSC 1 Battersea
02.03.94	Mark Legg W RTD 4 Solihull
16.03.94	Mark Elliot L PTS 6 Birmingham
27.04.94	Micky Hall W RSC 5 Solihull
17.05.94	Colin Dunne L PTS 6 Kettering

13.06.94	Tony Brown W RSC 4 Liverpool
11.10.94	Jason Rowland L RSC 4 Bethnal Green
22.11.94	Alan Temple L PTS 6 Bristol
08.03.95	Gareth Lawrence L PTS 6 Cardiff
30.03.95	P. J. Gallagher L PTS 6 Bethnal Green

Career: 19 contests, won 6, lost 13.

Simon Frailing

Hayes. *Born* London, 13 June, 1966
Lightweight. Ht. 5'7"
Manager D. Gunn

29.04.93	Bruce Ruegg DREW 6 Hayes
15.06.93	Bruce Ruegg L PTS 6 Hemel Hempstead
14.08.93	Mike Anthony Brown L RSC 4 Hammersmith
30.09.93	Norman Dhalie L PTS 6 Hayes
09.12.93	Andrew Reed W PTS 6 Watford
25.01.94	Craig Kelley L PTS 4 Piccadilly
10.03.94	Marco Fattore DREW 6 Watford
17.05.94	T. J. Smith L RSC 1 Kettering
03.03.95	Jason Lepre W PTS 6 Bracknell
25.05.95	Lewis Reynolds L CO 1 Reading

Career: 10 contests, won 2, drew 2, lost 6.

Chris Francis

Stepney. *Born* London, 23 October, 1968
Lightweight. Ht. 5'6"
Manager Self

02.10.91	Rick Dimmock W PTS 6 Barking
11.02.92	Paul Donaghey L CO 2 Barking
17.02.93	Jason Lepre W RSC 2 Bethnal Green
31.03.93	Steve Patton W CO 4 Bethnal Green
13.10.93	Anthony Wanza W RSC 2 Bethnal Green
27.05.94	Andrew Reed W PTS 6 Ashford
23.06.95	Brian Robb W RSC 1 Bethnal Green

Career: 7 contests, won 6, lost 1.

Dean Francis

Basingstoke. *Born* Basingstoke, 23 January, 1974
S. Middleweight. Ht. 5'10½"
Manager C. Sanigar

28.05.94	Darren Littlewood W PTS 4 Queensway
17.06.94	Martin Jolley W PTS 6 Plymouth
21.07.94	Horace Fleary W RSC 4 Tooting
02.09.94	Steve Osborne W RTD 4 Spitalfields
27.10.94	Tony Booth W CO 1 Bayswater
22.11.94	Darron Griffiths W RTD 1 Bristol
30.03.95	Paul Murray W RSC 2 Bethnal Green
25.05.95	Hunter Clay W RSC 8 Reading
16.06.95	Paul Murray W RTD 3 Southwark

Career: 9 contests, won 9.

Julius Francis

Woolwich. *Born* Peckham, 8 December, 1964
Southern Area Heavyweight Champion. Ht. 6'2"
Manager F. Maloney

23.05.93	Graham Arnold W RSC 5 Brockley
23.06.93	Joey Paladino W CO 4 Edmonton
24.07.93	Andre Tisdale W PTS 4 Atlantic City, USA
28.08.93	Don Sargent W RSC 2 Bismark, USA
01.12.93	John Keeton W PTS 4 Bethnal Green
27.04.94	Manny Burgo W PTS 4 Bethnal Green

25.05.94	John Ruiz L CO 4 Bristol
12.11.94	Conroy Nelson W RSC 4 Dublin
23.11.94	Gary Charlton W RSC 1 Piccadilly
23.02.95	Damien Caesar W RSC 8 Southwark
	(Vacant Southern Area Heavyweight Title)
27.04.95	Keith Fletcher W PTS 10 Bethnal Green
	(Southern Area Heavyweight Title Defence)
25.05.95	Steve Garber W PTS 8 Reading

Career: 12 contests, won 11, lost 1.

Andrew Furlong   Les Clark

Andrew Furlong

Hammersmith. *Born* Paddington, 29 July, 1967
L. Middleweight. Ht. 5'9½"
Manager Self

14.11.85	Robert Southey W PTS 6 Merton
22.11.85	Tony Richards W PTS 6 Longford
10.01.86	Bill Smith W PTS 6 Fulham
30.01.86	Marvin P. Gray W PTS 6 Merton
27.02.86	Barry Bacon W RSC 6 Merton
15.04.86	Willie Wilson W PTS 8 Merton
28.05.86	Billy Joe Dee W RSC 2 Lewisham
04.09.86	Les Remikie W PTS 8 Merton
22.10.86	Peppy Muire L RSC 2 Greenwich
20.11.86	Chubby Martin DREW 8 Merton
12.01.87	Chubby Martin W PTS 8 Ealing
22.01.87	Brian Sonny Nickels L PTS 8 Bethnal Green
25.02.87	Mark Dinnadge DREW 8 Lewisham
18.03.87	Tony Borg W PTS 8 Queensway
01.04.87	Frankie Lake W PTS 8 Southsea
30.04.87	Andrew Prescod W PTS 8 Bethnal Green
27.05.87	Wayne Weekes L RSC 1 Lewisham
25.09.87	Oliver Henry W RTD 5 Tooting
03.12.87	Eamonn McAuley W RTD 3 Belfast
18.01.88	Ian Honeywood L PTS 8 Mayfair
08.03.88	Neil Haddock W PTS 6 Holborn
19.09.88	Tony Richards L RSC 7 Mayfair
14.11.88	Joni Nyman L RSC 2 Helsinki, Finland
16.05.89	Ian John-Lewis W RSC 3 Wandsworth

12.06.89	Rocky Kelly L RSC 5 Battersea
11.10.89	Brian Robinson L PTS 6 Millwall
02.05.91	Delroy Waul L RSC 5 Northampton
30.06.91	Lee Crocker DREW 6 Southwark
12.02.92	Gary Pemberton W PTS 6 Wembley
25.03.92	Clay O'Shea DREW 6 Kensington
13.05.92	Clay O'Shea DREW 6 Kensington
16.06.92	Mickey Hughes L CO 1 Dagenham
02.10.92	Patrick Vungbo L RSC 8 Waregem, Belgium
10.04.93	Robin Reid L PTS 6 Swansea
20.05.94	Barry Thorogood W RSC 4 Acton
04.06.94	Robin Reid L RSC 2 Cardiff
18.11.94	Geoff McCreesh L PTS 6 Bracknell

Career: 37 contests, won 18, drew 5, lost 14.

Gypsy John Fury

Haslingden. *Born* Leiston, 22 May, 1964
Heavyweight. Ht. 6'3¾"
Manager F. Warren/N. Basso

28.04.87	Adam Fogerty L PTS 4 Halifax
07.10.87	Steve Garber W PTS 6 Burnley
10.11.87	Paul Sheldon W PTS 4 Batley
03.12.87	Mick Cordon W PTS 6 Leeds
23.02.88	Michael Murray W PTS 6 Oldham
28.03.88	Ian Priest W PTS 6 Stoke
26.09.88	Abner Blackstock W PTS 8 Leicester
13.02.89	Dave Hopkins DREW 6 Helsinki, Finland
21.06.89	Neil Malpass L PTS 10 Doncaster
	(Vacant Central Area Heavyweight Title)
02.06.90	Michael Murray W RTD 6 Manchester
16.02.91	Cesare di Benedetto W PTS 10 Thornaby
09.10.91	Henry Akinwande L CO 3 Manchester
	(Elim. British Heavyweight Title)
10.06.95	Steve Garber L CO 4 Manchester

Career: 13 contests, won 8, drew 1, lost 4.

Gypsy John Fury   Harry Goodwin

Carl Gaffney

Leeds. *Born* Leeds, 15 April, 1964
Heavyweight. Ht. 6'5"
Manager T. Callighan

12.05.84	Steve Abadom W RSC 3 Hanley
02.10.84	Theo Josephs W PTS 6 Leeds
23.01.85	Alphonso Forbes L CO 1 Solihull

25.03.85	Dave Madden W RSC 1 Huddersfield
30.05.85	Denroy Bryan W RSC 1 Halifax
21.11.85	Al Malcolm W PTS 8 Huddersfield
16.01.86	Joe Threlfall L CO 3 Preston
20.02.86	Chris Devine W RSC 8 Halifax
24.10.86	Damien Marignan L PTS 8 Guadalupe, FW1
01.12.86	Michael Simwelu L RSC 7 Arnhem, Holland
14.12.88	Keith Ferdinand W PTS 8 Bethnal Green
14.06.89	Rodolfo Marin L RSC 2 Madrid, Spain
25.10.89	Andrei Oreshkin L RSC 1 Wembley
02.05.91	Sean Hunter W PTS 6 Kensington
19.09.91	Michael Murray L RSC 8 Stockport
	(Vacant Central Area Heavyweight Title)
09.02.92	Steve Garber W PTS 6 Bradford
13.02.93	Brian Nielson L PTS 6 Randers, Denmark
26.03.93	Mikael Lindblad L RSC 2 Copenhagen, Denmark
13.10.93	Manny Burgo L PTS 6 Bethnal Green
21.12.93	Scott Welch L RSC 3 Mayfair
15.06.94	Jeff Pegues W DIS 2 Southwark
17.08.94	Clifton Mitchell L CO 1 Sheffield
13.12.94	Darren Corbett L RSC 1 Potters Bar
07.02.95	Kevin McBride L RSC 3 Ipswich
11.03.95	Neil Kirkwood L RSC 2 Barnsley
	(Vacant Central Area Heavyweight Title)

Career: 25 contests, won 10, lost 15.

Michael Gale

Leeds. *Born* Cardiff, 28 October, 1967
Cruiserweight. Central Area L.
Heavyweight Champion. Ht. 5'11"
Manager M. Duff

21.09.89	Dave Lawrence W RTD 4 Harrogate
13.11.89	Coco Collins W CO 1 Manchester
05.12.89	Randy B. Powell W RSC 1 Dewsbury
11.01.90	Cliff Curtis W RSC 2 Dewsbury
24.01.90	Andy Marlow W RSC 2 Sunderland
03.03.90	Peter Vosper W RSC 2 Wembley
11.04.90	Teo Arvizu W PTS 6 Dewsbury
18.10.90	Mick Queally W RSC 5 Dewsbury
15.11.90	Steve Osborne W PTS 6 Oldham
14.03.91	Carlos Christie W PTS 8 Middleton
21.03.91	David Haycock W RSC 2 Dewsbury
09.05.91	Steve Osborne W RSC 2 Leeds
13.06.91	Graham Burton W CO 4 Hull
27.06.91	Mark Bowen W PTS 8 Leeds
30.10.91	Denys Cronin DREW 8 Leeds
23.01.92	John Kaighin W PTS 8 York
08.04.92	Tony Booth W PTS 8 Leeds
29.10.92	Bobbi Joe Edwards W PTS 10 Leeds
	(Vacant Central Area L. Heavyweight Title)
07.04.93	Brent Kosolofski L RSC 9 Leeds
	(Vacant Commonwealth L. Heavyweight Title)
01.07.93	Tony Booth W PTS 8 York
07.10.93	John Kaighin W PTS 8 York
26.10.94	Bobbi Joe Edwards W PTS 8 Leeds

Career: 22 contests, won 20, drew 1, lost 1.

Jamie Gallagher

Northampton. *Born* Northampton, 16 June, 1970
Welterweight. Ht. 5'8"
Manager J. Cox

28.11.94	Steve Lynch W RSC 3 Northampton
15.03.95	Gary Beardsley L PTS 6 Stoke
03.04.95	Adam Baldwin L PTS 6 Northampton
22.06.95	Shaun O'Neill L PTS 6 Houghton le Spring

Career: 4 contests, won 1, lost 3.

(Patrick) P. J. Gallagher

Wood Green. *Born* Manchester, 14
February, 1973
Lightweight. Ht. 5'7"
Manager F. Maloney

15.09.93	John T. Kelly W RSC 2 Bethnal Green
13.10.93	Mike Morrison W PTS 4 Bethnal Green
01.12.93	Mark Antony W PTS 4 Bethnal Green
09.02.94	Simon Hamblett W RSC 1 Bethnal Green
29.03.94	Brian Coleman W PTS 6 Bethnal Green
15.06.94	Mark O'Callaghan W RSC 4 Southwark
29.09.94	Anthony Campbell W PTS 6 Bethnal Green
12.11.94	Karl Taylor W PTS 6 Dublin
23.01.95	David Thompson W RSC 1 Bethnal Green
30.03.95	Phil Found W PTS 6 Bethnal Green
25.05.95	Marco Fattore W RSC 5 Reading

Career: 11 contests, won 11.

Patrick Gallagher

Tottenham. *Born* Manchester, 23 July, 1971
Lightweight. Ht. 5'7½"
Manager B. Hearn

22.12.92	Karl Taylor W RSC 3 Mayfair
20.02.93	Joe Fannin W RTD 1 Earls Court
21.12.93	Karl Taylor W PTS 6 Mayfair
11.01.94	Mark Antony W RSC 3 Bethnal Green
15.03.94	Karl Taylor W PTS 6 Mayfair
07.11.94	Rudy Valentino W PTS 6 Bethnal Green
27.05.95	Paul Burke L PTS 8 Belfast

Career: 7 contests, won 6, lost 1.

Steve Garber

Bradford. *Born* Bradford, 20 June, 1962
Heavyweight. Ht. 6'6"
Manager Self

22.04.85	Mick Cordon DREW 6 Bradford
30.05.85	Mick Cordon L PTS 6 Blackburn
02.07.85	Joe Threlfall W RSC 2 Preston
03.10.85	Dave Shelton W PTS 4 Bradford
27.11.85	Mick Cordon W PTS 6 Bradford
06.02.86	Mick Cordon L PTS 6 Doncaster
27.04.86	Mick Cordon L PTS 6 Doncaster
22.05.86	Sean Daly W PTS 6 Horwich
18.09.86	Gary McConnell L PTS 6 Weston super Mare
25.09.86	Carl Timbrell W PTS 6 Wolverhampton
22.10.86	Dave Madden W PTS 4 Bradford
01.12.86	Tony Hallett W PTS 6 Nottingham
24.02.87	Gary McConnell L CO 1 Ilford
07.10.87	Gypsy John Fury L PTS 6 Burnley
18.01.88	Mick Cordon W PTS 6 Bradford
11.02.88	John Love L CO 1 Gravesend
21.03.88	Ted Shaw W CO 1 Leicester

22.04.88	Manny Burgo L PTS 6 Gateshead
23.05.88	Ted Shaw W CO 3 Bradford
26.09.88	Gifford Shillingford W RSC 4 Bradford
25.10.88	Paul Lister L PTS 6 Hartlepool
17.11.88	Michael Murray L PTS 6 Stockport
18.01.89	Peter Nyman W PTS 6 Kensington
19.05.89	Joe Threlfall W RSC 3 Gateshead
10.10.89	Lennox Lewis L CO 1 Hull
20.03.90	Chris Hubbert W RSC 1 Hartlepool
05.05.90	Knut Blin L PTS 6 Hamburg, Germany
12.11.90	David Jules W RSC 6 Bradford
30.11.90	Steve Gee W PTS 6 Birmingham
19.03.91	Al Malcolm W RSC 5 Birmingham
30.04.91	Michael Murray L CO 1 Stockport
31.05.91	Axel Schulz L CO 5 Berlin, Germany
10.10.91	Paul Lister L PTS 8 Gateshead
09.02.92	Carl Gaffney L PTS 6 Bradford
05.04.92	David Jules W RSC 4 Bradford
08.05.92	Alexandr Miroshnichenko L RSC 1 Waregem, Belgium
18.07.92	Henry Akinwande L RTD 2 Manchester
24.02.93	J. A. Bugner W RSC 6 Wembley
15.03.94	Scott Welch L RSC 4 Mayfair
21.05.94	Clifton Mitchell L CO 1 Belfast
30.07.94	Richard Bango L CO 1 Bethnal Green
21.02.95	Darren Corbett L PTS 6 Sunderland
25.05.95	Julius Francis L PTS 8 Reading
10.06.95	Gypsy John Fury W CO 4 Manchester

Career: 44 contests, won 20, drew 1, lost 23.

Steve Garber   Harry Goodwin

Dennis Gardner

Slough. *Born* Slough, 29 March, 1970
Welterweight. Ht. 5'10"
Manager W. Ball

18.11.94	Paul Salmon W RSC 1 Bracknell
20.01.95	Charlie Paine W RSC 1 Bethnal Green
03.03.95	Robbie Dunn W RSC 4 Bracknell
26.05.95	Dave Fallon W RSC 2 Norwich

Career: 4 contests, won 4.

Dennis Gardner   Les Clark

Des Gargano (Southern)

Manchester. *Born* Brighton, 20 December, 1960
S. Bantamweight. Ht. 5'5"
Manager J. Doughty

25.01.85	Sugar Gibiliru L PTS 4 Liverpool
18.03.85	Sugar Gibiliru L PTS 6 Liverpool
24.04.85	Glen McLaggon L PTS 6 Stoke
03.06.85	Anthony Wakefield DREW 6 Manchester
17.06.85	Anthony Wakefield W PTS 6 Manchester
03.10.85	Anthony Brown L PTS 6 Liverpool
13.10.85	Gary Maxwell L PTS 6 Sheffield
09.12.85	Robert Newbiggin W PTS 6 Nottingham
16.12.85	Gypsy Johnny W PTS 6 Bradford
24.02.86	Kevin Taylor L PTS 6 Bradford
01.04.86	Carl Cleasby L PTS 6 Leeds
07.04.86	Gerry McBride W PTS 6 Manchester
29.04.86	Pat Clinton L PTS 6 Manchester
23.09.86	David Ingram L PTS 6 Batley
24.11.86	Andrew Steadman L PTS 6 Leicester
03.12.86	Sean Murphy L PTS 6 Muswell Hill
15.12.86	Tony Heath L PTS 8 Loughborough
30.01.87	Nigel Crook L PTS 6 Kirkby
16.02.87	Pat Clinton L PTS 6 Glasgow
13.04.87	Jimmy Lee W PTS 6 Manchester
26.05.87	John Green L PTS 6 Oldham
19.10.87	John Green L PTS 6 Manchester
28.10.87	Paul Thornton W RSC 6 Stoke
09.11.87	Tony Heath L PTS 6 Leicester
26.01.88	Graham O'Malley L PTS 4 Hartlepool
23.03.88	Lambsy Kayani L PTS 6 Sheffield
29.03.88	Graham O'Malley L PTS 8 Marton
25.04.88	Ronnie Stephenson W PTS 8 Bradford
06.06.88	Darryl Pettit W PTS 6 Manchester
13.06.88	Joe Mullen L PTS 6 Glasgow
05.09.88	Wull Strike DREW 6 Glasgow
22.09.88	John Davison L PTS 8 Newcastle
29.09.88	John Davison L PTS 8 Sunderland
10.10.88	Shane Silvester L PTS 8 Edgbaston
18.10.88	Peter English L PTS 4 Oldham

28.10.88	Eyub Can L PTS 6 Copenhagen, Denmark
21.11.88	Ronnie Stephenson W PTS 6 Leicester
29.11.88	Chris Clarkson W PTS 6 Manchester
07.12.88	Renny Edwards L PTS 6 Aberavon
16.12.88	Jimmy Clark L PTS 6 Brentwood
14.02.89	Nigel Crook L PTS 10 Manchester
17.03.89	Jimmy Bredahl L PTS 6 Braedstrup, Denmark
17.04.89	Mark Priestley W PTS 8 Middleton
10.05.89	Mark Goult L PTS 8 Solihull
17.05.89	Mark Geraghty L PTS 8 Glasgow
12.06.89	Neil Parry W PTS 6 Manchester
11.07.89	Chris Clarkson L PTS 6 Batley
04.09.89	Ronnie Stephenson W PTS 6 Hull
11.09.89	Paul Dever W RSC 1 Manchester
20.09.89	Miguel Matthews W PTS 6 Stoke
05.10.89	Wayne Windle W PTS 6 Middleton
16.10.89	Wayne Windle L PTS 6 Manchester
31.10.89	Dave McNally L PTS 6 Manchester
10.11.89	Kruga Hydes L PTS 6 Liverpool
20.11.89	Dave Buxton L PTS 6 Leicester
30.11.89	Noel Carroll L PTS 6 Oldham
11.12.89	Joe Kelly L PTS 6 Bayswater
14.02.90	Danny Porter L PTS 6 Brentwood
06.03.90	Bradley Stone L PTS 6 Bethnal Green
17.03.90	John Lowey L RSC 6 Belfast
24.04.90	Jamie Morris W PTS 4 Stoke
09.05.90	Terry Collins L PTS 6 Kensington
16.05.90	Tony Doyle W PTS 6 Hull
11.06.90	Steve Armstrong W PTS 6 Manchester
05.09.90	John George L PTS 6 Stoke
01.10.90	Tony Smith W PTS 6 Cleethorpes
09.10.90	Brian Robb L PTS 6 Wolverhampton
22.10.90	John George L PTS 6 Cleethorpes
26.11.90	Tony Smith W PTS 8 Bury
03.12.90	Tony Smith W PTS 6 Cleethorpes
11.12.90	Stewart Fishermac W PTS 8 Evesham
16.01.91	Tony Smith W PTS 6 Stoke
06.02.91	Tim Driscoll L PTS 6 Bethnal Green
28.02.91	Carl Roberts W PTS 6 Bury
07.05.91	James Drummond L PTS 8 Glasgow
16.05.91	Jimmy Owens L RSC 2 Liverpool
19.08.91	Petteri Rissanen L PTS 4 Helsinki, Finland
02.10.91	Eric George L PTS 6 Solihull
24.10.91	Edward Cook L RSC 5 Glasgow
29.11.91	Harald Geier L DIS 8 Frohsdorf, Austria
31.01.92	Edward Cook L PTS 6 Glasgow
24.02.92	Colin Lynch L PTS 6 Coventry
04.03.92	Neil Armstrong L PTS 6 Glasgow
11.03.92	Dennis Oakes L PTS 6 Stoke
27.04.92	David Ramsden L PTS 6 Bradford
01.06.92	Mark Hargreaves L PTS 6 Manchester
08.06.92	David Ramsden L PTS 6 Bradford
07.10.92	Prince Nassem Hamed L RSC 4 Sunderland
20.11.92	Paul Lloyd L PTS 4 Liverpool
26.02.93	Alex Docherty W RSC 4 Irvine
04.04.93	Rowan Williams L PTS 4 Brockley
26.04.93	Wilson Docherty L PTS 6 Glasgow
01.06.93	Neil Parry W PTS 6 Manchester
09.09.93	James Murray L PTS 6 Glasgow
13.11.93	Richie Wenton L PTS 8 Cullompton
13.12.93	Tony Falcone L PTS 4 Bristol
17.02.94	Daryl McKenzie DREW 6 Bury
25.02.94	Peter Culshaw L PTS 6 Chester
15.03.94	Gary Marston L PTS 8 Stoke
02.06.94	Marty Chestnut W PTS 6 Middleton
20.10.94	Paul Quarmby W PTS 6 Middleton
05.12.94	Chip O'Neill L PTS 6 Houghton le Spring
23.01.95	Patrick Mullings L PTS 4 Bethnal Green

17.02.95	Spencer Oliver L PTS 4 Cumbernauld
03.03.95	Mark Bowers L RTD 2 Bracknell
18.05.95	Paul Quarmby W PTS 6 Middleton
04.06.95	Patrick Mullings L PTS 6 Bethnal Green
16.06.95	Paul Ingle L RSC 2 Southwark

Career: 108 contests, won 31, drew 3, lost 74.

Dermot Gascoyne

Sheffield. *Born* Alfreton, 23 April, 1967
Heavyweight. Ht. 6'5"
Manager F. Warren

17.12.92	John Harewood W RSC 5 Barking
03.02.93	Steve Stewart W RSC 4 Earls Court
10.04.93	Denroy Bryan W PTS 6 Swansea
23.10.93	Vance Idiens W RSC 4 Cardiff
17.02.94	John Keeton W RSC 1 Dagenham
09.04.94	Steve Yorath W CO 3 Mansfield
12.10.94	Keith Fletcher L PTS 6 Sheffield

Career: 7 contests, won 6, lost 1.

Terry Gaskin

Doncaster. *Born* Doncaster, 20 October, 1974
Bantamweight. Ht. 5'4"
Manager H. Hayes

28.03.94	Keith Knox L PTS 6 Musselburgh
09.05.94	Tiger Singh L RSC 2 Bradford
26.09.94	Ian Baillie W RSC 3 Bradford
29.10.94	Neil Parry L PTS 6 Cannock
28.11.94	Tiger Singh L PTS 6 Manchester
08.12.94	Ian Baillie W RTD 3 Hull
11.03.95	Neil Parry DREW 6 Barnsley
22.03.95	Neil Parry L PTS 8 Stoke
19.05.95	Shaun Hall L RSC 3 Leeds

Career: 9 contests, won 2, drew 1, lost 6.

Lou Gent

Streatham. *Born* London, 21 April, 1965
Former Undefeated WBC International
S. Middleweight Champion. Former
Undefeated Southern Area Cruiserweight
Champion. Ht. 5'10½"
Manager Self

18.09.84	Wes Taylor W PTS 6 Merton
05.02.85	Harry Andrews W PTS 6 Battersea
26.02.85	Lee White W PTS 6 Battersea
23.03.85	Simon Harris L PTS 6 Strand
30.04.85	Tee Jay DREW 6 Merton
12.09.85	Harry Andrews W RSC 2 Merton
25.10.85	Winston Burnett W PTS 6 Fulham
14.11.85	Winston Burnett W PTS 8 Merton
11.12.85	Serg Fame L RSC 2 Fulham
27.02.86	John Williams W RSC 4 Merton
20.03.86	Serg Fame L CO 2 Merton
16.06.86	Blaine Logsdon W PTS 8 Manchester
04.09.86	Chris Devine W RSC 6 Merton
16.10.86	Jerry Reed W RSC 7 Merton
20.11.86	Gypsy Carman W CO 1 Merton
29.01.87	Glazz Campbell W PTS 6 Merton
26.03.87	Danny Lawford L RSC 7 Merton
18.03.88	Abner Blackstock W RSC 5 Wandsworth
22.04.88	Glenn McCrory L RTD 8 Gateshead *(British & Commonwealth Cruiserweight Title Challenge)*
16.02.89	Lennie Howard W RSC 2 Battersea *(Vacant Southern Area Cruiserweight Title)*
26.04.89	Cyril Minnus W DIS 3 Battersea

93

Lou Gent (left) pictured here against Johnny Melfah   Les Clark

22.02.90	Gypsy Carman W PTS 10 Wandsworth *(Southern Area Cruiserweight Title Defence)*	
28.03.90	Johnny Nelson L CO 4 Bethnal Green *(British Cruiserweight Title Challenge)*	
18.10.90	Jose Seys W PTS 8 Wandsworth	
20.03.91	Derek Myers W RSC 7 Wandsworth *(Elim. British L. Heavyweight Title)*	
16.05.91	Gus Mendes W CO 8 Battersea	
30.10.91	Henry Wharton DREW 12 Leeds *(Commonwealth S. Middleweight Title Challenge)*	
25.02.92	Fidel Castro L PTS 12 Crystal Palace *(British S. Middleweight Title Challenge)*	
12.05.92	Johnny Melfah L RSC 3 Crystal Palace	
14.07.92	Simon Collins W RSC 5 Mayfair	
15.09.92	Karl Barwise W RSC 6 Crystal Palace	
16.02.93	Hunter Clay W PTS 12 Tooting *(WBC International S. Middleweight Title Challenge)*	
26.06.93	Nigel Benn L RSC 4 Earls Court *(WBC S. Middleweight Title Challenge)*	
28.07.94	Hunter Clay L TD 9 Tooting *(Vacant WBC International S. Middleweight Title)*	

Career: 34 contests, won 22, drew 2, lost 10.

Trevor George

Consett. *Born* Annfield Plain, 2 October, 1967
Lightweight. Ht. 5'7"
Manager Self

06.10.94	Paul Scott L PTS 6 Cramlington
13.10.94	Shaun O'Neill W RSC 6 Houghton le Spring
23.01.95	Garry Burrell W PTS 6 Glasgow
30.01.95	Leo Turner W PTS 6 Bradford
16.02.95	Dave Clavering L PTS 6 Bury

Career: 5 contests, won 3, lost 2.

Mark Geraghty

Glasgow. *Born* Paisley, 25 August, 1965
Scottish S. Featherweight Champion. Ht. 5'6"
Manager Self

14.11.88	Mark Priestley W PTS 6 Glasgow
27.01.89	Gordon Stobie W PTS 6 Durham
14.02.89	Gary Hickman L PTS 6 Sunderland
09.03.89	Chris Clarkson W PTS 6 Glasgow
20.03.89	Ian Johnson L PTS 6 Nottingham
24.04.89	Sean Hogg W PTS 6 Glasgow
17.05.89	Des Gargano W PTS 8 Glasgow
09.06.89	Jimmy Bredahl L PTS 6 Aarhus, Denmark
02.10.89	Steve Winstanley L PTS 6 Bradford
20.11.89	Gordon Shaw W RSC 4 Glasgow
22.01.90	Neil Leitch W PTS 8 Glasgow
19.03.90	Joe Donohoe L RSC 3 Glasgow
17.09.90	Peter Judson L PTS 8 Glasgow
08.10.90	Peter Judson L PTS 8 Glasgow
19.11.90	Tony Doyle W PTS 8 Glasgow
27.11.90	Muhammad Shaffique L PTS 8 Glasgow
06.03.91	Neil Leitch W PTS 10 Glasgow *(Vacant Scottish S. Featherweight Title)*
01.05.91	Pete Buckley L PTS 8 Solihull
03.06.91	Neil Leitch L PTS 8 Glasgow
23.09.91	Neil Leitch W PTS 10 Glasgow *(Scottish S. Featherweight Title Defence)*
09.10.91	Chris Clarkson W PTS 6 Glasgow
20.11.91	Tony Feliciello L RSC 4 Solihull
24.02.92	Colin Innes W PTS 8 Glasgow
18.03.92	Barrie Kelley W PTS 8 Glasgow
19.09.92	Micky Hall W PTS 6 Glasgow
19.10.92	Kevin Lowe W PTS 8 Glasgow
28.11.92	Alan Levene L PTS 6 Manchester
02.04.93	Medhi Labdouni L PTS 8 Fontenay Sous Bois, France
07.06.93	Karl Taylor L PTS 8 Glasgow
06.10.93	Miguel Matthews W PTS 6 York
10.04.94	Miguel Matthews W PTS 8 Glasgow

Career: 31 contests, won 18, lost 13.

Tony Gibbs

Barking. *Born* London, 20 January, 1964
Welterweight. Ht. 5'6¼"
Manager Self

08.10.87	Barry Messam W PTS 6 Bethnal Green
25.02.88	Mike Russell L PTS 6 Bethnal Green

08.03.88	David Lake W PTS 6 Holborn
13.04.88	David Lake W RSC 1 Gravesend
05.05.88	Mark Pearce L RSC 4 Bethnal Green
02.11.88	Gary Logan L PTS 6 Southwark
15.11.88	Tony Britland DREW 6 Piccadilly
30.11.88	Derek Grainger L CO 3 Southwark
13.03.89	Dennis Sullivan W PTS 6 Piccadilly
06.04.89	Davey Hughes L PTS 6 Cardiff
15.09.89	B. F. Williams L PTS 6 High Wycombe
28.09.89	Carlos Chase L PTS 6 Wandsworth
12.10.89	Lee Wicks L CO 2 Southwark
30.11.89	Ross Hale L PTS 6 Mayfair
03.04.90	Andy Robins W PTS 6 Southend
05.06.90	Tim Harmey L PTS 6 Eltham
18.10.90	Felix Kelly DREW 6 Wandsworth
16.11.90	Lindon Scarlett L PTS 6 Telford
08.05.91	Robert McCracken L CO 1 Kensington
20.11.91	Robert Wright L RTD 2 Solihull
02.04.92	Dean Hollington L CO 1 Basildon
16.05.94	Adrian Chase L PTS 6 Heathrow
30.07.94	A. M. Milton L CO 1 Bethnal Green

Career: 23 contests, won 5, drew 2, lost 16.

(Dramani) Sugar Gibiliru

Liverpool. *Born* Liverpool, 13 July, 1966
Lightweight. Former British S.
Featherweight Champion. Former
Undefeated Central Area S. Featherweight
& Lightweight Champion. Ht. 5'5½"
Manager S. Vaughan

30.11.84	Steve Benny L PTS 4 Liverpool
25.01.85	Des Gargano W PTS 4 Liverpool
04.02.85	Martin Power W RTD 3 Liverpool
18.03.85	Des Gargano W PTS 6 Liverpool
29.03.85	Craig Windsor L PTS 6 Liverpool
17.04.85	Carl Gaynor L PTS 6 Nantwich
29.04.85	Carl Gaynor L PTS 6 Liverpool
07.10.85	Martin Power W RSC 4 Liverpool
11.11.85	Nigel Senior W PTS 6 Liverpool
06.12.85	Anthony Brown L PTS 8 Liverpool
24.01.86	Floyd Havard L PTS 6 Muswell Hill
10.03.86	Brian Roche L PTS 8 Manchester
07.04.86	Muhammad Lovelock DREW 8 Manchester
24.05.86	Floyd Havard L PTS 8 Manchester
16.06.86	Brian Roche L PTS 8 Manchester
22.09.86	Carl Crook L PTS 6 Bradford
14.10.86	Muhammad Lovelock DREW 8 Manchester
17.11.86	Simon Eubank L PTS 8 Dulwich
20.11.86	Joey Jacobs L PTS 8 Bredbury
15.12.86	Carl Crook L PTS 8 Bradford
13.01.87	Edward Lloyd L PTS 8 Oldham
24.04.87	Dean Binch W CO 3 Liverpool
15.06.87	Muhammad Lovelock L PTS 8 Manchester
22.09.87	Ray Taylor L PTS 8 Oldham
16.11.87	Robert Harkin DREW 8 Glasgow
05.12.87	Glyn Rhodes L PTS 8 Doncaster
01.03.88	Pat Barrett DREW 8 Manchester
13.04.88	Peter Till L PTS 8 Wolverhampton
28.04.88	Mark Kelly DREW 6 Manchester
10.08.88	Jean-Charles Meuret L PTS 8 Geneva, Switzerland
28.09.88	Glyn Rhodes DREW 8 Solihull
01.12.88	Mark Kelly L PTS 6 Manchester
14.12.88	Andy Holligan L PTS 8 Kirkby
25.01.89	Ray Taylor L PTS 6 Solihull
11.04.89	Pat Barrett L CO 8 Oldham *(Central Area L. Welterweight Title Challenge)*

31.05.89 Tony Banks W CO 5 Manchester
21.06.89 Rudy Valentino L PTS 6 Eltham
19.09.89 Nigel Wenton L PTS 8 Belfast
16.11.89 Tony Foster L PTS 8 Manchester
30.01.90 Tony Foster W PTS 10 Manchester
(Vacant Central Area Lightweight
Title)
07.03.90 Peter Gabbitus W RTD 6 Doncaster
(Vacant Central Area S. Featherweight
Title)
01.05.90 Mark Reefer L RSC 5 Oldham
(Commonwealth S. Featherweight Title
Challenge)
07.07.90 Kris McAdam W PTS 8 Liverpool
19.11.90 Frankie Foster DREW 8 Manchester
17.12.90 Dean Bramhald W PTS 8 Manchester
29.01.91 Nigel Bradley W PTS 8 Stockport
30.04.91 Robert Dickie W RSC 9 Stockport
(British S. Featherweight Title
Challenge)
19.09.91 John Doherty L PTS 12 Stockport
(British S. Featherweight Title
Defence)
07.12.91 Paul Harvey L PTS 12 Manchester
(Commonwealth S. Featherweight Title
Challenge)
31.03.92 Frankie Foster W PTS 8 Stockport
27.06.92 Michael Ayers L RSC 6 Quinta do
Lago, Portugal
01.12.92 Ross Hale L RSC 1 Bristol
06.05.94 Norman Dhalie W RTD 5 Liverpool
31.10.94 Kelton McKenzie W PTS 6 Liverpool
25.03.95 Peter Judson L PTS 6 Chester
Career: 55 contests, won 16, drew 7, lost 32.

Shaun Gledhill

Manchester. *Born* Oldham, 22 April, 1976
L. Welterweight. Ht. 5'8"
Manager N. Basso

12.06.95 Tom Welsh L RSC 4 Manchester
Career: 1 contest, lost 1.

(Godfrey) G. G. Goddard

Alfreton. *Born* Swaziland, 6 April, 1966
S. Featherweight. Ht. 5'7"
Manager Self

22.11.90 Shaun Hickey W RTD 4 Ilkeston
17.01.91 Paul Chedgzoy W RSC 3 Alfreton
13.05.91 Finn McCool L PTS 6 Northampton
20.05.91 Finn McCool W PTS 6 Bradford
23.10.91 Chubby Martin L PTS 8 Stoke
04.02.92 Kevin Toomey L PTS 6 Alfreton
11.03.92 Micky Hall DREW 6 Solihull
28.04.92 Michael Clynch L RTD 4 Corby
09.07.92 Dave McHale L RTD 4 Glasgow
18.11.92 Ian McGirr L PTS 6 Solihull
23.02.93 Jonjo Irwin L RSC 8 Doncaster
25.06.93 Mike Anthony Brown L CO 2
Battersea
13.06.94 Keith Jones W PTS 6 Liverpool
21.07.94 Keith Jones W RSC 1 Battersea
17.10.94 Michael Hermon L PTS 6 Birmingham
07.12.94 Trevor Royal W RSC 6 Stoke
18.01.95 Muhammad Shaffique W RSC 2
Solihull
16.02.95 Michael Brodie L PTS 6 Bury
04.03.95 Brian Carr L PTS 8 Livingston
05.05.95 Michael Brodie L PTS 6 Swansea
Career: 20 contests, won 7, drew 1, lost 12.

Ray Golding

Birmingham. *Born* Birmingham, 27
August, 1966
L. Middleweight. Ht. 6'0"
Manager Self

09.02.93 Andy Peach W PTS 6 Wolverhampton
19.05.93 David Larkin L PTS 6 Sunderland
15.12.94 Shamus Casey W PTS 6 Evesham
Career: 3 contests, won 2, lost 1.

(Valentine) Val Golding

Croydon. *Born* Croydon, 9 May, 1964
S. Middleweight. Ht. 5'11"
Manager Self

17.07.89 Robbie Harron W RSC 2 Stanmore
05.10.89 Shamus Casey W PTS 6 Stevenage
12.12.89 Neil Munn W RSC 2 Brentford
14.04.90 Ian Strudwick L PTS 6 Kensington
22.09.90 Franki Moro W RSC 6 Kensington
15.10.90 Tod Nadon L RSC 6 Lewisham
04.09.91 Russell Washer W RTD 5 Bethnal
Green
29.10.91 Graham Jenner W RSC 3 Kensington
18.01.92 Quinn Paynter L RSC 7 Kensington
26.09.92 Kevin Sheeran L RSC 1 Earls Court
15.09.93 John Keeton W PTS 6 Ashford
27.05.94 Jerry Mortimer W PTS 6 Ashford
12.10.94 Eric Noi W PTS 6 Sheffield
06.05.95 Shaun Cummins L RSC 7 Shepton
Mallet
Career: 14 contests, won 9, lost 5.

Michael Gomez (Armstrong)

Manchester. *Born* Manchester, 21 June,
1977
S. Bantamweight. Ht. 5'5"
Manager F. Warren

10.06.95 Danny Ruegg W PTS 4 Manchester
Career: 1 contest, won 1.

Paul Goode

Northampton. *Born* Northampton, 8
September, 1962
S. Featherweight. Ht. 5'6"
Manager J. Cox

19.04.93 Tony Smith DREW 6 Manchester
01.06.93 Tony Smith L PTS 6 Manchester
07.02.94 Leo Turner L RSC 3 Bradford
13.10.94 Paul Quarmby L RSC 3 Houghton le
Spring
24.11.94 Colin Innes L PTS 6 Newcastle
05.12.94 Paul Quarmby L PTS 6 Houghton le
Spring
12.01.95 Paul Hamilton L RTD 1 Leeds
20.02.95 Paul Watson L RSC 1 Glasgow
15.05.95 Garry Burrell L RSC 1 Bradford
Career: 9 contests, drew 1, lost 8.

Steve Goodwin

Sheffield. *Born* Derby, 17 February, 1966
Midlands Area L. Middleweight Champion.
Ht. 5'11"
Manager Self

13.04.92 John Duckworth W PTS 6 Manchester
29.04.92 John Corcoran W PTS 8 Stoke
03.09.92 Steve McNess L PTS 6 Dunstable
29.09.92 Mark Dawson W RSC 1 Stoke

19.10.92 John Bosco L RSC 2 Mayfair
09.12.92 Mark Dawson L PTS 6 Mayfair
12.02.93 Said Bennajem L PTS 6 Aubervilliers,
France
12.05.93 Mark Dawson W PTS 10 Stoke
(Vacant Midlands Area L.
Middleweight Title)
28.07.93 Gary Stretch L PTS 6 Brixton
07.09.93 Wally Swift Jnr W RSC 7 Stoke
(Midlands Area L. Middleweight Title
Defence)
02.11.93 Lloyd Honeyghan L RSC 6 Southwark
25.05.94 Wally Swift Jnr L PTS 8 Stoke
10.02.95 Neville Brown L RSC 3 Birmingham
06.05.95 Robin Reid L CO 1 Shepton Mallet
Career: 14 contests, won 5, lost 9.

Allan Gray

Putney. *Born* Roehampton, 4 August, 1971
Welterweight. Ht. 5'9"
Manager D. Mancini/M. Duff

19.05.95 Darren Covill W PTS 6 Southwark
23.06.95 Wayne Jones W PTS 6 Bethnal Green
Career: 2 contests, won 2.

Allan Gray   Tony Fitch

Darren Greaves

Chesterfield. *Born* Chesterfield, 25 May,
1971
S. Bantamweight. Ht. 5'5"
Manager J. Gaynor

06.12.93 Graham McGrath DREW 6
Birmingham
16.12.93 Graham McGrath L PTS 6 Walsall
04.03.94 Danny Ruegg W PTS 6 Weston super
Mare
25.04.94 Ady Lewis L RSC 1 Bury
02.11.94 Graham McGrath L RSC 4
Birmingham
05.12.94 Graham McGrath L PTS 6 Birmingham
24.02.95 Anthony Hanna L RSC 5 Weston super
Mare
Career: 7 contests, won 1, drew 1, lost 5.

Dennis Griffin

Stepney. *Born* Stepney, 9 June, 1965
L. Welterweight. Ht. 5'9"
Manager M. Brennan

31.08.93 Trevor Royal W RSC 1 Croydon
09.12.93 Keith Marner L PTS 6 Watford
19.12.93 Dave Madden W RSC 1 Northampton
23.02.94 Adrian Chase L PTS 6 Watford
19.11.94 Danny Quacoe L RSC 5 Heathrow
Career: 5 contests, won 2, lost 3.

Paul Griffin

Dublin. *Born* Dublin, 3 June, 1971
Featherweight. Ht. 5'7"
Manager F. Warren

04.03.95 Chris Jickells W RSC 5 Livingston
10.06.95 Andrew Reed W RSC 5 Manchester
Career: 2 contests, won 2.

Darron Griffiths

Rhondda. *Born* Pontypridd, 11 February,
1972
Welsh S. Middleweight Champion. Ht. 6'0"
Manager Self

26.11.90 Colin Ford DREW 6 Mayfair
04.12.90 Kevin Adamson W RSC 4 Southend
23.01.91 Tony Booth DREW 6 Stoke
06.03.91 Barry Messam W PTS 6 Croydon
10.04.91 John Kaighin W PTS 6 Newport
25.04.91 Michael Graham W RSC 2 Mayfair
02.05.91 Carlton Myers W RTD 5 Kensington

21.10.91 John Ogiste W PTS 6 Mayfair
11.12.91 Adrian Wright W PTS 6 Stoke
22.01.92 Richard Okumu W PTS 8 Solihull
17.02.92 John Ogiste W RSC 5 Mayfair
29.04.92 Colin Manners DREW 8 Solihull
30.09.92 Colin Manners W PTS 10 Solihull
 (Elim. British Middleweight Title)
28.10.92 Antonio Fernandez W PTS 10 Cardiff
 (Elim. British Middleweight Title)
24.03.93 John Kaighin W RSC 6 Cardiff
 (Vacant Welsh S. Middleweight Title)
22.01.94 Carlos Christie W PTS 8 Cardiff
09.02.94 Paul Hitch W PTS 6 Bethnal Green
23.03.94 Karl Barwise W PTS 8 Cardiff
27.04.94 Ray Webb W RSC 6 Bethnal Green
 (Elim. British S. Middleweight Title)
15.06.94 Nigel Rafferty W RSC 4 Southwark
29.09.94 Ali Forbes L PTS 12 Bethnal Green
 *(Final Elim. British S. Middleweight
 Title)*
22.11.94 Dean Francis L RTD 1 Bristol
05.05.95 Wayne Ellis W PTS 10 Swansea
 (Welsh S. Middleweight Title Defence)
Career: 23 contests, won 18, drew 3, lost 2.

Tony Griffiths

Tottenham. *Born* Tower Hamlets, 16 April,
1969
S. Middleweight. Ht. 5'9½"
Manager B. Hearn

28.06.94 Tim Robinson W RSC 6 Mayfair
05.09.94 Mark Dawson L PTS 6 Brentwood
13.06.95 Andy Farr L RSC 4 Basildon
Career: 3 contests, won 1, lost 2.

Robert Grubb

Tipton. *Born* Stourbridge, 15 April, 1972
S. Featherweight. Ht. 5'4"
Manager Self

17.02.94 Paul Wynn L PTS 6 Walsall
07.04.94 Roger Brotherhood L PTS 6 Walsall
11.10.94 Chris Lyons L PTS 6 Wolverhampton
20.10.94 Andy Roberts DREW 6 Walsall
07.12.94 Fred Reeve L RSC 3 Stoke
09.02.95 Andy Roberts DREW 6 Doncaster
09.03.95 Andrew Smith DREW 6 Walsall
28.03.95 Andrew Smith L PTS 6
 Wolverhampton
14.06.95 Chris Aston L CO 1 Batley
Career: 9 contests, lost 6, drew 3.

Bobby Guynan

East Ham. *Born* Plaistow, 4 July, 1967
Lightweight. Ht. 5'9"
Manager Self

17.10.90 John O'Meara W RTD 2 Bethnal Green
26.11.90 Lee Fox L PTS 6 Bethnal Green
06.02.91 Lee Fox W PTS 6 Bethnal Green
26.03.91 Lee Fox L RTD 3 Bethnal Green
10.11.92 Mark Allen W RSC 2 Dagenham
30.01.93 Shaun Shinkwin W PTS 6 Brentwood
20.04.93 Norman Dhalie W PTS 6 Brentwood
26.06.93 Mike Morrison L PTS 4 Earls Court
29.11.93 Mike Morrison W PTS 6 Ingatestone
09.02.94 Mark Antony W DIS 5 Brentwood
09.07.94 Wayne Jones W PTS 6 Earls Court
05.09.94 Steve Burton L RTD 1 Brentwood
16.03.95 Jimmy Phelan L RSC 5 Basildon
Career: 13 contests, won 8, lost 5.

Tony Griffiths (right) forces Andy Farr to cover up at Basildon last June

Les Clark

Nigel Haddock
Llanelli. *Born* Llanelli, 8 August, 1966
S. Featherweight. Ht. 5'5½"
Manager Self

13.02.86	Paul Timmons L PTS 6 Digbeth
26.03.86	Paul Parry W PTS 6 Swansea
10.04.86	Ginger Staples W PTS 6 Weston super Mare
23.04.86	Nigel Senior W PTS 6 Stoke
19.05.86	Nigel Senior DREW 6 Nottingham
03.06.86	Albert Masih W RTD 3 Fulham
30.07.86	Tony Rahman W RSC 2 Ebbw Vale
01.10.86	Wayne Weekes L PTS 6 Lewisham
29.10.86	Nigel Senior W PTS 6 Ebbw Vale
26.11.86	Mark Reefer L RTD 3 Lewisham
15.04.87	Ginger Staples W RSC 5 Carmarthen
19.10.87	Gary Maxwell L PTS 8 Nottingham
05.11.87	John Maloney W RTD 4 Bethnal Green
18.11.87	Richie Foster W RSC 7 Bethnal Green
20.04.88	Patrick Kamy W PTS 6 Muswell Hill
02.11.88	Freddy Cruz L PTS 8 Paola, Italy
26.11.88	Maurizio Stecca L RTD 2 Forli, Italy
11.12.89	John Naylor W RSC 5 Nottingham
14.03.90	Kevin Pritchard DREW 6 Stoke
22.04.90	Ditau Molefyane L PTS 10 Spings, South Africa
30.03.93	Edward Lloyd W RTD 4 Cardiff
10.07.93	Alan Levene W RSC 5 Cardiff
30.11.93	Paul Harvey L RSC 3 Cardiff
20.05.94	Peter Harris L PTS 10 Neath *(Vacant Welsh Featherweight Title)*
19.11.94	Dave Anderson L PTS 6 Cardiff
12.04.95	Steve Burton L PTS 6 Llanelli

Career: 26 contests, won 13, drew 2, lost 11.

Mark Hale
Nuneaton. *Born* Nuneaton, 13 October, 1969
S. Middleweight. Ht. 5'11"
Manager Self

07.10.91	Andy Manning L PTS 6 Liverpool
07.11.91	Marc Rowley W PTS 6 Peterborough
15.01.92	Paul Murray W PTS 6 Stoke
25.03.92	Marc Rowley W PTS 6 Hinckley
11.05.92	Martin Jolley L PTS 6 Coventry
21.05.92	Tony Colclough DREW 6 Cradley Heath
01.06.92	Tony Colclough L PTS 6 Solihull
05.10.92	Martin Jolley L RSC 4 Bardon
16.03.93	Andrew Flute L RSC 2 Wolverhampton
11.05.93	Earl Ling W RSC 2 Norwich
08.12.93	Dean Ashton L RSC 1 Stoke
25.05.94	Steve Loftus L PTS 6 Stoke
06.09.94	Steve Loftus L PTS 6 Stoke
17.09.94	Eddie Knight L PTS 6 Crawley
12.10.94	Phil Ball W RSC 3 Stoke
07.11.94	Ryan Cummings L RSC 6 Bethnal Green
15.12.94	Darren Sweeney L PTS 6 Walsall
17.03.95	Frederik Alvarez L CO 1 Copenhagen, Denmark
26.04.95	Steve Loftus L PTS 6 Stoke
15.05.95	Dave Battey L PTS 6 Bradford

Career: 20 contests, won 5, drew 1, lost 14.

Eddie Haley
South Shields. *Born* South Shields, 25 August, 1965
L. Middleweight. Ht. 5'9"
Manager T. Callighan

06.06.94	Brian Dunn W PTS 6 Glasgow

25.10.94	Sven Hamer L RSC 4 Southwark
30.11.94	Roy Chipperfield W RSC 3 Solihull
23.01.95	Billy Collins L RSC 4 Glasgow
01.03.95	Gary Beardsley L RSC 1 Glasgow
27.04.95	Gary Silvester W RSC 2 Hull
19.05.95	James Lowther L RSC 5 Leeds

Career: 7 contests, won 3, lost 4.

Eddie Haley   Les Clark

Allan Hall
Darlington. *Born* Darlington, 16 November, 1969
L. Welterweight. Ht. 5'8"
Manager Self

10.10.89	Saturnin Cabanas W RSC 2 Hull
08.12.89	John Smith W RSC 2 Doncaster
22.02.90	Muhammad Lovelock W RSC 1 Hull
21.04.90	Darren Mount W PTS 6 Sunderland
09.05.90	George Jones W RSC 1 Kensington
22.05.90	Mohamed Ouhmad W PTS 6 Stockton
15.10.90	Marvin P. Gray W RSC 2 Lewisham
31.10.90	Gino de Leon W RSC 1 Crystal Palace
02.03.91	Steve Pollard W PTS 6 Darlington
06.04.91	Alan Peacock W PTS 6 Darlington
11.06.91	Abram Gumede W PTS 8 Leicester
25.04.92	Michael Driscoll W PTS 6 Manchester
25.06.92	Russell Mosley W PTS 6 San Diego, USA
11.07.92	Steve Barreras L RSC 5 Las Vegas, USA
11.09.92	Dave Pierre W PTS 10 Watford *(Elim. British L. Welterweight Title)*
14.01.93	Tony Foster W PTS 6 Mayfair
13.04.95	Nigel Bradley W RSC 2 Bloomsbury

Career: 17 contests, won 16, lost 1.

Micky Hall
Ludworth. *Born* Ludworth, 23 April, 1967
Lightweight. Ht. 5'8"
Manager T. Conroy

03.03.92	Mick Holmes W RSC 2 Houghton le Spring
11.03.92	G. G. Goddard DREW 6 Solihull
28.04.92	Jamie Davidson L PTS 6 Houghton le Spring

19.09.92	Mark Geraghty L PTS 6 Glasgow
12.10.92	Leo Turner W PTS 5 Bradford
18.11.92	Alan Ingle W RSC 3 Solihull
09.03.93	Kevin McKenzie L PTS 6 Hartlepool
17.04.93	John T. Kelly DREW 4 Washington
06.05.93	Brian Wright W PTS 6 Hartlepool
01.06.93	Kevin McKillan L PTS 6 Manchester
27.09.93	Paul Hughes W PTS 6 Manchester
04.10.93	Michael Alexander W CO 1 Bradford
12.11.93	Tony Foster L PTS 8 Hull
02.12.93	Kevin McKenzie W PTS 4 Hartlepool
10.02.94	Jimmy Phelan W PTS 6 Hull
02.03.94	Charlie Kane L RSC 2 Glasgow
27.04.94	Phil Found L RSC 5 Solihull
06.06.94	Kevin McKillan L PTS 6 Manchester
13.10.94	Charlie Paine W PTS 6 Houghton le Spring
05.12.94	T. J. Smith W RTD 3 Houghton le Spring
16.01.95	Tanveer Ahmed L RSC 4 Musselburgh
01.03.95	Alan Peacock L RSC 4 Glasgow
19.05.95	Steve Tuckett W RSC 2 Leeds
01.06.95	Steve McLevy W RSC 1 Musselburgh

Career: 24 contests, won 12, drew 2, lost 10.

Nick Hall
Darlington. *Born* Darlington, 9 November, 1968
Welterweight. Ht. 5'9"
Manager Self

14.09.89	Paul Charters W PTS 6 Motherwell
24.10.89	Paul Day L CO 4 Watford
21.03.90	Mark Antony W PTS 6 Solihull
03.04.90	Steve Griffith W RSC 2 Canvey Island
26.04.90	Michael Ayers L CO 3 Wandsworth
03.10.90	Mike Morrison W PTS 8 Solihull
18.10.90	Peter Till L PTS 6 Birmingham
03.11.93	Young Gully W RSC 2 Bristol
25.01.94	Nick Appiah W PTS 4 Piccadilly
25.10.94	Gary Logan DREW 8 Southwark

Career: 10 contests, won 6, drew 1, lost 3

Shaun Hall
Leeds. *Born* Leeds, 13 February, 1974
Bantamweight. Ht. 5'4"
Manager G. Lockwood

06.03.95	Steve Williams DREW 6 Bradford
19.05.95	Terry Gaskin W RSC 3 Leeds

Career: 2 contests, won 1, drew 1.

Simon Hamblett
Walsall Wood. *Born* Walsall, 10 October, 1966
Lightweight. Ht. 5'8"
Manager W. Tyler

24.02.92	Jamie Morris DREW 6 Coventry
11.03.92	Mark Antony L CO 1 Stoke
09.12.92	Mark Allen DREW 6 Stoke
09.02.93	Mark Allen L PTS 6 Wolverhampton
23.02.93	Mark Allen W PTS 6 Doncaster
19.04.93	Kevin McKillan L CO 2 Manchester
07.06.93	Robbie Sivyer L PTS 6 Walsall
13.10.93	Shaun Shinkwin L PTS 6 Watford
02.12.93	Paul Robinson L RSC 2 Walsall
09.02.94	P. J. Gallagher L RSC 1 Bethnal Green
07.04.94	Paul Bowen L PTS 6 Walsall
29.09.94	Peter Hickenbottom L RSC 5 Walsall
29.11.94	Mark Allen W PTS 6 Wolverhampton
09.03.95	Marc Smith W PTS 6 Walsall
18.03.95	Bernard McComiskey L RSC 1 Millstreet, Eire

Career: 15 contests, won 3, drew 2, lost 10.

Prince Nassem Hamed   Les Clark

11.05.94	Vincenzo Belcastro W PTS 12 Sheffield	

11.05.94 Vincenzo Belcastro W PTS 12 Sheffield
(European Bantamweight Title Challenge)
17.08.94 Antonio Picardi W RSC 3 Sheffield
(European Bantamweight Title Defence)
12.10.94 Freddy Cruz W RSC 6 Sheffield
(Vacant WBC International S. Bantamweight Title)
19.11.94 Laureano Ramirez W RTD 3 Cardiff
(WBC International S. Bantamweight Title Defence)
21.01.95 Armando Castro W RSC 4 Glasgow
(WBC S. Bantamweight Title Defence)
04.03.95 Sergio Liendo W RSC 2 Livingston
(WBC International S. Bantamweight Title Defence)
06.05.95 Enrique Angeles W CO 2 Shepton Mallet
(WBC International S. Bantamweight Title Defence)
Career: 18 contests, won 18.

Sven Hamer

Margate. *Born* Margate, 6 June, 1973
Middleweight. Ht. 5'11"
Manager F. Maloney

25.10.94 Eddie Haley W RSC 4 Southwark
07.11.94 Shamus Casey W PTS 4 Piccadilly
23.11.94 Andy Ewen W RSC 1 Piccadilly
20.12.94 Tony Velinor W RSC 4 Bethnal Green
24.01.95 Delroy Matthews L PTS 6 Piccadilly
Career: 5 contests, won 4, lost 1.

Sven Hamer   Les Clark

Paul Hamilton

Darlington. *Born* Darlington, 10 January, 1969
S. Featherweight. Ht. 5'7½"
Manager G. Lockwood

12.01.95 Paul Goode W RTD 1 Leeds
20.02.95 Marty Chestnut L PTS 6 Manchester
25.03.95 Colin Innes L PTS 6 Rothwell
27.04.95 Ram Singh L RSC 2 Hull
Career: 4 contests, won 1, lost 3.

Prince Nassem Hamed

Sheffield. *Born* Sheffield, 12 February, 1974
WBC International S. Bantamweight Champion. Former Undefeated European Bantamweight Champion. Ht. 5'3"
Manager B. Ingle

14.04.92 Ricky Beard W CO 2 Mansfield
25.04.92 Shaun Norman W RSC 2 Manchester
23.05.92 Andrew Bloomer W RSC 2 Birmingham
14.07.92 Miguel Matthews W RSC 3 Mayfair
07.10.92 Des Gargano W RSC 4 Sunderland
12.11.92 Pete Buckley W PTS 6 Liverpool
24.02.93 Alan Ley W CO 2 Wembley
26.05.93 Kevin Jenkins W RSC 3 Mansfield
24.09.93 Chris Clarkson W CO 2 Dublin
29.01.94 Pete Buckley W RSC 4 Cardiff
09.04.94 John Miceli W CO 1 Mansfield

Anthony Hanna

Birmingham. *Born* Birmingham, 22 September, 1974
Midlands Area Flyweight Champion. Ht. 5'6"
Manager Self

19.11.92	Nick Tooley L PTS 6 Evesham
10.12.92	Daren Fifield L RSC 6 Bethnal Green
11.05.93	Tiger Singh W PTS 6 Norwich
24.05.93	Lyndon Kershaw L PTS 6 Bradford
16.09.93	Chris Lyons W PTS 6 Southwark
06.10.93	Tiger Singh W PTS 6 Solihull
03.11.93	Mickey Cantwell L PTS 8 Bristol
25.01.94	Marty Chestnut W PTS 4 Piccadilly
10.02.94	Allan Mooney W RTD 1 Glasgow
13.04.94	Allan Mooney L PTS 6 Glasgow
22.04.94	Jesper David Jenson L PTS 6 Aalborg, Denmark
03.08.94	Paul Ingle L PTS 6 Bristol
01.10.94	Mark Hughes L PTS 4 Cardiff
30.11.94	Shaun Norman W PTS 10 Solihull
	(Vacant Midlands Area Flyweight Title)
24.02.95	Darren Greaves W RSC 5 Weston super Mare
06.03.95	Mark Hughes L PTS 6 Mayfair
27.04.95	Mickey Cantwell L PTS 6 Bethnal Green
05.05.95	Mark Cokely W RSC 4 Swansea
04.06.95	Mark Reynolds L PTS 10 Bethnal Green
	(Elim. British Flyweight Title)

Career: 19 contests, won 8, lost 11.

Dick Hanns-Kat (Katende-Kigula)

Stratford. *Born* Kampala, Uganda, 10 February, 1969
Welterweight. Ht. 5'10"
Manager B. Lynch

04.06.95	Darren Covill L RSC 3 Bethnal Green

Career: 1 contest, lost 1.

Dick Hanns-Kat   Les Clark

Japhet Hans

Leeds. *Born* Nigeria, 5 May, 1973
Middleweight. Ht. 5'11"
Manager P. Coleman

02.12.93	Jimmy Alston L PTS 6 Sheffield
28.02.94	Carl Smith L RSC 4 Manchester
24.05.94	Mark Jay W RSC 1 Sunderland
28.06.94	Darren Sweeney L PTS 6 Edgbaston
26.08.94	Ian Midwood-Tate L RSC 5 Barnsley

26.09.94	Brian Dunn W PTS 6 Cleethorpes
13.10.94	Dave Johnson L RSC 2 Houghton le Spring
12.12.94	Brian Dunn L PTS 6 Cleethorpes
20.02.95	Carl Harney L RSC 3 Manchester
06.04.95	Clinton Woods L RSC 3 Sheffield

Career: 10 contests, won 2, lost 8.

Dave Hardie

Glasgow. *Born* Glasgow 10 February, 1971
Bantamweight. Ht. 5'5"
Manager A. Morrison

28.11.91	Miguel Matthews W PTS 6 Glasgow
20.02.92	Shaun Norman W PTS 6 Glasgow
21.10.94	Dave Campbell W RTD 4 Glasgow
19.11.94	Neil Swain L RSC 2 Cardiff

Career: 4 contests, won 3, lost 1.

Mark Hargreaves

Burnley. *Born* Burnley, 13 September, 1970
S. Featherweight. Ht. 5'4"
Managers N. Basso/B. Myers

11.09.91	Dave Campbell W RSC 4 Stoke
23.10.91	Dave Martin W PTS 6 Stoke
10.02.92	Dennis Oakes L RSC 3 Liverpool
30.03.92	Ronnie Stephenson L PTS 6 Coventry
27.04.92	Ady Benton L PTS 6 Bradford
01.06.92	Des Gargano W PTS 6 Manchester
11.09.92	Shaun Anderson L PTS 6 Glasgow
07.10.92	Mike Deveney W RSC 7 Glasgow
14.10.92	Yusuf Vorajee W RSC 4 Stoke
19.11.92	Greg Upton W RSC 3 Evesham
28.11.92	John White L PTS 4 Manchester
20.01.93	Jonjo Irwin L RSC 4 Solihull
26.04.93	Mario Culpeper L PTS 6 Manchester
01.06.93	Paul Wynn W PTS 6 Manchester
01.12.93	Justin Murphy L RSC 4 Bethnal Green
19.03.94	Wayne McCullough L RSC 3 Millwall
06.06.94	Mike Deveney L PTS 6 Manchester
17.08.94	Duke McKenzie L RSC 3 Sheffield
22.09.94	Wayne Rigby L PTS 6 Bury
25.02.95	Colin McMillan L RSC 4 Millwall

Career: 20 contests, won 7, lost 13.

Carl Harney

Manchester. *Born* Manchester, 24 June, 1970
Middleweight. Ht. 6'1"
Manager Self

17.10.89	Shamus Casey W PTS 4 Oldham
18.10.90	Michael Clarke W PTS 6 Wandsworth
22.02.91	Mike Phillips L RSC 5 Manchester
31.05.91	Marvin OBrien L RSC 5 Manchester
29.05.92	Matthew Jones W RSC 6 Manchester
18.07.92	John Kaighin W PTS 6 Manchester
05.02.93	Gilbert Jackson L CO 3 Manchester
03.10.94	Dave Proctor W PTS 6 Manchester
28.11.94	John Duckworth W PTS 6 Manchester
20.02.95	Japhet Hans W RSC 3 Manchester
05.05.95	Lee Crocker L CO 4 Swansea

Career: 11 contests, won 7, lost 4.

Robert Harper

Doncaster. *Born* Doncaster, 1 April, 1969
S. Middleweight. Ht. 5'8"
Manager Self

16.09.93	Smokey Enison L RSC 1 Hull
02.12.93	Kevin Bailey L PTS 6 Sheffield
24.02.94	Dave Proctor L PTS 6 Hull
08.03.94	Chris Nurse L PTS 6 Edgbaston
25.04.94	Lee Blundell L RSC 2 Bury
25.01.95	Steve Loftus L PTS 6 Stoke
07.03.95	Andy McVeigh L RSC 5 Edgbaston
13.04.95	Russell Washer L PTS 6 Bloomsbury

26.05.95	Freddie Yemofio L PTS 6 Norwich
02.06.95	Michael Bowen L PTS 6 Bethnal Green
20.06.95	Barry Exton L PTS 6 Edgbaston

Career: 11 contests, lost 11.

Matthew Harris

Aldridge. *Born* Brownhills, 2 May, 1971
Bantamweight. Former Midlands Area S. Bantamweight Champion. Ht. 5'7"
Manager M. Shinfield

23.03.94	Yusuf Vorajee W PTS 6 Stoke
13.06.94	Marcus Duncan W RSC 1 Bradford
02.09.94	Karl Morling W CO 5 Spitalfields
	(Vacant Midlands Area S. Bantamweight Title)
05.10.94	Pete Buckley W PTS 6 Wolverhampton
30.11.94	Marty Chestnut W RSC 3 Wolverhampton
15.12.94	Kid McAuley W PTS 6 Evesham
10.02.95	Pete Buckley L RSC 6 Birmingham
	(Midlands Area S. Bantamweight Title Defence)
21.04.95	Chris Lyons W PTS 6 Dudley
19.05.95	John Armour L RSC 3 Southwark

Career: 9 contests, won 7, lost 2.

Peter Harris

Swansea. *Born* Swansea, 23 August, 1962
Welsh Featherweight Champion. Former British Featherweight Champion. Ht. 5'6½"
Manager Self

28.02.83	Dave Pratt L PTS 6 Birmingham
25.04.83	Jim Harvey DREW 6 Aberdeen
27.05.83	Brett Styles W PTS 8 Swansea
20.06.83	Danny Knaggs W PTS 6 Piccadilly
19.12.83	Kevin Howard W PTS 8 Swansea
06.02.84	Ivor Jones DREW 8 Bethnal Green
27.03.84	Johnny Dorey W RSC 6 Bethnal Green
13.06.84	Keith Wallace W PTS 8 Solihull
28.09.84	Ray Minus L PTS 10 Nassau, Bahamas
21.11.84	John Farrell L PTS 8 Solihull
20.03.85	Kid Sumali W PTS 8 Solihull
09.05.85	John Feeney L PTS 10 Warrington
09.11.85	Antoine Montero L PTS 10 Grenoble, France
26.03.86	Steve Pollard W RSC 3 Swansea
22.04.86	Roy Webb W RTD 8 Belfast
18.11.86	Kelvin Smart W PTS 10 Swansea
	(Vacant Welsh Featherweight Title)
30.04.87	Albert Parr W RSC 3 Newport
30.09.87	John Farrell W PTS 12 Solihull
	(Final Elim. British Featherweight Title)
15.12.87	Roy Williams W RSC 2 Cardiff
24.02.88	Kevin Taylor W PTS 12 Aberavon
	(Vacant British Featherweight Title)
18.05.88	Paul Hodkinson L RSC 12 Aberavon
	(British Featherweight Title Defence)
06.09.89	Paul Hodkinson L RSC 9 Aberavon
	(British & European Featherweight Title Challenge)
24.04.91	Colin Lynch W PTS 8 Aberavon
18.07.91	Steve Robinson L PTS 10 Cardiff
	(Welsh Featherweight Title Defence)
05.06.92	Stephane Haccoun L PTS 8 Marseille, France
22.12.92	Paul Harvey L PTS 8 Mayfair
21.12.93	Jonjo Irwin L PTS 6 Mayfair
20.05.94	Nigel Haddock W PTS 10 Neath
	(Vacant Welsh Featherweight Title)
27.08.94	Wilson Docherty L PTS 12 Cardiff
	(Penta-Continental Featherweight Title Challenge)
24.04.95	Wilson Docherty W PTS 10 Glasgow
	(Final Elim. British Featherweight Title)

Career: 30 contests, won 16, drew 2, lost 12.

Jason Hart (right) shown on his way to a points win over Andy Ewen at Crystal Palace last March   Les Clark

Jason Hart

Bromley. *Born* Beckenham, 23 January, 1970
Middleweight. Ht. 5'9½"
Manager Self

02.06.94	Paul Matthews L RSC 3 Tooting
28.07.94	Julian Eavis W PTS 6 Tooting
30.09.94	Freddie Yemofio W PTS 6 Bethnal Green
31.03.95	Andy Ewen W PTS 6 Crystal Palace

Career: 4 contests, won 3, lost 1.

Mark Haslam

Manchester. *Born* Bury, 20 October, 1969
L. Welterweight. Ht. 5'8"
Manager N. Basso/F. Warren

12.06.95 Steve Burton W PTS 6 Manchester
Career: 1 contest, won 1.

Robert Hay

Coatbridge. *Born* Coatbridge, 6 November, 1974
S. Bantamweight. Ht. 5'7"
Manager T. Gilmour

20.02.95	Muhammad Shaffique W RSC 2 Glasgow
24.04.95	Paul Quarmby W PTS 6 Glasgow
22.05.95	Marcus Duncan W RSC 3 Morecambe
05.06.95	Garry Burrell W PTS 6 Glasgow

Career: 4 contests, won 4.

Shaun Hendry

Leeds. *Born* Leeds, 30 March, 1971
Middleweight. Ht. 6'0"
Manager G. Lockwood

12.01.95	Jason Brown W CO 1 Leeds
30.01.95	Shamus Casey W PTS 6 Bradford
25.03.95	Mark Jay W RSC 2 Rothwell
06.06.95	Lawrence Ryan W RSC 1 Leicester

Career: 4 contests, won 4.

Michael Hermon

Birmingham. *Born* Birmingham, 29 April, 1968
S. Featherweight. Ht. 5'6"
Manager Self

04.03.94	Trevor Royal W PTS 6 Weston super Mare
17.10.94	G. G. Goddard W PTS 6 Birmingham
02.11.94	Hugh Collins W RSC 3 Solihull
04.03.95	Dave Anderson L PTS 8 Livingston
20.04.95	Gary Thornhill L RSC 6 Liverpool

Career: 5 contests, won 3, lost 2.

Sean Heron

Edinburgh. *Born* Edinburgh, 29 October, 1966
L. Heavyweight. Ht. 5'11"
Manager A. Morrison

09.11.87	Lindon Scarlett W PTS 6 Glasgow
03.12.87	Darren Hobson L PTS 8 Leeds
25.01.88	Gerry Richards W RTD 3 Birmingham
28.03.88	Steve Aquilina W PTS 8 Birmingham
14.04.88	Gary Finn W PTS 8 Piccadilly
23.05.88	Fidel Castro L RSC 4 Mayfair
10.10.88	Winston Burnett W PTS 8 Glasgow
25.05.89	Prince Rodney W PTS 6 Finsbury Park
21.03.90	Paul Burton W CO 1 Preston
01.05.90	Nigel Rafferty W RSC 2 Oldham
05.09.90	Karl Barwise W PTS 6 Brighton
18.11.90	Dave Owens W PTS 8 Birmingham
23.02.91	Johnny Melfah L PTS 8 Brighton

08.09.94	Steve Yorath W PTS 6 Glasgow
21.10.94	Nick Manners W PTS 6 Glasgow
18.11.94	Russell Washer W PTS 6 Glasgow
21.01.95	Simon McDougall W PTS 4 Glasgow

Career: 17 contests, won 14, lost 3.

Peter Hickenbottom

Great Wyrley. *Born* Walsall, 20 June, 1964
L. Welterweight. Ht. 5'8"
Manager Self

23.05.94	Shane Sheridan W PTS 6 Walsall
20.09.94	Simon Hamblett W RSC 5 Walsall
08.03.95	Jay Mahoney L PTS 6 Solihull

Career: 3 contests, won 2, lost 1.

Herbie Hide

Norwich. *Born* Nigeria, 27 August, 1971
Former WBO Heavyweight Champion.
Former Undefeated British, WBC
International & Penta-Continental
Heavyweight Champion. Ht. 6'1½"
Manager B. Hearn

24.10.89	L. A. Williams W CO 2 Bethnal Green
05.11.89	Gary McCrory W RTD 1 Kensington
19.12.89	Steve Osborne W RSC 6 Bethnal Green
27.06.90	Alek Penarski W RSC 3 Kensington
05.09.90	Steve Lewsam W RSC 4 Brighton
26.09.90	Jonjo Greene W RSC 1 Manchester
17.10.90	Gus Mendes W RSC 2 Bethnal Green
18.11.90	Steve Lewsam W RSC 1 Birmingham
29.01.91	Lennie Howard W RSC 1 Wisbech
09.04.91	David Jules W RSC 1 Mayfair
14.05.91	John Westgarth W RTD 4 Dudley
03.07.91	Tucker Richards W RSC 3 Brentwood
15.10.91	Eddie Gonzalez W CO 2 Hamburg, Germany
29.10.91	Chris Jacobs W RSC 1 Cardiff
21.01.92	Conroy Nelson W RSC 2 Norwich *(Vacant WBC International Heavyweight Title)*
03.03.92	Percell Davis W CO 1 Amsterdam, Holland
08.09.92	Jean Chanet W RSC 7 Norwich
06.10.92	Craig Peterson W RSC 7 Antwerp, Belgium *(WBC International Heavyweight Title Defence)*
12.12.92	James Pritchard W RSC 2 Muswell Hill
30.01.93	Juan Antonio Diaz W RSC 3 Brentwood *(Vacant Penta-Continental Heavyweight Title)*
27.02.93	Michael Murray W RSC 5 Dagenham *(Vacant British Heavyweight Title)*
11.05.93	Jerry Halstead W RSC 4 Norwich *(Penta-Continental Heavyweight Title Defence)*
18.09.93	Everett Martin W PTS 10 Leicester
06.11.93	Mike Dixon W RSC 9 Bethnal Green *(Penta-Continental Heavyweight Title Defence)*
04.12.93	Jeff Lampkin W RSC 2 Sun City, South Africa *(WBC International Heavyweight Title Defence)*
19.03.94	Michael Bentt W CO 7 Millwall *(WBO Heavyweight Title Challenge)*
11.03.95	Riddick Bowe L CO 6 Las Vegas, USA *(WBO Heavyweight Title Defence)*

Career: 27 contests, won 26, lost 1.

Tim Hill

North Shields. *Born* North Shields, 23
January, 1974
L. Welterweight. Ht. 5'9"
Manager T. Conroy

09.11.92	Fred Reeve W CO 4 Bradford
25.01.93	Michael Alexander L PTS 6 Bradford
22.02.93	Garry Burrell W PTS 6 Glasgow
29.03.93	Hugh Collins L PTS 6 Glasgow
08.11.93	Leo Turner W RTD 4 Bradford
17.02.94	Patrick Parton L PTS 6 Walsall
16.05.94	Robert Howard W CO 2 Morecambe
29.09.94	Garry Burrell W PTS 6 Tynemouth
13.10.94	John T. Kelly L PTS 6 Houghton le Spring
17.11.94	Chris Aston L PTS 6 Sheffield
16.03.95	Mark Allen W PTS 6 Sunderland

Career: 11 contests, won 6, lost 5.

Gary Hiscox

Dudley. *Born* Dudley, 25 May, 1970
L. Welterweight. Ht. 5'7¼"
Manager Self

14.10.92	Alan Ingle L PTS 6 Stoke
12.11.92	Shane Sheridan W PTS 6 Stafford
27.01.93	Dave Madden W PTS 6 Stoke
03.03.93	Erwin Edwards W PTS 6 Solihull
26.06.93	Mark Tibbs L RSC 4 Earls Court
28.10.93	Dean Bramhald W RSC 5 Walsall
04.11.93	Paul Hughes W PTS 6 Stafford
25.11.93	Mark Legg L RSC 3 Tynemouth
01.03.94	Gary Cogan W PTS 6 Dudley
29.09.94	Patrick Parton W PTS 6 Walsall
26.10.94	Steve Howden W RSC 4 Stoke
09.02.95	Cam Raeside W RSC 5 Doncaster
06.03.95	Neil Smith W PTS 6 Leicester
11.05.95	Anthony Maynard L RSC 4 Dudley

Career: 14 contests, won 10, lost 4.

Mick Hoban (Massie)

Burnley. *Born* Burnley, 25 July, 1967
Welterweight. Ht. 5'9"
Manager J. Doughty

19.04.89	Steve Booth L PTS 6 Doncaster
13.10.92	Danny Kett W PTS 6 Bury
07.12.92	Lee Soar W PTS 6 Manchester
15.02.93	Brian Wright W PTS 6 Manchester
28.06.93	Michael Alexander L PTS 6 Morecambe
13.09.93	Brian Coleman W PTS 6 Middleton
29.11.93	Pete Roberts W RSC 4 Manchester
19.01.94	Young Gully W RSC 3 Solihull
06.10.94	Hughie Davey L PTS 6 Cramlington

Career: 9 contests, won 6, lost 3.

Mike Holden

Manchester. *Born* Ashton under Lyme, 13
March, 1968
Heavyweight. Ht. 6'4"
Manager B. Hearn

| 04.10.94 | Gary Williams W RSC 4 Mayfair |
| 20.12.94 | Pat Passley L RTD 3 Bethnal Green |

Career: 2 contests, won 1, lost 1.

Mike Holden   Les Clark

Martin Holgate

Walthamstow. *Born* Waltham Forest, 24
November, 1968
L. Welterweight. Ht. 5'6½"
Manager F. Warren

| 02.06.95 | Adam Baldwin W PTS 6 Bethnal Green |

Career: 1 contest, won 1.

Martin Holgate   Les Clark

Andy Holligan

Liverpool. *Born* Liverpool, 6 June, 1967
Former British & Commonwealth L.
Welterweight Champion. Ht. 5'5¾"
Manager F. Warren

| 19.10.87 | Glyn Rhodes W PTS 6 Belfast |
| 03.12.87 | Jimmy Thornton W RTD 2 Belfast |

27.01.88	Andrew Morgan W RSC 5 Belfast
26.03.88	Tony Richards W RSC 2 Belfast
08.06.88	David Maw W RSC 1 Sheffield
19.10.88	Lenny Gloster W PTS 8 Belfast
14.12.88	Sugar Gibiliru W PTS 8 Kirkby
16.03.89	Jeff Connors W RSC 5 Southwark
19.09.89	Billy Buchanan W RSC 5 Belfast
25.10.89	Tony Adams W RSC 3 Wembley
26.09.90	Mike Durvan W CO 1 Mayfair
31.10.90	Eric Carroyez W RTD 2 Wembley
17.04.91	Pat Ireland W RSC 2 Kensington
16.05.91	Simon Eubank W RSC 2 Liverpool
20.06.91	Tony Ekubia W PTS 12 Liverpool *(British & Commonwealth L. Welterweight Title Challenge)*
28.11.91	Steve Larrimore W RSC 8 Liverpool *(Commonwealth L. Welterweight Title Defence)*
27.02.92	Tony McKenzie W RSC 3 Liverpool *(British & Commonwealth L. Welterweight Title Defence)*
15.09.92	Tony Ekubia W CO 7 Liverpool *(British & Commonwealth L. Welterweight Title Defence)*
07.10.92	Dwayne Swift W PTS 10 Sunderland
12.11.92	Mark Smith W PTS 10 Liverpool
26.05.93	Lorenzo Garcia W RSC 2 Mansfield
18.12.93	Julio Cesar Chavez L RTD 5 Puebla, Mexico *(WBC L. Welterweight Title Challenge)*
26.02.94	Massimo Bertozzi W CO 5 Earls Court
25.05.94	Ross Hale L RSC 3 Bristol *(British & Commonwealth L. Welterweight Title Defence)*
30.06.95	Tony Foster W CO 2 Liverpool

Career: 25 contests, won 23, lost 2.

Clayton Hollingsworth

Telford. *Born* Wolverhampton, 5 April,
1974
L. Welterweight. Ht. 5'7"
Manager D. Bradley

30.11.94	Shaba Edwards W PTS 6 Wolverhampton
10.02.95	Steve Howden W PTS 6 Birmingham
22.02.95	Shaba Edwards W PTS 6 Telford
20.04.95	Delroy Leslie L PTS 6 Mayfair

Career: 4 contests, won 3, lost 1.

Lloyd Honeyghan

Bermondsey. *Born* Jamaica, 22 April, 1960
Former Undefeated Commonwealth L.
Middleweight Champion. Former WBC
Welterweight Champion. Former
Undefeated WBA, IBF, British, European,
Commonwealth & Southern Area
Welterweight Champion. Ht. 5'8½"
Manager Self

08.12.80	Mike Sullivan W PTS 6 Kensington
20.01.81	Dai Davies W RSC 5 Bethnal Green
10.02.81	Dave Sullivan W PTS 6 Bethnal Green
16.11.81	Dave Finigan W RSC 1 Mayfair
24.11.81	Alan Cooper W RSC 4 Wembley
25.01.82	Dave Finigan W CO 2 Mayfair
09.02.82	Granville Allen W RSC 5 Kensington
02.03.82	Tommy McCallum W PTS 6 Kensington
15.03.82	Derek McKenzie W RSC 3 Mayfair
23.03.82	Dave Sullivan W PTS 6 Mayfair
18.05.82	Kostas Petrou W PTS 8 Bethnal Green
22.09.82	Kid Murray W RSC 3 Mayfair

101

22.11.82	Frank McCord W CO 1 Mayfair
18.01.83	Lloyd Hibbert W PTS 10 Kensington
	(Elim. British Welterweight Title)
01.03.83	Sid Smith W CO 4 Kensington
	(Southern Area Welterweight Title Challenge & Elim. British Welterweight Title)
05.04.83	Cliff Gilpin W PTS 12 Kensington
	(Vacant British Welterweight Title)
09.07.83	Kevin Austin W RSC 10 Chicago, USA
24.10.83	Harold Brazier W PTS 10 Mayfair
06.12.83	Cliff Gilpin W PTS 12 Kensington
	(British Welterweight Title Defence)
05.06.84	Roberto Mendez W RSC 8 Kensington
05.01.85	Gianfranco Rosi W CO 3 Perugia, Italy
	(European Welterweight Title Challenge)
12.02.85	R. W. Smith W RTD 6 Kensington
06.03.85	Roger Stafford W RSC 9 Kensington
30.08.85	Danny Paul W PTS 10 Atlantic City, USA
01.10.85	Ralph Twinning W RSC 4 Wembley
27.11.85	Sylvester Mittee W RSC 8 Muswell Hill
	(European Welterweight Title Defence. British & Commonwealth Welterweight Title Challenge)
20.05.86	Horace Shufford W RSC 8 Wembley
	(Final Elim. WBC Welterweight Title)
27.09.86	Don Curry W RTD 6 Atlantic City, USA
	(World Welterweight Title Challenge)
22.02.87	Johnny Bumphus W RSC 2 Wembley
	(IBF Welterweight Title Defence)
18.04.87	Maurice Blocker W PTS 12 Kensington
	(WBC Welterweight Title Defence)
30.08.87	Gené Hatcher W RSC 1 Marbella, Spain
	(WBC Welterweight Title Defence)
28.10.87	Jorge Vaca L TD 8 Wembley
	(WBC Welterweight Title Defence)
29.03.88	Jorge Vaca W CO 3 Wembley
	(WBC Welterweight Title Challenge)
29.07.88	Yung-Kil Chung W RSC 5 Atlantic City, USA
	(WBC Welterweight Title Defence)
05.02.89	Marlon Starling L RSC 9 Las Vegas, USA
	(WBC Welterweight Title Defence)
24.08.89	Delfino Marin W PTS 10 Tampa, USA
03.03.90	Mark Breland L RSC 3 Wembley
	(WBA Welterweight Title Challenge)
10.01.91	Mario Olmedo W RSC 4 Wandsworth
12.02.91	John Welters W RSC 1 Basildon
08.05.91	Darryl Anthony W CO 2 Kensington
22.04.92	Alfredo Ramirez W PTS 8 Wembley
13.05.92	Mick Duncan W RSC 2 Kensington
28.10.92	Carlo Colarusso W RSC 6 Kensington
30.01.93	Mickey Hughes W RSC 5 Brentwood
	(Commonwealth L. Middleweight Title Challenge)
26.06.93	Vinny Pazienza L RTD 10 Atlantic City, USA
02.11.93	Steve Goodwin W RSC 6 Southwark
26.02.94	Kevin Adamson W RSC 6 Earls Court
	(Commonwealth L. Middleweight Title Defence)
25.02.95	Adrian Dodson L RSC 3 Millwall

Career: 48 contests, won 43, lost 5.

Donnie Hood

Glasgow. *Born* Glasgow, 3 June, 1963
Former Undefeated WBC International & Scottish Bantamweight Champion. Ht. 5'5"
Manager Self

22.09.86	Stewart Fishermac W PTS 6 Glasgow
29.09.86	Keith Ward W PTS 6 Glasgow
08.12.86	Jamie McBride DREW 8 Glasgow
22.12.86	Keith Ward L PTS 8 Glasgow
27.01.87	Chris Clarkson W PTS 6 Glasgow
09.02.87	Danny Porter W RSC 4 Glasgow
24.02.87	Danny Lee W PTS 8 Glasgow
07.09.87	Kid Sumali W PTS 8 Glasgow
15.09.87	David Ingram L PTS 8 Batley
26.10.87	Jimmy Lee W PTS 8 Glasgow
25.11.87	Brian Holmes W PTS 10 Bellahouston
	(Vacant Scottish Bantamweight Title)
28.03.88	Nigel Crook W CO 2 Glasgow
12.05.88	Eyup Can L PTS 8 Copenhagen, Denmark
17.06.88	Fransie Badenhorst L RSC 7 Durban, South Africa
05.09.88	Gerry McBride W RTD 7 Glasgow
25.10.88	Graham O'Malley W RSC 9 Hartlepool
	(Elim. British Bantamweight Title)
06.03.89	Francisco Paco Garcia W RSC 6 Glasgow
28.03.89	John Vasquez W RSC 5 Glasgow
27.06.89	Ray Minus L RSC 6 Glasgow
	(Commonwealth Bantamweight Title Challenge)
22.01.90	Dean Lynch W PTS 8 Glasgow
26.03.90	Keith Wallace W RTD 8 Glasgow
	(Elim. British Bantamweight Title)
09.10.90	Samuel Duran W PTS 12 Glasgow
	(WBC International Bantamweight Title Challenge)
10.12.90	David Moreno W RSC 4 Glasgow
25.01.91	Dave Buxton W RSC 5 Shotts
05.03.91	Virgilio Openio W PTS 12 Glasgow
	(WBC International Bantamweight Title Defence)
31.05.91	Willie Richardson W PTS 8 Glasgow
24.09.91	Rocky Commey W PTS 12 Glasgow
	(WBC International Bantamweight Title Defence)
24.10.91	Vinnie Ponzio W PTS 8 Glasgow
14.03.92	Johnny Bredahl L RSC 7 Copenhagen, Denmark
	(Vacant European Bantamweight Title)
29.05.92	Pete Buckley W PTS 8 Glasgow
25.01.93	Drew Docherty L PTS 12 Glasgow
	(British Bantamweight Title Challenge)
11.03.94	Kid McAuley W PTS 8 Glasgow
02.03.95	Rowan Williams W PTS 8 Glasgow
21.04.95	Shaun Anderson L PTS 8 Glasgow

Career: 34 contests, won 25, drew 1, lost 8.

Johnny Hooks

Nottingham. *Born* North Shields, 9 March, 1968
L. Heavyweight. Ht. 6'1"
Manager J. Griffin

26.01.87	Young Gully L RSC 2 Nottingham
02.03.87	Jim Conley L RSC 2 Nottingham
18.02.94	Jim Pallatt W RSC 1 Leicester
07.04.94	Kevin Burton W PTS 6 Walsall
24.05.94	Dave Battey W PTS 6 Leicester
20.10.94	Neil Simpson L RSC 2 Walsall

Career: 6 contests, won 3, lost 3.

Glen Hopkins

Hetton. *Born* Easington, 8 November, 1974
Lightweight. Ht. 5'7"
Manager T. Conroy

05.12.94	John T. Kelly L PTS 6 Houghton le Spring
21.02.95	Ram Singh W RSC 1 Sunderland
11.05.95	Kid McAuley DREW 6 Sunderland
22.06.95	Niel Leggett L PTS 6 Houghton le Spring

Career: 4 contests, won 1, drew 1, lost 2.

Ron Hopley

Ripon. *Born* Ripon, 3 April, 1969
L. Middleweight. Ht. 5'8½"
Manager Self

27.11.91	William Beaton W RSC 2 Marton
23.01.92	Rick North W PTS 6 York
08.04.92	Steve Howden L PTS 6 Leeds
25.02.93	Rob Stevenson DREW 6 Bradford
07.04.93	Warren Stephens W PTS 6 Leeds
01.07.93	Rob Stevenson L PTS 6 York
07.10.93	Warren Bowers W PTS 6 York
28.02.94	Warren Bowers W RSC 1 Marton
26.10.94	Brian Dunn L PTS 6 Leeds

Career: 9 contests, won 5, drew 1, lost 3.

Lennie Howard

Chelmsford. *Born* Jamaica, 5 January, 1959
Cruiserweight. Ht. 6'1"
Manager Self

28.11.83	Paul Foster W CO 2 Southwark
16.02.84	Gypsy Carman W RTD 1 Basildon
27.03.84	Alex Romeo W PTS 6 Bethnal Green
19.04.84	Robbie Turner W RSC 4 Basildon
19.11.84	Stuart Robinson L PTS 8 Eltham
31.01.85	Romal Ambrose W CO 6 Basildon
28.03.85	Jerry Golden W RSC 2 Basildon
24.04.85	Geoff Rymer W PTS 6 Shoreditch
26.06.85	Hugh Johnson L PTS 8 Basildon
30.10.85	Glazz Campbell W PTS 8 Basildon
27.02.86	John Moody L RSC 6 Bethnal Green
	(Vacant Southern Area L. Heavyweight Title)
24.06.86	T. P. Jenkins W CO 4 Bethnal Green
23.10.86	John Moody L RSC 2 Basildon
	(Southern Area L. Heavyweight Title Challenge)
20.12.86	Richard Caramanolis L RSC 1 St Ouen, France
24.02.87	Noel Magee L RSC 1 Ilford
08.10.87	Derek Angol L RSC 5 Bethnal Green
17.02.88	John Williams W RSC 5 Bethnal Green
24.03.88	Sean Daly W RSC 6 Bethnal Green
21.04.88	Winston Burnett W PTS 6 Bethnal Green
06.06.88	Johnny Nelson L CO 2 Mayfair
28.10.88	Abner Blackstock W PTS 8 Brentwood
16.02.89	Lou Gent L RSC 2 Battersea
	(Vacant Southern Area Cruiserweight Title)
27.04.89	Magne Havnaa L RTD 3 Braedstrup, Denmark
06.06.89	Abner Blackstock W PTS 8 Chigwell
20.07.89	Francesco Terlizzi L PTS 6 Varese, Italy
02.10.89	Freddie Rafferty L PTS 10 Johannesburg, South Africa
16.12.89	Marcus Bott L CO 2 Pforzheim, Germany

26.09.90   Mick Queally L PTS 6 Mayfair
29.01.91   Herbie Hide L RSC 1 Wisbech
01.12.93   Denzil Browne L RSC 6 Kensington
26.01.94   Robert Norton L PTS 6 Birmingham
24.09.94   Paul Lawson L RSC 2 Wembley
Career: 32 contests, won 14, lost 18.

Robert Howard

Morecambe. *Born* Morecambe, 3 August, 1967
L. Welterweight. Ht. 5'9"
Manager F. Harrington

29.11.93   Scott Smith L PTS 6 Manchester
16.05.94   Tim Hill L CO 2 Morecambe
26.09.94   Ram Singh L PTS 6 Morecambe
Career: 3 contests, lost 3.

Steve Howden

Sheffield. *Born* Sheffield, 4 June, 1969
L. Welterweight. Ht. 5'8¾"
Manager Self

08.04.92   Ron Hopley W PTS 6 Leeds
01.06.92   Kevin McKillan L RSC 2 Manchester
07.07.92   Mike Morrison L CO 3 Bristol
01.10.92   Jimmy Reynolds L RTD 2 Telford
23.06.93   Shaba Edwards W RSC 1 Gorleston
11.08.93   Brian Coleman W RSC 4 Mansfield
30.11.93   Colin Anderson W PTS 6 Leicester
17.08.94   Rick North L PTS 6 Sheffield
23.09.94   Colin Dunne L CO 1 Bethnal Green
26.10.94   Gary Hiscox L RSC 4 Stoke
25.01.95   Mike Watson W RSC 2 Stoke
10.02.95   Clayton Hollingsworth L PTS 6 Birmingham
03.03.95   Danny Stevens L RSC 2 Bethnal Green
26.04.95   Mark Legg L RTD 2 Stoke
Career: 14 contests, won 5, lost 9.

John Hughes

Liverpool. *Born* Wrexham, 17 December, 1965
L. Middleweight. Ht. 5'7"
Manager D. Isaaman

02.06.94   Paolo Roberto L RSC 1 Tooting
02.07.94   Jon Stocks L RSC 1 Liverpool
Career: 2 contests, lost 2.

Mark Hughes

Swansea. *Born* Swansea, 8 July, 1971
Flyweight. Ht. 5'2"
Manager M. Duff

21.09.94   Graham McGrath W PTS 4 Cardiff
01.10.94   Anthony Hanna W PTS 4 Cardiff
06.03.95   Anthony Hanna W PTS 6 Mayfair
19.05.95   Shaun Norman W PTS 6 Southwark
Career: 4 contests, won 4.

Paul Hughes

Manchester. *Born* Manchester, 1 December, 1966
L. Welterweight. Ht. 5'8"
Manager N. Basso

09.10.91   Geoff Lawson W RSC 1 Marton
17.10.91   Tony Doyle W PTS 6 Mossley
13.11.91   Joey Moffat L RTD 4 Liverpool
01.06.92   Ty Zubair W PTS 6 Manchester
27.09.93   Micky Hall L PTS 6 Manchester
04.11.93   Gary Hiscox L PTS 6 Stafford

26.01.94   Chris Aston W PTS 6 Stoke
28.02.94   Michael Alexander L PTS 6 Manchester
15.07.94   Frankie Dewinter L PTS 6 Ieper, Belgium
20.02.95   Steve Tuckett L PTS 6 Manchester
Career: 10 contests, won 4, lost 6.

Norman Hutcheon

Leicester. *Born* Baillieston, 24 December, 1963
L. Middleweight. Ht. 5'8"
Manager J. Griffin

30.11.93   Prince Louis W PTS 6 Leicester
18.02.94   Balcar Singh W RSC 1 Leicester
24.05.94   Dennis Berry L RSC 2 Leicester
06.03.95   Andy Peach L RSC 2 Leicester
Career: 4 contests, won 2, lost 2.

Jason Hutson

Thame. *Born* London, 11 March, 1972
S. Featherweight. Ht. 5'6"
Manager Self

15.02.93   Marco Fattore L PTS 6 Mayfair
29.04.93   Vince Burns L RSC 1 Hayes
31.08.93   Ian Reid L RSC 6 Croydon
09.12.93   Marco Fattore DREW 6 Watford
07.10.94   Greg Upton L RSC 1 Taunton
25.10.94   Matt Brown L PTS 4 Southwark
19.11.94   Lewis Reynolds W RSC 2 Bracknell
20.01.95   Craig Kelley L RSC 2 Bethnal Green
17.03.95   Dennis H. Pedersen L RSC 4 Copenhagen, Denmark
Career: 9 contests, won 2, drew 1, lost 6.

Cordwell Hylton

Walsall. *Born* Jamaica, 20 September, 1958
Heavyweight. Former Midlands Area Cruiserweight Champion. Ht. 5'11"
Manager Self

22.09.80   Nigel Savery W PTS 6 Wolverhampton
30.10.80   Steve Fenton W CO 2 Wolverhampton
01.12.80   Liam Coleman L PTS 6 Wolverhampton
02.02.81   Steve Fenton W PTS 6 Nottingham
10.02.81   John O'Neill W RSC 6 Wolverhampton
16.03.81   Chris Lawson L RSC 5 Mayfair
13.04.81   Rupert Christie W RSC 5 Wolverhampton
11.05.81   Trevor Cattouse L PTS 8 Mayfair
05.10.81   Antonio Harris W PTS 8 Birmingham
30.11.81   Ben Lawlor W RSC 2 Birmingham
23.01.82   Chisanda Mutti L RSC 3 Berlin, Germany
16.02.82   Prince Mama Mohammed L PTS 8 Birmingham
19.03.82   Devon Bailey L RSC 2 Birmingham
24.05.82   Clive Beardsley W RSC 4 Nottingham
20.09.82   Keith Bristol NC 5 Wolverhampton
05.10.82   Alex Tompkins W PTS 8 Piccadilly
23.11.82   Winston Burnett W RSC 5 Wolverhampton
13.12.82   Steve Babbs L CO 1 Wolverhampton
15.02.83   Alek Pensarski W RSC 4 Wolverhampton
23.02.83   Devon Bailey L RSC 6 Mayfair
28.03.83   Gordon Stacey W RSC 1 Birmingham
25.04.83   Alex Tompkins W PTS 8 Southwark
19.05.83   Richard Caramanolis L CO 4 Paris, France
03.12.83   Andy Straughn L PTS 8 Marylebone

25.01.84   Romal Ambrose W RSC 3 Solihull
07.06.84   Roy Skeldon L CO 7 Dudley
01.12.84   Louis Pergaud L DIS 6 Dusseldorf, Germany
23.02.85   Chris Reid L CO 3 Belfast
25.04.85   Harry Andrews W PTS 6 Wolverhampton
05.06.85   Tony Wilson L CO 5 Kensington
12.10.87   Ivan Joseph L CO 6 Bow
24.02.88   Johnny Nelson L RSC 1 Sheffield
29.03.88   Eric Cardouza W CO 5 Wembley
05.05.88   Derek Angol L RSC 5 Wembley
19.09.88   Mike Aubrey L PTS 6 Mayfair
22.11.88   Crawford Ashley L CO 3 Basildon
02.02.89   Branko Pavlovic W RSC 2 Croydon
21.03.89   Abner Blackstock W CO 2 Wolverhampton
15.04.89   Alfredo Cacciatore L DIS 6 Vasto, Italy
21.05.89   Brendan Dempsey W PTS 8 Finsbury Park
12.08.89   Paul Muyodi L RTD 4 San Sepolcro, Italy
16.12.89   Lajos Eros L RSC 5 Milan, Italy
17.01.90   Mick Cordon W PTS 8 Stoke
08.02.90   Jim Peters W RSC 4 Southwark
08.03.90   Terry Dixon L PTS 8 Watford
25.04.90   Tee Jay L RSC 1 Millwall
13.06.90   Glazz Campbell W PTS 4 Manchester
31.10.90   Henry Maske L RSC 3 Wembley
12.02.91   Steve Lewsam W RSC 8 Wolverhampton
22.02.91   Bobbi Joe Edwards W RTD 6 Manchester
20.03.91   Roy Smith W RSC 7 Solihull
    (*Midland Area Cruiserweight Title Challenge*)
17.05.91   Neils H. Madsen L RSC 2 Copenhagen, Denmark
22.06.91   Norbert Ekassi L CO 5 Paris, France
16.09.91   Steve Lewsam L PTS 10 Cleethorpes
    (*Midlands Area Cruiserweight Title Defence*)
26.11.91   Tony Wilson L PTS 8 Wolverhampton
21.02.92   Markus Bott L PTS 8 Hamburg, Germany
06.03.92   Yuri Razumov DREW 6 Berlin, Germany
27.03.92   Jean-Marie Emebe W RSC 3 Creil, France
22.10.92   Chemek Saleta L RSC 4 Bethnal Green
25.02.93   Denzil Browne L PTS 8 Bradford
23.05.93   Wayne Llewelyn L PTS 6 Brockley
24.09.93   Cash McCullum DREW 8 Dublin
05.10.93   Scott Welch L RSC 1 Mayfair
03.11.93   John Ruiz L PTS 6 Bristol
29.01.94   Clifton Mitchell L RSC 1 Cardiff
03.03.94   Jacklord Jacobs L RSC 3 Ebbw Vale
15.04.94   Albert Call W RSC 4 Hull
    (*Vacant Midlands Area Cruiserweight Title*)
22.05.94   Wayne Llewelyn L CO 2 Crystal Palace
30.07.94   Jacklord Jacobs L RSC 4 Bethnal Green
05.12.94   John Foreman L PTS 10 Birmingham
    (*Midlands Area Cruiserweight Title Defence*)
21.04.95   Robert Norton L PTS 6 Dudley
19.05.95   Bruce Scott L RSC 1 Southwark
24.06.95   Wayne Buck L RSC 6 Cleethorpes
    (*Vacant Midlands Area Heavyweight Title*)
Career: 73 contests, won 27, drew 2, lost 43, no contest 1.

Nelson Ide

Leytonstone. *Born* Worthing, 24 July, 1969
Lightweight. Ht. 5'7"
Manager B. Lynch

16.03.95 Marc Smith W RSC 4 Basildon
04.06.95 Jimmy Singh W CO 1 Bethnal Green
Career: 2 contests, won 2.

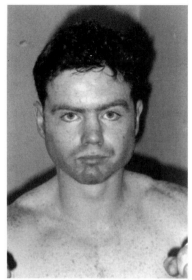

Nelson Ide   Les Clark

Vance Idiens

Cannock. *Born* Walsall, 9 June, 1962
Heavyweight. Ht. 6'4"
Manager W. Tyler

24.10.89 Mick Cordon W PTS 6
Wolverhampton
28.11.89 Ted Shaw W CO 1 Wolverhampton
06.12.89 Mick Cordon W PTS 6 Stoke
19.02.90 David Jules W PTS 6 Birmingham
22.03.90 Mick Cordon W PTS 6
Wolverhampton
24.05.90 Tucker Richards L RSC 5 Dudley
28.06.90 Paul Neilson W PTS 8 Birmingham
27.09.90 Paul Neilson W PTS 8 Birmingham
14.11.90 Paul Neilson L RSC 2 Doncaster
05.12.91 David Jules W RSC 4 Cannock
06.03.92 Mario Scheisser L RSC 1 Berlin,
Germany
09.12.92 David Jules W PTS 8 Stoke
11.03.93 Wayne Buck L PTS 8 Walsall
06.05.93 Joey Paladino W PTS 8 Walsall
19.05.93 John Harewood L CO 3 Sunderland
26.06.93 Justin Fortune L RSC 1 Keynsham
23.10.93 Dermot Gascoyne L RSC 4 Cardiff
14.03.94 Damien Caesar L RSC 4 Mayfair
14.04.94 Wayne Llewelyn L RSC 1 Battersea
05.12.94 Wayne Buck L PTS 6 Cleethorpes
Career: 20 contests, won 10, lost 10.

Paul Ingle

Scarborough. *Born* Scarborough, 22 June,
1972
S. Bantamweight. Ht. 5'5"
Manager F. Maloney

23.03.94 Darren Noble W RSC 3 Cardiff
27.04.94 Graham McGrath W PTS 4 Bethnal
Green
25.05.94 Neil Swain W CO 4 Bristol
03.08.94 Anthony Hanna W PTS 6 Bristol
24.11.94 Graham McGrath W PTS 6 Hull
23.02.95 Pete Buckley W PTS 8 Southwark
27.04.95 Pete Buckley W PTS 8 Bethnal Green
16.06.95 Des Gargano W RSC 2 Southwark
Career: 8 contests, won 8.

Nic Ingram

Northampton. *Born* Northampton, 3
October, 1972
L. Middleweight. Ht. 5'11"
Manager J. Cox

20.09.93 Mark Brogan W RSC 4 Northampton
04.11.93 Peter Reid L RSC 5 Stafford
08.03.94 Warren Stephens W PTS 6 Kettering
16.05.94 Roger Dean W RSC 3 Heathrow
27.05.94 Roy Dehara W PTS 6 Ashford
28.11.94 Peter Reid W PTS 6 Northampton
03.04.95 Stefan Scriggins L PTS 6 Northampton
12.06.95 John Stronach W PTS 6 Bradford
22.06.95 Robbie Bell L PTS 6 Houghton le
Spring
30.06.95 Danny Peters L RSC 6 Liverpool
Career: 10 contests, won 6, lost 4.

Colin Innes

Newcastle. *Born* Newcastle, 24 July, 1964
S. Featherweight. Ht. 5'6"
Manager N. Fawcett

10.09.90 Lee Christian W RSC 5 Northampton
24.09.90 Steve Armstrong W PTS 6 Manchester
08.10.90 Ervine Blake L PTS 6 Bradford
22.10.90 Steve Armstrong W RSC 6 Manchester
26.11.90 Carl Roberts L RSC 3 Bury
11.02.91 Steve Armstrong W PTS 6 Manchester
18.02.91 Ian McGirr L PTS 6 Glasgow
02.03.91 Tommy Smith W PTS 6 Darlington
28.03.91 Darryl Pettit W RTD 3 Alfreton
30.04.91 Noel Carroll L PTS 4 Stockport
19.09.91 Carl Roberts L PTS 4 Stockport
12.12.91 Tommy Smith L PTS 6 Hartlepool
24.02.92 Mark Geraghty L PTS 8 Glasgow
30.03.92 Chris Jickells L RSC 3 Bradford
28.05.92 Tommy Smith L PTS 6 Gosforth
05.10.92 Wayne Rigby L PTS 5 Manchester
18.11.92 Al Garrett DREW 6 Solihull
15.09.93 Chris Bennett DREW 6 Newcastle
25.11.93 Garry Burrell W PTS 6 Newcastle
06.12.93 Norman Dhalie L PTS 6 Bradford
24.01.94 Hugh Collins L PTS 6 Glasgow
03.03.94 Leo Turner DREW 6 Newcastle
21.04.94 Leo Turner W PTS 6 Gateshead
13.05.94 Rocky Ferrari L PTS 6 Kilmarnock
13.06.94 Leo Turner L PTS 6 Bradford
12.09.94 Kid McAuley L PTS 6 Doncaster
06.10.94 Chip O'Neill DREW 6 Cramlington
24.11.94 Paul Goode W PTS 6 Newcastle
24.02.95 Garry Burrell L PTS 6 Irvine
11.03.95 Trevor Sumner L PTS 6 Barnsley
25.03.95 Paul Hamilton W PTS 6 Rothwell
05.04.95 Ian McLeod L RSC 6 Irvine
11.05.95 Chip O'Neill L PTS 6 Sunderland
05.06.95 Paul Watson L RSC 4 Glasgow
Career: 34 contests, won 10, drew 4, lost 20.

(John) Jonjo Irwin

Doncaster. *Born* Denaby, 31 May, 1969
Penta-Continental S. Featherweight
Champion. All-Ireland Featherweight
Champion. Ht. 5'8"
Managers J. Rushton/B. Hearn

08.09.92 Kid McAuley W PTS 6 Doncaster
30.09.92 Miguel Matthews W PTS 6 Solihull
24.11.92 Colin Lynch W RSC 4 Doncaster
20.01.93 Mark Hargreaves W RSC 4 Solihull
23.02.93 G. G. Goddard W RSC 8 Doncaster
16.03.93 Kid McAuley W PTS 10 Mayfair
*(Vacant All-Ireland Featherweight
Title)*
28.04.93 Kevin Middleton L RSC 6 Solihull
06.10.93 Pete Buckley W PTS 8 Solihull
21.12.93 Peter Harris W PTS 8 Mayfair
22.01.94 Derek Amory L RSC 2 Belfast
10.05.94 Michael Armstrong W PTS 12
Doncaster
*(Vacant Penta-Continental
S. Featherweight Title)*
04.10.94 Harry Escott W PTS 12 Mayfair
*(Penta-Continental S. Featherweight
Title Defence)*
13.12.94 Bamana Dibateza W PTS 12 Potters
Bar
*(Penta-Continental S. Featherweight
Title Defence)*
30.06.95 Manuel Calvo W PTS 12 Doncaster
*(Inaugural WBO Continental
Featherweight Title)*
Career: 14 contests, won 12, lost 2.

Gilbert Jackson (Amponsan)

Battersea. *Born* Ghana, 21 August, 1970
L. Middleweight. Ht. 5'10"
Manager M. Duff

17.02.92 John Bosco L PTS 6 Mayfair
05.03.92 Tony Wellington W CO 2 Battersea
22.04.92 Russell Washer W PTS 6 Wembley
08.09.92 Paul Gamble W RSC 1 Norwich
05.02.93 Carl Harney W CO 3 Manchester
14.06.93 Lee Crocker W RSC 2 Bayswater
16.09.93 Alan Baptiste W RSC 5 Southwark
02.11.93 Ernie Loveridge W RTD 3 Southwark
01.12.93 Jerry Mortimer W RSC 3 Kensington
16.02.94 Chris Richards W RSC 2 Stevenage
14.03.94 Mark Atkins W PTS 6 Mayfair
13.04.94 Gordon Blair W RTD 1 Glasgow
23.09.94 Martin Jolley W CO 3 Bethnal Green
09.11.94 Chris Peters W RSC 3 Millwall
14.02.95 Chris Richards W RTD 2 Bethnal
Green
21.04.95 Paul Wesley W RSC 6 Dudley
(Elim. British L. Middleweight Title)
Career: 16 contests, won 15, lost 1.

(James) Jem Jackson

Birmingham. *Born* Birmingham, 22 March,
1970
Cruiserweight. Ht. 6'0"
Manager Self

28.03.94 Declan Faherty L RTD 5 Birmingham
12.12.94 Kevin Burton L RSC 4 Doncaster
Career: 2 contests, lost 2.

Gary Jacobs

Glasgow. *Born* Glasgow, 10 December, 1965
Former Undefeated European Welterweight Champion. Former Commonwealth Welterweight Champion. Former Undefeated British, WBC International & Scottish Welterweight Champion. Ht. 5'7½"
Manager M. Duff

20.05.85	John Conlan W PTS 6 Glasgow	
03.06.85	Nigel Burke W PTS 6 Glasgow	
12.08.85	Mike McKenzie W PTS 6 Glasgow	
07.10.85	Albert Buchanan W PTS 6 Cambuslang	
11.11.85	Tyrell Wilson W CO 5 Glasgow	
02.12.85	Dave Heaver W PTS 6 Glasgow	
10.02.86	Courtney Phillips W RSC 5 Glasgow	
10.03.86	Alistair Laurie W PTS 8 Glasgow	
14.04.86	Billy Cairns W PTS 8 Glasgow	
24.06.86	Dave Douglas L PTS 10 Glasgow	
	(Vacant Scottish Welterweight Title)	
15.09.86	Jeff Connors W RSC 3 Glasgow	
20.10.86	Kelvin Mortimer W RSC 5 Glasgow	
27.01.87	Dave Douglas W PTS 10 Glasgow	
	(Scottish Welterweight Title Challenge)	
24.02.87	Gary Williams W CO 7 Glasgow	
06.04.87	Robert Armstrong W RTD 5 Glasgow	
19.05.87	Gary Williams W RSC 3 Cumbernauld	
08.06.87	Tommy McCallum W RSC 5 Glasgow	
	(Scottish Welterweight Title Defence)	
26.11.87	Jeff Connors W PTS 8 Fulham	
24.02.88	Del Bryan W PTS 10 Glasgow	
	(Final Elim. British Welterweight Title)	
19.04.88	Wilf Gentzen W PTS 12 Glasgow	
	(Commonwealth Welterweight Title Challenge)	
06.06.88	Juan Alonzo Villa W RSC 5 Mayfair	
16.09.88	Javier Suazo W CO 10 Las Vegas, USA	
	(Vacant WBC International Welterweight Title)	
29.11.88	Richard Rova W CO 4 Kensington	
	(Commonwealth Welterweight Title Defence)	
14.02.89	Rocky Kelly W RTD 7 Wandsworth	
	(Commonwealth & WBC International Welterweight Title Defence)	
05.04.89	George Collins W PTS 12 Kensington	
	(Commonwealth & WBC International Welterweight Title Defence)	
27.06.89	Rollin Williams W RSC 1 Kensington	
27.08.89	James McGirt L PTS 10 New York, USA	
23.11.89	Donovan Boucher L PTS 12 Motherwell	
	(Commonwealth Welterweight Title Defence)	
26.04.90	Pascal Lorcy W RSC 2 Wandsworth	
09.05.90	Mike Durvan W CO 1 Kensington	
17.10.90	Mickey Hughes L CO 8 Bethnal Green	
05.03.91	Kenny Louis W CO 2 Glasgow	
20.11.91	Peter Eubank W PTS 8 Kensington	
20.02.92	Del Bryan W PTS 12 Glasgow	
	(British Welterweight Title Challenge)	
25.03.92	Tommy Small W RSC 2 Kensington	
22.04.92	Cirillo Nino W PTS 10 Wembley	
09.07.92	Robert Wright W RSC 6 Glasgow	
	(British Welterweight Title Defence)	
16.10.92	Ludovic Proto L PTS 12 Paris, France	
	(Vacant European Welterweight Title)	
06.02.93	Ludovic Proto W RTD 9 Paris, France	
	(European Welterweight Title Challenge)	
19.05.93	Horace Fleary W RTD 4 Sunderland	
22.09.93	Daniel Bicchieray W RSC 5 Wembley	
	(European Welterweight Title Defence)	
01.02.94	Tek Nkalankete W PTS 12 Paris, France	
	(European Welterweight Title Defence)	
13.04.94	Alessandro Duran W CO 8 Glasgow	
	(European Welterweight Title Defence)	
05.10.94	Rusty de Rouen W RSC 6 Wolverhampton	
09.11.94	Marcelo di Croce W PTS 10 Millwall	
04.03.95	Jose Miguel Fernandez W PTS 10 Atlantic City, USA	

Career: 46 contests, won 41, lost 5.

Jacklord Jacobs

Crystal Palace. *Born* Nigeria, 1 January, 1970
Cruiserweight. Ht. 6'1"
Manager M. Jacobs

03.03.94	Cordwell Hylton W RSC 3 Ebbw Vale	
30.07.94	Cordwell Hylton W RSC 4 Bethnal Green	
01.11.94	Bobby Anderson DREW 4 Las Vegas, USA	

Career: 3 contest, won 2, drew 1.

Lester Jacobs

Peckham. *Born* London, 29 January, 1962
Middleweight. Ht. 5'7"
Manager Self

01.03.89	Peter Vosper W PTS 6 Bethnal Green	
29.03.89	Reuben Thurley W RSC 4 Bethnal Green	
30.01.90	David Brown W PTS 6 Battersea	
12.09.90	Peter Gorny W RSC 2 Battersea	
18.10.90	Alan Pennington W RSC 2 Wandsworth	
20.03.91	Karl Barwise W PTS 6 Battersea	
16.05.91	Paul McCarthy W PTS 6 Battersea	
11.09.91	John Kaighin W RSC 2 Hammersmith	
05.03.92	John Kaighin W RSC 1 Battersea	
17.05.92	Marvin O'Brien W PTS 6 Harringay	
16.11.94	Stinger Mason W PTS 6 Bloomsbury	
23.02.95	Paul Murray W RSC 2 Southwark	
08.03.95	Mark Dawson W PTS 6 Bloomsbury	

Career: 13 contests, won 13.

John Janes

Cardiff. *Born* Worcester, 3 March, 1974
Welterweight. Ht. 5'7"
Manager D. Gardiner

29.11.94	Steve Burton W PTS 6 Cardiff	
25.01.95	Paul Dyer L PTS 6 Cardiff	
06.05.95	Sean Baker L PTS 4 Shepton Mallet	

Career: 3 contests, won 1, lost 2.

Mark Jay (Jackson)

Seaton Delaval. *Born* Newcastle, 4 April, 1969
Middleweight. Ht. 5'11"
Manager N. Fawcett

29.09.88	Tony Farrell W PTS 6 Sunderland	
22.11.88	Dave Whittle W PTS 6 Marton	
05.04.89	Lewis Welch L PTS 6 Halifax	
19.05.89	Mick Mulcahy W PTS 6 Gateshead	
25.09.89	Carlton Myers W PTS 6 Piccadilly	
21.10.89	Ian Thomas L RSC 5 Middlesbrough	
24.04.90	Ernie Loveridge L PTS 6 Stoke	
30.05.90	Trevor Meikle DREW 6 Stoke	
15.06.90	Trevor Meikle L RSC 5 Telford	
18.10.90	Phil Epton L PTS 6 Dewsbury	
19.11.90	John Mullen DREW 6 Glasgow	
29.11.90	Barry Messam L RSC 5 Sunderland	
09.10.91	Willie Quinn W PTS 6 Glasgow	
16.12.91	Tyrone Eastmond L PTS 6 Manchester	
20.01.92	Mick Duncan W PTS 6 Bradford	
24.02.92	David Radford W PTS 6 Bradford	
03.03.92	Dave Johnson L PTS 6 Houghton le Spring	
12.03.92	Gordon Blair DREW 8 Glasgow	
02.04.92	Jamie Robinson L PTS 6 Basildon	
25.04.92	Steve Foster L RSC 7 Manchester	
28.05.92	Shamus Casey W PTS 8 Gosforth	
24.09.92	Derek Wormald L RSC 5 Stockport	
01.12.92	Neil Patterson W PTS 6 Hartlepool	
17.12.92	Clay O'Shea L CO 1 Wembley	
09.03.93	Spencer Alton W RSC 4 Hartlepool	
29.04.93	Allan Grainger W RSC 3 Newcastle	
11.06.93	Tony Trimble W RSC 1 Gateshead	
15.09.93	John Duckworth L RSC 4 Newcastle	
02.12.93	Mark Cichocki L RSC 4 Hartlepool	
	(Northern Area L. Middleweight Title Challenge)	
03.03.94	Dave Whittle L PTS 8 Newcastle	
21.04.94	Shamus Casey W PTS 6 Gateshead	
24.05.94	Japhet Hans L RSC 1 Sunderland	
06.10.94	Spencer Alton W PTS 6 Cramlington	
23.11.94	Willie Quinn L RSC 1 Irvine	
16.01.95	Willie Quinn L RSC 2 Musselburgh	
02.03.95	Spencer Alton W PTS 6 Cramlington	
25.03.95	Shaun Hendry L RSC 2 Rothwell	

Career: 37 contests, won 15, drew 3, lost 19.

Andrew Jervis

Liverpool. *Born* Liverpool, 28 June, 1969
Welterweight. Ht. 5'11"
Manager Self

05.10.92	Rick North W PTS 6 Liverpool	
02.11.92	Shaun Martin W CO 2 Liverpool	
01.12.92	Cliff Churchward W PTS 6 Liverpool	
27.01.93	Mark Ramsey L PTS 6 Stoke	
22.02.93	Alan Williams W PTS 6 Liverpool	
29.03.93	Bullit Andrews W PTS 6 Liverpool	
09.06.93	Chris Mulcahy W PTS 6 Liverpool	
15.03.94	John Duckworth W PTS 6 Stoke	
25.05.94	Sean Baker DREW 4 Bristol	
04.06.94	Adrian Dodson L RSC 2 Cardiff	
17.08.94	Robin Reid L RSC 1 Sheffield	
26.10.94	David Larkin L CO 5 Leeds	
08.03.95	Howard Clarke L RSC 8 Solihull	
22.03.95	Andy Peach W PTS 6 Stoke	
03.04.95	Andy Davidson W CO 3 Manchester	
27.05.95	Neil Sinclair W RSC 3 Belfast	

Career: 16 contests, won 9, drew 1, lost 6.

Chris Jickells

Brigg. *Born* Scunthorpe, 26 March, 1971
S. Featherweight. Ht. 5'5"
Manager J. Rushton

18.11.91	Tony Smith W RSC 4 Manchester	
09.12.91	Al Garrett W RSC 2 Bradford	
15.01.92	Ronnie Stephenson L PTS 6 Stoke	
30.03.92	Colin Innes W RSC 3 Bradford	
29.04.92	Kevin Middleton W RSC 6 Solihull	
01.06.92	Dave McHale L RSC 4 Glasgow	
12.10.92	Ian McGirr W RSC 3 Bradford	
10.02.93	Kevin Middleton L CO 1 Lewisham	
07.06.93	Wilson Docherty L RSC 5 Glasgow	
02.11.93	Mark Bowers L RSC 3 Southwark	

21.03.94	Mike Deveney L RSC 5 Glasgow	
26.09.94	Dave Clavering L PTS 6 Morecambe	
11.10.94	Yifru Retta L PTS 6 Bethnal Green	
11.11.94	Dennis Holbaek Pedersen L PTS 6 Randers, Denmark	
23.11.94	Ian McLeod L PTS 6 Irvine	
04.02.95	Neil Swain L PTS 6 Cardiff	
04.03.95	Paul Griffin L RSC 5 Livingston	
30.06.95	Graham McGrath W PTS 4 Doncaster	

Career: 18 contests, won 6, lost 12.

Chris Jickells   Les Clark

James Jiora (Iwenjiora)

Otley. *Born* Nigeria, 6 April, 1968
L. Welterweight. Ht. 5'5"
Manager Self

07.06.87	Paul Kennedy W RSC 6 Bradford
15.09.87	Ian Murray W RSC 2 Batley
02.11.87	Michael Howell W RSC 3 Bradford
10.11.87	Marvin P. Gray L PTS 8 Batley
30.11.87	John Townsley W PTS 8 Nottingham
15.12.87	Paul Burke W PTS 4 Bradford
08.03.88	Rudy Valentino L PTS 6 Batley
26.01.89	Frankie Foster L PTS 6 Newcastle
20.02.89	Paul Bowen L PTS 6 Birmingham
20.03.89	Dean Dickinson W PTS 6 Bradford
31.03.89	Chris Bennett L PTS 6 Scarborough
11.07.89	Craig Walsh L PTS 8 Batley
05.12.89	Paul Charters L RSC 4 Dewsbury
11.01.90	Kid Sumali W PTS 4 Dewsbury
26.02.90	Brendan Ryan W PTS 6 Bradford
11.04.90	Rick Bushell L PTS 6 Dewsbury
29.11.90	Marvin P. Gray L PTS 8 Marton
13.06.91	David Thompson DREW 6 Hull
01.08.91	Chris Saunders L PTS 6 Dewsbury
09.10.91	John O. Johnson L PTS 6 Manchester
21.10.91	Charlie Kane L PTS 6 Glasgow
02.03.92	Carl Tilley L PTS 6 Marton
12.03.92	Alan McDowall L CO 2 Glasgow
13.06.94	Mark Allen W PTS 6 Bradford
24.10.94	Paul Scott W PTS 6 Bradford
05.12.94	Alan Peacock W PTS 6 Bradford

Career: 26 contests, won 11, drew 1, lost 14.

Dave Johnson

Boldon. *Born* Boldon, 10 August, 1972
Middleweight. Ht. 5'10"
Manager T. Conroy

13.05.91	Rocky Tyrell W PTS 6 Manchester
20.05.91	Griff Jones W PTS 6 Bradford
10.06.91	Tyrone Eastmond W PTS 6 Manchester
10.10.91	Shamus Casey W PTS 6 Gateshead
14.11.91	Shamus Casey W PTS 6 Gateshead
25.11.91	Mike Phillips L PTS 6 Liverpool
12.12.91	Mick Duncan W PTS 6 Hartlepool
03.03.92	Mark Jay W PTS 6 Houghton le Spring
28.04.92	Shaun McCrory DREW 6 Houghton le Spring
10.09.92	Spencer Alton W PTS 6 Sunderland
23.10.92	Griff Jones W PTS 6 Gateshead
17.04.93	Mike Phillips W PTS 6 Washington
11.06.93	Robert Riley W PTS 8 Gateshead
15.09.93	Darren Pilling W PTS 6 Newcastle
25.11.93	Dave Owens W PTS 8 Tynemouth
02.03.94	John Duckworth W PTS 8 Solihull
17.03.94	Peter Waudby L PTS 6 Lincoln
27.04.94	Barry Thorogood DREW 8 Solihull
24.05.94	Martin Jolley W PTS 6 Sunderland
13.10.94	Japhet Hans W RSC 2 Houghton le Spring
10.12.94	Derek Wormald DREW 8 Manchester
21.02.95	Vince Rose W PTS 8 Sunderland
01.03.95	Ernie Loveridge W PTS 6 Glasgow

Career: 23 contests, won 18, drew 3, lost 2.

Denny Johnson

Newcastle. *Born* Wallsend, 3 January, 1967
Welterweight. Ht. 5'8½"
Manager N. Fawcett

02.03.95	Wayne Shepherd W PTS 6 Cramlington
15.05.95	John Stronach L PTS 6 Bradford

Career: 2 contests, won 1, lost 1.

(Paul) John O. Johnson (Johnson)

Nottingham. *Born* Nottingham, 2 November, 1969
L. Welterweight. Ht. 5'5"
Manager W. Swift

29.08.91	Seth Jones W DIS 1 Oakengates
09.10.91	James Jiora W PTS 6 Manchester
24.10.91	Carl Hook L PTS 6 Dunstable
31.10.91	Darren Morris W PTS 6 Oakengates
26.11.91	Bernard Paul L PTS 6 Bethnal Green
22.01.92	Brian Coleman W PTS 6 Stoke
30.01.92	Chris Saunders W PTS 6 Southampton
20.02.92	Alan Peacock W PTS 6 Glasgow
09.03.92	Ricky Sackfield W PTS 6 Manchester
26.03.92	Davy Robb L PTS 6 Telford
03.06.92	Jason Barker W PTS 6 Newcastle under Lyme
09.09.92	Chris Saunders DREW 6 Stoke
05.10.92	Andreas Panayi L RTD 1 Liverpool
09.12.92	Jason Barker W PTS 8 Stoke
10.02.93	Dean Hollington L PTS 6 Lewisham
17.03.93	Jonathan Thaxton L PTS 6 Stoke
19.04.93	Billy McDougall L PTS 6 Stoke
10.03.94	Keith Marner L RSC 5 Watford
10.05.94	Mark Legg W RSC 6 Doncaster
11.06.94	Paul Knights W PTS 6 Bethnal Green
28.06.94	Andreas Panayi L RSC 5 Mayfair
30.09.94	Michael Ayers L RSC 3 Bethnal Green
23.02.95	Peter Richardson L RSC 5 Southwark

30.03.95	Richie Edwards L PTS 4 Bethnal Green
20.04.95	Carl Wright L PTS 6 Liverpool
13.05.95	Tanveer Ahmed L CO 3 Glasgow

Career: 26 contests, won 11, drew 1, lost 14.

Martin Jolley

Alfreton. *Born* Chesterfield, 22 November, 1967
S. Middleweight. Ht. 5'11½"
Manager M. Shinfield

10.03.92	Gypsy Johnny Price W RSC 3 Bury
06.04.92	Sean Byrne L RSC 6 Northampton
11.05.92	Mark Hale W PTS 6 Coventry
08.09.92	Brian McGloin W PTS 6 Doncaster
05.10.92	Mark Hale W RSC 4 Bardon
14.10.92	Carl Smallwood W PTS 6 Stoke
02.11.92	Bobby Mack L PTS 6 Wolverhampton
24.11.92	Phil Ball DREW 6 Doncaster
02.03.93	Mark McBiane W RSC 5 Derby
23.02.93	Phil Ball W RSC 5 Doncaster
12.05.93	Marvin O'Brien W PTS 6 Sheffield
08.06.93	Paul Hanlon W PTS 6 Derby
22.09.93	Nigel Rafferty L PTS 6 Chesterfield
29.10.93	Mads Larsen L CO 3 Korsoer, Denmark
02.12.93	Darren Littlewood L PTS 6 Evesham
17.03.94	Paul Hitch W RSC 2 Lincoln
25.04.94	Derek Wormald L RSC 4 Bury
24.05.94	Dave Johnson L PTS 6 Sunderland
17.06.94	Dean Francis L PTS 6 Plymouth
02.07.94	Glenn Catley L RSC 1 Keynsham
23.09.94	Gilbert Jackson L CO 3 Bethnal Green
24.10.94	Craig Joseph L PTS 6 Bradford
07.11.94	Mark Delaney L RSC 3 Bethnal Green
12.12.94	Darren Littlewood L PTS 6 Cleethorpes
20.12.94	Mark Delaney L RSC 4 Bethnal Green
17.02.95	Willie Quinn L CO 5 Cumbernauld
11.05.95	Darren Sweeney L PTS 6 Dudley
19.05.95	Steve McNess L PTS 6 Southwark
10.06.95	Robin Reid L CO 1 Manchester

Career: 29 contests, won 10, drew 1, lost 18.

Barry Jones

Cardiff. *Born* Cardiff, 3 May, 1974
Featherweight. Ht. 5'7"
Manager B. Aird

28.10.92	Conn McMullen W PTS 6 Cardiff
14.12.92	Miguel Matthews W PTS 6 Cardiff
27.01.93	Mike Deveney W PTS 6 Cardiff
24.03.93	Greg Upton W RSC 2 Mayfair
28.04.93	Kid McAuley W PTS 8 Solihull
09.10.93	John White W PTS 4 Manchester
10.11.93	Neil Swain W PTS 6 Ystrad
30.11.93	Pete Buckley W PTS 4 Cardiff
16.12.93	Elvis Parsley W PTS 6 Newport
22.01.94	Pete Buckley W PTS 6 Cardiff
27.08.94	Kelton McKenzie W PTS 6 Cardiff
25.05.95	Justin Murphy W PTS 10 Reading
	(Elim. British Featherweight Title)

Career: 12 contests, won 12.

Henry Jones

Pembroke. *Born* Haverfordwest, 23 December, 1975
Bantamweight. Ht. 5'0"
Manager G. Davies

17.06.95	Abdul Mannon W PTS 6 Cardiff

Career: 1 contest, won 1.

Keith Jones   Les Clark

Keith Jones

Bargoed. *Born* Bradwell, 4 December, 1968
S. Featherweight. Ht. 5'5¾"
Manager D. Gardiner

17.05.94	Abdul Mannon L PTS 6 Kettering
13.06.94	G. G. Goddard L PTS 6 Liverpool
21.07.94	G. G. Goddard L RSC 1 Battersea
12.09.94	Marco Fattore L PTS 6 Mayfair
29.09.94	Marlon Ward L PTS 4 Bethnal Green
21.10.94	James Murray L CO 3 Glasgow
27.11.94	Daniel Lutaaya L CO 1 Southwark

Career: 7 contests, lost 7.

Paul Jones

Sheffield. *Born* Sheffield, 19 November, 1966
WBO Continental L. Middleweight Champion. Former Undefeated Central Area L. Middleweight Champion. Ht. 6'0"
Manager B. Hearn

08.12.86	Paul Gillings W PTS 6 Liverpool
28.10.87	Pat Durkin W PTS 4 Sheffield
10.11.87	David Binns L PTS 6 Batley
11.01.88	Humphrey Harrison L PTS 8 Manchester
27.09.88	George Sponagle DREW 8 Halifax, Canada
07.12.88	Jimmy Thornton W PTS 6 Stoke
23.01.89	Donovan Boucher L DIS 6 Toronto, Canada
13.03.89	Dale Moreland W PTS 6 Toronto, Canada
30.03.89	Benoit Boudreau W PTS 10 Moncton, Canada
19.04.89	Tony Collier W CO 3 Toronto, Canada
06.06.89	George Sponagle L PTS 8 Halifax, Canada
06.09.89	Kid Ford W PTS 6 Mississouga, Canada
13.11.89	Ian Midwood-Tate W RSC 4 Manchester
08.12.89	Antoine Tarver L PTS 4 Doncaster

06.03.90	Antonio Fernandez W PTS 8 Stoke
22.03.90	Darren Pilling W RTD 7 Gateshead
26.04.90	Newton Barnett W PTS 8 Mayfair
20.05.90	Jim Beckett W CO 1 Sheffield
22.05.90	Wayne Ellis L PTS 6 St Albans
14.11.90	Jason Rowe W PTS 10 Sheffield
	(Central Area L. Middleweight Title Challenge)
12.03.91	Tony Velinor W PTS 8 Mansfield
16.08.91	Hugo Marinangelli L CO 2 Marbella, Spain
01.10.91	Simon Eubank W CO 6 Sheffield
14.04.92	Paul Lynch W RSC 3 Mansfield
19.05.92	Trevor Ambrose W PTS 6 Cardiff
02.06.92	Patrick Vungbo W PTS 10 Rotterdam, Holland
19.09.92	Ernie Loveridge W PTS 6 Glasgow
24.11.92	Paul Wesley L RSC 2 Doncaster
17.01.95	Julian Eavis W RSC 4 Worcester
06.03.95	Peter Waudby W PTS 6 Mayfair
14.04.95	Damien Denny W CO 1 Belfast
	(Inaugural WBO Continental L. Middleweight Title)

Career: 31 contests, won 22, drew 1, lost 8.

Seth Jones

Dyffryn. *Born* St Asaph, 9 February, 1968
Welterweight. Ht. 5'8¾"
Manager Self

29.08.91	John O'Johnson L DIS 1 Oakengates
19.09.91	Ricky Sackfield L RSC 1 Stockport
20.11.91	Jess Rundan W CO 4 Cardiff
09.12.91	Spencer McCracken L RSC 2 Brierley Hill
19.02.92	Paul Knights L RSC 5 Muswell Hill
31.03.92	Danny Kett W CO 1 Norwich
16.06.92	Paul Knights L PTS 6 Dagenham
26.09.92	Dave Lovell L RSC 4 Earls Court
01.12.92	Kevin McKenzie W RSC 3 Hartlepool
10.02.93	Jason Rowland L RSC 2 Lewisham
18.05.93	Shaun Cogan L RSC 2 Edgbaston
17.05.95	Gavin Barker L PTS 4 Ipswich
04.06.95	Richie Edwards L RSC 4 Bethnal Green

Career: 13 contests, won 3, lost 10.

Wayne Jones

Saltash. *Born* Halifax, 6 October, 1968
L. Welterweight. Ht. 5'8"
Manager N. Christian

13.11.93	Robbie Sivyer W PTS 6 Cullompton
14.01.94	Colin Dunne L RSC 3 Bethnal Green
04.03.94	Robbie Sivyer W PTS 6 Weston super Mare
17.06.94	Trevor Royal W PTS 6 Plymouth
09.07.94	Bobby Guynan L PTS 6 Earls Court
30.07.94	Sean Knight L RSC 2 Bethnal Green
01.10.94	Gareth Jordan L RSC 2 Cardiff
19.11.94	Adrian Chase L PTS 6 Heathrow
27.11.94	Everald Williams L RSC 2 Southwark
24.01.95	Brian Coleman W PTS 6 Piccadilly
18.02.95	Chris Barnett L RSC 5 Shepton Mallet
25.03.95	Danny Lutaaya L RSC 3 Millwall
09.05.95	Georgie Smith L RSC 3 Basildon
16.06.95	Lewis Reynolds L PTS 4 Southwark
23.06.95	Allan Gray L PTS 6 Bethnal Green

Career: 15 contests, won 4, lost 11.

Wesley Jones

Colwyn Bay. *Born* Rhuddlan, 13 November, 1974
L. Middleweight. Ht. 5'10¾"
Manager D. Davies

12.06.95	Lee Power L PTS 6 Bethnal Green

Career: 1 contest, lost 1.

Cham Joof

Brixton. *Born* London, 19 November, 1968
Southern Area Lightweight Champion. Ht. 5'8"
Managers F. Warren/C. Carew

22.02.93	Chris Saunders W PTS 4 Eltham
04.04.93	Anthony Wanza W RSC 2 Brockley
14.04.93	Mike Morrison W PTS 4 Kensington
23.05.93	Charles Shepherd L PTS 4 Brockley
25.06.93	Scott Smith W RTD 2 Battersea
14.08.93	Mark Allen W RSC 3 Hammersmith
20.01.94	Phil Found W RSC 1 Battersea
14.04.94	Brian Coleman W CO 3 Battersea
22.05.94	Felix Kelly W RSC 5 Crystal Palace
	(Southern Area Lightweight Title Challenge)
25.02.95	Tony Foster W PTS 8 Millwall
06.05.95	Karl Taylor L PTS 8 Shepton Mallet

Career: 11 contests, won 9, lost 2.

Gareth Jordan   Les Clark

Gareth Jordan

Monmouth. *Born* Usk, 19 December, 1971
Lightweight. Ht. 5'6¾"
Manager M. Duff

02.11.92	Con Cronin W RSC 2 Wolverhampton
04.12.92	Jason White W RSC 2 Telford
16.03.93	Lee Fox W RSC 3 Wolverhampton
26.05.93	Mark O'Callaghan W RSC 3 Mansfield
27.10.93	Dave Madden W RSC 5 West Bromwich
16.12.93	Phil Found W PTS 6 Newport
04.06.94	T. J. Smith W RSC 1 Cardiff
01.10.94	Wayne Jones W RSC 2 Cardiff

107

30.11.94	Kevin McKenzie W PTS 6 Wolverhampton
04.02.95	Mark O'Callaghan W RSC 2 Cardiff
21.04.95	Peter Till W PTS 6 Dudley

Career: 11 Contests, won 11.

Craig Joseph

Bradford. *Born* Bradford, 5 December, 1968
S. Middleweight. Ht. 6'0"
Manager Self

04.10.93	Pat McNamara W RSC 2 Bradford
07.02.94	Jimmy Tyers W PTS 6 Bradford
27.04.94	Chris Davies W PTS 6 Solihull
13.06.94	Spencer Alton W PTS 6 Bradford
24.10.94	Martin Jolley W PTS 6 Bradford
20.02.95	Ray Webb L PTS 6 Glasgow
26.04.95	Neil Simpson W PTS 6 Solihull

Career: 7 Contests, won 6, lost 1.

Peter Judson

Keighley. *Born* Keighley, 14 January, 1970
S. Featherweight. Ht. 5'7"
Managers F. Warren/N. Basso

24.04.89	Darryl Pettit DREW 6 Bradford
11.07.89	Neil Leitch W PTS 6 Batley
18.09.89	Phil Lashley W PTS 6 Mayfair
02.10.89	Stevie Woods L PTS 6 Bradford
22.11.89	Pete Buckley L PTS 6 Stafford
19.02.90	Phil Lashley W CO 6 Nottingham
08.03.90	Wayne Goult L PTS 6 Peterborough
19.03.90	Andrew Robinson W PTS 6 Grimsby
26.03.90	Wayne Marston W PTS 6 Nottingham
30.04.90	Derek Amory L PTS 6 Brierley Hill
09.05.90	Brian Robb W PTS 6 Solihull
04.06.90	Jamie McBride L PTS 8 Glasgow
17.09.90	Mark Geraghty W PTS 6 Glasgow
26.09.90	Carl Roberts W PTS 6 Manchester
08.10.90	Mark Geraghty L PTS 6 Glasgow
19.11.90	Russell Davison L PTS 8 Manchester
27.11.90	Rocky Lawlor W PTS 8 Wolverhampton
29.01.91	Russell Davison L PTS 10 Stockport
	(Vacant Central Area Featherweight Title)
21.02.91	Noel Carroll W PTS 8 Leeds
20.03.91	Colin Lynch W RTD 5 Solihull
01.05.91	Jimmy Owens L PTS 6 Liverpool
28.05.91	Scott Durham W PTS 6 Cardiff
24.09.91	Ian McGirr L PTS 6 Glasgow
11.11.91	Miguel Matthews W PTS 6 Stratford upon Avon
18.11.91	Jamie McBride DREW 6 Glasgow
09.02.92	Ceri Farrell W PTS 6 Bradford
05.04.92	Barrie Kelley W PTS 6 Bradford
14.11.92	J. T. Williams DREW 6 Cardiff
25.02.93	Dominic McGuigan DREW 6 Bradford
16.05.94	Carlos Chase W PTS 4 Heathrow
25.03.95	Sugar Gibiliru W PTS 6 Chester
06.05.95	Colin McMillan L PTS 8 Shepton Mallet

Career: 32 contests, won 17, drew 4, lost 11.

David Jules

Doncaster. *Born* Doncaster, 11 July, 1965
Heavyweight. Ht. 6'2"
Manager Self

12.06.87	Carl Timbrell W CO 5 Leamington
07.10.87	Carl Timbrell L RSC 3 Stoke
17.03.88	Peter Fury W RTD 2 Sunderland

21.03.88	Jess Harding L RSC 2 Bethnal Green
29.09.88	Gary McCrory L PTS 6 Sunderland
22.11.88	Gary McCrory L PTS 6 Marton
05.12.88	Denroy Bryan DREW 6 Dudley
18.01.89	Denroy Bryan W RSC 2 Stoke
22.02.89	Tony Hallett W RSC 1 Doncaster
19.04.89	Rocky Burton L RSC 3 Doncaster
11.11.89	Jimmy di Stolfo W RSC 1 Rimini, Italy
30.11.89	Biagio Chianese L RSC 2 Milan, Italy
19.02.90	Vance Idiens L PTS 6 Birmingham
07.05.90	Ramon Voorn L RSC 3 Arnhem, Holland
12.11.90	Steve Garber L RSC 6 Bradford
09.04.91	Herbie Hide L RSC 1 Mayfair
05.12.91	Vance Idiens L RSC 4 Cannock
24.02.92	Rocky Burton W CO 1 Coventry
05.04.92	Steve Garber L RSC 4 Bradford
08.09.92	Wayne Buck L RSC 3 Doncaster
09.12.92	Vance Idiens L PTS 8 Stoke
10.05.93	Steve Lewsam L CO 6 Cleethorpes
28.10.93	Joey Paladino L RSC 2 Walsall
10.12.94	Darren Corbett L RSC 1 Manchester
14.06.95	Martin Langtry L RSC 3 Batley

Career: 25 contests, won 6, drew 1, lost 18.

Justin Juuko

Millwall. *Born* Musaka, Uganda, 21 September, 1972
Lightweight. Ht. 5'7"
Manager D. Powell

18.03.91	Gilbert Diaz W RSC 3 Las Vegas, USA
26.03.91	Jorge Lopez W PTS 4 Las Vegas, USA
02.06.91	Kevin Childrey W RSC 2 Las Vegas, USA
12.06.91	Juan Carlos Lopez W CO 4 Irvine, USA
06.07.91	Norberto Bravo L RSC 2 Las Vegas, USA
29.10.91	Danny Gonzalez W RSC 1 Phoenix, USA
30.11.91	Ruben Rivera W RSC 5 Las Vegas, USA
14.02.92	Chris Crespin W RSC 3 Las Vegas, USA
28.03.92	Amador Martinez W RSC 2 Las Vegas, USA
24.05.92	Mario Lozano W CO 2 Las Vegas, USA
26.06.92	Victor Miranda T DRAW 2 Las Vegas, USA
21.08.92	Jose Manjarez W RSC 6 Las Vegas, USA
21.10.92	Roberto Torres W RSC 2 Las Vegas, USA
26.12.92	Roberto Torres W RSC 1 Las Vegas, USA
24.01.93	Cesar Guzman W CO 3 Lynwood, USA
24.02.93	Abe Gomez W PTS 8 Las Vegas, USA
17.04.93	Russell Mosley W CO 4 Sacramento, USA
28.11.93	Derek Amory W RSC 1 Southwark
09.02.94	Charles Shepherd W RSC 5 Bethnal Green
09.04.94	Bamana Dibateza W RSC 5 Mansfield
12.10.94	Juan Amando Reyes W PTS 8 Sheffield
18.02.95	Alberto Lopez W RTD 3 Shepton Mallet
13.05.95	Peter Till W RTD 4 Glasgow

Career: 23 contests, won 21, drew 1, lost 1.

Charlie Kane

Clydebank. *Born* Glasgow, 2 July, 1968
L. Welterweight. Ht. 5'10½"
Manager T. Gilmour

05.03.91	Dean Bramhald W RSC 6 Glasgow
21.10.91	James Jiora W PTS 6 Glasgow
24.02.92	Karl Taylor W PTS 8 Glasgow
10.12.92	Mick Mulcahy W RSC 2 Glasgow
07.11.93	Mick Mulcahy W RSC 2 Glasgow
25.11.93	John Smith W PTS 6 Tynemouth
02.03.94	Micky Hall W RSC 2 Glasgow
28.03.94	John Smith W PTS 6 Musselburgh
24.10.94	Shaun Cogan W PTS 10 Glasgow
	(Elim. British L. Welterweight Title)

Career: 9 contests, won 9.

Ray Kane

Dublin. *Born* Dublin, 4 June, 1968
Cruiserweight. Ht. 6'0"
Manager B. Eastwood

07.09.91	R. F. McKenzie W PTS 4 Belfast
11.12.91	Chris Coughlan W PTS 6 Dublin
28.04.93	John Kaighin W PTS 6 Dublin
05.05.93	Johnny Uphill W CO 2 Belfast
16.10.93	Jason McNeill W PTS 6 Belfast
12.03.94	Kent Davis W PTS 6 Cardiff
21.05.94	Nicky Wadman W PTS 6 Belfast
12.11.94	Steve Osborne W PTS 6 Dublin
14.04.95	Bobbi Joe Edwards W PTS 6 Belfast
27.05.95	Bobbi Joe Edwards W PTS 6 Belfast

Career: 10 contests, won 10.

(Sunday) Sandy Katerega

Canning Town. *Born* Uganda, 6 July, 1969
L. Middleweight. Ht. 5'6"
Manager B. Lynch

25.03.95	Julian Eavis W PTS 6 Millwall

Career: 1 contest, won 1.

(Nassim) Lambsy Kayani

Sheffield. *Born* Sheffield, 31 August, 1967
Welterweight. Ht. 5'8"
Manager G. Rhodes

15.09.86	Tony Carter W PTS 6 Manchester
14.10.86	Carl Cleasby W PTS 6 Manchester
01.12.86	Andrew Steadman L PTS 6 Manchester
26.01.87	Davey Hughes L PTS 6 Leamington
10.02.87	Andrew Steadman W RSC 5 Batley
02.03.87	Mitchell King W PTS 6 Nottingham
07.04.87	Simon Hunter DREW 4 Batley
24.04.87	Hugh Forde L PTS 8 Liverpool
31.07.87	Billy Cawley W PTS 6 Wrexham
30.09.87	Derek Amory DREW 8 Solihull
20.01.88	Derek Amory L PTS 8 Solihull
24.02.88	Paul Chedgzoy W PTS 4 Sheffield
23.03.88	Des Gargano W PTS 6 Sheffield
22.04.88	Pedro Silva W PTS 6 Lisbon, Portugal
12.06.95	Paul Scott W PTS 6 Bradford

Career: 15 contests, won 9, drew 2, lost 4.

John Keeton

Sheffield. *Born* Sheffield, 19 May, 1972
Cruiserweight. Ht. 6'0"
Manager B. Ingle

11.08.93	Tony Colclough W RSC 1 Mansfield
15.09.93	Val Golding L PTS 6 Ashford
27.10.93	Darren McKenna W RSC 3 Stoke
01.12.93	Julius Francis L PTS 4 Bethnal Green

19.01.94	Dennis Bailey W RTD 2 Stoke	
17.02.94	Dermot Gascoyne L RSC 1 Dagenham	
09.04.94	Eddie Knight W RTD 5 Mansfield	
11.05.94	John Rice W RSC 5 Sheffield	
02.06.94	Devon Rhooms W RSC 2 Tooting	
06.09.94	Mark Walker W RSC 5 Stoke	
24.09.94	Dirk Wallyn L CO 3 Middlekerke, Belgium	
26.10.94	Lee Archer W PTS 6 Stoke	
09.12.94	Bruce Scott L CO 2 Bethnal Green	
11.02.95	Rudiger May L PTS 6 Frankfurt, Germany	
06.03.95	Simon McDougall W RSC 5 Mayfair	

Career: 15 contests, won 9, lost 6.

Barrie Kelley

Llanelli. *Born* Llanelli, 14 February, 1972
Former Welsh S. Featherweight Champion.
Ht. 5'6"
Manager Self

16.10.90	Ervine Blake W PTS 6 Evesham	
21.11.90	Tony Falcone W PTS 6 Chippenham	
29.11.90	John O'Meara W RSC 5 Bayswater	
24.01.91	Martin Evans W PTS 6 Gorseinon	
18.02.91	Tony Falcone L RSC 6 Mayfair	
26.03.91	Dennis Adams W PTS 6 Bethnal Green	
18.07.91	Robert Smyth DREW 6 Cardiff	
16.09.91	Dominic McGuigan DREW 6 Mayfair	
14.10.91	Michael Armstrong L CO 4 Manchester	
20.11.91	Neil Haddock L PTS 6 Cardiff	
03.02.92	Noel Carroll L PTS 8 Manchester	
18.03.92	Mark Geraghty L PTS 8 Glasgow	
05.04.92	Peter Judson L PTS 6 Bradford	
30.09.92	Dean Bramhald W PTS 5 Solihull	
28.10.92	Derek Amory W PTS 6 Cardiff	
19.01.93	Edward Lloyd W PTS 10 Cardiff	
	(Vacant Welsh S. Featherweight Title)	
10.11.93	J. T. Williams L RTD 3 Ystrad	
	(Welsh S. Featherweight Title Defence)	
24.02.94	Peter Till L PTS 6 Walsall	
19.11.94	Marcus McCrae W PTS 6 Cardiff	
31.03.95	Mike Anthony Brown L RSC 2 Crystal Palace	
04.06.95	Paul Webster L RTD 1 Bethnal Green	

Career: 21 contests, won 9, drew 2, lost 10.

Craig Kelley   Les Clark

Craig Kelley

Llanelli. *Born* Swansea, 6 November, 1975
S. Featherweight. Ht. 5'8"
Manager B. Aird

25.01.94	Simon Frailing W PTS 4 Piccadilly	
25.02.94	John Sillo L PTS 6 Chester	
27.08.94	Dean Phillips L RSC 4 Cardiff	
20.01.95	Jason Hutson W RSC 2 Bethnal Green	
25.03.95	Gary Thornhill L PTS 6 Chester	

Career: 5 contests, won 2, lost 3.

John T. Kelly

Hartlepool. *Born* Hartlepool, 12 June, 1970
Lightweight. Ht. 5'7"
Manager T. Conroy

22.10.92	Tanveer Ahmed L PTS 6 Glasgow	
02.11.92	Kevin Lowe W PTS 6 Liverpool	
01.12.92	Wayne Rigby W PTS 6 Hartlepool	
15.02.93	Kevin McKillan L PTS 6 Manchester	
09.03.93	Michael Alexander W PTS 6 Hartlepool	
17.04.93	Micky Hall DREW 4 Washington	
06.05.93	Alan Graham W PTS 6 Hartlepool	
15.09.93	P. J. Gallagher L RSC 2 Bethnal Green	
02.12.93	Brian Wright W PTS 6 Hartlepool	
02.02.94	Dave McHale L CO 1 Glasgow	
13.04.94	Bradley Welsh L PTS 6 Glasgow	
06.10.94	Chris Aston DREW 6 Hull	
13.10.94	Tim Hill W PTS 6 Houghton le Spring	
24.11.94	Dominic McGuigan L PTS 6 Newcastle	
05.12.94	Glen Hopkins W PTS 6 Houghton le Spring	
16.01.95	Hugh Collins L PTS 6 Musselburgh	
16.02.95	Scott Walker L PTS 6 Bury	
06.03.95	Steve Tuckett L RSC 3 Bradford	
18.05.95	Wayne Rigby L PTS 6 Middleton	
22.06.95	Dave Madden W PTS 6 Houghton le Spring	

Career: 20 contests, won 8, drew 2, lost 10.

Lyndon Kershaw

Halifax. *Born* Halifax, 17 September, 1972
Flyweight. Ht. 5'6"
Manager T. Callighan

19.10.92	Stevie Woods W PTS 6 Glasgow	
14.12.92	Louis Veitch DREW 6 Bradford	
26.04.93	Golfraz Ahmed W PTS 6 Bradford	
24.05.93	Anthony Hanna W PTS 6 Bradford	
07.10.93	Louis Veitch W PTS 10 Hull	
	(Vacant Central Area Flyweight Title)	
06.12.93	Ian Baillie W PTS 6 Bradford	
02.03.94	Tiger Singh W PTS 6 Solihull	
27.04.94	Mark Cokely W PTS 6 Solihull	
09.05.94	Ian Baillie W PTS 6 Bradford	
15.06.94	Mickey Cantwell W PTS 8 Southwark	
02.11.94	Louis Veitch L PTS 10 Solihull	
	(Central Area Flyweight Title Challenge)	
13.01.95	Jesper D. Jensen L PTS 6 Aalborg, Denmark	
20.02.95	Keith Knox DREW 6 Glasgow	
08.03.95	Tiger Singh W PTS 6 Solihull	

Career: 14 contests, won 9, drew 2, lost 3.

Prince Kasi Kiahau

Doncaster. *Born* Doncaster, 3 October, 1967
L. Middleweight. Ht. 5'11"
Manager J. Rushton

12.10.93	Prince Louis W PTS 6 Wolverhampton	

24.11.93	Steve Levene W PTS 6 Solihull	
13.12.93	Rob Stevenson W RSC 3 Doncaster	
07.03.94	Steve Levene W RSC 3 Doncaster	
10.05.94	Billy McDougall W RTD 4 Doncaster	
12.09.94	Rick North W PTS 6 Doncaster	
12.10.94	Andy Peach W PTS 6 Doncaster	
30.11.94	Billy McDougall W PTS 6 Solihull	
12.12.94	Andy Peach W PTS 6 Doncaster	
28.03.95	David Bain L PTS 6 Wolverhampton	
05.05.95	Andy Peach W PTS 6 Doncaster	

Career: 11 contests, won 10, lost 1.

Paul King

Newcastle. *Born* Newcastle, 3 June, 1965
Northern Area Welterweight Champion.
Ht. 5'8½"
Manager Self

04.09.87	Willie MacDonald W PTS 6 Gateshead	
03.11.87	Mick Mason L PTS 6 Sunderland	
24.11.87	Mick Mason L PTS 6 Marton	
31.01.89	Jim Larmour W RTD 4 Glasgow	
27.02.90	Ian Thomas W PTS 6 Marton	
06.03.90	Mick Duncan W PTS 6 Newcastle	
15.11.90	Phil Epton W PTS 6 Oldham	
28.02.91	Dave Kettlewell W RSC 1 Sunderland	
21.03.91	Phil Epton W PTS 6 Dewsbury	
13.05.91	Shamus Casey L PTS 6 Northampton	
31.05.91	Gordon Blair L PTS 8 Glasgow	
09.10.91	Delroy Waul L RSC 6 Manchester	
29.09.92	Howard Clarke L PTS 6 Stoke	
16.03.93	Howard Clarke L PTS 6 Edgbaston	
29.04.93	Hughie Davey W PTS 6 Newcastle	
29.06.93	Howard Clarke L PTS 6 Edgbaston	
14.08.93	Gary Logan L CO 2 Hammersmith	
28.11.93	Gary Logan L CO 4 Southwark	
03.03.94	Hughie Davey W PTS 10 Newcastle	
	(Vacant Northern Area Welterweight Title)	
02.03.95	Peter Reid W RSC 3 Cramlington	
20.04.95	Craig Winter L RSC 4 Liverpool	
12.06.95	Derek Roche L PTS 6 Bradford	

Career: 22 contests, won 10, lost 12.

Neil Kirkwood

Barnsley. *Born* Barnsley, 30 November, 1969
Central Area Heavyweight Champion. Ht. 6'4"
Manager S. Doyle

17.03.94	Gary Williams W RSC 1 Lincoln	
16.05.94	Joey Paladino W RSC 2 Cleethorpes	
26.08.94	Shane Woollas W RSC 6 Barnsley	
11.03.95	Carl Gaffney W RSC 2 Barnsley	
	(Vacant Central Area Heavyweight Title)	

Career: 4 contests, won 4.

Eddie Knight

Ashford. *Born* Ashford, 4 October, 1966
L. Heavyweight. Ht. 5'11"
Manager Self

05.10.92	Shaun McCrory L PTS 6 Bristol	
29.10.92	Adrian Wright L PTS 6 Bayswater	
25.11.92	Julian Johnson L RSC 2 Mayfair	
15.09.93	Terry Duffus W PTS 6 Ashford	
09.04.94	John Keeton L RTD 5 Mansfield	
27.05.94	Lee Sara W CO 2 Ashford	
09.07.94	Mark Delaney L CO 4 Earls Court	
17.09.94	Mark Hale W PTS 6 Crawley	
13.12.94	Tim Robinson W RTD 2 Potters Bar	
09.05.95	Mark Delaney L RSC 2 Basildon	

Career: 10 contests, won 4, lost 6.

Eddie Knight   Les Clark

Paul Knights

Redhill. *Born* Redhill, 5 February, 1971
L. Welterweight. Ht. 5'10"
Manager B. Hearn

26.11.91 Steve Hearn W RSC 4 Bethnal Green
19.02.92 Seth Jones W RSC 5 Muswell Hill
16.06.92 Seth Jones W PTS 6 Dagenham
10.11.92 Alex Moffatt W CO 3 Dagenham
30.01.93 Dave Lovell W PTS 6 Brentwood
20.04.93 Mark Allen W PTS 6 Brentwood
26.06.93 Phil Found W PTS 4 Earls Court
28.09.93 Pat Delargy W RSC 3 Bethnal Green
11.01.94 Brian Coleman W RSC 4 Bethnal Green
09.02.94 Mark Allen W RSC 2 Brentwood
19.03.94 Alan Peacock W PTS 6 Millwall
11.06.94 John O. Johnson L PTS 6 Bethnal Green
17.09.94 Dewi Roberts W PTS 6 Crawley
17.02.95 Norman Dhalie W RTD 5 Crawley
16.03.95 Brian Coleman W RSC 2 Basildon
09.05.95 Alan Peacock W PTS 6 Basildon
Career: 16 contests, won 15, lost 1.

Keith Knox

Bonnyrigg. *Born* Edinburgh, 20 June, 1967
Flyweight. Ht. 5'3"
Manager T. Gilmour

04.03.94 Ian Bailie W CO 3 Irvine
28.03.94 Terry Gaskin W PTS 6 Musselburgh
20.09.94 Tiger Singh W PTS 6 Musselburgh
21.11.94 Neil Parry W PTS 6 Glasgow
16.01.95 Neil Parry W PTS 6 Musselburgh
20.02.95 Lyndon Kershaw DREW 6 Glasgow
05.04.95 Louis Veitch DREW 6 Irvine
Career: 7 contests, won 5, drew 2.

Kirkland Laing

Hackney. *Born* Jamaica, 20 June, 1954
L. Middleweight. Former British &
European Welterweight Champion. Ht. 5'9"
Manager Self

14.04.75 Joe Hannaford W CO 2 Nottingham

12.05.75 Liam White W PTS 8 Nottingham
29.09.75 Derek Simpson W PTS 8 Nottingham
25.11.75 Oscar Angus W PTS 6 Kensington
19.01.76 Terry Schofield W PTS 8 Nottingham
12.03.76 Charlie Cooper W PTS 8 Southend
13.04.76 Mike Manley W PTS 8 Southend
17.05.76 John Laine W RSC 3 Nottingham
22.09.76 Harry Watson W RSC 5 Mayfair
11.10.76 Jim Moore W RSC 2 Nottingham
22.11.76 Jim Montague W DIS 7 Birmingham
11.01.77 John Smith W PTS 10 Wolverhampton
08.03.77 Peter Morris DREW 10 Wolverhampton
16.11.77 Peter Morris W RSC 5 Solihull
27.09.78 Achille Mitchell W PTS 12 Solihull
(*Final Elim. British Welterweight Title*)
04.04.79 Henry Rhiney W RSC 10 Birmingham
(*British Welterweight Title Challenge*)
06.11.79 Des Morrison W PTS 8 Kensington
22.01.80 Salvo Nuciforo W RSC 6 Kensington
19.02.80 Colin Ward W RSC 5 Kensington
01.04.80 Colin Jones L RSC 9 Wembley
(*British Welterweight Title Defence*)
08.05.80 George Walker W PTS 8 Solihull
03.06.80 Curtis Taylor W RSC 7 Kensington
26.11.80 Joey Singleton W PTS 12 Solihull
(*Final Elim. British Welterweight Title*)
28.04.81 Colin Jones L RSC 9 Kensington
(*British Welterweight Title Challenge*)
18.11.81 Cliff Gilpin W PTS 12 Solihull
(*Final Elim. British Welterweight Title*)
09.02.82 Reg Ford L PTS 10 London
05.05.82 Joey Mack W CO 7 Solihull
04.09.82 Roberto Duran W PTS 10 Detroit, USA
10.09.83 Fred Hutchings L CO 10 Atlantic City, USA
27.11.84 Darwin Brewster W RSC 7 Wembley
12.02.85 Mosimo Maeleke W PTS 10 Kensington
14.03.85 Wo Lamani Wo W RSC 6 Leicester
16.06.85 Franki Moro W PTS 8 Bethnal Green
05.07.85 Brian Janssen L RTD 5 Brisbane, Australia
16.05.86 Mike Picciotti W PTS 10 Atlantic City, USA
17.09.86 Harry Theodossiadis W RSC 4 Kensington
14.03.87 Silvester Mittee W RSC 5 Southwark
(*Vacant British Welterweight Title*)
26.05.87 Marvin McDowell W RSC 1 Wembley
26.11.87 Rocky Kelly W RSC 5 Fulham
(*British Welterweight Title Defence*)
29.03.88 Sammy Floyd W PTS 8 Wembley
15.04.89 Nino la Rocca L PTS 12 Vasto, Italy
(*Vacant European Welterweight Title*)
15.11.89 George Collins W RSC 5 Reading
(*British Welterweight Title Defence*)
10.01.90 Buck Smith L RSC 7 Kensington
27.03.90 Trevor Smith W RSC 6 Mayfair
(*British Welterweight Title Defence*)
09.05.90 Antoine Fernandez W CO 2 Wembley
(*European Welterweight Title Challenge*)
10.10.90 Rocky Berg W RSC 2 Kensington
14.11.90 Patrizio Oliva L PTS 12 Campione d'Italia, Italy
(*European Welterweight Title Defence*)
16.01.91 Del Bryan L PTS 12 Kensington
(*British Welterweight Title Defence*)
16.04.91 Donovan Boucher L CO 9 Nottingham
(*Commonwealth Welterweight Title Challenge*)
17.02.93 Bozon Haule W RSC 3 Bethnal Green
31.03.93 Newton Barnett W PTS 8 Bethnal Green

23.06.93 Kevin Lueshing L RSC 5 Edmonton
(*Vacant Southern Area L. Middleweight Title*)
28.07.93 Dean Cooper W RSC 5 Brixton
15.09.93 Dave Maj W RSC 2 Ashford
30.09.94 Chris Peters W RSC 7 Bethnal Green
22.11.94 Glenn Catley L RSC 5 Bristol
Career: 56 contests, won 43, drew 1, lost 12.

Martin Langtry

Lincon. *Born* Hampstead, 22 May, 1964
Cruiserweight. Ht. 5'10"
Manager Self

29.04.93 Stevie R. Davies W RSC 2 Newcastle
12.05.93 Simon McDougall W PTS 6 Sheffield
20.09.93 John Pierre W PTS 6 Cleethorpes
13.12.93 Steve Osborne W PTS 6 Cleethorpes
17.03.94 Lee Archer W CO 4 Lincoln
26.08.94 Steve Osborne W PTS 8 Barnsley
26.04.95 Andrew Benson W PTS 6 Solihull
15.05.95 L. A. Williams W CO 2 Cleethorpes
14.06.95 David Jules W RSC 3 Batley
Career: 9 contests, won 9.

David Larkin

Leeds. *Born* Pontefract, 26 April, 1972
Middleweight. Ht. 5'10½"
Manager M. Duff

29.10.92 Rick North W PTS 6 Leeds
07.04.93 Cliff Churchward W RSC 4 Leeds
19.05.93 Ray Golding W PTS 6 Sunderland
01.07.93 David Sumner W CO 5 York
07.10.93 Lee Crocker W RSC 5 York
26.10.94 Andrew Jervis W CO 5 Leeds
03.03.95 Robert Peel L PTS 6 Bethnal Green
Career: 7 contests, won 6, lost 1.

Anthony Lawrence

Wolverhampton. *Born* West Bromwich, 9
October, 1963
L. Middleweight. Ht. 5'11"
Manager Self

07.12.88 Terry French L PTS 6 Stoke
18.01.89 Glyn Davies W RSC 3 Stoke
20.02.89 Martin Robinson L PTS 6 Birmingham
03.04.89 Mark Whitehouse L PTS 6 Manchester
08.05.89 Floyd Gibbs L RSC 3 Edgbaston
19.06.89 Trevor Meikle W PTS 6 Manchester
10.10.89 Reuben Thurley W PTS 6 Wolverhampton
25.10.89 Darren Parker W PTS 6 Stoke
19.02.90 Chris Walker W PTS 6 Nottingham
13.10.93 Scott Newman W PTS 6 Stoke
16.12.93 James McGee DREW 6 Walsall
26.01.94 Carl Smith W RSC 4 Stoke
24.02.94 Gary Osborne W RSC 3 Walsall
22.02.95 Rick North W PTS 6 Telford
19.05.95 Nicky Thurbin L PTS 6 Southwark
Career: 15 contests, won 9, drew 1, lost 5.

Gareth Lawrence

Gilfach Goch. *Born* Pontypridd, 1
February, 1975
S. Featherweight. Ht. 5'6½"
Manager D. Gardiner

25.01.95 Anthony Campbell W PTS 6 Cardiff
08.03.95 Phil Found W PTS 6 Cardiff
17.06.95 Dean Amory W RSC 2 Cardiff
Career: 3 contests, won 3.

Danny Lawson

Plymouth. *Born* Plymouth, 27 May, 1971
Bantamweight. Ht. 5'5¾"
Manager Self

17.06.94	Danny Ruegg W PTS 6 Plymouth
07.10.94	Jobie Tyers L PTS 6 Taunton
07.02.95	Mark Reynolds L PTS 4 Ipswich
06.05.95	Tony Falcone L RSC 2 Shepton Mallet

Career: 4 contest, won 1, lost 3.

Paul Lawson

Bethnal Green. *Born* Dundee, 2 December, 1966
Cruiserweight. Ht. 6'3"
Manager F. Maloney

15.09.93	Bobby Mack W PTS 4 Bethnal Green
13.10.93	Art Stacey W RSC 2 Bethnal Green
01.12.93	Des Vaughan W RSC 3 Bethnal Green
09.02.94	Nicky Wadman W RSC 1 Bethnal Green
29.03.94	Terry Duffus W RSC 1 Bethnal Green
15.06.94	Art Stacey W RSC 2 Southwark
24.09.94	Lennie Howard W RSC 2 Wembley
25.10.94	Newby Stevens W RSC 2 Southwark
13.12.94	Nigel Rafferty W RSC 4 Ilford
23.02.95	Chris Okoh L RSC 5 Southwark
	(Vacant Southern Area Cruiserweight Title)
17.05.95	Andrew Benson W RSC 2 Ipswich

Career: 11 contests, won 10, lost 1.

Mark Legg

South Shields. *Born* South Shields, 25 March, 1970
L. Welterweight. Ht. 5'9½"
Manager T. Callighan

28.02.92	Chris Aston W RSC 5 Irvine
17.03.92	Dean Hiscox W PTS 6 Wolverhampton
18.05.92	Charles Shepherd L PTS 6 Marton
24.09.92	Ricky Sackfield W PTS 6 Stockport
25.11.93	Gary Hiscox W RSC 3 Tynemouth
07.02.94	Erwin Edwards W RSC 6 Bradford
02.03.94	Phil Found L RTD 4 Solihull
10.05.94	John O. Johnson L RSC 6 Doncaster
02.11.94	Alan Peacock W PTS 6 Solihull
21.11.94	Steve McLevy L RSC 5 Glasgow
21.02.95	Bernard Paul L RSC 4 Sunderland
26.04.95	Steve Howden W RTD 2 Stoke
10.06.95	Juha Temonen L PTS 4 Pori, Finland

Career: 13 contests, won 7, lost 6.

Niel Leggett

Peterborough. *Born* Boreham, 10 December, 1966
Lightweight. Ht. 5'6"
Manager J. Cox

14.02.88	Jimmy Vincent W PTS 6 Peterborough
29.02.88	Steve Winstanley L PTS 6 Bradford
09.04.88	Paul Moylett L PTS 6 Bristol
17.04.88	Steve Winstanley DREW 6 Peterborough
05.09.88	Tony Dore L PTS 6 Glasgow
02.10.88	Mick Mulcahy DREW 6 Peterborough
10.10.88	Tony Dore L PTS 6 Glasgow
19.10.88	Nigel Wenton L RTD 2 Belfast
03.04.95	Andrew Smith W PTS 6 Northampton
22.06.95	Glen Hopkins W PTS 6 Houghton le Spring

Career: 10 contests, won 3, drew 2, lost 5.

Jason Lepre

Portsmouth. *Born* Portsmouth, 11 July, 1969
S. Featherweight. Ht. 5'10"
Manager J. Bishop

26.04.89	Alan Roberts W RTD 1 Southampton
09.05.89	Hugh Ruse W PTS 6 Southend
21.09.89	Darren Weller L RSC 3 Southampton
30.10.89	Steve Walker L CO 2 Piccadilly
23.05.91	Miguel Matthews W PTS 6 Southampton
16.12.91	Mark Loftus W PTS 6 Southampton
22.01.92	Kevin Simons W PTS 6 Cardiff
17.09.92	Con Cronin L PTS 6 Watford
29.10.92	Jason White L PTS 6 Hayes
17.02.93	Chris Francis L RSC 2 Bethnal Green
08.10.94	Stephen Smith L RSC 1 Halle, Germany
03.03.95	Simon Frailing L PTS 6 Bracknell

Career: 12 contests, won 5, lost 7.

Delroy Leslie

Carshalton. *Born* Jamaica, 22 February, 1970
L. Welterweight. Ht. 5'11½"
Manager M. Duff

29.04.93	Phil Found W PTS 6 Mayfair
14.06.93	Jason Barker W RTD 3 Bayswater
16.09.93	Jamie Davidson W PTS 6 Southwark
06.03.95	Shaun Cogan W RSC 1 Mayfair
20.04.95	Clayton Hollingsworth W PTS 6 Mayfair
23.06.95	Jonathan Thaxton L PTS 6 Bethnal Green

Career: 6 contests, won 5, lost 1.

Steve Levene

Birmingham. *Born* Birmingham, 23 August, 1969
L. Middleweight. Ht. 5'8½"
Manager Self

27.10.92	Steve Scott L RSC 1 Cradley Heath
07.12.92	Warren Stephens W CO 2 Birmingham
16.03.93	Alan Williams W RSC 1 Edgbaston
24.03.93	Sean Baker DREW 6 Belfast
19.04.93	Bullit Andrews W PTS 6 Northampton
18.05.93	Mark Antony L RSC 1 Edgbaston
06.09.93	Danny Peters L RSC 4 Liverpool
24.11.93	Prince Kasi Kiahau L PTS 6 Solihull
06.12.93	Bullit Andrews W RSC 6 Birmingham
17.02.94	Bullit Andrews W PTS 6 Walsall
07.03.94	Prince Kasi Kiahau L RSC 3 Doncaster
20.06.95	Paul Webb W PTS 6 Edgbaston

Career: 12 contests, won 6, drew 1, lost 5.

(Adrian) Ady Lewis

Bury. *Born* Bury, 31 May, 1975
Bantamweight. Ht. 4'10½"
Manager J. Doughty

25.04.94	Darren Greaves W RSC 1 Bury
02.06.94	Dave Campbell W RSC 1 Middleton
22.09.94	Neil Parry W RSC 3 Bury
21.11.94	Daryl McKenzie W RSC 4 Glasgow
17.01.95	Yusuf Vorajee W RSC 2 Worcester
16.02.95	Chip O'Neill W RSC 1 Bury
06.03.95	Mark Cokely W RSC 5 Mayfair
09.05.95	Pete Buckley W PTS 4 Basildon

Career: 8 contests, won 8.

Lennox Lewis

Crayford. *Born* London, 2 September, 1965
Former WBC Heavyweight Champion.
Former Undefeated British, European & Commonwealth Heavyweight Champion.
Ht. 6'4¾"
Manager F. Maloney

27.06.89	Al Malcolm W CO 2 Kensington
21.07.89	Bruce Johnson W RSC 2 Atlantic City, USA
25.09.89	Andrew Gerrard W RSC 4 Crystal Palace
10.10.89	Steve Garber W CO 1 Hull
05.11.89	Melvin Epps W DIS 2 Kensington
18.12.89	Greg Gorrell W RSC 5 Kitchener, Canada
31.01.90	Noel Quarless W RSC 2 Bethnal Green
22.03.90	Calvin Jones W CO 1 Gateshead
14.04.90	Mike Simwelu W CO 1 Kensington
09.05.90	Jorge Dascola W CO 1 Kensington
20.05.90	Dan Murphy W RSC 6 Sheffield
27.06.90	Ossie Ocasio W PTS 8 Kensington
11.07.90	Mike Acey W RSC 2 Mississuaga, Canada
31.10.90	Jean Chanet W RSC 6 Crystal Palace
	(European Heavyweight Title Challenge)
06.03.91	Gary Mason W RSC 7 Wembley
	(British Heavyweight Title Challenge. European Heavyweight Title Defence)
12.07.91	Mike Weaver W CO 6 Lake Tahoe, USA
30.09.91	Glenn McCrory W CO 2 Kensington
	(British & European Heavyweight Title Defence)
23.11.91	Tyrell Biggs W RSC 3 Atlanta, USA
01.02.92	Levi Billups W PTS 10 Las Vegas, USA
30.04.92	Derek Williams W RSC 3 Kensington
	(British & European Heavyweight Title Defence. Commonwealth Heavyweight Title Challenge)
11.08.92	Mike Dixon W RSC 4 Atlantic City, USA
31.10.92	Razor Ruddock W RSC 2 Earls Court
	(Final Elim. WBC Heavyweight Title & Commonwealth Heavyweight Title Defence)
08.05.93	Tony Tucker W PTS 12 Las Vegas, USA
	(WBC Heavyweight Title Defence)
01.10.93	Frank Bruno W RSC 7 Cardiff
	(WBC Heavyweight Title Defence)
06.05.94	Phil Jackson W RSC 8 Atlantic City
	(WBC Heavyweight Title Defence)
24.09.94	Oliver McCall L RSC 2 Wembley
	(WBC Heavyweight Title Defence)
13.05.95	Lionel Butler W RSC 5 Sacramento, USA
	(Elim. WBC Heavyweight Title)

Career: 27 contests, won 26, lost 1.

Steve Lewsam

Grimsby. *Born* Cleethorpes, 8 September, 1960
Former Undefeated Midlands Area Heavyweight Champion. Former Undefeated Midlands Area Cruiserweight Champion. Ht. 6'2"
Manager Self

22.11.82	Winston Wray W PTS 4 Liverpool

Lennox Lewis   Les Clark

Earl Ling   Les Clark

Earl Ling
Norwich. *Born* Kings Lynn, 9 March, 1972
S. Middleweight. Ht. 5'10"
Manager B. Lee

08.09.92 Eddie Collins W PTS 6 Norwich
11.05.93 Mark Hale L RSC 2 Norwich
12.12.94 Clinton Woods L RSC 5 Cleethorpes
Career: 3 contests, won 1, lost 2.

Darren Littlewood
Sheffield. *Born* Sheffield, 6 November, 1974
L. Heavyweight. Ht. 6'0"
Manager B. Ingle

24.11.93 Mark Smallwood L PTS 8 Solihull
02.12.93 Martin Jolley W PTS 6 Evesham
01.03.94 Joe Calzaghe L RSC 1 Dudley
28.05.94 Dean Francis L PTS 4 Queensway
17.08.94 Chris Woollas L RSC 4 Sheffield
26.10.94 John Duckworth W PTS 6 Stoke
24.11.94 Tim Robinson W PTS 6 Hull
12.12.94 Martin Jolley W PTS 6 Cleethorpes
23.01.95 Roland Ericsson W RSC 4 Bethnal
Green

Career: 9 contests, won 5, lost 4.

Darren Littlewood   Les Clark

07.11.83 Wes Taylor W PTS 6 Birmingham
22.11.83 Jerry Golden L RSC 5 Manchester
27.10.88 Paul Sheldon W PTS 6 Birmingham
01.12.88 Ian Carmichael W CO 2 Stafford
07.12.88 Chris Little W RSC 1 Stoke
16.02.89 Dave Lawrence W PTS 6 Stafford
08.05.89 Abner Blackstock DREW 8 Grimsby
04.09.89 Mick Cordon W PTS 8 Grimsby
04.12.89 Abner Blackstock W PTS 8 Grimsby
09.03.90 Dennis Bailey DREW 8 Grimsby
21.05.90 Dennis Bailey W PTS 8 Grimsby
05.09.90 Herbie Hide L RSC 4 Brighton
18.11.90 Herbie Hide L RSC 1 Birmingham
12.02.91 Cordwell Hylton L RSC 8
Wolverhampton
29.04.91 Dave Muhammed L PTS 8 Cleethorpes

16.09.91 Cordwell Hylton W PTS 10
Cleethorpes
*(Midlands Area Cruiserweight Title
Challenge)*
09.12.91 Tony Booth W PTS 8 Cleethorpes
04.06.92 Carl Thompson L RSC 8 Cleethorpes
(Vacant British Cruiserweight Title)
26.10.92 Tom Collins DREW 8 Cleethorpes
03.12.92 Eddie Smulders L CO 4 Rotterdam,
Holland
10.05.93 David Jules W CO 6 Cleethorpes
28.03.94 Wayne Buck W PTS 10 Cleethorpes
*(Vacant Midlands Area Heavyweight
Title)*
26.10.94 Denzil Browne L CO 2 Leeds
Career: 24 contests, won 13, drew 3, lost 8.

Wayne Llewelyn

Deptford. *Born* Greenwich, 20 April, 1970
Heavyweight. Ht. 6'3½"
Manager Self

18.01.92	Chris Coughlan W RSC 3 Kensington
30.03.92	Steve Stewart W RSC 4 Eltham
23.04.92	Gary Charlton W RSC 4 Eltham
10.12.92	Gary McCrory W RSC 2 Glasgow
23.05.93	Cordwell Hylton W PTS 6 Brockley
01.12.93	Manny Burgo W PTS 6 Bethnal Green
14.04.94	Vance Idiens W RSC 1 Battersea
22.05.94	Cordwell Hylton W CO 2 Crystal Palace
03.05.95	Mitch Rose W PTS 4 New York City, USA

Career: 9 contests, won 9.

Edward Lloyd   Les Clark

Edward Lloyd

Rhyl. *Born* St Asaph, 23 April, 1963
S. Featherweight. Ht. 5'7½"
Manager Self

07.02.83	Stan Atherton W PTS 6 Liverpool
14.02.83	Sammy Rodgers W RSC 4 Manchester
21.02.83	Paul Cook L RSC 1 Mayfair
27.04.83	Bobby Welburn W PTS 6 Rhyl
09.05.83	Jimmy Thornton L RSC 1 Manchester
16.09.83	Jim Paton L PTS 6 Rhyl
28.11.83	John Murphy L PTS 8 Rhyl
06.02.84	Paul Keers W PTS 6 Liverpool
06.03.84	Gary Felvus L PTS 8 Stoke
12.06.84	Mickey Brooks L RSC 6 St Helens
06.08.84	Henry Arnold W RSC 6 Aintree
15.10.84	Steve Griffith L RTD 4 Liverpool
05.12.84	Jaswant Singh Ark W RSC 2 Stoke
01.02.85	Andy Williams DREW 6 Warrington
29.03.85	Billy Laidman W RSC 2 Liverpool
10.04.85	Brian Roche L RSC 7 Leeds
20.05.85	Gary Flear L PTS 8 Nottingham
19.07.85	Stanley Jones DREW 10 Colwyn Bay
	(Vacant Welsh Lightweight Title)
10.02.86	Peter Bradley L PTS 8 Glasgow
06.03.86	Najib Daho L PTS 8 Manchester
24.11.86	Keith Parry L PTS 8 Cardiff
13.01.87	Sugar Gibiliru W PTS 8 Oldham

09.02.87	Craig Windsor W RSC 1 Cardiff
24.02.87	Alonzo Lopez W RTD 1 Marbella, Spain
31.10.87	Abdeselan Azowague W PTS 6 Marbella, Spain
30.11.87	Gary Maxwell L PTS 8 Nottingham
01.02.88	Colin Lynch L RTD 4 Northampton
11.02.92	Dewi Roberts W RSC 1 Cardiff
19.05.92	Mervyn Bennett W RSC 5 Cardiff
07.10.92	Steve Robinson L RTD 8 Barry
14.11.92	Carl Hook W PTS 6 Cardiff
19.01.93	Barrie Kelley L PTS 10 Cardiff
	(Vacant Welsh S. Featherweight Title)
30.03.93	Nigel Haddock L RTD 4 Cardiff
05.05.93	Francisco Arroyo L RTD 3 Belfast
18.12.93	Jyrki Vierela L PTS 8 Turku, Finland
25.02.94	Gary Thornhill DREW 6 Chester
14.04.94	Felix Kelly W RSC 6 Battersea
29.09.94	Floyd Havard L RSC 4 Bethnal Green
08.03.95	J. T. Williams DREW 10 Cardiff
	(Welsh S. Featherweight Title Challenge)

Career: 39 contests, won 15, drew 4, lost 20.

Paul Lloyd

Ellesmere Port. *Born* Bebington, 7
December, 1968
Central Area S. Bantamweight Champion.
Ht. 5'7"
Manager J. Hyland

25.09.92	Graham McGrath W RSC 3 Liverpool
23.10.92	Kid McAuley W PTS 4 Liverpool
20.11.92	Des Gargano W PTS 4 Liverpool
15.12.92	Glyn Shepherd W RSC 1 Liverpool
27.02.93	Miguel Matthews W PTS 6 Ellesmere Port
04.05.93	Andrew Bloomer W PTS 6 Liverpool
02.07.93	Ronnie Stephenson W RTD 1 Liverpool
30.10.93	Marty Chestnut W RSC 1 Chester
11.12.93	Gerald Shelton W RSC 3 Liverpool
25.02.94	Ady Benton W PTS 6 Chester
	(Vacant Central Area S. Bantamweight Title)
06.05.94	Pete Buckley W RTD 4 Liverpool
26.09.94	Chris Clarkson L RSC 4 Liverpool
25.03.95	Richie Wenton L RSC 5 Chester
	(British S. Bantamweight Title Challenge)
16.06.95	Garry Burrell W RSC 2 Liverpool

Career: 14 contests, won 12, lost 2.

Steve Loftus

Stoke. *Born* Stoke, 10 October, 1971
L. Heavyweight. Ht. 6'2½"
Manager Self

29.09.92	Bobby Mack L PTS 6 Stoke
21.10.92	Paul Murray W PTS 6 Stoke
09.12.92	Lee Prudden L PTS 6 Stoke
17.03.93	Chris Nurse L PTS 6 Stoke
12.05.93	Zak Goldman W PTS 6 Stoke
07.09.93	Greg Scott-Briggs L RSC 2 Stoke
01.12.93	Tony Colclough L PTS 6 Stoke
15.03.94	Tim Robinson W PTS 6 Stoke
25.05.94	Mark Hale W PTS 6 Stoke
06.09.94	Mark Hale W PTS 6 Stoke
16.11.94	Paul Murray L PTS 6 Bloomsbury
07.12.94	Paul Murray L PTS 6 Stoke
25.01.95	Robert Harper W PTS 6 Stoke
15.03.95	Pat Durkin W PTS 6 Stoke
26.04.95	Mark Hale W PTS 6 Stoke

Career: 15 contests, won 9, lost 6.

Gary Logan

Brixton. *Born* Lambeth, 10 October, 1968
Southern Area Welterweight Champion. Ht.
5'8¾"
Manager F. Maloney

05.10.88	Peppy Muire W RTD 3 Wembley
02.11.88	Tony Gibbs W PTS 6 Southwark
07.12.88	Pat Dunne W PTS 6 Piccadilly
12.01.89	Mike Russell W CO 1 Southwark
20.02.89	Dave Griffiths W RSC 5 Mayfair
29.03.89	Ronnie Campbell W PTS 6 Wembley
10.05.89	Tony Britland W CO 1 Kensington
07.06.89	Davey Hughes W CO 1 Wembley
24.08.89	Mike English W CO 2 Tampa, USA
04.10.89	Simon Eubank W PTS 6 Kensington
12.10.89	Jimmy Thornton W PTS 6 Southwark
08.11.89	Chris Blake L PTS 8 Wembley
10.01.90	Julian Eavis W PTS 8 Kensington
03.03.90	Anthony Joe Travis W CO 5 Wembley
09.05.90	Joseph Alexander W PTS 8 Wembley
13.09.90	Manuel Rojas W PTS 8 Watford
16.01.91	Julian Eavis W RSC 5 Kensington
18.02.91	Gordon Blair W CO 1 Mayfair
25.04.91	Trevor Ambrose W PTS 8 Mayfair
17.10.91	Des Robinson W PTS 8 Southwark
15.10.92	Mick Duncan W PTS 8 Lewisham
17.12.92	Roy Rowland W RSC 4 Wembley
	(Vacant Southern Area Welterweight Title)
23.05.93	Glyn Rhodes W CO 3 Brockley
25.06.93	Gordon Blair W RSC 6 Battersea
14.08.93	Paul King W CO 2 Hammersmith
28.11.93	Paul King W CO 4 Southwark
11.12.93	Horace Fleary W PTS 8 Dusseldorf, Germany
09.02.94	Graham Cheney L RSC 10 Bethnal Green
	(WBC International Welterweight Title Challenge)
29.09.94	Ojay Abrahams W PTS 10 Bethnal Green
	(Southern Area Welterweight Title Defence)
25.10.94	Nick Hall DREW 8 Southwark
02.06.95	Del Bryan L RSC 11 Bethnal Green
	(British Welterweight Title Challenge)

Career: 31 contests, won 27, drew 1, lost 3.

Patrick Loughran

Ballymena. *Born* Ballymena, 15 September,
1972
L. Welterweight. Ht. 5'6"
Manager Self

11.09.91	Kevin Lowe W PTS 6 Stoke
11.12.91	Keith Hardman W PTS 6 Stoke
11.03.92	Rick North W PTS 6 Stoke
07.07.92	Jason Barker W PTS 6 Bristol
24.03.93	Felix Kelly W PTS 6 Bristol
22.06.95	Dave Clark L PTS 6 Atlantic City, USA

Career: 6 contests, won 5, lost 1.

Prince Louis (Egbenoma)

Kings Lynn. *Born* Chelsea, 18 December,
1971
L. Middleweight. Ht. 5'10"
Manager G. Holmes

| 12.10.93 | Prince Kasi Kiahau L PTS 6 Wolverhampton |

30.11.93 Norman Hutcheon L PTS 6 Leicester
06.03.94 Danny Quacoe L RSC 2 Southwark
07.02.95 Chris Vassiliou W PTS 4 Ipswich
Career: 4 contests, won 1, lost 3.

Dave Lovell

Birmingham. *Born* Birmingham, 15 April, 1962
Welterweight. Ht. 5'7½"
Manager Self

25.03.92 Billy Robinson L PTS 6 Hinckley
29.04.92 Jason Barker W PTS 6 Stoke
26.09.92 Seth Jones W RSC 4 Earls Court
27.10.92 Spencer McCracken L PTS 4 Cradley Heath
18.11.92 Alan Peacock L PTS 6 Solihull
30.01.93 Paul Knights L PTS 6 Brentwood
22.02.93 Alan Peacock L PTS 8 Glasgow
01.04.93 Richard O'Brien L PTS 6 Evesham
24.09.93 Jimmy McMahon L PTS 6 Dublin
23.11.93 Sean Metherell W RSC 3 Kettering
26.01.94 Mark Elliot L PTS 6 Birmingham
17.02.94 Craig Fisher W RSC 2 Bury
01.03.94 Mark McCreath W RSC 5 Dudley
10.09.94 Paul Ryan L RSC 3 Birmingham
19.11.94 Michael Carruth L RSC 2 Cardiff
18.02.95 Sean Baker L PTS 6 Shepton Mallet
Career: 16 contests, won 5, lost 11.

Ernie Loveridge

Wolverhampton. *Born* Bromsgrove, 7 July, 1970
S. Middleweight. Former Undefeated Midlands Area Welterweight Champion. Ht. 5'10"
Manager P. Byrne

06.02.89 Ricky Nelson L RSC 6 Nottingham
17.04.89 Martin Robinson L PTS 4 Birmingham
08.05.89 Bullit Andrews W PTS 6 Edgbaston
05.06.89 Alan Richards L PTS 6 Birmingham
19.06.89 Ian Thomas DREW 6 Manchester
28.06.89 Barry Messam L PTS 6 Kenilworth
10.10.89 Matt Sturgess W RSC 1 Wolverhampton
25.10.89 Darren Mount L PTS 6 Stoke
11.12.89 Cliff Churchward W PTS 6 Birmingham
27.02.90 Julian Eavis W PTS 6 Evesham
14.03.90 Mickey Lerwill W PTS 6 Stoke
27.03.90 Eddie King W PTS 6 Wolverhampton
24.04.90 Mark Jay W PTS 6 Stoke
24.05.90 Mickey Lerwill DREW 6 Dudley
18.09.90 Ronnie Campbell W PTS 6 Wolverhampton
24.10.90 Trevor Meikle W PTS 6 Dudley
23.01.91 Cliff Churchward W PTS 6 Solihull
27.02.91 Ronnie Campbell W PTS 8 Wolverhampton
13.03.91 John Corcoran W RSC 4 Stoke
10.04.91 Julian Eavis DREW 8 Wolverhampton
14.05.91 Paul Murray W PTS 8 Dudley
05.06.91 Cliff Churchward W PTS 8 Wolverhampton
10.09.91 Gary Osborne W RSC 1 Wolverhampton
(Midlands Area Welterweight Title Challenge)
12.11.91 Mickey Lerwill W PTS 6 Wolverhampton
05.12.91 Jim Lawlor W PTS 8 Cannack
01.02.92 Michael Oliver W PTS 8 Birmingham

19.09.92 Paul Jones L PTS 6 Glasgow
01.10.92 Neville Brown L CO 4 Telford
20.01.93 Lee Crocker L PTS 6 Wolverhampton
17.02.93 Robert McCracken L CO 4 Bethnal Green
31.03.93 Kevin Lueshing L RSC 5 Bethnal Green
18.05.93 Antonio Fernandez L PTS 8 Edgbaston
10.07.93 Michael Smyth L RSC 6 Cardiff
09.10.93 Robin Reid L PTS 4 Manchester
02.11.93 Gilbert Jackson L RTD 3 Southwark
11.06.94 Mark Delaney L RSC 5 Bethnal Green
28.07.94 Dave Cranston L PTS 6 Tooting
17.08.94 Kevin Adamson L RSC 2 Sheffield
01.03.95 Dave Johnson L PTS 6 Glasgow
17.03.95 Mads Larsen L RSC 3 Copenhagen, Denmark
20.04.95 Danny Peters L PTS 6 Liverpool
05.06.95 Billy Collins L PTS 8 Glasgow
16.06.95 Craig Winter L PTS 6 Liverpool
Career: 43 contests, won 18, drew 3, lost 22.

James Lowther

Leeds. *Born* Leeds, 28 June, 1976
L. Middleweight. Ht. 5'11"
Manager G. Lockwood

12.01.95 Warren Stephens W CO 4 Leeds
25.03.95 Scott Doyle W PTS 6 Rothwell
16.05.95 Eddie Haley W RSC 5 Leeds
Career: 3 contests, won 3.

Kevin Lueshing　　　　Les Clark

Kevin Lueshing

Beckenham. *Born* Beckenham, 17 April, 1968
Welterweight. Former Undefeated Southern Area L. Middleweight Champion. Ht. 5'11"
Manager M. Jacobs

30.09.91 John McGlynn W RSC 2 Kensington
23.10.91 Julian Eavis W RSC 2 Bethnal Green
14.12.91 Trevor Meikle W CO 3 Bexleyheath
18.01.92 Simon Eubank W CO 4 Kensington
25.03.92 Tracy Jocelyn W RSC 3 Dagenham
30.04.92 Newton Barnett W PTS 6 Kensington
03.02.93 Ian Chantler W RSC 2 Earls Court

17.02.93 Leigh Wicks W PTS 6 Bethnal Green
31.03.93 Ernie Loveridge W RSC 5 Bethnal Green
14.04.93 Marty Duke W RSC 2 Kensington
23.06.93 Kirkland Laing W RSC 5 Edmonton
(Vacant Southern Area L. Middleweight Title)
03.03.94 Chris Saunders L RSC 4 Ebbw Vale
30.07.94 Dennis Berry W CO 2 Bethnal Green
25.10.94 Peter Waudby W RSC 2 Middlesbrough
17.06.95 Michael Smyth W RSC 3 Cardiff
(Final Elim. British Welterweight Title)
Career: 15 contests, won 14, lost 1.

Danny Lutaaya

Canning Town. *Born* Uganda, 23 December, 1971
S. Featherweight. Ht. 5'5½"
Manager D. Powell

17.10.94 Vince Burns W RSC 6 Mayfair
27.11.94 Keith Jones W CO 1 Southwark
23.01.95 Elvis Parsley L RSC 3 Bethnal Green
25.03.95 Wayne Jones W RSC 3 Millwall
16.06.95 Dean Phillips L RSC 2 Southwark
Career: 5 contests, won 3, lost 2.

Danny Lutaaya　　　　Les Clark

Craig Lynch

Edinburgh. *Born* Edinburgh, 22 July, 1974
Welterweight. Ht. 6'1"
Manager A. Morrison

13.05.95 James Clamp DREW 6 Glasgow
08.06.95 Gary Silvester W RSC 3 Glasgow
Career: 2 contests, won 1, drew 1.

Paul Lynch

Swansea. *Born* Swansea, 27 December, 1966
Welterweight. Ht. 5'11"
Manager Self

23.10.89 Darren Burford W PTS 6 Mayfair

16.11.89	Robbie Harron W PTS 6 Weston super Mare
20.12.89	Peter Reid W RSC 4 Swansea
08.03.90	Tony Booth W PTS 6 Watford
04.12.90	Ernie Noble W RSC 3 Southend
12.02.91	Roy Rowland W RTD 4 Basildon
01.10.91	Peter Manfredo L PTS 8 Providence, USA
12.02.92	Robert McCracken L RSC 4 Wembley
14.04.92	Paul Jones L RSC 3 Mansfield
16.02.93	Tony Velinor W PTS 8 Tooting
31.03.93	Kevin Sheeran L RSC 1 Barking
23.03.94	Robert Welin L PTS 6 Cardiff
31.03.94	Sean Baker W RSC 3 Bristol
11.05.94	Del Bryan L PTS 8 Sheffield
21.03.95	Dean Cooper W RSC 6 Swansea

Career: 15 contests, won 9, lost 6.

Steve Lynch

Rotherham. *Born* Maltby, 30 January, 1966
Welterweight. Ht 5'8"
Manager K. Richardson

06.10.94	Gary Silvester L PTS 6 Hull
28.11.94	Jamie Gallagher L RSC 3 Northampton

Career: 2 contests, lost 2.

Chris Lyons

Birmingham. *Born* Birmingham, 2
September, 1972
Featherweight. Ht. 5'9"
Manager Self

02.12.91	Ronnie Sephenson L PTS 6 Birmingham
09.12.91	Ronnie Stephenson L PTS 6 Cleethorpes
22.01.92	Dennis Oakes L RSC 3 Stoke
17.05.92	Dave Martin DREW 6 Harringay
08.09.92	Robert Braddock L CO 5 Doncaster
13.10.92	Paul Kelly W PTS 6 Wolverhampton
30.10.92	Paul Kelly W CO 1 Birmingham
17.12.92	Mark Bowers L CO 2 Wembley
08.03.93	Chip O'Neill L PTS 6 Leeds
22.04.93	Marcus Duncan L RSC 2 Bury
26.06.93	Tim Yeates L PTS 4 Earls Court
16.09.93	Anthony Hanna L PTS 6 Southwark
30.11.93	Kid McAuley L RSC 5 Wolverhampton
01.03.94	Marty Chestnut L PTS 6 Dudley
27.04.94	Marty Chestnut W RSC 3 Bethnal Green
06.05.94	John Sillo L RSC 3 Liverpool
15.06.94	Matt Brown L CO 3 Southwark
19.09.94	Daryl McKenzie L PTS 6 Glasgow
11.10.94	Robert Grubb W PTS 6 Wolverhampton
02.11.94	Daryl McKenzie L PTS 6 Solihull
16.11.94	Danny Ruegg L PTS 6 Bloomsbury
28.11.94	Andrew Bloomer W PTS 6 Northampton
24.01.95	Abdul Mannon L PTS 6 Piccadilly
07.02.95	Michael Edwards W PTS 6 Wolverhampton
21.04.95	Matthew Harris L PTS 6 Dudley

Career: 25 contests, won 6, drew 1, lost 18.

(Colin) Kid McAuley

Liverpool. *Born* Liverpool, 6 June, 1968
Lightweight. Ht. 5'6"
Manager J. Rushton

08.09.92	Jonjo Irwin L PTS 6 Doncaster

19.09.92	Alex Docherty L PTS 6 Glasgow
30.09.92	Yusuf Vorajee W PTS 6 Solihull
13.10.92	John White L PTS 4 Bury
23.10.92	Paul Lloyd L PTS 4 Liverpool
10.11.92	Michael Alldis L PTS 6 Dagenham
24.11.92	Miguel Matthews W PTS 6 Doncaster
12.12.92	Michael Alldis L CO 1 Muswell Hill
27.01.93	Yusuf Vorajee L RSC 5 Stoke
03.03.93	Kevin Middleton L PTS 8 Solihull
16.03.93	Jonjo Irwin L PTS 10 Mayfair
	(Vacant All-Ireland Featherweight Title)
28.04.93	Barry Jones L PTS 8 Solihull
14.05.93	Shaun Anderson L PTS 8 Kilmarnock
29.05.93	James Murray L PTS 6 Paisley
28.06.93	Carl Roberts W PTS 6 Morecambe
25.07.93	Mario Culpeper L PTS 6 Oldham
12.10.93	Elvis Parsley L PTS 6 Wolverhampton
30.11.93	Chris Lyons W RSC 5 Wolverhampton
22.01.94	Eamonn McAuley L PTS 6 Belfast
10.02.94	Tony Foster L RTD 4 Hull
11.03.94	Donnie Hood L PTS 8 Glasgow
27.04.94	Harry Escott L RTD 6 Solihull
02.06.94	Wayne Rigby L PTS 6 Middleton
10.06.94	Bradley Welsh L RTD 1 Glasgow
12.09.94	Colin Innes W PTS 6 Doncaster
30.11.94	Marco Fattore W PTS 6 Solihull
15.12.94	Matthew Harris L PTS 6 Evesham
09.02.95	Roger Brotherhood W PTS 6 Doncaster
17.02.95	Dean Pithie L RSC 3 Cumbernauld
28.03.95	Anthony Maynard L PTS 8 Wolverhampton
05.04.95	Hugh Collins L PTS 6 Irvine
13.04.95	Dean Pithie L RSC 1 Bloomsbury
11.05.95	Glen Hopkins DREW 6 Sunderland
18.05.95	Dave Clavering L PTS 6 Middleton
06.06.95	Neil Smith L RTD 1 Leicester

Career: 35 contests, won 7, drew 1, lost 27.

Kid McAuley   Les Clark

Kevin McBride

Clones. *Born* Monaghan, 10 May, 1973
Heavyweight. Ht. 6'5"
Manager F. Maloney

17.12.92	Gary Charlton DREW 6 Barking
13.02.93	Gary Williams W PTS 4 Manchester

15.09.93	Joey Paladino W CO 2 Bethnal Green
13.10.93	Chris Coughlan W PTS 4 Bethnal Green
01.12.93	John Harewood W RSC 3 Bethnal Green
06.05.94	Edgar Turpin W RSC 1 Atlantic City, USA
04.06.94	Roger Bryant W CO 1 Reno, USA
17.06.94	Stanley Wright W PTS 6 Atlantic City, USA
26.08.94	James Truesdale W RSC 3 Upper Marlboro, USA
24.09.94	Graham Arnold W RSC 2 Wembley
12.11.94	Dean Storey W RSC 3 Dublin
10.12.94	John Lamphrey W RSC 1 Portland, USA
07.02.95	Carl Gaffney W RSC 3 Ipswich
03.03.95	Carl McGrew W RSC 5 Boston, USA
22.04.95	Jimmy Harrison W RSC 1 Boston, USA
13.05.95	Atelea Kalhea W CO 1 Sacramento, USA

Carrer: 16 contests, won 15, drew 1.

Joe McCluskey

Croy. *Born* Glasgow, 13 March, 1970
L. Heavyweight. Ht. 6'0"
Manager Self

27.04.92	John Oxenham W PTS 4 Glasgow
09.07.92	Lee Prudden W PTS 6 Glasgow
25.01.93	Andy Manning W PTS 6 Glasgow
22.11.93	Jimmy Tyers W PTS 6 Glasgow
28.09.94	Dave Owens W PTS 6 Glasgow

Career: 5 contests, won 5.

Bernard McComiskey

Banbridge. *Born* Banbridge, 9 June, 1971
L. Welterweight. Ht. 5'7"
Manager Self

25.04.90	Lee Fox W RTD 3 Brighton
27.06.90	Stuart Rimmer W PTS 6 Kensington
22.09.90	Wayne Windle L PTS 6 Kensington
11.05.91	Sean Casey W RTD 3 Belfast
24.03.93	Trevor Royal W RSC 6 Belfast
18.06.93	Brian Wright W PTS 6 Belfast
22.01.94	Mike Morrison W PTS 6 Belfast
18.03.95	Simon Hamblett W RSC 1 Millstreet, Eire
14.04.95	Wayne Windle W RSC 5 Belfast

Career: 9 contests, won 8, lost 1.

Spencer McCracken

Birmingham. *Born* Birmingham, 8 August, 1969
Welterweight. Ht. 5'9"
Manager Self

15.10.91	Stuart Dunn DREW 6 Dudley
09.12.91	Seth Jones W RSC 2 Brierley Hill
27.10.92	Dave Lovell W PTS 4 Cradley Heath
07.12.92	Mark Antony W CO 1 Birmingham
22.02.93	Rick North W PTS 8 Birmingham
16.03.93	Ricky Mabbett W PTS 6 Edgbaston
18.05.93	Tony Britland W CO 1 Edgbaston
06.12.93	Jimmy Thornton W PTS 6 Birmingham
19.01.94	Julian Eavis W PTS 8 Solihull
28.03.94	Marty Duke W RSC 2 Birmingham
23.05.94	Ojay Abrahams W PTS 6 Walsall
25.10.94	Julian Eavis W PTS 6 Edgbaston
11.05.95	Tony Foster W PTS 6 Dudley
05.06.95	Stefan Scriggins L PTS 8 Birmingham

Career: 14 contests, won 12, drew 1, lost 1.

Marcus McCrae

Hackney. *Born* London, 13 November, 1969
S. Featherweight. Ht. 5'7"
Manager F. Warren

22.09.93	Miguel Matthews W PTS 6 Bethnal Green
10.11.93	Ian Reid W PTS 6 Bethnal Green
17.02.94	Thomas Bernard W RSC 1 Dagenham
04.06.94	Andrew Reed W PTS 6 Cardiff
01.10.94	Ceri Farrell W RTD 1 Cardiff
19.11.94	Barrie Kelley L PTS 6 Cardiff
25.02.95	Andrew Smith W RSC 4 Millwall

Career: 7 contests, won 6, lost 1.

Mark McCreath

Lincoln. *Born* Bradford, 30 May, 1964
Welterweight. Former Undefeated Benelux
Welterweight Champion. Ht. 5'8½"
Manager Self

11.05.89	Tom Heiskonen W RSC 6 Tallin, Estonia
01.11.89	Bianto Baekelandt W CO 2 Izegem, Belgium
29.11.89	Abdel Lahjar W RTD 4 Paris, France
09.12.89	Pierre Conan W RSC 4 Toul, France
10.02.90	Josef Rajic W PTS 6 Roulers, France
26.03.90	Eric Capoen W RSC 1 Nogent sur Marne, France
19.05.90	Mohammed Berrabah W RSC 6 Montpelier, France
11.08.90	Mohamed Oumad W RTD 5 Le cap d'Agde, France
05.09.90	Mehmet Demir W RSC 5 Belgrade, Yugoslavia
05.10.90	Patrick Vungbo L PTS 10 Waregem, Belgium
	(Vacant Belgium Welterweight Title)
17.04.91	Pat Barrett L RSC 6 Kensington
	(European L. Welterweight Title Challenge)
21.06.91	Freddy Demeulenaere W RSC 5 Waregem, Belgium
	(Vacant Benelux Welterweight Title)
30.04.92	Gary Barron W RSC 5 Mayfair
01.10.92	Chris Saunders W RSC 4 Telford
07.12.92	Gary Barron W RSC 5 Mayfair
06.03.93	Valery Kayumba L RSC 11 Levallois Perret, France
	(European L. Welterweight Title Challenge)
26.05.93	Peter Till W PTS 8 Mansfield
27.10.93	John Smith W RSC 7 West Bromwich
01.03.94	Dave Lovell L RSC 5 Dudley
23.07.94	Ahmed Katejev L RSC 6 Berlin, Germany
23.09.94	Jason Beard W PTS 6 Bethnal Green
10.02.95	Robert Wright W PTS 8 Birmingham

Career: 22 contests, won 17, lost 5.

Geoff McCreesh

Bracknell. *Born* Stockton, 12 June, 1970
Former Undefeated Southern Area L.
Middleweight Champion. Ht. 5'10"
Manager W. Ball

16.02.94	Tony Walton W PTS 6 Stevenage
12.03.94	Barry Thorogood W PTS 6 Cardiff
22.03.94	Mark Dawson W PTS 6 Bethnal Green
20.05.94	Robert Peel W RSC 2 Acton
02.07.94	Julian Eavis W PTS 4 Keynsham
18.11.94	Andrew Furlong W PTS 6 Bracknell
13.12.94	Ojay Abrahams W PTS 6 Potters Bar
20.01.95	Clay O'Shea W RSC 1 Bethnal Green
	(Vacant Southern Area L. Middleweight Title)
03.03.95	Dennis Berry L RTD 5 Bracknell

Career: 9 contests, won 8, lost 1.

Brian McDermott

Bradford. *Born* Wakefield, 10 March 1970
Heavyweight. Ht. 6'3"
T. Callighan

12.06.95	John Pierre W PTS 6 Bradford

Career: 1 contest, won 1.

Billy McDougall

Birmingham. *Born* Birmingham, 11 October, 1965
Welterweight. Ht. 5'10"
Manager Self

02.11.92	Jimmy Reynolds L PTS 6 Wolverhampton
19.11.92	Dean Carr W PTS 6 Evesham
07.12.92	Dean Carr W PTS 6 Birmingham
14.12.92	Kevin Mabbutt L RTD 4 Northampton
27.01.93	Jamie Morris W PTS 6 Stoke
22.02.93	Ernie Locke W PTS 6 Birmingham
29.04.93	Rob Stevenson DREW 6 Hull

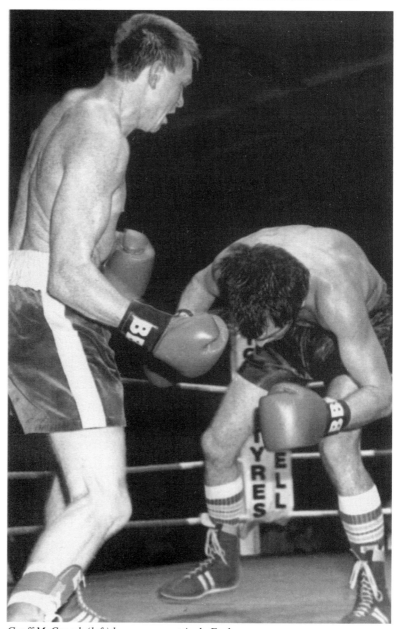

Geoff McCreesh (left) bangs away at Andy Furlong

Les Clark

06.05.93	Andy Peach W PTS 6 Walsall
23.06.93	Marty Duke L PTS 6 Gorleston
11.08.93	Paul Denton L PTS 6 Mansfield
02.12.93	Cam Raeside L RSC 5 Evesham
19.01.94	John O. Johnson W RSC 3 Stoke
08.02.94	Richard Swallow L PTS 6 Wolverhampton
16.02.94	Steve McNess L PTS 4 Stevenage
10.03.94	Danny Shinkwin DREW 4 Watford
10.05.94	Prince Kasi Kiahau L RTD 4 Doncaster
11.10.94	Nicky Thurbin L RSC 6 Bethnal Green
09.11.94	Peter Reid L PTS 6 Stafford
23.11.94	Brian Coleman L PTS 4 Piccadilly
30.11.94	Prince Kasi Kiahau L PTS 6 Solihull
15.12.94	Kenny Scott W RSC 3 Evesham
16.01.95	Tommy Quinn L CO 5 Musselburgh
24.02.95	Paul Salmon L PTS 6 Weston super Mare
24.04.95	Tommy Quinn L RSC 3 Glasgow

Career: 24 contests, won 7, drew 2, lost 15.

Billy McDougall Les Clark

Simon McDougall

Blackpool. *Born* Manchester, 11 July, 1968
L. Heavyweight. Ht. 5'10½"
Manager Self

14.11.88	Andrew Bravardo W CO 4 Manchester
16.01.89	Steve Osborne L PTS 6 Bradford
25.01.89	Steve Osborne L PTS 6 Stoke
20.02.89	Willie Connell W RSC 4 Bradford
04.04.89	Lee Woolis L PTS 6 Manchester
12.10.89	George Ferrie W PTS 6 Glasgow
30.11.89	Jimmy Cropper W PTS 6 Oldham
07.12.89	Sean O'Phoenix L PTS 6 Manchester
07.04.90	Eddie Smulders L PTS 6 Eindhoven, Holland
15.05.90	Terry French W PTS 4 South Shields
12.10.90	Ray Alberts L PTS 6 Cayenne, France
22.10.90	Glenn Campbell L RSC 4 Manchester
10.12.90	Morris Thomas W RSC 2 Bradford
28.01.91	Ian Henry W PTS 8 Bradford
28.02.91	Glenn Campbell L PTS 10 Bury
	(Central Area S. Middleweight Title Challenge)

23.04.91	Paul Burton L PTS 8 Evesham
10.05.91	Ian Henry L PTS 6 Gateshead
30.09.91	Doug Calderwood W RSC 4 Liverpool
10.10.91	Terry French L PTS 6 Gateshead
19.10.91	Andrea Magi L RSC 5 Terni, Italy
03.03.92	Paul Hitch L PTS 6 Houghton le Spring
11.03.92	Ian Henry L PTS 8 Solihull
30.03.92	Nigel Rafferty L PTS 8 Coventry
08.06.92	Mark McBiane W PTS 6 Bradford
06.10.92	Garry Delaney L PTS 8 Antwerp, Belgium
12.12.92	Garry Delaney L PTS 8 Muswell Hill
04.03.93	Alan Smiles L PTS 6 Glasgow
26.03.93	Roland Ericsson L RSC 5 Copenhagen, Denmark
17.04.93	Terry French L PTS 6 Washington
12.05.93	Martin Langtry L PTS 6 Sheffield
14.08.93	Mark Prince L PTS 6 Hammersmith
04.10.93	Bruce Scott L PTS 6 Mayfair
15.10.93	Christophe Girard L PTS 8 Romorantin, France
08.12.93	Stevie R. Davies W RSC 5 Hull
29.01.94	Ole Klemetsen L RTD 5 Cardiff
08.03.94	John Foreman W PTS 6 Edgbaston
11.05.94	Monty Wright W PTS 6 Stevenage
19.09.94	Stephen Wilson L RTD 3 Glasgow
21.01.95	Sean Heron L PTS 4 Glasgow
16.02.95	Glenn Campbell L PTS 6 Bury
06.03.95	John Keeton L RSC 5 Mayfair
17.04.95	Stefan Angehrn W RSC 5 Berne, Switzerland

Career: 42 contests, won 14, lost 28.

Alan McDowall

Renfrew. *Born* Renfrew, 29 September, 1967
Lightweight. Ht. 5'10"
Manager Self

24.09.91	Johnny Patterson W PTS 4 Glasgow
28.11.91	Johnny Patterson W PTS 6 Glasgow
31.01.92	Charles Shepherd W RSC 3 Glasgow
20.02.92	Mark O'Callaghan W PTS 6 Glasgow
12.03.92	James Jiora W CO 2 Glasgow
29.05.92	Karl Taylor W PTS 6 Glasgow
22.10.92	Robert Lloyd W RTD 4 Glasgow
30.04.93	Dean Bramhald W PTS 6 Glasgow
29.05.93	Rob Stewart DREW 6 Paisley
19.12.93	Dean Amory W PTS 8 Glasgow
10.06.94	Mark Antony W PTS 8 Glasgow
08.09.94	Peter Till L PTS 6 Glasgow

Career: 12 contests, won 10, drew 1, lost 1.

Steve McGovern

Bembridge. *Born* Newport, IOW, 17 April, 1969
Welterweight. Ht. 5'9"
Manager J. Bishop

21.09.89	Mike Morrison W PTS 6 Southampton
17.04.90	Justin Graham W PTS 6 Millwall
21.01.91	Mark Dinnadge W PTS 6 Crystal Palace
23.02.91	Tim Harmey W PTS 6 Brighton
23.04.91	Frank Harrington L PTS 6 Evesham
08.05.91	A.M.Milton W PTS 6 Millwall
16.12.91	Chris Mylan W PTS 8 Southampton
03.03.92	Tony Swift L RSC 4 Cradley Heath
27.10.92	Ricky Mabbett DREW 6 Leicester
29.04.93	Michael Dick W PTS 6 Hayes
23.06.93	Joel Ani W PTS 6 Edmonton

23.02.94	David Lake W PTS 6 Watford
17.12.94	Ahmet Katejev L RSC 4 Berlin, Germany
31.03.95	Maurice Forbes L PTS 6 Crystal Palace
19.04.95	Jason Beard L PTS 6 Bethnal Green
17.06.95	Michael Carruth L RSC 4 Cardiff

Career: 16 contests, won 10, drew 1, lost 5.

Mark McGowan

Plymouth. *Born* Plymouth, 5 February, 1972
L. Welterweight. Ht. 5'7½"
Manager D. Sullivan

10.06.95	Mark Winters L PTS 6 Manchester

Career: 1 contest, lost 1.

Graham McGrath

Warley. *Born* West Bromwich, 31 July, 1962
S. Bantamweight. Ht. 5'4"
Manager Self

21.05.92	Paul Kelly W RSC 2 Cradley Heath
01.06.92	Greg Upton L PTS 6 Solihull
09.07.92	Wilson Docherty L RSC 4 Glasgow
25.09.92	Paul Lloyd L RSC 3 Liverpool
02.11.92	Dennis Oakes L PTS 4 Liverpool
01.12.92	Leo Beirne L PTS 6 Liverpool
10.12.92	Shaun Anderson L PTS 6 Glasgow
14.01.93	Daren Fifield L PTS 4 Mayfair
21.01.93	Shaun Anderson L PTS 6 Glasgow
23.02.93	Ian Baillie W PTS 6 Kettering
29.03.93	Ian McLeod L PTS 6 Glasgow
19.04.93	Karl Morling L RSC 6 Northampton
23.06.93	Rowan Williams L PTS 4 Edmonton
02.07.93	Peter Culshaw L PTS 6 Liverpool
09.09.93	Shaun Anderson L PTS 6 Glasgow
28.09.93	John Sillo L PTS 6 Liverpool
06.10.93	Neil Parry DREW 6 York
21.10.93	James Murray L PTS 6 Glasgow
28.10.93	Greg Upton L PTS 8 Torquay
07.11.93	Alex Docherty L RSC 3 Glasgow
06.12.93	Darren Greaves DREW 6 Birmingham
16.12.93	Darren Greaves W PTS 6 Walsall
19.01.94	Gary White L PTS 6 Solihull
21.02.94	Ian McLeod L CO 6 Glasgow
21.03.94	Marcus Duncan L PTS 6 Bradford
28.03.94	Jason Morris W PTS 6 Birmingham
27.04.94	Paul Ingle L PTS 4 Bethnal Green
20.05.94	Mark Cokely W PTS 6 Neath
10.06.94	James Murray L PTS 8 Glasgow
08.09.94	Shaun Anderson L PTS 8 Glasgow
21.09.94	Mark Hughes L PTS 4 Cardiff
03.10.94	Michael Brodie L RSC 3 Manchester
02.11.94	Darren Greaves W RSC 4 Birmingham
24.11.94	Paul Ingle L PTS 6 Hull
05.12.94	Darren Greaves W PTS 6 Birmingham
13.12.94	Patrick Mullings L PTS 4 Ilford
18.01.95	Rowan Williams L CO 6 Solihull
	(Vacant Midlands Area Bantamweight Title)
14.02.95	Mark Bowers L PTS 6 Bethnal Green
09.03.95	Marty Chestnut L PTS 6 Walsall
20.03.95	Marty Chestnut W PTS 6 Birmingham
30.03.95	Patrick Mullings L RSC 3 Bethnal Green
11.05.95	Jon Pegg W PTS 6 Dudley
05.06.95	Jon Pegg W PTS 6 Birmingham
20.06.95	Jon Pegg W PTS 6 Edgbaston
30.06.95	Chris Jickells L PTS 4 Doncaster

Career: 45 contests, won 12, drew 2, lost 31.

Dominic McGuigan

Newcastle. *Born* Hexham, 13 June, 1963
Northern Area S. Featherweight Champion.
Ht. 5'6"
Manager N. Fawcett

10.10.89	Dave Buxton W PTS 6 Sunderland
24.01.90	John Milne DREW 6 Sunderland
20.03.90	Frankie Foster DREW 4 Hartlepool
21.04.90	Chris Bennett W PTS 6 Sunderland
22.05.90	Lester James L PTS 6 Stockton
16.09.91	Barrie Kelley DREW 6 Mayfair
28.11.91	John Milne W RTD 3 Glasgow
30.04.92	Kevin Lowe W RSC 6 Mayfair
15.05.92	Rene Walker L PTS 8 Augsburg, Germany
07.10.92	Harry Escott L RTD 5 Sunderland
12.11.92	Kevin Lowe W RSC 2 Liverpool
25.02.93	Peter Judson DREW 6 Bradford
27.03.93	Giorgio Campanella L RSC 3 Evian, France
19.05.93	J.T.Williams W PTS 6 Sunderland
03.06.93	Eugene Speed L CO 1 Marseille, France
21.10.93	John Stovin L PTS 6 Bayswater
02.12.93	Peter Till L RSC 2 Walsall
24.11.94	John T. Kelly W PTS 6 Newcastle
13.01.95	Dennis Holbaek Pedersen L PTS 6 Aalborg, Denmark
02.03.95	Frankie Foster W RSC 6 Cramlington
	(Northern Area S. Featherweight Title Challenge)

Career: 20 contests, won 8, drew 4, lost 8.

Dave McHale

Glasgow. *Born* Glasgow, 29 April, 1967
S. Featherweight. Ht. 5'7"
Manager Self

08.10.90	Sol Francis W RSC 2 Glasgow
25.11.91	Eddie Garbutt W RSC 1 Liverpool
30.03.92	Kevin Lowe W RSC 5 Glasgow
01.06.92	Chris Jickells W RSC 4 Glasgow
09.07.92	G. G. Goddard W RTD 4 Glasgow
19.10.92	Lee Fox W RSC 3 Glasgow
23.11.92	Karl Taylor W PTS 8 Glasgow
15.05.93	Miguel Matthews W RSC 4 Glasgow
02.02.94	John T. Kelly W CO 1 Glasgow
21.03.94	Frankie Foster W PTS 8 Glasgow
13.12.94	Floyd Havard L RSC 10 Ilford
	(British S. Featherweight Title Challenge)

Career: 11 contests, won 10, lost 1.

(Anthony) Daryl McKenzie

Paisley. *Born* Johnstone, 20 August, 1965
S. Bantamweight. Ht. 5'4"
Manager N. Sweeney

17.02.94	Des Gargano DREW 6 Bury
02.03.94	Al Garrett W PTS 6 Glasgow
25.04.94	Al Garrett L PTS 6 Glasgow
16.05.94	Marcus Duncan L PTS 6 Morecambe
19.09.94	Chris Lyons W PTS 6 Glasgow
26.09.94	Peter Culshaw L PTS 6 Liverpool
24.10.94	Jobie Tyers L PTS 6 Glasgow
02.11.94	Chris Lyons W PTS 6 Solihull
21.11.94	Ady Lewis L RSC 4 Glasgow

Career: 9 contests, won 3, drew 1, lost 5.

Duke McKenzie   Tony Fitch

Duke McKenzie

Croydon. *Born* Croydon, 5 May, 1963
Former Undefeated British Featherweight
Champion. Former WBO S. Bantamweight
& Bantamweight Champion. Former IBF
Flyweight Champion. Former Undefeated
British & European Flyweight Champion.
Ht. 5'7"
Manager Self

23.11.82	Charlie Brown W RSC 1 Wembley
24.01.83	Andy King W RSC 2 Mayfair
27.02.83	Dave Pierson W RSC 1 Las Vegas, USA
03.03.83	Gregorio Hernandez W RSC 3 Los Angeles, USA
19.03.83	Lupe Sanchez W CO 2 Reno, USA
18.10.83	Jerry Davis W RSC 2 Atlantic City, USA
22.11.83	Alain Limarola W PTS 6 Wembley
15.01.84	David Capo W PTS 4 Atlantic City, USA
23.05.84	Gary Roberts W CO 1 Mayfair
06.03.85	Julio Guerrero W PTS 8 Kensington
05.06.85	Danny Flynn W RSC 4 Kensington
	(Vacant British Flyweight Title)
16.10.85	Orlando Maestre W PTS 8 Kensington
19.02.86	Sonny Long W PTS 10 Kensington
20.05.86	Charlie Magri W RTD 5 Wembley
	(British Flyweight Title Defence & European Flyweight Title Challenge)
19.11.86	Lee Cargle W PTS 10 Atlantic City, USA
17.12.86	Piero Pinna W PTS 12 Acqui Terme, Italy
	(European Flyweight Title Defence)
24.03.87	Jose Manuel Diaz W PTS 8 Wembley
02.12.87	Juan Herrera W PTS 10 Wembley
09.03.88	Agapito Gomez W CO 2 Wembley
	(European Flyweight Title Defence)
04.05.88	Jose Gallegos W PTS 10 Wembley
05.10.88	Rolando Bohol W CO 11 Wembley
	(IBF Flyweight Title Challenge)
30.11.88	Artemio Ruiz W PTS 10 Southwark
08.03.89	Tony de Luca W RSC 4 Kensington
	(IBF Flyweight Title Defence)

07.06.89	Dave Boy McAuley L PTS 12 Wembley
	(IBF Flyweight Title Defence)
12.10.89	Dave Moreno W PTS 10 Southwark
08.11.89	Memo Flores W PTS 8 Wembley
30.09.90	Thierry Jacob L PTS 12 Calais, France
	(Vacant European Bantamweight Title)
10.01.91	Pete Buckley W RSC 5 Wandsworth
07.02.91	Julio Blanco W RSC 7 Watford
04.04.91	Chris Clarkson W RSC 5 Watford
30.06.91	Gaby Canizales W PTS 12 Southwark
	(WBO Bantamweight Title Challenge)
12.09.91	Cesar Soto W PTS 12 Wandsworth
	(WBO Bantamweight Title Defence)
25.03.92	Wilfredo Vargas W RSC 8 Kensington
	(WBO Bantamweight Title Defence)
13.05.92	Rafael del Valle L CO 1 Kensington
	(WBO Bantamweight Title Defence)
07.09.92	Pete Buckley W RTD 3 Bethnal Green
15.10.92	Jesse Benavides W PTS 12 Lewisham
	(WBO S. Bantamweight Title Challenge)
09.06.93	Daniel Jimenez L PTS 12 Lewisham
	(WBO S. Bantamweight Title Defence)
18.12.93	John Davison W RSC 4 Manchester
	(Vacant British Featherweight Title)
29.01.94	Marcelo Rodriguez W PTS 8 Cardiff
17.08.94	Mark Hargreaves W RSC 3 Sheffield
01.10.94	Steve Robinson L CO 9 Cardiff
	(WBO Featherweight Title Challenge)
28.04.95	Mehdi Labdouni L PTS 12 Fontenay sous Bois
	(European Featherweight Title Challenge)

Career: 42 contests, won 36, lost 6.

Kelton McKenzie

Leicester. *Born* Leicester, 18 September, 1968
S. Featherweight. Midlands Area
Featherweight Champion. Ht. 5'7"
Manager J. Griffin

18.10.90	Tony Silkstone L PTS 6 Dewsbury
29.11.90	Neil Leitch DREW 6 Marton
11.12.90	Sylvester Osuji W PTS 6 Evesham
21.01.91	J. T. Williams DREW 6 Crystal Palace
14.03.91	Craig Dermody L RSC 3 Middleton
01.05.91	Tim Yeates W PTS 6 Bethnal Green
17.06.91	Derek Amory W RSC 6 Edgbaston
05.11.91	Richard Woolgar W RSC 5 Leicester
22.01.92	Colin Lynch W RSC 5 Solihull
26.03.92	Brian Robb W RSC 4 Telford
29.04.92	Elvis Parsley W RSC 5 Solihull
	(Vacant Midlands Area Featherweight Title)
18.07.92	Steve Walker W CO 2 Manchester
27.10.92	Alan McKay L PTS 10 Cradley Heath
	(Elim. British Featherweight Title)
28.04.93	Richie Wenton L PTS 8 Dublin
19.05.93	Paul Harvey L RSC 7 Leicester
04.10.93	Mehdi Labdouni L PTS 8 Paris, France
10.05.94	Harry Escott L PTS 6 Doncaster
27.08.94	Barry Jones L PTS 6 Cardiff
31.10.94	Sugar Gibiliru L PTS 6 Liverpool
09.12.94	Yifru Retta L PTS 8 Bethnal Green
06.03.95	Wayne Rigby W PTS 8 Leicester
26.04.95	Charles Shepherd L RSC 7 Solihull

Career: 22 contests, won 9, drew 2, lost 11.

Kevin McKenzie

Hartlepool. *Born* Hartlepool, 18 October, 1968
L. Welterweight. Ht. 5'7½"
Manager Self

08.06.92 Jason Brattley W RTD 3 Bradford
21.09.92 Alan Ingle W PTS 6 Glasgow
22.10.92 Dave Anderson L RSC 3 Glasgow
01.12.92 Seth Jones L RSC 3 Hartlepool
09.03.93 Micky Hall W PTS 6 Hartlepool
17.04.93 Paul Charters L RSC 4 Washington
(Vacant Northern Area L.Welterweight Title)
13.09.93 Blue Butterworth W PTS 6 Middleton
02.12.93 Micky Hall L PTS 4 Hartlepool
02.02.94 Steve McLevy L PTS 6 Glasgow
28.02.94 Rocky Ferrari W PTS 6 Marton
18.04.94 Andy Davidson L RSC 1 Manchester
22.09.94 Kevin McKillan L PTS 6 Bury
25.10.94 A. M. Milton W PTS 4 Middlesbrough
23.11.94 Mark Breslin L PTS 6 Irvine
30.11.94 Gareth Jordan L PTS 6 Wolverhampton
17.02.95 Alan Peacock W PTS 6 Cumbernauld
02.03.95 Rocky Ferrari DREW 6 Glasgow
20.03.95 Alan Peacock W RSC 6 Glasgow
13.05.95 Gordon Blair L RTD 5 Glasgow
30.06.95 Tony Mock L PTS 6 Liverpool
Career: 20 contests, won 8, drew 1, lost 11.

(Roger) R. F. McKenzie

Croydon. *Born* Croydon, 3 October, 1965
Former Southern Area Heavyweight
Champion. Ht. 6'2"
Manager Self

31.01.89 Gerry Storey W PTS 6 Bethnal Green
24.09.90 Mark Bowen L RSC 1 Mayfair
29.11.90 Denzil Browne W PTS 6 Sunderland
12.02.91 Noel Magee L PTS 6 Belfast
21.03.91 Denzil Browne L PTS 6 Dewsbury
28.05.91 Steve Yorath L PTS 6 Cardiff
07.09.91 Ray Kane L PTS 4 Belfast
09.10.91 Denzil Browne W PTS 6 Manchester
28.10.91 Pedro van Raamsdonk W CO 7 Arnhem, Holland
12.12.91 Norbert Ekassi L RSC 3 Massy, France
14.03.92 Neils H. Madsen L PTS 6 Copenhagen, Denmark
25.04.92 Noel Magee L PTS 8 Belfast
31.10.92 Warren Richards DREW 6 Earls Court
13.02.93 Magne Havnaa W RTD 5 Randers, Denmark
31.03.93 Warren Richards W RSC 8 Bethnal Green
(Vacant Southern Area Heavyweight Title)
17.09.93 Brian Neilsen L PTS 6 Copenhagen, Denmark
13.10.93 James Oyebola L RSC 1 Bethnal Green
(Southern Area Heavyweight Title Defence)
11.12.93 Bernd Friedrich W RSC 2 Dusseldorf, Germany
25.03.94 Mark Hulstrom L PTS 6 Bernholme, Denmark
17.09.94 Scott Welch L RSC 1 Crawley
27.05.95 Darren Corbett W PTS 6 Belfast
Career: 21 contests, won 8, drew 1, lost 12.

Kevin McKillan

Manchester. *Born* Belfast, 1 March, 1969
Lightweight. Ht. 5'8"
Manager J. Doughty

28.10.91 Michael Byrne W PTS 6 Leicester
13.11.91 Barry Glanister W PTS 6 Liverpool
22.01.92 Sugar Boy Wright W PTS 6 Solihull
10.02.92 Jamie Davidson L PTS 6 Liverpool

11.03.92 Jamie Davidson DREW 6 Stoke
01.06.92 Steve Howden W RSC 2 Manchester
12.06.92 Floyd Churchill W PTS 6 Liverpool
25.09.92 John Smith W PTS 6 Liverpool
07.10.92 J. T. Williams L PTS 6 Barry
20.11.92 Steve Foran L PTS 6 Liverpool
15.02.93 John T. Kelly W PTS 6 Manchester
19.04.93 Simon Hamblett W CO 2 Manchester
26.04.93 Steve Walker DREW 8 Manchester
01.06.93 Micky Hall W PTS 6 Manchester
06.10.93 Norman Dhalie W RSC 1 Solihull
29.10.93 Soren Sondergaard L CO 2 Korsoer, Denmark
26.01.94 Dean Amory W PTS 8 Stoke
06.06.94 Micky Hall W PTS 6 Manchester
22.09.94 Kevin McKenzie W PTS 6 Bury
10.12.94 Tanveer Ahmed L PTS 6 Manchester
18.05.95 Shaun Stokes DREW 8 Middleton
Career: 21 contests, won 13, drew 3, lost 5.

Ian McLeod

Kilmarnock. *Born* Edinburgh, 11 June, 1969
Featherweight. Ht. 5'9"
Manager T. Gilmour

23.11.92 Robert Braddock DREW 6 Glasgow
29.03.93 Graham McGrath W PTS 6 Glasgow
21.02.94 Graham McGrath W CO 6 Glasgow
04.03.94 Chip O'Neill W RSC 2 Irvine
23.11.94 Chris Jickells W PTS 6 Irvine
05.04.95 Colin Innes W RSC 5 Irvine
Career: 6 contests, won 5, drew 1.

Steve McLevy

Glasgow. *Born* Glasgow, 23 September, 1972
L. Welterweight. Ht. 5'8"
Manager R. Watt

22.11.93 Dewi Roberts W RSC 1 Glasgow
02.02.94 Kevin McKenzie W PTS 6 Glasgow
28.03.94 Mark Antony W CO 1 Musselburgh
20.09.94 Dave Curtis W RTD 3 Musselburgh
21.11.94 Mark Legg W RSC 5 Glasgow
24.02.95 John Smith W PTS 6 Irvine
01.06.95 Micky Hall L RSC 1 Musselburgh
Career: 7 contests, won 6, lost 1.

Colin McMillan

Barking. *Born* London, 12 February, 1966
Former WBO Featherweight Champion.
Former Undefeated British & Commonwealth Featherweight Champion.
Ht. 5'5¼"
Manager Self

29.11.88 Mike Chapman W PTS 6 Battersea
10.12.88 Aldrich Johnson W PTS 6 Crystal Palace
31.01.89 Alan McKay L RSC 3 Bethnal Green
12.06.89 Miguel Matthews W RSC 3 Battersea
19.09.89 Graham O'Malley W PTS 8 Millwall
11.10.89 Marcel Herbert W PTS 6 Millwall
30.11.89 Sylvester Osuji W RSC 4 Barking
14.02.90 Vidal Tellez W RSC 2 Millwall
17.04.90 Jesus Muniz W PTS 8 Millwall
03.05.90 Steve Walker W PTS 6 Kensington
05.07.90 Tyrone Miller W CO 2 Greensville, USA
17.07.90 Malcolm Rougeaux W CO 1 Lake Charles, USA
25.09.90 Darren Weller W RSC 2 Millwall

10.10.90 Graham O'Malley W PTS 6 Millwall
12.11.90 Mark Holt W PTS 8 Norwich
05.03.91 Russell Davison W PTS 6 Millwall
26.04.91 Willie Richardson W PTS 8 Crystal Palace
22.05.91 Gary de Roux W RSC 7 Millwall
(British Featherweight Title Challenge)
03.07.91 Herbie Bivalacqua W RSC 3 Reading
04.09.91 Kevin Pritchard W RSC 7 Bethnal Green
(British Featherweight Title Defence)
29.10.91 Sean Murphy W PTS 12 Kensington
(British Featherweight Title Defence)
18.01.92 Percy Commey W PTS 12 Kensington
(Vacant Commonwealth Featherweight Title)
25.03.92 Tommy Valdez W CO 6 Dagenham
16.05.92 Maurizio Stecca W PTS 12 Muswell Hill
(WBO Featherweight Title Challenge)
26.09.92 Ruben Palacio L RSC 8 Earls Court
(WBO Featherweight Title Defence)
23.10.93 Steve Robinson L PTS 12 Cardiff
(WBO Featherweight Title Challenge)
04.02.95 Harry Escott W PTS 8 Cardiff
25.02.95 Mark Hargreaves W RSC 4 Millwall
06.05.95 Peter Judson W PTS 8 Shepton Mallet
Career: 29 contests, won 26, lost 3.

Colin McMillan   Les Clark

Conn McMullen

Carnlough. *Born* Larne, 21 June, 1967
Bantamweight. Ht. 5'6"
Manager Self

06.06.90 Ceri Farrell W RSC 5 Battersea
04.12.90 Neil Parry W RSC 2 Southend
12.11.91 Mark Loftus W PTS 6 Milton Keynes
28.10.92 Barry Jones L PTS 6 Cardiff
26.03.93 Neil Armstrong W RSC 5 Glasgow
05.05.93 Miguel Matthews DREW 6 Belfast
18.06.93 Wayne McCullough L RSC 3 Belfast
25.08.93 Anton Gilmore L PTS 8 Hammanskrall, South Africa
23.10.93 John Green W PTS 6 Cardiff
23.02.94 Tony Falcone DREW 4 Watford
29.03.94 Pete Buckley L PTS 6 Bethnal Green

119

11.06.94   Michael Alldis L PTS 8 Bethnal Green
09.07.94   Drew Docherty L PTS 8 Earls Court
07.10.94   Johnny Bredahl L PTS 8 Copenhagen, Denmark
04.11.94   Salim Medjkoune L PTS 8 Aubiere, France

Career: 15 contests, won 5, drew 2, lost 8.

Jason McNeill

Swansea. *Born* Bristol, 12 August, 1971
L. Heavyweight. Ht. 6'1"
Manager Self

03.10.91   Mark Pain L PTS 6 Burton
15.10.91   Tony Colclough L PTS 6 Dudley
28.11.91   Mark McBiane W PTS 6 Evesham
21.01.92   Gypsy Johnny Price L PTS 4 Stockport
11.03.92   Paul McCarthy W PTS 6 Cardiff
23.04.92   Abel Asinamali L CO 3 Eltham
07.09.92   Mark Baker L RSC 2 Glasgow
23.10.92   Paul Wright L RSC 1 Liverpool
06.02.93   Karl Mumford L PTS 6 Cardiff
22.02.93   Kenny Nevers L RSC 1 Eltham
10.04.93   Julian Johnson L PTS 6 Swansea
26.05.93   Graham Burton L RSC 3 Mansfield
16.10.93   Ray Kane L PTS 6 Belfast
03.11.93   Dale Nixon L RSC 1 Bristol
11.01.94   Mark Delaney L RSC 2 Bethnal Green
07.11.94   Luan Morena L RSC 5 Piccadilly

Career: 16 contests, won 2, lost 14.

Steve McNess   Les Clark

Steve McNess

Bethnal Green. *Born* Bow, 17 November, 1969
Middleweight. Ht. 5'10½"
Manager Self

22.04.92   Rick North W PTS 6 Wembley
13.05.92   Mark Verikios L RSC 5 Kensington
03.09.92   Steve Goodwin W PTS 6 Dunstable
28.10.92   Mark Dawson L RSC 2 Kensington
28.01.93   Steve Scott W PTS 6 Southwark
26.04.93   Bullit Andrews W RSC 3 Lewisham
15.06.93   Martin Rosamond L RSC 5 Hempstead
07.12.93   Robert Whitehouse W RSC 3 Bethnal Green

16.02.94   Billy McDougall W PTS 4 Stevenage
11.03.94   Tony Walton W PTS 4 Bethnal Green
11.10.94   Harry Dhami DREW 6 Bethnal Green
23.02.95   Julian Eavis W PTS 6 Southwark
25.03.95   Peter Vosper W RSC 5 Millwall
20.04.95   Spencer Alton W RSC 2 Mayfair
19.05.95   Martin Jolley W PTS 6 Southwark

Career: 15 contests, won 11, drew 1, lost 3.

Andy McVeigh

Birmingham. *Born* Moseley, 25 August, 1968
S. Middleweight. Ht. 5'8"
Manager P. Cowdell/R. Gray

02.11.94   Peter Varnarvas W RSC 3 Birmingham
09.11.94   Spencer Alton W RTD 3 Stafford
15.12.94   Dave Battey W RSC 3 Walsall
17.01.95   Paul Murray W PTS 6 Worcester
07.03.95   Robert Harper W RSC 5 Edgbaston
11.05.95   Neil Simpson W CO 2 Dudley
20.06.95   John Duckworth DREW 6 Edgbaston

Career: 7 contests, won 6, drew 1.

Dave Madden

Daventry. *Born* Birmingham, 18 June, 1967
L. Welterweight. Ht. 5'10"
Manager J. Cox

12.11.92   Blue Butterworth L RSC 2 Burnley
27.01.93   Gary Hiscox L PTS 6 Stoke
22.02.93   Kris McAdam L PTS 8 Glasgow
20.09.93   Lee Heggs W PTS 6 Northampton
27.10.93   Gareth Jordan L RSC 5 West Bromwich
19.12.93   Dennis Griffin L RSC 1 Northampton
10.03.94   Dave Fallon W PTS 6 Watford
16.05.94   Danny Quacoe L RSC 4 Heathrow
03.04.95   Ram Singh W PTS 6 Northampton
22.06.95   John T. Kelly L PTS 6 Houghton le Spring

Career: 10 contests, won 3, lost 7.

Jay Mahoney

Peterborough. *Born* Peterborough, 21 September, 1971
L. Welterweight. Ht 5'8"
Manager K. Whitney

05.12.94   Shaun O'Neill W PTS 6 Houghton le Spring
20.02.95   David Thompson W RSC 4 Manchester
08.03.95   Peter Hickenbottom W PTS 6 Solihull
03.04.95   Blue Butterworth W PTS 6 Manchester

Career: 4 contests, won 4.

Colin Manners

Leeds. *Born* Leeds, 4 July, 1962
Middleweight. Ht. 5'10"
Manager P. Byrne

26.04.90   Tony Booth L PTS 6 Halifax
27.09.90   Carlos Christie L PTS 6 Birmingham
18.10.90   Carlton Myers W CO 2 Dewsbury
25.10.90   Colin Ford L PTS 6 Bayswater
12.12.90   Tony Kosova W PTS 6 Leicester
31.01.91   Lee Crocker W PTS 6 Bredbury
18.02.91   John Ogiste L PTS 6 Mayfair
14.03.91   John Ogiste L PTS 8 Middleton
01.05.91   Darren Parker W CO 2 Solihull
05.06.91   Richard Carter W CO 1 Wolverhampton
03.09.91   Wayne Ellis W RSC 1 Cardiff
29.04.92   Darron Griffiths DREW 8 Solihull

14.07.92   Stan King W PTS 8 Mayfair
30.09.92   Darron Griffiths L PTS 10 Solihull
(Elim. British Middleweight Title)
23.02.93   Chris Pyatt L CO 3 Doncaster
15.07.93   Juan Medina Padilla L PTS 8 La Linea, Gibralter
19.01.94   Paul Busby DREW 8 Solihull
15.03.94   Paul Busby L PTS 8 Mayfair
11.05.94   Shaun Cummins W RSC 6 Sheffield
17.01.95   Antonio Fernandez L PTS 8 Worcester
04.02.95   Cornelius Carr L PTS 8 Cardiff
18.03.95   Sammy Storey L PTS 8 Millstreet, Eire

Career: 22 contests, won 8, drew 2, lost 12.

Colin Manners   Les Clark

Nick Manners

Leeds. *Born* Leeds, 23 November, 1966
S. Middleweight. Ht. 6'2"
Manager Self

18.10.90   Paul Murray W PTS 6 Dewsbury
13.12.90   John Kaighin W CO 3 Dewsbury
31.01.91   Terry Duffus W RSC 1 Bredbury
21.03.91   Marvin O'Brien W CO 2 Dewsbury
09.05.91   Peter Gorny W RSC 1 Leeds
27.06.91   Peter Vosper W RSC 1 Leeds
01.08.91   Tony Booth DREW 8 Dewsbury
30.10.91   Kevin Morton L PTS 8 Leeds
23.09.92   Lee Crocker W CO 1 Leeds
29.10.92   Ali Forbes L RSC 3 Leeds
25.02.93   Jason Fores W RSC 2 Bradford
01.04.93   Joe McKenzie W RSC 2 Leeds
21.10.94   Sean Heron L PTS 6 Glasgow

Career: 13 contests, won 9, drew 1, lost 3.

Abdul Mannon

Battersea. *Born* Bangladesh, 5 April, 1972
Featherweight. Ht. 5'3"
Manager T. Toole

08.03.94   Brian Eccles W RSC 2 Kettering
17.05.94   Keith Jones W PTS 6 Kettering
27.10.94   Marty Chestnut L DIS 2 Millwall
24.01.95   Chris Lyons W PTS 6 Piccadilly
08.06.95   Brian Carr L PTS 6 Glasgow
17.06.95   Henry Jones L PTS 6 Cardiff

Career: 6 contests, won 3, lost 3.

Keith Marner

Bracknell. *Born* Wokingham, 11 April, 1961
Former Southern Area L. Welterweight Champion. Ht. 5'8"
Manager Self

30.09.93	Ron Shinkwin W PTS 6 Hayes
09.12.93	Dennis Griffin W PTS 6 Watford
10.03.94	John O. Johnson W RSC 5 Watford
28.04.94	Gary Cogan W RSC 3 Mayfair
20.05.94	Chris Aston W PTS 8 Acton
02.09.94	Dewi Roberts W PTS 6 Spitalfields
18.11.94	Jonathan Thaxton W PTS 10 Bracknell *(Southern Area L. Welterweight Title Challenge)*
03.03.95	Scott Doyle W PTS 6 Bracknell
23.05.95	Bernard Paul L PTS 10 Potters Bar *(Southern Area L. Welterweight Title Defence)*

Career: 9 contests, won 8, lost 1.

Scott Marshall (Calow)

Nottingham. *Born* Mansfield, 6 July, 1973
L. Welterweight. Ht. 5'9"
Manager J. Ashton

02.03.95	James Montgomerie L PTS 6 Glasgow
16.03.95	Shaun O'Neill L RSC 3 Sunderland

Career: 2 contests, lost 2.

(Paul) Stinger Mason

Sheffield. *Born* Sheffield, 27 February, 1964
L. Heavyweight. Ht. 5'8"
Manager Self

19.04.89	Sean Stringfellow W PTS 6 Stoke
24.05.89	Andrew Flute L PTS 6 Hanley
16.11.89	Tony Lawrence DREW 4 Ilkeston
27.01.90	Ian Vokes W PTS 6 Sheffield
28.03.90	Cliff Curtis W PTS 6 Bethnal Green
20.05.90	Tony Hodge W CO 2 Sheffield
11.06.90	Glenn Campbell L RTD 5 Manchester
12.11.90	Adrian Wright L RSC 4 Stratford upon Avon
13.03.91	Mike Phillips DREW 6 Stoke
13.05.91	Doug Calderwood L CO 3 Manchester
23.10.91	Roger Wilson DREW 6 Stoke
11.11.91	Russell Washer W PTS 4 Stratford upon Avon
23.05.92	Paul Busby L RSC 2 Birmingham
28.09.92	Quinn Paynter L CO 1 Manchester
20.09.93	Stephen Wilson L RSC 6 Glasgow
10.11.93	Joe Calzaghe L RSC 1 Watford
15.03.94	Mark Dawson L RSC 6 Stoke
02.06.94	Luan Morena L PTS 6 Tooting
05.10.94	Lee Archer L PTS 6 Wolverhampton
16.11.94	Lester Jacobs L PTS 6 Bloomsbury
05.12.94	Jason Brown W RSC 2 Cleethorpes
13.12.94	Mark Baker L RSC 4 Ilford
23.01.95	Naveed Mirza W RSC 3 Bethnal Green
07.03.95	Justin Clements L RSC 4 Edgbaston

Career: 24 contests, won 7, drew 3, lost 14.

Delroy Matthews

Bromley. *Born* Dulwich 28 May, 1967
Middleweight. Ht. 5'11¼"
Manager J. Ryan

25.09.89	John Corcoran L CO 5 Crystal Palace
15.10.90	Nick Cope W RSC 1 Lewisham
26.11.90	Darren Murphy W RSC 2 Lewisham
30.09.91	Winston Tomlinson W RSC 4 Kensington
14.12.91	David Radford W CO 1 Bexleyheath
24.01.95	Sven Hamer W PTS 6 Piccadilly
27.04.95	Colin Pitters W RSC 2 Bethnal Green

Career: 7 contests, won 6, lost 1.

(Nicholas) Miguel Matthews

Ystalfera. *Born* Glanamman, 22 December, 1965
S. Bantamweight. Ht. 5'7"
Manager Self

21.09.88	Terry Collins L PTS 6 Basildon
28.09.88	Eugene Maloney DREW 6 Edmonton
25.10.88	Hugh Ruse L PTS 6 Pontadawe
15.11.88	Tommy Bernard W RSC 2 Chigwell
14.12.88	Richie Wenton L CO 2 Kirkby
14.02.89	Brian Robb W RSC 2 Wolverhampton
06.03.89	Mickey Markie L PTS 8 Northampton
21.03.89	Ronnie Stephenson DREW 6 Wolverhampton
11.04.89	Hugh Ruse W PTS 6 Aberavon
05.06.89	Lester James DREW 6 Birmingham

Miguel Matthews (right), not far short of 100 fights, has Michael Alldis in some difficulty on the ropes before going down on points

Les Clark

12.06.89 Colin McMillan L RSC 3 Battersea
06.09.89 Marcel Herbert L PTS 6 Aberavon
20.09.89 Des Gargano L PTS 6 Stoke
28.09.89 Steve Walker L PTS 6 Cardiff
17.10.89 Alan Roberts W PTS 6 Cardiff
24.10.89 Jimmy Clark L PTS 6 Watford
06.11.89 Mickey Markie DREW 8 Northampton
03.12.89 Johnny Bredahl L PTS 6 Copenhagen, Denmark
19.02.90 Mickey Markie L PTS 8 Kettering
27.02.90 Pete Buckley DREW 6 Evesham
21.03.90 Rocky Lawlor L PTS 8 Solihull
03.09.90 Derek Amory L PTS 6 Dudley
01.10.90 Pete Buckley L PTS 8 Cleethorpes
09.10.90 Pete Buckley W PTS 6 Wolverhampton
29.10.90 Pete Buckley L PTS 8 Birmingham
21.11.90 Jason Primera L PTS 8 Solihull
12.12.90 Paul Harvey L PTS 6 Basildon
19.12.90 Paul Forrest L PTS 6 Preston
07.03.91 Bradley Stone L RSC 4 Basildon
04.04.91 Mark Tierney L PTS 6 Watford
16.04.91 Craig Dermody L PTS 6 Nottingham
25.04.91 Bradley Stone L PTS 6 Basildon
23.05.91 Jason Lepre L PTS 6 Southampton
31.05.91 Danny Connelly L PTS 8 Glasgow
13.06.91 Tony Silkstone L PTS 6 Hull
24.06.91 Jimmy Owens L PTS 6 Liverpool
09.09.91 Moussa Sangare L RSC 5 Forges les Eux, France
09.10.91 Mark Loftus DREW 6 Manchester
24.10.91 Kevin Middleton L PTS 6 Dunstable
31.10.91 Brian Robb DREW 6 Oakengates
11.11.91 Peter Judson L PTS 6 Stratford on Avon
21.11.91 Craig Dermody L PTS 6 Burton
28.11.91 Dave Hardie L PTS 6 Glasgow
11.12.91 Jimmy Clark L PTS 6 Basildon
08.01.92 Ceri Farrell W PTS 6 Burton
31.01.92 John Green DREW 6 Manchester
20.02.92 Edward Cook L PTS 6 Glasgow
27.02.92 Craig Dermody L PTS 6 Liverpool
25.03.92 John Armour L PTS 6 Dagenham
01.06.92 Danny Porter L PTS 6 Glasgow
07.07.92 Tony Falcone L PTS 6 Bristol
14.07.92 Prince Nassem Hamed L RSC 3 Mayfair
30.09.92 Jonjo Irwin L PTS 6 Solihull
17.10.92 Mark Bowers L PTS 6 Wembley
24.11.92 Kid McAuley L PTS 6 Doncaster
14.12.92 Barry Jones L PTS 6 Cardiff
30.01.93 Tim Yeates L PTS 6 Brentwood
27.02.93 Paul Lloyd L PTS 6 Ellesmere Port
18.03.93 Kevin Middleton L PTS 6 Lewisham
17.04.93 Fabian Zavattini L PTS 6 Lausanne, Switzerland
05.05.93 Conn McMullen DREW 6 Belfast
15.05.93 Dave McHale L RSC 4 Glasgow
10.07.93 Russell Rees L PTS 6 Cardiff
22.09.93 Marcus McCrae L PTS 6 Bethnal Green
06.10.93 Mark Geraghty L PTS 6 York
30.10.93 Gary Thornhill L PTS 6 Chester
22.11.93 Ian McGirr L PTS 6 Glasgow
29.11.93 Tim Yeates DREW 6 Ingatestone
18.12.93 John White L PTS 6 Manchester
14.01.94 Kevin Middleton L PTS 6 Bethnal Green
28.01.94 Frederic Perez L PTS 8 Sete, France
10.04.94 Mark Geraghty L PTS 8 Glasgow
25.04.94 Hugh Collins L PTS 8 Glasgow
22.05.94 Mike Anthony Brown W RSC 5 Crystal Palace
06.06.94 Russell Davison W PTS 6 Glasgow

21.07.94 Mike Anthony Brown L PTS 6 Battersea
20.09.94 Drew Docherty L PTS 8 Musselburgh
17.02.95 Michael Alldis L PTS 8 Crawley
06.03.95 Michael Armstrong L PTS 6 Mayfair
Career: 79 contests, won 8, drew 10, lost 61.

Paul Matthews

Llanelli. *Born* Gorseinon, 26 September, 1968
Middleweight. Ht. 5'8"
Manager G. Davies

23.03.94 Steve Thomas W PTS 6 Cardiff
02.06.94 Jason Hart W RSC 3 Tooting
21.09.94 Peter Mitchell L PTS 6 Cardiff
11.11.94 Mads Larsen L RTD 4 Randers, Denmark
08.03.95 Barry Thorogood L PTS 4 Cardiff
12.04.95 Carl Winstone L PTS 6 Llanelli
06.05.95 Danny Ryan L PTS 6 Shepton Mallet
Career: 7 contests, won 2, lost 5.

David Maw

Sunderland. *Born* Sunderland, 14 January, 1967
L. Middleweight. Ht. 5'9½"
Manager Self

22.05.87 Kevin Plant W PTS 6 Peterlee
04.06.87 Dean Bramhald W PTS 6 Sunderland
04.09.87 Dean Bramhald W PTS 6 Gateshead
22.09.87 John Reid DREW 4 Oldham
16.10.87 Kevin Spratt L PTS 8 Gateshead
03.11.87 Jeff Connors W PTS 6 Sunderland
08.06.88 Andy Holligan L RSC 1 Sheffield
26.09.89 Steve Foran L PTS 8 Chigwell
10.10.89 Delroy Waul L PTS 4 Sunderland
14.10.91 Dave Maj W PTS 6 Manchester
08.12.94 Phil Epton W PTS 6 Hull
21.02.95 Hughie Davey L RSC 3 Sunderland
25.03.95 Craig Winter L RSC 3 Rothwell
22.06.95 Hughie Davey L PTS 6 Houghton le Spring
Career: 14 contests, won 6, drew 1, lost 7.

Anthony Maynard

Birmingham. *Born* Birmingham, 12 January, 1972
Lightweight. Ht. 5'8"
Managers P. Cowdell/R. Gray

17.10.94 Malcolm Thomas W PTS 6 Birmingham
02.11.94 Dean Phillips W PTS 6 Birmingham
25.01.95 Neil Smith L PTS 6 Stoke
07.02.95 Anthony Campbell W PTS 8 Wolverhampton
08.03.95 Scott Walker W PTS 6 Solihull
28.03.95 Kid McAuley W PTS 8 Wolverhampton
11.05.95 Gary Hiscox W RSC 4 Dudley
06.06.95 Richard Swallow L RSC 2 Leicester
Career: 8 contests, won 6, lost 2.

Shane Meadows

Wingate. *Born* Durham, 25 May, 1967
Heavyweight. Ht. 5'10"
Manager G. Robinson

28.02.94 Declan Faherty L CO 3 Marton
12.10.94 Clayton Brown L CO 1 Sheffield
Career: 2 contests, lost 2.

Trevor Meikle

Scunthorpe. *Born* Scunthorpe, 29 January, 1967
L. Middleweight. Ht. 5'9"
Manager K. Tate

16.05.89 Lewis Welch DREW 6 Halifax
12.06.89 Chris Mulcahy L PTS 6 Manchester
19.06.89 Anthony Lawrence L PTS 6 Manchester
11.07.89 Chris Mulcahy L PTS 6 Batley
10.10.89 Steve Hardman DREW 6 Manchester
23.10.89 Mick Mulcahy W PTS 6 Cleethorpes
06.11.89 Ian Thomas W PTS 6 Northampton
14.11.89 Cliff Churchward W PTS 6 Evesham
22.11.89 Cliff Churchward W PTS 6 Stafford
11.12.89 Barry Messam L CO 5 Nottingham
05.02.90 Malcolm Melvin L PTS 6 Brierley Hill
19.02.90 Gordon Blair L PTS 6 Glasgow
27.02.90 Dave Whittle DREW 8 Marton
14.03.90 Carlos Chase L PTS 6 Battersea
27.03.90 Barry Messam W PTS 6 Leicester
30.04.90 Young Gully L PTS 6 Brierley Hill
21.05.90 Frank Harrington L RSC 5 Hanley
30.05.90 Mark Jay DREW 6 Stoke
15.06.90 Mark Jay W RSC 5 Telford
14.09.90 Mickey Lerwill DREW 8 Telford
03.10.90 Jim Lawlor L PTS 6 Solihull
09.10.90 Pat Durkin W DIS 3 Liverpool
24.10.90 Ernie Loveridge L PTS 6 Dudley
06.11.90 Stuart Good L PTS 6 Southend
21.11.90 Jim Lawlor L PTS 6 Solihull
29.11.90 Dave Whittle L PTS 6 Marton
10.12.90 Kevin Spratt L PTS 6 Bradford
11.02.91 Steve Hardman L PTS 6 Manchester
21.02.91 Colin Sinnott W PTS 6 Leeds
27.02.91 Andreas Panayi W PTS 6 Wolverhampton
03.04.91 Mick Mulcahy W PTS 6 Manchester
10.04.91 Wayne Timmins L PTS 6 Wolverhampton
22.04.91 Nick Cope W RSC 2 Glasgow
01.05.91 Tommy Milligan L PTS 6 Liverpool
09.05.91 Tod Riggs L PTS 6 Leeds
03.06.91 Tommy Milligan L PTS 6 Glasgow
10.06.91 Chris Mulcahy DREW 6 Manchester
14.08.91 Efren Calamati L RSC 4 Alcamo, Italy
23.09.91 Alan Peacock W PTS 6 Glasgow
01.10.91 James McGee W PTS 6 Bedworth
05.11.91 Lee Ferrie L PTS 6 Leicester
25.11.91 Mark Kelly W PTS 8 Cleethorpes
05.12.91 Mickey Lerwill L PTS 6 Oakengates
14.12.91 Kevin Lueshing L CO 3 Bexleyheath
28.01.92 Alan Peacock L PTS 8 Piccadilly
29.02.92 Andre Kimbu L RTD 5 Gravelines, France
13.04.92 Crain Fisher L PTS 6 Manchester
30.04.92 B. F. Williams L PTS 6 Watford
14.09.92 Kevin Spratt W RSC 4 Bradford
23.10.92 Andreas Panayi L PTS 6 Liverpool
26.11.92 Willie Yeardsley W PTS 6 Hull
03.02.93 Derek Grainger L RSC 6 Earls Court
13.12.93 Rick North L PTS 6 Cleethorpes
22.05.94 Maurice Forbes L RTD 3 Crystal Palace
23.09.94 Clay O'Shea L RSC 1 Bethnal Green
Career: 55 contests, won 17, drew 6, lost 32.

Malcolm Melvin

Birmingham. *Born* Birmingham, 5 February, 1967
All-Ireland & Midlands Area L. Welterweight Champion. Ht. 5'7"
Manager Self

29.11.85   Steve Foster DREW 6 Ilkeston
04.12.85   Simon Collins L PTS 6 Stoke
24.03.86   Rocky McGran L PTS 6 Mayfair
10.04.86   Lincoln Pennant W PTS 6 Leicester
21.04.86   Malcolm Davies W PTS 6 Birmingham
07.05.86   Julian Monville W PTS 6 Solihull
19.01.88   Antonio Fernandez L RSC 4 Kings Heath
07.03.88   John Ellis L PTS 6 Piccadilly
03.12.89   Dave Jenkins W PTS 6 Birmingham
05.02.90   Trevor Meikle W PTS 6 Brierley Hill
22.02.90   Chris Saunders L PTS 4 Hull
19.03.90   Barry North W PTS 6 Brierley Hill
30.04.90   Andy Kent W RSC 5 Brierley Hill
04.06.90   Brendan Ryan L RSC 7 Edgbaston
03.09.90   Dave Jenkins W PTS 8 Dudley
13.11.90   Brendan Ryan W PTS 10 Edgbaston
    (Vacant Midlands Area L. Welterweight Title)
18.03.91   Carl Brasier W PTS 6 Piccadilly
17.06.91   Dean Bramhald W PTS 6 Edgbaston
21.05.92   Mark Kelly W PTS 8 Cradley Heath
05.10.92   Ross Hale L PTS 10 Bristol
    (Elim. British L. Welterweight Title)
17.11.92   Tusikoleta Nkalankete DREW 8 Paris, France
16.03.93   Shaun Cogan W PTS 10 Edgbaston
    (Vacant All-Ireland L. Welterweight Title & Midlands Area L. Welterweight Title Defence)
29.06.93   Mark Kelly W PTS 6 Edgbaston
24.11.93   Alan Peacock W PTS 8 Solihull
08.03.94   Julian Eavis W PTS 6 Edgbaston
28.06.94   John Smith W PTS 6 Edgbaston
18.02.95   Ross Hale L PTS 12 Shepton Mallet
    (British & Commonwealth Welterweight Title Challenge)
Career: 27 contests, won 17, drew 2, lost 8.

Ian Midwood-Tate

Huddersfield. *Born* Huddersfield, 9 December, 1968
L. Middleweight. Ht. 5.7½"
Manager Self

11.01.87   G. L. Booth L PTS 6 Manchester
13.06.88   Spencer Alton L PTS 6 Manchester
31.08.88   Spencer Alton W PTS 6 Stoke
12.09.88   Dave Andrews W RTD 4 Northampton
10.10.88   G. L. Booth W RTD 3 Manchester
21.11.88   Chris Mulcahy W CO 1 Leicester
16.05.89   John Corcoran L PTS 6 Halifax
13.11.89   Paul Jones L RSC 4 Manchester
11.11.91   Tyrone Eastmond L RSC 2 Bradford
26.08.94   Japhet Hans W RSC 5 Barnsley
Career: 10 contests, won 5, lost 5.

(John) Dusty Miller

Stepney. *Born* Islington, 25 February, 1962
L. Middleweight. Ht. 5'4½"
Manager B. Lynch

16.02.87   Jim Beckett L PTS 6 Mayfair
09.03.87   Barry Messam W CO 3 Mayfair
23.03.87   Roy Horn W PTS 6 Mayfair
09.04.87   Paul Deans L PTS 6 Bethnal Green
07.05.87   Lindon Scarlett L PTS 6 Bayswater
07.09.87   Paul Murray W RTD 4 Mayfair
08.10.87   Johnny Nanton W RSC 4 Bethnal Green
26.10.87   Kevin Thompson L PTS 4 Piccadilly
14.04.88   Manny Romain W CO 2 Piccadilly

05.05.88   Paul Seddon L CO 7 Bayswater
07.03.90   Chris Haydon L PTS 6 Croydon
03.05.90   Winston May L PTS 6 Kensington
19.04.95   Danny Stevens W RSC 3 Bethnal Green
27.04.95   Paolo Roberto W RSC 2 Bethnal Green
Career: 14 contests, won 7, lost 7.

(Alvin) Slick Miller

Doncaster. *Born* Doncaster, 12 May, 1968
Cruiserweight. Ht. 6'2"
Manager T. Petersen

28.04.94   Declan Faherty L RSC 2 Hull
06.10.94   Kent Davis L PTS 6 Hull
17.11.94   Graham Wassell L RSC 1 Sheffield
Career: 3 contests, lost 3.

(Alkis) A. M. Milton (Alkiviadov)

Streatham. *Born* London, 5 May, 1965
L. Welterweight. Ht. 5'3¾"
Manager Self

24.10.84   Kenny Watson L PTS 6 Mayfair
24.01.85   John Wilder W RTD 3 Streatham
04.02.85   John Faulkner L PTS 6 Lewisham
30.04.85   Kenny Watson W PTS 6 Merton
28.11.85   Brian Sonny Nickels L CO 4 Bethnal Green
04.09.86   Kevin Spratt DREW 6 Merton
19.11.87   Lee West L PTS 6 Wandsworth
10.05.88   Peter Hart L RSC 1 Tottenham
06.12.88   Shane Tonks W PTS 6 Southend
03.04.90   Dave Jenkins L PTS 6 Southend
25.09.90   Ray Newby W PTS 6 Millwall
12.11.90   Darren Morris W PTS 6 Norwich
08.05.91   Steve McGovern L PTS 6 Millwall
08.01.92   Darren Morris L PTS 6 Burton
31.10.92   Rick Bushell DREW 4 Earls Court
10.12.92   Brian Coleman DREW 4 Bethnal Green
17.02.93   Rick Bushell W RSC 1 Bethnal Green
31.03.93   Brian Coleman W PTS 4 Bethnal Green
23.06.93   Felix Kelly L CO 8 Edmonton
    (Vacant Southern Area Lightweight Title)
01.12.93   Brian Coleman W PTS 4 Bethnal Green
30.07.94   Tony Gibbs W CO 1 Bethnal Green
25.10.94   Kevin McKenzie L PTS 4 Middlesbrough
Career: 22 contests, won 9, drew 3, lost 10.

Naveed Mirza

Ilford. *Born* Pakistan, 29 July, 1971
S. Middleweight. Ht.5'11½"
Manager F. Maloney

23.01.95   Stinger Mason L RSC 3 Bethnal Green
Career: 1 contest, lost 1.

Clifton Mitchell

Sheffield. *Born* Derby, 29 October, 1965
Heavyweight. Ht. 6'2½"
Manager F. Warren

06.04.91   John Harewood W RSC 2 Darlington
01.08.91   John Harewood W CO 1 Dewsbury
03.10.91   Tucker Richards W PTS 6 Burton
21.11.91   Tucker Richards W RSC 6 Burton

Naveed Mirza   Les Clark

14.04.91   Michael Murray W RSC 8 Mansfield
16.03.93   Vivian Schwalger W CO 1 Wolverhampton
26.05.93   John Harewood W RSC 4 Mansfield
18.12.93   Jim Huffman W CO 3 Manchester
29.01.94   Cordwell Hylton W RSC 1 Cardiff
26.02.94   Jean Chanet W RSC 2 Earls Court
11.05.94   Emanuel Brites Camargo W RSC 1 Sheffield
21.05.94   Steve Garber W CO 1 Belfast
17.08.94   Carl Gaffney W CO 1 Sheffield
10.09.94   Jeff Williams W CO 1 Birmingham
19.11.94   James Oyebola L CO 4 Cardiff
    (WBC International Heavyweight Title Challenge & Vacant British Heavyweight Title)
Career: 15 contests, won 14, lost 1.

Peter Mitchell   Les Clark

Peter Mitchell

Southampton. *Born* Southampton, 26 May, 1967
Middleweight. Ht. 5'10½"
Manager J. Bishop

21.09.94	Paul Matthews W PTS 6 Cardiff	
12.10.94	Andy Ewen L PTS 6 Sheffield	
08.03.95	Paul Webb W RSC 1 Bloomsbury	
19.04.95	Nicky Thurbin L PTS 6 Bethnal Green	
02.06.95	Danny Ryan L PTS 6 Bethnal Green	

Career: 5 contests, won 2, lost 3.

Tony Mock

Liverpool. *Born* Liverpool, 3 May, 1969
Welterweight. Ht. 5'8"
Manager S. Vaughan

30.10.93	Tony Britland W PTS 6 Chester
11.12.93	Mark Antony W RSC 4 Liverpool
25.02.94	Mike Morrison W PTS 6 Chester
06.05.94	Scott Doyle W PTS 6 Liverpool
31.10.94	Charlie Paine W PTS 6 Liverpool
25.03.95	Floyd Churchill W PTS 6 Chester
30.06.95	Kevin McKenzie W PTS 6 Liverpool

Career: 7 contests, won 7.

James Montgomerie

Saltcoats. *Born* Irvine, 13 May, 1972
L. Welterweight. Ht. 5'7"
Manager A. Morrison/A. Melrose

02.03.95	Scott Marshall W PTS 6 Glasgow
21.04.95	Chris Aston W PTS 6 Glasgow

Career: 2 contests, won 2.

Karl Morling

Northampton. *Born* Douglas, IOM, 26
December, 1970
S. Bantamweight. Ht. 5'4"
Manager Self

15.10.90	Lee Christian W RSC 2 Kettering
22.10.90	Tony Falcone W PTS 6 Mayfair
31.01.91	Craig Dermody L RSC 3 Bredbury
02.05.91	Sol Francis W RSC 3 Northampton
13.05.91	Paul Wynn W RSC 2 Northampton
06.04.92	Norman Dhalie W PTS 6 Northampton
05.10.92	Robert Braddock W PTS 6 Northampton
14.12.92	Dean Lynch L RSC 4 Northampton
19.04.93	Graham McGrath W RSC 6 Northampton
01.12.93	John Armour L CO 3 Kensington
02.09.94	Matthew Harris L CO 5 Spitalfields
	(Vacant Midlands Area
	S. Bantamweight Title)

Career: 11 contests, won 7, lost 4.

Jason Morris

Birmingham. *Born* Birmingham, 28 May, 1972
Bantamweight. Ht. 5'2"
Manager Self

08.09.92	Jacob Smith L PTS 6 Manchester
22.02.93	Stevie Woods W CO 4 Glasgow
17.03.93	Gary Marston L PTS 6 Stoke
17.02.94	Marcus Duncan L RSC 6 Bury
28.03.94	Graham McGrath L PTS 6 Birmingham
12.12.94	Andy Roberts L PTS 6 Doncaster
05.05.95	Andy Roberts L PTS 6 Doncaster

Career: 7 contests, won 1, lost 6.

Jerry Mortimer

Islington. *Born* Mauritius, 22 June, 1962
S. Middleweight. Ht. 5'9"
Manager B. Aird

21.10.91	Steve Thomas L PTS 6 Mayfair
12.02.92	Darren Murphy W PTS 6 Watford
02.03.92	Lee Farrell W PTS 6 Merthyr
28.04.92	Stefan Wright L RSC 4 Corby
08.09.92	Robert Whitehouse W RSC 3 Southend
15.10.92	Russell Washer W RSC 5 Lewisham
14.12.92	Gareth Boddy W PTS 6 Cardiff
28.01.93	John Bosco L RSC 4 Southwark
09.03.93	Paul Smith W PTS 6 Bristol
01.12.93	Gilbert Jackson L RSC 3 Kensington
20.01.94	Dean Cooper L PTS 8 Battersea
24.02.94	Mark Smallwood L RSC 4 Walsall
10.03.94	Dale Nixon DREW 4 Bristol
26.04.94	Mark Baker L PTS 6 Bethnal Green
27.05.94	Val Golding L PTS 6 Ashford
30.09.94	Mark Delaney L RSC 3 Bethnal Green
31.03.95	Andy Wright L RSC 1 Crystal Palace

Career: 17 contests, won 6, drew 1, lost 10.

Johnny Moth (Buck)

Nottingham. *Born* Nottingham, 10 October, 1967
Cruiserweight. Ht. 5'9"
Manager M. Shinfield

08.06.93	Chris Harbourne DREW 6 Derby
25.01.95	Cliff Elden W PTS 6 Stoke

Career: 2 contests, won 1, drew 1.

Mick Mulcahy

Manchester. *Born* Rochdale, 9 May, 1966
L. Welterweight. Ht. 5'8"
Manager N. Basso

06.06.88	Nick Langley W RSC 5 Manchester
05.09.88	Johnny Walker W PTS 4 Glasgow
22.09.88	Frankie Foster L PTS 6 Newcastle
02.10.88	Niel Leggett DREW 6 Peterborough
25.10.88	Wayne Windle W PTS 6 Cottingham
03.11.88	Peter English L RSC 4 Manchester
12.12.88	Steve Taggart L PTS 6 Birmingham
25.01.89	Mark Tibbs L CO 1 Bethnal Green
23.02.89	Sean Conn W CO 1 Stockport
13.03.89	Dean Dickinson W PTS 6 Liecester
17.04.89	Neil Leitch W RSC 2 Middleton
19.05.89	Mark Jay L PTS 6 Gateshead
29.05.89	George Kerr L PTS 6 Dundee
12.06.89	Muhammad Shaffique L RSC 2 Manchester
11.09.89	Dave Croft W PTS 4 Manchester
19.09.89	Billy Couzens L PTS 6 Bethnal Green
03.10.89	Kevin Toomey W CO 5 Cottingham
13.10.89	Carl Wright L PTS 6 Preston
23.10.89	Trevor Meikle L PTS 6 Cleethorpes
31.10.89	Carl Wright L PTS 6 Manchester
10.11.89	Chris McReedy L PTS 6 Liverpool
20.11.89	Brendan Ryan L PTS 6 Leicester
04.12.89	Brian Cullen L PTS 8 Manchester
19.12.89	Errol McDonald L RSC 3 Bethnal Green
24.04.90	Brian Cullen L PTS 8 Stoke
22.10.90	Wayne Windle L PTS 4 Cleethorpes
12.11.90	Richard Joyce L RSC 6 Stratford upon Avon
12.12.90	Neil Porter DREW 6 Stoke
24.01.91	Robert McCracken L RSC 1 Brierley Hill
05.03.91	Darren Morris L PTS 6 Leicester

03.04.91	Trevor Meikle L PTS 6 Manchester
15.04.91	Andreas Panayi L RSC 2 Leicester
10.06.91	Mike Calderwood L PTS 6 Manchester
18.11.91	Benji Joseph L PTS 6 Manchester
28.11.91	B. K. Bennett L PTS 6 Evesham
05.12.91	Mark Elliot L RSC 2 Cannock
17.03.92	Bernard Paul L PTS 6 Mayfair
04.04.92	Michael Byrne W RSC 4 Cleethorpes
01.06.92	Jason Brattley L PTS 6 Manchester
11.09.92	Rocky Ferrari L PTS 6 Glasgow
25.09.92	Carl Wright L PTS 8 Liverpool
10.12.92	Charlie Kane L RSC 2 Glasgow
02.02.93	Shane Sheridan L PTS 6 Derby
19.03.93	Steve Walker L RSC 6 Manchester
01.06.93	Wayne Windle W PTS 6 Manchester
09.09.93	Martin Campbell L PTS 6 Glasgow
07.11.93	Charlie Kane L RSC 2 Glasgow
16.06.95	Paul Burns L RSC 3 Liverpool

Career: 48 contests, won 10, drew 2, lost 36.

Patrick Mullings

Harrow. *Born* Harlesden, 19 October, 1970
Bantamweight. Ht. 5'4½"
Manager F. Maloney

13.12.94	Graham McGrath W PTS 4 Ilford
23.01.95	Des Gargano W PTS 4 Bethnal Green
30.03.95	Graham McGrath W RSC 3 Bethnal Green
04.06.95	Des Gargano W PTS 6 Bethnal Green

Career: 4 contests, won 4.

Richard Munro (Smith)

Leeds. *Born* Sheffield, 27 December, 1967
S. Middleweight. Ht. 5'11"
Manager P. Coleman

11.03.95	David Radford L RSC 5 Barnsley

Career: 1 contest, lost 1.

Justin Murphy

Hove. *Born* Brighton, 21 February, 1974
Featherweight. Ht. 5'7"
Manager F. Maloney

15.09.93	Andrew Bloomer W PTS 4 Bethnal Green
13.10.93	Thomas Bernard W RSC 1 Bethnal Green
01.12.93	Mark Hargreaves W PTS 4 Bethnal Green
25.01.94	Jobie Tyers W RSC 3 Piccadilly
29.03.94	Tony Falcone W RSC 2 Bethnal Green
15.06.94	Mike Deveney W PTS 6 Southwark
23.11.94	Pete Buckley W PTS 4 Piccadilly
25.05.95	Barry Jones L PTS 10 Reading
	(Elim. British Featherweight Title)
16.06.95	Paul Webster L PTS 6 Southwark

Career: 9 contests, won 7, lost 2.

James Murray

Glasgow. *Born* Lanark, 7 December, 1969
Scottish Bantamweight Champion. Ht. 5'4"
Managers F. Warren/A. Morrison

26.03.93	L. C. Wilson W RSC 4 Glasgow
30.04.93	Dave Campbell W PTS 6 Glasgow
29.05.93	Kid McAuley W PTS 6 Paisley
09.09.93	Des Gargano W PTS 6 Glasgow
21.10.93	Graham McGrath W PTS 6 Glasgow
10.11.93	Paul Webster L PTS 4 Bethnal Green
10.02.94	Marty Chestnut W PTS 6 Glasgow

11.03.94	Paul Wynn W PTS 6 Glasgow
13.04.94	Pete Buckley W PTS 6 Glasgow
10.06.94	Graham McGrath W PTS 8 Glasgow
21.07.94	Dave Campbell W RSC 3 Edinburgh
21.10.94	Keith Jones W CO 3 Glasgow
18.11.94	Shaun Anderson W PTS 10 Glasgow
	(Vacant Scottish Bantamweight Title)
21.01.95	Louis Veitch W RSC 3 Glasgow
	(Scottish Bantamweight Title Defence)
21.04.95	Ady Benton W RSC 7 Glasgow
13.05.95	Danny Ruegg W PTS 6 Glasgow

Career: 16 contests, won 15, lost 1.

Michael Murray

Manchester. *Born* Preston, 3 September, 1964
Former Undefeated Central Area Heavyweight Champion. Ht. 6'1"
Manager J. Trickett

23.02.88	Gypsy John Fury L PTS 6 Oldham
28.04.88	Ian Nelson W RSC 6 Manchester
17.11.88	Steve Garber W PTS 6 Stockport
07.02.89	Rocky Burton W PTS 6 Manchester
10.05.89	Barry Ellis W RSC 3 Solihull
08.09.89	Noel Quarless L PTS 8 Liverpool
17.10.89	John Westgarth W RTD 4 Oldham
06.02.90	Al Malcolm W RSC 5 Oldham
02.06.90	Gypsy John Fury L RTD 6 Manchester
30.04.91	Steve Garber W CO 1 Stockport
19.09.91	Carl Gaffney W RSC 8 Stockport
	(Vacant Central Area Heavyweight Title)
15.10.91	Markus Bott W RSC 7 Hamburg, Germany
07.12.91	Steve Gee W RSC 7 Manchester
14.04.92	Clifton Mitchell L RSC 8 Mansfield
28.11.92	Ricky Sekorski W PTS 8 Manchester
27.02.93	Herbie Hide L RSC 5 Dagenham
	(Vacant British Heavyweight Title)
30.09.94	Terry Dunstan L PTS 8 Bethnal Green
10.12.94	Scott Welch L PTS 8 Manchester
23.02.95	Derek Williams W PTS 8 Southwark
17.05.95	John Ruiz L RSC 4 Ipswich

Career: 20 contests, won 12, lost 8.

Michael Murray Harry Goodwin

Paul Murray

Birmingham. *Born* Birmingham, 8 January, 1961
S. Middleweight. Ht. 5'9"
Manager P. Byrne

04.09.80	Gerry White W PTS 6 Morecambe
11.09.80	Graeme Ahmed L PTS 6 Hartlepool
29.09.80	Richard Wilson L PTS 6 Bedworth
08.10.80	Carl North W CO 2 Stoke
14.10.80	Steve McLeod W PTS 6 Wolverhampton
20.10.80	Steve Davies DREW 6 Birmingham
30.10.80	John Wiggins W PTS 6 Wolverhampton
07.11.80	Archie Salman L PTS 6 Cambuslang
18.11.80	John Wiggins L PTS 6 Shrewsbury
26.11.80	Mike Clemow L PTS 8 Stoke
08.12.80	John Wiggins L PTS 6 Nottingham
26.01.81	Errol Dennis W PTS 6 Edgbaston
16.03.81	Dennis Sheehan DREW 6 Nottingham
15.04.81	Nigel Thomas DREW 6 Evesham
28.05.81	Martin McGough L PTS 6 Edgbaston
09.07.81	Roger Guest L CO 8 Dudley
21.09.81	Gary Buckle DREW 6 Wolverhampton
07.10.81	Kostas Petrou W RSC 5 Solihull
13.10.81	Gary Buckle L PTS 6 Wolverhampton
24.11.81	Nick Riozzi W PTS 6 Wolverhampton
25.01.82	Martin McGough L RSC 4 Wolverhampton
22.02.82	Gary Buckle W PTS 8 Nottingham
10.03.82	Ron Pearce L PTS 8 Solihull
23.03.82	Errol Dennis L PTS 6 Wolverhampton
29.03.82	Tony Brown L PTS 6 Liverpool
07.04.82	Dennis Sheehan W PTS 6 Evesham
28.04.82	Lee Roy W CO 3 Burslem
17.05.82	Paul Costigan L PTS 8 Manchester
24.05.82	Dennis Sheehan DREW 6 Nottingham
07.06.82	Kostas Petrou L PTS 6 Edgbaston
13.09.82	Paul Costigan W PTS 6 Manchester
18.10.82	Kostas Petrou L RSC 5 Edgbaston
15.02.83	Bert Myrie L PTS 6 Wolverhampton
21.02.83	Steve Tempro L DIS 3 Edgbaston
01.03.83	Chris Pyatt L RTD 2 Kensington
17.05.83	T. P. Jenkins L PTS 6 Bethnal Green
23.06.83	Wayne Hawkins L PTS 6 Wolverhampton
19.09.83	Bert Myrie W PTS 8 Nottingham
26.10.83	Steve Henty L PTS 6 Stoke
14.11.83	Kid Sadler L PTS 8 Manchester
14.12.83	John Andrews L PTS 6 Stoke
19.03.84	Wayne Barker L PTS 8 Manchester
27.03.84	Rocky Kelly L RTD 5 Battersea
08.10.84	Gavin Stirrup L PTS 6 Manchester
26.01.87	Chris Walker L PTS 4 Bethnal Green
10.02.87	Chris Walker W PTS 4 Wolverhampton
16.02.87	Chris Galloway W PTS 6 Mayfair
24.02.87	Nicky Thorne L PTS 6 Wandsworth
03.08.87	Peter Elliott L PTS 6 Stoke
07.09.87	Dusty Miller L RTD 4 Mayfair
25.01.88	Paul Wesley L PTS 8 Birmingham
29.02.88	Paul Wesley DREW 8 Birmingham
14.03.88	Mickey Hughes L RSC 4 Mayfair
19.10.88	Geoff Calder NC 5 Evesham
26.10.88	Franki Moro L PTS 6 Stoke
05.12.88	Richard Carter L PTS 6 Dudley
24.01.89	Antonio Fernandez L PTS 6 Kings Heath
24.10.89	Andrew Flute L RSC 4 Wolverhampton
21.06.90	Spencer Alton L PTS 6 Alfreton
13.09.90	Nigel Rafferty L PTS 6 Watford
27.09.90	Nigel Rafferty DREW 6 Birmingham

09.10.90	Nigel Rafferty L PTS 6 Wolverhampton
18.10.90	Nick Manners L PTS 6 Dewsbury
29.10.90	Carlos Christie L PTS 6 Birmingham
16.12.90	Wayne Hawkins L PTS 6 Wolverhampton
28.01.91	Lee Prudden L PTS 6 Birmingham
06.02.91	Paul Walters DREW 6 Liverpool
27.02.91	Paul Busby L PTS 6 Wolverhampton
13.03.91	Lee Prudden DREW 6 Stoke
24.04.91	John Kaighin L PTS 6 Aberavon
14.05.91	Ernie Loveridge L PTS 8 Dudley
30.05.91	Robert McCracken L RSC 2 Birmingham
25.07.91	Tony Booth L PTS 6 Dudley
07.10.91	Antonio Fernandez L RSC 7 Birmingham
12.11.91	Lee Archer L PTS 6 Wolverhampton
05.12.91	Richard Carter L PTS 8 Cannock
17.12.91	Paul Busby L CO 3 Cardiff
15.01.92	Mark Hale L PTS 6 Stoke
06.02.92	John McKenzie L PTS 6 Peterborough
19.02.92	James F. Woolley W CO 4 Muswell Hill
26.03.92	Neville Brown L CO 3 Telford
05.10.92	Lee Archer L PTS 6 Bardon
13.10.92	Lee Archer L PTS 6 Wolverhampton
21.10.92	Steve Loftus L PTS 6 Stoke
23.11.92	John J. Cooke L CO 1 Coventry
17.06.93	Carl Smallwood L PTS 6 Bedworth
18.09.93	Zak Chelli W RSC 2 Leicester
02.12.93	Justin Clements W PTS 6 Walsall
19.03.94	Mark Delaney L CO 3 Millwall
17.06.94	Peter Vosper L PTS 8 Plymouth
02.07.94	Darren Dorrington L RSC 3 Keynsham
24.09.94	David Starie L RSC 2 Wembley
16.11.94	Steve Loftus W PTS 6 Bloomsbury
29.11.94	Mark Smallwood L PTS 8 Wolverhampton
07.12.94	Steve Loftus W PTS 6 Stoke
15.12.94	Neil Simpson L PTS 6 Walsall
17.01.95	Andy McVeigh L PTS 6 Worcester
23.02.95	Lester Jacobs L RSC 2 Southwark
30.03.95	Dean Francis L RSC 2 Bethnal Green
11.05.95	Andrew Flute L PTS 6 Dudley
16.06.95	Dean Francis L RTD 3 Southwark

Career: 101 contests, won 19, drew 9, lost 72, no contest 1.

Lee Murtagh

Leeds. *Born* Leeds, 30 September, 1973
L. Middleweight. Ht. 5'9¼"
Manager J. Celebanski

12.06.95	Dave Curtis W PTS 6 Bradford

Career: 1 contest, won 1.

George Naylor

Liverpool. *Born* Liverpool, 4 September, 1968
Lightweight. Ht. 5'7"
Manager S. Vaughan

25.09.92	Charles Shepherd L RSC 4 Liverpool
30.10.92	Dean Martin W PTS 6 Birmingham
20.11.92	Emlyn Rees W PTS 8 Liverpool
15.12.92	Renny Edwards L RSC 5 Liverpool
02.07.93	Bruce Ruegg W PTS 6 Liverpool
30.10.93	Paul Wynn W RSC 3 Chester
25.02.94	Steve Edwards W RTD 3 Chester
31.10.94	Jimmy Phelan W PTS 6 Liverpool
16.06.95	Norman Dhalie W PTS 6 Liverpool

Career: 9 contests, won 7, lost 2.

125

(Jimmy) Shea Neary

Liverpool. *Born* Liverpool, 18 May, 1968
L. Welterweight. Ht. 5'7½"
Managers B. Devine/J. Hyland

03.09.92	Simon Ford W RSC 1 Liverpool
05.10.92	Shaun Armstrong W RSC 6 Liverpool
02.11.92	Jason Barker W RSC 3 Liverpool
01.12.92	Chris Saunders W PTS 6 Liverpool
22.02.93	Vaughan Carnegie W RSC 1 Liverpool
29.03.93	John Smith W PTS 6 Liverpool
06.09.93	Wayne Shepherd W RTD 2 Liverpool
25.10.93	Mark Antony W RSC 1 Liverpool
13.06.94	Mark Pearce W RSC 4 Liverpool
07.12.94	Tony Foster W RSC 2 Stoke
25.01.95	John Smith W RSC 5 Stoke
15.03.95	Tony Swift W RSC 3 Stoke
16.06.95	Hugh Forde W RTD 6 Liverpool

Career: 13 contests, won 13.

Johnny Nelson

Sheffield. *Born* Sheffield, 4 January, 1967
WBF Heavyweight Champion. Former
WBF Cruiserweight Champion. Former
Undefeated British, European & Central
Area Cruiserweight Champion. Ht. 6'2"
Manager G. Steene

18.03.86	Peter Brown L PTS 6 Hull
15.05.86	Tommy Taylor L PTS 6 Dudley
03.10.86	Magne Havnaa L PTS 4 Copenhagen, Denmark
20.11.86	Chris Little W PTS 6 Bredbury
19.01.87	Gypsy Carman W PTS 6 Mayfair
02.03.87	Doug Young W PTS 6 Huddersfield
10.03.87	Sean Daly W RSC 1 Manchester
28.04.87	Brian Schumacher L PTS 8 Halifax
03.06.87	Byron Pullen W RSC 3 Southwark
14.12.87	Jon McBean W RSC 6 Edgbaston
01.02.88	Dennis Bailey L PTS 8 Northampton
24.02.88	Cordwell Hylton W RSC 1 Sheffield
25.04.88	Kenny Jones W CO 1 Liverpool
04.05.88	Crawford Ashley W PTS 8 Solihull
06.06.88	Lennie Howard W CO 2 Mayfair
31.08.88	Andrew Gerrard W PTS 8 Stoke
26.10.88	Danny Lawford W RSC 2 Sheffield *(Vacant Central Area Cruiserweight Title)*
04.04.89	Steve Mormino W RSC 2 Sheffield
21.05.89	Andy Straughn W CO 8 Finsbury Park *(British Cruiserweight Title Challenge)*
02.10.89	Ian Bulloch W CO 2 Hanley *(British Cruiserweight Title Defence)*
27.01.90	Carlos de Leon DREW 12 Sheffield *(WBC Cruiserweight Title Challenge)*
14.02.90	Dino Homsey W RSC 7 Brentwood
28.03.90	Lou Gent W CO 4 Bethnal Green *(British Cruiserweight Title Defence)*
27.06.90	Arthur Weathers W RSC 2 Kensington
05.09.90	Andre Smith W PTS 8 Brighton
14.12.90	Markus Bott W RSC 12 Karlsruhe, Germany *(Vacant European Cruiserweight Title)*
12.03.91	Yves Monsieur W RTD 8 Mansfield *(European Cruiserweight Title Defence)*
16.05.92	James Warring L PTS 12 Fredericksburg, USA *(IBF Cruiserweight Title Challenge)*
15.08.92	Norbert Ekassi L RSC 3 Ajaccio, France
29.10.92	Corrie Sanders L PTS 10 Morula, South Africa

30.04.93	Dave Russell W RSC 11 Melbourne, Australia *(WBF Cruiserweight Title Challenge)*
11.08.93	Tom Collins W RSC 1 Mansfield *(WBF Cruiserweight Title Defence)*
01.10.93	Francis Wanyama L DIS 10 Waregem, Belgium *(WBF Cruiserweight Title Defence)*
20.11.93	Jimmy Thunder W PTS 12 Auckland, New Zealand *(WBF Heavyweight Title Challenge)*
05.04.94	Henry Akinwande L PTS 10 Bethnal Green
05.11.94	Nikolai Kulpin W PTS 12 Bangkok, Thailand *(WBF Heavyweight Title Defence)*

Career: 36 contests, won 25, drew 1, lost 10.

Kenny Nevers

Hackney. *Born* Hackney, 10 August, 1967
L. Heavyweight. Ht. 5'11"
Manager B. Lynch

10.12.92	Hussain Shah L PTS 4 Bethnal Green
22.02.93	Jason McNeill W RSC 1 Eltham
04.04.93	Hussain Shah W RSC 4 Brockley
28.07.93	Paul McCarthy L PTS 4 Brixton
04.10.94	Neil Simpson L PTS 4 Mayfair
27.04.95	Luan Moreno L PTS 4 Bethnal Green
30.06.95	Chris Woollas W RSC 2 Doncaster

Career: 7 contests, won 3, lost 4.

Dale Nixon

Taunton. *Born* Exeter, 11 May, 1970
S. Middleweight. Ht. 6'2"
Manager C. Sanigar

09.03.93	Ian Vokes W RSC 2 Bristol
27.05.93	Chris Nurse W RSC 2 Bristol
26.06.93	Tim Robinson W RSC 2 Keynsham
03.11.93	Jason McNeill W RSC 1 Bristol
10.03.94	Jerry Mortimer DREW 4 Bristol
31.03.94	Steve Thomas DREW 4 Bristol
25.06.94	Robert Peel W PTS 6 Cullompton
07.10.94	Robert Peel W RSC 7 Taunton
06.05.95	Darren Ashton L RSC 4 Shepton Mallet

Career: 9 contests, won 6, drew 2, lost 1.

Darren Noble

South Shields. *Born* Newcastle, 2 October, 1969
Flyweight. Ht. 5'3"
Manager T. Callighan

21.10.93	Allan Mooney W PTS 6 Glasgow
23.03.94	Paul Ingle L RSC 3 Cardiff
26.04.95	Tiger Singh L PTS 6 Solihull

Career: 3 contests, won 1, lost 2.

Eric Noi

Manchester. *Born* Manchester, 12 May, 1967
S. Middleweight. Ht. 5'11"
Manager F. Warren

05.02.93	Tim Robinson W RSC 4 Manchester
19.03.93	Smokey Enison W RSC 5 Manchester
26.04.93	Karl Barwise W PTS 6 Manchester
28.05.93	Karl Barwise W RSC 4 Middleton
25.07.93	Horace Fleary W PTS 6 Oldham
18.12.93	Graham Jenner W CO 1 Manchester
02.06.94	Shamus Casey W PTS 6 Middleton

10.09.94	Tim Robinson W RSC 1 Birmingham
12.10.94	Val Golding L PTS 6 Sheffield

Career: 9 contests, won 8, lost 1.

Eric Noi   Harry Goodwin

Shaun Norman

Shepshed. *Born* Leicester, 1 April, 1970
Flyweight. Ht. 5'3"
Manager Self

11.11.91	Louis Veitch W RSC 5 Bradford
27.11.91	Dave Campbell L PTS 6 Marton
14.12.91	Mickey Cantwell L PTS 8 Bexley Heath
20.02.92	Dave Hardie L PTS 6 Glasgow
10.04.92	Neil Armstrong DREW 8 Glasgow
25.04.92	Prince Nassem Hamed L RSC 2 Manchester
16.06.92	Francis Ampofo L RSC 4 Dagenham
19.10.92	Alan Ley L PTS 6 Mayfair
23.11.92	Paul Weir L PTS 8 Glasgow
04.03.93	Neil Armstrong L RSC 8 Glasgow
21.10.93	Neil Armstrong L RSC 7 Glasgow
18.02.94	Vince Feeney L RSC 2 Leicester
24.05.94	Ian Baillie W RSC 2 Leicester
05.09.94	Ricky Beard W PTS 8 Brentwood
24.09.94	Mark Reynolds L PTS 4 Wembley
01.10.94	Robbie Regan L RSC 2 Cardiff
30.11.94	Anthony Hanna L PTS 10 Solihull *(Vacant Midlands Area Flyweight Title)*
04.03.95	Shaun Anderson L PTS 6 Livingston
15.03.95	Chris Thomas W RSC 2 Stoke
06.04.95	Adam Tate W RSC 6 Sheffield
26.04.95	Neil Parry DREW 6 Stoke
19.05.95	Mark Hughes L PTS 6 Southwark

Career: 22 contests, won 5, drew 2, lost 15.

Rick North

Grimsby. *Born* Grimsby, 2 February, 1968
Welterweight. Ht. 5'8½"
Manager B. Ingle

28.05.91	Michael Smyth L RSC 1 Cardiff
16.09.91	Eddie King W RSC 5 Cleethorpes
21.01.91	Steve Bricknell W PTS 6 Cleethorpes
11.11.91	Darren McInulty L PTS 6 Stratford upon Avon

09.12.91	Michael Byrne W RSC 2 Cleethorpes
23.01.92	Ron Hopley L PTS 6 York
19.02.92	Bernard Paul L PTS 6 Muswell Hill
11.03.92	Patrick Loughran L PTS 6 Stoke
22.04.92	Steve McNess L PTS 6 Wembley
03.06.92	Mark Dawson L PTS 6 Newcastle under Lyme
03.09.92	Andreas Panayi DREW 6 Liverpool
21.09.92	Hughie Davey DREW 6 Cleethorpes
05.10.92	Andrew Jervis L PTS 6 Liverpool
21.10.92	Jim Lawlor W PTS 6 Stoke
29.10.92	David Larkin L PTS 6 Leeds
20.11.92	Andreas Panayi L PTS 6 Liverpool
14.12.92	Lee Soar W PTS 6 Cleethorpes
27.01.93	Mark Dawson L PTS 8 Stoke
22.02.93	Spencer McCracken L PTS 8 Birmingham
09.03.93	Sean Baker L PTS 8 Bristol
14.04.93	Adrian Dodson L RTD 1 Kensington
27.05.93	Glenn Catley L PTS 4 Brisol
20.09.93	Dean Bramhald W PTS 6 Cleethorpes
30.09.93	Gary Osborne L PTS 6 Walsall
19.10.93	Chris Mulcahy DREW 6 Cleethorpes
27.10.93	Chris Mulcahy W PTS 6 Stoke
13.12.93	Trevor Meikle W PTS 6 Cleethorpes
26.01.94	Lindon Scarlett L RSC 6 Birmingham *(Vacant Midlands Area Welterweight Title)*
08.03.94	Kevin Mabbutt L PTS 6 Kettering
17.03.94	Dennis Berry W PTS 6 Lincoln
21.04.94	Dave Whittle L PTS 6 Gateshead
16.05.94	Dennis Berry L RSC 6 Cleethorpes
17.08.94	Steve Howden W PTS 6 Sheffield
06.09.94	Tony Brown DREW 6 Stoke
12.09.94	Prince Kasi Kiahau L PTS 6 Doncaster
12.10.94	Michael Carruth L PTS 6 Sheffield
26.10.94	Carl Smith DREW 6 Stoke
12.11.94	Damien Denny L PTS 6 Dublin
12.12.94	Richard O'Brien W PTS 6 Cleethorpes
25.01.95	Michael Smyth L DIS 4 Cardiff
22.02.95	Anthony Lawrence L PTS 6 Telford
02.06.95	Jim Webb L PTS 6 Bethnal Green

Career: 42 contests, won 11, drew 5, lost 26.

Robert Norton

Stourbridge. *Born* Dudley, 20 January, 1972
Cruiserweight. Ht. 6'2"
Manager D. Bradley

30.09.93	Stuart Fleet W CO 2 Walsall
27.10.93	Kent Davis W PTS 6 West Bromwich
02.12.93	Eddie Pyatt W RSC 2 Walsall
26.01.94	Lennie Howard W PTS 6 Birmingham
17.05.94	Steve Osborne W PTS 6 Kettering
05.10.94	Chris Woollas DREW 6 Wolverhampton
30.11.94	L. A. Williams W RSC 2 Wolverhampton
10.02.95	Newby Stevens W RSC 3 Birmingham
22.02.95	Steve Osborne W PTS 6 Telford
21.04.95	Cordwell Hylton W PTS 6 Dudley

Career: 10 contests, won 9, drew 1.

Chris Nurse

Birmingham. *Born* Birmingham, 17 May, 1968
S. Middleweight. Ht. 6'1"
Manager Self

24.11.92	Paul Hanlon L PTS 6 Wolverhampton
17.03.93	Steve Loftus L PTS 6 Stoke
01.04.93	Phil Ball DREW 6 Evesham

27.05.93	Dale Nixon L RSC 2 Bristol
30.11.93	Phil Ball W PTS 6 Wolverhampton
08.03.94	Robert Harper W PTS 6 Edgbaston
28.06.94	Richard Guy W RSC 3 Edgbaston
25.10.94	Kevin Burton L RSC 1 Edgbaston
15.12.94	Pat Durkin W PTS 6 Walsall

Career: 9 contests, won 5, drew 1, lost 3.

(David) Marvin O'Brien (Powell)

Leeds. *Born* Leeds, 3 September, 1966
S. Middleweight. Ht. 5'11"
Manager Self

31.01.90	Tony Hodge L RSC 3 Bethnal Green
04.04.90	Gary Osborne L CO 2 Stafford
07.09.90	Mike Phillips L RSC 1 Liverpool
12.11.90	Mike Phillips W PTS 6 Liverpool
17.01.91	Barry Messam L PTS 6 Alfreton
21.02.91	Russell Washer DREW 6 Walsall
02.03.91	Quinn Paynter DREW 6 Irvine
21.03.91	Nick Manners L CO 2 Dewsbury
31.05.91	Carl Harney W RSC 5 Manchester
24.06.91	Frank Eubanks L PTS 6 Liverpool
06.09.91	Cornelius Carr L RSC 7 Salemi, Italy
02.03.92	John Oxenham L PTS 6 Marton
26.03.92	John Ashton L PTS 8 Telford
05.04.92	Quinn Paynter L PTS 6 Bradford
17.05.92	Lester Jacobs L PTS 6 Harringay
20.11.92	Fran Harding L RSC 4 Liverpool
16.02.93	Andy Wright L PTS 6 Tooting
12.05.93	Martin Jolley L PTS 6 Sheffield
15.09.93	Paul Hitch L PTS 4 Newcastle
15.10.93	Bruno Girard L PTS 6 Romorantin, France
03.12.93	Mads Larsen L PTS 6 Randers, Denmark
02.02.94	Willie Quinn L PTS 6 Glasgow
06.06.94	Willie Quinn L RSC 4 Glasgow
20.10.94	Derek Wormald L PTS 6 Middleton
23.11.94	Mark Delaney L RTD 1 Irvine
18.01.95	Mark Smallwood L PTS 6 Solihull
07.02.95	David Starie L PTS 6 Ipswich
04.03.95	Robin Reid L RSC 6 Livingston
17.05.95	David Starie L RSC 5 Ipswich

Career: 29 contests, won 2, drew 2, lost 25.

Richard O'Brien

Alfreton. *Born* Chesterfield, 29 October, 1971
Welterweight. Ht. 5'10"
Manager Self

14.05.90	Finn McCool W RSC 3 Northampton
21.05.90	Andy Rowbotham W RSC 5 Bradford
21.06.90	Jim Lawlor DREW 6 Alfreton
15.10.90	Richard Swallow W RTD 1 Kettering
22.10.90	Crain Fisher L CO 3 Manchester
13.12.90	Mick Duncan L PTS 6 Hartlepool
17.01.91	Steve Hardman L PTS 6 Alfreton
11.02.91	Neil Porter W RSC 4 Manchester
21.02.91	Darren Morris W PTS 6 Walsall
28.03.91	Trevor Ambrose L RSC 1 Alfreton
21.10.91	Tony Connellan L PTS 8 Bury
21.11.91	Chris Mulcahy W RSC 2 Ilkeston
02.12.91	Tony Britland W RSC 2 Birmingham
04.02.92	Darren McInulty W PTS 4 Alfreton
03.03.92	Scott Doyle L PTS 4 Cradley Heath
21.05.92	Howard Clarke L CO 1 Cradley Heath
23.10.92	Hughie Davey L PTS 6 Gateshead
11.03.93	Andy Peach W PTS 6 Walsall
01.04.93	Dave Lovell W PTS 6 Evesham
12.05.93	Wayne Appleton L RTD 2 Sheffield
20.09.93	Kevin Mabbutt L PTS 6 Northampton

09.11.94	Mark Antony DREW 6 Stafford
12.12.94	Rick North L PTS 6 Cleethorpes

Career: 23 contests, won 10, drew 2, lost 11.

Mark O'Callaghan

Tunbridge Wells. *Born* Tunbridge Wells, 17 January, 1969
Lightweight. Ht. 5'7"
Manager Self

03.10.91	Chris Mylan DREW 6 Burton
24.10.91	Nicky Lucas W PTS 6 Dunstable
11.12.91	Richard Joyce L RSC 3 Stoke
20.02.92	Alan McDowall L PTS 6 Glasgow
12.11.92	Erwin Edwards L RSC 6 Bayswater
20.01.93	Sugar Boy Wright W CO 1 Wolverhampton
05.02.93	Nick Boyd L PTS 6 Manchester
18.03.93	Paul Denton L RSC 4 Lewisham
22.04.93	Trevor Royal W PTS 6 Mayfair
26.05.93	Gareth Jordan L RSC 3 Mansfield
22.09.93	Dean Hollington L CO 1 Wembley
07.12.93	Colin Dunne L RSC 1 Bethnal Green
15.06.94	P. J. Gallagher L RSC 4 Southwark
09.11.94	Colin Dunne L RSC 2 Millwall
04.02.95	Gareth Jordan L RSC 2 Cardiff
23.05.95	Andrew Reed L PTS 4 Potters Bar

Career: 16 contests, won 3, drew 1, lost 12.

Chris Okoh

Camberwell. *Born* Carshalton, 18 April, 1969
Southern Area Cruiserweight Champion. Ht. 6'2"
Manager D. Powell

16.03.93	Lee Prudden W PTS 6 Mayfair
10.07.93	Steve Yorath W PTS 6 Cardiff
28.09.93	Steve Osborne W RSC 5 Bethnal Green
06.11.93	Chris Henry W RSC 2 Bethnal Green
09.04.94	Art Stacey W PTS 6 Bethnal Green
17.09.94	Art Stacey W PTS 6 Crawley
23.02.95	Paul Lawson W RSC 5 Southwark *(Vacant Southern Area Cruiserweight Title)*

Career: 7 contests, won 7.

Spencer Oliver   Les Clark

127

Spencer Oliver

Finchley. *Born* Barnet, 27 March, 1975
Bantamweight. Ht. 5'4½"
Manager M. Jacobs/J. Spensley

17.02.95 Des Gargano W PTS 4 Cumbernauld
13.04.95 Marty Chestnut W RSC 4 Bloomsbury
23.05.95 Pete Buckley W PTS 4 Potters Bar
Career: 3 contest, won 3.

(Mike) Chip O'Neill

Sunderland. *Born* Sunderland, 10
December, 1963
Featherweight. Ht. 5'6½"
Manager Self

28.06.82 Charlie Brown L PTS 6 Bradford
20.09.82 Danny Flynn L PTS 2 Glasgow
07.03.83 Charlie Brown L RSC 3 Glasgow
28.04.92 Robert Braddock W PTS 6 Houghton le Spring
10.09.92 Vince Wilson W RSC 1 Sunderland
21.09.92 Ian McGirr L PTS 6 Glasgow
05.10.92 Phil Lashley W PTS 6 Manchester
09.11.92 Robert Braddock L RSC 3 Bradford
19.01.93 Russell Rees L RSC 1 Cardiff
08.03.93 Chris Lyons W PTS 6 Leeds
29.04.93 Paul Wynn L PTS 6 Newcastle
07.10.93 Fred Reeve W RSC 2 Hull
08.11.93 Ady Benton L RSC 5 Bradford
13.12.93 Paul Richards L PTS 6 Bristol
04.03.94 Ian McLeod L RSC 2 Irvine
24.05.94 Paul Wynn W PTS 6 Sunderland
06.10.94 Colin Innes DREW 6 Cramlington
20.10.94 Michael Brodie L CO 3 Middleton
05.12.94 Des Gargano W PTS 6 Houghton le Spring
16.02.95 Ady Lewis L RSC 1 Bury
25.03.95 Michael Alldis L RSC 2 Chester
11.05.95 Colin Innes W PTS 6 Sunderland
30.06.95 Gary Thornhill L RTD 3 Liverpool
Career: 23 contests, won 8, drew 1, lost 14.

Shaun O'Neill

Sunderland. *Born* Sunderland, 21
December, 1968
Welterweight. Ht. 5'9"
Manager T. Conroy

13.10.94 Trevor George W RSC 6 Houghton le Spring
05.12.94 Jay Mahoney L PTS 6 Houghton le Spring
16.03.95 Scott Marshall W RSC 3 Sunderland
11.05.95 Mark Allen W PTS 6 Sunderland
22.06.95 Jamie Gallagher W PTS 6 Houghton le Spring
Career: 5 contests, won 4, lost 1.

Gary Osborne

Walsall. *Born* Bloxwich, 24 August, 1963
Former Undefeated Midlands Area L.
Middleweight Champion. Former Midlands
Area Welterweight Champion. Ht. 5'10"
Manager Self

08.05.89 Peter Reid W CO 5 Edgbaston
22.03.90 Peter Reid W CO 1 Wolverhampton
04.04.90 Marvin O'Brien W CO 2 Stafford
24.05.90 Julian Eavis W PTS 6 Dudley
18.09.90 Paul Hanlon W RTD 2 Wolverhampton
17.10.90 Chris Richards W PTS 8 Stoke

06.12.90 Darren Morris W PTS 8 Wolverhampton
10.04.91 Mickey Lerwill W PTS 10 Wolverhampton
(Vacant Midlands Area Welterweight Title)
10.09.91 Ernie Loveridge L RSC 1 Wolverhampton
(Midlands Area Welterweight Title Defence)
17.03.92 Shamus Casey W RSC 5 Wolverhampton
(Vacant Midlands Area L. Middleweight Title)
28.04.92 Gary Pemberton W CO 3 Wolverhampton
07.06.93 Bullit Andrews W RSC 1 Walsall
30.09.93 Rick North W PTS 6 Walsall
24.02.94 Anthony Lawrence L RSC 3 Walsall
29.09.94 Mark Antony W RSC 2 Walsall
29.10.94 Warren Stephens W CO 1 Cannock
Career: 16 contests, won 14, lost 2.

Gary Osborne   Les Clark

Steve Osborne

Nottingham. *Born* Nottingham, 27 June, 1965
Cruiserweight. Ht. 5'9"
Manager Self

28.05.87 Gary Railton L PTS 6 Jarrow
09.06.87 Ian Bulloch L PTS 6 Manchester
24.09.87 Bobby Frankham L PTS 6 Glasgow
05.10.87 Ray Thomas L RSC 8 Piccadilly
14.12.87 Branko Pavlovic L RSC 3 Bedford
16.01.89 Simon McDougall W PTS 6 Bradford
25.01.89 Simon McDougall W PTS 6 Stoke
02.02.89 Dave Furneaux W CO 4 Southwark
13.02.89 Carl Thompson L PTS 6 Manchester
06.03.89 Jimmy Cropper W PTS 6 Manchester
05.04.89 Jimmy Cropper L PTS 6 Halifax
16.05.89 Henry Brewer W PTS 6 Halifax
12.06.89 Carl Thompson L PTS 8 Manchester
16.11.89 Dave Lawrence W PTS 6 Ilkeston
19.12.89 Herbie Hide L RSC 6 Bethnal Green
05.02.90 Dave Lawrence W PTS 8 Piccadilly
20.02.90 Rob Albon L PTS 6 Brentwood
03.03.90 Darren Westover L RSC 6 Wembley
15.11.90 Michael Gale L PTS 6 Oldham

08.12.90 Neils H. Madsen L RSC 6 Aalborg, Denmark
16.04.91 Art Stacey DREW 6 Nottingham
09.05.91 Michael Gale L RSC 2 Leeds
11.11.91 Art Stacey L PTS 6 Bradford
21.11.91 Bruce Scott L PTS 6 Burton
29.11.91 Maurice Core L PTS 6 Manchester
12.02.92 Phil Soundy L PTS 6 Wembley
12.11.92 Terry Dunstan L PTS 6 Bayswater
10.12.92 Ole Klemetsen L RSC 1 Bethnal Green
27.01.93 Darren McKenna L PTS 6 Stoke
22.02.93 Nicky Wadman L PTS 6 Eltham
26.04.93 Joe Frater W PTS 6 Cleethorpes
01.07.93 Denzil Browne L RSC 1 York
28.09.93 Chris Okoh L RSC 5 Bethnal Green
10.11.93 Monty Wright L RSC 3 Watford
13.12.93 Martin Langtry L PTS 6 Cleethorpes
28.03.94 Joe Frater W RSC 5 Cleethorpes
05.04.94 Bruce Scott L RSC 5 Bethnal Green
17.05.94 Robert Norton L PTS 6 Kettering
28.07.94 Devon Rhooms W PTS 6 Tooting
26.08.94 Martin Langtry L PTS 8 Barnsley
02.09.94 Dean Francis L RTD 4 Spitalfields
27.10.94 Phil Soundy L PTS 6 Millwall
12.11.94 Ray Kane L PTS 6 Dublin
26.11.94 Rudiger May L PTS 6 Wuppertal, Germany
05.12.94 Justin Clements L PTS 6 Birmingham
22.02.95 Robert Norton L PTS 6 Telford
03.03.95 Gypsy Carman L PTS 6 Bracknell
30.03.95 John Pettersen L PTS 4 Bethnal Green
02.06.95 Mark Prince L RSC 3 Bethnal Green
Career: 49 contests, won 10, drew 1, lost 38.

Clay O'Shea

Islington. *Born* London, 3 November, 1966
L. Middleweight. Ht. 6'0"
Manager D. Mancini

20.02.90 Carlton Myers W RSC 1 Brentford
14.03.90 Tony Grizzle W RSC 1 Kensington
04.10.90 Benji Good W CO 2 Bethnal Green
31.10.90 Remy Duverger W PTS 6 Wembley
04.04.91 Robert Peel W PTS 6 Watford
11.09.91 Shamus Casey W PTS 6 Hammersmith
26.09.91 Tony Wellington W CO 1 Dunstable
25.03.92 Andrew Furlong DREW 6 Kensington
13.05.92 Andrew Furlong DREW 6 Kensington
15.10.92 Steve Thomas W PTS 6 Lewisham
17.12.92 Mark Jay W CO 1 Wembley
28.01.93 Lee Crocker W RSC 1 Southwark
26.04.94 Steve Thomas W PTS 6 Bethnal Green
23.09.94 Trevor Meikle W RSC 1 Bethnal Green
09.11.94 Harry Dhami W PTS 6 Millwall
20.01.95 Geoff McCreesh L RSC 1 Bethnal Green
(Vacant Southern Area L. Middleweight Title)
Career: 16 contests, won 13, drew 2, lost 1.

Dave Owens

Castleford. *Born* Castleford, 11 December, 1954
L. Heavyweight. Former Undefeated
Central Area Middleweight Champion. Ht. 6'1"
Manager T. Petersen

12.05.76 Steve Heavisides W RSC 2 Bradford
08.06.76 Joe Jackson W PTS 4 Bradford

10.09.76	Carl McCarthy W CO 2 Digbeth
21.09.76	Steve Fenton W RSC 3 Bethnal Green
27.09.76	Neville Estaban DREW 6 Piccadilly
30.11.76	Owen Robinson W PTS 6 Leeds
20.04.77	Billy Hill W RSC 2 Manchester
27.04.77	Jim Moore W PTS 8 Bradford
15.05.77	Howard Mills W RSC 8 Manchester
10.07.77	Pat Brogan W RSC 9 Birmingham (Vacant Central Area Middleweight Title)
13.03.78	Paul Shutt W RSC 2 Nottingham
08.05.78	Howard Mills L RTD 4 Nottingham
04.09.78	Glen McEwan L CO 1 Wakefield
07.12.78	Torben Anderson L PTS 6 Copenhagen, Denmark
12.03.79	Romal Ambrose L PTS 8 Manchester
20.09.79	Dave Davies W CO 3 Liverpool
17.10.79	Jimmy Pickard W RSC 4 Piccadilly (Central Area Middleweight Title Defence)
29.04.80	Eddie Smith L CO 1 Stockport
12.08.80	Doug James L PTS 8 Gowerton
13.10.80	Earl Edwards L RSC 3 Windsor
03.09.85	Barry Ahmed DREW 6 Gateshead
20.09.85	Simon Harris W PTS 6 Longford
25.10.85	Nye Williams W PTS 8 Fulham
20.01.86	Tony Wilson L RSC 2 Mayfair
01.12.86	Pedro van Raamsdonk L CO 1 Arnhem, Holland
02.03.87	Peter Brown L PTS 8 Huddersfield
05.05.87	Shamus Casey W PTS 6 Leeds
18.11.87	John Foreman W RSC 5 Solihull
05.12.87	Darryl Ritchie L DIS 7 Doncaster
07.02.88	Brian Schumacher L CO 1 Stafford
28.11.88	John Foreman L CO 1 Edgbaston
31.01.89	Adam Cook DREW 6 Reading
13.03.89	James Wray L PTS 6 Glasgow
01.05.89	Jose Seys L RSC 6 Waregem, Belgium
20.11.89	Steve Williams DREW 6 Glasgow
19.12.89	Nicky Piper L CO 1 Gorleston
06.04.90	Everton Blake L RSC 6 Stevenage
14.05.90	Joe Frater W PTS 6 Cleethorpes
24.09.90	Sean O'Phoenix L PTS 8 Manchester
08.10.90	Darren McKenna W PTS 6 Leicester
29.10.90	Fidel Castro L PTS 6 Birmingham
18.11.90	Sean Heron L PTS 8 Birmingham
06.12.90	Gil Lewis L CO 2 Wolverhampton
17.02.91	Anton Josipovic L PTS 8 Prijedor, Yugoslavia
24.03.91	Christophe Girard L RSC 7 Vichy, France
23.04.91	Joe Frater W PTS 6 Evesham
27.05.91	Eddie Smulders L RSC 1 Rotterdam, Holland
14.11.91	Ian Henry L PTS 8 Gateshead
03.03.92	Terry French W CO 1 Houghton le Spring
26.03.92	Tony Booth L PTS 6 Hull
14.04.92	Martin Smith L PTS 6 Mansfield
26.10.92	Joe Frater W PTS 6 Cleethorpes
04.12.92	Bernard Bonzon L RSC 5 Geneva, Switzerland
06.03.93	Stephen Wilson L RSC 2 Glasgow
15.05.93	Willie Quinn L PTS 6 Glasgow
25.11.93	Dave Johnson L PTS 8 Tynemouth
28.03.94	Stephen Wilson L CO 2 Musselburgh
28.09.94	Joe McCluskey L PTS 6 Glasgow
25.10.94	David Starie L PTS 6 Southwark
05.12.94	Dave Battey L PTS 6 Cleethorpes
24.06.95	Neil Simpson L RSC 1 Cleethorpes

Career: 61 contests, won 21, drew 4, lost 36.

Charlie Paine (Bird)

Liverpool. *Born* Liverpool, 27 August, 1970
Welterweight. Ht. 5'7"
Manager Self

09.06.93	Delwyn Panayiotiou W PTS 6 Liverpool
13.10.94	Micky Hall L PTS 6 Houghton le Spring
31.10.94	Tony Mock L PTS 6 Liverpool
20.01.95	Dennis Gardner L RSC 1 Bethnal Green
23.02.95	Derek Roche L CO 1 Hull
30.06.95	Andreas Panayi L CO 1 Liverpool

Career: 6 contests, won 1, lost 5.

Charlie Paine   Les Clark

Joey Paladino

St Helens. *Born* Whiston, 29 August, 1965
Heavyweight. Ht. 6'6"
Manager N. Basso

06.05.93	Vance Idiens L PTS 8 Walsall
23.06.93	Julius Francis L CO 4 Edmonton
15.09.93	Kevin McBride L CO 2 Bethnal Green
28.10.93	David Jules W RSC 2 Walsall
06.11.93	Scott Welch L RSC 3 Bethnal Green
07.12.93	Damien Caesar L RSC 3 Bethnal Green
29.03.94	Graham Arnold W RSC 5 Wolverhampton
16.05.94	Neil Kirkwood L RSC 2 Cleethorpes
10.06.95	Gary Williams W PTS 6 Manchester

Career: 9 contests, won 3, lost 6.

Andreas Panayi

St Helens. *Born* Cyprus, 14 July, 1969
L. Welterweight. Ht. 5'6"
Manager B. Hearn

21.11.90	Trevor Ambrose L RSC 5 Solihull
04.02.91	Cliff Churchward W PTS 6 Leicester
12.02.91	Eddie King W CO 2 Wolverhampton
27.02.91	Trevor Meikle L PTS 6 Wolverhampton
15.04.91	Mick Mulcahy W RSC 2 Leicester
24.04.91	Darren Morris DREW 6 Stoke

11.09.91	Robert Riley W PTS 6 Stoke
30.09.91	Steve Hardman W RSC 5 Liverpool
23.10.91	Darren Morris W PTS 6 Stoke
25.11.91	Marvin P. Gray W PTS 8 Liverpool
11.12.91	Mark Kelly DREW 8 Stoke
11.03.92	Dean Bramhald L PTS 8 Stoke
14.05.92	Dave Maj W CO 6 Liverpool
03.09.92	Rick North DREW 6 Liverpool
05.10.92	John O. Johnson W RTD 1 Liverpool
23.10.92	Trevor Meikle W PTS 6 Liverpool
20.11.92	Rick North W PTS 6 Liverpool
15.12.92	Mark Kelly W PTS 6 Liverpool
27.01.93	Ross Hale W RSC 3 Cardiff
27.02.93	Darren McInulty W PTS 6 Ellesmere Port
04.05.93	Jimmy Thornton W CO 2 Liverpool
02.07.93	Mark Ramsey DREW 6 Liverpool
28.09.93	Hugh Forde W PTS 8 Liverpool
11.12.93	Bobby Butters W CO 3 Liverpool
09.04.94	Tony Swift L PTS 8 Bethnal Green
10.05.94	Shaun Cogan W RSC 7 Doncaster
11.06.94	Tony Swift W PTS 8 Bethnal Green
28.06.94	John O. Johnson W RSC 5 Mayfair
17.09.94	Sammy Fuentes L RSC 4 Crawley (Vacant Penta-Continental L. Welterweight Title)
11.02.95	Dingaan Thobela L CO 1 Hammanskraal, South Africa
20.04.95	John Smith W RSC 4 Liverpool
30.06.95	Charlie Paine W CO 1 Liverpool

Career: 32 contests, won 22, drew 4, lost 6.

Andreas Panayi   Les Clark

Neil Parry

Middlesbrough. *Born* Middlesbrough, 21 June, 1969
Flyweight. Ht. 5'5"
Manager T. Callighan

12.06.89	Des Gargano L PTS 6 Manchester
21.12.89	Kevin Jenkins L PTS 6 Kings Heath
31.01.90	Francis Ampofo L PTS 6 Bethnal Green
12.03.90	Paul Dever W PTS 6 Hull
19.03.90	James Drummond L RSC 4 Glasgow
27.11.90	Stevie Woods W PTS 6 Glasgow

04.12.90	Conn McMullen L RSC 2 Southend	
21.01.91	Stevie Woods L PTS 8 Glasgow	
06.02.91	Paul Dever W PTS 6 Liverpool	
05.03.91	Tony Smith DREW 6 Leicester	
24.04.91	Paul Dever DREW 6 Stoke	
17.05.91	Gary White L PTS 6 Bury	
03.06.91	Stevie Woods W RSC 2 Glasgow	
20.06.91	Tony Smith W PTS 6 Liverpool	
12.09.91	Mark Tierney L PTS 6 Wandsworth	
21.10.91	Neil Johnston L PTS 8 Glasgow	
27.01.92	Drew Docherty L RSC 4 Glasgow	
28.02.92	Stevie Woods W PTS 6 Irvine	
11.05.92	Tim Yeates L PTS 6 Piccadilly	
21.09.92	Paul Weir L RSC 4 Glasgow	
27.11.92	Eyup Can L PTS 6 Randers, Denmark	
25.01.93	Ady Benton L RSC 6 Bradford	
29.03.93	Louis Veitch L PTS 6 Glasgow	
01.06.93	Des Gargano L PTS 6 Manchester	
28.06.93	Marcus Duncan W RSC 2 Morecambe	
13.09.93	Marcus Duncan L PTS 6 Middleton	
06.10.93	Graham McGrath DREW 6 York	
25.10.93	James Drummond L RSC 2 Glasgow	
19.02.94	Harald Geier L CO 3 Hamburg, Germany	
22.09.94	Ady Lewis L RSC 3 Bury	
29.10.94	Terry Gaskin W PTS 6 Cannock	
21.11.94	Keith Knox L PTS 6 Glasgow	
16.01.95	Keith Knox L PTS 6 Musselburgh	
23.01.95	Ian Baillie W RTD 3 Glasgow	
11.03.95	Terry Gaskin DREW 6 Barnsley	
22.03.95	Terry Gaskin W PTS 8 Stoke	
26.04.95	Shaun Norman DREW 6 Stoke	
17.05.95	Mark Reynolds L PTS 6 Ipswich	
01.06.95	Rowan Williams L PTS 8 Musselburgh	

Career: 39 contests, won 10, drew 5, lost 24.

Elvis Parsley

Bloxwich. *Born* Walsall, 6 December, 1962
Featherweight. Ht. 5'7½"
Manager Self

04.06.90	Phil Lashley W RSC 3 Birmingham	
20.06.90	Mark Bates L CO 1 Basildon	
27.09.90	Andrew Robinson W RTD 3 Birmingham	
10.12.90	Karl Taylor W PTS 6 Birmingham	
18.02.91	Peter Campbell W RSC 3 Derby	
01.05.91	Neil Leitch W CO 2 Solihull	
20.05.91	Neil Smith L RSC 5 Leicester	
02.10.91	Muhammad Shaffique W CO 1 Solihull	
29.04.92	Kelton McKenzie L RSC 5 Solihull	
	(Vacant Midlands Area Featherweight Title)	
28.04.93	Dean Amory L PTS 6 Solihull	
12.10.93	Kid McAuley W PTS 6 Wolverhampton	
30.11.93	Mike Deveney W PTS 6 Wolverhampton	
16.12.93	Barry Jones L PTS 6 Newport	
05.04.94	Kevin Middleton W RSC 4 Bethnal Green	
23.01.95	Danny Lutaaya W RSC 3 Bethnal Green	
21.03.95	Floyd Havard L RSC 6 Swansea	

Career: 16 contests, won 10, lost 6.

Patrick Parton

Telford. *Born* Shifnal, 5 September, 1965
L. Welterweight. Ht. 5'11"
Manager D. Nelson

23.02.93	T. J. Smith L PTS 6 Kettering	
24.06.93	Shaun Shinkwin DREW 6 Watford	

17.02.94	Tim Hill W PTS 6 Walsall	
24.02.94	Malcolm Thomas W PTS 6 Walsall	
18.04.94	Mark Allen W PTS 6 Walsall	
23.05.94	Mark Allen W PTS 6 Walsall	
29.09.94	Gary Hiscox L PTS 6 Walsall	
09.03.95	Mark Allen W PTS 6 Walsall	
28.03.95	Shaun Stokes L CO 1 Wolverhampton	

Career: 9 contests, won 5, drew 1, lost 3.

Pat Passley

Edmonton. *Born* London, 10 October, 1965
Heavyweight. Ht. 6'4"
Manager F. Maloney

25.10.94	John Williams W PTS 4 Southwark	
20.12.94	Mike Holden W RTD 3 Bethnal Green	
07.02.95	Graham Arnold L RSC 3 Ipswich	
30.03.95	Keith Fletcher L RSC 6 Bethnal Green	

Career: 4 contests, won 2, lost 2.

Pat Passley   Les Clark

Bernard Paul

Tottenham. *Born* Mauritius, 22 October, 1965
Southern Area L. Welterweight Champion.
Ht. 5'7½"
Manager Self

01.05.91	Trevor Royal W CO 1 Bethnal Green	
04.06.91	Dave Jenkins W RSC 1 Bethnal Green	
24.09.91	Pat Delargy W RSC 5 Basildon	
26.10.91	Gordon Webster W RSC 4 Brentwood	
26.11.91	John O. Johnson W PTS 6 Bethnal Green	
19.02.92	Rick North W PTS 6 Muswell Hill	
17.03.92	Mick Mulcahy W PTS 6 Mayfair	
16.06.92	Brendan Ryan W CO 6 Dagenham	
13.10.92	Dean Bramhald DREW 6 Mayfair	
10.11.92	Ray Newby DREW 6 Dagenham	
12.12.92	Michael Driscoll L RSC 2 Muswell Hill	
20.04.93	Ray Newby DREW 6 Brentwood	
28.09.93	Dean Bramhald W PTS 8 Bethnal Green	
08.11.93	Shaun Cogan DREW 6 Bethnal Green	
11.01.94	Shaun Cogan L PTS 6 Bethnal Green	
09.07.94	Carlos Chase W RSC 2 Earls Court	

30.09.94	Richard Swallow L PTS 8 Bethnal Green	
13.12.94	Steve Burton W PTS 6 Potters Bar	
21.02.95	Mark Legg W RSC 4 Sunderland	
18.03.95	Jean Chiarelli W RTD 4 Millstreet, Eire	
23.05.95	Keith Marner W PTS 10 Potters Bar	
	(Southern Area L. Welterweight Title Challenge)	

Career: 21 contests, won 14, drew 4, lost 3.

Andy Peach

Bloxwich. *Born* Bloxwich, 1 August, 1971
Welterweight. Ht. 5'8"
Manager W. Tyler

27.10.92	Stuart Dunn L RSC 3 Leicester	
09.12.92	Jason Fores W PTS 6 Stoke	
09.02.93	Ray Golding L PTS 6 Wolverhampton	
11.03.93	Richard O'Brien L PTS 6 Walsall	
06.05.93	Billy McDougall L PTS 6 Walsall	
30.09.93	Ernie Locke L PTS 6 Walsall	
04.11.93	Dennis Berry L PTS 6 Stafford	
02.12.93	Ernie Locke L RTD 3 Walsall	
08.02.94	Brian Coleman L PTS 6 Wolverhampton	
04.03.94	Nicky Thurbin L PTS 6 Bethnal Green	
14.03.94	Howard Eastman L PTS 6 Mayfair	
18.04.94	Howard Clarke L PTS 6 Walsall	
28.04.94	Scott Doyle L PTS 6 Mayfair	
23.05.94	David Bain L RSC 6 Walsall	
26.08.94	Cam Raeside L PTS 6 Barnsley	
12.10.94	Prince Kasi Kiahau L PTS 6 Stoke	
25.10.94	Howard Clarke L RSC 3 Edgbaston	
29.11.94	Mark Antony W PTS 6 Wolverhampton	
12.12.94	Prince Kasi Kiahau L PTS 6 Doncaster	
18.01.95	John Stronach L RSC 5 Solihull	
06.03.95	Norman Hutcheon W RSC 2 Leicester	
22.03.95	Andrew Jervis L PTS 6 Stoke	
05.05.95	Prince Kasi Kiahau L PTS 6 Doncaster	
15.05.95	Brian Dunn W RSC 2 Cleethorpes	
23.05.95	Steve Roberts L RSC 3 Potters Bar	

Career: 25 contests, won 4, lost 21.

Alan Peacock

Cumbernauld. *Born* Glasgow, 17 February, 1969
L. Welterweight. Ht. 5'7"
Manager T. Gilmour

23.02.90	Gary Quigley W PTS 6 Irvine	
08.03.90	Gary Quigley W PTS 6 Glasgow	
29.05.90	John Ritchie W PTS 6 Glasgow	
11.06.90	Chris Mulcahy W RSC 3 Manchester	
17.09.90	John Ritchie W PTS 6 Glasgow	
09.10.90	Dave Anderson L RSC 3 Glasgow	
27.11.90	Stuart Rimmer W RSC 4 Glasgow	
11.02.91	Oliver Harrison L RSC 6 Glasgow	
18.03.91	Darren Mount W PTS 8 Glasgow	
27.03.91	Giovanni Parisi L PTS 6 Mestre, Italy	
06.04.91	Allan Hall L PTS 6 Darlington	
25.05.91	Giorgio Campanella L CO 1 Trezzano, Italy	
23.09.91	Trevor Meikle L PTS 6 Glasgow	
27.11.91	Dave Whittle L PTS 6 Marton	
28.01.92	Trevor Meikle W PTS 8 Piccadilly	
20.02.92	John O. Johnson L PTS 6 Glasgow	
04.03.92	Rob Stewart DREW 8 Glasgow	
12.03.92	Dave Whittle DREW 8 Glasgow	
30.03.92	Peter Bradley L PTS 8 Glasgow	

07.10.92	John Smith DREW 6 Glasgow
18.11.92	Dave Lovell W PTS 6 Solihull
22.02.93	Dave Lovell W PTS 8 Glasgow
23.03.93	Dean Bramhald L PTS 6 Wolverhampton
24.11.93	Malcolm Melvin L PTS 8 Solihull
21.02.94	John Smith W RSC 4 Glasgow
19.03.94	Paul Knights L PTS 6 Millwall
19.09.94	John Smith W PTS 8 Glasgow
02.11.94	Mark Legg L PTS 6 Solihull
21.11.94	Michael Alexander W RSC 1 Glasgow
05.12.94	James Jiora L PTS 6 Bradford
17.02.95	Kevin McKenzie L PTS 6 Cumbernauld
01.03.95	Micky Hall W RSC 6 Glasgow
20.03.95	Kevin McKenzie L RSC 6 Glasgow
09.05.95	Paul Knights L PTS 6 Basildon
22.05.95	Bobby Vanzie L RSC 1 Morecambe

Career: 35 contests, won 14, drew 3, lost 18.

Robert Peel

Llandovery. *Born* Birmingham, 11 January, 1969
Middleweight. Ht. 5'10"
Manager Self

24.01.91	John Kaighin W PTS 6 Gorseinon
12.02.91	John Kaighin W PTS 6 Cardiff
13.03.91	Andrew Flute L PTS 6 Stoke
04.04.91	Clay O'Shea L PTS 6 Watford
12.04.91	Adrian Wright L RSC 6 Willenhall
15.05.91	John Kaighin L PTS 8 Swansea
29.10.91	Jason Matthews L RSC 6 Cardiff
03.02.92	Warren Stowe L PTS 6 Manchester
02.03.92	Steve Thomas DREW 6 Merthyr
11.05.92	Steve Thomas L PTS 6 Llanelli
04.06.92	Darren Pilling L PTS 6 Burnley
28.10.92	Barry Thorogood L PTS 6 Cardiff
24.03.93	Russell Washer W PTS 6 Cardiff
27.05.93	Dean Cooper L PTS 6 Bristol
14.08.93	Ensley Bingham L RTD 3 Hammersmith
22.09.93	Adrian Dodson L CO 1 Bethnal Green
10.11.93	Barry Thorogood L PTS 6 Ystrad
20.05.94	Geoff McCreesh L RSC 2 Acton
25.06.94	Dale Nixon L PTS 6 Cullompton
07.10.94	Dale Nixon L RSC 7 Taunton
29.11.94	Barry Thorogood L PTS 10 Cardiff *(Vacant Welsh Middleweight Title)*
03.03.95	David Larkin W PTS 6 Bethnal Green
12.04.95	Barry Thorogood L RSC 8 Llanelli *(Welsh Middleweight Title Challenge)*
17.05.95	Andy Ewen L RSC 4 Ipswich

Career: 24 contests, won 4, drew 1, lost 19.

Jon Pegg

Birmingham. *Born* Marston Green, 10 June, 1974
Featherweight. Ht. 5'6"
Manager E. Cashmore

29.09.94	Michael Edwards W RSC 5 Walsall
25.10.94	Danny Ruegg L PTS 6 Edgbaston
07.12.94	Andrew Smith DREW 6 Stoke
07.02.95	Andrew Smith L PTS 6 Wolverhampton
11.05.95	Graham McGrath L PTS 6 Dudley
05.06.95	Graham McGrath L PTS 6 Birmingham
20.06.95	Graham McGrath L PTS 6 Edgbaston

Career: 7 contests, won 1, drew 1, lost 5.

Gary Pemberton

Cardiff. *Born* Cardiff, 15 May, 1960
L. Middleweight. Ht. 5'10"
Manager Self

10.09.86	Johnny Nanton W RSC 4 Muswell Hill
20.10.86	Alex Mullen L RSC 4 Glasgow
24.11.86	Shaun Cummins L RSC 6 Cardiff
28.01.87	Tommy Shiels L CO 1 Croydon
06.04.87	Paul McCarthy W RSC 4 Southampton
23.06.87	Shaun West L RSC 2 Swansea
28.09.87	Simon Paul W RSC 1 Dulwich
06.10.87	Danny Shinkwin W RSC 2 Southend
28.10.87	Mark Howell W PTS 6 Swansea
19.11.87	Steve Huxtable W RSC 4 Weston super Mare
01.03.88	Alex Romeo L RSC 3 Southend
14.04.88	Tony Britton DREW 8 Piccadilly
07.06.88	Winston Wray L PTS 6 Southend
04.10.88	Tony Cloak W RSC 1 Southend
25.10.88	Kevin Hayde L CO 4 Pontardawe
14.12.88	Crisanto Espana L RTD 1 Kirkby
01.03.89	Shaun Cummins L CO 2 Cardiff
19.08.89	Alan Richards W PTS 6 Cardiff
19.09.89	Ray Close L PTS 6 Belfast
25.09.89	Steve Craggs W CO 1 Leicester
11.10.89	Tony Collins L CO 1 Millwall
06.12.89	Jimmy McDonagh L RSC 2 Wembley
16.01.90	Jimmy Farrell L RSC 2 Cardiff
15.06.90	Chris Richards L RTD 1 Telford
13.09.90	B. K. Bennett W RSC 4 Watford
04.10.90	Brian Robinson L PTS 6 Bethnal Green
29.10.90	Tony Kosova W RSC 1 Nottingham
19.11.90	Carlo Colarusso L RSC 3 Cardiff
24.01.91	Carlo Colarusso L RSC 8 Gorseinon *(Vacant Welsh L Middleweight Title)*
10.04.91	Colin Pitters L RSC 3 Newport
01.10.91	Adrian Strachan L RSC 2 Sheffield
12.02.92	Andrew Furlong L PTS 6 Wembley
28.04.92	Gary Osborne L CO 3 Wolverhampton
22.10.92	Jamie Robinson L RSC 3 Bethnal Green
11.05.93	Vince Rose L PTS 6 Norwich
25.06.93	Miodrag Perunovic L RSC 4 Belgrade, Yugoslavia
30.11.93	Matthew Turner L RTD 3 Cardiff
03.08.94	Darren Dorrington L CO 4 Bristol

Career: 38 contests, won 11, drew 1, lost 26.

Danny Peters

Liverpool. *Born* Liverpool, 19 July, 1973
L. Middleweight. Ht. 5'10"
Manager Self

06.09.93	Steve Levene W RSC 4 Liverpool
25.10.93	Russell Washer W PTS 6 Liverpool
02.07.94	Spencer Alton W PTS 6 Liverpool
26.09.94	John Duckworth W PTS 6 Liverpool
20.04.95	Ernie Loveridge W PTS 6 Liverpool
30.06.95	Nic Ingram W RSC 6 Liverpool

Career: 6 contests, won 6.

Jimmy Phelan

Hull. *Born* London, 18 June, 1971
Lightweight. Ht. 5'9"
Manager M. Brooks

23.11.93	T. J. Smith L PTS 6 Kettering
16.12.93	Paul Bowen W PTS 6 Walsall
10.02.94	Micky Hall W PTS 6 Hull
11.10.94	Colin Dunne L PTS 6 Bethnal Green
31.10.94	George Naylor L PTS 6 Liverpool
16.03.95	Bobby Guynan W RSC 5 Basildon

Career: 6 contests, won 2, lost 4.

Jimmy Phelan   Les Clark

Dean Phillips

Swansea. *Born* Swansea, 1 February, 1976
S. Featherweight. Ht. 5'6"
Manager C. Breen

10.03.94	Paul Richards L PTS 6 Bristol
23.03.94	Phil Janes W RSC 1 Cardiff
27.08.94	Craig Kelley W RSC 4 Cardiff
21.09.94	Steve Edwards W RTD 4 Cardiff
02.11.94	Anthony Maynard L PTS 6 Birmingham
04.02.95	Greg Upton W PTS 6 Cardiff
04.03.95	Mike Deveney W PTS 8 Livingston
21.03.95	Bamana Dibateza W PTS 6 Swansea
16.06.95	Danny Lutaaya W RSC 2 Southwark

Career: 9 contests, won 7, lost 2.

Dean Phillips   Les Clark

(Warren) John Pierre

Newcastle. *Born* Newcastle, 22 April, 1966
Cruiserweight. Ht. 6'0"
Manager A. Walker

10.10.91	Gary Charlton W PTS 6 Gateshead
20.01.92	Art Stacey L PTS 6 Bradford
21.09.92	Albert Call L PTS 6 Cleethorpes
20.09.93	Martin Langtry L PTS 6 Cleethorpes
12.10.93	Richard Atkinson W PTS 6 Wolverhampton
21.10.93	Alan Smiles L PTS 6 Glasgow
08.12.93	Art Stacey L PTS 6 Hull
19.12.93	Alan Smiles DREW 6 Glasgow
25.10.94	Richard Bango L RSC 3 Middlesbrough
27.02.95	Kenley Price L PTS 6 Barrow
15.05.95	Declan Faherty L PTS 6 Bradford
12.06.95	Brian McDermott L PTS 6 Bradford

Career: 12 contests, won 2, drew 1, lost 9.

Michael Pinnock

Birmingham. *Born* Birmingham, 6 June, 1965
L. Heavyweight. Ht. 6'0"
Manager N. Nobbs

16.05.95	David Flowers L PTS 6 Leeds
13.06.95	Mark Snipe L PTS 6 Basildon
20.06.95	Darren Sweeney L PTS 8 Edgbaston

Career: 3 contests, lost 3.

Nicky Piper

Cardiff. *Born* Cardiff, 5 May, 1966
L. Heavyweight. Former Undefeated Penta-Continental S. Middleweight Champion.
Ht. 6'3"
Manager Self

06.09.89	Kevin Roper W CO 2 Aberavon
17.10.89	Gus Mendes W RSC 3 Cardiff
19.12.89	Dave Owens W CO 1 Gorleston
17.04.90	Darren McKenna W RTD 4 Millwall
22.05.90	Maurice Core DREW 6 St Albans
23.10.90	Paul McCarthy W RSC 3 Leicester
12.11.90	John Ellis W CO 1 Norwich
05.03.91	Johnny Held W RSC 3 Millwall
08.05.91	Serge Bolivard W RSC 1 Millwall
22.05.91	Martin Lopez W CO 1 Millwall
03.07.91	Simon Harris W RSC 1 Reading
04.09.91	Carl Thompson L RSC 3 Bethnal Green
29.10.91	Franki Moro W RSC 4 Kensington
20.11.91	Carlos Christie W CO 6 Cardiff
22.01.92	Frank Eubanks W PTS 10 Cardiff *(Elim. British S. Middleweight Title)*
11.03.92	Ron Amundsen W PTS 10 Cardiff
16.05.92	Larry Prather W PTS 8 Muswell Hill
25.07.92	Johnny Melfah W RSC 5 Manchester *(Elim. British S. Middleweight Title)*
12.12.92	Nigel Benn L RSC 11 Muswell Hill *(WBC S. Middleweight Title Challenge)*
13.02.93	Miguel Maldonado W PTS 12 Manchester *(Vacant Penta-Continental S. Middleweight Title)*
10.04.93	Chris Sande W RSC 9 Swansea *(Penta-Continental S. Middleweight Title Defence)*
10.07.93	Trevor Ambrose W RSC 5 Cardiff
23.10.93	Frank Rhodes DREW 8 Cardiff
29.01.94	Leonzer Barber L RSC 9 Cardiff *(WBO L. Heavyweight Title Challenge)*
21.09.94	Charles Oliver W RSC 5 Cardiff
19.11.94	Crawford Ashley L PTS 12 Cardiff *(Vacant British L. Heavyweight Title)*
17.06.95	Tim Bryan W RSC 1 Cardiff

Career: 27 contests, won 21, drew 2, lost 4.

Nicky Piper　　　　　　　　　　　　Les Clark

Dean Pithie

Coventry. *Born* Coventry, 18 January, 1974
S. Featherweight. Ht. 5'5"
Manager M. Jacobs/J. Spensley

17.02.95	Kid McAuley W RSC 3 Cumbernauld
13.04.95	Kid McAuley W RSC 1 Bloomsbury

Career: 2 contests, won 2.

Colin Pitters

Birmingham. *Born* Birmingham, 1 October, 1956
L. Middleweight. Ht. 6'3"
Manager Self

03.12.89	Des Robinson L PTS 6 Birmingham
21.12.89	Alan Richards W PTS 6 Kings Heath
13.02.90	Spencer Alton L PTS 6 Wolverhampton
27.03.90	Alan Richards L PTS 8 Wolverhampton
06.04.90	Trevor Ambrose L PTS 6 Telford
28.01.91	Lee Farrell W PTS 6 Birmingham
04.02.91	Barry Messam W PTS 6 Leicester
18.02.91	Richard Okumu W PTS 6 Birmingham
10.04.91	Gary Pemberton W RSC 3 Newport
24.04.91	Chris Richards W RSC 6 Stoke
20.09.91	Steve Foster L RTD 5 Manchester
31.10.91	Richie Woodhall L PTS 8 Oakengates
21.11.91	Neville Brown L RSC 3 Burton
15.04.94	Peter Waudby L PTS 8 Hull
03.08.94	Sean Baker W PTS 6 Bristol
10.09.94	Adrian Dodson L PTS 6 Birmingham
29.10.94	Neville Brown L CO 2 Cannock

07.03.95 Darren Sweeney L PTS 6 Edgbaston
27.04.95 Delroy Matthews L RSC 2 Bethnal Green

Career: 19 contests, won 7, lost 12.

Steve Pollard

Hull. *Born* Hull, 18 December, 1957
L. Welterweight. Former Central Area Featherweight Champion. Ht. 5'7"
Manager Self

28.04.80 Bryn Jones W PTS 6 Piccadilly
27.05.80 Pat Mallon W PTS 6 Glasgow
02.06.80 Andy Thomas W PTS 6 Piccadilly
02.10.80 Eddie Glass W PTS 6 Hull
03.11.80 Rocky Bantleman W CO 2 Piccadilly
01.12.80 Chris McCallum W PTS 6 Hull
17.02.81 Billy Laidman W PTS 6 Leeds
02.03.81 Bryn Jones W RSC 5 Piccadilly
30.03.81 John Sharkey L RSC 6 Glasgow
27.04.81 Ian McLeod L PTS 6 Piccadilly
01.06.81 Gary Lucas L PTS 8 Piccadilly
11.06.81 John Sharkey W PTS 8 Hull
08.03.82 Brian Hyslop DREW 8 Hamilton
22.04.82 Rocky Bantleman W RSC 8 Piccadilly
10.05.82 Lee Graham DREW 8 Piccadilly
26.05.82 Alan Tombs DREW 8 Piccadilly
23.09.82 Pat Doherty L PTS 8 Merton
26.10.82 Lee Halford L PTS 8 Hull
25.11.82 Kevin Howard L PTS 6 Sunderland
10.02.83 Keith Foreman L PTS 8 Sunderland
29.03.83 Steve Farnsworth W RSC 2 Hull
(Central Area Featherweight Title Challenge)
18.06.83 Andre Blanco W PTS 8 Izegem, Belgium
04.10.83 Jim McDonnell L RSC 5 Bethnal Green
22.11.83 Joey Joynson L PTS 8 Wembley
22.01.84 Jean-Marc Renard L PTS 8 Izegem, Belgium
13.11.84 Jim McDonnell L RSC 6 Bethnal Green
17.12.84 John Doherty L PTS 10 Bradford
(Central Area Featherweight Title Defence)
12.03.85 Mike Whalley L RSC 8 Manchester
20.01.86 Alex Dickson L RSC 7 Glasgow
10.03.86 Dave Savage L PTS 8 Glasgow
26.03.86 Peter Harris L RSC 3 Swansea
13.11.86 Dean Marsden L CO 7 Huddersfield
07.04.87 Darren Connellan W PTS 8 Batley
15.04.87 Paul Gadney L PTS 8 Lewisham
30.04.87 Gary Nickels L RSC 1 Wandsworth
22.09.87 Kevin Taylor L PTS 8 Oldham
18.11.87 Gary de Roux DREW 8 Peterborough
11.12.87 Gary Maxwell L PTS 8 Coalville
28.01.88 John Bennie L PTS 6 Bethnal Green
24.02.88 Craig Windsor L PTS 8 Glasgow
09.03.88 Peter Bradley L PTS 8 Bethnal Green
30.03.88 Scott Durham W PTS 8 Bethnal Green
25.04.88 Colin Lynch W PTS 8 Birmingham
18.05.88 John Bennie W PTS 8 Lewisham
30.08.88 Mike Chapman W PTS 8 Kensington
15.11.88 Tony Foster L RSC 3 Hull
17.01.89 Peter Bradley L PTS 8 Chigwell
31.05.89 Carl Crook L RSC 4 Manchester
04.09.89 Michael Armstrong L PTS 8 Hull
10.10.89 Tony Foster L RSC 3 Hull
22.03.90 Chris Bennett W PTS 4 Gateshead
07.04.90 Frankie Dewinter L PTS 6 St Elois Vyve, Belgium
20.05.90 Mark Ramsey L PTS 6 Sheffield

30.11.90 Shaun Cooper L PTS 6 Birmingham
11.02.91 Dave Anderson L PTS 6 Glasgow
02.03.91 Allan Hall L PTS 6 Darlington
05.12.91 Shaun Cogan L PTS 6 Oakengates
18.01.92 Ian Honeywood L PTS 6 Kensington
30.03.92 J. T. Williams W PTS 6 Eltham
30.04.92 Jason Rowland L RSC 2 Kensington
10.09.92 Paul Charters L RTD 5 Sunderland
16.10.92 Kevin Toomey L RSC 7 Hull
12.11.93 Kevin Toomey W PTS 8 Hull
24.11.94 Dave Curtis W RTD 4 Hull

Career: 64 contests, won 21, drew 4, lost 39.

Steve Pollard   Les Clark

Lee Power

Manchester. *Born* Manchester, 11 March, 1967
L. Middleweight. Ht. 5'11½"
Manager N. Basso

12.06.95 Wesley Jones W PTS 6 Manchester

Career: 1 contest, won 1.

Kenley Price

Liverpool. *Born* Liverpool, 30 December, 1965
Cruiserweight. Ht. 6'1½"
Manager S. Vaughan

15.12.92 Zak Goldman W RTD 2 Liverpool
27.02.93 Tony Colclough W RSC 5 Ellesmere Port
02.07.93 Paul McCarthy W PTS 6 Liverpool
30.10.93 Albert Call DREW 6 Chester
27.02.95 John Pierre W PTS 6 Barrow

Career: 5 contests, won 4, drew 1.

Mark Prince

Tottenham. *Born* London, 10 March, 1969
L. Heavyweight. Ht. 6'1"
Managers F. Warren/C. Carew

04.04.93 Bobby Mack W RSC 2 Brockley
23.05.93 John Kaighin W RSC 3 Brockley
25.06.93 Art Stacey W CO 2 Battersea
14.08.93 Simon McDougall W PTS 6 Hammersmith

20.01.94 Zak Chelli W CO 1 Battersea
14.04.94 John Foreman W CO 3 Battersea
21.07.94 Tony Booth W RSC 3 Battersea
25.02.95 Kofi Quaye W RSC 7 Millwall
02.06.95 Steve Osborne W RSC 3 Bethnal Green

Career: 9 contests, won 9.

(Paul) Dave Proctor

Leeds. *Born* Leeds, 25 August, 1972
S. Middleweight. Ht. 5'11"
Manager P. Coleman

24.02.94 Robert Harper W PTS 6 Hull
28.03.94 Tony Colclough W RSC 3 Birmingham
10.05.94 Phil Ball L PTS 6 Doncaster
03.10.94 Carl Harney L PTS 6 Manchester
17.11.94 Clinton Woods L PTS 6 Sheffield

Career: 5 contests, won 2, lost 3.

Chris Pyatt

Leicester. *Born* Islington, 3 July, 1963
Former WBO Middleweight Champion. Former Undefeated WBC International Middleweight Champion. Former European L. Middleweight Champion. Former Undefeated British & Commonwealth L. Middleweight Champion. Ht. 5'8½"
Manager Self

01.03.83 Paul Murray W RTD 2 Kensington
05.04.83 Billy Waith W RSC 8 Kensington
28.04.83 Lee Hartshorn W RSC 3 Leicester
27.09.83 Darwin Brewster W PTS 8 Wembley
08.10.83 Tyrone Demby W RSC 2 Atlantic City, USA
22.11.83 Tony Britton W RSC 4 Wembley
22.02.84 Judas Clottey W PTS 8 Kensington
15.03.84 Pat Thomas W PTS 10 Leicester
09.05.84 Franki Moro W CO 4 Leicester
23.05.84 Alfonso Redondo W RSC 3 Mayfair
16.10.84 John Ridgman W RSC 1 Kensington
16.11.84 Brian Anderson W PTS 12 Leicester
(Final Elim. British L. Middleweight Title)
12.02.85 Helier Custos W RSC 5 Kensington
05.06.85 Graeme Ahmed W RSC 3 Kensington
01.07.85 Mosimo Maeleke W RSC 6 Mayfair
23.09.85 Sabiyala Diavilia L RSC 4 Mayfair
19.02.86 Prince Rodney W CO 9 Kensington
(British L. Middleweight Title Challenge)
20.05.86 Thomas Smith W RSC 1 Wembley
17.09.86 John van Elteren W RSC 1 Kensington
(Vacant European L. Middleweight Title)
25.10.86 Renaldo Hernandez W RSC 3 Paris, France
28.01.87 Gianfranco Rosi L PTS 12 Perugia, Italy
(European L. Middleweight Title Defence)
18.04.87 Dennis Johnson W CO 2 Kensington
26.05.87 Sammy Floyd W RSC 2 Wembley
28.10.87 Gilbert Josamu W PTS 8 Wembley
28.05.88 Jose Duarte W RSC 4 Kensington
23.11.88 Eddie Hall W RSC 2 Bethnal Green
01.12.88 Knox Brown W RSC 2 Edmonton
14.12.88 Tyrone Moore W CO 1 Bethnal Green
15.02.89 Russell Mitchell W RSC 4 Bethnal Green
17.05.89 Daniel Dominguez W RSC 10 Millwall

The exciting Mark Prince (left), who aims to go one better than his father, Clarence, stopped Steve Osborne in three rounds last June
Les Clark

11.10.89	Wayne Harris W RSC 3 Millwall
25.04.90	Daniel Sclarandi W RSC 2 Millwall
23.10.90	John David Jackson L PTS 12 Leicester *(WBO L. Middleweight Title Challenge)*
05.11.91	Craig Trotter W PTS 12 Leicester *(Vacant Commonwealth L. Middleweight Title)*
01.02.92	Ambrose Mlilo W RSC 3 Birmingham *Commonwealth L. Middleweight Title Defence)*
31.03.92	Melvyn Wynn W CO 3 Norwich
28.04.92	James Tapisha W RSC 1 Wolverhampton *(Commonwealth L. Middleweight Title Defence)*
23.05.92	Ian Strudwick W PTS 10 Birmingham
27.10.92	Adolfo Caballero W CO 5 Leicester *(Vacant WBC International Middleweight Title)*
26.01.93	Danny Garcia W PTS 12 Leicester *(WBC International Middleweight Title Defence)*
23.02.93	Colin Manners W CO 3 Doncaster
16.03.93	Paul Wesley W PTS 10 Mayfair
10.05.93	Sumbu Kalambay W PTS 12 Leicester *(Vacant WBO Middleweight Title)*
18.09.93	Hugo Corti W CO 6 Leicester *(WBO Middleweight Title Defence)*
09.02.94	Mark Cameron W CO 1 Brentwood *(WBO Middleweight Title Defence)*
11.05.94	Steve Collins L RSC 5 Sheffield *(WBO Middleweight Title Defence)*
13.05.95	Anthony Ivory W PTS 8 Glasgow

Career: 47 contests, won 43, lost 4.

Danny Quacoe

Crawley. *Born* Hammersmith, 30 December, 1965
Welterweight. Ht. 5'10"
Manager H. Holland

22.10.92	Joel Ani L CO 1 Bethnal Green
28.11.93	Roger Dean W RSC 3 Southwark
06.03.94	Prince Louis W RSC 2 Southwark
16.05.94	Dave Madden W RSC 4 Heathrow
19.11.94	Dennis Griffin W RSC 5 Heathrow

Career: 5 contests, won 4, lost 1.

Danny Quacoe   Les Clark

Paul Quarmby

Hetton. *Born* Easington, 2 June, 1973
Featherweight. Ht. 5'6"
Manager T. Conroy

13.10.94	Paul Goode W RSC 3 Houghton le Spring
20.10.94	Des Gargano L PTS 6 Middleton
05.12.94	Paul Goode W PTS 6 Houghton le Spring
16.03.95	Paul Watson L RSC 3 Sunderland
24.04.95	Robert Hay L PTS 6 Glasgow
18.05.95	Des Gargano L PTS 6 Middleton
22.06.95	Andy Roberts W PTS 6 Houghton le Spring

Career: 7 contests, won 3, lost 4.

Tommy Quinn

Tranent. *Born* Edinburgh, 2 November, 1975
Welterweight. Ht. 5'11"
Manager T. Gilmour

16.01.95	Billy McDougall W CO 5 Musselburgh
20.03.95	Paul Scott W RSC 4 Glasgow
24.04.95	Billy McDougall W RSC 3 Glasgow
01.06.95	Wayne Shepherd W PTS 6 Musselburgh

Career: 4 contests, won 4.

Willie Quinn

Haddington. *Born* Edinburgh, 17 February, 1972
WBO Continental Middleweight Champion. Ht. 5'11½"
Manager T. Gilmour

09.10.91 Mark Jay L PTS 6 Glasgow
27.01.92 Hugh Fury W RSC 3 Glasgow
18.03.92 Andy Manning W PTS 6 Glasgow
30.03.92 John McKenzie W RSC 4 Glasgow
19.09.92 Martin Rosamond W RSC 4 Glasgow
25.01.93 Mike Phillips W PTS 6 Glasgow
06.03.93 Steve Thomas W RSC 4 Glasgow
15.05.93 Dave Owens W PTS 6 Glasgow
30.11.93 Russell Washer W PTS 6 Cardiff
02.02.94 Marvin O'Brien W PTS 6 Glasgow
28.03.94 Spencer Alton W RTD 3 Musselburgh
06.06.94 Marvin O'Brien W RSC 4 Glasgow
20.09.94 Shamus Casey W RSC 3 Musselburgh
23.11.94 Mark Jay W RSC 1 Irvine
16.01.95 Mark Jay W RSC 2 Musselburgh
17.02.95 Martin Jolley W CO 5 Cumbernauld
05.04.95 John Duckworth W PTS 8 Irvine
01.06.95 Paul Busby W RTD 8 Musselburgh
         (Inaugural WBO Continental Middleweight Title)
Career: 18 contests, won 17, lost 1.

David Radford

Hemsworth. *Born* Hemsworth, 30 May, 1969
Middleweight. Ht. 6'0"
Manager T. Callighan

27.03.90 Tommy Warde L CO 3 Leicester
09.05.90 Chris Micolczezyk W PTS 6 Solihull
21.05.90 Brian Keating W PTS 6 Bradford
28.06.90 Paul Hanlon W RSC 2 Birmingham
03.09.90 Andre Wharton L RSC 5 Dudley
16.01.91 Tony Kosova W PTS 6 Stoke
21.02.91 Kenny Tyson L PTS 6 Leeds
15.04.91 Paul Burton L RTD 1 Wolverhampton
13.05.91 Pete Bowman W CO 2 Manchester
02.12.91 Dave Binsteed W RSC 6 Liverpool
14.12.91 Delroy Matthews L CO 1 Bexleyheath
24.02.92 Mark Jay L PTS 6 Bradford
09.03.92 Tyrone Eastmond DREW 6 Manchester
25.04.92 Warren Stowe L RSC 3 Manchester
11.03.95 Richard Munro W RSC 5 Barnsley
28.04.95 Thomas Hansvoll L PTS 6 Randers, Denmark
Career: 16 contests, won 7, drew 1, lost 8.

Cam Raeside

Ilkeston. *Born* Canada, 7 May, 1968
Welterweight. Ht. 5'8"
Manager M. Shinfield

02.12.93 Billy McDougall W RSC 5 Evesham
18.02.94 Brian Coleman W PTS 6 Leicester
26.08.94 Andy Peach W PTS 6 Barnsley
09.02.95 Gary Hiscox L RSC 5 Doncaster
Career: 4 contests, won 3, lost 1.

Nigel Rafferty

Wolverhampton. *Born* Wolverhampton, 29 December, 1967
Midlands Area Cruiserweight Champion. Ht. 5'11"
Manager R. Gray

05.06.89 Carl Watson L PTS 6 Birmingham
28.06.89 Tony Hodge L PTS 6 Brentwood
06.07.89 Tony Hodge W PTS 6 Chigwell
04.09.89 Joe Frater L PTS 6 Grimsby
24.10.89 Paul Wesley W PTS 6 Wolverhampton
22.11.89 Paul Wesley W PTS 8 Stafford
28.11.89 Paul Wesley W PTS 6 Wolverhampton
04.12.89 Dean Murray W PTS 6 Grimsby

20.12.89 Paul Wright DREW 6 Kirkby
17.01.90 Gil Lewis L PTS 6 Stoke
31.01.90 Antoine Tarver L PTS 4 Bethnal Green
19.02.90 Paul Wesley W PTS 8 Birmingham
19.03.90 Terry Gilbey W PTS 6 Grimsby
01.05.90 Sean Heron L RSC 2 Oldham
13.09.90 Paul Murray W PTS 6 Watford
27.09.90 Paul Murray DREW 6 Birmingham
09.10.90 Paul Murray W PTS 6 Wolverhampton
24.10.90 Andrew Flute L CO 6 Dudley
27.11.90 Carlos Christie L PTS 6 Wolverhampton
06.12.90 Carlos Christie L PTS 6 Wolverhampton
28.01.91 Alan Richards DREW 8 Birmingham
04.03.91 Carlos Christie L PTS 8 Birmingham
26.03.91 Lee Prudden W PTS 6 Wolverhampton
13.05.91 Tony Behan W DIS 7 Birmingham
05.06.91 Lee Prudden W PTS 6 Wolverhampton
10.09.91 Paul Busby L RSC 2 Wolverhampton
20.11.91 Julian Johnson DREW 6 Cardiff
02.12.91 Kesem Clayton W PTS 8 Birmingham
21.01.92 Glenn Campbell L RSC 6 Stockport
30.03.92 Simon McDougall W PTS 8 Coventry
25.04.92 Sammy Storey L RSC 3 Belfast
16.06.92 Garry Delaney L CO 5 Dagenham
24.11.92 Graham Burton W PTS 8 Wolverhampton
02.12.92 John J. Cooke L PTS 6 Bardon
23.03.93 Stephen Wilson W RSC 3 Wolverhampton
14.04.93 Ole Klemetsen L RSC 2 Kensington
19.05.93 Zak Chelli L RSC 3 Leicester
22.09.93 Martin Jolley W PTS 6 Chesterfield
12.10.93 Carl Smallwood DREW 8 Wolverhampton
28.10.93 Lee Archer L PTS 8 Walsall
08.12.93 Darren Ashton L PTS 6 Stoke
26.01.94 Monty Wright L PTS 6 Birmingham
08.02.94 Greg Scott-Briggs W PTS 6 Wolverhampton
17.02.94 Glenn Campbell L RSC 7 Bury
18.04.94 Graham Burton W PTS 8 Walsall
23.05.94 Darren Ashton L PTS 6 Walsall
15.06.94 Darron Griffiths L RSC 4 Southwark
03.08.94 Leif Keiski L RSC 5 Bristol
20.10.94 John J. Cooke L RSC 7 Walsall
         (Midlands Area L. Heavyweight Title Challenge)
13.12.94 Paul Lawson L RSC 4 Ilford
20.03.95 John Foreman W PTS 10 Birmingham
         (Midlands Area Cruiserweight Title Challenge)
19.04.95 Bruce Scott L RSC 2 Bethnal Green
17.05.95 Ole Klemetsen L RSC 4 Ipswich
Career: 53 contests, won 20, drew 5, lost 28.

Mark Ramsey

Birmingham. *Born* Birmingham, 24 January, 1968
L. Welterweight. Ht. 5'7½"
Manager B. Ingle

15.11.89 Mick O'Donnell W RSC 1 Lewisham
08.12.89 Dave Pierre L RSC 2 Doncaster
22.02.90 Karl Taylor W RSC 4 Hull
10.04.90 George Jones W RSC 6 Doncaster
20.05.90 Steve Pollard W PTS 6 Sheffield
18.10.90 Neil Haddock L RSC 5 Birmingham
30.05.91 Colin Sinnott W PTS 6 Birmingham
05.12.91 Carl Hook W RSC 5 Oakengates
27.01.93 Andrew Jervis W PTS 6 Stoke
12.02.93 Reymond Deva W PTS 6 Aubervilliers, France

04.03.93 Dave Pierre L PTS 8 Peterborough
01.05.93 Vyacheslav Ianowski L PTS 8 Berlin, Germany
02.07.93 Andreas Panayi DREW 6 Liverpool
05.08.93 Jean Chiarelli W RSC 4 Ascona, Italy
01.10.93 Freddy Demeulenaere W RSC 3 Waregem, Belgium
26.03.94 James Osunsedo W RSC 4 Dortmund, Germany
07.05.94 Andrei Sinepupov L PTS 12 Dnepropetrousk, Ukraine
         (Vacant Penta-Continental Lightweight Title)
30.11.94 Mark Elliot W RSC 10 Wolverhampton
         (Elim. British L. Welterweight Title)
20.05.95 Ahmet Katejew L RTD 5 Hamburg, Germany
         (WBC International Welterweight Title Challenge)
Career: 19 contests, won 12, drew 1, lost 6.

(Peter) Andrew Reed

Potters Bar. *Born* Egham, 22 November, 1962
Lightweight. Ht. 5'7"
Manager Self

09.12.93 Simon Frailing L PTS 6 Watford
29.01.94 Russell Rees L PTS 6 Cardiff
08.03.94 T. J. Smith L PTS 6 Kettering
05.04.94 Anthony Campbell L PTS 6 Bethnal Green
28.04.94 Marco Fattore DREW 6 Mayfair
27.05.94 Chris Francis L PTS 6 Ashford
04.06.94 Marcus McCrae L PTS 6 Cardiff
29.09.94 Lewis Reynolds L PTS 4 Bethnal Green
16.11.94 Greg Upton L PTS 6 Bloomsbury
23.01.95 Matt Brown L PTS 4 Bethnal Green
25.02.95 Marcus McCrae L RSC 4 Millwall
23.05.95 Mark O'Callaghan W PTS 4 Potters Bar
10.06.95 Paul Griffin L RSC 5 Manchester
Career: 13 contests, won 1, drew 1, lost 11.

Andrew Reed   Les Clark

Fred Reeve

Hull. *Born* Hull, 14 April, 1969
Featherweight. Ht. 5'5½"
Manager M. Toomey

09.11.92	Tim Hill L CO 4 Bradford
14.12.92	Leo Turner L RSC 2 Bradford
19.03.93	Kevin Haidarah L RSC 2 Manchester
29.04.93	Marty Chestnut W PTS 6 Hull
07.10.93	Chip O'Neill L RSC 2 Hull
03.03.94	Ian Richardson L PTS 6 Newcastle
28.03.94	Dougie Fox W RSC 2 Cleethorpes
28.04.94	Ian Richardson L RSC 2 Hull
26.09.94	Jobie Tyers L PTS 6 Bradford
22.11.94	Tony Falcone L PTS 6 Bristol
07.12.94	Robert Grubb W RSC 3 Stoke
18.12.94	Brian Carr L CO 2 Glasgow
11.02.95	Stephen Smith L RSC 1 Frankfurt, Germany

Career: 13 contests, won 4, lost 9.

Robbie Regan

Cefn Forest. *Born* Caerphilly, 30 August, 1968
Former Undefeated British, European & Welsh Flyweight Champion. Ht. 5'4"
Manager D. Gardiner

19.08.89	Eric George DREW 6 Cardiff
06.03.90	Francis Ampofo W PTS 6 Bethnal Green
26.04.90	Kevin Downer W RSC 4 Merthyr
20.06.90	Dave McNally DREW 6 Basildon
19.11.90	Ricky Beard W RSC 6 Cardiff
21.12.90	Michele Poddighe DREW 6 Sassari, Italy
12.02.91	Kevin Jenkins W PTS 10 Cardiff *(Vacant Welsh Flyweight Title)*
28.05.91	Joe Kelly W PTS 12 Cardiff *(Vacant British Flyweight Title)*
03.09.91	Francis Ampofo L RSC 11 Cardiff *(British Flyweight Title Defence)*
17.12.91	Francis Ampofo W PTS 12 Cardiff *(British Flyweight Title Challenge)*
11.02.92	Juan Bautista W CO 1 Cardiff
19.05.92	James Drummond W RSC 9 Cardiff *(British Flyweight Title Defence)*
14.11.92	Salvatore Fanni W PTS 12 Cardiff *(European Flyweight Title Challenge)*
30.03.93	Danny Porter W RSC 3 Cardiff *(European Flyweight Title Defence)*
26.06.93	Adrian Ochoa W PTS 10 Earls Court
29.01.94	Michele Poddighe W PTS 10 Cardiff
12.03.94	Mauricio Bernal W PTS 8 Cardiff
01.10.94	Shaun Norman W RSC 2 Cardiff
19.11.94	Luigi Camputaro W PTS 12 Cardiff *(European Flyweight Title Challenge)*
17.06.95	Alberto Jimenez L RTD 9 Cardiff *(WBO Flyweight Title Challenge)*

Career: 20 contests, won 15, drew 3, lost 2.

Ian Reid

Balham. *Born* Lambeth, 30 August, 1972
S. Featherweight. Ht. 5'2"
Manager Self

30.03.93	Russell Rees L PTS 6 Cardiff
31.08.93	Jason Hutson W RSC 6 Croydon
10.11.93	Marcus McCrae L PTS 6 Bethnal Green
09.12.94	Mark Bowers L PTS 6 Bethnal Green
17.05.95	Michael Brodie L RSC 3 Ipswich

Career: 5 contests, won 1, lost 4.

Peter Reid

Derby. *Born* Derby, 19 February, 1966
Welterweight. Ht. 5'10½"
Manager Self

01.09.86	Andy Till L RSC 6 Ealing
10.10.86	John Davies L RSC 2 Gloucester
12.12.88	Mark Holden L RSC 4 Manchester
16.01.89	Steve Kiernan W PTS 6 Bradford
27.01.89	Frank Mobbs W PTS 4 Durham
22.02.89	Frank Mobbs W PTS 4 Bradford
01.03.89	Bullit Andrews W RSC 2 Stoke
08.05.89	Gary Osborne L CO 5 Edgbaston
26.09.89	Jim Beckett L PTS 8 Chigwell
13.11.89	Martin Robinson L PTS 6 Brierley Hill
20.12.89	Paul Lynch L RSC 4 Swansea
10.03.90	Martin Rosamond W RSC 6 Bristol
22.03.90	Gary Osborne L CO 1 Wolverhampton
18.10.90	Andrew Tucker L PTS 6 Hartlepool
29.10.90	Dean Cooper L RSC 1 Nottingham
21.11.91	Robert Riley W PTS 6 Ilkeston
04.12.91	Julian Eavis L PTS 6 Stoke
20.02.92	James Campbell L PTS 6 Oakengates
06.04.92	Kevin Mabbutt W PTS 6 Northampton
13.04.92	Dave Maj L CO 1 Manchester
04.06.92	Warren Bowers W RSC 2 Cleethorpes
12.11.92	Dean Hiscox W PTS 6 Stafford
19.10.93	Adey Allen W PTS 6 Cleethorpes
04.11.93	Nic Ingram W RSC 5 Stafford
08.12.93	Julian Eavis W PTS 6 Stoke
23.03.94	Julian Eavis W PTS 8 Stoke
16.05.94	Brian Dunn L RSC 4 Cleethorpes
09.11.94	Billy McDougall W PTS 6 Stafford
28.11.94	Nic Ingram L PTS 6 Northampton
07.12.94	Howard Clarke L PTS 8 Stoke
30.01.95	John Stronach W PTS 6 Bradford
07.02.95	David Bain W PTS 6 Wolverhampton
02.03.95	Paul King L RSC 3 Cramlington

Career: 33 contests, won 16, lost 17.

Robin Reid　　　　　　　Les Clark

Robin Reid

Warrington. Liverpool, 19 February, 1972
Middleweight. Ht. 5'9"
Manager F. Warren

27.02.93	Mark Dawson W RSC 1 Dagenham
06.03.93	Julian Eavis W RSC 2 Glasgow
10.04.93	Andrew Furlong W PTS 6 Swansea
10.09.93	Juan Garcia W PTS 6 San Antonio, USA
09.10.93	Ernie Loveridge W PTS 4 Manchester
18.12.93	Danny Juma DREW 6 Manchester
09.04.94	Kesem Clayton W RSC 1 Mansfield
04.06.94	Andrew Furlong W RSC 2 Cardiff
17.08.94	Andrew Jervis W RSC 1 Sheffield
19.11.94	Chris Richards W RSC 3 Cardiff
04.02.95	Bruno Westenberghs W RSC 1 Cardiff
04.03.95	Marvin O'Brien W RSC 6 Livingston
06.05.95	Steve Goodwin W CO 1 Shepton Mallet
10.06.95	Martin Jolley W CO 1 Manchester

Career: 14 contests, won 13, drew 1.

Robbie Regan (right) seen here winning the European title from Salvatore Fanni
Les Clark

Yifru Retta

Canning Town. *Born* Ethiopia, 24 September, 1971
S. Featherweight. Ht. 5'8½"
Managers T. Lawless/M. Duff

10.11.90	Paul Kaoma L RSC 4 Monsano, Italy
15.02.91	Branco Kuslakovic W PTS 4 Wiener Neustadt, Austria
01.03.91	Esteban Perez W PTS 6 Wiener Neustadt, Austria
05.07.91	Mauro Corrente L CO 4 Civitavecchia, Italy
14.06.93	Lee Fox W RTD 3 Bayswater
04.10.93	Vince Burns W PTS 6 Mayfair
07.12.93	Robert Braddock W RSC 2 Bethnal Green
04.03.94	Derek Amory W RSC 1 Bethnal Green
22.03.94	John Stovin W RSC 3 Bethnal Green
11.05.94	Bamana Dibateza W PTS 6 Stevenage
11.10.94	Chris Jickells W PTS 6 Bethnal Green
09.12.94	Kelton McKenzie W PTS 4 Bethnal Green
20.04.95	Carl Tilley W PTS 6 Mayfair

Career: 13 contests, won 11, lost 2.

Lewis Reynolds

Lambeth. *Born* Hatfield, 25 February, 1970
Lightweight. Ht. 5'8"
Manager D. Powell/F. Maloney

29.09.94	Andrew Reed W PTS 4 Bethnal Green
18.11.94	Jason Hutson L RSC 3 Bracknell
25.03.95	Vince Burns W RSC 3 Millwall
25.05.95	Simon Frailing W CO 1 Reading
16.06.95	Wayne Jones W PTS 4 Southwark

Career: 5 contests, won 4, lost 1.

Mark Reynolds

Sudbury. *Born* Sudbury, 27 July, 1969
Flyweight. Ht. 5'5½"
Manager F. Maloney

24.09.94	Shaun Norman W PTS 4 Wembley
12.11.94	Vince Feeney L PTS 6 Dublin
07.02.95	Danny Lawson W PTS 4 Ipswich
17.05.95	Neil Parry W PTS 6 Ipswich
04.06.95	Anthony Hanna W PTS 10 Bethnal Green
	(Elim. British Flyweight Title)

Career: 5 contests, won 4, lost 1.

Ryan Rhodes   Les Clark

Ryan Rhodes

Sheffield. *Born* Sheffield, 20 November, 1976
Middleweight. Ht. 5'8½"
Manager B. Ingle

04.02.95	Lee Crocker W RSC 2 Cardiff
04.03.95	Shamus Casey W CO 1 Livingston
06.05.95	Chris Richards W PTS 6 Shepton Mallet

Career: 3 contests, won 3.

Devon Rhooms

Sydenham. *Born* London, 24 July, 1965
Cruiserweight. Ht. 6'1"
Manager G. Steene

31.08.93	Steve Yorath W PTS 6 Croydon
02.12.93	Terry Dunstan L RSC 1 Sheffield
22.03.94	Phil Soundy L CO 2 Bethnal Green
02.06.94	John Keeton L RSC 2 Tooting
28.07.94	Steve Osborne L PTS 6 Tooting

Career: 5 contests, won 1, lost 4.

Chris Richards

Nottingham. *Born* Nottingham, 4 April, 1964
Middleweight. Ht. 5'5¼"
Manager Self

07.09.87	Darren Bowen W RSC 1 Mayfair
23.09.87	Shaun Cummins L PTS 6 Loughborough
13.10.87	Damien Denny L PTS 6 Windsor
03.11.87	Brian Robinson L PTS 6 Bethnal Green
18.01.88	Stan King W CO 5 Mayfair
29.01.88	Lou Ayres W RSC 3 Holborn
26.03.88	Terry Magee L PTS 8 Belfast
28.05.88	Tony Collins L RSC 3 Kensington
10.10.88	Antonio Fernandez L PTS 6 Edgbaston
23.11.88	Antonio Fernandez L PTS 6 Solihull
10.12.88	Terry Morrill L PTS 6 Crystal Palace
16.01.89	Mark Holden L DIS 3 Northampton
24.01.89	Ian Strudwick L PTS 6 Wandsworth
13.02.89	G. L. Booth W RSC 8 Manchester
10.03.89	Theo Marius L RSC 2 Brentwood
08.05.89	G. L. Booth W RSC 2 Manchester
22.05.89	B. K. Bennett L PTS 8 Mayfair
16.05.90	Mick Duncan L PTS 6 Hull
04.06.90	Antonio Fernandez L PTS 8 Edgbaston
15.06.90	Gary Pemberton W RTD 1 Telford
14.09.90	Shamus Casey W PTS 6 Telford
17.10.90	Gary Osborne L PTS 8 Stoke
13.11.90	Andrew Tucker W RSC 2 Hartlepool
13.12.90	Neville Brown L RSC 2 Dewsbury
13.02.91	Delroy Waul L PTS 6 Wembley
16.04.91	Paul Smith DREW 6 Nottingham
24.04.91	Colin Pitters L RSC 6 Stoke
26.11.91	Adrian Strachan L PTS 6 Bethnal Green
26.03.92	Glen Payton W PTS 6 Telford
18.06.92	Stefan Wright L PTS 6 Peterborough
18.07.92	Quinn Paynter L RSC 6 Manchester
06.10.92	Paul Busby L PTS 6 Antwerp, Belgium
13.12.93	Peter Waudby L PTS 6 Cleethorpes
16.02.94	Gilbert Jackson L RSC 2 Stevenage
25.04.94	Warren Stowe L PTS 6 Bury
25.05.94	Kevin Adamson L RSC 2 Stoke
27.10.94	Mark Baker L PTS 6 Millwall
19.11.94	Robin Reid L RSC 3 Cardiff
17.01.95	Andrew Flute L PTS 6 Worcester
14.02.95	Gilbert Jackson L RTD 2 Bethnal Green

(continued)

20.04.95	Paul Wright L PTS 6 Liverpool
06.05.95	Ryan Rhodes L PTS 6 Shepton Mallet
13.05.95	Cornelius Carr L RTD 3 Glasgow

Career: 43 contests, won 9, drew 1, lost 33.

Ian Richardson

Newcastle. *Born* Newcastle, 26 March, 1971
S. Featherweight. Ht. 5'6"
Manager N. Fawcett

06.12.93	Dean James W RSC 4 Bradford
03.03.94	Fred Reeve W PTS 6 Newcastle
28.04.94	Fred Reeve W PTS 6 Hull
09.05.94	Leo Turner DREW 6 Bradford
22.09.94	Dave Clavering L RSC 1 Bury
24.11.94	Leo Turner L RSC 6 Newcastle

Career: 6 contests, won 3, drew 1, lost 2.

Peter Richardson

Middlesbrough. *Born* Middlesbrough, 24 June, 1970
L. Welterweight. Ht. 5'9¼"
Manager F. Maloney

23.02.95	John O. Johnson W RSC 5 Southwark
27.04.95	Carl Roberts W RSC 1 Bethnal Green
25.05.95	Everald Williams W RSC 6 Reading

Career: 3 contests, won 3.

Wayne Rigby

Manchester. *Born* Manchester, 19 July, 1973
Lightweight. Ht. 5'6"
Manager J. Doughty

27.02.92	Lee Fox L PTS 6 Liverpool
08.06.92	Leo Turner W PTS 6 Bradford
02.07.92	Leo Turner W CO 5 Middleton
05.10.92	Colin Innes W PTS 6 Manchester
01.12.92	John T. Kelly L PTS 6 Hartlepool
02.06.94	Kid McAuley W PTS 6 Middleton
13.06.94	Chris Clarkson W PTS 6 Liverpool
22.09.94	Mark Hargreaves W PTS 6 Bury
06.03.95	Kelton McKenzie L PTS 8 Leicester
18.05.95	John T. Kelly W PTS 6 Middleton
05.06.95	Hugh Collins W RSC 4 Glasgow

Career: 11 contests, won 8, lost 3.

Brian Robb

Telford. *Born* Liverpool, 5 April, 1967
S. Featherweight. Ht. 5'6"
Manager Self

14.02.89	Miguel Matthews L RSC 2 Wolverhampton
27.03.90	Neil Leitch W PTS 6 Wolverhampton
09.05.90	Peter Judson L PTS 6 Solihull
22.05.90	Nicky Lucas W PTS 6 Canvey Island
20.06.90	Paul Harvey L PTS 6 Basildon
09.10.90	Des Gargano W PTS 6 Wolverhampton
24.10.90	Paul Harvey L RSC 2 Dudley
23.01.91	Jason Primera L RSC 7 Solihull
04.03.91	Pete Buckley L RSC 7 Birmingham
05.06.91	Pete Buckley L PTS 10 Wolverhampton
	(Vacant Midlands Area S. Featherweight Title)
29.08.91	Renny Edwards W PTS 6 Oakengates
31.10.91	Miguel Matthews DREW 6 Oakengates
05.12.91	Neil Leitch W CO 2 Oakengates
20.02.92	Pete Buckley L RSC 10 Oakengates
	(Midlands Area S. Featherweight Title Challenge)

26.03.92	Kelton McKenzie L RSC 4 Telford	
13.10.92	Paul Harvey L RSC 2 Mayfair	
04.12.92	Kevin Middleton L RSC 1 Telford	
22.02.95	Andrew Smith W PTS 6 Telford	
21.04.95	Andrew Smith DREW 6 Dudley	
23.06.95	Chris Francis L RSC 1 Bethnal Green	

Career: 20 contests, won 6, drew 2, lost 12.

Andy Roberts

Doncaster. *Born* Doncaster, 4 March, 1976
Flyweight. Ht. 5'3"
Manager J. Rushton

20.10.94 Robert Grubb DREW 6 Walsall
12.12.94 Jason Morris W PTS 6 Doncaster
09.02.95 Robert Grubb DREW 6 Doncaster
22.03.95 Michael Edwards L PTS 6 Stoke
06.04.95 Steve Williams L PTS 6 Sheffield
05.05.95 Jason Morris W PTS 6 Doncaster
22.06.95 Paul Quarmby L PTS 6 Houghton le Spring
30.06.95 Stefy Bull L PTS 4 Doncaster

Career: 8 contests, won 2, drew 2, lost 4.

Carl Roberts

Blackburn. *Born* Blackburn, 19 March, 1970
Lightweight. Ht. 5'7"
Manager B. Myers

26.09.90 Peter Judson L PTS 6 Manchester
22.10.90 Shaun Hickey W CO 4 Manchester
26.11.90 Colin Innes W RSC 3 Bury
17.12.90 Trevor Royal W PTS 6 Manchester
29.01.91 Derek Amory L PTS 4 Stockport
28.02.91 Des Gargano L PTS 6 Bury
03.04.91 Neil Leitch L RSC 6 Manchester
19.09.91 Colin Innes W PTS 4 Stockport
14.10.91 Kevin Lowe W PTS 6 Manchester
16.12.91 Robert Braddock W PTS 6 Manchester
10.03.92 Graham O'Malley L PTS 6 Bury
07.12.92 Mike Deveney L PTS 6 Manchester
15.02.93 Lee Fox W PTS 6 Manchester
25.02.93 Ian McGirr L PTS 6 Burnley
28.06.93 Kid McAuley L PTS 6 Morecambe
11.11.93 Brian Eccles W RSC 1 Burnley
19.01.94 Paul Bowen W PTS 6 Solihull
24.05.94 Liam Dineen L PTS 6 Sunderland
06.06.94 Alan Graham W PTS 6 Manchester
20.10.94 Leo Turner L RSC 3 Middleton
02.03.95 Peter Till L RSC 6 Glasgow
27.04.95 Peter Richardson L RSC 1 Bethnal Green

Career: 22 contests, won 10, lost 12.

Dewi Roberts

Bangor. *Born* Bangor, 11 September, 1968
L. Welterweight. Ht. 5'10"
Manager Self

28.11.91 Gavin Lane L PTS 6 Evesham
11.02.92 Edward Lloyd L RSC 1 Cardiff
11.05.92 Nigel Burder W CO 3 Llanelli
22.11.93 Steve McLevy L RSC 1 Glasgow
24.02.94 Paul Robinson W RSC 6 Walsall
04.03.94 Jason Rowland L RSC 1 Bethnal Green
17.06.94 Paul Dyer L PTS 6 Plymouth
25.06.94 Carl van Bailey W RSC 2 Cullompton
02.09.94 Keith Marner L PTS 6 Spitalfields
17.09.94 Paul Knights L PTS 6 Crawley
25.10.94 Everald Williams L PTS 6 Southwark
09.11.94 Jason Beard L RSC 4 Millwall
17.02.95 Georgie Smith L RSC 2 Crawley

Career: 13 contests, won 3, lost 10.

Steve Roberts, the latest West Ham prospect, hammers Andy Peach, prior to a third round stoppage win

Les Clark

Steve Roberts

West Ham. *Born* Newham, 3 December, 1972
Welterweight. Ht. 5'11"
Manager B. Hearn

16.03.95 Julian Eavis W PTS 6 Basildon
23.05.95 Andy Peach W RSC 3 Potters Bar
13.06.95 Robbie Dunn W RSC 3 Basildon

Career: 3 contests, won 3.

Jamie Robinson

West Ham. *Born* London, 12 September, 1968
L. Middleweight. Ht. 5'9"
Manager Self

17.08.90 Duke de Palma W PTS 4 Las Vegas, USA
04.10.90 Rodney Knox L RSC 1 Atlantic City, USA
23.10.91 Dave Whittle W RSC 4 Bethnal Green
13.11.91 Michael Oliver W PTS 6 Bethnal Green
11.02.92 Julian Eavis W PTS 6 Barking
02.04.92 Mark Jay W PTS 6 Basildon
22.10.92 Gary Pemberton W RSC 3 Bethnal Green
17.12.92 Lee Crocker W RTD 2 Barking
27.02.93 Russell Washer W PTS 6 Dagenham
31.03.93 John Duckworth W RSC 3 Barking
10.11.93 Stuart Dunn W PTS 6 Bethnal Green
17.02.94 Steve Scott W CO 2 Dagenham
21.09.94 Russell Washer L PTS 6 Cardiff

Career: 13 contests, won 11, lost 2.

Tim Robinson

Grimsby. *Born* Cleethorpes, 28 June, 1968
L. Heavyweight. Ht. 5'10"
Manager Self

21.09.92 Paul Hanlon L PTS 6 Cleethorpes
16.10.92 Griff Jones L RSC 3 Hull

14.12.92	Mohammed Malik W RSC 3 Cleethorpes	
14.01.93	Hussain Shah L PTS 4 Mayfair	
05.02.93	Eric Noi L RSC 4 Manchester	
10.05.93	Mark Smallwood L RSC 4 Cleethorpes	
26.06.93	Dale Nixon L RSC 2 Keynsham	
10.02.94	Phil Ball L PTS 6 Hull	
07.03.94	Phil Ball L PTS 6 Doncaster	
15.03.94	Steve Loftus L PTS 6 Stoke	
09.04.94	Mark Delaney L RSC 2 Bethnal Green	
28.06.94	Tony Griffiths L RSC 6 Mayfair	
10.09.94	Eric Noi L RSC 1 Birmingham	
11.10.94	Monty Wright L CO 1 Bethnal Green	
24.11.94	Darren Littlewood L PTS 6 Hull	
13.12.94	Eddie Knight L RTD 2 Potters Bar	
21.01.95	John Wilson L RSC 1 Glasgow	

Career: 17 contests, won 1, lost 16.

Derek Roche

Leeds. *Born* New Ross, 19 July, 1972
L. Middleweight. Ht. 5'9"
Manager J. Celebanski

26.09.94 Michael Alexander W RSC 6 Bradford
05.12.94 Shamus Casey W PTS 6 Bradford
30.01.95 Carl Smith W RSC 3 Bradford
23.02.95 Charlie Paine W CO 1 Hull
25.03.95 Rob Stevenson W PTS 6 Rothwell
12.06.95 Paul King W PTS 6 Bradford

Career: 6 contests, won 6.

Vince Rose

Tottenham. *Born* London, 9 July, 1968
L. Middleweight. Ht. 5'8"
Manager B. Hearn

13.10.92 Ojay Abrahams W RSC 3 Mayfair
14.11.92 Marty Duke W PTS 6 Cardiff
30.01.93 Ojay Abrahams DREW 6 Brentwood
11.05.93 Gary Pemberton W PTS 6 Norwich
11.01.94 Warren Stephens W PTS 6 Bethnal Green
09.02.94 Ojay Abrahams L PTS 6 Brentwood
28.06.94 Said Bennajem L PTS 6 Mayfair
27.08.94 Matthew Turner W RSC 4 Cardiff
07.11.94 Dennis Berry W PTS 6 Bethnal Green
21.02.95 Dave Johnson L PTS 8 Sunderland
14.04.95 Danny Juma L RSC 3 Belfast
23.06.95 Nicky Thurbin L PTS 10 Bethnal Green
(Vacant Southern Area L. Middleweight Title)

Career: 12 contests, won 6, drew 1, lost 5.

(Paul) Laurence Rowe (Page)

Manchester. *Born* Manchester, 26 March, 1972
L. Heavyweight. Ht. 5'11"
Manager N. Basso

06.06.94 Pat Durkin W PTS 6 Manchester
25.03.95 David Flowers L PTS 6 Rothwell

Career: 2 contests, won 1, lost 1.

Jason Rowland

West Ham. *Born* London, 6 August, 1970
L. Welterweight. Ht. 5'9¼"
Manager Self

19.09.89 Terry Smith W RSC 1 Millwall
15.11.89 Mike Morrison W PTS 6 Reading
14.02.90 Eamonn Payne W PTS 6 Millwall
17.04.90 Dave Jenkins W CO 1 Millwall

138

Jason Rowland (left) picked up win number 18 when stopping Richard Swallow inside two rounds last December Les Clark

22.05.90	Mike Morrison W PTS 6 St Albans
12.02.91	Vaughan Carnegie W PTS 6 Basildon
07.03.91	Vaughan Carnegie W CO 2 Basildon
11.12.91	Brian Cullen W RSC 4 Basildon
30.04.92	Steve Pollard W RSC 2 Kensington
17.12.92	Jimmy Vincent W PTS 6 Wembley
10.02.93	Seth Jones W RSC 2 Lewisham
18.03.93	John Smith W PTS 6 Lewisham
04.03.94	Dewi Roberts W RSC 1 Bethnal Green
26.04.94	Ray Hood W CO 1 Bethnal Green
12.09.94	Steve Burton W RSC 1 Mayfair
11.10.94	Phil Found W RSC 4 Bethnal Green
09.11.94	Floyd Churchill W RSC 2 Millwall
09.12.94	Richard Swallow W RSC 2 Bethnal Green
03.03.95	Nigel Bradley W RSC 3 Bethnal Green

Career: 19 contests, won 19.

Roy Rowland

West Ham. *Born* London, 19 May, 1967
Welterweight. Ht. 5'10"
Manager Self

29.10.86	Nick Lucas W PTS 6 Muswell Hill
03.12.86	Nick Meloscia W PTS 6 Muswell Hill
13.01.87	Ray Golding W PTS 6 Oldham
04.03.87	Andy Cox W RSC 3 Basildon
22.09.87	Brian Wareing W CO 1 Bethnal Green
03.11.87	Wil Halliday W RSC 1 Bethnal Green
02.12.87	Roy Callaghan W PTS 6 Kensington
09.03.88	Dave Haggarty W RSC 1 Bethnal Green
29.03.88	Nick Meloscia L RSC 1 Bethnal Green
07.09.88	Kelvin Mortimer W PTS 6 Reading
01.11.88	Kevin Hayde W PTS 6 Reading
25.01.89	Andy Tonks W RTD 1 Bethnal Green
15.02.89	Mike Russell W RSC 2 Bethnal Green
28.03.89	Paul Seddon W RSC 3 Bethnal Green
14.09.89	John Smith W RSC 3 Basildon
15.11.89	Lloyd Lee W PTS 8 Reading
25.04.90	Peter Eubank W RSC 8 Millwall
12.02.91	Paul Lynch L RTD 4 Basildon
06.06.91	Mark Kelly W RSC 4 Barking
02.10.91	Peter Eubank W PTS 8 Barking
25.03.92	Humphrey Harrison W CO 7 Dagenham

28.10.92	Darren Morris W RSC 2 Kensington
17.12.92	Gary Logan L RSC 4 Wembley
	(Vacant Southern Area Welterweight Title)
10.11.93	Peter Waudby L RSC 5 Watford
11.05.94	Julian Eavis W RSC 4 Stevenage
23.09.94	Paul Denton L RSC 5 Bethnal Green

Career: 26 contests, won 21, lost 5.

Trevor Royal

Bristol. *Born* Bristol, 8 May, 1962
Lightweight. Ht. 5'7"
Manager P. Dwyer

15.09.90	Dave Jenkins L RSC 4 Bristol
29.10.90	Peter Campbell L PTS 6 Nottingham
21.11.90	Gavin Fitzpatrick W PTS 6 Chippenham
08.12.90	Gavin Fitzpatrick W RSC 1 Bristol
17.12.90	Carl Roberts L PTS 6 Manchester
06.02.91	Steve Hearn DREW 6 Battersea
18.02.91	Felix Kelly L RSC 4 Windsor
03.04.91	Terry Riley W RTD 4 Bethnal Green
10.04.91	Robert Smyth L PTS 6 Newport
22.04.91	Kevin Toomey L PTS 6 Bradford
01.05.91	Bernard Paul L CO 1 Bethnal Green
10.06.91	Bobby Beckles L PTS 6 Manchester
09.03.93	Mike Morrison L PTS 6 Bristol
24.03.93	Bernard McComiskey L RSC 6 Belfast
22.04.93	Mark O'Callaghan L PTS 6 Mayfair
27.05.93	Greg Upton L CO 2 Bristol
	(Vacant Western Area S. Featherweight Title)
25.07.93	Nick Boyd L PTS 6 Oldham
31.08.93	Dennis Griffin L RSC 1 Croydon
04.03.94	Michael Hermon L PTS 6 Weston super Mare
28.03.94	Hugh Collins L RSC 2 Musselburgh
17.06.94	Wayne Jones L PTS 6 Plymouth
07.12.94	G. G. Goddard L RSC 6 Stoke
24.02.95	Stevie Bolt W RSC 5 Weston super Mare
05.06.95	Robbie Sivyer L CO 5 Birmingham

Career: 24 contests, won 4, drew 1, lost 19.

Danny Ruegg

Bournemouth. *Born* Poole, 28 November, 1974
S. Bantamweight. Ht. 5'5"
Manager J. Bishop

30.09.93	Johnny Simpson L PTS 6 Hayes
17.02.94	Paul Webster L PTS 4 Dagenham
04.03.94	Darren Greaves L PTS 6 Weston super Mare
17.06.94	Danny Lawson L PTS 6 Plymouth
25.10.94	Jon Pegg W PTS 6 Edgbaston
16.11.94	Chris Lyons W PTS 6 Bloomsbury
18.02.95	Tony Falcone L PTS 10 Shepton Mallet
	(Vacant Western Area S. Bantamweight Title)
13.05.95	James Murray L PTS 6 Glasgow
10.06.95	Michael Gomez L PTS 4 Manchester

Career: 9 contests, won 2, lost 7.

Danny Ryan

Donegal. *Born* Glasgow, 6 March, 1973
Middleweight. Ht. 5'10"
Manager F. Warren

06.05.95	Paul Matthews W PTS 6 Shepton Mallet
02.06.95	Peter Mitchell W PTS 6 Bethnal Green

Career: 2 contests, won 2.

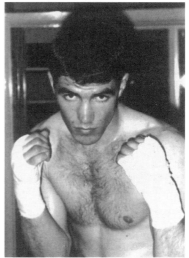

Danny Ryan Les Clark

Lawrence Ryan

Nuneaton. *Born* Kingston, 22 December, 1967
S. Middleweight. Ht. 5'10"
Manager J. Griffin

06.06.95	Shaun Hendry L RSC 1 Leicester

Career: 1 contest, lost 1.

Paul Ryan

Hackney. *Born* South Ockenham, 2 February, 1965
L. Welterweight. Ht. 5'8"
Manager F. Warren

26.09.91	Chris Mylan W PTS 6 Dunstable
18.01.92	Alex Sterling W RSC 4 Kensington
25.03.92	Michael Clynch W RSC 4 Dagenham
16.05.92	Greg Egbuniwe W RSC 4 Muswell Hill
26.09.92	Korso Aleain W CO 4 Earls Court
17.12.92	Rick Bushell W RSC 1 Barking
03.02.93	Neil Smith W RSC 1 Earls Court
27.02.93	Mike Morrison W PTS 6 Dagenham
15.09.93	Shaun Cogan W RSC 3 Ashford
10.11.93	Steve Phillips W RSC 3 Bethnal Green
17.02.94	Rob Stewart W RSC 4 Dagenham
09.04.94	Carl Wright W RSC 6 Mansfield
17.08.94	John Smith W RTD 2 Sheffield
10.09.94	Dave Lovell W RSC 3 Birmingham
09.11.94	Massimo Bertozzi W RSC 2 San Remo, Italy
04.02.95	George Wilson W RSC 4 Cardiff
25.02.95	Paul Denton W RSC 4 Millwall
13.05.95	Jorge Aquino W RSC 4 Glasgow

Career: 18 contests, won 18.

Ricky Sackfield

Salford. *Born* Birmingham, 11 April, 1967
Welterweight. Ht. 5'7"
Managers F. Warren/N. Basso

30.04.91	Willie Yeardsley W PTS 4 Stockport
19.09.91	Seth Jones W RSC 1 Stockport
21.10.91	Rob Stewart L PTS 6 Bury
21.01.92	David Thompson W CO 1 Stockport
03.02.92	Scott Doyle W PTS 6 Manchester
09.03.92	John O. Johnson L PTS 6 Manchester
31.03.92	Carl Wright L RSC 1 Stockport
24.09.92	Mark Legg L PTS 6 Stockport
15.02.93	Robert Lloyd W RSC 4 Manchester
26.03.93	Soren Sondergaard L RSC 2 Copenhagen, Denmark
12.06.95	Wayne Windle W PTS 6 Manchester

Career: 11 contests, won 6, lost 5.

Paul Salmon

Plymouth. *Born* Plymouth, 27 March, 1971
Welterweight. Ht. 5'9½"
Manager N. Christian

12.10.94	Anthony Huw Williams L RSC 4 Sheffield
18.11.94	Dennis Gardner L RSC 1 Bracknell
24.02.95	Billy McDougall W PTS 6 Weston super Mare
28.04.95	Frank Olsen L RSC 2 Randers, Denmark

Career: 4 contests, won 1, lost 3.

Chris Saunders

Barnsley. *Born* Barnsley, 15 August, 1969
Welterweight. Ht. 5'8"
Manager B. Ingle

22.02.90	Malcolm Melvin W PTS 4 Hull
10.04.90	Mike Morrison W PTS 6 Doncaster
20.05.90	Justin Graham W RSC 3 Sheffield
29.11.90	Ross Hale L PTS 6 Bayswater
05.03.91	Rocky Ferrari L PTS 4 Glasgow
19.03.91	Richard Woolgar W RSC 3 Leicester
26.03.91	Felix Kelly L PTS 6 Bethnal Green
17.04.91	Billy Schwer L RSC 1 Kensington
16.05.91	Richard Burton L PTS 6 Liverpool
06.06.91	Mark Tibbs W RSC 6 Barking
30.06.91	Billy Schwer L RSC 3 Southwark
01.08.91	James Jiora L PTS 6 Dewsbury
03.10.91	Gary Flear L PTS 6 Burton
24.10.91	Ron Shinkwin W PTS 6 Dunstable

21.11.91	Jason Matthews L RSC 4 Burton
30.01.92	John O. Johnson L PTS 6 Southampton
11.02.92	Eddie King W RSC 4 Wolverhampton
27.02.92	Richard Burton L PTS 10 Liverpool *(Vacant Central Area L. Welterweight Title)*
09.09.92	John O. Johnson DREW 6 Stoke
01.10.92	Mark McCreath L RSC 4 Telford
01.12.92	Shea Neary L PTS 6 Liverpool
22.02.93	Cham Joof L PTS 4 Eltham
16.03.93	Mark Elliot L PTS 6 Wolverhampton
26.04.93	Dean Hollington W RSC 5 Lewisham
23.10.93	Michael Smyth L PTS 6 Cardiff
02.12.93	Rob Stewart L PTS 4 Sheffield
03.03.94	Kevin Lueshing W RSC 4 Ebbw Vale
04.06.94	Jose Varela W CO 2 Dortmund, Germany
26.08.94	Julian Eavis W PTS 6 Barnsley
26.09.94	Julian Eavis W PTS 6 Cleethorpes
26.10.94	Lindon Scarlett W PTS 8 Leeds
17.12.94	Roberto Welin W RSC 7 Cagliari, Italy

Career: 32 contests, won 15, drew 1, lost 16.

Lindon Scarlett

Dudley. *Born* Dudley, 11 January, 1967
Midlands Area Welterweight Champion.
Ht. 5'10"
Manager M. Duff

22.04.87	Tommy Shiels L PTS 6 Kensington
07.05.87	Dusty Miller W PTS 6 Bayswater
09.11.87	Sean Heron L PTS 6 Glasgow
20.01.88	Simon Paul W PTS 6 Solihull
12.04.88	Ted Kershaw L RSC 7 Oldham
11.10.89	Carlo Colarusso W PTS 8 Stoke
22.11.89	Carlo Colarusso W PTS 8 Solihull
06.12.89	Julian Eavis W PTS 8 Stoke
14.02.90	Wayne Ellis DREW 6 Millwall
13.03.90	Romolo Casamonica L PTS 8 Milan, Italy
08.05.90	Mickey Lloyd L RSC 2 Brentford
18.10.90	Kevin Spratt W RSC 2 Birmingham
16.11.90	Tony Gibbs W PTS 6 Telford
19.03.91	Des Robinson W RSC 4 Birmingham
24.10.91	Razor Addo W PTS 8 Bayswater
22.01.92	Kelvin Mortimer W RSC 1 Solihull
08.02.92	Javier Castillejos L PTS 8 Madrid, Spain
23.05.92	Chris Peters DREW 8 Birmingham
15.02.93	Gordon Blair W CO 4 Mayfair
27.10.93	Chris Peters W PTS 8 West Bromwich
26.01.94	Rick North W RSC 6 Birmingham *(Vacant Midlands Area Welterweight Title)*
10.09.94	Del Bryan L PTS 12 Birmingham *(British Welterweight Title Challenge)*
26.10.94	Chris Saunders L PTS 8 Leeds

Career: 23 contests, won 13, drew 2, lost 8.

Bruce Scott

Hackney. *Born* Jamaica, 16 August, 1969
L. Heavyweight. Ht. 5'9½"
Manager M. Duff

25.04.91	Mark Bowen L PTS 6 Mayfair
16.09.91	Randy B. Powell W RSC 5 Mayfair
21.11.91	Steve Osborne W PTS 6 Burton
27.04.92	John Kaighin W CO 4 Mayfair
07.09.92	Lee Prudden W PTS 6 Bethnal Green
03.12.92	Mark Pain W RSC 5 Lewisham
15.02.93	Paul McCarthy W PTS 6 Mayfair
22.04.93	Sean O'Phoenix W RSC 3 Mayfair
14.06.93	John Oxenham W RSC 1 Bayswater

04.10.93	Simon McDougall W PTS 6 Mayfair
16.12.93	Bobby Mack W RSC 4 Newport
05.04.94	Steve Osborne W RSC 5 Bethnal Green
17.10.94	Bobbi Joe Edwards W PTS 8 Mayfair
09.12.94	John Keeton W CO 2 Bethnal Green
19.04.95	Nigel Rafferty W RSC 2 Bethnal Green
19.05.95	Cordwell Hylton W RSC 1 Southwark

Career: 16 contests, won 15, lost 1.

Kenny Scott

Chesterfield. *Born* Chesterfield, 23 April, 1967
Welterweight. Ht. 6'1"
Manager M. Shinfield

25.06.93	Maurice Forbes L RSC 2 Battersea
22.09.93	Colin Anderson L PTS 6 Chesterfield
03.11.93	Chris Pollock L PTS 6 Worcester
30.11.93	Adey Allen L PTS 6 Leicester
09.11.94	Brian Coleman W PTS 6 Stafford
15.12.94	Billy McDougall L RSC 3 Evesham
22.03.95	Shaun Stokes L RSC 1 Stoke

Career: 7 contests, won 1, lost 6.

Paul Scott

Newbiggin. *Born* Ashington, 27 November, 1969
L. Welterweight. Ht. 5'7"
Manager T. Conroy

06.10.94	Trevor George W PTS 6 Cramlington
24.10.94	James Jiora L PTS 6 Bradford
24.11.94	Ram Singh W PTS 6 Newcastle
20.03.95	Tommy Quinn L RSC 4 Glasgow
12.06.95	Lambsy Kayani L PTS 6 Bradford

Career: 5 contests, won 2, lost 3.

Greg Scott-Briggs

Chesterfield. *Born* Swaziland, 6 February, 1966
L. Heavyweight. Ht. 6'1"
Manager Self

04.02.92	Mark McBiane W PTS 6 Alfreton
03.03.92	Tony Colclough W RSC 2 Cradley Heath
30.03.92	Carl Smallwood L PTS 6 Coventry
27.04.92	Richard Atkinson L PTS 6 Bradford
28.05.92	Steve Walton W PTS 6 Gosforth
04.06.92	Joe Frater L PTS 6 Cleethorpes
30.09.92	Carl Smallwood L PTS 6 Solihull
17.03.93	Carl Smallwood L PTS 8 Stoke
26.04.93	Tony Colclough W RSC 4 Glasgow
08.06.93	Peter Flint W RSC 1 Derby
07.09.93	Steve Loftus W RSC 2 Stoke
22.09.93	Paul Hanlon W PTS 6 Chesterfield
04.11.93	Lee Archer L PTS 8 Stafford
24.11.93	Tony Colclough W PTS 6 Solihull
08.12.93	Lee Archer W RTD 6 Stoke
08.02.94	Nigel Rafferty L PTS 6 Wolverhampton
17.02.94	Lee Archer L PTS 8 Walsall
11.03.94	Monty Wright L CO 1 Bethnal Green
26.09.94	Dave Battey W RSC 4 Cleethorpes
11.10.94	Mark Smallwood L PTS 8 Wolverhampton
29.10.94	Mark Smallwood L PTS 6 Cannock
11.11.94	Thomas Hansvoll L PTS 4 Randers, Denmark
30.11.94	Monty Wright L PTS 6 Wolverhampton
06.03.95	Neil Simpson L RTD 5 Leicester

Career: 24 contests, won 10, lost 14.

Stefan Scriggins

Leicester. *Born* Leicester, 17 April, 1970
Welterweight. Ht. 6'2¼"
Manager C. Gunns

30.10.92	Bradley Mayo W PTS 10 Melbourne, Australia
05.12.92	Don Demezen W PTS 10 Lawnton, Australia
16.04.93	Danny Bellert W RSC 3 Strathpine, Australia
22.05.93	Danny Wilkinson W CO 1 Strathpine, Australia
10.07.93	Graham Cheney L PTS 10 Gold Coast, Australia
	(Australian Welterweight Title Challenge)
17.12.93	Bradley Mayo W DIS 6 Carrara, Australia
13.03.94	Sean Sullivan W PTS 8 Brighton, Australia
19.03.94	Paula Tuilau W PTS 10 Suva, Fiji
20.05.94	Luvthyo Kakaza L RSC 4 Capetown, South Africa
06.03.95	Gary Beardsley W PTS 6 Leicester
03.04.95	Nic Ingram W PTS 6 Northampton
05.06.95	Spencer McCracken W PTS 8 Birmingham

Career: 12 contests, won 10, lost 2.

Muhammad Shaffique

Huddersfield. *Born* Huddersfield, 19 February, 1969
S. Featherweight. Ht. 5'9"
Manager Self

07.02.89	Erwin Edwards W PTS 6 Southend
12.06.89	Mick Mulcahy W RSC 2 Manchester
12.12.89	Mick Moran L PTS 6 Brentford
05.02.90	Frankie Foster W PTS 6 Brierley Hill
12.11.90	Steve Walker L PTS 6 Stratford on Avon
27.11.90	Mark Geraghty W PTS 8 Glasgow
02.10.91	Elvis Parsley L CO 1 Solihull
28.11.94	Michael Brodie L RSC 2 Manchester
18.01.95	G. G. Goddard L RSC 2 Solihull
20.02.95	Robert Hay L RSC 2 Glasgow

Career: 10 contests, won 4, lost 6.

Charles Shepherd

Carlisle. *Born* Burnley, 28 June, 1970
Lightweight. Ht. 5'4"
Manager J. Doughty

28.10.91	Chris Aston W PTS 6 Leicester
31.01.92	Alan McDowall L RSC 3 Glasgow
18.05.92	Mark Legg W PTS 6 Marton
25.09.92	George Naylor W RSC 4 Liverpool
22.10.92	Didier Hughes L PTS 4 Bethnal Green
13.02.93	Nigel Wenton W PTS 8 Manchester
23.05.93	Cham Joof W PTS 4 Brockley
21.10.93	Karl Taylor W RTD 5 Bayswater
09.02.94	Justin Juuko L RSC 5 Bethnal Green
21.04.94	Tony Foster L PTS 10 Hull
	(Vacant Central Area Lightweight Title)
29.09.94	Frankie Foster W RSC 3 Tynemouth
08.03.95	Bamana Dibateza W PTS 8 Solihull
26.04.95	Kelton McKenzie W RSC 7 Solihull
23.05.95	Michael Ayers L RSC 3 Potters Bar
	(British Lightweight Title Challenge)

Career: 14 contests, won 9, lost 5.

Wayne Shepherd

Carlisle. *Born* Whiston, 3 June, 1959
Welterweight. Ht. 5'6"
Manager J. Doughty

07.10.91	Benji Joseph W PTS 6 Bradford
28.10.91	Noel Henry W PTS 6 Leicester
16.12.91	Dave Maj DREW 6 Manchester
03.02.92	Dave Maj L PTS 6 Manchester
30.03.92	Hughie Davey L PTS 6 Bradford
18.05.92	Dave Whittle W PTS 6 Marton
14.10.92	Richard Swallow L PTS 8 Stoke
31.10.92	George Scott L RSC 6 Earls Court
13.02.93	Delroy Waul L RSC 5 Manchester
31.03.93	Derek Grainger L RSC 4 Barking
11.06.93	Hughie Davey L PTS 6 Gateshead
06.09.93	Shea Neary L RTD 2 Liverpool
26.01.94	James McGee W PTS 6 Stoke
28.02.94	Craig Winter L PTS 6 Manchester
02.03.95	Denny Johnson L PTS 6 Cramlington
06.04.95	Shaun Stokes L PTS 6 Sheffield
22.05.95	Peter Varnavus W PTS 6 Morecambe
01.06.95	Tommy Quinn L PTS 6 Musselburgh

Career: 18 contests, won 5, drew 1, lost 12.

John Sillo (Sillitoe)

Liverpool. *Born* Oxford, 10 February, 1965
Featherweight. Ht. 5'5"
Manager S. Vaughan

28.09.93	Graham McGrath W PTS 6 Liverpool
11.12.93	Marty Chestnut W PTS 6 Liverpool
25.02.94	Craig Kelley W PTS 6 Chester
06.05.94	Chris Lyons W RSC 3 Liverpool
26.09.94	Pete Buckley W PTS 6 Liverpool
25.03.95	Garry Burrell W PTS 6 Chester
20.04.95	Pete Buckley W PTS 6 Liverpool

Career: 7 contests, won 7.

Gary Silvester

Hull. *Born* Hull, 6 June, 1974
Welterweight. Ht. 6'1"
Manager M. Toomey

06.10.94	Steve Lynch W PTS 6 Hull
27.04.95	Eddie Haley L RSC 2 Hull
08.06.95	Craig Lynch L RSC 3 Glasgow

Career: 3 contests, won 1, lost 2.

Neil Simpson

Coventry. *Born* London, 5 July, 1970
L. Heavyweight. Ht. 6'2"
Manager J. Griffin

04.10.94	Kenny Nevers W PTS 4 Mayfair
20.10.94	Johnny Hooks W RSC 2 Walsall
05.12.94	Chris Woollas L PTS 6 Cleethorpes
15.12.94	Paul Murray W PTS 6 Walsall
06.03.95	Greg Scott-Briggs W RTD 5 Leicester
17.03.95	Thomas Hansvoll L PTS 4 Copenhagen, Denmark
26.04.95	Craig Joseph L PTS 6 Solihull
11.05.95	Andy McVeigh L CO 2 Dudley
24.06.95	Dave Owens W RSC 1 Cleethorpes

Career: 9 contests, won 5, lost 4.

Neil Sinclair

Belfast. *Born* Belfast, 23 February, 1974
Welterweight. Ht. 5'10½"
Manager B. Hearn

14.04.95	Marty Duke W RSC 2 Belfast
27.05.95	Andrew Jervis L RSC 3 Belfast

Career: 2 contests, won 1, lost 1.

Jimmy Singh

Sheffield. *Born* Walsall, 15 October, 1971
S. Featherweight. Ht. 5'8"
Manager B. Ingle

04.06.95	Nelson Ide L CO 1 Bethnal Green

Career: 1 contest, lost 1.

(Raminderbir) Ram Singh

Wisbech. *Born* Crewe, 13 August, 1969
Lightweight. Ht. 5'11"
Manager B. Lee

06.06.94	Wahid Fats L RSC 3 Manchester
26.09.94	Robert Howard W PTS 6 Morecambe
17.11.94	Terry Whittaker L PTS 6 Sheffield
24.11.94	Paul Scott L PTS 6 Newcastle
05.12.94	Liam Dineen L PTS 6 Houghton le Spring
12.01.95	Steve Tuckett L RSC 6 Leeds
21.02.95	Glen Hopkins L RSC 1 Sunderland
03.04.95	Dave Madden L PTS 6 Northampton
27.04.95	Paul Hamilton W RSC 2 Hull
14.06.95	Terry Whittaker L PTS 6 Batley

Career: 10 contests, won 2, lost 8.

(Sukhdarshan) Tiger Singh (Mahal)

Peterborough. *Born* India, 28 October, 1970
Flyweight. Ht. 5'8"
Manager Self

10.12.92	Ian Baillie W PTS 6 Corby
11.05.93	Anthony Hanna L PTS 6 Norwich
06.10.93	Anthony Hanna L PTS 6 Solihull
28.10.93	Nick Tooley L PTS 6 Torquay
30.11.93	Vince Feeney L PTS 6 Leicester
02.03.94	Lyndon Kershaw L PTS 6 Solihull
09.05.94	Terry Gaskin W RSC 2 Bradford
20.09.94	Keith Knox L PTS 6 Musselburgh
28.11.94	Terry Gaskin W PTS 6 Manchester
08.03.95	Lyndon Kershaw L PTS 6 Solihull
26.04.95	Darren Noble W PTS 6 Solihull

Career: 11 contests, won 4, lost 7.

Robbie Sivyer

Alfreton. *Born* Chesterfield, 22 September, 1973
Lightweight. Ht. 5'9"
Manager J. Gaynor

26.04.93	Garry Burrell L PTS 6 Glasgow
07.06.93	Simon Hamblett W PTS 6 Walsall
29.06.93	Mark Allen L PTS 6 Edgbaston
22.09.93	John Stovin L PTS 6 Chesterfield
13.11.93	Wayne Jones L PTS 6 Cullompton
04.03.94	Wayne Jones L PTS 6 Weston super Mare
05.06.95	Trevor Royal W CO 5 Birmingham

Career: 7 contests, won 2, lost 5.

Trevor Small

Birmingham. *Born* Solihull, 26 February, 1968
Cruiserweight. Ht. 6'0"
Manager W. Swift

09.12.92	Sean O'Phoenix W PTS 6 Stoke
20.01.93	Art Stacey W PTS 6 Solihull
28.04.93	Tony Behan W PTS 6 Solihull
20.06.93	Albert Call DREW 6 Cleethorpes
06.10.93	Art Stacey W PTS 6 Solihull

02.11.93 Phil Soundy W RSC 6 Southwark
13.12.93 Albert Call L RSC 5 Cleethorpes
02.09.94 Andrew Benson L PTS 6 Spitalfields
20.12.94 Terry Dunstan L RTD 4 Bethnal Green
Career: 9 contests, won 5, drew 1, lost 3.

Mark Smallwood

Atherstone. *Born* Nuneaton, 30 January, 1975
S. Middleweight. Ht. 6'2"
Manager R. Gray

22.02.93 John Dempsey W CO 1 Bedworth
17.03.93 Sean Smith W RSC 1 Stoke
10.05.93 Tim Robinson W RSC 4 Cleethorpes
17.06.93 Phil Ball W RSC 1 Bedworth
24.11.93 Darren Littlewood W PTS 8 Solihull
24.02.94 Jerry Mortimer W PTS 6 Walsall
18.04.94 Gil Lewis W RSC 5 Walsall
23.05.94 Dean Ashton W RTD 3 Walsall
11.10.94 Greg Scott-Briggs W PTS 8 Wolverhampton
29.10.94 Greg Scott-Briggs W PTS 6 Cannock
29.11.94 Paul Murray W PTS 8 Wolverhampton
18.01.95 Marvin O'Brien W PTS 6 Solihull
Career: 12 contests, won 12.

Andrew Smith

Bedworth. *Born* Nuneaton, 15 February, 1975
Featherweight. Ht. 5'5"
Manager C. Gunns

20.05.94 Marc Smith DREW 6 Neath
16.09.94 Dennis Holbaek Pedersen L RSC 6 Aalborg, Denmark
07.12.94 Jon Pegg DREW 6 Stoke
07.02.95 Jon Pegg W PTS 6 Wolverhampton
22.02.95 Brian Robb L PTS 6 Telford
09.03.95 Robert Grubb DREW 6 Walsall
28.03.95 Robert Grubb W PTS 6 Wolverhampton
03.04.95 Niel Leggett L PTS 6 Northampton
21.04.95 Brian Robb DREW 6 Dudley
Career: 9 contests, won 2, drew 4, lost 3.

Carl Smith

Manchester. *Born* Hereford, 31 March, 1968
L. Middleweight. Ht. 5'9"
Manager N. Basso

29.11.93 Chris Mulcahy W CO 1 Manchester
26.01.94 Anthony Lawrence L RSC 4 Stoke
28.02.94 Japhet Hans W RSC 4 Manchester
18.04.94 Jimmy Alston L PTS 6 Manchester
06.06.94 Jimmy Alston DREW 6 Manchester
03.10.94 Peter Varnavas W RSC 2 Manchester
26.10.94 Rick North DREW 6 Stoke
30.01.95 Derek Roche L RSC 3 Bradford
25.03.95 Jon Stocks W PTS 6 Chester
12.06.95 John Duckworth L PTS 6 Manchester
Career: 10 contests, won 4, drew 2, lost 4.

Georgie Smith

Basildon. *Born* Basildon, 29 August, 1971
L. Welterweight. Ht. 5'10"
Manager B. Hearn

07.11.94 Malcolm Thomas W PTS 6 Bethnal Green
20.12.94 Stevie Bolt W RSC 2 Bethnal Green
17.02.95 Dewi Roberts W RSC 2 Crawley

16.03.95 Shaba Edwards W CO 2 Basildon
09.05.95 Wayne Jones W RSC 3 Basildon
13.06.95 Rudy Valentino W PTS 6 Basildon
Career: 6 contests, won 6.

Georgie Smith   Les Clark

John Smith

Liverpool. *Born* Liverpool, 13 October, 1959
L. Welterweight. Ht. 5'9"
Manager Self

26.06.86 Ray Golding W PTS 6 Edgbaston
22.09.86 John Townsley W PTS 6 Edgbaston
06.11.86 Robert Harkin L PTS 8 Glasgow
20.11.86 John Best L PTS 6 Bredbury
08.12.86 Gary Sommerville DREW 8 Edgbaston
18.03.87 John Best L RSC 2 Solihull
24.04.87 Brian Wareing L PTS 8 Liverpool
24.09.87 John Dickson L PTS 6 Glasgow
01.02.88 Peter Crook L PTS 6 Manchester
17.03.88 Mick Mason DREW 8 Sunderland
29.03.88 Paul Seddon W RSC 4 Marton
17.06.88 Gary Sommerville W RSC 5 Edgbaston
28.11.88 Gary Sommerville L PTS 8 Edgbaston
24.01.89 Mark Kelly L PTS 8 Kings Heath
22.03.89 John Davies L PTS 8 Solihull
17.07.89 Richard Adams W RSC 3 Stanmore
08.09.89 Muhammad Lovelock W PTS 6 Liverpool
14.09.89 Roy Rowland L RSC 3 Basildon
17.10.89 Jim Talbot L PTS 6 Oldham
25.10.89 Kevin Plant L PTS 6 Doncaster
10.11.89 Seamus O'Sullivan L PTS 6 Battersea
30.11.89 Dave Pierre L PTS 6 Mayfair
08.12.89 Allan Hall L RSC 2 Marton
29.01.90 Darren Mount L PTS 8 Liverpool
08.03.90 Dave Pierre L PTS 6 Peterborough
19.03.90 Brendan Ryan L PTS 6 Leicester
05.04.90 Darren Mount L PTS 8 Liverpool
04.05.90 Pete Roberts L PTS 6 Liverpool
24.09.90 Mark Dinnadge W RTD 2 Lewisham
09.10.90 Pete Roberts W PTS 8 Liverpool
13.11.90 Paul Charters L RSC 4 Hartlepool
21.01.91 Kris McAdam L PTS 6 Glasgow
07.02.91 Billy Schwer L RSC 2 Watford

26.03.91 Andrew Morgan L RSC 4 Wolverhampton
24.04.91 Andrew Morgan L PTS 6 Aberavon
16.05.91 Kevin Toomey L PTS 6 Liverpool
13.06.91 Kevin Toomey L PTS 6 Hull
25.07.91 Robert McCracken L RTD 1 Dudley
07.10.91 Pete Roberts L PTS 8 Liverpool
23.10.91 Dean Hollington L PTS 6 Bethnal Green
12.11.91 Mark Elliot L PTS 6 Wolverhampton
21.11.91 Richard Burton L PTS 6 Burton
02.12.91 Mike Calderwood DREW 8 Liverpool
19.12.91 Richard Burton L PTS 6 Oldham
01.02.92 George Scott L RSC 3 Birmingham
03.03.92 Paul Charters L PTS 8 Houghton le Spring
12.05.92 Ross Hale L CO 1 Crystal Palace
03.09.92 Chris Mulcahy DREW 6 Liverpool
25.09.92 Kevin McKillan L PTS 6 Liverpool
07.10.92 Alan Peacock DREW 6 Glasgow
12.11.92 Mark Tibbs L RSC 6 Bayswater
18.03.93 Jason Rowland L PTS 6 Lewisham
29.03.93 Shea Neary L PTS 6 Liverpool
13.09.93 Rob Stewart DREW 6 Middleton
22.09.93 Jonathan Thaxton L PTS 6 Wembley
27.10.93 Mark McCreath L RSC 7 West Bromwich
25.11.93 Charlie Kane L PTS 6 Tynemouth
21.02.94 Alan Peacock L RSC 4 Glasgow
28.03.94 Charlie Kane L PTS 6 Musselburgh
10.04.94 Kris McAdam W PTS 8 Glasgow
28.06.94 Malcolm Melvin L PTS 6 Edgbaston
17.08.94 Paul Ryan L RTD 2 Sheffield
19.09.94 Alan Peacock L PTS 8 Glasgow
28.09.94 Shaun Cogan L RSC 3 Glasgow
17.11.94 Nigel Bradley L PTS 6 Sheffield
29.11.94 Shaun Cogan L RSC 4 Cannock
25.01.95 Shea Neary L RSC 5 Stoke
24.02.95 Steve McLevy L PTS 6 Irvine
20.04.95 Andreas Panayi L RSC 4 Liverpool
12.06.95 Wahid Fats W CO 3 Manchester
Career: 70 contests, won 10, drew 6, lost 54.

Marc Smith

Swansea. *Born* Kingston, 31 August, 1974
Lightweight. Ht. 5'9"
Manager P. Boyce

20.05.94 Andrew Smith DREW 6 Neath
11.10.94 Mark Allen W PTS 6 Wolverhampton
20.10.94 Mark Allen L PTS 6 Walsall
09.03.95 Simon Hamblett L PTS 6 Walsall
16.03.95 Nelson Ide L RSC 4 Basildon
Career: 5 contests, won 1, drew 1, lost 3.

Neil Smith

Leicester. *Born* Leicester, 15 January, 1972
Lightweight. Ht. 6'1½"
Manager J. Griffin

13.12.90 Tony Silkstone L PTS 6 Dewsbury
06.02.91 Dennis Adams L PTS 6 Bethnal Green
14.03.91 John Naylor W RSC 6 Middleton
20.05.91 Elvis Parsley W RSC 5 Leicester
11.06.91 Lee Fox W PTS 6 Leicester
05.11.91 Neil Leitch W RSC 1 Leicester
04.02.92 Harry Escott L PTS 8 Alfreton
26.01.93 Norman Dhalie W PTS 4 Leicester
03.02.93 Paul Ryan L RSC 1 Earls Court
19.05.93 Dean Amory L PTS 6 Leicester
25.01.95 Anthony Maynard W PTS 6 Stoke
06.03.95 Gary Hiscox L PTS 6 Leicester
06.06.95 Kid McAuley W RTD 1 Leicester
Career: 13 contests, won 7, lost 6.

(Terry) T. J. Smith

Kettering. *Born* Kettering 17 October, 1967
Lightweight. Ht. 5'7½"
Manager C. Hogben

29.04.92	Floyd Churchill L RSC 2 Liverpool
10.12.92	Alan Graham L PTS 6 Corby
23.02.93	Patrick Parton W PTS 6 Kettering
29.03.93	Marco Fattore DREW 6 Mayfair
19.04.93	Lee Ryan W RSC 2 Northampton
18.05.93	Dean Martin W RSC 3 Kettering
23.11.93	Jimmy Phelan W PTS 6 Kettering
08.03.94	Andrew Reed W PTS 6 Kettering
17.05.94	Simon Frailing W RSC 1 Kettering
04.06.94	Gareth Jordan L RSC 1 Cardiff
05.12.94	Micky Hall W RTD 3 Houghton le Spring
21.02.95	Liam Dineen L PTS 6 Sunderland
05.04.95	Mark Breslin L PTS 6 Irvine
01.06.95	Mark Breslin L RSC 3 Musselburgh

Career: 14 contests, won 6, drew 1, lost 7.

Trevor Smith

Birmingham. *Born* Birmingham, 24
October, 1965
L. Welterweight. Ht. 5'8"
Manager E. Cashmore

04.02.95	Steve Burton W RSC 6 Cardiff
04.03.95	Mark Winters L PTS 6 Livingston
05.05.95	Shaun Stokes DREW 6 Doncaster

Career: 3 contests, won 1, drew 1, lost 1.

Michael Smyth

Rhoose. *Born* Caerphilly, 22 February,
1970
Welterweight. Ht. 5'9¾"
Manager D. Gardiner

02.05.91	Carl Brasier W RSC 2 Kensington
28.05.91	Rick North W RSC 1 Cardiff
18.07.91	Mike Morrison W RSC 2 Cardiff
03.09.91	Julian Eavis W PTS 6 Cardiff
20.11.91	Mike Russell W RSC 3 Cardiff
17.12.91	Julian Eavis W PTS 6 Cardiff
19.05.92	Ojay Abrahams W PTS 6 Cardiff

07.10.92	David Lake W CO 2 Barry
14.11.92	Des Robinson W PTS 6 Cardiff
10.07.93	Ernie Loveridge W RSC 6 Cardiff
23.10.93	Chris Saunders W PTS 6 Cardiff
12.03.94	Gordon Blair W RSC 4 Cardiff
21.07.94	Maurice Forbes W RSC 3 Battersea
24.09.94	Mike de Moss W RSC 1 Wembley
25.10.94	Scott Doyle W CO 1 Southwark
25.01.95	Rick North W DIS 4 Cardiff
17.06.95	Kevin Lueshing L RSC 3 Cardiff
	(Final Elim. British Welterweight Title)

Career: 17 contests, won 16, lost 1.

Mark Snipe

Brighton. *Born* Brighton, 9 March, 1972
L. Heavyweight. Ht. 6'1"
Manager P. Byrne

13.06.95	Michael Pinnock W PTS 6 Basildon

Career: 1 contest, won 1.

Phil Soundy

Basildon. *Born* Benfleet, 24 October, 1966
Cruiserweight. Ht. 5'11½"
Manager Self

04.10.89	Coco Collins W RSC 2 Basildon
24.10.89	Trevor Barry W RSC 1 Bethnal Green
14.02.90	Andy Balfe W RSC 3 Brentwood
28.03.90	Chris Coughlan W PTS 6 Bethnal Green
22.05.90	Cliff Curtis W PTS 6 Canvey Island
06.07.90	Steve Yorath W CO 3 Brentwood
12.09.90	Rob Albon W RSC 1 Bethnal Green
03.10.90	Steve Yorath W PTS 6 Basildon
12.12.90	David Haycock W RSC 3 Kensington
16.01.91	Chris Coughlan W PTS 6 Kensington
12.02.91	Gus Mendes W RSC 3 Basildon
07.03.91	Terry Duffus W RSC 2 Basildon
24.04.91	Steve Yorath L PTS 6 Basildon
11.09.91	Gus Mendes L RSC 3 Hammersmith
12.02.92	Steve Osborne W PTS 6 Wembley
22.04.92	Lee Prudden W RSC 5 Wembley
13.05.92	Tony Booth L PTS 6 Kensington
07.09.92	Dean Allen W RTD 4 Bethnal Green

28.10.92	Des Vaughan W RTD 4 Kensington
22.09.93	Art Stacey W PTS 6 Wembley
02.11.93	Trevor Small L RSC 6 Southwark
22.03.94	Devon Rhooms W CO 2 Bethnal Green
27.10.94	Steve Osborne W PTS 6 Millwall

Career: 23 contests, won 19, lost 4.

Jason Spurling

Swaffham. *Born* Kings Lynn, 11 December,
1971
L. Welterweight. Ht. 5'8"
Manager G. Holmes

17.05.95	Tom Welsh L PTS 4 Ipswich

Career: 1 contest, lost 1.

Jason Squire

Leicester. *Born* Leicester, 18 June, 1975
S. Bantamweight. Ht. 5'4½"
Manager J. Griffin

06.06.95	Michael Edwards W RSC 1 Leicester

Career: 1 contest, won 1.

(Mick) Art Stacey

Leeds. *Born* Leeds, 26 September, 1964
Cruiserweight. Ht. 6'0½"
Manager K. Tate

09.10.90	Trevor Barry DREW 6 Liverpool
06.11.90	Chris Coughlan W RSC 4 Southend
27.11.90	Allan Millett W PTS 6 Liverpool
21.02.91	Tony Lawrence W PTS 6 Leeds
18.03.91	Paul Gearon W RSC 1 Derby
16.04.91	Steve Osborne DREW 6 Nottingham
03.06.91	Dennis Afflick W PTS 6 Glasgow
11.11.91	Steve Osborne W PTS 6 Bradford
21.11.91	Gil Lewis L RSC 4 Stafford
20.01.92	John Pierre W PTS 8 Bradford
26.10.92	Ian Bulloch L PTS 6 Cleethorpes
27.11.92	Neils H. Madsen L PTS 8 Randers, Denmark
14.12.92	Albert Call L PTS 6 Cleethorpes
20.01.93	Trevor Small L PTS 6 Solihull
08.03.93	Lee Prudden DREW 6 Leeds
11.06.93	Ian Henry L PTS 6 Gateshead
25.06.93	Mark Prince L CO 2 Battersea
22.09.93	Phil Soundy L PTS 6 Wembley
06.10.93	Trevor Small L PTS 6 Solihull
13.10.93	Paul Lawson L RSC 2 Bethnal Green
25.11.93	Stevie R. Davies W PTS 6 Newcastle
08.12.93	John Pierre W PTS 6 Hull
17.03.94	Albert Call L PTS 6 Lincoln
09.04.94	Chris Okoh L PTS 6 Bethnal Green
21.04.94	Darren McKenna W PTS 6 Hull
11.05.94	Darren Westover L PTS 6 Stevenage
22.05.94	Owen Bartley L PTS 6 Crystal Palace
15.06.94	Paul Lawson L RSC 2 Southwark
17.09.94	Chris Okoh L PTS 6 Crawley
08.10.94	Rudiger May L PTS 6 Halle, Germany
17.10.94	John Foreman L PTS 8 Birmingham
18.11.94	Keith Fletcher L PTS 6 Bracknell
08.12.94	Declan Faherty W PTS 6 Hull
04.03.95	Terry Dunstan L CO 1 Livingston
27.04.95	Tony Booth L PTS 10 Hull
	(Vacant Central Area Cruiserweight Title)
26.05.95	Gypsy Carman L PTS 6 Norwich
08.06.95	John Wilson L PTS 6 Glasgow
23.06.95	Monty Wright L RSC 2 Bethnal Green

Career: 38 contests, won 11, drew 3, lost 24.

*Michael Smyth (right), seen here beating Maurice Forbes, later failed at the final
eliminator stage against Kevin Lueshing* Les Clark

143

David Starie

Bury St Edmunds. *Born* Bury St Edmunds, 11 June, 1974
S. Middleweight. Ht. 6'0"
Manager G. Holmes

24.09.94	Paul Murray W RSC 2 Wembley	
25.10.94	Dave Owens W PTS 6 Southwark	
07.02.95	Marvin O'Brien W PTS 6 Ipswich	
30.03.95	Mark Dawson W RSC 1 Bethnal Green	
17.05.95	Marvin O'Brien W RSC 5 Ipswich	

Career: 5 contests, won 5.

David Starie   Les Clark

Warren Stephens

Birmingham. *Born* Birmingham, 18 May, 1970
Welterweight. Ht. 6'0"
Manager Self

04.04.92	John Duckworth L RSC 5 Cleethorpes
21.05.92	Bullit Andrews L PTS 6 Cradley Heath
30.10.92	Bullit Andrews L PTS 6 Birmingham
23.11.92	Simon Fisher W PTS 6 Coventry
07.12.92	Steve Levene L CO 2 Birmingham
18.02.93	Rob Stevenson L PTS 6 Hull
07.04.93	Ron Hopley L PTS 6 Leeds
27.05.93	John Duckworth L RSC 5 Burnley
22.09.93	Norman Mitchell L PTS 6 Chesterfield
30.09.93	Nick Appiah L PTS 6 Hayes
03.11.93	Shamus Casey L PTS 6 Worcester
02.12.93	Scott Newman L DIS 4 Evesham
11.01.94	Vince Rose L PTS 6 Bethnal Green
16.02.94	Nicky Thurbin L PTS 6 Stevenage
08.03.94	Nic Ingram L PTS 6 Kettering
16.03.94	Carl van Bailey W PTS 6 Birmingham
29.03.94	David Bain L PTS 6 Wolverhampton
15.04.94	Brian Dunn L PTS 6 Hull
27.04.94	Jesse Keough L RSC 1 Bethnal Green
02.09.94	Roy Dehara L RSC 6 Spitalfields
11.10.94	David Bain L PTS 6 Wolverhampton
29.10.94	Gary Osborne L CO 1 Cannock
29.11.94	Brian Coleman L PTS 6 Wolverhampton
15.12.94	Dennis Berry L PTS 6 Evesham
12.01.95	James Lowther L CO 4 Leeds

Career: 25 contests, won 2, lost 23.

Danny Stevens

Bermondsey. *Born* Lambeth, 16 September, 1973
Welterweight. Ht. 5'10"
Manager T. Lawless

09.12.94	Brian Coleman W RTD 2 Bethnal Green
14.02.95	Roy Dehara W RSC 6 Bethnal Green
03.03.95	Steve Howden W RSC 2 Bethnal Green
19.04.95	Dusty Miller L RSC 3 Bethnal Green

Career: 4 contests, won 3, lost 1.

Danny Stevens   Les Clark

(Newbirth) Newby Stevens (Mukosi)

Paddington. *Born* Zimbabwe, 5 December, 1967
Cruiserweight. Ht. 6'2"
Manager Self

30.07.87	Black Bomber W PTS 4 Buluwayo, Zimbabwe
29.08.87	Sam Ringo Sithole W PTS 6 Buluwayo, Zimbabwe
28.11.87	Jabulaj Gombiro W DIS 1 Inkamo, Zimbabwe
25.05.88	Wild Mhere W PTS 6 Harare, Zimbabwe
09.10.88	Gilbert Mambo L RTD 3 Hwange, Zimbabwe
	(Zimbabwean L. Heavyweight Title Challenge)
28.01.89	Douglas Chinembiri L RTD 8 Harare, Zimbabwe
23.04.92	Warren Richards L CO 1 Eltham
26.04.94	Darren Westover L RSC 5 Bethnal Green
02.07.94	Kent Davis W PTS 6 Keynsham
25.10.94	Paul Lawson L RSC 2 Southwark
10.02.95	Robert Norton L RSC 3 Birmingham
26.05.95	Cliff Elden L RSC 3 Norwich

Career: 12 contests, won 5, lost 7.

Newby Stevens   Les Clark

Rob Stevenson

Hull. *Born* Hull, 16 March, 1971
L. Middleweight. Ht. 5'9"
Manager M. Brooks

28.11.91	Matt Mowatt L PTS 6 Hull
26.03.92	Steve Scott W PTS 6 Hull
04.04.92	Chris Mulcahy L PTS 8 Cleethorpes
29.04.92	Alan Williams W PTS 6 Liverpool
01.06.92	Chris Mulcahy L PTS 6 Manchester
13.10.92	Dean Hiscox L PTS 6 Wolverhampton
26.11.92	Steve Scott L PTS 6 Hull
18.02.93	Warren Stephens W PTS 6 Hull
25.02.93	Ron Hopley DREW 6 Bradford
29.04.93	Billy McDougall DREW 6 Hull
01.07.93	Ron Hopley W PTS 6 York
02.12.93	Ian Noble W PTS 6 Hartlepool
13.12.93	Prince Kasi Kiahau L RSC 5 Doncaster
24.02.94	David Sumner W PTS 6 Hull
24.02.95	Billy Collins L PTS 6 Irvine
25.03.95	Derek Roche L PTS 6 Rothwell

Career: 16 contests, won 6, drew 2, lost 8.

Jon Stocks

Liverpool. *Born* Liverpool, 22 January, 1969
L. Middleweight. Ht. 6'0½"
Manager S. Vaughan

14.02.91	Benji Good W PTS 6 Southampton
28.02.91	Kenny Tyson W PTS 6 Sunderland
02.07.94	John Hughes W RSC 1 Liverpool
31.10.94	Shamus Casey W PTS 6 Liverpool
27.02.95	Roy Chipperfield W RSC 3 Barrow
25.03.95	Carl Smith L PTS 6 Chester

Career: 6 contests, won 5, lost 1.

Shaun Stokes

Sheffield. *Born* Sheffield, 19 November, 1969
L. Welterweight. Ht. 5'7"
Manager J. Rushton

09.02.95	Gary Beardsley L RSC 3 Doncaster
22.03.95	Kenny Scott W RSC 1 Stoke

28.03.95 Patrick Parton W CO 1
Wolverhampton
06.04.95 Wayne Shepherd W PTS 6 Sheffield
05.05.95 Trevor Smith DREW 6 Doncaster
18.05.95 Kevin McKillan DREW 8 Middleton
Career: 6 contests, won 3, drew 2, lost 1.

John Stovin

Hull. *Born* Hull, 20 April, 1972
Lightweight. Ht. 6'0"
Manager M. Toomey

22.09.93 Robbie Sivyer W PTS 6 Chesterfield
07.10.93 Alan Graham W PTS 6 Hull
21.10.93 Dominic McGuigan W PTS 6
Bayswater
22.03.94 Yifru Retta L RSC 3 Bethnal Green
28.04.94 Norman Dhalie DREW 6 Hull
02.06.94 Nick Boyd L RSC 5 Middleton
21.07.94 Dave Anderson L CO 4 Edinburgh
Career: 7 contests, won 3, drew 1, lost 3.

John Stovin   Chris Bevan

Warren Stowe

Burnley. *Born* Burnley, 30 January, 1965
Middleweight. Former Undefeated Central
Area L. Middleweight Champion. Ht. 5'8"
Managers J. Doughty/T. Gilmour

21.10.91 Matt Mowatt W RSC 3 Bury
07.12.91 Griff Jones W RSC 6 Manchester
03.02.92 Robert Peel W PTS 6 Manchester
10.03.92 B. K. Bennett W PTS 6 Bury
25.04.92 David Radford W RSC 3 Manchester
04.06.92 Rob Pitters W PTS 8 Burnley
25.07.92 Shamus Casey W CO 2 Manchester
24.09.92 Mike Phillips W RSC 1 Stockport
12.11.92 Steve Thomas W RSC 1 Burnley
28.11.92 Julian Eavis W RSC 6 Manchester
25.02.93 Robert Riley W DIS 4 Burnley
*(Vacant Central Area L. Middleweight
Title)*
22.04.93 Leigh Wicks W PTS 6 Bury
27.05.93 Peter Waudby W PTS 6 Burnley
09.10.93 Paul Wesley L PTS 10 Manchester
(Elim. British L. Middleweight Title)

17.02.94 Rob Pitters W RSC 1 Bury
25.04.94 Chris Richards W PTS 6 Bury
22.09.94 Jimmy Alston W CO 4 Bury
17.01.95 Paul Busby L PTS 12 Worcester
*(Penta-Continental Middleweight Title
Challenge)*
Career: 18 contests, won 16, lost 2.

John Stronach

Keighley. *Born* Middlesbrough, 14
October, 1969
L. Middleweight. Ht. 5'10"
Manager J. Celebanski

26.04.93 Steve Scott W PTS 6 Bradford
24.10.94 Shamus Casey W PTS 6 Bradford
24.11.94 Hughie Davey L PTS 6 Newcastle
18.01.95 Andy Peach W RSC 5 Solihull
30.01.95 Peter Reid L PTS 6 Bradford
15.05.95 Denny Johnson W PTS 6 Bradford
12.06.95 Nic Ingram L PTS 6 Bradford
Career: 7 contests, won 4, lost 3.

Trevor Sumner

Sheffield. *Born* Sheffield, 26 August, 1963
S. Featherweight. Ht. 5'4"
Manager G. Rhodes

09.11.83 Ian Murray W RSC 5 Sheffield
14.11.83 Les Walsh L PTS 6 Manchester
05.12.83 Mike Whalley L CO 4 Manchester
29.02.84 Steve Enright W PTS 6 Sheffield
19.03.84 Les Walsh L PTS 8 Manchester
16.10.84 Dave Adam L PTS 6 Wolverhampton
11.03.95 Colin Innes W PTS 6 Barnsley
03.04.95 Russell Davison W PTS 6 Manchester
22.05.95 Garry Burrell W PTS 6 Morecambe
Career: 9 contests, won 5, lost 4.

Richard Swallow

Northampton. *Born* Northampton, 10
February, 1970
Welterweight. Ht. 5'8"
Manager J. Griffin

15.10.90 Richard O'Brien L RTD 1 Kettering
14.02.91 Dave Fallon W RSC 4 Southampton
06.03.91 Carl Brasier W PTS 6 Croydon
02.05.91 Mike Morrison W PTS 6 Northampton
24.03.92 Dean Bramhald W PTS 8
Wolverhampton
06.04.92 Dean Bramhald W PTS 6 Northampton
29.04.92 Chris Aston W RSC 3 Solihull
14.10.92 Wayne Shepherd W PTS 8 Stoke
24.11.92 Chris Mulcahy W PTS 6
Wolverhampton
20.01.93 Ray Newby W PTS 8 Solihull
03.03.93 Ray Newby L PTS 8 Solihull
11.06.93 Soren Sondergaard L RTD 3 Randers,
Denmark
08.02.94 Billy McDougall W PTS 6
Wolverhampton
30.09.94 Bernard Paul W PTS 8 Bethnal Green
31.10.94 Carl Wright L PTS 6 Liverpool
09.12.94 Jason Rowland L RSC 2 Bethnal Green
14.02.95 Jason Beard L PTS 6 Bethnal Green
17.03.95 Frank Olsen L RSC 1 Copenhagen,
Denmark
06.06.95 Anthony Maynard W RSC 2 Leicester
Career: 19 contests, won 12, lost 7.

Richard Swallow   Les Clark

Darren Sweeney

Birmingham. *Born* London, 3 March, 1971
Middleweight. Ht. 5'11"
Manager Self

28.06.94 Japhet Hans W PTS 6 Edgbaston
25.10.94 Dave Battey W CO 1 Edgbaston
15.12.94 Mark Hale W PTS 6 Walsall
07.03.95 Colin Pitters W PTS 6 Edgbaston
20.03.95 Carl Winstone W PTS 6 Birmingham
11.05.95 Martin Jolley W PTS 6 Dudley
20.06.95 Michael Pinnock W PTS 8 Edgbaston
Career: 7 contests, won 7.

(Richard) Clive Sweetland

Hendy. *Born* Swansea, 23 January, 1967
Welterweight. Ht. 5'11½"
Manager G. Davies

12.04.95 Tom Welsh L CO 2 Llanelli
Career: 1 contest, lost 1.

Tony Swift

Birmingham. *Born* Solihull, 29 June, 1968
L. Welterweight. Ht. 5'10"
Manager Self

25.09.86 Barry Bacon W PTS 6 Wolverhampton
06.10.86 Wil Halliday W PTS 6 Birmingham
23.10.86 Patrick Loftus W PTS 6 Birmingham
26.11.86 Adam Muir W PTS 6 Wolverhampton
08.12.86 George Baigrie W PTS 6 Birmingham
26.01.87 Dean Bramhald W PTS 8 Birmingham
04.03.87 Dean Bramhald W RSC 5 Dudley
25.03.87 Peter Bowen W PTS 8 Stafford
22.06.87 Peter Bowen W PTS 8 Stafford
07.10.87 Dean Bramhald W PTS 8 Stoke
19.10.87 Kevin Plant W PTS 8 Birmingham
02.12.87 Dean Bramhald W PTS 8 Stoke
16.03.88 Ron Shinkwin W PTS 8 Solihull
04.05.88 Kevin Plant DREW 8 Solihull
28.09.88 Kevin Plant DREW 8 Solihull
23.11.88 Lenny Gloster L PTS 8 Solihull
12.06.89 Humphrey Harrison W PTS 8
Manchester
28.11.89 Seamus O'Sullivan W RSC 1 Battersea

16.02.90	Ramses Evilio W PTS 6 Bilbao, Spain
30.05.90	Darren Mount W PTS 8 Stoke
05.09.90	Glyn Rhodes L RSC 7 Stoke
25.10.90	Jimmy Harrison L PTS 6 Battersea
19.04.91	Gary Barron DREW 8 Peterborough
12.11.91	Carlos Chase W PTS 6 Milton Keynes
03.03.92	Steve McGovern W RSC 4 Cradley Heath
10.04.92	Willie Beattie W PTS 10 Glasgow (Elim. British Welterweight Title)
29.09.92	Nigel Bradley W PTS 8 Stoke
05.10.93	Andrew Murray L RSC 6 Mayfair (Vacant Commonwealth Welterweight Title)
09.04.94	Andreas Panayi W PTS 8 Bethnal Green
11.06.94	Andreas Panayi L PTS 8 Bethnal Green
05.10.94	Mark Elliot L PTS 8 Wolverhampton
15.03.95	Shea Neary L RSC 3 Stoke

Career: 32 contests, won 22, drew 3, lost 7.

(Danny) Darren Swords (Muir)

Stockport. *Born* Manchester, 7 July, 1968
S. Middleweight. Ht. 5'9½"
Manager J. Doughty

22.09.94	Roy Chipperfield W PTS 6 Bury
05.12.94	Paul Clarkson W RSC 3 Bradford
16.02.95	Shamus Casey W PTS 6 Bury

Career: 3 contests, won 3.

(Somapat) Adam Tate (Sitiwatjana)

Sheffield. *Born* Bangkok, 3 October, 1968
Flyweight. Ht. 5'4"
Manager K. Tate

06.04.95	Shaun Norman L RSC 6 Sheffield

Career: 1 contest, lost 1.

Karl Taylor

Birmingham. *Born* Birmingham, 5 January, 1966
Midlands Area Lightweight Champion. Ht. 5'5"
Manager N. Nobbs

18.03.87	Steve Brown W PTS 6 Stoke
06.04.87	Paul Taylor L PTS 6 Southampton
12.06.87	Mark Begley W RSC 1 Leamington
18.11.87	Colin Lynch W RSC 4 Solihull
29.02.88	Peter Bradley L PTS 8 Birmingham
04.10.89	Mark Antony W CO 2 Stafford
30.10.89	Tony Feliciello L PTS 8 Birmingham
06.12.89	John Davison L PTS 8 Leicester
23.12.89	Regilio Tuur L RSC 2 Hoogvliet, Holland
22.02.90	Mark Ramsey L RSC 4 Hull
29.10.90	Steve Walker DREW 6 Birmingham
10.12.90	Elvis Parsley L PTS 6 Birmingham
16.01.91	Wayne Windle W PTS 8 Stoke
02.05.91	Billy Schwer L RSC 2 Northampton
25.07.91	Peter Till L RSC 4 Dudley (Midlands Area Lightweight Title Challenge)
24.02.92	Charlie Kane L PTS 8 Glasgow
28.04.92	Richard Woolgar W PTS 6 Wolverhampton
29.05.92	Alan McDowall L PTS 6 Glasgow
25.07.92	Michael Armstrong L RSC 3 Manchester
02.11.92	Hugh Forde L PTS 6 Wolverhampton
23.11.92	Dave McHale L PTS 8 Glasgow
22.12.92	Patrick Gallagher L RSC 3 Mayfair

13.02.93	Craig Dermody L RSC 5 Manchester
31.03.93	Craig Dermody W PTS 6 Barking
07.06.93	Mark Geraghty W PTS 8 Glasgow
13.08.93	Giorgio Campanella L CO 6 Arezzo, Italy
05.10.93	Paul Harvey W PTS 6 Mayfair
21.10.93	Charles Shepherd L RTD 5 Bayswater
21.12.93	Patrick Gallagher L PTS 6 Mayfair
09.02.94	Alan Levene W RSC 2 Brentwood
01.03.94	Shaun Cogan L PTS 6 Dudley
15.03.94	Patrick Gallagher L PTS 6 Mayfair
18.04.94	Peter Till W PTS 10 Walsall (Midlands Area Lightweight Title Challenge)
24.05.94	Michael Ayers DREW 8 Sunderland
12.11.94	P. J. Gallagher L PTS 6 Dublin
29.11.94	Dingaan Thobela W RSC 8 Cannock
31.03.95	Michael Ayers L RSC 8 Crystal Palace (British Lightweight Title Challenge)
06.05.95	Cham Joof W PTS 8 Shepton Mallet
23.06.95	Poli Diaz L PTS 8 Madrid, Spain

Career: 39 contests, won 13, drew 2, lost 24.

Alan Temple

Hartlepool. *Born* Hartlepool, 21 October, 1972
L. Welterweight. Ht. 5'8"
Manager F. Maloney

29.09.94	Stevie Bolt W CO 2 Bethnal Green
22.11.94	Phil Found W PTS 6 Bristol
07.02.95	Brian Coleman W PTS 6 Ipswich
27.04.95	Everald Williams L PTS 6 Bethnal Green

Career: 4 contests, won 3, lost 1.

Alan Temple   Les Clark

Jonathan Thaxton

Norwich. *Born* Norwich, 10 September, 1974
Former Southern Area L. Welterweight Champion. Ht. 5'6"
Manager B. Ingle

09.12.92	Scott Smith W PTS 6 Stoke
03.03.93	Dean Hiscox W PTS 6 Solihull

17.03.93	John O. Johnson W PTS 6 Stoke
23.06.93	Brian Coleman W PTS 8 Gorleston
22.09.93	John Smith W PTS 6 Wembley
07.12.93	Dean Hollington W RSC 3 Bethnal Green
10.03.94	B. F. Williams W RSC 4 Watford (Vacant Southern Area L. Welterweight Title)
18.11.94	Keith Marner L PTS 10 Bracknell (Southern Area L. Welterweight Title Defence)
26.05.95	David Thompson W RSC 6 Norwich
23.06.95	Delroy Leslie W PTS 6 Bethnal Green

Career: 10 contests, won 9, lost 1.

Chris Thomas

Sheffield. *Born* Merthyr Tydfil, 13 December, 1971
Flyweight. Ht. 5'3½"
Manager B. Ingle

15.03.95	Shaun Norman L RSC 2 Stoke

Career: 1 contest, lost 1.

(Lee) Malcolm Thomas

Llanelli. *Born* Swansea, 2 January, 1972
Welterweight. Ht. 5'6"
Manager D. Davies

24.02.94	Patrick Parton L PTS 6 Walsall
04.03.94	Colin Dunne L CO 1 Bethnal Green
20.05.94	Anthony Campbell L PTS 6 Acton
17.10.94	Anthony Maynard L PTS 6 Birmingham
07.11.94	Georgie Smith L PTS 6 Bethnal Green
08.03.95	Steve Burton L PTS 6 Cardiff

Career: 6 contests, lost 6.

Malcolm Thomas   Les Clark

Steve Thomas

Merthyr. *Born* Merthyr, 13 June, 1970
S. Middleweight. Ht. 6'0"
Manager Self

21.10.91	Jerry Mortimer W PTS 6 Mayfair

04.11.91 Andy Manning W PTS 6 Merthyr
02.03.92 Robert Peel DREW 6 Merthyr
08.04.92 Charlie Moore L RSC 3 Leeds
11.05.92 Robert Peel W PTS 6 Llanelli
07.10.92 Ray Price L PTS 6 Barry
15.10.92 Clay O'Shea L PTS 6 Lewisham
12.11.92 Warren Stowe L RSC 1 Burnley
19.01.93 Matthew Turner L PTS 6 Cardiff
06.02.93 Mike Phillips DREW 6 Cardiff
06.03.93 Willie Quinn L RSC 4 Glasgow
10.04.93 Darren Pullman DREW 6 Swansea
24.04.93 Andrew Flute L RSC 1 Birmingham
23.03.94 Paul Matthews L PTS 6 Cardiff
31.03.94 Dale Nixon DREW 4 Bristol
26.04.94 Clay O'Shea L PTS 6 Bethnal Green
25.05.94 Darren Dorrington L PTS 4 Bristol
02.06.94 Dave Cranston L PTS 6 Tooting
17.10.94 Mark Baker L RSC 5 Mayfair
28.11.94 Sean Byrne L PTS 6 Northampton
Career: 20 contests, won 3, drew 4, lost 13.

(Adrian) Carl Thompson

Manchester. *Born* Manchester, 26 May, 1964
Former Undefeated European, British & WBC International Cruiserweight Champion. Ht. 6'0"
Managers N. Basso/F. Warren

06.06.88 Darren McKenna W RSC 2 Manchester
11.10.88 Paul Sheldon W PTS 6 Wolverhampton
13.02.89 Steve Osborne W PTS 6 Manchester
07.03.89 Sean O'Phoenix W RSC 4 Manchester
04.04.89 Keith Halliwell W RSC 1 Manchester
04.05.89 Tenko Ernie W CO 4 Mayfair
12.06.89 Steve Osborne W PTS 8 Manchester
11.07.89 Peter Brown W RSC 5 Batley
31.10.89 Crawford Ashley L RSC 6 Manchester
(Vacant Central Area L. Heavyweight Title)
21.04.90 Francis Wanyama L PTS 6 St Amandsberg, Belgium
07.03.91 Terry Dixon W PTS 8 Basildon

01.04.91 Yawe Davis L RSC 2 Monaco, Monte Carlo
04.09.91 Nicky Piper W RSC 3 Bethnal Green
04.06.92 Steve Lewsam W RSC 8 Cleethorpes
(Vacant British Cruiserweight Title)
17.02.93 Arthur Weathers W CO 2 Bethnal Green
(Vacant WBC International Cruiserweight Title)
31.03.93 Steve Harvey W CO 1 Bethnal Green
25.07.93 Willie Jake W CO 3 Oldham
02.02.94 Massimiliano Duran W CO 8 Ferrara, Italy
(European Cruiserweight Title Challenge)
14.06.94 Akim Tafer W RSC 6 Epernay, France
(European Cruiserweight Title Defence)
10.09.94 Dionisio Lazario W RSC 1 Birmingham
13.10.94 Tim Knight W RSC 5 Paris, France
10.06.95 Ralf Rocchigiani L RSC 11 Manchester
(Vacant WBO Cruiserweight Title)
Career: 22 contests, won 18, lost 4.

David Thompson   Les Clark

David Thompson

Hull. *Born* Hull, 14 March, 1969
Lightweight. Ht. 5'8"
Manager M. Brooks

26.03.90 Mark Conley W PTS 4 Bradford
09.04.90 Andy Rowbotham W PTS 6 Manchester
26.04.90 Andy Rowbotham DREW 6 Manchester
21.05.90 Johnny Walker L CO 1 Bradford
01.11.90 Colin Sinnott L PTS 6 Hull
16.11.90 Carl Tilley L CO 1 Telford
17.12.90 Eddie King W PTS 6 Manchester
18.02.91 Barry North W PTS 6 Birmingham
25.02.91 Steve Winstanley W RTD 4 Bradford
28.03.91 Shane Sheridan L CO 5 Alfreton
17.05.91 Jason Brattley DREW 6 Bury
13.06.91 James Jiora DREW 6 Hull
30.06.91 Nicky Lucas W PTS 6 Southwark
25.07.91 Shaun Cogan L CO 1 Dudley
13.11.91 Mark Tibbs L PTS 6 Bethnal Green
28.11.91 Kevin Toomey L PTS 6 Hull
09.12.91 Chris Aston L PTS 6 Bradford

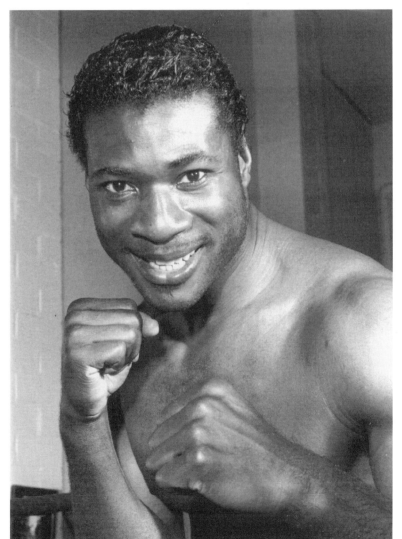

Carl Thompson   Harry Goodwin

147

21.01.92 Ricky Sackfield L CO 1 Stockport
30.03.92 Jason Brattley L PTS 6 Bradford
26.03.93 Tanveer Ahmed L PTS 6 Glasgow
09.12.94 Colin Dunne L RSC 3 Bethnal Green
23.01.95 P. J. Gallagher L RSC 1 Bethnal Green
20.02.95 Jay Mahoney L RSC 4 Manchester
26.05.95 Jonathan Thaxton L RSC 6 Norwich
Career: 24 contests, won 6, drew 3, lost 15.

Gary Thornhill

Liverpool. *Born* Liverpool, 11 February, 1968
S. Featherweight. Ht. 5'6½"
Manager S. Vaughan

27.02.93 Brian Hickey W CO 4 Ellesmere Port
02.07.93 Dougie Fox W CO 1 Liverpool
30.10.93 Miguel Matthews W PTS 6 Chester
01.12.93 Wayne Windle W PTS 6 Stoke
25.02.94 Edward Lloyd DREW 6 Chester
06.05.94 Derek Amory W RSC 1 Liverpool
25.03.95 Craig Kelley W PTS 6 Chester
20.04.95 Michael Hermon W RSC 6 Liverpool
30.06.95 Chip O'Neill W RTD 3 Liverpool
Career: 9 contests, won 8, drew 1.

Barry Thorogood

Cardiff. *Born* Cardiff, 1 December, 1972
Welsh Middleweight Champion. Ht. 6'0"
Manager D. Gardiner

28.10.92 Robert Peel W PTS 6 Cardiff
14.12.92 James Campbell W RSC 4 Cardiff
27.01.93 Russell Washer W PTS 6 Cardiff
24.03.93 Darren McInulty W PTS 6 Cardiff
28.04.93 Stuart Dunn L RSC 2 Solihull
13.09.93 Glenn Catley L PTS 4 Bristol
23.10.93 Mark Atkins W PTS 4 Cardiff
10.11.93 Robert Peel W PTS 6 Ystrad
29.01.94 Darren Dorrington DREW 6 Cardiff
02.03.94 Darren Pilling W PTS 6 Solihull
12.03.94 Geoff McCreesh L PTS 6 Cardiff
27.04.94 Dave Johnson DREW 8 Solihull
20.05.94 Andrew Furlong L RSC 4 Acton
17.10.94 Howard Eastman L RSC 6 Mayfair
29.11.94 Robert Peel W PTS 10 Cardiff
(*Vacant Welsh Middleweight Title*)
08.03.95 Paul Matthews W PTS 4 Cardiff
12.04.95 Robert Peel W RSC 8 Llanelli
(*Welsh Middleweight Title Defence*)
Career: 17 contests, won 10, drew 2, lost 5.

Nicky Thurbin

Ilford. *Born* Ilford, 26 October, 1971
Southern Area L. Middleweight Champion.
Ht. 5'10"
Manager M. Duff

07.12.93 John Rice W PTS 6 Bethnal Green
14.01.94 Delwyn Panayiotiou W RTD 3 Bethnal Green
16.02.94 Warren Stephens W PTS 6 Stevenage
04.03.94 Andy Peach W PTS 6 Bethnal Green
22.03.94 Carl Winstone W PTS 6 Bethnal Green
11.10.94 Billy McDougall W RSC 6 Bethnal Green
09.12.94 Julian Eavis W PTS 6 Bethnal Green
20.01.95 Marty Duke W PTS 6 Bethnal Green
19.04.95 Peter Mitchell W PTS 6 Bethnal Green
12.05.95 Marty Duke W RSC 3 Bethnal Green
19.05.95 Anthony Lawrence W PTS 6 Southwark
23.06.95 Vince Rose W PTS 10 Bethnal Green
(*Vacant Southern Area L. Middleweight Title*)
Career: 12 contests, won 12.

Peter Till

Bloxwich. *Born* Walsall, 19 August, 1963
Former Midlands Area Lightweight
Champion. Ht. 5'6"
Manager A. Morrison

25.04.85 Clinton Campbell W CO 1 Wolverhampton
23.05.85 J. J. Mudd W PTS 6 Dudley
17.10.85 Patrick Loftus W PTS 6 Leicester
14.11.85 Paul Wetter W RSC 3 Dudley
27.01.86 George Jones W PTS 8 Dudley
17.04.86 Tyrell Wilson W CO 5 Wolverhampton
15.05.86 Les Remikie W PTS 6 Dudley
03.06.86 Ray Newby L PTS 10 Wolverhampton
(*Vacant Midlands Area Lightweight Title*)
25.09.86 Gerry Beard DREW 8 Wolverhampton
26.11.86 Gerry Beard W CO 4 Wolverhampton
28.01.87 George Baigrie W PTS 8 Dudley
04.03.87 Carl Merrett W PTS 8 Dudley
30.03.87 Tony Richards L PTS 8 Birmingham
19.07.87 Aladin Stevens L CO 4 Johannesburg, South Africa
19.10.87 Dean Bramhald W PTS 8 Birmingham
24.11.87 Dean Bramhald W PTS 8 Wolverhampton
07.02.88 Michael Marsden W CO 1 Stafford
24.02.88 Neil Haddock W PTS 8 Aberavon
13.04.88 Sugar Gibiliru W PTS 8 Wolverhampton
14.06.88 Ray Newby W PTS 10 Dudley
(*Midlands Area Lightweight Title Challenge*)
22.09.88 Jim Moffat W RSC 4 Wolverhampton
10.11.88 George Jones W RSC 8 Wolverhampton
(*Midlands Area Lightweight Title Defence*)
02.02.89 Camel Touati W RSC 3 Wolverhampton
13.04.89 Phillipe Binante W RSC 3 Wolverhampton
21.12.89 Tony Richards L CO 8 Kings Heath
18.10.90 Nick Hall W PTS 6 Birmingham
30.11.90 Ray Newby W PTS 8 Birmingham
21.02.91 Paul Charters L RSC 6 Walsall
(*Elim. British Lightweight Title*)
31.05.91 Valery Kayumba L RSC 3 Grenoble, France
25.07.91 Karl Taylor W RSC 4 Dudley
(*Midlands Area Lightweight Title Defence*)
21.09.91 Michael Ayers L RSC 5 Tottenham
(*Elim. British Lightweight Title*)
09.12.91 Scott Doyle W CO 3 Brierley Hill
01.02.92 Michael Driscoll L RSC 3 Birmingham
17.03.92 Mark Reefer W RSC 3 Mayfair
04.06.92 Racheed Lawal L RSC 1 Randers, Denmark
15.08.92 Dingaan Thobela L RSC 9 Springs, South Africa
16.02.93 Errol McDonald L PTS 8 Tooting
26.05.93 Mark McCreath L PTS 8 Mansfield
02.12.93 Dominic McGuigan W RSC 2 Walsall
16.12.93 Norman Dhalie W PTS 8 Walsall
24.02.94 Barrie Kelley W PTS 6 Walsall
18.04.94 Karl Taylor L PTS 10 Walsall
(*Midlands Area Lightweight Title Defence*)
10.06.94 Dave Anderson L PTS 6 Glasgow
08.09.94 Alan McDowall W PTS 6 Glasgow
21.10.94 Dave Anderson L PTS 8 Glasgow
18.12.94 Dave Anderson L PTS 10 Glasgow
(*Elim. British Lightweight Title*)
02.03.95 Carl Roberts W RSC 6 Glasgow
21.04.95 Gareth Jordan L PTS 6 Dudley
13.05.95 Justin Juuko L RTD 4 Glasgow
Career: 49 contests, won 30, drew 1, lost 18.

Carl Tilley

Doncaster. *Born* Doncaster, 4 October, 1967
Lightweight. Ht. 5'6½"
Manager T. Petersen

04.09.90 Stuart Good W RSC 5 Southend
16.11.90 David Thompson W CO 1 Telford
13.05.91 Steve Winstanley W RTD 4 Marton
09.10.91 Bobby Beckles W RSC 4 Marton
02.03.92 James Jiora W PTS 6 Marton
30.04.92 Greg Egbuniwe L PTS 6 Kensington
15.09.92 Joey Moffat L PTS 6 Liverpool
26.09.94 Scott Walker L PTS 6 Morecambe
20.04.95 Yifru Retta L PTS 6 Mayfair
Career: 9 contests, won 5, lost 4.

Kevin Toomey

Hull. *Born* Hull, 19 September, 1967
Welterweight. Former Undefeated Central
Area Lightweight Champion. Ht. 5'9"
Manager Self

24.04.89 Chris Mulcahy L PTS 6 Bradford
04.09.89 Andy Rowbotham W RSC 1 Grimsby
03.10.89 Mick Mulcahy L CO 5 Cottingham
01.11.90 Joel Forbes W PTS 6 Hull
12.12.90 Andy Kent DREW 6 Leicester
24.01.91 Barry North W PTS 6 Brierley Hill
18.02.91 Andy Kent L RSC 5 Derby
22.04.91 Trevor Royal W PTS 6 Bradford
16.05.91 John Smith W PTS 6 Liverpool
13.06.91 John Smith W PTS 6 Hull
30.09.91 Mike Calderwood L RSC 2 Liverpool
28.11.91 David Thompson W PTS 6 Hull
10.12.91 Wayne Windle L PTS 6 Sheffield
04.02.92 G. G. Goddard W PTS 6 Alfreton
26.03.92 Wayne Windle W DIS 8 Hull
(*Central Area Lightweight Title Challenge*)
11.09.92 Dave Anderson L PTS 8 Glasgow
16.10.92 Steve Pollard W RSC 7 Hull
26.11.92 Dean Bramhald L PTS 10 Hull
(*Central Area Lightweight Title Defence*)
18.02.93 Dean Bramhald W PTS 10 Hull
(*Central Area Lightweight Title Challenge*)
29.04.93 Norman Dhalie W PTS 6 Hull
28.05.93 Phil Holliday L RSC 2 Johannesburg, South Africa
12.11.93 Steve Pollard L PTS 8 Hull
08.12.93 Chris Aston W PTS 6 Hull
09.02.94 Mark Tibbs L RSC 4 Bethnal Green
08.12.94 Tony Brown W PTS 6 Hull
23.02.95 Tony Brown L RSC 10 Hull
(*Vacant Central Area Welterweight Title*)
Career: 26 contests, won 14, drew 1, lost 11.

Joe Townsley

Cleland. *Born* Bellshill, 13 January, 1972
Welterweight. Ht. 5'9¼"
Manager T. Gilmour

20.03.95 Hughie Davey L PTS 6 Glasgow
05.04.95 Brian Dunn W RSC 3 Irvine
Career: 2 contests, won 1, lost 1.

Steve Tuckett

Wakefield. *Born* Leeds, 27 January, 1973
Lightweight. Ht. 5'9"
Manager G. Lockwood

12.01.95	Ram Singh W RSC 6 Leeds	
20.02.95	Paul Hughes W PTS 6 Manchester	
06.03.95	John T. Kelly W RSC 3 Bradford	
26.04.95	George Wilson W PTS 6 Solihull	
19.05.95	Micky Hall L RSC 2 Leeds	

Career: 5 contests, won 4, lost 1.

Leo Turner

Bradford. *Born* Bradford, 17 September, 1970
Lightweight. Ht. 5'9"
Manager J. Celebanski

08.06.92	Wayne Rigby L PTS 6 Bradford
02.07.92	Wayne Rigby L CO 5 Middleton
12.10.92	Micky Hall L RSC 5 Bradford
14.12.92	Fred Reeve W RSC 2 Bradford
25.01.93	Alan Graham L PTS 6 Bradford
08.11.93	Tim Hill L RTD 4 Bradford
07.02.94	Paul Goode W RSC 3 Bradford
03.03.94	Colin Innes DREW 6 Newcastle
21.04.94	Colin Innes L PTS 6 Gateshead
09.05.94	Ian Richardson DREW 6 Bradford
13.06.94	Colin Innes W PTS 6 Bradford
20.10.94	Carl Roberts W RSC 3 Middleton
24.11.94	Ian Richardson W RSC 6 Newcastle
30.01.95	Trevor George L PTS 6 Bradford

Career: 14 contests, won 5, drew 2, lost 7.

Matthew Turner

Rhoose. *Born* Cardiff, 20 September, 1968
L. Middleweight. Ht. 5'9"
Manager B. Hearn

19.01.93	Steve Thomas W PTS 6 Cardiff
30.03.93	Mark Dawson W PTS 6 Cardiff
19.05.93	Stuart Dunn L RSC 3 Leicester
30.11.93	Gary Pemberton W RTD 4 Cardiff
27.08.94	Vince Rose L RSC 4 Cardiff

Career: 5 contests, won 3, lost 2.

Jobie Tyers

Newcastle. *Born* Cleveland, 8 August, 1975
Bantamweight. Ht. 5'4"
Manager D. Gregory

27.10.93	Gary Marston L PTS 6 Stoke
25.01.94	Justin Murphy L RSC 3 Piccadilly
26.09.94	Fred Reeve W PTS 6 Bradford
07.10.94	Danny Lawson W PTS 6 Taunton
24.10.94	Daryl McKenzie W PTS 6 Glasgow

Career: 5 contests, won 3, lost 2.

Greg Upton

Teignmouth. *Born* Canada, 11 June, 1971
Western Area S. Featherweight Champion.
Ht. 5'5½"
Manager Self

28.11.91	Eunan Devenney W PTS 6 Evesham
29.04.92	Chris Morris W RSC 2 Liverpool
01.06.92	Graham McGrath W PTS 6 Solihull
19.11.92	Mark Hargreaves L RSC 3 Evesham
24.03.93	Barry Jones L RSC 2 Cardiff
27.05.93	Trevor Royal W CO 2 Bristol
	(Vacant Western Area S. Featherweight Title)
28.10.93	Graham McGrath W PTS 8 Torquay
03.03.94	Sean Knight L RSC 6 Ebbw Vale

25.06.94	Steve Edwards DREW 6 Cullompton
03.08.94	Pete Buckley W PTS 6 Bristol
07.10.94	Jason Hutson L RSC 1 Taunton
16.11.94	Andrew Reed W PTS 6 Bloomsbury
04.02.95	Dean Phillips L PTS 6 Cardiff
27.04.95	Paul Webster L RSC 1 Bethnal Green

Career: 14 contests, won 7, drew 1, lost 6.

Rudy Valentino (Isaacs)

Plumstead. *Born* London, 6 July, 1964
Lightweight. Ht. 5'6"
Manager Self

22.10.86	Mike Russell W PTS 6 Greenwich
26.11.86	Tim O'Keefe W PTS 6 Lewisham
19.03.87	Neil Haddock W PTS 6 Bethnal Green
30.04.87	Marvin P. Gray W PTS 6 Washington
15.09.87	Peter Crook L PTS 6 Kensington
18.11.87	Paul Burke L PTS 6 Bethnal Green
02.12.87	Mark Pearce W PTS 6 Piccadilly
18.01.88	John Dickson W PTS 6 Mayfair
08.03.88	James Jiora W PTS 6 Batley
05.04.88	Hugh Forde L RSC 2 Birmingham
18.05.88	Chubby Martin L RSC 5 Lewisham
08.02.89	Paul Moylett W PTS 6 Kensington
15.02.89	Richard Joyce L PTS 6 Stoke
24.04.89	Steve Topliss W PTS 6 Nottingham
21.06.89	Sugar Gibiliru W PTS 6 Eltham
04.09.89	Jose Tuominen L RSC 2 Helsinki, Finland
19.10.89	Harry Escott L RTD 4 Manchester
27.03.90	Peter Bradley L PTS 8 Mayfair
23.04.90	Lee Amass W RSC 4 Crystal Palace
28.05.90	Pierre Lorcy L PTS 8 Paris, France
20.10.90	Gianni di Napoli DREW 8 Leon, France
15.12.90	Angel Mona L PTS 8 Vichy, France
10.04.91	Marcel Herbert W RSC 3 Newport
	((Elim. British Lightweight Title)
17.07.91	Giovanni Parisi L PTS 8 Abbiategrasso, Italy
13.09.91	Giorgio Campanella L PTS 8 Gaggiano, Italy
19.02.92	Michael Ayers L RSC 7 Muswell Hill
	(Southern Area Lightweight Title Challenge & Elim. British Lightweight Title)
17.09.93	Soren Sondergaard L PTS 6 Copenhagen, Denmark
29.10.93	Racheed Lawal L CO 1 Korsoer, Denmark
04.10.94	Paul Burke L PTS 6 Mayfair
07.11.94	Patrick Gallagher L PTS 6 Bethnal Green
19.04.95	Colin Dunne L PTS 6 Bethnal Green
13.06.95	Georgie Smith L PTS 6 Basildon

Career: 32 contests, won 12, drew 1, lost 19.

Bobby Vanzie

Bradford. *Born* Bradford, 11 January, 1974
L. Welterweight. Ht. 5'5"
Manager J. Doughty

22.05.95	Alan Peacock W RSC 1 Morecambe

Career: 1 contest, won 1.

Peter Varnavas

Burnley. *Born* Burnley, 27 March, 1974
L. Middleweight. Ht. 5'6"
Manager B. Myers

03.10.94	Carl Smith L RSC 2 Manchester
02.11.94	Andy McVeigh L RSC 3 Birmingham
22.05.95	Wayne Shepherd L PTS 6 Morecambe

Career: 3 contests, lost 3.

Chris Vassiliou

Margate. *Born* Hitchin, 18 June, 1963
L. Middleweight. Ht. 5'11"
Manager P. Byrne

22.02.93	Darren Blackford L RSC 1 Eltham
26.06.93	Glenn Catley L CO 2 Keynsham
27.05.94	Harry Dhamie L RSC 5 Ashford
24.01.95	Robbie Dunn W PTS 6 Piccadilly
07.02.95	Prince Louis L PTS 4 Ipswich

Career: 5 contests, won 1, lost 4.

Louis Veitch

Preston. *Born* Glasgow, 9 March, 1963
Central Area Flyweight Champion. Ht. 5'2"
Manager J. McMillan

09.10.91	Tucker Thomas W RSC 4 Marton
11.11.91	Shaun Norman L RSC 5 Bradford
12.03.92	Neil Armstrong L PTS 6 Glasgow
10.04.92	Mark Robertson L PTS 6 Glasgow
16.05.92	Mickey Cantwell L PTS 6 Muswell Hill
09.07.92	Paul Weir L PTS 6 Glasgow
11.09.92	Neil Armstrong L PTS 6 Glasgow
26.10.92	Nick Tooley L PTS 6 Cleethorpes
14.12.92	Lyndon Kershaw DREW 6 Bradford
29.01.93	Neil Armstrong L PTS 6 Glasgow
10.02.93	Mickey Cantwell DREW 8 Lewisham
29.03.93	Neil Parry W PTS 6 Glasgow
29.05.93	Neil Armstrong L PTS 10 Paisley
07.10.93	Lyndon Kershaw W PTS 10 Hull
	(Vacant Central Area Flyweight Title)
22.11.93	James Drummond L PTS 8 Glasgow
02.02.94	Ian Baillie W RSC 1 Glasgow
25.03.94	Jesper David Jensen L PTS 6 Bornholme, Denmark
24.05.94	Vince Feeney L PTS 6 Leicester
02.11.94	Lyndon Kershaw W PTS 10 Solihull
	(Central Area Flyweight Title Defence)
21.01.95	James Murray L RSC 3 Glasgow
	(Scottish Bantamweight Title Challenge)
05.04.95	Keith Knox DREW 6 Irvine
14.06.95	Ady Benton W RSC 2 Batley

Career: 22 contests, won 6, drew 3, lost 13.

Tony Velinor

Stratford. *Born* London, 21 December, 1964
Middleweight. Ht. 5'8"
Manager Self

28.10.88	Robert Armstrong W RSC 4 Brentwood
22.11.88	Andy Tonks W RTD 1 Basildon
16.12.88	Kesem Clayton L RSC 2 Brentwood
25.01.89	Shamus Casey W RTD 3 Basildon
28.03.89	Ricky Nelson W RSC 4 Chigwell
26.05.89	Skip Jackson W RSC 2 Bethnal Green
19.09.89	Mark Howell W PTS 8 Bethnal Green
31.01.90	Shaun Cummins L PTS 8 Bethnal Green
22.05.90	Trevor Grant W PTS 6 Canvey Island
12.09.90	Ian Chantler L RSC 4 Bethnal Green
12.03.91	Paul Jones L PTS 8 Mansfield
03.07.91	Jason Rowe W RSC 1 Brentwood
11.05.92	Stan King L RSC 3 Piccadilly
16.02.93	Paul Lynch L PTS 8 Tooting
30.03.93	Carlo Colarusso L RSC 3 Cardiff
20.12.94	Sven Hamer L RSC 4 Bethnal Green

Career: 16 contests, won 8, lost 8.

Yusuf Vorajee

Coventry. *Born* Bradford, 21 August, 1969
Featherweight. Ht. 5'5½"
Manager P. Byrne

30.09.92	Kid McAuley L PTS 6 Solihull
14.10.92	Mark Hargreaves L RSC 4 Stoke
27.01.93	Kid McAuley W RSC 5 Stoke
03.03.93	Stewart Fishermac W RSC 2 Solihull
23.03.93	Garry Burrell W PTS 6 Wolverhampton
05.05.93	John White L PTS 6 Belfast
02.03.94	Mike Deveney L PTS 6 Solihull
23.03.94	Matthew Harris L PTS 6 Stoke
21.09.94	Neil Swain L RTD 1 Cardiff
17.01.95	Ady Lewis L RSC 6 Worcester

Career: 10 contests, won 3, lost 7.

Peter Vosper

Plymouth. *Born* Plymouth, 6 October, 1966
S. Middleweight. Ht. 5'10"
Manager N. Christian

15.02.89	Mark White W PTS 6 Bethnal Green
01.03.89	Lester Jacobs L PTS 6 Bethnal Green
29.03.89	George Moody L PTS 6 Bethnal Green
09.05.89	Tony Cloak W RSC 2 Plymouth
20.06.89	Spencer Alton W PTS 6 Plymouth
17.10.89	Spencer Alton DREW 8 Plymouth
30.11.89	Ray Webb L PTS 6 Southwark
03.03.90	Michael Gale L RSC 2 Wembley
26.04.90	Michael Clarke L PTS 6 Wandsworth
21.05.90	Chris Walker W RSC 2 Mayfair
26.09.90	Ali Forbes L PTS 6 Mayfair
12.04.91	Frank Eubanks L RSC 1 Manchester
30.05.91	Russell Washer W PTS 6 Mayfair
06.06.91	John Kaighin DREW 6 Barking
27.06.91	Nick Manners L RSC 1 Leeds
16.12.91	Paul McCarthy L PTS 6 Southampton
25.02.92	Roland Ericsson L RSC 6 Crystal Palace
01.12.92	John Kaighin L RSC 4 Bristol
13.11.93	Martin Rosamond W PTS 6 Cullompton
04.03.94	Cliff Churchward W PTS 8 Weston super Mare
17.06.94	Paul Murray W PTS 8 Plymouth
07.10.94	Darren Dorrington L RSC 6 Taunton (*Vacant Western Area S. Middleweight Title*)
13.01.95	Thomas Hansvoll L PTS 6 Aalborg, Denmark
17.02.95	Mark Delaney L RSC 1 Crawley
25.03.95	Steve McNess L RSC 5 Millwall
23.06.95	Howard Eastman L RSC 1 Bethnal Green

Career: 26 contests, won 8, drew 2, lost 16.

Nicky Wadman

Brighton. *Born* Brighton, 8 August, 1965
Cruiserweight. Ht. 6'1"
Manager Self

11.03.92	Julian Johnson W PTS 6 Cardiff
23.04.92	Mark McBiane W RSC 1 Eltham
26.09.92	Hussain Shah L RSC 4 Earls Court
29.01.93	Alan Smiles L PTS 6 Glasgow
22.02.93	Steve Osborne W PTS 6 Eltham
21.10.93	Bobby Mack L PTS 6 Bayswater
09.02.94	Paul Lawson L RSC 1 Bethnal Green
21.05.94	Ray Kane L PTS 6 Belfast
17.09.94	Rudiger May L PTS 4 Leverkusen, Germany
23.02.95	John Pettersen L RSC 3 Southwark
12.05.95	Monty Wright L CO 2 Bethnal Green
13.06.95	Darren Westover L RSC 1 Basildon

Career: 12 contests, won 3, lost 9.

Mark Walker

Warrington. *Born* Billinge, 10 May, 1966
Cruiserweight. Ht. 5'9"
Manager F. Britton

14.01.85	Shamus Casey W PTS 6 Manchester
01.02.85	Eddie Chatterton W RSC 6 Warrington
11.02.85	Terry Gilbey W RSC 6 Manchester
29.03.85	Eddie Chatterton L CO 4 Liverpool
03.06.85	Mal Kirk L PTS 6 Manchester
12.09.85	Chris Little L PTS 6 Manchester
07.10.85	Eddie Chatterton W PTS 8 Liverpool
04.11.85	Chris Little W PTS 6 Manchester
11.11.85	Rusty Torrance DREW 6 Liverpool
02.12.85	Steve Goodwin L RSC 7 Manchester
10.02.86	Ronnie Tucker DREW 6 Manchester
03.03.86	Shaun West W CO 1 Leicester
18.03.86	Sean O'Phoenix DREW 8 Hull
21.04.86	Ian Jackson L PTS 6 Bradford
06.09.94	John Keeton L RSC 5 Stoke

Career: 15 contests, won 6, drew 3, lost 6.

Scott Walker

Shaw. *Born* Oldham, 5 December, 1970
L. Welterweight. Ht. 5'5"
Manager J. Doughty

18.04.94	Paul Bowen W PTS 6 Manchester
02.06.94	Brian Coleman W CO 1 Middleton
26.09.94	Carl Tilley W PTS 6 Morecambe
28.11.94	Wahid Fats L RSC 4 Manchester
16.02.95	John T. Kelly W PTS 6 Bury
08.03.95	Anthony Maynard L PTS 6 Solihull
18.05.95	Mark Allen W RSC 2 Middleton

Career: 7 contests, won 5, lost 2.

Marlon Ward

Bethnal Green. *Born* Newham, 23 March, 1968
Featherweight. Ht. 5'5"
Manager F. Maloney

| 29.09.94 | Keith Jones W PTS 4 Bethnal Green |
| 07.11.94 | Pete Buckley W PTS 4 Piccadilly |

Career: 2 contests, won 2.

Marlon Ward   Les Clark

Russell Washer

Swansea. *Born* Swansea, 21 January, 1962
Middleweight. Ht. 5'10"
Manager Self

15.09.90	Dean Cooper L PTS 6 Bristol
02.10.90	Nick Gyaamie W RSC 4 Eltham
16.10.90	Wayne Panayiotiou W RSC 2 Evesham
29.10.90	Chris Walker L RSC 2 Nottingham
11.12.90	Matt Mowatt W RSC 6 Evesham
24.01.91	Wayne Panayiotiou W RSC 4 Gorseinon
21.02.91	Marvin O'Brien DREW 6 Walsall
19.03.91	Tony Meszaros L PTS 6 Birmingham
10.04.91	Andrew Flute L PTS 6 Wolverhampton
30.05.91	Peter Vosper L PTS 6 Mayfair
04.09.91	Val Golding L RTD 5 Bethnal Green
11.11.91	Stinger Mason L PTS 4 Stratford on Avon
20.11.91	Alan Richards L PTS 6 Cardiff
29.11.91	Ensley Bingham L RSC 4 Manchester
11.03.92	Lee Crocker L PTS 6 Cardiff
22.04.92	Gilbert Jackson L PTS 6 Wembley
11.05.92	Carlo Colarusso L RSC 5 Llanelli (*Welsh L. Middleweight Title Challenge*)
18.06.92	Tony Collins L RSC 2 Peterborough
03.09.92	John Bosco L RSC 2 Dunstable
05.10.92	Sean Byrne L PTS 6 Northampton
15.10.92	Jerry Mortimer L RSC 5 Lewisham
28.11.92	Paul Wright L PTS 8 Manchester
10.12.92	Abel Asinamali W PTS 6 Bethnal Green
27.01.93	Barry Thorogood L PTS 6 Cardiff
03.02.93	Kevin Sheeran L PTS 6 Earls Court
27.02.93	Jamie Robinson L PTS 6 Dagenham
24.03.93	Robert Peel L PTS 6 Cardiff
31.03.93	Kevin Adamson L PTS 6 Barking
10.04.93	Ray Price W RSC 4 Swansea
23.05.93	Darren Blackford W PTS 6 Brockley
23.06.93	Adrian Dodson L PTS 6 Edmonton
25.07.93	Steve Foster L PTS 6 Oldham
14.08.93	Quinn Paynter L RSC 4 Hammersmith
22.09.93	Kevin Adamson L PTS 6 Bethnal Green
25.10.93	Danny Peters L PTS 6 Liverpool
03.11.93	Darren Dorrington L PTS 4 Bristol
10.11.93	Kevin Sheeran L RSC 5 Bethnal Green
30.11.93	Willie Quinn L PTS 6 Cardiff
23.02.94	Robert Allen L RSC 4 Watford
21.09.94	Jamie Robinson W PTS 6 Cardiff
27.10.94	Darren Dorrington L PTS 8 Bayswater
18.11.94	Sean Heron L PTS 6 Glasgow
07.02.95	Andy Ewen L PTS 4 Ipswich
13.04.95	Robert Harper W PTS 6 Bloomsbury

Career: 44 contests, won 9, drew 1, lost 34.

Graham Wassell

Pontefract. *Born* Wakefield, 29 December, 1966
L. Heavyweight. Ht. 6'4"
Manager T. Callighan

13.11.90	Alan Gandy DREW 6 Edgbaston
21.10.91	Gypsy Johnny Price L RSC 5 Bury
16.10.92	Sean Smith W RSC 2 Hull
01.12.92	Cliff Taylor W PTS 6 Hartlepool
19.04.93	Gypsy Johnny Price L RSC 1 Manchester
17.11.94	Slick Miller W RSC 1 Sheffield

Career: 6 contests, won 3, drew 1, lost 2.

Mike Watson

Nottingham. *Born* Nottingham, 17
December, 1973
Welterweight. Ht. 5'9"
Manager W. Swift

25.01.95 Steve Howden L RSC 2 Stoke
08.03.95 Adam Baldwin W PTS 6 Bloomsbury
Career: 2 contests, won 1, lost 1.

Paul Watson

Coatbridge. *Born* Belshill, 8 January, 1976
Featherweight. Ht. 5'6"
Manager T. Gilmour

20.02.95 Paul Goode W RSC 1 Glasgow
16.03.95 Paul Quarmby W RSC 3 Sunderland
05.06.95 Colin Innes W RSC 4 Glasgow
Career: 3 contests, won 3.

Peter Waudby

Hull. *Born* Hull, 18 November, 1970
Middleweight. Ht. 5'10½"
Manager Self

21.09.92 Simon Fisher W RSC 2 Cleethorpes
16.10.92 Chris Mulcahy W RSC 4 Hull
14.12.92 Shamus Casey W PTS 6 Cleethorpes
10.05.93 Julian Eavis W PTS 6 Cleethorpes
27.05.93 Warren Stowe L PTS 6 Burnley
16.09.93 Shamus Casey W PTS 6 Hull
10.11.93 Roy Rowland W RSC 5 Watford
13.12.93 Chris Richards W PTS 6 Cleethorpes
17.03.94 Dave Johnson W PTS 6 Lincoln
15.04.94 Colin Pitters W PTS 8 Hull
16.05.94 Shamus Casey W PTS 6 Cleethorpes
25.10.94 Kevin Lueshing L RSC 2
               Middlesbrough
24.11.94 Shamus Casey W PTS 6 Hull
16.02.95 Derek Wormald DREW 6 Bury
06.03.95 Paul Jones L PTS 6 Mayfair
Career: 15 contests, won 11, drew 1, lost 3.

Delroy Waul

Manchester. *Born* Manchester, 3 May, 1970
WBU Global L. Middleweight Champion.
Ht. 6'1"
Manager D. Powell

29.05.89 Calum Rattray W PTS 6 Dundee
12.06.89 Calum Rattray W PTS 6 Glasgow
25.09.89 Jimmy Reynolds W RSC 4
               Birmingham
10.10.89 David Maw W PTS 4 Sunderland
05.12.89 Richard Adams W RSC 4 Dewsbury
11.01.90 Richard Adams W RSC 3 Dewsbury
22.10.90 Jim Talbot W RTD 3 Mayfair
15.11.90 Mike Russell W CO 1 Oldham
13.12.90 Kid Sylvester W RSC 6 Dewsbury
31.01.91 Kevin Hayde W RSC 4 Bredbury
13.02.91 Chris Richards W PTS 6 Wembley
14.03.91 Terry Morrill DREW 8 Middleton
02.05.91 Andrew Furlong W RSC 5
               Northampton
16.05.91 Paul Wesley W RSC 7 Liverpool
20.06.91 Gordon Blair L CO 2 Liverpool
09.10.91 Paul King W RSC 6 Manchester
19.12.91 Jason Rowe W RSC 4 Oldham
31.01.92 Patrick Vungbo L DIS 8 Waregem,
               Belgium
02.07.92 Jimmy Thornton W RSC 6 Middleton
13.02.93 Wayne Shepherd W RSC 5 Manchester
25.06.93 Bruno Wuestenberg L PTS 8 Brussels,
               Belgium
01.11.93 Lansana Diallo DREW 6 Izegem,
               Belgium

18.12.94 Patrick Vungbo L PTS 6 Vilvoorde,
               Belgium
18.01.95 Wayne Appleton W PTS 6 Solihull
27.05.95 Roberto Welin W PTS 12 Kiel,
               Germany
               *(Vacant WBU Global L. Middleweight
               Title)*
Career: 25 contests, won 19, drew 2, lost 4.

Jim Webb

Belfast. *Born* Belfast, 13 August, 1968
L. Middleweight. Ht. 5'6½"
Manager F. Warren

02.06.95 Rick North W PTS 6 Bethnal Green
Career: 1 contest, won 1.

Jim Webb   Les Clark

Paul Webb

Nuneaton. *Born* Nuneaton, 5 July, 1970
L. Middleweight. Ht. 5'11"
Manager C. Gunns

08.03.95 Peter Mitchell L RSC 1 Bloomsbury
11.05.95 Robbie Bell L PTS 6 Sunderland
20.06.95 Steve Levene L PTS 6 Edgbaston
Career: 3 contests, lost 3.

Ray Webb

Hackney. *Born* Hackney, 10 March, 1966
S. Middleweight. Ht. 5'11"
Manager Self

02.11.88 Doug Calderwood W RSC 6
               Southwark
12.01.89 Robert Gomez W RSC 1 Southwark
30.11.89 Peter Vosper W PTS 6 Southwark
06.04.90 Carlo Colarusso L PTS 6 Telford
15.09.90 Ray Close L PTS 8 Belfast
06.11.90 Ahmet Canbakis W PTS 6 Mayfair
08.12.90 Franck Nicotra L PTS 8 Ferrara, Italy
10.01.91 Carlos Christie W PTS 6 Wandsworth
27.03.91 Silvio Branco L PTS 8 Mestre, Italy
30.05.91 Karl Barwise W PTS 8 Mayfair
11.12.91 Ian Strudwick L CO 8 Basildon
               *(Vacant Southern Area S. Middleweight
               Title)*

06.03.92 Oleg Volkov L PTS 8 Berlin, Germany
28.11.93 Karl Barwise W PTS 6 Southwark
06.03.94 Trevor Ambrose W RSC 6 Southwark
27.04.94 Darron Griffiths L RSC 6 Bethnal
               Green
               (Elim. British S. Middleweight Title)
20.02.95 Craig Joseph W PTS 6 Glasgow
Career: 16 contests, won 9, lost 7.

Paul Webster

Barking. *Born* Doncaster, 26 December,
1974
S. Featherweight. Ht. 5'6"
Manager B. Lynch

22.09.93 Kevin Simons W RSC 2 Bethnal Green
10.11.93 James Murray W PTS 4 Bethnal Green
17.02.94 Danny Ruegg W PTS 4 Dagenham
23.01.95 Marty Chestnut W RSC 3 Bethnal
               Green
27.04.95 Greg Upton W RSC 1 Bethnal Green
04.06.95 Barrie Kelley W RTD 1 Bethnal Green
16.06.95 Justin Murphy W PTS 6 Southwark
Career: 7 contests, won 7.

Scott Welch

Brighton. *Born* Yarmouth, 21 April, 1968
Heavyweight. Ht. 6'2"
Manager F. Warren

08.09.92 John Williams W RSC 5 Norwich
06.10.92 Gary Williams W PTS 4 Antwerp,
               Belgium
23.02.93 Gary Charlton L RSC 3 Doncaster
11.05.93 Denroy Bryan W RSC 4 Norwich
29.06.93 John Harewood W RSC 5 Mayfair
18.09.93 Des Vaughan W RSC 2 Leicester
28.09.93 Gypsy Carman W RSC 3 Bethnal
               Green
05.10.93 Cordwell Hylton W RSC 1 Mayfair
06.11.93 Joey Paladino W RSC 3 Bethnal Green
30.11.93 Chris Coughlan W CO 1 Cardiff
21.12.93 Carl Gaffney W RSC 3 Mayfair
15.03.94 Steve Garber W RSC 4 Mayfair
06.05.94 James Oyebola L CO 5 Atlantic City,
               USA
               *(Vacant WBC International
               Heavyweight Title)*
17.09.94 R. F. McKenzie W RSC 1 Crawley
10.12.94 Michael Murray W PTS 8 Manchester
13.05.95 Eduardo Carranza W CO 1 Glasgow
Career: 16 contests, won 14, lost 2.

Bradley Welsh

Edinburgh. *Born* Edinburgh, 4 November,
1970
Lightweight. Ht. 5'10"
Manager Self

11.03.94 Brian Wright W PTS 6 Glasgow
13.04.94 John T. Kelly W PTS 6 Glasgow
13.05.94 Chris Bennett W RSC 3 Kilmarnock
10.06.94 Kid McAuley W RTD 1 Glasgow
21.07.94 Mark Allen W PTS 6 Edinburgh
Career: 5 contests, won 5.

Tom Welsh

Holyhead. *Born* Bangor, 13 March, 1968
Welterweight. Ht. 5'8¾"
Manager D. Davies

12.04.95 Clive Sweetland W CO 2 Llanelli
17.05.95 Jason Spurling W PTS 4 Ipswich
12.06.95 Shaun Gledhill W RSC 4 Manchester
Career: 3 contests, won 3.

Paul Webster (right), shown beating Danny Ruegg, remains unbeaten after seven contests

Les Clark

Paul Wesley

Birmingham. *Born* Birmingham, 2 May, 1962
L. Middleweight. Ht. 5'9"
Manager N. Nobbs

20.02.87	B. K. Bennett L PTS 6 Maidenhead
18.03.87	Darryl Ritchie DREW 4 Stoke
08.04.87	Dean Murray W PTS 6 Evesham
29.04.87	John Wright W PTS 4 Loughborough
12.06.87	Leon Thomas W RSC 2 Leamington
16.11.87	Steve McCarthy L CO 8 Southampton
25.01.88	Paul Murray W PTS 8 Birmingham
29.02.88	Paul Murray DREW 8 Birmingham
15.03.88	Johnny Williamson W CO 2 Bournemouth
09.04.88	Joe McKenzie W RSC 6 Bristol
10.05.88	Tony Meszaros W PTS 8 Edgbaston
21.03.89	Carlton Warren L CO 2 Wandsworth
10.05.89	Rod Douglas L CO 1 Kensington
24.10.89	Nigel Rafferty L PTS 6 Wolverhampton
22.11.89	Nigel Rafferty L PTS 8 Stafford
28.11.89	Nigel Rafferty L PTS 6 Wolverhampton
05.12.89	Ian Strudwick L PTS 6 Catford
24.01.90	Rocky Feliciello W PTS 6 Solihull
19.02.90	Nigel Rafferty L PTS 8 Birmingham
22.03.90	John Ashton L PTS 10 Wolverhampton *(Midlands Area Middleweight Title Challenge)*
17.04.90	Winston May DREW 8 Millwall

09.05.90	Alan Richards W PTS 8 Solihull
04.06.90	Julian Eavis W PTS 8 Birmingham
18.09.90	Shaun Cummins L RSC 1 Wolverhampton
17.10.90	Julian Eavis W PTS 6 Stoke
23.01.91	Wally Swift Jnr L PTS 10 Solihull *(Midlands Area L. Middleweight Title Challenge)*
20.03.91	Horace Fleary L RSC 5 Solihull
16.05.91	Delroy Waul L RSC 7 Liverpool
04.07.91	Neville Brown W RSC 1 Alfreton
31.07.91	Francesco dell'Aquila L PTS 8 Casella, Italy
03.10.91	Neville Brown L PTS 8 Burton
29.10.91	Tony Collins DREW 8 Kensington
03.03.92	Antonio Fernandez L PTS 10 Cradley Heath *(Vacant Midlands Area Middleweight Title)*
10.04.92	Jean-Charles Meuret L PTS 8 Geneva, Switzerland
03.06.92	Sumbu Kalambay L PTS 10 Salice Terme, Italy
29.10.92	Ian Strudwick W RSC 1 Bayswater
14.11.92	Paul Busby L PTS 8 Cardiff
24.11.92	Paul Jones W RSC 2 Doncaster
16.03.93	Chris Pyatt L PTS 10 Mayfair
04.06.93	Jacques le Blanc L PTS 10 Moncton, Canada
28.07.93	Antonio Fernandez L RSC 3 Brixton *(Midlands Area Middleweight Title Challenge)*

09.10.93	Warren Stowe W PTS 10 Manchester *(Elim. British L. Middleweight Title)*
09.02.94	Steve Collins L PTS 8 Brentwood
10.02.95	Robert McCracken L PTS 12 Birmingham *(British L. Middleweight Title Challenge)*
24.02.95	Scott Doyle W PTS 8 Weston super Mare
18.03.95	Crisanto Espana L PTS 6 Millstreet, Eire
21.04.95	Gilbert Jackson L RSC 6 Dudley *(Elim. British L. Middleweight Title)*

Career: 47 contests, won 16, drew 4, lost 27.

Darren Westover

Ilford. *Born* Plaistow, 3 September, 1963
Cruiserweight. Ht. 6'3"
Manager B. Hearn

04.10.89	Dave Furneaux W RSC 1 Kensington
25.10.89	David Haycock W RSC 2 Wembley
06.12.89	Kevin Roper W RSC 1 Wembley
03.03.90	Steve Osborne W RSC 6 Wembley
26.04.94	Newbirth Mukosi W RSC 5 Bethnal Green
11.05.94	Art Stacey W PTS 6 Stevenage
09.05.95	Rob Albon W RSC 2 Basildon
13.06.95	Nicky Wadman W RSC 1 Basildon

Career: 8 contests, won 8.

Terry Whittaker

Barnsley. *Born* Barnsley, 15 July, 1971
L. Welterweight. Ht. 5'6½"
Manager K. Tate

17.11.94 Ram Singh W PTS 6 Sheffield
14.06.95 Ram Singh W PTS 6 Batley
Career: 2 contests, won 2.

Dave Whittle

North Shields. *Born* North Shields, 19 May, 1966
L. Middleweight. Ht. 5'9"
Manager T. Conroy

22.11.88 Mark Jay L PTS 6 Marton
28.02.89 Tony Farrell W PTS 6 Marton
31.03.89 Seamus Sheridan W RSC 2 Scarborough
19.05.89 Chris Mulcahy L PTS 6 Gateshead
03.06.89 Ian Thomas W PTS 6 Stanley
13.12.89 Ian Thomas W PTS 6 Kirkby
27.02.90 Trevor Meikle DREW 8 Marton
04.06.90 Bullit Andrews W PTS 6 Edgbaston
29.11.90 Trevor Meikle W PTS 6 Marton
13.05.91 Barry Messam L PTS 6 Marton
23.10.91 Jamie Robinson L RSC 4 Bethnal Green
27.11.91 Alan Peacock W PTS 6 Marton
02.03.92 Jimmy Thornton L PTS 6 Marton

12.03.92 Alan Peacock DREW 8 Glasgow
14.04.92 Nigel Bradley L CO 3 Mansfield
18.05.92 Wayne Shepherd L PTS 6 Marton
17.03.93 Dean Hiscox W PTS 6 Stoke
11.06.93 Steve Scott W PTS 6 Gateshead
25.11.93 Bullit Andrews W PTS 6 Newcastle
03.03.94 Mark Jay W PTS 8 Newcastle
21.04.94 Rick North W PTS 6 Gateshead
26.09.94 Craig Winter L PTS 6 Liverpool
Career: 22 contests, won 12, drew 2, lost 8.

Anthony Huw Williams

Abercynon. *Born* Pontypridd, 21 November, 1967
Welterweight. Ht. 5'7"
Manager D. Gardiner

12.10.94 Paul Salmon W RSC 4 Sheffield
29.11.94 Scott Doyle W PTS 6 Cardiff
08.03.95 Paul Dyer L PTS 6 Cardiff
Career: 3 contests, won 2, lost 1.

Derek Williams

Peckham. *Born* Stockwell, 11 March, 1965
Former European & Commonwealth Heavyweight Champion. Ht. 6'5"
Manager F. Maloney

24.10.84 Tony Tricker W RSC 6 Mayfair
24.01.85 Mike Creasey W RSC 3 Streatham

11.02.85 Barry Ellis W RSC 2 Dulwich
25.03.85 Alphonso Forbes W RSC 2 Merton
20.09.85 Ron Ellis L PTS 8 Longford
30.01.86 Steve Gee W PTS 6 Merton
22.02.87 Steve Gee W PTS 6 Wembley
24.03.87 Andrew Gerrard W PTS 6 Wembley
25.06.87 Jess Harding W PTS 6 Bethnal Green
08.10.87 John Westgarth W RSC 7 Bethnal Green
28.01.88 Dave Garside W PTS 10 Bethnal Green
18.05.88 Mark Young W CO 4 Portsmouth
26.10.88 John Westgarth W RSC 2 Kensington
29.11.88 Young Haumona W CO 4 Kensington
          (Vacant Commonwealth Heavyweight Title)
14.02.89 Noel Quarless W CO 1 Wandsworth
05.04.89 Al Evans W RSC 2 Kensington
24.08.89 Mark Wills L PTS 8 New York, USA
05.12.89 Hughroy Currie W RSC 1 Catford
          (Vacant European Heavyweight Title. Commonwealth Heavyweight Title Defence)
03.02.90 Jean Chanet L PTS 12 St Didier, France
          (European Heavyweight Title Defence)
28.05.90 Jean Chanet L PTS 12 Paris, France
          (European Heavyweight Title Challenge)
01.05.91 Jimmy Thunder W RSC 2 Bethnal Green
          (Commonwealth Heavyweight Title Defence)

Derek William (left), seen covering up against Michael Murray, appears to be on the slide, without a win from his last five contests

Les Clark

30.09.91   David Bey W RTD 6 Kensington
18.01.92   Tim Anderson W RSC 1 Kensington
30.04.92   Lennox Lewis L RSC 3 Kensington
(Commonwealth Heavyweight Title Defence. British & European Heavyweight Title Challenge)
25.03.93   Bert Cooper L PTS 10 Atlantic City, USA
03.12.93   Jose Ribalta DREW 3 St Louis, USA
23.02.95   Michael Murray L PTS 8 Southwark
16.06.95   Keith Fletcher L RSC 5 Southwark
Career: 28 contests, won 19, drew 1, lost 8.

Everald Williams

Canning Town. *Born* Jamaica, 10 June, 1969
L. Welterweight. Ht. 5'9"
Manager J. Ryan

05.03.92   Korso Aleain W CO 6 Battersea
28.11.93   Michael Alexander W PTS 6 Southwark
06.03.94   Mike Morrison W PTS 4 Southwark
28.05.94   Steve Burton DREW 6 Queensway
29.09.94   Shaba Edwards W CO 1 Bethnal Green
25.10.94   Dewi Roberts W PTS 6 Southwark
17.11.94   Wayne Jones W RSC 2 Southwark
27.04.95   Alan Temple W PTS 6 Bethnal Green
25.05.95   Peter Richardson L RSC 6 Reading
Career: 9 contests, won 7, drew 1, lost 1.

Gary Williams

Nottingham. *Born* Nottingham, 25 September, 1965
Heavyweight, Ht. 5'11½"
Manager Self

27.04.92   Damien Caesar L RSC 4 Mayfair
07.09.92   J. A. Bugner L PTS 4 Bethnal Green
06.10.92   Scott Welch L PTS 4 Antwerp, Belgium
01.12.92   Kenny Sandison W PTS 6 Liverpool
27.01.93   Kenny Sandison W DREW 6 Stoke
13.02.93   Kevin McBride L PTS 4 Manchester
01.03.93   Ashley Naylor DREW 6 Bradford
29.03.93   Kevin Cullinane W RSC 2 Liverpool
26.04.93   Ashley Naylor W PTS 6 Bradford
21.07.93   Peter Smith L RSC 4 Marula, South Africa
08.12.93   Graham Arnold L PTS 6 Hull
02.02.94   Vincenzo Cantatore L CO 2 Ferrara, Italy
17.03.94   Neil Kirkwood L RSC 1 Lincoln
10.09.94   Clayton Brown L PTS 4 Birmingham
04.10.94   Mike Holden L RSC 4 Mayfair
13.12.94   Damien Caesar L RSC 2 Ilford
18.03.95   Darren Corbett DREW 6 Millstreet, Eire
06.05.95   Clayton Brown L PTS 4 Shepton Mallet
10.06.95   Joey Paladino L PTS 6 Manchester
Career: 19 contests, won 3, drew 3, lost 13.

(John) J. T. Williams

Cwmbran. *Born* Pontylottyn, 22 May, 1970
Welsh S. Featherweight Champion. Ht. 5'6¼"
Manager M. Jacobs

21.01.91   Kelton McKenzie DREW 6 Crystal Palace
10.04.91   Dave Buxton W PTS 8 Newport

28.05.91   Frankie Ventura W PTS 6 Cardiff
18.07.91   Billy Barton W PTS 6 Cardiff
22.01.92   Derek Amory W PTS 6 Cardiff
30.03.92   Steve Pollard L PTS 6 Eltham
07.10.92   Kevin McKillan W PTS 6 Barry
14.11.92   Peter Judson DREW 6 Cardiff
19.05.93   Dominic McGuigan L PTS 6 Sunderland
01.10.93   Neil Haddock L PTS 10 Cardiff
10.11.93   Barrie Kelley W RTD 3 Ystrad
(Welsh S. Featherweight Title Challenge)
03.03.94   Wayne Windle W RSC 3 Ebbw Vale
30.07.94   Tony Pep L RSC 1 Bethnal Green
(Commonwealth S. Featherweight Title Challenge)
08.03.95   Edward Lloyd DREW 10 Cardiff
(Welsh S. Featherweight Title Defence)
Career: 14 contests, won 7, drew 3, lost 4.

(Kirk) John Williams (Gibbon)

Birmingham. *Born* Birmingham, 26 October, 1963
Heavyweight. Ht. 6'2½"
Manager Self

12.02.85   Dougie Isles W RSC 5 South Shields
14.10.85   Alex Romeo W PTS 6 Birmingham
11.11.85   Roy Smith L RSC 2 Birmingham
27.02.86   Lou Gent L RSC 4 Merton
12.05.86   Blaine Logsdon L RSC 3 Manchester
15.09.86   Steve Williams L PTS 6 Glasgow
10.11.86   Simon Harris L PTS 6 Longford
27.01.87   Sean Daly L RSC 2 Manchester
19.01.88   Jon McBean W CO 3 Kings Heath
17.02.88   Lennie Howard L RSC 5 Bethnal Green
26.05.88   Gerry Storey W PTS 6 Bethnal Green
28.10.88   Magne Havnaa L RTD 4 Copenhagen, Denmark
23.10.89   Denroy Bryan DREW 6 Mayfair
21.02.90   Joe Egan L PTS 6 Belfast
03.03.90   Luigi Gaudiano L RSC 1 Pagani, Italy
24.09.90   Steve Yorath W PTS 6 Mayfair
26.11.90   Crawford Ashley L RSC 1 Mayfair
12.05.92   Gary Delaney L PTS 6 Crystal Palace
08.09.92   Scott Welch L RSC 5 Norwich
25.10.94   Pat Passley L PTS 4 Southwark
25.05.95   Keith Fletcher L RSC 2 Reading
Career: 21 contests, won 5, drew 1, lost 15.

(Lee) L. A. Williams

Blackwell. *Born* Caerphilly, 16 March, 1968
Heavyweight. Ht. 5'10"
Manager D. Gardiner

17.11.88   Ted Cofie L RSC 4 Ilkeston
15.09.89   Rob Albon DREW 6 High Wycombe
24.10.89   Herbie Hide L CO 2 Bethnal Green
16.12.93   Kent Davis L RSC 2 Newport
23.03.94   Darren Ashton L PTS 6 Stoke
07.04.94   John Foreman L RSC 7 Walsall
12.09.94   Monty Wright L RSC 1 Mayfair
30.11.94   Robert Norton L RSC 2 Wolverhampton
12.04.95   Darren Fearn L PTS 6 Llanelli
15.05.95   Martin Langtry L CO 2 Cleethorpes
Career: 10 contests, drew 1, lost 9.

Rowan Williams

Birmigham. *Born* Birmingham, 18 March, 1968
Midlands Area Bantamweight Champion. Ht. 5'5½"
Manager Self

17.02.93   Nick Tooley W PTS 4 Bethnal Green
04.04.93   Des Gargano W PTS 4 Brockley
23.06.93   Graham McGrath W PTS 4 Edmonton
01.10.93   Neil Swain L PTS 6 Cardiff
10.02.94   Neil Armstrong L PTS 6 Glasgow
11.11.94   Jesper D. Jensen L PTS 6 Randers, Denmark
18.01.95   Graham McGrath W CO 6 Solihull
(Vacant Midlands Area Bantamweight Title)
25.01.95   Neil Swain L PTS 6 Cardiff
02.03.95   Donnie Hood L PTS 8 Glasgow
20.04.95   Peter Culshaw L CO 6 Liverpool
01.06.95   Neil Parry W PTS 8 Musselburgh
Career: 11 contests, won 5, lost 6.

Rowan Williams   Les Clark

Steve Williams

Nottingham. *Born* Worksop, 11 October, 1968
Flyweight. Ht. 5'7"
Manager J. Ashton

06.03.95   Shaun Hall DREW 6 Bradford
06.04.95   Andy Roberts W PTS 6 Sheffield
Career: 2 contests, won 1, drew 1.

George Wilson

Camberwell. *Born* London, 7 April, 1966
Welterweight. Ht. 5'10"
Manager Self

18.06.92   Sean Cave L PTS 6 Peterborough
07.07.92   Erwin Edwards L RSC 4 Bristol
08.09.92   Erwin Edwards L RSC 3 Southend
16.02.93   Derrick Daniel W PTS 6 Tooting
23.02.93   Sean Metherell W PTS 6 Kettering
29.03.93   Joel Ani L PTS 6 Mayfair
21.06.93   Jamie Davidson W RSC 4 Swindon

03.11.93   Sean Baker L RSC 2 Bristol
26.02.94   Michael Carruth L PTS 6 Earls Court
29.03.94   Mark Tibbs L RSC 6 Bethnal Green
27.10.94   Paul Dyer L PTS 4 Bayswater
04.02.95   Paul Ryan L RSC 4 Cardiff
26.04.95   Steve Tuckett L PTS 6 Solihull
12.05.95   Mohamed Boualleg L RSC 6 Rouen, France

Career: 14 contests, won 3, lost 11.

John Wilson

Edinburgh. *Born* Edinburgh, 4 January, 1972
L. Heavyweight. Ht. 6'1"
Manager A. Morrison/F. Warren

18.11.94   Steve Yorath W PTS 6 Glasgow
18.12.94   Craig Byrne W RSC 2 Glasgow
21.01.95   Tim Robinson W RSC 1 Glasgow
04.03.95   Darren Ashton NC 3 Livingston
08.06.95   Art Stacey W PTS 6 Glasgow

Career: 5 contests, won 4, no contest 1.

Stephen Wilson

Wallyford. *Born* Edinburgh, 30 March, 1971
S. Middleweight. Ht. 6'0"
Manager T. Gilmour

23.11.92   Lee Prudden W PTS 6 Glasgow
25.01.93   Paul Smith W RSC 1 Glasgow
06.03.93   Dave Owens W RSC 2 Glasgow
23.03.93   Nigel Rafferty L RSC 3 Wolverhampton
07.06.93   Shamus Casey W PTS 6 Glasgow
20.09.93   Stinger Mason W RSC 6 Glasgow
21.02.94   Carlos Christie W RSC 2 Glasgow
28.03.94   Dave Owens W CO 2 Musselburgh
25.04.94   John J. Cooke W PTS 6 Bury
19.09.94   Simon McDougall W RTD 3 Glasgow
24.10.94   Paul Wright W PTS 10 Glasgow
           (Elim. British S. Middleweight Title)
20.03.95   Glenn Campbell W PTS 10 Glasgow
           (Final Elim. British S. Middleweight Title)

Career: 12 contests, won 11, lost 1.

Wayne Windle

Sheffield. *Born* Sheffield, 18 October, 1968
Former Central Area Lightweight Champion. Ht. 5'8"
Manager Self

25.10.88   Mick Mulcahy L PTS 6 Cottingham
17.11.88   Dave Pratt L PTS 6 Ilkeston
02.02.89   Jeff Dobson L RSC 6 Croydon
04.04.89   John Ritchie DREW 4 Sheffield
05.10.89   Des Gargano L PTS 6 Middleton
16.10.89   Des Gargano W PTS 6 Manchester
16.11.89   Noel Carroll L PTS 6 Manchester
04.12.89   Brendan Ryan DREW 6 Manchester
29.01.90   Mike Close W PTS 6 Liverpool
05.02.90   Mike Close W PTS 6 Brierley Hill
22.02.90   Bernard McComiskey W PTS 6 Kensington
12.03.90   Barry North W PTS 6 Hull
21.03.90   Neil Foran L PTS 6 Preston
29.05.90   Terry Collins L PTS 6 Bethnal Green
11.06.90   Muhammad Lovelock W PTS 6 Manchester
12.09.90   Brian Cullen W RSC 1 Stafford
08.10.90   Johnny Walker DREW 6 Leicester
22.10.90   Mick Mulcahy W PTS 4 Cleethorpes

14.11.90   Andy Robins W PTS 6 Sheffield
26.11.90   Michael Driscoll L RSC 3 Bethnal Green
16.01.91   Karl Taylor L PTS 8 Stoke
06.02.91   Felix Kelly L PTS 6 Bethnal Green
12.03.91   Mark Antony W CO 1 Mansfield
24.04.91   Steve Foran L CO 3 Preston
13.06.91   Pete Roberts W RSC 7 Hull
           (Vacant Central Area Lightweight Title)
16.08.91   Aukunun L PTS 6 Marbella, Spain
21.09.91   George Scott L CO 2 Tottenham
10.12.91   Kevin Toomey W PTS 6 Sheffield
26.03.92   Kevin Toomey L DIS 8 Hull
           (Central Area Lightweight Title Defence)
03.09.92   Billy Schwer L CO 1 Dunstable
20.01.93   Mark Elliot L CO 3 Wolverhampton
01.06.93   Mick Mulcahy L PTS 6 Manchester
01.12.93   Gary Thornhill L PTS 6 Stoke
03.03.94   J. T. Williams L RSC 3 Ebbw Vale
01.10.94   Dave Anderson L RSC 2 Cardiff
14.04.95   Bernard McComiskey L RSC 5 Belfast
12.06.95   Ricky Sackfield L PTS 6 Manchester

Career: 37 contests, won 12, drew 3, lost 22.

Carl Winstone

Newport. *Born* Pontypool, 21 December, 1967
Middleweight. Ht. 6'0"
Manager D. Gardiner

22.03.94   Nicky Thurbin L PTS 6 Bethnal Green
20.03.95   Darren Sweeney L PTS 6 Birmingham
12.04.95   Paul Matthews W PTS 6 Llanelli

Career: 3 contests, won 1, lost 2.

Craig Winter

Warrington. *Born* Aylesbury, 10 September, 1971
L. Middleweight. Ht. 5'10"
Managers R. Jones/T. Gilmour

19.12.93   Allan Logan W PTS 6 Glasgow
28.02.94   Wayne Shepherd W PTS 6 Manchester
18.04.94   John Duckworth W RSC 5 Manchester
26.09.94   Dave Whittle W PTS 6 Liverpool
10.12.94   Hughie Davey W PTS 6 Manchester
25.03.95   David Maw W RSC 3 Rothwell
20.04.95   Paul King W RSC 4 Liverpool
16.06.95   Ernie Loveridge W PTS 6 Liverpool

Career: 8 contests, won 8.

Mark Winters

Belfast. *Born* Antrim, 29 December, 1971
L. Welterweight. Ht. 5'8"
Manager F. Warren

04.03.95   Trevor Smith W PTS 6 Livingston
10.06.95   Mark McGowan W PTS 6 Manchester

Career: 2 contests, won 2.

Clinton Woods

Sheffield. *Born* Sheffield, 1 May, 1972
S. Middleweight. Ht. 6'2"
Manager K. Tate

17.11.94   Dave Proctor W PTS 6 Sheffield
12.12.94   Earl Ling W RSC 5 Cleethorpes
23.02.95   Paul Clarkson W RSC 1 Hull
06.04.95   Japhet Hans W RSC 3 Sheffield
15.05.95   Kevin Burton W PTS 6 Cleethorpes
14.06.95   Kevin Burton W RSC 6 Batley

Career: 6 contests, won 6.

Chris Woollas

Doncaster. *Born* Scunthorpe, 22 November, 1973
L. Heavyweight. Ht. 5'11"
Manager T. Petersen

17.08.94   Darren Littlewood W RSC 4 Sheffield
05.10.94   Robert Norton DREW 6 Wolverhampton
05.12.94   Neil Simpson W PTS 6 Cleethorpes
10.02.95   Monty Wright L RSC 4 Birmingham
30.06.95   Kenny Nevers L RSC 2 Doncaster

Career: 5 contests, won 2, drew 1, lost 2.

Shane Woollas

Doncaster. *Born* Scunthorpe, 28 July, 1972
Heavyweight. Ht. 6'2"
Manager T. Petersen

26.08.94   Neil Kirkwood L RSC 6 Barnsley

Career: 1 contest, lost 1.

Derek Wormald

Rochdale. *Born* Rochdale, 24 May, 1965
Middleweight. Ht. 5'10"
Managers J. Doughty/T. Gilmour

28.04.86   Dave Binsteed W RSC 2 Liverpool
20.05.86   Taffy Morris W PTS 6 Huddersfield
16.06.86   Claude Rossi W PTS 6 Manchester
23.09.86   Shamus Casey W PTS 8 Batley
16.10.86   Nigel Moore DREW 6 Merton
11.11.86   David Scere W RSC 3 Batley
25.11.86   Cliff Domville W RSC 4 Manchester
08.12.86   Martin McGough W RTD 4 Edgbaston
10.02.87   Manny Romain W CO 3 Batley
07.04.87   Tony Brown W RSC 6 Batley
28.04.87   Johnny Stone W RSC 1 Manchester
15.09.87   Sammy Sampson W PTS 10 Batley
09.02.88   Richard Wagstaff W RSC 6 Bradford
23.02.88   Judas Clottey W PTS 10 Oldham
12.04.88   John Ashton W RSC 4 Oldham
           (Elim. British L. Middleweight Title)
11.10.89   Gary Stretch L RSC 1 Millwall
           (British L. Middleweight Title Challenge)
24.09.92   Mark Jay W RSC 5 Stockport
27.05.93   Mark Dawson W RTD 5 Burnley
11.11.93   Paul Hitch W RSC 6 Burnley
25.04.94   Martin Jolley W RSC 4 Bury
20.10.94   Marvin O'Brien W PTS 6 Middleton
10.12.94   Dave Johnson DREW 8 Manchester
16.02.95   Peter Waudby DREW 6 Bury
30.06.95   Antonio Fernandez W PTS 10 Doncaster
           (Elim. British Middleweight Title)

Career: 24 contests, won 20, drew 3, lost 1.

Andy Wright

Tooting. *Born* Aldershot, 20 December, 1963
L. Heavyweight. Former Undefeated Southern Area S. Middleweight Champion. Ht. 5'11½"
Manager Self

20.03.86   Shamus Casey W RSC 4 Merton
15.04.86   J. J. Smith L PTS 6 Merton
28.05.86   Shamus Casey W PTS 6 Lewisham
04.09.86   Kevin Roper W CO 2 Merton
20.11.86   Winston Burnett W PTS 8 Merton
24.02.87   Nick Vardy W CO 1 Wandsworth

03.06.87 Simon Collins DREW 6 Southwark
24.09.87 Andy Till L RSC 2 Crystal Palace
01.12.87 Alex Romeo W RSC 2 Southend
14.12.87 Paul McCarthy W CO 3 Piccadilly
03.02.88 Steve McCarthy L RSC 4 Wembley
30.03.88 Errol Christie L CO 2 Bethnal Green
15.11.88 Darren Hobson L RSC 3 Hull
08.03.89 Ray Close L RSC 4 Belfast
20.03.91 Paul McCarthy W CO 5 Wandsworth
(Southern Area S. Middleweight Title Challenge)
22.10.91 John Kaighin DREW 6 Wandsworth
25.02.92 John Kaighin W PTS 6 Crystal Palace
16.02.93 Marvin O'Brien W PTS 6 Tooting
02.06.94 Hunter Clay L RSC 7 Tooting
31.03.95 Jerry Mortimer W RSC 1 Crystal Palace

Career: 20 contests, won 11, drew 2, lost 7.

Carl Wright

Liverpool. *Born* Liverpoool, 19 February, 1969
L. Welterweight. Ht. 5'7"
Manager S. Vaughan

13.10.89 Mick Mulcahy W PTS 6 Preston
31.10.89 Mick Mulcahy W PTS 6 Manchester
24.01.90 Mike Morrison W PTS 6 Preston
19.12.90 Julian Eavis W PTS 6 Preston
31.03.92 Ricky Sackfield W RSC 1 Stockport
14.05.92 Brendan Ryan W PTS 4 Liverpool
12.06.92 Dean Bramhald W PTS 6 Liverpool
15.09.92 Wayne Panayiotiou W RSC 2 Liverpool
25.09.92 Mick Mulcahy W PTS 8 Liverpool
12.11.92 Jim Lawlor W RSC 3 Liverpool
29.04.93 Marcel Herbert W PTS 8 Mayfair
09.04.94 Paul Ryan L RSC 6 Mansfield
31.10.94 Richard Swallow W PTS 6 Liverpool
27.02.95 Hugh Forde W PTS 6 Barrow
20.04.95 John O. Johnson W PTS 6 Liverpool

Career: 15 contests, won 14, lost 1.

Monty Wright

Biggleswade. *Born* Bedford, 1 November, 1969
L. Heavyweight. Ht. 5'9"
Managers M. Duff/T. Lawless

10.11.93 Steve Osborne W RSC 3 Watford
26.01.94 Nigel Rafferty W PTS 6 Birmingham
16.02.94 Bobby Mack W RSC 3 Stevenage
11.03.94 Greg Scott-Briggs W CO 1 Bethnal Green
05.04.94 Karl Barwise W PTS 6 Bethnal Green
11.05.94 Simon McDougall L PTS 6 Stevenage
12.09.94 L. A. Williams W RSC 1 Mayfair
11.10.94 Tim Robinson W CO 1 Bethnal Green
30.11.94 Greg Scott-Briggs W PTS 6 Wolverhampton
10.02.95 Chris Woollas W RSC 4 Birmingham
12.05.95 Nicky Wadman W CO 2 Bethnal Green
23.06.95 Art Stacey W RSC 2 Bethnal Green

Career: 12 contests, won 11, lost 1.

Paul Wright

Liverpool. *Born* Liverpool, 24 February, 1966
Middleweight. Ht. 5'9¾"
Manager S. Vaughan

13.10.89 Andy Balfe W RSC 1 Preston
31.10.89 John Tipping W RSC 1 Manchester

20.12.89 Nigel Rafferty DREW 6 Kirkby
13.04.92 Shaun McCrory W PTS 6 Manchester
14.05.92 Chris Walker W PTS 6 Liverpool
15.09.92 John Kaighin W DIS 5 Liverpool
23.10.92 Jason McNeill W RSC 1 Liverpool
28.11.92 Russell Washer W PTS 8 Manchester
05.02.93 Sean Smith W RSC 2 Manchester
22.04.93 Glenn Campbell L RSC 4 Bury
(Elim. British S. Middleweight Title & Central Area S. Middleweight Title Challenge)
06.09.93 Alan Baptiste W PTS 6 Liverpool
02.07.94 Shamus Casey W RSC 1 Liverpool
26.09.94 Carlos Christie W PTS 6 Liverpool
24.10.94 Stephen Wilson L PTS 10 Glasgow
(Elim. British S. Middleweight Title)
27.02.95 John Duckworth DREW 6 Barrow
20.04.95 Chris Richards W PTS 6 Liverpool

Career: 16 contests, won 12, drew 2, lost 2.

Robert Wright

Dudley. *Born* Dudley, 25 August, 1966
L. Middleweight. Ht. 5'11"
Manager M. Duff

16.05.88 Steve Hogg W PTS 6 Wolverhampton
14.06.88 Joff Pugh W RSC 5 Dudley
22.09.88 Martin Campbell W RSC 5 Wolverhampton
13.04.89 Steve Hogg W PTS 6 Wolverhampton
05.06.89 Dean Dickinson W RSC 4 Birmingham
10.10.89 Julian Eavis W PTS 8 Wolverhampton
11.12.89 Mike Russell W CO 1 Birmingham
20.03.90 Mickey Hughes L RSC 7 Norwich
16.11.90 Tony Britland W RSC 3 Telford
02.10.91 Chris Mulcahy W RSC 1 Solihull
20.11.91 Tony Gibbs W RTD 2 Solihull
26.11.91 Darren Dyer L RSC 3 Bethnal Green
15.01.92 Julian Eavis W PTS 8 Stoke
10.03.92 Errol McDonald W CO 3 Bury
17.03.92 Donovan Boucher L RSC 11 Mayfair
(Commonwealth Welterweight Title Challenge)
09.07.92 Gary Jacobs L RSC 6 Glasgow
(British Welterweight Title Challenge)
05.05.93 Sidney Msutu L PTS 10 Cape Town, South Africa
05.10.94 John Bosco W RSC 7 Wolverhampton
30.11.94 Harry Dhami W PTS 8 Wolverhampton
10.02.95 Mark McCreath L PTS 8 Birmingham

Career: 20 contests, won 14, lost 6.

Stefan Wright

Peterborough. *Born* Peterborough, 23 May, 1970
S. Middleweight. Ht. 5'10"
Manager P. De Freitas

22.10.90 John Kaighin W PTS 6 Peterborough
14.12.90 Shamus Casey W PTS 6 Peterborough
24.01.91 Andre Wharton L RSC 5 Brierley Hill
07.11.91 Gary Booker W PTS 6 Peterborough
28.04.92 Jerry Mortimer W RSC 4 Corby
18.06.92 Chris Richards W PTS 6 Peterborough
10.12.92 Paul McCarthy W PTS 6 Corby
04.03.93 Karl Barwise L RTD 5 Peterborough
13.05.95 Darren Ashton L PTS 6 Glasgow

Career: 9 contests, won 6, lost 3.

Paul Wynn

Newcastle. *Born* Newcastle, 23 March, 1972
S. Featherweight. Ht. 5'6"
Manager N. Fawcett

28.02.91 Tony Falcone L PTS 6 Sunderland
06.04.91 Tommy Smith L PTS 6 Darlington
13.05.91 Karl Morling L RSC 2 Northampton
29.04.93 Chip O'Neill W PTS 6 Newcastle
06.05.93 Tommy Smith W PTS 6 Hartlepool
01.06.93 Mark Hargreaves L PTS 6 Manchester
30.10.93 George Naylor L RSC 3 Chester
17.02.94 Robert Grubb W PTS 6 Walsall
11.03.94 James Murray L PTS 6 Glasgow
13.04.94 Shaun Anderson DREW 6 Glasgow
21.04.94 Alan Graham L PTS 6 Gateshead
13.05.94 Shaun Anderson W PTS 8 Kilmarnock
24.05.94 Chip O'Neill L PTS 6 Sunderland
10.06.94 Dennis Holbaek Pedersen L PTS 6 Kolding, Denmark
17.02.95 Hugh Collins L RSC 3 Cumbernauld
06.04.95 Roger Brotherhood L RSC 5 Sheffield
13.05.95 Brian Carr L RTD 2 Glasgow

Career: 17 contests, won 4, drew 1, lost 12.

Freddie Yemofio

Hayes. *Born* London, 15 July, 1969
S. Middleweight. Ht. 5'10"
Manager D. Gunn

31.08.93 Lee Sara L PTS 6 Croydon
30.09.93 Martin Rosamond L PTS 6 Hayes
20.05.94 Lee Blundell L RSC 6 Acton
30.09.94 Jason Hart L PTS 6 Bethnal Green
26.05.95 Robert Harper W PTS 6 Norwich

Career: 5 contests, won 1, lost 4.

Steve Yorath

Blackwood. *Born* Cardiff, 8 August, 1965
Cruiserweight. Ht. 6'2"
Manager D. Gardiner

21.11.85 Dai Davies L RSC 5 Blaenavon
13.03.86 John Ashton L CO 3 Alfreton
08.05.90 Rob Albon L PTS 6 Brentford
06.07.90 Phil Soundy L CO 3 Brentwood
17.09.90 Chris Coughlan W PTS 6 Cardiff
24.09.90 John Williams L PTS 6 Mayfair
03.10.90 Phil Soundy L PTS 6 Basildon
19.10.90 Neils H. Madsen L PTS 6 Skive, Denmark
15.04.91 Tony Colclough W PTS 6 Wolverhampton
24.04.91 Phil Soundy W PTS 6 Basildon
28.05.91 R. F. McKenzie W PTS 6 Cardiff
27.06.91 Denzil Browne L PTS 6 Leeds
21.01.92 Graham Arnold W PTS 6 Norwich
31.03.92 Graham Arnold L PTS 6 Norwich
18.05.92 Maro van Spaendonck L PTS 4 Valkenswaard, Holland
23.09.92 Denzil Browne L PTS 8 Leeds
25.11.92 Terry Dunstan L PTS 8 Mayfair
24.02.93 Derek Angol L RSC 5 Wembley
03.04.93 Biko Botowamungu L RSC 5 Vienna, Austria
10.07.93 Chris Okoh L PTS 6 Cardiff
31.08.93 Devon Rhooms L PTS 6 Croydon
04.10.93 Terry Dixon L RSC 4 Mayfair
09.04.94 Dermot Gascoyne L CO 3 Mansfield
27.08.94 Kent Davis W PTS 6 Cardiff
08.09.94 Sean Heron L PTS 6 Glasgow
18.11.94 John Wilson L PTS 6 Glasgow
27.11.94 Owen Bartley DREW 6 Southwark
25.01.95 Kent Davis L PTS 6 Cardiff

Career: 28 contests, won 6, drew 1, lost 21.

British Area Title Bouts during 1994-95

Central Area

Titleholders at 30 June 1995

Fly: Louis Veitch. **Bantam:** *vacant.* **S. Bantam:** Paul Lloyd. **Feather:** *vacant.* **S. Feather:** *vacant.* **Light:** Tony Foster. **L. Welter:** *vacant.* **Welter:** *vacant.* **L. Middle:** *vacant.* **Middle:** *vacant.* **S. Middle:** Glenn Campbell. **L. Heavy:** Michael Gale. **Cruiser:** Tony Booth. **Heavy:** Neil Kirkwood.

2 November 1994	Louis Veitch W PTS 10 Lyndon Kershaw, Solihull (Fly)
23 February 1995	Tony Brown W RSC 10 Kevin Toomey, Hull (Vacant Welter)
11 March 1995	Neil Kirkwood W RSC 2 Carl Gaffney, Barnsley (Vacant Heavy)
27 April 1995	Tony Booth W PTS 10 Art Stacey, Hull (Vacant Cruiser)

During the above period, Floyd Churchill (S. Feather) and Richard Burton (L. Welter) forfeited titles, while Tony Brown (Welter) and Warren Stowe (L. Middle) relinquished their crowns.

Midlands Area

Titleholders at 30 June 1995

Fly: Anthony Hanna. **Bantam:** Rowan Williams. **S. Bantam:** Pete Buckley. **Feather:** Kelton McKenzie. **S. Feather:** *vacant.* **Light:** Karl Taylor. **L. Welter:** Malcolm Melvin. **Welter:** Lindon Scarlett. **L. Middle:** Steve Goodwin. **Middle:** Antonio Fernandez. **S. Middle:** Carlos Christie. **L. Heavy:** John J. Cooke. **Cruiser:** Nigel Rafferty. **Heavy:** Wayne Buck.

2 September 1994	Matthew Harris W CO 5 Karl Morling, London (Vacant S. Bantam)
20 October 1994	John J. Cooke W RSC 7 Nigel Rafferty, Walsall (L. Heavy)
30 November 1994	Anthony Hanna W PTS 10 Shaun Norman, Solihull (Vacant Fly)
5 December 1994	Cordwell Hylton L PTS 10 John Foreman, Birmingham (Cruiser)
18 January 1995	Rowan Williams W CO 6 Graham McGrath, Solihull (Vacant Bantam)
10 February 1995	Matthew Harris L RSC 6 Pete Buckley, Birmingham (S. Bantam)
20 March 1995	John Foreman L PTS 10 Nigel Rafferty, Birmingham (Cruiser)
24 June 1995	Wayne Buck W RSC 6 Cordwell Hylton, Cleethorpes (Vacant Heavy)

During the above period, Pete Buckley (S. Feather) relinquished his title.

Northern Area

Titleholders at 30 June 1995

Fly: *vacant.* **Bantam:** *vacant.* **S. Bantam:** *vacant.* **Feather:** *vacant.* **S. Feather:** Dominic McGuigan. **Light:** *vacant.* **L. Welter:** *vacant.* **Welter:** Paul King. **L. Middle:** Mark Cichocki. **Middle:** *vacant.* **S. Middle:** *vacant.* **L. Heavy:** Terry French. **Cruiser:** *vacant.* **Heavy:** *vacant.*

2 March 1995	Frankie Foster L RSC 6 Dominic McGuigan, Tynemouth (S. Feather)

During the above period, Paul Charters (L. Welter) and Paul Lister (Heavy) retired.

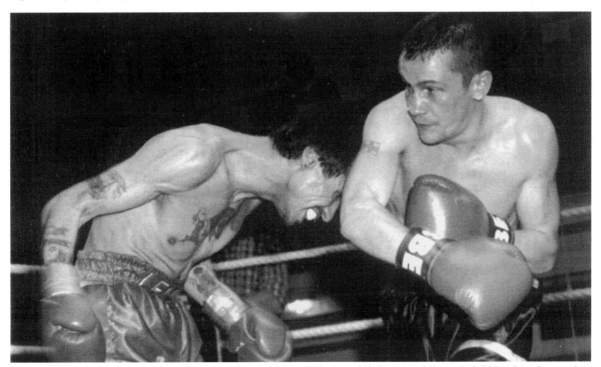

In a thrilling fight for the vacant Southern Area flyweight title, Ricky Beard (left) stopped Daren Fifield inside eight rounds

Les Clark

Bernard Paul (left) forces Keith Marner to cover up on his way to the Southern Area light-welter crown   Les Clark

Northern Ireland Area

Titleholders at 30 June 1995 - None.

Scottish Area

Titleholders at 30 June 1995

Fly: James Drummond. **Bantam:** James Murray. **S. Bantam:** *vacant.* **Feather:** *vacant.* **S. Feather:** Mark Geraghty. **Light:** Kris McAdam. **L. Welter:** *vacant.* **Welter:** *vacant.* **L. Middle:** *vacant.* **Middle:** *vacant.* **S. Middle:** *vacant.* **L. Heavy:** *vacant.* **Cruiser:** *vacant.* **Heavy:** *vacant.*

18 November 1994	James Murray W PTS 10 Shaun Anderson, Glasgow (Vacant Bantam)
21 January 1995	James Murray W RSC 3 Louis Veitch, Glasgow (Bantam)

During the above period, Willie Beattie (Welter) retired.

Southern Area

Titleholders at 30 June 1995

Fly: Ricky Beard. **Bantam:** *vacant.* **S. Bantam:** *vacant.* **Feather:** *vacant.* **S. Feather:** *vacant.* **Light:** Cham Joof. **L. Welter:** Bernard Paul. **Welter:** Gary Logan. **L. Middle:** Nicky Thurbin. **Middle:** *vacant.* **S. Middle:** *vacant.* **L. Heavy:** Garry Delaney. **Cruiser:** Chris Okoh. **Heavy:** Julius Francis.

29 September 1994	Gary Logan W PTS 10 Ojay Abrahams, London (Welter)
18 November 1994	Jonathan Thaxton L PTS 10 Keith Marner, Bracknell (L. Welter)
20 January 1995	Geoff McCreesh W RSC 1 Clay O'Shea, London (Vacant L. Middle)
23 February 1995	Julius Francis W RSC 8 Damien Caesar, London (Vacant Heavy)
23 February 1995	Chris Okoh W RSC 5 Paul Lawson, London (Vacant Cruiser)
30 March 1995	Ricky Beard W RSC 8 Daren Fifield, London (Vacant Fly)

27 April 1995	Julius Francis W PTS 10 Keith Fletcher, London (Heavy)
23 May 1995	Keith Marner L PTS 10 Bernard Paul, Potters Bar (L. Welter)
23 June 1995	Nicky Thurbin W PTS 10 Vince Rose, London (Vacant L. Middle)

During the above period, Ali Forbes (S. Middle) and James Oyebola (Heavy) relinquished titles, while W. O. Wilson (Middle) and John Graham (Cruiser) retired.

Welsh Area

Titleholders at 30 June 1995

Fly: *vacant.* **Bantam:** *vacant.* **S. Bantam:** *vacant.* **Feather:** Peter Harris. **S. Feather:** J. T. Williams. **Light:** Mervyn Bennett. **L. Welter:** *vacant.* **Welter:** *vacant.* **L. Middle:** Carlo Colarusso. **Middle:** Barry Thorogood. **S. Middle:** Darron Griffiths. **L. Heavy:** *vacant.* **Cruiser:** *vacant.* **Heavy:** Chris Jacobs.

29 November 1994	Barry Thorogood W PTS 10 Robert Peel, Cardiff (Vacant Middle)
8 March 1995	J. T. Williams DREW 10 Edward Lloyd, Cardiff (S. Feather)
12 April 1995	Barry Thorogood W RSC 8 Robert Peel, Llanelli (Middle)
5 May 1995	Darron Griffiths W PTS 10 Wayne Ellis, Swansea (S. Middle)

Western Area

Titleholders at 30 June 1995

Fly: *vacant.* **Bantam:** *vacant.* **S. Bantam:** Tony Falcone. **Feather:** *vacant.* **S. Feather:** Greg Upton. **Light:** *vacant.* **L. Welter:** *vacant.* **Welter:** *vacant.* **L. Middle:** Dean Cooper. **Middle:** *vacant.* **S. Middle:** Darren Dorrington. **L. Heavy:** *vacant.* **Cruiser:** *vacant.* **Heavy:** *vacant.*

7 October 1994	Darren Dorrington W RSC 6 Peter Vosper, Taunton (Vacant S. Middle)
18 February 1995	Tony Falcone W PTS 10 Danny Ruegg, Shepton Mallet (Vacant S. Bantam)

British Title Bouts during 1994-95

3 August 1994 Ross Hale 9.12¾ (England) W RSC 7 Hugh Forde 10.0 (England), Whitchurch Leisure Centre, Bristol (L. Welterweight Title). Referee: Mickey Vann. Although Hale's Commonwealth title was not at stake, with Forde not viewed as a credible challenger, the latter gave the champion all the trouble he could handle until one big punch sent him down to a stoppage defeat at 3.04 of the seventh round.

10 September 1994 Robert McCracken 10.13¼ (England) W PTS 12 Steve Foster 11.0 (England), National Exhibition Centre, Birmingham (L. Middleweight Title). On a night that both sets of fans disgraced themselves, McCracken, cut on the forehead as early as the second, did enough to justify John Coyle's 118-116½ decision. Foster looked dangerous at times, but was unable to make it pay.

10 September 1994 Del Bryan 10.4¾ (England) W PTS 12 Lindon Scarlett 10.5 (England), National Exhibition Centre, Birmingham (Welterweight Title). Starting after midnight, the fight lacked sparkle in the empty surrounds and, although the challenger tried everything he knew, he could not subdue the clever Bryan, who was well worth John Keane's 118½-117 points verdict.

20 September 1994 Francis Ampofo 7.13¾ (England) W RSC 3 James Drummond 8.0 (Scotland), Brunton Hall, Musselburgh (Flyweight Title). After making a bright start, the challenger picked up a bad cut over the right-eyebrow following a clash of heads at the end of the second and, from then on, was up against it. Despite the protestations of his corner, Drummond was pulled out by the referee, Mickey Vann, at 1.02 of round three, having being decked for a count of seven and offering little in the way of reply. By his victory, Ampofo also won the Lonsdale Belt outright.

19 November 1994 Crawford Ashley 12.7 (England) W PTS 12 Nicky Piper 12.7 (Wales), Ice Rink, Cardiff (Vacant L. Heavyweight Title). Fighting for the title vacated by Maurice Core the previous month, when he went forward to challenge for the European championship, both men gave it everything and more. At the finish it was the rapidly tiring Ashley who was the winner, taking John Coyle's 117½-116 points verdict after flooring (in the eighth) and inflicting a variety of cuts to Piper's face.

19 November 1994 James Oyebola 17.4½ (England) W CO 4 Clifton Mitchell 16.8 (England), Ice Rink, Cardiff (Vacant Heavyweight Title). Referee: Roy Francis. A dramatic finish, much against the run of play, and certainly out of the blue, saw Mitchell poleaxed for the full count by a straight-right at 0.58 of the fourth round. The title had been left vacant after Herbie Hide defeated Michael Bentt for the WBO crown last March.

23 November 1994 Drew Docherty 8.5 (Scotland) W PTS 12 Ady Benton 8.5 (England), Magnum Centre, Irvine (Bantamweight Title). Dominating the fight, Docherty won a Lonsdale Belt outright when receiving Roy Francis' 119-116½ verdict, a margin of five rounds that fully made up for his cornerman Pat Clinton's defeat at the hands of Benton seven months earlier. Although Benton always had a puncher's chance, there was only one man ever really in it.

29 November 1994 Neville Brown 11.5¾ (England) W RSC 9 Antonio Fernandez 11.5¼ (England), Chase Leisure Centre, Cannock (Middleweight Title). Both men were cut over both eyes, but that is where the similarities ended. Although the challenger went well for seven rounds, once Brown had imparted his will on his rival, the writing was on the wall. Under sustained pressure, Fernandez simply had no answers and was rescued by referee, Dave Parris, with 1.49 of the ninth round remaining, leaving the winner as the proud possessor of a Lonsdale Belt.

13 December 1994 Floyd Havard 9.3¾ (Wales) W RSC 10 Dave McHale 9.2½ (Scotland), The Island, Ilford (British S. Featherweight Title). Referee: John Keane. For the third time in successive British title fights, the winner went home with a Lonsdale Belt for keeps. This time it was the turn of Havard who, despite some difficulty in making the weight, forced a stoppage at 1.56 of the tenth round, having proved to be just too good in every department, apart from courage that is, for the gutsy challenger.

20 December 1994 Francis Ampofo 8.0 (England) W RSC 2 Daren Fifield 8.0 (England), York Hall, Bethnal Green (Flyweight Title). Once Ampofo realised that Fifield had neither the firepower or strength to hurt and extend him, the fight was as good as over. Decked after taking a heavy right-hander, and then going down again on both knees, the Commonwealth champion was saved from further punishment by referee, John Coyle, with 0.75 of the second round remaining.

21 January 1995 Dennis Andries 13.8 (England) W RSC 11 Denzil Browne 13.7¼ (England), Scottish Exhibition Centre, Glasgow (Vacant Cruiserweight Title). Fighting for the title vacated by Carl Thompson in February 1994, at the age of 41, the amazing Dennis Andries became the oldest man ever to win a British championship when he forced Paul Thomas to come to the aid of his by now defenceless rival at 2.09 of the penultimate round.

23 January 1995 Ali Forbes 11.13½ (England) W PTS 12 Fidel Castro 11.12¾ (England), York Hall, Bethnal Green (Vacant S. Middleweight Title). At the ripe old age of 33, and with just 13 professional fights behind him, Forbes' desire was the difference between winning or losing John Keane's 118-117½ points decision. The championship, vacated by Cornelius Carr at the end of December, was certainly within the grasp of Castro, but he failed to up his workrate at a critical stage of the contest and the chance to regain his old crown passed him by.

With just 13 pro bouts under his belt, Ali Forbes (right) narrowly outscored Fidel Castro (Smith) to win the vacant British super-middleweight title
Les Clark

23 January 1995   Michael Deveney 9.0 (Scotland) W PTS 12 Wilson Docherty 8.13½ (Scotland), Forte Crest Hotel, Glasgow (Vacant Featherweight Title). With Billy Hardy deciding to relinquish the title in December rather than defend, the two Scots were matched to contest the vacancy. In taking Dave Parris' 117½-117 points decision, Deveney proved that old fashioned jab-and-run tactics still have a place in the sport, while his harder-hitting rival, always looking to tee off, was outwitted in a contest that could still have gone either way.

10 February 1995   Robert McCracken 11.0 (England) W PTS 12 Paul Wesley 10.13 (England), Aston Villa Leisure Centre, Birmingham (L. Middleweight Title). Mickey Vann's scoreline of 117½-117 tells you how close Wesley came to pulling off a major upset, and there were still many who thought he had done just that. McCracken, who was never able to keep his game plan together for any concerted period, won the Lonsdale Belt outright on the result.

17 February 1995   Michael Ayers 9.8½ (England) W RSC 6 Paul Burke 9.8¾ (England), Leisure Centre, Crawley (Vacant Lightweight Title). Closing down Burke unremittingly, the more powerful Ayers gradually ground his man down and when the former was badly cut over the left-eye in the fourth the writing was on the wall. Bravely, Burke hung in before being rescued by Roy Francis at 2.54 of the sixth after a heavy left-hook sent him wobbling against the ropes defenceless. The two men had been matched when Billy Schwer relinquished the title in January to challenge for the IBF crown.

18 February 1995   Ross Hale 9.13¾ (England) W PTS 12 Malcolm Melvin 9.13 (England), Bath & West Country Showground, Shepton Mallet (L. Welterweight Title). Floored three times in the first, it was difficult to see Melvin progressing beyond the round. But progress he did and, although Hale collected Mickey Vann's decision along with a Lonsdale Belt for keeps with an emphatic 119½-115½ margin, he allowed his rival back into the fight. At the same time, his limitations were exposed against an opponent who boxed mainly on the retreat.

3 March 1995   Neville Brown 11.5½ (England) W RSC 7 Carlo Colarusso 11.4¾ (Wales), York Hall, Bethnal Green (Middleweight Title). Pressing forward continuously, Colarusso fought the only way he knew, but was met by a strangely subdued champion. It was only in the seventh that Brown woke up to the job at hand and started to let the punches go as the game Welshman walked onto them. Caught by a big right-hand, Colarusso was bowled over for a seven count and, on rising at 2.26, Dave Parris waved the fight off.

25 March 1995   Richie Wenton 8.8½ (England) W RSC 5 Paul Lloyd 8.9½ (England), Northgate Arena, Chester (S. Bantamweight Title). Despite being smashed to the canvas twice in the first, the brave Lloyd continued to take the fight to Wenton, as the pair met head-on and swopped punches. This could not last for ever and one of them had to go. In the event it was Lloyd who, after showing great determination to get up from a cracking left-hook delivery in the fifth, was stopped seconds later by referee, John Coyle, at 2.25 of the round.

31 March 1995   Michael Ayers 9.8¾ (England) W RSC 8 Karl Taylor 9.8¾ (England), National Sports Centre, Crystal Palace (Lightweight Title). As early as the second session Taylor was cut on the left-eye, before picking up similar damage under the other eye a round later. It was only Taylor's stout chin that kept him in the fight for so long but, by the eighth, there was only going to be one winner and looking a sorry state indeed he was led back to his corner by Paul Thomas after 56 seconds.

27 April 1995   Ali Forbes 11.13¾ (England) L PTS 12 Sammy Storey 12.0 (Ireland), York Hall, Bethnal Green (S. Middleweight). With two notches already on a Lonsdale Belt back in 1989, by his victory, Storey made the belt his own property. However, John Coyle's 118-117 points verdict appeared to flatter Forbes, who seemed to be running second best for at least two-thirds of the fight. There were no knockdowns and, although the champion hardly took a backward step, Storey's hand-speed won the day.

5 May 1995   Floyd Havard 9.1 (Wales) W CO 9 Michael Armstrong 9.1¼ (England), Brangwyn Hall, Swansea (S. Featherweight). After a difficult start, by the fifth, Havard had at last begun to find some rhythm and the former champion ended the session cut over the right-eye. Armstrong, though, was still forcing the fight, with the Welshman relying more on single blows and it was one of these, a terrific right-hook, that sent the former crashing to the deck to be counted out by John Keane at 2.41 of the ninth round.

13 May 1995   Dennis Andries 13.7¾ (England) L PTS 12 Terry Dunstan 13.6¼ (England), Kelvin Hall, Glasgow (Cruiserweight Title). Awarded the 118½-117 points decision by Paul Thomas, Dunstan won the title after just nine professional fights, a result that was hotly disputed by the loser following the fight. The new titleholder started well enough but, by the eighth round, he was blowing hard in the face of constant aggression and from that point onwards Andries pressed home the advantage, although not enough in the eyes of the referee.

23 May 1995   Michael Ayers 9.8¼ (England) W RSC 3 Charles Shepherd 9.7½ (England), Furzefield Leisure Centre, Potters Bar (Lightweight Title). Ayers, by his victory, proved to be a class or two above his tough rival, picking his man apart with the jab, cutting his left-eye, and dropping him with a booming right-hander. Following the knockdown, the end came at 0.50 of the third when Larry O'Connell rescued Shepherd, who was being hammered against the ropes without response. The win not only brought Ayers a Lonsdale Belt outright but, in achieving the feat within 95 days, he beat the previous record of 160 days set by Colin McMillan in 1991.

2 June 1995   Del Bryan 10.5½ (England) W RSC 11 Gary Logan 10.6½ (England), York Hall, Bethnal Green (Welterweight Title). Boxing cagily, his southpaw stance often bewildering the challenger, Bryan made a good start and carried it right through to the finish. Logan was never really able to make his aggression pay and he was swiftly (pun excused) countered more often than not and in the later stages, when being pounded without reply, Larry O'Connell came to his rescue at 1.15 of the 11th round. Now in his second spell as champion, the victory brought Bryan his second Lonsdale Belt, making him the ninth man during the season to win the belt outright.

Michael Ayers (left) hammered former champion, Paul Burke, to defeat when winning the vacant British lightweight title

Les Clark

Lord Lonsdale Challenge Belts: Outright Winners

The original belts were donated to the National Sporting Club by Lord Lonsdale and did not bear his name, the inscription reading, "The National Sporting Club's Challenge Belt." It was not until the British Boxing Board of Control was formed that the emblems were reintroduced and the belts became known as the Lord Lonsdale Challenge Belts. The first contest involving the BBBoC belt was Benny Lynch versus Pat Palmer for the flyweight title on 16 September 1936. To win a belt outright, a champion must score three title match victories at the same weight, not necessarily consecutively.

Outright Winners of the National Sporting Club's Challenge Belt, 1909-1935 (20)

FLYWEIGHT	Jimmy Wilde; Jackie Brown
BANTAMWEIGHT	Digger Stanley; Joe Fox; Jim Higgins; Johnny Brown; Johnny King
FEATHERWEIGHT	Jim Driscoll; Tancy Lee; Johnny Cuthbert; Nel Tarleton
LIGHTWEIGHT	Freddie Welsh
WELTERWEIGHT	Johnny Basham; Jack Hood
MIDDLEWEIGHT	Pat O'Keefe; Len Harvey; Jock McAvoy
L. HEAVYWEIGHT	Dick Smith
HEAVYWEIGHT	Bombardier Billy Wells; Jack Petersen

Outright Winners of the BBBoC Lord Lonsdale Challenge Belt, 1936-1995 (92)

FLYWEIGHT	Jackie Paterson; Terry Allen; Walter McGowan; John McCluskey; Hugh Russell; Charlie Magri; Pat Clinton; Robbie Regan; Francis Ampofo
BANTAMWEIGHT	Johnny King; Peter Keenan (2); Freddie Gilroy; Alan Rudkin; Johnny Owen; Billy Hardy; Drew Docherty
FEATHERWEIGHT	Nel Tarleton; Ronnie Clayton (2); Charlie Hill; Howard Winstone (2); Evan Armstrong; Pat Cowdell; Robert Dickie; Paul Hodkinson; Colin McMillan; Sean Murphy
S. FEATHERWEIGHT	Jimmy Anderson; John Doherty; Floyd Havard
LIGHTWEIGHT	Eric Boon; Billy Thompson; Joe Lucy; Dave Charnley; Maurice Cullen; Ken Buchanan; Jim Watt; George Feeney; Tony Willis; Carl Crook; Billy Schwer; Michael Ayers
L. WELTERWEIGHT	Joey Singleton; Colin Power; Clinton McKenzie (2); Lloyd Christie; Andy Holligan; Ross Hale
WELTERWEIGHT	Ernie Roderick; Wally Thom; Brian Curvis (2); Ralph Charles; Colin Jones; Lloyd Honeyghan; Kirkland Laing; Del Bryan (2)
L. MIDDLEWEIGHT	Maurice Hope; Jimmy Batten; Pat Thomas; Prince Rodney; Andy Till; Robert McCracken
MIDDLEWEIGHT	Pat McAteer; Terry Downes; Johnny Pritchett; Bunny Sterling; Alan Minter; Kevin Finnegan; Roy Gumbs; Tony Sibson; Herol Graham; Neville Brown
S. MIDDLEWEIGHT	Sammy Storey
L. HEAVYWEIGHT	Randy Turpin; Chic Calderwood; Chris Finnegan; Bunny Johnson; Tom Collins; Dennis Andries; Tony Wilson; Crawford Ashley
CRUISERWEIGHT	Johnny Nelson
HEAVYWEIGHT	Henry Cooper (3); Horace Notice; Lennox Lewis

NOTES: Jim Driscoll was the first champion to win an NSC belt outright, whilst Eric Boon later became the first champion to put three notches on a BBBoC belt.

Nel Tarleton and Johnny King are the only champions to have won both belts outright.

Freddie Welsh and Johnny King, each with just two notches on an NSC Lonsdale Belt, were allowed to keep their spoils after winning British Empire titles, while Walter McGowan and Charlie Magri, with one notch on a BBBoC Lonsdale Belt, kept their awards under the three years/no available challengers ruling.

Henry Cooper holds the record number of belts won by a single fighter, three in all.

Chris and Kevin Finnegan are the only brothers to have won belts outright.

Jim Higgins holds the record for winning an NSC belt outright in the shortest time, 279 days, whilst Michael Ayers won a BBBoC belt in just 95 days.

In 1994-95, a record for any one season, nine belts were won outright by Francis Ampofo, Drew Docherty, Floyd Havard, Michael Ayers, Ross Hale, Del Bryan, Robert McCracken, Neville Brown and Sammy Storey.

British Champions Since Gloves, 1878-1995

The listings below show the tenure of all British champions at each weight since gloves (two ounces or more) were introduced to British rings under Queensberry Rules. Although Charley Davis (147 lbs) had beaten Charlie Napper (140 lbs) with gloves in 1873, we start with Denny Harrington, who defeated George Rooke for both the English and world middleweight titles in London on 12 March 1878. We also make a point of ignoring competition winners, apart from Anthony Diamond who beat Dido Plumb for the middles title over 12 rounds, basically because full championship conditions of finish fights of three minute rounds were not applied. Another point worth bearing in mind, is that prior to the 1880s there were only three weights, heavy, middle and light. Anything above 154 lbs, the middleweight limit, was classified a heavyweight contest, whereas below, say 133 lbs, was considered to be a lightweight bout. Therefore, to put things into current perspective, in many cases, we have had to ascertain the actual poundage of fighters concerned and relate them to the modern weight classes. Another point worth remembering is that men born outside Britain, who won open titles in this country, are not recorded for fear of added confusion, and, although many of the champions or claimants listed before 1909, were no more than English titleholders, having fought for the "championship of England", for our purposes they carry the "British" label.

Prior to 1909, the year that the Lord Lonsdale Challenge Belt was introduced and weight classes subsequently standardised, poundages within divisions could vary quite substantially, thus enabling men fighting at different weights to claim the same "title" at the same time. A brief history of the weight fluctuations between 1891 and 1909, shows:

Bantamweight   With the coming of gloves, the division did not really take off until Nunc Wallace established himself at 112 lbs on beating (small) Bill Goode after nine rounds in London on 12 March 1889. Later, with Wallace fighting above the weight, Billy Plimmer was generally recognised as the country's leading eight stoner, following victories over Charles Mansford and Jem Stevens and became accepted as world champion when George Dixon, the number one in America's eyes, gradually increased his weight. In 1895 Pedlar Palmer took the British title at 112 lbs, but by 1900 he had developed into a 114 pounder. Between 1902 and 1904, Joe Bowker defended regularly at 116 lbs and in 1909 the NSC standardised the weight at 118 lbs, even though the USA continued for a short while to accept only 116 lbs.

Featherweight   Between 1886 and 1895, one of the most prestigious championship belts in this country was fought for at 126 lbs and although George Dixon was recognised in the USA as world featherweight champion, gradually moving from 114 to 122 lbs, no major international contests took place in Britain during the above period at his weight. It was only in 1895, when Fred Johnson took the British title at 120 lbs, losing it to Ben Jordan two years later, that we came into line with the USA. Ben Jordan became an outstanding champion, who, between 1898 and 1899, was seen by the NSC as world champion at 120 lbs. However, first Harry Greenfield, then Jabez White and Wil Curley, continued to claim the 126 lbs version of the British title and it was only in 1900, when Jack Roberts beat Curley, that the weight limit was finally standardised at nine stone.

Lightweight   Outstanding champions often carried their weights as they grew in size. A perfect example of this was Dick Burge, the British lightweight champion from 1891-1901, who gradually increased from 134 to 144 lbs, while still maintaining his right to the title. It was not until 1902 that Jabez White brought the division into line with the USA. Later, both White and then Goldswain, carried their weight up to 140 lbs and it was left to Johnny Summers to set the current limit of 135 lbs.

Welterweight   The presence of Dick Burge fighting from 134 to 144 lbs plus up until 1900, explains quite adequately why the welterweight division, although very popular in the USA, did not take off in this country until 1902. The championship was contested between 142 and 146 lbs in those days and was not really supported by the NSC, but by 1909 with their backing it finally became established at 147 lbs.

Note that the Lonsdale Belt notches (title bout wins) relate to NSC, 1909-1935, and BBBoC, 1936-1995.

Champions in **bold** are accorded national recognition.

*Undefeated champions (Includes men who may have forfeited their titles).

Title Holder	Lonsdale Belt Notches	Tenure	Title Holder	Lonsdale Belt Notches	Tenure	Title Holder	Lonsdale Belt Notches	Tenure
Flyweight (112 lbs)			Jimmy Wilde		1914-1915	Jackie Brown	3	1931-1935
Sid Smith		1911	**Joe Symonds**	1	1915-1916	**Benny Lynch***	2	1935-1938
Sid Smith	1	1911-1913	**Jimmy Wilde***	3	1916-1923	**Jackie Paterson**	4	1939-1948
Bill Ladbury		1913-1914	**Elky Clark***	2	1924-1927	**Rinty Monaghan***	1	1948-1950
Percy Jones*	1	1914	**Johnny Hill***	1	1927-1929	**Terry Allen**	1	1951-1952
Joe Symonds		1914	**Jackie Brown**		1929-1930	**Teddy Gardner***	1	1952
Tancy Lee	1	1914-1915	**Bert Kirby**	1	1930-1931	**Terry Allen***	2	1952-1954

163

Title Holder	Lonsdale Belt Notches	Tenure
Dai Dower*	1	1955-1957
Frankie Jones	2	1957-1960
Johnny Caldwell*	1	1960-1961
Jackie Brown	1	1962-1963
Walter McGowan*	1	1963-1966
John McCluskey*	3	1967-1977
Charlie Magri*	1	1977-1981
Kelvin Smart	1	1982-1984
Hugh Russell	3	1984-1985
Duke McKenzie*	2	1985-1986
Dave Boy McAuley*	1	1986-1988
Pat Clinton*	3	1988-1991
Robbie Regan	1	1991
Francis Ampofo	1	1991
Robbie Regan*	2	1991-1992
Francis Ampofo	3	1992-

Bantamweight (118 lbs)

Title Holder	Lonsdale Belt Notches	Tenure
Nunc Wallace*		1889-1891
Billy Plimmer		1891-1895
Tom Gardner		1892
Willie Smith		1892-1896
Nunc Wallace		1893-1895
George Corfield		1893-1895
Pedlar Palmer		1895-1900
George Corfield		1895-1896
Billy Plimmer		1896-1898
Harry Ware		1899-1900
Harry Ware		1900-1902
Andrew Tokell		1901-1902
Jim Williams		1902
Andrew Tokell		1902
Harry Ware		1902
Joe Bowker		1902-1910
Owen Moran		1905-1907
Digger Stanley		1906-1910
Digger Stanley	2	1910-1913
Bill Beynon	1	1913
Digger Stanley	1	1913-1914
Curley Walker*	1	1914-1915
Joe Fox*	3	1915-1917
Tommy Noble	1	1918-1919
Walter Ross*	1	1919-1920
Jim Higgins	3	1920-1922
Tommy Harrison		1922-1923
Bugler Harry Lake	1	1923
Johnny Brown*	3	1923-1928
Alf Pattenden	2	1928-1929
Johnny Brown		1928
Teddy Baldock		1928-1929
Teddy Baldock*	1	1929-1931
Dick Corbett	1	1931-1932
Johnny King	1	1932-1934
Dick Corbett*	1	1934
Johnny King	1+2	1935-1947
Jackie Paterson	2	1947-1949
Stan Rowan*	1	1949
Danny O'Sullivan	1	1949-1951
Peter Keenan	3	1951-1953
John Kelly	1	1953-1954
Peter Keenan	3	1954-1959
Freddie Gilroy*	4	1959-1963
Johnny Caldwell	1	1964-1965
Alan Rudkin	1	1965-1966
Walter McGowan	1	1966-1968
Alan Rudkin*	4	1968-1972
Johnny Clark*	1	1973-1974
Dave Needham	1	1974-1975
Paddy Maguire	1	1975-1977

Title Holder	Lonsdale Belt Notches	Tenure
Johnny Owen*	4	1977-1980
John Feeney	1	1981-1983
Hugh Russell	1	1983
Davy Larmour	1	1983
John Feeney	1	1983-1985
Ray Gilbody	2	1985-1987
Billy Hardy*	5	1987-1991
Joe Kelly	1	1992
Drew Docherty	3	1992-

S. Bantamweight (122 lbs)

Title Holder	Lonsdale Belt Notches	Tenure
Richie Wenton	2	1994-

Featherweight (126 lbs)

Title Holder	Lonsdale Belt Notches	Tenure
Bill Baxter		1884-1891
Harry Overton		1890-1891
Billy Reader		1891-1892
Fred Johnson		1891-1895
Harry Spurden		1892-1895
Jack Fitzpatrick		1895-1897
Fred Johnson		1895-1897
Harry Greenfield		1897-1899
Ben Jordan*		1897-1900
Jabez White		1899-1900
Wil Curley		1900-1901
Jack Roberts		1901-1902
Wil Curley		1902-1903
Ben Jordan*		1902-1905
Joe Bowker*		1905
Johnny Summers		1906
Joe Bowker		1905-1906
Jim Driscoll		1906-1907
Spike Robson*		1906-1907
Jim Driscoll*	3	1907-1913
Spike Robson		1907-1910
Ted Kid Lewis*	1	1913-1914
Llew Edwards*	1	1915-1917
Charlie Hardcastle	1	1917
Tancy Lee*	3	1917-1919
Mike Honeyman	2	1920-1921
Joe Fox*	1	1921-1922
George McKenzie	2	1924-1925
Johnny Curley	2	1925-1927
Johnny Cuthbert	1	1927-1928
Harry Corbett	1	1928-1929
Johnny Cuthbert	2	1929-1931
Nel Tarleton	1	1931-1932
Seaman Tommy Watson	2	1932-1934
Nel Tarleton	3	1934-1936
Johnny McGrory*	1	1936-1938
Jim Spider Kelly	1	1938-1939
Johnny Cusick	1	1939-1940
Nel Tarleton*	3	1940-1947
Ronnie Clayton	6	1947-1954
Sammy McCarthy	1	1954-1955
Billy Spider Kelly	1	1955-1956
Charlie Hill	3	1956-1959
Bobby Neill	1	1959-1960
Terry Spinks	2	1960-1961
Howard Winstone*	7	1961-1969
Jimmy Revie	2	1969-1971
Evan Armstrong	2	1971-1972
Tommy Glencross	1	1972-1973
Evan Armstrong*	2	1973-1975
Vernon Sollas	1	1975-1977
Alan Richardson	2	1977-1978
Dave Needham	2	1978-1979
Pat Cowdell*	3	1979-1982
Steve Sims*	1	1982-1983

Title Holder	Lonsdale Belt Notches	Tenure
Barry McGuigan*	2	1983-1986
Robert Dickie*	3	1986-1988
Peter Harris	1	1988
Paul Hodkinson*	3	1988-1990
Sean Murphy	2	1990-1991
Gary de Roux	1	1991
Colin McMillan*	3	1991-1992
John Davison*	1	1992-1993
Sean Murphy*	1	1993
Duke McKenzie*	1	1993-1994
Billy Hardy*	1	1994
Michael Deveney	1	1995-

S. Featherweight (130 lbs)

Title Holder	Lonsdale Belt Notches	Tenure
Jimmy Anderson*	3	1968-1970
John Doherty	1	1986
Pat Cowdell	1	1986
Najib Daho	1	1986-1987
Pat Cowdell	1	1987-1988
Floyd Havard	1	1988-1989
John Doherty	1	1989-1990
Joey Jacobs	1	1990
Hugh Forde	1	1990
Kevin Pritchard	1	1990-1991
Robert Dickie	1	1991
Sugar Gibiliru	1	1991
John Doherty	1	1991-1992
Michael Armstrong	1	1992
Neil Haddock	2	1992-1994
Floyd Havard	3	1994-

Lightweight (135 lbs)

Title Holder	Lonsdale Belt Notches	Tenure
Dick Burge		1891-1897
Harry Nickless		1891-1894
Tom Causer		1894-1897
Tom Causer		1897
Dick Burge*		1897-1901
Jabez White		1902-1906
Jack Goldswain		1906-1908
Johnny Summers		1908-1909
Freddie Welsh	1	1909-1911
Matt Wells	1	1911-1912
Freddie Welsh*	1	1912-1919
Bob Marriott*	1	1919-1920
Ernie Rice	1	1921-1922
Seaman Nobby Hall		1922-1923
Harry Mason*		1923-1924
Ernie Izzard	2	1924-1925
Harry Mason		1924-1925
Harry Mason*	1	1925-1928
Sam Steward		1928-1929
Fred Webster		1929-1930
Al Foreman*	1	1930-1932
Johnny Cuthbert		1932-1934
Harry Mizler		1934
Jackie Kid Berg		1934-1936
Jimmy Walsh	1	1936-1938
Dave Crowley	1	1938
Eric Boon	3	1938-1944
Ronnie James*	1	1944-1947
Billy Thompson	3	1947-1951
Tommy McGovern	1	1951-1952
Frank Johnson*	1	1952-1953
Joe Lucy	1	1953-1955
Frank Johnson	1	1955-1956
Joe Lucy	2	1956-1957
Dave Charnley*	3	1957-1965
Maurice Cullen*	4	1965-1968

Title Holder	Lonsdale Belt Notches	Tenure
Ken Buchanan*	2	1968-1971
Willie Reilly*	1	1972
Jim Watt		1972-1973
Ken Buchanan*	1	1973-1974
Jim Watt*	2	1975-1977
Charlie Nash*	1	1978-1979
Ray Cattouse	2	1980-1982
George Feeney*	3	1982-1985
Tony Willis	3	1985-1987
Alex Dickson	1	1987-1988
Steve Boyle*	2	1988-1990
Carl Crook	5	1990-1992
Billy Schwer	1	1992-1993
Paul Burke	1	1993
Billy Schwer	2	1993-1995
Michael Ayers	3	1995-

L. Welterweight (140 lbs)

Title Holder	Lonsdale Belt Notches	Tenure
Des Rea	1	1968-1969
Vic Andreetti*	2	1969-1970
Des Morrison	1	1973-1974
Pat McCormack	1	1974
Joey Singleton	3	1974-1976
Dave Boy Green*	1	1976-1977
Colin Power*	2	1977-1978
Clinton McKenzie	1	1978-1979
Colin Power	1	1979
Clinton McKenzie	5	1979-1984
Terry Marsh*	1	1984-1986
Tony Laing*	1	1986
Tony McKenzie	2	1986-1987
Lloyd Christie	3	1987-1989
Clinton McKenzie*	1	1989
Pat Barrett*	2	1989-1990
Tony Ekubia	1	1990-1991
Andy Holligan	3	1991-1994
Ross Hale	3	1994-

Welterweight (147 lbs)

Title Holder	Lonsdale Belt Notches	Tenure
Charlie Allum		1903-1904
Charlie Knock		1904-1906
Curly Watson*		1906-1910
Young Joseph		1908-1910
Young Joseph	1	1910-1911
Arthur Evernden		1911-1912
Johnny Summers		1912
Johnny Summers	2	1912-1914
Tom McCormick		1914
Matt Wells*		1914
Johnny Basham	3	1914-1920
Matt Wells		1914-1919
Ted Kid Lewis		1920-1924
Tommy Milligan*		1924-1925
Hamilton Johnny Brown		1925
Harry Mason		1925-1926
Jack Hood*	3	1926-1934
Harry Mason		1934
Pat Butler*		1934-1936
Dave McCleave		1936
Jake Kilrain	1	1936-1939
Ernie Roderick	5	1939-1948
Henry Hall	1	1948-1949
Eddie Thomas	2	1949-1951
Wally Thom	1	1951-1952
Cliff Curvis*	1	1952-1953
Wally Thom	2	1953-1956
Peter Waterman*	2	1956-1958
Tommy Molloy	2	1958-1960
Wally Swift	1	1960

Title Holder	Lonsdale Belt Notches	Tenure
Brian Curvis*	7	1960-1966
Johnny Cooke	2	1967-1968
Ralph Charles*	3	1968-1972
Bobby Arthur	1	1972-1973
John H. Stracey*	1	1973-1975
Pat Thomas	2	1975-1976
Henry Rhiney	2	1976-1979
Kirkland Laing	1	1979-1980
Colin Jones*	3	1980-1982
Lloyd Honeyghan*	2	1983-1985
Kostas Petrou	1	1985
Sylvester Mittee	1	1985
Lloyd Honeyghan*	1	1985-1986
Kirkland Laing	4	1987-1991
Del Bryan	2	1991-1992
Gary Jacobs*	2	1992-1993
Del Bryan	4	1993-

L. Middleweight (154 lbs)

Title Holder	Lonsdale Belt Notches	Tenure
Larry Paul	2	1973-1974
Maurice Hope*	3	1974-1977
Jimmy Batten	3	1977-1979
Pat Thomas	3	1979-1981
Herol Graham*	2	1981-1983
Prince Rodney*	1	1983-1984
Jimmy Cable	2	1984-1985
Prince Rodney	2	1985-1986
Chris Pyatt*	1	1986
Lloyd Hibbert*	1	1987
Gary Cooper	1	1988
Gary Stretch*	2	1988-1990
Wally Swift Jnr	2	1991-1992
Andy Till	3	1992-1994
Robert McCracken	3	1994-

Middleweight (160 lbs)

Title Holder	Lonsdale Belt Notches	Tenure
Denny Harrington		1876-1880
William Sheriff*		1880-1883
Bill Goode		1887-1890
Toff Wall*		1890
Ted Pritchard*		1890-1895
Ted White		1893-1895
Ted White*		1895-1896
Anthony Diamond*		1898
Dick Burge*		1898-1900
Jack Palmer		1902-1903
Charlie Allum		1905-1906
Pat O'Keefe		1906
Tom Thomas	1	1906-1910
Jim Sullivan*	1	1910-1912
Jack Harrison*	1	1912-1913
Pat O'Keefe	2	1914-1916
Bandsman Jack Blake	1	1916-1918
Pat O'Keefe*	1	1918-1919
Ted Kid Lewis		1920-1921
Tom Gummer	1	1920-1921
Gus Platts		1921
Johnny Basham*		1921
Ted Kid Lewis	2	1921-1923
Johnny Basham		1921
Roland Todd*		1923-1925
Roland Todd		1925-1927
Tommy Milligan	1	1926-1928
Frank Moody		1927-1928
Alex Ireland		1928-1929
Len Harvey	5	1929-1933
Jock McAvoy*	3+2	1933-1944
Ernie Roderick	1	1945-1946
Vince Hawkins	1	1946-1948

Title Holder	Lonsdale Belt Notches	Tenure
Dick Turpin	2	1948-1950
Albert Finch	1	1950
Randy Turpin*	1	1950-1954
Johnny Sullivan	1	1954-1955
Pat McAteer*	3	1955-1958
Terry Downes	1	1958-1959
John Cowboy McCormack	1	1959
Terry Downes*	2	1959-1962
George Aldridge	1	1962-1963
Mick Leahy	1	1963-1964
Wally Swift	1	1964-1965
Johnny Pritchett*	4	1965-1969
Les McAteer	1	1969-1970
Mark Rowe	1	1970
Bunny Sterling	4	1970-1974
Kevin Finnegan*	1	1974
Bunny Sterling*	1	1975
Alan Minter*	3	1975-1977
Kevin Finnegan	1	1977
Alan Minter*	1	1977-1978
Tony Sibson	1	1979
Kevin Finnegan*	1	1979-1980
Roy Gumbs	3	1981-1983
Mark Kaylor	1	1983-1984
Tony Sibson*	1	1984
Herol Graham*	1	1985-1986
Brian Anderson	1	1986-1987
Tony Sibson*	1	1987-1988
Herol Graham	4	1988-1992
Frank Grant	2	1992-1993
Neville Brown	4	1993-

S. Middleweight (168 lbs)

Title Holder	Lonsdale Belt Notches	Tenure
Sammy Storey	2	1989-1990
James Cook*	1	1990-1991
Fidel Castro	2	1991-1992
Henry Wharton*	1	1992-1993
James Cook	1	1993-1994
Cornelius Carr*	1	1994
Ali Forbes	1	1995
Sammy Storey	1	1995-

L. Heavyweight (175lbs)

Title Holder	Lonsdale Belt Notches	Tenure
Dennis Haugh		1913-1914
Dick Smith	2	1914-1916
Harry Reeve*	1	1916-1917
Dick Smith*	1	1918-1919
Boy McCormick*	1	1919-1921
Jack Bloomfield*	1	1922-1924
Tom Berry	1	1925-1927
Gipsy Daniels*	1	1927
Frank Moody	1	1927-1929
Harry Crossley	1	1929-1932
Jack Petersen	1	1932
Len Harvey*	1	1933-1934
Eddie Phillips		1935-1937
Jock McAvoy	1	1937-1938
Len Harvey	2	1938-1942
Freddie Mills*	1	1942-1950
Don Cockell	2	1950-1952
Randy Turpin*	1	1952
Dennis Powell	1	1953
Alex Buxton	2	1953-1955
Randy Turpin*	1	1955
Ron Barton*	1	1956
Randy Turpin*	2	1956-1958
Chic Calderwood*	4	1960-1966
Young John McCormack	2	1967-1969
Eddie Avoth	2	1969-1971

Title Holder	Lonsdale Belt Notches	Tenure
Chris Finnegan	2	1971-1973
John Conteh*	2	1973-1974
Johnny Frankham	1	1975
Chris Finnegan*	1	1975-1976
Tim Wood	1	1976-1977
Bunny Johnson*	3	1977-1981
Tom Collins	3	1982-1984
Dennis Andries*	5	1984-1986
Tom Collins*	1	1987
Tony Wilson	3	1987-1989
Tom Collins*	1	1989-1990
Steve McCarthy*	1	1990-1991
Crawford Ashley*	3	1991-1992
Maurice Core*	2	1992-1994
Crawford Ashley	1	1994-

Cruiserweight (190 lbs)

Title Holder	Lonsdale Belt Notches	Tenure
Sam Reeson*	1	1985-1986
Andy Straughn	1	1986-1987
Roy Smith	1	1987
Tee Jay	1	1987-1988
Glenn McCrory*	2	1988
Andy Straughn	1	1988-1989
Johnny Nelson*	3	1989-1991
Derek Angol*	2	1991-1992
Carl Thompson*	1	1992-1994
Dennis Andries	1	1995
Terry Dunstan	1	1995-

Heavyweight (190 lbs +)

Title Holder	Lonsdale Belt Notches	Tenure
Tom Allen*		1878-1882
Charlie Mitchell*		1882-1894
Jem Smith		1889-1891
Ted Pritchard		1891-1895
Jem Smith*		1895-1896
George Chrisp		1901
Jack Scales		1901-1902
Jack Palmer		1903-1906
Gunner Moir		1906-1909
Iron Hague		1909-1910
P.O. Curran		1910-1911
Iron Hague		1910-1911
Bombardier Billy Wells	3	1911-1919
Joe Beckett*	1	1919
Frank Goddard	1	1919
Joe Beckett		1919
Joe Beckett*	1	1919-1923
Frank Goddard		1923-1926
Phil Scott*		1926-1931
Reggie Meen		1931-1932
Jack Petersen	3	1932-1933
Len Harvey		1933-1934
Jack Petersen		1934-1936
Ben Foord		1936-1937
Tommy Farr*	1	1937-1938
Len Harvey*	1	1938-1942

Title Holder	Lonsdale Belt Notches	Tenure
Jack London	1	1944-1945
Bruce Woodcock	2	1945-1950
Jack Gardner	1	1950-1952
Johnny Williams	1	1952-1953
Don Cockell*	1	1953-1956
Joe Erskine	2	1956-1958
Brian London	1	1958-1959
Henry Cooper*	9	1959-1969
Jack Bodell	1	1969-1970
Henry Cooper	1	1970-1971
Joe Bugner	1	1971
Jack Bodell	1	1971-1972
Danny McAlinden	1	1972-1975
Bunny Johnson	1	1975
Richard Dunn	2	1975-1976
Joe Bugner*	1	1976-1977
John L. Gardner*	2	1978-1980
Gordon Ferris	1	1981
Neville Meade	1	1981-1983
David Pearce*	1	1983-1985
Hughroy Currie	1	1985-1986
Horace Notice*	4	1986-1988
Gary Mason	2	1989-1991
Lennox Lewis*	3	1991-1993
Herbie Hide*	1	1993-1994
James Oyebola	1	1994-

Sammy Storey (right) regained his British super-middleweight title when outscoring the champion, Ali Forbes, last April

Les Clark

Commonwealth Title Bouts during 1994-95

All of last season's title bouts are shown in date order and give the boxers' respective weights, along with the scorecard, if going to a decision. There is also a short summary of any bout that involved a British contestant and British officials, where applicable, are listed.

30 July 1994   Tony Pep 9.2 (Canada) W RSC 1 J. T. Williams 9.3½ (Wales), York Hall, Bethnal Green (S. Featherweight Title). The champion was just too powerful for Williams, who was rescued by John Coyle at 0.92 after being decked for the second time.

23 August 1994   John Armour 8.5¼ (England) W RSC 11 Shaun Anderson 8.6 (Scotland), York Hall, Bethnal Green (Bantamweight Title). Although comfortably ahead at the time of the stoppage, Armour once again picked up plenty of facial damage. The challenger, a late substitute for the Kenyan, Steve Mwema, was stopped at 1.47 of the 11th round when virtually unable to see out of his right-eye, but he had not been floored and it was only his inability to influence Roy Francis' scorecard that prompted the timely intervention.

30 August 1994   Garry Delaney 12.6 (England) W CO 2 Arigoma Chiponda 12.4 (Zimbabwe), York Hall, Bethnal Green (Vacant L. Heavyweight Title). The above pairing was made following Brent Kosolofski forfeiting the title in July for failing to defend within the stipulated time. Unfortunately, the African was way out of his depth, and it would be just a matter of time before a big right-hand sent him crashing to be counted out by John Keane at the 1.53 mark of the second round.

5 October 1994   Richie Woodhall 11.4 (England) W PTS 12 Jacques le Blanc 11.4 (Canada), Civic Hall, Wolverhampton (Middleweight Title). Referee: Dave Parris. Boxing his way to a clear 120-114½ points victory, Woodhall eased his way back after seven months out of the ring with an injury to his right-hand, but never looked like knocking his man over.

15 October 1994   Billy Hardy 8.13¾ (England) W PTS 12 Stanford Ngcebeshe 9.0 (South Africa), Sun City, South Africa (Featherweight Title). The first Commonwealth title fight to be held in South Africa for 34 years, saw Hardy win with scores of 118-112, 117-112 and 115-114. There

Daren Fifield (right) spars for an opening against Francis Ampofo. The British flyweight champion, Ampofo, added the Commonwealth title to his collection in round two   Les Clark

167

were no knockdowns and, despite the challenger carrying a nasty cut over the left-eye from the fourth round and boxing negatively from then onwards, he somehow held out.

23 October 1994   Henry Wharton 11.13½ (England) W CO 1 Sipho Moyo 11.9¾ (Zimbabwe), Town Hall, Leeds (S. Middleweight Title). Referee: Roy Francis. All over at 0.38 of the first, the challenger crashed to defeat, a tremendous left-hook to the body doing the damage.

30 October 1994   Leo Young 10.13¼ (Australia) W PTS 12 Fitzgerald Bruney 10.10¾ (Canada), Tweed Heads, Australia (Vacant L. Middleweight Title). The title had become vacant when Lloyd Honeghan was stripped of it in July for failing to defend against a recognised challenger within the stipulated period.

30 November 1994   Richie Woodhall 11.5¾ (England) W RSC 11 Art Serwano 11.5¾ (Uganda), Civic Hall, Wolverhampton (Middleweight Title). The game Ugandan was rescued by John Coyle at 2.05 of the 11th round, having been on the receiving end throughout. What was surprising though was that while Woodhall was totally on top, often landing several punches without reply, he lacked the power to bring the fight to a summary conclusion far earlier.

20 December 1994   Daren Fifield 8.0 (England) L RSC 2 Francis Ampofo 8.0 (England), York Hall, Bethnal Green (Flyweight Title). Referee: John Coyle. For a summary, see under British Title Bouts, 1994-95.

14 February 1995   John Armour 8.5½ (England) W RSC 7 Tsitsi Sokutu 8.6 (South Africa), York Hall, Bethnal Green (Bantamweight Title). Dropped by a straight-left in the fourth, Armour fought back to stop his fellow southpaw two rounds later, but not before he had been further hurt. Showing great spirit in what had become a gruelling fight, the champion, behind on the referee's scorecard, refused to be phased and put Sokutu down at the end of the sixth. He followed that up by dropping his man again, early in the seventh, prior to forcing Roy Francis to rescue the South African at 0.50 of the round.

18 February 1995   Ross Hale 9.13¾ (England) W PTS 12 Malcolm Melvin 9.13 (England), Bath & West Country Showground, Shepton Mallet (L. Welterweight Title). Referee: Mickey Vann. Scorecard: 119½-115½. For a summary, see under British Title Bouts, 1994-95.

21 February 1995   Billy Hardy 9.0 (England) W RSC 11 Percy Commey 8.11¾ (Ghana), Crowtree Leisure Centre, Sunderland (Featherweight Title). Having been hammered relentlessly all night, although not floored, the challenger was rescued by Larry O'Connell at 1.28 of the 11th round. This was Hardy's fourth successful defence of the title and it was probably his most emphatic yet, with the lanky Ghanaian unable to find any form of respite.

26 February 1995   Andrew Murray 10.6 (Guyana) W RTD 10 Alain Bosimenu 10.5 (Canada), Georgetown, Guyana (Welterweight Title).

6 March 1995   Francis Ampofo 7.13¾ (England) L CO 12 Danny Ward 7.13 (South Africa), Grosvenor House, Mayfair (Flyweight Title). As the first South African to win the Commonwealth title since 1962, the slick-moving Ward certainly proved worthy of the recognition that will come his way, having clearly outboxed the champion round-after-round before applying the finishing touches. Ampofo was counted out by referee, Dave Parris, at 0.47 of the final session after being driven across the ring by a two-fisted attack and put down by a heavy right to the head.

12 April 1995   Neil Swain 8.8¼ (Wales) W RSC 10 Mike Parris 8.10 (Guyana), Leisure Centre, Llanelli (Inaugural S. Bantamweight Title). Referee: Dave Parris. Swain swarmed all over the 37-year-old visitor and it was a good job for the youngster that the veteran did not carry a potent punch, especially in the early stages, as he often left himself open to the counter. Worried that he might not make the trip, Swain took it easy in the latter part of the fight until coming on strong in the tenth and driving his man around the ring to force a stoppage at 1.53 of the round.

6 May 1995   Ross Hale 9.13 (England) W RSC 4 Shaun Cogan (England), Bath & West Country Showground, Shepton Mallet (L. Welterweight Title). Down twice and cut by the side of his left-eye, Cogan, an 11th hour replacement for Hale's original opponent, Razor Addo, did particularly well in the first two rounds before being eventually ground down and rescued by Paul Thomas after 1.32 of the fourth had elapsed. With Commonwealth billing only, the British championship was not at stake, but, had Hale lost, that title would have been effected also.

9 May 1995   Garry Delaney 12.6¾ (England) L RTD 7 Noel Magee 12.6¾ (Ireland), Festival Hall, Basildon (L. Heavyweight Title). Referee: John Keane. When retiring on his stool after seven rounds with a damaged left-hand, Delaney, also cut on both eyes, not only lost his unbeaten record but his title as well. Injuries apart, it was Magee's night as he confidently negated Delaney's best work, never allowing the champion to get his punches off, and was well ahead at the finish.

12 May 1995   Billy Schwer 9.8½ (England) W RSC 11 Stephen Chungu 9.6¾ (Zambia), York Hall, Bethnal Green (Lightweight Title). Out in front for several rounds, it was only when Schwer knocked him down in the fifth did Chungu begin to lose some of his composure. It still took the champion several more rounds to get on top, but when a short left-hook deposited the African on the canvas in round 11, the fight was called off by referee, Mickey Vann, when he arose.

Commonwealth Champions, 1908-1995

Over the years, record books, including this one, have continued to show Jim Driscoll's 15 round points win over the Australian, Charlie Griffin, at the NSC on 24 February 1908 for the featherweight title, as being the first recorded Empire title fight. I assume that was because for the first time a belt was authorised to be presented to the winner. However, there were many earlier fighters, such as the great Peter Jackson (Australia), who knocked out Frank Slavin in the tenth round at the NSC on 30 May 1892 in a contest billed for the British, Australian, Imperial (Empire) and World titles, along with men such as Jem Hall (Australia) and Dan Creedon (New Zealand), who should also be accorded similar status. Harold Alderman, the well-known boxing historian, and a specialist in the field of research covering the early period of gloved fighting onwards, is currently putting together a list of fights previously not seen in record books that carried Imperial title billing. Hopefully, this will be available in time for the 1997 edition of the Yearbook. For the record, it was not until July 1954 that an exploratory meeting, held in London, led to a body being set up and named as the British Commonwealth and Empire Board, which was duly formed during its inaugural meeting at the BBBoC on 12 October 1954. At that meeting, Great Britain, South Africa, Trinidad, British Guyana, Canada, Nigeria, New Zealand and Australia, were all represented and a Championship Committee issued their list of champions, recognising Don Cockell (Heavy), Randy Turpin (L. Heavy), Johnny Sullivan (Middle), Barry Brown (Welter), Billy Spider Kelly (Feather) and Jake Tuli (Fly), with the Light and Bantamweight divisions seen as vacant. Earlier, pressure had been mounting because countries outside of Britain often felt that their best fighters were not getting a fair crack of the whip. Matters were finally brought to a head when Stadiums Ltd (Melbourne), who ran the sport in Australia, decided to support two of their own, Al Bourke (from 12 December 1952) and Pat Ford (from 28 August 1953 to 9 April 1954 and 2 July 1954). The situations were finally resolved when Bourke retired in December 1954 and Ford in June 1955. Known then as the British Empire title, it became the Commonwealth title in 1970.

COMMONWEALTH COUNTRY CODE
A = Australia; BAH = Bahamas; BAR = Barbados; BER = Bermuda; C = Canada; E = England; F = Fiji; GH = Ghana; GU = Guyana; I = Ireland; J = Jamaica; K = Kenya; N = Nigeria; NZ = New Zealand; NI = Northern Ireland; PNG = Papua New Guinea; SA = South Africa; SAM = Samoa; S = Scotland; T = Tonga; TR = Trinidad; U = Uganda; W = Wales; ZA = Zambia; ZI = Zimbabwe.

Champions in **bold** denote those recognised by the British Commonwealth and Empire Board (1954)

*Undefeated champions (Includes men who may have forfeited their titles)

Title Holder	Country	Tenure	Title Holder	Country	Tenure	Title Holder	Country	Tenure
Flyweight (112 lbs)			Dick Corbett	E	1930-1932	Nel Tarleton*	E	1940-1947
Elky Clark*	S	1924-1927	Johnny King	E	1932-1934	Tiger Al Phillips	E	1947
Jackie Paterson	S	1940-1948	Dick Corbett*	E	1934	Ronnie Clayton	E	1947-1951
Rinty Monaghan*	NI	1948-1950	Jim Brady	S	1941-1945	Roy Ankrah	GH	1951-1954
Teddy Gardner	E	1952	Jackie Paterson	S	1945-1949	**Billy Spider Kelly**	NI	1954-1955
Jake Tuli	SA	1952-1954	Stan Rowan	E	1949	**Hogan Kid Bassey***	N	1955-1957
Dai Dower*	W	1954-1957	Vic Toweel	SA	1949-1952	**Percy Lewis**	TR	1957-1960
Frankie Jones	S	1957	Jimmy Carruthers*	A	1952-1954	**Floyd Robertson**	GH	1960-1967
Dennis Adams*	SA	1957-1962	Peter Keenan	S	1955-1959	**John O'Brien**	S	1967
Jackie Brown	S	1962-1963	**Freddie Gilroy***	NI	1959-1963	**Johnny Famechon***	A	1967-1969
Walter McGowan*	S	1963-1969	**Johnny Caldwell***	NI	1964-1965	**Toro George**	NZ	1970-1972
John McCluskey	S	1970-1971	**Alan Rudkin**	E	1965-1966	**Bobby Dunne**	A	1972-1974
Henry Nissen	A	1971-1974	**Walter McGowan**	S	1966-1968	**Evan Armstrong**	S	1974
Big Jim West*	A	1974-1975	**Alan Rudkin**	E	1968-1969	**David Kotey***	GH	1974-1975
Patrick Mambwe	ZA	1976-1979	**Lionel Rose***	A	1969	**Eddie Ndukwu**	N	1977-1980
Ray Amoo	N	1980	**Alan Rudkin***	E	1970-1972	**Pat Ford***	GU	1980-1981
Steve Muchoki	K	1980-1983	**Paul Ferreri**	A	1972-1977	**Azumah Nelson***	GH	1981-1985
Keith Wallace*	E	1983-1984	**Sulley Shittu***	GH	1977-1978	**Tyrone Downes***	BAR	1986-1988
Richard Clarke*	J	1986-1987	**Johnny Owen***	W	1978-1980	**Thunder Aryeh**	GH	1988-1989
Nana Yaw Konadu*	GH	1987-1989	**Paul Ferreri**	A	1981-1986	**Oblitey Commey**	GH	1989-1990
Alfred Kotey*	GH	1989-1993	**Ray Minus***	BAH	1986-1991	**Modest Napunyi**	K	1990-1991
Francis Ampofo*	E	1993	**John Armour**	E	1992-	**Barrington Francis***	C	1991
Daren Fifield	E	1993-1994				**Colin McMillan***	E	1992
Francis Ampofo	E	1994-1995	**S. Bantamweight (122 lbs)**			**Billy Hardy**	E	1992-
Danny Ward	SA	1995-	**Neil Swain**	W	1995-			
						S. Featherweight (130 lbs)		
Bantamweight (118 lbs)			**Featherweight (126 lbs)**			**Billy Moeller**	A	1975-1977
Jim Higgins	S	1920-1922	Jim Driscoll*	W	1908-1913	**Johnny Aba***	PNG	1977-1982
Tommy Harrison	E	1922-1923	Llew Edwards*	W	1915-1917	**Langton Tinago**	ZI	1983-1984
Bugler Harry Lake	E	1923	Johnny McGrory*	S	1936-1938	**John Sichula**	ZA	1984
Johnny Brown	E	1923-1928	Jim Spider Kelly	NI	1938-1939	**Lester Ellis***	A	1984-1985
Teddy Baldock*	E	1928-1930	Johnny Cusick	E	1939-1940	**John Sichula**	ZA	1985-1986

Title Holder	Country	Tenure
Sam Akromah	GH	1986-1987
John Sichula	ZA	1987-1989
Mark Reefer*	E	1989-1990
Thunder Aryeh	GH	1990-1991
Hugh Forde	E	1991
Paul Harvey	E	1991-1992
Tony Pep	C	1992-

Lightweight (135 lbs)

Title Holder	Country	Tenure
Freddie Welsh*	W	1912-1914
Al Foreman	E	1930-1933
Jimmy Kelso	A	1933
Al Foreman*	E	1933-1934
Laurie Stevens*	SA	1936
Arthur King	C	1948-1951
Frank Johnson	E	1953
Pat Ford	A	1953-1954
Ivor Germain	BAR	1954
Pat Ford*	A	1954-1955
Johnny van Rensburg	SA	1955-1956
Willie Toweel	SA	1956-1959
Dave Charnley	E	1959-1962
Bunny Grant	J	1962-1967
Manny Santos*	NZ	1967
Love Allotey	GH	1967-1968
Percy Hayles*	J	1968-1975
Jonathan Dele	N	1975-1977
Lennox Blackmore	GU	1977-1978
Hogan Jimoh	N	1978-1980
Langton Tinago	ZI	1980-1981
Barry Michael	A	1981-1982
Claude Noel	T	1982-1984
Graeme Brooke	A	1984-1985
Barry Michael	A	1985-1986
Langton Tinago	ZI	1986-1987
Mo Hussein	E	1987-1989
Pat Doherty	E	1989
Najib Daho	E	1989-1990
Carl Crook	E	1990-1992
Billy Schwer	E	1992-1993
Paul Burke	E	1993
Billy Schwer	E	1993-

L. Welterweight (140 lbs)

Title Holder	Country	Tenure
Joe Tetteh	GH	1972-1973
Hector Thompson	A	1973-1977
Baby Cassius Austin	A	1977-1978
Jeff Malcolm	A	1978-1979
Obisia Nwankpa	N	1979-1983
Billy Famous*	N	1983-1986
Tony Laing	E	1987-1988
Lester Ellis	A	1988-1989
Steve Larrimore	BAH	1989
Tony Ekubia	E	1989-1991
Andy Holligan	E	1991-1994
Ross Hale	E	1994-

Welterweight (147 lbs)

Title Holder	Country	Tenure
Johnny Summers	E	1912-1914
Tom McCormick	I	1914
Matt Wells	E	1914-1919
Johnny Basham	W	1919-1920
Ted Kid Lewis	E	1920-1924
Tommy Milligan*	S	1924-1925
Eddie Thomas	W	1951
Wally Thom	E	1951-1952
Cliff Curvis	W	1952
Gerald Dreyer	SA	1952-1954
Barry Brown	NZ	1954
George Barnes	A	1954-1956
Darby Brown	A	1956
George Barnes	A	1956-1958
Johnny van Rensburg	SA	1958
George Barnes	A	1958-1960
Brian Curvis*	W	1960-1966
Johnny Cooke	E	1967-1968
Ralph Charles*	E	1968-1972
Clyde Gray	C	1973-1979
Chris Clarke	C	1979
Clyde Gray*	C	1979-1980
Colin Jones*	W	1981-1984
Sylvester Mittee	E	1984-1985
Lloyd Honeyghan*	E	1985-1986
Brian Janssen	A	1987
Wilf Gentzen	A	1987-1988
Gary Jacobs	S	1988-1989
Donovan Boucher	C	1989-1992
Eamonn Loughran*	NI	1992-1993
Andrew Murray	GU	1993-

L. Middleweight (154 lbs)

Title Holder	Country	Tenure
Charkey Ramon*	A	1972-1975
Maurice Hope*	E	1976-1979
Kenny Bristol	GU	1979-1981
Herol Graham*	E	1981-1984
Ken Salisbury	A	1984-1985
Nick Wilshire	E	1985-1987
Lloyd Hibbert	E	1987
Troy Waters*	A	1987-1991
Chris Pyatt*	E	1991-1992
Mickey Hughes	E	1992-1993
Lloyd Honeyghan*	E	1993-1994
Leo Young	A	1994-

Middleweight (160 lbs)

Title Holder	Country	Tenure
Ted Kid Lewis	E	1922-1923
Roland Todd*	E	1923-1925
Len Johnson*	E	1926
Tommy Milligan	S	1926-1928
Alex Ireland	S	1928-1929
Len Harvey	E	1929-1933
Jock McAvoy*	E	1933-1939
Ron Richards*	A	1940-1941
Bos Murphy	NZ	1948
Dick Turpin	E	1948-1949
Dave Sands*	A	1949-1952
Randy Turpin*	E	1952-1954
Al Bourke*	A	1952-1954
Johnny Sullivan	E	1954-1955
Pat McAteer	E	1955-1958
Dick Tiger	N	1958-1960
Wilf Greaves	C	1960
Dick Tiger*	N	1960-1962
Gomeo Brennan	BAH	1963-1964
Tuna Scanlon*	NZ	1964
Gomeo Brennan	BAH	1964-1966
Blair Richardson*	C	1966-1967
Milo Calhoun	J	1967
Johnny Pritchett*	E	1967-1969
Les McAteer	E	1969-1970
Mark Rowe	E	1970
Bunny Sterling	E	1970-1972
Tony Mundine*	A	1972-1975
Monty Betham	NZ	1975-1978
Al Korovou	A	1978
Ayub Kalule*	U	1978-1980
Tony Sibson*	E	1980-1983
Roy Gumbs	E	1983
Mark Kaylor	E	1983-1984
Tony Sibson*	E	1984-1988
Nigel Benn	E	1988-1989
Michael Watson*	E	1989-1991
Richie Woodhall	E	1992-

S. Middleweight (168 lbs)

Title Holder	Country	Tenure
Rod Carr	A	1989-1990
Lou Cafaro*	A	1990-1991
Henry Wharton	E	1991-

L. Heavyweight (175 lbs)

Title Holder	Country	Tenure
Jack Bloomfield*	E	1923-1924
Tom Berry	E	1927
Gipsy Daniels*	W	1927
Len Harvey	E	1939-1942
Freddie Mills*	E	1942-1950
Randy Turpin*	E	1952-1955
Gordon Wallace	C	1956-1957
Yvon Durelle*	C	1957-1959
Chic Calderwood*	S	1960-1966
Bob Dunlop*	A	1968-1970
Eddie Avoth	W	1970-1971
Chris Finnegan	E	1971-1973
John Conteh*	E	1973-1974
Steve Aczel	A	1975
Tony Mundine	A	1975-1978
Gary Summerhays	C	1978-1979
Lottie Mwale	ZA	1979-1985
Leslie Stewart*	TR	1985-1987
Willie Featherstone	C	1987-1989
Guy Waters*	A	1989-1993
Brent Kosolofski*	C	1993-1994
Garry Delaney	E	1994-1995
Noel Magee	I	1995-

Cruiserweight (190 lbs)

Title Holder	Country	Tenure
Stewart Lithgo	E	1984
Chisanda Mutti	ZA	1984-1987
Glenn McCrory*	E	1987-1989
Apollo Sweet	A	1989
Derek Angol*	E	1989-1993
Francis Wanyama	U	1994-

Heavyweight (190 lbs +)

Title Holder	Country	Tenure
Tommy Burns	C	1910
P.O. Curran	I	1911
Dan Flynn	I	1911
Bombardier Billy Wells	E	1911-1919
Joe Beckett*	E	1919-1923
Phil Scott	E	1926-1931
Larry Gains	C	1931-1934
Len Harvey	E	1934
Jack Petersen	W	1934-1936
Ben Foord	SA	1936-1937
Tommy Farr*	W	1937-1938
Len Harvey*	E	1939-1942
Jack London	E	1944-1945
Bruce Woodcock	E	1945-1950
Jack Gardner	E	1950-1952
Johnny Williams	W	1952-1953
Don Cockell*	E	1953-1956
Joe Bygraves	J	1956-1957
Joe Erskine	W	1957-1958
Brian London	E	1958-1959
Henry Cooper	E	1959-1971
Joe Bugner	E	1971
Jack Bodell	E	1971-1972
Danny McAlinden	NI	1972-1975
Bunny Johnson	E	1975
Richard Dunn	E	1975-1976
Joe Bugner	E	1976-1977
John L. Gardner*	E	1978-1981
Trevor Berbick*	C	1981-1986
Horace Notice*	E	1986-1988
Derek Williams	E	1988-1992
Lennox Lewis*	E	1992-1993
Henry Akinwande	E	1993-

European Title Bouts during 1994-95

All of last season's title bouts are shown in date order and give the boxers' respective weights, along with the scorecard, if going to a decision. There is also a short summary of any bout that involved a British contestant and British officials, where applicable, are listed.

20 July 1994   Agostino Cardamone 11.4½ (Italy) W RSC 7 Neville Brown 11.4½ (England), Solfra, Italy (Middleweight Title). Floored in the second and twice more in the seventh, there was no way back for Brown and the fight was called off at 1.38 of the round.

23 July 1994   Henry Akinwande 16.4 (England) W RSC 7 Mario Schiesser 15.7 (Germany), Berlin, Germany (Heavyweight Title). Having been comprehensively outboxed, the German, heavily floored by a combination of punches, only just managed to beat the count before being rescued by the referee at 1.22 of the seventh round.

23 July 1994   Javier Castillejos 10.13 (Spain) W RTD 8 Ludovic Proto 10.12 (France), Boiro, Spain (L. Middleweight Title). Referee: Roy Francis.

3 August 1994   Luigi Camputaro 7.12¾ (Italy) W PTS 12 Daren Fifield 7.13¾ (England), Whitchurch Leisure Centre, Bristol (Flyweight Title). Scorecards: 118-111, 117-111, 118-110. Lacking the power needed to back his man up, Fifield bravely lasted the course, somehow surviving two bad cuts and a knockdown in the ninth round.

17 August 1994   Prince Nassem Hamed 8.5½ (England) W RSC 3 Antonio Picardi 8.5 (Italy), Hillsborough Leisure Centre, Sheffield (Bantamweight Title). Far more disciplined this time round, Hamed took the Italian apart, scoring three knockdowns before the referee wisely brought things to a close at 1.23 of the third.

9 September 1994   Stefano Zoff 8.13¼ (Italy) L PTS 12 Mehdi Labdouni 8.13½ (France), Fontenay sous Bois, France (Featherweight Title). Scorecards: 117-114, Larry O'Connell 116-114, 116-113.

7 October 1994   Jacobin Yoma 9.3 (France) W PTS 12 Jimmy Bredahl 9.4 (Denmark), Copenhagen, Denmark (S. Featherweight Title). Scorecards: 119-111, 119-111, 118-112.

8 October 1994   Frederic Seillier 11.13¾ (France) W RSC 9 Bernard Bonzon 11.13 (Switzerland), Berck sur Mer, France (S. Middleweight Title). Referee: Paul Thomas.

25 October 1994   Fabrice Tiozzo 12.7 (France) W RSC 4 Maurice Core 12.7 (England), Besancon, France (L. Heavyweight Title). Cut above the right-eye and down three times, twice in the third and again in the fourth, Core, backed up in a corner shipping punishment, was rescued by the referee after his trainer, Jimmy Tibbs, threw in the towel.

9 November 1994   Agostino Cardamone 11.5½ (Italy) W PTS 12 Shaun Cummins 11.5 (England), San Remo, Italy (Middleweight Title). Scorecards: 119-109, 118-110, 117-111. Dropped heavily in the eighth, Cardamone somehow

survived an extremely tough fight, something that was not borne out by the judges' scores. The Englishman proved to be a dangerous opponent right up to the final bell, despite suffering from a variety of bad cuts.

Shaun Cummins, the British challenger, put up a great display in his European middleweight title fight against Agostino Cardamone   Les Clark

11 November 1994   Khalid Rahilou 9.12¾ (France) W RTD 2 Gert Bo Jacobsen 9.13¾ (Denmark). Randers, Denmark (L. Welterweight Title). Referee: John Coyle.

19 November 1994   Luigi Camputaro 7.13 (Italy) L PTS 12 Robbie Regan 7.13 (Wales), Ice Rink, Cardiff (Flyweight Title). Scorecards: 113-116, 115-114, 115-113. In a desperately close fight, with both men cut around their eyes, it was only when Regan started to concentrate on the body during the latter stages that the tide began to turn his way. However, unable to find a finishing punch, having a point deducted for low blows in the ninth round could have cost the Welshman dearly.

4 December 1994   Racheed Lawal 9.8½ (Denmark) L RSC 9 Jean Baptist-Mendy 9.8¾ (France), Thiais, France (Lightweight Title).

171

10 December 1994   Frederic Seillier 11.12¾ (France) DREW 12 Graciano Rocchigiani 11.12¾ (Germany), Berlin, Germany (S. Middleweight Title). Scorecards: John Keane 115-115, 114-113, 113-116. Seillier vacated the title in April to concentrate on challenging Frank Lilles for the WBA crown.

17 December 1994   Jose Luis Navarro 10.6½ (Spain) W RSC 10 Del Bryan 10.3 (England), Cordoba, Spain (Vacant Welterweight Title). Moving forward remorselessly, and never taking a backward step, the Spaniard gradually wore Bryan down before forcing him to take two standing counts immediately prior to the tenth round stoppage. The title became vacant in October after Gary Jacobs decided to concentrate on a WBC match against Pernell Whitaker.

3 January 1995   Javier Castillejos 10.10½ (Spain) L RSC 9 Laurent Boudouani 10.12 (France), Epernay, France (L. Middleweight Title).

17 January 1995   Alexander Gurov 13.6½ (Ukraine) W RSC 1 Norbert Ekassi 13.4¾ (France), Levallois Perret, France (Vacant Cruiserweight Title). Referee: Larry O'Connell. The title became vacant in November when Carl Thompson forfeited same due to sickness.

4 February 1995   Khalid Rahilou 9.13¼ (France) W RSC 7 Patrick Ballesta 9.13¼ (France), Castelnau le Lez, France (L. Welterweight Title).

14 February 1995   Jean-Baptiste Mendy 9.7¾ (France) W PTS 12 Oleg Martchenko 9.8 (Russia), Thiais, France (Lightweight Title). Scorecards: 118-111, 118-111, 118-111.

17 February 1995   Jose Luis Navarro 10.7 (Spain) W RSC 5 Jose Ramon Escriche 10.6 (Spain), Cordoba, Spain (Welterweight Title).

22 February 1995   Richie Woodhall 11.5¼ (England) W RSC 9 Silvio Branco 11.5¼ (Italy), Ice Rink, Telford (Vacant Middleweight Title). After putting Branco down in the third and cutting his left-eyebrow a round later, Woodhall showed his fans that he was not just a "Fancy Dan" when proceeding to give the visitor a right going-over. Both men's left-eyes were swollen by the ninth, but, by then, Woodhall was in total command and was blasting away when the referee jumped in to rescue the Italian at 1.36 on the clock. The title had become vacant when Agostino Cardamone relinquished it December 1994 in order to go for the WBC championship, with this fight serving as an eliminator.

5 March 1995   Fabrice Tiozzo 12.6½ (France) W RSC 4 Noel Magee 12.4½ (Ireland), Vitrolles, France (L. Heavyweight Title). Outgunned for four rounds, it was only a matter of time before the heavy punching champion caught up with Magee. The fourth was to prove fatal for the Irishman as he was floored twice and rescued by the referee, who called the proceedings off halfway through the round.

14 March 1995   Alexander Gurov 13.7½ (Ukraine) L CO 3 Patrice Aouissi 13.4¾ (France), Levallois Perret, France (Cruiserweight Title). Judge: John Coyle.

1 April 1995   Jose Luis Navarro 10.5¼ (Spain) L RSC 8 Valery Kayumba 10.6 (France), Levallois Perret, France (Welterweight Title).

6 April 1995   Vincenzo Belcastro 8.8¾ (Italy) W PTS 12 Sergei Devakov 8.8¾ (Ukraine), Alassio, Italy (Inaugural S. Bantamweight Title). Referee: Mickey Vann. Scorecards: 116-114. 118-112. 117-114.

11 April 1995   Zeljko Mavrovic 15.4¾ (Croatia) W RSC 11 Christophe Bizot 15.12¾ (France), Levallois Perret, France (Vacant Heavyweight Title). Henry Akinwande had vacated the championship last February when deciding to make his base in the USA, in order to concentrate on getting a world title shot.

19 April 1995   John Armour 8.6 (England) W RSC 8 Antonio Picardi 8.6 (Italy), York Hall, Bethnal Green (Vacant Bantamweight Title). The pairing was made after Prince Nassem Hamed relinquished the title in February to move up to super-bantam. Although always in charge, unlike Hamed, Armour did not have the power to flatten his man, having to rely on wearing him down instead. The finish came following a clash of heads (Armour picked up a bad cut by the right-eye), which left Picardi turning his back on his rival and the referee calling it off with 2.32 of the eighth round on the clock.

28 April 1995   Mehdi Labdouni 9.0 (France) W PTS 12 Duke McKenzie 9.0 (England), Fontenay sous Bois, France (Featherweight Title). Scorecards: 120-114, 118-113, 117-112. Although never hurt by the champion, McKenzie failed to take any risks, merely content to box on the retreat when he should have been looking to pick up the pace and make his better boxing count. In a dull affair, it was not one of Labdouni's better nights either, but he at least forced the fight.

28 April 1995   Khalid Rahilou 9.13 (France) W RSC 9 Gert Bo Jacobsen 9.13¼ (Denmark), Randers, Denmark (L. Welterweight Title). Judge: Dave Parris.

6 May 1995   Eddy Smulders 12.6¾ (Holland) W PTS 12 Christophe Girard 12.5½ (France), Romarantin, France (Vacant L. Heavyweight Title). Scorecards: (Referee) John Coyle 117-111, 117-113, 118-112. Fabrice Tiozzo had relinquished the title in April to prepare for his crack at the WBC crown held by Mike McCallum.

10 June 1995   Luigi Camputaro 7.13 (Italy) DREW 12 Salvatore Fanni 7.13¾ (Italy), Guspini, Italy (Vacant Flyweight Title). The title became vacant when Robbie Regan gave it up in May to challenge Alberto Jimenez for the WBO crown. Scorecards: 116-113, 115-115, 115-115.

27 June 1995   Laurent Boudouani 10.12½ (France) W RSC 6 Patrick Vungbo 10.13 (Belgium), Levallois Perret, France (L. Middleweight Title). Referee: Roy Francis.

European Champions, 1909-1995

Prior to 1946, the championship was contested under the auspices of the International Boxing Union, re-named that year as the European Boxing Union (EBU). The IBU had come into being when Victor Breyer, a Paris-based journalist and boxing referee who later edited the Annuaire du Ring (first edition in 1910), warmed to the idea of an organisation that controlled boxing right across Europe, regarding rules and championship fights between the champions of the respective countries. He first came to London at the end of 1909 to discuss the subject with the NSC, but went away disappointed. However, at a meeting between officials from Switzerland and France in March 1912, the IBU was initially formed and, by June of that year, had published their first ratings. By April 1914, Belgium had also joined the organisation, although it would not be until the war was over that the IBU really took off. Many of the early champions shown on the listings were the result of promoters, especially the NSC, billing their own championship fights. Although the (French dominated) IBU recognised certain champions, prior to being re-formed in May 1920, they did not find their administrative "feet" fully until other countries such as Italy (1922), Holland (1923), and Spain (1924), produced challengers for titles. Later in the 1920s, Germany (1926), Denmark (1928), Portugal (1929) and Romania (1929) also joined the fold. Unfortunately, for Britain, its representatives (Although the BBBoC, as we know it today, was formed in 1929, an earlier attempt to form a Board of Control had been initiated in April 1918 by the NSC and it was that body who were involved here) failed to reach agreement on the three judges' ruling, following several meetings with the IBU early in 1920 and, apart from Elky Clark (fly), Ernie Rice and Alf Howard (light), and Jack Hood (welter), who conformed to that stipulation, fighters from these shores would not be officially recognised as champions until the EBU was formed in 1946. This led to British fighters claiming the title after beating IBU titleholders, or their successors, under championship conditions in this country. The only men who did not come into this category were Kid Nicholson (bantam), and Ted Kid Lewis and Tommy Milligan (welter), who defeated men not recognised by the IBU. For the record, the first men recognised and authorised, respectively, as being champions of their weight classes by the IBU were: Sid Smith and Michel Montreuil (fly), Charles Ledoux (bantam), Jim Driscoll and Louis de Ponthieu (feather), Freddie Welsh and Georges Papin (light), Georges Carpentier and Albert Badoud (welter), Georges Carpentier and Ercole Balzac (middle), Georges Carpentier and Battling Siki (light-heavy and heavy).

EUROPEAN COUNTRY CODE

AU = Austria; BEL = Belgium; CRO = Croatia; CZ = Czechoslovakia; DEN = Denmark; E = England; FIN = Finland; FR = France; GER = Germany; GRE = Greece; HOL = Holland; HUN = Hungary; ITA = Italy; LUX = Luxembourg; NI = Northern Ireland; NOR = Norway; POR = Portugal; ROM = Romania; RUS = Russia; S = Scotland; SP = Spain; SWE = Sweden; SWI = Switzerland; TU = Turkey; UK = Ukraine; W = Wales; YUG = Yugoslavia.

Champions in **bold** denote those recognised by the IBU/EBU

*Undefeated champions (Includes men who may have forfeited their titles)

Title Holder	Country	Tenure	Title Holder	Country	Tenure	Title Holder	Country	Tenure
Flyweight (112 lbs)			Louis Skena*	FR	1953-1954	Tommy Harrison	E	1921-1922
Sid Smith	E	1913	**Nazzareno Giannelli**	ITA	1954-1955	**Charles Ledoux**	FR	1922-1923
Bill Ladbury	E	1913-1914	**Dai Dower**	W	1955	Bugler Harry Lake	E	1923
Percy Jones*	W	1914	**Young Martin**	SP	1955-1959	Johnny Brown	E	1923-1928
Joe Symonds	E	1914	**Risto Luukkonen**	FIN	1959-1961	**Henry Scillie***	BEL	1925-1928
Tancy Lee	S	1914-1916	**Salvatore Burruni***	ITA	1961-1965	Kid Nicholson*	E	1928
Jimmy Wilde	W	1914-1915	**Rene Libeer***	FR	1965-1966	Teddy Baldock*	E	1928-1931
Jimmy Wilde*	W	1916-1923	**Fernando Atzori**	ITA	1967-1972	**Domenico Bernasconi**	ITA	1929
Michel Montreuil	BEL	1923-1925	**Fritz Chervet***	SWI	1972-1973	**Carlos Flix**	SP	1929-1931
Elky Clark	S	1925-1927	**Fernando Atzori**	ITA	1973	**Lucien Popescu**	ROM	1931-1932
Victor Ferrand	SP	1927	**Fritz Chervet***	SWI	1973-1974	**Domenico Bernasconi***	ITA	1932
Emile Pladner	FR	1928-1929	**Franco Udella**	ITA	1974-1979	**Nicholas Biquet**	BEL	1932-1935
Johnny Hill*	S	1928-1929	**Charlie Magri***	E	1979-1983	**Maurice Dubois**	SWI	1935-1936
Eugene Huat*	FR	1929	**Antoine Montero***	FR	1983-1984	**Joseph Decico**	FR	1936
Emile Degand	BEL	1929-1930	**Charlie Magri***	E	1984-1985	**Aurel Toma***	ROM	1936-1937
Kid Oliva	FR	1930	**Franco Cherchi**	ITA	1985	**Nicholas Biquet***	BEL	1937-1938
Lucien Popescu	ROM	1930-1931	**Charlie Magri**	E	1985-1986	**Aurel Toma**	ROM	1938-1939
Jackie Brown	E	1931-1935	**Duke McKenzie***	E	1986-1988	**Ernst Weiss**	AU	1939
Praxile Gyde	FR	1932-1935	**Eyup Can***	TU	1989-1990	**Gino Cattaneo**	ITA	1939-1941
Benny Lynch*	S	1935-1938	**Pat Clinton***	S	1990-1991	**Gino Bondavilli***	ITA	1941-1943
Kid David*	BEL	1935-1936	**Salvatore Fanni**	ITA	1991-1992	**Jackie Paterson**	S	1946
Ernst Weiss	AU	1936	**Robbie Regan***	W	1992-1993	**Theo Medina**	FR	1946-1947
Valentin Angelmann*	FR	1936-1938	**Luigi Camputaro**	ITA	1993-1994	**Peter Kane**	E	1947-1948
Enrico Urbinati*	ITA	1938-1943	**Robbie Regan***	W	1994-1995	**Guido Ferracin**	ITA	1948-1949
Raoul Degryse	BEL	1946-1947				**Luis Romero**	SP	1949-1951
Maurice Sandeyron	FR	1947-1949	**Bantamweight (118 lbs)**			**Peter Keenan**	S	1951-1952
Rinty Monaghan*	NI	1949-1950	Joe Bowker	E	1910	**Jean Sneyers***	BEL	1952-1953
Terry Allen	E	1950	Digger Stanley	E	1910-1912	**Peter Keenan**	S	1953
Jean Sneyers*	BEL	1950-1951	**Charles Ledoux**	FR	1912-1921	**John Kelly**	NI	1953-1954
Teddy Gardner*	E	1952	Bill Beynon	W	1913	**Robert Cohen***	FR	1954-1955

173

Title Holder	Country	Tenure
Mario D'Agata	ITA	1955-1958
Piero Rollo	ITA	1958-1959
Freddie Gilroy	NI	1959-1960
Pierre Cossemyns	BEL	1961-1962
Piero Rollo	ITA	1962
Alphonse Halimi	FR	1962
Piero Rollo	ITA	1962-1963
Mimoun Ben Ali	SP	1963
Risto Luukkonen*	FIN	1963-1964
Mimoun Ben Ali	SP	1965
Tommaso Galli	ITA	1965-1966
Mimoun Ben Ali	SP	1966-1968
Salvatore Burruni*	ITA	1968-1969
Franco Zurlo	ITA	1969-1971
Alan Rudkin	E	1971
Agustin Senin*	SP	1971-1973
Johnny Clark*	E	1973-1974
Bob Allotey	SP	1974-1975
Daniel Trioulaire	FR	1975-1976
Salvatore Fabrizio	ITA	1976-1977
Franco Zurlo	ITA	1977-1978
Juan Francisco Rodriguez	SP	1978-1980
Johnny Owen*	W	1980
Valerio Nati	ITA	1980-1982
Giuseppe Fossati	ITA	1982-1983
Walter Giorgetti*	ITA	1983-1984
Ciro de Leva*	ITA	1984-1986
Antoine Montero	FR	1986-1987
Louis Gomis*	FR	1987-1988
Fabrice Benichou	FR	1988
Vincenzo Belcastro*	ITA	1988-1990
Thierry Jacob*	FR	1990-1992
Johnny Bredahl*	DEN	1992
Vincenzo Belcastro	ITA	1993-1994
Prince Nassem Hamed*	E	1994-1995
John Armour	E	1995-

S. Bantamweight (122 lbs)

Title Holder	Country	Tenure
Vincenzo Belcastro	ITA	1995-

Featherweight (126 lbs)

Title Holder	Country	Tenure
Young Joey Smith	E	1911
Jean Poesy	FR	1911-1912
Jim Driscoll*	W	1912-1913
Ted Kid Lewis*	E	1913-1914
Louis de Ponthieu*	FR	1919-1920
Arthur Wyns	BEL	1920-1922
Billy Matthews	E	1922
Eugene Criqui*	FR	1922-1923
Edouard Mascart	FR	1923-1924
Charles Ledoux	FR	1924
Henri Hebrans	BEL	1924-1925
Antonio Ruiz	SP	1925-1928
Luigi Quadrini	ITA	1928-1929
Knud Larsen	DEN	1929
Jose Girones*	SP	1929-1934
Maurice Holtzer*	FR	1935-1938
Phil Dolhem	BEL	1938-1939
Lucien Popescu	ROM	1939-1941
Ernst Weiss	AU	1941
Gino Bondavilli	ITA	1941-1945
Ermanno Bonetti*	ITA	1945-1946
Tiger Al Phillips	E	1947
Ronnie Clayton	E	1947-1948
Ray Famechon	FR	1948-1953
Jean Sneyers	BEL	1953-1954
Ray Famechon	FR	1954-1955
Fred Galiana	SP	1955-1956
Cherif Hamia*	FR	1957-1958
Sergio Caprari	ITA	1958-1959
Gracieux Lamperti	FR	1959-1962

Title Holder	Country	Tenure
Alberto Serti	ITA	1962-1963
Howard Winstone*	W	1963-1967
Jose Legra*	SP	1967-1968
Manuel Calvo	SP	1968-1969
Tommaso Galli	ITA	1969-1970
Jose Legra*	SP	1970-1972
Gitano Jiminez	SP	1973-1975
Elio Cotena	ITA	1975-1976
Nino Jimenez	SP	1976-1977
Manuel Masso	SP	1977
Roberto Castanon*	SP	1977-1981
Salvatore Melluzzo	ITA	1981-1982
Pat Cowdell*	E	1982-1983
Loris Stecca*	ITA	1983
Barry McGuigan*	NI	1983-1985
Jim McDonnell*	E	1985-1987
Valerio Nati*	ITA	1987
Jean-Marc Renard*	BEL	1988-1989
Paul Hodkinson*	E	1989-1991
Fabrice Benichou	FR	1991-1992
Maurizio Stecca	ITA	1992-1993
Herve Jacob	FR	1993
Maurizio Stecca	ITA	1993
Stephane Haccoun	FR	1993-1994
Stefano Zoff	ITA	1994
Medhi Labdouni	FR	1994-

S. Featherweight (130 lbs)

Title Holder	Country	Tenure
Tommaso Galli	ITA	1971-1972
Domenico Chiloiro	ITA	1972
Lothar Abend	GER	1972-1974
Sven-Erik Paulsen*	NOR	1974-1976
Roland Cazeaux	FR	1976
Natale Vezzoli	ITA	1976-1979
Carlos Hernandez	SP	1979
Rodolfo Sanchez	SP	1979
Carlos Hernandez	SP	1979-1982
Cornelius Boza-Edwards*	E	1982
Roberto Castanon	SP	1982-1983
Alfredo Raininger	ITA	1983-1984
Jean-Marc Renard	BEL	1984
Pat Cowdell*	E	1984-1985
Jean-Marc Renard*	BEL	1986-1987
Salvatore Curcetti	ITA	1987-1988
Piero Morello	ITA	1988
Lars Lund Jensen	DEN	1988
Racheed Lawal	DEN	1988-1989
Daniel Londas*	FR	1989-1991
Jimmy Bredahl*	DEN	1992
Regilio Tuur	HOL	1992-1993
Jacobin Yoma	FR	1993-

Lightweight (135 lbs)

Title Holder	Country	Tenure
Freddie Welsh	W	1909-1911
Matt Wells	E	1911-1912
Freddie Welsh*	W	1912-1914
Georges Papin	FR	1920-1921
Ernie Rice	E	1921-1922
Seaman Nobby Hall	E	1922-1923
Harry Mason*	E	1923-1926
Fred Bretonnel	FR	1924
Lucien Vinez	FR	1924-1927
Luis Rayo*	SP	1927-1928
Aime Raphael	FR	1928-1929
Francois Sybille	BEL	1929-1930
Alf Howard	E	1930
Harry Corbett	E	1930-1931
Francois Sybille	BEL	1930-1931
Bep van Klaveren	HOL	1931-1932
Cleto Locatelli	ITA	1932

Title Holder	Country	Tenure
Francois Sybille	BEL	1932-1933
Cleto Locatelli*	ITA	1933
Francois Sybille	BEL	1934
Carlo Orlandi*	ITA	1934-1935
Enrico Venturi*	ITA	1935-1936
Vittorio Tamagnini	ITA	1936-1937
Maurice Arnault	FR	1937
Gustave Humery*	FR	1937-1938
Aldo Spoldi*	ITA	1938-1939
Karl Blaho	AU	1940-1941
Bruno Bisterzo	ITA	1941
Ascenzo Botta	ITA	1941
Bruno Bisterzo	ITA	1941-1942
Ascenzo Botta	ITA	1942
Roberto Proietti	ITA	1942-1943
Bruno Bisterzo	ITA	1943-1946
Roberto Proietti*	ITA	1946
Emile Dicristo	FR	1946-1947
Kid Dussart	BEL	1947
Roberto Proietti	ITA	1947-1948
Billy Thompson	E	1948-1949
Kid Dussart	BEL	1949
Roberto Proietti*	ITA	1949-1950
Pierre Montane	FR	1951
Elis Ask	FIN	1951-1952
Jorgen Johansen	DEN	1952-1954
Duilio Loi*	ITA	1954-1959
Mario Vecchiatto	ITA	1959-1960
Dave Charnley*	E	1960-1963
Conny Rudhof*	GER	1963-1964
Willi Quatuor	GER	1964-1965
Franco Brondi	ITA	1965
Maurice Tavant	FR	1965-1966
Borge Krogh	DEN	1966-1967
Pedro Carrasco*	SP	1967-1969
Miguel Velazquez	SP	1970-1971
Antonio Puddu	ITA	1971-1974
Ken Buchanan*	S	1974-1975
Fernand Roelandts	BEL	1976
Perico Fernandez*	SP	1976-1977
Jim Watt*	S	1977-1979
Charlie Nash*	NI	1979-1980
Francisco Leon	SP	1980
Charlie Nash	NI	1980-1981
Joey Gibilisco	ITA	1981-1983
Lucio Cusma	ITA	1983-1984
Rene Weller	GER	1984-1986
Gert Bo Jacobsen*	DEN	1986-1988
Rene Weller*	GER	1988
Policarpo Diaz*	SP	1988-1990
Antonio Renzo	ITA	1991-1992
Jean-Baptiste Mendy*	FR	1992-1994
Racheed Lawal	DEN	1994
Jean-Baptiste Mendy	FR	1994-

L. Welterweight (140 lbs)

Title Holder	Country	Tenure
Olli Maki*	FIN	1964-1965
Juan Sombrita-Albornoz	SP	1965
Willi Quatuor*	GER	1965-1966
Conny Rudhof	GER	1967
Johann Orsolics	AU	1967-1968
Bruno Arcari*	ITA	1968-1970
Rene Roque	FR	1970-1971
Pedro Carrasco*	SP	1971-1972
Roger Zami	FR	1972
Cemal Kamaci	TU	1972-1973
Toni Ortiz	SP	1973-1974
Perico Fernandez*	SP	1974
Jose Ramon Gomez-Fouz	SP	1975
Cemal Kamaci*	TU	1975-1976
Dave Boy Green*	E	1976-1977

Gary Jacobs, who vacated the European welter title last October, is seen here outpointing Marcelo di Croce   Les Clark

Title Holder	Country	Tenure	Title Holder	Country	Tenure	Title Holder	Country	Tenure
Primo Bandini	ITA	1977	Robert Villemain*	FR	1947-1948	Antoine Fernandez	FR	1989-1990
Jean-Baptiste Piedvache	FR	1977-1978	Livio Minelli	ITA	1949-1950	Kirkland Laing	E	1990
Colin Power	E	1978	Michele Palermo	ITA	1950-1951	Patrizio Oliva*	ITA	1990-1992
Fernando Sanchez	SP	1978-1979	Eddie Thomas	W	1951	Ludovic Proto	FR	1992-1993
Jose Luis Heredia	SP	1979	Charles Humez*	FR	1951-1952	Gary Jacobs*	S	1993-1994
Jo Kimpuani*	FR	1979-1980	Gilbert Lavoine	FR	1953-1954	Jose Luis Navarro	SP	1994-1995
Giuseppe Martinese	ITA	1980	Wally Thom	E	1954-1955	Valery Kayumba	FR	1995-
Antonio Guinaldo	SP	1980-1981	Idrissa Dione	FR	1955-1956			
Clinton McKenzie	E	1981-1982	Emilio Marconi	ITA	1956-1958	**L. Middleweight (154 lbs)**		
Robert Gambini	FR	1982-1983	Peter Waterman*	E	1958	Bruno Visintin	ITA	1964-1966
Patrizio Oliva*	ITA	1983-1985	Emilio Marconi	ITA	1958-1959	Bo Hogberg	SWE	1966
Terry Marsh*	E	1985-1986	Duilio Loi*	ITA	1959-1963	Yolande Leveque	FR	1966
Tusikoleta Nkalankete	FR	1987-1989	Fortunato Manca*	ITA	1964-1965	Sandro Mazzinghi*	ITA	1966-1968
Efren Calamati	ITA	1989-1990	Jean Josselin	FR	1966-1967	Remo Golfarini	ITA	1968-1969
Pat Barrett*	E	1990-1992	Carmelo Bossi	ITA	1967-1968	Gerhard Piaskowy	GER	1969-1970
Valery Kayumba	ITA	1992-1993	Fighting Mack	HOL	1968-1969	Jose Hernandez	SP	1970-1972
Christian Merle	FR	1993-1994	Silvano Bertini	ITA	1969	Juan Carlos Duran	ITA	1972-1973
Valery Kayumba	FR	1994	Jean Josselin	FR	1969	Jacques Kechichian	FR	1973-1974
Khalid Rahilou	FR	1994-	Johann Orsolics	AU	1969-1970	Jose Duran	SP	1974-1975
			Ralph Charles	E	1970-1971	Eckhard Dagge	GER	1975-1976
Welterweight (147 lbs)			Roger Menetrey	FR	1971-1974	Vito Antuofermo	ITA	1976
Young Joseph	E	1910-1911	John H. Stracey*	E	1974-1975	Maurice Hope*	E	1976-1978
Georges Carpentier*	FR	1911-1912	Marco Scano	ITA	1976-1977	Gilbert Cohen	FR	1978-1979
Albert Badoud*	SWI	1915-1921	Jorgen Hansen	DEN	1977	Marijan Benes	YUG	1979-1981
Johnny Basham	W	1919-1920	Jorg Eipel	GER	1977	Louis Acaries	FR	1981
Ted Kid Lewis*	E	1920-1924	Alain Marion	FR	1977-1978	Luigi Minchillo*	ITA	1981-1983
Piet Hobin*	BEL	1921-1925	Jorgen Hansen	DEN	1978	Herol Graham*	E	1983-1984
Billy Mack	E	1923	Josef Pachler	AU	1978	Jimmy Cable	E	1984
Tommy Milligan*	S	1924-1925	Henry Rhiney	E	1978-1979	Georg Steinherr*	GER	1984-1985
Mario Bosisio*	ITA	1925-1928	Dave Boy Green	E	1979	Said Skouma*	FR	1985-1986
Leo Darton	BEL	1928	Jorgen Hansen*	DEN	1979-1981	Chris Pyatt	E	1986-1987
Alf Genon	BEL	1928-1929	Hans-Henrik Palm	DEN	1982	Gianfranco Rosi*	ITA	1987
Gustave Roth	BEL	1929-1932	Colin Jones*	W	1982-1983	Rene Jacquot*	FR	1988-1989
Adrien Aneet	BEL	1932-1933	Gilles Elbilia*	FR	1983-1984	Edip Secovic	AU	1989
Jack Hood*	E	1933	Gianfranco Rosi	ITA	1984-1985	Giuseppe Leto	ITA	1989
Gustav Eder*	GER	1934-1936	Lloyd Honeyghan*	E	1985-1986	Gilbert Dele*	FR	1989-1990
Felix Wouters	BEL	1936-1938	Jose Varela	GER	1986-1987	Said Skouma	FR	1991
Saverio Turiello	ITA	1938-1939	Alfonso Redondo	SP	1987	Mourad Louati	HOL	1991
Marcel Cerdan*	FR	1939-1942	Mauro Martelli*	SWI	1987-1988	Jean-Claude Fontana	FR	1991-1992
Ernie Roderick	E	1946-1947	Nino la Rocca	ITA	1989	Laurent Boudouani	FR	1992-1993

Title Holder	Country	Tenure
Bernard Razzano	FR	1993-1994
Javier Castillejos	SP	1994-1995
Laurent Boudouani	FR	1995-

Middleweight (160 lbs)

Title Holder	Country	Tenure
Georges Carpentier*	FR	1912-1918
Ercole Balzac	FR	1920-1921
Gus Platts	E	1921
Johnny Basham	W	1921
Ted Kid Lewis	E	1921-1923
Roland Todd	E	1923-1924
Ted Kid Lewis	E	1924-1925
Bruno Frattini	ITA	1924-1925
Tommy Milligan	S	1925-1928
Rene Devos*	BEL	1926-1927
Barthelemy Molina	FR	1928
Alex Ireland	S	1928-1929
Mario Bosisio	ITA	1928
Leone Jacovacci	ITA	1928-1929
Len Johnson*	E	1928-1929
Marcel Thil	FR	1929-1930
Mario Bosisio	ITA	1930-1931
Poldi Steinbach	AU	1931
Hein Domgoergen*	GER	1931-1932
Ignacio Ara*	SP	1932-1933
Gustave Roth	BEL	1933-1934
Marcel Thil	FR	1934-1938
Edouard Tenet	FR	1938
Bep van Klaveren	HOL	1938
Anton Christoforidis	GRE	1938-1939
Edouard Tenet*	FR	1939
Josef Besselmann*	GER	1942-1943
Marcel Cerdan	FR	1947-1948
Cyrille Delannoit	BEL	1948
Marcel Cerdan*	FR	1948
Cyrille Delannoit	BEL	1948-1949
Tiberio Mitri*	ITA	1949-1950
Randy Turpin	E	1951-1954
Tiberio Mitri	ITA	1954
Charles Humez	FR	1954-1958
Gustav Scholz*	GER	1958-1961
John Cowboy McCormack	S	1961-1962
Chris Christensen	DEN	1962
Laszlo Papp*	HUN	1962-1965
Nino Benvenuti*	ITA	1965-1967
Juan Carlos Duran	ITA	1967-1969
Tom Bogs	DEN	1969-1970
Juan Carlos Duran	ITA	1970-1971
Jean-Claude Bouttier*	FR	1971-1972
Tom Bogs*	DEN	1973
Elio Calcabrini	ITA	1973-1974
Jean-Claude Bouttier	FR	1974
Kevin Finnegan	E	1974-1975
Gratien Tonna*	FR	1975
Bunny Sterling	E	1976
Angelo Jacopucci	ITA	1976
Germano Valsecchi	ITA	1976-1977
Alan Minter	E	1977
Gratien Tonna*	FR	1977-1978
Alan Minter*	E	1978-1979
Kevin Finnegan	E	1980
Matteo Salvemini	ITA	1980
Tony Sibson*	E	1980-1982
Louis Acaries	FR	1982-1984
Tony Sibson*	E	1984-1985
Ayub Kalule	DEN	1985-1986
Herol Graham	E	1986-1987
Sumbu Kalambay*	ITA	1987
Pierre Joly	FR	1987-1988
Christophe Tiozzo*	FR	1988-1989
Francesco dell' Aquila	ITA	1989-1990
Sumbu Kalambay*	ITA	1990-1993
Agostino Cardamone*	ITA	1993-1994
Richie Woodhall	E	1995-

S. Middleweight (168 lbs)

Title Holder	Country	Tenure
Mauro Galvano	ITA	1990-1991
James Cook	E	1991-1992
Franck Nicotra*	FR	1992
Vincenzo Nardiello	ITA	1992-1993
Ray Close*	NI	1993
Vinzenzo Nardiello	ITA	1993-1994
Frederic Seillier*	FR	1994-1995

L. Heavyweight (175 lbs)

Title Holder	Country	Tenure
Georges Carpentier	FR	1913-1922
Battling Siki	FR	1922-1923
Emile Morelle	FR	1923
Raymond Bonnel	FR	1923-1924
Louis Clement	SWI	1924-1926
Herman van T'Hof	HOL	1926
Fernand Delarge	BEL	1926-1927
Max Schmeling*	GER	1927-1928
Michele Bonaglia*	ITA	1929-1930
Ernst Pistulla*	GER	1931-1932
Adolf Heuser*	GER	1932
John Andersson*	SWE	1933
Martinez de Alfara	SP	1934
Marcel Thil*	FR	1934-1935
Merlo Preciso	ITA	1935
Hein Lazek	AU	1935-1936
Gustave Roth	BEL	1936-1938
Adolf Heuser*	GER	1938-1939
Luigi Musina*	ITA	1942-1943
Freddie Mills*	E	1947-1950
Albert Yvel	FR	1950-1951
Don Cockell*	E	1951-1952
Conny Rux*	GER	1952
Jacques Hairabedian	FR	1953-1954
Gerhard Hecht	GER	1954-1955
Willi Hoepner	GER	1955
Gerhard Hecht	GER	1955-1957
Artemio Calzavara	ITA	1957-1958
Willi Hoepner	GER	1958
Erich Schoeppner*	GER	1958-1962
Giulio Rinaldi	ITA	1962-1964
Gustav Scholz*	GER	1964-1965
Giulio Rinaldi	ITA	1965-1966
Piero del Papa	ITA	1966-1967
Lothar Stengel	GER	1967-1968
Tom Bogs*	DEN	1968-1969
Yvan Prebeg	YUG	1969-1970
Piero del Papa	ITA	1970-1971
Conny Velensek	GER	1971-1972
Chris Finnegan	E	1972
Rudiger Schmidtke	GER	1972-1973
John Conteh*	E	1973-1974
Domenico Adinolfi	ITA	1974-1976
Mate Parlov*	YUG	1976-1977
Aldo Traversaro	ITA	1977-1979
Rudi Koopmans	HOL	1979-1984
Richard Caramonolis	FR	1984
Alex Blanchard	HOL	1984-1987
Tom Collins	E	1987-1988
Pedro van Raamsdonk	HOL	1988
Jan Lefeber	HOL	1988-1989
Eric Nicoletta	FR	1989-1990
Tom Collins*	E	1990-1991
Graciano Rocchigiani*	GER	1991-1992
Eddie Smulders	HOL	1993-1994
Fabrice Tiozzo*	FR	1994-1995
Eddy Smulders	HOL	1995-

Cruiserweight (190 lbs)

Title Holder	Country	Tenure
Sam Reeson*	E	1987-1988
Angelo Rottoli	ITA	1989
Anaclet Wamba*	FR	1989-1990
Johnny Nelson*	E	1990-1992
Akim Tafer*	FR	1992-1993
Massimiliano Duran	ITA	1993-1994
Carl Thompson*	E	1994
Alexander Gurov	UK	1995
Patrice Aouissi	FR	1995-

Heavyweight (190 lbs +)

Title Holder	Country	Tenure
Georges Carpentier	FR	1913-1922
Battling Siki*	FR	1922-1923
Erminio Spalla	ITA	1923-1926
Paolino Uzcudun*	SP	1926-1928
Pierre Charles	BEL	1929-1931
Hein Muller	GER	1931-1932
Pierre Charles	BEL	1932-1933
Paolino Uzcudun	SP	1933
Primo Carnera*	ITA	1933-1935
Pierre Charles	BEL	1935-1937
Arno Kolblin	GER	1937-1938
Hein Lazek	AU	1938-1939
Adolf Heuser	GER	1939
Max Schmeling*	GER	1939-1941
Olle Tandberg	SWE	1943
Karel Sys*	BEL	1943-1946
Bruce Woodcock*	E	1946-1949
Joe Weidin	AU	1950-1951
Jack Gardner	E	1951
Hein Ten Hoff	GER	1951-1952
Karel Sys	BEL	1952
Heinz Neuhaus	GER	1952-1955
Franco Cavicchi	ITA	1955-1956
Ingemar Johansson*	SWE	1956-1959
Dick Richardson	W	1960-1962
Ingemar Johansson*	SWE	1962-1963
Henry Cooper*	E	1964
Karl Mildenberger	GER	1964-1968
Henry Cooper*	E	1968-1969
Peter Weiland	GER	1969-1970
Jose Urtain	SP	1970
Henry Cooper	E	1970-1971
Joe Bugner	E	1971
Jack Bodell	E	1971
Jose Urtain	SP	1971-1972
Jurgen Blin	GER	1972
Joe Bugner*	E	1972-1975
Richard Dunn	E	1976
Joe Bugner*	E	1976-1977
Jean-Pierre Coopman	BEL	1977
Lucien Rodriguez	FR	1977
Alfredo Evangelista	SP	1977-1979
Lorenzo Zanon*	SP	1979-1980
John L. Gardner*	E	1980-1981
Lucien Rodriguez	FR	1981-1984
Steffen Tangstad	NOR	1984-1985
Anders Eklund	SWE	1985
Frank Bruno*	E	1985-1986
Steffen Tangstad*	NOR	1986
Alfredo Evangelista	SP	1987
Anders Eklund	SWE	1987
Francesco Damiani*	ITA	1987-1989
Derek Williams	E	1989-1990
Jean Chanet	FR	1990
Lennox Lewis*	E	1990-1992
Henry Akinwande*	E	1993-1995
Zeljko Mavrovic	CRO	1995-

A-Z of Current World Champions

by Eric Armit

Shows the record since 1 July 1994, plus career summary, for all men holding IBF, WBA, WBC and WBO titles as at 30 June 1995. The author has also produced a pen-portrait of those who first won titles between 1 July 1994 and 30 June 1995. Incidentally, the place name given is the respective boxer's domicile and may not necessarily be his birthplace, while all nicknames are shown where applicable. Not included are fighters such as Michael Carbajal (WBO-L. Fly), Mike McCallum (WBC-L. Heavy), Harold Mestre (IBF-Bantam), and Francisco Tejedor (IBF-Fly), who won and lost, forfeited or relinquished titles during the period.

Hector Acero-Sanchez

Santo Domingo, Dominican Republic. *Born* 18 March, 1966
WBC S. Bantamweight Champion. Former Dominican S. Bantamweight Champion

A classy, slick boxer, with excellent defensive skills, and a good punch, he was one of seven kids born in conditions of abject poverty in the Santo Domingo slum area known as Devil's Island. Started boxing at the age of ten and won the Dominican national title three times as an amateur before turning professional in 1989 as a bantamweight. Unbeaten in his first 23 contests, he collected the Dominican super-bantamweight crown in May 1990 by knocking out Francisco Alvarez in six rounds. Dropped his title in September 1991 when he was knocked out in 11 rounds by world-rated Jose Garcia and to progress his career he moved to New York in 1993, acquiring a millionaire backer. Won the New York State title in his first fight in the USA with a points win over unpredictable Darryl Pinckney and retained it with a split decision in a tough match with unbeaten Ishmael Sanders. The tough matches continued as he fought a majority draw with highly touted Eddie Croft and then lost to world-rated Frankie Toledo, who took a unanimous verdict as Hector failed to come to terms with his rival's southpaw style. He was selected as a safe opponent for WBC champion, Tracy Patterson, but shocked the champion with a second round knockdown and staged a strong finish to lift the title on a split decision. Scored a good points win over Barrington Francis in a non-title bout and then showed class by clearly out boxing former WBA champion, Julio Gervacio, in his first title defence. His second defence, though, was a different proposition and Hector looked lucky to retain his title with a draw against veteran, Daniel Zaragoza. Smooth skills have drawn comparisons with Wilfred Benitez, but it is early days to make any definitive judgement and he looked ordinary against Zaragoza. Not a big puncher, despite his 20 quick wins.

26.08.94	Tracy Harris Patterson W PTS 12 Atlantic City *(WBC S. Bantamweight Title Challenge)*
28.10.94	Barrington Francis W PTS 10 Bushkill
11.03.95	Julio Gervacio W PTS 12 Atlantic City *(WBC S. Bantamweight Title Defence)*
02.06.95	Daniel Zaragoza DREW 12 Ledyard *(WBC S. Bantamweight Title Defence)*

Career: 37 contests, won 32, drew 3, lost 2.

Yuri (Ebihara) Arbachakov

Kemerova, Armenia. *Born* 22 October, 1966
WBC Flyweight Champion. Former Undefeated Japanese Flyweight Champion

01.08.94	Hugo Soto W CO 8 Tokyo *(WBC Flyweight Title Defence)*
30.01.95	Oscar Arciniega W PTS 12 Sapporo *(WBC Flyweight Title Defence)*

Career: 20 contests, won 20.

Marco Antonio (The Baby Faced Assassin) Barrera

Mexico City, Mexico. *Born* 17 January, 1974
WBO S. Bantamweight Champion. Former Undefeated Mexican & NABF S. Flyweight Champion

Comes from a boxing family, his brother Jorge is a professional, Marco was introduced to boxing at the age of seven by one of his uncles. Won the Mexican Golden Gloves light-flyweight title as an amateur in 1988 and turned professional in November 1989 when just 15-years-old. Originally a southpaw, before his uncle converted him to orthodox, he was matched early with some tough opposition, but breezed through with no problems and won the vacant Mexican super-flyweight title in April 1992 by outpointing world-rated Josefinao Suarez. Made three successful defences in the same year beating good class opponents Jose Montiel, Mike Espinoza and Esteban Ayala, inside the distance. Stopped Facundo Rodriguez and decisioned Noe Santillan in defences in 1993 and, in August 1993, collected the vacant NABF title by outpointing Eduardo

Yuri Arbachakov

Ramirez. Matched with Argentinian Carlos Salazar in a final eliminator to find a challenger for the WBC title in Buenos Aires in April 1994, Marco failed to make the weight. The bout went ahead at catchweights and he easily outpointed Salazar. Moved up two divisions and made his mark at super-bantamweight by halting the former WBA bantamweight champion, Eddie Cook, in two rounds in December 1994. Won the WBO title in March, when he overcame an early cut to take a unanimous decision over Daniel Jimenez, and must have sent a shiver through the division in the way he dismissed Frankie Toledo in two rounds with devastating body punches in his first defence. 5' 7" tall, cool, and a gifted boxer-puncher, with a good chin, Barrera is still only 21 and could be one of the stars of the future. He has 25 wins inside the distance.

15.08.94	Israel Gonzalez W RSC 8 Los Angeles
22.10.94	Jesus Sarabia W RSC 3 Las Vegas
03.12.94	Eddie Cook W RSC 8 Las Vegas
31.03.95	Daniel Jimenez W PTS 12 Los Angeles
	(WBO S. Bantamweight Title Challenge)
02.06.95	Frankie Toledo W RSC 2 Ledyard
	(WBO S. Bantamweight Title Defence)
Career: 36 contests, won 36.	

Nigel (Dark Destroyer) Benn

Ilford, England. *Born* 22 January, 1964
WBC S. Middleweight Champion.
Former WBO & Commonwealth Middleweight Champion

Note: Full record will be found in the Current British-Based Champions: Career Records' Section.

Mbulelo Botile

East London, South Africa. *Born* 23 July, 1972
IBF Bantamweight Champion. Former Undefeated South African Bantamweight Champion

A stable-mate of IBF super-bantamweight champion, Vuyani Bungu, and former champion, Welcome Ncita, he started boxing in the Duncan Township at the age of 12 and turned professional in July 1989 at the age of 17. His obvious talent made it difficult to get fights and he was confined to two or three bouts a year in the Cape area. Although a change of management did not bring more action, it did give him the chance to train full-time and work with Bungu and Ncita. The improvement since then has been amazing. With only 11 fights behind him, he faced the much more experienced former IBF title challenger, Derrick Whiteboy, in May 1994, and took the South African title with a clear points victory. Scored two more victories during the year, decisioning the Mexican veteran, Javier Diaz, and outpointing Puerto Rican prospect, Jose Ayala. In March 1995 he halted the Central American champion, Eddie Saenz, and then won the IBF title by outclassing Colombian, Harold Mestre, stopping him in two rounds. The 5' 5" tall Botile is a good boxer and an excellent counter puncher who still has a lot ot learn. Has eight inside the distance wins.

15.10.94	Javier Diaz W PTS 10 Laredo
19.11.94	Jose Ayala W PTS 10 Hammanskraal
04.03.95	Eddie Saenz W RSC 4 Hammanskraal
29.04.95	Harold Mestre W RSC 2 Johannesburg
	(IBF Bantamweight Title Challenge)
Career: 16 contests, won 16.	

Riddick (Big Daddy) Bowe

New York, USA. *Born* 10 August, 1967
WBO Heavyweight Champion.
Former IBF & WBA Heavyweight Champion. Former Undefeated WBC & WBC Con Am Heavyweight Champion

13.08.94	Buster Mathis NC 4 Atlantic City
03.12.94	Larry Donald W PTS 12 Las Vegas
11.03.95	Herbie Hide W CO 6 Las Vegas
	(WBO Heavyweight Title Challenge)
17.06.95	Jorge Luis Gonzales W CO 6 Las Vegas
	(WBO Heavyweight Title Defence)
Career: 40 contests, won 38, lost 1, no contest 1.	

Lonnie Bradley

New York, USA. *Born* 16 September, 1968
WBO Middleweight Champion

Born in Charleston, South Carolina, but living in Harlem, Lonnie is the first world champion from that area since Sugar Ray Robinson. 5' 11" tall, with a 76 inch reach, he had 69 amateur fights with 62 victories. Won the New York Golden Gloves championship in 1990, '91 and '92, and was also National Golden Gloves champion in 1992, but failed to make the Olympic team, losing to Raul Marquez in the trials. Turning professional in November 1992, he made a smart move by taking on Dave Wolf as his manager and ex-boxer, Bobby Cassidy, as his trainer. Fought initially for the Madison Square Garden group, but had to become a road warrior when they closed their doors, keeping busy with a series of bouts around America. Scored a significant victory and lifted the New York State title when he took a majority decision over Ron Morgan in August 1994. Won every round against tough Mexican, Luiz Vazquez, in January, but had to climb off the floor to decision Apolinar Hernandez in March. Was matched with hard-punching David Mendez for the vacant WBO crown after Steve Collins relinquished the title and then stopped the Mexican in the last round to become champion. Lonnie is a compact boxer with a stiff jab, and his good combination punching has given him 17 inside the distance victories.

07.08.94	Ronnie Morgan W PTS 10 Callicoon
07.11.94	Matthew Charleston W RSC 2 Los Angeles
03.01.95	Karl Willis W RSC 3 Las Vegas
30.01.95	Luis Vazquez W RSC 5 Los Angeles
03.03.95	Apolinar Hernandez W PTS 10 Hauppauge
19.05.95	David Mendez W RSC 12 Jean
	(Vacant WBO Middleweight Title)
Career: 21 contests, won 21.	

Lonnie Bradley

Vuyani (The Beast) Bungu

Mdantsane, South Africa. *Born* 26 February, 1967
IBF S. Bantamweight Champion. Former Undefeated South African S. Bantamweight Champion

Takes his nickname from John Mugabi. Turned professional in April 1987 and came through some tough tests in Township bouts, winning the Cape title in June 1988, when stopping Sexon Ngqayimbanya, and rising to top contender position in the national rankings. Challenged Fransie Badenhorst for the South African crown in August 1989, but fought with careless aggression and was floored three times. Although he had Badenhorst down, Vuyani faded in the late rounds and lost on points. He faced Fransie again in May 1990 and this time boxed his way to a clear victory to take the title. Defended his throne by flooring Lunga Dundu twice and halting him in nine rounds in June 1991, but lost for the second time when the American southpaw, Freddie Norwood, decisioned him on a trip to Italy in April 1992. Vuyani returned to domestic business with successful defences against Segigi Nekile and June Siko and then challenged the unbeaten Kennedy McKinney for the IBF title in August 1994. Despite being given no chance, Vuyani proved to be too strong and busy for the champion and took the title on an easy decision. Has had three easy defences, winning comfortably on points over light-punching Felix Camacho, the limited Indonesian, Nurhuda, and Colombian, Victor Llerena. Vuyani has emerged from the shadow of his stable-mate, Welcome Ncita, who previously held the IBF title, and has impressed with his body punching. Is 5' 5" tall.

20.08.94	Kennedy McKinney W PTS 12 Hammanskraal *(IBF S. Bantamweight Title Challenge)*
19.11.94	Felix Camacho W PTS 12 Hammanskraal *(IBF S. Bantamweight Title Defence)*
04.03.95	Mohammed Al Haji Nurhuda W PTS 12 Hammanskraal *(IBF S. Bantamweight Title Defence)*
29.04.95	Victor Llerena W PTS 12 Johannesburg *(IBF S. Bantamweight Title Defence)*
Career: 29 contests, won 27, lost 2.	

Jorge Castro

Jorge (Locomotora) Castro

Puerto Deseado, Argentine. *Born* 18 August, 1967
WBA Middleweight Champion. Former Undefeated Argentinian & South American L. Middleweight Champion

Unorthodox, undisciplined and courageous, with plenty of natural talent, but too little dedication, Jorge is one of the busiest of world-class fighters with over 100 fights in eight years. Lost only two of 55 amateur contests and beat the world champion, Cuban, Carlos Garcia. Turned professional in February 1987 and fought two draws in his first seven fights, but did not lose until June 1989 when he was outpointed by veteran, Lorenzo Garcia, in fight number 40. Won the Argentinian light-middleweight title in April 1989, knocking out Hugo Marinangeli in four rounds, but relinquished the title without making a defence. Took the South American title in October 1990, halting Marinangeli in 12 rounds, and retained it in March 1991 with a first round kayo of dangerous Miguel Arroyo. Regained the Argentinian title in April 1991 by beating Mario Gaston in eight rounds, but, at the end of the year, Jorge was unsuccessful in a try at the WBC title when he was easily outpointed by Terry Norris. Failed to make the weight for a defence of his Argentinian title in April 1992 and moved up to middleweight, where he lost a wide decision to Roy Jones in June 1992, prior to winning his next 23 bouts. Faced Reggie Johnson for the vacant WBA title in Argentina in August 1994 and the venue was significant as Jorge seemed fortunate to receive a disputed split decision over the Texan. Made an easy defence in November, by knocking out veteran, Alex Ramos in two rounds, and then faced former champion, John David Jackson, in December. In the year's most dramatic finish, an exhausted, cut, dazed, and seemingly defenceless champion, produced a wild left-hook in the ninth to turn the fight around, flooring Jackson three times to retain his crown. Made hard work of his defence against Anthony Andrews, suffering a flash knockdown and was only slightly ahead when he caught up with his challenger in the final round. The Argentinian has hardly ever trained for a fight, but gets by on strength and ability and has registered 68 quick wins in his 103 fights.

08.07.94	Francisco Bobadilla W PTS 10 Comodoro Rivadavia
17.07.94	Royan Hammond W CO 4 Buenos Aires
12.08.94	Reggie Johnson W PTS 12 Tucuman *(Vacant WBA Middleweight Title)*
05.11.94	Alex Ramos W CO 2 Caleta Oliva *(WBA Middleweight Title Defence)*
10.12.94	John David Jackson W RSC 9 Monterrey *(WBA Middleweight Title Defence)*
27.05.95	Anthony Andrews W RSC 12 Fort Lauderdale *(WBA Middleweight Title Defence)*
Career: 103 contests, won 97, drew 2, lost 4.	

Antonio (Goloso) Cermeno

Miranda, Venezuela. *Born* 6 March, 1969
WBA S. Bantamweight Champion. Former Undefeated Latin American S. Bantamweight Champion

Very tall for his weight at 5' 10" and, not surprisingly, likes to fight at a distance, he is strong and a good puncher. Won a gold medal in the 1989 Central American championships before turning professional in September 1990 and initially boxing at super-featherweight. Showed his potential in his seventh fight in October 1991 when he decisioned the experienced and dangerous Jesus Flores and fought his way to the top of the WBA ratings in August 1993 when he lifted the Latin American super-bantamweight crown by halting Venezuelan champion, Ramon Guzman, in four rounds. Travelled to Korea in December 1993 to face the unbeaten local fighter Jae-Won Choi in a final eliminator, but their styles did not mix and after a disappointing bout the verdict went to Choi. Antonio kept busy in 1994 with four wins, but it took some political in-fighting before he was given a shot at Wilfredo Vasquez in May. Keeping the veteran champion on the outside throughout the fight, he hurt him in the third round and finished strongly to take a clear decision. The Vasquez camp lodged an official protest over confusion in the scoring, but it was dismissed and Antonio was crowned as champion. Despite his 15 inside the distance wins, he is not considered a big puncher and his jerky style is not pretty, but he is tough and difficult to beat.

05.11.94	Felix Guzman W RSC 2 Los Teques
13.05.95	Wilfredo Vasquez W PTS 12 Bayamon *(WBA S. Bantamweight Title Challenge)*
Career: 23 contests, won 22, lost 1.	

Julio Cesar (Super Star) Chavez

Ciudad Obregon, Mexico. *Born* 12 July, 1962
WBC L. Welterweight Champion. Former Undefeated IBF L. Welterweight Champion. Former Undefeated WBC & WBA Lightweight Champion. Former Undefeated WBC S. Featherweight Champion

17.09.94	Meldrick Taylor W RSC 8 Las Vegas *(WBC L. Welterweight Title Defence)*
10.12.94	Tony Lopez W RSC 10 Monterrey *(WBC L. Welterweight Title Defence)*
08.04.95	Giovanni Parisi W PTS 12 Las Vegas *(WBC L. Welterweight Title Defence)*
Career: 95 contests, won 93, drew 1, lost 1.	

Hi-Yong Choi

Pusan, South Korea. *Born* 13 September, 1965
WBA L. Flyweight Champion. Former WBA M. Flyweight Champion. Former Undefeated OPBF M. Flyweight Champion

Former outstanding amateur who turned professional in July 1987 and went straight into the eight round class. Won the vacant OPBF mini-flyweight title in only his fourth fight, outpointing fellow-countryman, Sam-Joong Lee, in April 1988 and made two successful defences before lifting the WBA crown in February 1991, when outscoring Bong-Jun Kim in a bout which saw both fighters on the floor. The decision was so controversial that the WBA ordered a rematch. Choi made a voluntary defence with a points verdict over Filipino, Sugar Ray Mike, in June and then settled the controversy be decisioning Kim again in October. Defended his title again, halting Yuichi Hosono and knocking out Rommel Lawas, but lost it in October 1992 when dropping a close verdict to Hideyuki Ohashi in Japan. Choi was then inactive for 14 months and returned as a light-flyweight. After three wins he challenged "Leo" Gamez for the WBA title and by building up an early lead against the tiny Venezuelan, and holding off the champion's strong finish, he took the title on points. Choi is a fast, busy fighter, but not a big puncher.

27.08.94	Mongkhonchai Satheragym W PTS 10 Kangrun
04.02.95	Silvio Gamez W PTS 12 Ulsan *(WBA L. Flyweight Title Challenge)*
Career: 19 contests, won 18, lost 1.	

Daorung (MP-Petroleum) Chuwatana

Uttaradit, Thailand. *Born* 1 April, 1968
WBA Bantamweight Champion. Former Undefeated OPBF & Thai Bantamweight Champion

As with many Thai fighters, Daorung has boxed under different names, reflecting his gym or sponsors, and fought as Daorung Technicut at one stage. The hard-punching, busy south-paw, is a former stablemate of the great Kaosai Galaxy and turned professional back in 1985. Although dropping early decisions to top Thais, Noree Jockygym and Petch Donjadee, those were his only losses in his first 30 bouts. Won the Thai bantamweight

title in November 1989 when out-pointing Choocherd Eausampan, but suffered his only inside the distance loss in June 1990 when he was knocked out by Eun-Shik Lee in Korea. Returned to Korea again in October 1991 where he beat Yong-Chun Min on a technical decision to win the OPBF title. Made three successful defences of his OPBF title and also scored victories over former world champions, Rolando Bohol and Tacy Macalos, to earn a shot at the WBA crown. In July 1994, Daorung won the title in controversial circumstances when the champion, John Michael Johnson, suffered a bad cut in the first round which seemed to have been caused by a clash of heads, and the fight was given to Daorung on a retirement. His first defence in November against Korean, In-Shik Koh, was also ended by a cut, this time to Daorung, and he retained his title on a technical decision. Had a tough time with fellow-countryman, Lakhin CP Gym, in May, before holding on to his crown with a draw. Has 33 wins inside the distance.

17.07.94	John Michael Johnson W RTD 1 Uttaradit *(WBA Bantamweight Title Challenge)*
20.11.94	In-Shik Koh W TD 5 Bangkok *(WBA Bantamweight Title Defence)*
27.05.95	Lakhin CP Gym DREW 12 Bangkok *(WBA Bantamweight Title Defence)*
Career: 62 contests, won 55, drew 3, lost 4.	

Al (Ice) Cole

Suffern, USA. *Born* 21 April, 1964
IBF Cruiserweight Champion. Former Unbeaten USBA Cruiserweight Champion

23.07.94	Nate Miller W PTS 12 Bismark *(IBF Cruiserweight Title Defence)*
18.03.95	Mike Dixon W RTD 8 Pensacola
24.06.95	Uriah Grant W PTS 12 Atlantic City *(IBF Cruiserweight Title Defence)*
Career: 28 contests, won 27, lost 1.	

Steve Collins

Dublin, Ireland. *Born* 21 July, 1964
WBO S. Middleweight Champion. Former Undefeated WBO, All-Ireland, USBA and Penta-Continental Middleweight Champion

Note: Full record will be found in the Current British-Based Champions: Career Records' section.

Carl (The Squirrel) Daniels

St Louis, USA. *Born* 26 August, 1970
WBA L. Middleweight Champion

A well-schooled, southpaw fighter, Carl has put on weight over the years. In 1987 he was World Junior flyweight champion and also won the National Golden Gloves title at the same weight that year. In 1988, he won the United States' amateur title at featherweight, but failed to make the US Olympic team and turned professional in November 1988 at the age of 18. Won his first five fights on points and then his next 13 inside the distance. Kept up a very busy schedule against mediocre opposition, winning the Missouri State title in September 1990 by halting Gary Williams and also beat Wilbur Kigundu and Daniel Sclarandi. Challenged Terry Norris for the WBC crown in February 1992 as a 10-1 outsider, but hurt Norris in the second round and fought well until being stopped in the ninth round, his left-eye completely closed. Scored a good unanimous verdict over world-rated Curtis Summitt in April 1992 and floored and outpointed classy Louis Howard in March 1993. Briefly moved up to middleweight, but was eventually matched with the strong Dominican, Julio Cesar Green, for the vacant WBA light-middleweight title, flooring and battering his opponent to take the decision, along with the crown. A sharp and accurate puncher, but not a big hitter, he is still improving. Has stopped 22 opponents.

29.08.94	Robert Cameron W CO 1 Louisville
22.02.95	Sergio Medina W PTS 12 Rochester
08.04.95	James Mason W RTD 2 Las Vegas
16.06.95	Julio Cesar Green W PTS 12 Lyon
	(Vacant WBA L. Middleweight Title)
Career: 36 contests, won 35, lost 1.	

Oscar de la Hoya

Montebello, USA. *Born* 4 February, 1973
IBF & WBO Lightweight Champion.
Former Undefeated WBO S. Featherweight Champion

29.07.94	Jorge Paez W CO 2 Las Vegas
	(Vacant WBO Lightweight Title)
18.11.94	Carl Griffith W RSC 3 Las Vegas
	(WBO Lightweight Title Defence)
10.12.94	John Avila W RSC 9 Los Angeles
	(WBO Lightweight Title Defence)
18.02.95	Juan Molina W PTS 12 Las Vegas
	(WBO Lightweight Title Defence)
06.05.95	Rafael Ruelas W RSC 2 Las Vegas
	(WBO Lightweight Title Defence &
	IBF Lightweight Title Challenge)
Career: 18 contests, won 18.	

George Foreman

Marshall, USA. *Born* 10 January, 1949
IBF Heavyweight Champion. Former Undefeated WBA Heavyweight Champion. Former World Heavyweight Champion

05.11.94	Michael Moorer W CO 10 Las Vegas
	(IBF & WBA Heavyweight Title Challenge)
22.04.95	Axel Schulz W PTS 12 Las Vegas
	(IBF Heavyweight Title Defence)
Career: 78 contests, won 74, lost 4.	

Sammy (Mangany) Fuentes

Loiza, Puerto Rico. *Born* 18 February, 1964
WBO L. Welterweight Champion.
Former Undefeated Penta-Continental L. Welterweight Champion

A 5' 9" tall, flat-footed, aggressive switch-hitter, who has had a number of lows and highs in his career, Sammy turned professional in November 1982 in Puerto Rico but lost an early bout to future WBA lightweight champion, Juan Nazario, in August 1983. Later that year, in December, on a trip to Trinidad, he was disqualified for a low blow against Fitzroy Davidson. Moved to the United States in 1985 and scored good wins over Othal Dixon and the former IBF lightweight champion, Harry Arroyo, knocking him out in seven rounds in October 1985. He swung downwards in 1986 as he was beaten in three consecutive fights, being outpointed by Frankie Warren and stopped by both Frankie Randall and Roger Mayweather. Sammy bounced back with a fifth round kayo of Tony Martin in December 1987, before being halted in a round by Fred Pendleton in February 1988. The Inglewood Forum tournament gave him another chance in 1989 and he took it, with wins over Vince

Releford, Santos Cardona, John Montes and Rodolfo Aguilar. Faced Julio Cesar Chavez for the WBC light-welterweight title in November 1989, but took a beating and retired after ten rounds. After losing five of his next seven bouts, including a first round stoppage at the hands of Konstantin Tszyu, he seemed on the way to becoming just a trial horse until stopping Andreas Panayi in September 1994 to win the Penta-Continental title. That gave his career a boost and he took his big chance when he was called in as a substitute and won the vacant WBO crown by halting Fidel Avendano in two rounds. Overcoming an early cut to floor and easily outpoint Hector Lopez in his first defence, he is a dangerous and erratic performer who is unlikely to reign for long.

15.08.94	Gilberto Flores W CO 1 Los Angeles
17.09.94	Andreas Panayi W RSC 4 Crawley
07.11.94	David Ojeda W RSC 5 Los Angeles
03.12.94	Daniel Hernandez W RTD 6 Las Vegas
20.02.95	Fidel Avendano W RSC 2 Los Angeles
	(Vacant WBO L. Welterweight Title)
10.06.95	Hector Lopez W PTS 12 Las Vegas
	(WBO L. Welterweight Title Defence)
Career: 45 contests, won 31, drew 1, lost 13.	

Alejandro (Little Cobra) Gonzalez

Guadalajara, Mexico. *Born* 11 August, 1973
WBC Featherweight Champion.
Former Undefeated WBC International Featherweight Champion

Lanky, 5' 8" tall, aggressive box-puncher with a fluid style and a hard punch, Alejandro turned professional in April 1988 at the age of 14. Lost a decision in his third fight and was stopped by the more experienced Josefino Suarez in May 1990, but is unbeaten since then. His first 16 fights were all in Guadalajara, and he made a big impression when he fought in Mexico City in 1991, scoring four wins over good opposition. Won the vacant WBC International featherweight title in February 1992, battering Harold Rhodes so badly that he could not answer the bell for the ninth round. Made three defences in 1992 against Paquito Openo, Claudio Martinet and Lupe Gutierrez, all ending on second round knockouts.

Continued his progress in 1993 with a points win over Ulises Chong in a title bout and a second round stoppage of former WBA bantamweight champion, Luisito Espinosa. Took on the top contender, Cesar Soto, in a WBC eliminator in the latter's hometown in August 1994 and won clearly on points, despite the split decision. He was still a big outsider for his challenge to unbeaten Kevin Kelley in January, but was a revelation as he outclassed Kelley and climbed off the floor to force a tenth round stoppage. Made a successful defence against former WBA and WBO super-bantamweight champion, Louie Espinosa, winning on points, and showed his power in June with a nine round crushing of tough Tony Green. Has 26 quick wins and, at the age of 21, he looks set for a long reign. Has the talent to move up and win a world title at more than one weight.

06.08.94	Cesar Soto W PTS 12 Juarez
04.11.94	Eduardo Montes W RSC 3 Guadalajara
07.01.95	Kevin Kelley W RTD 10 San Antonio *(WBC Featherweight Title Challenge)*
31.03.95	Louie Espinosa W PTS 12 Los Angeles *(WBC Featherweight Title Defence)*
02.06.95	Tony Green W RSC 9 Ledyard *(WBC Featherweight Title Defence)*
Career: 39 contests, won 37, lost 2.	

Humberto (Chiquita) Gonzalez

Mexico City, Mexico. *Born* 25 March, 1966
WBC & IBF L. Flyweight Champion. Former Undefeated Mexican L. Flyweight Champion

08.07.94	Armando Diaz W RSC 3 Los Angeles
10.09.94	Juan Domingo Cordoba W RTD 7 Lake Tahoe *(WBC & IBF L. Flyweight Title Defence)*
12.11.94	Michael Carbajal W PTS 12 Mexico City *(WBC & IBF L. Flyweight Title Defence)*
31.03.95	Jesus Zuniga W CO 5 Los Angeles *(WBC & IBF L. Flyweight Title Defence)*
Career: 43 contests, won 41, lost 2.	

Miguel (Angel) Gonzalez

Ensenada, Mexico. *Born* 15 November, 1970
WBC Lightweight Champion. Former Undefeated WBC International Lightweight Champion

06.08.94	Leavander Johnson W RSC 8 Juarez *(WBC Lightweight Title Defence)*
13.12.94	Calvin Grove W RTD 5 Albuquerque *(WBC Lightweight Title Defence)*
25.04.95	Ricardo Silva W PTS 12 South Padre Island *(WBC Lightweight Title Defence)*
02.06.95	Marty Jakubowski W PTS 12 Ledyard *(WBC Lightweight Title Defence)*
Career: 37 contests, won 37.	

Harold Grey

Arjona Bolivar, Colombia. *Born* 20 December, 1971
IBF S. Flyweight Champion

5' 7" tall, long-armed, busy stylist with a good punch, who came out of nowhere to pick up the IBF title. His brother Ernesto is also a professional. Although a good, if not outstanding amateur before joining the paid ranks in November 1990, he showed power in his early fights, winning his first six, all inside three rounds. However, the opposition remained modest and he had not even challenged for the national title or fought outside Colombia, before being given a shot at the IBF champion, Julio Borboa, in August. Had a four inch reach advantage over the Mexican, who was making his sixth title defence, and used it well to keep the fight at a distance. Both fighters were cut, but Harold, who had never gone beyond six rounds, held off a strong finish by Borboa to take a narrow split decision. Had a tough time in his first defence against the experienced Vincenzo Belcastro in Italy and had to climb off the canvas to retain his crown with a split verdict. The defence against fellow-Colombian, Orlando Tobon, was slightly easier as his work in the early rounds helped him to a unanimous points decision and he repeated his victory over Borboa, although again it was close. His 15 quick wins are deceptive as they were largely scored over very modest opposition and, because his victories over Borboa and Belcastro were not totally convincing, Harold still has to prove his true class.

29.08.94	Julio Borboa W PTS 12 Los Angeles *(IBF S. Flyweight Title Challenge)*
17.12.94	Vincenzo Belcastro W PTS 12 Cagliari *(IBF S. Flyweight Title Defence)*
18.03.95	Orlando Tobon W PTS 12 Cartagena *(IBF S. Flyweight Title Defence)*
24.06.95	Julio Cesar Borboa W PTS 12 Cartagena *(IBF S. Flyweight Title Defence)*
Career: 20 contests, won 20.	

Genaro (Chicanito) Hernandez

Los Angeles, USA. *Born* 10 May, 1966
WBA S. Featherweight Champion

12.11.94	Jimmy Garcia W PTS 12 Mexico City *(WBA S. Featherweight Title Defence)*
31.03.95	Jorge Paez W RSC 8 Los Angeles
Career: 33 contests, won 32, drew 1.	

Virgil (Sugar) Hill

Williston, USA. *Born* 18 January, 1964
WBA L. Heavyweight Champion. Former Undefeated WBC International & Con Am L. Heavyweight Champion

23.07.94	Frank Tate W PTS 12 Bismark *(WBA L. Heavyweight Title Defence)*
01.04.95	Crawford Ashley W PTS 12 Stateline *(WBA L. Heavyweight Title Defence)*
Career: 41 contests, won 40, lost 1.	

Bernard (The Executioner) Hopkins

Philadelphia, USA. *Born* 15 January 1965
IBF Middleweight Champion. Former Undefeated USBA Middleweight Champion

Born in the tough north-Philadelphia district that spawned many good fighters, his uncle Art McCloud was a professional, Bernard started boxing in his mid-teens. Had a good record as an amateur, but walked away from boxing for a while after failing to make the US team for the 1984 Olympics and spent some time working as a roofer and some time in jail. Turned professional in October 1988, but lost his first paid fight to Clinton Mitchell, at which point he disappeared again until 1990. On his return, his heavy-punching quickly made him a local favourite and he added colour by coming into the ring dressed in a cloak and wearing an executioner's mask. Illustrated what a dangerous fighter he had become with a four round destruction of Dennis Milton in January 1992 and, at the end of the year, won the USBA crown by halting Wayne Powell in just 21 seconds. Retained his title in February 1993 with a unanimous verdict over Gilbert Baptist, although unsuccessful in a fight for the vacant IBF middleweight title in May when Roy Jones easily outboxed him. Bernard made three defences of his USBA title, beating Roy Ritchie, Wendell Hall and Lupe Aquino, and then had a shot at the vacant IBF title again. This time, despite being floored twice, he looked unlucky to only get a draw in a tough scrap with Ecuadorian, Segundo Mercado, in Quito in December 1994. Bernard made no mistake in their return fight and halted Mercado in seven rounds to win the title. A sinewy 6' 0", he hits hard as his 20 quick wins attest, but is capable of some ordinary performances, while his work sometimes lacks variety.

17.12.94	Segundo Mercado DREW 12 Quito
	(Vacant IBF Middleweight Title)
29.04.95	Segundo Mercado W RSC 7
	Landover
	(Vacant IBF Middleweight Title)
Career: 30 contests, won 27, drew 1, lost 2.	

Eddie (Boy Wonder) Hopson

St Louis, USA. *Born* 30 June, 1971
IBF S. Featherweight Champion.
Former Undefeated NABF
S. Featherweight Champion

Southpaw. 5' 4" tall, and a member of the Main Events team, along with Pernell Whitaker and Juan Molina, Eddie takes his nickname from Robin in the Batman series and sometimes wears a cape into the ring, celebrating his victories with back flips. As a 17-year-old, he won the National Golden Gloves title at featherweight in 1988, but lost controversially to Kelcie Banks in the box-offs for the US Olympic team, having beaten Banks twice in the trials. Turned professional with Lou Duva in February 1989, after 71 wins in 85 bouts as an amateur, but also continued his High School education at the same time and was brought along slowly. Sidelined by a bicep injury in 1990, he still made good progress, scoring 21 wins to the end of 1993, including victories over Alvaro Bohorquez and Jesus Pool in good learning fights. Won the vacant NABF super-featherweight title in January 1994 with a unanimous verdict over Alexis Perez and defended it in August with a technical points win over Angel Aldama in a rough brawl. Faced his biggest test in October against experienced Troy Dorsey, overcoming a rough period in the middle of the fight to win on a unanimous decision. When

his stablemate, Molina, relinquished the IBF title, Ed was matched with Moises Pedroza and knocked out the Colombian in round seven. He is a fast-handed, slick fighter, with a darting, ducking style, which is effective but not always pretty, and there are still questions to be answered over his chin. Has stopped 13 opponents.

23.08.94	Angel Aldama W TD 10 Forth Worth
	(NABF S. Featherweight Title Defence)
27.10.94	Troy Dorsey W PTS 12 Washington
	(NABF S. Featherweight Title Defence)
22.04.95	Moises Pedroza W CO 7 Atlantic City
	(Vacant IBF S. Featherweight Title)
Career: 26 contests, won 26.	

Eddie Hopson

Julian Jackson

St Thomas, Virgin Islands. *Born* 12 September, 1960
WBC Middleweight Champion.
Former Undefeated WBA
L. Middleweight Champion. Former Undefeated WBC Con Am
L. Middleweight Champion

17.12.94	Luis Buitron W RSC 3 Quito
17.03.95	Agostino Cardamone W RSC 2
	Worcester
	(Vacant WBC Middleweight Title)
Career: 54 contests, won 51, lost 3.	

Alberto (Raton) Jimenez

Mexico City, Mexico. *Born* 8 April, 1969

WBO Flyweight Champion. Former Undefeated Mexican Flyweight Champion

One of a family of nine children, he had no interest in boxing until he was 16 when he was encouraged to take up the sport by his uncle who had fought as an amateur. Only boxed for one year as an amateur, before becoming a professional in June 1988. Although held to a draw by Enrique Jupiter in February 1989 and losing on a disqualification to Mauricio Aceves in July, eight consecutive stoppage wins in 1990 took him to the top of the Mexican ratings and a seventh round defeat of experienced Willy Salazar in March 1991 earned him a shot at the national title. Floored Gonzalo Villalobos four times and stopped him in the fourth round to win the crown in June 1991. In October he challenged Muangchai Kitikasem for the WBC title in Thailand and floored the champion heavily in the third round. The bell saved Kitikasem, who boxed his way to a points victory. Alberto scored five more quick wins, before finding Mark Johnson too smart for him in May 1993. Beat former WBO super-flyweight champion, Jose Quirino, in three rounds in November 1993, but was held to a split decision by clever Arthur Johnson in May 1994. His second chance at a world title came in February when he battered brave Jacob Matlala to defeat in eight rounds to become WBO champion and he certainly showed his class in his defence against Robbie Regan, who was forced to retire after nine rounds. An aggressive little fighter, who is a good body puncher, he has accounted for 25 victims within the distance.

10.10.94	Mauro Diaz T Draw 3 Los Angeles
11.02.95	Jacob Matlala W RSC 8
	Hammanskraal
	(WBO Flyweight Title Challenge)
17.06.95	Robbie Regan W RTD 9 Cardiff
	(WBO Flyweight Title Defence)
Career: 34 contests, won 29, drew 2, lost 3.	

Tom (Boom Boom) Johnson

Evansville, USA. *Born* 15 July, 1964
IBF Featherweight Champion. Former Undefeated WBA Americas Featherweight Champion

183

22.10.94	Francisco Segura W PTS 12 Atlantic City
	(IBF Featherweight Title Defence)
28.01.95	Manuel Medina W PTS 12 Atlantic City
	(IBF Featherweight Title Defence)
26.04.95	Victor Laureano W RSC 2 Auburn Hills
28.05.95	Eddie Croft W PTS 12 South Padre Island
	(IBF Featherweight Title Defence)

Career: 43 contests, won 40, drew 1, lost 2.

Roy Jones Jnr

Pensacola, USA. *Born* 16 January, 1969
IBF S. Middleweight Champion. Former Undefeated IBF & WBC Con Am Middleweight Champion

18.11.94	James Toney W PTS 12 Las Vegas
	(IBF S. Middleweight Title Challenge)
18.03.95	Antoine Byrd W RSC 1 Pensacola
	(IBF S. Middleweight Title Defence)
24.06.95	Vinny Pazienza W RSC 6 Atlantic City
	(IBF S. Middleweight Title Defence)

Career: 29 contests, won 29.

Hiroshi Kawashima

Hiroshi (Untouchable) Kawashima

Tokushima, Japan. *Born* 27 March, 1970
WBC S. Flyweight Champion. Former Undefeated Japanese S. Flyweight Champion

07.08.94	Carlos Salazar W PTS 12 Tokyo
	(WBC S. Flyweight Title Defence)
18.01.95	Jose Luis Bueno W PTS 12 Yokohama
	(WBC S. Flyweight Title Defence)
24.05.95	Seung-Koo Lee W PTS 12 Yokohama
	(WBC S. Flyweight Title Defence)

Career: 20 contests, won 17, drew 1, lost 2.

Alfred (Cobra) Kotey

Accra, Ghana. *Born* 3 June, 1968
WBO Bantamweight Champion. Former Undefeated Commonwealth Flyweight Champion

The son of a fisherman, he comes from the Ga tribe which has produced many of Ghana's best fighters. Competed in the 1988 Olympic Games and won 51 of his 55 amateur bouts, prior to turning professional in November 1988 and winning the vacant Commonwealth flyweight title in his sixth fight when stopping George Foreman. Retained his title with a points victory over Danny Porter in July 1990, but then moved his base to Philadelphia in 1991. Scored five quick wins over mediocre opposition, before being taken the distance in successive fights by experienced Mexicans, Francisco Montiel, Armando Diaz and Alex Sanabria. In November 1992 he faced little known Julio Cesar Borboa and lost his unbeaten record when the Mexican turned out to be a classy fighter who outboxed him to win a split decision on his way to becoming IBF champion. After a long period of inactivity, he moved to England and joined the KO Pro group, returning to action by outpointing Chris Clarkson in March 1994 and then flooring and outpointing Puerto Rican, Rafael del Valle, to win the WBO title in July. Outclassed tough Mexican, Armando Castro, in his first defence, and destroyed Drew Docherty in four rounds in February for hs 13th win inside the distance.

30.07.94	Rafael del Valle W PTS 12 London
	(WBO Bantamweight Title Challenge)
25.10.94	Armando Castro W PTS 12 Middlesbrough
	(WBO Bantamweight Title Defence)
17.02.95	Drew Docherty W RSC 4 Cumbernauld
	(WBO Bantamweight Title Defence)

Career: 21 contests, won 20, lost 1.

Hyung-Chul Lee

Chunnahbokdo, South Korea. *Born* 13 December, 1969
WBA S. Flyweight Champion. Former Undefeated South Korean S. Flyweight Champion

Turned professional in October 1987 with very little amateur experience and lost three of his first four fights. Found some form to run up six victories, but was then sent to Japan as an easy opponent for future WBA champion, David Griman, in August 1990. Lee cut the classy Venezuelan and impressed the Japanese fans, although losing the decision. Brought back to Japan in November to test Tomoki Morikawa, winning on points, he next picked up the Korean super-flyweight title in April 1991 by knocking out Chan-Woo Park in three rounds, retaining it in July with a second round stoppage of Keun-Ho Kim. Concentrated on imported opponents after that, scoring seven more wins, with only one minor scare, when having to come off the canvas to outpoint Julius Tarona. Was an outsider when he challenged the unbeaten Katsuya Onizuka for the WBA title in Japan in September 1994 but, despite being badly shaken in the third, his relentless pressure finally overwhelmed the champion, who was stopped in round nine. Defending against Tomonori Tamura in February, the challenger's corner threw in the towel in the last round with their fighter badly battered. Lee is a tough, durable, pressure fighter, who wears his opponents down and has shown steady improvement after a rocky start.

18.09.94	Kaysuya Onizuka W RSC 9 Tokyo
	(WBA S. Flyweight Title Challenge)
25.02.95	Tomonori Tamura W RSC 12 Pusan
	(WBA S. Flyweight Title Defence)

Career: 23 contests, won 19, lost 4.

Frank Lilles

Syracuse, USA. *Born* 15 February, 1965
WBA S. Middleweight Champion. Former Undefeated NABF S. Middleweight Champion

6' 3" tall southpaw. An outstanding amateur who was National Golden Gloves champion at welterweight in 1985 and United States champion at light-middleweight in 1987 and 1988, he beat fighters such as Roy Jones and Gerald McClellan, before losing to the former in the Olympic trials in 1988. Turned professional with Kronk in November 1988, but his fourth fight ended on a double disqualification which was later ruled a no-contest. Moved his base to California in 1991 and scored good wins over Ralph Ward and Rollin Williams. Lost his unbeaten record in July 1992 when his old amateur foe, Tim Littles, out-pointed him in a challenge for the USBA super-middleweight title. Three months later, however, Frank picked up the vacant NABF crown as he overcame a shower of low blows to halt tough Merqui Sosa in the 12th round. After a couple of more wins, Frank travelled down to Tucuman in Argentina in August to challenge Steve Little for the WBA title and won a clear decision in a poor fight. In his first defence he withstood a late finish by former champion, Michael Nunn, to win a unanimous decision and then outclassed former European titleholder, Frederic Seillier, battering him to defeat in six rounds. The shaven headed, goateed champion is a solid puncher and has stopped or knocked out 17 of his victims, but lacks the colour of IBF champion, Roy Jones.

12.08.94	Steve Little W PTS 12 Tucuman *(WBA S. Middleweight Title Challenge)*
17.12.94	Michael Nunn W PTS 12 Quito *(WBA S. Middleweight Title Defence)*
27.05.95	Frederic Seillier W RSC 6 Fort Lauderdale *(WBA S. Middleweight Title Defence)*
Career: 29 contests, won 27, lost 1, no contest 1.	

Ricardo (Finito) Lopez

Cuernavaca, Mexico. *Born* 25 July, 1967
WBC M. Flyweight Champion.
Former Undefeated WBC Con Am M. Flyweight Champion

17.09.94	Yodsing Saenmorokot W RSC 1 Las Vegas *(WBC M. Flyweight Title Defence)*
12.11.94	Javier Varguez W RSC 8 Mexico City *(WBC M. Flyweight Title Defence)*
10.12.94	Yamil Caraballo W RSC 1 Monterrey *(WBC M. Flyweight Title Defence)*
01.04.95	Andy Tabanas W RSC 12 Stateline *(WBC M. Flyweight Title Defence)*
Career: 40 contests, won 40.	

Eamonn Loughran

Ballymena, Ireland. *Born* 5 June, 1970
WBO Welterweight Champion.
Former Undefeated Commonwealth Welterweight Champion

Note: Full record will be found in the Current British-Based Champions: Career Records' section.

Oliver (The Atomic Bull) McCall

Chicago, USA. *Born* 21 April, 1965
WBC Heavyweight Champion

Muscular, 6' 2" tall, and with a 81 inch reach, Oliver spent many years as a sparring partner with Mike Tyson and, at one time, his only claim to fame was to have floored the champion in the

Oliver McCall   Les Clark

gym. Has also acted as Frank Bruno's sparring partner in the past. Married with four daughters and one son, he was born and brought up on the tough south-side of Chicago. Was a good basketball player and it was when he got into a fight during a basketball game that he took up boxing in 1982. Never really made it to the top as an amateur, although he was twice Chicago Golden Gloves champion and claimed 31 wins in 32. In between fights he used to work as a roofer for his stepfather's company. Turned pro in November 1985 and was trained by Joe Frazier, but lost in his second fight to a real no-hoper, Joey Christjohn. Found some form after that and won his next ten, until being beaten on points over six rounds by cagey Mike Hunter in January 1988. Had Buster Douglas hurt in their July 1989 fight, before losing a unanimous decision. Lost again in November 1990 when he was beaten on a split decision by the current WBA cruiserweight champion, Orlin Norris. Bounced back in April 1991, stopping previously unbeaten Bruce Seldon in nine rounds, and challenged Tony Tucker for the NABF title in June 1992, but lost clearly in a very poor contest. Once again he bounced back when breaking the nose of Francesco Damiani and halting him in eight rounds in April 1993. His contract with Don King helped him to get a shot at Lennox Lewis for the WBC title, and Oliver pulled off a big upset when he beat Lewis to the punch in the second round and floored and halted him. Had his limitations shown up when veteran, Larry Holmes, had little trouble in lasting the distance in their April title fight, even though Oliver won clearly. He is strong, with a hard right-hand punch, but has limited skills. Has 18 wins inside the distance.

24.09.94	Lennox Lewis W RSC 2 Wembley *(WBC Heavyweight Title Challenge)*
08.04.95	Larry Holmes W PTS 12 Las Vegas *(WBC Heavyweight Title Defence)*
Career: 31 contests, won 26, lost 5.	

Henry Maske

Trevenbrietzen, Germany. *Born* 6 January, 1964
IBF L. Heavyweight Champion

08.10.94	Iran Barkley W RTD 9 Halle *(IBF L. Heavyweight Title Defence)*
11.02.95	Egerton Marcus W PTS 12 Frankfurt *(IBF L. Heavyweight Title Defence)*
27.05.95	Graciano Rocchigiani W PTS 12 Dortmund *(IBF L. Heavyweight Title Defence)*
Career: 27 contests, won 27.	

Dariusz Michalczewski

Hamburg, Germany. *Born* Poland 5 May, 1968
WBO L. Heavyweight Champion. Former Undefeated WBO Cruiserweight Champion. Former Undefeated IBF Intercontinental & German International L. Heavyweight Champion

Born in Gdansk, Dariusz was an outstanding amateur and won a bronze medal at middleweight for Poland in the 1968 European Junior championships, beating current top professional, Fabrice Tiozzo, on the way. He then defected to West Germany and won a gold medal in the 1991 Senior European championships, defeating the current European cruiserweight champion, Patrice Aoussi, in the competition. Turned professional in September 1991 and stopped his first nine opponents. Beat Steve McCarthy in September 1992, when the Englishman was thrown out in the third round for butting, and faced a good test in former WBA title challenger, Mike Peak, in December, coming through with a clear points verdict. Won the German International light-heavyweight title in February 1993 with a tenth round kayo of useful Saidi Ali and the vacant IBF Intercontinental crown in September 1993 with a points victory over veteran, Mwehu Beya. Made a successful defence of his IBF title in November, when forcing former WBC title challenger, Sergio Merani, to retire after ten rounds and then challenged Leonzer Barber for the WBO title in September 1994. Despite the stadium lights going out during the fight, and Dariusz suffering a cut, he proved too busy and fast for Barber and took the title on a clear, unanimous decision. Although a natural light-heavyweight, he moved up to cruiser and collected the WBO title in that division, flooring the champion, Nestor Giovannini, in the

ninth and knocking him out in the tenth. Dariusz soon relinquished the cruiserweight crown and continued to defend his light-heavyweight title. Almost came to grief in March against hard-punching Roberto Dominguez as he was floored for the first time as an amateur or a professional in the opening round and badly hurt in the second, before flattening the Spaniard with a left-hook just a few moments later. Had less trouble with Paul Carlo in May, knocking out the St Louis fighter in round four. Is a good boxer and a hard puncher, but the Dominguez fight has put a question mark over his chin. Has either stopped or knocked out 21 opponents.

10.09.94	Leonzer Barber W PTS 12 Hamburg *(WBO L. Heavyweight Title Challenge)*
17.12.94	Nestor Giovannini W CO 10 Hamburg *(WBO Cruiserweight Title Challenge)*
11.03.95	Roberto Dominguez W CO 2 Cologne *(WBO L. Heavyweight Title Defence)*
20.05.95	Paul Carlo W CO 4 Hamburg *(WBO L. Heavyweight Title Defence)*
Career: 27 contests, won 27.	

Orzubek (Gussie) Nazarov

Kant, Russia. *Born* 30 August, 1966
WBA Lightweight Champion. Former Undefeated OPBF & Japanese Lightweight Champion

10.12.94	Joey Gamache W RSC 2 Portland *(WBA Lightweight Title Defence)*
15.05.95	Won Park W CO 2 Tokyo *(WBA Lightweight Title Defence)*
Career: 21 contests, won 21.	

Orzubek Nazarov

Orlin (Boscoe Bear) Norris

Lubbock, USA. *Born* 4 October, 1965
WBA Cruiserweight Champion.
Former Undefeated NABF
Cruiserweight Champion. Former
NABF Heavyweight Champion

02.07.94	Arthur Williams W RSC 3 Las Vegas *(WBA Cruiserweight Title Defence)*
12.11.94	James Heath W CO 2 Mexico City *(WBA Cruiserweight Title Defence)*
18.03.95	Adolpho Washington W PTS 12 Worcester *(WBA Cruiserweight Title Defence)*
Career: 47 contests, won 43, lost 3, no decision 1.	

Vince Pettway

Baltimore, USA. *Born* 9 November,
1965
IBF L. Middleweight Champion.
Former Undefeated USBA
L. Middleweight Champion

One of boxings nice people, Vince is a
devout Christian who has stuck with
the same manager since he first began
boxing. Got into the sport after he was
sent to a gym by a neighbour when he
was being bullied on the tough streets
of East Baltimore. The gym was run
by Mack Lewis, who is a boxing
legend in Maryland, and Mack is still
his manager. Had almost 200 amateur
fights, but failed to make the US team
for the 1984 Olympics, due to a hand
injury which ruled him out of the
trials, and turned professional in
February 1984. Won his first 17 fights,
15 inside the distance, before losing on
a stoppage to George Leach in April
1986, after coming in as a late
substitute. Scored eight more wins,
until being knocked out by Javier
Suazo in six rounds in April 1988.
Again he bounced back with a good
run, including victories over Luis
Santana and James Hughes, although it
looked as though he was going
nowhere when he suffered back-to-
back stoppage losses to Victor Davis
and Steve Johnson. Picked up the
vacant USBA light-middleweight title
in February 1992 with a points victory
over tough Gilbert Baptist and retained
his crown in May 1993 by flooring
and halting the Canadian, Dan Sherry,
in 11 rounds. Was then inactive for
almost ten months before challenging
Gianfranco Rosi for the IBF title in
March 1994. Vince suffered a disputed
knockdown in the first round, but was
fighting on even terms when the
Italian was badly cut by a clash of
heads and the bout was declared a
technical draw. In their return contest,
in September, Vince dominated all the
way and knocked out Rosi with a great
combination in the fourth round.
Scored a dramatic victory in his April
defence against former champion,
Simon Brown, as he bounced back
from two knockdowns to flatten the
Jamaican with a tremendous left-hook.
The 5' 7" champion is very quick and a
terrific hitter, although his own chin
and stamina are questionable. Has 31
wins by stoppages or knockouts, but
his four losses have also come inside
the distance.

17.09.94	Gianfranco Rosi W CO 4 Las Vegas *(IBF L. Middleweight Title Challenge)*
29.04.95	Simon Brown W CO 6 Landover *(IBF L. Middleweight Title Defence)*
Career: 44 contests, won 38, drew 1, lost 4, no contest 1.	

Chana Porpaoin

Petchaboon, Thailand. *Born* 25 March,
1966
WBA M. Flyweight Champion.
Former Undefeated Thai M. Flyweight
Champion

Chana Porpaoin

27.08.94	Keun-Young Kang W PTS 12 Phatthalung
	(WBA M. Flyweight Title Defence)
05.11.94	Manuel Herrera W PTS 12 Hat Yai
	(WBA M. Flyweight Title Defence)
28.01.95	Jin-Ho Kim W PTS 12 Bangkok
	(WBA M. Flyweight Title Defence)
Career: 34 contests, won 34.	

Ike (Bazooka) Quartey

Accra, Ghana. *Born* 27 November, 1969
WBA Welterweight Champion.
Former Undefeated Ghanaian, African Boxing Council and WBC International Welterweight Champion

01.10.94	Alberto Cortes W RSC 5 Carpentras
	(WBA Welterweight Title Defence)
04.02.95	Bobby Butters W RSC 3 Castelnau le Lez
04.03.95	Jung-Oh Park W RSC 4 Atlantic City
	(WBA Welterweight Title Defence)
Career: 30 contests, won 30.	

Frankie (The Surgeon) Randall

Morristown, USA. *Born* 25 September, 1961
WBA L. Welterweight Champion.
Former WBC L. Welterweight Champion

Earned his place in ring history as the first man to defeat the great Julio Cesar Chavez. Born in Birmingham, Alabama, although moving to Tennessee as a kid, he started boxing at the age of nine and had 236 amateur fights, but lost to Joe Manley in US Olympic trials in 1980. Turned professional in February 1983 and won his first 23, including victories over Jerome Artis and Fred Pendleton, before losing his unbeaten record to Edwin Rosario at Bethnal Green in June 1985. Frankie came off the floor to dominate the early sessions, but then faded in the last rounds of a great fight to drop a close decision. Stopped Sammy Fuentes in two rounds in May 1986 and drew with Pendleton for the vacant USBA lightweight title in July. By 1987, he had risen to the top contender's position, but blew his chance when he was knocked out cold in two rounds by a left-hook from Primo Ramos in a bout for the vacant NABF

crown that October. Frankie bounced back with some good wins in 1988 and '89, including a points victory over Olympic gold medal winner, James Page, but his career seemed to be over in 1990 when he was jailed for dealing drugs. However, on his release in 1991, he jumped straight back with a victory against Rodolfo Aguilar and, in January 1993, gained revenge over Edwin Rosario when he came in as a late substitute and halted his old opponent in seven rounds. Shocked the boxing fraternity in January 1994 when, as a 15-1 outsider, he floored and outpointed Julio Cesar Chavez to lift the WBC title. Lost the championship to Chavez in controversial circumstances in May 1994 when the Mexican was cut and awarded a technical decision. Frankie came back in style four months later, climbing off the canvas to easily outpoint Juan Martin Coggi and become WBA champion. He then demolished the useful Rodney Moore in seven rounds to retain his title in December, but struggled with the clever Venezuelan, Jose Barbosa, and only took a split verdict. Frankie is 5' 7" tall, with a 72 inch reach, and is a classy fighter with a hard punch. Has overcome many personal problems, having risen from sweeping floors in Don King's gym to become recognised as a one of the most skilful boxers around. His 40 wins inside the distance show his power.

17.09.94	Juan Martin Coggi W PTS 12 Las Vegas
	(WBA L. Welterweight Title Challenge)
10.12.94	Rodney Moore W RSC 7 Monterrey
	(WBA L. Welterweight Title Defence)
16.06.95	Jose Barbosa W PTS 12 Lyon
	(WBA L. Welterweight Title Defence)
Career: 56 contests, won 52, drew 1, lost 3.	

Steve Robinson

Cardiff, Wales. *Born* 13 December, 1968
WBO Featherweight Champion.
Former Undefeated Welsh & Penta-Continental Featherweight Champion

Note: Full record will be found in the Current British-Based Champions: Career Records' section.

Ralf Rocchigiani

Rheinhauser, Germany. *Born* 13 March, 1963
WBO Cruiserweight Champion.
Former German Cruiserweight Champion

Brother of the former IBF super-middleweight champion, Graciano, their father was Italian and won the national amateur title at welterweight in 1958. Ralf lost only 15 of 100 amateur fights and won a bronze medal at the European Junior championships, before turning professional in November 1983. Mainly boxed at cruiserweight, although often moving down to light-heavyweight, or even up to heavyweight, when a title opportunity arose. Lost and drew with Manfred Jassman for the German light-heavyweight title in early bouts, but won the cruiserweight crown in August 1985 by knocking out Josef Kossman. Challenged for the European light-heavyweight title in October 1986 and was outpointed by Alex Blanchard. Tried again in April 1989, but this time fought a draw with the champion, Jan Lefeber, and later lost to Markus Bott on points, in May 1991, while challenging for the German heavyweight title. Given a shot at the WBO cruiserweight title in October 1992, he lost a close points decision to Tyrone Booze. His career seemed to be going nowhere when he was held to a draw by Tony Booth in May 1993 and lost his German title to Torsten May in May 1994, before receiving a lucky break when the WBO nominated him to face Carl Thompson for their vacant title. Ralf was behind on points, but fighting strongly, when Thompson suffered a dislocated shoulder and was stopped in 11 rounds. A strong, but limited fighter, Ralf will need careful matching if he is to retain his title.

12.02.95	Terry Wright W PTS 8 Hamburg
10.06.95	Carl Thompson W RSC 11 Manchester
	(Vacant WBO Cruiserweight Title)
Career: 49 contests, won 34, drew 7, lost 8.	

Eloy Rojas

Caracas, Venezuela. *Born* 25 March, 1967
WBA Featherweight Champion.
Former Undefeated Venezuelan and Latin American Featherweight Champion

11.09.94	Samart Payakaroon W CO 8 Trang
	(WBA Featherweight Title Defence)
03.12.94	Luis Mendoza W PTS 12 Bogota
	(WBA Featherweight Title Defence)
27.05.95	Yung-Kyun Park W PTS 12 Seoul
	(WBA Featherweight Title Defence)
Career: 33 contests, won 31, drew 1, lost 1.	

Danny (Kid Dynamite) Romero

Albuquerque, USA. *Born* 12 July, 1974
IBF Flyweight Champion. Former Undefeated NABF Flyweight & S. Flyweight Champion

A 5' 5" power-house, Danny has slammed his way to becoming the first American world flyweight champion for 50 years. Boxing is a family matter for the Romero's, his father started to train him when he was just five years old and two of his uncles work in his corner. Was the US National Junior Olympic champion in 1989 and 1990 and, after winning 127 of his 132 fights, he turned professional in August 1992 at the age of 18. Five of his first seven contests ended in one round wins, which drew the attention of the big promoters, and Danny signed with the Top Rank group at the end of 1993, also acquiring a set of sponsors calling themselves Kid Dynamite Enterprises. Picked up the vacant NABF crown in May 1994, when flooring former amateur star, Brian Lonon, three times and halting him in round two. Knocked out ex-Mexican champion, Hugo Torres, in three rounds in a defence in May and went on to outpoint world-rated Manuel Herrera in September. Moved up to super-flyweight in October and decisioned tough Marcos Pacheco to lift the vacant NABF title, prior to successfully defending his crown in November, disposing of Domingo Sosa in just 66 seconds. Faced the classy Colombian, Francisco Tejedor, in a challenge for the IBF flyweight

title in April 1995 and proved too powerful for the champion, flooring him in the last round to take a unanimous decision. A hard hitter with both hands, and a particularly good body puncher, Romero has 21 quick wins to his credit and could have a great future ahead of him.

03.08.94	Facundo Rodriguez W RSC 1 Albuquerque
09.09.94	Manuel Herrera W RSC 12 Los Angeles
	(NABF Flyweight Title Defence)
12.10.94	Marcos Pacheco W PTS 12 Albuquerque
	(Vacant NABF S. Flyweight Title)
18.11.94	Domingo Sosa W RSC 1 Las Vegas
	(NABF S. Flyweight Title Defence)
08.12.94	Andres Cazares W CO 1 Albuquerque
10.02.95	Javier Cintron W CO 3 Albuquerque
22.04.95	Francisco Tejedor W PTS 12 Las Vegas
	(IBF Flyweight Title Challenge)
Career: 24 contests, won 24.	

Gabriel Ruelas

La Yerba, Mexico. *Born* 23 July, 1970
WBC S. Featherweight Champion.
Former Undefeated NABF S. Featherweight Champion

One of a family of 14 children, his brother Rafael is a former IBF lightweight champion. Started fighting at the Ten Goose gym at the age of 12 and turned professional just two months after his 18th birthday. Won his first 21 fights, before losing his unbeaten record against Jeff Franklin in unfortunate circumstances, in April 1990. Gabriel was winning the fight when he suffered a broken elbow in the seventh round and was forced to retire. There were some doubts as to whether he would box again, but he returned 14 months later and showed he was still dangerous with a first round kayo of Fili Montoya in June 1991. Collected the vacant NABF super-featherweight title in July by flooring, and easily outpointing, Aaron Lopez, and successfully defended it with victories over Alvaro Bohorquez and Jorge Palomares. Challenged Azumah Nelson for the WBC title in February 1993, but showed the great African too much respect and a good last round enabled the champion to retain his title on a majority verdict.

Gabriel was given a second chance in September against new champion, "Jesse" James Leija, and, in a fight which saw both boxers on the floor, Gabriel finished the stronger and clinched the title with a last round knockdown. Made an impressive first defence when flooring Fred Liberatore with the first punch he threw and halting him in two rounds. His next defence, against Jimmy Garcia, had a tragic end as the young Colombian took a heavy beating before being stopped in the eleventh round and dying from the injuries received in the fight. It now remains to be seen what effect this has had on Gabriel. 5' 7" tall, and a good boxer, with a hard left-hook, he has halted or kayoed 23 opponents.

17.09.94	James Leija W PTS 12 Las Vegas
	(WBC S. Featherweight Title Challenge)
28.01.95	Fred Liberatore W RTD 2 Las Vegas
	(WBC S. Featherweight Title Defence)
06.05.95	Jimmy Garcia W RSC 11 Las Vegas
	(WBC S. Featherweight Title Defence)
Career: 43 contests, won 41, lost 2.	

Alex (Nene) Sanchez

Playa Ponce, Puerto Rico. *Born* 6 May, 1973
WBO M. Flyweight Champion

13.08.94	Carlos Juan Rodriquez W CO 1 Bayamon
	(WBO M. Flyweight Title Defence)
10.09.94	Oscar Andrade W RSC 4 Hamburg
	(WBO M. Flyweight Title Defence)
01.11.94	Pablo Tiznado W PTS 10 San Juan
28.01.95	Rafael Orozco W PTS 12 Las Vegas
	(WBO M. Flyweight Title Defence)
27.02.95	Ventura Mendivil W RSC 2 Condado
04.05.95	Fernando Martinez W CO 1 Ponce
15.06.95	Arturo Valdes W RSC 3 Condado
Career: 21 contests, won 21.	

Luis Santana

Dominican Republic. *Born* 19 November, 1958
WBC L. Middleweight Champion.
Former NABF Welterweight Champion

The only fighter to win two consecutive world title fights whilst on the canvas, he also won a court case against the Californian Commission after they banned him for failing one of their medical tests. A tough slugger, who was one of the best amateur fighters produced by the Dominican Republic, Luis won 80 out of 88 fights, was four times national champion and won a bronze medal in the World Military championships. Turned professional in the United States in December 1981 and lost only two of his first 29 bouts. Destroyed in two rounds by Milton McCrory in May 1985, he came back to win the vacant NABF welterweight crown in November 1986, halting Allen Braswell. Dropped the title to Tommy Ayers in March 1987, being stopped in a four round war, but regained it in January when battering Sean O'Sullivan to defeat in 11 rounds. Made two successful defences, before losing the title to Derrick Kelly in January 1989. Although beaten again in 1989 by Aaron Davis, and then Vince Pettway, he was still given a shot at the IBF welterweight title in November, but took a bad beating before losing on points to Simon Brown. Was stopped by Glenwood Brown for the USBA belt in February 1990, outpointed by Cristano Espana for the WBC International championship in February 1991, and then lost to Vinny Pazienza in December. Despite only registering a couple of meaningless wins, and being inactive for a year, he was awarded a shot at Terry Norris for the WBC light-middleweight title in November 1994. Santana was laid out by a rabbit punch in the fifth round and awarded the title on a disqualification. In the return bout, in April 1995, Norris was thrown out again after knocking Luis out with a punch that landed well after the bell. A very lucky champion, Luis was over the hill before he won the title and is unlikely to reign for long.

12.11.94	Terry Norris W DIS 5 Mexico City
	(WBC L. Middleweight Title
	Challenge)
08.04.95	Terry Norris W DIS 3 Las Vegas
	(WBC L. Middleweight Title Defence)
Career: 57 contests, won 40, drew 2, lost 15.	

Bruce (The Atlantic City Express) Seldon

Atlantic City, USA. *Born* 30 January, 1967
WBA Heavyweight Champion.
Former IBF Intercontinental Heavyweight Champion

6' 3" tall. A good boxer with a fast jab, Bruce tends to be an arm puncher and his chin is still considered suspect. Went from street gang battles in Atlantic City to armed robbery and was sentenced to ten years in jail as a 15-year-old in 1982. Joined the boxing programme in jail and went on to win the super-heavyweight championship for the Jersey State jails. Released early in 1986, he turned professional in October 1988 and won his first 18 fights, and included Osvaldo Ocasio, David Bey and Jose Ribalta among his list of victims. Suffered a big set-back in April 1991, when floored three times and stopped in nine rounds by Oliver McCall, Bruce claimed that personal problems had prevented him from training for this fight. However, he had no excuses for his next loss in August 1991, Riddick Bowe putting him down twice and knocking him out in the first round. A points victory over Jesse Ferguson in January 1992 won Bruce the IBF Intercontinental title, but, in October, he lost a wide decision to Tony Tubbs. Seven stoppage wins in a row, including a victory over Greg

Page, and the help of Don King, landed Bruce a shot at the vacant WBA title against Tony Tucker last April. Bruce was narrowly ahead on all cards when Tucker, unable to continue due to a closed left-eye, was forced to retire. Has 28 wins inside the distance, but most of these were against poor opposition.

02.07.94	Tui Toia W RSC 3 Las Vegas
17.12.94	Bill Corrigan W CO 1 Quito
08.04.95	Tony Tucker W RTD 7 Las Vegas
	(Vacant WBA Heavyweight Title)
Career: 35 contests, won 32, lost 3.	

Saen Sorploenchit

Phatumthani, Thailand. *Born* 15 May, 1972
WBA Flyweight Champion

25.09.94	Yong-Kang Kim W PTS 12
	Kanchanaburi
	(WBA Flyweight Title Defence)
25.12.94	Danny Nunez W RSC 11 Rayong
	(WBA Flyweight Title Defence)
07.05.95	Evangelio Perez W PTS 12
	Songkhla
	(WBA Flyweight Title Defence)
Career: 22 contests, won 22.	

Ratanapol Sowvoraphin

Dankoonthod, Thailand. *Born* 6 June, 1973
IBF M. Flyweight Champion. Former Undefeated IBF Intercontinental M. Flyweight Champion

Ratanapol Sowvoraphin

13.08.94	Marcelino Bolivar W RSC 4 Buriram
	(IBF M. Flyweight Title Defence)
12.11.94	Carlos Rodriguez W RSC 3 Khonkaen
	(IBF M. Flyweight Title Defence)
25.02.95	Jerry Pahayahay W RSC 3 Bangkok
	(IBF M. Flyweight Title Defence)
20.05.95	Oscar Flores W RSC 2 Chiang Mai
	(IBF M. Flyweight Title Defence)
Career: 25 contests, won 22, drew 1, lost 2.	

Johnny (Tap Tap) Tapia

Albuquerque, USA. *Born* 13 February, 1967
WBO S. Flyweight Champion. Former Undefeated USBA & NABF S. Flyweight Champion

A young man who has had a constant battle with drug addiction, his mother was murdered when he was just eight and his father abandoned him. Found his way for a while, through boxing, and won the National Golden Gloves light-flyweight title in 1983 at just 16-years-of-age, and again at flyweight in 1985. He then disappeared from the scene until his professional debut in March 1988, when he was held to a draw by Efren Chavez. A busy schedule kept him out of trouble for a while, and he defeated good opponents such as future WBA champion, John Michael Johnson, and Mexican, Jesus Chong. Won the Vacant USBA title in May 1990, halting Roland Gomez in 11 rounds, and made successful defences against Jose Felix Montiel, Luigi Camputaro and Santiago Caballero. Unfortunately, he failed a drugs test after the Caballero fight in October 1990 and was banned from fighting. Failed four more tests in the next two years and was constantly in trouble with the police, before finally returning to the ring in March 1994. Won the vacant NABF super-flyweight title in July by knocking out Oscar Aguilar in two rounds and floored and halted Henry Martinez in October to become the WBO champion. Easily defeated the durable Argentinian, Jose Rafael Sosa, in his first defence, but was most fortunate to retain the title when Mexican, Ricardo Vargas, suffered a bad cut in a clash of heads and the judges voted a draw. A good boxer, and a pressure fighter, the spectre of drugs still hangs over his future, but he has performed miracles to come back as he has, his accurate punching accounting for 18 opponents inside the distance.

15.07.94	Oscar Aguilar W CO 2 Phoenix
	(Vacant NABF S. Flyweight Title)
12.10.94	Henry Martinez W RSC 11 Albuquerque
	(Vacant WBO S. Flyweight Title)
08.12.94	Rolando Bohol W CO 2 Albuquerque
10.02.95	Jose Rafael Sosa W PTS 12 Albuquerque
	(WBO S. Flyweight Title Defence)
06.05.95	Ricardo Vargas T DRAW 8 Las Vegas
	(WBO S. Flyweight Title Defence)
Career: 31 contests, won 29, drew 2.	

Fabrice Tiozzo

Saint Denis, France. *Born* 8 May, 1969
WBC L. Heavyweight Champion. Former Undefeated European & French L. Heavyweight Champion

The younger brother of Christophe, a former WBA super-middleweight champion, Fabrice won a silver medal in the World Junior championships in 1987, and the French senior title in 1988. Turned professional in New York, in November 1988, and then returned to France to continue his career. Made steady progress and, in June 1991, won the French title by beating the former European champion, Eric Nicoletta, in the final of the annual tournament. His manager was only released from a spell in jail two hours before the bout, but Fabrice floored Nicoletta and dominated the action. Continued his winning ways with victories over good opposition, such as Tony Wilson and Ramzi Hassan, although he had to climb off the floor to decision the Syrian. Challenged Virgil Hill for the WBA crown in April 1993 and looked to be booked for an early defeat when floored in each of the first two rounds, but battled his way back into the fight to lose a split verdict. Fabrice was floored again, when challenging Eddy Smulders for the European title in March 1994, but he put the Dutchman down twice and halted him in round seven. Made two defences, beating both Maurice Core and Noel Magee inside the distance, and then used his youth and strength to decision Mike McCallum and lift the WBC crown, flooring the great Jamaican for the first time in his career. 6' 1" tall, he is an upright stylist with a good jab and left-hook, has a hard right-hand punch and although being floored a few times, he has never been stopped. Is always well conditioned.

13.08.94	Tim St Clair W RSC 5 Pacavas les Flots
25.10.94	Maurice Core W RSC 4 Besancon
	(European L. Heavyweight Title Defence)
05.03.95	Noel Magee W RSC 4 Vitrolles
	(European L. Heavyweight Title Defence)
16.06.95	Mike McCallum W PTS 12 Lyon
	(WBC L. Heavyweight Title Challenge)
Career: 33 contests, won 32, lost 1.	

Felix Trinidad

Cupoy Alto, Puerto Rico. *Born* 10 January, 1973
IBF Welterweight Champion

17.09.94	Yori Boy Campas W RSC 4 Las Vegas
	(IBF Welterweight Title Defence)
10.12.94	Oba Carr W RSC 8 Monterrey
	(IBF Welterweight Title Defence)
08.04.95	Roger Turner W RSC 2 Las Vegas
	(IBF Welterweight Title Defence)
Career: 26 contests, won 26.	

Konstantin (Kostya) Tszyu

Serov, Russia. *Born* 19 September, 1969
IBF L. Welterweight Champion

Started boxing in Russia at the age of nine and was a brilliant amateur, being the Russian champion five times, the European Junior champion at featherweight in 1986, a bronze medalist in the 1989 World Championships, and European lightweight champion in 1989 and 1991. He also won the World title in 1991. Losing just three of 272 fights, his victory in the World Championships attracted the Australian promoter, Bill Mordey, who brought

Kostya to Sydney where he turned professional in March 1992, being an immediate success. In only his fourth fight, in July 1992, he outclassed former world champion, Juan Laporte, who just about lasted the distance. Two fights later he destroyed future WBO champion, Sammy Fuentes, inside a round, and, in June 1993, he knocked out Roberto Rivera in 87 seconds, before flooring and easily decisioning the former WBA light-weight champion, Livingston Bramble, in his tenth bout. Made his American debut in January 1994, but was not impressive, needing a strong finish to decision the tough Mexican, Hector Lopez. Back in Australia, he turned on the class again with a seventh round stoppage of experienced Puerto Rican survivor, Angel Hernandez, and a four round destruction of the highly-rated Dominican, Pedro Sanchez. Lifted the IBF title in January by stopping Jake Rodriguez in six rounds. Rodriguez, a tough southpaw, was on the floor five times and was totally outclassed. With his plaited pony-tail and earring, the 5'7" Kostya may look eccentric but is a dangerous stalker who fights with controlled ferocity before exploding with real power in both hands. He also shows amazing polish for a boxer with just 15 professional bouts and less than 75 rounds of fighting behind him. However, he struggled against oldie, Roger Mayweather, and can be frustrated by good boxers.

29.08.94	Pedro Sanchez W RSC 4 Melbourne
28.01.95	Jake Rodriguez W RSC 6 Las Vegas
	(IBF L. Welterweight Title Challenge)
25.06.95	Roger Mayweather W PTS 12 Newcastle
	(IBF L. Welterweight Title Defence)

Career: 15 contests, won 15.

Regilio (Turbo) Tuur

Paramaribo, Surinam. *Born* 12 August, 1967
WBO S. Featherweight Champion. Former European S. Featherweight Champion

One of ten children, he moved to Holland when he was four-years-old and his father, who boxed in the 1970s, introduced Regilio to the fight game when he was 14. Claiming 92 victories in 98 amateur fights, he won a bronze medal in the 1987 European Championships, but really made his name in the 1988 Olympics when he knocked out the American favourite, Kelcie Banks, in just 110 seconds. Moved to the United States in January 1989 to join the Madison Square Garden group and turned professional in July, scoring eight victories before being outpointed by the elusive Fernando Rodriquez in January 1990. A couple of fights later he was held to a draw by Jacobin Yoma, but then ran up 20 wins in a row, beating useful Moussa Sanagre and staging a strong finish to give him a points victory over former IBF super-bantamweight champion, Jose Sanabria. Suffered his second defeat in March 1992 when he was outboxed by former world champion, Calvin Grove, and lost on points in a New York State title fight. Won the vacant European title in December, with a very close decision over old foe, Yoma, and retained it with an easy third round stoppage of Italian, Michele la Fratta. Faced Yoma again in June 1993, this time in the Frenchman's hometown, and lost his title in another hotly contested bout. Bounced back to decision Eugene Speed for the vacant WBO crown in September 1994, despite being badly cut. Has outpointed Tony Pep and halted an outclassed Pete Taliaferro in defences so far. 5' 7" tall, Regilio is an aggressive fighter, with a good left-hook, and has accounted for 25 opponents inside the distance.

24.09.94	Eugene Speed W PTS 12 Rotterdam
	(Vacant WBO S. Featherweight Title)
11.03.95	Tony Pep W PTS 12 Groningen
	(WBO S. Featherweight Title Defence)
17.06.95	Pete Taliaferro W RSC 5 New Orleans
	(WBO S. Featherweight Title Defence)

Career: 43 contests, won 39, drew 1, lost 3.

Anaclet Wamba

Saint Brieuc, France. *Born* 6 January, 1960
WBC Cruiserweight Champion. Former Undefeated European Cruiserweight Champion

14.07.94	Adolpho Washington DREW 12 Monaco
	(WBC Cruiserweight Title Defence)
11.11.94	Charles Dixon W CO 1 Tucuman
03.12.94	Marcelo Dominguez W PTS 12 Salta
	(WBC Cruiserweight Title Defence)
30.12.94	Perfecto Gonzalez W RSC 4 Pointe a Pitre

Career: 49 contests, won 46, drew 1, lost 2.

Paul Weir

Irvine, Scotland. *Born* 16 September, 1967
WBO L. Flyweight Champion. Former WBO M. Flyweight Champion

Note: Full record will be found in the Current British-Based Champions: Career Records Section.

Pernell (Sweet Pea) Whitaker

Norfolk, USA. *Born* 2 January, 1964
WBC Welterweight Champion. Former Undefeated WBA L. Middleweight Champion. Former Undefeated IBF L. Welterweight Champion. Former Undefeated IBF, WBA & WBC Lightweight Champion. Former Undefeated NABF & USBA Lightweight Champion

01.10.94	James McGirt W PTS 12 Norfolk
	(WBC Welterweight Title Defence)
04.03.95	Julio Cesar Vasquez W PTS 12 Atlantic City
	(WBA L. Middleweight Title Challenge)

Career: 37 contests, won 35, drew 1, lost 1.

Yasuei Yakushiji

Tsukumi, Japan. *Born* 22 July, 1968
WBC Bantamweight Champion. Former Undefeated Japanese Bantamweight Champion

31.07.94	Jung-Il Byun W RTD 11 Nagoya
	(WBC Bantamweight Title Defence)
04.12.94	Joichiro Tatsuyoshi W PTS 12 Nagoya
	(WBC Bantamweight Title Defence)
02.04.95	Cuauhtemoc Gomez W PTS 12 Tokyo
	(WBC Bantamweight Title Defence)

Career: 27 contests, won 24, drew 1, lost 2.

World Title Bouts during 1994-95

All of last season's title bouts for the IBF, WBA, WBC and WBO are shown in date order and give the boxers' respective weights, along with the scorecard if going to a decision. There is also a short summary of any bout that involved a British contestant, and British officials, where applicable, are listed. There were 184 title bouts in all, a far cry from the days of not so long ago when you were lucky if there were 20.

2 July 1994   Wilfredo Vasquez 8.9 (Puerto Rico) W RSC 2 Jae-Won Choi 8.10 (South Korea), Las Vegas, USA (WBA S. Bantamweight Title).

2 July 1994   Orlin Norris 13.6 (USA) W RSC 3 Arthur Williams 13.8 (USA), Las Vegas, USA (WBA Cruiserweight Title).

9 July 1994   Chris Eubank 12.0 (England) W PTS 12 Mauricio Amaral 11.12 (Brazil), Olympia, Earls Court (WBO S. Middleweight Title). Scorecards: 116-114, 116-113, 115-113. This was the first fight in Eubank's so-called "world tour", comprising eight title defences in a year, and one that he should have won with ease. However, he struggled to assert any kind of authority over his rival and once again did just enough to keep his championship.

14 July 1994   Anaclet Wamba 13.7$\frac{1}{2}$ (France) DREW 12 Adolpho Washington 13.7$\frac{3}{4}$ (USA), Monaco, Monte Carlo (WBC Cruiserweight Title). Referee: Mickey Vann. Scorecards: 115-115, Larry O'Connell 116-116, 116-114.

15 July 1994   Josue Camacho 7.8$\frac{1}{2}$ (Puerto Rico) L PTS 12 Michael Carbajal 7.10 (USA), Phoenix, USA (WBO L. Flyweight Title). Scorecards: 108-119, 108-119, Roy Francis 110-119. Carbajal vacated the title in October after deciding to have a crack at Humberto Gonzalez's IBF/WBC championships.

17 July 1994   John Michael Johnson 8.5 (USA) L RTD 1 Daorung Chuwatana 8.5$\frac{1}{2}$ (Thailand), Uttaradit, Thailand (WBA Bantamweight Title).

23 July 1994   Al Cole 13.7 (USA) W PTS 12 Nate Miller 13.8 (USA), Bismark, USA (IBF Cruiserweight Title). Scorecards: 117-111, 117-111, 115-113.

23 July 1994   Jeff Harding 12.6 (Australia) L PTS 12 Mike McCallum 12.6$\frac{1}{2}$ (USA), Bismark, USA (WBC L. Heavyweight Title). Scorecards: 114-115, 113-116, 113-115.

23 July 1994   Virgil Hill 12.6$\frac{1}{2}$ (USA) W PTS 12 Frank Tate 12.6$\frac{1}{2}$ (USA), Bismark, USA (WBA L. Heavyweight Title). Scorecards: 119-108, 119-107, 118-110.

24 July 1994   Zack Padilla 10.0 (USA) W RTD 9 Juan Laporte 10.0 (Puerto Rico), Los Angeles, USA (WBO L. Welterweight Title). Padilla was forced to retire from the ring in September after suffering an aneurysm when sparring in the gym.

25 July 1994   Verno Phillips 11.0 (USA) W RSC 7 Jaime Llanes 11.0 (Mexico), Los Angeles, USA (WBO L. Middleweight Title).

29 July 1994   James Toney 12.0 (USA) W CO 12 Charles Williams 11.13$\frac{1}{2}$ (USA), Las Vegas, USA (IBF S. Middleweight Title).

29 July 1994   Oscar de la Hoya 9.9 (USA) W CO 2 Jorge Paez 9.8$\frac{1}{2}$ (Mexico), Las Vegas, USA (Vacant WBO Lightweight Title). The Italian, Giovanni Parisi, had relinquished the title in May.

30 July 1994   Rafael del Valle 8.6 (Puerto Rico) L PTS 12 Alfred Kotey 8.3$\frac{3}{4}$ (Ghana), York Hall, Bethnal Green (WBO Bantamweight Title). Referee: Dave Parris. Scorecards: Paul Thomas 111-116, 111-118, 112-116.

31 July 1994   Yasuei Yakushiji 8.5$\frac{1}{2}$ (Japan) W RTD 11 Jung-Il Byun 8.6 (South Korea), Nagoya, Japan (WBC Bantamweight Title).

1 August 1994   Yuri Arbachakov 8.0 (Russia) W CO 8 Hugo Soto 8.0 (Argentine), Tokyo, Japan (WBC Flyweight Title).

6 August 1994   Miguel Gonzalez 9.8 (Mexico) W RSC 8 Leavander Johnson 9.6$\frac{1}{2}$ (USA), Juarez, Mexico (WBC Lightweight Title). Referee: Mickey Vann.

7 August 1994   Hiroshi Kawashima 8.3 (Japan) W PTS 12 Carlos Salazar 8.3 (Argentine), Tokyo, Japan (WBC S. Flyweight Title). Scorecards: 118-110, 117-113, 115-113.

12 August 1994   Steve Little 12.0 (USA) L PTS 12 Frank Lilles 11.12$\frac{1}{4}$ (USA), Tucuman, Argentine (WBA S. Middleweight Title). Scorecards: 114-116, 113-118, 112-118.

12 August 1994   Jorge Castro 11.5$\frac{3}{4}$ (Argentine) W PTS 12 Reggie Johnson 11.5$\frac{3}{4}$ (USA) Tucuman, USA (Vacant WBA Middleweight Title). Scorecards: 116-114, 116-114, 115-116. John David Jackson (USA) forfeited the title in May for taking a non-title fight without having the WBA'S authorisation.

13 August 1994   Alex Sanchez 7.7 (Puerto Rico) W CO 1 Carlos Juan Rodriguez 7.7 (Dominican Republic), Bayamon, Puerto Rico (WBO M. Flyweight Title).

13 August 1994   Ratanapol Sowvoraphin 7.7 (Thailand) W RSC 4 Marcelino Bolivar 7.7 (Venezuela), Buriram, Thailand (IBF M. Flyweight Title).

20 August 1994   Kennedy McKinney 8.9$\frac{3}{4}$ (USA) L PTS 12 Vuyani Bungu 8.9$\frac{3}{4}$ (South Africa), Temba, South Africa (IBF S. Bantamweight Title). Scorecards: 111-117, 112-116, 112-116.

21 August 1994   Julio Cesar Vazquez 10.11 (Argentine) W PTS 12 Ronald Wright 10.12$\frac{3}{4}$ (USA), St Jean de Luz, France (WBA L. Middleweight Title). Scorecards: 115-110, 114-110, 113-110.

26 August 1994   Tracy Harris Patterson 8.10 (USA) L PTS 12 Hector Acero-Sanchez 8.10 (Dominican Republic) Atlantic City, USA (WBC S. Bantamweight Title). Scorecards: 115-112, 113-114, 113-114.

27 August 1994   Jake Rodriquez 10.0 (USA) W RTD 9 George Scott 9.13$^1/_2$ (Sweden), Bushkill, USA (IBF L. Welterweight Title).

27 August 1994   Chris Eubank 12.0 (England) W RSC 7 Sammy Storey 12.0 (Ireland), International Arena, Cardiff (WBO S. Middleweight Title). Eubank's first inside-the-distance win in ten fights saw him stop Storey at 1.0 of the seventh round. The Irishman, who had twisted his ankle when put down in the sixth, was rescued by Dave Parris following two more counts after his leg continued to give way. Scotsman, Billy Rafferty, was one of the judges.

27 August 1994   Chana Porpaoin 7.7 (Thailand) W PTS 12 Keun-Young Kang 7.6$^3/_4$ (South Korea), Phatthalung, Thailand (WBA M. Flyweight Title). Scorecards: 120-110, 119-112, 119-110.

29 August 1994   Julio Cesar Borboa 8.3 (Mexico) L PTS 12 Harold Grey 8.3 (Colombia), Los Angeles, USA (IBF S. Flyweight Title). Scorecards: 117-111, 113-114, 112-116.

3 September 1994   Daniel Jimenez 8.9$^1/_4$ (Puerto Rico) W CO 1 Harold Geier 8.9$^1/_4$ (Austria), Wiener Neustadt, Austria (WBO S. Bantamweight Title).

10 September 1994   Humberto Gonzalez 7.10 (Mexico) W RTD 7 Juan Domingo Cordoba 7.9 (Argentine), Lake Tahoe, USA (WBC/IBF L. Flyweight Title).

10 September 1994   Leonzer Barber 12.6 (USA) L PTS 12 Dariusz Michalczewski 12.6 (Germany), Hamburg, Germany (WBO L. Heavyweight Title). Scorecards: 109-117, 111-116, 111-116.

10 September 1994   Alex Sanchez 7.7 (Puerto Rico) W RSC 4 Oscar Andrade 7.7 (Mexico), Hamburg, Germany (WBO M. Flyweight Title).

10 September 1994   Nigel Benn 11.13$^1/_4$ (England) W PTS 12 Juan Carlos Gimenez 11.13$^1/_2$ (Paraguay), National Exhibition Centre, Birmingham (WBC S. Middleweight Title). Scorecards: 119-115, 118-112, 117-112. This was a lacklustre contest by Benn's exciting standards, although that was hardly surprising when you consider the "punch-ups" outside the ring that broke his concentration during the fourth round. Although the trouble had subsided by the fifth, the champion failed to find any real rhythm and had to be content with his third distance fight in a row.

11 September 1994   Eloy Rojas 8.13$^1/_2$ (Venezuela) W CO 8 Samart Payakaroon 9.0 (Thailand), Trang, Thailand (WBA Featherweight Title).

17 September 1994   Gianfranco Rosi 11.0 (Italy) L CO 4 Vince Pettway 10.13 (USA), Las Vegas, USA (IBF L. Middleweight Title). Judge: Roy Francis.

17 September 1994   Felix Trinidad 10.6$^1/_2$ (Puerto Rico) W RSC 4 Yori Boy Campas 10.6$^1/_2$ (Mexico), Las Vegas, USA (IBF Welterweight Title).

17 September 1994   Julio Cesar Chavez 10.0 (Mexico) W RSC 8 Meldrick Taylor 10.0 (USA), Las Vegas, USA (WBC L. Welterweight Title).

17 September 1994   Juan Martin Coggi 10.0 (Argentine) L PTS 12 Frankie Randall 10.0 (USA), Las Vegas (WBA L. Welterweight Title). Scorecards: 109-115, 108-116, 108-116.

17 September 1994   James Leija 9.4 (USA) L PTS 12 Gabriel Ruelas 9.4 (USA), Las Vegas (WBC S. Featherweight Title). Scorecards: 111-115, 109-115, 108-116.

17 September 1994   Ricardo Lopez 7.7 (Mexico) W RSC 1 Yodsingh Saengmorokot 7.7 (Thailand), Las Vegas, USA (WBC M. Flyweight Title).

18 September 1994   Katsuya Onizuka 8.3 (Japan) L RSC 9 Hyung-Chul Lee 8.3 (South Korea), Tokyo, Japan (WBA S. Flyweight Title). Referee: John Coyle.

24 September 1994   Regilio Tuur 9.3$^3/_4$ (Holland) W PTS 12 Eugene Speed 9.3 (USA), Rotterdam, Holland (Vacant WBO S. Featherweight Title). Scorecards: 118-110, 118-108, 117-109. The title had become vacant in June after Oscar de la Hoya decided to move up to lightweight to contest the vacant WBO crown with Jorge Paez.

24 September 1994   Kevin Kelley 9.0 (USA) W RSC 2 Jose Vida Ramos 8.13 (Dominican Republic), Atlantic City, USA (WBC Featherweight Title).

24 September 1994   Lennox Lewis 17.0 (England) L RSC 2 Oliver McCall 16.7 (USA), The Arena, Wembley (WBC Heavyweight Title). In one of the biggest upsets seen in a British ring, and there has been a few of those, Lewis was caught by a right-hander that can only be termed a "sucker" punch. Although getting to his feet before the count was completed, he was clearly in no position to defend himself, according to most good judges, and the referee called the action off after 0.31 of the second round.

25 September 1994   Saen Sorploenchit 8.0 (Thailand) W PTS 12 Yong-Kang Kim 8.0 (South Korea), Kanchanaburi, Thailand (WBA Flyweight Title). Scorecards: 119-109, 118-109, 118-109.

1 October 1994   Nestor Giovannini (Argentine) W RTD 6 Larry Carlisle (USA), Buenos Aires, Argentine. Although billed as a cruiserweight title defence for Giovannini by the promoter, the fight was not sanctioned as one by the WBO.

1 October 1994   Ike Quartey 10.4$^3/_4$ (Ghana) W RSC 5 Alberto Cortes 10.6 (Argentine), Carpentras, France (WBA Welterweight Title).

1 October 1994   Pernell Whitaker 10.7 W PTS 12 James McGirt 10.6 (USA), Norfolk, USA (WBC Welterweight Title). Scorecards: 118-112, 117-112, 117-110.

1 October 1994   Steve Robinson 8.13$\frac{1}{2}$ (Wales) W CO 9 Duke McKenzie 8.13$\frac{3}{4}$ (England), National Ice Rink, Cardiff (WBO Featherweight Title). Although Robinson was ahead on all three judges' cards at the finish, including that of our own Dave Parris, McKenzie's neat boxing had made things difficult for him. The punch that brought the fight to an end was a tremendous short left-hook to the body which dropped McKenzie to his knees to be counted out by Roy Francis at 2.50 of the ninth round.

8 October 1994   Henry Maske 12.6$\frac{1}{4}$ (Germany) W RTD 9 Iran Barkley 12.3$\frac{1}{2}$ (USA), Halle, Germany (IBF L. Heavyweight Title).

9 October 1994   Silvio Gamez 7.9$\frac{1}{2}$ (Venezuela) W RSC 6 Phichitnoi Sitbangprachan 7.9$\frac{1}{2}$ (Thailand), Bangkok, Thailand (WBA L. Flyweight Title).

12 October 1994   Johnny Tapia 8.2$\frac{1}{2}$ (USA) W RSC 11 Henry Martinez 8.3 (USA), Albuquerque, USA (Vacant WBO S. Flyweight Title). Title vacated when Johnny Bredahl relinquished in August, following the WBO being outlawed in Denmark.

13 October 1994   Wilfredo Vasquez 8.7 (Puerto Rico) W PTS 12 Juan Polo Perez 8.5$\frac{1}{2}$ (Colombia), Levallois Perret, France (WBA S. Bantamweight Title). Scorecards: 116-112, 116-111, 115-112.

15 October 1994   Chris Eubank 12.0 (England) W PTS 12 Dan Schommer 11.12$\frac{1}{2}$ (USA), Sun City, South Africa (WBO S. Middleweight Title). Scorecards: 117-113, 116-114, 116-113. This was yet another Eubank fight which could have slipped away from him due to lack of effort. At times the 34-year-old challenger outboxed the champion with ease and it could have only been his lack of aggression that failed to influence the judges. Even allowing for that, many were surprised with the scoreline in Eubank's favour.

15 October 1994   Jacob Matlala 7.12$\frac{1}{2}$ (South Africa) W PTS 12 Domingo Lucas 7.11$\frac{3}{4}$ (Philippines), Sun City, South Africa (WBO Flyweight Title). Scorecards: Paul Thomas 118-110, Roy Francis 119-110, 118-110.

15 October 1994   Orlando Canizales 8.6 (USA) W PTS 12 Sergio Reyes 8.5$\frac{3}{4}$ (USA), Laredo, USA (IBF Bantamweight Title). Scorecards: 116-111, 115-112, 114-113. In making his 16th consecutive successful defence of the IBF title, and disregarding the no-decision contest against Derrick Whiteboy (19/6/93), the champion finally broke Manuel Ortiz's divisional record. Canizales relinquished the title in December when moving up a weight division to challenge Wilfredo Vasquez for the WBA crown.

22 October 1994   Tom Johnson 9.0 (USA) W PTS 12 Francisco Segura 8.13$\frac{1}{2}$ (USA), Atlantic City, USA (IBF Featherweight Title). Scorecards: 118-110, 118-110, 117-111.

25 October 1994   Alfred Kotey 8.5$\frac{1}{2}$ (Ghana) W PTS 12 Armando Castro 8.5$\frac{3}{4}$ (Mexico), Town Hall, Middlesbrough (WBO Bantamweight Title). Scorecards: 120-108, 120-108, 119-111.

5 November 1994   Michael Moorer 15.12 (USA) L CO 10 George Foreman 17.12 (USA), Las Vegas, USA (IBF/WBA Heavyweight Titles). By his victory, the 46-year-old Foreman became the oldest man ever to win the heavyweight title, but was stripped of the WBA version of the championship in March 1995 when failing to take on that organisation's leading challenger.

5 November 1994   Jorge Castro 11.5$\frac{1}{2}$ (Argentine) W CO 2 Alex Ramos 11.5$\frac{3}{4}$ (USA), Caleta Oliva, Argentine (WBA Middleweight Title).

5 November 1994   Chana Porpaoin 7.7 (Thailand) W PTS 12 Manuel Herrera 7.5$\frac{3}{4}$ (Dominican Republic), Hat Yai, Thailand (WBA M. Flyweight Title), Scorecards: 115-113, 115-112, 112-114.

9 November 1994   Verno Phillips 10.13$\frac{3}{4}$ (USA) W PTS 15 Santos Cardona 10.12$\frac{1}{2}$ (Puerto Rico), New Orleans, USA (WBO L. Middleweight Title). Scorecards: 116-110, 116-112, 114-113.

11 November 1994   Julio Cesar Vasquez 10.13$\frac{3}{4}$ (Argentine) W PTS 12 Tony Marshall 10.8$\frac{1}{4}$ (USA), Tucuman, Argentina (WBA L. Middleweight Title). Scorecards: 119-112, 118-110, 117-111.

12 November 1994   Ratanapol Sowvoraphin 7.7 (Thailand) W RSC 3 Carlos Rodriguez 7.7 (Venezuela), Khonkaen, Thailand (IBF M. Flyweight Title).

12 November 1994   Ricardo Lopez 7.7 (Mexico) W RSC 8 Javier Varguez 7.6$\frac{3}{4}$ (Mexico) Mexico City, Mexico (WBC M. Flyweight Title).

12 November 1994   Humberto Gonzalez 7.9$\frac{1}{2}$ (Mexico) W PTS 12 Michael Carbajal 7.10 (USA), Mexico City, Mexico (WBC/IBF L. Flyweight Title). Referee: Larry O'Connell. Scorecards: 117-114, 116-113, 114-114.

12 November 1994   Genaro Hernandez 9.4 (USA) W PTS 12 Jimmy Garcia 9.4 (Colombia), Mexico City, Mexico (WBA S. Featherweight Title). Scorecards: 120-107, 119-109, 117-109.

12 November 1994   Terry Norris 10.11 (USA) L DIS 5 Luis Santana 10.12$\frac{1}{2}$ (Dominican Republic), Mexico City, Mexico (WBC L. Middleweight Title).

12 November 1994   Orlin Norris 13.5$\frac{3}{4}$ (USA) W CO 2 James Heath 13.5$\frac{3}{4}$ (USA), Mexico City, Mexico (WBA Cruiserweight Title).

18 November 1994   James Toney 11.13 (USA) L PTS 12 Roy Jones 12.0 (USA), Las Vegas, USA (IBF S. Middleweight Title). Scorecards: 108-119, 109-118, 110-117.

18 November 1994   Oscar de la Hoya 9.9 (USA) W RSC 3 Carl Griffith 9.9 (USA), Las Vegas (WBO Lightweight Title).

19 November 1994   Vuyani Bungu 8.9³/₄ (South Africa) W PTS 12 Felix Camacho 8.10 (Puerto Rico), Hammanskraal, South Africa (IBF S. Bantamweight Title). Scorecards: 119-110, 118-111, 117-111.

20 November 1994   Daorung Chuwatana 8.6 (Thailand) W TD 5 In-Shik Koh 8.6 (South Korea), Bangkok, Thailand (WBA Bantamweight Title). Scorecards: 40-36, 40-37, 39-37.

23 November 1994   Paul Weir 7.10 (Scotland) W PTS 12 Paul Oulden 7.10 (South Africa), Magnum Centre, Irvine (Vacant WBO L. Flyweight Title). Scorecards: 119-110, 117-111, 116-112. Having lost his WBO mini-flyweight crown earlier in the year, Weir came through resoundingly on all three judges' scorecards to pick up another title, three pounds higher up the weight scale. Although Oulden came forward throughout, he was picked off smartly, while never being given the opportunity to land his heavier punches, and, at the final bell, was a well outsmarted fighter.

26 November 1994   Juan Molina 9.4 (Puerto Rico) W CO 10 Wilson Rodriguez 9.3 (Dominican Republic), Bayamon, Puerto Rico (IBF S. Featherweight Title). Molina vacated title in January 1995 in order to step up a division and take a match with Oscar de la Hoya.

3 December 1994   Anaclet Wamba 13.8 (France) W PTS 12 Marcelo Dominguez 13.6³/₄ (Argentine), Salta, Argentine (WBC Cruiserweight Title). Referee: Mickey Vann. Scorecards: 116-115, 115-113, 114-114.

3 December 1994   Eloy Rojas 9.0 (Venezuela) W PTS 12 Luis Mendoza 8.13³/₄ (Colombia), Bogota, Colombia (WBA Featherweight Title). Scorecards: 117-111, 116-114, 115-113.

4 December 1994   Yasuei Yakushiji 8.5³/₄ (Japan) W PTS 12 Joichiro Tatsuyoshi 8.5¹/₄ (Japan), Nagoya, Japan (WBC Bantamweight Title). Scorecards: 116-112, 115-114, 114-114.

10 December 1994   Jorge Castro 11.6 (Argentine) W RSC 9 John David Jackson 11.6 (USA), Monterrey, Mexico (WBA Middleweight Title).

10 December 1994   Julio Cesar Chavez 10.0 (Mexico) W RSC 10 Tony Lopez 9.13 (USA), Monterrey, Mexico (WBC L. Welterweight Title).

10 December 1994   Frankie Randall 10.0 (USA) W RSC 7 Rodney Moore 9.13 (USA), Monterrey, Mexico (WBA L. Welterweight Title).

10 December 1994   Felix Trinidad 10.6¹/₂ (Puerto Rico) W RSC 8 Oba Carr 10.5 (USA), Monterrey, Mexico (IBF Welterweight Title).

10 December 1994   Ricardo Lopez 7.6 (Mexico) W RSC 1 Yamil Caraballo 7.6 (Colombia), Monterrey, Mexico (WBC M. Flyweight Title).

10 December 1994   Orzubek Nazarov 9.8 (Russia) W RSC 2 Joey Gamache 9.9 (USA), Portland, USA (WBA Lightweight Title). Referee: John Coyle.

10 December 1994   Oscar de la Hoya 9.9 (USA) W RSC 9 John Avila 9.9 (USA), Los Angeles, USA (WBO Lightweight Title).

10 December 1994   Chris Eubank 12.0 (England) W PTS 12 Henry Wharton 11.13³/₄ (England), G-Mex Centre, Manchester (WBO S. Middleweight Title). Scorecards: Paul Thomas 115-113, Roy Francis 118-112, 116-112. Following recent unimpressive title defences, this was much better from Eubank. Granted that Wharton's style was "tailor made" for the champion's counter-punches, but at last the fans were able to get a glimpse of the skills that had won him the championship in the first place. The courageous Wharton not only finished well beaten, but also unable to see out of his badly swollen left-eye.

10 December 1994   Eamonn Loughran 10.6¹/₂ (Ireland) W TD 4 Manning Galloway 10.6 (USA), G-Mex Centre, Manchester (WBO Welterweight Title). Scorecards: 40-37, 39-37, 39-37. With only four rounds completed, and with both men badly cut, especially so the challenger, the fight went to the judges' cards before a punch could be thrown at the start of the fifth. The trouble had started when the awkward Galloway and Loughran clashed heads in the second, leaving the former badly cut on the right-eye and the champion on the forehead. However, when Galloway was cut over the left-eye in the third, with Loughran well on top, it was apparent to all and sundry that the end was imminent.

13 December 1994   Miguel Gonzalez 9.8¹/₂ (Mexico) W RTD 5 Calvin Grove 9.7¹/₂ (USA), Alberquerque, USA (WBC Lightweight Title).

17 December 1994   Nestor Giovannini 13.0 (Argentine) L CO 10 Dariusz Michalczewski 12.13 (Germany), Hamburg, Germany (WBO Cruiserweight Title). Michalczewski vacated the title in January 1995 after failing to secure a defence against Thomas Hearns and deciding to continue as WBO light-heavyweight champion.

17 December 1994   Frank Lilles 11.13 (USA) W PTS 12 Michael Nunn 12.0 (USA), Quito, Ecuador (WBA S. Middleweight Title). Scorecards: 117-111, 115-112, 114-113.

17 December 1994   Bernard Hopkins 11.3 (USA) DREW 12 Segundo Mercado 11.4 (Eucador), Quito, Ecuador (Vacant IBF Middleweight Title). Scorecards: 114-111, 114-116, 113-113. Roy Jones vacated title on 18 November after beating James Toney for the S. Middleweight crown.

17 December 1994   Harold Grey 8.3 (Colombia) W PTS 12 Vincenzo Belcastro 8.3 (Italy), Cagliari, Italy (IBF S. Flyweight Title). Scorecards: 115-113, 115-112, 113-114.

25 December 1994   Saen Sorploenchit 8.0 (Thailand) W RSC 11 Danny Nunez 8.0 (Dominican Republic), Rayong, Thailand (WBA Flyweight Title).

7 January 1995   Kevin Kelley 9.0 (USA) L RTD 10 Alejandro Gonzalez 9.0 (Mexico), San Antonio, USA (WBC Featherweight Title).

7 January 1995   Wifredo Vasquez 8.10 (Puerto Rico) W PTS 12 Orlando Canizales 8.9$^{1}/_{2}$ (USA), San Antonio, USA (WBA S. Bantamweight Title). Scorecards: 116-115, 115-113, 113-117.

18 January 1995   Hiroshi Kawashima 8.2$^{1}/_{2}$ (Japan) W PTS 12 Jose Luis Bueno 8.3 (Mexico), Yokohama, Japan (WBC S. Flyweight Title). Scorecards: 118-109, 116-111, 115-114.

21 January 1995   Harold Mestre 8.6 (Colombia) W RSC 8 Juvenal Berrio 8.6 (Colombia), Cartagena, Colombia (Vacant IBF Bantamweight Title).

28 January 1995   Chana Porpaoin 7.7 (Thailand) W PTS 12 Jin-Ho Kim 7.7 (South Korea), Bangkok, Thailand (WBA M. Flyweight Title). Scorecards: 118-112, 118-112, 117-112.

28 January 1995   Rafael Ruelas 9.9 (USA) W RTD 8 Billy Schwer 9.8 (England), Las Vegas, USA (IBF Lightweight Title). Unfortunate to be cut so early in the fight, his left-eyebrow was gashed in the third, Schwer was always in contention and made Ruelas work hard for his win. When another bad wound opened up over the challenger's right-eye in the fifth session, the writing was on the wall. However, Schwer responded magnificently in taking the fight to the champion and it was only when his cornerman, Dennie Mancini, was unable to stem the flow of blood, the referee, on the advice of the doctor, stopped it. Dave Parris, one of the judges, had Ruelas leading by just two rounds at the finish.

28 January 1995   Alex Sanchez 7.7 (Puerto Rico) W PTS 12 Rafael Orozco 7.6 (Mexico), Las Vegas, USA (WBO M. Flyweight Title). Scorecards: 116-111, 116-110, 115-111.

28 January 1995   Jake Rodriguez 9.13$^{1}/_{2}$ (USA) L RSC 6 Konstantin Tszyu 9.13 (Russia), Las Vegas, USA (IBF L. Welterweight Title).

28 January 1995   Gabriel Ruelas 9.3$^{1}/_{2}$ (USA) W RTD 2 Fred Liberatore 9.3$^{1}/_{2}$ (USA), Las Vegas, USA (WBC S. Featherweight Title).

28 January 1995   Tom Johnson 8.13$^{3}/_{4}$ (USA) W PTS 12 Manuel Medina 8.13 (Mexico), Atlantic City, USA (IBF Featherweight Title). Scorecards: 116-112, 116-112, 115-113.

30 January 1995   Yuri Arbachakov 7.13$^{1}/_{4}$ (Russia) W PTS 12 Oscar Arciniega 7.12$^{1}/_{2}$ (Mexico), Sapporo, Japan (WBC Flyweight Title). Scorecards: 116-113, 116-112, 116-112.

3 February 1995   Verno Phillips 10.12$^{1}/_{2}$ (USA) W PTS 12 Santos Cardona 10.13 (Puerto Rico), Bushkill, USA (WBO L. Middleweight Title). Scorecards: 116-112, 115-113, 113-115.

4 February 1995   Steve Robinson 8.13$^{1}/_{2}$ (Wales) W PTS 12 Domingo Damigella 8.13$^{1}/_{2}$ (Argentine), National Ice Rink, Cardiff (WBO Featherweight Title). Scorecards: 116-113, 115-113, 115-113. With a challenger who was always on the move, apart from the early stages, Robinson found his man a difficult target to pin down and ultimately had to settle for a points win. While it was not a convincing victory, in the main, the Welshman was the aggressor, despite feeling sluggish, and Damigella did not have the power needed to dislodge him.

4 February 1995   Silvio Gamez 7.9$^{1}/_{4}$ (Venezuela) L PTS 12 Hi-Yong Choi 7.9$^{3}/_{4}$ (South Korea), Ulsan, South Korea (WBA L. Flyweight Title). Scorecards: 114-118, 114-115, 112-116.

10 February 1995   Johnny Tapia 8.3$^{3}/_{4}$ (USA) W PTS 12 Jose Rafael Sosa 8.2$^{1}/_{2}$ (Argentine), Albuquerque, USA (WBO S. Flyweight Title). Scorecards: 120-107, 118-109, 117-110.

11 February 1995   Henry Maske 12.6 (Germany) W PTS 12 Egerton Marcus 12.5$^{1}/_{4}$ (Canada), Frankfurt, Germany (IBF L. Heavyweight Title). Scorecards: 118-110, 118-110, 118-111.

11 February 1995   Jacob Matlala 7.12$^{1}/_{2}$ (South Africa) L RSC 8 Alberto Jimenez 7.12$^{1}/_{4}$ (Mexico), Hammanskraal, South Africa (WBO Flyweight Title). Judge: Roy Francis.

17 February 1995   Alfred Kotey 8.5$^{1}/_{4}$ (Ghana) W RSC 4 Drew Docherty 8.6 (Scotland), Tryst Centre, Cumbernauld (WBO Bantamweight Title). On paper, it was always going to be an uphill struggle for the game Docherty and that is exactly how it turned out. The Scot certainly gave it his best shot, although it proved to be his undoing. Backing Kotey against the ropes in the third, he took a cracking right on the jaw that sent him down for an eight count, before gamely rising to slug it out for the remainder of the session. That weakened him considerably and, on coming out for the fourth on shaky legs, he was eventually felled by two more heavy right-handers, the referee stopping the count at five to call a halt at 0.50 of the round.

18 February 1995   Francisco Tejedor 7.13$^{1}/_{2}$ (Colombia) W RTD 7 Jose Luis Zepeda 7.13$^{1}/_{2}$ (Mexico), Cartagena, Colombia (Vacant IBF Flyweight Title). Pichit Sithbangprachan (Thailand) relinquished the title last October due to extended inactivity.

18 February 1995   Oscar de la Hoya 9.9 (USA) W PTS 12 Juan Molina 9.8 (Puerto Rico), Las Vegas, USA (WBO Lightweight Title). Scorecards: 117-110, 116-111, 116-111.

20 February 1995   Sammy Fuentes 9.13$^{1}/_{2}$ (Puerto Rico) W RSC 2 Fidel Avendano 9.12 (Mexico), Los Angeles, USA (Vacant WBO L. Welterweight Title).

197

25 February 1995   Ratanapol Sowvoraphin 7.5³/₄ (Thailand) W RSC 3 Jerry Pahayahay 7.5³/₄ (Philippines), Bangkok, Thailand (IBF M. Flyweight Title).

25 February 1995   Hyung-Chul Lee 8.3 (South Korea) W RSC 12 Tomonori Tamura 8.2³/₄ (Japan), Pusan, South Korea (WBA S. Flyweight Title).

25 February 1995   Nigel Benn 12.0 (England) W CO 10 Gerald McClellan 11.11 (USA), London Arena, Millwall (WBC S. Middleweight Title). One of the greatest fights ever seen in Britain, unfortunately saw McClellan carried from the ring unconscious. It must be said that without the ringside medical care available on the night, it is doubtful whether the American would still be with us. However, as at today, he continues to make progress, following life-saving operations to remove blood-clots carried out immediately after the fight. The fight itself was memorable. In a one-sided first round, Benn was knocked out of the ring, cut, and on the verge of defeat. That he pulled the fight round was remarkable in itself. Although the champion was down again in the eighth, McClellan was now struggling himself, his gumshield constantly hanging from his mouth, and in the ninth it was his turn to be floored. Two more counts in the tenth saw him counted out at 1.46 of the round, prior to his collapse. By his victory, Benn proved he need fear nobody and can look forward to taking his place alongside men such as Randy Turpin, when the history books are updated.

25 February 1995   Mike McCallum 12.6 (Jamaica) W RSC 7 Carl Jones 12.3 (USA), London Arena, Millwall (WBC L. Heavyweight Title). Referee: Larry O'Connell. Judges: Mickey Vann, John Keane.

4 March 1995   Julio Cesar Vasquez 10.13³/₄ (Argentine) L PTS 12 Pernell Whitaker 10.13³/₄ (USA), Atlantic City, USA (WBA L. Middleweight Title). Scorecards: 110-116, 110-118, 107-118. Whitaker relinquished title soon afterwards to concentrate on his welterweight crown.

4 March 1995   Ike Quartey 10.7 (Ghana) W RSC 4 Jung-Oh Park 10.7 (South Korea), Atlantic City, USA (WBA Welterweight Title).

4 March 1995   Vuyani Bungu 8.9¹/₂ (South Africa) W PTS 12 Mohammed Al Haji Nurhuda 8.9³/₄ (Indonesia), Hammanskraal, South Africa (IBF S. Bantamweight Title). Scorecards: 119-109, 119-109, 118-110.

9 March 1995   Regilio Tuur 9.3¹/₂ (Holland) W PTS 12 Tony Pep 9.3³/₄ (Canada), Groningen, Holland (WBO S. Featherweight Title). Scorecards: 119-109, 117-112, 117-111.

11 March 1995   Herbie Hide 15.4 (England) L CO 6 Riddick Bowe 17.3 (USA), Las Vegas, USA (WBO Heavyweight Title). To give away more than two stone to a puncher like Bowe was almost suicidal, but to Hide's lasting credit he fought on until it was impossible to continue. Floored for six counts, before being counted out at 2.25 of round six, the Britisher can look back in pride on his gutsy performance, but, if he is to make further inroads at this level, he will need to build himself up further.

11 March 1995   Dariusz Michalczewski 12.5³/₄ (Germany) W CO 2 Roberto Dominguez 12.5¹/₄ (Spain), Cologne, Germany (WBO L. Heavyweight Title).

11 March 1995   Hector Acero-Sanchez 8.10 (Dominican Republic) W PTS 12 Julio Gervacio 8.10 (Puerto Rico), Atlantic City, USA (WBC S. Bantamweight Title). Scorecards: 118-110, 117-111, 115-113.

17 March 1995   Julian Jackson 11.6 (USA) W RSC 2 Agostino Cardamone 11.6 (Italy), Worcester, USA (Vacant WBC Middleweight Title). Having problems in making the weight, Gerald McClellan vacated the title last January after landing a title fight at super-middleweight against Nigel Benn.

18 March 1995   Orlin Norris 13.8 (USA) W PTS 12 Adolpho Washington 13.8 (USA), Worcester, USA (WBA Cruiserweight Title). Scorecards: 114-113, 114-113, 114-113.

18 March 1995   Harold Grey 8.3 (Colombia) W PTS 12 Orlando Tobon 8.3 (Colombia), Cartagena, Colombia (IBF S. Flyweight Title). Scorecards: 117-111, 116-112, 114-114.

18 March 1995   Chris Eubank 11.13³/₄ (England) L PTS 12 Steve Collins 11.13³/₄ (Ireland), Millstreet, Ireland (WBO S. Middleweight Title). Scorecards: Roy Francis 114-116, 113-114, 111-115. This fight will be remembered as the one in which Collins was accused by the champion as having been under hypnosis. Whether or not that was the case, Collins certainly outflanked his rival and, apart from when floored in the tenth, he looked to be a clear winner. Eubank was forced to work for each minute of every round as the Irishman took the fight to him and was found wanting.

18 March 1995   Roy Jones 11.13¹/₂ (USA) W RSC 1 Antoine Byrd 11.13¹/₂ (USA), Pensacola, USA (IBF S. Middleweight Title).

31 March 1995   Humberto Gonzalez 7.10 (Mexico) W CO 5 Jesus Zuniga 7.9 (Colombia), Los Angeles, USA (WBC/IBF L. Flyweight Titles).

31 March 1995   Alejandro Gonzalez 9.0 (Mexico) W PTS 12 Louie Espinosa 9.0 (USA), Los Angeles, USA (WBC Featherweight Title). Scorecards: 117-111, 117-110, 116-112.

31 March 1995   Daniel Jimenez 8.8¹/₂ (Puerto Rico) L PTS 12 Marco Antonio Barrera 8.8¹/₂ (Mexico), Los Angeles, USA (WBO S. Bantamweight Title). Scorecards: 110-117, 111-116, 112-115.

1 April 1995   Virgil Hill 12.7 (USA) W PTS 12 Crawford Ashley 12.6 (England), Stateline, USA (WBA L. Heavyweight Title). Scorecards: 118-110, 118-110, 117-113. Although both men finished battered and bruised, it really had not been that kind of fight and, while showing plenty of heart in surviving a tough last round, Ashley had not produced nearly enough work that would normally be expected of a challenger trying to lift a title.

1 April 1995   Ricardo Lopez 7.6 (Mexico) W RSC 12 Andy Tabanas 7.7 (Philippines), Stateline, USA (WBC M. Flyweight Title).

2 April 1995   Yasuei Yakushiji 8.5^3/$_4$ (Japan) W PTS 12 Cuauhtemoc Gomez 8.5^1/$_2$ (Mexico), Tokyo, Japan (WBC Bantamweight Title). Scorecards: 117-111, 116-112, 114-114.

5 April 1995   Paul Weir 7.10 (Scotland) W PTS 12 Ric Magramo 7.10 (Philippines), Magnum Leisure Centre, Irvine (WBO L. Flyweight Title). Scorecards: 118-112. 118-109, 116-112. Under strict instructions to box to plan, in order to conserve his injured right-hand, Weir did just that as he left-jabbed his way to a relatively easy points victory. Diagnosed as having tendon damage to the right-wrist, the champion will be looking to have the problem ironed out before climbing back into the ring.

8 April 1995   Bruce Seldon 16.12 (USA) W RTD 7 Tony Tucker 17.5 (USA), Las Vegas, USA (Vacant WBA Heavyweight Title).

8 April 1995   Julio Cesar Chavez 10.0 (Mexico) W PTS 12 Giovanni Parisi 9.13 (Italy), Las Vegas, USA (WBC L. Welterweight Title). Scorecards: 120-108, 118-109, 118-109.

8 April 1995   Luis Santana 10.13 (Dominican Republic) W DIS 3 Terry Norris 10.13 (USA), Las Vegas, USA (WBC L. Middleweight Title).

8 April 1995   Oliver McCall 16.7 (USA) W PTS 12 Larry Holmes 16.12 (USA), Las Vegas, USA (WBC Heavyweight Title). Scorecards: 115-112, 115-114, 114-113.

8 April 1995   Felix Trinidad 10.7 (Puerto Rico) W RSC 2 Roger Turner 10.7 (USA), Las Vegas, USA (IBF Welterweight Title).

22 April 1995   Francisco Tejedor 7.13 (Colombia) L PTS 12 Danny Romero 8.0 (USA), Las Vegas, USA (IBF Flyweight Title). Scorecards: 112-116, 112-115, 111-116.

22 April 1995   George Foreman 18.4 W PTS 12 Axel Schulz 15.11 (Germany), Las Vegas, USA (IBF Heavyweight Title). Scorecards: 115-113, 115-113, 114-114.

22 April 1995   Eddie Hopson 9.2 (USA) W CO 7 Moises Pedroza 9.4 (Colombia), Atlantic City, USA (Vacant IBF S. Featherweight Title).

25 April 1995   Miguel Gonzalez 9.8^1/$_2$ (Mexico) W PTS 12 Ricardo Silva 9.6^1/$_2$ (Argentine), South Padre Island, USA (WBC Lightweight Title). Scorecards: 119-109, 118-110, 118-110.

29 April 1995   Vince Pettway 10.12^1/$_4$ (USA) W CO 6 Simon Brown 11.0 (USA), Landover, USA (IBF L. Middleweight Title).

29 April 1995   Bernard Hopkins 11.4 (USA) W RSC 7 Segundo Mercado 11.6 (Ecuador), Landover, USA (Vacant IBF Middleweight Title).

29 April 1995   Harold Mestre 8.5^3/$_4$ (Colombia) L RSC 2 Mbulelo Botile 8.5^1/$_4$ (South Africa), Johannesburg, South Africa (IBF Bantamweight Title).

29 April 1995   Vuyani Bungu 8.10 (South Africa) W PTS 12 Victor Llerena 8.9^1/$_2$ (Colombia), Johannesburg, South Africa (IBF S. Bantamweight Title). Scorecards: 120-105, 118-108, 114-111.

6 May 1995   Oscar de la Hoya 9.8^3/$_4$ (USA) W RSC 2 Rafael Ruelas 9.9 (USA), Las Vegas, USA (WBO/IBF Lightweight Titles).

6 May 1995   Gabriel Ruelas 9.4 (USA) W RSC 11 Jimmy Garcia 9.3^1/$_2$ (Colombia), Las Vegas, USA (WBC S. Featherweight Title). Following the fight, Garcia went into a coma and later passed away following surgery for brain damage.

6 May 1995   Johnny Tapia 8.3 (USA) T DRAW 8 Ricardo Vargas 8.2 (Mexico), Las Vegas, USA (WBO S. Flyweight Title). Scorecards: 68-64, 66-66, 66-66.

7 May 1995   Saen Sorploenchit 7.13^1/$_2$ (Thailand) W PTS 12 Evangelio Perez 7.13^1/$_2$ (Panama), Songkhla, Thailand (WBA Flyweight Title). Scorecards: 117-111, 116-114, 116-113.

13 May 1995   Wifredo Vasquez 8.10 (Puerto Rico) L PTS 12 Antonio Cermeno 8.10 (Venezuela), Bayamon, Puerto Rico (WBA S. Bantamweight Title). Scorecards: 114-116, 114-116, 114-115.

15 May 1995   Orzubek Nazarov 9.9 (Russia) W CO 2 Won Park 9.9 (South Korea), Tokyo, Japan (WBA Lightweight Title).

17 May 1995   Verno Phillips 11.0 (USA) L PTS 12 Gianfranco Rosi 10.12^3/$_4$ (Italy), Perugia, Italy (WBO L. Middleweight Title). Referee: Paul Thomas. Scorecards: 113-115, 112-116, 114-116. Rosi forfeited title in June, having tested positive for amphetamines after the fight.

19 May 1995   Lonnie Bradley 11.6 (USA) W RSC 12 David Mendez 11.5 (Mexico), Jean, USA (Vacant WBO Middleweight Title). Steve Collins had vacated title following his victory over Chris Eubank for the WBO S. Middleweight Title.

20 May 1995   Dariusz Michalczewski 12.4^3/$_4$ (Germany) W CO 4 Paul Carlo 12.6^1/$_4$ (USA), Hamburg, Germany (WBO L. Heavyweight Title).

20 May 1995   Ratanapol Sowvoraphin 8.6^1/$_2$ (Thailand) W RSC 2 Oscar Flores 8.7 (Colombia), Chiang Mai, Thailand (IBF M. Flyweight Title).

24 May 1995   Hiroshi Kawashima 8.3 (Japan) W PTS 12 Seung-Koo Lee 8.2^3/$_4$ (South Korea), Yokohama, Japan (WBC S. Flyweight Title). Scorecards: 117-112, 116-111, 116-111.

27 May 1995   Eamonn Loughran 10.7 (Ireland) ND 3 Angel Beltre 10.5^3/$_4$ (Dominican Republic), King's Hall, Belfast (WBO Welterweight Title). Thinking that

Loughran had retained his title by a third round stoppage, the fans were probably surprised to find out the next morning that the verdict had been changed to that of no-decision. The end came at 2.23 of the third round when an accidental head clash left Beltre, seeping blood from a badly cut right-eyebrow, unable to continue. At the closure, British judge, Paul Thomas, had both men even.

27 May 1995   Henry Maske 12.6 (Germany) W PTS 12 Graciano Rocchigiani 12.5^1/$_2$ (Germany), Dortmund, Germany (IBF L. Heavyweight Title). Scorecards: 117-111, 116-113, 116-113.

27 May 1995   Daorung Chuwatana 8.6 (Thailand) DREW 12 Lakhin CP Gym 8.6 (Thailand), Bangkok, Thailand (WBA Bantamweight Title). Scorecards: 116-114, 115-115, 114-115.

27 May 1995   Frank Lilles 11.12^1/$_4$ (USA) W RSC 6 Frederic Seillier 11.13 (France), Fort Lauderdale, USA (WBA S. Middleweight Title).

27 May 1995   Jorge Castro 11.5^3/$_4$ (Argentine) W RSC 12 Anthony Andrews 11.4^1/$_4$ (Guyana), Fort Lauderdale, USA (WBA Middleweight Title).

27 May 1995   Eloy Rojas 8.13^3/$_4$ (Venezuela) W PTS 12 Yung-Kyun Park 9.0 (South Korea), Seoul, South Korea (WBA Featherweight Title). Scorecards: 118-109, 114-113, 113-114. Referee: John Coyle.

28 May 1995   Tom Johnson 8.13^1/$_2$ (USA) W PTS 12 Eddie Croft 8.13 (USA), South Padre Island, USA (IBF Featherweight Title). Scorecards: 120-108, 120-109, 119-109.

2 June 1995   Marco Antonio Barrera 8.10 (Mexico) W RSC 2 Frankie Toledo 8.9^3/$_4$ (USA), Ledyard, USA (WBO S. Bantamweight Title).

2 June 1995   Hector Acero-Sanchez 8.9^1/$_2$ (Dominican Republic) DREW 12 Daniel Zaragoza 8.10 (Mexico), Ledyard, USA (WBC S. Bantamweight Title). Scorecards: 114-112, 114-114, 114-114.

2 June 1995   Alejandro Gonzalez 9.0 (Mexico) W RSC 9 Tony Green 8.12^1/$_4$ (USA), Ledyard, USA (WBC Featherweight Title).

2 June 1995   Miguel Gonzalez 9.9 (Mexico) W PTS 12 Marty Jakubowski 9.8^1/$_4$ (USA), Ledyard, USA (WBC Lightweight Title). Scorecards: 120-109, 120-108, 119-109. Referee: Mickey Vann.

10 June 1995   Ralf Rocchigiani 13.5^1/$_2$ (Germany) W RSC 11 Carl Thompson 13.6 (England), G-Mex Centre, Manchester (Vacant WBO Cruiserweight Title). Well ahead on the judges' scorecards, the unfortunate Thompson dislocated his right shoulder in the tenth round. Earlier, the German, badly cut in the fourth, had put Thompson down twice in the fifth, only for the British fighter to smash his rival to the floor near the end of the session. By now, Rocchigiani's face was a bloody mess, but somehow his

seconds kept him in the fight. The fateful tenth saw Thompson on the floor, seemingly without taking a punch, but in the 11th, having been floored and in considerable pain, the referee pulled him out at 0.38 of the round.

10 June 1995   Sammy Fuentes 10.0 (Puerto Rico) W PTS 12 Hector Lopez 9.13^1/$_2$ (Mexico), Las Vegas, USA (WBO L. Welterweight Title). Scorecards: 114-111, 113-112, 112-113.

16 June 1995   Mike McCallum 12.6^1/$_4$ (Jamaica) L PTS 12 Fabrice Tiozzo 12.6^1/$_4$ (France), Lyon, France (WBC L. Heavyweight Title). Scorecards: John Keane 112-116, 112-115, 113-116.

16 June 1995   Carl Daniels 10.13^1/$_2$ (USA) W PTS 12 Julio Cesar Green 10.13^3/$_4$ (Dominican Republic), Lyon, France (Vacant WBA L. Middleweight Title). Scorecards: 119-107, 118-108, 115-111.

16 June 1995   Frankie Randall 10.0 (USA) W PTS 12 Jose Barbosa 9.13^1/$_2$ (Venezuela), Lyon, France (WBA L. Welterweight Title). Scorecards: 119-111, 116-114, 114-116.

17 June 1995   Alberto Jimenez 7.13^1/$_2$ (Mexico) W RTD 9 Robbie Regan 7.13^3/$_4$ (Wales), National Ice Rink, Cardiff (WBO Flyweight Title). While Gimenez proved to be one of the better fighters to have visited these shores, Regan, up against it right from the opening bell, showed courage beyond the call of duty, before being humanely retired by his corner. Although there were no knockdowns, the little Welshman finished with damage to both eyes and was never in with a real chance as the Mexican rattled in punches to both head and body, clearly dominating the proceedings.

17 June 1995   Riddick Bowe 17.5 (USA) W CO 6 Jorge Luis Gonzalez 16.13 (Cuba), Las Vegas, USA (WBO Heavyweight Title).

17 June 1995   Regilio Tuur 9.4 (Holland) W RSC 5 Pete Taliaferro 9.4 (USA), New Orleans, USA (WBO S. Featherweight Title).

24 June 1995   Al Cole 13.8 (USA) W PTS 12 Uriah Grant 13.6 (Jamaica), Atlantic City, USA (IBF Cruiserweight Title). Scorecards: 118-110, 117-111, 117-111.

24 June 1995   Roy Jones 12.0 (USA) W RSC 6 Vinny Pazienza 12.0 (USA), Atlantic City, USA (IBF S. Middleweight Title).

24 June 1995   Harold Grey 8.3 (Colombia) W PTS 12 Julio Cesar Borboa 8.2^1/$_2$ (Mexico), Cartagena, Colombia (IBF S. Flyweight Title). Scorecards: 116-112, 115-114, 113-115.

25 June 1995   Konstantin Tszyu 9.13^1/$_2$ (Russia) W PTS 12 Roger Mayweather 10.0 (USA), Newcastle, Australia (IBF L. Welterweight Title). Scorecards: 119-109, 118-110, 118-110.

The Old Man and the Rock

by Derek O'Dell

In February 1994, boxing lost one of its most underrated former heavyweight champions. "Jersey" Joe Walcott was 80 when he died and over a quarter of those four-score years were spent in earning a living with his fists.

It surprises me that the Walcott saga has never appeared in book form. There was enough drama, upset, excitement and pathos to assuage the requirements of half a dozen biographers, but nobody has taken up the opportunity to record one of the most poignant tales of the heavyweight division.

My first glimpse of him was on film in 1947, when the highlights of his first encounter with the great Joe Louis were shown on a newsreel at my local cinema. Even after allowing for the sharp decline in the "Brown Bomber's" skills, due to rust accumulated after war-time inactivity, it was clear that Walcott was a class act. He had a technical mastery of his craft that could never have appeared overnight, yet he was, to the general public, an unknown. The New York State Athletic Commission rated him a rank outsider, and, at first, recognised the fight as being no more than an exhibition, before conferring full championship status to it after a public outcry. Throughout history, a heavyweight champion's title has been at stake every time he has entered the ring.

Walcott had come up the hard way. On his record are several losses to what was, to those who knew of his capabilities, inferior opposition. With a large family to feed, he accepted many fights as a late substitute when he was not in shape. On one occasion, he'd gone for so long without a decent meal, that a body punch, thrown by a run-of-the-mill heavyweight, put him down for the full count. I suspect that some other losses came after reminders that his role was that of "opponent" and, as such, he was not in there to win. Prejudice against dark-skinned athletes – especially those who aspired to heavyweight boxing honours – was rife. They seldom dominated the headlines on sports pages. No – I've not overlooked that Joe Louis was of the same ethnic stock as Walcott, but he had long been accepted because of his exemplary public relations' record. Despite that, the ghosts of the Jack Johnson era still lingered. It was grossly unfair and unethical, but we British should not throw stones; it was 1948 before the iniquitous colour-bar was rescinded over here. Louis, a great man outside the ring, was instrumental in emancipating boxers of his race, and his greatness *inside* the ring was the reason for the long odds against Walcott.

In the eyes of most ringsiders and of the referee, "Jersey" Joe, who dropped Louis for two counts, was a clear winner. What mattered was the verdicts of the two judges who scored in favour of the champion. Louis tried to leave the ring before the decision was announced. His post-fight speech epitomised his honesty: "I'm not the fighter I was but there ain't gonna be no argument next time. I'll get him".

And next time he did "get him", but victory came only after 11 rounds in which Louis, trailing on points and embarrassed by his inability to fathom Walcott's style, had to climb off the deck to knock out his adversary. "Jersey" Joe fell into the trap that had snared Billy Conn back in 1941. He thought that he had the champion beaten and came down off his toes, planted his feet, and slugged it out. Louis struck. He was a deadly finisher and with a barrage redolent of his vintage years, he put Walcott down and out.

The search began for a new challenger, but eight months later, Louis announced his retirement and the National Boxing Association quickly paired Walcott with Ezzard Charles in a match for the vacant crown. The NYSAC recognised it as being the first in a series of eliminators, but, in reality, this was done to gain enough time to persuade Louis to change his mind. The old champion had other plans. He teamed up with Jim Norris and Arthur Wirtz to form the International Boxing Club, which eventually promoted the NBA approved Charles-Walcott clash.

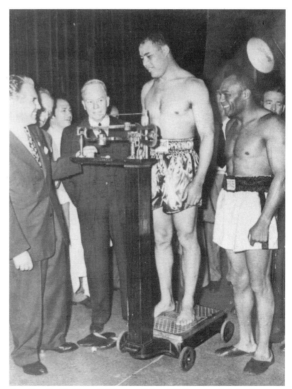

Joe Louis (left) and "Jersey" Joe Walcott weigh in for their first clash on 5 December 1947

Charles won on points but didn't exactly set the world on fire in so doing. Louis watched the proceedings from a ringside seat, from the safe confines of which he became convinced that he still had enough ability to see off the man who had unsurped his throne. He was wrong! Charles beat him – or rather the shadow of what had been Joe Louis – and the NYSAC then conferred their recognition. There was a political angle to this; both American bodies wanted the championship to remain in the States. In June 1950, some three months before Charles trimmed Louis, Lee Savold beat Bruce Woodcock in London and the fight carried a world championship label that was recognised by the British Boxing Board of Control. Savold never defended his title. Instead of cashing in, he remained inactive for a year and then rather unwisely, crossed gloves with Joe Louis, who disposed of him easily in six rounds. Louis' victory placed the British authorities in an embarrassing situation and further complicated the lineage of the heavyweight championship. The man who cleared up the mess turned out to be the ubiquitous "Jersey" Joe Walcott!

The year 1951 was a watershed for boxing. In the autumn, Louis was sent into permanent retirement when he was stopped by the rising prospect, Rocky Marciano. In July, Walcott, who was 37, upset huge odds when he knocked out Ezzard Charles with one of the hardest single punches ever thrown. He'd been on top throughout the fight which he brought to a sensational dénouement in the seventh round with a pile-driving left-hook. For a man who had lost twice to Charles and twice to Louis in fights that bore a world-championship tag, and who was regarded as being a "nearly" fighter, it was a remarkable and emotional victory – easily the most important of his long career. After 21 years of punching for pay, Walcott was champion and the title was not a fragmented one, but a version that was to be recognised world-wide. Yet his greatest performance – a career-best showing that surpassed that in which he destroyed Charles – was yet to come. In it, he was to lose his title, but not before he'd given a brilliant exhibition of fistic skills, stamina and accurate hitting in one of the best heavyweight fights of all-time.

The man who deposed Walcott was Rocky Marciano, an unbeaten Italian-American who had ended Joe Louis' career in 1951 when he, Marciano, was still an apprentice at his trade. Subsequently, he lost credibility when struggling to beat a former victim of Louis – the veteran Lee Savold, then regained his prestige by quickly disposing of Gino Buonvino and Bernie Reynolds. In late 1952, he moved into the number one contender's spot by impressively knocking out the highly-regarded Harry Matthews. Walcott then had a viable challenger and the pairing of this undefeated slugger with the polished and ringwise champion was an immediate box-office success. It pitted experience against tremendous power, ringcraft against durability, and technique against punch.

Search the record books from the beginning of gloved boxing, or back further to the bare-knuckle era, and you will not find another instance of a 38-year-old man matching the performance that Walcott gave that night. The old guy was magnificent. His timing, speed, hitting power and accuracy were superb. He showed a pride in his work, in his adaptability that is the hallmark of the great champions. Yet I thought he was committing fistic suicide when he came out at the first bell with both barrels blazing. Toe-to toe slugging was Marciano's métier, but he was the one who came off worse. The fight was only a minute old when a left-hook dumped him on the canvas! It was a duplicate of the punch that had separated Ezzard Charles from his senses, and from his title, but the effect was short-lived on Marciano who was up at "two" and fighting back so hard as the round ended, that he had Walcott backing off. You knew then that this was going to be one of the great fights – one of the classic confrontations, and so it turned out to be.

Marciano seemed to have a steel implant in his jaw. He was generally out-boxed and took some hefty blows that would have finished a lesser man, but he kept forcing the pace and made the older man fight hard *all* the time. Walcott could never coast nor relax his concentration. He had to dig deep into his bag of tricks, but what an assortment he had in that bag! In mid-ring he was the boss. There he could enfilade Marciano and side-step his rushes, but when forced back to the ropes by his tireless and persistent adversary, he had to call on all his 22-years' experience to survive. For 12 rounds his defence was sound. Nothing of devastating effect penetrated that barrier of gloves, elbows and shoulders. Walcott was in sight of a clear points win when, just over half a minute into the 13th round, he came off the ropes the wrong way – straight into the trajectory of a tremendous right-cross. This was the first serious mistake that "Jersey" Joe had made all night, and the moment that Marciano had awaited with the patience of a saint. As soon as that punch landed, we knew that the fight was over. Walcott froze; his left arm caught in the middle rope until his head drooped low enough to free him from that web. He was completely out and slowly keeled forward like sugar running out of a split bag. Reviewing his career in 1956, Marciano had no hesitation in naming that punch as being the best one that he ever landed. He also paid Walcott the compliment of having given him the hardest fight of his entire career. He was champion for four years during which he eradicated much of the clumsiness still evident when he gained the title. He defended against the best men around, most of whom were never the same force again, and retired unbeaten in 49 fights. He often fought when incapacitated by a painful back condition, despite which, he went on to become one of the mightiest fighters of modern times.

Having suffered a points defeat at the hands of Ezzard Charles on 7 March 1951, "Jersey" Joe Walcott (right) upset the form book with a seventh round kayo of the heavyweight champion some four months later

A boxer's style is influenced by his physique. Those of standard build can learn the basics and progress from that point, but Marciano was under six feet tall and the possessor of the shortest reach of any heavyweight champion. It was fortunate that he came under the tutelage of trainer Charlie Goldman before his pro career began to lift off. Now, I knew something about Goldman. I'd seen a lot of him in the gym when he came over here with Cesar Brion and Nick Barone. He was a genius. I've never seen a better trainer and it is possible that without the analytical wisdom and patience of this man, Marciano may never have achieved what he did.

Instead of teaching Marciano to box behind the jab, Goldman concentrated on perfecting Rocky's balance and from that came leverage. He taught him to nullify a taller opponent's reach by weaving beneath it and then to go for the body. He taught him how to cut off the ring from a back-pedalling adversary, to conserve strength, to concentrate and to appreciate the value of being in top condition. Goldman built a solid sub-strata on which the tremendously strong and dedicated Marciano was formed. He didn't teach him to punch, he didn't have to. That was an asset that aroused Goldman's interest when he first appraised the raw material presented to him in 1949, and so well did his charge use that asset, that only four men ever took him the distance. The others were sent home early. He defended his title against good men like Ezzard Charles, Roland LaStarza and Don Cockell, then rang down the curtain on a great career by stopping Archie Moore in another of boxing's great fights. He'd honed off the rough edges in his style long before then and had too much power, strength and determination for "Ancient Archie".

Marciano retired and the championship went into decline. The IBC, which had promoted all of the Rock's championship fights, was disbanded following an investigation into what was termed "monopolistic practices". Monopolies have continued to the present day. They can be curtailed for a while, but never stopped. The *real* reason for the vendetta against the IBC, was that its henchman, Jim Norris, was a close friend of the gangster, Frankie Carbo, who'd been a thorn in the side of every boxing commission since the war.

A hiatus followed in which the standard of heavyweight boxing and the way in which it was presented, went into decline. As a prominent world champion ruefully remarked: "With the IBC in control, we got fights and we got paid." It was not until another great boxer, Muhammad Ali, emerged in 1964, that the division regained its old appeal and entered a new golden age, but that is a whole story in itself. The object of *this* exercise is to pay tribute to "Jersey" Joe Walcott and also to Rocky Marciano for giving us that epic battle 42 years ago. I saw the action in a newsreel cinema which had the customary hour's entertainment running continuously, and sat through four showings of the fight before the manager quietly and firmly suggested to me that I had had my money's worth. Like the two protagonists on the big screen, we parted on good terms. He too was a fight fan and he too had viewed the action many times. A video tape of that fight rests on the shelf above me. I am glad to say that after 50 years of watching fights, I have not become so blasé that the action on that tape fails to thrill me, and the fight still rates as one of the best of my time.

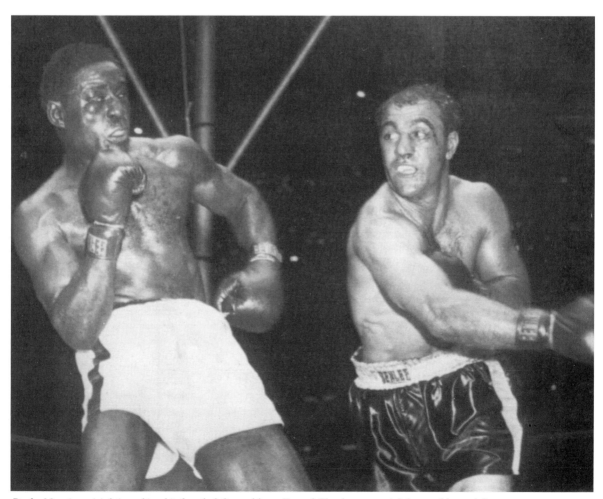

Rocky Marciano (right), making his fourth defence, blasts Ezzard Charles to an eighth round kayo defeat

World Title Bouts (L. Welterweight to Heavyweight) Since Gloves

In trying not to repeat myself too much, but for the benefit of new readers, this is the second of two instalments relating to every championship bout contested under Queensberry Rules (gloves and three minute rounds) that has been reported in record books as such, along with recent discoveries, since the introduction of two ounce gloves. Not included among the title listings, are fights with bare-knuckles, heavy driving gloves, or skin-tights, although these will be mentioned in the introduction to each weight class if they involved the succession.

Although last year's Yearbook did not clarify the first recognised gloved title bouts in the bantam, feather and lightweight divisions, that will be remedied in the 1997 edition, plus any new discoveries relating to fights already listed, plus many new ones which should be recognised as involving world championships in one way or another. These will include fights with championships billing which have never appeared in record books before, and whenever a champion or genuine claimant genuinely risked their title or claim, mainly in the no-decision era. Also, for reasons of space, an unofficial "Black" heavyweight title listing from the first George Godfrey through to Joe louis, has had to be shelved until the 1997 edition.

If one overlooks the no-decision era in America, which allowed boxers to ply their wares, with prize-fighting banned in many States, right through to the early 1930s, then one is merely ignoring the true development of world championship boxing as we know it today. However, while Georges Carpentier (light-heavy), Al McCoy, Mike O'Dowd (middles), Jack Britton (welter) and Benny Leonard (light), were all successful in claiming their titles, via no-decision bouts of ten rounds or more in duration, George Chip (middle) was the exception to the rule, achieving his recognition following two six round Pittsburgh club fights. Incidentally, the only way a champion could lose his title in a no-decision bout was if he failed to stipulate that his rival came in over the weight and was beaten inside the distance. Having scoured the American papers for announced weights, there are few available, especially for six round fights in Philadelphia, and one must assume that agreements between the fighters were normally in place. Where the prospective challenger's weight has been made available, and falls within the weight class, I have faithfully recorded it. Also, with weights not being standardised prior to 1920, a championship class fighter in Europe, for example, could find himself in a different weight division when campaigning in America. Another problem was in respect to the distinct lack of Boxing Commissions. The New York State Athletic Commission, properly formed in 1920, was the first of its kind in America, whilst the British Boxing Board of Control was not formed until 1929, although the NSC and leading promoters were working together from the early 1920s.

Without a true understanding of the sport's background, like myself for many years, you would probably think that the lists of champions and championship fights you occasionally see are gospel. Consider then, that all champions prior to say 1920 received their recognition from little more than various clubs and groups of people throughout the world of boxing and, above all, from the pressmen who covered the sport. Although many of the great fighters fought their way to the top, there were others who mainly owed their fame to a vociferous manager, false records, their own referees, betting syndicates, etc, etc.

Bearing all that in mind, it is hardly surprising when you read the American newspapers covering those early years, not only is there disagreement right across the country as to who is a champion and who is not, in many instances the weight classes become confused. For example, Tommy Ryan, weighing 152 lbs, was billed in a welter title defence in 1899 against Jack Moffatt, even though he had last made the weight class limit of 142 lbs some four years earlier and, at the time, was perceived to be a middleweight. A common occurrence in those days was for the better known fighters to carry their excess poundage right into the next weight class and still be recognised as champion of their former division.

What the British Boxing Yearbook team continues to do is to go back in time to research the papers across the world in an effort to assemble information in the way it was originally reported. Where we have found discrepancies in certain fights between the way it really was and the way they have since been portrayed, often due to over-zealous tidying up down the ages, we have made due note.

As in last Year's Yearbook, I would like to thank all those without whose help this extensive undertaking would not have been possible. With the expertise of Professor Luckett Davis and Harold Alderman, who are again properly thanked within the acknowledgements, Bob Soderman and Hy Rosenberg, on the other side of the Atlantic, and Bill Matthews and Derek O'Dell, here in Britain, the work continues to bear fruit. There are still, would you believe, more than 500 American fights between 1890 and 1930 still to assess, many not covered by the national newspapers, and I was heartened recently when Herb Goldman, the former editor of the Ring Record Book and the newly appointed editor of Boxing Illustrated in New York, agreed to utilise his resources in attempting to track some of these down. Herb, an old friend of mine, has long been in search of the truth regarding the early pioneering days of championship boxing, and work continues.

Country Code (Codes relate to place of domicile, not necessarily birthplace)
A-Australia; ARG-Argentina; ARM-Armenia; AU-Austria; BAH-Bahamas; BAR-Barbados; BEL-Belgium; BR-Brazil; C-Canada; CH-Chile; COL-Colombia; CR-Costa Rica; CUB-Cuba; CZ-Czechoslovakia; DEN-Denmark; DOM-Dominican Republic; EC-Ecuador; FIN-Finland; FR-France; GB-Great Britain; GER-Germany; GH-Ghana; GRE-Greece; GU-Guyana; HA-Hawaii; HOL-Holland; I-Ireland; IC-Ivory Coast; INDON-Indonesia; ITA-Italy; J-Jamaica; JAP-Japan; K-Kenya; MEX-Mexico; MOR-Morocco; N-Nigeria; NIC-Nicaragua; NOR-Norway; NZ-New Zealand; PAN-Panama; PAR-Paraguay; PE-Peru; PH-Philippines; PNG-Papua New Guinea; PR-Puerto Rico; SA-South Africa; SK-South Korea; SP-Spain; SWE-Sweden; SWI-Switzerland; TH-Thailand; TO-Togo; TR-Trinidad; TUN-Tunisia; U-Uganda; UR-Uruguay; USA-United States of America; VEN-Venezuela; YUG-Yugoslavia; ZA-Zambia.

Light-Welterweight (140 lbs)

Came into being in 1922 when Pinkey Mitchell was proclaimed world champion on 15 November, after the result of a "poll" taken by a weekly boxing magazine in Minneapolis called the Boxing Blade. Also known as the junior-welterweight and super-lightweight division, it was not until 1926 that the National Boxing Association gave it their support, followed by New York in 1927. Mitchell only defended his "title" in no-decision affairs, against Bud Logan in Milwaukee on 1 January 1923, Harvey Thorpe in Milwaukee on 13 April 1923, Nate Goldman in Philadelphia on 9 July 1923, Bobby Harper in Portland on 8 April 1924 and Al van Ryan in Sioux City on 10 June 1924, apart from boxing a ten round draw against Joe Simonich in Portland on 25 April 1924, in which Simonich failed to make the weight, before facing Mushy Callahan under the auspices of the NBA. Earlier, it had been thought that Mitchell had lost his title by a seventh round disqualification against Jimmy Herring in Detroit on 27 March 1925, but it has recently been discovered that Herring agreed to come into the fight at 145 lbs.

21.09.26 Mushy Callahan (USA) W PTS 10 Pinkey Mitchell (USA), Los Angeles - NBA

22.10.26 Mushy Callahan (USA) W CO 2 Charlie Pitts (A), Los Angeles - NBA. *Not recorded in the Ring Record Book as a title fight, the Los Angeles Times (newspaper) reported, without mention of weights, that seldom does a champion risk his championship honours in an ordinary affair against a man from his own weight class such as Callahan did tonight.*

14.03.27 Mushy Callahan (USA) W CO 2 Andy Divodi (USA), New York City - NBA/NY

31.05.27 Mushy Callahan (USA) W PTS 10 Spug Myers (USA), Chicago - NBA/NY

28.05.29 Mushy Callahan (USA) W CO 3 Fred Mahan (USA), Los Angeles - NBA/NY

18.02.30 Jackie Kid Berg (GB) W RTD 10 Mushy Callahan (USA), Albert Hall, London - NBA. *Following the decision by the NYSAC on 1 January 1930 not to recognise "Junior" weight classes in future and the fact that the BBBoC also did not acknowledge the ten stone division, while billed as a title fight, it had gone ahead with the support of the NBA, only.*

Jackie Kid Berg, England's world junior-lightweight champion

04.04.30 Jackie Kid Berg (GB) W PTS 10 Joe Glick (USA), New York City. *Although unable to be billed as a championship fight in New York, Berg always considered his title to be on the line when his opponent made the weight. The Ring Magazine fully supported this notion and with Glick weighing 137¼ lbs, recognised it as a title fight.*

29.05.30 Jackie Kid Berg (GB) W RSC 4 Al Delmont (USA), Newark - NBA

11.06.30 Jackie Kid Berg (GB) W PTS 10 Herman Perlick (USA), Long Island. *With Perlick weighing 138½ lbs, Berg's title was at stake.*

07.08.30 Jackie Kid Berg (GB) W PTS 10 Kid Chocolate (CUB), New York City. *The title was at stake with Berg weighing 135 lbs to Chocolate's 124.*

03.09.30 Jackie Kid Berg (GB) W PTS 10 Buster Brown (USA), Newark - NBA

18.09.30 Jackie Kid Berg (GB) W PTS 10 Joe Glick (USA), Long Island. *Berg's title was up for grabs, with Glick weighing-in at 139 lbs.*

10.10.30 Jackie Kid Berg (GB) W PTS 10 Billy Petrolle (USA), New York City. *Petrolle weighed 137 lbs and would have undoubtedly claimed Berg's title had he won.*

13.01.31 Jackie Kid Berg (GB) W PTS 10 Goldie Hess (USA), Chicago - NBA

30.01.31 Jackie Kid Berg (GB) W PTS 10 Herman Perlick (USA), New York City. *Another New York "title defence" saw Berg risk his crown yet again against Perlick, who scaled 139 lbs.*

10.04.31 Jackie Kid Berg (GB) W PTS 10 Billy Wallace (USA), Detroit - NBA

24.04.31 Tony Canzoneri (USA) W CO 3 Jackie Kid Berg (GB), Chicago - NBA. *Following the fight, Berg claimed he had been contracted to contest the lightweight title, only, and that his light-welterweight crown was safe because different titles at different weights could not be at stake during the same bout. That did not wear with the NBA, even though Berg had been forced to reduce to 135 lbs in order to challenge Canzoneri. However, support again came in the shape of the prestigious Ring Magazine and Berg continued to style himself as champion.*

08.05.31 Jackie Kid Berg (GB) W PTS 10 Tony Herrera (USA), New York City. *Recognised by the Ring Magazine as champion, everytime Berg allowed an opponent to come to the ring inside 140 lbs and wherever he fought, that recognition was always technically at stake. For this one, Berg weighed 137¾ lbs to Herrera's 138½.*

18.05.31 Jackie Kid Berg (GB) W PTS 10 Ray Kiser (USA), Pittsburgh. *Berg weighed 137½ lbs to Kiser's 138½.*

22.06.31 Jackie Kid Berg (GB) W RSC 8 Tony Lambert (USA), Newark. *Berg weighed 139 lbs to Lambert's 140.*

25.06.31 Tony Canzoneri (USA) W PTS 10 Herman Perlick (USA), New Haven. *With Perlick scaling 140 lbs to Canzoneri's 134, the latter's newly won NBA recognised title would have been at stake although there was no mention of that being the case in the New York Times (newspaper) report of the fight.*

13.07.31 Tony Canzoneri (USA) W PTS 10 Cecil Payne (USA), Los Angeles - NBA

24.07.31 Jackie Kid Berg (GB) W CO 7 Teddy Watson (USA), Jersey City. *Both men were announced as being inside 139 lbs.*

27.07.31 Jackie Kid Berg (GB) W PTS 10 Phillie Griffin (USA), Newark. *Berg weighed 138 lbs to Griffin's 140.*

04.08.31 Jackie Kid Berg (GB) W PTS 10 Jimmy McNamara (USA), New York City. *Berg weighed 137 lbs to McNamara's 138.*

10.09.31 Tony Canzoneri (USA) W PTS 15 Jackie Kid Berg (GB), New York City. *This was billed as a lightweight defence, but given the logic of the NBA, although fought at a contracted weight five pounds below the light-welter mark and in a State that failed to recognise the 140 lbs division, Canzoneri's title was at stake.*

20.11.31 Tony Canzoneri (USA) W PTS 15 Kid Chocolate (CUB), New York City. *A billed lightweight title fight, saw Canzoneri's 140 lbs championship belt also at stake.*

29.10.31 Tony Canzoneri (USA) W PTS 10 Phillie Griffin (USA), Newark - NBA

14.12.31 Jackie Kid Berg (GB) W RSC 5 Marius Baudry (FR), Albert Hall, London. *Billed as a title bout, but only supported by the Ring Magazine, who still recognised Berg as the rightful champion.*

18.01.32 Johnny Jadick (USA) W PTS 10 Tony Canzoneri (USA), Philadelphia - NBA

01.04.32 Jackie Kid Berg (GB) DREW 10 Sammy Fuller (USA), New York City. *Berg weighed 138½ lbs to Fuller's 136¼.*

20.05.32 Sammy Fuller (USA) W PTS 12 Jackie Kid Berg (GB), New York City. *With Berg still recognised by the Ring Magazine and Fuller weighing 138 lbs, the Englishman's claim to the title passed to the winner.*

18.07.32 Johnny Jadick (USA) W PTS 10 Tony Canzoneri (USA), Philadelphia - NBA. *On 20 September 1932, the NBA also*

decided not to recognise the "junior" divisions in future, although independent States such as Pennsylvania, California, Illinois and Louisiana, plus Washington, Florida, Missouri and Ohio, were happy to support their own champions or contests taking place on home territory.

20.02.33 Battling Shaw (MEX) W PTS 10 Johnny Jadick (USA), New Orleans - LOUISIANA

17.04.33 Battling Shaw (MEX) W PTS 10 Tommy Grogan (USA), New Orleans - LOUISIANA. *The New Orleans Daily Picayune (newspaper), in the pre-fight build up, referred to the fact that Shaw's title would be on the line and that Grogan was a dangerous challenger who had twice troubled Tony Canzoneri and, in his last outing, had given Barney Ross a run for his money. We may never know if the title was ever intended to be involved or whether the match was contracted at catchweights, but, with Grogan weighing in at 143^1/$_2$ lbs to Shaw's 138^3/$_4$, we can be sure that this was no championship fight.*

27.04.33 Cleto Locatelli (ITA) W PTS 10 Jackie Kid Berg (GB), Albert Hall, London. *Having returned home from America and with both men inside 140 lbs, promoter, Jeff Dickson, billed this one as a title defence for Berg. However, whatever claim he might have had after the Canzoneri fights had been well and truly lost against Fuller and, following this defeat, the title was never brought up again as far as both Berg and Locatelli were concerned.*

21.05.33 Tony Canzoneri (USA) W PTS 10 Battling Shaw (MEX), New Orleans - LOUISIANA

23.06.33 Barney Ross (USA) W PTS 10 Tony Canzoneri (USA), Chicago - ILLINOIS. *Ross also won Canzoneri's lightweight title at the same time, with both men inside 135 lbs.*

26.07.33 Barney Ross (USA) W RSC 6 Johnny Farr (USA), Kansas City - ILLINOIS/MISSOURI

12.09.33 Barney Ross (USA) W PTS 15 Tony Canzoneri (USA), New York City. *Billed as a lightweight title fight, although outside the jurisdiction of the Illinois State Commission, Ross' light-welterweight belt was also at stake.*

17.11.33 Barney Ross (USA) W PTS 10 Sammy Fuller (USA), Chicago - ILLINOIS. *With the result, Fuller finally lost his claim to be recognised as the rightful titleholder.*

07.02.34 Barney Ross (USA) W PTS 12 Pete Nebo (USA), New Orleans - ILLINOIS/LOUISIANA

05.03.34 Barney Ross (USA) DREW 10 Frankie Klick (USA), San Francisco - ILLINOIS/CALIFORNIA

27.03.34 Barney Ross (USA) W PTS 10 Bobby Pacho (USA), Los Angeles - ILLINOIS/CALIFORNIA

10.12.34 Barney Ross (USA) W PTS 12 Boby Pacho (USA), Cleveland - ILLINOIS/OHIO

28.01.35 Barney Ross (USA) W PTS 10 Frankie Klick (USA), Miami - ILLINOIS/FLORIDA

09.04.35 Barney Ross (USA) W PTS 12 Harry Woods (USA), Seattle - ILLINOIS/WASHINGTON. *Ross relinquished the Illinois version of the title after regaining the world welterweight crown in June 1935 and the weight class went into hibernation until Maxie Berger resurrected it in Montreal some four years later.*

05.07.39 Maxie Berger (C) W PTS 10 Wesley Ramey (USA), Montreal - CANADA. *Billed as a world title fight and recognised as such by the Montreal Boxing Commission, who recommended that the NBA revive the weight class, Berger weighed 139^3/$_4$ lbs to Ramey's 132^3/$_4$. Berger failed to capitalise on his newly gained title and soon after moved up to welter.*

28.10.40 Harry Weekly (USA) W PTS 15 Jerome Conforto (USA), New Orleans - LOUISIANA

27.06.41 Harry Weekly (USA) W PTS 10 Carmelo Fenoy (USA), Birmingham - LOUISIANA/ALABAMA

28.07.41 Harry Weekly (USA) W PTS 15 Baby Breese (USA), New Orleans - LOUISIANA

20.10.41 Harry Weekly (USA) W CO 5 Ervin Berlier (USA), New Orleans - LOUISIANA. *Weekly was inducted into the US Army in May 1942 and his claim to the title was abandoned. With the weight class clearly out of favour, and with war raging throughout the world, it would be another four years before there was further activity.*

29.04.46 Tippy Larkin (USA) W PTS 12 Willie Joyce (USA), Boston - MASSACHUSETTS

13.09.46 Tippy Larkin (USA) W PTS 12 Willie Joyce (USA), New York City - NY/MASSACHUSETTS. *Larkin forfeited NY/Massachusetts recognition following a fourth round defeat by Ike Williams in a non-title bout on 20 June 1947 (New York City) and the weight class fell into disuse.*

21.04.54 Freddie Dawson (USA) W PTS 15 George Barnes (A), Sydney. *Billed for the Junior-welterweight title by the Australian Boxing Club, Dawson came in at 142 lbs and was forced to pay a forfeit.*

Nobody, even in Australia, took the fight seriously, recognising it for what it was, in putting money on the gate.

12.06.59 Carlos Ortiz (USA) W RTD 2 Kenny Lane (USA), New York City - NBA

04.02.60 Carlos Ortiz (USA) W CO 10 Battling Torres (MEX), Los Angeles - NBA

15.06.60 Carlos Ortiz (PR) W PTS 15 Duillio Loi (ITA), San Francisco - NBA

01.09.60 Duillio Loi (ITA) W PTS 15 Carlos Ortiz (PR), Milan - NBA

10.05.61 Duillio Loi (ITA) W PTS 15 Carlos Ortiz (PR), Milan - NBA

21.10.61 Duillio Loi (ITA) DREW 15 Eddie Perkins (USA), Milan - NBA

14.09.62 Eddie Perkins (USA) W PTS 15 Duillio Loi (ITA), Milan - NBA

15.12.62 Duillio Loi (ITA) W PTS 15 Eddie Perkins (USA), Milan - NBA. *Duillio Loi retired as undefeated champion in January 1963.*

21.03.63 Roberto Cruz (PH) W CO 1 Battling Torres (MEX), Los Angeles - WBA

15.06.63 Eddie Perkins (USA) W PTS 15 Roberto Cruz (PH), Manila - WBA

04.01.64 Eddie Perkins (USA) W RSC 13 Yoshinori Takahashi (JAP), Tokyo - WBA

18.04.64 Eddie Perkins (USA) W PTS 15 Bunny Grant (J), Kingston - WBA

18.01.65 Carlos Hernandez (VEN) W PTS 15 Eddie Perkins (USA), Caracas - WBA

15.05.65 Carlos Hernandez (VEN) W RSC 4 Mario Rossito (COL), Maracaibo - WBA

10.07.65 Carlos Hernandez (VEN) W CO 3 Percy Hayles (J), Kingston - WBA

30.04.66 Sandro Lopopolo (ITA) W PTS 15 Carlos Hernandez (VEN), Rome - WBA

21.10.66 Sandro Lopopolo (ITA) W RSC 7 Vicente Rivas (VEN), Rome - WBA

30.04.67 Paul Fujii (USA) W RTD 2 Sandro Lopopolo (ITA), Tokyo - WBA

16.11.67 Paul Fujii (USA) W CO 4 Willi Quatuor (GER), Tokyo - WBA

12.12.68 Nicolino Loche (ARG) W RTD 9 Paul Fujii (USA), Tokyo - WBA

14.12.68 Pedro Adigue (PH) W PTS 15 Adolph Pruitt (USA), Quezon City - WBC

03.05.69 Nicolino Loche (ARG) W PTS 15 Carlos Hernandez (VEN), Buenos Aires - WBA

11.10.69 Nicolino Loche (ARG) W PTS 15 Joao Henrique (BR), Buenos Aires - WBA

01.02.70 Bruno Arcari (ITA) W PTS 15 Pedro Adigue (PH), Rome - WBC

16.05.70 Nicolino Loche (ARG) W PTS 15 Adolph Pruitt (USA), Buenos Aires - WBA

10.07.70 Bruno Arcari (ITA) W DIS 6 Rene Roque (FR), Lignano - WBC

30.10.70 Bruno Arcari (ITA) W CO 3 Raymundo Dias (BR), Genoa - WBC

06.03.71 Bruno Arcari (ITA) W PTS 15 Joao Henrique (BR), Rome - WBC

03.04.71 Nicolino Loche (ARG) W PTS 15 Domingo Barrera (SP), Buenos Aires - WBA

26.06.71 Bruno Arcari (ITA) W RSC 9 Enrique Jana (ARG), Palermo - WBC

10.10.71 Bruno Arcari (ITA) W CO 10 Domingo Barrera (SP), Genoa - WBC

11.12.71 Nicolino Loche (ARG) W PTS 15 Antonio Cervantes (COL), Buenos Aires - WBA

10.03.72 Alfonso Frazer (PAN) W PTS 15 Nicolino Loche (ARG), Panama City - WBA

10.06.72 Bruno Arcari (ITA) W CO 12 Joao Henrique (BR), Genoa - WBC

17.06.72 Alfonso Frazer (PAN) W RTD 4 Al Ford (C), Panama City - WBA

28.10.72 Antonio Cervantes (COL) W CO 10 Alfonso Frazer (PAN), Panama City - WBA

02.12.72 Bruno Arcari (ITA) W PTS 15 Costa Azevedo (BR), Turin - WBC

16.02.73 Antonio Cervantes (COL) W PTS 15 Josua Marquez (PR), San Juan - WBA

17.03.73 Antonio Cervantes (COL) W RTD 9 Nicolino Loche (ARG), Maracay - WBA

19.05.73 Antonio Cervantes (COL) W RSC 5 Alfonso Frazer (PAN), Panama City - WBA

08.09.73 Antonio Cervantes (COL) W RSC 5 Carlos Giminez (ARG), Bogota - WBA

01.11.73 Bruno Arcari (ITA) W CO 5 Jorgen Hansen (DEN), Copenhagen - WBC. *Billed as a title fight, Arcari's title was safeguarded after Hansen came to the ring one pound overweight.*

04.12.73 Antonio Cervantes (COL) W PTS 15 Lion Furuyama (JAP), Panama City - WBA

16.02.74 Bruno Arcari (ITA) W DIS 8 Tony Ortiz (SP), Turin - WBC.

Arcari relinquished WBC version of the title in August 1974, due to weight making difficulties.

02.03.74 Antonio Cervantes (COL) W CO 6 Chang-Kil Lee (SK), Cartagena - WBA

27.07.74 Antonio Cervantes (COL) W CO 2 Victor Ortiz (PR), Cartagena - WBA

21.09.74 Perico Fernandez (SP) W PTS 15 Lion Furuyama (JAP), Rome - WBC

26.10.74 Antonio Cervantes (COL) W CO 8 Shinchi Kadoto (JAP), Tokyo - WBA

19.04.74 Perico Fernandez (SP) W CO 9 Joao Henrique (BR), Barcelona - WBC

17.05.75 Antonio Cervantes (COL) W PTS 15 Esteban de Jesus (PR), Panama City - WBA

15.07.75 Saensak Muangsurin (TH) W RTD 8 Perico Fernandez (SP), Bangkok - WBC

15.11.75 Antonio Cervantes (COL) W RTD 7 Hector Thompson (A), Panama City - WBA

25.01.76 Saensak Muangsurin (TH) W PTS 15 Lion Furuyama (JAP), Tokyo - WBC

06.03.76 Wilfred Benitez (PR) W PTS 15 Antonio Cervantes (COL), San Juan - WBA

31.05.76 Wilfred Benitez (PR) W PTS 15 Emiliano Villa (COL), San Juan - WBA

30.06.76 Miguel Velasquez (SP) W DIS 4 Saensak Muangsurin (TH), Madrid - WBC

16.10.76 Wilfred Benitez (PR) W RSC 3 Tony Petronelli (USA), San Juan - WBA. *Benitez forfeited WBA recognition in December 1976 for failing to defend against Antonio Cervantes.*

29.10.76 Saensak Muangsurin (TH) W RSC 2 Miguel Velasquez (SP), Segovia - WBC

05.01.77 Saensak Muangsurin (TH) W RSC 15 Monroe Brooks (USA), Chiang - WBC

02.04.77 Saensak Muangsurin (TH) W CO 6 Guts Ishimatsu (JAP), Tokyo - WBC

17.06.77 Saensak Muangsurin (TH) W PTS 15 Perico Fernandez (SP), Madrid - WBC

25.06.77 Antonio Cervantes (COL) W RSC 5 Carlos Giminez (ARG), Maracaibo - WBA

03.08.77 Wilfred Benitez (PR) W RSC 15 Guerrero Chavez (C), New York City - NY. *As the number one contender for the world welterweight title, although still officially holding the New York version of the light-welterweight crown, it was clear that Wilfred Benitez wouldn't make ten stone again following a six round stoppage win over Randy Shields on 25 August 1978 (New York City) and after the fight he announced that in future he would only fight at a higher poundage.*

20.08.77 Saensak Muangsurin (TH) W RSC 6 Mike Everett (USA), Roi-Et - WBC

22.10.77 Saensak Muangsurin (TH) W PTS 15 Saoul Mamby (USA), Korat - WBC

05.11.77 Antonio Cervantes (COL) W PTS 15 Adriano Marrero (DOM), Maracay - WBA

29.12.77 Saensak Muangsurin (TH) W RTD 13 Jo Kimpuani (FR), Chanthabun - WBC

08.04.78 Saensak Muangsurin (TH) W CO 13 Francisco Moreno (VEN), Hat Yai - WBC

28.04.78 Antonio Cervantes (COL) W CO 6 Tonga Kiatvayupakdi (TH), Udon - WBA

26.08.78 Antonio Cervantes (COL) W RSC 9 Norman Sekgapane (SA), Botswana - WBA

30.12.78 Sang-Hyun Kim (SK) W CO 13 Saensak Muangsurin (TH), Seoul - WBC

18.01.79 Antonio Cervantes (COL) W PTS 15 Miguel Montilla (DOM), New York City - WBA

03.06.79 Sang-Hyun Kim (SK) W PTS 15 Fitzroy Guisseppi (TR), Seoul - WBC

25.08.79 Antonio Cervantes (COL) W PTS 15 Kwang-Min Kim (SK), Seoul - WBA

04.10.79 Sang-Hyun Kim (SK) W CO 11 Masahiro Yokai (JAP), Tokyo - WBC

23.02.80 Saoul Mamby (USA) W CO 14 Sang-Hyun Kim (SK), Seoul - WBC

29.03.80 Antonio Cervantes (COL) W RSC 7 Miguel Montilla (DOM), Cartegena - WBA

07.07.80 Saoul Mamby (USA) W RSC 13 Esteban de Jesus (PR), Bloomington - WBC

02.08.80 Aaron Pryor (USA) W CO 4 Antonio Cervantes (COL), Cincinnati - WBA

02.10.80 Saoul Mamby (USA) W PTS 15 Maurice Watkins (USA), Las Vegas - WBC

22.11.80 Aaron Pryor (USA) W RSC 6 Gaetan Hart (USA), Cincinnati - WBA

12.06.81 Saoul Mamby (USA) W PTS 15 Jo Kimpuani (FR), Detroit - WBC

27.06.81 Aaron Pryor (USA) W RSC 2 Lennox Blackmore (GU), Las Vegas - WBA

29.08.81 Saoul Mamby (USA) W PTS 15 Thomas Americo (INDON), Jakarta - WBC

14.11.81 Aaron Pryor (USA) W RSC 7 Dujuan Johnson (USA), Cleveland - WBA

20.12.81 Saoul Mamby (USA) W PTS 15 Obisia Nwankpa (N), Lagos - WBC

21.03.82 Aaron Pryor (USA) W RSC 12 Miguel Montilla (DOM), Atlantic City - WBA

26.06.82 Leroy Haley (USA) W PTS 15 Saoul Mamby (USA), Cleveland - WBC

04.07.82 Aaron Pryor (USA) W RSC 6 Akio Kameda (JAP), Cincinnati - WBA

20.10.82 Leroy Haley (USA) W PTS 15 Juan Giminez (ARG), Cleveland - WBC

12.11.82 Aaron Pryor (USA) W RSC 14 Alexis Arguello (NIC), Miami - WBA

13.02.83 Leroy Haley (USA) W PTS 12 Saoul Mamby (USA), Cleveland - WBC

02.04.83 Aaron Pryor (USA) W RSC 3 Sang-Hyun Kim (SK), Atlantic City - WBA

18.05.83 Bruce Curry (USA) W PTS 12 Leroy Haley (USA), Las Vegas - WBC

07.07.83 Bruce Curry (USA) W RSC 7 Hidekazu Akai (JAP), Osaka - WBC

09.09.83 Aaron Pryor (USA) W CO 10 Alexis Arguello (NIC), Las Vegas - WBA. *Aaron Pryor relinquished WBA version of title and was proclaimed IBF champion in January 1984.*

19.10.83 Bruce Curry (USA) W PTS Leroy Haley (USA), Las Vegas - WBC

22.01.84 Johnny Bumphus (USA) W PTS 15 Lorenzo Garcia (ARG), Atlantic City - WBA

29.01.84 Bill Costello (USA) W RSC 10 Bruce Curry (USA), Beaumont - WBC

01.06.84 Gene Hatcher (USA) W RSC 11 Johnny Bumphus (USA), Buffalo - WBA

22.06.84 Aaron Pryor (USA) W PTS 15 Nicky Furlano (C), Toronto - IBF

15.07.84 Bill Costello (USA) W PTS 12 Ronnie Shields (USA), Kingston, NY - WBC

03.11.84 Bill Costello (USA) W PTS 12 Saoul Mamby (USA), Kingston, NY - WBC

15.12.84 Gene Hatcher (USA) W PTS 15 Ubaldo Sacco (ARG), Fort Worth - WBA

16.02.85 Bill Costello (USA) W PTS 12 Leroy Haley (USA), Kingston, NY - WBC

02.03.85 Aaron Pryor (USA) W PTS 15 Gary Hinton (USA), Atlantic City - IBF. *Aaron Pryor forfeited IBF recognition in December 1985 due to inactivity.*

21.07.85 Ubaldo Sacco (ARG) W RSC 9 Gene Hatcher (USA), Campione - WBA

21.08.85 Lonnie Smith (USA) W RSC 8 Bill Costello (USA), New York City - WBC

15.03.86 Patrizio Oliva (ITA) W PTS 15 Ubaldo Sacco (ARG), Monaco - WBA

26.04.86 Gary Hinton (USA) W PTS 15 Antonio Reyes Cruz (DOM), Lucca - IBF

05.05.86 Rene Arredondo (MEX) W RSC 5 Lonnie Smith (USA), Los Angeles - WBC

24.07.86 Tsuyoshi Hamada (JAP) W CO 1 Rene Arredondo (MEX), Tokyo - WBC

06.09.86 Patrizio Oliva (ITA) W RSC 3 Brian Brunette (USA), Naples - WBA

30.10.86 Joe Manley (USA) W CO 10 Gary Hinton (USA), Hartford - IBF

02.12.86 Tsuyoshi Hamada (JAP) W PTS 12 Ronnie Shields (USA), Tokyo - WBC

10.01.87 Patrizio Oliva (ITA) W PTS 15 Rodolfo Gonzalez (MEX), Agrigento - WBA

04.03.87 Terry Marsh (GB) W RSC 10 Joe Manley (USA), Festival Hall Super Tent, Basildon - IBF

01.07.87 Terry Marsh (GB) W RTD 6 Akio Kameda (JAP), Albert Hall, London - IBF. *Terry Marsh retired as undefeated IBF champion in September 1987.*

04.07.87 Juan M. Coggi (ARG) W CO 3 Patrizio Oliva (ITA), Ribera - WBA

22.07.87 Rene Arredondo (MEX) W RSC 6 Tsuyoshi Hamada (JAP), Tokyo - WBC

12.11.87 Roger Mayweather (USA) W RSC 6 Rene Arredondo (MEX), Los Angeles - WBC

14.02.88 James McGirt (USA) W RSC 12 Frankie Warren (USA), Corpus Christi - IBF

24.03.88 Roger Mayweather (USA) W CO 3 Mauricio Aceves (MEX), Los Angeles - WBC

07.05.88 Juan M. Coggi (ARG) W CO 2 Sang-Ho Lee (SK), Roseto - WBA

06.06.88 Roger Mayweather (USA) W PTS 12 Harold Brazier (USA), Las Vegas - WBC

31.07.88 James McGirt (USA) W CO 1 Howard Davis (USA), New York City - IBF

03.09.88 Meldrick Taylor (USA) W RSC 12 James McGirt (USA), Atlantic City - IBF

22.09.88 Roger Mayweather (USA) W RSC 12 Rodolfo Gonzalez (MEX), Los Angeles - WBC

07.11.88 Roger Mayweather (USA) W PTS 12 Vinny Pazienza (USA), Las Vegas - WBC

21.01.89 Juan M. Coggi (ARG) W PTS 12 Harold Brazier (USA), Vasto - WBA

21.01.89 Meldrick Taylor (USA) W RSC 7 John Meekins (USA), Atlantic City - IBF

06.03.89 Hector Camacho (PR) W PTS 12 Ray Mancini (USA), Reno - WBO

29.04.89 Juan M. Coggi (ARG) W PTS 12 Akinobu Hiranaka (JAP), Vasto - WBA

13.05.89 Julio Cesar Chavez (MEX) W RTD 10 Roger Mayweather (USA), Los Angeles - WBC

11.09.89 Meldrick Taylor (USA) W PTS 12 Courtney Hooper (USA), Atlantic City - IBF

18.11.89 Julio Cesar Chavez (MEX) W RSC 10 Sammy Fuentes (USA), Las Vegas - WBC

16.12.89 Julio Cesar Chavez (MEX) W CO 3 Alberto Cortes (ARG), Mexico City - WBC

03.02.90 Hector Camacho (PR) W PTS 12 Vinny Pazienza (USA), Atlantic City - WBO

17.03.90 Julio Cesar Chavez (MEX) W RSC 12 Meldrick Taylor (USA), Las Vegas - IBF/WBC

24.03.90 Juan M. Coggi (ARG) W PTS 12 Jose Luis Ramirez (MEX), Arjaccio - WBA

11.08.90 Hector Camacho (PR) W PTS 12 Tony Baltazar (USA), Stateline - WBO

17.08.90 Loreta Garza (USA) W PTS 12 Juan M. Coggi (ARG), Nice - WBA

01.12.90 Loreta Garza (USA) W DIS 11 Vinny Pazienza (USA), Sacramento - WBA

08.12.90 Julio Cesar Chavez (MEX) W RSC 3 Kyung-Duk Ahn (SK), Atlantic City - IBF/WBC

23.02.91 Greg Haugen (USA) W PTS 12 Hector Camacho (PR), Las Vegas - WBO. *Greg Haugen forfeited title in March 1991 when failing post-fight drug test.*

18.03.91 Julio Cesar Chavez (MEX) W RSC 4 John Duplessis (USA), Las Vegas - IBF/WBC. *Julio Cesar Chavez relinquished IBF version of title in April 1991 rather than defend against Rafael Pineda on a Bob Arum promotion.*

18.05.91 Hector Camacho (PR) W PTS 12 Greg Haugen (USA), Reno - WBO. *Hector Camacho forfeited WBO version of title in March 1992 after failing to comply with the WBO's terms and conditions.*

14.06.91 Edwin Rosario (PR) W RSC 3 Loreta Garza (USA), Sacramento - WBA

14.09.91 Julio Cesar Chavez (MEX) W PTS 12 Lonny Smith (USA), Las Vegas - WBC

07.12.91 Rafael Pineda (COL) W RSC 9 Roger Mayweather (USA), Reno - IBF

10.04.92 Julio Cesar Chavez (MEX) W CO 5 Angel Hernandez (PR), Mexico City - WBC

10.04.92 Akinobu Hiranaka (JAP) W RSC 1 Edwin Rosario (PR), Mexico City - WBA

22.05.92 Rafael Pineda (COL) W RSC 7 Clarence Coleman (USA), Mexico City - IBF

30.06.92 Carlos Gonzalez (MEX) W RSC 2 Jimmy Paul (USA), Los Angeles - WBO

18.07.92 Pernell Whitaker (USA) W PTS 12 Rafael Pineda (COL), Las Vegas - IBF. *Pernell Whitaker relinquished IBF version of title on becoming WBC welterweight champion in March 1993.*

01.08.92 Julio Cesar Chavez (MEX) W RSC 4 Frankie Mitchell (USA), Las Vegas - WBC

09.09.92 Morris East (PH) W RSC 11 Akinobu Hiranaka (JAP), Tokyo - WBA

12.09.92 Julio Cesar Chavez (MEX) W PTS 12 Hector Camacho (PR), Las Vegas - WBC

09.11.92 Carlos Gonzalez (MEX) W RTD 6 Lorenzo Smith (USA), Los Angeles - WBO

14.12.92 Carlos Gonzalez (MEX) W RSC 1 Rafael Ortiz (DOM), Mexico City - WBO

13.01.93 Juan M. Coggi (ARG) W RSC 8 Morris East (PH), Mar del Plata - WBA

20.02.93 Julio Cesar Chavez (MEX) W RSC 5 Greg Haugen (USA), Mexico City - WBC. *Fighting in front of his own fans, and not forgetting that there were three other world title bouts on the same bill, Nelson v Ruelas (S. Feather), Norris v Blocker (L. Middle) and Nunn v Morgan (S. Middle), Chavez was the main reason for the world record turnout of 136,000 people who crowded into the Aztec Stadium.*

22.03.93 Carlos Gonzalez (MEX) W RSC 1 Tony Baltazar (USA), Los Angeles - WBO

10.04.93 Juan M. Coggi (ARG) W RSC 7 Jose Rivera (PR), Mar del Plata - WBA

08.05.93 Julio Cesar Chavez (MEX) W RSC 6 Terrence Alli (GU), Las Vegas - WBC

15.05.93 Charles Murray (USA) W PTS 12 Rodney Moore (USA), Atlantic City - IBF

07.06.93 Zack Padilla (USA) W PTS 12 Carlos Gonzalez (MEX), Las Vegas - WBO

23.06.93 Juan M. Coggi (ARG) W CO 5 Hiroyuki Yoshino (JAP), Tokyo - WBA

24.07.93 Charles Murray (USA) W PTS 12 Juan Laporte (PR), Atlantic City - IBF

13.08.93 Juan M. Coggi (ARG) W PTS 12 Jose Barboza (VEN), Buenos Aires - WBA

24.09.93 Juan M. Coggi (ARG) W RSC 10 Guillermo Cruz (MEX), Tucuman - WBA

19.11.93 Charles Murray (USA) W RTD 5 Courtney Hooper (USA), Atlantic City - IBF

19.11.93 Zack Padilla (USA) W RTD 7 Efrem Calamati (ITA), Arezzo - WBO

16.12.93 Zack Padilla (USA) W PTS 12 Ray Oliveira (USA), Ledyard - WBO

17.12.93 Juan M. Coggi (ARG) W RSC 7 Eder Gonzalez (COL), Tucuman - WBA

18.12.93 Julio Cesar Chavez (MEX) W RTD 5 Andy Holligan (GB), Puebla - WBC

29.01.94 Frankie Randall (USA) W PTS 12 Julio Cesar Chavez (MEX), Las Vegas - WBC

13.02.94 Jake Rodriguez (USA) W PTS 12 Charles Murray (USA), Atlantic City - IBF

18.03.94 Juan M. Coggi (ARG) W RSC 3 Eder Gonzalez (COL), Las Vegas - WBA

18.04.94 Zack Padilla (USA) W RTD 6 Harold Miller (USA), Rotterdam - WBO

21.04.95 Jake Rodriquez (USA) W PTS 12 Ray Oliveira (USA), Ledyard - IBF

07.05.94 Julio Cesar Chavez (MEX) W TD 8 Frankie Randall (USA), Las Vegas - WBC

Welterweight (147 lbs)

Adapted from horse racing terminology, the "welter" division first came into being in America in order to bridge the gap between light and middle and was initially set at 142 lbs. Paddy Duffy is generally recognised as being the first bare-knuckle champion under London Prize Ring Rules, after beating Bob Lyons by a 11th round kayo in April 1884 (Boston). Having successfully defended the title against Bill Young, via a second round kayo win in March 1886 (Baltimore), he next claimed to be the division's first Queensberry Rules' champion after knocking out Billy McMillan in the 17th round at Fort Foote on 30 October 1888. However, that was with skin-tight gloves and he was matched to meet Tom Meadows at the California Athletic Club in San Francisco, a venue recognised for its use of gloves.

29.03.89 Paddy Duffy (USA) W DIS 45 Tom Meadows (A), San Francisco. *According to the Sporting Life (newspaper), this was a title fight, but the San Francisco Chronicle (newspaper) only made mention of it as a contest at 142 lbs between Duffy (139) and Meadows (141½), with both men using small lace-up gloves. Incidentally, although Meadows was billed out of Australia, he had actually* *been born in England. For Duffy, it would be his last fight as he tragically contracted tuberculosis, passing away at the early age of 26 on 19 July 1890. On Duffy's untimely demise, there emerged several claimants, the most notable being Tommy Ryan, Con Doyle, Danny Needham and, a year or two later, Mysterious Billy Smith.*

16.02.91 Tommy Ryan (USA) W CO 76 Danny Needham (USA), Minneapolis. *Ryan (139 lbs) admitted prior to the fight that if he was to be a world champion, Needham (137½ lbs) would have to be eliminated, just as Con Doyle (knocked out in 28 rounds) had been in Shelby on 6 September 1890. Although there was no title billing as such, the Chicago Tribune (newspaper) reported it as being the greatest glove (four ounce) fight seen in the USA up to that time, while the New Orleans Daily Picayune (newspaper) supported Ryan's claim to be recognised as the American champion on the result. Incidentally, I believe this is the first time that a record book has picked up Ryan's early claim to this title.*

09.08.91 Tommy Ryan (USA) W CO 3 Billy McMillan (USA), Richardson. *Billed at 144 lbs for the not very well defined welterweight title. Well, that was how the Chicago Tribune (newspaper) saw it, with both men inside the weight.*

13.12.91 Tommy Ryan (USA) W CO 14 Frank Howson (GB), Chicago. *According to the New York Herald and Sporting Life (newspapers), this fight was billed for the world welter title at 144 lbs with four ounce gloves in use.*

14.12.92 Mysterious Billy Smith (USA) W CO 14 Danny Needham (USA), San Francisco. *With no title billing given in the San Francisco Chronicle (newspaper), the Ring Record Book tells us it was following his victory over Needham (143) that Smith (142) first laid claim to the 142 lbs championship. Needham had been claiming the title after Ryan was forced through illness to pull out of a defence against him in New Orleans on 1 March 1892, leaving Jack Burke to be substituted. Although he defeated Burke (136 lbs) on points, while weighing in himself at 142 lbs, he had already been beaten by Ryan and, prior to his fight with Smith, had also lost at the hands of the Australian, George Dawson, inside 29 rounds at San Francisco on 26 July of that year. While Needham's claim was relatively weak, recognition for Smith was undoubtedly strengthened after Tommy Ryan failed to put in an appearance for a prospective defence against Dawson, in New Orleans on 3 March 1893. Strangely enough, within a few months and without any further ring activity, apart from a couple of six-round exhibition bouts (against Ryan and Al O'Brien), the 25-year-old Dawson retired to become the boxing coach at the Chicago Athletic Club, a position he held until 1924.*

17.04.93 Mysterious Billy Smith (USA) W CO 2 Tom Williams (A), Brooklyn. *According to the San Francisco Chronicle and New York Herald (newspapers), this was an advertised title bout to a finish, with both men articled to make 140 lbs. Although Williams came to the ring with a win over fellow-Australian, George Dawson, the 142 lbs welterweight championship would only be settled after Smith met Tommy Ryan.*

26.07.94 **Tommy Ryan** (USA) W PTS 20 Mysterious Billy Smith (USA), Minneapolis *(142 lbs).*

18.01.95 **Tommy Ryan** (USA) W RSC 3 Nonpareil Jack Dempsey (USA), Brooklyn. *With the welterweight limit set at 142 lbs, Ryan weighed in at 145. However, with Dempsey tipping the beam at 142, the title would have been at stake. That was to be Dempsey's last contest and less than a year later he was dead, the victim of tuberculosis.*

27.05.95 **Tommy Ryan** (USA) NC 18 Mysterious Billy Smith (USA), Brooklyn. *Scheduled for 45 rounds at 142 lbs, the fight was halted after interference from the police in both the 11th and 18th rounds. Both men were inside the weight.*

02.03.96 Kid McCoy (USA) W CO 15 Tommy Ryan (USA), Long Island. *Early editions of the Ring Record Book showed this to be a welterweight title defence for Ryan, but since it came to light that both Ryan and McCoy were articled to come into the ring inside 154 lbs, it is now accepted that it was the welterweight champion's middleweight title claim which was at stake and, as such, the fight is also listed in that division.*

25.11.96 Tommy Ryan (USA) W DIS 9 Mysterious Billy Smith (USA), Long Island. *Following his defeat at the hands of Kid McCoy, it is doubtful whether Ryan had much credibility as welterweight champion from then on, especially when you take into account the fact that he was no longer able to make 142 lbs. The Boston Post (newspaper) report, with no weights given, made no mention of this fight involving the title, while the Mirror of Life (newspaper) reported it being at catchweights.*

23.12.96 Tommy Ryan (USA) W CO 4 Bill Payne (USA), Syracuse. *The Philadelphia Item (newspaper) reported the fight but said nothing about it involving the championship, even though it is listed in the Ring Record Book as such, albeit without mention of weights.*

Payne had fought Jim Butler in Brooklyn four days earlier, which was hardly what you would expect of a man about to challenge for the title, while the Buffalo Courier (newspaper) did not even cover it.

24.02.97 Tommy Ryan (USA) W CO 9 Tom Tracy (A), Syracuse. *Although recorded in the Ring Record Book as involving the championship, with Ryan leaning towards the middleweight ranks, Prof. Luckett Davis unearthed the following extract from the Philadelphia Item (newspaper) report. According to the Item, the match was made at 145 lbs, with Ryan scaling 144 lbs to Tracy's 139, but, had the latter won, he would almost certainly claimed the "popular" 142 lbs title.*

17.03.97 George Green (USA) W CO 12 Mysterious Billy Smith (USA), Carson City. *With Tommy Ryan inexorably moving towards the middleweight ranks, according to the Police Gazette (newspaper) and despite the absence of weights, Green claimed the title following his victory over former champion, Smith.*

26.08.97 Joe Walcott (USA) W CO 18 George Green (USA), San Francisco. *Although no weights were given, the Police Gazette (newspaper) said that this was "practically" a championship affair, while the San Francisco Chronicle (newspaper) claimed: "the contest was being treated with all the consideration due to a title fight" and labelled it as a battle for welter honours. With his victory, Walcott took over Green's title claim.*

14.04.98 Mysterious Billy Smith (USA) DREW 25 Joe Walcott (USA), Bridgeport. *Shown in the Boxing News Annual as a title fight, the Boston Post (newspaper) reported it to be a catchweight contest with neither man to exceed 148 lbs.*

13.06.98 Tommy Ryan (USA) W RSC 14 Tommy West (USA), New York City. *Listed as a welterweight defence for Ryan in the Ring Record Book, the Articles of Agreement called for a bout at catchweights, with Ryan coming in at 146 lbs to West's 152. Although this contest had no bearing on the "popular" title, Ryan continued to call himself champion (listed under middleweight, also).*

29.07.98 Mysterious Billy Smith (USA) W PTS 25 George Green (USA), New York City. *Regarded as a title fight by the 1985 Ring Record Book (later removed), Smith, who scaled 147 lbs to Green's 146, would not be generally recognised until he defeated Matty Matthews at 142 lbs.*

27.08.98 **Mysterious Billy Smith** (USA) W PTS 25 Matty Matthews (USA), New York City. *Scheduled for 25 rounds, the New York Herald (newspaper) reported that both men were inside the agreed 142 lbs, and, on the result, Smith became generally recognised as the new leader of the weight class. Meanwhile, Ryan was still claiming the championship at 150 lbs and continued to defend as such.*

05.09.98 **Mysterious Billy Smith** (USA) DREW 25 Andy Walsh (USA), Brooklyn. *Recorded in the Ring Record Book as a title fight, it was contested at 145 lbs, three pounds above the recognised limit.*

03.10.98 **Mysterious Billy Smith** (USA) W CO 20 Jim Judge (USA), Scranton. *Removed from the 1984 Ring Record Book as a title fight, and with no mention that the championship was at stake in either the Philadelphia Item or Chicago Tribune (newspaper) reports, there appears to be nothing on record to suggest that the championship was involved, other than a later date remark attributed to Judge, claiming that he was inside 140 lbs on the night.*

07.10.98 **Mysterious Billy Smith** (USA) W PTS 25 Charley McKeever (USA), New York City. *While there was no mention of it being a title clash in the New York Herald (newspaper) report, both men were announced as being inside the championship limit of 142 lbs.*

06.12.98 **Mysterious Billy Smith** (USA) W PTS 20 Joe Walcott (USA), New York City. *Billed for the 145 lbs title, it should not be considered as a defence of Smith's "popular" crown.*

12.12.98 Bobby Dobbs (USA) W RTD 8 Dick Burge (GB), People's Palace, Newcastle. *Advertised as being for the world 144 lbs title, at the time there was no recognised welterweight division in Britain, with Burge having carried his national lightweight title up in weight.*

24.01.99 **Mysterious Billy Smith** (USA) W CO 14 Billy Edwards (A), New York City. *Made at 147 lbs, this should not be seen as a "popular" title defence for Smith.*

22.02.99 Bobby Dobbs (USA) NC 1 Joe McDonald (GB), Wellington Palace, Glasgow. *Billed as a defence of Dobbs' 144 lbs title, the fight was halted when the police climbed into the ring and arrested both men for assault. Earlier, McDonald, having only his second contest, should have been disqualified when he was knocked out of the ring and helped back in again.*

01.03.99 Bobby Dobbs (USA) W CO 2 Joe McDonald (GB), Standard Theatre, Gateshead. *At this point in time, Dobbs' 144 lbs title claim did not even make an impact in Britain, let alone America,* *and was quickly forgotten.*

10.03.99 **Mysterious Billy Smith** (USA) W RSC 14 George Lavigne (USA), San Francisco. *Weights (lbs): Smith (142), Lavigne (139).*

30.06.99 **Mysterious Billy Smith** (USA) DREW 20 Charley McKeever (USA), New York City. *Recorded as a title fight in the Ring Record Book, there was no mention of that being the case in the New York Herald (newspaper), while the New York Times (newspaper) reported it to be at catchweights.*

04.08.99 **Mysterious Billy Smith** (USA) DREW 25 Andy Walsh (USA), Brooklyn. *Listed in the 1985 Ring Record Book as title fight (later removed), the New York Herald (newspaper) stated that both men were inside the allotted 150 lbs. On that basis, the 142 lbs title was not involved.*

31.08.99 Tommy Ryan (USA) W PTS 20 Jack Moffatt (USA), Dubuque. *Billed as a welterweight title defence for Ryan (listed under middleweights, also), with both men scaling 152 lbs, it was really his middleweight claim that was at stake had Moffatt won.*

08.11.99 **Mysterious Billy Smith** (USA) W PTS 20 Charley McKeever (USA), New York City. *Another fight for Smith listed by the Ring Record Book as involving the title, the New York Herald (newspaper) reported it to be at catchweights, with Smith weighing 145 lbs to McKeever's 144.*

15.01.00 Rube Ferns (USA) W DIS 21 Mysterious Billy Smith (USA), Buffalo. *In a match made at 145 lbs, Ferns, who had been floored 15 times, was declared the winner by disqualification. However, the weight class was still recognised as being 142 lbs in America and Ferns would have to wait another eight months before being accorded full recognition.*

26.01.00 Mysterious Billy Smith (USA) W CO 22 Frank McConnell (USA), New York City. *Listed as a title fight in the Ring Record Book, according to the New York Herald (newspaper) report, it was scheduled for 25 rounds at 148 lbs.*

22.02.00 Rube Ferns (USA) W PTS 20 Mike Donovan (USA), Buffalo. *Advertised as a world title fight at 145 lbs, according to the Buffalo Courier (newspaper).*

17.04.00 Matty Matthews (USA) W CO 19 Mysterious Billy Smith (USA), New York City *(142 lbs).*

24.05.00 Rube Ferns (USA) W CO 1 Jack Bennett (GB), Toronto. *Calling himself the welter champion after beating Mysterious Billy Smith at 145 lbs, Ferns defended his claim against Bennett at 142 lbs in a fight billed for the title.*

05.06.00 Eddie Connolly (C) W PTS 25 Matty Matthews (USA), Brooklyn. *With both men inside 140 lbs, the Canadian won the title. Prior to the 1986-87 Ring Record Book, there had never been mention of Connolly being champion, something that was remedied following research on the welterweight succession carried out by Prof. Luckett Davis.*

13.08.00 **Rube Ferns** (USA) W RTD 15 Eddie Connolly (C), Buffalo. *The Buffalo Courier (newspaper) stated that the title changed hands on the result, with both men weighing under 140 lbs.*

30.08.00 **Rube Ferns** (USA) W PTS 15 Matty Matthews (USA), Detroit *(142 lbs).*

03.09.00 Jack Everhardt (USA) W DIS 10 Tommy Ireland (GB), Wonderland, London. *Scheduled for 20 (two minute) rounds and billed for the world 140 lbs title, with full championship conditions not applied, it could not be taken seriously.*

16.10.00 Matty Matthews (USA) W PTS 15 Rube Ferns (USA), Detroit. *Made at 140 lbs, although the recognised limit was set at 142 lbs, both men were inside the weight on the night of the fight.*

29.04.01 Matty Matthews (USA) W PTS 20 Tom Couhig (USA), Detroit. *Weights (lbs): Matthews (139½), Couhig (139).*

24.05.01 Rube Ferns (USA) W CO 10 Matty Matthews (USA), Toronto *(142 lbs).*

23.09.01 **Rube Ferns** (USA) W CO 9 Frank Erne (USA), Fort Erie. *The Sporting Life (newspaper), here in Britain, and the Philadelphia Item (newspaper), reported that the contest had been made at 142 lbs, with both men on the weight.*

28.11.01 **Rube Ferns** (USA) W PTS 15 Charley Thurston (USA), Detroit. *Although no weights were given, the Chicago Tribune (newspaper) stated that Ferns made a successful defence against "Dutch" Thurston, while the Philadelphia Item (newspaper) made no mention of any championship billing.*

18.12.01 **Joe Walcott** (USA) W RSC 5 Rube Ferns (USA), Fort Erie. *Scheduled for 20 rounds, both men were inside the stipulated 142 lbs and the title changed hands.*

29.05.02 Rube Ferns (USA) W CO 3 Owen Zeigler (USA), Joplin. *According to certain sources, although this writer has been unable to obtain confirmation, this was a title fight at 145 lbs and scheduled for 20 rounds. Bill Matthews' "smashing" little book, The English Boxing Champions, tells us that Zeigler had won the American title by kayoing Eddie Connolly in two rounds at Hartford on 29 November 1900. However, the Chicago Tribune*

(newspaper) report of the above fight merely stated that Zeigler, a last minute substitute for Jack Daly at 138 lbs, caused an upset. Certainly, if Zeigler later claimed the 145 lbs title, he lost it here to Ferns.

21.06.02 Eddie Connolly (C) W PTS 15 Pat Daley (GB), NSC, London. *Billed for the world 144 lbs title.*

23.06.02 **Joe Walcott** (USA) W PTS 15 Tommy West (USA), NSC, London. *Although listed in the Ring Record Book as a title fight and advertised as such, it was, in fact, articled and contested at catchweights. With West's best fighting poundage at this time somewhere between 152 and 158, it was small wonder that the weights were not announced. After the fight, Walcott challenged the winner of the Ryan v Gorman so-called middleweight title bout that took place the following day.*

15.09.02 Tom Woodley (GB) W PTS 11 Eddie Connolly (C), Wonderland, London. *Originally scheduled for ten (two minute) rounds to decide the world 140 lbs title, regardless of the fact that it was not contested under full championship conditions, another round was thrown in for good measure.*

20.11.02 Jim Maloney (GB) W PTS 20 Bobby Dobbs (USA), National Athletic Club, London. *Given world championship billing at 138 lbs, a weight six pounds below the accepted welterweight limit in Britain, it received no support whatsoever.*

22.12.02 Matty Matthews (USA) W PTS 10 Rube Ferns (USA), Pittsburgh. *Following the above contest between two former titleholders at 145 lbs, Matthews claimed the "white" version of the title. Regardless of the result, Walcott continued to be generally recognised as the lineal champion.*

26.01.03 Eddie Connolly (C) W PTS 15 Tom Woodley (GB), NSC, London. *Billed for the world 146 lbs title, with the welterweight limit standing at 144 lbs in Britain and 142 in America. Following one more bout in England, Connolly went home.*

01.04.03 **Joe Walcott** (USA) DREW 20 Billy Woods (USA), Los Angeles. *Listed as a title fight in the Ring Record Book, according to the Los Angeles Times (newspaper) report, it was an ordinary fight between two "black" men with no disclosure of weights.*

27.04.03 Rube Ferns (USA) W RSC 19 Matty Matthews (USA), Fort Erie. *Ferns, calling himself the "white" welterweight champion, once again laid claim to the title following his victory at 145 lbs, but received scant support.*

28.05.03 Martin Duffy (USA) W CO 13 Rube Ferns (USA), Louisville. *Scheduled for 20 rounds at 142 lbs, the Chicago Tribune (newspaper) confirmed the billing to be for the American welterweight title. Not generally recognised as a championship bout, Duffy merely took over the mantle of Ferns' "white" title claim.*

25.08.03 Martin Duffy (USA) W PTS 10 Matty Matthews (USA), Fort Huron. *According to the Chicago Tribune (newspaper) report, this was billed for the "white" title at 145 lbs.*

31.08.03 Martin Duffy (USA) DREW 10 Gus Gardner (USA), Fort Huron. *Also shown in some quarters as an American championship fight, the Chicago Tribune (newspaper) reported that, with Gardner outweighed by some 15 lbs, it was a catchweight contest.*

15.02.04 Jack Clancy (USA) W PTS 15 Pat Daley (GB), NSC, London. *Billed for the world 146 lbs title.*

26.02.04 Martin Duffy (USA) W PTS 20 Rube Ferns (USA), Hot Springs. *Shown occasionally as a "White" title defence, although there was no mention of that or of the weights in the Chicago Tribune (newspaper) report of the fight.*

22.04.04 Honey Mellody (USA) W CO 4 Martin Duffy (USA), Chicago. *Not a title bout, just a "typical" Chicago six rounder of the day, but, with the result, went Duffy's "white" title claim. Mellody weighed 142 lbs to Duffy's 147½.*

29.04.04 Dixie Kid (USA) W DIS 20 Joe Walcott (USA), San Francisco. *Weighing in at 144½ lbs, Walcott, winning easily, was disqualified for no discernable reason. Later, the contest was disregarded as a title bout and Walcott continued as champion when it was discovered that the referee had placed a bet on the Dixie Kid (138 lbs). At the same time, due to the chicanery involved, the Kid was accorded no recognition whatsoever and his career faltered when he was sent to prison for offences committed outside the ring.*

02.05.04 Jack Clancy (USA) W PTS 10 Peter Brown (GB), Wonderland, London. *Scheduled for ten (two minute) rounds and billed for the 144 lbs title, it should not be recognised as such, with full championship conditions not applied.*

12.05.04 Dixie Kid (USA) DREW 20 Joe Walcott (USA), San Francisco. *Removed from the Ring Record Book in 1986, this has now been exposed as a fight that never took place.*

14.05.04 Jack Clancy (USA) W PTS 20 Bobby Dobbs (USA), Ginnett's Circus, Newcastle. *In a match made at 142 lbs and billed for the world title, Clancy came in at 144, with Dobbs scaling 140.*

04.06.04 Jack Clancy (USA) W CO 3 Charlie Allum (GB), Ginnett's Circus, Newcastle. *Billed for the world 146 lbs title.*

05.09.04 Joe Walcott (USA) DREW 15 Sam Langford (USA), Manchester, USA. *Refusing to accept the loss to the Dixie Kid, Walcott signed Articles of Agreement for a title defence at 142 lbs against the much feared Sam Langford. The Boston Post (newspaper) failed to publish weights, other than remarking four days earlier that, although Walcott was still three pounds over the limit, he expected to be well inside on the night. There was nothing mentioned of Langford.*

12.09.04 Jack Clancy (USA) DREW 20 Bobby Dobbs (USA), Ginnett's Circus, Newcastle. *Billed for the world 144 lbs championship, the title was vacated on Clancy returning to America.*

26.09.04 Young Peter Jackson (USA) W CO 3 Charlie Knock (GB), Wonderland, London. *Although billed as a welterweight title fight at 148 lbs, it was way above the weight limit of the day, and, with two minute rounds in place, full championship conditions were not applied.*

30.09.04 Joe Walcott (USA) DREW 20 Joe Gans (USA), San Francisco. *Weights (lbs): Walcott (141), Gans (137). In October 1904, Walcott accidentally shot himself through the right hand (his friend and fellow boxer, Nelson Hall, was killed by the same bullet) and was forced out of the ring until mid-1906.*

14.11.04 Buddy Ryan (USA) W CO 1 Honey Mellody (USA), Chicago. *Reported as a ten round championship fight by the Chicago Tribune (newspaper), with both fighters inside 142 lbs, Ryan took over Mellody's "white" title claim.*

04.07.05 Buddy Ryan (USA) W CO 11 George Hurberts (USA), Butte. *Reported in the Chicago Tribune (newspaper) as a defence of Ryan's title claim, it was scheduled for 20 rounds.*

19.07.05 Buddy Ryan (USA) W RTD 20 George Petersen (USA), San Francisco. *The San Francisco Chronicle (newspaper) reported it as being a battle for the championship between Ryan, the recognised American titleholder, and Petersen, the Californian champion with a win over Jack Clancy under his belt. Although billed as such, but with no weights announced, at best it would have been Ryan's "white" title claim that was at stake.*

25.08.05 Jimmy Gardner (USA) W RTD 15 Buddy Ryan (USA), San Francisco. *While not reporting this as a title fight, the San Francisco Chronicle (newspaper) described Ryan as world champion, with both men agreeing to make 142 lbs. The finish came when Ryan, on the floor after being hit in the solar-plexus, unsuccessfully tried to claim a foul. All bets were called off, but that did not stop Gardner claiming the "white" title after his victory.*

24.11.05 Mike Twin Sullivan (USA) W PTS 20 Jimmy Gardner (USA), San Francisco. *At face value, one would have thought the "white" title passed to Sullivan on the result, but, according to the San Francisco Chronicle (newspaper), while recognising Gardner as the "legitimate" holder of the "white" title, the match went ahead at catchweights.*

19.01.06 Joe Gans (USA) W CO 15 Mike Twin Sullivan (USA), San Francisco. *According to the Philadelphia Item and San Francisco Chronicle (newspapers), the fight was for a version of the title with Articles of Agreement calling for the men to come into the ring at 142 lbs.*

17.03.06 Joe Gans (USA) W CO 5 Mike Twin Sullivan (USA), Los Angeles. *Although billed as a title fight, Sullivan came in six pounds over the limit and, on Walcott announcing his comeback, Gans moved back to the lightweight division.*

10.07.06 Joe Walcott (USA) W CO 8 Jack Dougherty (USA), Chelsea. *On Walcott's comeback, the Boston Post (newspaper) reported the fight as being for the title, with both men inside the required 142 lbs.*

03.09.06 Joe Thomas (USA) W CO 11 Honey Mellody (USA), Chelsea. *This was a 15 round non-title fight at 145 lbs, but, following Mellody's sensational victory over Joe Walcott in his very next contest, Thomas retrospectively laid claim to the championship on the basis of the above result.*

29.09.06 Joe Walcott (USA) DREW 20 Billy Rhodes (USA), Kansas City. *As in Walcott v Dougherty, Articles of Agreement were signed for Walcott's title to be at stake and for both men to make 142 lbs. Incidentally, neither of these bouts were listed in record books over the years as title fights.*

16.10.06 Honey Mellody (USA) W PTS 15 Joe Walcott (USA), Chelsea. *Although billed as a title bout, the fact that they were contracted to meet at 145 lbs did not please everyone. The general concensus among the pressmen was that only a return at 142 lbs would satsify all concerned and the pair met again just six weeks later.*

29.11.06 **Honey Mellody** (USA) W RSC 12 Joe Walcott (USA), Chelsea (142 lbs).

08.01.07 **Honey Mellody** (USA) W PTS 15 Terry Martin (USA), Augusta.

With championship billing given at 145 lbs, the Boston Post (newspaper) stated that, although the "popular" title was not strictly involved, if Martin won he would follow precedent and claim the title.

11.02.07 **Honey Mellody** (USA) W RSC 4 Willie Lewis (USA), Valley Falls. *Advertised as a title fight at 142 lbs, it turned out that Articles of Agreement had been signed for the contest to go on at 147 lbs and it was at that weight the two men weighed in.*

23.04.07 Mike Twin Sullivan (USA) W PTS 20 Honey Mellody (USA), Los Angeles. *Although billed as a title fight at 145 lbs, Mellody claimed that the championship had not been on the line because the officials had allowed the challenger to weigh-in close on 150 lbs. This explanation was accepted by some, but not by others, with much support for Sullivan in California. Regardless of this defeat, Mellody continued to be referred to by the Boston Post (newspaper) as the 142 lbs champion.*

04.07.07 Joe Thomas (USA) DREW 20 Stanley Ketchel (USA), Marysville. *Shown in Boxing News Annuals as a middles title fight (see under middleweight listings, also), it neither involved that or the welterweight championship. Although the San Francisco Chronicle (newspaper) reported that Thomas almost lost his welter title to Ketchel in this fight, it was a fallacy, with the weights recorded as 150 lbs and 147, respectively.*

01.11.07 Frank Mantell (USA) W CO 15 Honey Mellody (USA), Dayton. *Billed as a title fight, according to the Boston Post (newspaper), it was contested at 145 lbs. The Post went on to say: "the result was such a fluke that it was to laugh". However, fluke or not, Mellody, by his inability to defend at 142 lbs, would not be considered as a champion from hereon.*

01.11.07 Mike Twin Sullivan (USA) W PTS 20 Frank Fields (USA), Goldfield. *According to the Ring Record Book, Sullivan defended the "Californian" version of the title in this fight. However, there is no mention in either the San Francisco Chronicle or Los Angeles Times (newspapers) of that being the case.*

27.11.07 Mike Twin Sullivan (USA) W CO 13 Kid Farmer (USA), Los Angeles. *Listed in the Ring Record Book as a title fight, the Los Angeles Times (newspaper), at some stage, advertised it as being a title fight but made no mention of the fighters' weights, while the San Francisco Chronicle (newspaper) reported it being a 20 round contest at catchweights.*

23.01.08 Harry Lewis (USA) W CO 3 Frank Mantell (USA), New Haven. *Billed and advertised as a 12 round championship fight at 145 lbs, according to the Boston Post (newspaper), the paper went on to say that Lewis had a lot of backers after his win and quickly laid claim to the 142 lbs title also. The Post also stated, that despite all statements given to the press, it was a good 10-1 bet that Lewis never came in a low as 142 lbs against Mantell and his claim to that title should be disregarded. However, the Philadelphia Item (newspaper), reported that both men weighed in at 142 lbs. On the statements made in the Boston Post, Prof. L. V. Davis, who researched the subject, says: "It sounds like the sort of empty gossip that abounded in those days." You takes your pick!*

26.03.08 Harry Lewis (USA) W PTS 15 Terry Martin (USA), Baltimore. *According to the Ring Record Book, this was a billed championship bout, while the Philadelphia Item (newspaper) merely stated that it assumed the character of a title fight. With no weights recorded, one should remain sceptical. My guess would be that the fight was made at either 145 or 147 lbs.*

20.04.08 Harry Lewis (USA) W CO 4 Honey Mellody (USA), Boston. *Listed in the Ring Record Book as a title fight, the Boston Post (newspaper) stated that the contest did not involve the championship, with both men weighing in at 147 lbs. Early in 1910, Lewis took his version of the title to Europe.*

23.04.08 Mike Twin Sullivan (USA) W PTS 25 Jimmy Gardner (USA), Los Angeles. *Reported as a so-called championship fight by the Los Angeles Times (newspaper), both men made the 142 lbs required of them, with Gardner down to 141½ the day before. Following the fight, Sullivan relinquished his claim to the title due to increasing weight problems.*

07.11.08 Jimmy Gardner (USA) W PTS 15 Jimmy Clabby (USA), New Orleans. *Billed for the vacant 142 lbs title, Gardner weighed 142 lbs, while Clabby scaled 138.*

26.11.08 Jimmy Gardner (USA) DREW 20 Jimmy Clabby (USA), New Orleans. *According to the New Orleans Daily Picayune (newspaper), Gardner was defending the 142 lbs championship. Early in 1909, Gardner moved into the middleweight ranks, thus leaving his claim to the title vacant.*

26.05.09 Willie Lewis (USA) W CO 3 Andrew Jeptha (GB), Villiers Street Arena, London. *Although billed as a title fight at 147 lbs over 20 rounds, it was not widely recognised as one in Britain. Earlier, following the NSC's initiative, the weight limit for the division was set at 147 lbs in Britain and recognised elsewhere in the world other than America, who remained at 142 lbs.*

19.02.10 Harry Lewis (USA) DREW 25 Willie Lewis (USA), Paris - GB/FRANCE. *With the formation of the IBU currently being proposed and with Harry Lewis bringing his title claim from America, this was accepted as a title fight in Europe at 147 lbs. For the record, both men were announced as being inside the weight at the 2.0 pm weigh-in.*

23.04.10 Harry Lewis (USA) DREW 25 Willie Lewis (USA), Paris - GB/FRANCE *(147 lbs).*

04.05.10 Harry Lewis (USA) W CO 3 Peter Brown (GB), Paris - GB/FRANCE *(147 lbs).*

05.05.10 Jimmy Clabby (USA) ND-W PTS 10 Dixie Kid (USA), New York City. *After receiving the "press" decision over the Kid, who still saw himself as champion, Clabby claimed the title, while the loser moved his base to Europe.*

27.06.10 Harry Lewis (USA) W RTD 7 Young Joseph (GB), Wonderland, London - GB/FRANCE *(147 lbs).*

05.09.10 Jimmy Clabby (USA) W CO 13 Guy Buckles (USA), Sheridan. *Following this win over the man from Nebraska in an advertised championship bout, and with Harry Lewis operating in Europe, Clabby strengthened his claim on the USA version of the title before joining the exodus of American boxers campaigning abroad by leaving for Australia. That is what the Ring Record Book tells us, but the fight was not even reported in the Chicago Tribune (newspaper) and should be ignored until the fighters' weights are uncovered.*

02.11.10 Jimmy Clabby (USA) W RSC 7 Bob Bryant (A), Sydney. *While recorded in the Ring Record Book as a world title (Australian version) fight, the Sydney Daily Telegraph (newspaper) made no mention of that, although describing Clabby as probably being the best welter in the world at that moment in time. For the record, it was a catchweight contest, with Clabby weighing in at 146 lbs to Bryant's 150.*

26.12.10 Jimmy Clabby (USA) W CO 1 Gus Devitt (NZ), Brisbane. *Although billed as a title fight and scheduled for 20 rounds, according to the Brisbane Daily Mail (newspaper) it was made at 154 lbs with both men spot on. That being the case, and with the welterweight limit outside America standing at 147 lbs, this does not hold up as a title fight. In April 1911, Clabby relinquished the so-called Australian version of the title and moved up to middleweight.*

25.01.11 Harry Lewis (USA) W CO 4 Johnny Summers (GB), Olympia, London. *Billed as a title bout at 144 lbs, it was tarnished by the fact that after initially refusing to weigh in, Lewis was found to scale 148¾ lbs. For the record, Summers came in at 140¾ lbs. A few weeks later, Lewis announced that, in the future, he would be fighting in the middleweight division and promptly laid claim to that title, also.*

03.07.11 Blink McCloskey (USA) W DIS 3 Dixie Kid (USA), Wonderland, London. *Billed by the promoter as a title match at 147 lbs, it was not seen as one throughout Britain and McCloskey received no recognition as such, especially after weighing in two pounds over the limit.*

09.11.11 Dixie Kid (USA) W CO 2 Johnny Summers (GB), The Stadium, Liverpool. *Billed for the world title at 142 lbs, which the Dixie Kid still claimed, both men were announced as being inside the weight. With Harry Lewis now perceived to be a middleweight, the Kid was generally recognised in Britain as champion.*

18.01.12 Harry Lewis (USA) W RSC 8 Dixie Kid (USA), The Stadium, Liverpool. *Although listed as a welterweight title fight in Jack Solomons' International Boxing Annual, it most definitely was not. Made at the middleweight limit of 158 lbs, it was articled as being at catchweights and carried no title billing.*

01.04.12 Ray Bronson (USA) W PTS 15 Clarence English (USA), St Joseph. *With all the top Americans campaigning abroad, Bronson laid claim to the title following his win over English. Later, Bronson would put up forfeit without takers, to fight anyone for the title in America at 145 lbs ringside.*

24.04.12 Dixie Kid (USA) W RTD 11 George Bernard (FR), Paris - GB/FRANCE. *Billed over 20 rounds for the world 147 lbs title, with both men inside the weight, Bernard was dropped writhing in agony in the 10th round, wherepon the referee, Willie Lewis, disqualified the Kid after the bell had already rung to get the 11th underway. Later, on being examined by three doctors, Bernard was found to show no trace of having being fouled and the decision was overturned.*

04.10.12 Marcel Thomas (FR) W PTS 15 Dixie Kid (USA), Paris - FRANCE. *In a title match made at 147 lbs, with both men announced as having made the weight, the Kid, who had been recognised by the IBU as champion since June 1912, gave way to the Frenchman.*

16.07.13 Mike Glover (USA) ND-W PTS 10 Young Hickey (USA), New York City. *Glover laid claim to the 142 lbs title after receiving the "press" decision.*

22.07.13 Mike Glover (USA) W RSC 4 Marcel Thomas (FR), Boston. *Although both Glover and Thomas had a reasonable claim to the title, it was not billed as a championship fight and no weights were given. However, the Boston Post (newspaper) stated: "this was as near a title fight as you will get" and, following the result, Thomas was effectively eliminated from the title chase.*

10.12.13 Mike Gibbons (USA) ND-W CO 2 Clarence Ferns (USA), New Orleans. *Although a ten round no-decision fight, it was billed for the title. However, with Gibbons weighing 147 lbs to Ferns' 146, with the limit still at 142 (3.0 pm weigh-in) or 145 (ringside) in America, it received scant recognition. Ferns had been claiming the title since twice defeating Guy Buckles in 1912.*

01.01.14 Waldemar Holberg (DEN) W PTS 20 Ray Bronson (USA), Melbourne. *Bronson (146¾), who had been claiming the title, met Holberg (143½) in a fight given championship billing at 147 lbs by the leading Melbourne promoter.*

24.01.14 Tom McCormick (GB) W DIS 6 Waldemar Holberg (DEN), Melbourne. *Weights (lbs): McCormick (145¼), Holberg (145¼). This contest, along with Holberg v Bronson, was billed as a championship bout at 147 lbs by the local promoter, but was not recognised as such in Sydney, the power base of Australian boxing, and an elimination series was set up there to determine a world champion at the weight.*

14.02.14 Tom McCormick (GB) W CO 1 Johnny Summers (GB), Sydney. *Recorded in most record books as a title fight, it was, in effect, a semi-final leg of the elimination series. For the record, McCormick came in at 145¾ lbs, while Summers scaled 143¼.*

28.02.14 Matt Wells (GB) W RSC 7 Ray Bronson (USA), Sydney. *According to the Jack Solomons' International Boxing Annual, this was a title bout. However, the Sydney Daily Telegraph (newspaper) makes no mention of that and it should be seen as the second semi-final leg of the elimination series.*

21.03.14 Matt Wells (GB) W PTS 20 Tom McCormick (GB), Sydney - AUSTRALIA. *The final leg of the elimination tournament saw both Wells and McCormick scaling 146 lbs. McCormick had just eight more bouts before rejoining the British army and being killed in action on the Western Front in June 1916.*

30.06.14 Johnny Summers (GB) DREW 20 Harry Stone (USA), Olympia, London - GB. *With many of the top Britishers fighting abroad, Summers was matched against leading American, Stone, to contest the 147 lbs title. For the record, both men comfortably made the weight, but the result was inconclusive.*

18.07.14 Kid Graves (USA) ND-W CO 2 Johnny Alberts (USA), Brooklyn. *Following the scheduled ten-rounder, the final of a competition run by the ABA (American Boxing Association) to find a new champion, and having earlier eliminated Soldier Bartfield and Mike Glover in no-decision "press" wins, Graves laid claim to the title, but was not taken too seriously. This view was vindicated later when he was deemed by the press to have been outscored in ten round no-decision bouts against future champions, Jack Britton and Ted Kid Lewis, on 30 January 1915 (Brooklyn) and 9 June 1915 (New York City), respectively.*

01.06.15 Mike Glover (USA) W PTS 12 Matt Wells (GB), Boston. *Recorded in the Ring Record Book as a title fight, there was no mention of that being the case in the Boston Daily Globe (newspaper), although the Boston Post (newspaper) claimed that both men were inside 142 lbs and stated: "by all the rules in boxing, Glover should now hold the Australian version of the title. However, it would appear that historians over the years have tried to tidy up the descent of the welterweight title without sufficient evidence to be on safe ground.*

22.06.15 Jack Britton (USA) W PTS 12 Mike Glover (USA), Boston. *As in Wells v Glover, the fight was not advertised as involving the title and the weights were not declared. Looking back, it may seem to be yet another revision of history to accept Britton as world welterweight champion at that time, as he was still interested in getting his hands on the lightweight crown. Glover, however, had just 11 more contests before passing away at the age of 26 on 11 July 1917.*

31.08.15 Ted Kid Lewis (GB) W PTS 12 Jack Britton (USA), Boston. *According to Lewis, it was not billed as a title bout and Britton refused to weigh-in. At this stage of his career, Lewis was also looking for a crack at lightweight champion, Freddie Welsh, and had arranged for the contest to be made at 135 lbs. He is quoted as saying in his memoirs that Nat Fleischer got it wrong in the Ring Record Book.*

27.09.15 Ted Kid Lewis (GB) W PTS 12 Jack Britton (USA), Boston. *Again, the fight was not billed for the title and, after Britton weighed in at 136½ lbs, Lewis refused to get on the scales.*

26.10.15 **Ted Kid Lewis** (GB) W PTS 12 Joe Mandot (USA), Boston. *Recorded in the Ring Record Book as a title defence, according to Lewis, he had yet to claim the championship at this point in time.*

02.11.15 Ted Kid Lewis (GB) W PTS 12 Milburn Saylor (USA), Boston. *As above.*

23.11.15 Ted Kid Lewis (GB) W CO 1 Jimmy Duffy (USA), Boston. *Another fight recorded in the Ring Record Book as a title defence, in Lewis' own words it was at catchweights and did not involve the championship as he had yet to claim it.*

28.12.15 **Ted Kid Lewis** (GB) ND-W PTS 10 Willie Ritchie (USA), New York City. *Although a no-decision contest, it was billed for the 142 lbs welterweight championship of the world, with the Englishman, who had recently claimed the title after failing to get a crack at Freddie Welsh for the lightweight crown, styled as champion. Interestingly, the State of New York's Rules and Regulations at the time called for a welterweight limit of 145 lbs at 3.0 pm and the pre fight weigh-in saw Lewis scaling 139¼ to Ritchie's 143¾.*

17.01.16 **Ted Kid Lewis** (GB) ND-W PTS 10 Kid Graves (USA), Milwaukee. *Graves weighed 142 lbs, while Lewis came in at 140½.*

20.01.16 **Ted Kid Lewis** (GB) ND-L PTS 10 Jack Britton (USA), Buffalo. *Britton weighed 144¾ lbs to Lewis' 142½.*

15.02.16 **Ted Kid Lewis** (GB) ND-L PTS 10 Jack Britton (USA), Brooklyn. *Britton weighed 143½ lbs, while Lewis tipped the beam at 141½.*

21.02.16 Eddie Moha (USA) W DIS 11 Kid Graves (USA), Dayton. *Although Graves had dropped press decisions to both Ted Kid Lewis and Jack Britton, he was still claiming the title. Following this result, Moha himself laid claim to the title and had some backing until being kayoed by Lewis in 13 rounds at Dayton on 24 May 1916.*

01.03.16 **Ted Kid Lewis** (GB) W PTS 20 Harry Stone (USA), New Orleans. *Postponed from 28 February due to heavy rain, with both men articled to come to the ring inside 142 lbs, Lewis scaled 142 to Stone's 139.*

24.04.16 **Jack Britton** (USA) W PTS 20 Ted Kid Lewis (GB), New Orleans. *In a match made at 145 lbs, both men came in on the limit.*

06.06.16 **Jack Britton** (USA) W PTS 12 Mike O'Dowd (USA), Boston. *According to the Boston Post (newspaper) report, this was a battle for titular honours, while the Boston Daily Globe (newspaper) failed to indicate that the title was at stake. With O'Dowd fighting as a middleweight, and in the absence of any weights, in all probability it was merely an over the weight clash between the welterweight champion and a man who was less than 18 months away from winning the 158 lbs crown. Incidentally, O'Dowd had earlier claimed the title at 147 lbs to no avail.*

05.09.16 **Jack Britton** (USA) ND-W PTS 10 Joe Welling (USA), Buffalo. *Welling weighed 134½ lbs.*

17.10.16 **Jack Britton** (USA) W PTS 12 Ted Kid Lewis (GB), Boston. *The Boston Post (newspaper) classed it as a title fight, but failed to list any weights, while according to Lewis, with both men inside the limit, the title was at stake.*

14.11.16 **Jack Britton** (USA) DREW 12 Ted Kid Lewis (GB), Boston. *Scheduled for 12 rounds, there was no mention in the Boston Post (newspaper) that the title was up for grabs and no weights were indicated. Although Lewis makes no mention of it as such in his biography, it seems fairly safe to assume that he was inside the limit.*

21.11.16 **Jack Britton** (USA) W PTS 12 Charley White (USA), Boston. *According to the Boston Post (newspaper), the Articles of Agreement called for the two men to be inside 142 lbs at 3.0 pm on the day of the fight. After the paper went on to say that Britton scaled 144½ lbs to White's 136½, had the latter won the title would have changed hands.*

01.01.17 **Jack Britton** (USA) ND-W PTS 10 Jimmy Duffy (USA), Buffalo. *Although no weights were given, one has to assume that both men were inside the championship limit after the Toronto Daily Main (newspaper) reported that Britton successfully held on to his title.*

26.03.17 **Jack Britton** (USA) ND-L PTS 10 Ted Kid Lewis (GB), Cleveland. *Recorded in various published title listings as involving the title, heavy research to date has failed to uncover either weights or billing. The same conditions apply where asterisked (*).*

19.05.17 **Jack Britton** (USA) ND-L PTS 10 Ted Kid Lewis (GB), Toronto. *Both men agreed to be inside 142 lbs (3.0 pm weigh-in).*

06.06.17 **Jack Britton** (USA) ND-DREW 10 Ted Kid Lewis (GB), St Louis *

14.06.17 **Jack Britton** (USA) ND-DREW 10 Ted Kid Lewis (GB), New York City. *Lewis weighed 144¼ lbs.*

25.06.17 **Ted Kid Lewis** (GB) W PTS 20 Jack Britton (USA), Dayton. *Both men were inside the agreed 142 lbs at 3.0 pm on the day of the fight.*

04.07.17 **Ted Kid Lewis** (GB) ND-L PTS 15 Johnny Griffiths (USA), Akron *

31.08.17 **Ted Kid Lewis** (GB) ND-W CO 1 Albert Badoud (SWI), New York City. *Recorded in early Ring Record Books as a no-decision title fight, although Badoud had challenged Lewis at every turn, he came into the ring at 152 lbs in order to protect his European title.*

24.10.17 **Ted Kid Lewis** (GB) DREW 4 Battling Ortega (MEX), Emeryville. *Shown in the 1981 Ring Record Book as a fight where the title was at stake, it should not have been so, with Lewis conceding around 20 lbs to his rival in a contest of just four rounds duration.*

13.11.17 **Ted Kid Lewis** (GB) W PTS 4 Johnny McCarthy (USA), San Francisco. *Mistakenly shown as a four round stoppage title win for Lewis in the 1983 Boxing Encyclopedia, in fact, it was little more than an exhibition bout.*

17.12.17 **Ted Kid Lewis** (GB) ND-W PTS 12 Bryan Downey (USA), Columbus. *Although no weights were disclosed, the Chicago Tribune (newspaper) reported that Downey was challenging for the title.*

17.05.18 **Ted Kid Lewis** (GB) W PTS 20 Johnny Tillman (USA), Denver *(142 lbs at 3.0 pm).*

04.07.18 **Ted Kid Lewis** (GB) ND-W PTS 20 Johnny Griffiths (USA), Akron *

25.09.18 **Ted Kid Lewis** (GB) ND-W PTS 8 Benny Leonard (USA), Newark. *Leonard weighed 130¼ lbs.*

10.03.19 **Ted Kid Lewis** (GB) ND-DREW 8 Johnny Griffiths (USA), Memphis *

17.03.19 **Jack Britton** (USA) ND-W CO 9 Ted Kid Lewis (GB), Canton. *In a no-decision bout scheduled for 12 rounds, Lewis was knocked down nine times before being counted out and Britton successfully claimed the title on the result. Prior to the fight, Lewis, suffering from anaemia, had been told by doctors to take a complete rest from boxing, but his management team stupidly disregarded the advice. Also, with the championship weight in America fluctuating between 142 and 145 lbs, regardless of whether a 3.0 pm or ringside weigh-in, Lewis should have realised that Britton, who weighed 144½ lbs on the night, would be accepted as champion if he won inside the distance.*

24.03.19 **Jack Britton** (USA) ND-W PTS 10 Jack Perry (USA), Pittsburgh. *The day before the fight, the Pittsburgh Daily Gazette (newspaper) claimed that Britton was already down to 142 lbs, while Perry was expected to comfortably make his normal fighting weight of 140.*

06.05.19 **Jack Britton** (USA) ND-W PTS 10 Johnny Griffiths (USA), Buffalo. *Recorded in the 1984 Ring Record Book as a no-decision title fight, the Buffalo Boxing Record gave Britton as 145½ lbs and Griffiths at 147. However, at this point in time, the weight class limit in America was recognised as being 145 lbs.*

19.05.19 **Jack Britton** (USA) ND-W PTS 10 Joe Welling (USA), Syracuse. *Both men were inside 142 lbs at the 6.0 pm weigh-in, according to the Chicago Tribune (newspaper) report on the fight.*

04.07.19 **Jack Britton** (USA) ND-W PTS 15 Johnny Griffiths (USA), Canton *

28.07.19 **Jack Britton** (USA) ND-W PTS 8 Ted Kid Lewis (GB), Jersey City. *According to the New York Herald (newspaper) report, both men were inside 145 lbs at the 3.0 pm weigh-in.*

07.08.19 Jack Britton (USA) ND-DREW 12 Johnny Griffiths (USA), Denver *

05.11.19 **Jack Britton** (USA) ND-DREW 10 Johnny Tillman (USA), Detroit *

01.12.19 **Jack Britton** (USA) ND-W CO 11 Billy Ryan (USA), Canton *

09.12.19 **Jack Britton** (USA) ND-W PTS 10 Steve Latzo (USA), Johnstown *

31.05.20 **Jack Britton** (USA) ND-W PTS 15 Johnny Griffiths (USA), Akron *

02.06.20 **Jack Britton** (USA) ND-W PTS 8 Young Joe Borrell (USA), Philadelphia. *With both men inside 145 lbs, the title was at risk.*

23.08.20 **Jack Britton** (USA) DREW 12 Lou Bogash (USA), Bridgeport. *Although shown as a title fight in the Ring Record Book, there was nothing in the Boston Daily Globe (newspaper) to indicate that it was. However, with both men inside 147 lbs, now universally recognised as the welterweight limit, Britton's title was undoubtedly at stake.*

03.09.20 **Jack Britton** (USA) ND-W PTS 10 Johnny Tillman (USA), Cleveland *

06.09.20 **Jack Britton** (USA) ND-W PTS 10 Ray Bronson (USA), Cedar Point *

06.12.20 **Jack Britton** (USA) ND-W PTS 10 Pinkey Mitchell (USA), Milwaukee. *Outweighed by nearly five pounds, Mitchell, who would later be proclaimed the first junior-welter champion, was inside 147 lbs.*

07.02.21 **Jack Britton** (USA) W PTS 15 Ted Kid Lewis (GB), New York City

17.05.21 **Jack Britton** (USA) ND-W PTS 10 Johnny Tillman (USA), Des Moines *

03.06.21 **Jack Britton** (USA) DREW 10 Dave Shade (USA), Portland. *Taking place in Milwaukee, a suburb of Portland, Oregon, the Morning Oregonian (newspaper) advertised it as a title fight, even though the match was made at 150 lbs. Although no weights were announced, unofficially, Shade was known to be 142 lbs, while Britton was expected to come to the ring at 145 lbs.*

08.06.21 **Jack Britton** (USA) DREW 10 Frank Barrieau (C), Vancouver. *Recorded in the Ring Record Book as taking place in Portland on 10 June 1921, according to the Vancouver Daily Province (newspaper), like Britton v Shade, it was a billed title fight. This match was also made at 150 lbs and both men were over the class limit of 147 lbs, with Britton scaling 147½ to the Canadian's 149½.*

18.07.21 **Jack Britton** (USA) ND-W PTS 12 Mickey Walker (USA), Newark. *Walker weighed 145 lbs.*

17.02.22 **Jack Britton** (USA) DREW 15 Dave Shade (USA), New York City

05.05.22 **Jack Britton** (USA) ND-W PTS 10 Cowboy Padgett (USA), Omaha. *Although not disclosing weights, the Vancouver Daily Province (newspaper) reported that Britton retained his title in this one.*

26.06.22 **Jack Britton** (USA) W DIS 13 Benny Leonard (USA), New York City. *One of the great unsolved mysteries of the ring, saw lightweight champion, Leonard, ruled out for hitting the already floored Britton for no apparent reason. However, information to hand years later, suggests that Leonard had no intention of winning the welterweight title and getting disqualified without loss of face seemed to be his best way out.*

10.10.22 **Jack Britton** (USA) W PTS 12 Jimmy Kelly (USA), Havana. *Overlooked as a title fight in all the record books I have come across over the years, that omission can at last be remedied. According to the Havana Post (newspaper), this was a billed championship match with Britton weighing 144 lbs to Kelly's 147.*

01.11.22 **Mickey Walker** (USA) W PTS 15 Jack Britton (USA), New York City

23.02.23 **Mickey Walker** (USA) ND-W PTS 10 Johnny Griffiths (USA), Scranton. *According to the New York Times (newspaper) report of the fight, Walker's title was up for grabs in this one.*

22.03.23 **Mickey Walker** (USA) ND-W PTS 12 Pete Latzo (USA), Newark. *Latzo weighed 144½ lbs.*

03.05.23 **Mickey Walker** (USA) ND-W CO 6 Morrie Schlaiffer (USA), Chicago. *The Chicago Tribune (newspaper) reported this at 147 lbs, with Walker's welter crown being the prize if Schlaiffer could score an inside the distance win. After repeated requests for Walker to defend his title against Dave Shade had failed, the NYSAC stripped him on 6 June 1923 and proclaimed Shade as champion.*

27.07.23 **Jimmy Jones** (USA) W PTS 10 Dave Shade (USA), Boston. *Jones is shown in the Ring Record Book as having won the NYSAC and Massachusetts' version of the title and the Boxing Blade reported "whatever claim Shade had was lost on 27 July." However, the nearest clue this writer could find as to whether it was a billed championship bout came in the shape of a headline in the Boston Post (newspaper) on the day of the fight stating that "Shade defends his title tonight", although there was nothing in the report to suggest that was the case. Both men were inside the weight, with Shade scaling 143 lbs' 145½.*

24.08.23 **Dave Shade** (USA) W PTS 15 Georgie Ward (USA), New York City. *According to the Boston Post (newspaper), prior to Shade v Jones, a New York promoter had signed up Shade and Ward to contest the NYSAC version of the title, a statement backed up in the March 1951 edition of Ring Magazine. We now know that Shade had already lost his claim in the offices of the NYSAC on 31 July and the above fight would have carried an "unofficial" title tag, only.*

08.10.23 **Mickey Walker** (USA) ND-NC 9 Jimmy Jones (USA), Newark - NBA. *With Walker carrying an injured hand, the pair were thrown out for not trying. Three days later, both men were suspended by the NYSAC, who also rescinded Jones' title claim. Incidentally, for this fight Jones weighed 145¾ lbs, while Walker came in at 148.*

26.10.23 **Dave Shade** (USA) W PTS 15 Bermondsey Billy Wells (GB), New York City. *Earlier thought to be a defence of Shade's NYSAC title, it is now recognised that Shade no longer held that at this time. That is supported by a statement from Leo Flynn,*

Shade's manager, in the New York Times on the day of the fight saying "his boxer will lay claim to the welterweight championship if successful tonight and defend it against all-comers." The following day, the NYSAC announced that it was no longer their intention to make champions by proclamation, but, in order to compel champions to defend their titles, they would be suspended until doing so. Going back to the fight, Shade weighed 146 lbs to Wells' 145.

02.06.24 Mickey Walker (USA) W PTS 10 Lew Tendler (USA), Philadelphia - NBA

01.10.24 Mickey Walker (USA) W CO 6 Bobby Barrett (USA), Philadelphia - NBA

24.08.25 **Mickey Walker** (USA) ND-W PTS 10 Sailor Friedman (USA), Chicago. *According to the Chicago Tribune (newspaper), both men were inside 147 lbs.*

21.09.25 Mickey Walker (USA) W PTS 15 Dave Shade (USA), New York City

25.11.25 **Mickey Walker** (USA) ND-W PTS 12 Sailor Friedman (USA), Newark. *Friedman weighed 144 lbs against Walker's 146½.*

20.05.26 Pete Latzo (USA) W PTS 10 Mickey Walker (USA), Scranton

29.06.26 **Pete Latzo** (USA) ND-W CO 5 Willie Harmon (USA), Newark. *Harmon weighed 144¼ lbs.*

09.07.26 Pete Latzo (USA) W DIS 4 George Levine (USA), New York City

03.06.27 Joe Dundee (USA) W PTS 15 Pete Latzo (USA), New York City

13.07.27 **Joe Dundee** (USA) W PTS 10 Billy Drako (USA), Cincinnati. *Not recorded in the Ring Record Book as a title fight, the Cincinnati Enquirer (newspaper) tell us it was advertised as such, with both men inside 147 lbs.*

07.07.28 **Joe Dundee** (USA) W RTD 8 Hilario Martinez (SP), Barcelona. *Although listed as a championship fight within Dundee's record in the Ring Record Book, it is not recorded as such in the title bout listings. According to the 1929 Everlast Annual, no one, excepting the Spanish fans, perhaps, took the advance championship advertising seriously as it was contested over ten rounds when 15 was the order of the day and that the report in the August 1928 issue of Ring Magazine clearly stated that it was at catchweights. That last point was substantiated when a Spanish newspaper claimed that Dundee (78.3 kg) and Martinez (77 kg) had both been well over the middleweight limit.*

30.08.28 **Young Jack Thompson** (USA) W RSC 2 Joe Dundee (USA), Chicago. *Although recorded in the Boxing News Annual as a title fight, it was, in fact, a catchweight contest at 148 lbs. Incidentally, Thompson actually weighed 143 lbs. Following the fight, however, Dundee forfeited NBA recognition when persistently refusing to defend against either Thompson or the leading contender, Jackie Fields, who were subsequently matched for the vacant NBA title.*

25.03.29 Jackie Fields (USA) W PTS 10 Young Jack Thompson (USA), Chicago - NBA

25.07.29 Jackie Fields (USA) W DIS 2 Joe Dundee (USA), Detroit

09.05.30 Young Jack Thompson (USA) W PTS 15 Jackie Fields (USA), Detroit

05.09.30 **Tommy Freeman** (USA) W PTS 15 Young Jack Thompson (USA), Cleveland. *After becoming champion, for some reason or another, the Boxing News Annual recorded five of Freeman's next seven contests as title fights. For the record, they were specifically stated as being non-title catchweight bouts by the Chicago Tribune (newspaper) and Ring Magazine. The five fights in question are listed below.*

09.01.31 **Tommy Freeman** (USA) W PTS 10 Pete August (USA), Hot Springs

26.01.31 **Tommy Freeman** (USA) W PTS 10 Eddie Murdock (USA), Oklahoma City

05.02.31 **Tommy Freeman** (USA) W RSC 5 Duke Trammel (USA), Memphis

09.02.31 **Tommy Freeman** (USA) W RSC 5 Al Kober (USA), New Orleans

01.03.31 **Tommy Freeman** (USA) W PTS 10 Alfredo Gaona (MEX), Mexico City

14.04.31 **Young Jack Thompson** (USA) W RTD 12 Tommy Freeman (USA), Cleveland

23.10.31 **Lou Brouillard** (C) W PTS 15 Young Jack Thompson (USA), Boston

28.01.32 Jackie Fields (USA) W PTS 10 Lou Brouillard (C), Chicago

22.02.33 **Young Corbett III** (USA) W PTS 10 Jackie Fields (USA), San Francisco

29.05.33 **Jimmy McLarnin** (USA) W CO 1 Young Corbett III (USA), Los Angeles

28.05.34 **Barney Ross** (USA) W PTS 15 Jimmy McLarnin (USA), New York City

17.09.34 Jimmy McLarnin (USA) W PTS 15 Barney Ross (USA), New York City

28.05.35 Barney Ross (USA) W PTS 15 Jimmy McLarnin (USA), New York City

27.11.36 Barney Ross (USA) W PTS 15 Izzy Jannazzo (USA), New York City

23.09.37 Barney Ross (USA) W PTS 15 Ceferino Garcia (PH), New York City. *Barney Ross forfeited IBU recognition in January 1938, when that authority decided to recognise the winner of the Felix Wouters v Gustav Eder European title bout, as world champion.*

16.02.38 Felix Wouters (BEL) W PTS 15 Gustav Eder (GER), Brussels - IBU. *During an international boxing convention held in Rome in May 1938, which was attended by many of the leading authorities within the sport, the IBU agreed to refuse to recognise all individually-made world champions, including their own Felix Wouters, in an effort to stand by one universally acknowledged champion, who, in turn, would have to concede to regular defences decided by the new Federation.*

31.05.38 Henry Armstrong (USA) W PTS 15 Barney Ross (USA), New York City

25.11.38 Henry Armstrong (USA) W PTS 15 Ceferino Garcia (PH), New York City

05.12.38 Henry Armstrong (USA) W RSC 3 Al Manfredo (USA), Cleveland

10.01.39 Henry Armstrong (USA) W PTS 10 Baby Arizmendi (MEX), Los Angeles

04.03.39 Henry Armstrong (USA) W RSC 4 Bobby Pacho (USA), Havana

16.03.39 Henry Armstrong (USA) W CO 1 Lew Feldman (USA), St Louis. *Although the title was at stake, with Armstrong weighing 135 lbs to Feldman's 134, it was also a lightweight championship match.*

31.03.39 Henry Armstrong (USA) W CO 12 Davey Day (USA), New York City

25.05.39 Henry Armstrong (USA) W PTS 15 Ernie Roderick (GB), Harringay Arena, London

09.10.39 Henry Armstrong (USA) W RSC 4 Al Manfredo (USA), Des Moines

13.10.39 Henry Armstrong (USA) W CO 2 Howard Scott (USA), Minneapolis

20.10.39 Henry Armstrong (USA) W CO 3 Richie Fontaine (USA), Seattle

24.10.39 Henry Armstrong (USA) W PTS 10 Jimmy Garrison (USA), Los Angeles

30.10.39 Henry Armstrong (USA) W RSC 4 Bobby Pacho (USA), Denver

11.12.39 Henry Armstrong (USA) W CO 7 Jimmy Garrison (USA), Cleveland

04.01.40 Henry Armstrong (USA) W CO 5 Joe Ghnouly (USA), St Louis

24.01.40 Henry Armstrong (USA) W RSC 9 Pedro Montanez (PR), New York City

26.04.40 Henry Armstrong (USA) W RSC 7 Paul Junior (C), Boston

24.05.40 Henry Armstrong (USA) W RSC 5 Ralph Zanelli (USA), Boston

21.06.40 Henry Armstrong (USA) W RSC 3 Paul Junior (C), Portland

17.07.40 Henry Armstrong (USA) W RTD 6 Lew Jenkins (USA), New York City. *Although both men were inside the weight, this was a contracted non-title bout and the championship was not involved as may have been reported on occasion.*

23.09.40 Henry Armstrong (USA) W CO 4 Phil Furr (USA), Washington

04.10.40 Fritzie Zivic (USA) W PTS 15 Henry Armstrong (USA), New York City. *Following Fritzie Zivic's victory over Henry Armstrong, the Maryland Boxing Commission ruled that until he gave the Cocoa Kid a shot at the title they would fail to recognise him as champion.*

14.10.40 Izzy Jannazzo (USA) W PTS 15 Cocoa Kid (USA), Baltimore - MARYLAND

17.01.41 Fritzie Zivic (USA) W RSC 12 Henry Armstrong (USA), New York City - NY

14.04.41 Izzy Jannazzo (USA) W PTS 15 Jimmy Leto (USA), Baltimore - MARYLAND. *Izzy Jannazzo forfeited Maryland's version of the title, following a defeat at the hands of Coley Welch on 14 November 1941.*

29.07.41 Red Cochrane (USA) W PTS 15 Fritzie Zivic (USA), Newark - NY

01.02.46 Marty Servo (USA) W CO 4 Red Cochrane (USA), New York City. *Lined up to defend his title against Sugar Ray Robinson, Marty Servo suffered an injured nose in training and, on refusing to accede to a new date, the New York Boxing Commission stripped him. Servo then announced his retirement on 25 September 1946 and Robinson was nominated to contest the vacant crown against the NBA representative, Tommy Bell. There* was no need for a series of eliminators as Robinson was the outstanding challenger, while Bell was the only fighter available at the time, prepared to take him on.*

20.12.46 Sugar Ray Robinson (USA) W PTS 15 Tommy Bell (USA), New York City

24.06.47 Sugar Ray Robinson (USA) W RSC 8 Jimmy Doyle (USA), Cleveland. *Jimmy Doyle died in hospital 17 hours after the fight, having lapsed into a coma and failing to survive an operation.*

19.12.47 Sugar Ray Robinson (USA) W RSC 6 Chuck Taylor (USA), Detroit

28.06.48 Sugar Ray Robinson (USA) W PTS 15 Bernard Docusen (USA), Chicago

11.07.49 Sugar Ray Robinson (USA) W PTS 15 Kid Gavilan (CUB), Philadelphia

09.08.50 Sugar Ray Robinson (USA) W PTS 15 Charlie Fusari (USA), Jersey City. *Sugar Ray Robinson relinquished title on becoming world middleweight champion in February 1951 and the NBA selected Johnny Bratton to fight Charlie Fusari for their version of the championship, while New York named Kid Gavilan as their representative. At the same time, the EBU promoted their champion, Charles Humez, and it was only when he gave up the European title at the end of February 1952, due to increasing weight problems, that the title was unified.*

14.03.51 Johnny Bratton (USA) W PTS 15 Charlie Fusari (USA), Chicago - NBA

18.05.51 Kid Gavilan (CUB) W PTS 15 Johnny Bratton (USA), New York City - NBA/NY

29.08.51 Kid Gavilan (CUB) W PTS 15 Billy Graham (USA), New York City - NBA/NY

04.02.52 Kid Gavilan (CUB) W PTS 15 Bobby Dykes (USA), Miami - NBA/NY

07.07.52 Kid Gavilan (CUB) W RSC 11 Gil Turner (USA), Philadelphia

05.10.52 Kid Gavilan (CUB) W PTS 15 Billy Graham (USA), Havana

11.02.53 Kid Gavilan (CUB) W RTD 9 Chuck Davey (USA), Chicago

18.09.53 Kid Gavilan (CUB) W PTS 15 Carmen Basilio (USA), Syracuse

13.11.53 Kid Gavilan (CUB) W PTS 15 Johnny Bratton (USA), Chicago

20.10.54 Johnny Saxton (USA) W PTS 15 Kid Gavilan (CUB), Philadelphia

01.04.55 Tony de Marco (USA) W RSC 14 Johnny Saxton (USA), Boston

10.06.55 Carmen Basilio (USA) W RSC 12 Tony de Marco (USA), Syracuse

30.11.55 Carmen Basilio (USA) W RSC 12 Tony de Marco (USA), Boston

14.03.56 Johnny Saxton (USA) W PTS 15 Carmen Basilio (USA), Chicago

12.09.56 Carmen Basilio (USA) W RSC 9 Johnny Saxton (USA), Syracuse

22.02.57 Carmen Basilio (USA) W CO 2 Johnny Saxton (USA), Cleveland. *Carmen Basilio relinquished the title on becoming world middleweight champion in September 1957 and a World Championship Commission was set up to organise a series of eliminators. In the meantime, Tony de Marco was matched to contest the Massachusetts version of the title with Virgil Akins.*

29.10.57 Virgil Akins (USA) W CO 14 Tony de Marco (USA), Boston - MASSACHUSETTS

21.01.58 Virgil Akins (USA) W RSC 12 Tony de Marco (USA), Boston - MASSACHUSETTS. *With these last two contests being part of the elimination series, the semi-final legs saw Virgil Akins kayo Isaac Logart in the sixth on 21 March 1958 (New York City) and Vince Martinez win on points over 12 rounds against Gil Turner on 14 January 1958 (Philadelphia). Earlier, in a quarter-final pairing, Isaac Logart had outscored Gaspar Ortega over 12 rounds on 6 December 1957 in Cleveland.*

05.06.58 Virgil Akins (USA) W RSC 4 Vince Martinez (USA), St Louis

05.12.58 Don Jordan (USA) W PTS 15 Virgil Akins (USA), Los Angeles

24.04.59 Don Jordan (USA) W PTS 15 Virgil Akins (USA), St Louis

10.07.59 Don Jordan (USA) W PTS 15 Denny Moyer (USA), Portland

27.05.60 Benny Kid Paret (CUB) W PTS 15 Don Jordan (USA), Las Vegas

10.12.60 Benny Kid Paret (CUB) W PTS 15 Federico Thompson (PAN), New York City

01.04.61 Emile Griffith (USA) W CO 13 Benny Kid Paret (CUB), Miami

03.06.61 Emile Griffith (USA) W RSC 12 Gaspar Ortega (MEX), Los Angeles

30.09.61 Benny Kid Paret (CUB) W PTS 15 Emile Griffith (USA), New York City

24.03.62 Emile Griffith (USA) W RSC 12 Benny Kid Paret (CUB), New York City. *After being battered to the floor, Benny Paret failed to regain conciousness and died in hospital ten days later.*

13.07.62 Emile Griffith (USA) W PTS 15 Ralph Dupas (USA), Las Vegas

08.12.62 **Emile Griffith** (USA) W RTD 9 Jorge Fernandez (ARG), Las Vegas

21.03.63 **Luis Rodriguez** (CUB) W PTS 15 Emile Griffith (USA), Los Angeles

08.06.63 **Emile Griffith** (USA) W PTS 15 Luis Rodriguez (CUB), New York City

12.06.64 **Emile Griffith** (USA) W PTS 15 Luis Rodriguez (CUB), Las Vegas

22.09.64 **Emile Griffith** (USA) W PTS 15 Brian Curvis (GB), The Arena, Wembley

30.03.65 **Emile Griffith** (USA) W PTS 15 Jose Stable (CUB), New York City

10.12.65 **Emile Griffith** (USA) W PTS 15 Manuel Gonzalez (USA), New York City. *When Emile Griffith relinquished the title in April 1966 on becoming world middleweight champion, the NBA immediately set up a match between Curtis Cokes, who had stopped Luis Rodriguez in the 15th round of an eliminator on 6 July 1966 in New Orleans, and Manuel Gonzalez, for their version of the championship. New York agreed to recognise a fight between the winner of the NBA tournament and European champion, Jean Josselin.*

06.08.66 Willie Ludick (SA) W PTS 15 Jean Josselin (FR), Johannesburg - SOUTH AFRICA

24.08.66 Curtis Cokes (USA) W PTS 15 Manuel Gonzalez (USA), New Orleans - WBA

28.11.66 Curtis Cokes (USA) W PTS 15 Jean Josselin (FR), Dallas - WBA/WBC

07.12.66 Charlie Shipes (USA) W RSC 10 Percy Manning (USA), Hayward - CALIFORNIA

19.05.67 Curtis Cokes (USA) W RSC 10 Francois Pavilla (FR), Dallas - WBA/WBC

02.10.67 Curtis Cokes (USA) W RSC 8 Charlie Shipes (USA), Oakland - WBA/WBC

16.04.68 **Curtis Cokes** (USA) W RSC 5 Willie Ludick (SA), Dallas

21.10.68 **Curtis Cokes** (USA) W PTS 15 Ramon la Cruz (ARG), New Orleans

18.04.69 **Jose Napoles** (CUB) W RSC 13 Curtis Cokes (USA), Los Angeles

29.06.69 **Jose Napoles** (CUB) W RTD 10 Curtis Cokes (USA), Mexico City

17.10.69 **Jose Napoles** (CUB) W PTS 15 Emile Griffith (USA), Los Angeles

15.02.70 **Jose Napoles** (CUB) W RSC 15 Ernie Lopez (USA), Los Angeles

03.12.70 **Billy Backus** (USA) W RSC 4 Jose Napoles (CUB), Syracuse

04.06.71 **Jose Napoles** (CUB) W RSC 8 Billy Backus (USA), Los Angeles

14.12.71 **Jose Napoles** (CUB) W PTS 15 Hedgemon Lewis (USA), Los Angeles

28.03.72 **Jose Napoles** (CUB) W CO 7 Ralph Charles (GB), The Arena, Wembley

10.06.72 **Jose Napoles** (CUB) W RSC 2 Adolph Pruitt (USA), Monterrey. *Having failed to get Jose Napoles to give Billy Backus a return, following the latter's win on points over 12 rounds against Danny McAloon in Syracuse on 14 April 1972, the New York Boxing Commission announced that they had matched Backus against Hedgemon Lewis for their version of the title.*

16.06.72 Hedgemon Lewis (USA) W PTS 15 Billy Backus (USA), Syracuse - NY

08.12.72 Hedgemon Lewis (USA) W PTS 15 Billy Backus (USA), Syracuse - NY

28.02.73 Jose Napoles (CUB) W CO 7 Ernie Lopez (USA), Los Angeles - WBA/WBC

23.06.73 Jose Napoles (CUB) W PTS 15 Roger Menetrey (FR), Grenoble - WBA/WBC

22.09.73 Jose Napoles (CUB) W PTS 15 Clyde Gray (C), Toronto - WBA/WBC

03.08.74 **Jose Napoles** (CUB) W RSC 9 Hedgemon Lewis (USA), Mexico City

14.12.74 **Jose Napoles** (CUB) W CO 3 Horacio Saldano (ARG), Mexico City

30.03.75 **Jose Napoles** (CUB) W TD 12 Armando Muniz (MEX), Acapulco. *In May 1975, after hearing the news that Jose Napoles was handing back his WBA belt in order to concentrate on defending the WBC title, the WBA announced that a Clyde Gray v Angel Espada contest would be for their version of the vacant title.*

28.06.75 Angel Espada (PR) W PTS 15 Clyde Gray (C), San Juan - WBA

12.07.75 Jose Napoles (CUB) W PTS 15 Armando Muniz (MEX), Mexico City - WBC

11.10.75 Angel Espada (PR) W PTS 15 Johnny Gant (USA), San Juan - WBA

06.12.75 John H. Stracey (GB) W RSC 6 Jose Napoles (CUB), Mexico City - WBC

20.03.76 John H. Stracey (GB) W RSC 10 Hedgemon Lewis (USA), The Arena, Wembley - WBC

22.06.76 Carlos Palomino (MEX) W RSC 12 John H. Stracey (GB), The Arena, Wembley - WBC

17.07.76 Pipino Cuevas (MEX) W RSC 2 Angel Espada (PR), Mexicali - WBA

27.10.76 Pipino Cuevas (MEX) W CO 2 Shoji Tsujimoto (JAP), Kanazawa - WBA

22.01.77 Carlos Palomino (MEX) W RSC 15 Armando Muniz (MEX), Los Angeles - WBC

12.03.77 Pipino Cuevas (MEX) W CO 2 Miguel Campanino (ARG), Mexico City - WBA

14.06.77 Carlos Palomino (MEX) W CO 11 Dave Boy Green (GB), The Arena, Wembley - WBC

06.08.77 Pipino Cuevas (MEX) W CO 2 Clyde Gray (C), Los Angeles - WBA

13.09.77 Carlos Palomino (MEX) W PTS 15 Everaldo Azevedo (BR), Los Angeles - WBC

19.11.77 Pipino Cuevas (MEX) W RSC 11 Angel Espada (PR), San Juan - WBA

10.12.77 Carlos Palomino (MEX) W CO 13 Jose Palacios (MEX), Los Angeles - WBC

11.02.78 Carlos Palomino (MEX) W CO 7 Ryu Sorimachi (JAP), Las Vegas - WBC

04.03.78 Pipino Cuevas (MEX) W RSC 9 Harold Weston (USA), Los Angeles - WBA

18.03.78 Carlos Palomino (MEX) W RSC 9 Mimoun Mohatar (MOR), Las Vegas - WBC

20.05.78 Pipino Cuevas (MEX) W RSC 1 Billy Backus (USA), Los Angeles - WBA

27.05.78 Carlos Palomino (MEX) W PTS 15 Armando Muniz (MEX), Los Angeles - WBC

09.09.78 Pipino Cuevas (MEX) W RSC 2 Pete Ranzany (USA), Sacramento - WBA

14.01.79 Wilfred Benitez (PR) W PTS 15 Carlos Palomino (MEX), San Juan - WBC

29.01.79 Pipino Cuevas (MEX) W RSC 2 Scott Clark (USA), Los Angeles - WBA

25.03.79 Wilfred Benitez (PR) W PTS 15 Harold Weston (USA), San Juan - WBC

30.07.79 Pipino Cuevas (MEX) W PTS 15 Randy Shields (USA), Chicago - WBA

30.11.79 Sugar Ray Leonard (USA) W RSC 15 Wilfred Benitez (PR), Las Vegas - WBC

08.12.79 Pipino Cuevas (MEX) W RSC 10 Angel Espada (PR), Los Angeles - WBA

31.03.80 Sugar Ray Leonard (USA) W CO 4 Dave Boy Green (GB), Landover - WBC

06.04.80 Pipino Cuevas (MEX) W CO 5 Harold Volbrecht (SA), Houston - WBA

20.06.80 Roberto Duran (PAN) W PTS 15 Sugar Ray Leonard (USA), Montreal - WBC

02.08.80 Thomas Hearns (USA) W RSC 2 Pipino Cuevas (MEX), Detroit - WBA

25.11.80 Sugar Ray Leonard (USA) W RTD 8 Roberto Duran (PAN), New Orleans - WBC

06.12.80 Thomas Hearns (USA) W CO 6 Luis Primera (VEN), Detroit - WBA

28.03.81 Sugar Ray Leonard (USA) W RSC 10 Larry Bonds (USA), Syracuse - WBC

25.04.81 Thomas Hearns (USA) W RSC 12 Randy Shields (USA), Phoenix - WBA

25.06.81 Thomas Hearns (USA) W RSC 4 Pablo Baez (USA), Houston - WBA

16.09.81 **Sugar Ray Leonard** (USA) W RSC 14 Thomas Hearns (USA), Las Vegas

15.02.82 **Sugar Ray Leonard** (USA) W RSC 3 Bruce Finch (USA), Reno. *Sugar Ray Leonard relinquished title on announcing his retirement in November 1982 and the WBA lined up Don Curry, who had won a final eliminator on points over 12 rounds against Marlon Starling at Atlantic City on 23 October 1982, to fight Jun-Sok Hwang for their version of the championship. Meanwhile, the WBC set up Colin Jones v Milton McCrory to contest their title.*

13.02.83 Don Curry (USA) W PTS 15 Jun-Sok Hwang (SK), Fort Worth - WBA

19.03.83 Milton McCrory (USA) DREW 12 Colin Jones (GB), Reno - WBC

13.08.83 Milton McCrory (USA) W PTS 12 Colin Jones (GB), Las Vegas - WBC

03.09.83 Don Curry (USA) W RSC 1 Roger Stafford (USA), Marsala - WBA

14.01.84 Milton McCrory (USA) W RSC 6 Milton Guest (USA), Detroit - WBC

04.02.84 Don Curry (USA) W PTS 15 Marlon Starling (USA), Atlantic City - WBA/IBF

15.04.84 Milton McCrory (USA) W RSC 6 Gilles Ebilia (FR), Detroit - WBC

21.04.84 Don Curry (USA) W RTD 7 Elio Diaz (VEN), Fort Worth - WBA/IBF

22.09.84 Don Curry (USA) W RSC 6 Nino la Rocca (ITA), Monaco - WBA/IBF

19.01.85 Don Curry (USA) W RSC 4 Colin Jones (GB), National Exhibition Centre, Birmingham - WBA/IBF

09.03.85 Milton McCrory (USA) W PTS 12 Pedro Vilella (PR), Paris - WBC

14.07.85 Milton McCrory (USA) W RSC 3 Carlos Trujillo (PAN), Monaco - WBC

06.12.85 **Don Curry** (USA) W CO 2 Milton McCrory (USA), Las Vegas

09.03.86 **Don Curry** (USA) W CO 2 Eduardo Rodriguez (PAN), Fort Worth

27.09.86 **Lloyd Honeyghan** (GB) W RTD 6 Don Curry (USA), Atlantic City. *Following his shock victory, Honeyghan relinquished the WBA version of the title in December 1986 after being told that his first defence would be against their number one challenger, the white South African, Harold Volbrecht. Honeyghan refused the edict on the grounds of the organisation's attitude towards apartheid and the WBA matched Volbrecht against Mark Breland for their version of the title.*

06.02.87 Mark Breland (USA) W CO 7 Harold Volbrecht (SA), Atlantic City - WBA

22.02.87 Lloyd Honeyghan (GB) W RSC 2 Johnny Bumphus (USA), Grand Hall, Wembley - IBF/WBC

18.04.87 Lloyd Honeyghan (GB) W PTS 12 Maurice Blocker (USA), Albert Hall, London - IBF/WBC

22.08.87 Marlon Starling (USA) W CO 11 Mark Breland (USA), Columbia - WBA

30.08.87 Lloyd Honeyghan (GB) W RSC 1 Gene Hatcher (USA), Marbella - IBF/WBC. *All over after 45 seconds of the opening round, Honeyghan holds the record as the quickest winner of a world title bout.*

28.10.87 Jorge Vaca (MEX) W TD 8 Lloyd Honeyghan (GB), Grand Hall, Wembley - IBF/WBC. *Jorge Vaca forfeited IBF recognition due to the duration of the bout being over 12 rounds and not 15, as required by that body.*

05.02.88 Marlon Starling (USA) W PTS 12 Fujio Ozaki (JAP), Atlantic City - WBA

29.03.88 Lloyd Honeyghan (GB) W CO 3 Jorge Vaca (MEX), The Arena, Wembley - WBC

16.04.88 Marlon Starling (USA) DREW 12 Mark Breland (USA), Las Vegas - WBA

23.04.88 Simon Brown (USA) W RSC 14 Tyrone Trice (USA), Berck sur Mer - IBF

16.07.88 Simon Brown (USA) W RSC 3 Jorge Vaca (MEX), Kingston - IBF

29.07.88 Tomas Molinares (COL) W CO 6 Marlon Starling (USA), Atlantic City - WBA. *Tomas Molinares forfeited WBA recognition in January 1989 when unable to make the weight.*

29.07.88 Lloyd Honeyghan (GB) W RSC 5 Yung-Kil Chung (SK), Atlantic City - WBC

14.10.88 Simon Brown (USA) W PTS 12 Mauro Martelli (SWI), Lausanne - IBF

05.02.89 Mark Breland (USA) W RSC 1 Seung-Soon Lee (SK), Las Vegas - WBA

05.02.89 Marlon Starling (USA) W RSC 9 Lloyd Honeyghan (GB), Las Vegas - WBC

18.02.89 Simon Brown (USA) W RSC 3 Jorge Maysonet (PR), Budapest - IBF

22.04.89 Mark Breland (USA) W RSC 5 Rafael Pineda (COL), Atlantic City - WBA

27.04.89 Simon Brown (USA) W CO 7 Al Long (USA), Washington - IBF

08.05.89 Genaro Leon (MEX) W CO 1 Danny Garcia (PR), Santa Ana - WBO. *Genaro Leon relinquished WBO version of title in October 1989 in order to try for a crack at one of the other organisation's crowns.*

15.09.89 Marlon Starling (USA) W PTS 12 Yung-Kil Chung (SK), Hartford - WBC

20.09.89 Simon Brown (USA) W RSC 2 Bobby Jo Brown (USA), Rochester - IBF

13.10.89 Mark Breland (USA) W RSC 2 Mauro Martelli (SWI), Geneva - WBA

09.11.89 Simon Brown (USA) W PTS 12 Luis Santana (DOM), Springfield - IBF

10.12.89 Mark Breland (USA) W RSC 4 Fujio Ozaki (JAP), Tokyo - WBA

15.12.89 Manning Galloway (USA) W PTS 12 Al Hamza (USA), Yabucoa - WBO

03.03.90 Mark Breland (USA) W RSC 3 Lloyd Honeyghan (GB), The Arena, Wembley - WBA

01.04.90 Simon Brown (USA) W RSC 10 Tyrone Trice (USA), Washington - IBF

08.07.90 Aaron Davis (USA) W CO 9 Mark Breland (USA), Reno - WBA

19.08.90 Maurice Blocker (USA) W PTS 12 Marlon Starling (USA), Reno - WBC

25.08.90 Manning Galloway (USA) W PTS 12 Nika Khumalo (SA), Lewiston - WBO

19.01.91 Meldrick Taylor (USA) W PTS 12 Aaron Davis (USA), Atlantic City - WBA

15.02.91 Manning Galloway (USA) W RTD 8 Gert Bo Jacobsen (DEN), Randers - WBO

18.03.91 Simon Brown (USA) W RSC 10 Maurice Blocker (USA), Las Vegas - IBF/WBC. *Simon Brown relinquished IBF version of title in May 1991 to challenge for the WBC crown.*

17.05.91 Manning Galloway (USA) W RTD 7 Racheed Lawal (DEN), Copenhagen - WBO

01.06.91 Meldrick Taylor (USA) W PTS 12 Luis Garcia (VEN), Palm Springs - WBA

15.09.91 Manning Galloway (USA) W PTS 12 Jeff Malcolm (A), Broadbeach - WBO

04.10.91 Maurice Blocker (USA) W PTS 12 Glenwood Brown (USA), Atlantic City - IBF

29.11.91 James McGirt (USA) W PTS 12 Simon Brown (USA), Las Vegas - WBC

14.12.91 Manning Galloway (USA) W PTS 12 Nika Khumalo (SA), Cape Town - WBO

18.01.92 Meldrick Taylor (USA) W PTS 12 Glenwood Brown (USA), Philadelphia - WBA

25.06.92 James McGirt (USA) W PTS 12 Patrizio Oliva (ITA), Naples - WBC

25.07.92 Manning Galloway (USA) W PTS 12 Pat Barrett (GB), G-Mex Centre, Manchester - WBO

28.08.92 Maurice Blocker (USA) W PTS 12 Luis Garcia (VEN), Atlantic City - IBF

31.10.92 Crisanto Espana (VEN) W RSC 8 Meldrick Taylor (USA), Earls Court Arena, London - WBA

27.11.92 Manning Galloway (USA) NC 1 Gert Bo Jacobsen (DEN), Randers - WBO

12.01.93 James McGirt (USA) W PTS 12 Genaro Leon (MEX), New York City - WBC

12.02.93 Gert Bo Jacobsen (DEN) W PTS 12 Manning Galloway (USA), Randers - WBO. *Owing to an illness, Gert Bo Jacobsen relinquished the WBO version of title in October 1993, the week before he was due to defend against Eamonn Loughran.*

06.03.93 Pernell Whitaker (USA) W PTS 12 James McGirt (USA), New York City - WBC

05.05.93 Crisanto Espana (VEN) W PTS 12 Rodolfo Aguilar (PAN), Ulster Hall, Belfast - WBA

19.06.93 Felix Trinidad (PR) W CO 2 Maurice Blocker (USA), San Diego - IBF

06.08.93 Felix Trinidad (PR) W RSC 1 Luis Garcia (VEN), Bayamon - IBF

10.09.93 Pernell Whitaker (USA) DREW 12 Julio Cesar Chavez (MEX), San Antonio - WBC

09.10.93 Crisanto Espana (VEN) W RSC 10 Donovan Boucher (C), Old Trafford, Manchester - WBA

16.10.93 Eamonn Loughran (GB) W PTS 12 Lorenzo Smith (USA), King's Hall, Belfast - WBO

23.10.93 Felix Trinidad (PR) W CO 10 Anthony Stephens (USA), Fort Lauderdale - IBF

22.01.94 Eamonn Loughran (GB) W PTS 12 Alessandro Duran (ITA), King's Hall, Belfast - WBO

29.01.94 Felix Trinidad (PR) W PTS 12 Hector Camacho (PR), Las Vegas - IBF

09.04.94 Pernell Whitaker (USA) W PTS 12 Santos Cardona (PR), Norfolk - WBC

04.06.94 Ike Quartey (GH) W RSC 11 Crisanto Espana (VEN), Paris - WBA

Light-Middleweight (154 lbs)

Recognised by the amateurs since 1951, because the weight gap between welter and middle was too great, it was initiated in 1962 by the World Boxing Association and the Austrian Boxing Board of Control. Also known as the super-welter and junior middleweight division, the Austrians supported a contest between Americans, Teddy Wright and world welterweight champion, Emile Griffith (who was having difficulty making 147 lbs), while the WBA promoted the claims of Denny Moyer and Joey Giambra.

17.10.62 Emile Griffith (USA) W PTS 15 Teddy Wright (USA), Vienna - AUSTRIA

20.10.62 Denny Moyer (USA) W PTS 15 Joey Giambra (USA), Portland - WBA

03.02.63 Emile Griffith (USA) W RSC 9 Chris Christensen (DEN), Copenhagen - AUSTRIA. *Immediately following the fight, Emile Griffith gave up the Austrian version of the title to concentrate on his welterweight crown, instead.*

19.02.63 Denny Moyer (USA) W PTS 15 Stan Harrington (USA), Honolulu - WBA

29.04.63 Ralph Dupas (USA) W PTS 15 Denny Moyer (USA), New Orleans - WBA

17.06.63 Ralph Dupas (USA) W PTS 15 Denny Moyer (USA), Baltimore - WBA

07.09.63 Sandro Mazzinghi (ITA) W CO 9 Ralph Dupas (USA), Milan - WBA

02.12.63 Sandro Mazzinghi (ITA) W RSC 13 Ralph Dupas (USA), Sydney - WBA

03.10.64 Sandro Mazzinghi (ITA) W CO 12 Tony Montano (USA), Genoa - WBA. *Although billed as a championship bout, Montano came into the ring two pounds overweight and couldn't have won the title even if victorious.*

11.12.64 Sandro Mazzinghi (ITA) W PTS 15 Fortunato Manca (ITA), Rome - WBA

18.06.65 Nino Benvenuti (ITA) W CO 6 Sandro Mazzinghi (ITA), Milan - WBA

17.12.65 Nino Benvenuti (ITA) W PTS 15 Sandro Mazzinghi (ITA), Rome - WBA

25.06.66 Ki-Soo Kim (SK) W PTS 15 Nino Benvenuti (ITA), Seoul - WBA

17.12.66 Ki-Soo Kim (SK) W PTS 15 Stan Harrington (USA), Seoul - WBA

03.10.67 Ki-Soo Kim (SK) W PTS 15 Freddie Little (USA), Seoul - WBA

25.05.68 Sandro Mazzinghi (ITA) W PTS 15 Ki-Soo Kim (SK), Milan - WBA

25.10.68 Sandro Mazzinghi (ITA) NC 9 Freddie Little (USA), Rome - WBA. *Tired and badly cut-up, Mazzinghi did not come out for the ninth round and the referee declared a no-contest on the grounds that he had acted under EBU rules. Actually, the rules specifically stated that in the event of injuries, the referee could call a halt prior to the second half of the eighth round. The title was declared vacant in January 1969 after Mazzinghi had failed to sign for a return contest.*

17.03.69 Freddie Little (USA) W PTS 15 Stan Hayward (USA), Las Vegas - WBA

09.09.69 Freddie Little (USA) W CO 2 Hisao Minami (JAP), Osaka - WBA

20.03.70 Freddie Little (USA) W PTS 15 Gerhard Piaskowy (GER), Berlin - WBA

09.07.70 Carmelo Bossi (ITA) W PTS 15 Freddie Little (USA), Monza - WBA

29.04.71 Carmelo Bossi (ITA) DREW 15 Jose Hernandez (SP), Madrid - WBA

31.10.71 Koichi Wajima (JAP) W PTS 15 Carmelo Bossi (ITA), Tokyo - WBA

07.05.72 Koichi Wajima (JAP) W CO 1 Domenico Tiberia (ITA), Tokyo - WBA

03.10.72 Koichi Wajima (JAP) W CO 3 Matt Donovan (TR), Tokyo - WBA

09.01.73 Koichi Wajima (JAP) DREW 15 Miguel de Oliveira (BR), Tokyo - WBA

19.04.73 Koichi Wajima (JAP) W PTS 15 Ryu Sorimachi (JAP), Osaka - WBA

14.08.73 Koichi Wajima (JAP) W RTD 12 Silvani Bertini (ITA), Sapporo - WBA

05.02.74 Koichi Wajima (JAP) W PTS 15 Miguel de Oliveira (BR), Tokyo - WBA

03.06.74 Oscar Albarado (USA) W CO 15 Koichi Wajima (JAP), Tokyo - WBA

08.10.74 Oscar Albarado (USA) W RSC 7 Ryu Sorimachi (JAP), Tokyo - WBA

21.01.75 Koichi Wajima (JAP) W PTS 15 Oscar Albarado (USA), Tokyo - WBA

07.05.75 Miguel de Oliveira (BR) W PTS 15 Jose Duran (SP), Monaco - WBC

07.06.75 Jae-Do Yuh (SK) W RSC 7 Koichi Wajima (JAP), Kitakyushi - WBA

11.11.75 Jae-Do Yuh (SK) W RSC 6 Masahiro Misako (JAP), Shizuoka - WBA

13.11.75 Elisha Obed (BAH) W RTD 10 Miguel de Oliveira (BR), Paris - WBC

17.02.76 Koichi Wajima (JAP) W CO 15 Jae-Do Yuh (SK), Tokyo - WBA

28.02.76 Elisha Obed (BAH) W CO 2 Tony Gardner (USA), Nassau - WBC

25.04.76 Elisha Obed (BAH) W PTS 15 Sea Robinson (IC), Abidjan - WBC

18.05.76 Jose Duran (SP) W CO 14 Koichi Wajima (JAP), Tokyo - WBA

18.06.76 Eckhard Dagge (GER) W RTD 10 Elisha Obed (BAH), Berlin - WBC

18.09.76 Eckhard Dagge (GER) W PTS 15 Emile Griffith (USA), Berlin - WBC

08.10.76 Miguel Castellini (ARG) W PTS 15 Jose Duran (SP), Madrid - WBA

05.03.77 Eddie Gazo (NIC) W PTS 15 Miguel Castellini (ARG), Managua - WBA

15.03.77 Eckhard Dagge (GER) DREW 15 Maurice Hope (GB), Berlin - WBC

07.06.77 Eddie Gazo (NIC) W RSC 11 Koichi Wajima (JAP), Tokyo - WBA

06.08.77 Rocky Mattioli (ITA) W CO 5 Eckhard Dagge (GER), Berlin - WBC

13.09.77 Eddie Gazo (NIC) W PTS 15 Kenji Shibata (JAP), Tokyo - WBA

18.12.77 Eddie Gazo (NIC) W PTS 15 Chae-Keun Lim (SK), Inchon - WBA

11.03.78 Rocky Mattioli (ITA) W CO 7 Elisha Obed (BAH), Melbourne - WBC

14.05.78 Rocky Mattioli (ITA) W RSC 5 Jose Duran (SP), Pescara - WBC

09.08.78 Masashi Kudo (JAP) W PTS 15 Eddie Gazo (NIC), Akita - WBA

13.12.78 Masashi Kudo (JAP) W PTS 15 Ho-In Joo (SK), Osaka - WBA

04.03.79 Maurice Hope (GB) W RTD 8 Rocky Mattioli (ITA), San Remo - WBC

13.03.79 Masashi Kudo (JAP) W PTS 15 Manuel Gonzalez (USA), Tokyo - WBA

20.06.79 Masashi Kudo (JAP) W RSC 12 Manuel Gonzalez (USA), Yokkaichi - WBA

25.09.79 Maurice Hope (GB) W RSC 7 Mike Baker (USA), The Arena, Wembley - WBC

24.10.79 Ayub Kalule (U) W PTS 15 Masashi Kudo (JAP), Akita - WBA

06.12.79 Ayub Kalule (U) W PTS 15 Steve Gregory (USA), Copenhagen - WBA

17.04.80 Ayub Kalule (U) W RTD 11 Emiliano Villa (COL), Copenhagen - WBA

12.06.80 Ayub Kalule (U) W PTS 15 Marijan Benes (YUG), Randers - WBA

12.07.80 Maurice Hope (GB) W RSC 11 Rocky Mattioli (ITA), Grand Hall, Wembley - WBC

06.09.80 Ayub Kalule (U) W PTS 15 Bushy Bester (SA), Aarhus - WBA

26.11.80 Maurice Hope (GB) W PTS 15 Carlos Herrera (ARG), Grand Hall Wembley - WBC

24.05.81 Wilfred Benitez (PR) W CO 12 Maurice Hope (GB), Las Vegas - WBC

25.06.81 Sugar Ray Leonard (USA) W RSC 9 Ayub Kalule (U), Houston - WBA. *Sugar Ray Leonard relinquished WBA version of title in July 1981 to concentrate on unifying the welterweight division.*

07.11.81 Tadashi Mihara (JAP) W PTS 15 Rocky Fratto (USA), Rochester - WBA

14.11.81 Wilfred Benitez (PR) W PTS 15 Carlos Santos (PR), Las Vegas - WBC

30.01.82 Wilfred Benitez (PR) W PTS 15 Roberto Duran (PAN), Las Vegas - WBC

02.02.82 Davey Moore (USA) W RSC 6 Tadashi Mihara (JAP), Tokyo - WBA

26.04.82 Davey Moore (USA) W CO 5 Charlie Weir (SA), Johannesburg - WBA

17.07.82 Davey Moore (USA) W RSC 10 Ayub Kalule (U), Atlantic City - WBA

03.12.82 Thomas Hearns (USA) W PTS 15 Wilfred Benitez (PR), New Orleans - WBC

29.01.83 Davey Moore (USA) W CO 4 Gary Guiden (USA), Atlantic City - WBA

16.06.83 Roberto Duran (PAN) W RSC 8 Davey Moore (USA), New York City - WBA. *Roberto Duran relinquished WBA version of title in June 1984 to challenge Marvin Hagler for the world middleweight crown.*

11.02.84 Thomas Hearns (USA) W PTS 12 Luigi Minchillo (ITA), Detroit - WBC

11.03.84 Mark Medal (USA) W RSC 5 Earl Hargrove (USA), Atlantic City - IBF

15.06.84 Thomas Hearns (USA) W CO 2 Roberto Duran (PAN), Las Vegas - WBC

15.09.84 Thomas Hearns (USA) W RSC 3 Fred Hutchings (USA), Saginaw - WBC

19.10.84 Mike McCallum (J) W PTS 15 Sean Mannion (USA), New York City - WBA

02.11.84 Carlos Santos (PR) W PTS 15 Mark Medal (USA), New York City - IBF

01.12.84 Mike McCallum (J) W RSC 14 Luigi Minchillo (ITA), Milan - WBA

01.06.85 Carlos Santos (PR) W PTS 15 Louis Acaries (FR), Paris - IBF. *Carlos Santos forfeited IBF recognition in February 1986 for failing to defend against Davey Moore.*

28.07.85 Mike McCallum (J) W RSC 8 David Braxton (USA), Miami - WBA

04.06.86 Buster Drayton (USA) W PTS 15 Carlos Santos (PR), East Rutherford - IBF

23.06.86 Thomas Hearns (USA) W RSC 8 Mark Medal (USA), Las Vegas - WBC. *Thomas Hearns relinquished WBC version of title in September 1986 due to difficulty making the weight.*

23.08.86 Mike McCallum (J) W RSC 2 Julian Jackson (USA), Miami - WBA

24.08.86 Buster Drayton (USA) W RSC 10 Davey Moore (USA), Juan les Pins - IBF

25.10.86 Mike McCallum (J) W CO 9 Said Skouma (FR) Paris - WBA

05.12.86 Duane Thomas (USA) W RSC 3 John Mugabi (U), Las Vegas - WBC

27.03.87 Buster Drayton (USA) W RTD 10 Said Skouma (FR), Cannes - IBF

19.04.87 Mike McCallum (J) W RSC 10 Milton McCrory (USA), Phoenix - WBA

27.06.87 Matthew Hilton (C) W PTS 15 Buster Drayton (USA), Montreal - IBF

12.07.87 Lupe Aquino (MEX) W PTS 12 Duane Thomas (USA), Bordeaux - WBC

18.07.87 Mike McCallum (J) W CO 5 Don Curry (USA), Las Vegas - WBA. *Mike McCallum relinquished WBA version of title in September 1987 to campaign in the middleweight division.*

02.10.87 Gianfranco Rosi (ITA) W PTS 12 Lupe Aquino (MEX), Perugia - WBC

16.10.87 Matthew Hilton (C) W RTD 2 Jack Callahan (USA), Atlantic City - IBF

21.11.87 Julian Jackson (USA) W RSC 3 In-Chul Baek (SK), Las Vegas - WBA

03.01.88 Gianfranco Rosi (ITA) W RSC 7 Duane Thomas (USA), Genoa - WBC

08.07.88 Don Curry (USA) W RTD 9 Gianfranco Rosi (ITA), San Remo - WBC

30.07.88 Julian Jackson (USA) W RSC 3 Buster Drayton (USA), Atlantic City - WBA

04.11.88 Robert Hines (USA) W PTS 12 Matthew Hilton (C), Las Vegas - IBF

08.12.88 John David Jackson (USA) W RTD 7 Lupe Aquino (MEX), Detroit - WBO

05.02.89 Darrin van Horn (USA) W PTS 12 Robert Hines (USA), Atlantic City - IBF

11.02.89 Rene Jacquot (FR) W PTS 12 Don Curry (USA), Grenoble - WBC

25.02.89 Julian Jackson (USA) W CO 8 Francisco de Jesus (BR), Las Vegas - WBA

22.04.89 John David Jackson (USA) W RSC 8 Steve Little (USA), Detroit - WBO

08.07.89 John Mugabi (U) W RSC 1 Rene Jacquot (FR), Paris - WBC

15.07.89 Gianfranco Rosi (ITA) W PTS 12 Darrin van Horn (USA), Atlantic City - IBF

30.07.89 Julian Jackson (USA) W RSC 2 Terry Norris (USA), Atlantic City - WBA. *Julian Jackson relinquished WBA version of title in September 1990 in order to challenge for the vacant WBC crown.*

27.10.89 Gianfranco Rosi (ITA) W PTS 12 Troy Waters (A), St Vincent - IBF

17.02.90 John David Jackson (USA) NC 11 Martin Camara (FR), Deauville - WBO

31.03.90 Terry Norris (USA) W CO 1 John Mugabi (U), Tampa - WBC

14.04.90 Gianfranco Rosi (ITA) W RSC 7 Kevin Daigle (USA), Monaco - IBF

13.07.90 Terry Norris (USA) W PTS 12 Rene Jacquot (FR), Annecy - WBC

21.07.90 Gianfranco Rosi (ITA) W PTS 12 Darrin van Horn (USA), Marino - IBF

23.11.90 John David Jackson (USA) W PTS 12 Chris Pyatt (GB), Granby Halls, Leicester - WBO

30.11.90 Gianfranco Rosi (ITA) W PTS 12 Rene Jacquot (FR), Marsala - IBF

09.02.91 Terry Norris (USA) W PTS 12 Sugar Ray Leonard (USA), New York City - WBC

23.02.91 Gilbert Dele (FR) W RSC 7 Carlos Elliott (USA), Point a Pitre - WBA

16.03.91 Gianfranco Rosi (ITA) W PTS 12 Ron Amundsen (USA), St Vincent - IBF

05.05.91 Gilbert Dele (FR) W PTS 12 Jun-Suk Hwang (SK), Paris - WBA

01.06.91 Terry Norris (USA) W CO 8 Don Curry USA, Palm Springs - WBC

13.07.91 Gianfranco Rosi (ITA) W PTS 12 Glenn Wolfe (USA), Avezzano - IBF

20.07.91 John David Jackson (USA) W PTS 12 Tyrone Trice (USA), McKee City - WBO

16.08.91 Terry Norris (USA) W RSC 1 Brett Lally (USA), San Diego - WBC

03.10.91 Vinnie Pazienza (USA) W RSC 12 Gilbert Dele (FR), Providence - WBA. *Vinnie Pazienza relinquished WBA version of title in October 1992 when an injury stopped him from defending inside the deadline.*

21.11.91 Gianfranco Rosi (ITA) W PTS 12 Gilbert Baptist (USA), Perugia - IBF

13.12.92 Terry Norris (USA) W PTS 12 Jorge Castro (ARG), Paris - WBC

22.02.92 Terry Norris (USA) W RSC 9 Carl Daniels (USA), San Diego - WBC

09.04.92 Gianfranco Rosi (ITA) W RSC 6 Angel Hernandez (SP), Celano - IBF

09.05.92 Terry Norris (USA) W RSC 4 Meldrick Taylor (USA), Las Vegas - WBC

09.06.92 John David Jackson (USA) W RTD 9 Pat Lawlor (USA), San Francisco - WBO

11.07.92 Gianfranco Rosi (ITA) W PTS 12 Gilbert Dele (FR), Monaco - IBF

19.12.92 John David Jackson (USA) W RTD 10 Michele Mastrodonato (ITA), San Severo - WBO. *John David Jackson relinquished WBO version of title in July 1993 due to difficulty making the weight.*

21.12.92 Julio Cesar Vasquez (ARG) W RSC 1 Hitoshi Kamiyama (JAP), Buenos Aires - WBA

20.01.93 Gianfranco Rosi (ITA) W PTS 12 Gilbert Dele (FR), Avoriaz - IBF

20.02.93 Terry Norris (USA) W RSC 2 Maurice Blocker (USA), Mexico City - WBC

22.02.93 Julio Cesar Vasquez (ARG) W CO 1 Aquilino Asprilla (PAN), Mar del Plata - WBA

24.04.93 Julio Cesar Vasquez (ARG) W PTS 12 Javier Castillejos (SP), Madrid - WBA

19.06.93 Terry Norris (USA) W RTD 3 Troy Waters (A), San Diego - WBC

10.07.93 Julio Cesar Vasquez (ARG) W PTS 12 Alejandro Ugueto (VEN), Tucuman - WBA

21.08.93 Julio Cesar Vasquez (ARG) W PTS 12 Aaron Davis (USA), Monaco - WBA

10.09.93 Terry Norris (USA) W RSC 1 Joe Gatti (USA), San Antonio - WBC

30.10.93 Verno Phillips (USA) W RSC 7 Lupe Aquino (MEX), Phoenix - WBO

18.12.93 Simon Brown (USA) W CO 4 Terry Norris (USA), Puebla - WBC

22.01.94 Julio Cesar Vasquez (ARG) W PTS 12 Juan Medina Padilla (SP), Alma Ata - WBA

29.01.94 Simon Brown (USA) W PTS 12 Troy Waters (A), Las Vegas - WBC

04.03.94 Gianfranco Rosi (ITA) T DRAW 6 Vince Pettway (USA), Las Vegas - IBF

04.03.94 Julio Cesar Vasquez (ARG) W RSC 2 Arman Picar (PH), Las Vegas - WBA

08.04.94 Julio Cesar Vasquez (ARG) W PTS 12 Ricardo Nunez (ARG), Tucuman - WBA

07.05.94 Terry Norris (USA) W PTS 12 Simon Brown (USA), Las Vegas - WBC

21.05.94 Julio Cesar Vasquez (ARG) W RSC 10 Ahmet Dottuev (RUS), King's Hall, Belfast - WBA

Middleweight (160 lbs)

The first recognised champion under the Marquis of Queensberry Rules was England's Denny Harrington, although the weight class can be traced as far back as 1786 when Richard Humphries defeated Sam Martin. Harrington, wearing "big" gloves, won the vacant title in London on 12 March 1878, following a six round kayo victory over the American champion, George Rooke, who had emigrated from Ireland at the age of 19. After that he successfully defended in London against Florrie Barnett (second round kayo on 26 May 1879) and Alf Greenfield (18th round disqualification on 27 November 1879), before losing to William Sherriff after 11 hours and 44 minutes at Lapworth on 17 December 1880. However, with Sherriff remaining inactive, the Irish-born Jack "The Nonpareil" Dempsey won the American version of the title on 3 February 1886, beating Jack Fogarty by a 27th round kayo in New York. He retained his crown by defeating George LaBlanche (13th round kayo at Larchmont on 4 March 1886) and Johnny Reagan (45th round stoppage in Manhasset on 13 December 1887), prior to losing in a return match against LaBlanche. The Ring Record Book shows Dempsey winning the title on 30 July 1884 when beating George Fulljames by a 22nd round kayo at Great Kill, New York, following the latter claiming the championship earlier that year. In his book, English Boxing Champions, Bill Matthews refutes that as being ridiculous when explaining that after losing to Dempsey, with neither man exceeding ten stone, Fulljames was defeated by Harry Gilmore for the Canadian featherweight crown! While Harrington had only been recognised as champion in England, Dempsey was accorded similar status in America, although, right up until his second fight with LaBlanche, the Irish-born fighter had made his reputation wearing either skin-tight or driving gloves. Billed for the 154 lbs world title at the Californian Athletic Club, San Francisco, on 27 August 1889, Dempsey v LaBlanche should have achieved significance as the division's first title fight with gloves (five ounce) on American soil. Instead, the fight's notoriety stemmed from a blow, named the pivot punch and subsequently made illegal, which started out as a left-hook that missed its mark until a swivel on the heel brought LaBlanche's elbow back with full force on Dempsey's jaw to register a 32nd round kayo. Although the fight was made famous by the "pivot punch", what has often been overlooked is the fact that LaBlanche, at 161 lbs, failed to make the required weight and therefore no title was ultimately involved.

18.02.90 Nonpareil Jack Dempsey (USA) W RSC 28 Billy McCarthy (A), San Francisco. *It is my opinion that this fight should be recognised as the first "modern" middleweight title bout, with Dempsey weighing 147½ lbs to the English-born McCarthy's 152½, even though there was scandal surrounding the regulation five ounce gloves. The fight, delayed when it was discovered that the air had been let out of the gloves, finally went ahead with more stuffing inserted and weighing in the region of three to four ounces.*

14.01.91 Bob Fitzsimmons (A) W CO 13 Nonpareil Jack Dempsey (USA), New Orleans. Weights (lbs): Fitzsimmons (150½), Dempsey (147½).

20.08.92 Jim Hall (A) W CO 4 Ted Pritchard (GB), The Sussex Downs, Nr Brighton. *With Bob Fitzsimmons recognised as world champion at 154 lbs. Hall and Pritchard were matched for the British version of the title at 160 lbs. Incidentally, both men weighed 157 lbs.*

03.03.93 Bob Fitzsimmons (A) W CO 4 Jim Hall (A), New Orleans. *Although billed as a title match, with both men accepting it as such, the above contest should not be recognised as involving the championship. Fitzsimmons weighed in at a massive 167 lbs to his opponent's 163½ and it was now clear that he would be unable to make 154 lbs again without losing strength. Bearing that in mind and taking advantage of the champion's privilege of the day in being able to carry the weight to suit his own convenience, he successfully named 158 lbs as the new class limit.*

26.09.94 Bob Fitzsimmons (A) W CO 2 Dan Creedon (NZ), New Orleans. *Weights (lbs): Fitzsimmons (156), Creedon (157). By early 1896, it was clear that Fitzsimmons, unable to make 158 lbs anymore, had set his sights on the heavyweight title, even though he continued to call himself the middleweight champion, and Tommy Ryan, who had already beaten the former titleholder, Nonpareil Jack Dempsey, claimed the crown.*

08.10.94 Frank Craig (USA) W CO 2 John O'Brien (GB), NSC, London - GB. *Billed for the British version of the world 158 lbs title, it was Craig's debut in England. Earlier, Craig had claimed the world*

title after all the American white middleweights refused to fight him in anything other than four rounders.

17.12.94 Frank Craig (USA) W CO 1 Ted Pritchard (GB), Central Hall, London - GB. *Billed for the British version of the world 158 lbs title.*

14.10.95 Dan Creedon (NZ) W PTS 20 Frank Craig (USA), NSC, London - GB. *After winning the British version of the world 158 lbs title, Creedon left for America.*

02.03.96 Kid McCoy (USA) W CO 15 Tommy Ryan (USA), Long Island. *A fight made famous by the fact that McCoy, Ryan's old sparring partner, tricked the welterweight (see under that weight class, also) champion into taking him on at 154 lbs by claiming he was out of condition. Following this, the famous expression: "the real McCoy" was coined, but, with Fitzsimmons still considered champion in some quarters, the winner would not be generally recognised.*

18.05.96 Kid McCoy (USA) W DIS 6 Mysterious Billy Smith (USA), Boston. *Reported in the Boston Post (newspaper) as being to a decision over 15 rounds and for the championship of their class, Smith scaled 150 lbs to McCoy's 153. Following the bout, McCoy stated he would immediately be issuing a challenge to Bob Fitzsimmons, who he still recognised as champion.*

26.12.96 Kid McCoy (USA) W CO 9 Billy Doherty (A), Johannesburg. *Billed as a world title fight at 158 lbs, McCoy scaled 156 to Doherty's 158. Although McCoy was recognised in South Africa as champion, in America, Bob Fitzsimmons was still generally perceived to be the titleholder.*

17.12.97 Kid McCoy (USA) W PTS 15 Dan Creedon (NZ), Long Island. *According to the New York Herald (newspaper), the official announcement that McCoy weighed 155½ lbs to Creedon's 157, brought the two men together inside the championship limit, yet, in the very next breath, it went on to say both looked bigger than the given weights and that the contest had been made at catchweights and was therefore not a legitimate title fight. Following the contest, with McCoy electing to campaign among the heavies, Tommy Ryan reclaimed the title.*

25.02.98 Tommy Ryan (USA) W CO 18 George Green (USA), San Francisco. *Recorded as a middleweight title bout in Gilbert Odd's splendid 1983 Boxing Encyclopedia, according to the San Francisco Chronicle (newspaper) report of the day, it was a catchweight contest between the welterweight champion and a man some seven pounds heavier. However, with both men obviously inside 158 lbs, had Ryan lost, it would have been a massive dent to his middleweight title claim.*

13.06.98 Tommy Ryan (USA) W RSC 14 Tommy West (USA), New York City. *Listed as a welterweight title defence for Ryan in the Ring Record Book (see under that weight class, also), the Articles of Agreement specifically called for a catchweight contest and, with Ryan weighing 146 lbs to West's 152 and claiming to be the 150 lbs champion, it had more bearing on the eventual middleweight lineage.*

24.10.98 Tommy Ryan (USA) W PTS 20 Jack Bonner (USA), Brooklyn. *According to the New York Herald (newspaper) report of the fight, Ryan (149) v Bonner (158) involved the 158 lbs title. The Ring Record Book lists this contest as being for the vacant title and, with Fitzsimmons and McCoy continuing to fight out of the weight class, even though the former still saw himself as the middleweight champion, from that moment in time, Ryan proved himself to be the outstanding man at the weight.*

31.08.99 Tommy Ryan (USA) W PTS 20 Jack Moffatt (USA), Dubuque. *Billed as a welterweight title defence for Ryan (see under that weight class also), with both men weighing 152 lbs, according to the Chicago Tribune (newspaper), it was effectively Ryan's middleweight claim that was at stake here.*

18.09.99 Tommy Ryan (USA) W RSC 10 Frank Craig (USA), Brooklyn. *The New York Herald (newspaper) stated that both men were candidates for middleweight honours and were to meet at 158 lbs. Unfortunately, Craig failed to make the weight. Following the fight, Ryan challenged Kid McCoy to a fight at 154 lbs, knowing his rival would have difficulty in making it. McCoy declined the offer, stating that 158 lbs was the middleweight limit and that he still recognised Fitzsimmons as champion.*

15.10.00 Charley McKeever (USA) W PTS 15 Dido Plumb (GB), NSC, London. *Billed for the world title at 152 lbs, with Tommy Ryan considered to be the champion, the result carried no weight on the other side of the Atlantic.*

27.11.00 Tommy Ryan (USA) W PTS 6 Kid Carter (USA), Chicago. *The Chicago Tribune (newspaper) reported that while this could hardly be classified as a championship match, both men were inside 158 lbs at the 6.0 pm weigh-in.*

04.03.01 Tommy Ryan (USA) W RTD 17 Tommy West (USA), Louisville (158 lbs).

04.07.01 George Gardner (USA) W RSC 3 Jack Moffatt (USA), San Francisco. *Advertised for the middleweight title at 159 lbs, according to the San Francisco Chronicle (newspaper), Gardner (158) and Moffatt (156) failed to conform to the Articles of Agreement when they weighed in only four hours before the fight. Despite that, with Ryan now generally recognised as champion, there would have been little support for Gardner outside California.*

19.08.01 Jack O'Brien (USA) W CO 6 Dido Plumb (GB), Ginnett's Circus, Newcastle. *Billed for the British version of the 154 lbs title, fights like this today would be seen as eliminators.*

10.10.01 George Green (USA) W DIS 6 Tommy Ryan (USA), Kansas City. *Occasionally mentioned in passing as a title bout, although it has to be said, in the main, unsupported, the Philadelphia Item (newspaper) report gave no indication that the championship may have been involved and continued to refer to Ryan as the champion. There was also no mention that it was a title fight in the Chicago Tribune (newspaper), merely that it was scheduled for ten rounds or until a decision was reached. The fight itself saw Ryan winning easily until accidentally striking Green with his knee.*

27.01.02 Jack O'Brien (USA) W DIS 3 Charley McKeever (USA), The County Athletic Club, London. *After successfully defending his British version of the 154 lbs title, O'Brien returned to America to seek a fight with Tommy Ryan.*

30.01.02 **Tommy Ryan** (USA) W CO 7 George Green (USA), Kansas City. *Again, sometimes referred to as a title fight, it was not even reported in either the Philadelphia Item or Boston Daily Globe (newspapers) boxing columns, while the Chicago Tribune (newspaper) made no mention of any championship involvement.*

31.01.02 Jack Root (USA) W DIS 7 George Gardner (USA), San Francisco. *According to the Chicago Tribune (newspaper), this was advertised as a middleweight title fight, despite Tommy Ryan being recognised as the lineal champion and the Articles of Agreement calling for a contest at catchweights. Regardless of that, neither man was inside 158 lbs and they would eventually meet to decide the championship of the newly created light-heavyweight class.*

24.06.02 **Tommy Ryan** (USA) W CO 3 Johnny Gorman (USA), NSC, London. *Listed as a world title bout in the Ring Record Book, the Articles of Agreement called for catchweights. However, the newspaper reports of the day gave it as a championship fight, with Ryan scaling 151 lbs to Gorman's 158.*

15.09.02 **Tommy Ryan** (USA) W CO 6 Kid Carter (USA), Fort Erie *(158 lbs)*. *In April 1905, it was falsely rumoured that Ryan was to finally defend his title against Jack O'Brien at 154 lbs. O'Brien had been chasing the 35-year-old champion for several years, but Ryan had always resisted him on the grounds that he would only defend the middleweight title at 154 lbs and not at 158, conveniently overlooking his fights against Tommy West and Carter. That proposed match fell through, however, and Ryan's protege, Hugo Kelly, took on O'Brien instead. Made at 158 lbs, although it is doubtful whether O'Brien made the weight, Kelly outpointed his man over ten rounds on 25 April 1905 (Indianapolis). Early in 1906, it was reported that Ryan had posted a forfeit to meet O'Brien at 158 lbs, with the weigh-in to be at ringside, but, with O'Brien now eyeing up the heavyweight title, this also fell through. Meanwhile, having been inactive for over a year and seemingly at the end of his career, Ryan handed the crown to Kelly, the man he had been coaching to succeed him. Kelly was immediately challenged by another claimant, Jack Twin Sullivan, who had already outpointed him over 20 rounds in Kansas City on 6 April 1904. Several years later, when admitting that the great majority of his fights had been fixed, Jack O'Brien was quoted as saying: "when I boxed Tommy Ryan in Philadelphia on 27 January 1904, he tricked me by threatening to pull out of our six round no-decision affair at the last moment unless I deposited £1,000 to be forfeited in case he was knocked out. Rather than having the match called off I complied with his wishes. Also, in the Hugo Kelly match we had agreed in advance that neither should try for a kayo and that the referee should call a draw. We put up a clever exhibition and I felt I had clearly outpointed Kelly, so you could imagine my surprise when the decision was awarded to my opponent. I decided there and then I would have nothing more to do with Ryan and that is why a title fight between us ultimately never came off".*

09.03.06 Hugo Kelly (USA) DREW 20 Jack Twin Sullivan (USA), Los Angeles. *Made at 158 lbs, with both men inside the weight according to the Los Angeles Times (newspaper), the two leading claimants came together with a view to settling their championship dispute.*

10.05.07 Hugo Kelly (USA) DREW 20 Jack Twin Sullivan (USA), Los Angeles. *Reported by the Los Angeles Times (newspaper) to have*

involved the championship, there was no mention of weights, although it would seem reasonably safe to assume that both men were inside 158 lbs.

04.07.07 Stanley Ketchel (USA) DREW 20 Joe Thomas (USA), Marysville. *Shown in Boxing News Annuals, although rectified in their Winter Special of 1979, as a title fight, it was not. Earlier, Thomas (150 lbs) had claimed the welterweight (see under that weight class, also) title after Honey Mellody, who he had beaten on 3 September 1906, had become champion when relieving Joe Walcott of his laurels. However, for this go, both he and Ketchel (147 lbs) were fighting at 150 lbs without having any bearing on either championship.*

02.09.07 Stanley Ketchel (USA) W CO 32 Joe Thomas (USA), San Francisco. *Scheduled for 45 rounds, with both men to be inside 150 lbs, there was no title billing according to the San Francisco Chronicle (newspaper).*

12.12.07 Stanley Ketchel (USA) W PTS 20 Joe Thomas (USA), San Francisco. *Another Ketchel v Thomas scrap shown as a title fight in the Boxing News Annual, it was only by beating Thomas that the former became a contender. There was no mention of any championship involvement in the San Francisco Chronicle (newspaper), only that the match had been made at 155 lbs.*

30.12.07 Hugo Kelly (USA) DREW 10 Billy Papke (USA), Milwaukee. *On perusing the Chicago Tribune (newspaper) report of the fight, there was no mention of a title or weights, only the statement that it was not over the championship route. It did say, however, that the winner of this fight would be bound to have a good claim on the title.*

22.02.08 Stanley Ketchel (USA) W CO 1 Mike Twin Sullivan (USA), San Francisco. *Another fight thought by the Boxing News Annual to have involved one version of the title or other, there was nothing in the San Francisco Chronicle (newspaper) to suggest that was the case. Made at 154 lbs, Sullivan was thought to weigh in the region of 149/151 lbs.*

16.03.08 Billy Papke (USA) W PTS 10 Hugo Kelly (USA), Milwaukee. *The Philadelphia Item (newspaper) report said: "the winner would be entitled to the best claim to the middleweight title", while, according to the Chicago Tribune (newspaper), with both men inside 158 lbs, "Papke eliminated Kelly from the championship race".*

09.05.08 Stanley Ketchel (USA) W CO 20 Jack Twin Sullivan (USA), San Francisco. *Reckoned by the Ring Record Book to be for the vacant title, there was no mention of that in the San Francisco Chronicle (newspaper), apart from the fact that both Sullivan and Ketchel were already claiming it. For the record, it was scheduled for 35 rounds, with both men required to make 156 lbs.*

04.06.08 **Stanley Ketchel** (USA) W PTS 10 Billy Papke (USA), Milwaukee. *Recognised by the Chicago Tribune (newspaper) as the first championship battle for close on six years and, with both men inside 158 lbs, this should now be accepted as being for the vacant title.*

31.07.08 **Stanley Ketchel** (USA) W CO 3 Hugo Kelly (USA), San Francisco. *With both men inside 158 lbs, the San Francisco Chronicle (newspaper) said: "just one punch snuffed out Kelly's title aspirations for good".*

18.08.08 **Stanley Ketchel** (USA) W CO 2 Joe Thomas (USA), San Francisco. *Listed as a title fight in the Ring Record Book, according to the San Francisco Chronicle (newspaper), the fight was at catchweights, with Thomas scaling 172 lbs to Ketchel's 168.*

07.09.08 **Billy Papke** (USA) W RSC 12 Stanley Ketchel (USA), Los Angeles *(158 lbs)*.

26.11.08 **Stanley Ketchel** (USA) W CO 11 Billy Papke (USA), San Francisco *(158 lbs)*.

26.03.09 **Stanley Ketchel** (USA) ND-W PTS 10 Jack O'Brien (USA), New York City. *Mistakenly recorded in the 1985 Ring Record Book as being a fight where the title was at risk, it was, in fact, made at 160 lbs.*

02.06.09 **Stanley Ketchel** (USA) ND-W CO 4 Tony Caponi (USA), Schnectady. *Recorded in the 1985 Ring Record Book as a title risk, the Chicago Tribune (newspaper) reported that Caponi weighed 160 lbs (two pounds over the class limit), while Ketchel scaled somewhere between 165 and 170 lbs.*

09.06.09 **Stanley Ketchel** (USA) ND-W CO 3 Jack O'Brien (USA), Philadelphia. *Again contested at catchweights and only over six rounds at that, Ketchel's title could not have been at risk as implied in the 1985 Ring Record Book.*

05.07.09 **Stanley Ketchel** (USA) W PTS 20 Billy Papke (USA), San Francisco *(158 lbs)*. *In January 1910, it was announced that Ketchel was relinquishing the title due to increased weight and, on hearing the news, Billy Papke, who was campaigning abroad, claimed the crown.*

19.03.10 Billy Papke (USA) W CO 3 Willie Lewis (USA), Paris. *With Papke claiming the title, the leading French promoters matched him against fellow American, Willie Lewis, giving the fight championship billing at 158 lbs. At the weigh-in, Papke scaled 156½ lbs to Lewis' 155. Immediately afterwards, Ketchel decided to stay in the middleweight division.*

23.03.10 Stanley Ketchel (USA) ND-DREW 6 Frank Klaus (USA), Pittsburgh. *Klaus weighed 157 lbs.*

27.05.10 Stanley Ketchel (USA) ND-W CO 2 Willie Lewis (USA), New York City. *Lewis weighed 148 lbs, with Ketchel spot on the limit at 158.*

10.06.10 Stanley Ketchel (USA) ND-W CO 5 Jim Smith (USA), New York City. *For some reason or other, the Ring Record Book decided to show the above fight as involving the title, although it was later rectified. According to the Los Angeles Times (newspaper), it was at catchweights, with Smith the heavier man by some eight pounds. On 15 October 1910, Ketchel was murdered and Billy Papke reclaimed the title.*

26.10.10 Billy Papke (USA) W CO 6 Ed Williams (USA), Sydney. *According to the Sydney Daily Telegraph (newspaper), this was to be the first middleweight title bout held in Australia. However, following the fight, after Papke had scaled 160 lbs to Williams' 158, and with both men inside the British class limit, the same newspaper stated that Papke's title had not been at stake.*

11.02.11 Cyclone Johnny Thompson (USA) W PTS 20 Billy Papke (USA), Sydney. *Prior to the fight, the Sydney Daily Telegraph (newspaper) referred to Papke as the champion, but there was no mention of this having involved the championship and the paper went on to say that Papke held all the advantages in height, weight and reach. Reports from an unknown source have Papke scaling 165 lbs to Thompson's 158, with the match made at catchweights. That aside, the reason for Thompson's claim appears to stem from the fact that he weighed 153¼ lbs after the fight. Meanwhile, Papke continued to style himself as champion and, before leaving Sydney, avenged an earlier defeat by Dave Smith when knocking the Australian out in seven rounds on 11 March 1911 at 165 lbs.*

22.02.11 Harry Lewis (USA) W PTS 25 Blink McCloskey (USA), Paris. *Lewis had stopped McCloskey rather unsatisfactorily in three rounds on 1 February (Paris) and undertook to do a better job this time round. Although carrying no title billing and with no weights given, Lewis laid claim to the middleweight title after the fight.*

03.05.11 Leo Houck (USA) W PTS 20 Harry Lewis (USA), Paris. *Having claimed the title, Lewis found himself challenged by Houck, who had been unsuccessful in seeking a match with British champion, Jim Sullivan, and had twice bettered Lewis back home. Unable to avoid the challenge, Lewis met Houck at 158 lbs in a bout given championship billing. While Lewis scaled a low 147 lbs (the welterweight limit), Houck, allowed to weigh-in privately, was announced as being within the agreed target. Supported by the Philadelphia Public Ledger (newspaper), Houck promptly laid claim to the title, but, outside a few quarters of Paris, he found himself virtually ignored.*

08.06.11 Billy Papke (USA) W RTD 9 Jim Sullivan (GB), The Paladium, London - GB. *Made at 158 lbs and billed for the title, both men were announced as being inside the agreed limit.*

27.07.11 Cyclone Johnny Thompson (USA) ND-W PTS 10 Willie Lewis (USA), New York City. *Shown in the 1981 Ring Record Book as involving Thompson's title claim, had Lewis, who was at least 20 lbs lighter than his rival, won there is no doubt that he would have re-established himself as a contender.*

17.08.11 Cyclone Johnny Thompson (USA) ND-L PTS 10 Frank Klaus (USA), New York City. *The New York Times (newspaper) reported that Thompson was still claiming the title and that both men were announced as being inside 158 lbs. From hereon, though, Thompson was not considered a threat and he had soon moved up to light-heavy.*

22.08.11 Billy Papke (USA) ND-L PTS 10 Sailor Burke (USA), New York City. *Without giving weights, both the New York Times and Tribune (newspapers) implied that this fight involved Papke's title claim.*

31.10.11 Bob Moha (USA) W PTS 12 Billy Papke, (USA), Boston. *Reported in the Boston Daily Globe (newspaper) as a title fight, the Boston Post (newspaper) merely referred to it as a 12-rounder with the title in prospect. The Post went on to say: "younger fans got their first view of an out and out fake". Although Moha laid claim to the title, with no weights given and the spectators left with a bad taste in the mouth, it was not taken too seriously.*

13.12.11 Georges Carpentier (FR) W PTS 20 Harry Lewis (USA), Paris. *Given world title billing at 158 lbs by the promoters, despite Lewis' recent losses to Leo Houck and George Gunther, the affair*

was ultimately invalidated when Carpentier came in half an ounce over the weight.

22.02.12 Frank Mantell (USA) W PTS 20 Billy Papke (USA), San Francisco. *According to the San Francisco Chronicle (newspaper), as in Klaus v Petroskey, this fight was part of an elimination tournament. Afterwards, the Philadelphia Item (newspaper) reported "that whatever claim Papke had to the title is now the undisputed property of Mantell". However, while Papke continued to claim the title, even though he had failed to make 158 lbs on the day of the fight, his cause was now considerably lacking support in America.*

22.02.12 Frank Klaus (USA) W PTS 20 Sailor Petroskey (USA), San Francisco. *Occasionally listed as a title fight, it was merely part of an elimination series which ultimately saw Klaus lift the title.*

29.02.12 Georges Carpentier (FR) W CO 2 Jim Sullivan (GB), Monaco. *Made at 160 lbs and recognised by many as the first European middleweight title fight, Carpentier weighed 155 to Sullivan's 157. Years later it was recognised by the Ring Record Book as having involved the championship (later removed) and, according to the Mirror of Life immediately prior to the fight, both men were claiming the world title even though there was no official backing as such. Following this, I think we can accept that Carpentier had as strong a claim as any of the other leading contenders.*

23.03.12 Frank Klaus (USA) W PTS 20 Jack Dillon (USA), Daly City. *Shown in some publications as a title fight, in fact, it was yet another unofficial eliminator which saw Klaus progressing further, while Dillon went on to claim the light-heavyweight title just two months later.*

30.03.12 Frank Mantell (USA) W PTS 20 Jack Herrick (USA), Los Angeles. *Listed in Boxing News Annuals as a title fight, the Los Angeles Times (newspaper) reported the contest as being another round in the elimination series at 158 lbs. Mantell, whose title claim was on the line for this one, having beaten Billy Papke, lost much credibility in putting up a poor display and, although victorious again, he was not widely accepted as being championship material.*

03.04.12 Georges Carpentier (FR) W PTS 20 George Gunther (A), Paris. *Carpentier, having won the European crown by knocking out Jim Sullivan, was next matched to defend his new 160 lbs belt against fellow Frenchman, Marcel Moreau. Unfortunately, Moreau was injured in training and, in hunting around for a replacement, the promoters brought in George Gunther at ten days notice. Gunther had been claiming the world title since November 1911 after repeated challenges to Billy Papke had been turned down. However, with the promoters sticking to their original billing, as an Australian he was hardly eligible to contest the European crown. Nevertheless, with Carpentier weighing 158¼ lbs to Gunther's 158, this should be seen as a legitimate title fight or at second best, a defence of Gunther's claim. Regardless of billing, following the fight, Carpentier would be recognised throughout France as a world champion of sorts.*

10.05.12 Georges Carpentier (FR) W CO 6 Hubert Roc (FR), Marseilles. *Although shown as a title fight in the Ring Record Books of the early 1980s, before being removed, with Roc being the ex-heavyweight champion of France it was an overweight contest.*

22.05.12 Georges Carpentier (FR) W PTS 20 Willie Lewis (USA), Paris - FFSB. *Given world title billing at 160 lbs, and supported by the French Federation Society of Boxing, both men were announced as being inside the weight. The FFSB were one of two groups in France trying to control boxing, the other being the French Federation of Boxing Professionals (FFBP).*

24.06.12 Frank Klaus (USA) W DIS 19 Georges Carpentier (FR), Dieppe - FFSB. *Billed for the 160 lbs title and fighting for the biggest purse yet seen in a French ring (80,000 Francs), Klaus was announced as being well inside the weight, while Carpentier was said to have scaled 159 lbs. Later, it was discovered that the scales were weighing some four pounds light, a discovery that appeared to suit the Frenchman who was already experiencing problems in making 160 lbs.*

29.06.12 Billy Papke (USA) W RSC 16 Marcel Moreau (FR), Paris - FFBP. *Billed for the title at 160 lbs, Papke made the weight at the second attempt, while Moreau came in at 157¾ lbs.*

09.09.12 Frank Klaus (USA) W DIS 4 Marcel Moreau (FR), Aix les Bains. *Mistakenly shown as a title fight in early record books, it was just another case of anything you can do I can do better, when this fight was announced. Although Klaus was supported by the FFSB, this one carried no championship billing, no mention of weights, and was cut from 20 rounds to 15.*

23.10.12 Billy Papke (USA) W DIS 17 Georges Carpentier (FR), Paris - FFBP. *Billed for the title at 160 lbs, Carpentier weighed in spot on the mark, while Papke scaled 161 lbs. The fight went ahead, with Papke paying £200 forfeit. Afterwards, despite the result, Carpentier was handed the title but refused to accept it on the* *grounds that he would no longer be fighting at 160 lbs. Following that announcement, Papke was reinstated as champion, while in America, the New York boxing authority, in refusing to recognise him, put their weight behind Frank Mantell.*

04.12.12 Billy Papke (USA) W RTD 7 George Bernard (FR), Paris - FFBP. *An extremely unsatisfactory affair, with more than a hint that the Frenchman had been drugged, saw Bernard sound asleep in his corner and unable to be revived in time to answer the bell. The fight had been advertised as involving Papke's title claim and Bernard scaled 157 lbs to the American's 159.*

09.01.13 Jack Dillon (USA) W PTS 15 Frank Mantell (USA), Thornton. *Shown in the Australian Ring Magazine as a title fight, in reality it was a catchweight contest between a man already claiming the light-heavyweight crown and one who saw himself as the middleweight champion.*

19.02.13 Frank Mantell (USA) DREW 20 Jeff Smith (USA), Paris. *Although shown in the Jack Solomons' International Boxing Annual as a championship bout, this carried no title billing. However, a French paper said prior to the fight: "If Smith wins he will have a genuine claim to the New York version of the title".*

05.03.13 Frank Klaus (USA) W DIS 15 Billy Papke (USA), Paris. *Recognised by all authorities, within reason, except the NY commission, who still supported Frank Mantell, this was billed as a title fight at 160 lbs, with both men scaling 159 lbs.*

02.04.13 Jeff Smith (USA) W CO 11 Adrien Hogan (FR), Paris. *Although shown in some quarters as being a title fight, it was not billed as such, and was part of an elimination series to find Klaus' next opponent.*

14.04.13 Pat O'Keefe (GB) W PTS 20 Frank Mantell (USA), The Ring, London. *Billed as a title fight at 160 lbs, with both men announced as being within the limit, O'Keefe showed no interest in Mantell's NY version of the title, preferring to go his own way.*

24.05.13 Frank Klaus (USA) ND-W PTS 6 Eddie McGoorty (USA), Pittsburgh - USA. *Both Klaus and McGoorty weighed 158 lbs.*

01.07.13 Frank Klaus (USA) W CO 3 Jimmy Gardner (USA), Boston - USA. *Prior to the fight, Gardner claimed that if he did not win the title this would be his final appearance in the ring. Although there was no mention of the championship in the Boston Post (newspaper) report, one can only assume that Gardner was safely inside 158 lbs and that Klaus' title was therefore automatically at stake.*

29.09.13 Frank Klaus (USA) ND-L PTS 10 Eddie McGoorty (USA), Milwaukee - USA. *McGoorty weighed 157¾ lbs.*

11.10.13 George Chip (USA) ND-W CO 6 Frank Klaus (USA), Pittsburgh - USA. *This was not billed as a title bout as it was only a six round no-decision affair, but the championship was deemed to have changed hands after Klaus was counted out. In a situation such as this, the only way a champion could lose his crown, unless he stipulated a poundage above the limit of the weight class, was if he failed to last the distance, and it was on this basis that Chip received recognition as champion. However, on closer scrutiny, Chip weighed 161½ lbs and Klaus 163, respectively, and the former's recognition almost certainly stemmed from the return.*

12.10.13 Joe Borrell (USA) ND-W RSC 5 Harry Lewis (USA), Philadelphia. *With both men inside 158 lbs, Borrell claimed the title after this no-decision contest win, but received little or no support at all and moved his base to Europe.*

15.11.13 George Chip (USA) ND-L PTS 6 Leo Houck (USA), Philadelphia - USA. *Advertised as involving the title, despite the absence of weights in the Philadelphia Inquirer (newspaper) report of the fight.*

15.11.13 Jeff Smith (USA) W PTS 20 George Bernard (FR), Paris. *Billed for the title at 160 lbs, Bernard (real christian name, Croesus) scaled 159½ lbs, while it was announced that Smith was also inside the 160 mark. After the fight, with Klaus back in America, the promoters awarded Smith a championship belt and proclaimed him to be the new champion.*

25.11.13 George Chip (USA) ND-W PTS 10 Tim O'Neill (USA), Racine - USA. *Chip had claimed the title at 160 lbs and this match was made at that weight, with O'Neill having a two pound advantage at 159.*

23.12.13 George Chip (USA) ND-W CO 5 Frank Klaus (USA), Pittsburgh - USA. *According to the Chicago Tribune (newspaper), Chip scaled 160 lbs to Klaus' 162½ and, by his victory, he was generally recognised as the champion in America, even though the class limit remained at 158 lbs in America. This was on the basis that Klaus had first won recognition as champion at 160 lbs.*

01.01.14 Eddie McGoorty (USA) W CO 1 Dave Smith (USA), Sydney - AUSTRALIA. *Chip was not recognised outside America and, with many of the leading fighters at the weight campaigning abroad, the Australian authorities declared the title vacant, matching McGoorty (158 lbs) against Smith (158 lbs) at 160 lbs for their version of the title.*

12.01.14 George Chip (USA) ND-W PTS 10 Gus Christie (USA), Milwaukee - USA. *Both men were reckoned to be inside 158 lbs at the 3.0 pm weigh-in.*

19.01.14 George Chip (USA) ND-W RSC 2 Tim O'Neill (USA), Grand Rapids - USA. *Both men were articled to meet at 160 lbs.*

26.01.14 George Chip (USA) ND-W PTS 6 Joe Borrell (USA), Philadelphia - USA. *According to the Philadelphia Public Ledger (newspaper), both men were inside 158 lbs.*

07.02.14 Eddie McGoorty (USA) W PTS 20 Pat Bradley (A), Sydney - AUSTRALIA. *Weights (lbs): McGoorty (158), Bradley (158).*

26.02.14 Joe Borrell (USA) W PTS 15 George Bernard (FR), The Stadium, Liverpool. *Although this was billed as a championship bout at 160 lbs by the promoter, with both men inside the weight, it was not generally recognised as one, even in Britain.*

14.03.14 Jeff Smith (USA) W PTS 20 Eddie McGoorty (USA), Sydney - AUSTRALIA. *Weights (lbs): Smith (157¾), McGoorty (159). The initial decision was given in McGoorty's favour, but it proved to be so unpopular that it was later rescinded by the officials in charge.*

07.04.14 Al McCoy (USA) ND-W CO 1 George Chip (USA), Brooklyn - USA. *As in the contests between Chip and Frank Klaus, this was not a billed title bout, but the championship was deemed to have changed hands following the result. Although a ten round no-decision affair, McCoy received recognition as the first southpaw champion in boxing history as he had weighed in at 156 lbs and, with no weight stipulation in force, it barely mattered that Chip scaled 162½ lbs.*

13.04.14 Jeff Smith (USA) W CO 16 Pat Bradley (A), Sydney - AUSTRALIA. *Weights (lbs): Smith (157½), Bradley (157¼).*

20.04.14 Joe Borrell (USA) NC 4 Bandsman Blake (GB), The Ring, London. *Although billed as a title bout at 160 lbs, and with both men announced as having made the weight, it was not generally recognised as one in Britain .*

08.05.14 Al McCoy (USA) ND-W CO 1 George Pearsall (USA), South Norwalk - USA. *Recorded in various published title listings as involving the title, heavy research to date has failed to uncover weight or billing. The same conditions apply where (*).*

21.05.14 Al McCoy (USA) ND-L PTS 10 Billy Murray (USA), New York City - USA. *Murray weighed 157 lbs, while McCoy came in at 154½.*

06.06.14 Jeff Smith (USA) W PTS 20 Jimmy Clabby (USA), Sydney - AUSTRALIA. *Weights (lbs): Smith (156¾), Clabby (153¼).*

11.06.14 Al McCoy (USA) ND-L PTS 10 Billy Murray (USA), New York City - USA. *McCoy scaled 157 lbs to Murray's 158.*

13.10.14 Al McCoy (USA) ND-W CO 5 Willie Lewis (USA), Brooklyn - USA. *Lewis weighed 157¼ lbs, with McCoy half a pound heavier at 157¾.*

19.10.14 Al McCoy (USA) ND-L PTS 10 Knockout Brennan (USA), Buffalo. *Brennan weighed 157 lbs to McCoy's 158.*

06.11.14 Jimmy Clabby (USA) W PTS 20 George Chip (USA), San Francisco. *Occasionally mentioned as a championship fight, it was described in the San Francisco Chronicle (newspaper) as another step in the settlement of the title at 158 lbs. With both men inside 158 lbs, Clabby said afterwards that he saw himself not only as the American champion, but world leader, also. Taken in context, Chip had lost his claim to Al McCoy and was trying hard to get back into contention, while Clabby had recently been turned back by Jeff Smith for the Australian version of the title.*

10.11.14 Al McCoy (USA) ND-DREW 10 Soldier Bartfield (USA), Brooklyn - USA. *Bartfield weighed 146 lbs.*

28.11.14 Mick King (A) W PTS 20 Jeff Smith (USA), Sydney - AUSTRALIA. *Weights (lbs): King (157¼), Smith (157).*

11.12.14 Al McCoy (USA) ND-W PTS 10 Italian Joe Gans (USA), New York City. *Gans weighed 157 lbs.*

22.12.14 Al McCoy (USA) ND-L PTS 10 Soldier Bartfield (USA), Brooklyn. *Both men were inside the 158 lbs mark, with McCoy weighing 156 to Bartfield's 146¾.*

26.12.14 Jeff Smith (USA) W PTS 20 Mick King (A), Sydney - AUSTRALIA. *Weights (lbs): Smith (158), King (154).*

23.01.15 Jeff Smith (USA) W DIS 5 Les Darcy (A), Sydney - AUSTRALIA. *Weights (lbs): Smith (160), Darcy (155).*

23.01.15 Al McCoy (USA) ND-W PTS 10 Billy Grupp (USA), New York City - USA*

25.01.15 Al McCoy (USA) ND-W PTS 6 Joe Borrell (USA), Philadelphia - USA. *Although Borrell, at 158¼ lbs, was a shade over the American middleweight limit, had he won inside the distance, he would have undoubtedly claimed the 160 lbs version. Incidentally, McCoy weighed 156 lbs.*

16.02.15 Al McCoy (USA) ND-W PTS 10 Al Thiel (USA), Brooklyn. *Shown in the 1981 Ring Record Book as a fight where McCoy's title claim was at stake, in truth it should not have been, with Thiel weighing-in at 160¼ lbs.*

20.02.15 Jeff Smith (USA) W PTS 20 Mick King (A), Melbourne - AUSTRALIA. *Weights (lbs): Smith (158½), King (156½).*

23.03.15 Al McCoy (USA) ND-L PTS 10 Silent Martin (USA), Brooklyn - USA. *The Chicago Tribune (newspaper) reported that Martin, inside the limit, gave McCoy a nine pound handicap in the weights and an artistic trimming to boot.*

06.04.15 Al McCoy (USA) ND-L PTS 10 George Chip (USA), Brooklyn - USA. *Chip, at 159¼ lbs, was trying to regain his 160 lbs title claim from McCoy, who was the lighter man by two pounds.*

04.05.15 Al McCoy (USA) ND-L PTS 10 Jimmy Clabby (USA), Brooklyn - USA. *Both men were inside the championship limit, with McCoy scaling 157¼ and Clabby 154¼ lbs, respectively.*

22.05.15 Les Darcy (A) W DIS 2 Jeff Smith (USA), Sydney - AUSTRALIA. *Weights (lbs): Darcy (159), Smith (159).*

31.05.15 Al McCoy (USA) ND-DREW 10 Silent Martin (USA), Brooklyn - USA. *McCoy, at 157½ lbs, again successfully defended his title claim against Martin, who came in at 155.*

12.06.15 Les Darcy (A) W RTD 10 Mick King (A), Sydney - AUSTRALIA. *Weights (lbs): Darcy (159), King (159).*

31.07.15 Les Darcy (A) W RSC 15 Eddie McGoorty (USA), Sydney - AUSTRALIA. *Weights (lbs): Darcy (159), McGoorty (159½).*

04.09.15 Les Darcy (A) W PTS 20 Billy Murray (USA), Sydney - AUSTRALIA. *Weights (lbs): Darcy (159), Murray (160).*

09.09.15 Al McCoy (USA) ND-L PTS 10 Young Ahearn (GB), Brooklyn - USA. *Ahearn weighed 154 lbs as opposed to McCoy at 157½.*

11.09.15 Mike Gibbons (USA) ND-W PTS 10 Packey McFarland (USA), Brooklyn. *Following the above fight at 154 lbs, Gibbons laid claim to the title but, despite adding Young Ahearn, Jeff Smith and Jack Dillon, to his impressive list of "press" victories, he was unable to coax Al McCoy into the ring and his claim ultimately fizzled out. The Andrews Record Books tell us that other Americans who laid claim to the title over the next two or three years with little success included Bob Moha, George Brown and later, Harry Greb, who would have to wait a little longer.*

09.10.15 Les Darcy (USA) W RTD 6 Fred Dyer (GB), Sydney - AUSTRALIA. *Weights (lbs): Darcy (159), Dyer (150).*

23.10.15 Al McCoy (USA) ND-DREW 10 Soldier Bartfield (USA), Brooklyn - USA*

23.10.15 Les Darcy (A) W PTS 20 Jimmy Clabby (USA), Sydney - AUSTRALIA. *Weights (lbs): Darcy (159¼), Clabby (153¾).*

13.11.15 Al McCoy (USA) ND-DREW 10 Zulu Kid (USA), Brooklyn - USA. *The Zulu Kid weighed 157 lbs.*

25.11.15 Al McCoy (USA) ND-L PTS 15 Silent Martin (USA), Waterbury - USA *

01.01.16 Al McCoy (USA) ND-L PTS 10 Young Ahearn (GB), Brooklyn - USA. *Ahearn weighed 156 lbs.*

20.01.16 Al McCoy (USA) ND-L PTS 10 George Chip (USA), Brooklyn - USA. *Chip weighed 157¼ lbs.*

21.03.16 Al McCoy (USA) ND-W PTS 10 Leo Benz (USA), Brooklyn - USA. *Benz weighed 156 lbs.*

17.04.16 Al McCoy (USA) ND-L PTS 10 Al Thiel (USA), New York City - USA *

13.05.16 Les Darcy (A) W RTD 5 Alex Costica (ROM), Sydney - AUSTRALIA. *Weights (lbs): Darcy (158), Costica (154¼).*

26.06.16 Al McCoy (USA) W PTS 15 Hugh Ross (USA), Bridgeport. *Deleted as a title bout from the 1987 Ring Record Book, and with nothing in the Boston Daily Globe or Boston Post (newspapers) to suggest the championship was involved, the likelyhood was that it was fought at catchweights.*

09.09.16 Les Darcy (A) W PTS 20 Jimmy Clabby (USA), Sydney - AUSTRALIA. *Weights (lbs): Darcy (159¼), Clabby (153¼).*

30.09.16 Les Darcy (A) W CO 9 George Chip (USA), Sydney - AUSTRALIA. *Weights (lbs): Darcy (159½), Chip (159½). Les Darcy left the Australian version of the title vacant on 24 May 1917 when he died of pneumonia.*

30.04.17 Al McCoy (USA) ND-L PTS 10 Harry Greb (USA), Pittsburgh - USA. *According to the Pittsburgh Daily Gazette (newspaper), Greb said he would be inside 160 lbs. However, with the limit standing at 158 lbs, it is doubtful whether the title claim was on the line.*

14.11.17 Mike O'Dowd (USA) ND-W CO 6 Al McCoy (USA), Brooklyn. *As in the contests between George Chip v Frank Klaus and McCoy v Chip, this was not billed as a championship fight, but the title was deemed to have changed hands with no additional weight stipulation in force and McCoy failing to last the distance. Although McCoy came in over the weight at 162 lbs, O'Dowd was*

one pound inside the limit at 157. O'Dowd was generally recognised as champion at this point in time.

24.11.17 Mike O'Dowd (USA) ND-W PTS 6 Jack McCarron (USA), Philadelphia. *The Philadelphia Inquirer (newspaper) stated that as both boys were within the weight class, had McCarron won inside the distance he could well have claimed the title.*

15.12.17 Mike O'Dowd (USA) ND-W PTS 6 Billy Kramer (USA), Philadelphia. *Although no weights were given, the Philadelphia Inquirer (newspaper) reported that O'Dowd staked his title against Kramer in this one.*

25.02.18 Mike O'Dowd (USA) ND-W PTS 10 Harry Greb (USA), St Paul*

17.07.19 Mike O'Dowd (USA) ND-W CO 3 Al McCoy (USA), St Paul. *Recorded in Boxing News Annuals as being a title fight, according to the New York Times (newspaper) report, it was a catchweight contest with McCoy "many" pounds over the limit.*

11.08.19 Mike O'Dowd (USA) ND-W PTS 10 Jackie Clark (USA), Syracuse. *At the 6.0 pm weigh-in, both O'Dowd and Clark were inside 158 lbs.*

22.08.19 Mike O'Dowd (USA) ND-L PTS 8 Jack Britton (USA), Newark. *Britton weighed 146 lbs, with O'Dowd scaling 155.*

01.09.19 Mike O'Dowd (USA) ND-W PTS 10 Ted Kid Lewis (GB), Syracuse *

19.09.19 Mike O'Dowd (USA) ND-W PTS 10 Soldier Bartfield (USA), St Paul *The New York Times (newspaper), without giving weights, claimed that Bartfield was outweighed by some ten pounds. That pointer alone would have seen him well inside 158 lbs.*

29.09.19 Mike O'Dowd (USA) ND-W PTS 8 Augie Ratner (USA), Jersey City. *Ratner weighed 154 lbs.*

06.11.19 Mike O'Dowd (USA) ND-W CO 2 Billy Kramer (USA), Paterson. *Spot on the 160 lbs mark, had he won, Kramer would probably have claimed that version of the title, while O'Dowd scaled 164 lbs.*

10.11.19 Mike O'Dowd (USA) ND-W CO 2 Jimmy O'Hagen (USA), Detroit. *The Chicago Tribune (newspaper) acknowledged O'Hagen as the challenger, despite the omission of weights.*

21.11.19 Mike O'Dowd (USA) ND-DREW 10 Mike Gibbons (USA), St Paul. *According to the New York Times (newspaper), both men entered the ring inside 158 lbs.*

20.01.20 Mike O'Dowd (USA) W RSC 3 Tommy Murphy (USA), Boston. *Included in the title listings because the Chicago Tribune (newspaper) showed the fight to have been made at 150 lbs. However, because O'Dowd at that stage of his career was scaling between 158 and 165 lbs, this one needs to be further researched.*

01.03.20 Mike O'Dowd (USA) ND-W CO 2 Jack McCarron (USA), Philadelphia *

30.03.20 Mike O'Dowd (USA) W CO 5 Joe Eagan (USA), Boston. *Recorded in the Ring Record Book as a title fight, the Boston Daily Globe (newspaper) made clear that the championship was not involved. However, according to Boston Post (newspaper), Eagan was inside the limit and the title was at stake.*

06.05.20 Johnny Wilson (USA) W PTS 12 Mike O'Dowd (USA), Boston. *Announced from the ring as a title fight, Wilson, spot on the American limit at 158 lbs and amid much protestation, was generally recognised as champion after his defeat of O'Dowd (159½ lbs).*

01.07.20 Johnny Wilson (USA) W PTS 12 Soldier Bartfield (USA), Newark. *Bartfield weighed no more than 151 lbs according to the New York Times (newspaper), who went on to say that Wilson, in his first defence, outweighed his challenger by at least seven pounds.*

09.12.20 Johnny Wilson (USA) ND-L PTS 10 George Robinson (USA), Montreal. *According to the Montreal Herald (newspaper) report of the fight, despite the absence of weights, the championship was within an ace of changing hands when Wilson was sent crashing to the floor within seconds of the start. He recovered to lose the "press" verdict.*

17.01.21 Johnny Wilson (USA) ND-W PTS 10 Joe Chip (USA), Pittsburgh. *Following a dispute over who should referee, according to the Pittsburgh Daily Gazette (newspaper), Wilson threatened to withdraw. At that juncture, Chip, said to be inside the weight limit, stated that if the champion pulled out he would lay claim to the title. The fight then went ahead as planned.*

10.02.21 Johnny Wilson (USA) ND-W CO 2 Navy Rostan (USA), Kenosha. *The New York Times (newspaper) gave this one as title fight scheduled for ten rounds.*

17.03.21 Johnny Wilson (USA) W PTS 15 Mike O'Dowd (USA), New York City. *This was the first middleweight title fight under Walker Law, which had gone into effect from 24 May 1920 to govern boxing in New York and, at the same time, brought the weight class into line with the rest of the world at 160 lbs.*

25.05.21 **Johnny Wilson** (USA) ND-W PTS 10 Joe Chip (USA), Detroit. *Both men weighed 158 lbs.*

27.07.21 Johnny Wilson (USA) ND-W DIS 7 Bryan Downey (USA), Cleveland. *After the contest came to an end, when the referee disqualified Downey (154 lbs), the Ohio Boxing Commission refused to accept the decision and declared Downey the winner by a kayo. The referee, who had been brought in to protect Wilson (165 lbs), claimed he had disqualified Downey for attempting to hit the champion while he was down, but Wilson had already been decked three times and appeared well beaten at the time. Although no authority other than Ohio recognised Downey as champion, the NYSAC took due note before eventually deciding to declare the title vacant.*

05.09.21 Johnny Wilson (USA) ND-DREW 12 Bryan Downey (USA), Jersey City. *Downey weighed 154¹/₂ lbs to Wilson's 159.*

22.02.22 Bryan Downey (USA) W PTS 12 Frank Carbone (USA), Canton - OHIO

15.05.22 Bryan Downey (USA) W PTS 12 Mike O'Dowd (USA), Columbus - OHIO

04.07.22 **Johnny Wilson** (USA) ND-W CO 4 Al de Maris (USA), Rutland. *The Chicago Tribune (newspaper) reported that Wilson could only draw some 500 people to Vermont's first ever world title fight. However, they failed to mention the contestants' weights and the fact that Wilson was not recognised as champion by the NYSAC or Ohio.*

14.08.22 Dave Rosenberg (USA) W PTS 15 Phil Krug (USA), New York City - NY

18.09.22 Jock Malone (USA) W PTS 12 Bryan Downey (USA), Columbus - OHIO

30.11.22 Mike O'Dowd (USA) W DIS 8 Dave Rosenberg (USA), Brooklyn - NY

09.01.23 Lou Bogash (USA) W RSC 11 Charlie Nashert (USA), New York City. *Recorded in the Ring Record Book as being for the New York version of the title, and with O'Dowd still recognised as champion, evidence uncovered by Bob Soderman from the New York Times (newspaper) makes clear that it was not recognised by the NYSAC.*

16.03.23 Jock Malone (USA) ND-W CO 1 Mike O'Dowd (USA), St Paul. *Recorded as a title bout by the Boxing News Annual, it involved neither the New York or Ohio versions of the title and O'Dowd retired immediately afterwards.*

24.07.23 Jock Malone (USA) W PTS 12 Anthony Downey (USA), Columbus. *Prior to 1986, the Ring Record Book had shown a fight between Malone and Bryan (not Anthony) Downey on this date as being for the Ohio verson of the title. However, diligent research by boxing historians uncovered the fact that once Downey had lost to Malone on 18 September 1922, the title was soon forgotten. Incidentally, Anthony was Bryan's younger brother.*

31.08.23 **Harry Greb** (USA) W PTS 15 Johnny Wilson (USA), New York City

04.10.23 **Harry Greb** (USA) ND-W PTS 10 Jimmy Darcy (USA), Pittsburgh. *At some time or other recorded in the Ring Record Book as involving the title, the Pittsburgh Gazette (newspaper) stated the day before: "If Darcy, who is down to weight, can score a kayo there will be a new champion crowned". Following the fight, the same paper recorded Darcy's weight as being 165 lbs, five pounds over the limit, with Greb making 163.*

03.12.23 **Harry Greb** (USA) W PTS 10 Bryan Downey (USA), Pittsburgh. *This contest effectively unified the title and was recognised as such, even though Greb weighed 161 lbs to Downey's 158¹/₂.*

18.01.24 **Harry Greb** (USA) W PTS 15 Johnny Wilson (USA), New York City

24.03.24 **Harry Greb** (USA) W RSC 12 Fay Kaiser (USA), Baltimore. *Although a contracted title bout, an oversight saw Greb, believing it to be a catchweight contest, weigh-in at 173 lbs. Obviously, the Maryland Boxing Commission took a firm stance, but, with Kaiser (158¹/₂) willing to accept the weight difference and with the promoter anxious for the fight to go ahead, they demanded that Greb put his title at stake. Thus, under threat of suspension, Greb, his weight announced as being 159¹/₂ lbs, was compelled to enter the ring.*

26.06.24 **Harry Greb** (USA) W PTS 15 Ted Moore (GB), New York City

02.07.25 **Harry Greb** (USA) W PTS 15 Mickey Walker (USA), New York City

13.11.25 **Harry Greb** (USA) W PTS 15 Tony Marullo (USA), New Orleans. *Although billed as a world title fight, both the Ring Record Book and the New Orleans Daily Picayune (newspaper) report show Greb as weighing 169 lbs to Marullo's 168, with middleweight limit set at 160.*

26.02.26 **Tiger Flowers** (USA) W PTS 15 Harry Greb (USA), New York City

19.08.26 **Tiger Flowers** (USA) W PTS 15 Harry Greb (USA), New York City

03.12.26 **Mickey Walker** (USA) W PTS 10 Tiger Flowers (USA), Chicago. *On 16 November 1927, just over 13 months after Harry Greb had died, Flowers followed him when failing to recover from an eye operation.*

30.06.27 **Mickey Walker** (USA) W CO 10 Tommy Milligan (GB), Olympia, London

05.06.28 **Mickey Walker** (USA) ND-W PTS 10 Jock Malone (USA), St Paul. *The Los Angeles Times (newspaper) gave this as a match made at 160 lbs. On the day of the fight, the paper said that Malone was already inside the weight, whilst Walker still had a few pounds left to shed.*

21.06.28 **Mickey Walker** (USA) W PTS 10 Ace Hudkins (USA), Chicago

29.10.29 **Mickey Walker** (USA) W PTS 10 Ace Hudkins (USA), Los Angeles

30.07.30 **Mickey Walker** (USA) W CO 3 Willie Oster (USA), Newark. *Inadvertently recorded by the Boxing News Annual as being a title fight, it was not, with Walker weighing 163 lbs to Oster's 168. From then on, Walker would concentrate on the heavyweight division and relinquished his title in June 1931.*

25.08.31 Gorilla Jones (USA) W PTS 10 Tiger Thomas (USA), Milwaukee. *Listed in the Boxing News Annual as a title fight, it was merely one of the preliminary bouts in the NBA tournament held to find a new champion. Following that win, Jones repeated the dose over Clyde Chastain, George Nicholls, Frankie O'Brien and Henry Firpo, to reach the final. The other finalist, Oddone Piazza, had an easier path, whipping Paul Rojas and drawing with Firpo, before getting a bye at the semi-final stage when O'Brien was unavailable.*

25.01.32 Gorilla Jones (USA) W RSC 6 Oddone Piazza (ITA), Milwaukee - NBA

26.04.32 Gorilla Jones (USA) W PTS 12 Young Terry (USA), Trenton - NBA

11.06.32 Marcel This (FR) W DIS 11 Gorilla Jones (USA), Paris - IBU. *Not recognised as a title fight by the NBA, Jones lost credibility with that body when losing.*

04.07.32 Marcel Thil (FR) W PTS 15 Len Harvey (GB), White City, London - IBU

21.11.32 Ben Jeby (USA) W PTS 15 Chick Devlin (USA), New York City. *Recorded as a title fight in Boxing News Annuals, it was merely the final leg of the NYSAC elimination tournament. On 13 October 1932, in New York City, Jeby had knocked out Paul Pirrone inside six rounds, with Devlin and Battaglia drawing over ten rounds. Following Jeby v Devlin, the winner and Battaglia were matched to contest New York's version of the vacant title.*

13.01.33 Ben Jeby (USA) W RSC 12 Frank Battaglia (C), New York City - NY

30.01.33 Gorilla Jones (USA) W CO 7 Sammy Slaughter (USA), Cleveland. *The NBA, who were still viewing the result of the Marcel Thil v Jones verdict with some suspicion, matched Jones and Slaughter for their version of the American, not to be confused with world, title as recorded in the Boxing News Annual. However, any hopes the NBA had of promoting the winner's claims further, were abandoned following Jones' six round no-contest with Ben Jeby on 19 April 1933 in the same city.*

17.03.33 Ben Jeby (USA) DREW 15 Vince Dundee (USA), New York City - NY

10.07.33 Ben Jeby (USA) W PTS 15 Young Terry (USA), Newark - NY. *Advertised as being for the title, the fight went ahead on NBA territory under full championship conditions with the NBA turning a "blind eye" when recognising Terry to be a deserving challenger.*

28.07.33 Vearl Whitehead (USA) W DIS 10 Gorilla Jones (USA), Los Angeles. *According to the Milwaukee Journal (27 October 1933), the Californian Boxing Committee decided to recognise Whitehead as world champion on the basis of the above win. However, on the very same day as that announcement, Whitehead was outpointed over ten rounds in Los Angeles by another Californian, Chick Devlin. Whether that changed anything or not soon became irrelevant, when, within two months of that date, all but one of the Committee had been removed from office.*

09.08.33 Lou Brouillard (C) W CO 7 Ben Jeby (USA), New York City - NY/NBA

21.08.33 Teddy Yarosz (USA) W PTS 10 Vince Dundee (USA), Pittsburgh - PENNSYLVANIA

02.10.33 Marcel Thil (FR) W PTS 15 Kid Tunero (CUB), Paris - IBU

30.10.33 Vince Dundee (USA) W PTS 15 Lou Brouillard (C), Boston - NY/NBA

08.12.33 Vince Dundee (USA) W PTS 15 Andy Callahan (USA), Boston - NY/NBA

12.02.34 Teddy Yarosz (USA) W PTS 15 Jimmy Smith (USA), Pittsburgh - PENNSYLVANIA

26.02.34 Marcel Thil (FR) W PTS 15 Ignacio Ara (SP), Paris - IBU

06.04.34 Teddy Yarosz (USA) W PTS 12 Ben Jeby (USA), Pittsburgh - PENNSYLVANIA

01.05.34 Vince Dundee (USA) W PTS 15 Al Diamond (USA), Paterson - NY/NBA

03.05.34 Marcel Thil (FR) W PTS 15 Gustav Roth (BEL), Paris - IBU

14.08.34 Young Corbett III (USA) W PTS 10 Mickey Walker (USA), San Francisco. *Billed for the Pacific Coast title, with both men inside 160 lbs, the promoters attached an "unofficial" world championship tag to it in order to draw the customers.*

11.09.34 Teddy Yarosz (USA) W PTS 15 Vince Dundee (USA), Pittsburgh - NY/NBA

15.10.34 Marcel Thil (FR) DREW 15 Carmelo Candel (FR), Paris - IBU

04.05.35 Marcel Thil (FR) W RTD 14 Kid Jaks (CZ), Paris - IBU

03.06.35 Marcel Thil (FR) W PTS 15 Ignacio Ara (SP), Madrid - IBU

28.06.35 Marcel Thil (FR) W PTS 10 Carmelo Candel (FR), Paris. *Recorded in the Boxing News Annual as a title fight, it could not be considered as such. Although both men were presumably inside the weight limit, full championship conditions were not applied, with 15 rounds being the recognised title distance in Europe at the time.*

19.09.35 Babe Risko (USA) W PTS 15 Teddy Yarosz (USA), Pittsburgh - NY/NBA

20.01.36 Marcel Thil (FR) W DIS 4 Lou Brouillard (C), Paris - IBU

10.02.36 Babe Risko (USA) W PTS 15 Tony Fisher (USA), Newark - NY/NBA

11.07.36 Freddie Steele (USA) W PTS 15 Babe Risko (USA), Seattle - NY/NBA

01.01.37 Freddie Steele (USA) W PTS 10 Gorilla Jones (USA), Milwaukee - NY/NBA

15.02.37 Marcel Thil (FR) W DIS 6 Lou Brouillard (C), Paris - IBU

19.02.37 Freddie Steele (USA) W PTS 15 Babe Risko (USA), New York City - NY/NBA

11.05.37 Freddie Steele (USA) W CO 3 Frank Battaglia (C), Seattle - NY/NBA

11.09.37 Freddie Steele (USA) W CO 4 Ken Overlin (USA), Seattle - NY/NBA

23.09.37 Fred Apostoli (USA) W RSC 10 Marcel Thil (FR), New York City. *Although recorded as a championship fight in the Ring Record Book, in order to protect Freddie Steele, whom the NYSAC recognised as champion, the two men were asked to sign an agreement that the above fight would not involve the world title. Fought under championship conditions, following Apostoli's victory and the subsequent retirement of Thil, the American was recognised as champion in Europe. Next, the NYSAC called for Apostoli and Steele to get together. Finally, the pair met in an overweight scrap on 7 January 1938 (New York City), with Apostoli winning on a ninth round kayo. However, Steele continued to avoid his number one challenger and signed to meet Carmen Barth, instead.*

19.02.38 Freddie Steele (USA) W RTD 7 Carmen Barth (USA) Cleveland - NY/NBA

01.04.38 Fred Apostoli (USA) W PTS 15 Glen Lee (USA), New York City. *With Freddie Steele still recognised in New York and the IBU giving their backing to a forthcoming European championship fight between Edouard Tenet and Josef Besselmann as being for their version of the world title, Apostoli defended his "crown" in New York. Yet again recorded as a title bout in the Ring Record Book, full championship conditions did not apply with Apostoli weighing in at 160³/₄ lbs. Finally, in May 1938, Steele was stripped of his New York title belt for continuing to refuse Apostoli a crack at it and the latter was eventually matched against Young Corbett III to decide a new champion.*

07.04.38 Edouard Tenet (FR) W RTD 12 Josef Besselmann (GER), Berlin - IBU. *During an international Boxing Convention held in Rome in May 1938, which was attended by many leading authorities within the sport, the IBU agreed to refuse to recognise all individually-made world champions, including their own Edouard Tenet, in an effort to stand by one universally acknowledged champion, who, in turn, would have to concede to regular defences decided by the new Federation.*

26.07.38 Al Hostak (USA) W CO 1 Freddie Steele (USA), Seattle - NBA

01.11.38 Solly Krieger (USA) W PTS 15 Al Hostak (USA), Seattle - NBA

18.11.38 Fred Apostoli (USA) W RSC 8 Young Corbett III (USA), New York City - NY

27.06.39 Al Hostak (USA) W RSC 4 Solly Krieger (USA), Seattle - NBA

02.10.39 Ceferino Garcia (PH) W RSC 7 Fred Apostoli (USA), New York City - NY

11.12.39 Al Hostak (USA) W CO 1 Eric Seelig (GER), Cleveland - NBA

23.12.39 Ceferino Garcia (PH) W CO 13 Glen Lee (USA), Manila - NY

01.03.40 Ceferino Garcia (PH) DREW 10 Henry Armstrong (USA), Los Angeles. *Although billed as a title fight and given Californian backing, there was no championship at stake as it was not supported by the NYSAC, who recognised Garcia as champion. There were two good reasons why that was the case. At that time, New York Title bouts were of 15 rounds duration, whereas, this was contested over ten stanzas and under the rules of boxing a champion was entitled to defend at the class limit, but, for this go against the welterweight king, Garcia was contracted to come in at 152 lbs. Even allowing for the fact that Garcia came to the ring weighing 153¹/₂ lbs, it should be seen as a handicap match rather than a title fight. Armstrong weighed 142 lbs.*

23.05.40 Ken Overlin (USA) W PTS 15 Ceferino Garcia (PH), New York City - NY

19.07.40 Tony Zale (USA) W RTD 13 Al Hostak (USA), Seattle - NBA

01.11.40 Ken Overlin (USA) W PTS 15 Steve Belloise (USA), New York City - NY

13.12.40 Ken Overlin (USA) W PTS 15 Steve Belloise (USA), New York City - NY

21.02.41 Tony Zale (USA) W CO 14 Steve Mamakos (USA), Chicago - NBA

09.05.41 Billy Soose (USA) W PTS 15 Ken Overlin (USA), New York City - NY. *After winning the NY version of the title, Soose never defended it, mainly due to increasing weight problems and, following a ten round points defeat at the hands of Georgie Abrams in New York on 30 July 1941, he was stripped. Following that action, it was Abrams who went forward for a unification fight against Tony Zale.*

28.05.41 Tony Zale (USA) W CO 2 Al Hostak (USA), Chicago - NBA

28.11.41 Tony Zale (USA) W PTS 15 Georgie Abrams (USA), New York City

27.09.46 **Tony Zale** (USA) W CO 6 Rocky Graziano (USA), New York City

16.07.47 **Rocky Graziano** (USA) W RSC 6 Tony Zale (USA), Chicago. *With Graziano under suspension in New York for failing to report an attempted bribe, the return encounter with Zale had gone ahead in Chicago. The NBA, apparently oblivious to any other reasons why Graziano should be banned, were therefore shocked, shortly after he had won the championship under their jurisdiction, to find out that he had gone absent without leave during the war before being given a dishonourable discharge. In line with their own rules, the NBA were then forced to release a statement saying that they rejected any participant in boxing who had not fulfilled his trust to his country. However, following a favourable poll among associated NBA States, with the NYSAC still sitting on the sidelines, the third Graziano v Zale fight was eventually accepted by New Jersey.*

10.06.48 **Tony Zale** (USA) W CO 3 Rocky Graziano (USA), Newark

21.09.48 **Marcel Cerdan** (FR) W RSC 12 Tony Zale (USA), Jersey City

16.06.49 **Jake la Motta** (USA) W RTD 10 Marcel Cerdan (FR), Detroit. *With la Motta and Cerdan matched in a return, the latter was killed in a plane crash over the Azores on 27 October 1949, while on his way to America for the fight. By now, Sugar Ray Robinson was recognised as the outstanding challenger and, in May 1950, following la Motta's inability to sign for a defence, Pennsylvania decided to match the welterweight champion against Frenchman, Robert Villemain, for their version of the title.*

05.06.50 Sugar Ray Robinson (USA) W PTS 15 Robert Villemain (FR), Philadelphia - PENNSYLVANIA

12.07.50 Jake la Motta (USA) W PTS 15 Tiberio Mitri (ITA), New York City - NY/NBA

25.08.50 Sugar Ray Robinson (USA) W CO 1 Jose Basora (PR), Scranton - PENNSYLVANIA

13.09.50 Jake la Motta (USA) W CO 15 Laurent Dauthuille (FR), Detroit - NY/NBA

26.10.50 Sugar Ray Robinson (USA) W CO 12 Carl Bobo Olson (USA), Philadelphia - PENNSYLVANIA

14.02.51 **Sugar Ray Robinson** (USA) W RSC 13 Jake la Motta (USA), Chicago

10.07.51 **Randy Turpin** (GB) W PTS 15 Sugar Ray Robinson (USA), Earls Court Arena, London

12.09.51 **Sugar Ray Robinson** (USA) W RSC 10 Randy Turpin (GB), New York City

13.03.52 **Sugar Ray Robinson** (USA) W PTS 15 Carl Bobo Olson (USA), San Francisco

16.04.52 **Sugar Ray Robinson** (USA) W CO 3 Rocky Graziano (USA), Chicago. *Sugar Ray Robinson relinquished his title on announcing his retirement in December 1952 and it was agreed by the NBA and New York that the winner of a series of eliminating bouts, to decide the champion of America, should fight the victor* *of a European title bout between Randy Turpin (England) and Charles Humez (France) for the vacant crown. Carl Bobo Olson duly won the American title, beating Paddy Young on points over 15 rounds in New York City on 19 June 1953, but prior to that Britain had stated that it would recognise the winner of the Turpin v Humez fight as world champion.*

09.06.53 Randy Turpin (GB) W PTS 15 Charles Humez (FR), White City, London - GB

21.10.53 **Carl Bobo Olson** (USA) W PTS 15 Randy Turpin (GB), New York City

02.04.54 **Carl Bobo Olson** (USA) W PTS 15 Kid Gavilan (CUB), Chicago

20.08.54 **Carl Bobo Olson** (USA) W PTS 15 Rocky Castellani (USA), San Francisco

15.12.54 **Carl Bobo Olson** (USA) W RSC 11 Pierre Langlois (FR), San Francisco

09.12.55 **Sugar Ray Robinson** (USA) W CO 2 Carl Bobo Olson (USA), Chicago

18.05.56 **Sugar Ray Robinson** (USA) W CO 4 Carl Bobo Olson (USA), Los Angeles

02.01.57 **Gene Fullmer** (USA) W PTS 15 Sugar Ray Robinson (USA), New York City

01.05.57 **Sugar Ray Robinson** (USA) W CO 5 Gene Fullmer (USA), Chicago

23.09.57 **Carmen Basilio** (USA) W PTS 15 Sugar Ray Robinson (USA), New York City

25.03.58 **Sugar Ray Robinson** (USA) W PTS 15 Carmen Basilio (USA), Chicago. *Having remained inactive for over a year and been given a deadline by the NBA to sign for a defence against Carmen Basilio by 25 April 1959, Robinson ignored the edict and was stripped at the beginning of May. At that juncture, the NBA declared the title vacant and matched Basilio with Gene Fullmer for their version of the title.*

28.08.59 Gene Fullmer (USA) W RSC 14 Carmen Basilio (USA), San Francisco - NBA

04.12.59 Gene Fullmer (USA) W PTS 15 Spider Webb (USA), Logan - NBA

22.01.60 Paul Pender (USA) W PTS 15 Sugar Ray Robinson (USA), Boston - NY/EBU

20.04.60 Gene Fullmer (USA) DREW 15 Joey Giardello (USA), Bozeman - NBA

10.06.60 Paul Pender (USA) W PTS 15 Sugar Ray Robinson (USA), Boston - NY/EBU

29.06.60 Gene Fullmer (USA) W RSC 12 Carmen Basilio (USA), Salt Lake City - NBA

03.12.60 Gene Fullmer (USA) DREW 15 Sugar Ray Robinson (USA), Los Angeles - NBA

14.01.61 Paul Pender (USA) W RSC 7 Terry Downes (GB), Boston - NY/EBU

04.03.61 Gene Fullmer (USA) W PTS 15 Sugar Ray Robinson (USA), Las Vegas - NBA

22.04.61 Paul Pender (USA) W PTS 15 Carmen Basilio (USA), Boston - NY/EBU

11.07.61 Terry Downes (GB) W RTD 9 Paul Pender (USA), The Arena, Wembley - NY/EBU

05.08.61 Gene Fullmer (USA) W PTS 15 Florentino Fernandez (CUB), Ogden - NBA

09.12.61 Gene Fullmer (USA) W CO 10 Benny Kid Paret (CUB), Las Vegas - NBA

07.04.62 Paul Pender (USA) W PTS 15 Terry Downes (GB), Boston - NY/EBU. *Paul Pender forfeited NY/EBU recognition in November 1962 for failing to defend within stipulated period.*

23.10.62 Dick Tiger (N) W PTS 15 Gene Fullmer (USA), San Francisco - NBA

23.02.63 Dick Tiger (N) DREW 15 Gene Fullmer (USA), Las Vegas - NBA

10.08.63 Dick Tiger (N) RTD 7 Gene Fullmer (USA), Ibadan, Nigeria

07.12.63 Joey Giardello (USA) W PTS 15 Dick Tiger (N), Atlantic City

14.12.64 **Joey Giardello** (USA) W PTS 15 Ruben Carter (USA), Philadelphia

21.10.65 Dick Tiger (N) W PTS 15 Joey Giardello (USA), New York City

25.04.66 **Emile Griffith** (USA) W PTS 15 Dick Tiger (N), New York City

13.07.66 **Emile Griffith** (USA) W PTS 15 Joey Archer (USA), New York City

23.01.67 **Emile Griffith** (USA) W PTS 15 Joey Archer (USA), New York City

17.04.67 **Nino Benvenuti** (ITA) W PTS 15 Emile Griffith (USA), New York City

29.09.67 **Emile Griffith** (USA) W PTS 15 Nino Benvenuti (ITA), New York City

04.03.68 **Nino Benvenuti** (ITA) W PTS 15 Emile Griffith (USA), New York City

14.12.68 **Nino Benvenuti** (ITA) W PTS 15 Don Fullmer (USA), San Remo

04.10.69 **Nino Benvenuti** (ITA) W DIS 7 Fraser Scott (USA), Naples

22.11.69 **Nino Benvenuti** (ITA) W CO 1 Luis Rodriguez (CUB), Rome

23.05.70 **Nino Benvenuti** (ITA) W CO 8 Tom Bethea (USA), Umag

07.11.70 **Carlos Monzon** (ARG) W CO 12 Nino Benvenuti (ITA), Rome

08.05.71 **Carlos Monzon** (ARG) W RSC 3 Nino Benvenuti (ITA), Monaco

25.09.71 **Carlos Monzon** (ARG) W RSC 14 Emile Griffith (USA), Buenos Aires

04.03.72 **Carlos Monzon** (ARG) W RSC 5 Denny Moyer (USA), Rome

17.06.72 **Carlos Monzon** (ARG) W RTD 12 Jean-Claude Bouttier (FR), Colombes

19.08.72 **Carlos Monzon** (ARG) W RSC 5 Tom Bogs (DEN), Copenhagen

11.11.72 **Carlos Monzon** (ARG) W PTS 15 Bennie Briscoe (USA), Buenos Aires

02.06.73 **Carlos Monzon** (ARG) W PTS 15 Emile Griffith (USA), Monaco

29.09.73 **Carlos Monzon** (ARG) W PTS 15 Jean-Claude Bouttier (FR), Paris

09.02.74 **Carlos Monzon** (ARG) W RTD 6 Jose Napoles (CUB), Paris. *When Carlos Monzon forfeited WBC recognition in April 1974 for failing to arrange a defence against Rodrigo Valdez within the stipulated period, the latter was matched with Bennie Briscoe in order to find a successor.*

25.05.74 Rodrigo Valdez (COL) W CO 7 Bennie Briscoe (USA), Monaco - WBC

05.10.74 Carlos Monzon (ARG) W CO 7 Tony Mundine (A), Buenos Aires - WBA

30.11.74 Rodrigo Valdez (COL) W CO 11 Gratien Tonna (FR), Paris - WBC

31.05.75 Rodrigo Valdez (COL) W RSC 8 Ramon Mendez (ARG), Cali - WBC

30.06.75 Carlos Monzon (ARG) W RSC 10 Tony Licata (USA), New York City - WBA

16.08.75 Rodrigo Valdez (COL) W PTS 15 Rudy Robles (MEX), Cartagena - WBC

13.12.75 Carlos Monzon (ARG) W CO 5 Gratien Tonna (FR), Paris - WBA

28.03.75 Rodrigo Valdez (COL) W RTD 4 Nessim Cohen (FR), Paris - WBC

26.06.76 **Carlos Monzon** (ARG) W PTS 15 Rodrigo Valdez (COL), Monaco

30.07.77 **Carlos Monzon** (ARG) W PTS 15 Rodrigo Valdez (COL), Monaco. *Carlos Monzon retired as undefeated champion in August 1977, when the WBA forced him to vacate their portion of the title, after he failed to agree terms for a championship contest against Rodrigo Valdez. With the WBA supporting Bennie Briscoe and the WBC backing Valdez, neither body saw the need for an eliminator.*

05.11.77 **Rodrigo Valdez** (COL) W PTS 15 Bennie Briscoe (USA), Campione

26.11.77 Marvin Hagler (USA) W CO 12 Mike Colbert (USA), Boston - MASSACHUSETTS. *The billing was more in protest that Hagler had not been considered for an elimination series, following the retirement of Monzon, and proved to be a one off.*

22.04.78 **Hugo Corro** (ARG) W PTS 15 Rodrigo Valdez (COL), San Remo

05.08.78 **Hugo Corro** (ARG) W PTS 15 Ronnie Harris (USA), Buenos Aires

11.11.78 **Hugo Corro** (ARG) W PTS 15 Rodrigo Valdez (COL), Buenos Aires

30.06.79 **Vito Antuofermo** (ITA) W PTS 15 Hugo Corro (ARG), Monaco

30.11.79 **Vito Antuofermo** (ITA) DREW 15 Marvin Hagler (USA), Las Vegas

16.03.80 **Alan Minter** (GB) W PTS 15 Vito Antuofermo (ITA), Las Vegas

28.06.80 **Alan Minter** (GB) W RTD 8 Vito Antuofermo (ITA), The Arena, Wembley

27.09.80 **Marvin Hagler** (USA) W RSC 3 Alan Minter (GB), The Arena, Wembley

17.01.81 **Marvin Hagler** (USA) W RSC 8 Fully Obelmejias (VEN), Boston

13.06.81 **Marvin Hagler** (USA) W RTD 4 Vito Antuofermo (ITA), Boston

03.10.81 **Marvin Hagler** (USA) W RSC 11 Mustafa Hamsho (USA), Rosemont

07.03.82 **Marvin Hagler** (USA) W RSC 1 Caveman Lee (USA), Atlantic City

30.10.82 **Marvin Hagler** (USA) W RSC 5 Fully Obelmejias (VEN), San Remo

11.02.83 **Marvin Hagler** (USA) W RSC 6 Tony Sibson (GB), Worcester

27.05.83 **Marvin Hagler** (USA) W CO 4 Wilford Scypion (USA),

Alan Minter: world middleweight champion, 1980

Derek Rowe (Photos) Ltd

Providence. *The fight was not sanctioned by either the WBA or the WBC, but was organised by a new body calling themselves the USA International Boxing Association. However, because Hagler was recognised universally as the undisputed champion and Scypion was a worthy challenger, the fight was given credence by all bar the offices of the WBA and WBC.*

10.11.83 **Marvin Hagler** (USA) W PTS 15 Roberto Duran (PAN), Las Vegas

30.03.84 **Marvin Hagler** (USA) W RSC 10 Juan Domingo Roldan (ARG), Las Vegas

19.10.84 **Marvin Hagler** (USA) W RSC 3 Mustafa Hamsho (USA), New York City

16.04.85 **Marvin Hagler** (USA) W RSC 3 Thomas Hearns (USA), Las Vegas

10.03.86 **Marvin Hagler** (USA) W CO 11 John Mugabi (U), Las Vegas. *Marvin Hagler forfeited WBA recognition in February 1987 for failing to meet Herol Graham within the stipulated period and subsequently signing for a defence against Sugar Ray Leonard.*

06.04.87 Sugar Ray Leonard (USA) W PTS 12 Marvin Hagler (USA), Las Vegas - WBC. *Following the fight, the IBF stated that they were vacating the title because they could not lend their support to Leonard, while, on 26 May, Herol Graham forfeited his chance of crack at the WBA title when losing his European title to Sumbu Kalambay on points over 12 rounds at Wembley. A short while later, in June, all versions of the title were left vacant after Leonard announced that he was giving up the WBC belt in order to take a long break from boxing. With the division in turmoil, Iran Barkley, who had earlier been matched against Michael Olajide for the IBF title, was finally booked to meet Kalambay for the WBA crown, on the proviso that the winner gave Mike McCallum first crack and, with matches made between Thomas Hearns v Juan Domingo Roldan (WBC) and Olajide v Frank Tate (IBF), the championship would be split three ways.*

10.10.87 Frank Tate (USA) W PTS 15 Michael Olajide (C), Las Vegas - IBF

23.10.87 Sumbu Kalambay (ITA) W PTS 15 Iran Barkley (USA), Livorno - WBA

29.10.87 Thomas Hearns (USA) W CO 4 Juan Domingo Roldan (ARG), Las Vegas - WBC

07.02.88 Frank Tate (USA) W CO 10 Tony Sibson (GB), Stafford - IBF

01.03.88 Sumbu Kalambay (ITA) W PTS 12 Mike McCallum (J), Pesaro - WBA

06.06.88 Iran Barkley (USA) W RSC 3 Thomas Hearns (USA), Las Vegas - WBC

12.06.88 Sumbu Kalambay (ITA) W PTS 12 Robbie Sims (USA), Ravenna - WBA

28.07.88 Michael Nunn (USA) W RSC 9 Frank Tate (USA), Las Vegas - IBF

04.11.88 Michael Nunn (USA) W CO 8 Juan Domingo Roldan (ARG), Las Vegas - IBF

08.11.88 Sumbu Kalambay (ITA) W RSC 7 Doug de Witt (USA), Monaco - WBA. *Sumbu Kalambay forfeited WBA recognition in March 1989 when failing to sign for defence against Herol Graham.*

24.02.89 Roberto Duran (PAN) W PTS 12 Iran Barkley (USA), Atlantic City - WBC

25.03.89 Michael Nunn (USA) W CO 1 Sumbu Kalambay (ITA), Las Vegas - IBF

18.04.89 Doug de Witt (USA) W PTS 12 Robbie Sims (USA), Atlantic City - WBO

10.05.89 Mike McCallum (J) W PTS 12 Herol Graham (GB), Albert Hall, London - WBA

14.08.89 Michael Nunn (USA) W PTS 12 Iran Barkley (USA), Reno - IBF

07.12.89 Sugar Ray Leonard (USA) W PTS 12 Roberto Duran (PAN), Las Vegas - WBC. *Although billed for the WBC super-middles title held by Leonard, and made at 162 lbs (six pounds below the championship limit), both men were inside 160 lbs. Technically, Duran's WBC middles title was also at stake and, following the result, should have been declared vacant. However, the champion was stripped in January 1990 for failing to give a written undertaking to defend.*

15.01.90 Doug de Witt (USA) W RTD 11 Matthew Hilton (C), Atlantic City - WBO

03.02.90 Mike McCallum (J) W PTS 12 Steve Collins (I), Boston - WBA

14.04.90 Michael Nunn (USA) W PTS 12 Marlon Starling (USA), Las Vegas - IBF

14.04.90 Mike McCallum (J) W CO 11 Michael Watson (GB), Albert Hall, London - WBA

29.04.90 Nigel Benn (GB) W RSC 8 Doug de Witt (USA), Atlantic City - WBO

18.08.90 Nigel Benn (GB) W RSC 1 Iran Barkley (USA), Las Vegas - WBO

18.10.90 Michael Nunn (USA) W RSC 10 Don Curry (USA), Paris - IBF

18.11.90 Chris Eubank (GB) W RSC 9 Nigel Benn (GB), Exhibition Centre, Birmingham - WBO

24.11.90 Julian Jackson (USA) W CO 4 Herol Graham (GB), Benalmadena - WBC

23.02.91 Chris Eubank (GB) W TD 10 Dan Sherry (C), Conference Centre, Brighton - WBO

01.04.91 Mike McCallum (J) W PTS 12 Sumbu Kalambay (ITA), Monaco - WBA. *Mike McCallum forfeited WBA recognition in December 1991 when challenging James Toney for the IBF version of title.*

18.04.91 Chris Eubank (GB) W RSC 6 Gary Stretch (GB), Olympia, London - WBO

10.05.91 James Toney (USA) W RSC 11 Michael Nunn (USA), Davenport - IBF

22.06.91 Chris Eubank (GB) W PTS 12 Michael Watson (GB), Earls Court Exhibition Centre, London - WBO. *Chris Eubank relinquished WBO version of title in July 1991 in order to challenge for the vacant WBO super-middleweight crown.*

29.06.91 James Toney (USA) W PTS 12 Reggie Johnson (USA), Las Vegas - IBF

14.09.91 Julian Jackson (USA) W CO 1 Dennis Milton (USA), Las Vegas - WBC

12.10.91 James Toney (USA) W RSC 4 Francisco Dell' Aquila (ITA), Monaco - IBF

20.11.91 Gerald McClellan (USA) W RSC 1 John Mugabi (U), Albert Hall, London - WBO. *Gerald McClellan relinquished WBO version of title in March 1993 to challenge for the WBC crown.*

13.12.91 James Toney (USA) DREW 12 Mike McCallum (J), Atlantic City - IBF

08.02.92 James Toney (USA) W PTS 12 Dave Tiberi (USA), Atlantic City - IBF

15.02.92 Julian Jackson (USA) W CO 1 Ismael Negron (USA), Las Vegas - WBC

10.04.92 Julian Jackson (USA) W RSC 5 Ron Collins (USA), Mexico City - WBC

11.04.92 James Toney (USA) W PTS 12 Glenn Wolfe (USA), Las Vegas - IBF

22.04.92 Reggie Johnson (USA) W PTS 12 Steve Collins (I), East Rutherford - WBA

01.08.92 Julian Jackson (USA) W PTS 12 Thomas Tate (USA), Las Vegas - WBC

29.08.92 James Toney (USA) W PTS 12 Mike McCallum (J), Reno - IBF. *James Toney relinquished IBF version of title on becoming that body's super-middleweight champion in February 1993.*

27.10.92 Reggie Johnson (USA) W PTS 12 Lamar Parks (USA), Houston - WBA

19.01.93 Reggie Johnson (USA) W RSC 8 Ki-Yun Song (SK), Boise - WBA

04.05.93 Reggie Johnson (USA) W PTS 12 Wayne Harris (GU), Denver - WBA

08.05.93 Gerald McClellan (USA) W RSC 5 Julian Jackson (USA), Las Vegas - WBC

19.05.93 Chris Pyatt (GB) W PTS 12 Sumbu Kalambay (ITA), Granby Halls, Leicester - WBO

22.05.93 Roy Jones (USA) W PTS 12 Bernard Hopkins (USA), Washington - IBF

06.08.93 Gerald McClellan (USA) W CO 1 Jay Bell (USA), Bayamon - WBC

18.09.93 Chris Pyatt (GB) W CO 6 Hugo Corti (ARG), Granby Halls, Leicester - WBO

01.10.93 John David Jackson (USA) W PTS 12 Reggie Johnson (USA), Buenos Aires - WBA. *John David Jackson was stripped of the WBA version of the crown for accepting a non-title fight without having the body's authorisation.*

09.02.94 Chris Pyatt (GB) W RSC 1 Mark Cameron (SA), International Hall, Brentwood - WBO

04.03.94 Gerald McClellan (USA) W RSC 1 Gilbert Baptist (USA), Las Vegas - WBC

07.05.94 Gerald McClellan (USA) W RSC 1 Julian Jackson (USA), Las Vegas - WBC

11.05.94 Steve Collins (I) W RSC 5 Chris Pyatt (GB), Ponds Forge Centre, Sheffield - WBO

27.05.94 Roy Jones (USA) W RSC 2 Thomas Tate (USA), Las Vegas - IBF

Super-Middleweight (168 lbs)

One of the most recent divisions, it took a long while in coming, probably due to the more prestigious middleweight title. Introduced, as we know it, by the International Boxing Federation in 1984, as a means of furthering fighters' opportunities, it was, in truth, sorely needed, with a 15 lb weight differential holding many good men back. Although the IBF are to be given credit for developing it to full international status, "world" titles at 168 lbs, even if little known, had been in existance previously. On 3 April 1967 in Salt Lake City, and supported by the State Boxing Commission, Don Fullmer (USA) won Utah's version of the title, beating Joe Hopkins (USA) by a knockout in the sixth round. Fullmer then made successful defences against fellow Americans, Luis Garduna (by a kayo in round two in Missoula on 22 June 1967) and Carl Moore (outpointed over ten rounds in Phoenix on 20 February 1968), before losing a ten round points decision to Doyle Baird (USA) in Cleveland on 29 October 1969. Baird showed no interest in preserving his newly won honours and moved up to light-heavy, eventually challenging Vicente Rondon for the WBA version. Five years later, Danny Brewer (USA), backed by Ohio, claimed their version of the title. However, he lost all three championship contests he participated in. Bill Douglas (USA) knocked him out in the second round of their fight in Columbus on 27 November 1974, but had no interest in the title whatsoever and moved on immediately, while Jesse Burnett (USA) kayoed him twice. After being beaten in the third round on 28 November 1975 (Edmonton) and then in the seventh on 3 May 1976 (Stockton), Brewer finally called it a day, while Burnett went on to contest both the WBC light-heavy and cruiser titles in 1977 and 1983, respectively. Apart from the World Athletic Association, a minority group who named a champion in 1982, it was left to the IBF to announce Murray Sutherland and Ernie Singletary as the nominations for their first ever championship contest.

28.03.84 Murray Sutherland (C) W PTS 15 Ernie Singletary (USA), Atlantic City - IBF

22.07.84 Chong-Pal Park (SK) W CO 11 Murray Sutherland (C), Seoul - IBF

02.01.85 Chong-Pal Park (SK) W CO 2 Roy Gumbs (GB), Seoul - IBF

30.06.85 Chong-Pal Park (SK) W PTS 15 Vinnie Curto (USA), Seoul - IBF

11.04.86 Chong-Pal Park (SK) W CO 15 Vinnie Curto (USA), Los Angeles - IBF

06.07.86 Chong-Pal Park (SK) TD 2 Lindell Holmes (USA), Chungju - IBF

14.09.86 Chong-Pal Park (SK) W PTS 15 Marvin Mack (USA), Pusan - IBF

25.01.87 Chong-Pal Park (SK) W RSC 15 Doug Sam (A), Seoul - IBF

03.05.87 Chong-Pal Park (SK) W PTS 15 Lindell Holmes (USA), Inchon - IBF

26.07.87 Chong-Pal Park (SK) W RSC 4 Emmanuel Otti (U), Kwangju - IBF. *Chong-Pal Park relinquished IBF version of title immediately prior to fighting Jesus Gallardo for the vacant WBA crown.*

06.12.87 Chong-Pal Park (SK) W RSC 2 Jesus Gallardo (MEX), Seoul - WBA

01.03.88 Chong-Pal Park (SK) W CO 5 Polly Pasieron (INDON), Chungju - WBA

12.03.88 Graciano Rocchigiani (GER) W RSC 8 Vince Boulware (USA), Dusseldorf - IBF

23.05.88 Fully Obelmejias (VEN) W PTS 12 Chong-Pal Park (SK), Suanbao - WBA

03.06.88 Graciano Rocchigiani (GER) W PTS 15 Nicky Walker (USA), Berlin - IBF

07.10.88 Graciano Rocchigiani (GER) W RTD 11 Chris Reid (USA), Berlin - IBF

07.11.88 Sugar Ray Leonard (USA) W RSC 9 Don Lalonde (C), Las Vegas - WBC

14.11.88 Thomas Hearns (USA) W PTS 12 James Kinchen (USA), Las Vegas - WBO

27.01.89 Graciano Rocchigiani (GER) W PTS 12 Thulani Malinga (SA), Berlin - IBF. *Graciano Rocchigiani relinquished IBF version of title in September 1989 due to continuing weight problems.*

27.05.89 In-Chul Baek (SK) W RSC 11 Fully Obelmejias (VEN), Seoul - WBA

12.06.89 Sugar Ray Leonard (USA) DREW 12 Thomas Hearns (USA), Las Vegas - WBC

08.10.89 In-Chul Baek (SK) W RSC 11 Ronnie Essett (USA), Seoul - WBA

07.12.89 Sugar Ray Leonard (USA) W PTS 12 Roberto Duran (PAN), Las Vegas - WBC. *Sugar Ray Leonard relinquished WBC version of title in August 1990 saying he was too light to defend.*

13.01.90 In-Chul Baek (SK) W RSC 7 Yoshiaki Tajima (JAP), Seoul - WBA

27.01.90 Lindell Holmes (USA) W PTS 12 Frank Tate (USA), New Orleans - IBF

30.03.90 Chrisophe Tiozzo (FR) W RSC 6 In-Chul Baek (SK), Lyon - WBA

28.04.90 Thomas Hearns (USA) W PTS 12 Michael Olajide (C), Atlantic City - WBO. *Thomas Hearns relinquished WBO version of title in April 1991 to concentrate on a WBA light-heavyweight challenge against Virgil Hill.*

19.07.90 Lindell Holmes (USA) W RSC 9 Carl Sullivan (USA), Seattle - IBF

20.07.90 Christophe Tiozzo (FR) W RSC 8 Paul Whittaker (USA), Aries - WBA

23.11.90 Christophe Tiozzo (FR) W RSC 2 Danny Morgan (USA), Cergy Pontoise - WBA

15.12.90 Mauro Galvano (ITA) W PTS 12 Dario Matteoni (ARG), Monaco - WBC

16.12.90 Lindell Holmes (USA) W PTS 12 Thulani Malinga (SA), Marino - IBF

07.03.91 Lindell Holmes (USA) W PTS 12 Antoine Byrd (USA), Madrid - IBF

05.04.91 Victor Cordoba (PAN) W RSC 9 Christophe Tiozzo (FR), Marseille - WBA

18.05.91 Darrin van Horn (USA) W CO 11 Lindell Holmes (USA), Verbania - IBF

27.07.91 Mauro Galvano (ITA) W PTS 12 Ronnie Essett (USA), Capo d'Orlando - WBC

17.08.91 Darrin van Horn (USA) W RSC 3 John Jarvis (USA), Irvine - IBF

21.09.91 Chris Eubank (GB) W RSC 12 Michael Watson (GB), White Hart Lane, London - WBO

13.12.91 Victor Cordoba (PAN) W RSC 11 Vincenzo Nardiello (ITA), Paris - WBA

10.01.92 Iran Barkley (USA) W RSC 2 Darrin van Horn (USA), New York City - IBF

01.02.92 Chris Eubank (GB) W PTS 12 Thulani Malinga (SA), National Indoor Centre, Birmingham - WBO

06.02.92 Mauro Galvano (ITA) W PTS 12 Juan Carlos Gimenez (PAR), Marino - WBC

25.04.92 Chris Eubank (GB) W CO 3 John Jarvis (USA), G-Mex Leisure Centre, Manchester - WBO

27.06.92 Chris Eubank (GB) W PTS 12 Ronnie Essett (USA), Quinta do Lago - WBO

12.09.92 Michael Nunn (USA) W PTS 12 Victor Cordoba (PAN), Las Vegas - WBA

19.09.92 Chris Eubank (GB) W PTS 12 Tony Thornton (USA), Scottish Exhibition Centre, Glasgow - WBO

03.10.92 Nigel Benn (GB) W RTD 3 Mauro Galvano (ITA), Marino - WBC

28.11.92 Chris Eubank (GB) W PTS 12 Juan Carlos Gimenez (PAR), G-Mex Centre, Manchester - WBO

12.12.92 Nigel Benn (GB) W RSC 11 Nicky Piper (GB), Alexandra Palace, London - WBC

30.01.93 Michael Nunn (USA) W PTS 12 Victor Cordoba (PAN), Memphis - WBA

13.02.93 James Toney (USA) W RTD 9 Iran Barkley (USA), Las Vegas - IBF

20.02.93 Michael Nunn (USA) W CO 1 Danny Morgan (USA), Mexico City - WBA

20.02.93 Chris Eubank (GB) W PTS 12 Lindell Holmes (USA), Olympia National Hall, London - WBO

06.03.93 Nigel Benn (GB) W PTS 12 Mauro Galvano (ITA), Scottish Exhibition Centre, Glasgow - WBC

23.04.93 Michael Nunn (USA) W RSC 6 Crawford Ashley (GB), Memphis - WBA

15.05.93 Chris Eubank (GB) DREW 12 Ray Close (GB), Scottish Exhibition Centre, Glasgow - WBO

26.06.93 Nigel Benn (GB) W RSC 4 Lou Gent (GB), Olympia National Hall, London - WBC

09.10.93 Nigel Benn (GB) DREW 12 Chris Eubank (GB), Old Trafford, Manchester - WBC/WBO

29.10.93 James Toney (USA) W PTS 12 Tony Thornton (USA), Tulsa - IBF

18.12.93 Michael Nunn (USA) W PTS 12 Merqui Sosa (DOM), Puebla - WBA

05.02.94 Chris Eubank (GB) W PTS 12 Graciano Rocchigiani (GER), Berlin - WBO

26.02.94 Nigel Benn (GB) W PTS 12 Henry Wharton (GB), Earls Court Arena, London - WBC

26.02.94 Steve Little (USA) W PTS 12 Michael Nunn (USA), Earls Court Arena, London - WBA

05.03.94 James Toney (USA) W RSC 4 Tim Littles (USA), Los Angeles - IBF

21.05.94 Chris Eubank (GB) W PTS 12 Ray Close (GB), King's Hall, Belfast - WBO

Light-Heavyweight (175 lbs)

Originated in America, following a series of articles written by Lou Houseman, a newspaperman based in Chicago who also managed a stable of fighters on the side, the division was first "thought up" in 1899. Although Houseman is mainly remembered for steering his own fighter, Jack Root, to the "title", he first promoted a fight between Joe Choynski (158 lbs) and the Australian, Jim Ryan (152 lbs), in Dubuque on 18 August 1899, as being for the vacant light-heavyweight championship. Choynski won on points over 20 rounds and next time out successfully "defended" against another Australian, Jim Hall, who was knocked out in the seventh round on 25 September 1899 (Louisville). However, at no stage did Choynski seriously see himself as the light-heavyweight champion and, while his fourth round kayo defeat at the hands of Kid McCoy on 12 January 1900 (New York City) saw both men inside 175 lbs, it was not billed as a title match and was not considered to be one. The next three years saw no further "title" action, but it did see the rise of two young fighters, George Gardner and Jack Root, who, although quickly growing out of the middleweight ranks, were a bit on the small side to tangle with the "big fellows", but were ideally suited to an interim division. They first met up in an advertised middleweight title bout at San Francisco on 31 January 1902, but neither man was able to get down to 158 lbs. Although Root won on a seventh round disqualification, Gardner got his revenge when kayoing the former inside 17 heats on 18 August 1902 (Salt Lake City), with both men inside 165 lbs. While the stage was now set to offer titular opportunities to men between 158 and 175 lbs, it would be nearly 20 years before the weight class became generally accepted.

22.04.03 Jack Root (USA) W PTS 10 Kid McCoy (USA), Detroit. *Generally recognised as being the division's first title fight, even if it was only billed for the American 175 lbs championship, Root* tipped the beam at 168 lbs, whereas McCoy came in at 173 lbs. The famous referee, George Siler, writing in the Chicago Tribune (newspaper), said: "There was really no necessity to advertise the fight as a championship bout as the new light-heavyweight class should only be seen as a maverick and, as such, have no standing".

13.05.03 George Gardner (USA) W PTS 12 Marvin Hart (USA), Louisville. *Following this win in another billed championship bout, this time at 170 lbs, Gardner and Root were matched to effectively decide the vacant title. For the record, the Chicago Tribune (newspaper) stated that Hart, had no realistic "claim" to the title in scaling 176 lbs to Gardner's 168.*

04.07.03 George Gardner (USA) W PTS 20 Jack Root (USA), Fort Erie. *With the first two so-called championship contests decided at 175 and 170 lbs, respectively, this one was made at 165 lbs. The Chicago Tribune (newspaper) claimed that, with three days to go, both men were already down to the weight give or take a couple of pounds.*

25.11.03 Bob Fitzsimmons (A) W PTS 20 George Gardner (USA), San Francisco - USA. *Although the Articles of Agreement called for the men to make 168 lbs, according to the San Francisco Chronicle (newspaper), Gardner came in at 170, while Fitzsimmons was spot on. Gardner was a good fighter, but had hardly set the world on fire, whereas Fitzsimmons, who became the first man to win three titles at different weights at the final bell, gave the light-heavyweight division a certain air of respectability. That aside, the new weight class was still generally considered to be nothing more than a short stop-gap between the prestigious middle and heavyweight ranks and also one with no fixed weight limit at that moment in time.*

20.12.05 Jack O'Brien (USA) W RTD 13 Bob Fitzsimmons (A), San Francisco. *Weights (lbs): O' Brien (164), Fitzsimmons (165). With both men well inside 175 lbs, it appears, that over a period of time, historians have wrongly assumed the above contest to have been for the light-heavyweight title, when, in fact, it was one of a series of eliminators to decide the heavyweight crown (see under that weight class, also). It would also be a revision of history to say that O'Brien ever claimed the title and he continued to operate in the heavyweight division.*

28.11.06 Jack O'Brien (USA) DREW 20 Tommy Burns (C), Los Angeles. *The above contest was billed as deciding the heavyweight championship, but because both men were inside 175 lbs, with O'Brien scaling 163½ lbs to Burns' 172, over the years, record compilers, who saw O'Brien as the light-heavyweight boss, logged it as a title defence (see under heavyweight listings, also).*

08.05.07 Tommy Burns (C) W PTS 20 Jack O'Brien (USA), Los Angeles. *Billed for the world heavyweight title (see under those listings, also), some record books, including the TS Andrews, saw this as deciding the light-heavy issue as well. However, with Burns scaling 180 lbs and the weight limit recognised as being no more than 175 lbs, would explain why Burns never laid claim to the title.*

15.08.11 Sam Langford (USA) ND-W RSC 5 Jack O'Brien (USA), New York City. *On the basis of this victory, Langford was recognised by the IBU as the world 170 lbs champion when they first published their ratings in June 1912, but there is no record of him being the least bit interested in the "title" around this time, the newly formed New York State Athletic Commission announced that they would recognise the weight class, but at 165 lbs, and Fireman Jim Flynn promptly laid claim to the title, without ever bothering to defend it.*

28.05.12 Jack Dillon (USA) ND-W CO 3 Hugo Kelly (USA), Indianapolis. *Dillon claimed the title following his defeat of Kelly, but the result met with little interest and even less acceptance. Of course, Dillon was a great fighter and it would be nice to fill in interruptions in the lineage of champions, but that is revising history and the weight class, which had been dormant since 1905, remained in the doldrums. Although Dillon continued to defend his "title" at 175 lbs in billed championship bouts (see below), there was no nationwide recognition and that should be depicted as such.*

14.04.14 Jack Dillon (USA) W PTS 12 Battling Levinsky (USA), Butte. *According to the Ring Record Book, and supported by the Andrews Record Book, this was recognised in some States as being for the vacant 175 lbs title.*

28.04.14 Jack Dillon (USA) W PTS 10 Al Norton (USA), Kansas City

15.06.14 Jack Dillon (USA) W PTS 12 Bob Moha (USA), Butte

03.07.14 Jack Dillon (USA) W PTS 10 Sailor Petroskey (USA), Kansas City

25.04.16 Jack Dillon (USA) W PTS 15 Battling Levinsky (USA), Kansas City

17.10.16 Jack Dillon (USA) ND-W PTS 10 Tim O'Neill (USA), Brooklyn. *O'Neill weighed 172 lbs.*

24.10.16 Battling Levinsky (USA) W PTS 12 Jack Dillon (USA), Boston. *Following Dillon's first loss for over four years, Levinsky, who had begun his professional career as Barney Williams, claimed the title. Although neither man weighed in, according to the Andrews Record Book, Levinsky was conveniently considered to have made the stipulated 175 lbs. The Boston Daily Globe (newspaper) report of the fight said Dillon lost because his hands were in bad shape from fighting too frequently, while in summing up, Prof. L. V. Davis makes the point that Dillon certainly did not behave like a champion defending a valuable title. In the meantime, Levinsky was hardly perceived to be a world champion and the light-heavyweight division remained away from the public eye.*

16.10.17 Kid Norfolk, (USA) W PTS 12 Billy Miske (USA), Boston. *Although in some quarters it is said that Kid Norfolk claimed the title following this win, that information should be discarded. According to the Boston Evening Globe (newspaper) report, both men weighed at least 175 lbs, a statement compounded with no proof that either man actually weighed in. However, when Norfolk boxed Harry Wills for the coloured heavyweight title on 2 March 1922 (New York City), he was billed as the black light-heavyweight champion.*

11.08.19 Battling Levinsky (USA) ND-W PTS 8 Clay Turner (USA), Jersey City - USA. *Both men were inside the 175 lbs mark, with Levinsky scaling 173 to Turner's 170.*

12.10.20 Georges Carpentier (FR) ND-W CO 4 Battling Levinsky (USA), Jersey City. *When promoter, Tex Rickard, was looking for a way to build Carpentier into a main attraction, and a worthy opponent for Jack Dempsey, he hit upon the idea of reviving the light-heavyweight class, which was, in fact, the ideal weight division for the Frenchman. Although a decision could not be given, it was advertised as a championship battle and finally gave the 175 lbs title international recognition, with Carpentier acknowledged as champion. Later, on 13 January 1922, when Carpentier was competing among the heavyweights and the Americans looking to find a successor, Gene Tunney won the vacant USA title, beating Levinsky on points over 12 rounds in New York City.*

11.05.22 Georges Carpentier (FR) W CO 1 Ted Kid Lewis (GB), Olympia, London. *Twelve days after the Frenchman's victory, Gene Tunney was parted from the American title on 23 May 1922, when Harry Greb outpointed him over 15 rounds in New York City.*

24.09.22 Battling Siki (FR) W CO 6 Georges Carpentier (FR), Paris. *After counting Carpentier out, the referee announced that he had disqualified Siki for tripping his opponent over, but the verdict was so unpopular that an hour later the judges overruled the decision and declared Siki the winner. Outside the ring, Siki's behaviour was eccentric to say the least and there was even more emphasis placed on the American title. Two 15 round fights that took place in New York City, saw Harry Greb outscore Tommy Loughran on 30 January 1923, before losing the American title in reverse fashion to Gene Tunney on 23 February 1923.*

17.03.23 Mike McTigue (USA) W PTS 20 Battling Siki (FR), Dublin. *Siki, the recipient of a "dodgy" decision, should have lost his title on the scales when refusing to weigh-in, knowing full well he was over the limit. Following the fight, and in view of his inability to declare his weight, the IBU stripped Siki of his European title. Incidentally, on 15 December 1925, Siki, who had the habit of walking his pet lion through the streets of New York City, was found shot to death in the gutter.*

25.06.23 Mike McTigue (USA) ND-L PTS 8 Tommy Loughran (USA), Philadelphia. *Loughran weighed 161 lbs, while McTigue made 164¹/₂. On 31 July 1923, Gene Tunney successfully defended the American title, following a 12 round points win over Dan O'Dowd (175 lbs) in Long Island City.*

02.08.23 Mike McTigue (USA) ND-W PTS 12 Tommy Loughran (USA), West New York. *Loughran weighed 166 lbs to McTigue's 163¹/₂.*

04.10.23 Mike McTigue (USA) DREW 10 Young Stribling (USA), Columbus. *Not shown in the Ring Record Book as a title fight because of the disgraceful circumstances surrounding the contest and the fact that no weights were announced. It appeared that Stribling (165 lbs) won eight of the ten rounds, with McTigue (162 lbs), it was claimed, being forced at gunpoint to fight on even though he had suffered a broken hand. The referee first called a draw, then changed it to a win for Stribling when intimidated by the crowd, which included hooded Ku Klux Klansmen. Afterwards, when safely back home, he refuted his second decision and the fight remains on record as a draw. Some two months later, on 10 December 1923, in New York City, Gene Tunney retained his American title when outpointing Harry Greb over 15 rounds, but, following the fight, he decided to relinquish his belt in order to concentrate on the heavyweight division.*

31.03.24 Mike McTigue (USA) ND-L PTS 12 Young Stribling (USA),

Newark. *Stribling weighed 165 lbs as opposed to McTigue at 166¹/₂.*

07.01.25 Mike McTigue (USA) ND-L PTS 12 Mickey Walker (USA), Newark. *McTigue, at 160 lbs, outweighed the challenger by a whopping 11¹/₄ lbs.*

30.05.25 Paul Berlenbach (USA) W PTS 15 Mike McTigue (USA), New York City.

13.07.25 Paul Berlenbach (USA) ND-NC 9 Tony Marullo (USA), Newark. *Billed as a 12 round no-decision fight for the championship, both men were thrown out for not trying. For the record, Berlenbach scaled 173¹/₂ lbs, with Marullo weighing in at 166¹/₂.*

11.09.25 Paul Berlenbach (USA) W RSC 11 Jimmy Slattery (USA), New York City.

11.12.25 Paul Berlenbach (USA) W PTS 15 Jack Delaney (C), New York City.

10.06.26 Paul Berlenbach (USA) W PTS 15 Young Stribling (USA), New York City.

16.07.26 Jack Delaney (C) W PTS 15 Paul Berlenback (USA), Brooklyn.

10.12.26 Jack Delaney (C) W CO 3 Jamaica Kid (USA), Waterbury, *Not listed in the Ring Record Book as a title fight, it was, in fact, scheduled for 15 rounds of championship boxing. The Kid initially weighed in at 180 lbs, but was given nearly three hours to weight reduce before coming in at 175 lbs to Delaney's 172¹/₂. Later, when Delaney relinquished the title in June 1927 to campaign as a heavyweight, the NBA matched Jimmy Slattery and Maxie Rosenbloom for their version of the championship, while former champion, Mike McTigue, claimed the New York crown.*

30.08.27 Jimmy Slattery (USA) W PTS 10 Maxie Rosenbloom (USA), Hartford - NBA.

07.10.27 Tommy Loughran (USA) W PTS 15 Mike McTigue (USA), New York City - NY.

12.12.27 Tommy Loughran (USA) W PTS 15 Jimmy Slattery (USA), New York City.

06.01.28 Tommy Loughran (USA) W PTS 15 Leo Lomski (USA), New York City.

01.06.28 Tommy Loughran (USA) W PTS 15 Pete Latzo (USA), Brooklyn.

16.07.28 Tommy Loughran (USA) W PTS 10 Pete Latzo (USA), Wilkes Barre.

28.03.29 Tommy Loughran (USA) W PTS 10 Mickey Walker (USA), Chicago.

18.07.29 Tommy Loughran (USA) W PTS 15 James J. Braddock (USA), New York City. *When Tommy Loughran relinquished his title in September 1929, in order to campaign as a heavyweight, the New York State Athletic Commission matched the local favourite, Jimmy Slattery, against Lou Scozza for their version of the title. Scozza had knocked out K.O. Brown inside seven rounds in Buffalo on 1 November 1929, while Slattery outpointed Maxie Rosenbloom over ten rounds in Buffalo on 25 November 1929 in the other semi-final leg. Although Rosenbloom was eliminated from the competition, he had beaten Slattery just six weeks earlier and was supported by the NBA in his quest for a return.*

10.02.30 Jimmy Slattery (USA) W PTS 15 Lou Scozza (USA), Buffalo - NY.

25.06.30 Maxie Rosenbloom (USA) W PTS 15 Jimmy Slattery (USA), Buffalo.

22.10.30 Maxie Rosenbloom (USA) W RSC 11 Abe Bain (USA), New York City.

15.05.31 Maxie Rosenbloom (USA) W PTS 10 Don Petrin (USA), Los Angeles. *The Los Angeles Times (newspaper) stated that although both men were announced as being 170 lbs, Rosenbloom looked considerably bigger. There had been nothing in the build up to the fight to suggest that the title was involved and, if it was, it was not recognised outside of California. On 6 June 1931, the NBA withdrew recognition from Maxie Rosenbloom and decided to set up an elimination tournament to find a worthier champion. The move, apparently a political one, came about after Rosenbloom, a ten round points non-title victim of Billy Jones on 6 April 1931 (Pittsburgh), had failed to make an official defence within the stipulated six month regulation period. With wins over Don Petrin, Charley Belanger, Lou Scozza and Jones, George Nicholls was matched against Dave Maier, a man who had already beaten Nicholls, and defeated Rosenbloom, Abie Bain and Mike Mandell, during the same period.*

05.08.31 Maxie Rosenbloom (USA) W PTS 15 Jimmy Slattery (USA), Brooklyn - NY.

18.03.32 George Nichols (USA) W PTS 10 Dave Maier (USA), Chicago - NBA.

31.05.32 Lou Scozza (USA) W PTS 10 George Nicholls (USA), Buffalo. *Incorrectly recorded as an NBA title fight in the Boxing News*

Annual, Scozza went on to challenge the New York champion, Maxie Rosenbloom, in a contest that many thought had unified the title. In truth, Scozza did not represent the NBA and Nicholls remained their champion. However, after losing three of his next four fights, the NBA stripped Nicholls of his belt and declared the title vacant in December 1932.

14.07.32 Maxie Rosenbloom (USA) W PTS 15 Lou Scozza (USA), Buffalo - NY

22.02.33 Maxie Rosenbloom (USA) W PTS 10 Al Stillman (USA), St Louis. *According to the 1934 Post Record Book, the fight was billed as a title bout, but, although both men scaled inside the weight limit, Rosenbloom was only recognised as the champion by New York at the time and the contest was outside their jurisdiction. However, had he lost, the NYSAC could well have declared the title vacant.*

01.03.33 Bob Goodwin (USA) W PTS 10 Joe Knight (USA), Palm Beach - NY

10.03.33 Maxie Rosenbloom (USA) W PTS 15 Ad Heuser (GER), New York City - NY

24.03.33 **Maxie Rosenbloom** (USA) W RSC 4 Bob Godwin (USA), New York City

03.11.33 **Maxie Rosenbloom** (USA) W PTS 15 Mickey Walker (USA), New York City

05.02.34 **Maxie Rosenbloom** (USA) DREW 15 Joe Knight (USA), Miami

16.11.34 **Bob Olin** (USA) W PTS 15 Maxie Rosenbloom (USA), New York City. *Bob Olin forfeited both IBU and Canadian recognition in August 1935 when ignoring the claims of their representatives.*

05.09.35 Al McCoy (C) W PTS 15 Joe Knight (USA), Montreal - CANADA. *Almost three months later, on 29 November 1935, Al McCoy was outpointed over ten rounds by Jock McAvoy in New York City and lost the opportunity to challenge the new champion, John Henry Lewis. Instead, it was the Englishman who was offered a shot at the title, with the French-Canadian eventually moving up to heavyweight.*

17.09.35 Hein Lazek (AU) W DIS 13 Merlo Preciso (ITA), Vienna - IBU

31.10.35 John Henry Lewis (USA) W PTS 15 Bob Olin (USA), St Louis - USA/GB

25.02.36 Hein Lazek (AU) W CO 6 Reinus de Boer (HOL), Vienna - IBU

13.03.36 John Henry Lewis (USA) W PTS 15 Jock McAvoy (GB), New York City - USA/GB

03.08.36 Hein Lazek (AU) W CO 9 Emil Olive (FR), Vienna - IBU

01.09.36 Gustav Roth (BEL) W PTS 15 Hein Lazek (AU), Vienna - IBU

29.10.36 Gustav Roth (BEL) W PTS 15 Adolph Witt (GER), Berlin - IBU

09.11.36 John Henry Lewis (USA) W PTS 15 Len Harvey (GB), The Arena, Wembley - USA/GB

12.01.37 Gustav Roth (BEL) DREW 15 Antonio Rodriguez (BR), Rio de Janeiro - IBU

24.03.37 Gustav Roth (BEL) W PTS 15 Merlo Preciso (ITA), Brussels - IBU

01.05.37 Gustav Roth (BEL) W PTS 15 John Andersson (SWE), Antwerp - IBU

03.06.37 John Henry Lewis (USA) W RSC 8 Bob Olin (USA), St Louis - USA/GB

01.12.37 Gustav Roth (BEL) DREW 15 Karel Sys (BEL), Brussels - IBU

21.01.38 Gustav Roth (BEL) W PTS 15 Joseph Besselmann (GER), Berlin - IBU

25.03.38 Ad Heuser (GER) W CO 7 Gustav Roth (BEL), Berlin - IBU. *During an international boxing convention held in Rome in May 1938, which was attended by many leading authorities within the sport (not including the New York State Athletic Commission who couldn't agree to designate any part of its function to a foreign body as it was ruled by State legislative law), the IBU agreed to refuse to recognise all individually made world champions, including their own Ad Heuser, in an effort to stand by one universally acknowledged champion, who, in turn, would have to concede to regular defences decided by the new Federation.*

25.04.38 John Henry Lewis (USA) W CO 4 Emilio Martinez (USA), Minneapolis - USA/GB. *On 27 July 1938, John Henry Lewis forfeited NY recognition when refusing to fight in the "Empire City".*

28.10.38 John Henry Lewis (USA) W PTS 15 Al Gainer (USA), New Haven - NBA/GB. *John Henry Lewis was forced to retire on 19 June 1939, due to failing eyesight and, with the NBA already supporting the claims of Billy Conn, Britain decided to recognise a match between their own Len Harvey and Jock McAvoy as being for their version of the title.*

29.11.38 Tiger Jack Fox (USA) W PTS 15 Al Gainer (USA), New York City. *Recorded by the Boxing News Annual as being for the NYSAC version of the vacant title, in fact, it was merely a semi-final leg, with the winner going forward to meet Melio Bettina, who drew a bye, in the final round.*

03.02.39 Melio Bettina (USA) W RSC 9 Tiger Jack Fox (USA), New York City - NY

10.07.39 Len Harvey (GB) W PTS 15 Jock McAvoy (GB), White City, London - GB

13.07.39 Billy Conn (USA) W PTS 15 Melio Bettina (USA), New York City - NY/NBA

25.09.39 Billy Conn (USA) W PTS 15 Melio Bettina (USA), Pittsburgh - NY/NBA

17.11.39 Billy Conn (USA) W PTS 15 Gus Lesnevich (USA), New York City - NY/NBA

05.06.40 Billy Conn (USA) W PTS 15 Gus Lesnevich (USA), Detroit - NY/NBA. *In December 1940, with Conn concentrating on the heavyweight division, the NBA withdrew recognition from him in favour of a match between Anton Christoforidis and Melio Bettina for their version of the vacant title.*

13.01.41 Anton Christoforidis (GRE) W PTS 15 Melio Bettina (USA), Cleveland - NBA. *Following Christoforidis' win and the news in March 1941 that NY had stripped Conn and were supporting the claims of Gus Lesnevich, the pair were matched for the American version of the title.*

22.05.41 Gus Lesnevich (USA) W PTS 15 Anton Christoforidis (GRE), New York City - NY/NBA

26.08.41 Gus Lesnevich (USA) W PTS 15 Tami Mauriello (USA), New York City - NY/NBA

14.11.41 Gus Lesnevich (USA) W PTS 15 Tami Mauriello (USA), New York City - NY/NBA. *With Gus Lesnevich inactive between March 1942 and January 1946, due to military service, Ohio initiated a light-heavyweight "duration" title. It was won by Jimmy Bivins, who outscored Anton Christoforidis over 15 rounds in Cleveland on 26 February 1943, but not before Ezzard Charles and Joey Maxim had been eliminated in the earlier stages. His one and only defence came when he knocked out Lloyd Marshall inside 13 rounds in Cleveland on 8 June 1943, but, although he remained unbeaten during the period, he was unable to get a crack at Lesnevich, following the latter's return to the ring.*

20.06.42 Freddie Mills (GB) W CO 2 Len Harvey (GB), White Hart Lane, London - GB

14.05.46 Gus Lesnevich (USA) W RSC 10 Freddie Mills (GB), Harringay Arena, London

28.02.47 Gus Lesnevich (USA) W RSC 10 Billy Fox (USA), New York City

05.03.48 Gus Lesnevich (USA) W CO 1 Billy Fox (USA), New York City

26.07.48 Freddie Mills (GB) W PTS 15 Gus Lesnevich (USA), White City, London

24.01.50 Joey Maxim (USA) W CO 10 Freddie Mills (GB), Earls Court, London

22.08.51 Joey Maxim (USA) W PTS 15 Bob Murphy (USA), New York City

25.06.52 Joey Maxim (USA) W RTD 13 Sugar Ray Robinson (USA), New York City. *Maxim was suspended by the NYSAC in September 1952 for his failure to honour a contract made with the London promoter, Jack Solomons, which called for him to meet the winner of Randy Turpin v Don Cockell. Just days prior to Maxim v Moore, New York lifted the suspension when Turpin, who had stopped Cockell inside 11 rounds on 10 June 1952 (London), announced that he had relinquished his British light-heavyweight crown in order to concentrate on regaining the world middleweight title.*

17.12.52 Archie Moore (USA) W PTS 15 Joey Maxim (USA), St Louis

24.06.53 Archie Moore (USA) W PTS 15 Joey Maxim (USA), Ogden

27.01.54 Archie Moore (USA) W PTS 15 Joey Maxim (USA), Miami

11.08.54 Archie Moore (USA) W RSC 14 Harold Johnson (USA), New York City

22.06.55 Archie Moore (USA) W CO 3 Carl Bobo Olson (USA), New York City

05.06.56 Archie Moore (USA) W RSC 10 Yolande Pompey (TR), Harringay Arena, London

20.09.57 Archie Moore (USA) W RSC 7 Tony Anthony (USA), Los Angeles

10.12.58 Archie Moore (USA) W CO 11 Yvon Durelle (C), Montreal

12.08.59 Archie Moore (USA) W CO 3 Yvon Durelle (C), Montreal. *When Archie Moore forfeited NBA recognition in October 1960, the Association had initially planned an elimination series involving Erich Schoeppner v Chic Calderwood and Harold Johnson v Willie Pastrano. However, with Schoeppner more intent on a match with Moore, Calderwood pulling out through injury and then Pastrano being outpointed over ten rounds by Jesse Bowdry on 27 December (Miami Beach), a straight NBA title bout between Johnson and Bowdry was the next best option.*

07.02.61 Harold Johnson (USA) W RSC 9 Jesse Bowdry (USA), Miami - NBA

24.04.61 Harold Johnson (USA) W RSC 2 Von Clay (USA), Philadelphia - NBA

10.06.61 Archie Moore (USA) W PTS 15 Giulio Rinaldi (ITA), New York City - NY/EBU. *Archie Moore forfeited NY/EBU recognition in February 1962 for failing to defend against either Harold Johnson or Doug Jones.*

29.08.61 Harold Johnson (USA) W PTS 15 Eddie Cotton (USA), Seattle - NBA

12.05.62 **Harold Johnson** (USA) W PTS 15 Doug Jones (USA), Philadelphia

23.06.62 **Harold Johnson** (USA) W PTS 15 Gustav Scholz (GER), Berlin

01.06.63 **Willie Pastrano** (USA) W PTS 15 Harold Johnson (USA), Las Vegas. *Following several good wins, especially one over Sixto Rodriguez, Henry Hank was lined up to challenge Harold Johnson for the world title in June 1963. Unfortunately, the Michigan man was injured just prior to the contest and Willie Pastrano stepped in to relieve Johnson of his crown. In October 1963, when a Pastrano v Hank (now fully fit) match was not forthcoming, the Michigan Boxing Federation decided to hold their own version of the championship and brought in a leading contender, Eddie Cotton, to face the local man.*

29.10.63 Eddie Cotton (USA) W PTS 15 Henry Hank (USA), Flint - MICHIGAN. *Eddie Cotton forfeited Michigan recognition after a ten rounds defeat at the hands of Johnny Persol in New York City on 21 February 1964.*

10.04.64 **Willie Pastrano** (USA) W RSC 5 Greg Peralta (ARG), New Orleans

30.11.64 **Willie Pastrano** (USA) W RSC 11 Terry Downes (GB), Belle Vue, Manchester

30.03.65 **Jose Torres** (PR) W RSC 9 Willie Pastrano (USA), New York City

21.05.66 **Jose Torres** (PR) W PTS 15 Wayne Thornton (USA), New York City

15.08.66 **Jose Torres** (PR) W PTS 15 Eddie Cotton (USA), Las Vegas

15.10.66 **Jose Torres** (PR) W CO 2 Chic Calderwood (GB), San Juan

16.12.66 **Dick Tiger** (N) W PTS 15 Jose Torres (PR), New York City

16.05.67 **Dick Tiger** (N) W PTS 15 Jose Torres (PR), New York City

17.11.67 **Dick Tiger** (N) W RSC 12 Roger Rouse (USA), Las Vegas

24.05.68 **Bob Foster** (USA) W CO 4 Dick Tiger (N), New York City

23.01.69 **Bob Foster** (USA) W RSC 1 Frankie de Paula (USA), New York City

24.05.69 **Bob Foster** (USA) W RSC 4 Andy Kendall (USA), Springfield

04.04.70 **Bob Foster** (USA) W RSC 3 Roger Rouse (USA), Missoula

27.06.70 **Bob Foster** (USA) W CO 10 Mark Tessman (USA), Baltimore. *Bob Foster forfeited WBA recognition in December 1970 for consistently failing to defend his title against top-rated contenders. Those were the words of the WBA, who, shortly after, announced that a match had been arranged between the two leading challengers, Jimmy Dupree and Vicente Rondon, for the Association's version of the title.*

27.02.71 Vicente Rondon (VEN) W RSC 6 Jimmy Dupree (USA), Caracas - WBA

02.03.71 Bob Foster (USA) W CO 4 Hal Carroll (USA), Scranton - WBC

24.04.71 Bob Foster (USA) W PTS 15 Ray Anderson (USA), Tampa - WBC

05.06.71 Vicente Rondon (VEN) W CO 1 Piero del Papa (ITA), Caracas - WBA

21.08.71 Vicente Rondon (VEN) W PTS 15 Eddie Jones (USA), Caracas - WBA

26.10.71 Vicente Rondon (VEN) W RSC 12 Gomeo Brennan (BAH), Miami - WBA

29.10.71 Bob Foster (USA) W RSC 8 Tommy Hicks (USA), Scranton - WBC

15.12.71 Vicente Rondon (VEN) W CO 8 Doyle Baird (USA), Cleveland - WBA

16.12.71 Bob Foster (USA) W RSC 3 Brian Kelly (USA), Oklahoma City - WBC

07.04.72 **Bob Foster** (USA) W CO 2 Vicente Rondon (VEN), Miami

27.06.72 **Bob Foster** (USA) W CO 4 Mike Quarry (USA), Las Vegas

Bob Foster, the world light-heavyweight champion (1968-1974), is seen here snuffing out the brave challenge of England's Chris Finnegan

26.09.72 **Bob Foster** (USA) W CO 14 Chris Finnegan (GB), The Arena, Wembley

21.08.73 **Bob Foster** (USA) W PTS 15 Pierre Fourie (SA), Alburquerque

01.12.73 **Bob Foster** (USA) W PTS 15 Pierre Fourie (SA), Johannesburg

17.06.74 **Bob Foster** (USA) DREW 15 Jorge Ahumada (ARG), Alburquerque. *Bob Foster relinquished the title on announcing his retirement in September 1974 and, while the WBC supported the claims of John Conteh (beat Chris Finnegan on points over 15 rounds on 21 May 1974 at Wembley) and Jorge Ahumada (beat Angel Oquendo over 12 rounds on 29 July 1974 in New York City), who had both come through eliminating bouts, the WBA backed Victor Galindez and Len Hutchins in a straight fight for their version of the title.*

01.10.74 John Conteh (GB) W PTS 15 Jorge Ahumada (ARG), The Arena, Wembley - WBC

07.12.74 Victor Galindez (ARG) W RTD 12 Len Hutchins (USA), Buenos Aires - WBA

11.03.75 John Conteh (GB) W RSC 5 Lonnie Bennett (USA), The Arena, Wembley - WBC

07.04.75 Victor Galindez (ARG) W PTS 15 Pierre Fourie (SA), Johannesburg - WBA

30.06.75 Victor Galindez (ARG) W PTS 15 Jorge Ahumada (ARG), New York City - WBA

13.09.75 Victor Galindez (ARG) W PTS 15 Pierre Fourie (SA), Johannesburg - WBA

28.03.76 Victor Galindez (ARG) W RTD 3 Harald Skog (NOR), Oslo - WBA

22.05.76 Victor Galindez (ARG) W CO 15 Richie Kates (USA), Johannesburg - WBA

05.10.76 Victor Galindez (ARG) W PTS 15 Kosie Smith (SA), Johannesburg - WBA

09.10.76 John Conteh (GB) W PTS 15 Yaqui Lopez (USA), Copenhagen - WBC

05.03.77 John Conteh (GB) W RSC 3 Len Hutchins (USA), The Stadium, Liverpool - WBC. *John Conteh forfeited WBC version of title in May 1977 when he withdrew from a scheduled defence against Miguel Cuello.*

21.05.77 Miguel Cuello (ARG) W CO 9 Jesse Burnett (USA), Monaco - WBC

18.06.77 Victor Galindez (ARG) W PTS 15 Richie Kates (USA), Rome - WBA

17.09.77 Victor Galindez (ARG) W PTS 15 Yaqui Lopez (USA), Rome - WBA

20.11.77 Victor Galindez (ARG) W PTS 15 Mustapha Muhammad (USA), Turin - WBA

07.01.78 Mate Parlov (YUG) W CO 9 Miguel Cuello (ARG), Milan - WBC

06.05.78 Victor Galindez (ARG) W PTS 15 Yaqui Lopez (USA), Reggio - WBA

17.06.78 Mate Parlov (YUG) W PTS 15 John Conteh (GB), Belgrade - WBC

15.09.78 Mike Rossman (USA) W RSC 13 Victor Galindez (ARG), New Orleans - WBA

02.12.78 Marvin Johnson (USA) W RSC 10 Mate Parlov (YUG), Marsala - WBC

05.12.78 Mike Rossman (USA) W RSC 6 Aldo Traversaro (ITA), Philadelphia - WBA

14.04.79 Victor Galindez (ARG) W RTD 9 Mike Rossman (USA), New Orleans - WBA

22.04.79 Matt Saad Muhammad (USA) W RSC 8 Marvin Johnson (USA), Indianapolis - WBC. *Prior to winning the title, Matthew Saad Muhammad was known as Matt Franklin, the name he was christened with.*

18.08.79 Matt Saad Muhammad (USA) W PTS 15 John Conteh (GB), Atlantic City - WBC

30.11.79 Marvin Johnson (USA) W RSC 11 Victor Galindez (ARG), New Orleans - WBA

29.03.80 Matt Saad Muhammad (USA) W RSC 4 John Conteh (GB), Atlantic City - WBC

31.03.80 Mustapha Muhammad (USA) W RSC 11 Marvin Johnson (USA), Knoxville - WBA. *Following the earlier example of Matt Franklin, the new champion changed his name from Eddie Gregory to that of Mustapha Muhammad.*

11.05.80 Matt Saad Muhammad (USA) W RSC 5 Louis Pergaud (FR), Halifax - WBC

13.07.80 Matt Saad Muhammad (USA) W RSC 14 Yaqui Lopez (USA), McAfee - WBC

20.07.80 Mustapha Muhammad (USA) W RSC 10 Jerry Martin (USA), McAfee - WBA

28.11.80 Matt Saad Muhammad (USA) W CO 4 Lotte Mwale (U), San Diego - WBC

29.11.80 Mustapha Muhammad (USA) W RSC 3 Rudi Koopmans (HOL), Los Angeles- WBA

28.02.81 Matt Saad Muhammad (USA) W RSC 11 Vonzell Johnson (USA), Atlantic City - WBC

25.04.81 Matt Saad Muhammad (USA) W CO 9 Murray Sutherland (C), Atlantic City - WBC

18.07.81 Michael Spinks (USA) W PTS 15 Mustapha Muhammad (USA), Las Vegas - WBA

26.09.81 Matt Saad Muhammad (USA) W RSC 11 Jerry Martin (USA), Atlantic City - WBC

07.11.81 Michael Spinks (USA) W RSC 7 Vonzell Johnson (USA), Atlantic City - WBA

19.12.81 Dwight Muhammad Qawi (USA) W RSC 10 Matt Saad Muhammad (USA), Atlantic City - WBC

13.02.82 Michael Spinks (USA) W RSC 6 Mustapha Wasajja (U), Atlantic City - WBA

21.03.82 Dwight Muhammad Qawi (USA) W RSC 6 Jerry Martin (USA), Las Vegas - WBC

11.04.82 Michael Spinks (USA) W RSC 8 Murray Sutherland (C), Atlantic City - WBA

12.06.82 Michael Spinks (USA) W RSC 8 Jerry Celestine (USA), Atlantic City - WBA

07.08.82 Dwight Muhammad Qawi (USA) W RSC 6 Matt Saad Muhammad (USA), Philadelphia - WBC. *Before this fight, Dwight Muhammad Qawi boxed as Dwight Braxton, his given birthname.*

18.09.82 Michael Spinks (USA) W RSC 9 Johnny Davis (USA), Atlantic City - WBA

20.11.82 Dwight Muhammad Qawi (USA) W RSC 11 Eddie Davis (USA), Atlantic City - WBC

18.03.83 **Michael Spinks** (USA) W PTS 15 Dwight Muhammad Qawi (USA), Atlantic City

25.11.83 **Michael Spinks** (USA) W RSC 10 Oscar Rivadeneyra (PERU), Vancouver

25.02.84 **Michael Spinks** (USA) W PTS 12 Eddie Davis (USA), Atlantic City

23.02.85 **Michael Spinks** (USA) W RSC 3 David Sears (USA), Atlantic City

06.06.85 **Michael Spinks** (USA) W RSC 8 Jim MacDonald (USA), Las Vegas. *Michael Spinks relinquished title on winning the IBF heavyweight crown in September 1985.*

10.12.85 J. B. Williamson (USA) W PTS 12 Prince Muhammad (GH), Los Angeles - WBC

21.12.85 Slobodan Kacar (YUG) W PTS 15 Mustafa Muhammad (USA), Pesaro - IBF

09.02.86 Marvin Johnson (USA) W RSC 7 Leslie Stewart (TR), Indianapolis - WBA

30.04.86 Dennis Andries (GB) W PTS 12 J. B. Williamson (USA), Picketts Lock Leisure Centre, London - WBC

06.09.86 Bobby Czyz (USA) W RSC 5 Slobodan Kacar (YUG), Las Vegas - IBF

10.09.86 Dennis Andries (GB) W RSC 9 Tony Sibson (GB), Alexandra Pavilion, London - WBC

20.09.86 Marvin Johnson (USA) W RSC 13 Jean-Marie Emebe (FR), Indianapolis - WBA

26.12.86 Bobby Czyz (USA) W RSC 1 David Sears (USA), West Orange - IBF

21.02.87 Bobby Czyz (USA) W CO 2 Willie Edwards (USA), Atlantic City - IBF

07.03.87 Thomas Hearns (USA) W RSC 10 Dennis Andries (GB), Detroit - WBC. *Thomas Hearns relinquished WBC version of title in August 1987 to challenge for the vacant WBC middleweight crown.*

03.05.87 Bobby Czyz (USA) W RSC 6 Jim MacDonald (USA), Atlantic City - IBF

23.05.87 Leslie Stewart (TR) W RTD 8 Marvin Johnson (USA), Port of Spain - WBA

05.09.87 Virgil Hill (USA) W RSC 4 Leslie Stewart (TR), Atlantic City - WBA

29.10.87 Charles Williams (USA) W RTD 9 Bobby Czyz (USA), Las Vegas - IBF

21.11.87 Virgil Hill (USA) W PTS 12 Rufino Angulo (FR), Paris - WBA

27.11.87 Don Lalonde (C) W RSC 2 Eddie Davis (USA), Port of Spain - WBC

03.04.88 Virgil Hill (USA) W RSC 11 Jean-Marie Emebe (FR), Bismark - WBA

29.05.88 Don Lalonde (C) W RSC 5 Leslie Stewart (TR), Port of Spain - WBC

06.06.88 Virgil Hill (USA) W PTS 12 Ramzi Hassan (USA), Las Vegas - WBA

10.06.88 Charles Williams (USA) W RTD 11 Richard Caramanolis (FR), Annecy - IBF

21.10.88 Charles Williams (USA) W RSC 3 Rufino Angulo (FR), Villenevue d'Ornon - IBF

07.11.88 Sugar Ray Leonard (USA) W RSC 9 Don Lalonde (C), Las Vegas - WBC. *Also billed for the vacant WBC super-middleweight title, Lalonde, who entered the ring at 167 lbs (one pound inside the limit), should not have been forced to put his 175 lbs crown on the line at the same time. The situation went some way to righting itself when Leonard relinquished the championship following the fight, in order to concentrate on defending his lighter belt.*

11.11.88 Virgil Hill (USA) W RSC 10 Willie Featherstone (C), Bismark - WBA

03.12.88 Michael Moorer (USA) W RSC 5 Ramzi Hassan (USA), Cleveland - WBO

14.01.89 Michael Moorer (USA) W RSC 2 Victor Claudio (PR), Detroit - WBO

19.02.89 Michael Moorer (USA) W RSC 6 Frankie Swindell (USA), Monessen - WBO

21.02.89 Dennis Andries (GB) W RSC 5 Tony Willis (USA), Tucson - WBC

04.03.89 Virgil Hill (USA) W PTS 12 Bobby Czyz (USA), Bismark - WBA

22.04.89 Michael Moorer (USA) W RSC 1 Freddie Delgado (PR), Detroit - WBO

27.05.89 Virgil Hill (USA) W RSC 7 Joe Lasisi (N), Bismark - WBA

24.06.89 Jeff Harding (A) W RSC 12 Dennis Andries (GB), Atlantic City - WBC

25.06.89 Charles Williams (USA) W RSC 10 Bobby Czyz (USA), Atlantic City - IBF

25.06.89 Michael Moorer (USA) W RSC 8 Leslie Stewart (TR), Atlantic City - WBO

24.10.89 Jeff Harding (A) W RTD 2 Tom Collins (GB), Brisbane - WBC

24.10.89 Virgil Hill (USA) W RSC 1 James Kinchen (USA), Bismark - WBA

16.11.89 Michael Moorer (USA) W RSC 1 Jeff Thompson (USA), Atlantic City - WBO

22.12.89 Michael Moorer (USA) W RSC 6 Mike Sedillo (USA), Detroit - WBO

07.01.90 Charles Williams (USA) W RSC 8 Frankie Swindell (USA), Atlantic City - IBF

03.02.90 Michael Moorer (USA) W RSC 9 Marcellus Allen (USA), Atlantic City - WBO

25.02.90 Virgil Hill (USA) W PTS 12 David Vedder (USA), Bismark - WBA

18.03.90 Jeff Harding (A) W RSC 11 Nestor Giovannini (ARG), Atlantic City - WBC

28.04.90 Michael Moorer (USA) W CO 1 Mario Melo (ARG), Atlantic City - WBO

07.07.90 Virgil Hill (USA) W PTS 12 Tyrone Frazier (USA), Bismark - WBA

28.07.90 Dennis Andries (GB) W CO 7 Jeff Harding (A), Melbourne - WBC

10.10.90 Dennis Andries (GB) W RTD 4 Sergio Merani (ARG), Albert Hall, London - WBC

15.12.90 Michael Moorer (USA) W CO 8 Danny Lindstrom (C), Pittsburgh - WBO. *Michael Moorer relinquished WBO version of title in April 1991 to campaign as a heavyweight.*

06.01.91 Virgil Hill (USA) W PTS 12 Mike Peak (USA), Bismark - WBA

12.01.91 Charles Williams (USA) W PTS 12 Mwehu Beya (ITA), St Vincent - IBF

19.01.91 Dennis Andries (GB) W PTS 12 Guy Waters (A), Adelaide - WBC

20.04.91 Charles Williams (USA) W RSC 2 James Kinchen (USA), Atlantic City - IBF

09.05.91 Leonzer Barber (USA) W RTD 5 Tom Collins (GB), Town Hall, Leeds - WBO

03.06.91 Thomas Hearns (USA) W PTS 12 Virgil Hill (USA), Las Vegas - WBA

20.07.91 Charles Williams (USA) W CO 3 Vince Boulware (USA), San Remo - IBF

11.09.91 Jeff Harding (A) W PTS 12 Dennis Andries (GB), Hammersmith Odeon, London - WBC

19.10.91 Charles Williams (USA) W RSC 2 Freddie Delgado (PR), Williamsburg - IBF

07.01.92 Leonzer Barber (USA) W PTS 12 Anthony Hembrick (USA), Detroit - WBO

20.03.92 Iran Barkley (USA) W PTS 12 Thomas Hearns (USA), Las Vegas - WBA. *Iran Barkley relinquished WBA version of title in April 1992 to concentrate on defending his IBF super-middleweight crown.*

05.06.92 Jeff Harding (A) W RSC 8 Christophe Tiozzo (FR), Marseille - WBC

29.09.92 Virgil Hill (USA) W PTS 12 Frank Tate (USA), Bismark - WBA

03.12.92 Jeff Harding (A) W PTS 12 David Vedder (USA), St Jean de Luz - WBC. *Ruled out by a cut-eye a week before defending his WBC crown against Mike McCallum, Jeff Harding had to sit it out while the former stopped Randall Yonker in the fifth round on 4 March 1994 (Las Vegas) to win the "interim title".*

20.02.93 Virgil Hill (USA) W TD 11 Adolpho Washington (USA), Fargo - WBA

27.02.93 Leonzer Barber (USA) W PTS 12 Mike Sedillo (USA), Beijing - WBO

20.03.93 Henry Maske (GER) W PTS 12 Charles Williams (USA), Dusseldorf - IBF

03.04.93 Virgil Hill (USA) W PTS 12 Fabrice Tiozzo (FR), Levallois Perret - WBA

28.08.93 Virgil Hill (USA) W PTS 12 Sergio Merani (ARG), Bismark - WBA

18.09.93 Henry Maske (GER) W PTS 12 Anthony Hembrick (USA), Dusseldorf - IBF

29.09.93 Leonzer Barber (USA) W PTS 12 Andrea Magi (ITA), Pesaro - WBO

09.11.93 Virgil Hill (USA) W RSC 10 Saul Montana (USA), Bismark - WBA

11.12.93 Henry Maske (GER) W PTS 12 David Vedder (USA), Dusseldorf - IBF

17.12.93 Virgil Hill (USA) W PTS 12 Guy Waters (A), Minot - WBA

29.01.94 Leonzer Barber (USA) W RSC 9 Nicky Piper (GB), Ice Rink, Cardiff - WBO

26.03.94 Henry Maske (GER) W RSC 9 Ernesto Magdaleno (USA), Dortmund - IBF

04.06.94 Henry Maske (GER) W PTS 12 Andrea Magi (ITA), Dortmund - IBF

Cruiserweight (190 lbs)

A name that was once used to describe light-heavyweights, and emanating from the description of battleships of a lighter build rather than of maximum size, the division came into being in 1979 when the World Boxing Council introduced it in order to give more opportunity to men too light to take on full-blown heavies. Also known as the junior-heavyweight division, the WBC introduced it at 190 lbs. In order to find a champion, the WBC set up eliminators involving Marvin Camel v David Cabrera and Mate Parlov v Tony Mundine. And, after knocking Cabrera out in the third round on 30 August 1979 in McAllen, Camel went through to fight Parlov, who outscored Mundine over 12 rounds in Gorizia on 26 September 1979.

08.12.79 Marvin Camel (USA) DREW 15 Mate Parlov (YUG), Split - WBC

31.03.80 Marvin Camel (USA) W PTS 15 Mate Parlov (YUG), Las Vegas - WBC

25.11.80 Carlos de Leon (PR) W PTS 15 Marvin Camel (USA), New Orleans - WBC

13.02.82 Ossie Ocasio (PR) W PTS 15 Robbie Williams (SA), Johannesburg - WBA

24.02.82 Carlos de Leon (PR) W RSC 8 Marvin Camel (USA), Atlantic City - WBC

27.06.82 S. T. Gordon (USA) W RSC 2 Carlos de Leon (PR), Cleveland - WBC. *The winner, Gordon, who scaled 189 lbs, claimed he was unaware until shortly before the fight that the WBC had recently increased the weight class limit from 190 lbs to 195. Had he known, he said, he would have obviously come in heavier.*

15.12.82 Ossie Ocasio (PR) W PTS 15 Young Joe Louis (USA), Chicago - WBA

16.02.83 S. T. Gordon (USA) W RSC 8 Jesse Burnett (USA), East Rutherford - WBC

20.05.83 Ossie Ocasio (PR) W PTS 15 Randy Stephens (USA), Las Vegas - WBA

21.05.83 Marvin Camel (USA) W RSC 9 Rick Sekorski (USA), Billings - IBF

17.07.83 Carlos de Leon (PR) W PTS 12 S. T. Gordon (USA), Las Vegas - WBC

21.09.83 Carlos de Leon (PR) W RSC 4 Yaqui Lopez (USA), San Jose - WBC

13.12.83 Marvin Camel (USA) W RSC 5 Rod MacDonald (C), Halifax - IBF

09.03.84 Carlos de Leon (PR) W PTS 12 Anthony Davis (USA), Las Vegas - WBC

05.05.84 Ossie Ocasio (PR) W RSC 15 John Odhiambo (U), San Juan - WBA

02.06.84 Carlos de Leon (PR) W PTS 12 Bash Ali (N), Oakland - WBC

06.10.84 Lee Roy Murphy (USA) W RSC 14 Marvin Camel (USA), Billings - IBF

01.12.84 Piet Crous (SA) W PTS 15 Ossie Ocasio (PR), Sun City - WBA

20.12.84 Lee Roy Murphy (USA) W RSC 12 Young Joe Louis (USA), Chicago - IBF

30.03.85 Piet Crous (SA) W RSC 3 Randy Stephens (USA), Sun City - WBA

06.06.85 Alfonso Ratliff (USA) W PTS 12 Carlos de Leon (PR), Las Vegas - WBC

27.07.85 Dwight Muhammad Qawi (USA) W CO 11 Piet Crous (SA), Sun City - WBA

21.09.85 Bernard Benton (USA) W PTS 12 Alfonso Ratliff (USA), Las Vegas - WBC

19.10.85 Lee Roy Murphy (USA) W CO 12 Chisanda Mutti (ZA), Monaco - IBF

22.03.86 Carlos de Leon (PR) W PTS 12 Bernard Benton (USA), Las Vegas - WBC

23.03.86 Dwight Muhammad Qawi (USA) W RSC 6 Leon Spinks (USA), Reno - WBA

19.04.86 Lee Roy Murphy (USA) W CO 9 Dorcey Gaymon (USA), San Remo - IBF

12.07.86 Evander Holyfield (USA) W PTS 15 Dwight Muhammad Qawi (USA), Atlanta - WBA

10.08.86 Carlos de Leon (PR) W RSC 8 Michael Greer (USA), Giardini Naxos - WBC

25.10.86 Rickey Parkey (USA) W RSC 10 Lee Roy Murphy (USA), Marsala - IBF

14.02.87 Evander Holyfield (USA) W RSC 7 Henry Tillman (USA), Reno - WBA

21.02.87 Carlos de Leon (PR) W RTD 4 Angelo Rottoli (ITA), Bergamo - WBC

28.03.87 Rickey Parkey (USA) W RSC 12 Chisanda Mutti (ZA), Camaiore - IBF

15.05.87 Evander Holyfield (USA) W RSC 3 Rickey Parkey (USA), Las Vegas - IBF/WBA

15.08.87 Evander Holyfield (USA) W RSC 11 Ossie Ocasio (PR), St Tropez - IBF/WBA

05.12.87 Evander Holyfield (USA) W CO 4 Dwight Muhammad Qawi (USA), Atlantic City - IBF/WBA

22.01.88 Carlos de Leon (PR) W PTS 12 Jose Mario Flores (UR), Atlantic City - WBC

09.04.88 **Evander Holyfield** (USA) W RSC 8 Carlos de Leon (PR), Las Vegas. *Prior to the fight, the WBC stipulated 195 lbs as being the division's limit, while the IBF and WBA agreed on 190 lbs. However, with both men inside 190 lbs all three titles were at stake and, from then on, the poundage would be standardised. There was such a paucity of talent around that when Evander Holyfield, the only champion to unify the weight division, relinquished his title in November 1988 in order to campaign as a heavyweight, the three major organisations were hard pressed to find a championship bout of any consequence, let alone be in a position to organise elimination tournaments.*

25.03.89 Taoufik Belbouli (FR) W RSC 8 Michael Greer (USA), Casablanca - WBA. *Taoufik Belbouli relinquished WBA version of title in August 1989 following a long-term knee injury.*

17.05.89 Carlos de Leon (PR) W RSC 9 Sam Reeson (GB), London Arena, London - WBC

03.06.89 Glenn McCrory (GB) W PTS 12 Patrick Lumumba (K), Louisa Centre, Stanley - IBF

21.10.89 Glenn McCrory (GB) W CO 11 Siza Makhatini (SA), Eston Leisure Centre, Middlesbrough - IBF

28.11.89 Robert Daniels (USA) W PTS 12 Dwight Muhammad Qawi (USA), Noget Sur Marne - WBA

03.12.89 Boone Pultz (USA) W PTS 12 Magne Havnaa (NOR), Copenhagen - WBO

27.01.90 Carlos de Leon (PR) DREW 12 Johnny Nelson (GB), City Hall, Sheffield - WBC

22.03.90 Jeff Lampkin (USA) W CO 3 Glenn McCrory (GB), Leisure Centre, Gateshead - IBF

17.05.90 Magne Havnaa (NOR) W RSC 5 Boone Pultz (USA), Aars - WBO

19.07.90 Robert Daniels (USA) W PTS 12 Craig Bodzianowski (USA), Seattle - WBA

27.07.90 Masimilliano Duran (ITA) W DIS 11 Carlos de Leon (PR), Capo d'Orlando - WBC

29.07.90 Jeff Lampkin (USA) W CO 8 Siza Makhatini (SA), St Petersburg - IBF. *Jeff Lampkin relinquished IBF version of title in July 1991 on signing with promoter, Don King.*

22.11.90 Robert Daniels (USA) DREW 12 Taoufik Belbouli (FR), Madrid - WBA

08.12.90 Masimilliano Duran (ITA) W DIS 12 Anaclet Wamba (FR), Ferrara - WBC

08.12.90 Magne Havnaa (NOR) W PTS 12 Daniel Netto (ARG), Aalborg - WBO

15.02.91 Magne Havnaa (NOR) W PTS 12 Tyrone Booze (USA), Randers - WBO. *Magne Havnaa relinquished WBO version of title in February 1992 due to increasing weight problems.*

09.03.91 Bobby Czyz (USA) W PTS 12 Robert Daniels (USA), Atlantic City - WBA

20.07.91 Anaclet Wamba (FR) W RSC 11 Masimilliano Duran (ITA), Palermo - WBC

09.08.91 Bobby Czyz (USA) W PTS 12 Bash Ali (N), Atlantic City - WBA

06.09.91 James Warring (USA) W CO 1 James Pritchard (USA), Salemi - IBF

15.11.91 James Warring (USA) W CO 5 Donnell Wingfield (USA), Roanoke - IBF

13.12.91 Anaclet Wamba (FR) W RSC 11 Masimilliano Duran (ITA), Paris - WBC

08.05.92 Bobby Czyz (USA) W PTS 12 Don Lalonde (C), Las Vegas - WBA. *Bobby Czyz forfeited WBA version of title in September 1993 due to inactivity.*

16.05.92 James Warring (USA) W PTS 12 Johnny Nelson (GB), Fredericksburg - IBF

13.06.92 Anaclet Wamba (FR) W RSC 5 Andrei Rudenko (CIS), Levallois Perret - WBC

25.07.92 Tyrone Booze (USA) W CO 7 Derek Angol (GB), G-Mex Centre, Manchester - WBO

30.07.92 Al Cole (USA) W PTS 12 James Warring (USA), Stanhope - IBF

02.10.92 Tyrone Booze (USA) W PTS 12 Ralf Rocchigiani (GER), Berlin - WBO

16.10.92 Anaclet Wamba (FR) W PTS 12 Andrew Maynard (USA), Paris - WBC

13.02.93 Marcus Bott (GER) W PTS 12 Tyrone Booze (GER), Hamburg - WBO

28.02.93 Al Cole (USA) W PTS 12 Uriah Grant (USA), Atlantic City - IBF

06.03.93 Anaclet Wamba (FR) W PTS 12 David Vedder (USA), Levallois Perret - WBC

26.06.93 Nester Giovannini (ARG) W PTS 12 Marcus Bott (GER), Hamburg - WBO

16.07.93 Al Cole (USA) W PTS 12 Glenn McCrory (GB), Moscow - IBF

16.10.93 Anaclet Wamba (FR) W RTD 7 Akim Tafer (FR), Levallois Perret - WBC

06.11.93 Orlin Norris (USA) W RSC 6 Marcelo Figueroa (ARG), Paris - WBA

17.11.93 Al Cole (USA) W RSC 5 Vince Boulware (USA), Atlantic City - IBF

20.11.93 Nestor Giovannini (ARG) W PTS 12 Marcus Bott (GER), Hamburg - WBO

04.03.94 Orlin Norris (USA) W PTS 12 Arthur Williams (USA), Las Vegas - WBA

Heavyweight (190 lbs+)

Known as the richest prize in sport, the history of the heavyweight division takes us right back to 1719 when James Figg was recognised as champion of the London Prize Ring. The first man to challenge the world's heavyweights with gloves was Tom Allen, who, a year earlier, in 1876, had lost his bare-knuckle title in America to fellow-Englishman, Joe Goss, after being disqualified in the 21st round. In a fight advertised as being the first at heavyweight under Queensberry Rules, Allen forced Tomkin Gilbert to retire inside seven rounds in London on 29 October 1877, and defended the title against Charley Davis (won on a fifth round disqualification at Cambridge Heath on 29 October 1878) and Jem Stewart (drew over 25 rounds in London on 22 April 1879), before retiring. Incidentally, although gloves were in use for Allen v Gilbert, three minute rounds were not applied and, on that basis, the fight could not have been contested under Queensberry Rules. The other two bouts conformed though. However, while these fights were billed for the championship and there was no denying that Allen had been a leading bare-knuckle man in his prime, he was fast approaching 40-years-of-age and the above opposition could hardly be considered top-class. Meanwhile, in America, it was John L. Sullivan who claimed to preside over the last bare-knuckle fighters of the day, having won the American title when knocking out Paddy Ryan in the ninth round at Mississippi City on 7 February 1882. Sullivan went on to defend that title when drawing against Charlie Mitchell over 39 rounds (Chantilly, France on 10 March 1888) and stopping Jake Kilrain in the 75th session (Richburg, Mississippi, on 8 July 1889) of a fight that pulled the curtains down on the bare-fist era once and for all. While Sullivan might have been seen as the bare-knuckle champion of the world, and there were many who disputed that, especially on this side of the Atlantic, he should never be given credence as the first champion with gloves, despite beating Dominic McCaffrey on points over six rounds (Cincinatti on 29 August 1885) for what was "loosely" termed the vacant Queensberry Rules' world title. That privilege should be accorded to Paddy Slavin, the holder of the Australian Queensberry Rules' title following his victory over Bill Farnan, who met the American, Joe McAuliffe, a man who had been matched to fight Sullivan with gloves, only for the latter to pull out.

27.09.90 Frank Slavin (A) W CO 2 Joe McAuliffe (USA), Ormonde Club, London. *In a match made with four ounce gloves, Slavin won the Police Gazette championship belt.*

16.06.91 Frank Slavin (A) W RSC 9 Jake Kilrain (USA), Hoboken. *Slavin defended the championship belt with the same conditions applying as above. He had initially gone to America for the purpose of challenging John L. Sullivan, but took on Kilrain after being told by the "great" man himself that he had retired and on learning that leading contenders, James J. Corbett and Peter Jackson, were already matched to fight.*

30.05.92 Peter Jackson (A) W CO 10 Frank Slavin (A), NSC, London. *Although only billed for the championships of England and Australia, by his victory Jackson took over Slavin's claim. Unfortunately for Jackson, who was born in the West Indies and recognised as the "black" champion after beating George Godfrey in 1888, Sullivan continually ignored his challenges, preferring to put up a "colour bar" instead. Eventually, when coming out of "hibernation", it was James J. Corbett who grasped the opportunity, while Jackson remained inactive for six years. Sadly, after returning to the ring for three more contests, he fell victim to the ravages of consumption on 13 July 1901.*

07.09.92 James J. Corbett (USA) W CO 21 John L. Sullivan (USA), New Orleans

25.01.94 James J. Corbett (USA) W CO 3 Charlie Mitchell (GB), Jacksonville. *After two failed attempts to stage a defence of his title against Bob Fitzsimmons, in Texas and Arkansas, Corbett decided to spend some time persuing an acting career. The pair had actually signed articles on 11 October 1894, with a side bet of $10,000 and the largest purse ever to be paid, winner take all. However, it would be two and a half years before they would eventually meet.*

11.11.95 Peter Maher (USA) W CO 1 Steve O'Donnell (A), Long Island. *After Maher had kayoed O'Donnell, one of the champion's regular sparring partners, Corbett jumped into the ring, announced his retirement, and awarded the title to the winner. Corbett admitted afterwards that he had been wrong in reacting in this peculiar fashion, but, angry with Fitzsimmons for allowing himself to be talked out of their prospective fight in Hot Springs and continually making derogatory remarks, he decided on teaching his rival a lesson.*

21.02.96 Bob Fitzsimmons (A) W CO 1 Peter Maher (USA), Couhuahua. *Most people thought a champion should lose his title in the ring and, with the public refusing to recognise Fitzsimmons, Corbett was talked out of retirement and contracts were duly signed in September 1896. Even when Fitzsimmons was disqualified in the eighth round against Tom Sharkey on 2 December in San Francisco, the victim of a diabolical decision inflicted by the famous Marshall, Wyatt Earp, everybody knew who was the better man and his forthcoming fight with Corbett continued to attract a great deal of interest.*

17.03.97 Bob Fitzsimmons (A) W CO 14 James J. Corbett (USA), Carson City. *After recovering from a long-count in the sixth round (Corbett and his manager claimed it was at least 13 seconds), Fitzsimmons kayoed the champion with his famous "solar plexus punch", a left-hook to that region of the body.*

09.06.99 James J. Jeffries (USA) W CO 11 Bob Fitzsimmons (A), Brooklyn. *Jeffries won the championship after just 12 contests, a record he shared with James J. Corbett, but history shows him to have drawn the "colour bar", an action which precluded great fighters, such as Jack Johnson, getting the chance to fight for the title during his tenure.*

03.11.99 James J. Jeffries (USA) W PTS 25 Tom Sharkey (USA), Brooklyn

06.04.00 James J. Jeffries (USA) W CO 1 Jack Finnegan (USA), Detroit

11.05.00 James J. Jeffries (USA) W CO 23 James J. Corbett (USA), Brooklyn

15.11.01 James J. Jeffries (USA) W RTD 5 Gus Ruhlin (USA), San Francisco

25.07.02 James J. Jeffries (USA) W CO 8 Bob Fitzsimmons (A), San Francisco

14.08.03 James J. Jeffries (USA) W CO 10 James J. Corbett (USA), San Francisco

26.08.04 James J. Jeffries (USA) W CO 2 Jack Munroe (USA), San Francisco. *Jeffries relinquished the title on announcing his retirement as undefeated champion in May 1905, having run out of worthy "white" opposition, and nominated the winner of a match between Marvin Hart and Jack Root as his successor. At the same time, Jack O'Brien, Bob Fitzsimmons, Al Kaufmann and Tommy Burns, all laid claim to the title.*

03.07.05 Marvin Hart (USA) W RSC 12 Jack Root (USA), Reno. *Although Jim Jeffries refereed and gave his belt to the winner, nobody was fooled and Hart was never really accepted as champion. In truth, this fight and the ones that followed should be seen as eliminators and it would not be until Burns defeated O'Brien that a champion was generally recognised.*

27.10.05 Jack O'Brien (USA) W CO 17 Al Kaufmann (USA), San Francisco. *Not recognised as a title bout within the record books and not indicated as being one in the Philadelphia Item (newspaper) fight report. However, it had as much right to title billing as Hart v Root in the scramble for the heavyweight crown.*

20.12.05 Jack O'Brien (USA) W CO 13 Bob Fitzsimmons (A), San Francisco. *As in O'Brien v Kaufmann, this bout does not find its way into the record books as a title fight, but it was regarded by "certain sporting men" as a championship scrap based on the theory that the title reverted to Fitzsimmons on Jeffries' retirement.*

23.02.06 Tommy Burns (C) W PTS 20 Marvin Hart (USA), Los Angeles. *Although billed as a championship fight, Burns, at 5'7", the shortest man to win the title, received scant recognition as the winner.*

02.10.06 Tommy Burns (C) W CO 15 Jim Flynn (USA), Los Angeles

28.11.06 Tommy Burns (C) W DREW 20 Jack O'Brien (USA), Los Angeles. *According to O'Brien, the fight was pre-arranged with Burns to be drawn. "The promoter, McCarey, had figured it out that, if we fought a spirited draw, he could bill the return match during fiesta week and make a small fortune by charging top prices".*

08.05.07 Tommy Burns (C) W PTS 20 Jack O'Brien (USA), Los Angeles. *Burns was generally recognised as champion from hereon. More to the point, O'Brien was just not up to the task, especially following revelations afterwards that he had offered Burns the winner's end of the purse to take a dive in the 11th round. Fearing that O'Brien would not accept the fight under any other circumstances and wishing to prove himself the better man, Burns agreed to his terms, but had no intention whatsoever of complying with them. According to Burns, he had made up his mind to "double cross" his opponent at the onset and immediately reported the matter to the promoter. At that stage, the decision was made to get both men into the ring before calling all bets off and leaving O'Brien to face the music.*

04.07.07 Tommy Burns (C) W CO 1 Bill Squires (A), Los Angeles

02.12.07 Tommy Burns (C) W CO 10 Gunner Moir (GB), NSC, London

10.02.08 Tommy Burns (C) W CO 4 Jack Palmer (GB), Wonderland, London

17.03.08 Tommy Burns (C) W CO 1 Jem Roche (GB), Dublin

18.04.08 Tommy Burns (C) W CO 5 Jewey Smith (GB), Paris

13.06.08 Tommy Burns (C) W CO 8 Bill Squires (A), Paris

24.08.08 Tommy Burns (C) W CO 13 Bill Squires (A), Sydney

02.09.08 Tommy Burns (C) W CO 6 Bill Lang (A), Melbourne

26.12.08 Jack Johnson (USA) W RSC 14 Tommy Burns (C), Sydney. *The black champion for close on six years, Johnson had been unable to force a match with Burns and followed the Canadian first to England and then to Australia. Finally cornered, Burns eventually accepted a $30,000 guarantee from promoter, Snowy Baker, a huge sum for those days, and Rushcutters Bay was set aside as the venue. With the action underway and the crowd at fever pitch, it was the police, not the referee, who stopped the contest to save a badly battered Burns. Johnson had steadfastly refused to land a kayo blow and beat up the champion badly. He had also taunted him incessantly.*

19.05.09 Jack Johnson (USA) ND-DREW 6 Jack O'Brien (USA), Philadelphia

24.05.09 Sam Langford (USA) W CO 4 Iron Hague (GB), NSC, London. *Following Johnson's win over Burns, the champion failed to honour an agreement to fight Langford at the NSC and the proprietors matched the latter with the new British champion, Iron Hague, for their version of the world title. However, outside of the Club, Langford was not recognised.*

30.06.09 Jack Johnson (USA) ND-W PTS 6 Tony Ross (USA), Pittsburgh

09.09.09 **Jack Johnson** (USA) ND-W PTS 10 Al Kaufmann (USA), San Francisco

16.10.09 **Jack Johnson** (USA) W CO 12 Stanley Ketchel (USA), Los Angeles. *An historic battle, with both men agreeing to a no-knockdown clause, saw Ketchel floor his rival in the 12th round, only for the angry Johnson to rise quickly and smash in a powerful blow that took Ketchel out of the fight immediately.*

04.07.10 **Jack Johnson** (USA) W RSC 15 James J. Jeffries (USA), Reno. *Jeffries was coaxed out of retirement on the grounds that he was expected to win for the white race and put Johnson firmly in his place. Unfortunately for his supporters, six years out of the ring and at the age of 35, the weary Jeffries was not up to the task.*

04.07.12 **Jack Johnson** (USA) W RSC 9 Jim Flynn (USA), Las Vegas. *Towards the end of 1912, Johnson fled to France after being charged with "transporting a white woman for immoral purposes". The American public were outraged and, while the Government looked for a way to bring Johnson back to America for trial and fearful of having another "black" champion, a "white" tournament was set up in the interim. At this stage, Johnson was recognised as champion only in Europe.*

01.01.13 Luther McCarty (USA) W CO 18 Al Palzer (USA), Los Angeles. *This was the final of the white tournament and followed wins by McCarty over Al Kaufmann and Jim Flynn and Palzer's third round kayo of the British champion, Bombardier Billy Wells. McCarty risked his newly won title in no-decision fights against Jim Flynn (Six rounds in Philadelphia on 16 April 1913) and Frank Moran (Ten rounds in New York City on 30 April 1913), but came through unscathed.*

24.05.13 Arthur Pelkey (C) W CO 1 Luther McCarty (USA), Calgary. *McCarty's first proper title defence as white champion ended in tragedy when, failing to regain consciousness, he was pronounced dead following a haemorrhaging of the brain.*

19.12.13 Jack Johnson (USA) DREW 10 Jim Johnson (USA), Paris - IBU. *Scheduled for 20 rounds, Jack Johnson claimed a broken arm at the end of the tenth, whereupon the referee hurriedly offered up a drawn decision. The fight had been the first where two black men had contested the heavyweight title and the result was strange to say the least.*

01.01.14 Gunboat Smith (USA) W CO 5 Arthur Pelkey (C), San Francisco. *White title fight.*

27.06.14 Jack Johnson (USA) W PTS 20 Frank Moran (USA), Paris. *By now, Johnson was only recognised in certain parts of Europe and was virtually into semi-retirement, living the "gay" life and squandering his fortune.*

16.07.14 Georges Carpentier (FR) W DIS 6 Gunboat Smith (USA), Olympia, London. *White title fight. Following the outbreak of war in Europe, Carpentier relinquished the white title in favour of military service, and, much to the chagrin of Smith, it was Jess Willard, a man he had already defeated and one with no outstanding record to speak of, who challenged Jack Johnson following the latter's move to South America.*

05.04.15 **Jess Willard** (USA) W CO 26 Jack Johnson (USA), Havana. *To his dying day, Johnson insisted that he had been forced to throw the fight and would often point to a picture of himself on the canvas shading his eyes from the sun as his proof. Although there has always been doubt, Johnson's story has never been proved one way or the other and remains one of boxing's great mysteries.*

25.03.16 **Jess Willard** (USA) ND-W PTS 10 Frank Moran (USA), New York City

04.07.19 **Jack Dempsey** (USA) W RTD 3 Jess Willard (USA), Toledo. *Willard was knocked down a record seven times in the opening round and Dempsey actually left the ring feeling he had already won, only to be called back to finish the job. Incidentally, although taking place in Ohio, a State more accustomed to contests of a no-decision variety, Dempsey v Willard was billed for 12 rounds of boxing with a points verdict to be given if neccessary. Tex Rickard took the fight to Toledo when he discovered that under Ohio law at the time, it was up to the local authority, not the Governor, whether boxing took place within the state.*

06.09.20 **Jack Dempsey** (USA) ND-W CO 3 Billy Miske (USA), Benton Harbor. *This affair left a nasty taste in the mouth when it was later learned that Miske was already dying from "Bright's Disease". Although he knew his rival had been ill, there was never any proof that Dempsey ever realised it was terminal and he was exonerated from any blame after the unfortunate Miske died on 1 January 1924.*

14.12.20 **Jack Dempsey** (USA) W CO 12 Bill Brennan (USA), New York City

02.07.21 **Jack Dempsey** (USA) ND-W CO 4 Georges Carpentier (FR), Jersey City. *Although a decision could not be rendered in New Jersey at that time, it was billed as a title fight and has achieved*

lasting fame as being the first million dollar gate. By defending his title under no-decision conditions, Dempsey forced the Frenchman to look for a kayo victory and thus negated his shrewd boxing skills.

04.07.23 **Jack Dempsey** (USA) W PTS 15 Tommy Gibbons (USA), Shelby. *Famous for the fact that the town went bankrupt in staging the fight, having guaranteed the champion $300,000.*

14.09.23 **Jack Dempsey** (USA) W CO 2 Angel Firpo (ARG), New York City. *Just three minutes and 57 seconds of fighting, saw Firpo floored seven times in the first and twice in the second, before a short right-uppercut ended his challenge. However, Dempsey himself was decked twice in the first round, including being knocked out of the ring, and, if the champion had not been illegally helped back in again, Firpo would surely have won. Later, with Dempsey serving a suspension applied by the New York State Athletic Commission for avoiding a fight with the outstanding negro of the day, Harry Wills, promoter, Tex Rickard, was forced to move the champion's first defence for over three years to Philadelphia. Several abortive attempts had been made to bring Wills and Dempsey together, but to no avail, and a claim that the Governor of New York had not desired a mixed match was strongly refuted.*

23.09.26 **Gene Tunney** (USA) W PTS 10 Jack Dempsey (USA), Philadelphia. *The outstanding challenger had well earned the opportunity to face Dempsey by beating Georges Carpentier on a 15th round stoppage on 24 July 1924, before knocking out Tommy Gibbons in the 12th round of a final eliminator on 5 June 1925, with both fights held in New York City. Fought in a rainstorm, Tunney adapted to the prevailing conditions far better than Dempsey, who was sorely ring-rusty, and the title changed hands.*

22.09.27 **Gene Tunney** (USA) W PTS 10 Jack Dempsey (USA), Chicago. *A fight made famous for what became known for "the long count" after it was estimated that Tunney was on the canvas for at least 14 seconds during the seventh round. However, with the referee refusing to take up the count until Dempsey went to a neutral corner, the champion managed to struggle to his feet in time to continue.*

26.07.28 **Gene Tunney** (USA) W RSC 11 Tom Heeney (NZ), New York City. *A few days after the fight, on 31 July, Tunney announced his retirement and an elimination tournament was ordered by both the NBA and NYSAC. The leading promoter, Tex Rickard, immediately got busy and went to Miami to set up a fight between Jack Sharkey and Young Stribling, but while there he was taken ill and died, following an operation to remove an appendix. Former champion, Jack Dempsey, was drafted in to help the promotion along and the fight eventually took place, with Sharkey winning on points over ten rounds on 27 February 1929. Meanwhile, the German, Max Schmeling, who had already beaten Joe Monte, Joe Sekyra and Pietro Corri since landing in the USA, knocked out Johnny Risko inside nine rounds on 1 February 1929 in New York City, before outscoring Paolino Uzcudun over 15 sessions on 27 June 1929 at the same venue. New York next recognised an American title fight between Sharkey and the former light-heavyweight champion, Tommy Loughran, won by the former, following a third round kayo on 26 September 1929, as a semi-final leg of their newly proposed tournament. Chairman, William Muldoon's idea was for Phil Scott, who had outpointed Vittorio Campolo over ten rounds three days earlier, also in New York City, to meet Schmeling in the other semi. However, those plans were well and truly scuppered due to a maze of contractual agreements and instead of Sharkey meeting the winner of Scott v Schmeling in New York City for the vacant title, he went back to Miami to kayo Scott in three rounds on 27 February 1930, while Schmeling spent a year on the sidelines awaiting his big moment.*

12.06.30 **Max Schmeling** (GER) W DIS 4 Jack Sharkey (USA), New York City. *On Schmeling becoming the first man to win the heavyweight title while sitting on the floor, the NYSAC only confirmed his position as champion on the proviso that he would have to give Sharkey a return, while the NBA went along with the verdict. However, early in 1931, Schmeling, inactive since winning the title, forfeited NBA recognition in favour of Young Stribling. The NBA reasoned that Stribling, who had been beaten on a debatable points decision over ten rounds by Sharkey in the elimination series, and had since defeated several of the leading contenders, was equally deserving a shot at the title.*

03.07.31 **Max Schmeling** (GER) W RSC 15 Young Stribling (USA), Cleveland. *Nineteen days later, on 22 July in Brooklyn, Jack Sharkey put his American title up for grabs against Mickey Walker, but could only manage a political draw over 15 rounds, with the latter seeming a clear winner. Although not a good result for Sharkey, the NYSAC still went ahead, and matched him to fight Primo Carnera for their version of the world title in Brooklyn on 12 October 1931. Incensed by that action, the promoters at*

Madison Square Garden, who had Schmeling under contract to defend the title, applied for and won an injunction against the NYSAC on the grounds that Sharkey v Carnera could not be billed as a world championship fight. The fight went ahead as planned, with Sharkey winning on points over 15 rounds and shortly afterwards contracts were signed for a match with Schmeling.

21.06.32 Jack Sharkey (USA) W PTS 15 Max Schmeling (GER), Long Island

29.06.33 Primo Carnera (ITA) W CO 6 Jack Sharkey (USA), Long Island. *In a fight made famous because of the "phantom punch", a right uppercut that nobody saw land cleanly, Sharkey became the first heavyweight champion to lose his title in his first defence.*

22.10.33 Primo Carnera (ITA) W PTS 15 Paolino Uzcudun (SP), Rome

01.03.34 Primo Carnera (ITA) W PTS 15 Tommy Loughran (USA), Miami

14.06.34 Max Baer (USA) W RSC 11 Primo Carnera (ITA), Long Island. *In May 1935, Baer, apparently not interested in the claims of the European champion, Pierre Charles, forfeited IBU recognition.*

13.06.35 James J. Braddock (USA) W PTS 15 Max Baer (USA), Long Island. *Dubbed the "Cinderella Man", Braddock, in winning the title, provided one of the greatest upsets in the history of the division. Prior to that, he had been in virtual retirement, before coming back to shock the up-and-coming Corn Griffin and future light-heavyweight champion, John Henry Lewis. However, the fight that secured his championship challenge was a 15 round points victory over Art Lasky in a final eliminator on 22 March 1935 in New York City.*

02.10.35 George Godfrey (USA) W PTS 15 Pierre Charles (BEL), Brussels - IBU. *Godfrey, who had initially gone to Europe on a wrestling tour, gained nothing by his win and both he and his manager were suspended indefinitely by the IBU for "irregular conduct". Back in America, and just one fight later, his career came to an end when he was stopped inside eight rounds by Hank Hankinson on 10 August 1937 (Los Angeles).*

22.06.37 Joe Louis (USA) W CO 8 James J. Braddock (USA), Chicago. *Earlier, the NYSAC had ordered Braddock to defend his title against Max Schmeling, following the German's 12 round kayo win over Louis on 19 June 1936. But, when Braddock, inactive for two years, decided to fight Louis for promoter, Mike Jacobs, instead, the next move appeared to be with the NYSAC. However, they fudged it. While Braddock was fined just $1,000, Schmeling was happy enough to go along with an offer from the new champion, for a return match within 12 months. In victory, Louis was the first coloured champion since Jack Johnson.*

30.08.37 Joe Louis (USA) W PTS 15 Tommy Farr (GB), New York City

23.02.38 Joe Louis (USA) W CO 3 Nathan Mann (USA), New York City. *This fight marked the start of what came to be known as the "bum of the month" battles as Louis took on a series of defences in double-quick time.*

01.04.38 Joe Louis (USA) W CO 5 Harry Thomas (USA), Chicago

22.06.38 Joe Louis (USA) W CO 1 Max Schmeling (GER), New York City. *In avenging the only defeat on his record, Louis destroyed Schmeling in just over two minutes of fighting. The fight was made famous by the fact that whether he liked it or not, Schmeling was used for Nazi propaganda purposes by Adolph Hitler.*

25.01.39 Joe Louis (USA) W RSC 1 John Henry Lewis (USA), New York City. *Forgetting Jack Johnson v Battling Jim Johnson in 1913, which was not generally recognised as a title fight, this meeting was the first occasion that the official championship was contested between negroes.*

17.04.39 Joe Louis (USA) W CO 1 Jack Roper (USA), Los Angeles

28.06.39 Joe Louis (USA) W RSC 4 Tony Galento (USA), New York City. *Galento, made famous by his "I'll moider der bum" comments and called "two ton Tony" in support of his roly-poly appearance, actually floored Louis before being banged out.*

20.09.39 Joe Louis (USA) W CO 11 Bob Pastor (USA), Detroit

09.02.40 Joe Louis (USA) W PTS 15 Arturo Godoy (CH), New York City

29.03.40 Joe Louis (USA) W CO 2 Johnny Paychek (USA), New York City

20.06.40 Joe Louis (USA) W RSC 8 Arturo Godoy (CH), New York City

16.12.40 Joe Louis (USA) W RTD 6 Al McCoy (C), Boston

31.01.41 Joe Louis (USA) W CO 5 Red Burman (USA), New York City

17.02.41 Joe Louis (USA) W CO 2 Gus Dorazio (USA), Philadelphia

21.03.41 Joe Louis (USA) W RSC 13 Abe Simon (USA), Detroit

08.04.41 Joe Louis (USA) W RSC 9 Tony Musto (USA), St Louis

23.05.41 Joe Louis (USA) W DIS 7 Buddy Baer (USA), Washington. *Baer became the first man to fight for the title that was once held by his brother.*

18.06.41 Joe Louis (USA) W CO 13 Billy Conn (USA), New York City. *Conn was just a few minutes away from victory when he took the fight to Louis and was kayoed for his temerity.*

29.09.41 Joe Louis (USA) W RSC 6 Lou Nova (USA), New York City

09.01.42 Joe Louis (USA) W CO 1 Buddy Baer (USA), New York City

27.03.42 Joe Louis (USA) W CO 6 Abe Simon (USA), New York City. *With Joe Louis joining the army in June 1942, first Maryland and then Ohio decided to set up a "duration" championship. First into the arena came Big Boy Brown, a cousin of Joe Louis, and also from Detroit, who outpointed Lou Brooks over 15 rounds on 23 November 1942 (Baltimore), and he cemented that result with a ten round points win in the same town against Pat Comiskey on 21 December 1942. Although that fight was probably not billed as such, the Ring correspondent claimed it as a successful defence. Meanwhile, in Columbus on 29 December 1942, Harry Bobo, an army corporal stationed at Camp Lee, outscored Buddy Walker over ten rounds to win the Ohio version of the title. Matters came to a head when the two men met in Baltimore on 25 January 1943, with Bobo winning on points over 15 rounds. The title changed hands after Lee Q. Murray stopped Bobo in the eighth round on 9 August 1943, but he ceased to be recognised after being outpointed over ten rounds by Jimmy Bivins on 1 December 1943 and 29 February 1944; the last three named fights taking place in Baltimore. Neither of the Murray v Bivins fights were billed as involving the "duration" title, but were considered as such. Earlier, on 12 March 1943, Bivins had outpointed Tami Mauriello over ten rounds in New York City for what was thought at the time to be the NYSAC version of the title, although that billing never quite materialised. At this stage of his career, Bivins, rated the world's number one in two weight divisions, was inactive for over a year on military service after joining up on 1 March 1944, and, with the "duration" title getting such bad publicity, the public quickly lost interest. Bivins eventually came back to run up an unbeaten sequence of 12, including a draw against Melio Bettina, but he eventually forfeited any title aspirations he may have had after losing three on the trot in 1946 to Jersey Joe Walcott, Lee Q. Murray and Ezzard Charles.*

19.06.46 Joe Louis (USA) W CO 8 Billy Conn (USA), New York City

18.09.46 Joe Louis (USA) W CO 1 Tami Mauriello (USA), New York City

05.12.47 Joe Louis (USA) W PTS 15 Jersey Joe Walcott (USA), New York City

25.06.48 Joe Louis (USA) W CO 11 Jersey Joe Walcott (USA), New York City. *When Joe Louis relinquished his title on announcing his retirement as undefeated champion, the NBA immediately matched the foremost two challengers, Jersey Joe Walcott and Ezzard Charles, who had outpointed Joey Maxim over 15 rounds of an eliminator on 28 February 1949 in Cincinnati, to meet for their version of the title. But, with Joe Louis embarking on a busy schedule of exhibitions, New York, who felt the championship should only be decided after a series of eliminators, kept their options open. Meanwhile, the British, angry that the European champion, Bruce Woodcock, did not figure in America's plans, matched him with Lee Savold for the BBBoC version of the title.*

22.06.49 Ezzard Charles (USA) W PTS 15 Jersey Joe Walcott (USA), Chicago - NBA

10.08.49 Ezzard Charles (USA) W RSC 7 Gus Lesnevich (USA), New York City - NBA. *Surprisingly, the fight took place in New York, a State where Charles was not even recognised as world champion. However, he was supported by the remaining 47 States of America under the banner of the NBA.*

14.10.49 Ezzard Charles (USA) W CO 8 Pat Valentino (USA), San Francisco - NBA

06.06.50 Lee Savold (USA) W RTD 4 Bruce Woodcock (GB), White City, London - GB

15.08.50 Ezzard Charles (USA) W RSC 14 Freddie Beshore (USA), Buffalo - NBA. *Still not supported by the NYSAC, Charles made another defence of the NBA title on their territory and afterwards signed to fight Joe Louis, who was returning from summary retirement, with the winner to be recognised by all the American authorities.*

27.09.50 Ezzard Charles (USA) W PTS 15 Joe Louis (USA), New York City - NY/NBA

05.12.50 Ezzard Charles (USA) W CO 11 Nick Barone (USA), Cincinnati - NY/NBA

12.01.51 Ezzard Charles (USA) W RSC 10 Lee Oma (USA), New York City - NY/NBA

07.03.51 Ezzard Charles (USA) W PTS 15 Jersey Joe Walcott (USA), Detroit - NY/NBA

30.05.51 Ezzard Charles (USA) W PTS 15 Joey Maxim (USA), Chicago - NY/NBA.

15.06.51 Joe Louis (USA) W CO 6 Lee Savold (USA), New York City. *Although the contest was fought in America, it was under championship conditions and, with the result, the BBBoC recognised Louis as champion. However, following an eighth round*

kayo at the hands of Rocky Marciano on 26 October 1951, Louis finally called it a day and retired.

18.07.51 Jersey Joe Walcott (USA) W CO 7 Ezzard Charles (USA), Pittsburgh - NY/NBA

05.06.52 **Jersey Joe Walcott** (USA) W PTS 15 Ezzard Charles (USA), Philadelphia

23.09.52 **Rocky Marciano** (USA) W CO 13 Jersey Joe Walcott (USA), Philadelphia

15.05.53 **Rocky Marciano** (USA) W CO 1 Jersey Joe Walcott (USA), Chicago

24.09.53 **Rocky Marciano** (USA) W RSC 11 Roland la Starza (USA), New York City

17.06.54 **Rocky Marciano** (USA) W PTS 15 Ezzard Charles (USA), New York City

17.09.54 **Rocky Marciano** (USA) W CO 8 Ezzard Charles (USA), New York City

16.05.55 **Rocky Marciano** (USA) W RSC 9 Don Cockell (GB), San Francisco

21.09.55 **Rocky Marciano** (USA) W CO 9 Archie Moore (USA), New York City. *Rocky Marciano retired as undefeated champion in April 1956 and, with Archie Moore recognised by both the NBA and EBU as the leading challenger, having already eliminated Nino Valdez on points over 15 rounds in Las Vegas on 2 May 1955, in order to find his opponent, the NYSAC set up another eliminator between Floyd Patterson and Tommy Jackson, won on points by the former over 12 rounds on 8 June 1956 in New York City.*

25.07.56 Archie Moore (USA) W RSC 7 James J. Parker (C), Toronto. *Although Moore was already matched against Floyd Patterson for the vacant title, the promoter insisted on billing the above as a championship contest. Fortunately, the Canadian Boxing Federation saw sense and refused to give their official backing.*

30.11.56 **Floyd Patterson** (USA) W CO 5 Archie Moore (USA), Chicago

29.07.57 **Floyd Patterson** (USA) W RSC 10 Tommy Jackson (USA), New York City

22.08.57 **Floyd Patterson** (USA) W CO 6 Pete Rademacher (USA), Seattle. *Rademacher, the 1956 Olympic champion, made history by becoming the first man to contest a world heavyweight title when making his professional debut.*

18.08.58 **Floyd Patterson** (USA) W RTD 12 Roy Harris (USA), Los Angeles

01.05.59 **Floyd Patterson** (USA) W CO 11 Brian London (GB), Indianapolis

26.06.59 **Ingemar Johansson** (SWE) W RSC 3 Floyd Patterson (USA), New York City

20.06.60 **Floyd Patterson** (USA) W CO 5 Ingemar Johansson (SWE), New York City. *In winning, Patterson became the first man to regain the heavyweight title.*

13.03.61 **Floyd Patterson** (USA) W CO 6 Ingemar Johansson (SWE), Miami

04.12.61 **Floyd Patterson** (USA) W CO 4 Tom McNeeley (USA), Toronto

25.09.62 **Sonny Liston** (USA) W CO 1 Floyd Patterson (USA), Chicago

22.07.63 **Sonny Liston** (USA) W CO 1 Floyd Patterson (USA), Las Vegas

25.02.64 **Muhammad Ali** (USA) W RTD 6 Sonny Liston (USA), Miami. *Muhammad Ali, having changed his name from that of Cassius Clay, was stripped by the WBA in September 1964, due to his decision to go ahead with a return fight with Sonny Liston, and plans were made to set up an elimination tournament. Following a fight between Doug Jones and George Chuvalo on 2 October (New York City), which produced an 11th round stoppage win for the latter, four men, Chuvalo, Ernie Terrell, Cleveland Williams and Floyd Patterson, were named for the semi-final legs. However, Patterson had already been matched against Chuvalo, which broke a WBA regulation and, although the winner (Patterson outpointed Chuvalo over 12 rounds on 1 February 1965 in New York City) was promised first crack at the new champion, it was Williams and Terrell who were selected to contest the vacant title. Unfortunately, for Williams, he was put out of action when suffering bullet wounds during a scuffle with a policeman and was replaced by the next logical contender, Eddie Machen.*

05.03.65 Ernie Terrell (USA) W PTS 15 Eddie Machen (USA), Chicago - WBA

25.05.65 Muhammad Ali (USA) W CO 1 Sonny Liston (USA), Lewiston - WBC

01.11.65 Ernie Terrell (USA) W PTS 15 George Chuvalo (C), Toronto - WBA

22.11.65 Muhammad Ali (USA) W RSC 12 Floyd Patterson (USA), Las Vegas - WBC

29.03.66 Muhammad Ali (USA) W PTS 15 George Chuvalo (C), Toronto - WBC

21.05.66 Muhammad Ali (USA) W RSC 6 Henry Cooper (GB), Highbury Stadium, London - WBC

28.06.66 Ernie Terrell (USA) W PTS 15 Doug Jones (USA), Houston - WBA

06.08.66 Muhammad Ali (USA) W CO 3 Brian London (GB), Earls Court, London - WBC

10.09.66 Muhammad Ali (USA) W RSC 12 Karl Mildenberger (GER), Frankfurt - WBC

14.11.66 Muhammad Ali (USA) W RSC 3 Cleveland Williams (USA), Houston - WBC

06.02.67 Muhammad Ali (USA) W PTS 15 Ernie Terrell (USA), Houston

22.03.67 **Muhammad Ali** (USA) W CO 7 Zora Folley (USA), New York City. *In April 1967, Muhammad Ali forfeited his title when he refused to serve in the US army and a series of eliminators got underway to determine a new champion. The WBA announced that eight men, namely, Thad Spencer, Jimmy Ellis, Oscar Bonavena, Jerry Quarry, Ernie Terrell, Leotis Martin, Karl Mildenberger and Floyd Patterson, would compete, while the WBC were happy to have a straight final between Joe Frazier and Buster Mathis. Of the successful quarter-finalists, Ellis outpointed Bonavena over 12 rounds on 2 December 1967 (Louisville) and Quarry stopped Spencer in the 12th round (Oakland) on 3 February 1968, and would meet in the final.*

04.03.68 Joe Frazier (USA) W RSC 11 Buster Mathis (USA), New York City - WBC

27.04.68 Jimmy Ellis (USA) W PTS 15 Jerry Quarry (USA), Oakland - WBA

24.06.68 Joe Frazier (USA) W RTD 2 Manuel Ramos (MEX), New York City - WBC

14.09.68 Jimmy Ellis (USA) W PTS 15 Floyd Patterson (USA), Stockholm - WBA

10.12.68 Joe Frazier (USA) W PTS 15 Oscar Bonavena (ARG), Philadelphia - WBC

22.04.69 Joe Frazier (USA) W CO 1 Dave Zyglewicz (USA), Houston - WBC

23.06.69 Joe Frazier (USA) W RSC 7 Jerry Quarry (USA), New York City - WBC

16.02.70 **Joe Frazier** (USA) W RTD 4 Jimmy Ellis (USA), New York City

18.11.70 **Joe Frazier** (USA) W CO 2 Bob Foster (USA), Detroit

08.03.71 **Joe Frazier** (USA) W PTS 15 Muhammad Ali (USA), New York City

15.01.72 **Joe Frazier** (USA) W RSC 4 Terry Daniels (USA), New Orleans

26.05.72 **Joe Frazier** (USA) W RSC 4 Ron Stander (USA), Omaha

22.01.73 **George Foreman** (USA) W RSC 2 Joe Frazier (USA), Kingston

01.09.73 **George Foreman** (USA) W CO 1 Jose Roman (PR), Tokyo

26.03.74 **George Foreman** (USA) W RSC 2 Ken Norton (USA), Caracas

30.10.74 **Muhammad Ali** (USA) W CO 8 George Foreman (USA), Kinshasa

24.03.75 **Muhammad Ali** (USA) W RSC 15 Chuck Wepner (USA), Cleveland

16.05.75 **Muhammad Ali** (USA) W RSC 11 Ron Lyle (USA), Las Vegas

01.07.75 **Muhammad Ali** (USA) W PTS 15 Joe Bugner (GB), Kuala Lumpur

01.10.75 **Muhammad Ali** (USA) W RTD 14 Joe Frazier (USA), Manila

20.02.76 **Muhammad Ali** (USA) W CO 5 Jean-Pierre Coopman (BEL), San Juan

30.04.76 **Muhammad Ali** (USA) W PTS 15 Jimmy Young (USA), Landover

25.05.76 **Muhammad Ali** (USA) W RSC 5 Richard Dunn (GB), Munich

28.09.76 **Muhammad Ali** (USA) W PTS 15 Ken Norton (USA), New York City

16.05.77 **Muhammad Ali** (USA) W PTS 15 Alfredo Evangelista (SP), Landover

29.09.77 **Muhammad Ali** (USA) W PTS 15 Earnie Shavers (USA), New York City

15.02.78 **Leon Spinks** (USA) W PTS 15 Muhammad Ali (USA), Las Vegas. *Leon Spinks forfeited WBC recognition in March 1978 for not being prepared to defend against their leading contender, Ken Norton, who had been promised first crack at the winner. Norton, having won a final eliminator when outscoring Jimmy Young over 15 rounds on 5 November 1977 (Las Vegas), was immediately proclaimed champion on the basis of that victory. To qualify as his first challenger, Larry Holmes outscored Earnie Shavers over 12 rounds of a WBC final eliminator, held in Las Vegas on 25 March 1978.*

09.06.78 Larry Holmes (USA) W PTS 15 Ken Norton (USA), Las Vegas - WBC

15.09.78 Muhammad Ali (USA) W PTS 15 Leon Spinks (USA), New Orleans - WBA. *Muhammad Ali relinquished WBA version of the title on announcing his retirement in June 1979 and an elimin-*

ating series was set up to find the next champion. In the first semi-final leg, John Tate (USA) stopped Kallie Knoetze (SA) inside eight rounds in Mabatho on 2 June 1979, while the second, held in Monte Carlo on 24 June 1979, saw Gerrie Coetzee (SA) force the referee to come to the rescue of Leon Spinks (USA) in the first.

10.11.78 Larry Holmes (USA) W CO 7 Alfredo Evangelista (SP), Las Vegas - WBC

23.03.79 Larry Holmes (USA) W RSC 7 Ossie Ocasio (PR), Las Vegas - WBC

22.06.79 Larry Holmes (USA) W RSC 12 Mike Weaver (USA), New York City - WBC

28.09.79 Larry Holmes (USA) W RSC 11 Earnie Shavers (USA), Las Vegas - WBC

20.10.79 John Tate (USA) W PTS 15 Gerrie Coetzee (SA), Pretoria - WBA

03.02.80 Larry Holmes (USA) W CO 6 Lorenzo Zanon (ITA), Las Vegas - WBC

31.03.80 Mike Weaver (USA) W CO 15 John Tate (USA), Knoxville - WBA

31.03.80 Larry Holmes (USA) W RSC 8 Leroy Jones (USA), Las Vegas - WBC

07.07.80 Larry Holmes (USA) W RSC 7 Scott Ledoux (USA), Minneapolis - WBC

02.10.80 Larry Holmes (USA) W RTD 10 Muhammad Ali (USA), Las Vegas - WBC

25.10.80 Mike Weaver (USA) W CO 13 Gerrie Coetzee (SA), Sun City - WBA

11.04.81 Larry Holmes (USA) W PTS 15 Trevor Berbick (C), Las Vegas - WBC

12.06.81 Larry Holmes (USA) W RSC 3 Leon Spinks (USA), Detroit - WBC

03.10.81 Mike Weaver (USA) W PTS 15 James Tillis (USA), Rosemont - WBA

06.11.81 Larry Holmes (USA) W RSC 11 Renaldo Snipes (USA), Pittsburgh - WBC

11.06.82 Larry Holmes (USA) W RSC 13 Gerry Cooney (USA), Las Vegas - WBC

26.11.82 Larry Holmes (USA) W PTS 15 Tex Cobb (USA), Houston - WBC

10.12.82 Michael Dokes (USA) W RSC 1 Mike Weaver (USA), Las Vegas - WBA

27.03.83 Larry Holmes (USA) W PTS 12 Lucien Rodriguez (FR), Scranton - WBC

20.05.83 Michael Dokes (USA) DREW 15 Mike Weaver (USA), Las Vegas - WBA

20.05.83 Larry Holmes (USA) W PTS 12 Tim Witherspoon (USA), Las Vegas - WBC

10.09.83 Larry Holmes (USA) W RSC 5 Scott Frank (USA), Atlantic City - WBC

23.09.83 Gerrie Coetzee (SA) W CO 10 Michael Dokes (USA), Richfield - WBA

25.11.83 Larry Holmes (USA) W RSC 1 Marvis Frazier (USA), Las Vegas - WBC. *Larry Holmes relinquished the WBC version of the title on being proclaimed IBF champion in December 1983 and Tim Witherspoon, who had stopped James Tillis in one round on 23 September 1983 (Richfield), and Greg Page, having outscored Renaldo Snipes on 20 May 1983 (Las Vegas), were selected to contest the vacancy.*

09.03.84 Tim Witherspoon (USA) W PTS 12 Greg Page (USA), Las Vegas - WBC

31.08.84 Pinklon Thomas (USA) W PTS 12 Tim Witherspoon (USA), Las Vegas - WBC

09.11.84 Larry Holmes (USA) W RSC 12 James Smith (USA), Las Vegas - IBF

01.12.84 Greg Page (USA) W CO 8 Gerrie Coetzee (SA), Sun City - WBA

15.03.85 Larry Holmes (USA) W RSC 10 David Bey (USA), Las Vegas - IBF

29.04.85 Tony Tubbs (USA) W PTS 15 Greg Page (USA), Buffalo - WBA

20.05.85 Larry Holmes (USA) W PTS 15 Carl Williams (USA), Reno - IBF

15.06.85 Pinklon Thomas (USA) W CO 8 Mike Weaver (USA), Las Vegas - WBC

21.09.85 Michael Spinks (USA) W PTS 15 Larry Holmes (USA), Las Vegas - IBF

17.01.86 Tim Witherspoon (USA) W PTS 15 Tony Tubbs (USA), Atlanta - WBA

22.03.86 Trevor Berbick (C) W PTS 12 Pinklon Thomas (USA), Las Vegas - WBC

19.04.86 Michael Spinks (USA) W PTS 15 Larry Holmes (USA), Las Vegas - IBF

19.07.86 Tim Witherspoon (USA) W RSC 11 Frank Bruno (GB), The Stadium, Wembley - WBA

06.09.86 Michael Spinks (USA) W RSC 4 Steffen Tangstad (NOR), Las Vegas - IBF. *Michael Spinks forfeited the IBF version of the title*

in February 1987 after refusing to defend against Tony Tucker and signing to meet Gerry Cooney, instead.

22.11.86 Mike Tyson (USA) W RSC 2 Trevor Berbick (C), Las Vegas - WBC

12.12.86 James Smith (USA) W RSC 1 Tim Witherspoon (USA), New York City - WBA

07.03.87 Mike Tyson (USA) W PTS 12 James Smith (USA), Las Vegas - WBA/WBC

30.05.87 Mike Tyson (USA) W RSC 6 Pinklon Thomas (USA), Las Vegas - WBA/WBC

30.05.87 Tony Tucker (USA) W RSC 10 James Douglas (USA), Las Vegas - IBF

15.06.87 Michael Spinks (USA) W RSC 5 Gerry Cooney (USA), Atlantic City. *Not supported by any of the commissions, but billed for "the peoples' world heavyweight championship", following his victory, Spinks remained inactive until facing Mike Tyson for the undisputed title.*

01.08.87 **Mike Tyson** (USA) W PTS 12 Tony Tucker (USA), Las Vegas

16.10.87 **Mike Tyson** (USA) W RSC 7 Tyrell Biggs (USA), Atlantic City

22.01.88 **Mike Tyson** (USA) W RSC 4 Larry Holmes (USA), Atlantic City

21.03.88 **Mike Tyson** (USA) W RSC 2 Tony Tubbs (USA), Tokyo

27.06.88 **Mike Tyson** (USA) W CO 1 Michael Spinks (USA), Atlantic City

25.02.89 **Mike Tyson** (USA) W RSC 5 Frank Bruno (GB), Las Vegas. *In their wisdom, the WBO decided to support the winner of a Francesco Damiani v Johnny du Plooy bout as their champion.*

06.05.89 Francesco Damiani (ITA) W CO 3 Johnny du Plooy (SA), Syracuse - WBO

21.07.89 Mike Tyson (USA) W RSC 1 Carl Williams (USA), Atlantic City - IBF/WBA/WBC

16.12.89 Francesco Damiani (ITA) W RTD 2 Daniel Netto (ARG), Cesena - WBO

11.02.90 James Douglas (USA) W CO 10 Mike Tyson (USA), Tokyo - IBF/WBA/WBC

25.10.90 Evander Holyfield (USA) W CO 3 James Douglas (USA), Las Vegas - IBF/WBA/WBC

11.01.91 Ray Mercer (USA) W CO 9 Francesco Damiani (ITA), Atlantic City - WBO

19.04.91 Evander Holyfield (USA) W PTS 12 George Foreman (USA), Atlantic City - IBF/WBA/WBC

18.10.91 Ray Mercer (USA) W RSC 5 Tommy Morrison (USA), Atlantic City - WBO. *Ray Mercer forfeited title in January 1992 when refusing to defend against Michael Moorer.*

23.11.91 Evander Holyfield (USA) W RSC 7 Bert Cooper (USA), Atlanta - IBF/WBA/WBC

15.05.92 Michael Moorer (USA) W RSC 5 Bert Cooper (USA), Atlantic City - WBO. *Michael Moorer relinquished WBO version of title in February 1993 in order to make himself available to challenge either Bowe or Lewis.*

19.06.92 Evander Holyfield (USA) W PTS 12 Larry Holmes (USA), Las Vegas - IBF/WBA/WBC

13.11.92 Riddick Bowe (USA) W PTS 12 Evander Holyfield (USA), Las Vegas - IBF/WBA/WBC. *Riddick Bowe forfeited WBC version of the title in December 1992 when failing to sign for a defence against their leading contender, Lennox Lewis. Lewis, who had stopped Razor Ruddock inside two rounds on 31 October 1992 (Earls Court, London) in a final eliminator, was immediately proclaimed WBC champion.*

27.02.93 Riddick Bowe (USA) W RSC 1 Michael Dokes (USA), New York City - WBA/IBF

08.05.93 Lennox Lewis (GB) W PTS 12 Tony Tucker (USA), Las Vegas - WBC

22.05.93 Riddick Bowe (USA) W RSC 2 Jesse Ferguson (USA), Washington - WBA/IBF

07.06.93 Tommy Morrison (USA) W PTS 12 George Foreman (USA), Las Vegas - WBO

30.08.93 Tommy Morrison (USA) W RTD 4 Tim Tomashek (USA), Kansas City - WBO. *Following the fight, the WBO withdrew title status after overruling their supervisor and deciding that Tomashek, a last minute replacement, was not of championship class.*

01.10.93 Lennox Lewis (GB) W RSC 7 Frank Bruno (GB), Arms Park, Cardiff - WBC

29.10.93 Michael Bentt (USA) W RSC 1 Tommy Morrison (USA), Tulsa - WBO

06.11.93 Evander Holyfield (USA) W PTS 12 Riddick Bowe (USA), Las Vegas - WBA/IBF

19.03.94 Herbie Hide (GB) W CO 7 Michael Bentt (USA), The New Den, London - WBO

22.04.94 Michael Moorer (USA) W PTS 12 Evander Holyfield (USA), Las Vegas - WBA/IBF

06.05.94 Lennox Lewis (GB) W RSC 8 Phil Jackson (USA), Atlantic City - WBC

World Champions Since Gloves, 1891-1995

As I stated in last year's listings, much research on world championship boxing has been, and continues to be, carried out. Also, I explained that many men, especially in America, did not have enough backing to warrant a strong enough claim, and if we tried to list all the claimants there would just not be the space available. However, for our purposes, I have started with the first of the internationally acclaimed champions for the six original weights, bantam, feather, light, welter, middle and heavy.

Bantam: After the Canadian claimant, George Dixon, had moved up to feather, and with the popular weight being allowed to increase from 105 up to 110 lbs, the English champion, Billy Plimmer, knocked out Tommy Kelly, the best America had to offer, in ten rounds at Coney Island on 9 May 1892.

Feather: George Dixon, who moved up from bantam, and consolidated his claim with a win over the Australian, Abe Willis, in 1891, is generally accepted as champion after kayoing the British titleholder, Fred Johnson, inside 14 rounds at the Coney Island Athletic Club, Brooklyn, on 27 June 1892.

Light: With the division recognised at 133 lbs, the American champion, Jack McAuliffe, had carried his weight to 134$\frac{1}{2}$ lbs in his first defence with gloves against Jimmy Carroll, who succumbed to a 47th round kayo in San Francisco on 21 March 1890. While Carroll continued to claim the title at 133 lbs, without much backing, McAuliffe's great rival, Jem Carney, was beaten on an 11th round disqualification in London on 25 May 1891. By his victory, at 133 lbs, Burge claimed the English version of the title and eventually met McAuliffe's American successor, George Lavigne, in the first truly international glove fight at lightweight, albeit at 137 lbs. That was conveniently overlooked after Lavigne (134) knocked Burge out in the 17th round at the NSC on 1 June 1896 to claim the title.

Welter: The first recorded claimant with gloves was Paddy Duffy, by dint of his victory over Tom Meadows in 1889, but, following his early death on 19 July 1890, the leading protagonists at 142 lbs appear to be Tommy Ryan and Mysterious Billy Smith. Although many would recognise Smith as champion after his victory over Danny Needham in 1892, Ryan appears on paper to have had a better and longer claim, having defeated Con Doyle (1890), Danny Needham (1891), Billy McMillan (1891) and Frank Howson (1891). However, the division finally gained credibility when Ryan outpointed Smith over 20 rounds at Minneapolis on 26 July 1894 to become its clear leader.

Middle: The famous Jack (The Nonpareil) Dempsey carried the USA 154 pounders through the transitional period from bare-fists, driving gloves and skin-tight gloves, to those of the two to five ounce variety, allowing for a spot of tampering, with his 28th round stoppage win over Australian Billy McCarthy in San Francisco on 18 February 1890. However, Bob Fitzsimmons in best recognised as the division's first international champion, following his 13th round stoppage of the Irish-American in New Orleans on 14 January 1891.

Heavy: Although Frank Slavin won the English and Australian version of the title, beating Joe McAuliffe and Jake Kilrain, before losing his claim to the legendary Peter Jackson on 30 May 1892, because the coloured Australian was inactive for the next six years, most people would accept James J. Corbett, following his 21st round kayo of the bare-knuckle king, John L. Sullivan, in New Orleans on 7 September 1892, as being the division's first international champion with gloves.

Championship Status Code:

AU = Austria; AUST = Australia; CALIF = California; CAN = Canada; EBU = European Boxing Union; FR = France; GB = Great Britain; IBF = International Boxing Federation; IBU = International Boxing Union; ILL = Illinois; LOUIS = Louisiana; MARY = Maryland; MASS = Massachusetts; NBA = National Boxing Association; NY = New York; PEN = Pennsylvania; SA = South Africa; TBC = Territorial Boxing Commission; USA = United States; WBA = World Boxing Association; WBC = World Boxing Council; WBO = World Boxing Organisation.

Champions in **bold** are accorded universal recognition.

* Undefeated champions (Does not include men who forfeited titles).

Title Holder	Birthplace	Tenure	Status	Title Holder	Birthplace	Tenure	Status
M. Flyweight (105 lbs)				Fahlan Lukmingkwan	Thailand	1990-1992	IBF
Kyung-Yung Lee*	S Korea	1987-1988	IBF	Ricardo Lopez	Mexico	1990-	WBC
Hiroki Ioka	Japan	1987-1988	WBC	Hi-Yon Choi	S Korea	1991-1992	WBA
Silvio Gamez*	Venezuela	1988-1989	WBA	Manny Melchor	Philippines	1992	IBF
Samuth Sithnaruepol	Thailand	1988-1989	IBF	Hideyuki Ohashi	Japan	1992-1993	WBA
Napa Kiatwanchai	Thailand	1988-1989	WBC	Ratanapol Sowvoraphin	Thailand	1992-	IBF
Bong-Jun Kim	S Korea	1989-1991	WBA	Chana Porpaoin	Thailand	1993-	WBA
Nico Thomas	Indonesia	1989	IBF	Paul Weir*	Scotland	1993-1994	WBO
Rafael Torres	Dom Republic	1989-1992	WBO	Alex Sanchez	Puerto Rico	1993-	WBO
Eric Chavez	Philippines	1989-1990	IBF				
Jum-Hwan Choi	S Korea	1989-1990	WBC	**L. Flyweight (108 lbs)**			
Hideyuki Ohashi	Japan	1990	WBC	Franco Udella	Italy	1975	WBC

Title Holder	Birthplace	Tenure	Status
Jaime Rios	Panama	1975-1976	WBA
Luis Estaba	Venezuela	1975-1978	WBC
Juan Guzman	Dom Republic	1976	WBA
Yoko Gushiken	Japan	1976-1981	WBA
Freddie Castillo	Mexico	1978	WBC
Sor Vorasingh	Thailand	1978	WBC
Sun-Jun Kim	S Korea	1978-1980	WBC
Shigeo Nakajima	Japan	1980	WBC
Hilario Zapata	Panama	1980-1982	WBC
Pedro Flores	Mexico	1981	WBA
Hwan-Jin Kim	S Korea	1981	WBA
Katsuo Tokashiki	Japan	1981-1983	WBA
Amado Ursua	Mexico	1982	WBC
Tadashi Tomori	Japan	1982	WBC
Hilario Zapata	Panama	1982-1983	WBC
Jung-Koo Chang*	S Korea	1983-1988	WBC
Lupe Madera	Mexico	1983-1984	WBA
Dodie Penalosa	Philippines	1983-1986	IBF
Francisco Quiroz	Dom Republic	1984-1985	WBA
Joey Olivo	USA	1985	WBA
Myung-Woo Yuh	S Korea	1985-1991	WBA
Juan-Hwan Choi	S Korea	1987-1988	IBF
Tacy Macalos	Philippines	1988-1989	IBF
German Torres	Mexico	1988-1989	WBC
Yul-Woo Lee	S Korea	1989	WBC
Muangchai Kitikasem	Thailand	1989-1990	IBF
Jose de Jesus	Puerto Rico	1989-1992	WBO
Humberto Gonzalez	Mexico	1989-1990	WBC
Michael Carbajal	USA	1990-1991	IBF
Rolando Pascua	Philippines	1990-1991	WBC
Melchor Cob Castro	Mexico	1991	WBC
Humberto Gonzalez	Mexico	1991-1993	WBC
Hiroki Ioka	Japan	1991-1992	WBA
Josue Camacho	Puerto Rico	1992-1994	WBO
Myung-Woo Yuh*	S Korea	1992-1993	WBA
Michael Carbajal	USA	1993-1994	IBF/WBC
Silvio Gamez	Venezuela	1993-1995	WBA
Humberto Gonzalez	Mexico	1994-	WBC/IBF
Michael Carbajal*	USA	1994	WBO
Paul Weir	Scotland	1994-	WBO
Hi-Yong Choi	S Korea	1995-	WBA

Flyweight (112 lbs)

Title Holder	Birthplace	Tenure	Status
Sid Smith	England	1913	GB/IBU
Bill Ladbury	England	1913-1914	GB/IBU
Percy Jones	Wales	1914	GB/IBU
Tancy Lee	Scotland	1915	GB/IBU
Joe Symonds	England	1915-1916	GB/IBU
Jimmy Wilde	Wales	1916	GB/IBU
Jimmy Wilde	Wales	1916-1923	
Pancho Villa*	Philippines	1923-1925	
Fidel la Barba*	USA	1925-1927	
Pinky Silverburg	USA	1927	NBA
Johnny McCoy	USA	1927-1928	CALIF
Frankie Belanger	Canada	1927-1928	NBA
Izzy Schwartz	USA	1927-1929	NY
Newsboy Brown	Russia	1928	CALIF
Frankie Genaro	USA	1928-1929	NBA
Johnny Hill	Scotland	1928-1929	GB/CALIF
Emile Pladner	France	1929	NBA/IBU
Frankie Genaro	USA	1929-1931	NBA/IBU
Midget Wolgast	USA	1930-1935	NY
Young Perez	Tunisia	1931-1932	NBA/IBU
Jackie Brown	England	1932-1935	NBA/IBU
Benny Lynch	Scotland	1935-1937	NBA
Small Montana	Philippines	1935-1937	NY/CALIF
Valentin Angelmann	France	1936-1937	IBU
Benny Lynch	Scotland	1937	
Peter Kane*	England	1938-1939	
Little Dado	Philippines	1938-1939	CALIF
Little Dado	Philippines	1939-1942	NBA/CALIF

Title Holder	Birthplace	Tenure	Status
Jackie Paterson	Scotland	1943-1947	
Jackie Paterson	Scotland	1947-1948	GB/NY
Rinty Monaghan	Ireland	1947-1948	NBA
Rinty Monaghan*	Ireland	1948-1950	
Terry Allen	England	1950	
Dado Marino	Hawaii	1950-1952	
Yoshio Shirai	Japan	1952-1954	
Pascual Perez	Argentina	1954-1960	
Pone Kingpetch	Thailand	1960-1962	
Fighting Harada	Japan	1962-1963	
Pone Kingpetch	Thailand	1963	
Hiroyuki Ebihara	Japan	1963-1964	
Pone Kingpetch	Thailand	1964-1965	
Salvatore Burruni	Italy	1965	
Salvatore Burruni	Italy	1965-1966	WBC
Horacio Accavallo*	Argentina	1966-1968	WBA
Walter McGowan	Scotland	1966	WBC
Chartchai Chionoi	Thailand	1966-1969	WBC
Efren Torres	Mexico	1969-1970	WBC
Hiroyuki Ebihara	Japan	1969	WBA
Bernabe Villacampo	Philippines	1969-1970	WBA
Chartchai Chionoi	Thailand	1970	WBC
Berkerk Chartvanchai	Thailand	1970	WBA
Masso Ohba*	Japan	1970-1973	WBA
Erbito Salavarria	Philippines	1970-1971	WBC
Betulio Gonzalez	Venezuela	1972	WBC
Venice Borkorsor*	Thailand	1972-1973	WBC
Chartchai Chionoi	Thailand	1973-1974	WBA
Betulio Gonzalez	Venezuela	1973-1974	WBC
Shoki Oguma	Japan	1974-1975	WBC
Susumu Hanagata	Japan	1974-1975	WBA
Miguel Canto	Mexico	1975-1979	WBC
Erbito Salavarria	Philippines	1975-1976	WBA
Alfonso Lopez	Panama	1976	WBA
Guty Espadas	Mexico	1976-1978	WBA
Betulio Gonzalez	Venezuela	1978-1979	WBA
Chan-Hee Park	S Korea	1979-1980	WBC
Luis Ibarra	Panama	1979-1980	WBA
Tae-Shik Kim	S Korea	1980	WBA
Shoji Oguma	Japan	1980-1981	WBC
Peter Mathebula	S Africa	1980-1981	WBA
Santos Lacial	Argentina	1981	WBA
Antonio Avelar	Mexico	1981-1982	WBC
Luis Ibarra	Panama	1981	WBA
Juan Herrera	Mexico	1981-1982	WBA
Prudencio Cardona	Colombia	1982	WBC
Santos Laciar*	Argentina	1982-1985	WBA
Freddie Castillo	Mexico	1982	WBC
Eleonicio Mercedes	Dom Republic	1982-1983	WBC
Charlie Magri	Tunisia	1983	WBC
Frank Cedeno	Philippines	1983-1984	WBC
Soon-Chun Kwon	S Korea	1983-1985	IBF
Koji Kobayashi	Japan	1984	WBC
Gabriel Bernal	Mexico	1984	WBC
Sot Chitalada	Thailand	1984-1988	WBC
Hilario Zapata	Panama	1985-1987	WBA
Chong-Kwan Chung	S Korea	1985-1986	IBF
Bi-Won Chung	S Korea	1986	IBF
Hi-Sup Shin	S Korea	1986-1987	IBF
Fidel Bassa	Colombia	1987-1989	WBA
Dodie Penalosa	Philippines	1987	IBF
Chang-Ho Choi	S Korea	1987-1988	IBF
Rolando Bohol	Philippines	1988	IBF
Yong-Kang Kim	S Korea	1988-1989	WBC
Elvis Alvarez*	Colombia	1989	WBO
Duke McKenzie	England	1988-1989	IBF
Sot Chitalada	Thailand	1989-1991	WBC
Dave McAuley	Ireland	1989-1992	IBF
Jesus Rojas	Venezuela	1989-1990	WBA
Yul-Woo Lee	S Korea	1990	WBA
Isidro Perez	Mexico	1990-1992	WBO

Title Holder	Birthplace	Tenure	Status
Yukihito Tamakuma	Japan	1990	WBA
Muangchai Kitikasem	Thailand	1991-1992	WBC
Elvis Alvarez	Colombia	1991	WBA
Yong-Kang Kim	S Korea	1991-1992	WBA
Pat Clinton	Scotland	1992-1993	WBO
Rodolfo Blanco	Colombia	1992	IBF
Yuri Arbachakov	Russia	1992-	WBC
Aquiles Guzman	Venezuela	1992	WBA
Pichit Sitbangprachan*	Thailand	1992-1994	IBF
David Griman	Venezuela	1992-1994	WBA
Jacob Matlala	S Africa	1993-1995	WBO
Saen Sowploenchit	Thailand	1994-	WBA
Alberto Jimenez	Mexico	1995-	WBO
Francisco Tejedor	Colombia	1995	IBF
Danny Romero	USA	1995-	IBF

S. Flyweight (115 lbs)

Title Holder	Birthplace	Tenure	Status
Rafael Orono	Venezuela	1980-1981	WBC
Chul-Ho Kim	S Korea	1981-1982	WBC
Gustavo Ballas	Argentine	1981	WBA
Rafael Pedroza	Panama	1981-1982	WBA
Jiro Watanabe	Japan	1982-1984	WBA
Rafael Orono	Venezuela	1982-1983	WBC
Payao Poontarat	Thailand	1983-1984	WBC
Joo-Do Chun	S Korea	1983-1985	IBF
Jiro Watanabe	Japan	1984-1986	WBC
Elly Pical	Indonesia	1985-1986	IBF
Kaosai Galaxy*	Thailand	1984-1991	WBA
Cesar Polanco	Dom Republic	1986	IBF
Gilberto Roman	Mexico	1986-1987	WBC
Elly Pical	Indonesia	1986-1987	IBF
Santos Laciar	Argentine	1987	WBC
Tae-Il Chang	S Korea	1987	IBF
Jesus Rojas	Colombia	1987-1988	WBC
Elly Pical	Indonesia	1987-1989	IBF
Gilberto Roman	Mexico	1988-1989	WBC
Jose Ruiz	Puerto Rico	1989-1992	WBO
Juan Polo Perez	Colombia	1989-1990	IBF
Nana Yaw Konadu	Ghana	1989-1990	WBC
Sung-Il Moon	S Korea	1990-1993	WBC
Robert Quiroga	USA	1990-1993	IBF
Jose Quirino	Mexico	1992	WBO
Katsuya Onizuka	Japan	1992-1994	WBA
Johnny Bredahl*	Denmark	1992-1994	WBO
Julio Cesar Borboa	Mexico	1993-1994	IBF
Jose Luis Bueno	Mexico	1993-1994	WBC
Hiroshi Kawashima	Japan	1994-	WBC
Harold Grey	Colombia	1994-	IBF
Hyung-Chul Lee	S Korea	1994-	WBA
Johnny Tapia	USA	1994-	WBO

Bantamweight (118 lbs)

Title Holder	Birthplace	Tenure	Status
Billy Plimmer	England	1892-1895	
Pedlar Palmer	England	1895-1899	
Terry McGovern*	USA	1899-1900	
Harry Forbes	USA	1901-1903	USA
Frankie Neil	USA	1903-1904	USA
Joe Bowker	England	1903-1904	GB
Joe Bowker*	England	1904-1905	
Jimmy Walsh*	USA	1905-1907	USA
Owen Moran*	England	1907	GB
Monte Attell	USA	1909-1910	USA
Frankie Conley	Italy	1910-1911	USA
Digger Stanley	England	1910-1912	GB/IBU
Johnny Coulon	Canada	1911-1914	USA
Charles Ledoux	France	1912-1913	GB/IBU
Eddie Campi	USA	1913-1914	IBU
Kid Williams	Denmark	1914	IBU
Kid Williams	Denmark	1914-1917	
Pete Herman	USA	1917-1920	
Joe Lynch	USA	1920-1921	

Title Holder	Birthplace	Tenure	Status
Pete Herman	USA	1921	
Johnny Buff	USA	1921-1922	
Joe Lynch	USA	1922-1924	
Abe Goldstein	USA	1924	
Eddie Martin	USA	1924-1925	
Charlie Rosenberg	USA	1925-1927	
Bud Taylor*	USA	1927-1928	NBA
Teddy Baldock	England	1927	GB
Willie Smith	S Africa	1927-1929	GB
Bushy Graham*	Italy	1928-1929	NY
Al Brown	Panama	1929-1931	NY/IBU
Pete Sanstol	Norway	1931	NBA
Al Brown	Panama	1931-1932	
Speedy Dado	Philippines	1932-1933	CALIF
Al Brown	Panama	1932-1934	NY/NBA/IBU
Young Tommy	Philippines	1933	CALIF
Speedy Dado	Philippines	1933	CALIF
Baby Casanova	Mexico	1933-1934	CALIF
Al Brown	Panama	1934-1935	NY/IBU
Sixto Escobar	Puerto Rico	1934	CAN
Sixto Escobar	Puerto Rico	1934-1935	NBA
Lou Salica	USA	1935	CALIF
Baltazar Sangchilli	Spain	1935	NY/IBU
Baltazar Sangchilli	Spain	1935-1936	IBU
Lou Salica	USA	1935	NBA/NY
Sixto Escobar	Puerto Rico	1935-1936	NBA/NY
Tony Marino	USA	1936	IBU
Sixto Escobar	Puerto Rico	1936-1937	
Harry Jeffra	USA	1937-1938	
Sixto Escobar	Puerto Rico	1938	
Sixto Escobar	Puerto Rico	1938	NY/NBA
Al Brown	Panama	1938	IBU
Star Frisco	Philippines	1938	AUSTR
Sixto Escobar	Puerto Rico	1938-1939	
Georgie Pace	USA	1939-1940	NBA
Lou Salica	USA	1939-1940	CALIF
Lou Salica	USA	1940-1942	
Kenny Lindsay	Canada	1941-1943	CAN
Lou Salica	USA	1941-1942	NY/NBA
Manuel Ortiz	USA	1942-1945	NY/NBA
Kui Kong Young	Hawaai	1943	TBC
Rush Dalma	Philippines	1943-1945	TBC
Manuel Ortiz	USA	1945-1947	
Harold Dade	USA	1947	
Manuel Ortiz	USA	1947-1950	
Vic Toweel	S Africa	1950-1952	
Jimmy Carruthers*	Australia	1952-1954	
Robert Cohen	Algeria	1954	
Robert Cohen	Algeria	1954-1956	NY/EBU
Raton Macias	Mexico	1955-1957	NBA
Mario D'Agata	Italy	1956-1957	NY/ EBU
Alphonse Halimi	Algeria	1957	NY/EBU
Alphonse Halimi	Algeria	1957-1959	
Joe Becerra*	Mexico	1959-1960	
Alphonse Halimi	Algeria	1960-1961	EBU
Eder Jofre	Brazil	1960-1962	NBA
Johnny Caldwell	Ireland	1961-1962	EBU
Eder Jofre	Brazil	1962-1965	
Fighting Harada	Japan	1965-1968	
Lionel Rose	Australia	1968-1969	
Ruben Olivares	Mexico	1969-1970	
Chuchu Castillo	Mexico	1970-1971	
Ruben Olivares	Mexico	1971-1972	
Rafael Herrera	Mexico	1972	
Enrique Pinder	Panama	1972	
Enrique Pinder	Panama	1972-1973	WBC
Romeo Anaya	Mexico	1973	WBA
Rafael Herrera	Mexico	1973-1974	WBC
Arnold Taylor	S Africa	1973-1974	WBA
Soo-Hwan Hong	S Korea	1974-1975	WBA
Rodolfo Martinez	Mexico	1974-1976	WBC

Title Holder	Birthplace	Tenure	Status
Alfonso Zamora	Mexico	1975-1977	WBA
Carlos Zarate	Mexico	1976-1979	WBC
Jorge Lujan	Panama	1977-1980	WBA
Lupe Pintor*	Mexico	1979-1983	WBC
Julian Solis	Puerto Rico	1980	WBA
Jeff Chandler	USA	1980-1984	WBA
Albert Davila	USA	1983-1985	WBC
Richard Sandoval	USA	1984-1986	WBA
Satoshi Shingaki	Japan	1984-1985	IBF
Jeff Fenech*	Australia	1985-1987	IBF
Daniel Zaragoza	Mexico	1985	WBC
Miguel Lora	Colombia	1985-1988	WBC
Gaby Canizales	USA	1986	WBA
Bernardo Pinango*	Venezuela	1986-1987	WBA
Takuya Muguruma	Japan	1987	WBA
Kelvin Seabrooks	USA	1987-1988	IBF
Chan-Yung Park	S Korea	1987	WBA
Wilfredo Vasquez	Puerto Rico	1987-1988	WBA
Kaokor Galaxy	Thailand	1988	WBA
Orlando Canizales*	USA	1988-1994	IBF
Sung-Il Moon	S Korea	1988-1989	WBA
Raul Perez	Mexico	1988-1991	WBC
Israel Contrerras*	Venezuela	1989-1991	WBO
Kaokor Galaxy	Thailand	1989	WBA
Luisito Espinosa	Philippines	1989-1991	WBA
Greg Richardson	USA	1991	WBC
Gaby Canizales	USA	1991	WBO
Duke McKenzie	England	1991-1992	WBO
Joichiro Tatsuyoshi*	Japan	1991-1992	WBC
Israel Contrerras	Venezuela	1991-1992	WBA
Eddie Cook	USA	1992	WBA
Victor Rabanales	Mexico	1992-1993	WBC
Rafael del Valle	Puerto Rico	1992-1994	WBO
Jorge Eliecer Julio	Colombia	1992-1993	WBA
Il-Jung Byun	S Korea	1993	WBC
Junior Jones	USA	1993-1994	WBA
Yasuei Yakushiji	Japan	1993-	WBC
John Michael Johnson	USA	1994	WBA
Daorung Chuwatana	Thailand	1994-	WBA
Alfred Kotey	Ghana	1994-	WBO
Harold Mestre	Colombia	1995	IBF
Mbulelo Botile	S Africa	1995-	IBF

S. Bantamweight (122 lbs)

Title Holder	Birthplace	Tenure	Status
Rigoberto Riasco	Panama	1976	WBC
Royal Kobayashi	Japan	1976	WBC
Doug-Kyun Yum	S Korea	1976-1977	WBC
Wilfredo Gomez*	Puerto Rico	1977-1983	WBC
Soo-Hwan Hong	S Korea	1977-1978	WBA
Ricardo Cardona	Colombia	1978-1980	WBA
Leo Randolph	USA	1980	WBA
Sergio Palma	Argentine	1980-1982	WBA
Leonardo Cruz	Dom Republic	1982-1984	WBA
Jaime Garza	USA	1983-1984	WBC
Bobby Berna	Philippines	1983-1984	IBF
Loris Stecca	Italy	1984	WBA
Seung-In Suh	S Korea	1984-1985	IBF
Victor Callejas	Puerto Rico	1984-1986	WBA
Juan Meza	Mexico	1984-1985	WBC
Ji-Won Kim*	S Korea	1985-1986	IBF
Lupe Pintor	Mexico	1985-1986	WBC
Samart Payakarun	Thailand	1986-1987	WBC
Louie Espinosa	USA	1987	WBA
Seung-Hoon Lee*	S Korea	1987-1988	IBF
Jeff Fenech*	Australia	1987-1988	WBC
Julio Gervacio	Dom Republic	1987-1988	WBA
Bernardo Pinango	Venezuela	1988	WBA
Daniel Zaragoza	Mexico	1988-1990	WBC
Jose Sanabria	Venezuela	1988-1989	IBF
Juan J. Estrada	Mexico	1988-1989	WBA
Fabrice Benichou	Spain	1989-1990	IBF

Title Holder	Birthplace	Tenure	Status
Kenny Mitchell	USA	1989	WBO
Valerio Nati	Italy	1989-1990	WBO
Jesus Salud	USA	1989-1990	WBA
Welcome Ncita	S Africa	1990-1992	IBF
Paul Banke	USA	1990	WBC
Orlando Fernandez	Puerto Rico	1990-1991	WBO
Luis Mendoza	Colombia	1990-1991	WBA
Pedro Decima	Argentine	1990-1991	WBC
Kiyoshi Hatanaka	Japan	1991	WBC
Jesse Benavides	USA	1991-1992	WBO
Daniel Zaragoza	Mexico	1991-1992	WBC
Raul Perez	Mexico	1991-1992	WBA
Thierry Jacob	France	1992	WBC
Wilfredo Vasquez	Puerto Rico	1992-1995	WBA
Tracy Harris Patterson	USA	1992-1994	WBC
Duke McKenzie	England	1992-1993	WBO
Kennedy McKinney	USA	1992-1994	IBF
Daniel Jimenez	Puerto Rico	1993-1995	WBO
Vuyani Bungu	S Africa	1994-	IBF
Hector Acero-Sanchez	Dom Republic	1994-	WBC
Marco Antonio Barrera	Mexico	1995-	WBO
Antonio Cermeno	Venezuela	1995-	WBA

Featherweight (126 lbs)

Title Holder	Birthplace	Tenure	Status
George Dixon	Canada	1892-1896	
Frank Erne	USA	1897	
George Dixon	Canada	1897	
Solly Smith	USA	1897-1898	
Solly Smith	USA	1898	USA
Ben Jordan	England	1898-1899	GB
Dave Sullivan	Ireland	1898	USA
George Dixon	Canada	1899-1900	USA
Eddie Santry	USA	1899-1900	GB
Terry McGovern	USA	1900	USA
Terry McGovern	USA	1900-1901	
Young Corbett II	USA	1901-1903	
Abe Attell	USA	1903-1909	
Abe Attell	USA	1909-1912	USA
Jim Driscoll	Wales	1909-1912	GB
Jim Driscoll*	Wales	1912-1913	GB/IBU
Johnny Kilbane	USA	1912-1913	USA
Johnny Kilbane	USA	1913-1922	
Johnny Kilbane	USA	1922-1923	NBA
Johnny Dundee	Italy	1922-1923	NY
Eugene Criqui	France	1923	
Johnny Dundee*	Italy	1923-1924	
Kid Kaplan*	Russia	1925-1926	
Honeyboy Finnegan	USA	1926-1927	MASS
Benny Bass	Russia	1927-1928	NBA
Tony Canzoneri	USA	1927-1928	NY
Tony Canzoneri	USA	1928	
Andre Routis	France	1928-1929	
Bat Battalino	USA	1929-1932	
Tommy Paul	USA	1932-1933	NBA
Kid Chocolate*	Cuba	1932-1933	NY
Baby Arizmendi	Mexico	1932-1933	CALIF
Freddie Miller	USA	1933-1936	NBA
Baby Arizmendi	Mexico	1934-1936	NY
Baby Arizmendi	Mexico	1935-1936	NY/MEX
Petey Sarron	USA	1936-1937	NBA
Henry Armstrong	USA	1936-1937	CALIF
Mike Belloise	USA	1936	NY
Maurice Holtzer	France	1937-1938	IBU
Henry Armstrong*	USA	1937-1938	NBA/NY/CALIF
Leo Rodak	USA	1938-1939	MARY
Joey Archibald	USA	1938-1939	NY
Joey Archibald	USA	1939-1940	
Joey Archibald	USA	1940	NY
Jimmy Perrin	USA	1940	LOUIS
Harry Jeffra	USA	1940-1941	NY/MARY
Petey Scalzo	USA	1940-1941	NBA

Title Holder	Birthplace	Tenure	Status
Joey Archibald	USA	1941	NY/MARY
Richie Lemos	USA	1941	NBA
Chalky Wright	Mexico	1941-1942	NY/MARY
Jackie Wilson	USA	1941-1943	NBA
Willie Pep	USA	1942-1946	NY
Jackie Callura	Canada	1943	NBA
Phil Terranova	USA	1943-1944	NBA
Sal Bartolo	USA	1944-1946	NBA
Willie Pep	USA	1946-1948	
Sandy Saddler	USA	1948-1949	
Willie Pep	USA	1949-1950	
Sandy Saddler*	USA	1950-1957	
Hogan Kid Bassey	Nigeria	1957-1959	
Davey Moore	USA	1959-1963	
Sugar Ramos	Cuba	1963-1964	
Vicente Saldivar*	Mexico	1964-1967	
Raul Rojas	USA	1967-1968	WBA
Howard Winstone	Wales	1968	WBC
Jose Legra	Cuba	1968-1969	WBC
Shozo Saijyo	Japan	1968-1971	WBA
Johnny Famechon	France	1969-1970	WBC
Vicente Saldivar	Mexico	1970	WBC
Kuniaki Shibata	Japan	1970-1972	WBC
Antonio Gomez	Venezuela	1971-1972	WBA
Clemente Sanchez	Mexico	1972	WBC
Ernesto Marcel*	Panama	1972-1974	WBA
Jose Legra	Cuba	1972-1973	WBC
Eder Jofre	Brazil	1973-1974	WBC
Ruben Olivares	Mexico	1974	WBA
Bobby Chacon	USA	1974-1975	WBC
Alexis Arguello*	Nicaragua	1974-1977	WBA
Ruben Olivares	Mexico	1975	WBC
David Kotey	Ghana	1975-1976	WBC
Danny Lopez	USA	1976-1980	WBC
Rafael Ortega	Panama	1977	WBA
Cecilio Lastra	Spain	1977-1978	WBA
Eusebio Pedroza	Panama	1978-1985	WBA
Salvador Sanchez*	Mexico	1980-1982	WBC
Juan Laporte	Puerto Rico	1982-1984	WBC
Min-Keun Chung	S Korea	1984-1985	IBF
Wilfredo Gomez	Puerto Rico	1984	WBC
Azumah Nelson*	Ghana	1984-1987	WBC
Barry McGuigan	Ireland	1985-1986	WBA
Ki-Yung Chung	S Korea	1985-1986	IBF
Steve Cruz	USA	1986-1987	WBA
Antonio Rivera	Puerto Rico	1986-1987	IBF
Antonio Esparragoza	Venezuela	1987-1991	WBF
Calvin Grove	USA	1988	IBF
Jeff Fenech*	Australia	1988-1989	WBC
Jorge Paez	Mexico	1988-1990	IBF
Maurizio Stecca	Italy	1989-1992	WBO
Louie Espinosa	USA	1989-1990	WBO
Jorge Paez*	Mexico	1990-1991	IBF/WBO
Marcos Villasana	Mexico	1990-1991	WBC
Kyun-Yung Park	S Korea	1991-1993	WBA
Troy Dorsey	USA	1991	IBF
Maurizio Stecca	Italy	1991-1992	WBO
Manuel Medina	Mexico	1991-1993	IBF
Paul Hodkinson	England	1991-1993	WBC
Colin McMillan	England	1992	WBO
Ruben Palacio	Colombia	1992-1993	WBO
Tom Johnson	USA	1993-	IBF
Steve Robinson	Wales	1993-	WBO
Gregorio Vargas	Mexico	1993	WBC
Kevin Kelley	USA	1993-1995	WBC
Eloy Rojas	Venezuela	1993-	WBA
Alejandro Gonzalez	Mexico	1995-	WBC

S. Featherweight (130 lbs)

Title Holder	Birthplace	Tenure	Status
Johnny Dundee	Italy	1921-1923	NY
Jack Bernstein	USA	1923	NBA/NY

Title Holder	Birthplace	Tenure	Status
Johnny Dundee	Italy	1923-1924	NBA/NY
Kid Sullivan	USA	1924-1925	NBA/NY
Mike Ballerino	USA	1925	NBA/NY
Tod Morgan	USA	1925-1929	NBA/NY
Benny Bass	Russia	1929	NBA/NY
Benny Bass	Russia	1929-1931	NBA
Kid Chocolate	Cuba	1931-1933	NBA
Frankie Klick*	USA	1933-1934	NBA
Sandy Saddler*	USA	1949-1950	OHIO
Harold Gomes	USA	1959-1960	
Flash Elorde	Philippines	1960-1967	NBA
Yoshiaki Numata	Japan	1967	WBA
Hiroshi Kobayashi	Japan	1967-1971	WBA
Rene Barrientos	Philippines	1969-1970	WBC
Yoshiaki Numata	Japan	1970-1971	WBC
Alfredo Arredondo	Mexico 1971-1974		WBC
Ricardo Arredondo	Mexico	1971-1974	WBC
Ben Villaflor	Philippines	1972-1973	WBA
Kuniaki Shibata	Japan	1973	WBA
Ben Villaflor	Philippines	1973-1976	WBA
Kuniaki Shibata	Japan	1974-1975	WBA
Alfredo Escalera	Puerto Rico	1975-1978	WBC
Sam Serrano	Puerto Rico	1976-1980	WBA
Alexis Arguello*	Nicaragua	1978-1980	WBC
Yasutsune Uehara	Japan	1980-1981	WBA
Rafael Limon	Mexico	1980-1981	WBC
Cornelius Boza-Edwards	Uganda	1981	WBC
Sam Serrano	Puerto Rico	1981-1983	WBA
Roland Navarrete	Philippines	1981-1982	WBC
Rafael Limon	Mexico	1982	WBC
Bobby Chacon	USA	1982-1983	WBC
Roger Mayweather	USA	1983-1984	WBA
Hector Camacho*	Puerto Rico	1983-1984	WBC
Rocky Lockridge	USA	1984-1985	WBA
Hwan-Kil Yuh	S Korea	1984-1985	IBF
Julio Cesar Chavez*	Mexico	1984-1987	WBC
Lester Ellis	England	1985	IBF
Wilfredo Gomez	Puerto Rico	1985-1986	WBA
Barry Michael	England	1985-1987	IBF
Alfredo Layne	Panama	1986	WBA
Brian Mitchell*	S Africa	1986-1991	WBA
Rocky Lockridge	USA	1987-1988	IBF
Azumah Nelson	Ghana	1988-1994	WBC
Tony Lopez	USA	1988-1989	IBF
Juan Molina*	Puerto Rico	1989	WBO
Juan Molina	Puerto Rico	1989-1990	IBF
Kamel Bou Ali	Tunisia	1989-1992	WBO
Tony Lopez	USA	1990-1991	IBF
Joey Gamache*	USA	1991	WBA
Brian Mitchell*	S Africa	1991-1992	IBF
Genaro Hernandez	USA	1991-	WBA
Juan Molina*	Puerto Rico	1992-1995	IBF
Daniel Londas	France	1992	WBO
Jimmy Bredahl	Denmark	1992-1994	WBO
Oscar de la Hoya*	USA	1994	WBO
James Leija	USA	1994	WBC
Gabriel Ruelas	USA	1994-	WBC
Regilio Tuur	Holland	1994-	WBO
Eddie Hopson	USA	1995-	IBF

Lightweight (135 lbs)

Title Holder	Birthplace	Tenure	Status
George Lavigne	USA	1896-1899	
Frank Erne	Switzerland	1899-1902	
Joe Gans	USA	1902-1904	
Jimmy Britt	USA	1904-1905	
Battling Nelson	Denmark	1905-1906	
Joe Gans	USA	1906-1908	
Battling Nelson	Denmark	1908-1910	
Ad Wolgast	USA	1910-1912	
Willie Ritchie	USA	1912	
Freddie Welsh	Wales	1912-1914	GB

Title Holder	Birthplace	Tenure	Status
Willie Ritchie	USA	1912-1914	USA
Freddie Welsh	Wales	1914-1917	
Benny Leonard*	USA	1917-1925	
Jimmy Goodrich	USA	1925	NY
Rocky Kansas	USA	1925-1926	
Sammy Mandell	USA	1926-1930	
Al Singer	USA	1930	
Tony Canzoneri	USA	1930-1933	
Barney Ross*	USA	1933-1935	
Tony Canzeroni	USA	1935-1936	
Lou Ambers	USA	1936-1938	
Henry Armstrong	USA	1938-1939	
Lou Ambers	USA	1939-1940	
Sammy Angott	USA	1940-1941	NBA
Lew Jenkins	USA	1940-1941	NY
Sammy Angott*	USA	1941-1942	
Beau Jack	USA	1942-1943	NY
Slugger White	USA	1943	MARY
Bob Montgomery	USA	1943	NY
Sammy Angott	USA	1943-1944	NBA
Beau Jack	USA	1943-1944	NY
Bob Montgomery	USA	1944-1947	NY
Juan Zurita	Mexico	1944-1945	NBA
Ike Williams	USA	1945-1947	NBA
Ike Williams	USA	1947-1951	
Jimmy Carter	USA	1951-1952	
Lauro Salas	Mexico	1952	
Jimmy Carter	USA	1952-1954	
Paddy de Marco	USA	1954	
Jimmy Carter	USA	1954-1955	
Wallace Bud Smith	USA	1955-1956	
Joe Brown	USA	1956-1962	
Carlos Ortiz	Puerto Rico	1962-1965	
Ismael Laguna	Panama	1965	
Carlos Ortiz	Puerto Rico	1965-1968	
Carlos Teo Cruz	Dom Republic	1968-1969	
Mando Ramos	USA	1969-1970	
Ismael Laguna	Panama	1970	
Ken Buchanan	Scotland	1970-1971	
Ken Buchanan	Scotland	1971-1972	WBA
Pedro Carrasco	Spain	1971-1972	WBC
Mando Ramos	USA	1972	WBC
Roberto Duran	Panama	1972-1978	WBA
Chango Carmona	Mexico	1972	WBC
Rodolfo Gonzalez	Mexico	1972-1974	WBC
Guts Ishimatsu	Japan	1974-1976	WBC
Esteban de Jesus	Puerto Rico	1976-1978	WBC
Roberto Duran*	Panama	1978-1979	
Jim Watt	Scotland	1979-1981	WBC
Ernesto Espana	Venezuela	1979-1980	WBA
Hilmer Kenty	USA	1980-1981	WBA
Sean O'Grady	USA	1981	WBA
Alexis Arguello*	Nicaragua	1981-1983	WBC
Claude Noel	Trinidad	1981	WBA
Arturo Frias	USA	1981-1982	WBA
Ray Mancini	USA	1982-1984	WBA
Edwin Rosario	Puerto Rico	1983-1984	WBC
Charlie Brown	USA	1984	IBF
Harry Arroyo	USA	1984-1985	IBF
Livingstone Bramble	USA	1984-1986	WBA
Jose Luis Ramirez	Mexico	1984-1985	WBC
Jimmy Paul	USA	1985-1986	IBF
Hector Camacho*	Puerto Rico	1985-1987	WBC
Edwin Rosario	Puerto Rico	1986-1987	WBA
Greg Haugen	USA	1986-1987	IBF
Vinnie Pazienza	USA	1987-1988	IBF
Jose Luis Ramirez	Mexico	1987-1988	WBC
Julio Cesar Chavez	Mexico	1987-1988	WBA
Greg Haugen	USA	1988-1989	IBF
Julio Cesar Chavez*	Mexico	1988-1989	WBA/WBC
Maurizio Aceves	Mexico	1989-1990	WBO

Title Holder	Birthplace	Tenure	Status
Pernell Whitaker	USA	1989	IBF
Edwin Rosario	Puerto Rico	1989-1990	WBA
Pernell Whitaker	USA	1989-1990	IBF/WBC
Juan Nazario	Puerto Rico	1990	WBA
Pernell Whitaker*	USA	1990-1992	IBF/WBC/WBA
Dingaan Thobela*	S Africa	1990-1992	WBO
Joey Gamache	USA	1992	WBA
Giovanni Parisi*	Italy	1992-1994	WBO
Tony Lopez	USA	1992-1993	WBA
Miguel Gonzalez	Mexico	1992-	WBC
Fred Pendleton	USA	1993-1994	IBF
Dingaan Thobela	S Africa	1993	WBA
Orzubek Nazarov	Russia	1993-	WBA
Rafael Ruelas	USA	1994-	IBF
Oscar de la Hoya	USA	1994-	WBO

L. Welterweight (140 lbs)

Title Holder	Birthplace	Tenure	Status
Mushy Callahan	USA	1926-1929	NBA/NY
Mushy Callahan	USA	1929-1930	NBA
Jackie Kid Berg	England	1930-1931	NBA
Tony Canzoneri	USA	1931-1932	NBA
Johnny Jadick	USA	1932	NBA
Johnny Jadick	USA	1932-1933	PEN
Battling Shaw	Mexico	1933	LOUIS
Tony Canzoneri	USA	1933	LOUIS
Barney Ross*	USA	1933-1935	ILL
Maxie Berger	Canada	1939	CAN
Harry Weekly	USA	1940-1942	LOUIS
Tippy Larkin*	USA	1946-1947	MASS/NY
Carlos Oritz	Puerto Rico	1959-1960	NBA
Duilio Loi	Italy	1960-1962	NBA
Eddie Perkins	USA	1962	NBA
Duilio Loi*	Italy	1962-1963	NBA
Roberto Cruz	Philippines	1963	WBA
Eddie Perkins	USA	1963-1965	WBA
Carlos Hernandez	Venezuela	1965-1966	WBA
Sandro Lopopolo	Italy	1966-1967	WBA
Paul Fujii	Hawaii	1967-1968	WBA
Nicolino Loche	Argentine	1968-1972	WBA
Pedro Adigue	Philippines	1968-1970	WBC
Bruno Arcari*	Italy	1970-1974	WBC
Alfonso Frazer	Panama	1972	WBA
Antonio Cervantes	Colombia	1972-1976	WBA
Perico Fernandez	Spain	1974-1975	WBC
Saensak Muangsurin	Thailand	1975-1976	WBC
Wilfred Benitez	USA	1976	WBA
Miguel Velasquez	Spain	1976	WBC
Saensak Muangsurin	Thailand	1976-1978	WBC
Antonio Cervantes	Colombia	1977-1980	WBA
Wilfred Benitez*	USA	1977	NY
Sang-Hyun Kim	S Korea	1978-1980	WBC
Saoul Mamby	USA	1980-1982	WBC
Aaron Pryor*	USA	1980-1983	WBA
Leroy Haley	USA	1982-1983	WBC
Bruce Curry	USA	1983-1984	WBC
Johnny Bumphus	USA	1984	WBA
Bill Costello	USA	1984-1985	WBC
Gene Hatcher	USA	1984-1985	IBF
Aaron Pryor	USA	1984-1985	IBF
Ubaldo Sacco	Argentine	1985-1986	WBA
Lonnie Smith	USA	1985-1986	WBC
Patrizio Oliva	Italy	1986-1987	WBA
Gary Hinton	USA	1986	IBF
Rene Arredondo	Mexico	1986	WBC
Tsuyoshi Hamada	Japan	1986-1987	WBC
Joe Manley	USA	1986-1987	IBF
Terry Marsh*	England	1987	IBF
Juan M. Coggi	Argentine	1987-1990	WBA
Rene Arredondo	Mexico	1987	WBC
Roger Mayweather	USA	1987-1989	WBC
James McGirt	USA	1988	IBF

Title Holder	Birthplace	Tenure	Status
Meldrick Taylor	USA	1988-1990	IBF
Hector Camacho	Puerto Rico	1989-1991	WBO
Julio Cesar Chavez	Mexico	1989-1990	WBC
Julio Cesar Chavez	Mexico	1990-1991	IBF/WBC
Loreto Garza	USA	1990-1991	WBA
Greg Haugen	USA	1991	WBO
Hector Camacho*	Puerto Rico	1991-1992	WBO
Edwin Rosario	Puerto Rico	1991-1992	WBA
Julio Cesar Chavez	Mexico	1991-1994	WBC
Rafael Pineda	Colombia	1991-1992	IBF
Akinobu Hiranaka	Japan	1992	WBA
Carlos Gonzalez	Mexico	1992-1993	WBO
Pernell Whitaker*	USA	1992-1993	IBF
Morris East	Philippines	1992-1993	WBA
Juan M. Coggi	Argentine	1993-1994	WBA
Charles Murray	USA	1993-1994	IBF
Zack Padilla*	USA	1993-1994	WBO
Jake Rodriguez	USA	1994-1995	IBF
Frankie Randall	USA	1994	WBC
Julio Cesar Chavez	Mexico	1994-	WBC
Frankie Randall	USA	1994-	WBA
Konstantin Tszyu	Russia	1995-	IBF
Sammy Fuentes	Puerto Rico	1995-	WBO

Welterweight (147 lbs)

Title Holder	Birthplace	Tenure	Status
Tommy Ryan*	USA	1894-1898	
Mysterious Billy Smith	USA	1898-1900	
Matty Matthews	USA	1900-1901	
Eddie Connolly	USA	1900	
Rube Ferns	USA	1900	
Matty Matthews	USA	1900-1901	
Joe Walcott	Barbados	1901-1906	
Honey Mellody	USA	1906-1907	
Harry Lewis	USA	1910-1912	GB/FR
Jimmy Clabby	USA	1910-1912	AUSTR
Matt Wells	England	1914-1915	AUSTR
Ted Kid Lewis	England	1915-1916	
Jack Britton	USA	1916-1917	
Ted Kid Lewis	England	1917-1919	
Jack Britton	USA	1919-1922	
Mickey Walker	USA	1922-1923	
Mickey Walker	USA	1923-1925	NBA
Dave Shade	USA	1923	NY
Jimmy Jones	USA	1923	NY/MASS
Mickey Walker	USA	1925-1926	
Pete Latzo	USA	1926-1927	
Joe Dundee	Italy	1927-1929	
Joe Dundee	Italy	1929	NY
Jackie Fields	USA	1929	NBA
Jackie Fields	USA	1929-1930	
Young Jack Thompson	USA	1930	
Tommy Freeman	USA	1930-1931	
Young Jack Thompson	USA	1931	
Lou Brouillard	Canada	1931-1932	
Jackie Fields	USA	1932-1933	
Young Corbett III	Italy	1933	
Jimmy McLarnin	Ireland	1933-1934	
Barney Ross	USA	1934	
Jimmy McLarnin	Ireland	1934-1935	
Barney Ross	USA	1935-1938	
Barney Ross	USA	1938	NY/NBA
Felix Wouters	Belgium	1938	IBU
Henry Armstrong	USA	1938-1940	
Fritzie Zivic	USA	1940-1941	
Fritzie Zivic	USA	1940-1941	NY/NBA
Izzy Jannazzo	USA	1940-1941	MARY
Red Cochrane	USA	1941	NY/NBA
Red Cochrane	USA	1941-1946	
Marty Servo	USA	1946	
Sugar Ray Robinson*	USA	1946-1951	
Johnny Bratton	USA	1951	NBA

Title Holder	Birthplace	Tenure	Status
Kid Gavilan	Cuba	1951-1952	NBA/NY
Kid Gavilan	Cuba	1952-1954	
Johnny Saxton	USA	1954-1955	
Tony de Marco	USA	1955	
Carmen Basilio	USA	1955-1956	
Johnny Saxton	USA	1956	
Carmen Basilio*	USA	1956-1957	
Virgil Akins	USA	1957-1958	MASS
Virgil Akins	USA	1958	
Don Jordan	Dom Republic	1958-1960	
Benny Kid Paret	Cuba	1960-1961	
Emile Griffith	Virgin Islands	1961	
Benny Kid Paret	Cuba	1961-1962	
Emile Griffith	Virgin Islands	1962-1963	
Luis Rodriguez	Cuba	1963	
Emile Griffith*	Virgin Islands	1963-1966	
Willie Ludick	S Africa	1966-1968	SA
Curtis Cokes	USA	1966-1968	WBA/WBC
Curtis Cokes	USA	1966-1967	WBA
Charley Shipes	USA	1966-1967	CALIF
Curtis Cokes	USA	1968-1969	
Jose Napoles	Cuba	1969-1970	
Billy Backus	USA	1970-1971	
Jose Napoles	Cuba	1971-1975	
Jose Napoles	Cuba	1972-1974	WBA/WBC
Hedgemon Lewis	USA	1972-1974	NY
Jose Napoles	Cuba	1974-1975	
Jose Napoles	Cuba	1975	WBC
Angel Espada	Puerto Rico	1975-1976	WBA
John H. Stracey	England	1975-1976	WBC
Carlos Palomino	Mexico	1976-1979	WBC
Pipino Cuevas	Mexico	1976-1980	WBA
Wilfred Benitez	USA	1979	WBC
Sugar Ray Leonard	USA	1979-1980	WBC
Roberto Duran	Panama	1980	WBC
Thomas Hearns	USA	1980-1981	WBA
Sugar Ray Leonard	USA	1980-1981	WBC
Sugar Ray Leonard*	USA	1981-1982	
Don Curry	USA	1983-1984	WBA
Milton McCrory	USA	1983-1985	WBC
Don Curry	USA	1984-1985	WBA/IBF
Don Curry	USA	1985-1986	
Lloyd Honeyghan	Jamaica	1986	
Lloyd Honeyghan	Jamaica	1986-1987	WBC/IBF
Mark Breland	USA	1987	WBA
Marlon Starling	USA	1987-1988	WBA
Jorge Vaca	Mexico	1987-1988	WBC
Lloyd Honeyghan	Jamaica	1988-1989	WBC
Simon Brown	Jamaica	1988-1991	IBF
Tomas Molinares	Colombia	1988	WBA
Mark Breland	USA	1989-1990	WBA
Marlon Starling	USA	1989-1990	WBC
Genaro Leon*	Mexico	1989	WBO
Manning Galloway	USA	1989-1993	WBO
Aaron Davis	USA	1990-1991	WBA
Maurice Blocker	USA	1990	WBC
Meldrick Taylor	USA	1991-1992	WBA
Simon Brown	Jamaica	1991	WBC/IBF
Simon Brown	Jamaica	1991	
Maurice Blocker	USA	1991-1993	IBF
James McGirt	USA	1991-1993	WBC
Crisanto Espana	Venezuela	1992-1994	WBA
Gert Bo Jacobsen*	Denmark	1993	WBO
Pernell Whitaker	USA	1993-	WBC
Felix Trinidad	Puerto Rico	1993-	IBF
Eamonn Loughran	Ireland	1993-	WBO
Ike Quartey	Ghana	1994-	WBA

L. Middleweight (154 lbs)

Title Holder	Birthplace	Tenure	Status
Emile Griffith*	USA	1962-1963	AU
Denny Moyer	USA	1962-1963	WBA

Title Holder	Birthplace	Tenure	Status
Ralph Dupas	USA	1963	WBA
Sandro Mazzinghi	Italy	1963-1965	WBA
Nino Benvenuti	Italy	1965-1966	WBA
Ki-Soo Kim	S Korea	1966-1968	WBA
Sandro Mazzinghi	Italy	1968-1969	WBA
Freddie Little	USA	1969-1970	WBA
Carmelo Bossi	Italy	1970-1971	WBA
Koichi Wajima	Japan	1971-1974	WBA
Oscar Albarado	USA	1974-1975	WBA
Koichi Wajima	Japan	1975	WBA
Miguel de Oliveira	Brazil	1975	WBC
Jae-Do Yuh	S Korea	1975-1976	WBA
Elisha Obed	Bahamas	1975-1976	WBC
Koichi Wajima	Japan	1976	WBA
Jose Duran	Spain	1976	WBA
Eckhard Dagge	Germany	1976-1977	WBC
Miguel Castellini	Argentine	1976-1977	WBA
Eddie Gazo	Nicaragua	1977-1978	WBA
Rocky Mattioli	Italy	1977-1979	WBC
Masashi Kudo	Japan	1978-1979	WBA
Maurice Hope	Antigua	1979-1981	WBC
Ayub Kalule	Uganda	1979-1981	WBA
Wilfred Benitez	USA	1981-1982	WBC
Sugar Ray Leonard*	USA	1981	WBA
Tadashi Mihara	Japan	1981-1982	WBA
Davey Moore	USA	1982-1983	WBA
Thomas Hearns*	USA	1982-1986	WBC
Roberto Duran*	Panama	1983-1984	WBA
Mark Medal	USA	1984	IBF
Mike McCallum*	Jamaica	1984-1987	WBA
Carlos Santos	Puerto Rico	1984-1986	IBF
Buster Drayton	USA	1986-1987	IBF
Duane Thomas	USA	1986-1987	WBC
Matthew Hilton	Canada	1987-1988	IBF
Lupe Aquino	Mexico	1987	WBC
Gianfranco Rosi	Italy	1987-1988	WBC
Julian Jackson*	Virgin Islands	1987-1990	WBA
Don Curry	USA	1988-1989	WBC
Robert Hines	USA	1988-1989	IBF
John David Jackson*	USA	1988-1993	WBO
Darrin van Horn	USA	1989	IBF
Rene Jacqot	France	1989	WBC
John Mugabi	Uganda	1989-1990	WBC
Gianfranco Rosi	Italy	1989-1994	IBF
Terry Norris	USA	1990-1993	WBC
Gilbert Dele	France	1991	WBA
Vinnie Pazienza*	USA	1991-1992	WBA
Julio Cesar Vasquez	Argentine	1992-1995	WBA
Verno Phillips	USA	1993-1995	WBO
Simon Brown	USA	1993-1994	WBC
Terry Norris	USA	1994	WBC
Vince Pettway	USA	1994-	IBF
Luis Santana	Dom Republic	1994-	WBC
Pernell Whitaker*	USA	1995	WBA
Gianfranco Rosi	Italy	1995	WBO
Carl Daniels	USA	1995-	WBA

Middleweight (160 lbs)

Title Holder	Birthplace	Tenure	Status
Bob Fitzsimmons*	England	1891-1897	
Kid McCoy*	USA	1897-1898	
Tommy Ryan*	USA	1898-1907	
Stanley Ketchel	USA	1908	
Billy Papke	USA	1908	
Stanley Ketchel*	USA	1908-1910	
Billy Papke	USA	1911-1912	GB
Georges Carpentier	France	1912	IBU
Billy Papke	USA	1912-1913	IBU
Frank Klaus	USA	1913	IBU
George Chip	USA	1913-1914	USA
Eddie McGoorty	USA	1914	AUSTR
Jeff Smith	USA	1914	AUSTR
Al McCoy	USA	1914-1917	USA
Mick King	Australia	1914	AUSTR
Jeff Smith	USA	1914-1915	AUSTR
Les Darcy*	Australia	1915-1917	AUSTR
Mike O'Dowd	USA	1917-1920	
Johnny Wilson	USA	1920-1922	
Johnny Wilson	USA	1922-1923	NBA
Bryan Downey	USA	1922	OHIO
Dave Rosenberg	USA	1922	NY
Jock Malone	USA	1922-1923	OHIO
Mike O'Dowd	USA	1922-1923	NY
Harry Greb	USA	1923-1926	
Tiger Flowers	USA	1926	
Mickey Walker*	USA	1926-1931	
Gorilla Jones	USA	1931-1932	NBA
Marcel Thil	France	1932-1937	IBU
Ben Jeby	USA	1933	NY
Lou Brouillard	Canada	1933	NY/NBA
Teddy Yarosz	USA	1933-1934	PENN
Vince Dundee	USA	1933-1934	NY/NBA
Teddy Yarosz	USA	1934-1935	NY/NBA
Babe Risko	USA	1935-1936	NY/NBA
Freddie Steele	USA	1936-1938	NY/NBA
Freddie Steele	USA	1938	NBA
Fred Apostoli	USA	1937-1938	IBU
Fred Apostoli	USA	1937-1939	NY
Edouard Tenet	France	1938	IBU
Al Hostak	USA	1938	NBA
Solly Krieger	USA	1938-1939	NBA
Al Hostak	USA	1939-1940	NBA
Ceferino Garcia	Philippines	1939-1940	NY
Ken Overlin	USA	1940-1941	NY
Tony Zale	USA	1940-1941	NBA
Billy Soose	USA	1941	NY
Tony Zale	USA	1941-1947	
Rocky Graziano	USA	1947-1948	
Tony Zale	USA	1948	
Marcel Cerdan	Algeria	1948-1949	
Jake la Motta	USA	1949-1950	
Jake la Motta	USA	1950-1951	NY/NBA
Sugar Ray Robinson	USA	1950-1951	PEN
Sugar Ray Robinson	USA	1951	
Randy Turpin	England	1951	
Sugar Ray Robinson*	USA	1951-1952	
Randy Turpin	England	1953	EBU
Carl Bobo Olson	Hawaii	1953-1955	
Sugar Ray Robinson	USA	1955-1957	
Gene Fullmer	USA	1957	
Sugar Ray Robinson	USA	1957	
Carmen Basilio	USA	1957-1958	
Sugar Ray Robinson	USA	1958-1959	
Sugar Ray Robinson	USA	1959-1960	NY/EBU
Gene Fullmer	USA	1959-1962	NBA
Paul Pender	USA	1960-1961	NY/EBU
Terry Downes	England	1961-1962	NY/EBU
Paul Pender	USA	1962-1963	NY/EBU
Dick Tiger	Nigeria	1962-1963	NBA
Dick Tiger	Nigeria	1963	
Joey Giardello	USA	1963-1965	
Dick Tiger	Nigeria	1965-1966	
Emile Griffith	Virgin Islands	1966-1967	
Nino Benvenuti	Italy	1967	
Emile Griffith	Virgin Islands	1967-1968	
Nino Benvenuti	Italy	1968-1970	
Carlos Monzon	Argentine	1970-1974	
Carlos Monzon	Argentine	1974-1976	WBA
Rodrigo Valdez	Colombia	1974-1976	WBC
Carlos Monzon	Argentine	1976-1977	
Carlos Monzon*	Argentine	1977	WBA
Rodrigo Valdez	Colombia	1977-1978	
Hugo Corro	Argentine	1978-1979	

Title Holder	Birthplace	Tenure	Status
Vito Antuofermo	Italy	1979-1980	
Alan Minter	England	1980	
Marvin Hagler	USA	1980-1987	
Marvin Hagler	USA	1987	WBC/IBF
Sugar Ray Leonard	USA	1987	WBC
Frank Tate	USA	1987-1988	IBF
Sumbu Kalambay	Zaire	1987-1989	WBA
Thomas Hearns	USA	1987-1988	WBC
Iran Barkley	USA	1988-1989	WBC
Michael Nunn	USA	1988-1991	IBF
Roberto Duran	Panama	1989-1990	WBC
Doug de Witt	USA	1989-1990	WBO
Mike McCallum	Jamaica	1989-1991	WBA
Nigel Benn	England	1990	WBO
Chris Eubank*	England	1990-1991	WBO
Julian Jackson	Virgin Islands	1990-1993	WBC
James Toney*	USA	1991-1993	IBF
Gerald McClellan*	USA	1991-1993	WBC
Reggie Johnson	USA	1992-1993	WBA
Gerald McClellan*	USA	1993-1995	WBC
Chris Pyatt	England	1993-1994	WBO
Roy Jones*	USA	1993-1994	IBF
John David Jackson	USA	1993-1994	WBA
Steve Collins*	Ireland	1994-1995	WBO
Jorge Castro	Argentine	1994-	WBA
Julian Jackson	Virgin Islands	1995-	WBC
Bernard Hopkins	USA	1995-	IBF
Lonnie Bradley	USA	1995-	WBO

Nigel Benn (left) and the ill-fated Gerald McClellan pose before their epic super-middleweight title fight   Les Clark

S. Middleweight (168 lbs)

Title Holder	Birthplace	Tenure	Status
Murray Sutherland	Scotland	1984	IBF
Chong-Pal Park*	S Korea	1984-1987	IBF
Chong-Pal Park	S Korea	1987-1988	WBA
Graciano Rocchigiani*	Germany	1988-1989	IBF
Fully Obelmejias	Venezuela	1988-1989	WBA
Sugar Ray Leonard*	USA	1988-1990	WBC
Thomas Hearns*	USA	1988-1991	WBO
In-Chul Baek	S Korea	1989-1990	WBA

Title Holder	Birthplace	Tenure	Status
Lindell Holmes	USA	1990-1991	IBF
Christophe Tiozzo	France	1990-1991	WBA
Mauro Galvano	Italy	1990-1992	WBC
Victor Cordoba	Panama	1991-1992	WBA
Darrin van Horn	USA	1991-1992	IBF
Chris Eubank	England	1991-1995	WBO
Iran Barkley	USA	1992-1993	IBF
Michael Nunn	USA	1992-1994	WBA
Nigel Benn	England	1992	WBC
James Toney	USA	1993-1994	IBF
Steve Little	USA	1994	WBA
Frank Lilles	USA	1994-	WBA
Roy Jones	USA	1994-	IBF
Steve Collins	Ireland	1995-	WBO

L. Heavyweight (175 lbs)

Title Holder	Birthplace	Tenure	Status
Jack Root	Austria	1903	USA
George Gardner	Ireland	1903	USA
Bob Fitzsimmons	England	1903-1905	USA
Jack Dillon	USA	1912-1916	USA
Battling Levinsky	USA	1916-1920	USA
Georges Carpentier	France	1920-1922	
Battling Siki	Senegal	1922-1923	
Mike McTigue	Ireland	1923-1925	
Paul Berlenbach	USA	1925-1926	
Jack Delaney*	Canada	1926-1927	
Jimmy Slattery	USA	1927	NBA
Tommy Loughran	USA	1927	NY
Tommy Loughran*	USA	1927-1929	
Jimmy Slattery	USA	1930	NY
Maxie Rosenbloom	USA	1930-1931	
Maxie Rosenbloom	USA	1931-1933	NY
George Nichols	USA	1932	NBA
Bob Godwin	USA	1933	NBA
Maxie Rosenbloom	USA	1933-1934	
Bob Olin	USA	1934-1935	
Al McCoy	Canada	1935	CAN
Bob Olin	USA	1935	NY/NBA
John Henry Lewis	USA	1935-1938	NY/NBA
Hein Lazek	Austria	1935-1936	IBU
Gustav Roth	Belgium	1936-1938	IBU
Ad Heuser	Germany	1938	IBU
John Henry Lewis*	USA	1938	
Melio Bettina	USA	1939	NY
Len Harvey	England	1939-1942	GB
Billy Conn	USA	1939-1940	NY/NBA
Anton Christoforidis	Greece	1941	NBA
Gus Lesnevich	USA	1941-1946	NY/NBA
Freddie Mills	England	1942-1946	GB
Gus Lesnevich	USA	1946-1948	
Freddie Mills	England	1948-1950	
Joey Maxim	USA	1950-1952	
Archie Moore	USA	1952-1960	
Archie Moore	USA	1960-1962	NY/EBU
Harold Johnson	USA	1961-1962	NBA
Harold Johnson	USA	1962-1963	
Willie Pastrano	USA	1963-1965	
Jose Torres	Puerto Rico	1965-1966	
Dick Tiger	Nigeria	1966-1968	
Bob Foster	USA	1968-1971	
Bob Foster	USA	1971-1972	WBC
Vicente Rondon	Venezuela	1971-1972	WBA
Bob Foster*	USA	1972-1974	
John Conteh	England	1974-1977	WBC
Victor Galindez	Argentine	1974-1978	WBA
Miguel Cuello	Argentine	1977-1978	WBC
Mate Parlov	Yugoslavia	1978	WBC
Mike Rossman	USA	1978-1979	WBA
Marvin Johnson	USA	1978-1979	WBC
Victor Galindez	Argentine	1979	WBA
Matt Saad Muhammad	USA	1979-1981	WBC

Title Holder	Birthplace	Tenure	Status
Marvin Johnson	USA	1979-1980	WBA
Mustafa Muhammad	USA	1980-1981	WBA
Michael Spinks	USA	1981-1983	WBA
Dwight Muhammad Qawi	USA	1981-1983	WBC
Michael Spinks*	USA	1983-1985	
J. B. Williamson	USA	1985-1986	WBC
Slobodan Kacar	Yugoslavia	1985-1986	IBF
Marvin Johnson	USA	1986-1987	WBA
Dennis Andries	Guyana	1986-1987	WBC
Bobby Czyz	USA	1986-1987	IBF
Thomas Hearns*	USA	1987	WBC
Leslie Stewart	Trinidad	1987	WBA
Virgil Hill	USA	1987-1991	WBA
Charles Williams	USA	1987-1993	IBF
Don Lalonde	Canada	1987-1988	WBC
Sugar Ray Leonard*	USA	1988	WBC
Michael Moorer*	USA	1988-1991	WBO
Dennis Andries	Guyana	1989	WBC
Jeff Harding	Australia	1989-1990	WBC
Dennis Andries	England	1990-1991	WBC
Thomas Hearns	USA	1991-1992	WBA
Leonzer Barber	USA	1991-1994	WBO
Jeff Harding	Australia	1991-1994	WBC
Iran Barkley*	USA	1992	WBA
Virgil Hill	USA	1992-	WBA
Henry Maske	Germany	1993-	IBF
Mike McCallum	Jamaica	1994-1995	WBC
Dariusz Michalczewski	Germany	1994-	WBO
Fabrice Tiozzo	France	1995-	WBC

Cruiserweight (190 lbs)

Title Holder	Birthplace	Tenure	Status
Marvin Camel	USA	1979-1980	WBC
Carlos de Leon	Puerto Rico	1980-1982	WBC
Ossie Ocasio	Puerto Rico	1982-1984	WBA
S. T. Gordon	USA	1982-1983	WBC
Marvin Camel	USA	1983-1984	IBF
Carlos de Leon	Puerto Rico	1983-1985	WBC
Lee Roy Murphy	USA	1984-1986	IBF
Piet Crous	S Africa	1984-1985	WBA
Alfonso Ratliff	USA	1985	WBC
Dwight Muhammad Qawi	USA	1985-1986	WBA
Bernard Benton	USA	1985-1986	WBC
Carlos de Leon	Puerto Rico	1986-1988	WBC
Rickey Parkey	USA	1986-1987	IBF
Evander Holyfield	USA	1986-1987	WBA
Evander Holyfield	USA	1987-1988	WBA/IBF
Evander Holyfield*	USA	1988	
Taoufik Belbouli*	France	1989	WBA
Carlos de Leon	Puerto Rico	1989-1990	WBC
Glenn McCrory	England	1989-1990	IBF
Robert Daniels	USA	1989-1991	WBA
Boone Pultz	USA	1989-1990	WBO
Jeff Lampkin*	USA	1990-1991	IBF
Magne Havnaa*	Norway	1990-1992	WBO
Masimilliano Duran	Italy	1990-1991	WBC
Bobby Czyz	USA	1991-1993	WBA
Anaclet Wamba	France	1991-	WBC
James Warring	USA	1991-1992	IBF
Tyrone Booze	USA	1992-1993	WBO
Al Cole	USA	1992-	IBF
Markus Bott	Germany	1993	WBO
Nestor Giovannini	Argentine	1993-1994	WBO
Orlin Norris	USA	1993-	WBA
Dariusz Michalczewski*	Germany	1994-1995	WBO
Ralf Rocchigiani	Germany	1995-	WBO

Heavyweight (190 lbs +)

Title Holder	Birthplace	Tenure	Status
James J. Corbett	USA	1892-1897	
Bob Fitzsimmons	England	1897-1899	
James J. Jeffries*	USA	1899-1905	
Marvin Hart	USA	1905-1906	

Title Holder	Birthplace	Tenure	Status
Tommy Burns	Canada	1906-1908	
Jack Johnson	USA	1908-1915	
Jess Willard	USA	1915-1919	
Jack Dempsey	USA	1919-1926	
Gene Tunney*	USA	1926-1928	
Max Schmeling	Germany	1930-1932	
Jack Sharkey	USA	1932-1933	
Primo Carnera	Italy	1933-1934	
Max Baer	USA	1934-1935	
James J. Braddock	USA	1935	
James J. Braddock	USA	1935-1936	NY/NBA
George Godfrey	USA	1935-1936	IBU
James J. Braddock	USA	1936-1937	
Joe Louis*	USA	1937-1949	
Ezzard Charles	USA	1949-1951	NBA
Lee Savold	USA	1950-1951	GB/EBU
Ezzard Charles	USA	1951	
Jersey Joe Walcott	USA	1951-1952	
Rocky Marciano*	USA	1952-1956	
Floyd Patterson	USA	1956-1959	
Ingemar Johansson	Sweden	1959-1960	
Floyd Patterson	USA	1960-1962	
Sonny Liston	USA	1962-1964	
Muhammad Ali	USA	1964-1965	
Muhammad Ali	USA	1965-1967	WBC
Ernie Terrell	USA	1965-1967	WBA
Muhammad Ali	USA	1967	
Joe Frazier	USA	1968-1970	WBC
Jimmy Ellis	USA	1968-1970	WBA
Joe Frazier	USA	1970-1973	
George Foreman	USA	1973-1974	
Muhammad Ali	USA	1974-1978	
Leon Spinks	USA	1978	
Leon Spinks	USA	1978	WBA
Larry Holmes*	USA	1978-1983	WBC
Muhammad Ali*	USA	1978-1979	WBA
John Tate	USA	1979-1980	WBA
Mike Weaver	USA	1980-1982	WBA
Michael Dokes	USA	1982-1983	WBA
Gerrie Coetzee	S Africa	1983-1984	WBA
Tim Witherspoon	USA	1984	WBC
Pinklon Thomas	USA	1984-1986	WBC
Larry Holmes	USA	1984-1985	IBF
Greg Page	USA	1984-1985	WBA
Tony Tubbs	USA	1985-1986	WBA
Michael Spinks	USA	1985-1987	IBF
Tim Witherspoon	USA	1986	WBA
Trevor Berbick	Jamaica	1986	WBC
Mike Tyson	USA	1986-1987	WBC
James Smith	USA	1986-1987	WBA
Mike Tyson	USA	1987	WBA/WBC
Tony Tucker	USA	1987	IBF
Mike Tyson	USA	1987-1989	
Mike Tyson	USA	1989-1990	IBF/WBA/WBC
Francesco Damiani	Italy	1989-1991	WBO
James Douglas	USA	1990	IBF/WBA/WBC
Evander Holyfield	USA	1990-1992	IBF/WBA/WBC
Ray Mercer	USA	1991-1992	WBO
Michael Moorer*	USA	1992-1993	WBO
Riddick Bowe	USA	1992	IBF/WBA/WBC
Riddick Bowe	USA	1992-1993	IBF/WBA
Lennox Lewis	England	1992-1994	WBC
Tommy Morrison	USA	1993	WBO
Michael Bentt	USA	1993-1994	WBO
Evander Holyfield	USA	1993-1994	WBA/IBF
Herbie Hide	England	1994-1995	WBO
Michael Moorer	USA	1994	WBA/IBF
Oliver McCall	USA	1994-	WBC
George Foreman	USA	1994-1995	WBA/IBF
Riddick Bowe	USA	1995-	WBO
George Foreman	USA	1995-	IBF
Bruce Seldon	USA	1995-	WBA

Highlights from the 1994-95 Amateur Season

by David Prior

The four international championship events produced a notable collection of 16 medals for the home nations, including four golds in the Commonwealth Games, and two more of the same hue during the more recent European U19 title event.

The 1994 Commonwealth Games in Victoria, Canada, in August 1994, saw double gold for Northern Ireland when Neil Sinclair (welterweight) and Jim Webb (light-middle) took top honours in their weight divisions. Coincidentally, their splendid efforts equalled the two titles achieved by Barry McGuigan and Gerry Hamill in 1978, also in Canada (Edmonton). The Irish triumph continued at silver, with Martin Reneghan (lightweight) and Mark Winters (light-welter).

There was gold for England too when Peter Richardson, so long at the fringe of international title status, won the light-welterweight title. He was joined by Spencer Oliver, who earned silver at bantamweight, flyweight, Danny Costello, and super-heavyweight, Danny Williams, who both won third-place medals.

Paul Shepherd became Scotland's fifth champion at the flyweight limit, following in the footsteps of Hugh Riley, Dick Currie, Jackie Brown and Bobby Mallon. In Victoria, this division produced a tripartite meeting of Damaen Kelly, Danny Costello and Shepherd - Kelly lost to Costello, who was then beaten by the Scottish gold medallist. There were two more awards for Scotland – John Wilson (light-heavyweight) in the silver category and Joe Townsley who won bronze at light-middleweight.

Jason Cook from Wales was also among the medals with silver in the featherweight division.

African countries, so long the dominating factor in the Games, had to be content with three champions (two for Kenya and one for Nigeria), Australia made title status at bantamweight, while the host country, Canada, made it to the winner's rostrum on four occasions.

Something new in the judging/scoring scenario – complaints that some of the decisions were a result of racism (instead of incompetence). And there were cries of "foul" when the round-by-round scores, shown on national television and on ringside monitors, were passed on to the corners. Officialdom may well have to take this one on board, either to somehow prevent the unofficial passage of scores, or to make public the points tally as bouts progress.

The Canadian event also marked the retirement of respected BBC television commentator, Harry Carpenter, so long an integral part of boxing – amateur and professional.

A former World Junior gold medallist, Alan Vaughan, at last realised his potential at senior level when winning the ABA light-welter title. He is seen here (left) beating Dwayne Ashley at the semi-final stage

Steve Parkin

Back in Europe, in Istanbul, Turkey (September), the gold standard for boxers from England, Ireland, Scotland and Wales again proved elusive in the World U19 championships, and there was not even silver or bronze. The Cubans, as usual, monopolised the event, having an incredible seven champions, with the remaining five top places being shared between Turkey (two), Romania, Italy and Finland (one each).

Moving on to 1995, it was the turn of the World seniors in Berlin in May and, yet again, it was a blank score-sheet for boxers from over here. So far, and since the championships began in 1974, only Ireland's Tommy Corr, Michael Carruth and Damean Kelly have won anything, all bronze medals.

By any standards to collect four gold medals in an international title event would be classed as "excellent" for most countries, but in Cuban terms it might just get a "not bad" label. In Tampere in 1993 they had eight champions; in Berlin it was four, but three of them – Hector Vinent, Ariel Hernandez and Felix Savon – were already Olympic titleholders from Barcelona. It was, in fact, heavyweight Saxon's fifth World senior title win. Other champions in Berlin came mainly from Eastern Europe – two each for Bulgaria, Romania and Russia, with Germany and the USA completing matters at one apiece.

It was better news from Siofok, Hungary, in June, when hard-punching heavyweight, Cathal O'Grady, won gold for Ireland and Scott Harrison did the same for Scotland at featherweight. It was Ireland's first title success at the event and Scotland's second (following Billy Lauder in 1976), and, for the history-minded fans, the two 1995 gold medals were the first to come across the English and Irish Channels since Errol Christie did the trick for England in 1982. Scotland's Gerald Murphy took silver at light-welterweight and Neil Linford, from England, won bronze in the light-middle division.

The 12 international team fixtures were mainly a cross-matching of the four home countries, with Denmark and the USA (versus England) and Italy and Holland (against Ireland), being the only foreign opposition. England lost to Denmark (8-4), to the USA (5-4) and, for the first time in 20 years, to Scotland (4-3), while an U19 meet against Scotland ended all square at 4-4. It was a good season for Wales with wins over Ireland (6-3) and Scotland, twice (5-3, and 4-3), although a third match saw Scotland win 6-3. Scotland lost to Ireland (6-4), while their Select team beat an Ulster Select 3-1. Ireland's programme was completed with a 6-3 loss to Italy and a 5-3 win over Holland.

The Liverpool Festival of Amateur Boxing, held for the second time, was again a huge success (108 boxers from 15 countries), with gold for England's Michael Jones and Matthew Ellis. There was also silver for England and eight bronze, and a bronze for Ireland. Scotland and Wales were absent. Russia came top (three gold medals), with two each for Ukraine, Germany and Australia, and one for Hungary.

In other international affairs, Ireland's Paul Stephens was a gold medallist in the European U16 tournament in Greece, in October. His fellow team-members, Michael Andrews and Patrick Walsh, won silver, while Michael

Dillon was a bronze medallist. From England, James Rooney (silver) and Michael Hunter (bronze) completed what was a successful international outing for the two countries.

Also in October, Paul Griffin (Ireland) won gold in the Tammer multi-national and then, in the following April/May, Jason Cook from Wales, earned a bronze medal in the Italia Cup.

Lack of finance was the reason for the cancellation of the Golden Gloves U17 tournament in Cardiff (June); it had been an extremely successful event since 1989. For the same reason the inaugural Great Britain and Ireland invitation championships, also scheduled for Cardiff in June, for boxers from Ireland, Scotland, and Wales, was called off. England had declined to take part. In Dublin the host country was once again well clear of their competitors in the Gaelic Youth championships.

Here and there, across the world, our boxing policemen took time out from fighting crime to "fight" their rivals in the World Police championships in Denver (August), and, in October, Cuba travelled to Ledyard, Connecticut to trounce the Americans 10-2, to make it 17 wins from 18. In the same month, the "Met" won comfortably against a New York Police team for the John Banham Challenge Cup.

For the future, boxing was confirmed for the 2000 Sydney Olympics, including a possible competition for the ladies, it will be ten ounce gloves for all seniors from January 1996 and 5 x 2 minute rounds for international events from January 1997. Two points (instead of three) will be now deducted for a warning in computer scored contests. On the home front (in England), discussions were held about the formation of a National Boxing League.

The new look ABA Championships (which produced nine new titleholders), again an all-England affair following the withdrawal of Scotland and Wales last season, ended for the third consecutive year at the National Indoor Arena in Birmingham on 12 April. The earlier than usual date (May) had been adopted to avoid the run-up to the World senior championships in Berlin.

The main changes involved revised pairings in the quarter-finals – London v CSBA, Southern v North-East Counties, Western v North-West Counties and the Midlands v East/Home Counties – which were drawn out of the hat and which stand for two seasons. A fresh draw will be made for 1997-98. There were also separate semi-finals at Portsmouth and Doncaster on different days and another first was the use of the computer scoring system for the semi-finals and finals.

Four of the 1994 defending champions made it to the finals, with flyweight Danny Costello (Hollington) and Kelly Oliver (Bracebridge) triumphant again. Costello stopped Delroy Spencer (Pleck) in the middle round to become a double titleholder, while Oliver set up a new post-war record by winning at light-heavyweight for the fourth time. Harry Mitchell had done the same in the 1920s. Oliver stopped James Branch (Repton Cedar Street) in the third round after an exciting encounter and later announced his intention to move over to the paid ranks. The light-fly supremo from last year, Gary Jones (Sefton), met Darren Fox in a re-run of their 1994 final, but, this time, it was Fox the winner on points. That win brought the Royal Air Force back on to the championship list for the first time since 1974 when Neville Meade took the heavyweight division. The fourth champion from last year, super-heavyweight, Danny Watts (Army), was ruled out at the start of the second round against Rod Allen (Preston & Fulwood). The reason, a punch (a left) which landed on target, but after the bell had signalled the end of the first round. In the light-middleweight division the 1994 titleholder, Wayne Alexander (Lynn), lost in the preliminary stages leaving Army boxer, Chris Bessey, the champion with a points win over Mick Barker (St Paul's). Bessey had been the welterweight titleholder in 1993. Another Army boxer, Kevin Short, who had won the welterweight division in 1994, was eliminated by Patrick Wright (Repton Cedar Street) in the quarter-finals. Wright made it to the finals but was outpointed by Darlington's Michael Hall, who thus joined older brother, Alan, who won twice, in 1988 and in 1989, at light-welterweight. The other reigning 1994 champions – Spencer Oliver, Dean Pithie, Andy Green, Alan Temple and David Starie – all turned to the paid ranks, while Steve Burford retired. At bantamweight, newcomer Noel Wilders (Five Towns) won on points over Owen Spensley (Royal Air Force), who had lost to Danny Costello in the 1994 flyweight final. The featherweight title was captured by David Burrows (Benchill), who stopped Michael Gibbons (South Bank) just 14 seconds into the middle round (on a cut eye). Little-known Roy Rutherford (Bell Green) won after an exciting nine minutes with Andrew McLean (Hylton Castle) to take the honours at lightweight in only his tenth bout, an all-time record. The successful return of Huyton light-welterweight, Alan Vaughan, was completed in style with his first ABA senior title; the loser, after a gallant battle, was Lance Crosby (St Paul's), who was stopped in the third. Vaughan, a World U19 gold medallist in 1990, had been inactive since the 1992 Barcelona Olympics. There was a one-punch finish for middleweight Jason Matthews (Crown & Manor), who kayoed Gary Grounds (Phil Thomas School of Boxing) in the opening session. Matthews was impressive throughout his title campaign, his sixth, but has now made his paid debut. There was another convincing win in the heavyweight final when Matthew Ellis (Blackpool & Fylde) pounded Fola Okesola (Lynn) into a second round defeat. Ellis had looked good in his preliminary outings.

Earlier, (17 February) in the Irish ABA finals at the National Stadium in Dublin, there were just two 1994 titleholders – flyweight Damaen Kelly (Holy Trinity) and Crumlin's Glen Stephens (lightweight) – completing the double. Their respective opponents were Brendan Walsh (Darndale) and Martin Reneghan (Keady). Paul Douglas (Holy Family/Golden Gloves) won his fifth title (this time at super-heavyweight) with a points decision over namesake George Douglas from South Meath. Nine new champions were produced. At light-fly, Jim Prior, another from Darndale, outpointed Colin Moffat (Holy Family), while Willie Valentine (St Saviour's) outscored Donal

Fola Okesola (left) was no match for Matthew Ellis, who stormed to the 1995 ABA heavyweight crown with a second round stoppage   Steve Parkin

Hosford (Greenmount) at bantamweight. St Patricks' Adrian Patterson took the featherweight crown with a points decision over Terry Carlyle (Sacred Heart) and moving up to light-welterweight it was Glen McClarnon (Clann Eireann) in front of Billy Walsh (St Colman's) after three rounds. Declan Higgins (Fermoy) won at light-middleweight, outpointing Michael Roche (Sunnyside) and Brian Magee (Holy Trinity) won (also on points) against former champion, Denis Galvin (St Saviour's), in the middleweight category. Stephen Kirk (Cairn Lodge) became the light-heavyweight champion, when he decisioned Sunnyside's Gordon Joyce, and the new heavyweight number one was James Clancy (Kilfenora), with a former champion (at light-heavy), Mark Sutton from St Saviour's, on the wrong end of a points decison against him. Finally, Neil Sinclair (Holy Family/Golden Gloves) reversed a 1994 finals loss to Neil Gough (St Paul's) for the welterweight division.

It was almost a similar story in the Welsh championships at the Institute of Sport in Cardiff (2 March) when six new names were added to the record books. With no entries at light-fly, it was first, flyweight Chris Williams (Highfields) who outscored Khalid Ali (Splott Adventure), followed by Ian Turner (Heads of Valley) and David Morris (Roath Youth) at bantam and featherweight, respectively. Andrew Greenaway (Trelewis) lost on points to Turner, but Anthony Fletcher (Newtown) was stopped in a round by Morris. Jason Samuels (Grange Catholics) won for the first time (light-middleweight) by outpointing Sean Pepperall (Vale and the Royal Air Force) and it was a similar title debut for Scott Gammer (Pembroke Dock), who was successful in the light-heavyweight category. Gammer's bout with Sean Pritchard (Fleur de Lys) was stopped in the second round when Pritchard sustained a badly cut nose with the Pembroke man, ahead at the time, declared the winner on points. At heavyweight, it was also a first-time championship win for Timothy Redmond, (Idris) with a decision over Steven Donaldson (Highfields), but it was more of the same for super-heavyweight, Kevin McCormack, doubling up for Coed Eva and the Royal Navy. McCormack established an all-time Welsh record by winning his ninth title, this time by default when Paul Lazenby (Newport Sports) failed to turn up. Middleweight Grant Briggs (Pontypridd & District) and Andrew Robinson (Pennar) both retained their 1994 titles. Briggs halted Nigel Trinder (Coed Eva) in the opening round, but light-welterweight, Robinson, travelled the full route to outpoint Martin Hall from Cwmbran. Last year's featherweight champion, Jason Cook (Maesteg), moved up to lightweight to win that division in the first round against Alwyn Evans (Carmarthen). It was his third title, as it was for Paul Samuels (Crindau Harlequins), who won, this time at welterweight, with a points decision over Anthony Smith (Highfields).

On 23 March at the Monklands Time Capsule in Coatbridge it was the turn of Scotland's best to try for titles. It was the same again (as in 1994) for flyweight Paul Shepherd (Sparta), who outpointed Lee Munro from Dennistoun; for lightweight Jamie Coyle (Bannockburn), with a similar win over Malcolm Gowans (Selkirk), and also for perennial Jim Pender (St Francis), who again monopolised the light-welterweight division. He outpointed Graham McLevy (Clydeview). Triple super-heavyweight champion in past years, Colin Brown from Gartcosh, came down to heavyweight and won his fourth title with a third round stoppage of Paul Reilly (Dalry). Following the pattern of brand new champions in Ireland and Wales (and later in England), there were seven new titleholders in Scotland, including a Forgewood double for Lawrence Murphy and Gordon Seal. Murphy won at light-middleweight with a points decision over Barry Laidlaw (Cardenden), while super-heavy, Gordon Seal, had a similar win over John Cowie (Bannockburn). Craig Lynch (Sparta) and Lee Powles (St Francis) could not repeat the title wins of clubmates Paul Shepherd and Jim Pender. Lynch went out on points to John Docherty (Portobello) in the welterweight division, with a similar loss for Powles against Tony Wright (Newharthill) at middleweight. At bantamweight, Andrew Brennan (Barn) won against Scott Dixon (Sydney Street) on points, as did Scott Harrison (Phoenix Calton) over Alston Buchanan (Army) at feather-weight. Light-heavyweight Rodney Campbell (Greenock) won that division; it was another points win – against Steve Topen (Lochee). In view of Scotland's tradition for producing good "little men", it was perhaps surprising that there were no entries in the light-flyweight division.

With a new minimum age limit for senior boxers (they have to be at least 19 in the year of a ABA title bid), there was a change in the format of the Junior ABA title event (which was for 15/16 year-olds). Now entitled the Youth

championships it is for boxers aged 17/18 years. There was no change in the structure of the Schoolboy and NABC-CYP championships.

The inaugural ABA Youth finals held at the Bracknell Leisure Centre (13 May) saw 11 champions in Class 5 (boxers born 1978) and ten in Class 6 (boxers born 1987), and included wins for Richard Hatton (Sale West), Neil Linford (Belgrave) and James Rooney (Hartlepool Catholic Boys), while Gary Dove, Michael Lomax and Danny Tokeley completed a trio of wins for West Ham.

In Torquay (4 March), 86 boxers competed for 32 schools titles in four age categories, ranging from 32 kg in the Junior "A" division to 75 kg in the Senior class. There were, as usual, many promising young boxers in action, including Bobby Beck (Repton Cedar Street), Tony Dodson (Gemini), Martin Power (St Pancras), Delroy Pryce (Newbridge), and Richard Hatton (Sale West), who all won for the third time. The hard punching Hatton had a very good season; he won all three U19 titles. Later it was reported that future Schoolboy championships were likely to be all-England affairs (with Welsh boxers excluded), arising from an agreement between the SABA and the ABAE on the future structure of Schoolboy boxing.

The NABC-CYP Class "A" and "B" finals were combined and staged as an open tournament at the Granby Halls in Leicester (7 January), with Patrick Mowbray (Dockers, Belfast) selected as the "best stylist" in Class "B". It was the first time that boxers from Northern Ireland had entered the event for nearly 30 years. Other Class "B" awards went to John Smith, RAF Uxbridge (best runner-up), and James Rooney, Hartlepool Catholic Boys (best winner). Class "A" trophies were awarded to Terry Driscoll (best winner) and Ricky Mann (best runner-up), both from Newham, and to Nicky Cook, Hornchurch & Elm Park (best stylist). At the London Hilton (9 January), the Class "C" finals produced another special award for a Northern Ireland boxer, Liam Cunningham (Saints), as "best stylist". Sam Mullins, Downside (most courageous), Micky Bush, Newham (best winner), and Michael O'Gara, Old Vic (best runner-up), received the other trophies.

ABAE statistics for 1994-95 showed a slight increase in the number of officials, from 569 in 1993-94 to 574. Other registrations moved down, slightly – clubs from 613 to 606, and coaches from 1247 to 1208. There was, however, a noticeable decrease in the number of senior boxers (4256 to 3634) and juniors (3240 to 2900).

And so to 1995-96, when the whole of the amateur boxing world will be focused on the Olympic Games in Atlanta (20 July to 4 August). It seems only yesterday that it was Barcelona! In Atlanta there will be a maximum entry of 364 boxers (there were 24 boxers in the first Olympics in St Louis in 1904), achieved by a series of world-wide qualifying tournaments as in 1992. For boxers from England, the only way to get to Atlanta is to reach the quarter-finals of the 1996 European senior championships in Copenhagen (28 March to 6 April). That in itself is a formidable task.

(David Prior writes on amateur boxing in Boxing News/Amateur Boxing Scene.)

ABA National Championships, 1994-95

Southern Counties v North-East Counties

Southern Counties

Hampshire, Kent, Surrey & Sussex Divisions   The Leisure Centre, Bexhill on Sea - 11 & 18 February
L. Fly: no entries. **Fly:** *semi-finals:* M. Bell (Brighton) wo, T. Craig (Basingstoke) w pts N. Bell (Brighton); *final:* M. Bell w pts T. Craig. **Bantam:** *final:* J. McLean (Basingstoke) w pts R. Stoneman (Medway GG). **Feather:** *final:* M. Wright (St Mary's) wo. **Light:** *final:* D. Lavender (Foley) w rsc 2 P. Bedford (Basingstoke). **L. Welter:** *prelims:* J. Newton (Seaford) wo, P. Milsom (Southampton) wo, R. Cox (Brighton) wo, A. Martin (Foley) wo, T. Bayrack (Crawley) wo, G. Shorter (Shepway) wo, M. Bloomfield (St Leonards) w co 2 L. Hutton (Working), A. Elcock (Camberley) w pts G. Moriano (Camberley); *quarter finals:* J. Newton w rsc 1 P. Milsom, R. Cox w rsc 2 A. Martin, T. Bayrack w pts G. Shorter, M. Bloomfield w pts A. Elcock; *semi-finals:* M. Bloomfield w pts T. Bayrack, J. Newton w rsc 2 R. Cox; *final:* J. Newton w rsc 2 M. Bloomfield. **Welter:** *quarter-finals:* J. Godsell (Westree) wo, P. Miles (Foley) w pts S. Sheeran, D. Stannard (Crawley) w pts W. Rothwell (Westree), P. Larner (Bognor) w pts J. Honey (Basingstoke); *semi-finals:* P. Miles w rsc 1 J. Godsell, P. Larner w pts D. Stannard; *final:* P. Miles w pts P. Larner. **L. Middle:** *quarter-finals:* J. Cole (Cowes Medina) wo, D. Goddard (Foley) wo, A. Wilkes (Broadstairs) wo, A. Gilbert (Crawley) w pts A. Coppard (Crawley); *semi-finals:* J. Cole w pts D. Goddard, A. Wilkes w pts A. Gilbert; *final:* J. Cole w pts A. Wilkes. **Middle:** *quarter-finals:* A. Wilford (Faversham) wo, D. Guilfoyle (Crawley) wo, S. James (Broadstairs) w pts J. Fletcher (Woking), M. Galea (Foley) w pts C. Voysey (Cowes Medina); *semi-finals:* M. Galea w pts S. James, A. Wilford w rtd 2 D. Guilfoyle; *final:* M. Galea (Foley) w pts A. Wilford. **L. Heavy:** *final:* G. Townsend (West Hill) wo. **Heavy:** *semi-finals:* G. Russell (Shepway) w dis 1 G. Scraggs (West Hill), D. Whitman (Woking) wo F. Booker (Seaford); *final:* G. Russell w pts D. Whitman. **S. Heavy:** *final:* M. Alexander (Southampton) w pts M. Brown (Ryde).

North East Counties

North-East Division   The Leisure Centre, Gateshead - 3 & 10 February
L. Fly: no entries. **Fly:** no entries. **Bantam:** *final:* C. Gray (Longbenton) wo. **Feather:** *final:* M. Gibbons (South Bank) w pts S. Grant (Aycliffe). **Light:** *final:* A. McLean (Hylton Castle) w pts G. Williams (Hartlepool BW). **L. Welter:** *final:* K. Scott (Newbiggin) w pts B. Wrightson (Lambton Street). **Welter:** *semi-finals:* M. Hall (Darlington) wo, J. Green (Phil Thomas SOB) w pts M. McLean (Hylton Castle); *final:* M. Hall w pts J. Green. **L. Middle:** *quarter-finals:* S. McCready (Birtley) wo, M. Lumley (Lambton Street) wo, J. Donaghue (Phil Thomas SOB) wo, I. Cooper (Hartlepool Catholic) w pts J. Spencer (Wellington); *semi-finals:* S. McCready w pts M. Lumley, J. Donaghue w pts I. Cooper; *final:* J. Donaghue w pts S. McCready. **Middle:** *semi-finals:* G. Grounds (Phil Thomas SOB) w pts A. Rowbotham (Hartlepool BW), G. Smith (Hartlepool Catholic) w pts R. Pink (Wellington); *final:* G. Grounds w pts G. Smith. **L. Heavy:** *semi-finals:* M. Smith (Hartlepool Catholic) w rsc 1 R. Aldridge (Old Vic), M. Thompson (Spennymoor) w pts S. Bowes (Consett);

final: M. Smith wo M. Thompson. **Heavy:** *final:* K. Duke (Sunderland) w pts J. Brown (Phil Thomas SOB). **S. Heavy:** *final:* G. McGhin (Sunderland) wo.

Yorkshire & Humberside Divisions   The Dome, Barnsley - 10 February & The Irish Centre, Leeds - 24 February
L. Fly: no entries. **Fly:** *final:* M. Cairns (St Paul's) wo. **Bantam:** *final:* N. Wilders (Five Towns) wo. **Feather:** *final:* J. Whittaker (Halifax) wo. **Light:** *quarter-finals:* J. Darlow (Barnsley) wo, N. Wilders (Five Towns) wo, G. Williams (St Patrick's) wo, T. Bradley (Unity) w pts B. Turner (Bradford Police); *semi-finals:* J. Darlow w rsc 2 N. Wilders, G. Williams w rsc 2 T. Bradley; *final:* G. Williams w rsc 3 J. Darlow. **L. Welter:** *semi-finals:* M. Johnson (Full Flow) wo, L. Crosby (St Paul's) w pts F. Hogg (St Patrick's); *final:* L. Crosby w pts M. Johnson. **Welter:** *semi-finals:* J. Witter (Bradford Police) w rsc 2 A. Wharton (Scarborough), G. Matsell (Hull Fish Trades) w pts W. Christian (Full Flow); *final:* G. Matsell w dis 3 J. Witter. **L. Middle:** *semi-finals:* M. Barker (St Paul's) w rsc 1 L. Murtagh (Hunslet), L. Moorhouse (Sedbergh) w rsc 1 B. Moss (Hull Fish Trades); *final:* M. Barker w pts L. Moorhouse. **Middle:** *semi-finals:* S. Smith (Burmantofts) w rsc 3 K. Robertshaw (Hunslet), D. Smillie (Sedbergh) w rsc 1 M. Thompson (Wombwell); *final:* D. Smillie w rsc 3 S. Smith. **L. Heavy:** *semi-finals:* D. Rees (Sedbergh) wo, G. Biglin (North Hull) w pts H. Wood (Keighley); *final:* G. Biglin w rsc 1 D. Rees. **Heavy:** *final:* M. Asfar (Sedbergh) w rsc 2 C. Nicholson (White Rose). **S. Heavy:** *final:* G. Fitzgerald (Plant Works) wo.

North-East Counties Finals   The Leisure Centre, Gateshead - 3 March
L. Fly: no entries. **Fly:** M. Cairns (St Paul's) wo. **Bantam:** N. Wilders (Five Towns) w pts C. Gray (Longbenton). **Feather:** M. Gibbons (South Bank) w pts J. Whittaker (Halifax). **Light:** A. McLean (Hylton Castle) w dis 3 G. Williams (St Patrick's). **L. Welter:** L. Crosby (St Paul's) w rsc 1 K. Scott (Newbiggin). **Welter:** M. Hall (Darlington) w pts G. Matsell (Hull Fish Trades). **L. Middle:** M. Barker (St Paul's) w pts J. Donaghue (Phil Thomas SOB). **Middle:** G. Grounds (Phil Thomas SOB) w rsc 1 D. Smillie (Sedbergh). **L. Heavy:** G. Biglin (North Hull) w pts M. Smith (Hartlepool Catholic). **Heavy:** K. Duke (Sunderland) w pts M. Asfar (Sedbergh). **S. Heavy:** G. McGhin (Sunderland) w pts G. Fitzgerald (Plant Works).

Southern Counties v North-East Counties

The Rothwell Sports Centre, Oulton - 18 March
L. Fly: no entries. **Fly:** M. Cairns (St Paul's) w rsc 3 M. Bell (Brighton). **Bantam:** N. Wilders (Five Towns) w pts J. McLean (Basingstoke). **Feather:** M. Gibbons (South Bank) w pts M. Wright (St Mary's). **Light:** A. McLean (Hylton Castle) w co 1 D. Lavender (Foley). **L. Welter:** L. Crosby (St Paul's) w rsc 3 J. Newton (Seaford). **Welter:** M. Hall (Darlington) w pts P. Miles (Foley). **L. Middle:** M. Barker (St Paul's) w pts J. Coles (Cowes Medina). **Middle:** G. Grounds (Phil Thomas SOB) w rtd 1 M. Galea (Foley). **L. Heavy:** G. Biglin (North Hull) w pts G. Townsend (West Hill). **Heavy:** K. Duke w rtd 1 G. Russell (Shepway). **S. Heavy:** G. McGhin (Sunderland) wo M. Alexander (Southampton).

Western Counties v North-West Counties

Western Counties

Northern Division   The South-West Electricity Social Club, Bristol - 25 February

L. Fly: no entries. **Fly:** no entries. **Bantam:** *final:* M. Braden (Walcot) wo. **Feather:** *final:* S. Lucas (Walcot) w pts D. Thompson (Empire). **Light:** *final:* M. Kane (Watchet) wo. **L. Welter:** *final:* F. Davies (Viking) w pts T. Knowles (Malmesbury). **Welter:** *semi-finals:* J. Turley (Penhill) wo, D. Kelly (Bronx) w pts E. McCrae (Walcot); *final:* J. Turley w rsc 2 D. Kelly. **L. Middle:** *quarter-finals:* C. Powell (National Smelting) wo, I. McDonald (Kingswood) wo, D. Holder (Gloucester) wo, L. McCrae (Walcot) w pts A. Derrick (Taunton); *semi-finals:* C. Powell w pts I. McDonald, L. McCrae w rtd 2 D. Holder; *final:* L. McCrae w pts C. Powell. **Middle:** *final:* S. Ford (Malmesbury) wo. **L. Heavy:** *final:* P. Rogers (Penhill) w rtd 2 G. Lee (Synwell). **Heavy:** *semi-finals:* P. Lewis (Taunton) wo, P. Day (Walcot) w rsc 3 D. Poulson (Bronx); *final:* P. Day w pts P. Lewis. **S. Heavy:** *final:* H. Williams (Bronx) w pts K. Oputu (St George).

Southern Division   The Haven Holiday Centre, Weymouth - 11 February

L. Fly: no entries. **Fly:** *final:* D. Barriball (Launceston) wo. **Bantam:** no entries. **Feather:** *final:* S. Gawron (Devonport) wo. **Light:** *semi-finals:* I. Dytham (Weymouth) w pts D. Maton (Poole), L. Willock (Paignton) w pts C. McBurnie (Pisces); *final:* I. Dytham w rsc 2 L. Willock. **L. Welter:** *semi-finals:* M. Pickard (Weymouth), J. Hudson (Lymptsone) w pts R. Petherick (Dawlish); *final:* J. Hudson w pts M. Pickard. **Welter:** *semi-finals:* J. Batten (Launceston) wo, J. Simmons (Saxon) w co 1 N. Western (Torbay); *final:* J. Simmons w pts J. Batten. **L. Middle:** no entries. **Middle:** *final:* E. Stuart (Leonis) wo. **L. Heavy:** *quarter-finals:* A. Stables (Devonport) wo, J. Jones (Launceston) wo, M. Dunlop (Leonis), R. Mann (Torbay) w pts N. Hickey (Bideford); *semi-finals:* R. Mann w pts A. Stables, J. Jones w pts M. Dunlop; *final:* R. Mann w pts J. Jones. **Heavy:** *semi-finals:* D. Keenor (Barnstaple) wo, N. Hosking (Devonport) w pts J. Teaves (Torbay); *final:* N. Hosking w pts D. Keenor. **S. Heavy:** *semi-finals:* N. Kendall (Appolo) wo, J. Smith (Poole) w pts S. Mann (Torbay); *final:* N. Kendall w pts J. Smith.

Western Counties Finals   The Barnstaple Hotel, Barnstaple - 4 March

L. Fly: no entries. **Fly:** D. Barriball (Launceston) wo. **Bantam:** M. Braden (Walcot) wo. **Feather:** S. Lucas (Walcot) w co 2 S. Gawron (Devonport). **Light:** I. Dytham (Weymouth) w rsc 2 M. Kane (Watchet). **L. Welter:** J. Hudson (Lympstone) wo F. Davies (Viking). **Welter:** J. Simmons (Saxon) w pts J. Turley (Penhill). **L. Middle:** L. McCrae (Walcot) wo. **Middle:** E. Stuart (Leonis) w pts S. Ford (Malmesbury). **L. Heavy:** P. Rogers (Penhill) w pts R. Mann (Torbay). **Heavy:** P. Day (Walcot) w co 1 N. Hosking (Devonport). **S. Heavy:** N. Kendall (Apollo) wo H. Williams (Bronx).

North-West Counties

East Lancashire & Cheshire Division   The Pembroke Halls, Walkden - 3 & 17 February & Everton Park Sports Centre, Liverpool - 10 February

L. Fly: no entries. **Fly:** *final:* N. Wilkes (Mottram & Hattersley) wo. **Bantam:** *final:* S. Bell (Bredbury) wo. **Feather:** *final:* D. Burrows (Benchill) wo. **Light:** *semi-finals:* E. Nevins (Benchill) wo, G. Hibbert (Gallagher) w rsc 1 R. Francis (Preston & Fulwood); *final:* G. Hibbert w pts E. Nevins. **L. Welter:** *final:* M. Sewell (Workington) w pts J. McGirl (Benchill). **Welter:** *semi-finals:* A. Golding (Bolton) w rsc 2 I. Andrew (Boarshaw), B. Gonzalez (Preston Red Rose) w pts J. Barrow (Preston & Fulwood); *final:* B. Gonzalez w co 1 A. Golding. **L. Middle:** *quarter-finals:* J. Aikenhead (Sale West) wo, T. Feno (Bredbury) wo, D. Bateman (Moss Side) wo, P. Street (Bredbury) w co 2 M. Porter (Northside); *semi-finals:* D. Bateman w pts P. Street, J. Aikenhead w pts T. Feno; *final:* J. Aikenhead w pts D. Bateman. **Middle:** *quarter-finals:* S. Keith (Fox) wo, J. Whiteside (Preston Red Rose) wo, S. Battle (Halliwell) wo, P. Heneghan (Moss Side) w rsc 2 D. Richards (Barrow); *semi-finals:* P. Heneghan w rsc 2 S. Keith, J. Whiteside w rsc 1 S. Battle; *final:* J. Whiteside w pts P. Heneghan. **L. Heavy:** *final:* G. Williams (Collyhurst & Moston) w pts N. Harrison (Bolton). **Heavy:** *semi-finals:* J. Quayson (Moss Side) wo, M. Ellis (Blackpool & Fylde) w pts M. Levy (Collyhurst & Moston); *final:* M. Ellis w pts J. Quayson. **S. Heavy:** *final:* R. Allen (Preston & Fulwood) wo.

West Lancashire & Cheshire Division   Everton Part Sports Centre, Liverpool - 10 & 17 February

L. Fly: *final:* G. Jones (Sefton) wo. **Fly:** *final:* C. Toohey (Gemini) w pts D. Vlasman (Gemini). **Bantam:** *semi-finals:* L. Eedle (Gemini) wo, M. Parker (Kirkby) w pts A. Mulholland (Transport); *final:* L. Eedle w pts M. Parker. **Feather:** *semi-finals:* A. Moon (Kirkby) w pts C. Pennington (St Helens), C. Ainscough (Transport) w pts D. Burke (Salisbury); *final:* A. Moon w pts C. Ainscough. **Light:** *semi-finals:* J. Farrell (Marsh Lane) wo, E. Roberts (Gemini) w pts T. Peacock (Salisbury); *final:* J. Farrell w co 1 Eddie Roberts. **L. Welter:** *semi-finals:* J. Vlasman (Gemini) wo, A. Vaughan (Huyton) w pts J. Mellor (Transport); *final:* A. Vaughan w pts J. Vlasman. **Welter:** *final:* M. Jones (Rotunda) w pts G. Ryder (Kirkby). **L. Middle:** *semi-finals:* J. Jones (Sefton) w pts L. Burns (Gemini), R. Hill (Knowsley Vale) w pts R. Turner (Warrington); *final:* J. Jones w rsc 3 R. Hill. **Middle:** *final:* R. Burns (Gemini) w pts L. Malloy (Tuebrook). **L. Heavy:** *semi-finals:* J. Naylor (Rotunda) w co 2 L. Cuddy (Kirkdale), T. Smith (Long Lane) w pts C. Smith (Golden Star); *final:* J. Naylor w pts T. Smith. **Heavy:** no entries. **S. Heavy:** no entries.

North-West Counties Finals   Everton Park Sports Centre, Liverpool - 3 March

L. Fly: G. Jones (Sefton) wo. **Fly:** C. Toohey (Gemini) w pts N. Wilkes (Mottram & Hattersley). **Bantam:** L. Eedle (Gemini) w pts S. Bell (Bredbury). **Feather:** D. Burrows (Benchill) w pts A. Moon (Kirkby). **Light:** G. Hibbert (Gallagher) w pts J. Farrell (Marsh Lane). **L. Welter:** A. Vaughan (Huyton) w rsc 1 M. Sewell (Warrington). **Welter:** M. Jones (Rotunda) w pts B. Gonzalez (Preston Red Rose). **L. Middle:** J. Jones (Sefton) w pts J. Aikenhead (Sale West). **Middle:** J. Whiteside (Preston Red Rose) w pts R. Burns (Gemini). **L. Heavy:** G. Williams (Collyhurst & Moston) w pts J. Naylor (Rotunda). **Heavy:** M. Ellis (Blackpool & Fylde) wo. **S. Heavy:** R. Allen (Preston & Fulwood) wo.

Western Counties v North-West Counties

The Whitchurch Sports Centre, Bristol - 18 March

L. Fly: G. Jones (Sefton) wo. **Fly:** C. Toohey (Gemini) w pts D. Barriball (Launceston). **Bantam:** L. Eedle (Gemini) w pts M. Braden (Walcot). **Feather:** D. Burrows (Benchill) w pts S. Lucas (Walcot). **Light:** G. Hibbert (Gallagher) w rsc 1 I. Dytham (Weymouth). **L. Welter:** A. Vaughan (Huyton) w rtd 1 J. Hudson (Lympstone). **Welter:** M. Jones (Rotunda) w pts J. Simmons

(Saxon). **L. Middle:** J. Jones (Sefton) w pts L. McCrae (Walcot). **Middle:** E. Stuart (Leonis) w pts J. Whiteside (Preston Red Rose). **L. Heavy:** P. Rogers (Penhill) w rsc 2 J. Naylor (Rotunda) - replaced G. Williams (Collyhurst & Moston). **Heavy:** M. Ellis (Blackpool & Fylde) w pts P. Day (Walcot). **S. Heavy:** R. Allen (Preston & Fulwood) w rsc 1 N. Kendall (Apollo).

Midland Counties v Eastern Counties / Home Counties

Midland Counties

Derbyshire Division   The Moorways Stadium, Derby - 10 January
L. Fly: no entries. **Fly:** no entries. **Bantam:** no entries. **Feather:** *final:* C. Spacie (St Michael's) wo. **Light:** *final:* D. Billing (Trinity) wo. **L. Welter:** *final:* D. Ashley (Merlin) wo. **Welter:** *final:* G. Lowe (Derby) w pts C. Pridmore (South Normanton). **L. Middle:** *final:* K. Gibbons (Derby) wo. **Middle:** D. Grafton (Bolsover) wo. **L. Heavy:** no entries. **Heavy:** *final:* A. Aziz (Derby) w pts J. Oakes (Draycott). **S. Heavy:** no entries.

Leicester, Rutland & Northamptonshire Division   The Heathfield Sports & Social Club, Northampton - 19 January
L. Fly: no entries. **Fly:** no entries. **Bantam:** *final:* J. Squires (Belgrave) w pts A. Pope (Wellingborough). **Feather:** *final:* P. Neale (Alexton) wo. **Light:** *final:* A. Thomas (Wellingborough) wo. **L. Welter:** *final:* A. Bosworth (Henry Street) wo. **Welter:** no entries. **L. Middle:** *final:* A. Foster (Henry Street) wo. **Middle:** *final:* C. Williams (Belgrave) wo. **L. Heavy:** *final:* S. Beasley (Northampton) wo. **Heavy:** *final:* R. McLeod (Wellingborough) wo. **S. Heavy:** no entries.

Nottinghamshire & Lincolnshire Division   The Miners' Social Club, Harworth - 14 January
L. Fly: No entries. **Fly:** no entries. **Bantam:** *final:* E. Pickering (RHP) wo. **Feather:** *final:* C. Greaves (RHP) wo. **Light:** *final:* K. Gerowski (Cotgrave) w pts N. Exton (Burton Arms). **L. Welter:** *final:* R. Walker (Huthwaite) wo. **Welter:** *semi-finals:* J. Khaliq (Meadows & Ruddington) wo, R. Briggs-Price (Radford) w pts J. Dean (Lincoln); *final:* J. Khaliq w rsc 2 R. Briggs-Price. **L. Middle:** no entries. **Middle:** *final:* B. Exton (Burton Arms) w pts A. Lovelace (Boston). **L. Heavy:** *final:* K. Oliver (Bracebridge) wo. **Heavy:** *semi-finals:* N. Williamson (Bulwell) wo, A. Dowling (Bracebridge) w pts S. Curtis (Bingham); *final:* A. Dowling w co 2 N. Williamson. **S. Heavy:** *final:* D. Castle (Radford) wo.

Warwickshire Division   Kersley Colliery Social Club, Coventry - 27 January
L. Fly: no entries. **Fly:** no entries. **Bantam:** *final:* G. Payne (Bell Green) wo. **Feather:** *final:* R. Evatt (Triumph) wo. **Light:** *final:* R. Rutherford (Bell Green) wo. **L. Welter:** *final:* I. Carroll (Triumph) w pts S. Walford (Bell Green). **Welter:** no entries. **L. Middle:** *final:* A. Payne (Bell Green) wo. **Middle:** *final:* S. Bendall (Triumph) wo. **L. Heavy:** *final:* J. Twite (Triumph) wo. **Heavy:** *final:* D. Bendall (Triumph) wo. **S. Heavy:** no entries.

Midland Counties (North Zone) Semi-Finals & Finals   Clifton Entertainment Centre, Nottingham - 23 January, Glenville's Nite Spot, Northampton - 6 February & Pennine Hotel, Derby - 18 February
L. Fly: no entries. **Fly:** no entries. **Bantam:** *semi-finals:* E. Pickering (RHP) wo, G. Payne (Bell Green) wo J. Squires (Belgrave); *final:* E. Pickering w pts G. Payne. **Feather:** *semi-*

finals: C. Spacie (St Michael's) w pts C. Greaves (RHP), R. Evatt (Triumph) w rsc 1 P. Neale (Alexton); *final:* R. Evatt w co 1 C. Spacie. **Light:** *semi-finals:* D. Billing (Trinity) w pts K. Gerowski (Cotgrave), R. Rutherford (Bell Green) w rsc 3 A. Thomas (Wellingborough); *final:* R. Rutherford w pts D. Billing. **L. Welter:** *semi-finals:* D. Ashley (Merlin) w pts R. Walker (Huthwaite), A. Bosworth (Henry Street) w pts I. Carroll (Triumph); *final:* D. Ashley w pts A. Bosworth. **Welter:** *final:* J. Khaliq (Meadows & Ruddington) w rsc 3 G. Lowe (Derby). **L. Middle:** *semi-finals:* K. Gibbons (Derby) wo, A. Foster (Henry Street) w pts A. Payne (Bell Green); *final:* K. Gibbons w pts A. Foster. **Middle:** *semi-finals:* S. Bendall (Triumph) w pts C. Williams (Belgrave), D. Grafton (Bolsover) w pts B. Exton (Burton Arms); *final:* S. Bendall w pts D. Grafton. **L. Heavy:** *semi-finals:* K. Oliver (Bracebridge) wo, J. Twite (Triumph) w pts S. Beasley (Northampton); *final:* K. Oliver w pts J. Twite. **Heavy:** *semi-finals:* A. Dowling (Bracebridge) w pts A. Aziz (Derby), R. Bendall (Triumph) w co 1 R. McLeod (Wellingborough); *final:* A. Dowling w pts R. Bendall. **S. Heavy:** *final:* D. Castle (Radford) wo.

Birmingham Division   The Irish Centre, Digbeth - 22 January
L. Fly: no entries. **Fly:** no entries. **Bantam:** *final:* I. Hussain (Birmingham) wo. **Feather:** *final:* S. Michael (Birmingham) wo. **Light:** no entries. **L. Welter:** no entries. **Welter:** *final:* J. Scanlon (Birmingham) wo. **L. Middle:** *final:* C. Underhill (Birmingham) w pts G. Harris (Rover). **Middle:** no entries. **L. Heavy:** *final:* L. Page (Birmingham) wo. **Heavy:** *final:* K. Hitchens (Birmingham) wo. **S. Heavy:** no entries.

North Staffordshire Division   Bidds Country & Western Club, Longton - 6 January
L. Fly: no entries. **Fly:** no entries. **Bantam:** no entries. **Feather:** no entries. **Light:** no entries. **L. Welter:** no entries. **Welter:** *final:* C. Chadwick (Hulton Abbey) wo. **L. Middle:** *final:* M. Gaylor (Burton) w co 1 K. Flowers (Orme). **Middle:** *final:* E. Bengry (Stoke) wo. **L. Heavy:** *semi-finals:* C. Morgan (Queensbery) w pts P. Scope (Burton), J. Steele (Brownhills) w pts I. Thomas (Queensbery); *final:* C. Morgan w pts J. Steele. **Heavy:** *final:* R. Francis (Orme) wo. **S. Heavy:** no entries.

South Staffordshire Division   The Gala Baths, West Bromwich - 3 February, The Saddlers' Club, Walsall - 16 February & The Penns Hall Hotel, Sutton Coldfield - 20 February
L. Fly: no entries. **Fly:** *final:* D. Spencer (Pleck) wo. **Bantam:** *final:* N. Read (Tipton) wo. **Feather:** no entries. **Light:** *quarter-finals:* G. Reid (Wolverhampton) wo, S. Cockayne (Wednesbury) wo, C. Allen (Scotland's) wo, C. Foxall (Silver Street) w pts M. Bowen (Tipton); *semi-finals:* G. Reid w co 1 S. Cockayne, C. Allen w co 1 C. Foxall; *final:* C. Allen w pts G. Reid. **L. Welter:** *final:* M. Fox (Pleck) w pts M. Richards (Wednesbury). **Welter:** *final:* P. Nightingale (Wednesbury) w pts R. Caulder (Silver Street). **L. Middle:** *final:* P. Garrett (Wednesbury) w pts M. Bamford (Silver Street). **Middle:** *semi-finals:* A. Mason (Wolverhampton) w co 1 D. Smith (Wednesbury), S. Martin (Wolverhampton) w rsc 2 A. Gardiner (Wolverhampton); *final:* S. Martin w pts A. Mason. **L. Heavy:** no entries. **Heavy:** *final:* A. Wilson (Wolverhampton) w pts M. Pugh (Silver Street). **S. Heavy:** *final:* B. Summers (Wednesbury) wo.

West Mercia Division   The Childes Sports Centre, Cleobury Mortimer - 21 January
L. Fly: no entries. **Fly:** no entries. **Bantam:** no entries. **Feather:** no entries. **Light:** no entries. **L. Welter:** no entries. **Welter:** no

entries. **L. Middle:** *final:* J. Adams (Warley) w pts G. Richards (Windmill). **Middle:** *final:* T. Broadbridge (Warley) wo. **L. Heavy:** *final:* N. Raxter (Droitwich) wo. **Heavy:** no entries. **S. Heavy:** no entries.

Midland Counties (South Zone) Semi-Finals & Finals   Bidds Country & Western Club, Longton - 27 January & 23 February & Castle Vale Residents' Club, Birmingham - 18 February
L. Fly: no entries. **Fly:** *final:* D. Spencer (Pleck) wo. **Bantam:** *final:* I. Hussain (Birmingham) w pts N. Read (Tipton). **Feather:** *final:* S. Michael (Birmingham) wo. **Light:** *final:* C. Allen (Scotland's) wo. **L. Welter:** *final:* M. Fox (Pleck) wo. **Welter:** *semi-finals:* C. Chadwick (Hulton Abbey) wo, J. Scanlon (Birmingham) w pts P. Nightingale (Wednesbury); *final:* J. Scanlon w rsc 2 C. Chadwick. **L. Middle:** *semi-finals:* C. Underhill (Birmingham) w pts M. Bamford (Silver Street) - replaced P. Garrett (Wednesbury), J. Adams (Warley) w pts M. Gaylor (Burton); *final:* J. Adams w rsc 2 C. Underhill. **Middle:** *semi-finals:* S. Martin (Wolverhampton) wo; E. Bengry (Stoke) w pts T. Broadbridge (Warley); *final:* S. Martin w pts E. Bengry. **L. Heavy:** *semi-finals:* L. Page (Birmingham) wo, N. Raxter (Droitwich) w co 1 C. Morgan (Queensberry); *final:* L. Page w pts N. Raxter. **Heavy:** *sem-finals:* R. Francis (Orme) wo, K. Hitchens (Birmingham) w co 2 A. Wilson (Wolverhampton); *final:* K. Hitchens w pts R. Francis. **S. Heavy:** *final:* B. Summers (Wednesbury) wo.

Midland Counties Finals   Garrington's Sports & Social Club, Bromsgrove - 11 March
L. Fly: no entries. **Fly:** D. Spencer (Pleck) wo. **Bantam:** E. Pickering (RHP) w pts I. Hussain (Birmingham). **Feather:** R. Evatt (Triumph) w rtd 2 S. Michael (Birmingham). **Light:** R. Rutherford (Bell Green) w pts C. Allen (Scotland's). **L. Welter:** D. Ashley (Merlin) w rsc 3 M. Fox (Pleck). **Welter:** J. Scanlon (Birmingham) w pts J. Khaliq (Meadows & Ruddington). **L. Middle:** K. Gibbons (Derby) w pts J. Adams (Warley). **Middle:** S. Bendall (Triumph) w pts S. Martin (Wolverhampton). **L. Heavy:** K. Oliver (Bracebridge) wo L. Page (Birmingham). **Heavy:** A. Dowling (Bracebridge) w pts K. Hitchens (Birmingham). **S. Heavy:** B. Summers (Wednesbury) w dis 2 D. Castle (Radford).

Eastern Counties v Home Counties

Eastern Counties

Essex Division   The Civic Hall, Grays - 13 January
L. Fly: no entries. **Fly:** no entries. **Bantam:** *final:* D. Adams (Colchester)wo. **Feather:** *final:* D. Dainty (Canvey) wo. **Light:** *final:* S. Rogan (Belhus Park) wo. **L. Welter:** *final:* A. Hussain (Chalvedon) w pts M. Saliu (Colchester). **Welter:** *final:* A. Sims (Canvey) wo. **L. Middle:** *final:* D. Sharpe (Halstead) wo. **Middle:** *final:* R. Hadley (Canvey) w pts J. Veal (Rayleigh Mill). **L. Heavy:** *final:* D. George (Belhus Park) wo. **Heavy:** *final:* S. Honeywell (Rayleigh Mill) wo. **S. Heavy:** no entries.

Mid -Anglia Division   The Guildhall, Cambridge - 29 January
L. Fly: no entries. **Fly:** no entries. **Bantam:** no entries. **Feather:** no entries. **Light:** no entries. **L. Welter:** no entries. **Welter:** no entries. **L. Middle:** *final:* L. Baxter (Chatteris) wo. **Middle:** *final:* M. Redhead (Cambridge & Soham) w rsc 1 A. Beaumont (Howard Mallet). **L. Heavy:** no entries. **Heavy:** *final:* R. Hardy (Cambridge & Soham) wo. **S. Heavy:** no entries.

Norfolk Division   The Royal British Legion Hall, Norwich - 20 January
L. Fly: no entries. **Fly:** no entries. **Bantam:** no entries. **Feather:** no entries. **Light:** no entries. **L. Welter:** *final:* S. Garner (Dereham) w pts J. Spurling (Kings Lynn). **Welter:** *final:* S. Johnstone (Norwich Lads) w pts J. Fitzgerald (Norwich City). **L. Middle:** *final:* K. Elliott (Norwich Lads) w pts J. Cobb (Aylesham). **Middle:** *final:* M. Rodgers (Aylesham) w pts C. Saunders (Norwich City). **L. Heavy:** *final:* A. Gray (Yarmouth) w rsc 3 J. Nicholls (Aylesham). **Heavy:** *final:* S. Thompson (Yarmouth) w rsc 2 C. Bell (Norwich City). **S. Heavy:** no entries.

Suffolk Division   The Corn Exchange, Bury St Edmunds - 21 January
L. Fly: no entries. **Fly:** no entries. **Bantam:** no entries. **Feather:** *final:* R. McKenzie (Ipswich) wo. **Light:** *final:* M. Hawthorne (Lowestoft) wo. **L. Welter:** *final:* D. James (Bury St Edmunds) w pts W. Asker (Hurstlea & Kerridge). **Welter:** no entries. **L. Middle:** *final:* N. Burwood (Lowestoft) wo. **Middle:** *final:* A. Cook (Triple A) wo. **L. Heavy:** no entries. **Heavy:** *final:* S. Potter (Ipswich) w co 1 J. Goodchild (Sudbury). **S. Heavy:** *final:* I. Davey (Ipswich) w co 2 P. King (Lowestoft).

Eastern Counties Semi-Finals & Finals   The Focus Youth Club, Peterborough - 11 February
L. Fly: no entries. **Fly:** no entries. **Bantam:** *final:* D. Adams (Colchester) wo. **Feather:** *final:* D. Dainty (Canvey) w rtd 1 R. McKenzie (Ipswich). **Light:** *final:* M. Hawthorne (Lowestoft) w co 2 S. Rogan (Belhus Park). **L. Welter:** *semi-finals:* S. Garner (Dereham) wo, D. James (Bury St Edmunds) w pts A. Hussain (Chalvedon); *final:* D. James w pts S. Garner. **Welter:** *final:* A. Sims (Canvey) w pts S. Johnstone (Norwich Lads). **L. Middle:** *semi-finals:* K. Elliott (Norwich Lads) w pts L. Baxter (Chatteris), N. Burwood (Lowestoft) w pts D. Sharpe (Halstead); *final:* N. Burwood w pts K. Elliott. **Middle:** *semi-finals:* A. Cook (Triple A) w pts M. Rodgers (Aylesham), M. Redhead (Cambridge & Soham) w pts R. Hadley (Canvey); *final:* M. Redhead w pts A. Cook. **L. Heavy:** *final:* A. Gray (Yarmouth) w pts D. George (Belhus Park). **Heavy:** *semi-finals:* S. Honeywell (Rayleigh Mill) wo S. Thompson (Yarmouth), R. Hardy (Cambridge & Soham) w rsc 1 S. Potter (Ipswich). **S. Heavy:** *final:* I. Davey (Ipswich) wo.

Home Counties

Bedfordshire, Hertfordshire & North Buckinghamshire & Oxfordshire, Berkshire & South Buckinghamshire Divisions   Molin's Recreation Club, Saunderton - 11 February
L. Fly: *final:* J. Locke (Henley) wo. **Fly:** no entries. **Bantam:** no entries. **Feather:** *final:* D. Maher (Marlow) w pts L. Dibstall (Wolvercote). **Light:** *final:* A. McBeal (Hitchin) wo. **L. Welter:** *final:* A. Tomlin (Bedford) w pts J. Grant (Didcot). **Welter:** *final:* K. McCarthy (Bedford) w pts A. Smith (Watford). **L. Middle:** *semi-finals:* S. Wright (Sandy) w pts M. Browning (Watford), J. Liles (Chesham) w rsc 3 E. Randall (Bushey); *final:* S. Wright w pts J. Liles. **Middle:** *final:* C. Marshall (Stevenage) w co 1 I. Rowe (Hitchin). **L. Heavy:** *semi-finals:* P. Watts (Henley) wo, R. Baptiste (Lewsey Centre) w pts S. Green (Farley); *final:* P. Watts w pts R. Baptiste. **Heavy:** no entries. **S. Heavy:** *final:* M. Sprott (Bulmershe) w co 1 P. Reading (Hitchin).

Eastern Counties v Home Counties

Molin's Recreation Club, Saunderton - 4 March
L. Fly: J. Locke (Henley) wo. **Fly:** no entries. **Bantam:** D. Adams

(Colchester) wo. **Feather:** D. Dainty (Canvey) w pts D. Maher (Marlow). **Light:** M. Hawthorne w rtd 2 A. McBeal (Hitchin). **L. Welter:** D. James (Bury St Edmunds) w pts A. Tomlin (Bedford). **Welter:** K. McCarthy (Bedford) w pts A. Sims (Canvey). **L. Middle:** N. Burwood (Lowestoft) w pts S. Wright (Sandy). **Middle:** C. Marshall (Stevenage) w co 2 M. Redhead (Cambridge & Soham). **L. Heavy:** P. Watts (Henley) w rsc 3 A. Gray (Yarmouth). **Heavy:** R. Hardy (Cambridge & Soham) wo. **S. Heavy:** M. Sprott (Bulmershe) w pts I. Davey (Ipswich).

Midland Counties v Eastern Counties / Home Counties

Garrington's Sports & Social Club - 18 March

L. Fly: J. Locke (Henley) wo. **Fly:** D. Spencer (Pleck) wo. **Bantam:** D. Adams (Colchester) w pts E. Pickering (RHP). **Feather:** R. Evatt (Triumph) wo D. Dainty (Canvey). **Light:** R. Rutherford (Bell Green) w pts M. Hawthorne (Lowestoft). **L. Welter:** D. Ashley (Merlin) w pts D. James (Bury St Edmunds). **Welter:** K. McCarthy (Bedford) w rsc 2 J. Scanlon (Birmingham). **L. Middle:** K. Gibbons (Derby) w rtd 2 N. Burwood (Lowestoft). **Middle:** C. Marshall (Stevenage) w pts S. Bendall (Triumph). **L. Heavy:** J. Oliver (Bracebridge) w pts P. Watts (Henley). **Heavy:** A. Dowling (Bracebridge) w rsc 2 R. Hardy (Cambridge & Soham). **S. Heavy:** M. Sprott (Bulmershe) w dis 2 B. Summers (Wednesbury).

London v Combined Services

London

North-East Division   York Hall, Bethnal Green - 9 February
L. Fly no entries. **Fly:** *final:* M. Cahill (Lion) wo. **Bantam:** *final:* L. Jared (Gator) w pts M. Bush (Newham). **Feather:** *final:* S. Murray (Newham) wo. **Light:** *semi-finals:* K. Wing (Repton) wo, D. Happe (Repton) w pts S. O'Donnell (Alma); *final:* K. Wing wo D. Happe. **L. Welter:** *semi-finals:* P. Swinney (Repton) w pts A. Cesay (Repton), M. Riviere (Newham) w rsc 3 G. Turner (Hornchurch & Elm Park); *final:* P. Swinney w pts M. Riviere. **Welter:** *final:* P. Wright (Repton) wo. **L. Middle:** *semi-finals:* E. Monteith (Gator) w pts C. Houliston (Alma), R. Maguire (Hornchurch & Elm Park) w pts L. Omar (Repton); *final:* R. Maguire w rsc 2 E. Monteith. **Middle:** *quarter-finals:* A. Lowe (Repton) wo, J. Ratcliffe (Alma) wo, C. Baker (Waltham Forest) w rsc 3 N. Clark (Newham), J. Matthews (Crown & Manor) w dis 1 B. Allen (St Monica's); *semi-finals:* A. Lowe w pts J. Ratcliffe, J. Matthews w rsc 1 C. Baker; *final:* J. Matthews w pts A. Lowe. **L. Heavy:** *final:* J. Branch (Repton) w co 2 B. Kalombo (West Ham). **Heavy:** *semi-finals:* E. Crawford (Repton) wo, D. Negus (Five Star) w rsc 3 S. Lukacs (Newham); *final:* D. Negus w pts E. Crawford. **S. Heavy:** *final:* J. Beecroft (Gator) wo.

North-West Division   The Irish Centre, Tottenham - 2 February & The Town Hall, Battersea - 7 February
L. Fly: no entries. **Fly:** *final:* R. Ramzan (St Patrick's) wo. **Bantam:** *final:* M. Alexander (Islington) w pts C. Beeby (Northolt). **Feather:** *final:* T. Mongan (Trojan Police) w rsc 2 D. Stipour (All Stars). **Light:** *final:* D. Brown (St Patrick's) wo. **L. Welter:** *semi-finals:* J. Hall (St Patrick's) w pts A. Hunt (Northolt), B. Kelly (Dale) w pts I. Beaumont (St Patrick's); *final:* J. Hall w pts B. Kelly. **Welter:** *final:* J. Nevin (Northolt) w co 1 A. Lazarus (St Patrick's). **L. Middle:** *semi-finals:* O. Newman (Hanwell) wo, D. Odangkara (Trojan Police) w pts M. Scott

(Islington); *final:* D. Odangkara w pts O. Newman. **Middle:** *quarter-finals:* G. Reyniers (St Patrick's) w rsc 3 D. Johnson (Islington), E. Gayle (St Pancras) w rsc 2 T. Hrela (Islington), E. Gordiano (Islington) w pts C. Ifekoya (Ruislip), S. Tobin (All Stars) w pts T. Owoh (All Stars); *semi-finals:* E. Gayle w pts G. Reyniers, S. Tobin w pts E. Giordano; *final:* S. Tobin w pts E. Gayle. **L. Heavy:** *final:* B. Lesley (Islington) w co 3 C. Fry (Islington). **Heavy:** *semi-finals:* C. Prince (New Enterprise) w pts I. Ajose (All Stars), P. Lawrence (Hayes) w pts J. Young (All Stars); *final:* C. Prince w rsc 2 P. Lawrence. **S. Heavy:** *final:* A. Harrison (Islington) wo.

South-East Division   The Crook Log Sports Centre, Bexleyheath - 4 February & York Hall, Bethnal Green - 9 February
L.Fly: no entries. **Fly:** *final:* D. Costello (Hollington) wo. **Bantam:** *final:* D. Easton (New Addington) wo. **Feather:** *semi-finals:* B. May (Lynn) w pts E. Lam (Fitzroy Lodge), S. Oates (Fitzroy Lodge) w pts A. Graham (New Peckham); *final:* B. May w pts S. Oates. **Light:** *final:* J. Alldis (Lynn) wo. **L. Welter:** *semi-finals:* A. Rossiter (St Joseph's) wo, C. Stanley (Fitzroy Lodge) w rsc 2 D. Banjo (Lynn); *final:* A. Rossiter w pts C. Stanley. **Welter:** *final:* M. Reigate (Croydon) wo. **L. Middle:** *final:* W. Alexander (Lynn) wo, S. Fearon (Lynn) w dis 2 M. Coney (St Peter's); *final:* W. Alexander w rsc 1 S. Fearon. **Middle:** *final:* N. Travis (Fitzroy Lodge) w dis 1 S. Johnson (Lynn). **L. Heavy:** *final:* M. Thomas (Hollington) wo. **Heavy:** *quarter-finals:* F. Okesola (Lynn) wo, K. Mitchell (Lynn) wo, T. Callum (Lynn) w pts S. Hewitt (Fitzroy Lodge), W. Gibson (St Peter's) w pts D. Williams (New Addington); *semi-finals:* F. Okesola w rsc 1 K. Mitchell, W. Gibson w pts T. Callum; *final:* F. Okesola w rsc 1 W. Gibson. **S. Heavy:** *final:* H. Senior (Lynn) w pts D. Williams (Lynn).

South-West Division   The Town Hall, Battersea - 7 February
L. Fly: no entries. **Fly:** *final:* S. Mallon (Tolworth) wo. **Bantam:** no entries. **Feather:** no entries. **Light:** *final:* F. Wilson (Battersea) w pts P. Nicholas (Balham). **L. Welter:** no entries. **Welter:** *final:* G. Eastman (Battersea) w rsc 3 R. Chambers (Balham). **L. Middle:** *final:* R. Williams (Earlsfield) wo. **Middle:** *final:* C. Campbell (Earlsfield) wo. **L. Heavy:** *final:* D. Gibbs (British Police) w pts F. Annan (Battersea). **Heavy:** *final:* N. Eastwood (Kingston) w pts T. Clark (Balham). **S. Heavy:** no entries.

London Semi-Finals & Finals   York Hall, Bethnal Green - 23 February & 2 March
L. Fly: no entries. **Fly:** *semi-finals:* D. Costello (Hollington) w rsc 2 M. Cahill (Lion), S. Mallon (Tolworth) w pts R. Ramzan (St Patrick's); *final:* D. Costello w co 1 S. Mallon. **Bantam:** *semi-finals:* L. Jared (Gator) wo, M. Alexander (Islington) w pts D. Easton (New Addington); *final:* L. Jared w pts M. Alexander. **Feather:** *semi-finals:* S. Murray (Newham) w, S. Oates (Fitzroy Lodge) - replaced B. May (Lynn) w co 2 T. Mongan (Trojan Police); *final:* S. Murray w rsc 3 S. Oates. **Light:** *semi-finals:* K. Wing (Repton) w pts D. Brown (St Patrick's), J. Alldis (Lynn) w dis 3 F. Wilson (Battersea); *final:* K. Wing w pts J. Alldis. **L. Welter:** *semi-finals:* P. Swinney (Repton) wo, J. Hall (St Patrick's) w pts A. Rossiter (St Joseph's); *final:* J. Hall w pts P. Swinney. **Welter:** *semi-finals:* P. Wright (Repton) w pts M. Reigate (Croydon), G. Eastman (Battersea) w co 2 J. Nevin (Northolt); *final:* P. Wright w rsc 2 G. Eastman. **L. Middle:** *semi-finals:* R. Williams (Earlsfield) w rsc 2 R. Maguire (Hornchurch & Elm Park), W. Alexander (Lynn) w co 1 D. Odangkara (Trojan Police); *final:* R. Williams w pts W. Alexander. **Middle:** *semi-finals:* J. Matthews (Crown & Manor) w rsc 1 S. Tobin (All Stars),

N. Travis (Fitzroy Lodge) w rsc 3 C. Campbell (Earlsfield); *final:* J. Matthews w rsc 3 N. Travis. **L. Heavy:** *semi-finals:* M. Thomas (Hollington) w pts D. Gibbs (British Police), J. Branch (Repton) w pts B. Lesley (Islington); *final:* J. Branch w dis 3 M. Thomas. **Heavy:** *semi-finals:* F. Okesola (Lynn) w rsc 1 E. Crawford (Repton) - replaced D. Negus (Five Star), C. Prince (New Enterprise) w rsc 1 N. Eastwood (Tolworth); *final:* F. Okesola w rsc 2 C. Prince. **S. Heavy:** *semi-finals:* H. Senior (Lynn) wo, A. Harrison (Islington) w rsc 2 J. Beecroft (Gator); *final:* A. Harrison w pts H. Senior.

Combined Services

RAF, RN & Army Championships   RAF Locking, Weston super Mare - 2 March

L. Fly: *final:* D. Fox (RAF) wo. **Fly:** no entries. **Bantam:** *semi-finals:* D. Dugan (Army) wo, O. Spensley (RAF) w pts S. Donley (RN); *final:* O. Spensley w rsc 3 D. Dugan. **Feather:** *final:* P. Williams (Army) w rtd 2 J. Kilkenny (RN). **Light:** *final:* V. Powell (Army) wo. **L. Welter:** *semi-finals:* K. Bennett (Army) wo, S. Mackay (Army) w pts P. Harris (RN); *final:* K. Bennett w pts S. Mackay. **Welter:** *semi-finals:* S. Whyte (RN) wo, K. Short (Army) w rsc 2 W. Davies (RAF); *final:* K. Short w rsc 3 S. Whyte. **L. Middle:** *final:* C. Beesey (Army) wo. **Middle:** *final:* J. Ollerhead (Army) wo. **L. Heavy:** *final:* M. Quirey (Army) wo. **Heavy:** *final:* V. Jones (Army) w pts L. Kerry (RN). **S. Heavy:** *final:* D. Watts (Army) w rsc 1 P. Fiske (RAF).

London v Combined Services

The Military Boxing Centre, Aldershot - 18 March

L. Fly: D. Fox (RAF) wo. **Fly:** D. Costello (Hollington) wo. **Bantam:** O. Spensley (RAF) w pts L. Jared (Gator). **Feather:** P. Williams (Army) w rsc 3 S. Murray (Newham). **Light:** V. Powell (Army) w co 3 J. Alldis (Lynn) - replaced K. Wing (Repton). **L. Welter:** K. Bennett (Army) w pts J. Hall (St Patrick's). **Welter:** P. Wright (Repton) w pts K. Short (Army). **L. Middle:** C. Bessey (Army) w pts R. Williams (Earlsfield). **Middle:** J. Matthews (Crown & Manor) w pts J. Ollerhead (Army). **L. Heavy:** J. Branch (Repton) w pts M. Quirey (Army). **Heavy:** F. Okesola (Lynn) w co 3 V. Jones (Army). **S. Heavy:** D. Watts (Army) w pts A. Harrison (Islington).

English ABA Semi-Final & Finals

HMS Nelson, Portsmouth - 28 March, The Dome, Doncaster - 29 March & The National Indoor Arena, Birmingham - 12 April

L. Fly: *semi-finals:* G. Jones (Sefton) wo, D. Fox (RAF) w rsc 2 J. Locke (Henley); *final:* D. Fox w pts G. Jones. **Fly:** *semi-finals:* D. Spencer (Pleck) w pts M. Cairns (St Paul's), D. Costello (Hollington) w rsc 1 C. Toohey (Gemini); *final:* D. Costello w rsc 2 D. Spencer. **Bantam:** *semi-finals:* N. Wilders (Five Towns) w pts D. Adams (Colchester), O. Spensley (RAF) w pts L. Eedle (Gemini); *final:* N. Wilders w co 3 O. Spensley. **Feather:** *semi-finals:* M. Gibbons (South Bank) w pts R. Evatt (Triumph), D. Burrows (Benchill) w rsc 2 P. Williams (Army); *final:* D. Burrows w rsc 2 M. Gibbons. **Light:** *semi-finals:* R. Rutherford (Bell Green) w pts G. Hibbert (Gallagher), A. McLean (Hylton Castle)

w pts V. Powell (Army); *final:* R. Rutherford w pts A. McLean. **L. Welter:** *semi-finals:* A. Vaughan (Huyton) w rsc 2 D. Ashley (Merlin), L. Crosby (St Paul's) w pts K. Bennett (Army); *final:* A. Vaughan w rsc 3 L. Crosby. **Welter:** *semi-finals:* M. Hall (Darlington) w pts M. Jones (Rotunda), P. Wright (Repton) w pts K. McCarthy (Bedford); *final:* M. Hall w pts P. Wright. **L. Middle:** *semi-finals:* M. Barker (St Paul's) w pts K. Gibbons (Derby), C. Bessey (Army) w pts J. Jones (Sefton); *final:* C. Beesey w pts M. Barker. **Middle:** *semi-finals:* G. Grounds (Phil Thomas SOB) w pts C. Marshall (Stevenage), J. Matthews (Crown & Manor) w pts E. Stuart (Leonis); *final:* J. Matthews w co 1 G. Grounds. **L. Heavy:** *semi-finals:* K. Oliver (Bracebridge) w rsc 3 G. Biglin (North Hull), J. Branch (Repton) w pts P. Rogers (Penhill); *final:* K. Oliver w rsc 3 J. Branch. **Heavy:** *semi-finals:* M. Ellis (Blackpool & Fyldes) w rsc 1 A. Dowling (Bracebridge), F. Okesola (Lynn) w rsc 3 K. Duke (Sunderland); *final:* M. Ellis w rsc 2 F. Okesola. **S. Heavy:** *semi-finals:* R. Allen (Preston & Fulwood) w rsc 3 M. Sprott (Bulmershe), D. Watts (Army) w co 1 G. McGhin (Sunderland); *final:* R. Allen w dis 1 D. Watts.

Danny Costello (Hollington), the two-time ABA flyweight champion   Steve Parkin

Irish Championships, 1994-95

Senior Tournament

The National Stadium, Dublin - 10, 11 & 17 February
L. Fly: *final:* J. Prior (Darndale, Dublin) w pts C. Moffat (Holy Family, Belfast). **Fly:** *semi-finals:* D. Kelly (Holy Trinity, Belfast) wo, B. Walsh (Darndale, Dublin) w pts M. Wells (Midland/White City, Belfast); *final:* D. Kelly w pts B. Walsh. **Bantam:** *quarter-finals:* W. Valentine (St Saviour's, Dublin) w pts T. Hamilton (St Saviour's. Dublin), D. McKenna (Holy Family, Drogheda) w pts M. Murphy (St Paul's, Waterford), D. Hosford (Greenmount, Cork) w pts T. Waite (Cairn Lodge, Belfast), O. Duddy (Coleraine, Derry) w pts D. Lowry (Albert Foundry, Belfast); *semi-finals:* W. Valentine w pts D. McKenna, D. Hosford w pts O. Duddy; *final:* W. Valentine w pts D. Hosford. **Feather:** *semi-finals:* A. Patterson (St Patrick's, Newry) w pts F. Eade (St Anne's, Westport), T. Carlyle (Sacred Heart, Belfast) w pts J. Conlon (Holy Trinity, Belfast); *final:* A. Patterson w pts T. Carlyle. **Light:** *quarter-finals:* G. Stephens (Crumlin, Dublin) w pts S. Cowman (St Paul's, Waterford), M. Dillon (Golden Cobra, Dublin) w pts J. McEvoy (Edenmore, Dublin), M. Reneghan (Keady, Armagh) w pts J. Morrissey (Sunnyside, Cork), E. Bolger (Wrexford CBS) w pts E. McEnearney (Dealgan, Dundalk); *semi-finals:* G. Stephens w pts M. Dillon, M. Reneghan w rsc 3 E. Bolger; *final:* G. Stephens w pts M. Reneghan. **L. Welter:** *quarter-finals:* W. Walsh (St Colman's, Cork) wo, F. Carruth (Drimnagh, Dublin) wo, S. Barrett (Rylane, Cork) w co 1 J. Breen (St Ibar's, Wrexford), G. McClarnon (Clann Eirann, Lurgan) w pts S. McCann (Holy Family, Belfast); *semi-finals:* G. McClarnon w pts S. Barrett, W. Walsh w pts F. Carruth; *final:* G. McClarnon w pts W. Walsh. **Welter:** *semi-finals:* N. Gough (St Paul's, Waterford) wo, N. Sinclair (Holy Family, Belfast) w pts W. Egan (Neilstown, Dublin); *final:* N. Sinclair w pts N. Gough. **L. Middle:** *prelims:* S. Gibson (Immaculata, Belfast) wo, S. McCluskey (Docker's Belfast) wo, D. Higgins (Fermoy, Cork) wo, J. Payne (Tramore, Waterford) wo, J. Kelly (Sean McDermott's, Manorhamilton, Leitrim) wo, M. McBride (Edenderry, Offaly) wo, E. Fisher (Holy Trinity, Belfast) wo, M. Roche (Sunnyside, Cork) w pts T. Roche (St Luke's, Dublin); *quarter-finals:* S. Gibson w pts S. McCluskey, D. Higgins w pts J. Payne, J. Kelly w pts M. McBride, M. Roche w pts E. Fisher; *semi-finals:* D. Higgins w rsc 3 S. Gibson, M. Roche w pts J. Kelly; *final:* D. Higgins w pts M. Roche. **Middle:** *quarter-finals:* D. Galvin (St Saviour's, Dublin) wo, R. Fox (Phibsboro, Dublin) w pts J. McBride (Edenderry, Offaly), J. Rock (CIE, Dublin) w rtd 2 K. Walsh (St Colman's, Cork), B. Magee (Holy Trinity, Belfast) w pts T. Donnelly (Mark Heaghney's, Tyrone); *semi-finals:* D. Galvin w pts R. Fox, B. Magee w pts J. Rock; *final:* B. Magee w pts D. Galvin. **L. Heavy:** *quarter-finals:* G. Joyce (Sunnyside, Cork) wo, S. Lawlor (Grangecon, Kildare) wo, A. Sheerin (Swinford, Mayo) w pts S. Collier (Loch Gorman, Wexford), S. Kirk (Cairn Lodge, Belfast) w co 1 G. Hyde (Sunnyside, Cork); *semi-finals:* G. Joyce w pts S. Lawlor, S. Kirk w pts A. Sheerin; *final:* S. Kirk w pts G. Joyce. **Heavy:** *prelims:* M. Sutton (St Saviour's, Dublin) wo, T. Clifford (Rylane, Cork) wo, N. Okasili (Clonoe, Tyrone) wo, T. Brady (Galway) wo, P. Deane (Ballina, Mayo) wo; D. Griffin (Castleisland, Kerry) wo, J. Clancy (Kilfenora, Clare) w pts D. Cowley (St Michan's, Dublin), J. Kiely (Limerick City) w pts P. Doran (Phibsboro, Dublin); *quarter-finals:* M. Sutton w pts T. Clifford, N. Okasili w pts T. Brady, P. Deane w pts D. Griffin, J. Clancy w pts J. Kiely; *semi-finals:* M. Sutton w rsc 3 N. Okasili, J. Clancy w pts P. Deane; *final:* J. Clancy w pts M. Sutton. **S. Heavy:** *semi-finals:* P. Douglas (Holy Family, Belfast) wo, G. Douglas (South Meath, Meath) w pts D. Ward (Ballymun, Dublin); *final:* P. Douglas w pts G. Douglas.

Intermediate Finals

The National Stadium, Dublin - 9 December
L. Fly: N. Bowman (St Anne's, Westport) w pts J. Stacey (Crumlin, Dublin). **Fly:** B. Walsh (Darndale, Dublin) w rsc 3 J. Simpson (St Paul's, Waterford). **Bantam:** D. Lowry (Albert Foundry, Belfast) w pts C. O'Neill (Bracken, Dublin). **Feather:** F. Eade (St Anne's, Westport) w pts T. Hamilton (St Saviour's, Dublin). **Light:** O. Monteith (Carrickmore, Tyrone) w pts R. Bowe (Docker's, Belfast). **L. Welter:** A. Dunne (St Saviour's, Dublin) w pts G. McClarnon (Clann Eirann, Lurgan). **Welter:** R. Brannigan (Docker's, Belfast) w pts J. Harkin (Dunfanaghy, Donegal). **L. Middle:** D. Higgins (Fermoy, Cork) w pts J. Kelly (Sean McDermott's, Manorhamilton, Leitrim). **Middle:** B. Crowley (Ennis, Clare) w pts J. Gillen (St Michan's Dublin). **L. Heavy:** H. McNally (Randalstown, Antrim) w rsc 3 B. O'Riorden (Rylane, Cork). **Heavy:** C. O'Grady (St Saviour's, Dublin) w pts D. Ward (Galway). **S. Heavy:** D. Walsh (Knocknagoshel, Kerry).

Junior Finals

The National Stadium, Dublin - 5 May
L. Fly: N. Bowman (St Anne's, Westport) w pts D. Sweetman (Golden Cobra, Dublin). **Fly:** D. Cullen (Edenderry, Offaly) w pts N. Haslett (St Mochta's, Dublin). **Bantam:** D. Hyland (Golden Cobra, Dublin) w co 1 C. McAllister (Oliver Plunkett's, Belfast). **Feather:** E. Lecumber (Portlaoise, Laios) w pts M. Dillon (Golden Cobra, Dublin). **Light:** P. Mowbray (Docker's, Belfast) w pts P. Walsh (St Colman's, Cork). **L. Welter:** F. Barrett (Olympic, Galway) w pts J. Keohane (Durgarvan, Waterford). **Welter:** K. Cumiskey (Tralee, Kerry) w pts F. O'Brien (Ballyduff, Kerry). **L. Middle:** P. Keogh (Inner City, Dublin) w pts P. Daly (St Colman's, Cork). **Middle:** A. Kelly (Brosna, Offaly) w pts P. O'Brien (Kilcullen, Kildare). **L. Heavy:** T. Crampton (St Broughan's, Offaly) w pts P. Walsh (Rosmuc, Galway). **Heavy:** C. O'Grady (St Saviour's, Dublin) w rsc 2 D. Hoary (Portumna, Galway). **S. Heavy:** B. McGinley (Keady, Armagh) wo.

Irish Senior Titles: Record Championship Wins

10: Jim O'Sullivan, 1980-1990. **9:** Gerry O'Colmain, 1943-1952; Harry Perry, 1952-1962. **8:** Mick Dowling, 1968-1975; Ernie Smyth, 1932-1940. **7:** Jack Chase, 1926-1932; Jim McCourt, 1963-1972. **6:** Brian Byrne, 1954-1967; Matt Flanagan, 1925-1931; Paddy Hughes, 1929-1935; Kieran Joyce, 1983-1988; Frank Kerr, 1932-1938; Mick McKeon, 1945-1951; Tommy Milligan, 1950-1955; W. J. Murphy, 1924-1932; Jack O'Driscoll, 1924-1934; Ando Reddy, 1951-1961; Billy Walsh, 1983-1991. **5:** Willie Byrne, 1959-1963; Paul Douglas, 1989-1995; Paul Fitzgerald, 1982-1988; Dennis Galvin, 1989-1994; Dick Hearns, 1933-1938; Brendan McCarthy, 1967-1971; Charlie Nash, 1970-1975. **4:** Ken Beattie, 1977-1982; Paul Buttimer, 1987-1993; Michael Carruth, 1987-1992; Dave Connell, 1946-1951; Peter Crotty, 1949-1952; Gordon Ferris, 1973-1977; Paul Griffin, 1991-1994; Gordon Joyce, 1986-1994; Joe Lawlor, 1986-1991; Eamonn McCusker, 1965-1969; Jack O'Rourke, 1963-1971; Danno Power, 1958-1962; Phil Sutcliffe, 1977-1985; Eddie Treacy, 1961-1969; T. J. Tubridy, 1912-1923.

Scottish Championships, 1994-95

The Monklands Time Capsule, Coatbridge - 4 & 23 March, The Fairfield Workmen's Club, Glasgow - 13 March & The Hydro, Dunblane - 17 March

L. Fly: no entries. **Fly:** *semi-finals:* P. Shepherd (Sparta) w pts W. Logue (Phoenix Calton), L. Munro (Dennistoun) w pts J. Davidson (Bannockburn); *final:* P. Shepherd w pts L. Munro. **Bantam:** *final:* A. Brennan (Barn) w pts S. Dickson (Sydney Street). **Feather:** *quarter-finals:* S. Harrison (Phoenix Calton) wo, T. McDermott (Croy) wo, A. McKinnon (Portobello) w pts R. Silverstein (Selkirk), A. Buchanan (Army) w rsc 2 A. Kidd (Meadowbank); *semi-finals:* S. Harrison w pts T. McDermott, A. Buchanan w pts A. McKinnon; *final:* S. Harrison w pts A. McKinnon. **Light:** *prelims:* K. Stuart (Elgin) wo, A. Lindie (Paisley) wo; M. Gowans (Selkirk) wo; J. Lees (Aberdeen) wo; R. McPhee (Glenboig) wo; B. Wilkie (Barn) wo; J. Coyle (Bannockburn) wo; K. Armstrong (Hasties) w pts L. Sharp (Phoenix); *quarter-finals:* R. McPhee w pts B. Wilkie, J. Coyle w pts K. Armstrong, K. Stuart w pts A. Lindie, M. Gowans w pts J. Lees; *semi-finals:* M. Gowans w pts K. Stuart, J. Coyle w pts R. McPhee; *final:* J. Coyle w pts M. Gowans. **L. Welter:** *prelims:* G. Murphy (Forgewood) wo, G. McLevy (Clydeview) wo; G. Fernie (Bonnyrigg) wo, C. McCann (Sparta) wo, J. Pender (St Francis) wo, D. Evans (Barn) wo, J. Gardner (Army) w pts W. Leckie (Haddington), G. Howett (Lochee) w pts A. Weir (GCT); *quarter-finals:* J. Pender w pts D. Evans, G. McLevy w pts G. Fernie, G. Howett w pts J. Gardner, G. Murphy w pts C. McCann; *semi-finals:* G. McLevy w pts G. Murphy, J. Pender w pts J. Howett; *final:* J. Pender w pts G. McLevy. **Welter:** *prelims:* C. McNeil (Springside) wo, K. McCartney (Portobello) wo, C. Lynch (Sparta) wo, S. Kelly (Dennistoun) wo, R. Beattie (Kingkorth) wo, I. McEwan (Clydebank) wo, J. Docherty (Portobello) w rsc 2 C. Summers (Belahouston), P. Munro (Lochee) w pts J. Millar (Stirling); *quarter-finals:* J. Docherty w rsc 1 P. Munro, C. Lynch w pts S. Kelly, C. McNeil w pts K. McCartney, I. McEwan w rsc 3 R. Beattie; *semi-finals:* C. Lynch w pts C. McNeill, J. Docherty w rsc 1 I. McEwan; *final:* J. Docherty w pts C. Lynch. **L. Middle:** *prelims:* L. Murphy (Forgewood) wo, M. Fleming (Denbeath) wo, A. Craig (Aberdeen) wo, B. Laidlaw (Cardenden) wo, J. Kane (Forgewood) wo, J. Gilhaney (Cleland) w pts A. Howett (Lochee), J. Heaney (Croy) w pts R. Mackie (Hayton), M. Flynn (Blantyre) w pts J. Norman (Arbroath); *quarter-finals:* L. Murphy w rsc 2 M. Fleming, A. Craig w pts J. Kane, B. Laidlaw w pts J. Gilhaney, J. Heaney w pts M. Flynn; *semi-finals:* L. Murphy w pts A. Craig, B. Laidlaw w pts J. Heaney; *final:* L. Murphy w pts B. Laidlaw. **Middle:** *prelims:* S. Docherty (Arbroath) wo, L. Powles (St Francis) wo, J. Usher (North West) wo, J. Daley (Bannockburn) wo, P. Grainger (Sparta) w rsc 2 G. Millard (Meadowbank), A. Wright (Newarthill) w pts S. McFarlane (Cleland), R. Hughes (Partick) w pts D. Stewart (Dunfermline), P. Murphy (Springhill) w pts J. Day (Montrose); *quarter-finals:* L. Powles w pts S. Docherty, J. Usher w pts J. Daley, A. Wright w rsc 3 P. Grainger, R. Hughes w pts P. Murphy; *semi-finals:* A. Wright w rsc 2 R. Hughes, L. Powles w rsc 3 J. Usher; *final:* A. Wright w pts L. Powles. **L. Heavy:** *prelims:* A. Khan (St Francis) wo, M. Fleming (Denbeath) wo, C. Templeton (GCT) wo, S. Topen (Lochee) wo, W. Cane (Four Isles) w rsc 3 M. Todd (Wellmeadow), A. Kelly (Meadowbank) w rsc 1 D. McNeill (Gartcosh), R. Campbell (Port Glasgow) w pts M. Sangster (Clovenstone), S. Kerr (St Francis) w pts I. Borden (Leith); *quarter-finals:* A. Kelly w pts W. Cane, M. Fleming w pts C. Templeton, S. Topen w dis 2 A. Khan, R. Campbell w pts S. Kerr; *semi-finals:* S. Topen w rsc 3 M. Fleming, R. Campbell wo A. Kelly; *final:* R. Campbell w pts S. Topen. **Heavy:** *quarter-finals:* J. Reilly (Lochee) wo, C. Brown (Gartcosh) wo, G. Ramsay (Arbroath) wo, J. Brown (Hawick) w pts P. Reilly (Dalray); *semi-finals:* C. Brown w rsc 2 J. Reilly, P. Reilly w rsc 3 G. Ramsay; *final:* C. Brown w rsc 3 P. Reilly. **S. Heavy:** *quarter-finals:* G. Seal (Forgewood) wo, J. Akinlami (Larkhall) wo, J. Cowie (Bannockburn) wo, S. McGuire (Glenrothes) w rsc 3 J. Williams (North West); *semi-finals:* G. Seal w pts J. Akinlami, J. Cowie w rsc 2 S. McGuire; *final:* G. Seal w pts J. Cowie.

Two-time Scottish flyweight champion, Paul Shepherd, is seen here being floored by England's Paul Ingle, now a successful pro.

Les Clark

Welsh Championships, 1994-95

The Afan Lido, Port Talbot - 4 February, The Tynewydd Labour Club, Treherbert - 15 February, The Leisure Centre, Ebbw Vale - 17 February & The Institute of Sport, Cardiff - 2 March

L. Fly: no entries. **Fly:** *final:* C. Williams (Highfield) w pts K. Ali (Splott). **Bantam:** *semi-finals:* A. Greenaway (Gelligaer) wo, I. Turner (Heads of Valleys) w pts R. Vowles (Llanharan); *final:* I. Turner w pts A. Greenaway. **Feather:** *semi-finals:* A. Fletcher (Newtown) wo, D. Morris (Roath) w rsc 2 H. Jones (Pembroke); *final:* D. Morris w rsc 1 A. Fletcher. **Light:** *quarter-finals:* J. Cook (Maesteg) wo, A. Evans (Carmarthen) wo, D. James (Highfield) wo, J. Davies (Cwmgors) w rsc 2 K. Evans (Newtown), *semi-finals:* A. Evans w co 3 D. James, J. Cook w rsc 1 J. Davies; *final:* J. Cook w rsc 1 A. Evans. **L. Welter:** *prelims:* M. Hall (Cwmbran) wo, C. Howells (Vale) wo, L. Winney (Teifi Valley) wo, J. Shoaib (Prince of Wales), N. Robinson (Prince of Wales), A. Robinson (Pennar) w rsc 1 P. Bailey (Coed Eva), J. Cheal (Whitland) w rsc 2 P. Goldsmith (Cwmcarn), L. Butler (Llanharan) w pts H. Janes (Highfield); *quarter-finals:* L. Winney wo J. Cheal, J. Shoaib w rsc 1 N. Robinson, M. Hall w pts C. Howells, A. Robinson w dis 1 L. Butler; *semi-finals:* M. Hall wo J. Shoaib, A. Robinson w co 3 L. Winney; *final:* A. Robinson w pts M. Hall. **Welter:** *quarter-finals:* J. Hall (Torfaen) w pts J. Thomas (Army), P. Samuels (Crindau) w rsc 1 A. Mitchell (Wrexham), P. Killian (Cwmcarn) w pts C. Rees (Garw Valley), A. Smith (Highfield) w rsc 3 K. Thomas (Pentwyn); *semi-finals:* A. Smith w pts P. Killian, P. Samuels w rsc 1 J. Hall; *final:* P. Samuels w pts A. Smith. **L. Middle:** *quarter-finals:* J. Samuels (Grange) wo, W. Jones (Idris) w rsc 2 A. Kerr (Army), A. Coffey (Colcot) w pts G. Harvey (St Joseph's), S. Pepperall (Vale) w pts G. Lockett (Pontypool & Panteg); *semi-finals:* J. Samuels w co 3 A. Coffey, S. Pepperall w pts W. Jones; *final:* J. Samuels w pts S. Pepperall. **Middle:** *quarter-finals:* G. Briggs (Pontypridd) wo, R. Phillips (Carmarthen) wo, N. Trinder (Coed Eva) wo, S. Stradling (Rhoose) w pts J. Rees (Trostre); *semi-finals:* N. Trinder w pts R. Phillips, G. Briggs w pts S. Stradling; *final:* G. Briggs w rsc 1 N. Trinder. **L. Heavy:** *prelims:* K. Evans (Carmarthen) wo, M. Durani (St Joseph's) wo, S. Gammer (Pembroke) w rsc 2 R. Higgs (Crindau), M. Rowland (Aberaman) w pts A. Barren (Vale), L. Hogan (Mold) w pts M. McCorley (Pontypridd), S. Pritchard (Fleur de Lys) w rsc 1 M. Jones (Porthcawl & Pyle), A. Holloway (Rhoose) w pts M. Vowles (Llanharan), H. Williams (Newtown) w rsc 2 D. Jones (Kyber Colts); *quarter-finals:* K. Evans w pts M. Durani, S. Pritchard w rsc 1 H. Williams, S. Gammer w co 1 M. Rowland, L. Hogan w rsc 2 A. Holloway; *semi-finals:* S. Gammer w pts K. Evans, S. Pritchard w pts L. Hogan; *final:* S. Gammer w pts S. Pritchard. **Heavy:** *prelims:* B. McCormack (Coed Eva) wo, B. Ludlow (All Saints) wo, S. Donaldson (Highfield) wo, S. Onytwu (RAOB Swansea) wo, H. Hartt (Preseli) wo, G. Paders (Crindau) wo, T. Redman (Idris) wo, D. Pippin (Newport) w rsc 3 C. Croft (Penarth); *quarter-finals:* B. McCormack w pts B. Ludlow, S. Donaldson w pts S. Onytwu, H. Hartt w pts G. Paders, T. Redman w pts D. Pippin; *semi-finals:* S. Donaldson w dis 3 B. McCormack, T. Redman w dis 2 H. Hartt; *final:* T. Redman w pts S. Donaldson. **S. Heavy:** *semi-finals:* K. McCormack (Coed Eva) w pts J. Davidson (Trostre), P. Lazenby (Newport) w rsc 2 S. White (Trelewis); *final:* K. McCormack wo P. Lazenby.

Jason Cook   Les Clark

British and Irish International Matches and Championships, 1994-95

Internationals

England (4) v Denmark (8)   Esbjerg, Denmark - 7 October
(English names first): **Fly:** O. Spensley l pts M. Mellenburg.
Feather: D. Burke w pts R. Idrissi. **Light:** T. Peacock w pts E.
Jensen; I. Smith l pts M. Eraslam. **L. Welter:** G. Smith l pts T.
Damgaard; P. Swinney l pts L. Pedersen. **Welter:** P. Wright l pts
F. Olsen; M. Hall l pts H. Al; P. Miles l rsc 1 C. Bladt. **L. Middle:**
W. Alexander l pts P. Andersen. **Middle:** S. Bendall w pts J. Laut.
L. Heavy: P. Rogers w pts M. Jasperson.

**Young England (4) v Young Scotland (4)   Tatton Park,
Knutsford - 17 October**
(English names first): **Fly:** W. Toohey l pts S. Dixon; D. Costello
w pts M. Crossan. **Bantam:** A. Crockett l pts A. Arthur; E.
Pickering w pts J. Davidson. **Feather:** S. Hodgson l pts F. Kerr.
Light: C. Wall l pts J. Coyle. **Welter:** J. Donaghue w pts A.
Wolecki. **L. Middle:** N. Linford w rsc 1 M. Black.

**Ireland (6) v Scotland (4)   Holy Family ABC, Drogheda - 6
November**
(Irish names first): **Fly:** J. Prior w pts M. Crossan. **Bantam:** D.
McKenna w co 1 L. Munro; B. Walsh l pts J. Davidson; M.
McQuillan l pts P. Shepherd. **L. Welter:** W. Walsh w rsc 3 J.
Pender; S. McCann w pts D. Evans; E. Bolger l pts M. Gowans.
Welter: T. Dunne w pts M. Black. **L. Middle:** S. Keeler w pts R.
Beattie; M. McBride l pts B. Laidlaw.

**Wales (6) v Ireland (3)   Holme View Leisure Centre, Barry -
18 November**
(Welsh names first): **Fly:** C. Williams w pts D. Cullen; J. Thomas
w co 1 M. McQuillan. **Feather:** T. Janes l pts G. Palmer. **L.
Welter:** H. Janes l pts T. Dunne; L. Winney w pts M. Dillon.
Welter: K. Thomas w co 2 S. Barrett. **Middle:** G. Briggs w rsc 1
R. Dooris. **L. Heavy:** L. Ratti l pts G. Joyce; P. Collins w pts P.
Doran.

*Mick Barker (left), seen here against Chris Bessey in this year's ABA light-middleweight final, made his international debut
for England on 13 February 1995, knocking out Scotland's Craig Lynch in the first round*   Steve Parkin

England (4) v USA (5)   Hilton Hotel, London - 21 November
Fly: D. Costello l pts J. Vega. **Bantam:** D. Easton l rtd 3 A. Johnson. **Feather:** M. Wright w pts R. Caban. **L. Welter:** J. Vlasman l co 1 A. Miller. **Welter:** J. Donaghue w pts J. Magallanez. **Middle:** S. Bendall l pts R. Simms. **L. Heavy:** P. Rogers w pts B. Mitchell. **Heavy:** M. Ellis w pts J. Cruz. **S. Heavy:** H. Senior l pts C. Shufford.

Scotland (3) v Ulster (1)   Earl Grey Hotel, Dundee - 1 December
(Scottish names first): **Bantam:** P. Shepherd w pts T. Waite. **Light:** J. Coyle w pts M. Reneghan. **Welter:** A. Wolecki w pts G. McNicholl. **Middle:** D. Flintoff l pts B. Kerr.

England (3) v Scotland (4)   Royal Lancaster Hotel, London - 13 February
(English names first): **Bantam:** G. Nicette l pts P. Shepherd. **Light:** G. Hibbert l rtd 2 J. Coyle. **L. Welter:** G. Stanley w co 2 G. Howett. **Welter:** R. McDonagh l rsc 1 C. McNeill; M. Barker w co 1 C. Lynch. **L. Middle:** W. Alexander w rsc 1 J. Gilhaney; T. Taylor l pts B. Laidlaw.

Ireland (3) v Italy (6)   National Stadium, Dublin - 24 February
(Irish names first): **L. Fly:** J. Prior l pts A. Cipriani; D. Sweetman l pts S. Digrazia. **Feather:** A. Patterson w pts G. Sannella. **Light:** G. Stephens w pts R. Verzolini. **L. Welter:** G. McClarnon l pts C. Giantamassi. **Welter:** N. Gough w pts P. Buonanno. **L. Middle:** D. Higgins l pts A. Perugino. **L. Heavy:** S. Collier l pts P. Aurino. **S. Heavy:** P. Douglas l co 1 P. Vidoz.

Wales (5) v Scotland (3)   Springfield Hotel, Holywell - 31 March
(Welsh names first): **Fly:** C. Williams w rsc 1 L. Munro. **L. Welter:** J. Shield l pts J. Coyle. **Welter:** A. Smith w pts J. Docherty. **L. Middle:** D. Haines l rsc 3 M. Flynn. **Middle:** S. Stradling w pts M. Fleming. **L. Heavy:** S. Thomas l rsc 3 A. Fleming. **Heavy:** T. Redman w pts W. Cane. **S. Heavy:** M. Rice w co 3 G. Seal.

Ireland (5) v Holland (3)   National Stadium, Dublin - 7 April
(Irish names first): **Light:** G. Stephens l pts A. Santana. **L. Welter:** G. McClarnon w pts N. Amine; T. Dunne w rtd 3 E. Atta. **L. Middle:** D. Higgins l pts O. Delibas. **Middle:** B. Magee w pts E. van den Heuvel. **L. Heavy:** S. Collier w pts D. Stolegraaf. **S. Heavy:** P. Douglas w pts H. de Kiefer; G. Douglas l pts P. Bouley.

Scotland (6) v Wales (3)   Fairfield Workmen's Club, Glasgow - 18 April
Bantam: S. Dixon w pts J. Thomas. **Light:** R. McPhee w pts J. Gethin. **L. Welter:** G. McLevy w pts P. Killian. **Welter:** C. McNeill w pts D. Haines. **L. Middle:** L. Murphy w pts J. Samuels; J. Gilhaney l pts W. Jones. **Middle:** R. Hughes l rsc 3 S. Stradling. **L. Heavy:** W. Cane l pts S. Gammer. **Heavy:** C. Brown w rsc 2 P. Timms.

Scotland (3) v Wales (4)   Earl Grey Hotel, Dundee - 20 April
(Scottish names first): **Feather:** A. Kidd l pts J. Gethin. **Light:** J. Coyle w pts J. Cook. **L. Welter:** J. Pender w pts P. Killian. **L. Middle:** B. Laidlaw l pts J. Samuels; A. Craig w pts D. Haines. **Middle:** L. Powles l co 1 S. Stradling. **L. Heavy:** S. Topen l pts S. Gammer.

Championships

World Juniors   Istanbul, Turkey - 8 to 18 September
Fly: K. Ali (Wales) l pts B. Nikolov (Bulgaria). **Bantam:** J. Davidson (Scotland) l rsc 2 G. Peradze (Uzbekistan). **Feather:** P. Watson (Scotland) w pts D. Abramovitsch (Israel), l rtd 3 L. Alvaraz (Cuba). **Light:** J. Coyle (Scotland) l rsc 3 T. Kalimor (Kazakhstan); D. Happe (England) l dis 3 F. Vargas (USA). **L. Welter:** J. Hare (Scotland) l pts M. Macovei (Romania); S. Rees (Wales) l pts H. Hak-Soo (S. Korea); J. Docherty (Scotland) l rsc 2 M. Ghenov (Moldova); T. Dunne (Ireland) w pts N. Kasenov (Kyrgyzstan), l pts H. Cexeubaev (Kazakhstan). **Welter:** D. Devers (Ireland) w pts G. Torvisco (Spain), l rsc 1 M. Rodriguez (Cuba); B. Tyrell (England) l rsc 2 T. Csala (Hungary), w co 2 G. Bonaparte (Romania), l rsc 1 M. Rodriguez (Cuba). **L. Middle:** L. Murphy (Scotland) l pts F. Kazanic (Slovakia). **Middle:** B. Crowley (Ireland) l pts M. Bahri (Algeria). **L. Heavy:** C. O'Grady (Ireland) l pts S. Mikharlov (Uzbekistan).

World Seniors   Berlin, Germany - 6 to 14 May
Fly: J. Thomas (Wales) l pts H. Mostafa (Egypt); P. Shepherd (Scotland) l pts B. Jumadilov (Kazakhstan); D. Kelly (Ireland) w pts S. Villareal (Argentine), withdrew v G. Farkas (Hungary); D. Costello (England) w pts A. Bravo (USA), l pts J. Turunen (Finland). **Feather:** D. Burke (England) w pts S. Vagasky (Slovakia), l pts U. Ibragimov. **Light:** G. Stephens (Ireland) l pts P. Rojas (Cuba). **L. Welter:** J. Pender (Scotland) l pts O. Urkal (Germany). **Welter:** N. Gough (Ireland) l pts K. Kauramaeki (Finland); J. Donaghue (England) l pts P. Buonanno (Italy). **L. Middle:** L. Murphy (Scotland) l pts A. Fetahovic (Bosnia). **Middle:** B. Magee (Ireland) l pts D. Eigenbrodt (Germany); G. Briggs (Wales) l pts M. Borbashev (Kyrghzstan). **S. Heavy:** D. Williams (England) l pts A. Levin (Sweden).

European Juniors   Sifok, Hungary - 19 to 25 June
L. Fly: N. Bowman (Ireland) l pts I. Kummerow (Germany); J. Booth (England) l pts C. Rodriguez (France). **Fly:** C. Williams (Wales) l pts A. Sabbakhov (Russia); J. Davidson (Scotland) l pts R. Walstad (Norway); D. Cullen (Ireland) l pts A. Ramazyan (Armenia). **Bantam:** J. Rooney (England) w pts R. Raphael (Slovakia), l pts A. Loutsenko (Ukraine); D. Hyland (Ireland) w pts A. Leonov (Russia), l pts D. Uchkov (Bulgaria). **Feather:** M. McDonagh (England) l pts A. Ercin (Turkey); E. Lecumber (Ireland) w pts A. Pliopa (Lithuania), l co 1 I. Goriunov (Russia); S. Harrison (Scotland) w pts T. Papp (Germany), w rtd 3 A. Jonas (Hungary), w pts Y. Zaoui (France), w pts I. Goriunov (Russia). **Light:** D. Dunnion (Wales) l pts G. Trunca (Lithuania); P. Mowbray (Ireland) w pts R. Klucar (Slovakia), w pts G. Trunca (Lithuania), l pts L. Konecny (Czechoslovakia). **L. Welter:** F. Barrett (Ireland) w pts A. Avdalian (Armenia), l pts V. Senchenko (Ukraine); G. Murphy (Scotland) w pts A. Stoda (Estonia), w pts M. Lokes (Russia), w pts V. Grouchak (Moldova), l pts B. Ulusoy (Turkey). **Welter:** K. Cumiskey (Ireland) l pts C. Perugino (Italy); R. Dakin-Weston (Wales) w pts R. Lumberg (Finland), l pts O. Bouts (Ukraine). **L. Middle:** N. Linford (England) w pts P. Keogh (Ireland), w pts A. Tikkanen (Finland), l pts C. D'Alessandro (Italy). **Middle:** A. Kelly (Ireland) l pts V. Hasoiya (Israel). **Heavy:** T. Crampton (Ireland) l rtd 1 O. Stoukalo (Ukraine). **Heavy:** C. O'Grady (Ireland) w rsc 1 A. Gueorguiev (Bulgaria), w pts J. Golla (Germany), w co 1 I. Tzavaras (Greece), w rsc 2 M. Dantus (Romania).

British Junior Championship Finals, 1994-95

National Association of Boy's Clubs

Granby Halls, Leicester - 7 January

Class A: 42 kg: N. Cook (Hornchurch & Elm Park) w pts H. Johnson (Pontypool & Panteg). 45 kg: S. Burke (Salisbury) w pts J. O'Sullivan (Medway GG). 48 kg: J. Chambers (Highfield) w pts D. Hayde (Splott). 51 kg: T. Driscoll (Newham) w pts P. Croll (St Paul's). 54 kg: J. Fethon (Kingston, Hull) w pts R. Mann (Newham). 57 kg: S. Smith (St Joseph's) wo T. Poulson (Tuebrook). 60 kg: T. James (Eltham) w pts S. Reagan (Salisbury). 63.5 kg: S. Swales (Phil Thomas' SOB) w rsc 1 E. Fitzgerald (Lynn). 67 kg: A. Larkins (Bracknell) w pts G. McAnaney (Lambton Street). 71 kg: P. Souter (Newham) w pts G. Drinkwater (Belgrave).

Class B: 45 kg: S. Groves (Tower Hill) w pts G. Dove (West Ham). 48 kg: D. Tokeley (West Ham) w pts C. Johanneson (Burmantofts). 51 kg: J. Rooney (Hartlepool Catholic) w pts G. Alger (Eltham). 54 kg: S. Hodgson (Shildon) w co 1 A. Thomas (Canvey). 57 kg: L. Daws (Rosehill) w pts A. Kelly (Darlington). 60 kg: G. Earl (Luton High Town) w pts R. Denton (Sheffield). 63.5 kg: P. Mowbray (Dockers) w pts J. Smith (RAF Uxbridge). 67 kg: R. Hatton (Sale West) w pts A. Coates (Medway GG). 71 kg: G. Hutchon (Dale) w pts R. Rooney (Croxteth). 74 kg: G. Diggins (Foley) w pts M. Fenton (Belgrave). 77 kg: no entries.

Hilton Hotel, Mayfair - 9 January

Class C: 48 kg: L. Cunningham (Saints) w pts S. Mullins (Downside). 51 kg: J. Martin (Canvey) w pts M. O'Gara (Old Vic). 54 kg: M. Bush (Newham) w co 2 K. Roberts (Gemini). 57 kg: M. Armstrong (Collyhurst & Moston) w pts M. Bolger (Lynn). 60 kg: S. Glasser (Paignton) w rsc 2 R. McPhee (West Hull). 63.5 kg: C. Wall (Gemini) w pts B. Scott (Camberley). 67 kg: B. Bangher (Bedford) wo J. Gould (Wednesbury). 71 kg: G. Lockett (Pontypool & Panteg) w rsc 1 E. McDermott (Northolt). 75 kg: P. Loughran (Luton Irish) w pts J. Dolan (Plains Farm). 81 kg: G. Johnson (Bracebridge) w pts S. St John (Berry). 91 kg: S. Smith (Hurstleigh & Kerridge) w pts D. Coates (Highfield).

Schools

Riviera Centre, Torquay - 4 March

Class 1: 32 kg: S. McDonald (St Joseph's) w pts G. Pickin (Llansamlet). 34 kg: J. Evans (Maesteg) w rsc 1 D. Wilson (Triple A). 36 kg: R. Eccleston (Everton Red Triangle) w pts D. Langley (Hollington). 39 kg: J. Doherty (Dale) w pts G. Howe (Shildon). 42 kg: M. O'Donnell (Dale) w pts D. Richards (Highfields). 45 kg: N. Evans (Maesteg) w pts L. Beavis (Dale). 48 kg: C. Masterson (Coventry Colliery) w pts P. McDonagh (St Monica's). 51 kg: S. Gorman (Bulkington) w rsc 2 S. Trigg (Bronx). 54 kg: D. Spensley (Aycliffe) w pts A. Milton (East Ham). 57 kg: P. Buchanan (Teams) w pts W. Slate (Five Star).

Class 2: 36 kg: M. Maitchell (Darlington) w pts D. Cook (Hornchurch & Elm Park). 39 kg: B. Tokely (West Ham) w pts J. Garforth (Batley & Dewsbury). 42 kg: W. Stratford (Splott) w pts J. Convoy (St Mary's). 45 kg: M. Burke (Newham) w rsc 1 M. White (Porthcawl). 48 kg: T. Shaw (Sporting Ring) w pts T. McDonagh (Collyhurst & Moston). 51 kg: D. Thomas (Hartlepool Catholic) w pts H. Rahman

(Bushey). 54 kg: J. Kiely (Repton) w pts I. Hennigan (Salisbury). 57 kg: D. Smith (Partington) w rsc 3 G. Smith (Foley). 60 kg: S. Price (Pinewood Starr) w pts D. Smith (Willenhall). 63 kg: L. Fields (Tower Hill) w co 1 T. Wilton (Aylesham). 66 kg: R. Davies (Croeserw) w rsc 1 R. Welch (Cambridge & Soham).

Class 3: 39 kg: R. Nelson (Batley & Dewsbury) w pts S. Symes (West Hill). 42 kg: N. Cook (Hornchurch & Elm Park) w pts J. O'Sullivan (Bracebridge). 45 kg: C. Solway (West Hull) w pts L. O'Reilly (St Mary's). 48 kg: M. Gallagher (Islington) w pts D. Mulholland (Transport). 51 kg: M. Power (St Pancras) w pts G. Winstone (Aberbargoed). 54 kg: J. Spence (Cotgrave) w pts B. Morgan (Canvey). 57 kg: M. Knowles (Bury) w pts M. Hickman (Titchfield). 60 kg: S. Reagan (Salisbury) w pts M. McLean (County). 63 kg: G. McAnaney (Lambton Street) w pts T. James (Eltham). 66 kg: A. Hindley (St Paul's) w pts L. Coates (Medway GG). 69 kg: A. Dodson (Gemini) w rsc 2 R. Mirza (Ruskin).

Class 4: 42 kg: D. Taylor (Bulmershe) w co 3 H. Johnson (Pontypool & Panteg). 45 kg: S. Miller (St Paul's) w pts J. O'Sullivan (Medway GG). 48 kg: D. Pryce (Newbridge) w pts T. Utting (St Mary's). 51 kg: T. Driscoll (Newham) w pts T. Rowley (Hartlepool BW). 54 kg: W. Connors (Splott) w pts R. Mann (Newham). 57 kg: C. Adams (Gilfach Goch) w pts S. Smith (St Joseph's). 60 kg: R. Beck (Repton) w pts M. Walters (Highfields). 63.5 kg: D. Brown (March) w rsc 3 S. Swales (Phil Thomas SOB). 67 kg: R. Hatton (Sale West) w rsc 1 K. Chaffer (Taunton). 71 kg: R. Rooney (Croxteth) w pts S. Lee (West Ham). 75 kg: P. Souter (Newham) w pts T. Iqbal (Bradford Police).

ABA Youth

Leisure Centre, Bracknell - 13 May

Class 5: 42 kg: no entries. 45 kg: G. Dove (West Ham) w pts S. Groves (Tower Hill). 48 kg: J. Hegney (Castle Vale) w co 1 C. Johannson (Burmantofts). 51 kg: D. Tokely (West Ham) w pts J. Bunney (Lingdale). 54 kg: J. Rooney (Hartlepool Catholic) w rsc 3 S. Gethin (Wednesbury). 57 kg: C. Skelton (South Bank) w pts K. Fox (Bracebridge). 60 kg: A. Kelly (Darlington) w pts N. Lee (Repton). 63.5 kg: M. Lomax (West Ham) w pts J. Idris (Birmingham). 67 kg: R. Hatton (Sale West) wo R. Padley (Haworth Colliery). 71 kg: A. Coates (Medway GG) w pts R. Brown (March). 75 kg: G. Diggins (Foley) w rsc 3 D. Robinson (Willy Freund). 81 kg: H. Smith (Avalon) w pts J. Smith (Foley). 91 kg: no entries.

Class 6: 45 kg: no entries. 48 kg: S. Green (Islington) w pts S. Warbrick (Gemini). 51 kg: J. Booth (Radford) w pts G. Wood (Brighton). 54 kg: S. Morgan (Farley) w pts C. Rumble (St Mary's). 57 kg: M. McDonagh (Lynn) w pts S. Conway (Batley & Dewsbury). 60 kg: L. Daws (Rosehill) w pts A. Berkley (Synwell). 63.5 kg: B. Scott (Camberley) w pts J. Gallagher (Islington). 67 kg: D. Oliver (Silver Street) w pts M. Jennings (Preston Red Rose). 71 kg: N. Linford (Belgrave) w rsc 2 C. Johnson (Southampton). 75 kg: S. Whatley (South Norwood) w pts L. Bailey (Colchester). 81 kg: S. St John (Berry) wo. 91 kg: no entries.

ABA Champions, 1881-1995

Darren Fox (RAF), ABA light-flyweight champion for 1995   Steve Parkin

L. Flyweight
1971 M. Abrams
1972 M. Abrams
1973 M. Abrams
1974 C. Magri
1975 M. Lawless
1976 P. Fletcher
1977 P. Fletcher
1978 J. Dawson
1979 J. Dawson
1980 T. Barker
1981 J. Lyon
1982 J. Lyon
1983 J. Lyon
1984 J. Lyon
1985 M. Epton
1986 M. Epton
1987 M. Epton
1988 M. Cantwell
1989 M. Cantwell
1990 N. Tooley
1991 P. Culshaw
1992 D. Fifield
1993 M. Hughes
1994 G. Jones
1995 D. Fox

Flyweight
1920 H. Groves
1921 W. Cuthbertson
1922 E. Warwick
1923 L. Tarrant
1924 E. Warwick
1925 E. Warwick
1926 J. Hill
1927 J. Roland
1928 C. Taylor
1929 T. Pardoe
1930 T. Pardoe
1931 T. Pardoe
1932 T. Pardoe
1933 T. Pardoe
1934 P. Palmer
1935 G. Fayaud
1936 G. Fayaud
1937 P. O'Donaghue
1938 A. Russell
1939 D. McKay
1944 J. Clinton
1945 J. Bryce
1946 R. Gallacher
1947 J. Clinton
1948 H. Carpenter
1949 H. Riley
1950 A. Jones
1951 G. John
1952 D. Dower
1953 R. Currie
1954 R. Currie
1955 D. Lloyd
1956 T. Spinks
1957 R. Davies
1958 J. Brown
1959 M. Gushlow
1960 D. Lee
1961 W. McGowan
1962 M. Pye
1963 M. Laud

1964 J. McCluskey
1965 J. McCluskey
1966 P. Maguire
1967 S. Curtis
1968 J. McGonigle
1969 D. Needham
1970 D. Needham
1971 P. Wakefield
1972 M. O'Sullivan
1973 R. Hilton
1974 M. O'Sullivan
1975 C. Magri
1976 C. Magri
1977 C. Magri
1978 G. Nickels
1979 R. Gilbody
1980 K. Wallace
1981 K. Wallace
1982 J. Kelly
1983 S. Nolan
1984 P. Clinton
1985 P. Clinton
1986 J. Lyon
1987 J. Lyon
1988 J. Lyon
1989 J. Lyon
1990 J. Armour
1991 P. Ingle
1992 K. Knox
1993 P. Ingle
1994 D. Costello
1995 D. Costello

Bantamweight
1884 A. Woodward
1885 A. Woodward
1886 T. Isley
1887 T. Isley
1888 H. Oakman
1889 H. Brown
1890 J. Rowe
1891 E. Moore
1892 F. Godbold
1893 E. Watson
1894 P. Jones
1895 P. Jones
1896 P. Jones
1897 C. Lamb
1898 F. Herring
1899 A. Avent
1900 J. Freeman
1901 W. Morgan
1902 A. Miner
1903 H. Perry
1904 H. Perry
1905 W. Webb
1906 T. Ringer
1907 E. Adams
1908 H. Thomas
1909 J. Condon
1910 W. Webb
1911 W. Allen
1912 W. Allen
1913 A. Wye
1914 W. Allen
1919 W. Allen
1920 G. McKenzie
1921 L. Tarrant
1922 W. Boulding

1923 A. Smith
1924 L. Tarrant
1925 A. Goom
1926 F. Webster
1927 E. Warwick
1928 J. Garland
1929 F. Bennett
1930 H. Mizler
1931 F. Bennett
1932 J. Treadaway
1933 G. Johnston
1934 A. Barnes
1935 L. Case
1936 A. Barnes
1937 A. Barnes
1938 J. Pottinger
1939 R. Watson
1944 R. Bissell
1945 P. Brander
1946 C. Squire
1947 D. O'Sullivan
1948 T. Proffitt
1949 T. Miller
1950 K. Lawrence
1951 T. Nicholls
1952 T. Nicholls
1953 J. Smillie
1954 J. Smillie
1955 G. Dormer
1956 O. Reilly
1957 J. Morrissey
1958 H. Winstone
1959 D. Weller
1960 F. Taylor
1961 P. Benneyworth
1962 P. Benneyworth
1963 B. Packer
1964 B. Packer
1965 R. Mallon
1966 J. Clark
1967 M. Carter
1968 M. Carter
1969 M. Piner
1970 A. Oxley
1971 G. Turpin
1972 G. Turpin
1973 P. Cowdell
1974 S. Ogilvie
1975 S. Ogilvie
1976 J. Bambrick
1977 J. Turner
1978 J. Turner
1979 R. Ashton
1980 R. Gilbody
1981 P. Jones
1982 R. Gilbody
1983 J. Hyland
1984 J. Hyland
1985 S. Murphy
1986 S. Murphy
1987 J. Sillitoe
1988 K. Howlett
1989 K. Howlett
1990 P. Lloyd
1991 D. Hardie
1992 P. Mullings
1993 R. Evatt
1994 S. Oliver
1995 N. Wilders

Featherweight
1881 T. Hill
1882 T. Hill
1883 T. Hill
1884 E. Hutchings
1885 J. Pennell
1886 T. McNeil
1887 J. Pennell
1888 J. Taylor
1889 G. Belsey
1890 G. Belsey
1891 F. Curtis
1892 F. Curtis
1893 T. Davidson
1894 R. Gunn
1895 R. Gunn
1896 R. Gunn
1897 N. Smith
1898 P. Lunn
1899 J. Scholes
1900 R. Lee
1901 C. Clarke
1902 C. Clarke
1903 J. Godfrey
1904 C. Morris
1905 H. Holmes
1906 A. Miner
1907 C. Morris
1908 T. Ringer
1909 A. Lambert
1910 C. Houghton
1911 H. Bowers
1912 G. Baker
1913 G. Baker
1914 G. Baker
1919 G. Baker
1920 J. Fleming
1921 G. Baker
1922 E. Swash
1923 E. Swash
1924 A. Beavis
1925 A. Beavis
1926 R. Minshull
1927 F. Webster
1928 F. Meachem
1929 F. Meachem
1930 J. Duffield
1931 B. Caplan
1932 H. Mizler
1933 J. Walters
1934 J. Treadaway
1935 E. Ryan
1936 J. Treadaway
1937 A. Harper
1938 C. Gallie
1939 C. Gallie
1944 D. Sullivan
1945 J. Carter
1946 P. Brander
1947 S. Evans
1948 P. Brander
1949 H. Gilliland
1950 P. Brander
1951 J. Travers
1952 P. Lewis
1953 P. Lewis
1954 D. Charnley
1955 T. Nicholls
1956 T. Nicholls

269

1957 M. Collins
1958 M. Collins
1959 G. Judge
1960 P. Lundgren
1961 P. Cheevers
1962 B. Wilson
1963 A. Riley
1964 R. Smith
1965 K. Buchanan
1966 H. Baxter
1967 K. Cooper
1968 J. Cheshire
1969 A. Richardson
1970 D. Polak
1971 T. Wright
1972 K. Laing
1973 J. Lynch
1974 G. Gilbody
1975 R. Beaumont
1976 P. Cowdell
1977 P. Cowdell
1978 M. O'Brien
1979 P. Hanlon
1980 M. Hanif
1981 P. Hanlon
1982 H. Henry
1983 P. Bradley
1984 K. Taylor
1985 F. Havard
1986 P. Hodkinson
1987 P. English
1988 D. Anderson
1989 P. Richardson
1990 B. Carr
1991 J. Irwin
1992 A. Temple
1993 J. Cook
1994 D. Pithie
1995 D. Burrows

Lightweight
1881 F. Hobday
1882 A. Bettinson
1883 A. Diamond
1884 A. Diamond
1885 A. Diamond
1886 G. Roberts
1887 J. Hair
1888 A. Newton
1889 W. Neale
1890 A. Newton
1891 E. Dettmer
1892 E. Dettmer
1893 W. Campbell
1894 W. Campbell
1895 A. Randall
1896 A. Vanderhout
1897 A. Vanderhout
1898 H. Marks
1899 H. Brewer
1900 G. Humphries
1901 A. Warner
1902 A. Warner
1903 H. Fergus
1904 M. Wells
1905 M. Wells
1906 M. Wells
1907 M. Wells
1908 H. Holmes
1909 F. Grace
1910 T. Tees
1911 A. Spenceley
1912 R. Marriott

1913 R. Grace
1914 R. Marriott
1919 F. Grace
1920 F. Grace
1921 G. Shorter
1922 G. Renouf
1923 G. Shorter
1924 W. White
1925 E. Viney
1926 T. Slater
1927 W. Hunt
1928 F. Webster
1929 W. Hunt
1930 J. Waples
1931 D. McCleave
1932 F. Meachem
1933 H. Mizler
1934 J. Rolland
1935 F. Frost
1936 F. Simpson
1937 A. Danahar
1938 T. McGrath
1939 H. Groves
1944 W. Thompson
1945 J. Williamson
1946 E. Thomas
1947 C. Morrissey
1948 R. Cooper
1949 A. Smith
1950 R. Latham
1951 R. Hinson
1952 F. Reardon
1953 D. Hinson
1954 G. Whelan
1955 S. Coffey
1956 R. McTaggart
1957 J. Kidd
1958 R. McTaggart
1959 P. Warwick
1960 R. McTaggart
1961 P. Warwick
1962 B. Whelan
1963 B. O'Sullivan
1964 J. Dunne
1965 A. White
1966 J. Head
1967 T. Waller
1968 J. Watt
1969 H. Hayes
1970 N. Cole
1971 J. Singleton
1972 N. Cole
1973 T. Dunn
1974 J. Lynch
1975 P. Cowdell
1976 S. Mittee
1977 G. Gilbody
1978 T. Marsh
1979 G. Gilbody
1980 G. Gilbody
1981 G. Gilbody
1982 J. McDonnell
1983 K. Willis
1984 A. Dickson
1985 E. McAuley
1986 J. Jacobs
1987 M. Ayers
1988 C. Kane
1989 M. Ramsey
1990 P. Gallagher
1991 P. Ramsey
1992 D. Amory
1993 B. Welsh

1995 R. Rutherford

L. Welterweight
1951 W. Connor
1952 P. Waterman
1953 D. Hughes
1954 G. Martin
1955 F. McQuillan
1956 D. Stone
1957 D. Stone
1958 R. Kane
1959 R. Kane
1960 R. Day
1961 B. Brazier
1962 B. Brazier
1963 R. McTaggart
1964 R. Taylor
1965 R. McTaggart
1966 W. Hiatt
1967 B. Hudspeth
1968 E. Cole
1969 J. Stracey
1970 D. Davies
1971 M. Kingwell
1972 T. Waller
1973 N. Cole
1974 P. Kelly
1975 J. Zeraschi
1976 C. McKenzie
1977 J. Douglas
1978 D. Williams
1979 E. Copeland
1980 A. Willis
1981 A. Willis
1982 A. Adams
1983 D. Dent
1984 D. Griffiths
1985 I. Mustafa
1986 J. Alsop
1987 A. Holligan
1988 A. Hall
1989 A. Hall
1990 J. Pender
1991 J. Matthews
1992 D. McCarrick
1993 P. Richardson
1994 A. Temple
1995 A. Vaughan

Welterweight
1920 F. Whitbread
1921 A. Ireland
1922 E. White
1923 P. Green
1924 P. O'Hanrahan
1925 P. O'Hanrahan
1926 B. Marshall
1927 H. Dunn
1928 H. Bone
1929 T. Wigmore
1930 F. Brooman
1931 J. Barry
1932 D. McCleave
1933 P. Peters
1934 D. McCleave
1935 D. Lynch
1936 W. Pack
1937 D. Lynch
1938 C. Webster
1939 R. Thomas
1944 H. Hall
1945 R. Turpin
1946 J. Ryan

1947 J. Ryan
1948 M. Shacklady
1949 A. Buxton
1950 T. Ratcliffe
1951 J. Maloney
1952 J. Maloney
1953 L. Morgan
1954 N. Gargano
1955 N. Gargano
1956 N. Gargano
1957 R. Warnes
1958 B. Nancurvis
1959 J. McGrail
1960 C. Humphries
1961 A. Lewis
1962 J. Pritchett
1963 J. Pritchett
1964 M. Varley
1965 P. Henderson
1966 P. Cragg
1967 D. Cranswick
1968 A. Tottoh
1969 T. Henderson
1970 T. Waller
1971 D. Davies
1972 T. Francis
1973 T. Waller
1974 T. Waller
1975 W. Bennett
1976 C. Jones
1977 C. Jones
1978 E. Byrne
1979 J. Frost
1980 T. Marsh
1981 T. Marsh
1982 C. Pyatt
1983 R. McKenley
1984 M. Hughes
1985 E. McDonald
1986 D. Dyer
1987 M. Elliot
1988 M. McCreath
1989 M. Elliot
1990 A. Carew
1991 J. Calzaghe

1992 M. Santini
1993 C. Bessey
1994 K. Short
1995 M. Hall

L. Middleweight
1951 A. Lay
1952 B. Foster
1953 B. Wells
1954 B. Wells
1955 B. Foster
1956 J. McCormack
1957 J. Cunningham
1958 S. Pearson
1959 S. Pearson
1960 W. Fisher
1961 J. Gamble
1962 J. Lloyd
1963 A. Wyper
1964 W. Robinson
1965 P. Dwyer
1966 T. Imrie
1967 A. Edwards
1968 E. Blake
1969 T. Imrie
1970 D. Simmonds
1971 A. Edwards
1972 L. Paul
1973 R. Maxwell
1974 R. Maxwell
1975 A. Harrison
1976 W. Lauder
1977 C. Malarkey
1978 E. Henderson
1979 D. Brewster
1980 J. Price
1981 E. Christie
1982 D. Milligan
1983 R. Douglas
1984 R. Douglas
1985 R. Douglas
1986 T. Velinor
1987 N. Brown
1988 W. Ellis
1989 N. Brown

Noel Wilders (Five Towns), the 1995 ABA bantamweight champion   Steve Parkin

David Burrows (right) on his way to a second round stoppage win over Michael Gibbons in the 1995 ABA featherweight final

Steve Parkin

1990 T. Taylor	1909 W. Child	1953 R. Barton	1989 S. Johnson	1951 G. Walker
1991 T. Taylor	1910 R. Warnes	1954 K. Phillips	1990 S. Wilson	1952 H. Cooper
1992 J. Calzaghe	1911 W. Child	1955 F. Hope	1991 M. Edwards	1953 H. Cooper
1993 D. Starie	1912 E. Chandler	1956 R. Redrup	1992 L. Woolcock	1954 A. Madigan
1994 W. Alexander	1913 W. Bradley	1957 P. Burke	1993 J. Calzaghe	1955 D. Rent
1995 C. Bessey	1914 H. Brown	1958 P. Hill	1994 D. Starie	1956 D. Mooney
	1919 H. Mallin	1959 F. Elderfield	1995 J. Matthews	1957 T. Green
Middleweight	1920 H. Mallin	1960 R. Addison		1958 J. Leeming
1881 T. Bellhouse	1921 H. Mallin	1961 J. Caiger	**L. Heavyweight**	1959 J. Ould
1882 A. H. Curnick	1922 H. Mallin	1962 A. Matthews	1920 H. Franks	1960 J. Ould
1883 A. J. Curnick	1923 H. Mallin	1963 A. Matthews	1921 L. Collett	1961 J. Bodell
1884 W. Brown	1924 J. Elliot	1964 W. Stack	1922 H. Mitchell	1962 J. Hendrickson
1885 M. Salmon	1925 J. Elliot	1965 W. Robinson	1923 H. Mitchell	1963 P. Murphy
1886 W. King	1926 F. P. Crawley	1966 C. Finnegan	1924 H. Mitchell	1964 J. Fisher
1887 R. Hair	1927 F. P. Crawley	1967 A. Ball	1925 H. Mitchell	1965 E. Whistler
1888 R. Hair	1928 F. Mallin	1968 P. McCann	1926 D. McCorkindale	1966 R. Tighe
1889 G. Sykes	1929 F. Mallin	1969 D. Wallington	1927 A. Jackson	1967 M. Smith
1890 J. Hoare	1930 F. Mallin	1970 J. Conteh	1928 A. Jackson	1968 R. Brittle
1891 J. Steers	1931 F. Mallin	1971 A. Minter	1929 J. Goyder	1969 J. Frankham
1892 J. Steers	1932 F. Mallin	1972 F. Lucas	1930 J. Murphy	1970 J. Rafferty
1893 J. Steers	1933 A. Shawyer	1973 F. Lucas	1931 J. Petersen	1971 J. Conteh
1894 W. Sykes	1934 J. Magill	1974 D. Odwell	1932 J. Goyder	1972 W. Knight
1895 G. Townsend	1935 J. Magill	1975 D. Odwell	1933 G. Brennan	1973 W. Knight
1896 W. Ross	1936 A. Harrington	1976 E. Burke	1934 G. Brennan	1974 W. Knight
1897 W. Dees	1937 M. Dennis	1977 R. Davies	1935 R. Hearns	1975 M. Heath
1898 G. Townsend	1938 H. Tiller	1978 H. Graham	1936 J. Magill	1976 G. Evans
1899 R. Warnes	1939 H. Davies	1979 N. Wilshire	1937 J. Wilby	1977 C. Lawson
1900 E. Mann	1944 J. Hockley	1980 M. Kaylor	1938 A. S. Brown	1978 V. Smith
1901 R. Warnes	1945 R. Parker	1981 B. Schumacher	1939 B. Woodcock	1979 A. Straughn
1902 E. Mann	1946 R. Turpin	1982 J. Price	1944 E. Shackleton	1980 A. Straughn
1903 R. Warnes	1947 R. Agland	1983 T. Forbes	1945 A. Watson	1981 A. Straughn
1904 E. Mann	1948 J. Wright	1984 B. Schumacher	1946 J. Taylor	1982 G. Crawford
1905 J. Douglas	1949 S. Lewis	1985 D. Cronin	1947 A. Watson	1983 A. Wilson
1906 A. Murdock	1950 P. Longo	1986 N. Benn	1948 D. Scott	1984 A. Wilson
1907 R. Warnes	1951 E. Ludlam	1987 R. Douglas	1949 *Declared no contest*	1985 J. Beckles
1908 W. Child	1952 T. Gooding	1988 M. Edwards	1950 P. Messervy	1986 J. Moran

1987 J. Beckles	1897 G. Townsend	1928 J. L. Driscoll	1959 D. Thomas	1986 E. Cardouza
1988 H. Lawson	1898 G. Townsend	1929 P. Floyd	1960 L. Hobbs	1987 J. Moran
1989 N. Piper	1899 F. Parks	1930 V. Stuart	1961 W. Walker	1988 H. Akinwande
1990 J. McCluskey	1900 W. Dees	1931 M. Flanagan	1962 R. Dryden	1989 H. Akinwande
1991 A. Todd	1901 F. Parks	1932 V. Stuart	1963 R. Sanders	1990 K. Inglis
1992 K. Oliver	1902 F. Parks	1933 C. O'Grady	1964 C. Woodhouse	1991 P. Lawson
1993 K. Oliver	1903 F. Dickson	1934 P. Floyd	1965 W. Wells	1992 S. Welch
1994 K. Oliver	1904 A. Horner	1935 P. Floyd	1966 A. Brogan	1993 P. Lawson
1995 K. Oliver	1905 F. Parks	1936 V. Stuart	1967 P. Boddington	1994 S. Burford
	1906 F. Parks	1937 V. Stuart	1968 W. Wells	1995 M. Ellis
Heavyweight	1907 H. Brewer	1938 G. Preston	1969 A. Burton	
1881 R. Frost-Smith	1908 S. Evans	1939 A. Porter	1970 J. Gilmour	
1882 H. Dearsley	1909 C. Brown	1944 M. Hart	1971 L. Stevens	**S. Heavyweight**
1883 H. Dearsley	1910 F. Storbeck	1945 D. Scott	1972 T. Wood	1982 A. Elliott
1884 H. Dearsley	1911 W. Hazell	1946 P. Floyd	1973 G. McEwan	1983 K. Ferdinand
1885 W. West	1912 R. Smith	1947 G. Scriven	1974 N. Meade	1984 R. Wells
1886 A. Diamond	1913 R. Smith	1948 J. Gardner	1975 G. McEwan	1985 G. Williamson
1887 E. White	1914 E. Chandler	1949 A. Worrall	1976 J. Rafferty	1986 J. Oyebola
1888 W. King	1919 H. Brown	1950 P. Toch	1977 G. Adair	1987 J. Oyebola
1889 A. Bowman	1920 R. Rawson	1951 A. Halsey	1978 J. Awome	1988 K. McCormack
1890 J. Steers	1921 R. Rawson	1952 E. Hearn	1979 A. Palmer	1989 P. Passley
1891 V. Barker	1922 T. Evans	1953 J. Erskine	1980 F. Bruno	1990 K. McCormack
1892 J. Steers	1923 E. Eagan	1954 B. Harper	1981 A. Elliott	1991 K. McCormack
1893 J. Steers	1924 A. Clifton	1955 D. Rowe	1982 H. Hylton	1992 M. Hopper
1894 H. King	1925 D. Lister	1956 D. Rent	1983 H. Notice	1993 M. McKenzie
1895 W. E. Johnstone	1926 T. Petersen	1957 D. Thomas	1984 D. Young	1994 D. Watts
1896 W. E. Johnstone	1927 C. Capper	1958 D. Thomas	1985 H. Hylton	1995 R. Allen

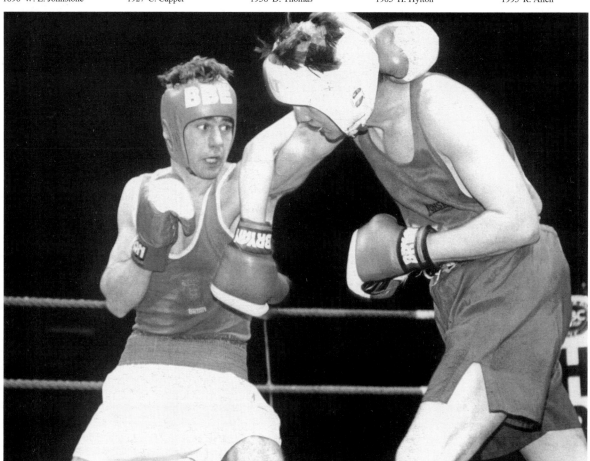

In outpointing Patrick Wright to become the 1995 ABA welter champion, Michael Hall (left) emulated his elder brother, Allan, who also won titles two years in succession

Steve Parkin

International Amateur Champions, 1904-1995

Shows all Olympic, World, European & Commonwealth champions since 1904. British silver and bronze medal winners are shown throughout, where applicable.

Country Code

ARG = Argentine; ARM = Armenia; AUS = Australia; AUT = Austria; AZE = Azerbaijan; BEL = Belgium; BUL = Bulgaria; CAN = Canada; CEY = Ceylon (now Sri Lanka); CI = Channel Islands; CUB = Cuba; DEN = Denmark; DOM = Dominican Republic; ENG = England; ESP = Spain; EST = Estonia; FIJ = Fiji Islands; FIN = Finland; FRA = France; GBR = United Kingdom; GDR = German Democratic Republic; GEO = Georgia; GER = Germany (but West Germany only from 1968-1990); GHA = Ghana; GUY = Guyana; HOL = Netherlands; HUN = Hungary; IRL = Ireland; ITA = Italy; JAM = Jamaica; JPN = Japan; KEN = Kenya; LIT = Lithuania; MEX = Mexico; NKO = North Korea; NIG = Nigeria; NIR = Northern Ireland; NOR = Norway; NZL = New Zealand; POL = Poland; PUR = Puerto Rico; ROM = Romania; RUS = Russia; SAF = South Africa; SCO = Scotland; SKO = South Korea; SR = Southern Rhodesia; STV = St Vincent; SWE = Sweden; TCH = Czechoslovakia; TUR = Turkey; UGA = Uganda; UKR = Ukraine; URS = USSR; USA = United States of America; VEN = Venezuela; WAL = Wales; YUG = Yugoslavia; ZAM = Zambia.

Olympic Champions, 1904-1992

St Louis, USA - 1904

Fly: G. Finnegan (USA). **Bantam:** O. Kirk (USA). **Feather:** O. Kirk (USA). **Light:** H. Spangler (USA). **Welter:** A. Young (USA). **Middle:** C. May (USA). **Heavy:** S. Berger (USA).

London, England - 1908

Bantam: H. Thomas (GBR). **Feather:** R. Gunn (GBR). **Light:** F. Grace (GBR). **Middle:** J.W.H.T. Douglas (GBR). **Heavy:** A. Oldman (GBR).
Silver medals: J. Condon (GBR), C. Morris (GBR), F. Spiller (GBR), S. Evans (GBR).
Bronze medals: W. Webb (GBR), H. Rodding (GBR), T. Ringer (GBR), H. Johnson (GBR), R. Warnes (GBR), W. Philo (GBR), F. Parks (GBR).

Antwerp, Belgium - 1920

Fly: F. Genaro (USA). **Bantam:** C. Walker (SAF). **Feather:** R. Fritsch (FRA). **Light:** S. Mossberg (USA). **Welter:** T. Schneider (CAN). **Middle:** H. Mallin (GBR). **L. Heavy:** E. Eagan (USA). **Heavy:** R. Rawson (GBR).
Silver medal: A. Ireland (GBR).
Bronze medals: W. Cuthbertson (GBR), G. McKenzie (GBR), H. Franks (GBR).

Paris, France - 1924

Fly: F. la Barba (USA). **Bantam:** W. Smith (SAF). **Feather:** J. Fields (USA). **Light:** H. Nielson (DEN). **Welter:** J. Delarge (BEL). **Middle:** H. Mallin (GBR). **L. Heavy:** H. Mitchell (GBR). **Heavy:** O. von Porat (NOR).
Silver medals: J. McKenzie (GBR), J. Elliot (GBR).

Amsterdam, Holland - 1928

Fly: A. Kocsis (HUN). **Bantam:** V. Tamagnini (ITA). **Feather:** B. van Klaveren (HOL). **Light:** C. Orlando (ITA). **Welter:** E. Morgan (NZL). **Middle:** P. Toscani (ITA). **L. Heavy:** V. Avendano (ARG). **Heavy:** A. Rodriguez Jurado (ARG).

Los Angeles, USA - 1932

Fly: I. Enekes (HUN). **Bantam:** H. Gwynne (CAN). **Feather:** C. Robledo (ARG). **Light:** L. Stevens (SAF). **Welter:** E. Flynn (USA). **Middle:** C. Barth (USA). **L. Heavy:** D. Carstens (SAF). **Heavy:** A. Lovell (ARG).

Berlin, West Germany - 1936

Fly: W. Kaiser (GER). **Bantam:** U. Sergo (ITA). **Feather:** O. Casanova (ARG). **Light:** I. Harangi (HUN). **Welter:** S. Suvio (FIN). **Middle:** J. Despeaux (FRA). **L. Heavy:** R. Michelot (FRA). **Heavy:** H. Runge (GER).

London, England - 1948

Fly: P. Perez (ARG). **Bantam:** T. Csik (HUN). **Feather:** E. Formenti (ITA). **Light:** G. Dreyer (SAF). **Welter:** J. Torma (TCH). **Middle:** L. Papp (HUN). **L. Heavy:** G. Hunter (SAF). **Heavy:** R. Iglesas (ARG).
Silver medals: J. Wright (GBR), D. Scott (GBR).

Helsinki, Finland - 1952

Fly: N. Brooks (USA). **Bantam:** P. Hamalainen (FIN). **Feather:** J. Zachara (TCH). **Light:** A. Bolognesi (ITA). **L. Welter:** C. Adkins (USA). **Welter:** Z. Chychla (POL). **L. Middle:** L. Papp (HUN). **Middle:** F. Patterson (USA). **L. Heavy:** N. Lee (USA). **Heavy:** E. Sanders (USA).
Silver medal: J. McNally (IRL).

Melbourne, Australia - 1956

Fly: T. Spinks (GBR). **Bantam:** W. Behrendt (GER). **Feather:** V. Safronov (URS). **Light:** R. McTaggart (GBR). **L. Welter:** V. Jengibarian (URS). **Welter:** N. Linca (ROM). **L. Middle:** L. Papp (HUN). **Middle:** G. Schatkov (URS). **L. Heavy:** J. Boyd (USA). **Heavy:** P. Rademacher (USA).
Silver medals: T. Nicholls (GBR), F. Tiedt (IRL).
Bronze medals: J. Caldwell (IRL), F. Gilroy (IRL), A. Bryne (IRL), N. Gargano (GBR), J. McCormack (GBR).

Rome, Italy - 1960

Fly: G. Torok (HUN). **Bantam:** O. Grigoryev (URS). **Feather:** F. Musso (ITA). **Light:** K. Pazdzior (POL). **L. Welter:** B. Nemecek (TCH). **Welter:** N. Benvenuti (ITA). **L. Middle:** W. McClure (USA). **Middle:** E. Crook (USA). **L. Heavy:** C. Clay (USA). **Heavy:** F. de Piccoli (ITA).
Bronze medals: R. McTaggart (GBR), J. Lloyd (GBR), W. Fisher (GBR).

Tokyo, Japan - 1964

Fly: F. Atzori (ITA). **Bantam:** T. Sakurai (JPN). **Feather:** S. Stepashkin (URS). **Light:** J. Grudzien (POL). **L. Welter:** J. Kulej (POL). **Welter:** M. Kasprzyk (POL). **L. Middle:** B. Lagutin (URS). **Middle:** V. Popenchenko (URS). **L. Heavy:** C. Pinto (ITA). **Heavy:** J. Frazier (USA).
Bronze medal: J. McCourt (IRL).

Mexico City, Mexico - 1968

L. Fly: F. Rodriguez (VEN). **Fly:** R. Delgado (MEX). **Bantam:** V. Sokolov (URS). **Feather:** A. Roldan (MEX). **Light:** R. Harris (USA). **L. Welter:** J. Kulej (POL). **Welter:** M. Wolke (GDR). **L. Middle:** B. Lagutin (URS). **Middle:** C. Finnegan (GBR). **L. Heavy:** D. Poznyak (URS). **Heavy:** G. Foreman (USA).

Munich, West Germany - 1972

L. Fly: G. Gedo (HUN). **Fly:** G. Kostadinov (BUL). **Bantam:** O. Martinez (CUB). **Feather:** B. Kusnetsov (BUL). **Light:** J. Szczepanski (POL). **L. Welter:** R. Seales (USA). **Welter:** E. Correa (CUB). **L. Middle:** D. Kottysch (GER). **Middle:** V. Lemeschev (URS). **L. Heavy:** M. Parlov (YUG). **Heavy:** T. Stevenson (CUB).
Bronze medals: R. Evans (GBR), G. Turpin (GBR), A. Minter (GBR).

Montreal, Canada - 1976

L. Fly: J. Hernandez (CUB). **Fly:** L. Randolph (USA). **Bantam:** Y-J. Gu (NKO). **Feather:** A. Herrera (CUB). **Light:** H. Davis (USA). **L. Welter:** R. Leonard (USA). **Welter:** J. Bachfield (GDR). **L. Middle:** J. Rybicki (POL). **Middle:** M. Spinks (USA). **L. Heavy:** L. Spinks (USA). **Heavy:** T. Stevenson (CUB).
Bronze medal: P. Cowdell (GBR).

Moscow, USSR - 1980

L. Fly: S. Sabirov (URS). **Fly:** P. Lessov (BUL). **Bantam:** J. Hernandez (CUB). **Feather:** R. Fink (GDR). **Light:** A. Herrera (CUB). **L. Welter:** P. Oliva (ITA). **Welter:** A. Aldama (CUB). **L. Middle:** A. Martinez (CUB). **Middle:** J. Gomez (CUB). **L. Heavy:** S. Kacar (YUG). **Heavy:** T. Stevenson (CUB).
Bronze medals: H. Russell (IRL), A. Willis (GBR).

Los Angeles, USA - 1984

L. Fly: P. Gonzalez (USA). **Fly:** S. McCrory (USA). **Bantam:** M. Stecca (ITA). **Feather:** M. Taylor (USA). **Light:** P. Whitaker (USA). **L. Welter:** J. Page (USA). **Welter:** M. Breland (USA). **L. Middle:** F. Tate (USA). **Middle:** J-S. Shin (SKO). **L. Heavy:** A. Josipovic (YUG). **Heavy:** H. Tillman (USA). **S. Heavy:** T. Biggs (USA).
Bronze medal: B. Wells (GBR).

Seoul, South Korea - 1988

L. Fly: I. Mustafov (BUL). **Fly:** H-S. Kim (SKO). **Bantam:** K. McKinney (USA). **Feather:** G. Parisi (ITA). **Light:** A. Zuelow (GDR). **L. Welter:** V. Yanovsky (URS). **Welter:** R. Wangila (KEN). **L. Middle:** S-H. Park (SKO). **Middle:** H. Maske (GDR). **L. Heavy:** A. Maynard (USA). **Heavy:** R. Mercer (USA). **S. Heavy:** L. Lewis (CAN).
Bronze medal: R. Woodhall (GBR).

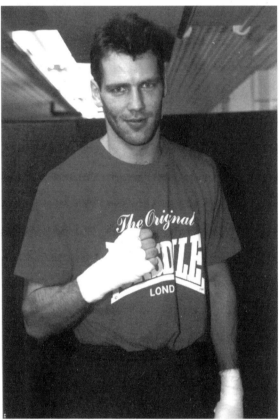

The former European, World and Olympic champion, Henry Maske   Les Clark

Barcelona, Spain - 1992

L. Fly: R. Marcelo (CUB). **Fly:** C-C. Su (NKO). **Bantam:** J. Casamayor (CUB). **Feather:** A. Tews (GER). **Light:** O. de la Hoya (USA). **L. Welter:** H. Vinent (CUB). **Welter:** M. Carruth (IRL). **L. Middle:** J. Lemus (CUB). **Middle:** A. Hernandez (CUB). **L. Heavy:** T. May (GER). **Heavy:** F. Savon (CUB). **S. Heavy:** R. Balado (CUB).
Silver medal: W. McCullough (IRL).
Bronze medal: R. Reid (GBR).

World Champions, 1974-1995

Havana, Cuba - 1974

L. Fly: J. Hernandez (CUB). **Fly:** D. Rodriguez (CUB). **Bantam:** W. Gomez (PUR). **Feather:** H. Davis (USA). **Light:** V. Solomin (URS). **L.**

Welter: A. Kalule (UGA). **Welter:** E. Correa (CUB). **L. Middle:** R. Garbey (CUB). **Middle:** R. Riskiev (URS). **L. Heavy:** M. Parlov (YUG). **Heavy:** T. Stevenson (CUB).

Belgrade, Yugoslavia - 1978

L. Fly: S. Muchoki (KEN). **Fly:** H. Strednicki (POL). **Bantam:** A. Horta (CUB). **Feather:** A. Herrera (CUB). **Light:** D. Andeh (NIG). **L. Welter:** V. Lvov (URS). **Welter:** V. Rachkov (URS). **L. Middle:** V. Savchenko (URS). **Middle:** J. Gomez (CUB). **L. Heavy:** S. Soria (CUB). **Heavy:** T. Stevenson (CUB).

Munich, West Germany - 1982

L. Fly: I. Mustafov (BUL). **Fly:** Y. Alexandrov (URS). **Bantam:** F. Favors (USA). **Feather:** A. Horta (CUB). **Light:** A. Herrera (CUB). **L. Welter:** C. Garcia (CUB). **Welter:** M. Breland (USA). **L. Middle:** A. Koshkin (URS). **Middle:** B. Comas (CUB). **L. Heavy:** P. Romero (CUB). **Heavy:** A. Jagubkin (URS). **S. Heavy:** T. Biggs (USA).
Bronze medal: T. Corr (IRL).

Reno, USA - 1986

L. Fly: J. Odelin (CUB). **Fly:** P. Reyes (CUB). **Bantam:** S-I. Moon (SKO). **Feather:** K. Banks (USA). **Light:** A. Horta (CUB). **L. Welter:** V. Shishov (URS). **Welter:** K. Gould (USA). **L. Middle:** A. Espinosa (CUB). **Middle:** D. Allen (USA). **L. Heavy:** P. Romero (CUB). **Heavy:** F. Savon (CUB). **S. Heavy:** T. Stevenson (CUB).

Moscow, USSR - 1989

L. Fly: E. Griffin (USA). **Fly:** Y. Arbachakov (URS). **Bantam:** E. Carrion (CUB). **Feather:** A. Khamatov (URS). **Light:** J. Gonzalez (CUB). **L. Welter:** I. Ruzinkov (URS). **Welter:** F. Vastag. **L. Middle:** I. Akopokhian (URS). **Middle:** A. Kurniavka (URS). **L. Heavy:** H. Maske (GDR). **Heavy:** F. Savon (CUB). **S. Heavy:** R. Balado (CUB).
Bronze medal: M. Carruth (IRL).

Sydney, Australia - 1991

L. Fly: E. Griffin (USA). **Fly:** I. Kovacs (HUN). **Bantam:** S. Todorov (BUL). **Feather:** K. Kirkorov (BUL). **Light:** M. Rudolph (GER). **L. Welter:** K. Tsziu (URS). **Welter:** J. Hernandez (CUB). **L. Middle:** J. Lemus (CUB). **Middle:** T. Russo (ITA). **L. Heavy:** T. May (GER). **Heavy:** F. Savon (CUB). **S. Heavy:** R. Balado (CUB).

Tampere, Finland - 1993

L. Fly: N. Munchian (ARM). **Fly:** W. Font (CUB). **Bantam:** A. Christov (BUL). **Feather:** S. Todorov (BUL). **Light:** D. Austin (CUB). **L. Welter:** H. Vinent (CUB). **Welter:** J. Hernandez (CUB). **L. Middle:** F. Vastag (ROM). **Middle:** A. Hernandez (CUB). **L. Heavy:** R. Garbey (CUB). **Heavy:** F. Savon (CUB). **S. Heavy:** R. Balado (CUB).
Bronze medal: D. Kelly (IRL).

Berlin, Germany - 1995

L. Fly: D. Petrov (BUL). **Fly:** Z. Lunka (GER). **Bantam:** R. Malachbekov (RUS). **Feather:** S. Todorov (BUL). **Light:** L. Doroftel (ROM). **L. Welter:** H. Vinent (CUB). **Welter:** J. Hernandez (CUB). **L. Middle:** F. Vastag (ROM). **Middle:** A. Hernandez (CUB). **L. Heavy:** A. Tarver (USA). **Heavy:** F. Savon (CUB). **S. Heavy:** A. Lezin (RUS).

World Junior Champions, 1979-1994

Yokohama, Japan - 1979

L. Fly: R. Shannon (USA). **Fly:** P. Lessov (BUL). **Bantam:** P-K. Choi (SKO). **Feather:** Y. Gladychev (URS). **Light:** R. Blake (USA). **L. Welter:** I. Akopokhian (URS). **Welter:** M. McCrory (USA). **L. Middle:** A. Mayes (USA). **Middle:** A. Milov (URS). **L. Heavy:** A. Lebedev (URS). **Heavy:** M. Frazier (USA).
Silver medals: N. Wilshire (ENG), D. Cross (ENG).
Bronze medal: I. Scott (SCO).

Santa Domingo, Dominican Republic - 1983

L. Fly: M. Herrera (DOM). **Fly:** J. Gonzalez (CUB). **Bantam:** J. Molina (PUR). **Feather:** A. Miesses (DOM). **Light:** A. Beltre (DOM). **L. Welter:** A. Espinoza (CUB). **Welter:** M. Watkins (USA). **L. Middle:** U. Castillo (CUB). **Middle:** R. Batista (CUB). **L. Heavy:** O. Pought (USA). **Heavy:** A. Williams (USA). **S. Heavy:** L. Lewis (CAN).

Bucharest, Romania - 1985
L. Fly: R-S. Hwang (SKO). Fly: T. Marcelica (ROM). Bantam: R. Diaz (CUB). Feather: D. Maeran (ROM). Light: J. Teiche (GDR). L. Welter: W. Saeger (GDR). Welter: A. Stoianov (BUL). L. Middle: M. Franek (TCH). Middle: O. Zahalotskih (URS). L. Heavy: B. Riddick (USA). Heavy: F. Savon (CUB). S. Heavy: A. Prianichnikov (URS).

Havana, Cuba - 1987
L. Fly: E. Paisan (CUB). Fly: C. Daniels (USA). Bantam: A. Moya (CUB). Feather: G. Iliiyasov (URS). Light: J. Hernandez (CUB). L. Welter: L. Mihai (ROM). Welter: F. Vastag (ROM). L. Middle: A. Lobsyak (URS). Middle: W. Martinez (CUB). L. Heavy: D. Yeliseyev (URS). Heavy: R. Balado (CUB). S. Heavy: L. Martinez (CUB).
Silver medal: E. Loughran (IRL).
Bronze medal: D. Galvin (IRL).

San Juan, Puerto Rico - 1989
L. Fly: D. Petrov (BUL). Fly: N. Monchai (FRA). Bantam: J. Casamayor (CUB). Feather: C. Febres (PUR). Light: A. Acevedo (PUR). L. Welter: E. Berger (GDR). Welter: A. Hernandez (CUB). L. Middle: L. Bedey (CUB). Middle: R. Garbey (CUB). L. Heavy: R. Alvarez (CUB). Heavy: K. Johnson (CAN). S. Heavy: A. Burdiantz (URS).
Silver medals: E. Magee (IRL), R. Reid (ENG), S. Wilson (SCO).

Lima, Peru - 1990
L. Fly: D. Alicea (PUR). Fly: K. Pielert (GDR). Bantam: K. Baravi (URS). Feather: A. Vaughan (ENG). Light: J. Mendez (CUB). L. Welter: H. Vinent (CUB). Welter: A. Hernandez (CUB). L. Middle: A. Kakauridze (URS). Middle: J. Gomez (CUB). L. Heavy: B. Torsten (GDR). Heavy: I. Andreev (URS). S. Heavy: J. Quesada (CUB).
Bronze medal: P. Ingle (ENG).

Montreal, Canada - 1992
L. Fly: W. Font (CUB). Fly: J. Oragon (CUB). Bantam: N. Machado (CUB). Feather: M. Stewart (CAN). Light: D. Austin (CUB). L. Welter: O. Saitov (RUS). Welter: L. Brors (GER). L. Middle: J. Acosta (CUB). Middle: I. Arsangaliev (RUS). L. Heavy: S. Samilsan (TUR). Heavy: G. Kandeliaki (GEO). S. Heavy: M. Porchnev (RUS).
Bronze medal: N. Sinclair (IRL).

Istanbul, Turkey - 1994
L. Fly: J. Turunen (FIN). Fly: A. Jimenez (CUB). Bantam: J. Despaigne (CUB). Feather: D. Simion (ROM). Light: L. Diogenes (CUB). L. Welter: V. Romero (CUB). Welter: E. Aslan (TUR). L. Middle: G. Ledsvanys (CUB). Middle: M. Genc (TUR). L. Heavy: P. Aurino (ITA). Heavy: M. Lopez (CUB). S. Heavy: P. Carrion (CUB).

European Champions, 1924-1993

Paris, France - 1924
Fly: J. McKenzie (GBR). Bantam: J. Ces (FRA). Feather: R. de Vergnie (BEL). Light: N. Nielsen (DEN). Welter: J. Delarge (BEL). Middle: H. Mallin (GBR). L. Heavy: H. Mitchell (GBR). Heavy: O. von Porat (NOR).

Stockholm, Sweden - 1925
Fly: E. Pladner (FRA). Bantam: A. Rule (GBR). Feather: P. Andren (SWE). Light: S. Johanssen (SWE). Welter: H. Nielsen (DEN). Middle: F. Crawley (GBR). L. Heavy: T. Petersen (DEN). Heavy: B. Persson (SWE).
Silver medals: J. James (GBR), E. Viney (GBR), D. Lister (GBR).

Berlin, Germany - 1927
Fly: L. Boman (SWE). Bantam: K. Dalchow (GER). Feather: F. Dubbers (GER). Light: H. Domgoergen (GER). Welter: R. Caneva (ITA). Middle: J. Christensen (NOR). L. Heavy: H. Muller (GER). Heavy: N. Ramm (SWE).

Amsterdam, Holland - 1928
Fly: A. Kocsis (HUN). Bantam: V. Tamagnini (ITA). Feather: B. van Klaveren (HOL). Light: C. Orlandi (ITA). Welter: R. Galataud (FRA). Middle: P. Toscani (ITA). L. Heavy: E. Pistulla (GER). Heavy: N. Ramm (SWE).

Budapest, Hungary - 1930
Fly: I. Enekes (HUN). Bantam: J. Szeles (HUN). Feather: G. Szabo (HUN). Light: M. Bianchini (ITA). Welter: J. Besselmann (GER). Middle: C. Meroni (ITA). L. Heavy: T. Petersen (DEN). Heavy: J. Michaelson (DEN).

Los Angeles, USA - 1932
Fly: I. Enekes (HUN). Bantam: H. Ziglarski (GER). Feather: J. Schleinkofer (GER). Light: T. Ahlqvist (SWE). Welter: E. Campe (GER). Middle: R. Michelot (FRA). L. Heavy: G. Rossi (ITA). Heavy: L. Rovati (ITA).

Budapest, Hungary - 1934
Fly: P. Palmer (GBR). Bantam: I. Enekes (HUN). Feather: O. Kaestner GER). Light: E. Facchini (ITA). Welter: D. McCleave (GBR). Middle: S. Szigetti (HUN). L. Heavy: P. Zehetmayer (AUT). Heavy: G. Baerlund (FIN).
Bronze medal: P. Floyd (GBR).

Milan, Italy - 1937
Fly: I. Enekes (HUN). Bantam: U. Sergo (ITA). Feather: A. Polus (POL). Light: H. Nuremberg (GER). Welter: M. Murach (GER). Middle: H. Chmielewski (POL). L. Heavy: S. Szigetti (HUN). Heavy: O. Tandberg (SWE).

Dublin, Eire - 1939
Fly: J. Ingle (IRL). Bantam: U. Sergo (ITA). Feather: P. Dowdall (IRL). Light: H. Nuremberg (GER). Welter: A. Kolczyski (POL). Middle: A. Raedek (EST). L. Heavy: L. Musina (ITA). Heavy: O. Tandberg (SWE).
Bronze medal: C. Evenden (IRL).

Dublin, Eire - 1947
Fly: L. Martinez (ESP). Bantam: L. Bogacs (HUN). Feather: K. Kreuger (SWE). Light: J. Vissers (BEL). Welter: J. Ryan (ENG). Middle: A. Escudie (FRA). L. Heavy: H. Quentemeyer (HOL). Heavy: G. O'Colmain (IRL).
Silver medals: J. Clinton (SCO), P. Maguire (IRL), W. Thom (ENG), G. Scriven (ENG).
Bronze medals: J. Dwyer (SCO), A. Sanderson (ENG), W. Frith (SCO), E. Cantwell (IRL), K. Wyatt (ENG).

Oslo, Norway - 1949
Fly: J. Kasperczak (POL). Bantam: G. Zuddas (ITA). Feather: J. Bataille (FRA). Light: M. McCullagh (IRL). Welter: J. Torma (TCH). Middle: L. Papp (HUN). L. Heavy: G. di Segni (ITA). Heavy: L. Bene (HUN).
Bronze medal: D. Connell (IRL).

Milan, Italy - 1951
Fly: A. Pozzali (ITA). Bantam: V. Dall'Osso (ITA). Feather: J. Ventaja (FRA). Light: B. Visintin (ITA). L. Welter: H. Schelling (GER). Welter: Z. Chychla (POL). L. Middle: L. Papp (HUN). Middle: S. Sjolin (SWE). L. Heavy: M. Limage (BEL). Heavy: G. di Segni (ITA).
Silver medal: J. Kelly (IRL).
Bronze medals: D. Connell (IRL), T. Milligan (IRL), A. Lay (ENG).

Warsaw, Poland - 1953
Fly: H. Kukier (POL). Bantam: Z. Stefaniuk (POL). Feather: J. Kruza (POL). Light: V. Jengibarian (URS). L. Welter: L. Drogosz (POL). Welter: Z. Chychla (POL). L. Middle: B. Wells (ENG). Middle: D. Wemhoner (GER). L. Heavy: U. Nietchke (GER). Heavy: A. Schotzikas (URS).
Silver medal: T. Milligan (IRL).
Bronze medals: J. McNally (IRL), R. Barton (ENG).

Berlin, West Germany - 1955
Fly: E. Basel (GER). Bantam: Z. Stefaniuk (POL). Feather: T. Nicholls (ENG). Light: H. Kurschat (GER). L. Welter: L. Drogosz (POL). Welter: N. Gargano (ENG). L. Middle: Z. Pietrzykowski (POL). Middle: G. Schatkov (URS). L. Heavy: E. Schoeppner (GER). Heavy: A. Schotzikas (URS).

Prague, Czechoslovakia - 1957
Fly: M. Homberg (GER). Bantam: O. Grigoryev (URS). Feather: D. Venilov (BUL). Light: K. Pazdzior (POL). L. Welter: V. Jengibarian (URS). Welter: M. Graus (GER). L. Middle: N. Benvenuti (ITA). Middle: Z. Pietrzykowski (POL). L. Heavy: G. Negrea (ROM). Heavy: A. Abramov (URS).
Bronze medals: R. Davies (WAL), J. Morrissey (SCO), J. Kidd (SCO), F. Teidt (IRL).

Lucerne, Switzerland - 1959
Fly: M. Homberg (GER). **Bantam:** H. Rascher (GER). **Feather:** J. Adamski (POL). **Light:** O. Maki (FIN). **L. Welter:** V. Jengibarian (URS). **Welter:** L. Drogosz (POL). **L. Middle:** N. Benvenuti (ITA). **Middle:** G. Schatkov (URS). **L. Heavy:** Z. Pietrzykowski (POL). **Heavy:** A. Abramov (URS).
Silver medal: D. Thomas (ENG).
Bronze medals: A. McClean (IRL), H. Perry (IRL), C. McCoy (IRL), H. Scott (ENG).

Belgrade, Yugoslavia - 1961
Fly: P. Vacca (ITA). **Bantam:** S. Sivko (URS). **Feather:** F. Taylor (ENG). **Light:** R. McTaggart (SCO). **L. Welter:** A. Tamulis (URS). **Welter:** R. Tamulis (URS). **L. Middle:** B. Lagutin (URS). **Middle:** T. Walasek (POL). **L. Heavy:** G. Saraudi (ITA). **Heavy:** A. Abramov (URS).
Bronze medals: P. Warwick (ENG), I. McKenzie (SCO), J. Bodell (ENG).

Moscow, USSR - 1963
Fly: V. Bystrov (URS). **Bantam:** O. Grigoryev (URS). **Feather:** S. Stepashkin (URS). **Light:** J. Kajdi (HUN). **L. Welter:** J. Kulej (POL). **Welter:** R. Tamulis (URS). **L. Middle:** B. Lagutin (URS). **Middle:** V. Popenchenko (URS). **L. Heavy:** Z. Pietrzykowski (POL). **Heavy:** J. Nemec (TCH).
Silver medal: A. Wyper (SCO).

Berlin, East Germany - 1965
Fly: H. Freisdadt (GER). **Bantam:** O. Grigoryev (URS). **Feather:** S. Stepashkin (URS). **Light:** V. Barranikov (URS). **L. Welter:** J. Kulej (POL). **Welter:** R. Tamulis (URS). **L. Middle:** V. Ageyev (URS). **Middle:** V. Popenchenko (URS). **L. Heavy:** D. Poznyak (URS). **Heavy:** A. Isosimov (URS).
Silver medal: B. Robinson (ENG).
Bronze medals: J. McCluskey (SCO), K. Buchanan (SCO), J. McCourt (IRL).

Rome, Italy - 1967
Fly: H. Skrzyczak (POL). **Bantam:** N. Giju (ROM). **Feather:** R. Petek (POL). **Light:** J. Grudzien (POL). **L. Welter:** V. Frolov (URS). **Welter:** B. Nemecek (TCH). **L. Middle:** V. Ageyev (URS). **Middle:** M. Casati (ITA). **L. Heavy:** D. Poznyak (URS). **Heavy:** M. Baruzzi (ITA).
Silver medal: P. Boddington (ENG).

Bucharest, Romania - 1969
L. Fly: G. Gedo (HUN). **Fly:** C. Ciuca (ROM). **Bantam:** A. Dumitrescu (ROM). **Feather:** L. Orban (HUN). **Light:** S. Cutov (ROM). **L. Welter:** V. Frolov (URS). **Welter:** G. Meier (GER). **L. Middle:** V. Tregubov (URS). **Middle:** V. Tarasenkov (URS). **L. Heavy:** D. Poznyak (URS). **Heavy:** I. Alexe (ROM).
Bronze medals: M. Dowling (IRL), M. Piner (ENG), A. Richardson (ENG), T. Imrie (SCO).

Madrid, Spain - 1971
L. Fly: G. Gedo (HUN). **Fly:** J. Rodriguez (ESP). **Bantam:** T. Badar (HUN). **Feather:** R. Tomczyk (POL). **Light:** J. Szczepanski (POL). **L. Welter:** U. Beyer (GDR). **Welter:** J. Kajdi (HUN). **L. Middle:** V. Tregubov (URS). **Middle:** J. Juotsiavitchus (URS). **L. Heavy:** M. Parlov (YUG). **Heavy:** V. Tchernishev (URS).
Bronze medals: N. McLaughlin (IRL), M. Dowling (IRL), B. McCarthy (IRL), M. Kingwell (ENG), L. Stevens (ENG).

Belgrade, Yugoslavia - 1973
L. Fly: V. Zasypko (URS). **Fly:** C. Gruescu (ROM). **Bantam:** A. Cosentino (FRA). **Feather:** S. Forster (GDR). **Light:** S. Cutov (ROM). **L. Welter:** M. Benes (YUG). **Welter:** S. Csjef (HUN). **L. Middle:** A. Klimanov (URS). **Middle:** V. Lemechev (URS). **L. Heavy:** M. Parlov (YUG). **Heavy:** V. Ulyanich (URS).
Bronze medal: J. Bambrick (SCO).

Katowice, Poland - 1975
L. Fly: A. Tkachenko (URS). **Fly:** V. Zasypko (URS). **Bantam:** V. Rybakov (URS). **Feather:** T. Badari (HUN). **Light:** S. Cutov (ROM). **L. Welter:** V. Limasov (URS). **Welter:** K. Marjaama (FIN). **L. Middle:** W. Rudnowski (POL). **Middle:** V. Lemechev (URS). **L. Heavy:** A. Klimanov (URS). **Heavy:** A. Biegalski (POL).
Bronze medals: C. Magri (ENG), P. Cowdell (ENG), G. McEwan (ENG).

Halle, East Germany - 1977
L. Fly: H. Srednicki (POL). **Fly:** L. Blazynski (POL). **Bantam:** S. Forster (GDR). **Feather:** R. Nowakowski (GDR). **Light:** A. Rusevski (YUG). **L. Welter:** B. Gajda (POL). **Welter:** V. Limasov (URS). **L. Middle:** V. Saychenko (URS). **Middle:** I. Shaposhnikov (URS). **L. Heavy:** D. Kvachadze (URS). **Heavy:** E. Gorstkov (URS).
Bronze medal: P. Sutcliffe (IRL).

Cologne, West Germany - 1979
L. Fly: S. Sabirov (URS). **Fly:** H. Strednicki (POL). **Bantam:** N. Khrapzov (URS). **Feather:** V. Rybakov (URS). **Light.** V. Demianenko (URS). **L. Welter:** S. Konakbaev (URS). **Welter:** E. Muller (GER). **L. Middle:** M. Perunovic (YUG). **Middle:** T. Uusiverta (FIN). **L. Heavy:** A. Nikolyan (URS). **Heavy:** E. Gorstkov (URS). **S. Heavy:** P. Hussing (GER).
Bronze medal: P. Sutcliffe (IRL).

Tampere, Finland - 1981
L. Fly: I. Mustafov (BUL). **Fly:** P. Lessov (BUL). **Bantam:** V. Miroschnichenko (URS). **Feather:** R. Nowakowski (GDR). **Light:** V. Rybakov (URS). **L. Welter:** V. Shisov (URS). **Welter:** S. Konakvbaev (URS). **L. Middle:** A. Koshkin (URS). **Middle:** J. Torbek (URS). **L. Heavy:** A Krupin (URS). **Heavy:** A. Jagupkin (URS). **S. Heavy:** F. Damiani (ITA).
Bronze medal: G. Hawkins (IRL).

Varna, Bulgaria - 1983
L. Fly: I. Mustafov (BUL). **Fly:** P. Lessov (BUL). **Bantam:** Y. Alexandrov (URS). **Feather:** S. Nurkazov (URS). **Light:** E. Chuprenski (BUL). **L. Welter:** V. Shishov (URS). **Welter:** P. Galkin (URS). **L. Middle:** V. Laptev (URS). **Middle:** V. Melnik (URS). **L. Heavy:** V. Kokhanovski (URS). **Heavy:** A. Jagubkin (URS). **S. Heavy:** F. Damiani (ITA).
Bronze medal: K. Joyce (IRL).

Budapest, Hungary - 1985
L. Fly: R. Breitbarth (GDR). **Fly:** D. Berg (GDR). **Bantam:** L. Simic (YUG). **Feather:** S. Khachatrian (URS). **Light:** E. Chuprenski (BUL). **L. Welter:** S. Mehnert (GDR). **Welter:** I. Akopokhian (URS). **L. Middle:** M. Timm (GDR). **Middle:** H. Maske (GDR). **L. Heavy:** N. Shanavasov (URS). **Heavy:** A. Jagubkin (URS). **S. Heavy:** F. Somodi (HUN).
Bronze medals: S. Casey (IRL), J. Beckles (ENG).

Turin, Italy - 1987
L. Fly: N. Munchyan (URS). **Fly:** A. Tews (GDR). **Bantam:** A. Hristov (BUL). **Feather:** M. Kazaryan (URS). **Light:** O. Nazarov (URS). **L. Welter:** B. Abadjier (BUL). **Welter:** V. Shishov (URS). **L. Middle:** E. Richter (GDR). **Middle:** H. Maske (GDR). **L. Heavy:** Y. Vaulin (URS). **Heavy:** A. Vanderlijde (HOL). **S. Heavy:** U. Kaden (GDR).
Bronze medal: N. Brown (ENG).

Athens, Greece - 1989
L. Fly: I.Mustafov (BUL). **Fly:** Y. Arbachakov (URS). **Bantam:** S. Todorov (BUL). **Feather:** K. Kirkorov (BUL). **Light:** K. Tsziu (URS). **L. Welter:** I. Ruznikov (URS). **Welter:** S. Mehnert (GDR). **L. Middle:** I. Akopokhian (URS). **Middle:** H. Maske (GDR). **L. Heavy:** S. Lange (GDR). **Heavy:** A. Vanderlijde (HOL). **S. Heavy:** U. Kaden (GDR).
Bronze Medal: D. Anderson (SCO).

Gothenburg, Sweden - 1991
L. Fly: I. Marinov (BUL). **Fly:** I. Kovacs (HUN). **Bantam:** S. Todorov (BUL). **Feather:** P. Griffin (IRL). **Light:** V. Nistor (ROM). **L. Welter:** K. Tsziu (URS). **Welter:** R. Welin (SWE). **L. Middle:** I. Akopokhian (URS). **Middle:** S. Otke (GER). **L. Heavy:** D. Michalczewski (GER). **Heavy:** A. Vanderlijde (HOL). **S. Heavy:** E. Beloussov (URS).
Bronze medals: P. Weir (SCO), A. Vaughan (ENG).

Bursa, Turkey - 1993
L. Fly: D. Petrov (BUL). **Fly:** R. Husseinov (AZE). **Bantam:** R. Malakhbetov (RUS). **Feather:** S. Todorov (BUL). **Light:** J. Bielski (POL). **L. Welter:** N. Suleymanogiu (TUR). **Welter:** V. Karpaclauskas (LIT). **L. Middle:** F. Vastag (ROM). **Middle:** D. Eigenbrodt (GER). **L. Heavy:** I. Kshinin (RUS). **Heavy:** G. Kandelaki (GEO). **S. Heavy:** S. Rusinov (BUL).
Bronze medals: P. Griffin (IRL), D. Williams (ENG), K. McCormack (WAL).

Note: Gold medals were awarded to the Europeans who went the furthest in the Olympic Games of 1924, 1928 & 1932.

European Junior Champions, 1970-1995

Miskolc, Hungary - 1970
L. Fly: Gluck (HUN). **Fly:** Z. Kismeneth (HUN). **Bantam:** A. Levitschev (URS). **Feather:** Andrianov (URS). **Light:** L. Juhasz (HUN). **L. Welter:** K. Nemec (HUN). **Welter:** Davidov (URS). **L. Middle:** A. Lemeschev (URS). **Middle:** N. Anfimov (URS). **L. Heavy:** O. Sasche (GDR). **Heavy:** J. Reder (HUN).
Bronze medals: D. Needham (ENG), R. Barlow (ENG), L. Stevens (ENG).

Bucharest, Romania - 1972
L. Fly: A. Turei (ROM). **Fly:** Condurat (ROM). **Bantam:** V. Solomin (URS). **Feather:** V. Lvov (URS). **Light:** S. Cutov (ROM). **L. Welter:** K. Pierwieniecki (POL). **Welter:** Zorov (URS). **L. Middle:** Babescu (ROM). **Middle:** V. Lemeschev (URS). **L. Heavy:** Mirounik (URS). **Heavy:** Subutin (URS).
Bronze medals: J. Gale (ENG), R. Maxwell (ENG), D. Odwell (ENG).

Kiev, Russia - 1974
L. Fly: A. Tkachenko (URS). **Fly:** V. Rybakov (URS). **Bantam:** C. Andreikovski (BUL). **Feather:** V. Sorokin (URS). **Light:** V. Limasov (URS). **L. Welter:** N. Sigov (URS). **Welter:** M. Bychkov (URS). **L. Middle:** V. Danshin (URS). **Middle:** D. Jende (GDR). **L. Heavy:** K. Dafinoiu (ROM). **Heavy:** K. Mashev (BUL).
Silver medal: C. Magri (ENG).
Bronze medals: G. Gilbody (ENG), K. Laing (ENG).

Izmir, Turkey - 1976
L. Fly: C. Seican (ROM). **Fly:** G. Khratsov (URS). **Bantam:** M. Navros (URS). **Feather:** V. Demoianeko (URS). **Light:** M. Puzovic (YUG). **L. Welter:** V. Zverev (URS). **Welter:** K. Ozoglouz (TUR). **L. Middle:** W. Lauder (SCO). **Middle:** H. Lenhart (GER). **L. Heavy:** I. Yantchauskas (URS). **Heavy:** B. Enjenyan (URS).
Silver medal: J. Decker (ENG).
Bronze medals: I. McLeod (SCO), N. Croombes (ENG).

Dublin, Ireland - 1978
L. Fly: R. Marx (GDR). **Fly:** D. Radu (ROM). **Bantam:** S. Khatchatrian (URS). **Feather:** H. Loukmanov (URS). **Light:** P. Oliva (ITA). **L. Welter:** V. Laptiev (URS). **Welter:** R. Filimanov (URS). **L. Middle:** A. Beliave (URS). **Middle:** G. Zinkovitch (URS). **L. Heavy:** I. Jolta (ROM). **Heavy:** P. Stoimenov (BUL).
Silver medals: M. Holmes (IRL), P. Hanlon (ENG), M. Courtney (ENG).
Bronze medals: T. Thompson (IRL), J. Turner (ENG), M. Bennett (WAL), J. McAllister (SCO), C. Devine (ENG).

Rimini, Italy - 1980
L. Fly: A. Mikoulin (URS). **Fly:** J. Varadi (HUN). **Bantam:** F. Rauschning (GDR). **Feather:** J. Gladychev (URS). **Light:** V. Shishov (URS). **L. Welter:** R. Lomski (BUL). **Welter:** T. Holonics (GDR). **L. Middle:** N. Wilshire (ENG). **Middle:** S. Laptiev (URS). **L. Heavy:** V. Dolgoun (URS). **Heavy:** V. Tioumentsev (URS). **S. Heavy:** S. Kormihtsine (URS).
Bronze medals: N. Potter (ENG), B. McGuigan (IRL), M. Brereton (IRL), D. Cross (ENG).

Schwerin, East Germany - 1982
L. Fly: R. Kabirov (URS). **Fly:** I. Filchev (BUL). **Bantam:** M. Stecca (ITA). **Feather:** B. Blagoev (BUL). **Light:** E. Chakimov (URS). **L. Welter:** S. Mehnert (GDR). **Welter:** T. Schmitz (GDR). **L. Middle:** B. Shararov (URS). **Middle:** E. Christie (ENG). **L. Heavy:** Y. Waulin (URS). **Heavy:** A. Popov (URS). **S. Heavy:** V. Aldoshin (URS).
Silver medal: D. Kenny (ENG).
Bronze medal: O. Jones (ENG).

Tampere, Finland - 1984
L. Fly: R. Breitbart (GDR). **Fly:** D. Berg (GDR). **Bantam:** K. Khdrian (URS). **Feather:** O. Nazarov (URS). **Light:** C. Furnikov (BUL). **L. Welter:** W. Schmidt (GDR). **Welter:** K. Doinov (BUL). **L. Middle:** O. Volkov (URS). **Middle:** R. Ryll (GDR). **L. Heavy:** G. Peskov (URS). **Heavy:** R. Draskovic (YUG). **S. Heavy:** L. Kamenov (BUL).
Bronze medals: J. Lowey (IRL), F. Harding (ENG), N. Moore (ENG).

Copenhagen, Denmark - 1986
L. Fly: S. Todorov (BUL). **Fly:** S. Galotian (URS). **Bantam:** D. Drumm (GDR). **Feather:** K. Tsziu (URS). **Light:** G. Akopkhian (URS). **L. Welter:** F. Vastag (ROM). **Welter:** S. Karavayev (URS). **L. Middle:** E. Elibaev (URS). **Middle:** A. Kurnabka (URS). **L. Heavy:** A. Schultz (GDR). **Heavy:** A. Golota (POL). **S. Heavy:** A. Prianichnikov (URS).

Gdansk, Poland - 1988
L. Fly: I. Kovacs (HUN). **Fly:** M. Beyer (GDR). **Bantam:** M. Aitzanov (URS). **Feather:** M. Rudolph (GDR). **Light:** M. Shaburov (URS). **L. Welter:** G. Campanella (ITA). **Welter:** D. Konsun (URS). **L. Middle:** K. Kiselev (URS). **Middle:** A. Rudenko (URS). **L. Heavy:** O. Velikanov (URS). **Heavy:** A. Ter-Okopian (URS). **S. Heavy:** E. Belusov (URS).
Bronze medals: P. Ramsey (ENG), M. Smyth (WAL).

Usti Nad Labem, Czechoslovakia - 1990
L. Fly: Z. Paliani (URS). **Fly:** K. Pielert (GDR). **Bantam:** K. Baravi (URS). **Feather:** P. Gvasalia (URS). **Light:** J. Hildenbrandt (GDR). **L. Welter:** N. Smanov (URS). **Welter:** A. Preda (ROM). **L. Middle:** A. Kakauridze (URS). **Middle:** J. Schwank (GDR). **L. Heavy:** Iljin (URS). **Heavy:** I. Andrejev (URS). **S. Heavy:** W. Fischer (GDR).
Silver medal: A. Todd (ENG).
Bronze medal: P. Craig (ENG).

Edinburgh, Scotland - 1992
L. Fly: M. Ismailov (URS). **Fly:** F. Brennfuhrer (GER). **Bantam:** S. Kuchler (GER). **Feather:** M. Silantiev (URS). **Light:** S. Shcherbakov (URS). **L. Welter:** O. Saitov (URS). **Welter:** H. Kurlumaz (TUR). **L. Middle:** Z. Erdie (HUN). **Middle:** V. Zhirov (URS). **L. Heavy:** D. Gorbachev (URS). **Heavy:** L. Achkasov (URS). **S. Heavy:** A. Mamedov (URS).
Silver medals: M. Hall (ENG), B. Jones (WAL).
Bronze medals: F. Slane (IRL), G. Stephens (IRL), C. Davies (WAL).

Salonika, Greece - 1993
L. Fly: O. Kiroukhine (UKR). **Fly:** R. Husseinov (AZE). **Bantam:** M. Kulbe (GER). **Feather:** E. Zakharov (RUS). **Light:** O. Sergeev (RUS). **L. Welter:** A. Selihanov (RUS). **Welter:** O. Kudinov (UKR). **L. Middle:** E. Makarenko (RUS). **Middle:** D. Droukovski (RUS). **L. Heavy:** A. Voida (RUS). **Heavy:** V. Klitchko (UKR). **S. Heavy:** A. Moiseev (RUS).
Bronze medal: D. Costello (ENG).

Sifok, Hungary - 1995
L. Fly: D. Gaissine (RUS). **Fly:** A. Kotelnik (UKR). **Bantam:** A. Loutsenko (UKR). **Feather:** S. Harrison (SCO). **Light:** D. Simon (ROM). **L. Welter:** B. Ulusoy (TUR). **Welter:** O. Bouts (UKR). **L. Middle:** O. Bukalo (UKR). **Middle:** V. Plettnev (RUS). **L. Heavy:** A. Derevtsov (RUS). **Heavy:** C. O'Grady (IRL). **S. Heavy:** D. Savvine (RUS).
Silver medal: G. Murphy (SCO).
Bronze medal: N. Linford (ENG).

Note: The age limit for the championships were reduced from 21 to 19 in 1976.

Commonwealth Champions, 1930-1994

Hamilton, Canada - 1930
Fly: W. Smith (SAF). **Bantam:** H. Mizler (ENG). **Feather:** F. Meacham (ENG). **Light:** J. Rolland (SCO). **Welter:** L. Hall (SAF). **Middle:** F. Mallin (ENG). **L. Heavy:** J. Goyder (ENG). **Heavy:** V. Stuart (ENG).
Silver medals: T. Pardoe (ENG), T. Holt (SCO).
Bronze medals: A. Lyons (SCO), A. Love (ENG), F. Breeman (ENG).

Wembley, England - 1934
Fly: P. Palmer (ENG). **Bantam:** F. Ryan (ENG). **Feather:** C. Cattarall (SAF). **Light:** L. Cook (AUS). **Welter:** D. McCleave (ENG). **Middle:** A. Shawyer (ENG). **L. Heavy:** G. Brennan (ENG). **Heavy:** P. Floyd (ENG).
Silver medals: A. Barnes (WAL), J. Jones (WAL), F. Taylor (WAL), J. Holton (SCO).
Bronze medals: J. Pottinger (WAL), T. Wells (SCO), H. Moy (ENG), W. Duncan (NIR), J. Magill (NIR), Lord D. Douglas-Hamilton (SCO).

Melbourne, Australia - 1938
Fly: J. Joubert (SAF). **Bantam:** W. Butler (ENG). **Feather:** A. Henricus (CEY). **Light:** H. Groves (ENG). **Welter:** W. Smith (AUS). **Middle:** D. Reardon (WAL). **L. Heavy:** N. Wolmarans (SAF). **Heavy:** T. Osborne (CAN).
Silver medals: J. Watson (SCO), M. Dennis (ENG).
Bronze medals: H. Cameron (SCO), J. Wilby (ENG).

Auckland, New Zealand - 1950
Fly: H. Riley (SCO). **Bantam:** J. van Rensburg (SAF). **Feather:** H. Gilliland (SCO). **Light:** R. Latham (ENG). **Welter:** T. Ratcliffe (ENG). **Middle:** T. van Schalkwyk (SAF). **L. Heavy:** D. Scott (ENG). **Heavy:** F. Creagh (NZL).
Bronze medal: P. Brander (ENG).

Vancouver, Canada - 1954
Fly: R. Currie (SCO). **Bantam:** J. Smillie (SCO). **Feather:** L. Leisching (SAF). **Light:** P. van Staden (SR). **L. Welter:** M. Bergin (CAN). **Welter:** N. Gargano (ENG). **L. Middle:** W. Greaves (CAN). **Middle:** J. van de Kolff (SAF). **L. Heavy:** P. van Vuuren (SAF). **Heavy:** B. Harper (ENG).
Silver medals: M. Collins (WAL), F. McQuillan (SCO).
Bronze medals: D. Charnley (ENG), B. Wells (ENG).

Cardiff, Wales - 1958
Fly: J. Brown (SCO). **Bantam:** H. Winstone (WAL). **Feather:** W. Taylor (AUS). **Light:** R. McTaggart (SCO). **L. Welter:** H. Loubscher (SAF). **Welter:** J. Greyling (SAF). **L. Middle:** G. Webster (SAF). **Middle:** T. Milligan (NIR). **L. Heavy:** A. Madigan (AUS). **Heavy:** D. Bekker (SAF).
Silver medals: T. Bache (ENG), M. Collins (WAL), J. Jordan (NIR), R. Kane (SCO), S. Pearson (ENG), A. Higgins (WAL), D. Thomas (ENG).
Bronze medals: P. Lavery (NIR), D. Braithwaite (WAL), R. Hanna (NIR), A. Owen (SCO), J. McClory (NIR), J. Cooke (ENG), J. Jacobs (ENG), B. Nancurvis (ENG), R. Scott (SCO), W. Brown (WAL), J. Caiger (ENG), W. Bannon (SCO), R. Pleace (WAL).

Perth, Australia - 1962
Fly: R. Mallon (SCO). **Bantam:** J. Dynevor (AUS). **Feather:** J. McDermott (SCO). **Light:** E. Blay (GHA). **L. Welter:** C. Quartey (GHA). **Welter:** W. Coe (NZL). **L. Middle:** H. Mann (CAN). **Middle:** M. Calhoun (JAM). **L. Heavy:** A. Madigan (AUS). **Heavy:** G. Oywello (UGA).
Silver medals: R. McTaggart (SCO), J. Pritchett (ENG).
Bronze medals: M. Pye (ENG), P. Benneyworth (ENG), B. Whelan (ENG), B. Brazier (ENG), C. Rice (NIR), T. Menzies (SCO), H. Christie (NIR), A. Turmel (CI).

Kingston, Jamaica - 1966
Fly: S. Shittu (GHA). **Bantam:** E. Ndukwu (NIG). **Feather:** P. Waruinge (KEN). **Light:** A. Andeh (NIG). **L. Welter:** J. McCourt (NIR). **Welter:** E. Blay (GHA). **L. Middle:** M. Rowe (ENG). **Middle:** J. Darkey (GHA). **L. Heavy:** R. Tighe (ENG). **Heavy:** W. Kini (NZL).
Silver medals: P. Maguire (NIR), R. Thurston (ENG), R. Arthur (ENG), T. Imrie (SCO).
Bronze medals: S. Lockhart (NIR), A. Peace (SCO), F. Young (NIR), J. Turpin (ENG), D. McAlinden (NIR).

Edinburgh, Scotland - 1970
L. Fly: J. Odwori (UGA). **Fly:** D. Needham (ENG). **Bantam:** S. Shittu (GHA). **Feather:** P. Waruinge (KEN). **Light:** A. Adeyemi (NIG). **L. Welter:** M. Muruli (UGA). **Welter:** E. Ankudey (GHA). **L. Middle:** T. Imrie (SCO). **Middle:** J. Conteh (ENG). **L. Heavy:** F. Ayinla (NIG). **Heavy:** B. Masanda (UGA).
Silver medals: T. Davies (WAL), J. Gillan (SCO), D. Davies (WAL), J. McKinty (NIR).
Bronze medals: M. Abrams (ENG), A. McHugh (SCO), D. Larmour (NIR), S. Oglivie (SCO), A. Richardson (ENG), T. Joyce (SCO), P. Doherty (NIR), J. Rafferty (SCO), L. Stevens (ENG).

Christchurch, New Zealand - 1974
L. Fly: S. Muchoki (KEN). **Fly:** D. Larmour (NIR). **Bantam:** P. Cowdell (ENG). **Feather:** E. Ndukwu (NIG). **Light:** A. Kalule (UGA). **L. Welter:** O. Nwankpa (NIG). **Welter:** M. Muruli (UGA). **L. Middle:** L. Mwale (ZAM). **Middle:** F. Lucas (STV). **L. Heavy:** W. Knight (ENG). **Heavy:** N. Meade (ENG).
Silver medals: E. McKenzie (WAL), A. Harrison (SCO).
Bronze medals: J. Bambrick (SCO), J. Douglas (SCO), J. Rodgers (NIR), S. Cooney (SCO), R. Davies (ENG), C. Speare (ENG), G. Ferris (NIR).

Edmonton, Canada - 1978
L. Fly: S. Muchoki (KEN). **Fly:** M. Irungu (KEN). **Bantam:** B. McGuigan (NIR). **Feather:** A. Nelson (GHA). **Light:** G. Hamill (NIR). **L. Welter:** W. Braithwaite (GUY). **Welter:** M. McCallum (JAM). **L. Middle:** K. Perlette (CAN). **Middle:** P. McElwaine (AUS). **L. Heavy:** R. Fortin (CAN). **Heavy:** J. Awome (ENG).
Silver medals: J. Douglas (SCO), K. Beattie (NIR), D. Parkes (ENG), V. Smith (ENG).
Bronze medals: H. Russell (NIR), M. O'Brien (ENG), J. McAllister (SCO), T. Feal (WAL).

Brisbane, Australia - 1982
L. Fly: A. Wachire (KEN). **Fly:** M. Mutua (KEN). **Bantam:** J. Orewa (NIG). **Feather:** P. Konyegwachie (NIG). **Light:** H. Khalili (KEN). **L. Welter:** C. Ossai (NIG). **Welter:** C. Pyatt (ENG). **L. Middle:** S. O'Sullivan (CAN). **Middle:** J. Price (ENG). **L. Heavy:** F. Sani (FIJ). **Heavy:** W. de Wit (CAN).
Silver medals: J. Lyon (ENG), J. Kelly (SCO), R. Webb (NIR), P. Hanlon (ENG), J. McDonnell (ENG), N. Croombes (ENG), H. Hylton (ENG).
Bronze medals: R. Gilbody (ENG), C. McIntosh (ENG), R. Corr (NIR).

Edinburgh, Scotland - 1986
L. Fly: S. Olson (CAN). **Fly:** J. Lyon (ENG). **Bantam:** S. Murphy (ENG). **Feather:** B. Downey (CAN). **Light:** A. Dar (CAN). **L. Welter:** H. Grant (CAN). **Welter:** D. Dyer (ENG). **L. Middle:** D. Sherry (CAN). **Middle:** R. Douglas (ENG). **L. Heavy:** J. Moran (ENG). **Heavy:** J. Peau (NZL). **S. Heavy:** L. Lewis (CAN).
Silver medals: M. Epton (ENG), R. Nash (NIR), P. English (ENG), N. Haddock (WAL), J. McAlister (SCO), H. Lawson (SCO), D. Young (SCO), A. Evans (WAL).
Bronze medals: W. Docherty (SCO), J. Todd (NIR), K. Webber (WAL), G. Brooks (SCO), J. Wallace (SCO), C. Carleton (NIR), J. Jacobs (ENG), B. Lowe (NIR), D. Denny (NIR), G. Thomas (WAL), A. Mullen (SCO), G. Ferrie (SCO), P. Tinney (NIR), B. Pullen (WAL), E. Cardouza (ENG), J. Oyebola (ENG), J. Sillitoe (CI).

Auckland, New Zealand - 1990
L. Fly: J. Juuko (UGA). **Fly:** W. McCullough (NIR). **Bantam:** S. Mohammed (NIG). **Feather:** J. Irwin (ENG). **Light:** G. Nyakana (UGA). **L. Welter:** C. Kane (SCO). **Welter:** D. Defiagbon (NIG). **L. Middle:** R. Woodhall (ENG). **Middle:** C. Johnson (CAN). **L. Heavy:** J. Akhasamba (KEN). **Heavy:** G. Onyango (KEN). **S. Heavy:** M. Kenny (NZL).
Bronze medals: D. Anderson (SCO), M. Edwards (ENG), P. Douglas (NIR).

A current professional favourite, Wayne McCullough, won gold for Northern Ireland at flyweight in the 1990 Commonwealth Games　　Les Clark

Victoria, Canada - 1994
L. Fly: H. Ramadhani (KEN). **Fly:** P. Shepherd (SCO). **Bantam:** R. Peden (AUS). **Feather:** C. Patton (CAN). **Light:** M. Strange (CAN). **L. Welter:** P. Richardson (ENG). **Welter:** N. Sinclair (NIR). **L. Middle:** J. Webb (NIR). **Middle:** R. Donaldson (CAN). **L. Heavy:** D. Brown (CAN). **Heavy:** O. Ahmed (KEN). **S. Heavy:** D. Dokiwari (NIG).
Silver medals: S. Oliver (ENG), J. Cook (WAL), M. Reneghan (NIR), M. Winters (NIR), J. Wilson (SCO).
Bronze medals: D. Costello (ENG), J. Townsley (SCO), D. Williams (ENG).

Directory of Ex-Boxers' Associations

by Ron Olver

BIRMINGHAM Founded 1985. Disbanded. Re-formed 1995. HQ: Emerald Club, Green Lane, Birmingham. Ernie Cashmore (P); Paddy Maguire(C); Bobby Sexton (T); Tom Byrne(S).

BOURNEMOUTH Founded 1980. HQ: Mallard Road Bus Services Social Club, Bournemouth. Dai Dower (P); Peter Fay (C); Percy Singer (T); Ken Wells (VC); Les Smith (S), Flat L, 592 Charminster Road, Bournemouth BH8 9SL.

CORK Founded 1973. HQ: Acra House, Maylor Street, Cork. Johnny Fitzgerald (P & C); John Cronin (VC); Eamer Coughlan (T); Tim O'Sullivan (S & PRO), Acra House, Maylor Street, Dublin.

CORNWALL Founded 1989. HQ: St Austell British Legion and Redruth British Legion in alternate months. Roy Coote (P); Stan Cullis (C); Len Magee (VC); Jimmy Miller (T); John Soloman (S), 115 Albany Road, Redruth.

CROYDON Founded 1982. HQ: The Prince Of Wales, Thornton Heath. Tom Powell, BEM (P); Bill Goddard (C); Martin Olney (VC); Morton Lewis (T); Gilbert Allnutt (S), 37 Braemar Avenue, Thornton Heath, Croydon CR9 7RJ.

EASTERN AREA Founded 1973. HQ: Norfolk Dumpling, Cattle Market, Hall Road, Norwich. Brian Fitzmaurice (P); Alfred Smith (C); Clive Campling (VC); Eric Middleton (T & S), 48 City Road, Norwich NR1 3AU.

IPSWICH Founded 1970. HQ: Flying Horse, Waterford Road, Ipswich. Alby Kingham (P); Frank Webb (C); Vic Thurlow (T); Nigel Wheeler (PRO & S); 20 Stratford Road, Ipswich 1PL 6OF.

IRISH Founded 1973. HQ: National Boxing Stadium, South Circular Road, Dublin. Maxie McCullagh (P); Jack O'Rourke (C); Willie Duggan (VC); Tommy Butler (T); Denis Morrison (S), 55 Philipsburgh Terrace, Marino, Dublin.

KENT Founded 1967. HQ: Chatham WMC, New Road, Chatham. Teddy Bryant (P); Bill Warner (C); Mick Smith (VC); Fred Atkins (T); Ray Lambert (PRO); Paul Nihill MBE, (S), 59 Balfour Road, Rochester, Kent.

LEEDS Founded 1952. HQ: North Leeds WMC, Burmantofts, Lincoln Green, Leeds 9. Johnny Durkin (P); Kevin Cunningham (C); Frankie Brown (VC); Alan Alster (T); Steve Butler (PRO); Malcolm Bean (S), 11 Crawshaw Gardens, Pudsey, Leeds LS28 7 BW

LEFT-HOOK CLUB Betty Faux (S), 144 Longmoor Lane, Aintree, Liverpool. No regular meetings. Formed specifically with the aim of holding functions to raise money in order to help former boxers in need.

LEICESTER Founded 1972. HQ: Belgrave WMC, Checketts Road, Leicester. Pat Butler (P); Mick Greaves (C); Mrs Rita Jones (T); Norman Jones (S), 60 Dumbleton Avenue, Leicester LE3 2EG.

LONDON Founded 1971. HQ; St Pancras Conservative Club, Argyle Street, London. Jack Powell (P); Micky O'Sullivan (C); Andy Williamson (VC); Ron Olver (PRO); Ray Caulfield (T); Mrs Mary Powell (S), 36 St Peters Street, Islington, London N1 8JT.

MANCHESTER Founded 1968. HQ: British Rail Social Club, Store Street, Manchester. Jackie Braddock (Life P); Jack Jamieson (P); Tommy Proffitt (C); Jack Edwards (VC); Eddie Lillis (T); Jackie Moran (S), 4 Cooper House, Boundary Lane, Hulme, Manchester.

MERSEYSIDE (Liverpool) Founded 1973. HQ: Queens Hotel, Derby Square, Liverpool. Johnny Cooke (P); Terry Riley (C); Jim Boyd (VC); Jim Jenkinson (T); Billy Davies (S), 7 Rockford Walk, Southdene, Kirkby, Liverpool.

NORTHAMPTONSHIRE Founded 1981. HQ: Exclusive Club, Gold Street, Northampton. Tony Perrett (P); Pat Boyle (C); Keith Hall (S), 29 Sydney Street, Kettering, Northants NN16 0HZ.

NORTHERN FEDERATION Founded 1974. Several member EBAs. Annual Gala. Eddie Monahan (S), 16 Braemar Avenue, Marshside, Southport.

NORTHERN IRELAND Founded 1970. HQ: Ulster Sports Club, Belfast. J. Bradbury (P); Freddie Gilroy (C); Sammy Cosgrove (PRO); J. Garrett (T); Al Gibson (S), 900 Crumlin Road, Belfast.

NORTH STAFFS & SOUTH CHESHIRE Founded 1969. HQ: The Saggar Makers Bottom Knocker, Market Place, Burslem, Stoke on Trent. Tut Whalley (P); Roy Simms (VC); Les Dean (S); John Greatbach (T); Billy Tudor (C & PRO), 133 Sprinkbank Road, Chell Heath, Stoke on Trent, Staffs ST6 6HW.

NORWICH HQ: West End Retreat, Brown Street, Norwich. Les King (P); John Pipe (C); Jack Wakefield (T); Dick Sadd (S), 76 Orchard Street, Norwich.

NOTTINGHAM Founded 1979. HQ: The Lion Hotel, Clumber Street, Nottingham. Frank Parkes (P); Frank Hayes (C); John Kinsella (T); Jim Shrewsbury (S), 219 Rosecroft Drive, Nottingham NG5 6EL.

NOTTS & DERBY Founded 1973. Dick Johnson (S & PRO), 15 Church Street, Pinxton, Nottingham.

PLYMOUTH Founded 1982. HQ: Exmouth Road Social Club, Stoke, Plymouth. George Borg (P); Tom Pryce-Davies (C); Doug Halliday (VC); Arthur Willis (T); Buck Taylor (S), 15 Greenbank Avenue, St Judes, Plymouth PL4 9BT.

PRESTON Founded 1973. HQ: County Arms Hotel, Deepdale Road, Preston. Albert Bradley (P); Brian Petherwick (C); Frank Brown (T); Ted Sumner (S), 7 Kew Gardens, Penwortham, Preston PR1 0DR.

READING Founded 1977. HQ: Salisbury Club, Kings Road, Reading. Roland Dakin (P); Bob Pitman (C); Arnold Whatmore (T); Bob Sturgess (S).

ST HELENS Founded 1983. HQ: Travellers Rest Hotel, Crab Street, St Helens. George Thomas (C); Jimmy O'Keefe (VC); Tommy McNamara (T); Paul Britch (S), 40 Ashtons Green Drive, Parr, St Helens.

SEFTON Founded 1975. HQ: St Benet's Parochial Club, Netherton, Bootle. Alf Lunt (T); Johnny Holmes (S); 41 Higher End Park, Sefton, Bootle.

SLOUGH Founded 1973. HQ: Luton Arndale Centre Social Club. Max Quartermain (P); Jack Bridge (C); Charlie Knight (T); Ernie Watkins (S), 5 Sunbury Road, Eton, Windsor.

SQUARE RING Founded 1978. HQ: Torquay Social Club. George Pook (P); Maxie Beech (VC); Johnny Mudge (S); Jim Banks (T); Paul King (C), 10 Pine Court Apartments, Middle Warberry Road, Torquay.

SUNDERLAND Founded 1959. HQ: Hendon Gardens, Sunderland. Bert Ingram (P); Terry Lynn (C); Joe Riley (PRO); Les Simm (S), 21 Orchard Street, Pallion, Sunderland SR4 6QL.

SUSSEX Founded 1974. HQ: Brighton & Hove Sports & Social Club, Conway Street, Hove. Geoff Williams (P); Bert Hollows (C); Harry Parkinson (T); John Ford (S), 69 Moyne Close, Hove, Sussex.

SWANSEA & SOUTH WEST WALES Founded 1983. HQ: Villiers Arms, Neath Road, Hafod, Swansea. Cliff Curvis (P); Gordon Pape (C); Ernie Wallis (T); Len Smith (S), Cockett Inn, Cockett, Swansea SA2 0GB.

TRAMORE Founded 1981. HQ: Robinson Bar, Main Street, Tramore, Co Waterford. T. Flynn (P); J. Dunne (C); C. O'Reilly (VC); W. Hutchinson (T); N. Graham (PRO); Pete Graham (S), 3 Riverstown, Tramore.

TYNESIDE Founded 1970. HQ: The Swan Public House, Heworth. Billy Charlton (P); Maxie Walsh (C); Gordon Smith (VC); Malcolm Dinning (T); Bill Wilkie (S & PRO), 60 Calderdale Avenue, Walker, Newcastle NE6 4HN.

WELSH Founded 1976. HQ: Rhydyfelin Rugby Club, Pontypridd, Mid Glamorgan. Syd Worgan (P & S); Terry Pudge (C); Howard Winstone (VC); Llew Miles (T & PRO), 7 Edward Street, Miskin, Mountain Ash, Mid Glamorgan.

The above information is set at the time of going to press and no responsibility can be taken for any changes in officers or addresses of HQs that may happen between then and publication and/or have not been notified to me.

ABBREVIATIONS

P - President. C - Chairman. VC - Vice Chairman. T - Treasurer. S - Secretary. PRO - Public Relations and/or Press Officer.

Ron Olver (left) receives the Boxing Writers' Club Special Award from Chairman, Tony Bodley, at the Savoy Hotel last April

Derek Rowe (Photos) Ltd

Obituaries

by Ron Olver

It is impossible to list everyone, but I have again done my best to include final tributes for as many of the well-known boxers and other familiar names within the sport, who have passed away since the 1995 Yearbook was published. We honour them and will remember them.

ABRAMS Georgie *From* Roanoke, Virginia, USA. *Born* 11 November 1918. *Died* 14 July 1994. *Pro* 1937-1948. Outpointed by Tony Zale for the world middleweight title (1941), he lost ten of his 61 bouts, with most of his wins coming on points. Defeated Teddy Yarosz, Lou Brouillard, Billy Soose, Cocoa Kid, Izzy Jannazzo, Coley Welch and Steve Belloise. Also met Sugar Ray Robinson, Fred Apostoli, and Marcel Cerdan.

AKEEM Kid *Born* Akeem Anifowoshe in Nigeria. *Died* December 1994 aged 26. Challenged Robert Quiroga for the IBF light-flyweight title on 15 June 1991, having been unbeaten in 23 fights, but failed to get the decision in a fight that, according to many present, could have gone either way. However, as the verdict was announced, the Kid collapsed and later suffered permanent damage, despite an operation to remove a blood clot from his brain. Banned from boxing, but still hoping to make a comeback, he was deported back to Nigeria after turning to drugs and dealing cocaine. Sadly, he collapsed and died at his Lagos home, his dream of a return to the ring unfulfilled.

ALVEREZ Elvis *Born* Colombia. Shot dead in July 1995 aged 30. A pro since 1983, he won the national super-flyweight title in 1986 and the Latin American flyweight crown in 1988, before going on to outpoint Miguel Mercedes for the vacant WBO flyweight championship in March 1989. Having relinquished that title, he took over the WBA version from Yukihito Tamakuma in March 1991, losing it less than three months later to Yong-Kang Kim. Carried on with little success, and was surprisingly given a crack at WBA bantamweight champion, Junior Jones, being outscored in January 1994. A southpaw, Elvis also had a solid win over future WBO and WBA bantam champion, Israel Contrerras.

AMBERS Lou *Born* Herkimer, New York, 8 November 1913. *Died* 25 April 1995. Real name Luigi Guiseppe D'Ambrosio. Nicknamed the "Herkimer Hurricane". *Pro* 1932-1941. Won vacant world lightweight title by beating Tony Canzoneri (1936). This avenged Lou's defeat by Tony in a championship fight the previous year. Retained title against Canzoneri (1937), Pedro Montanez (1937), before losing to Henry Armstrong (1938). Regained it from Armstrong (1939), but later lost it to Lew Jenkins (1940). Defeated only eight times in 100 fights, Lou was elected to the Boxing Hall of Fame in 1964.

ANKRAH Roy Surname sometimes spelt "Ankarah." *From* Gold Coast (now Ghana). *Born* 25 December 1925.

Died 28 May 1995. Turned pro in the 1940s, when it was reported that he won every Gold Coast title from flyweight to welter. Joined Royal West African Frontier Force during World War II, and was part of the boxing squad, headed by Freddie Mills, which toured and gave exhibitions to the troops in India. Freddie planned to bring him to Britain, but, when the war ended, Roy returned home to work as a motor mechanic. However, when Freddie was boxing in Glasgow, local manager, Joe McKean, asked him how good Roy was. On Freddie's recommendation, Joe brought Roy to Britain, and he made his debut in 1950. He gained immediate success, his only defeat to May 1952 being a disqualification against Jimmy Murray for a careless blow,

Lou Ambers

281

after having floored Jimmy several times. Important wins over Luis Romero and Tony Lombard brought him an Empire title fight against Ronnie Clayton, which he won on points (1951) and in a return, Roy stopped Ronnie in round 13 (1952). In a match billed as a final eliminator for the world featherweight title, Roy was outpointed by Ray Famechon (1952). Had two bouts with Billy Kelly in Belfast (1954), the first being a non-title ten-rounder, which he won on points, but the return was for Roy's title, and Billy took the decision. Also in 1954, Roy was beaten by Sammy McCarthy and Robert Cohen. Returned home, and didn't fight again until 1959 in the Gold Coast, when he won two and lost one. In later years he helped with the administration of the sport in his own country, and was also trainer of their amateur teams in important events like the Olympics and Commonwealth Games. His "perpetual motion" style endeared him to British fight fans, who dubbed him "The Black Flash" and he was a great ambassador for the sport.

AWOME Joe *From* Birmingham and Golders Green. *Born* 25 July 1933. *Died* January 1995. Boxed for Woking BC as an amateur and in 1978 won the ABA heavyweight title, beating two previous champions, John Rafferty and Glen Adair. Represented England in the 1978 Commonwealth Games, and won the gold medal. Also beat top German, Peter Hussing, in an England v West Germany match. Turned pro in 1979, and his career comprised 12 bouts (nine wins and three defeats), with every contest ending inside the distance. Victims were Clive Beardsley, Alan Bagley (twice), Ron McLean, Reg Long, Austin Okoye, Glen Adair, Ricky James and Manny Gabriel and he was beaten by Ron McLean, Stan McDermott and Neil Malpass. On retiring, he became general manager of the pop group *The Jam,* led by Paul Weller.

BARONET Ernie *Born* Durban, South Africa, 7 November 1936. *Died* August 1994. Won the South African Featherweight title in 1958, beating Graham van der Walt in his third recorded fight. Lost it and regained it in fights with Charlie Els the following year, before travelling to Britain for three contests in 1960. After losing to Con Mount Bassie, Paddy Kelly and Gordon Blakey, he went home and I can only find two more contests for him, the last being an eight round points win over Homicide Kunutu in Salisbury, Rhodesia in June 1961. Father of the ill-fated light-welterweight, Brian, who died on 17 June 1988, three days after being knocked out by Kenny Vice.

BARTLETT Ray *From* Stockwell. *Died* 14 August 1995 aged 70. Well-known as the former competition secretary of the Fitzroy Lodge, Fisher and Repton ABCs, as a member of the first-named, he worked closely with Vic Andreetti senior and Bill Chevalley. Always a great influence in helping amateurs who wanted to turn pro, the boxer who gave him most satisfaction was Dave Charnley and Ray remained his advisor until the day the former British, Commonwealth, and European lightweight champion retired. Dave thought so highly of Ray that when

he challenged Joe Brown for the world title in Houston, Texas, he even paid Ray's expenses for the pleasure of his company. Worked as a news vendor near St Paul's right up until his death.

BIRTLEY Jackie *From* Northampton. *Died* 27 January 1995 aged 63. A member of the British Boxing Writers' Club and of the Northampton EBA, he was also chief of *Northants Press,* and contributor to many newspapers and periodicals, including *Boxing News.* An author, his books included stories on Freddie Mills and Randolph Turpin.

BLISS Alf *From* Croydon. *Died* 11 January 1995. A former manager, among those he looked after were Charlie Bint, Jim and Johnny Toohig, Sid Hart and George Kelly. Never worried about the financial side, and all his boxers received their purses IN FULL. Was a founder-member of Croydon EBA and held the posts of assistant secretary and welfare officer. For the previous seven years he had been suffering from heart problems, during which he had a by-pass operation. Three days before his death he attended a meeting of the London Ex-Boxers' Association, and later, when out walking, collapsed from yet another heart attack.

BUCKINGHAM Snowy *Born* Hackney, London. *Died* 25 February 1995 aged 93. His christian name was "Sydney", but his nickname came from his having blond hair. Snowy's first taste of boxing came when former fighter and film star, Alf Goddard, took him to the Blackfriars Ring. Fascinated by the work of the cornermen, he became a "regular" at various gyms, picking up pointers on training and conditioning methods. Soon became a licensed trainer, and among those he looked after were Eddie Phillips, Charlie Belanger, George Cook, Larry Gains, Walter Neusel, Bob Olin, Archie Sexton, Jack Hyams, Peter Waterman, Ron Hinson, Yolande Pompey and Lew Lazar. An accepted expert "cuts-man", manager Jack King asked Snowy to look at a young lad named Sammy McCarthy, which was the start of a great partnership. When Sammy retired he became a manager, signing up Terry Spinks, and Snowy became Terry's trainer.

CARTER Jimmy *From* Aiken, South Carolina, USA. *Born* 15 December 1923. *Died* 21 September 1994. *Pro* 1946-1960. Won world lightweight title by stopping Ike Williams (1951), and retained it against Art Aragon later that year. He again retained it by beating Lauro Salas, but then lost it to Salas a month later (1952), before regaining it from the Mexican, also in 1952. Had three more successful defences in 1953, stopping Tommy Collins, George Araujo and Armand Savoie, but the following year lost the title to Paddy DeMarco, prior to stopping DeMarco in a rematch. In 1955 he lost the championship to Wallace Bud Smith and was beaten in the return. That was his last shot, although he continued to box for another five years, beating Don Jordan and Lauro Salas. In 1957, Jimmy came to Britain and was outpointed by Willie Toweel. Was only beaten three times inside the distance in 120 fights and had only been boxing for just over 12 months when he drew with the great Sandy Saddler.

COLPITTS Jackie *Born* Prudhoe, 4 September 1926. *Died* April 1995. *Pro* 1952-1956. Beat Dave Underwood, Bob Batey, Vic Glover, Billy Taylor, John Watson, Jock McCready, Jimmy Ford and Brian Jelley and drew with Al Sharpe. Also met Don McTaggart, Neville Tetlow and Johnny Miller.

COMMEY Rocky *From* Ghana. *Died* August 1995 aged 25 after being hit by a vehicle whilst doing roadwork. First came to notice as a challenger for Donnie Hood's WBC International bantamweight title back in September 1991. Inexperienced, with only eight contests under his belt, Rocky pushed the Scot all the way, despite two late knockdowns.

CURTIS Steve *Born* Cardiff, 26 December 1948. *Died* 28 October 1994. Was ABA flyweight champion (1967) and, as a pro, he won the Welsh bantamweight title, beating Glyn Davies for the vacant crown (1969). Also beat Johnny Fitzgerald, Sammy Vernon and Glyn Davies in a non-title fight.

DARNELL Les *From* Sunderland. *Died* May 1995 aged 66. Real surname was Quenet, and he was the second son of Les, who boxed in the 1920s under the ring-name of Gus Hughes. Boxed as an amateur for Lambton Street BC before turning pro in 1949, a career that lasted until 1951. Victims included Ernie Vickers, Eddie Carroll, Joe Myers, Eric Hague, Johnny Fitzpatrick, Dave Parker, Jimmy Muirhead, Johnny Cross and Roy Davies. Was a self-made millionaire, starting as a joiner, buying, renovating, and selling property. He married the daughter of former Sunderland featherweight, the late, great, Tom Smith.

DAVIES David Stanley *From* Hafodyrynys, Crumlin, Wales. *Died* 4 January 1995 aged 87. Granted a referee's licence (Class B) in 1949 and was later promoted to Class A, prior to retiring at 65 as per regulations. Returned in 1975-76 as a member of the new non-financially interested Welsh Area Council and in 1980 became its chairman, before being elected as the Council's Representative Steward in 1988. Retiring from the Council in 1992 due to ill-health, by trade he was a gas engineer and manager.

GALLIE Cyril *Born* Cardiff, 19 January 1920. *Died* 17 January 1995. His father formed Cardiff Gas BC and made Cyril join at the age of 13, with brother Alf as his trainer. At that age he won the Welsh Schoolboy title at five stones. Won five successive ABA titles, the Junior in 1935/6/7 and the Senior in 1938/9. During World War II was a Staff Sergeant PTI and represented the Army several times, winning two titles. A pro between 1944 and 1948, Cyril beat Harry Lazar, Jimmy Watson, Dick Shields, Johnny McManus, Jimmy Molloy and Battling Hai. Went to America in 1946, having ten bouts, winning seven, his victims including Pat Scanlon, Patsy Giovanelli, and Joey D'Amato. Returned to Britain a year later, beating Joe Cassidy, but losing to Henry Hall and Yrgo Piitulainen. In 1948, he defeated Bob Burniston in an eliminator for the Welsh welterweight title, before losing to Ric Sanders. Emigrated to America in 1957, only to return home a year later. Became a member of the Welsh EBA in 1976 and was chairman in 1979.

GARCIA Jimmy *Born* Colombia. *Died* May 1995 aged 23, following brain surgery after being stopped by Gabriel Ruelas in the 11th round of a WBC super-featherweight title challenge. Having taken a steady beating throughout, he could have been pulled out much earlier. Prior to the fight, he brought a 35-31 (17)-4 record to the ring, but, markedly, had dropped a lopsided points decision to Genaro Hernandez the previous November, when challenging for the WBA version of the championship.

GREYVENSTEIN Chris *From* Cape Town, South Africa. *Died* 6 May 1995 aged 64. Collapsed and died following a luncheon to mark his retirement from the *Cape Times,* of which he was Managing Editor. He was also Consultant Editor of the South African *Boxing World.* Was considered to be a world authority on boxing and was the author of many books, including *The Fighter,* which was considered to be a definitive history of South African boxing and, indeed, one of the best books ever written on the sport. He also wrote *Springbok Saga,* the finest book ever published on South African rugby.

HENDERSON Earl *Born* Trinidad, 13 August 1957. *Died* in London on 9 June 1995. Also known as Abdul Malik Saddiq, his Muslim name. Never turned pro, winning the ABA light-middleweight title in 1978, defeating four internationals on the way, and representing England five times. Brought up in Reading, it was with the local club that he made his reputation as a classy box-fighter after making his debut at the age of 16 in 1974.

HORRIDGE Joe *Born* Walsden, near Rochdale, 19 February 1915. *Died* 14 March 1995. Had no amateur experience, before boxing as a pro between 1931 and 1937. His favourite venue was Royton, and he boxed around 50 contests there. Commenced 1934 with an unbeaten run of 14, and was soon meeting champions like Ronnie James, Johnny McGrory and Johnny King. In a busy career, his victims included Dave Finn, Jackie Stayton, Sandy McEwan, Packey McFarland, Arley Hollingsworth, Joe Myers, Mick Howard, Ernie Upton, Jimmy Griffiths, Dick Titley, Billy Cakewell and Cyclone Jarvie. He retired in March 1937, and coached at the local Hamer Youth Club. While helping the war effort at an engineering firm during World War II, he boxed on a few booths, including those of Bert Hughes and Harry Kid Furness. Had to leave his job through arthritis, eventually becoming a member of Manchester EBA. Enjoyed snooker, and, in later years, cribbage and dominoes at the local club. His best friend and former fighter, Frankie "Boy" Holt, said: "Joe proudly claimed that he was only floored three times in his whole career."

HUGHES Jesse James *From* Mobile, USA. Murdered on 16 July 1995, just 19 days after beating Nick Rupa. Having spent time in prison for holding up drug dealers, while disguised as a policeman, he first came to notice when beating Anthony Stephens in the last minute to win the USBA welterweight title. Game as a pebble, and easily recognised by his black vest and cowboy hat, he followed that up with a kayo defence over Britain's Adrian Stone.

HUGHES Paddy *From* Dublin. *Died* September 1994 aged 80. As a member of the Corinthian BC, he collected six national senior titles at flyweight (1929-30), bantamweight (1931-32) and featherweight (1933 and '35). Represented Ireland at the 1932 Olympics, and later won a Tailtean Games title. Was employed by the *Irish Press* Newspaper.

JOHN Gerald *From* Slough. *Died* 27 October 1994 aged 60. As a member of Slough Centre BC, Gerald won the ABA flyweight title in 1951 and reached the final the following year, only to be outpointed by Dai Dower. Six years later, while in the Royal Air Force, he again reached the final, but was outscored by Jackie Brown. Made ten appearances in international representative matches and was a founder-member of Pinewood Starr, which started as Bracknell Boys, then Clark Eaton. Retired from coaching in 1989 because of arthritis.

JONES Eric *Born* Coalville, 19 June 1913. *Died* December 1994. Started as an amateur with Coalville Scouts, before boxing as a pro between 1929 and 1944. In only his third bout, he drew with Len Wickwar, winning the return the following year, and remaining unbeaten until April 1930. He averaged around 20 fights per year, most of them being in Leicester. In 1932 he made his London debut on the same bill at Wimbledon Stadium which featured Jack Petersen winning the British heavyweight title by knocking out Reggie Meen. Eric beat Herbie Hill. When scheduled to box in Rushden, he was involved in a motor-cycle accident on the way, and was unconscious when they picked him up. Nevertheless, he insisted on going through with the fight, and, not surprisingly, was beaten by Ronnie Summerton. Then, in 1934, he was walking to the hall at Burslem when he was bitten by a dog. After treatment he boxed Jack Lilley and won on points. To end 1936 he tackled Jimmy Warnock and Benny Lynch within three weeks, losing both. In 1937 he was stopped by Dave Keller in a final eliminator for the Southern Area flyweight title, and, in 1939, beat Johnny Griffiths for the vacant Southern Area title. Eric had one-round wins over Bert Kirby, Percy Dexter, Charlie Hazel and Len Wickwar and beat South African champion, Alec Knight. Among his other victims were Tut Whalley, Billy Nash, Johnny Boom, Les Johnson and Paddy Ryan. He also met Frank Bonser (seven times), George Marsden (five times), Jackie Brown and Jackie Paterson, the latter being a final eliminator for the British title, which Jackie won. During World War II, Eric helped to make Spitfire undercarriages before taking out a manager's licence. A member of Leicester EBA, he was an engineer at Loughborough until 1977.

JURY Jimmy *Born* Plymouth, 7 September 1914. Real first name "Cyril." *Died* 25 November 1994. Boxed on the booths at the age of 15, and was a full-time professional at 16. In 1938, he met Jack Thompson five times in three months, drawing the first, losing the next two and winning the last two, one of which was for the West of England lightweight title. Before World War II he beat George Pook, Jimmy Bitmead and Dick Wheller. Attached to the 21st Company RAMC, he beat Garry Roche, Jacky Bart, Cliff Saunders and Paddy O'Leary, and somehow crammed nearly 20 bouts into 1944. Victims included Ivor Simpson, Ted Duffy, Tommy Foxall, Ken Barrett, Darkie Sullivan and Billy Hawkins. He also met Dave Crowley, Dave Finn, Johnny Molloy and Tommy Davies, and, going into 1945, beat Jack Watkins and Hughie Smith, while drawing with Tommy Foxall and Jimmy Bryan. In 1946, he stopped Bob Hickey, Dennis Rebbeck and Hughie Smith in successive fights, along with Ivor Roberts and Les Haycox. He never avoided the top men, meeting Billy Thompson, Peter Fallon, Roy Coote, Reg Quinlan, Hal Bagwell, Stan Hawthorne and Bert Hornby, and, in 1947, beat Harry Legge and Tommy Shaw. Jimmy's final bout was in 1949, when he was outpointed by Tommy Shaw in a final eliminator for the Western Area welterweight title. Retired to become a trainer, looking after the likes of Ebe Mensah and Con Mount-Bassie. Arrived in Bournemouth in 1945, where he worked for the local Corporation as a painter and decorator, before retiring in 1979 and moving to Pontyclun, mid-Glamorgan. Was a member of both the Bournemouth EBA and Welsh EBA.

KELLY Cyclone *From* Manchester. *Died* June 1995 aged 83. *Pro* 1928-1941. Met the following champions, Rinty Monaghan (twice), Jim Brady (twice), John Cusick, Peter Kane and Bert Kirby. Later became a prominent member of Manchester EBA.

KESTRELL Doug *Born* Trealaw, Rhondda, June 1914. *Died* February 1995. Brothers Frank and Alby were both top professionals and Doug turned pro in 1929. In 1935, he met world featherweight champion, Freddie Miller, losing on points. Doug was quoted as saying: "When we were on the boat back from Belfast to Liverpool, referee, Jack Smith, told me there was only a quarter of a point in it." In 1936, he met another world champion in Jackie Wilson, again being outpointed in a close encounter. Also boxed British champions, Bert Kirby, Dick Corbett, Johnny McGrory, Dave Crowley, Ronnie James and Harry Mizler. During World War II, Doug served with the 63rd Searchlight Regiment and had quite a few bouts as an amateur. He explained: "My family name is Cheverton, and I had to box under that name in the Army, but I never took advantage of my pro experience." He did not continue his career after the war and later helped to found the Welsh Ex-Boxers' Association, of which he became Chairman. In a busy career, his victims included, Eddie Davies, Griff Williams, Johnny Griffiths, Ellis Ashurst, Harry Edwards, Jimmy Chinn, Boy Edge, Benny Thackray, Arley Hollingsworth, Bert Kirby, Spike Robinson, Frank McAloran, George Marsden, Stan Jehu and Mick Carney.

KRAY Ronnie *Born* Bethnal Green in 1934. *Died* in March 1995. Far more famous for his gangland activities than he ever was for achievements in boxing, Ronnie turned pro in 1951 aged 17, along with his identical twin, Reggie. With their elder brother Charlie one fight away from retirement, the twins, both lightweights, set out on a career that would last less than five months. Ronnie beat Bernie Long (twice), Bobbie Edwards and Charlie Godsell, before losing to Doug Sherlock and Bill Sliney, while Reggie had seven fights, winning them all, including two victories over his brother's victor, Bill Sliney. Following National Service, Ronnie (and Reggie) never returned to the ring, but always maintained a keen interest in the sport.

LA CHANCE Maurice (Lefty) *Born* Lisbon Falls, Maine, USA, 1921. *Died* May 1994. French-Canadian feather-weight whose pro career ran from 1940 to 1950. Mixed in good company, beating Davy Crawford, Charley Cabey Lewis, Larry Bolvin, Phil Terranova, Carlos Chavez and Tony LaBua, but losing to Ike Williams, Sal Bartolo, Bernie Docuson, Chico Morales, Willie Pep, Jackie Graves, Danny Webb and Bobby Ruffin.

LAKE Charlie *Born* Catford, 9 July 1933. *Died* 22 December 1994. As an amateur, Charlie won Southern Counties and Services titles under his real name of Chidgey. As a pro, between 1955 and 1962, he beat Dudley Cox, Jackie Hughes, Mick Endley and Vic Harrison, and also drew with George Lavery and Dudley Cox. Started the Herne Bay and Horton Lodge BCs in Kent. Later trained his sons Dean and Dave, when they turned pro. The latter is still boxing.

LAWLOR Seaman Jim *Born* Halifax, 7 May 1912. *Died* 8 June 1995. *Pro* 1932-1939. His father was Irish, as were his grandfather and great-grandfather, who were both bare-knuckle fighters. Father died in World War I and mother shortly afterwards. Both were only in their 20s. Then his grandmother died and he was brought up by an aunt and uncle. Joined the Navy at 15-years-of-age and started to box, winning, among others, the welterweight champion-ship of the Mediterranean Fleet. Married Rose in 1935, and, by the end of that year, Jim had taken part in around 50 fights, including a win over former champion, Harry Mason. He was bought out of the Navy by Corinthian Promotions Ltd, who offered him a job as a boxing instructor at the famous Green Man gym at Blackheath. When Corinthian went into liquidation, Jim became proprietor of the Green Man. An excellent box-fighter, he outpointed Albert Danahar, Herbie Fraser, Jack McKnight, Roy Mills and Chuck Parker. In 1936, he kayoed Chris Dawson in 75 seconds at Norwich, then travelled 500 miles to Plymouth to outpoint "Battling" Charlie Parkin the following night, for which feat he was awarded a coveted Boxing News Certificate of Merit. Also kayoed "Tiger" Bob Ennis in 17 seconds and George Rose in 25 seconds. On the outbreak of World War II, he was recalled to the Navy, where he had a few fights and, afterwards, returned to Yorkshire, before eventually coming back to Lowestoft.

Worked in printing and tailoring, then in a stainless steel factory, before becoming a boxing instructor at Woodhouse Grove, a private school in Apperley Bridge, near Bradford. After his autobiography was published in 1975, a limited edition of 500 copies, he sent a couple of his poems to Muhammad Ali, to which the champ replied – Jim, your poems are great." Jim's career spanned some hundred fights, of which he won half inside the distance.

LEVINE Georgie *Born* New York City, USA, 1903. *Died* May 1994. As an American-Hebrew welterweight, he challenged Pete Latzo for the world title on 9 July 1926, losing on a fourth round disqualification. Fought world champions such as Jack Britton, Joe Dundee (twice), Tommy Freeman (twice), Pinkey Mitchell and Latzo (twice) and, apart from the title shot, always managed to go the distance. He also won and lost against Sergeant Sammy Baker, beat Andy DiVodi and drew with Canada Lee.

MACPHERSON Stewart Myles *Born* Winnipeg, Canada, 29 October 1908. *Died* April 1995. Joined the BBC in 1937, and was a leading radio commentator on boxing, ice hockey and other sports. Too old to join up in World War II, Stewart returned to Winnipeg and became sports editor of a local station. A few months later he received a cable from the BBC inviting him to join their war reporting unit and he was assigned to the RAF, filing an account of a bombing raid over Cologne and a report about Arnhem, among many others. After the war, he covered the Oxford and Cambridge Boat Race, and was question master of the quiz programmes *Twenty Questions* and *Ignorance Is Bliss*. In 1949, Stewart moved to North America, running a sports stadium in Winnipeg and, in 1960, starting CJAY, a small TV station. All this after arriving in London with just two pounds and ten shillings in his pocket.

MANCINI Tony *Born* 30 November 1932. *Died* June 1995. *Pro* 1950-1962. Had two shots at the Southern Area welterweight title, losing the first to champion, Albert Carroll (1960), then beating Carroll (1961), before relinquishing the title. Came from the famous Mancini family, who have been involved as boxers, trainers, managers and promoters, starting with Alf Mancini, who, in 1928, was outpointed by Jack Hood for the British welterweight title. Tony's career was in two parts, as he was out of the ring for five years because of hand injuries. During his enforced retirement, he became a manager-trainer and looked after middleweight, Maxie Beech. After winning the Southern Area title he met champion, Brian Curvis, for the British and Empire championships, the fight being stopped when Tony sustained eye injuries. He then became a manager, looking after top men like Ivan Whiter, Eric Blake and Vic Moore, all of whom won Southern Area titles. In recent years, Tony enjoyed working with Tony Burke, Bruce Scott, Jason Beard and Howard Eastman, etc.

MATTHEWS Jimmy *From* Belfast. *Died* November 1994. As a member of the St John Bosco BC, won the Ulster senior flyweight title in 1953 and 1954, also winning the national senior flyweight title in 1954. Before emigrating to New Zealand, and later going to America, he turned pro in 1954, beating Pete Holberg on points. Had six contests in 1955, before departing and continuing his career, beating Bobby Robinson, Jim Loughrey, Tommy Emberson and Don Armagh, but lost to Loughrey and Jimmy Quinn.

MILLSON Ken *From* Doncaster. *Born* 1 September 1929. *Died* 19 September 1994. *Pro* 1950-1954. Beat Derek John, Charlie Howe, Geoff Heath, Ted Dexter, Ivan Hutton and Sammy Milsom. Also met Al Allotey, Johnny Barton and Terry Gooding. Unbeaten in his first 12 contests, he lost just four from 24, finishing on a high note with an eight round points win over Johnny Smith.

MONZON Carlos *Born* Argentina, 7 August 1942. *Died* 8 January 1995 in a car crash. Spent the last five years of his life serving a jail sentence for the murder of Alicia Muniz, having been found guilty on 3 July 1989, and sentenced to 11 years. At the time of the crash he was on a permitted home visit, pending parole, and was driving two friends, one of whom died. Had the reputation of living "in the fast lane", but, as a boxer, was one of the all-time greats. *Pro* 1963-1977. Won Argentinian and South American middleweight titles, before stopping Nino Benvenuti for the world title (1970). There were successful defences against Benvenuti and Emile Griffith (1971), Denny Moyer, Jean-Claude Bouttier, Tom Bogs and Bennie Briscoe (1972), Griffith and Briscoe (1972), Griffith and Bouttier (1973), Jose Napoles and Tony Mundine (1974), Tony Licata and Gratien Tonna (1975), Rodrigo Valdez (1976 and 1977), after which he retired. He lost only three of 101 contests, and was never stopped. In 1974, the WBC took away his title for not signing for a defence against Rodrigo Valdez, but he retained the WBA version, and his two subsequent fights with Valdez were for the undisputed crown.

MOORE Rees *Born* Mardy, Wales, 17 June 1925. *Died* 2 April 1995. First name was "Cyril", but he preferred to box under his second name. His family had moved to Luton when he was very young, and there he remained. Had 75 bouts with a local amateur club, before turning pro in April 1948. His first big scalp was Jim Wellard, whom Rees beat in 1949, in his 16th bout. Also in 1949, he was outpointed by Gwyn Williams in an eliminator for the Welsh welterweight title. Won the title in 1953, beating Dennis Rowley and successfully defended against Eric Davies (1955) and Eddie Williams (1956), before losing it to Les Morgan (1957). Had around 80 bouts in nine years, and among his victims were Johnny Sullivan, Tommy Jones, Stan Hawthorne, Alf Danahar, and Laurie Buxton. In three contests with Paul King, he lost the first two and won the third, which gave him a British rating of number five in the welterweight division. Retired in 1957.

MOY Harry *Born* Walworth, London, 1913. *Died* November 1994. Harry was a top participant at soccer, athletics and swimming, the latter as a representative of his employers, publishers J. M. Dent & Sons Ltd. Started boxing at the age of 12 at the Lomond Grove LCC School, Camberwell, and only a damaged hand robbed him of a Schoolboy title at 5st 7lb. On leaving school, he joined the Cambridge House Boys Club, and was also a junior member of the Cornwall Club, Blackfriars, before signing up with Lynn BC at the age of 18. Was beaten by Frank Frost in the final of the South-East London Divisionals (1932-33), and the following year, after beating Frank, he was adjudged the loser against Phil Grace in the second series, with his rival admitting that he had been lucky. Nicknamed "Turkey", in the Empire Games' trials of 1934, Harry qualified by beating Frank Frost and A. Waklin, having won 52 out of 72 bouts at that stage of his career, and went on to win a bronze medal at Wembley. Later, he moved to Letchworth, where he was a neighbour of Peter Cragg. Also became a member of the London Ex-Boxers' Association.

MUTTI Chisanda *Born* Lusaka, Zambia, 14 February 1957. *Died* July 1995 aged 38. Reported to have had a dozen bouts locally before tackling Frankie Lucas in Lusaka (1978), losing in nine rounds. Outpointed by Tony Sibson for the Commonwealth middleweight title in 1980, two months later, he beat Eddie Smith. Was twice beaten by fellow-countryman, Lotte Mwale (1982 and 1983), before winning the Commonwealth cruiser crown by beating Stuart Lithgo (1984). Having outpointed Tom Collins (1985), he then lost to Lee Roy Murphy (1985) for the IBF cruiser crown, Evander Holyfield and Rickey Parkey, in another crack at the IBF title. Based in Germany, he retained the Commonwealth title by beating Dave Russell, before losing it to Glenn McCrory (1987).

ODWELL George *Born* City of London Hospital in 1911. *Died* 11 July 1995. *Pro* 1930-1945. Had over 200 fights, with one of the highest stoppage records in the world. Twice beat Kid Berg, twice kayoed Len Wickwar, each time in two rounds and, in the short space of three months, defeated lightweight champion, Jimmy Walsh, in an overweight bout, drew with George Daly, was outpointed by Dave Crowley in an eliminator for the Southern Area lightweight title, and by Norman Snow for the Southern Area welter crown. In 1933, he won all 22 bouts, 16 inside the distance, and from May 1932 to the end of 1933, won all 41 contests. He and Stella were married in 1930, and later they took over the Locomotive pub in Camden Town. Sadly, Stella died in 1946, leaving him with three sons, George, Billy and Jimmy. In 1949, he remarried, to Rosina, and there were three children, Dennis, David and Patricia. Of the five sons, only Jimmy wasn't connected with boxing. In World War II he was a PTI in the RASC, winning the Western Command middleweight title, but, after losing on points to Henry Hall, it was time to call it a day. George became a scrap-metal merchant after the Locomotive was sold and, in 1952, he was invited to train Phil Coren's stable, later becoming trainer of the stable belonging to his old manager, Jack Burns. Also coached

Langham BC and Inns Of Court (Gainsford) BC. In 1956, he became a warehouseman in the "print", and, after retiring in 1976, he and Rosina went to live in Westcliff, before coming back to reside in North London.

PHILLIPS Eddie *Born* Bow, London, 1909. *Died* 2 March 1995. Came into boxing by accident. Was a coach driver who regularly took boxers and fans from Aldgate to shows at the Rochester Casino, but one night in December 1929 one of the fighters didn't turn up and Eddie agreed to come in as a substitute, boxing a draw with Reg Palmer. He became a regular at the lunch-hour tests at the Old Stadium Club, Holborn, and in a return at Rochester he knocked out Reg Palmer. Unbeaten until April 1932, when he met Bill Partridge for the unofficial championship of Bow, Eddie forgot to duck and was kayoed in round two. In March 1933, he met middleweight champion, Len Harvey, in a final eliminator for the British light-heavyweight title. The result was a draw. In June 1933, these two met again, this time for the vacant title, Len winning on points. When the title again became vacant, Eddie outpointed Tommy Farr, the third time he had beaten Tommy. In 1935, he again met Harvey, this time in an eliminator for the heavyweight crown, Len winning on points. By now, Eddie was having weight problems, and, in 1937, he was kayoed by Jock McAvoy, thus losing his British light-heavyweight title. When the heavyweight crown became vacant, Eddie lost to Len Harvey on a disqualification. There were two "fights" with Jack Doyle. In the first, 1938, Jack missed with a left-swing, went clean through the ropes and was counted out and the following year, Eddie kayoed him in 145 seconds. With the coming of World War II, Eddie joined the RAF, but was discharged on medical grounds. That was in 1942, and was thought to be the end of his boxing career. However, in September 1945, he came back to outpoint Olle Tandberg at the Royal Albert Hall and then retired to become a publican. Sadly, several years ago, following an illness, he became house-bound.

PREBEG Yvan *Born* Yosipdol, Yugoslavia, 25 August 1938. *Died* in Zagreb in June 1995. The first Yugoslav boxer to win the European title, Yvan outpointed Welshman, Eddie Avoth, over 15 rounds in June 1969, to win the light-heavyweight belt. Lost the title to Piero del Papa in February 1970 and two fights later had retired. Beat Lion Ven, Peter Gumpert, Buddy Turman and Dave Bailey, but lost to Gustav Scholz, Gert van Heerden, Pekka Kokkonen, Karl Mildenberger, and our own Jack Bodell.

PULLUM Bill *From* Croydon. *Died* 10 December 1994. A Schoolboy champion, Bill turned pro in his teens, meeting among others, George Daly. Around 1937 he became Britain's youngest promoter. At that time, he managed *Health & Strength* magazine, which had just been bought by his father, W. A. Pullum, the nine-stone weight-lifting champion of the world. Later became Advertising Manager of *Exchange & Mart,* before ill-health brought about a move to Eastbourne. Was president of Sussex EBA.

RAFFERTY Billy *Born* Glasgow, Scotland, 14 August 1933. *Died* October 1994. As an amateur, Billy represented Scotland v England and as a pro, between 1956 and 1962, he beat Jake Tuli, Terry Spinks, Len Reece, George Dormer, Graham van der Walt and George Bowes. Had two bouts with Freddie Gilroy, the first, in 1960, being for Freddie's British, European and Commonwealth bantamweight titles, injuries prompting a stoppage in the champion's favour in round 13. The second, in 1962, was for Gilroy's British and Commonwealth crowns and Billy was kayoed in round 12, after which he announced his retirement. Owned a house in Stewarton Ayrshire, a blacksmith's business in Glasgow, and had been involved with the Stars Organisation for Spastics' committee since 1962. His death came in tragic circumstances. On a cruise holiday, and having stopped off at Miami, as always a fitness fanatic, he went for a run and had a heart attack.

RIORDAN John *From* Dublin. *Died* July 1995. A member of Crumlin BC, and later St Mary's BC, he won an Irish senior light-heavyweight title in 1966, also representing Ireland at international level. A fireman, attached to Tara Street Fire Department, in the city centre, he was a member of the Irish Boxers' Mutual Benefit Association.

ROSS Billy *From* Methil, Scotland. *Died* 1995 aged 72. A coal miner, he turned pro in 1943 and met tough opposition like Tommy Armour and Cyril Wills. For many years was a coach and trainer at East Wemyss BC and Western BC.

SCOTT Charley *Born* Philadelphia, USA, 12 November 1936. *Died* November 1994. Came from nowhere at the beginning of 1959 to the number one welterweight challenger's spot in October of that year. Charley had been on the verge of retiring, but victories over Isaac Logart (twice), Ralph Dupas and Garnett "Sugar" Hart, put him in line for a crack at champion, Don Jordan. Instead of sitting on his laurels, he surprisingly took on Benny Paret, twice losing to the Cuban, before going down at the hands of Virgil Akins, Ralph Dupas (twice), and returning to virtual obscurity after being outpointed over ten rounds in February 1961 by Denny Moyer.

SHAW Battling *Born* Neuvo Lardeo, Mexico, 21 October 1910. *Died* September 1994. Our incomplete record has him with 66 fights (15 losses) between 1927 and 1938. Won the world junior-lightweight title from Johnny Jadick in February 1933, but lost it to Tony Canzoneri in his first defence. Most of his fights from 1932 were in New Orleans, where he became a great favourite. Beat men such as Joe Ghnouly, Davey Abad, Ervin Berlier and Tommy Grogan, before going on the downward slide and losing the last nine contests we have recorded for him.

SICHULA John *Born* Zambia, 4 February 1955. *Died* October 1994. Our earliest record shows him turning pro in 1982 and winning the African super-feather title in 1983, prior to beating Langton Tinago for the Commonwealth 130 lbs championship. Did not taste defeat until his 19th bout, when he lost the Commonwealth crown to Lester Ellis in November 1984. Recovered the title on knocking out Haste Sankissa the following year, but lost both that and the African belt to Sam Akromah in October 1986. Regaining the championship, he made successful defences against Akromah and John Farrell, before dropping it, once and for all, to Mark Reefer in September 1989. His best win, certainly on paper, came when he kayoed Lester Ellis in four rounds (1985).

SIMPSON Billy *From* Birkenhead. *Born* 1911. *Died* 1994. Real name was Owen Thomas Jones, but he adopted the ring name after substituting for a boxer named Billy Simpson in his second pro fight. Managed by Jim Turner, the other local hero was Charlie Smith, the two meeting three times in 1934, in the short space of six weeks. Smith won the first, Simpson the second and Smith the "rubber" match, all three bouts going the full distance, 37 rounds altogether. Billy joined the RAF in 1939 as an air gunner and later became a parachute instructor, making 67 jumps. Becoming a referee in 1944, after the war he was invited to re-enlist in the RAF to take charge of their boxing teams. In 1952 he left Birkenhead for Blackpool, continuing to referee, and retired from the RAF in 1959. Having joined the UK Atomic Energy Authority at Springfields, near Preston, Billy finally retired in 1972, but due to ill-health he moved to Staveley, near Kendal, to be near one of his daughters.

STRANGE Billy *From* Stanton Hill. *Died* 16 May 1995 aged 80. *Pro* 1928-1951. Beat Tiger Bert Ison, Billy Gibbons, Arthur Hill and Charlie Chetwin, and went the distance with champion, Harry Mason (1936). First entry into boxing was in a "battle royal", when five boxers were in the ring together, punching away until only one was left. That one was Billy. Also had two bouts on the same night (1935), outpointing Charlie Thompson and then Bob Barlow.

STRYDOM Lou *Born* Pretoria, South Africa, 24 April 1931. *Died* 14 December 1994. *Pro* 1950-1960. Having won the vacant South African heavyweight title, when beating George Bissett (1952), the following year he had three fights with Johnny Arthur, all for the same title, and lost all three. Came to Britain in 1952, beating George Stern and Paddy Slavin, but lost to Stern (disqualification), Jock McVicar and George Nuttall. Numbered men like Giorgio Milan, Reg Andrews, Freddie Vorster, Archie Smith, Mike Oberholzer (two wins, two defeats) among his victims and met champions Gawie De Klerk, Stan Lotriet, and Austrian, Joe Weidin.

TARONE Jordan *Died* December 1994. *Pro* 1940-1949. Met many of the top welterweights of the day such as Freddie Simpson, Roy Davies, Ginger Ward, Willie Whyte,

Laurie Buxton, Gwyn Williams, Les Allen and Jeff Tite. Was a member of the London Ex-Boxers' Association.

TOWEEL Frazer *Born* South Africa. *Died* 10 June 1995. The youngest of the famous fighting Toweel brothers, in a career of some 30 contests he was beaten by only two men, Stoffel Steyn and Willie Ludick, who defeated him on six occasions, and thwarted his ambitions to win a national title. Their fights were reported as "classics" in the 1960s. Beat good men like Charlie Els, three times, Bobbie Scanlon, a high-ranking American, and top British fighters, Tony Smith and Sammy McSpadden. Emigrated to Australia on retiring.

WARD Dai "Ginger" *From* Merthyr Tydfil, before moving to Crewe. *Died* 7 December 1994 at the age of 74. *Pro* 1938-1954. Met Len Wickwar, Tommy Armour, Willie Whyte, Gwyn Williams, Ric Sanders, Dennis Chadwick, Chris Adcock, Eddie Cardew and Alan Wilkins. Beat Mick Gibbons and had a good win over Ric Sanders. Career was temporarily halted by World War II, during which he served on HMS Rodney, and was awarded the Malta and Russian Medals for services in the Mediterranean and Arctic.

WILDING Ray *From* Northwich, Cheshire. *Born* 6 September 1929. *Died* 23 May 1995. *Pro* 1947-1956. Beat George Nuttall, Martin Thornton, Harry Painter, Peter Bell, Terry O'Connor, Ron Raynor, Nick Fisher, Don Scott and Len Bennett. Won an open heavyweight competition at Watford, knocking out Charlie Scott in the final. Became Central Area heavyweight title (1950) by stopping Frank Bell, and, in doing so, gained a *Boxing News* Certificate of Merit. Sparred with American, Lee Savold, when he came to Britain, and the latter's manager, "Squire" Bill Daly, invited him back to the States, where he also sparred with Rocky Marciano and Cesar Brion. Won several fights in America, returning home to successfully defend his Central Area title by stopping Frank Bell, but, after defeats by Werner Wiegand and Charley Norkus, Ray eventually retired in 1956 to take up permanent residence in New Jersey. Started his own waterproofing business, which turned out to be the best and longest established in the area. Inducted into the New Jersey Hall of Fame in 1995, Ray made annual visits to relatives in Northwich and became a member of the London Ex-Boxers' Association. Out of 50 bouts, he won 34 inside the distance and was once widely tipped for world title honours.

WILLIAMS Robbie *Born* South Africa, 27 October 1953. Committed suicide in September 1994. A former South African heavyweight champion, he was outpointed (split decision) over 15 rounds by Ossie Ocasio in a contest for the inaugural WBA cruiser title in February 1982. Never quite made it, with wins over Jimmy Abbott, Kallie Knoetze and Ron Ellis, being the pick of his victories.

Leading BBBoC License Holders: Names and Addresses

Licensed Promoters

Billy Aird
The Golden Gloves
346 Seaside
Eastbourne
East Sussex BN22 7RJ

Michael Andrew
38 Kennedy Avenue
Laindon West
Basildon
Essex

Anglo Swedish Promotions
11 Whitcomb Street
London
WC2H 7HA

John Ashton
1 Charters Close
Kirkby in Ashfield
Nottinghamshire
NG17 8PF

Teresa Breen
31 Penlan Road
Treboeth
Swansea

Pat Brogan
112 Crewe Road
Haslington
Crewe
Cheshire

Harry Burgess
25 Calthorpe Street
London WC1X 0JX

Bruce Burrows
126 Ferndale Road
Swindon
Wiltshire

Roy Cameron
36/8 Birbeck Road
Acton
London W3 6BQ

Carlton Carew
18 Mordaunt Street
Stockwell
London SW9 9RB

Champion Enterprises
Frank Maloney
99 Middlesex Street
London E1 7DA

Pat Cowdell
129a Moat Road
Oldbury
Warley
West Midlands

John Cox
11 Fulford Drive
Links View
Northampton

Shaun Doyle
15 Jermyn Croft
Dodworth
Barnsley
South Yorkshire

Dragon Boxing Promotions
Kevin Hayde
93 St Mary's Street
Cardiff
South Wales
CF1 1DW

Eastwood Promotions
Bernard Eastwood
Eastwood House
2-4 Chapel Lane
Belfast 1
Northern Ireland

James Evans
88 Windsor Road
Bray
Berkshire

Evesham Sporting Club
Mike Goodall
Schiller
Gibbs Lane
Offenham
Evesham

Norman Fawcett
4 Wydsail Place
Gosforth
Newcastle upon Tyne
NE3 4QP

John Forbes
5 Durham Road
Sedgefield
Stockton on Tees
Cleveland TS21 3DW

Joe Frater
The Cottage
Main Road
Grainthorpe
Louth
Lincolnshire

Dai Gardiner
13 Hengoed Hall Drive
Cefn Hengoed
Hengoed
Mid Glamorgan
CF8 7JW

Anthony Gee
35 Greville Street
Hatton Garden
London EC1

Harold Gorton
Gorton House
4 Hollius Road
Oldham
Lancashire

Ron Gray
Ingrams Oak
19 Hatherton Road
Cannock
Staffordshire

Johnny Griffin
26 Christow Street
Leicester
Leicestershire LE1 2GN

Clive Hall
23 Linnett Drive
Barton Seagrave
Kettering
Northamptonshire

David Harris
16 Battle Crescent
St Leonards on Sea
Sussex

Dennis Hobson
The Lodge
Stone Lane
Woodhouse
Sheffield
Yorkshire S13 7BR

Steve Holdsworth
85 Sussex Road
Watford
Hertfordshire
WD2 5HR

Harry Holland
12 Kendall Close
Feltham
Middlesex

Hull & District Sporting Club
Mick Toomey
25 Purton Grove
Bransholme
Hull HU7 4QD

John Hyland
9 The Old Quarry
Woolton
Liverpool
L25 6RS

Alma Ingle
26 Newman Road
Wincobank
Sheffield S9 1LP

Owen McMahon
3 Atlantic Avenue
Belfast BT15 2HN

McMahon Promotions
17c Lewisham Park
London SE13 6QZ
and
60 Stapleton Road
Easton
Bristol

Matchroom
Barry Hearn
10 Western Road
Romford
Essex RM1 3JT

Alan Matthews (Special Licence)
256 Lodge Avenue
Dagenham
Essex RM8 2HF

Midland Sporting Club
D. L. Read
Ernest & Young
Windsor House
3 Temple Row
Birmingham
B2 5LA

Katherine Morrison
5 Abercromby Drive
Glasgow G40

National Promotions
National House
60-66 Wardour Street
London W1V 3HP

North Staffs Sporting Club
J Baddeley
29 Redwood Avenue
Stone
Staffordshire ST15 0DB

Michael O'Brien
39 Clydesdale Mount
Byker
Newcastle upon Tyne
NE6 2EN

Peacock Promotions
Anthony Bowers
Peacock Gym
Caxton Street North
Canning Town
London

Steve Pollard
269 Hessle Road
Hull
East Yorkshire
HU3 4BE

Quensberry Yeo Ltd (Special Licence)
1 Concorde Drive
5(c) Business Centre
Clevedon
Avon BS21 6UH

Ringside Promotions
Ken Whitney
38 Shakespeare Way
Corby
Northamptonshire
NN17 2ND

Gus Robinson
Stranton House
Westview Road
Hartlepool
TS24 0BB

Round One Boxing Promotions
Dave Furneaux
251 Embankment Road
Prince Rock
Plymouth
Cornwall
PL4 9JH

Christine Rushton
20 Alverley Lane
Balby
Doncaster
Yorkshire
DN4 9AS

St Andrews Sporting Club
Tommy Gilmour
Anderson Suite
Forte Crest Hotel
Bothwell Street
Glasgow
G2 7EN

Chris Sanigar
147 Two Mile Hill Road
Kingswood
Bristol
Avon
BS15 1BH

Mike Shinfield
126 Birchwood Lane
Somercotes
Derbyshire DE55 4NF

Brian Snagg
The Heath Hotel
Green Hill Road
Allerton
Liverpool

John Spensley
The Black Swan Hotel
Tremholme Bar
Near Stokesley
North Yorkshire
DL6 3JY

Sporting Club of Wales
Paul Boyce
79 Church Street
Britton Ferry
Neath SA11 2TU

Sportsman Promotions
Frank Quinlan
Hollinthorpe Low Farm
Swillington Lane
Leeds
Yorkshire
LS26 8BZ

Tara Promotions
Jack Doughty
Grains Road
Shaw
Oldham
Lancashire
OL2 8JB

Team Promotions
David Gregory
Contract House
Split Crow Road
Gateshead
Tyne and Wear

Jack Trickett
Acton Court Hotel
187 Buxton Road
Stockport
Cheshire

UK Pro Box Promotions
David Matthews
22 Copt Royd Grove
Yeadon
Leeds
Yorkshire LS19 7HQ

Stephen Vaughan
43-45 Pembroke Place
Liverpool L3 5PH

Frank Warren
Centurion House
Bircherley Green
Hertford
Hertfordshire SG14 1AP

Winning Combination
Annette Conroy
144 High Street East
Sunderland
Tyne and Wear
SR1 2BL

Wolverhampton Sporting Club
J R Mills
24 Perton Road
Wightwick
Wolverhampton
Staffordshire WV6 8DN

Yorkshire Executive Sporting Club
John Celebanski
The Bungalow
Clayton Golf Club
Thornton View Road
Bradford
Yorkshire

Licensed Managers

Billy Aird
The Golden Gloves
346 Seaside
Eastbourne
East Sussex
BN22 7RJ

Isola Akay
129 Portnall Road
Paddington
London
W9 3BN

John Ashton
1 Charters Close
Kirkby in Ashfield
Nottinghamshire
NG17 8PF

Mike Atkinson
9 Tudor Road
Ainsdale
Southport
Lancashire
PR8 2RU

Don Austin
14 Winchat Road
Broadwaters
Thamesmead
London
SE28 0DZ

Billy Ball
6 Copse Close
Marlow
Buckinghamshire
SL7 2NY

Nat Basso
38 Windsor Road
Prestwich
Lancashire
M25 8FF

John Baxter
6 Havencrest Drive
Leicester
LE5 2AG

Lance Billany
32 Beaconsfield
Carrs Meadow
Withernsea
North Humberside
HU19 2EP

Jack Bishop
76 Gordon Road
Fareham
Hampshire
PO16 7SS

Abner Blackstock
23 Alice Street
Pill
Newport
Gwent
South Wales

Gerald Bousted
4 Firlands Road
Barton
Torquay
Devon
TQ2 8EW

Paul Boyce
Brynamlwg
2 Pant Howell Ddu
Ynysmerdy
Briton Ferry
Neath SA11 2TU

David Bradley
Dallicote Cottage
Worfield
Shropshire
WV15 5PC

Colin Breen
31 Penlan Road
Treboeth
Swansea
West Glamorgan

Mike Brennan
2 Canon Avenue
Chadwell Heath
Romford
Essex

Fred Britton
71 Henrietta Street
Leigh
Lancashire WN7 1LH

Pat Brogan
112 Crewe Road
Haslington
Cheshire

Michael Brooks
114 Gildane
Orchard Park Estate
Hull HU6 9AY

Harry Burgess
25 Calthorpe Street
London
WC1X 0JX

Winston Burnett
6 Faber Way
City Gardens
Sloper Road
Grangetown
Cardiff CF1 8DN

Paddy Byrne
70 Benfield Way
Portslade by Sea
Sussex BN4 2DL

Pat Byrne
16 Barbridge Close
Bulkington
Warwickshire
CV12 9PW

Trevor Callighan
40 Prescott Street
Halifax
West Yorkshire
HX1 2QW

Carlton Carew
18 Mordaunt Street
Brixton
London SW9 9RB

Ernie Cashmore
18 North Drive
Handsworth
Birmingham
B20 8SX

John Celebanski
The Bungalow
Clayton Golf Club
Thornton View Road
Bradford
Yorkshire

John Cheshire
38 Achilles Close
St James Place
Rolls Road
London SE1

Nigel Christian
80 Alma Road
Plymouth
Devon
PL3 4HU

Peter Coleman
29 The Ring Road
Leeds
Yorkshire
LS14 1NH

Roger Colson
63 Amwell Street
Roseberry Avenue
London EC1

William Connelly
72 Clincart Road
Mount Florida
Glasgow G42

Tommy Conroy
144 High Street East
Sunderland
Tyne and Wear

George Cooper
16 Robin Hood Green
St Mary Cray
Orpington
Kent

Chris Coughlan
27 Maes Yr Haf
Llansamlet
Swansea
Wales SA7 9ST

Pat Cowdell
129a Moat Road
Oldbury
Warley
West Midlands
B68 8EE

John Cox
11 Fulford Drive
Links View
Northampton NN2 7NX

Bingo Crooks
37 Helming Drive
Danehust Estate
Wolverhampton
West Midlands
WV1 2AF

David Davies
10 Bryngelli
Carmel
Llanelli
Dyfed SA14 7EL

Glyn Davies
63 Parc Brynmawr
Felinfoel
Llanelli
Dyfed SA15 4PG

John Davies
5 Welsh Road
Garden City
Deeside
Clwyd
Wales

Ronnie Davies
3 Vallensdean Cottages
Hangleton Lane
Portslade
Sussex

Brian Dawson
30 Presdales Drive
Ware
Hertfordshire
SG12 9NN

Peter Defreitas
17 Ramsay Road
London E7 9EN

Brendan Devine
12 Birkdale Close
Clubmoor
Liverpool L6 0DL

Jack Doughty
Lane End Cottage
Golden Street
Shaw
Lancashire
OL2 8LY

Shaun Doyle
15 Jermyn Croft
Dodworth
Barnsley
South Yorkshire
S75 3LR

Phil Duckworth
The Hampton Hotel
Longclose Lane
Richmond Hill
Leeds LS9 8NP

Mickey Duff
National House
60-66 Wardour Street
London W1V 3HP

Pat Dwyer
93 Keir Hardie Avenue
Bootle
Liverpool 20
Merseyside
L20 0DN

Bernard Eastwood
Eastwood House
2-4 Chapel Lane
Belfast 1
Northern Ireland

George Evans
14 Donald Street
Abercanaid
Merthyr Tydfil
Glamorgan

Greg Evans
21 Portman Road
Liverpool
Merseyside
L15 2HH

Jack Evans
Morlee House
Hanbury Road
Pontypool
Monmouth

Michael Fawcett
44 Rawstone Walk
Plaistow
London E13

Norman Fawcett
4 Wydsail Place
Gosforth
Newcastle upon Tyne
NE3 4QP

Colin Flute
84 Summerhill Road
Coseley
West Midlands
WV14 8RE

Dai Gardiner
13 Hengoed Hall Drive
Cefn Hengoed
Mid Glamorgan

John Gaynor
7 Westhorne Fold
Counthill Drive
Brooklands Road
Crumpsall
Manchester
M8 6JN

Tommy Gilmour
Forte Crest Hotel
Bothwell Street
Glasgow
G2 7EN

Ron Gray
Ingrams Oak
19 Hatherton Road
Cannock
Staffordshire

Dave Gregory
10 Mill Farm Road
Hamsterley Mill
Nr Rowlands Gill
Tyne & Wear

Johnny Griffin
26 Christow Street
Leicester LE1 2GN

Dick Gunn
43 Moray Avenue
Hayes
Middlesex OB3 2AY

Carl Gunns
Flat 2
Heathcliffe
469 Loughborough
Road
Birstall
Leicester LE4 0DS

Billy Hardy
24 Dene Park
Castletown
Sunderland
SR5 3AG

Frank Harrington
178 Kingsway
Heysham
Lancashire
LA3 2EG

Kevin Hayde
93 St Mary Street
Cardiff
CF1 1DW

Howard Hayes
16 Hyland Crescent
Warmsworth
Doncaster
South Yorkshire
DN4 9JS

Teddy Haynes
The Henry Cooper
516 Old Kent Road
London SE1 5BA

Patrick Healy
1 Cranley Buildings
Brookes Market
Holborn
London EC1

Barry Hearn
Matchroom
10 Western Road
Romford
Essex RM1 3JT

George Hill
52 Hathaway
Marton
Blackpool
Lancashire
FY4 4AB

Mick Hill
35 Shenstone House
Aldrington Road
London
SW16 1TL

Clive Hogben
44 Polwell Lane
Barton Seagrave
Kettering
Northamptonshire
NN15 6UA

Steve Holdsworth
85 Sussex Road
Watford
Hertfordshire
WD2 5HR

Harry Holland
12 Kendall Close
Feltham
Middlesex

Gordon Holmes
New Cottage
Watton Road
Hingham
Norfolk
NR9 4NN

Lloyd Honeyghan
22 Risborough
Deacon Way
Walworth Road
London SE17

John Hyland
401 Grafton Street
Liverpool

Brendan Ingle
26 Newman Road
Wincobank
Sheffield S9 1LP

Derek Isaamen
179 Liverpool Road
South
Maghill
Liverpool
L31 8AA

Mike Jacobs
The Penthouse Suite
Duke Street House
50 Duke Street
London W1M 5DS

Colin Jones
1 Brookfield Close
Penyrheol
Gorseinon
Swansea
SA4 2GW

Richard Jones
1 Churchfields
Croft
Warrington
Cheshire WA3 7JR

Duncan Jowett
Cedarhouse
Caplethill Road
Paisley
Strathclyde
Scotland

Billy Kane
17 Bamburn Terrace
Byker
Newcastle upon Tyne
NE6 2GH

Johnny Kramer
115 Crofton Road
Plaistow
London E13

Terry Lawless
4 Banyards
Off Nelmes Way
Emerson Park
Hornchurch
Essex

Buddy Lee
The Walnuts
Roman Bank
Leverington
Wisbech
Cambridgeshire

Paul Lister
7 Murrayfield
Seghill
Northumberland

Graham Lockwood
106 Burnside Avenue
Skipton
Yorkshire
BB23 2DB

Brian Lynch
53 Hall Lane
Upminster
Essex

Pat Lynch
Gotherinton
68 Kelsey Lane
Balsall Common
Near Coventry
West Midlands

Glenn McCrory
Holborn
35 Station Road
Stanley
Co Durham
DH9 0JL

Bobby McEwan
302 Langside Road
Glasgow

Jim McMillan
21 Langcliffe Road
Preston
Lancashire
PR2 6UE

Charlie Magri
48 Tavistock Gardens
Seven Kings
Ilford
Essex
IG3 1BE

Frank Maloney
Champion Enterprises
99 Middlesex Street
London E1 7DA

Dennie Mancini
16 Rosedew Road
Off Fulham Palace Road
London W6 9ET

Terry Marsh
141 Great Gregorie
Basildon
Essex

Arthur Melrose
33 Easterhill Street
Glasgow
G32 8LN

Tommy Miller
128 Clapton Mount
King Cross Road
Halifax
West Yorkshire

Glyn Mitchell
28 Furneaux Road
Milehouse
Plymouth
Devon

Carl Moorcroft
108 Stuart Road
Crosby
Liverpool 23

Alex Morrison
39 Armour Street
Glasgow
G33 5EX

Graham Moughton
1 Hedgemans Way
Dagenham
Essex RM9 6DB

James Murray
87 Spean Street
Glasgow G44 4DS

Herbert Myers
The Lodge
Lower House Lane
Burnley
Lancashire

David Nelson
29 Linley Drive
Stirchley Park
Telford
Shropshire
TF3 1RQ

Paul Newman
8 Teg Close
Downs Park Estate
Portslade
Sussex
BN41 2GZ

Norman Nobbs
364 Kings Road
Kingstanding
Birmingham
B44 0UG

Bob Paget
8 Masterman House
New Church Road
London SE5 7HU

George Patrick
84 Wooler Road
Edmonton
London N18 2JS

Terry Petersen
54 Green Leafe Avenue
Wheatley Hills
Doncaster
South Yorkshire
DN2 5RF

Steve Pollard
35 Gorthorpe
Orchard Park Estate
Hull HU6 9EY

Ricky Porter
73 County Road
Swindon
Wiltshire

Dean Powell
10 Cuddington
Deacon Way
Heygate Estate
Walworth
London SE17 1SP

Glyn Rhodes
8 Valentine Crescent
Shine Green
Sheffield
S5 0NW

Ken Richardson
15 East Walk
North Road Estate
Retford
Nottinghamshire
DN22 7YF

Fred Rix
14 Broom Road
Shirley
Croydon
Surrey
CR0 8NE

Gus Robinson
Stranton House
Westview Road
Hartlepool
TS24 0BB

John Rushton
20 Alverley Lane
Balby
Doncaster
DN4 9AS

Joe Ryan
22a Glenarm Road
Clapton
London E5 0LZ

Kevin Sanders
19 Whittington
Off Parnwell Way
Peterborough
Cambridgeshire

Chris Sanigar
147 Two Mile Hill Road
Kingswood
Bristol BS15 1BH

Kevin Sheehan
84 Amesbury Circus
Bells Lane Estate
Nottingham
NG8 6DH

Mike Shinfield
126 Birchwood Lane
Somercotes
Derbyshire DE55 4NE

Steve Sims
9 High Street
Newport
Gwent

Len Slater
78 Sutcliffe Avenue
Nunsthorpe
Grimsby
Lincolnshire

Andy Smith
Valandra
19 St Audreys Lane
St Ives
Cambridgeshire

Darkie Smith
21 Northumberland House
Gaisford Street
London NW5

John Smith
6 Kildare Road
Chorlton
Manchester M21 1YR

Brian Snagg
The Heath Hotel
Green Hill Road
Allerton
Liverpool

Les Southey
Oakhouse
Park Way
Hillingdon
Middlesex

John Spensley
The Black Swan Hotel
Tremholme Bar
Near Stokesley
North Yorkshire DL6 3JY

Ken Squires
27 University Close
Syston
Leicestershire
LE7 2AY

Greg Steene
11 Whitcomb Street
London WC2H 7HA

Danny Sullivan
29 Mount Gould
Avenue
Mount Gould
Plymouth
Devon PL4 9HA

Norrie Sweeney
3 Saucehill Terrace
Paisley
Scotland PA2 6SY

Wally Swift
Grove House
54 Grove Road
Knowle
Solihull
West Midlands B93 0PJ

Amos Talbot
70 Edenfield Road
Rochdale OL11 5AE

Keith Tate
214 Dick Lane
Tyersal
Bradford BD4 8JH

Glenroy Taylor
95 Devon Close
Perivale
Middlesex

Eddie Thomas
Runnington
Penydarren Park
Merthyr Tydfil
Mid Glamorgan

Jimmy Tibbs
44 Gylingdune Gardens
Seven Kings
Essex

Terry Toole
8 Conningsby Gardens
South Chingford
London
E4 9BD

Mick Toomey
25 Purton Grove
Bransholme
Hull
HU7 4QD

Jack Trickett
Acton Court Hotel
187 Buxton Road
Stockport
Cheshire

Frankie Turner
Matchroom
10 Western Road
Essex
RM1 3JT

Bill Tyler
Northcroft House
Chorley
Lichfield
Staffordshire
WS13 8DL

Danny Urry
26 Nella Road
Hammersmith
London W6

Stephen Vaughan
43-45 Pembroke Place
Liverpool
L3 5PH

Alan Walker
47 Consett Road
Castleside
Consett
Durham
DH8 9QL

Frank Warren
Centurion House
Bircherley Green
Hertford
Hertfordshire
SG14 1AP

Robert Watt
32 Dowanhill Street
Glasgow G11

Ken Whitney
38 Shakespeare Way
Corby
Northamptonshire
NN17 2ND

William Wigley
4 Renfrew Drive
Wollaton
Nottinghamshire
NG8 2FX

Mick Williamson
34a St Marys Grove
Cannonbury
London N1

Tex Woodward
Spanorium Farm
Berwick Lane
Compton Greenfield
Bristol
BS12 3RX

Frank Maloney, the manager of Lennox Lewis
Les Clark

Licensed Matchmakers

Nat Basso
38 Windsor Road
Prestwich
Lancashire
M25 8FF

Harry Burgess
25 Calthorpe Street
London WC1

David Davies
10 Byrngelli
Carmel
Llanelli
Dyfed
SA14 7EL

David Davis
179 West Heath Road
Hampstead
London NW3

Mickey Duff
National House
60-66 Wardour Street
London W1 3HP

Ernie Fossey
26 Bell Lane
Brookmans Park
Hertfordshire

John Gaynor
7 Westhorne Fold
Counthill Drive
Brooklands Road
Crumpsall
Manchester
M8 6JN

Tommy Gilmour
Fort Crest Hotel
Bothwell Street
Glasgow
G2 7EN

Ron Gray
Ingrams Oak
19 Hatherton Road
Cannock
Staffordshire

Patrick Healy
1 Cranley Buildings
Brookes Market
Holborn
London EC1

Bobby Holder
17 Merredene Street
Brixton
London
SW9 6LR

Steve Holdsworth
85 Sussex Road
Watford
Herts
WD2 5HR

Terry Lawless
4 Banyards
Off Nelmes Way
Emerson Park
Hornchurch
Essex

Graham Lockwood
106 Burnside Avenue
Skipton
N. Yorkshire
BD23 2DB

Frank Maloney
99 Middlesex Street
London
E1 7DA

Dennie Mancini
16 Rosedew Road
Off Fulham Palace Road
Hammersmith
London
W6 9ET

Tommy Miller
128 Clapton Mount
King Cross Road
Halifax
West Yorkshire

Chris Moorcroft
17 Cambrian Drive
Prostatyn
Clwyd
LL19 9RN

Alex Morrison
39 Armour Street
Glasgow
G33 5EX

Norman Nobbs
364 Kings Road
Kingstanding
Birmingham
B44 0UG

Ricky Porter
Angelique Guest House
73 County Road
Swindon
Wiltshire

Dean Powell
10 Cuddington
Deacon Way
Heygate Estate
Walworth
London
SE17 1SP

Len Slater
78 Sutcliffe Avenue
Nunsthorpe
Grimsby
Lincolnshire

Darkie Smith
21 Northumberland
  House
Gaisford Street
London NW5

Terry Toole
8 Conningsby Gardens
South Chingford
London
E4 9BD

Frank Turner
10 Western Road
Romford
Essex
RM1 3JT

Licensed Referees

Class 'B'

Kenneth Curtis	Southern Area
Keith Garner	Central Area
Mark Green	Southern Area
Jeffrey Hinds	Southern Area
Al Hutcheon	Scottish Area
David Irving	Northern Ireland
Ian John-Lewis	Southern Area
Marcus McDonnell	Southern Area
Philip Moyse	Midlands Area
Roy Snipe	Central Area
Grant Wallis	Western Area

Class 'A'

Ivor Bassett	Welsh Area
Arnold Bryson	Northern Area
Phil Cowsill	Central Area
Richard Davies	Southern Area
Roddy Evans	Welsh Area
Anthony Green	Central Area
Ron Hackett	Central Area
Michael Heatherwick	Welsh Area
Wynford Jones	Welsh Area
Denzil Lewis	Western Area
Len Mullen	Scottish Area
Terry O'Connor	Midlands Area
James Pridding	Midlands Area
Reg Thompson	Southern Area
Lawrence Thompson	Northern Area
Anthony Walker	Southern Area
Gerald Watson	Northern Area
Barney Wilson	Northern Ireland

Class 'A' Star

John Coyle	Midlands Area
Roy Francis	Southern Area
John Keane	Midlands Area
Larry O'Connell	Southern Area
Dave Parris	Southern Area
Paul Thomas	Midlands Area
Mickey Vann	Central Area

Licensed Timekeepers

Alan Archbald	Northern Area
Roy Bicknell	Midlands Area
Roger Bowden	Western Area
John Breward	Northern Area
Neil Burder	Welsh Area
Ivor Campbell	Welsh Area
Frank Capewell	Central Area
Robert Edgeworth	Southern Area
Harry Foxall	Midlands Area
Eric Gilmour	Scottish Area
Brian Heath	Midlands Area
Ken Honiball	Western Area
Winston Hughes	Midlands Area
Albert Kelleher	Northern Area
Michael McCann	Southern Area
Norman Maddox	Midlands Area

Gordon Pape	Welsh Area
Daniel Peacock	Southern Area
Barry Pinder	Central Area
Raymond Rice	Southern Area
Tommy Rice	Southern Area
Colin Roberts	Central Area
James Russell	Scottish Area
Nick White	Southern Area

Licensed Ringwhips

Bob Ainsley-Matthews	Southern Area
George Andrews	Central Area
Robert Brazier	Southern Area
Albert Brewer	Southern Area
Steve Butler	Central Area
Theodore Christian	Western Area
John Davis	Southern Area
Ernie Draper	Southern Area
Colin Gallagher	Central Area
Danny Gill	Midlands Area
Chris Gilmore	Scottish Area
Mike Goodall	Midlands Area
Simon Goodall	Midlands Area
Peter Gray	Midlands Area
Arran Lee Grinnell	Midlands Area
David Hall	Central Area
Thomas Hallett	Northern Area
John Hardwick	Southern Area
Keith Jackson	Midlands Area
Philip Keen	Central Area
Fred Little	Western Area
Alun Martin	Welsh Area
James McGinnis	Scottish Area
Tommy Miller (Jnr)	Central Area
Linton O'Brien	Northern Area
Dennis Pinching	Southern Area
Sandy Risley	Southern Area
John Vary	Southern Area
Paul Wainwright	Northern Area
James Wallace	Scottish Area
James Whitelaw	Scottish Area
John Whitelaw	Scottish Area

Inspectors

Alan Alster	Central Area
Michael Barnett	Central Area
Don Bartlett	Midlands Area
John Braley	Midlands Area
Fred Breyer	Southern Area
David Brown	Western Area
Ray Chichester	Welsh Area
Geoff Collier	Midlands Area
Jaswinder Dhaliwal	Midlands Area
Les Dean	Midlands Area
Robert Edgar	Central Area
Phil Edwards	Central Area

Kevin Fulthorpe	Welsh Area
Bob Galloway	Southern Area
John Hall	Central Area
Freddie King	Southern Area
Bob Lonkhurst	Southern Area
Ken Lyas	Southern Area
Tom McElkinney	Northern Area
Stuart Meiklejohn	Central Area
David Ogilvie	Northern Area
Charlie Payne	Southern Area
Fred Potter	Northern Area
Les Potts	Midlands Area
David Renicke	Western Area
Bob Rice	Midlands Area
Bert Smith	Central Area
David Stone	Southern Area
Charlie Thurley	Southern Area
John Toner	Northern Ireland
Nigel Underwood	Midlands Area
Ernie Wallis	Welsh Area
Robert Warner	Central Area
P. J. White	Southern Area
Clive Williams	Western Area
Geoff Williams	Midlands Area
David Wilson	Southern Area
Harry Woods	Scottish Area

BOB MEE'S BRITISH BOXING RECORDS 1996

Publication date February 1st.

All records up to December 31st, 1995 1993, 1994, and 1995 editions still available.

Inquiries: Bob Mee, 1 Lodge Farm, Snitterfield, Stratford upon Avon, Warwicks CV37 0LR

Larry O' Connell (Class 'A' Star Referee)

Wishes

The British Boxing Board of Control Yearbook

every success

O'CONNELL & YARDLEY

L. D. O'CONNELL F.I.P.G.   TERENCE A. YARDLEY   K. O'CONNELL
ENGRAVERS

5 Mill Street, London W1R 9TF. Telephone: 0171-499 6414 Fax: 0171-495 3963

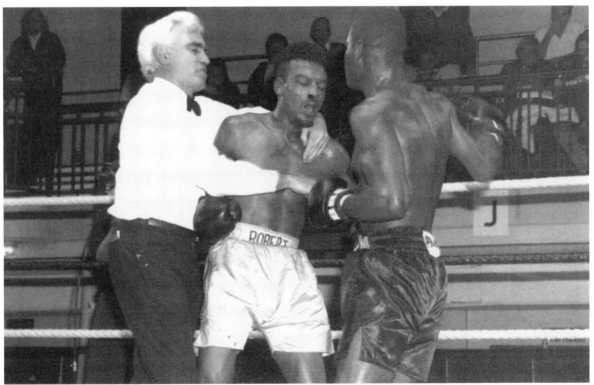

Larry O'Connell (left) rescues a brave Robert Wright from the fists of Darren Dyer in November 1991   Les Clark

CHRIS SANIGAR
"BRISTOL BOYS"
INTERNATIONAL BOXING
147 TWO MILE HILL ROAD KINSWOOD BRISTOL BS15 1BH
Tel. 01179-496699   0831-359978   Fax 01179-496700
__PROMOTIONS__   __MANAGEMENT__   __TRAINING__

WINNING COMBINATION

Tel: (0191) 567 6871
Fax: (0191) 565 2581
Mobile: (0305) 434457

Tommy Conroy - Manager and Trainer
Annette Conroy - First North-East Lady Promoter
Matchmaker: Graham Lockwood (01805) 434457
Trainers: Charlie Armstrong and Malcolm Gates

144 High Street East, East End
Sunderland, Tyne & Wear,
SR1 2BL

Tommy Conroy's Sunderland Based Stable

Ian Henry (Gateshead) Light-Heavyweight
Dave Johnson (Boldon) Middleweight
Micky Johnson (Newcastle) Middleweight
Robbie "Boy" Bell (Sunderland) Light-Middleweight
Mark Cichoki (Hartlepool) Light-Middleweight
Micky Hall (Ludworth) Lightweight
John T. Kelly (Hartlepool) Lightweight
Chip O'Neill (Sunderland) Featherweight
Hughie Davey (Wallsend) Welterweight
Glen Hopkins (Hetton-le-Hole) Light-Welterweight
Alan Graham (Newcastle) Lightweight
Tim Hill (Whitley Bay) Lightweight
Liam Dineen (Peterlee) Lightweight
Paul Quarmby (Hetton-le-Hole) Super-Bantamweight
Paul Scott (Newbiggin) Light-Welterweight
Shaun O'Neill (Sunderland) Light-Welterweight

NOBLE ART PROMOTIONS LTD
GREG STEENE & BRUCE BAKER
INTERNATIONAL PROMOTERS, MANAGERS,
MATCHMAKERS AND AGENTS

BOXERS MANAGED BY GREG STEENE:

HUNTER CLAY....................FORMER WBC INTERNATIONAL SUPER-MIDDLEWEIGHT CHAMPION

ANDY WRIGHT..................FORMER UNDEFEATED SOUTHERN AREA SUPER-MIDDLEWEIGHT CHAMPION

HORACE FLEARY ....GERMAN INTERNATIONAL SUPER-MIDDLEWEIGHT CHAMPION

JAKE KILRAIN ....SUPER-MIDDLEWEIGHT

BRIAN GENTRY ....LIGHTWEIGHT

GODFREY SEMPAYA ....LIGHT-WELTERWEIGHT

ROBERT NJIE.....................WELTERWEIGHT

TRAINERS
CASEY McCULLUM, TREVOR CATTOUSE, KARL BARWISE AND GERRY CONTEH (USA)

ANY UNATTACHED PROFESSIONALS OR SERIOUS AMATEURS SEEKING FIRST CLASS TRAINING AND MANAGEMENT, PLEASE CONTACT THE BELOW NUMBER

871 High Road, North Finchley, London N12 8QA
Telephone: 0171 839 4532   Fax: 0171 839 4367
Company Reg. No. 02840916

DAI GARDINER BOXING STABLE
SPONSORED BY
EMPRESS CAR SALES

Prince of Wales Industrial Estate, Cwmcarn, Gwent.
Gym Tel: 01495 248885   Home Tel: 01443 812971

BOXERS

STEVE ROBINSON	FEATHERWEIGHT. WBO CHAMPION
ROBBIE REGAN	FLYWEIGHT. UNDEFEATED EUROPEAN CHAMPION
NEIL SWAIN	SUPER-BANTAMWEIGHT. COMMONWEALTH CHAMPION
MICHAEL SMYTH	WELTERWEIGHT
MERVYN BENNETT	LIGHTWEIGHT. WELSH CHAMPION
BARRY THOROGOOD	MIDDLEWEIGHT. WELSH CHAMPION
J. T. WILLIAMS	SUPER-FEATHERWEIGHT. WELSH CHAMPION
DARREN FEARN	HEAVYWEIGHT
L. A. WILLIAMS	HEAVYWEIGHT
EDDIE LLOYD	SUPER-FEATHERWEIGHT
JOHN JANES	WELTERWEIGHT
PHIL FOUND	LIGHT-WELTERWEIGHT
HARRY WOODS	FLYWEIGHT
JASON PAUL MATTHEWS	WELTERWEIGHT
ANDREW BLOOMER	SUPER-BANTAMWEIGHT
GARETH LAWRENCE	SUPER-FEATHERWEIGHT
CARLOS GILES	LIGHT-MIDDLEWEIGHT
CARL WINSTONE	LIGHT-MIDDLEWEIGHT

LICENCED MANAGER & PROMOTER: DAI GARDINER

TRAINERS: Ronnie Rush - Roy Agland - Pat Chidgey
Eddie Green - Gary Thomas - Bob Avoth
EXECUTIVE ASSISTANT: Wayne Elliott
Tel: 01633 284818   Fax: 01633 278889

ST. ANDREW'S SPORTING CLUB
EXCLUSIVE GENTLEMEN'S CLUB
AND
THE HOME OF SCOTTISH BOXING

1995-96 Fixture List

Monday 18th September 1995

Monday 23th October

Monday 20th November

Monday 11th December
(Ladies Night - Dinner & Dance)

Monday 22nd January 1996

Monday 19th February

Monday 18th March

Monday 22nd April

Monday 3rd June

Team 1995-96

Light Flyweight
Paul Weir - WBO World Champion

Flyweight
Keith Knox - ABA Champion, Undefeated

Bantamweight
Drew Docherty - British Champion
James Drummond

Super-Bantamweight
Richard Vowles - New Pro
Robert Hay - Undefeated

Featherweught
Billy Hardy - Commonwealth Champion
Ian McLeod - Undefeated Paul Watson - Undefeated
Wilson Docherty

Super-Featherweight
Davy McHale   Hugh Collins   Gary Burrell

Lightweight
Mark Breslin - Undefeated

Welterweight
John Docherty - New Pro
Joe Townsley   Tommy Quinn

Light -Middleweight
Billy Collins - Undefeated

Middleweight
Willie Quinn - WBO Continental Champion

Super-Middleweight
Stephen Wilson

Cruiserweight
Colin Brown - New Pro

Administrative Offices and Club Room
**Forte Crest,
Bothwell Street, Glasgow G2 7EN
Telephone: 0141-248 5461 and 0141-248 2656
Fax: 0141-221 8986   Telex: 77440**

DIRECTOR: TOMMY GILMOUR JNR.

Robson Books Ltd

Bolsover House
5-6 Clipstone Street
London W1P 8LE

Tel: 0171-323-1223
Fax: 0171-636-0798

Muhammad Ali

"Robson Books have rapidly become the foremost
publishers of boxing books in the country."

Boxing Monthly

List includes:

BOXING BABYLON
Behind the Shadowy World
of the Prize Ring
Nigel Collins

CHAMPIONS OF THE RING
The Lives and Times of
Boxing's Heavyweight Heroes
Gerald Suster

LONSDALE'S BELT: The Story
of Boxing's Greatest Prize
John Harding

LIGHTNING STRIKES: The Lives
and Times of Boxing's Lightweight
Heroes
Gerald Suster

MUHAMMAD ALI: His Life and Times
Thomas Hauser

MEN OF STEEL: The Lives and Times
of Boxing's Middleweight Champions
Peter Walsh

IN THIS CORNER . . . !
Forty World Champions Tell Their
Stories
Peter Heller

**BOXING'S STRANGEST
FIGHTS**
Graeme Kent

JACK KID BERG
John Harding

JACK DEMPSEY:
The Manassa Mauler
Randy Roberts

**THE LONSDALE BOXING
MANUAL**
David James

TED KID LEWIS
Morton Lewis

MUHAMAD ALI: A Thirty
Year Journey
Howard Bingham

TYSON: In and Out
of the Ring
Peter Heller

RINGMASTERS
Great Boxing Trainers
Talk About Their Art
Dave Anderson

ALSO PUBLISHED BY ROBSON BOOKS
Biographies of Joe Louis, John L Sullivan, Papa Jack,
Primo 'Man Mountain' Carnera, Rocky Marciano, Sugar Ray Leonard,
Sugar Ray Robinson . . . and many more.